Ancient Methone
2003–2013

UCLA COTSEN INSTITUTE OF ARCHAEOLOGY PRESS
Monumenta Archaeologica

Volume 48

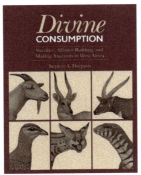

Divine Consumption: Sacrifice, Alliance Building, and Making Ancestors in West Africa

By Stephen A. Dueppen

Volume 47

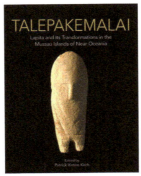

Talepakemalai: Lapita and Its Transformations in the Mussau Islands of Near Oceania

Edited by Patrick Vinton Kirch

Volume 46

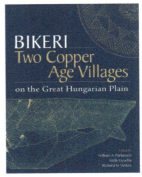

Bikeri: Two Copper Age Villages on the Great Hungarian Plain

Edited by William A. Parkinson, Attila Gyucha, and Richard W. Yerkes

Volume 45

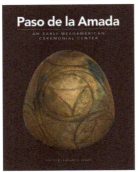

Paso de la Amada: An Early Mesoamerican Ceremonial Center

Edited by Richard G. Lesure

Volume 44

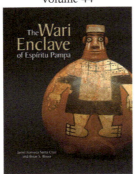

The Wari Enclave of Espíritu Pampa

By Javier Fonseca Santa Cruz and Brian S. Bauer

Volume 43

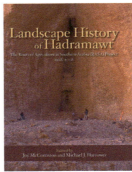

Landscape History of Hadramawt: The Roots of Agriculture in Southern Arabia (RASA) Project 1998–2008

Edited by Joy McCorriston and Michael J. Harrower

Volume 42

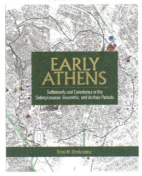

Early Athens: Settlements and Cemeteries in the Submycenaean, Geometric, and Archaic Periods

By Eirini M. Dimitriadou

Volume 41

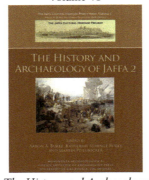

The History and Archaeology of Jaffa 2

Edited by Aaron A. Burke, Katherine Strange Burke, and Martin Peilstöcker

Volume 40

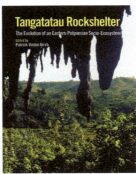

Tangatatau Rockshelter: The Evolution of an Eastern Polynesian Socio-Ecosystem

Edited by Patrick Vinton Kirch

See page 1445 for a complete list of volumes in the Cotsen Institute of Archaeology Monumenta Archaeologica series.

Ancient Methone
2003–2013

Excavations by Matthaios Bessios, Athena Athanassiadou, and Konstantinos Noulas

Volume 1

Edited by
Sarah P. Morris and John K. Papadopoulos

With contributions by (in alphabetical order)
Athena Athanassiadou, Matthaios Bessios, Angelos Boufalis, Brian Damiata,
Elissavet Dotsika, Styliana Galiniki, Despina Ignatiadou, Petros Karalis,
Alexandra Kasseri, Antonis Kotsonas, Alexandra Livarda, Antonio Longinelli,
Ioannis Manos, Samantha L. Martin, Sarah P. Morris, Vanessa Muros, Marianna Nikolaidou,
Konstantinos Noulas, Niki Oikonomaki, John K. Papadopoulos, Vaso Papathanasiou,
Seth Pevnick, Llorenç Picornell-Gelabert, John Southon, Maria Tolia-Christakou,
Sevi Triantaphyllou, Yannis Z. Tzifopoulos, Trevor Van Damme, Anastasia Vasileiadou,
Samuel Verdan, Rena Veropoulidou, and Ioannis Vlastaridis

Monumenta Archaeologica 49
UCLA COTSEN INSTITUTE OF ARCHAEOLOGY PRESS

THE COTSEN INSTITUTE OF ARCHAEOLOGY PRESS is the publishing unit of the Cotsen Institute of Archaeology at UCLA, a premier research organization dedicated to the creation, dissemination, and conservation of archaeological knowledge and heritage. It is home to both the Interdepartmental Archaeology Graduate Program and the UCLA/Getty Program in the Conservation of Cultural Heritage. The Cotsen Institute provides a forum for innovative faculty research, graduate education, and public programs at UCLA in an effort to positively impact the academic, local and global communities. Established in 1973, the Cotsen Institute is at the forefront of archaeological research, education, conservation and publication, and is an active contributor to interdisciplinary research at UCLA.

THE COTSEN INSTITUTE OF ARCHAEOLOGY PRESS specializes in producing high-quality academic volumes in nine different series, including *Monumenta Archaeologica, Monographs, World Heritage and Monuments, Cotsen Advanced Seminars,* and *Ideas, Debates, and Perspectives*. Through a generous endowment by Lloyd E. Cotsen, longtime Institute volunteer and benefactor, the Press makes the fruits of archaeological research accessible to scholars, professionals, students, and the general public. Our archaeological publications receive critical acclaim in both academic communities and the public at large.

THE COTSEN INSTITUTE OF ARCHAEOLOGY AT UCLA
Willeke Wendrich, Director
Aaron A. Burke, Editor-in-Chief
Randi Danforth, Publications Director
Deidre Brin, Digital Publications Director

EDITORIAL BOARD
Willeke Wendrich	Africa (Ex officio member)
Li Min	East Asia
John K. Papadopoulos	Mediterranean Basin
Gregson Schachner	North America–Southwest
Ellen J. Pearlstein	Conservation of Indigenous and Archaeological Materials
Sharon E. J. Gerstel	Medieval and Early Modern Mediterranean Archaeology
Richard G. Lesure	North America–Mesoamerica
Aaron A. Burke	West Asia–Near East
Randi Danforth	Ex officio member

Edited by Jody Baboukis
Designed by Sally Boylan

The publication of this volume was made possible by a grant from the Institute for Aegean Prehistory and the Steinmetz Chair Endowment in Classical Archaeology and Material Culture at UCLA.

Library of Congress Cataloging-in-Publication Data

Names: Morris, Sarah P., 1954- editor. | Papadopoulos, John K., 1958- editor.
Title: Ancient Methone, 2003-2013 : excavations by Matthaios Bessios, Athena Athanassiadou, and Konstantinos Noulas / edited by Sarah P. Morris and John K. Papadopoulos.
Other titles: Excavations by Matthaios Bessios, Athena Athanassiadou, and Konstantinos Noulas
Description: [Los Angeles, California] : The Cotsen Institute of Archaeology Press, [2022] | Series: Monumenta archaeologica ; 49 |
Identifiers: LCCN 2022021422 | ISBN 9781950446285 (v. 1 ; hardback) | ISBN 9781950446285 (v. 2 ; hardback) | ISBN 9781950446339 (v. 1 ; ebook) | ISBN 9781950446339 (v. 2 ; ebook)
Classification: LCC DF901.M54 A53 2022 | DDC 938--dc23/eng/20220822
LC record available at https://lccn.loc.gov/2022021422

Copyright ©2023 Regents of the University of California
All rights reserved. Printed in the United States of America

FRONTISPIECE
Sketch of Methone, September 12, 2012, by Anne Hooton,
looking east across the archaeological site, with the Thermaic Gulf beyond,
including the delta of the Haliakmon River and Mt. Chortiatis in the distance

CONTENTS

VOLUME 1

Preface and Acknowledgments *Sarah P. Morris and John K. Papadopoulos*		ix
List of Contributors		xi
Abbreviations		xv
List of Illustrations		xvii
List of Tables		xxvii

INTRODUCTION

Introduction:	The Ancient Methone Archaeological Project *John K. Papadopoulos and Sarah P. Morris* (with contributions by *Antonis Kotsonas*)	3
Chapter 1	Excavations at Methone (2003–2013) *Matthaios Bessios, Athena Athanassiadou, and Konstantinos Noulas*	19
Chapter 2	Methone in Ancient Sources *Yannis Z. Tzifopoulos*	49
Chapter 3	At the Water's Edge *Samantha L. Martin*	75

PART I. METHONE BEFORE ERETRIA: THE LATE NEOLITHIC THROUGH EARLY IRON AGE SETTLEMENT

Chapter 4	The Neolithic and Early Bronze Age Settlement and Pottery *Marianna Nikolaidou*	97
Chapter 5	The Middle and Late Bronze Age Pottery *Trevor Van Damme*	199

Chapter 6	The Late Bronze Age Cemetery *Sarah P. Morris, Sevi Triantaphyllou, and Vaso Papathanasiou (with contributions by John K. Papadopoulos, Vanessa Muros, Brian Damiata, and John Southon)*	239
Chapter 7	The Early Iron Age Settlement and Pottery: An Overview *John K. Papadopoulos*	323

PART II. TRADE, INDUSTRY, AND LIFEWAYS IN EARLY IRON AGE METHONE: THE HYPOGEION

Chapter 8	The Excavation of the Hypogeion *Matthaios Bessios*	387
Chapter 9	Catalogue of Select Pottery from the Hypogeion *Matthaios Bessios*	407
Chapter 10	Lifeways and Foodways in Iron Age Methone: A Perishable Material Culture Approach *Alexandra Livarda, Rena Veropoulidou, Anastasia Vasileiadou, and Llorenç Picornell-Gelabert*	471
Chapter 11	Inscriptions, Graffiti/Dipinti, and (Trade)Marks at Methone (ca. 700 B.C.) *Yannis Z. Tzifopoulos*	487
Chapter 12	Why Was Methone Colonized? Transport Amphoras and the Economics of Greek Colonization Between History and Archaeology *Antonis Kotsonas*	499
Chapter 13	Metallurgical Activity at Methone: The Evidence of the Stone Artifacts from the Hypogeion *Ioannis Manos and Ioannis Vlastaridis*	529
Chapter 14	Metallurgical Ceramics from the Hypogeion *Samuel Verdan*	545
Chapter 15	Metal Finds from the Hypogeion *John K. Papadopoulos*	563
Chapter 16	Clay Textile Tools from Methone: Spindlewhorls and Loomweights from the Hypogeion *Sarah P. Morris*	661
Chapter 17	Cut Sherd Disks from the Hypogeion *John K. Papadopoulos*	677

VOLUME 2

PART III. METHONE IN THE ARCHAIC AND CLASSICAL PERIODS

Chapter 18	Building A on the East Hill of Ancient Methone *Samantha L. Martin*	691
Chapter 19	a) Pottery Workshops of Ancient Methone *Matthaios Bessios*	721
	b) Archaic Pottery from the Acropolis (West Hill) of Ancient Methone *Matthaios Bessios and Konstantinos Noulas*	725
Chapter 20	The Role of Methone in the Macedonian Timber Trade *Angelos Boufalis*	735
Chapter 21	Trade in the Archaic North Aegean: Transport Amphoras from the West Hill of Methone *Alexandra Kasseri*	771
Chapter 22	The East Greek Fine Pottery *John K. Papadopoulos*	797
Chapter 23	a) Selected Attic Black-figure and Red-figure Pottery from Methone *Seth Pevnick*	857
	b) An Attic Red-figure Cup by the Bonn Painter from Methone *Maria Tolia-Christakou*	874
Chapter 24	Terracotta Lamps *John K. Papadopoulos*	879
Chapter 25	Early Glass in Methone *Despina Ignatiadou (with a contribution by Elissavet Dotsika, Petros Karalis, and Antonio Longinelli)*	897
Chapter 26	Metal Objects in Archaic and Classical Methone: Acropolis and Its East Slope, the Agora, and the South Harbor Area *John K. Papadopoulos*	953
Chapter 27	Jewelry Molds from Methone in the Archaeological Museum of Thessaloniki (Stamatios Tsakos Collection) *Styliana Galiniki*	1107
Chapter 28	The Lead Sling Bullets from Methone: Warfare (Un)inscribed *Angelos Boufalis, Niki Oikonomaki, and Yannis Z. Tzifopoulos*	1141
Chapter 29	The Ancient Agora of Methone: Pottery from the Destruction Layer *Athena Athanassiadou*	1239

ΠΕΡΙΛΗΨΗ (Greek Summary)	1323
Bibliography	1351
Concordances	1415
Index	1429

PREFACE AND ACKNOWLEDGMENTS

Sarah P. Morris and John K. Papadopoulos

The genesis of this volume resulted from the generosity of Matthaios Bessios, Athena Athanassiadou, and Konstantinos Noulas, in responding to an initiative by Yannis Tzifopoulos to share the discoveries made at ancient Methone since 2003 with the wider public which these finds deserved. The first stage of this dissemination was the publication of the important early inscriptions from the Hypogeion;[1] this coincided with an international conference bringing together philologists, linguists, historians, and archaeologists in 2012 to explore these discoveries more fully,[2] followed by an exhibit of the early inscriptions at the Archaeological Museum of Thessaloniki.[3] At the invitation of Manthos Bessios, the next stage of research at Methone brought in the University of California at Los Angeles, represented by John Papadopoulos and Sarah Morris, to assemble a team of specialists to do justice to the wide spectrum of spectacular finds from excavations conducted between 2003 and 2013, and began in 2012 with a collaborative study permit issued by the Greek Ministry of Culture. This volume, delayed in part by the onset of new field research in 2014 that formed another component of our collaboration,[4] is the result of our research since 2012 and 2013. In addition to the many individuals thanked in each chapter of this volume, we are grateful to a great number of individuals and institutions who helped the Ancient Methone Archaeology Project (AMAP) reach its goals.

The Pieria Ephoreia (formerly, since 2004, KZ´ Ephoreia) has hosted both field research and study seasons devoted to this project since 2012, at its storage facilities in Makrygialos, and assisted with both personnel and equipment in every season. The entire team is grateful to our successive Ephors (Efi Poulaki-Pantermali, Elena Papastavrou, and Christos Gatzolis) for permission to conduct fieldwork and study seasons, to our co-directors for arranging their summer schedules around team seasons, and to the staff for providing services on site and in the *apotheke* (especially Christos Avramidis, Charilaos Karanikas, Ioannis Moschos, Ioannis Moschou, Konstantinos Athanassiadis, and Iordanis Poimenidis). Security staff for study seasons at the Makrygialos storage facility graciously allowed for extended hours, thanks to guards Nikos Kalitsios and the late Vassilis Danielidis, while the Makrygialos middle school (*gymnasion*) provided extra workspace and restrooms under its successive principals. Since 2012, we have been assisted annually and ably by archaeologist Stamatia Kordanouli in field survey, cataloguing, washing pottery and shells, and assistance to photographers and illustrators in the documentation of finds: our profound thanks are expressed to her. Additional assistance was provided in 2012 by Maria Karanika. Since 2015, Annette Dukes has served as registrar, driver, base manager, informal photographer, and project angel; no season could have run smoothly without her generosity, patience, team spirit, and archaeological skills.

The heroic task of conservation was headed since 2012 by Vanessa Muros of UCLA, assisted over the years by students from the UCLA-Getty MA Program in Conservation of Archaeological and Ethnographic Materials (Brittany Dolph, Carinne Tzadik, Heather White, Marci Burton, and

Lindsay Ocal), as well as Megan O'Connor and Ciarán Lavelle (2013); during field excavation and post-excavation study seasons, we were joined by Chrysanthe Pantages (2015–2019), Anna Weiss (2014), Dr. Wendy Reade (2016), Nefeli Theocharous (2018), and Alekos Tsiogkas (2018–2019). Photography was performed by Ian Coyle (2012–2014) and Jeffrey Vanderpool (2015–2020); the latter also edited many illustrations and worked tirelessly on our images. Many of our digital illustrations were edited with skill and patience by Myles Chykerda. Illustrations of artifacts were prepared by Anne Hooton (2012–2021), Fani Skyvalida (2012–2013), and Tina Ross (2014–2019), and in the field by Hooton and Ross working together with the excavators (2014–2017).

Study seasons and research were funded initially by UCLA through the Steinmetz Chair in Classical Archaeology and Material Culture at UCLA, the Cotsen Institute of Archaeology in Ahmanson Field Research grants, and the Steinmetz Family Foundation through travel grants for UCLA graduate students in archaeology. Since 2015, a Collaborative Research Grant from the National Endowment for the Humanities (RZ 230604-15) supported all aspects of study and field research for this project, including graduate student research fellowships, travel and honoraria for professional staff, off-season processing and analysis of artifacts and ecofacts, and recurring expenses for travel, accommodation, and supplies for annual study seasons. Additional funding was provided by the Loeb Classical Library Foundation (2015–2016), the Keck Foundation (through the generosity of James S. Economou) in 2014 and 2016, and Michael and Jamie Lynton. Analytic Instruments S.A., Greece, lent valuable equipment (a Bruker pXRF) for analysis in conservation to the project in 2012 and 2013.

The communities of Methone and Nea Agathoupolis, and their respective leaders (Antonios Boubouras and the late Paschalis Papadopoulos), hosted and supported us in myriad ways, not least with their interest and enthusiasm for the project and their hospitality to our team. In particular, the Agathones of Nea Agathoupolis provided enthusiasm and refreshment to our field team since 2014, and inspired our restoration of the abandoned train station as their cultural center.[5] Ioannis Emmanuelidis and his family provided housing, hospitality, and myriad support services to our team every year, along with other local hosts (Spyros Papadopoulos and family) and family kitchens (Giorgios Chalkidis and Renia Eleutheriadou). The Olympus Festival graciously included the Methone project and its directors in their lecture program in 2015, and its then-Festival director, Nikos Paschaloudis, former head of the Pieria Forestry Service, also facilitated field trips and research on the forest resources of Pieria, and provided essential information and documents for Chapter 20.

The editors and contributors to this volume collectively thank the two anonymous reviewers of this volume whose careful reading and comments have greatly improved the final result. We are also grateful to Randi Danforth, the Director of the Publications Office of the Cotsen Institute of Archaeology at UCLA, to Johanna Baboukis for her meticulous copy-editing of this volume, and to Sally Boylan for the page layout and design.

We are grateful to everyone who contributed to this volume in myriad ways and, most of all, for the fact that since its inception, this project and publication was a true *synergasia*—a collaboration—in every sense of the word.

NOTES

1 Bessios, Tzifopoulos, and Kotsonas 2012.
2 Published as Strauss Clay, Malkin, and Tzifopoulos 2017b.
3 Tzifopoulos 2013.
4 Morris et al. 2020.
5 For which see Morris et al. 2020, pp. 717–719.

LIST OF CONTRIBUTORS

Athena Athanassiadou is department head of Prehistoric and Classical Antiquities and Museums of the Ephoreia of Antiquities of Pieria.

Matthaios Bessios was, for many years, the head of archaeological sites, monuments, and field research in the Ephoreia of Antiquities of Pieria.

Angelos Boufalis is an archaeologist and a research associate in the Epigraphy & Papyrology Laboratory, Aristotle University of Thessaloniki, where he received his PhD in Classics in 2020. His research focuses on Greek epigraphy, the history and archaeology of the Archaic and Classical periods, and ethnography.

Brian Damiata is a geophysicist who conducts subsurface prospection of archaeological sites, ^{14}C AMS and stable isotope analyses of ancient skeletal and faunal specimens for chronological and paleodiet reconstructions, and paleo-climate studies of coastal sites. He is an associated researcher of the Cotsen Institute of Archaeology, Los Angeles, California.

Elissavet Dotsika is Director of Research at the Stable Isotope Unit at the Institute of Nanoscience and Nanotechnology, National Center for Scientific Research Demokritos, Agia Paraskevi, Athens, with scientific fields in Material and Environmental Isotope Geochemistry and stable isotope analysis of inorganic and organic materials, water, sulfates, and geological and natural materials.

Styliana Galiniki is an archaeologist and head of the Department of Stonework and Sculpture, Wall Paintings, and Mosaics Collections, Archaeological Museum of Thessaloniki.

Despina Ignatiadou is Head Curator and head of the Department of Sculpture, National Archaeological Museum, Athens, and formerly Head Curator in the Department of Metalwork, Archaeological Museum of Thessaloniki. She holds a postgraduate degree in the Conservation of Antiquities from the University of London, and a PhD on Classical colorless glass from the Aristotle University of Thessaloniki.

Petros Karalis is a PhD candidate in the Geology Department, National and Kapodistrian University of Athens, with research interests in the traceability of raw materials of glass, food, palaeoclimate, and palaeodiet with stable isotopes. His work for this project was based at the Institute of Nanoscience and Nanotechnology, National Center for Scientific Research Demokritos, Agia Paraskevi, Athens.

Alexandra Kasseri holds a DPhil in archaeology from the Faculty of Classics, University of Oxford, where she completed her thesis on Archaic trade in the north Aegean, with a focus on ancient Methone.

Antonis Kotsonas is associate professor of Mediterranean history and archaeology at the Institute for the Study of the Ancient World, New York University. He specializes in material culture and socioeconomic history, and co-directs the Lyktos Archaeological Project in Crete.

Alexandra Livarda is a Ramón y Cajal Researcher at the Catalan Institute of Classical Archaeology, Tarragona, Spain, where she co-directs the bioarchaeology research line of the Landscape Archaeology Research Group (GIAP). She specializes in archaeobotany and the archaeology of food.

Antonio Longinelli is in the Dipartimento di Scienze della Terra, University of Parma, Parma, Italy.

Ioannis Manos is an archaeologist specializing in ancient stone artifacts in the Ephoreia of Paleoanthropology and Speleology, Ministry of Culture and Sports (northern Greece office, Thessaloniki).

Samantha Martin is associate professor in the School of Architecture, Planning and Environmental Policy at University College Dublin, where her research and teaching focus on the built environment of Classical antiquity and the phenomenology of landscapes.

Sarah Morris is a Classical philologist and Aegean archaeologist who has worked on field projects in Israel, Turkey, Albania, and Greece, with research interests in prehistoric Greek and Near Eastern archaeology. She is Steinmetz professor in the Department of Classics and Cotsen Institute of Archaeology, University of California, Los Angeles, California.

Vanessa Muros is a conservator and laboratory director at the Cotsen Institute of Archaeology, University of California, Los Angeles, California.

Marianna Nikolaidou holds a PhD from the Aristotle University of Thessaloniki, and is an associate researcher at the Cotsen Institute of Archaeology, University of California, Los Angeles.

Konstantinos Noulas is an archaeologist in the Ephoreia of Antiquities of Pieria, Katerini, Greece.

Niki Oikonomaki belongs to the scientific and laboratory teaching staff and is a member of the Epigraphy and Papyrology Laboratory in the Department of Classics, Aristotle University of Thessaloniki. Her teaching and research interests focus on ancient Greek and Latin epigraphy, historiography, ancient literacy, and epic poetry.

John K. Papadopoulos is distinguished professor of archaeology and classics in the Department of Classics and Cotsen Institute of Archaeology, University of California, Los Angeles. He has conducted fieldwork and research in Australia, Greece, southern Italy, and Albania, and since July 1, 2022 is the Director of the Excavations in the Athenian Agora.

Vaso Papathanasiou received her MA in the Department of History and Archaeology, Aristotle University of Thessaloniki and specializes in bioarchaeology.

Seth Pevnick holds a PhD in Archaeology from UCLA and is curator of Greek and Roman art at the Cleveland Museum of Art and a specialist in Greek vase painting.

Llorenç Picornell-Gelabert holds a PhD from the University of Barcelona, Spain, and focuses on the archaeological study of human–environment interactions and archaeobotany (charcoal analysis-anthracology) in the Mediterranean and Africa. He is a lecturer, ArqueoUIB, in the Department of Historical Sciences and Art Theory, University of the Balearic Islands, Palma, Mallorca.

John Southon is a research scientist in the Department of Earth System Science (School of Physical Sciences), and cofounder and director of the W. M. Keck–Carbon Cycle Accelerator Mass Spectrometry Facility at the University of California, Irvine in the Earth System Science Department.

Maria Tolia-Christakou is a curator in the Department of Vases, Metalwork, and Minor Arts, National Archaeological Museum, Athens.

Sevi Triantaphyllou is a bioarchaeologist and associate professor of archaeology, and co-director of the Toumba Thessalonikis excavations in the Department of History and Archaeology, Aristotle University of Thessaloniki.

Yannis Tzifopoulos is professor of Greek and epigraphy and director of the Epigraphy and Papyrology Lab in the Department of Philology at Aristotle University of Thessaloniki.

Trevor Van Damme holds a PhD in Archaeology from UCLA and teaches in the Department of Greek and Roman Studies, University of Victoria in Canada.

Anastasia Vasileiadou completed an MA in the Department of History and Archaeology, Aristotle University of Thessaloniki and specializes in paleo-faunal material.

Samuel Verdan is research leader at the Swiss School of Archaeology in Greece, where he conducts pottery studies and collaborates in the exploration of the sanctuary of Artemis at Amarynthos (Euboia). He is also based at the Institut d'Archéologie et des Sciences de l'Antiquité ASA, University of Lausanne, Switzerland.

Rena Veropoulidou is based at the Museum of Byzantine Culture, Hellenic Ministry of Culture and Sports, Thessaloniki, and is a former research fellow at the M. H. Wiener Laboratory for Archaeological Science, American School of Classical Studies, Athens, Greece.

Ioannis Vlastaridis is a geologist and geotechician in the Ephoreia of Paleoanthropology and Speleology, Ministry of Culture and Sports (northern Greece office, Thessaloniki).

ABBREVIATIONS

In addition to standard references (e.g., periodic table of elements), abbreviations of titles (Bibliography), and those defined in text (e.g., Chapter 6 appendix, Chapter 25 analysis)

A.D.	Anno Domini
ASL	above sea level
B.C.	Before Christ
BG	black-glaze
B.P.	before the present
cm	centimeters
D.	depth
DD	destruction deposit
Diam.	diameter
DRL	*Deckrandlampen* [covered-rim lamps]: Scheibler lamp type
DSL	(Scheibler lamp type)
EBA	Early Bronze Age
ed.	edited by, or edition
EG	Early Geometric
EIA	Early Iron Age
EPG	Early Protogeometric
ext.	exterior
Fig(s).	figures (in ms.)
FM	Furumark motif
FN	Final Neolithic
fr, frr	fragment(s)
FS	Furumark shape
g	gram
H.	height
HM	handmade

HPD	Highest Probability Density
HT	Howland Type (lamp)
int.	interior
kg	kilogram
km	kilometer
KSL	*Knickschulterlampen* [angled-shoulder lamps]: Scheibler lamp type
L.	length
LBA	Late Bronze Age
LG	Late Geometric
LH	Late Helladic
LN	Late Neolithic
LPG	Late Protogeometric
m	meters (all dimensions in meters, unless otherwise specified)
MBA	Middle Bronze Age
ME	μίκρο εύρημα (= SF: small find)
MG	Middle Geometric
MH	Middle Helladic
mm	millimeters
MN	Middle Neolithic
MPG	Middle Protogeometric
NH	neck-handled
N/R	not recoverable
P./p.	preserved
PG	Protogeometric
PSC	pendent semi-circle (skyphos/i)
pXRF	portable X-ray fluorescence [instrument]
SF	small find
SOS	Distinctive amphora decoration resembling the Greek letters ΣΟΣ
SPG	Subprotogeometric
RSL	*Rundschulterlampen* [rounded-shoulder lamps]: Scheibler lamp type
T	toichos (Wall)
Th.	thickness
W.	width
WM	wheelmade
Wt.	weight
XRF	X-ray fluorescence

LIST OF ILLUSTRATIONS

Volume 1

Frontispiece	Sketch of Methone, looking east across the archaeological site, with the Thermaic Gulf beyond, including the delta of the Haliakmon River and Mt. Chortiatis in the distance
I.1.	Map of northern Greece showing Methone in relation to other ancient sites
I.2.	Contour map of ancient Methone showing the extent of ancient (prehistoric through Classical) and Macedonian (Hellenistic and Roman) occupation
I.3.	The Thermaic Gulf based on the ASTER 30 m contour map
I.4.	Boat trip up the Haliakmon River in the summer of 2012
I.5.	The Haliakmon Gorge, taken from the Monastery of St. John the Baptist
I.6.	Ancient Methone in February 2012
I.7.	Bronze statue of Philip II erected at modern Methone and Nea Agathoupolis in 2010
I.8.	a) Aerial view taken by drone from above the West Hill; b) The bird tower immediately to the north-northeast of ancient Methone, built as part of the Natura 2000 program of the European Union
1.1.	Google Earth view of the area of ancient and Macedonian Methone, showing the location of the various land holdings (plot numbers)
1.2.	Plan of the northeast section of the East Hill as it survives today, showing the location of the prehistoric (Late Neolithic and Early Bronze) defensive ditches and the Hypogeion
1.3.	General view of the Hypogeion, with wall no. 5
1.4.	General view of the Hypogeion
1.5.	Section showing the stratigraphy of the Hypogeion and its various primary phases
1.6.	Spouted Euboian krater with pierced floor, serving as strainer
1.7.	Skyphos of Euboian manufacture
1.8.	East Greek "bird kotyle"
1.9.	Protocorinthian kotyle
1.10.	Attic spouted krater, attributed to the Painter of Athens 897
1.11.	Phoenician amphoras from the Hypogeion
1.12.	Fragmentary Aiolian/Lesbian drinking cup with incised, post-firing inscription
1.13.	Fragmentary Lesbian amphora with incised, post-firing inscription on the neck
1.14.	Ivory seal
1.15.	Fragments of clay mold
1.16.	Stone molds for jewelry
1.17.	Clay crucible for bronzeworking

1.18.	Gold melting plate of clay
1.19.	Small clay crucible
1.20.	Bellows nozzles
1.21.	Plan of the agora of ancient Methone
1.22.	View of the agora from west, showing Building A
1.23.	View from west of Building A in the agora, showing portion of a polygonal wall from the earliest phase of the building
1.24.	View from north of the later phases of Building A, showing mud-brick walls on a stone socle
1.25.	A selection of pottery from the destruction deposit of the agora
1.26.	Underground tunnel dug by the Methonaians in the later Classical period as part of their defense system against the siege of Philip II in 354 B.C. (Plot 245, West Hill)
1.27.	Late Bronze Age Tomb 9 in Plot 245 on the West Hill
1.28.	Selection of wheelmade and painted, as well as handmade, pottery deposited in Late Bronze Age tombs
1.29.	The jewelry from Tomb 10 in Plot 229 on the West Hill, including ornaments made of gold, amber, semi-precious stone, animal bone, and terracotta
1.30.	The solitary Late Bronze Age cremation, Tomb 8 in Plot 229, showing cinerary urn and cremated remains
1.31.	View from east of the Early Iron Age fortification trench in Plot 245
1.32.	View of one of the Ephoreia trenches in Plot 229
1.33.	Plan of the buildings uncovered at the top of the West Hill
1.34.	Two amphoras of the Archaic period
1.35.	Archaic Corinthian plate
1.36.	Two stone molds from the West Hill of Methone
1.37.	Elephant ivory debitage from the West Hill
1.38.	Inscription recording the alliance between Athens and Methone
1.39.	Google Earth plan showing the locations of ancient Methone, Macedonian Methone, the "Melissia" cemetery, and the settlement and cemetery at Palaiokatachas
1.40.	Cist tomb at "Melissia" cemetery northwest of Methone
1.41.	Euboian Late Protogeometric oinochoe
1.42.	Body fragment, Attic Middle Geometric amphora
2.1.	The four decrees of the Athenian boule and demos dated to the decade of 430–420 B.C. recording the alliance between Athens and Methone
3.1.	Map of "site walks" in and around Methone
3.2.	Map of excursion by boat in the Haliakmon River Delta
3.3.	Boat's-eye views toward Nea Agathoupolis and the site of Methone
3.4.	Profile sketch of Methone
3.5.	Pierian ridge from present-day shoreline east of Methone
3.6.	Contour map of Methone
3.7.	Map of towns and foothills in the vicinity of Methone and the Haliakmon River
3.8.	Two views toward the Voras mountain range and Mt. Paiko
3.9.	Mt. Chortiatis from the coast between Methone and Makrygialos at sunrise
3.10.	Mt. Olympos: drone aerial view
3.11.	Shoreline movement over time
3.12.	Wind rose diagrams showing the prevailing wind direction and strength throughout the year
3.13.	Sightline from the agora of Methone and Building A, toward the ancient shoreline and harbor of Methone
3.14.	Aerial view of Methone in 2014

LIST OF ILLUSTRATIONS

xxi

3.15.	Fishing hut in the Haliakmon River Delta
4.1.	Aerial view of the Ephoreia excavations on the East Hill
4.2.	General topography of the excavations with prehistoric pottery plotted on the areas of recovery
4.3.	Topographic plan of the northeast area of the excavation, with the prehistoric ditches and the Hypogeion
4.4.	Prehistoric incised sherds from the Hypogeion
4.5.	Late Neolithic polished sherd from the Hypogeion
4.6.	Late Neolithic ceramic fabrics (macroscopic close-ups)
4.7.	Final Neolithic ceramic fabrics (macroscopic close-ups)
4.8.	Early Bronze Age finer fabrics (macroscopic close-ups)
4.9.	Early Bronze Age coarser fabrics (macroscopic close-ups)
4.10.	Late Neolithic monochrome burnished/polished pottery: **4/1**
4.11.	Late Neolithic monochrome burnished/polished pottery: **4/2**
4.12.	Late Neolithic decorated, medium to fine pottery: **4/3**
4.13.	Late Neolithic decorated, medium to fine pottery: **4/4**
4.14.	Late Neolithic decorated, medium to fine pottery: **4/5**
4.15.	Late Neolithic decorated, medium to fine pottery: **4/6**
4.16.	Late Neolithic decorated, medium to fine pottery: **4/7**
4.17.	Late Neolithic decorated, medium to fine pottery: **4/8**
4.18.	Late Neolithic decorated, medium to fine pottery: **4/9**
4.19.	Late Neolithic decorated, medium to fine pottery: **4/10**
4.20.	Late Neolithic cooking vessels: **4/11**
4.21.	Late Neolithic cooking vessels: **4/12**
4.22.	Late Neolithic miscellaneous (burnisher): **4/13**
4.23.	Final Neolithic monochrome/mottled burnished, open vessels: **4/14**
4.24.	Final Neolithic monochrome/mottled burnished, open vessels: **4/15**
4.25.	Final Neolithic monochrome/mottled burnished, open vessels: **4/16**
4.26.	Final Neolithic monochrome/mottled burnished, open vessels: **4/17**
4.27.	Final Neolithic monochrome/mottled burnished, open vessels: **4/18**
4.28.	Final Neolithic monochrome/mottled burnished, open vessels: **4/19**
4.29.	Final Neolithic monochrome/mottled burnished, open vessels: **4/20**
4.30.	Final Neolithic monochrome/mottled burnished, open vessels: **4/21**
4.31.	Final Neolithic monochrome/mottled burnished, open vessels: **4/22**
4.32.	Final Neolithic monochrome/mottled burnished, open vessels: **4/23**
4.33.	Final Neolithic monochrome/mottled burnished, open vessels: **4/24**
4.34.	Final Neolithic monochrome/mottled burnished, open vessels: **4/25**
4.35.	Final Neolithic incised, medium to fine pottery: **4/26**
4.36.	Final Neolithic incised, medium to fine pottery: **4/27**
4.37.	Final Neolithic incised, medium to fine pottery: **4/28**
4.38.	Final Neolithic utility forms, medium to coarse: **4/29**
4.39.	Final Neolithic utility forms, medium to coarse: **4/30**
4.40.	Final Neolithic utility forms, medium to coarse: **4/31**
4.41.	Final Neolithic utility forms, medium to coarse: **4/32**
4.42.	Final Neolithic miscellaneous (spindlewhorl, bead, or button): **4/33**
4.43.	Early Bronze Age decorated fine pottery: **4/34**
4.44.	Early Bronze Age decorated fine pottery: **4/35**
4.45.	Early Bronze Age monochrome bowls, medium to large sized: **4/36**
4.46.	Early Bronze Age monochrome bowls, medium to large sized: **4/37**
4.47.	Early Bronze Age monochrome bowls, medium to large sized: **4/38**
4.48.	Early Bronze Age monochrome bowls, medium to large sized: **4/39**
4.49.	Early Bronze Age monochrome bowls, medium to large sized: **4/40**
4.50.	Early Bronze Age monochrome bowls, medium to large sized: **4/41**

4.51.	Early Bronze Age monochrome bowls, medium to large sized: **4/42**
4.52.	Early Bronze Age small open vessels: **4/43**
4.53.	Early Bronze Age small open vessels: **4/44**
4.54.	Early Bronze Age small open vessels: **4/45**
4.55.	Early Bronze Age small open vessels: **4/46**
4.56.	Early Bronze Age small open vessels: **4/47**
4.57.	Early Bronze Age closed vessels, fine to medium: **4/48**
4.58.	Early Bronze Age closed vessels, fine to medium: **4/49**
4.59.	Early Bronze Age storage containers, medium-fine to coarse: **4/50**
4.60.	Early Bronze Age storage containers, medium-fine to coarse: **4/51**
4.61.	Early Bronze Age storage containers, medium-fine to coarse: **4/52**
4.62.	Early Bronze Age storage containers, medium-fine to coarse: **4/53**
4.63.	Early Bronze Age storage containers, medium-fine to coarse: **4/54**
4.64.	Early Bronze Age cooking/utility forms: **4/55**
4.65.	Early Bronze Age cooking/utility forms: **4/56**
4.66.	Early Bronze Age cooking/utility forms: **4/57**
4.67.	Early Bronze Age cooking/utility forms: **4/58**
4.68.	Early Bronze Age cooking/utility forms: **4/59**
4.69.	Early Bronze Age cooking/utility forms: **4/60**
5.1.	Middle Bronze Age Minyan/Imitation Minyan, closed vessels: **5/1, 5/2**
5.2.	Middle Bronze Age Minyan/Imitation Minyan, closed vessels: **5/3**
5.3.	Middle Bronze Age Minyan/Imitation Minyan, closed vessels: **5/4, 5/5**
5.4.	Middle Bronze Age Minyan/Imitation Minyan, closed vessels: **5/6, 5/7**
5.5.	Middle Bronze Age Minyan/Imitation Minyan, open vessels: **5/8**
5.6.	Middle Bronze Age Minyan/Imitation Minyan, open vessels: **5/9, 5/10**
5.7.	Middle Bronze Age Minyan/Imitation Minyan, open vessels: **5/11, 5/12**
5.8.	Middle Bronze Age Minyan/Imitation Minyan, open vessels: **5/13, 5/14**
5.9.	Middle Bronze Age Minyan/Imitation Minyan, open vessels: **5/15, 5/16**
5.10.	Middle Bronze Age Minyan/Imitation Minyan, open vessels: **5/17, 5/18**
5.11.	Middle Bronze Age–Late Bronze Age, handmade, closed vessels: **5/19, 5/20, 5/21**
5.12.	Middle Bronze Age–Late Bronze Age, handmade, closed vessels: **5/22**
5.13.	Middle Bronze Age–Late Bronze Age, handmade, closed vessels: **5/23**
5.14.	Middle Bronze Age–Late Bronze Age, handmade, open vessels: **5/24, 5/25**
5.15.	Middle Bronze Age–Late Bronze Age, handmade, open vessels: **5/26, 5/27**
5.16.	Middle Bronze Age–Late Bronze Age, handmade, open vessels: **5/28, 5/29**
5.17.	Late Bronze Age Mycenaean, closed vessels: **5/30, 5/31, 5/32**
5.18.	Late Bronze Age Mycenaean kylikes
5.19.	Late Bronze Age Mycenaean kylikes: **5/33, 5/34, 5/35**
5.20.	Late Bronze Age Mycenaean kylikes: **5/36, 5/3, 5/38**
5.21.	Late Bronze Age Mycenaean, other open vessels: **5/39, 5/40**
5.22.	Late Bronze Age Mycenaean, other open vessels: **5/41, 5/42**
5.23.	Late Bronze Age Mycenaean, other open vessels: **5/43, 5/44, 5/45**
5.24.	Late Bronze Age–Early Iron Age matt-painted, closed vessels: **5/46, 5/47**
5.25.	Late Bronze Age–Early Iron Age matt-painted, closed vessels: **5/48, 5/49, 5/50**
5.26.	Late Bronze Age–Early Iron Age matt-painted, open vessels: **5/51, 5/52, 5/53**
5.27.	Late Bronze Age–Early Iron Age matt-painted, open vessels: **5/54, 5/55, 5/56**
6.1.	Ancient Methone: The acropolis area
6.2.	Methone Plot 245: Tombs 1–18
6.3.	Methone West Hill (acropolis): Plot 229, Tomb 3, with inset of Tombs 4–9
6.4.	Methone Plot 245, Tomb 1
6.5.	Plot 245, Tomb 1: **6/1**, alabastron; **6/2**, alabastron, straight-sided; **6/3**, handmade footed kantharos

6.6.	Plot 245, Tomb 1: **6/4**, handmade matt-painted jar; **6/5**, bronze pin; **6/6α–δ**, **6/7**, beads of bone, glass, and bronze; **6/6α**; **6/6δ**; **6/7**
6.7.	Methone Plot 245, Tomb 2; **6/8**, bronze knife
6.8.	Methone Plot 245, Tomb 3: **6/8**, bronze knife; **6/9**, straight-sided alabastron; bone pins: **6/10α**, **6/10β**, **6/10γ**, **6/10α–6/10γ**, **6/11**
6.9.	Methone Plot 245, Tomb 4
6.10.	Methone Plot 245, Tomb 5
6.11.	Plot 245, Tomb 5: **6/12**, rounded alabastron; **6/13**, rounded alabastron; **6/14**, rounded alabastron; **6/15**, handmade jar
6.12.	Plot 245, Tomb 5: **6/16**, bronze pin (*Rollenkopfnadel*); **6/17**, bronze pin/needle; **6/16** and **6/17**, bronze needle/pin; **6/18α** and **6/18β**, bronze spiral rings; **6/19α**, **6/19β**, **6/19γ**, spindlewhorls, beads, or buttons.
6.13.	Plot 245, Tomb 5: **6/20α**, amber bead; **6/20β**, amber bead; **6/20α** and **6/20β**, amber beads; **6/21**, necklace of glass and stone beads; showing additional beads and fragments
6.14.	Plot 245, Tomb 6: **6/24**, small handmade cup or jar
6.15.	Methone Plot 245, Tomb 7: **6/25α–β**, bronze spiral rings; **6/26**, bone pin.
6.16.	Methone Plot 245, Tombs 7 and 8: **6/27**, small handmade vessel with feeding spout (*thelastron*)
6.17.	Methone Plot 245, Tomb 9: **6/28**, amphoriskos; **6/29**, alabastron
6.18.	Methone Plot 245, Tomb 9: **6/30**, rounded alabastron; **6/31**, bone pin.
6.19.	Methone Plot 245, Tomb 10
6.20.	Methone Plot 245, Tomb 11: **6/32**, bronze ring (earring?)
6.21.	Methone Plot 245, Tomb 12: **6/33**; **6/34**, two spindlewhorls, beads, or buttons
6.22.	Methone Plot 245, Tomb 13: **6/35**, one-handled cup
6.23.	Methone Plot 245, Tomb 14
6.24.	Methone Plot 245, Tomb 15: **6/36**, amphoriskos
6.25.	Methone Plot 245, Tomb 16
6.26.	Plot 245, Tomb 16: **6/37**, handmade kantharos with spur handles; **6/38α**, blue glass bead; **6/38β**, opaque white bead; **6/38γ**, small bronze spiral; **6/39**, bronze knife fragment
6.27.	Methone Plot 245, Tomb 17: **6/40**, small handleless jar
6.28.	Methone Plot 245, Tomb 18: **6/41**, small handleless jar
6.29.	Methone Plot 245, Tomb 18: **6/42**, bronze pin frr; **6/43α**; **6/43β**; **6/43γ**; **6/44**
6.30.	Methone Plot 229, Tomb 1
6.31.	Methone Plot 229, Tomb 3
6.32.	Methone Plot 229, Tomb 4
6.33.	Methone Plot 229, Tomb 4: **6/45**, rounded alabastron; **6/46**, amphoriskos; **6/47**, bronze knife; **6/48** bone pin
6.34.	Methone Plot 229, Tombs 5, 6 and 7
6.35.	Methone Plot 229, Tomb 8: **6/49** (ΜΕΘ 4068), handmade jar or amphora; d) **6/50**, clay spindlewhorl, bead, or button
6.36.	Methone Plot 229, Tomb 10
6.37.	Methone Plot 229, Tomb 10: **6/51**, small handleless jar; **6/52**, small handleless jar; **6/53**, small banded handleless jar
6.38.	Methone Plot 229, Tomb 10: **6/54**, rounded alabastron; **6/55**, local handmade alabastron
6.39.	Methone Plot 229, Tomb 10: **6/56**, north Aegean handmade jug with cutaway neck; small finds
6.40.	Methone Plot 229, Tomb 10: **6/57**, bone pin; **6/58**, bone pin; clay spindlewhorls, beads, or buttons; **6/59**; **6/60**; **6/61**; **6/62**; **6/63**; **6/64**; **6/65**, bronze spiral ring

6.41.	Methone Plot 229, Tomb 10 **6/66**, amber bead; **6/67α**, gold coiled wire bead; **6/67β**, gold coiled wire bead; **6/67γ**, sardonyx/carnelian bead; **6/67δ**, sardonyx/carnelian bead
6.42.	Methone Plot 229, Tomb 10: **6/67ζ**, amber bead; **6/67η**, amber bead; **6/67θ**, amber bead
6.43.	Methone Plot 229, Tomb 10: **6/68α**; **6/68β**, pair of gold wire earrings
6.44.	Methone, West Hill (unstratified): **6/69**, gold pendant ornament; **6/70**, sardonyx/carnelian bead
6.45.	Chronological distribution of calibrated dates indicating absolute chronology
7.1.	Wheelmade and painted closed vessels: **7/1, 7/2**
7.2.	Wheelmade and painted closed vessels: **7/3, 7/4**
7.3.	Wheelmade and painted closed vessel: **7/5**
7.4.	Wheelmade and painted closed vessels: **7/6, 7/7, 7/8**
7.5.	Wheelmade and painted closed vessels: **7/9, 7/10**
7.6.	Wheelmade and painted closed vessels: **7/11, 7/12**
7.7.	Wheelmade and painted open vessels: **7/13, 7/14, 7/15, 7/16, 7/17**
7.8.	Wheelmade and painted open vessels: **7/18, 7/19**
7.9.	Wheelmade and painted open vessels: **7/20, 7/21**
7.10.	Handmade burnished closed vessels: **7/22, 7/23, 7/24**
7.11.	Handmade burnished closed vessels: **7/25, 7/26**
7.12.	Handmade burnished closed vessels: **7/27, 7/28**
7.13.	Handmade burnished open vessels: **7/29, 7/30**
7.14.	Handmade burnished open vessels: **7/31, 7/32, 7/33**
7.15.	Handmade burnished open vessels: **7/34, 7/35, 7/36**
7.16.	Handmade burnished open vessels: **7/37, 7/38**
7.17.	Handmade burnished open vessels: **7/39, 7/40**
7.18.	Handmade burnished open vessels: **7/41, 7/42**
7.19.	Handmade burnished open vessels: **7/43, 7/44, 7/45**
7.20.	Handmade burnished open vessel: **7/46**
7.21.	Handmade burnished open vessels: **7/47, 7/48, 7/49**
7.22.	Fragments with incised decoration: **7/50, 7/51**
7.23.	Miscellaneous, sieves/strainers: **7/52, 7/53**
7.24.	Miscellaneous, terracotta burnisher: **7/54**
7.25.	Cooking pottery: **7/55, 7/56**
7.26.	Cooking pottery, tripod legs: **7/57, 7/58**
7.27.	Pithos fragments: **7/59, 7/60**
8.1.	Map showing the settlements of ancient Methone and "Macedonian Methone"
8.2.	The site of ancient Methone from the northwest
8.3.	Plan of the summit of the East Hill
8.4.	The Hypogeion during excavation
8.5.	The Hypogeion: traces of wooden beams in a layer of greenish clay
8.6.	Hypogeion: beam imprint in the northeast corner
8.7.	Stratigraphic section of the Hypogeion
8.8.	The Hypogeion floor
8.9.	Hypogeion, Phase I
8.10.	Hypogeion, Phase I
8.11.	Hypogeion stratigraphy of Phase I
8.12.	Hypogeion, Phase II
8.13.	Hypogeion, Phase II
8.14.	Hypogeion, Phase III
8.15.	Hypogeion, Phase III
8.16.	Plan of wall T.14, as found within the area of the Hypogeion

8.17.	Wall T.14 from the north and south sides
8.18.	Hypogeion, wall T.5 from the north side
8.19.	Hypogeion, detail, from the north
9.1.	Attic MG II amphora body fr, **9/1**; Euboian LG I skyphos rim fr, **9/2**; Euboian LG I skyphos, **9/3**
9.2.	Fragmentary Euboian skyphoi, **9/4**, **9/5**, **9/6** (the cup of Hakesandros)
9.3.	Fragmentary Corinthian kotylai, **9/7**, **9/8**, **9/9**, **9/10**
9.4.	Fragmentary Corinthian kotylai, **9/11**, **9/12**, **9/13**
9.5.	Fragmentary Corinthian kotylai, **9/14**, **9/15**, **9/16**, **9/17**
9.6.	Fragments of Thapsos Class skyphoi, **9/18**, **9/19**
9.7.	Fragmentary Corinthian kotylai, **9/20**, **9/21**, **9/22**
9.8.	Complete and fragmentary Corinthian kotylai, **9/23**, **9/24**, **9/25**, **9/26**
9.9.	Fragmentary Corinthian kotylai, **9/27**, **9/28**, **9/29**, **9/30**
9.10.	Fragmentary Corinthian kotylai, **9/31**, **9/32**, **9/33**
9.11.	Fragmentary Corinthinan krater, **9/34**, and fragments of Corinthian lids, **9/35** and **9/36**
9.12.	Fragmentary Attic krater attributed to the Painter or Workshop of Athens 897, **9/37**
9.13.	Fragments of an Attic krater, **9/38**, attributed to the Painter or Workshop of Athens 897
9.14.	Fragmentary krater, **9/39**, stylistically related to the Workshop of the Painter of Athens 897
9.15.	Fragments of krater, **9/40**, stylistically related to the Workshop of the Painter of Athens 897
9.16.	Fragmentary krater, **9/41**, stylistically related to the Attic Lion Painter
9.17.	Fragments of an Attic amphora, **9/42**, and an Attic oinochoe, **9/43**
9.18.	Euboian or Euboian-style open vessels, cup (**9/44**) and skyphoi (**9/45**, **9/46**, **9/47**)
9.19.	Euboian or Euboian-style skyphoi, including conical skyphoi, **9/48**, **9/49**, **9/50**
9.20.	Euboian or Euboian-style skyphoi, including conical skyphoi, **9/51**, **9/52**, **9/53**, **9/54**
9.21.	Euboian or Euboian-style kotyle (**9/55**) and krater (**9/56**)
9.22.	Euboian or Euboian-style krater, **9/57**
9.23.	Fragmentary Euboian or Euboian-style krater, **9/58**
9.24.	Euboian or Euboian-style large skyphos, **9/59**
9.25.	Euboian oinochoe, **9/60**
9.26.	Fragmentary Euboian lid, **9/61**
9.27.	Fragmentary Euboian krater, **9/62**
9.28.	Local waster fragments, **9/63**, and fragmentary local oinochoe (production discard), **9/64**
9.29.	Fragmentary local kotylai, **9/65**, **9/66**, **9/67**
9.30.	Fragmentary local kotylai, **9/68**, **9/69**, **9/70**
9.31.	Fragmentary local skyphoi, **9/71**, **9/72**, **9/73**
9.32.	Fragmentary local skyphoi, **9/74**, **9/75**, **9/76**
9.33.	Local skyphoi, **9/77**, **9/78**, **9/79**
9.34.	Fragmentary local skyphoi, **9/80**, **9/81**, **9/82**
9.35.	Spouted krater, perhaps Euboian, **9/83**
9.36.	Fragmentary spouted krater, likely Euboian, **9/84**
9.37.	Local skyphoi, **9/85**, **9/86**, **9/87**
9.38.	Local skyphoi with tall rims, **9/88**, **9/89**, **9/90**
9.39.	Fragmentary local skyphoi, **9/91**, **9/92**
9.40.	Fragmentary East Greek oinochoai, **9/93**, **9/94**
9.41.	Fragmentary local skyphos, **9/95**

9.42.	Fragmentary base, Corinthian oinochoe, **9/96**
9.43.	Fragmentary Ionian cup (*Knickrandschale*), **9/97**, and base fragment Corinthian spherical aryballos, **9/98**
10.1.	Examples of cutmarks on ribs recovered from Trench 032 of the Hypogeion
10.2.	*Cerastoderma glaucum* shells
10.3.	*Cerastoderma glaucum* artifacts from the Hypogeion
11.1.	Amphora, unknown provenance, **11/1**, ca. 700 B.C.
11.2.	Antekydes amphora, **11/2**, ca. 700 B.C.
11.3.	Drinking cup from the Thermaic Gulf, **11/3**, ca. 700 B.C.; Epige[nes] drinking cup, **11/4**, ca. 730–720 B.C.; Euboian drinking cup, **11/5**, ca. 730–720 B.C.
11.4.	Hakesandros: Euboian drinking cup, **11/6**, ca. 730–720 B.C.
11.5.	Philion mug from Lesbos, **11/7**, ca. 730 B.C.
11.6.	Letter shapes on vessel, **11/1–11/7**
11.7.	Tataie's lekythos from Cumae (Kyme). Protocorinthian aryballos/lekythos
11.8.	The Dipylon oinochoe
11.9.	The inscription on Nestor's cup from Pithekoussai
12.1.	Vintage poster of Carlsberg beer
12.2.	Thermaic amphoras from the Hypogeion
12.3.	The distribution of Thermaic amphoras in the north Aegean and in the Mediterranean
12.4.	Lesbian amphoras from the Hypogeion
12.5.	Samian amphoras from the Hypogeion
12.6.	Chian amphoras from the Hypogeion
12.7.	Milesian amphoras from the Hypogeion
12.8.	Attic SOS amphora from the Hypogeion
12.9.	Euboian SOS amphora from the Hypogeion
12.10.	Corinthian amphoras from the Hypogeion
12.11.	Coated amphoras of indeterminate provenance from the Hypogeion
12.12.	Amphoras of indeterminate provenance from the Hypogeion, with thick lip and undercutting
13.1.	a) Stratigraphic projection of stone macroartifacts from the Hypogeion at Methone (numbers indicate the quantity of lithic macroartifacts in each successive level). b) histogram showing the number of macrolithic objects by depth.
13.2.	Neolithic axe, **13/1**
13.3.	Marble pebble, **13/2**
13.4.	Stone object, **13/3** (ΜΕΘ 606), made from a pyroclastic rock
13.5.	Passive hammering tool, **13/4** (ΜΕΘ 565), made of marble
13.6.	A multifunctional tool, **13/5**
13.7.	Passive hammering tools: **13/6**, **13/7**, both made of amphibolite
13.8.	Marble percussion tool, **13/8**
13.9.	Amphibolite percussion tool, **13/9**
13.10.	Amphibolite percussion tool, **13/10**
13.11.	Quern of coarse-grained material (diorite), **13/11**
13.12.	Polisher/whetstone, **13/12**
13.13.	Clay mass formation containing inclusions of crushed quartz, **13/13**
13.14.	Tools used for the decoration of metal surfaces, **13/14**, **13/15**, **13/16**, **13/17**
13.15.	Fine-grained raw material (of unknown stone), **13/18**
14.1.	Large crucible used for bronze melting and casting
14.2.	Tuyère ends
14.3.	Lost-wax mold of a bronze pendant (so-called "jug stopper"); bronze pendant ("jug-stopper") of unknown provenance; bronze pendant of unknown provenance
14.4.	Lost-wax mold fragment for a biconical bead

14.5.	Gold melting plate
14.6.	Gold melting plate
14.7.	Gold melting plate fragment
14.8.	Gold melting plate with large gold globule and ingot impression
14.9.	Two pieces probably belonging to the same gold ingot, hammered and cut
14.10.	Lower surface of a large gold ingot from the Geometric hoard found in Eretria
14.11.	Small crucible perhaps used for lead melting
15.1.	Bronze pendant, **15/1**
15.2.	Bronze spectacle fibulae, **15/2, 15/3, 15/4, 15/5**
15.3.	Bronze violin-bow fibulae, **15/6, 15/7**
15.4.	Bronze arched fibulae, **15/8, 15/9**
15.5.	Beaded fibula, **15/10**
15.6.	Island fibula with one bead on arch, **15/11**
15.7.	Fibula with decorative element on arch, **15/12**
15.8.	"Phrygian" fibulae, **15/13, 15/14, 15/15**
15.9.	Bronze fibula a navicella, **15/16**
15.10.	Catchplate of bronze fibula, **15/17**
15.11.	Bronze *Rollenkopfnadeln*, **15/18, 15/19, 15/20**
15.12.	Bronze pin with coiled spiral head, **15/21**
15.13.	Bronze *Keulenkopfnadeln* with incised decoration, **15/22**
15.14.	Variant of a *Blattkopfnadel*, **15/23**
15.15.	Bronze pin with small head, **15/24**
15.16.	Bronze pin with beaded head, **15/25**
15.17.	Bronze pins of uncertain type, **15/26, 15/27**
15.18.	Bronze beads, **15/28, 15/29**
15.19.	Bronze finger rings, ear- or hairrings, **15/30, 15/31, 15/32**
15.20.	Bronze *krikoi*, **15/33, 15/34**
15.21.	Bronze spiral ornament, **15/35**
15.22.	Bronze tutuli, **15/36, 15/37, 15/38, 15/39, 15/40**
15.23.	Bronze tutuli, **15/41, 15/42, 15/43**
15.24.	Unidentified bronze object, possible large tutulus, **15/44**
15.25.	Bronze needles, **15/45, 15/46, 15/47**
15.26.	Possible bronze needle rather than attachment, **15/48**
15.27.	Bronze disk (perhaps from pin), **15/49**
15.28.	Bronze chains and related, **15/50, 15/51**
15.29.	Miniature bronze double axe, **15/52**
15.30.	Solid bronze cube, possible weight or ingot, **15/53**
15.31.	Bronze knife, **15/54**
15.32.	Small bronze cone (arrowhead?), **15/55**
15.33.	Bronze clamp/binding sheaths, **15/56**
15.34.	Bronze nails, **15/57, 15/58**
15.35.	Small bronze pin associated with hinged object, **15/59**
15.36.	Bronze hooked object other than fishhook, **15/60**
15.37.	Length of bronze wire, **15/61**
15.38.	Bronze rods, strips, and related, **15/62, 15/63, 15/64**
15.39.	Bronze rods, strips, and related, **15/65, 15/66, 15/67, 15/68, 15/69**
15.40.	Bronze sheet and wider strips of bronze, **15/70, 15/71, 15/72, 15/73, 15/74**
15.41.	Iron spearhead, **15/75**, and iron sockets probably associated with spearheads, **15/76, 15/77**
15.42.	Iron arrowhead, **15/78**
15.43.	Iron blades (larger and smaller knives), **15/79, 15/80, 15/81, 15/82, 15/83**
15.44.	Iron blades (larger and smaller knives), **15/84, 15/85, 15/86**
15.45.	Narrow iron blades (knives), **15/87, 15/88**

15.46.	Iron axes/adzes, **15/89, 15/90**
15.47.	Iron axes/adzes or hammers, and related, **15/91, 15/92**
15.48.	Iron chisels (and related), **15/93, 15/94**
15.49.	Iron chisels (and related), **15/95, 15/96, 15/97**
15.50.	Fragmentary iron metalworker's tongs or poker, **15/98**
15.51.	Related fragmentary iron tongs or poker, **15/99**
15.52.	Athenian black-figure amphora, attributed to the Plousios Painter
15.53.	Iron tack, **15/100**
15.54.	Fragmentary iron wire or iron shaft fragments in the form of spirals and rings, **15/101, 15/102**
15.55.	Iron "fish-shaped" attachment(?), **15/103**
15.56.	Lead fishnet weights, **15/104, 15/105, 15/106**
15.57.	Lead mending clamp, **15/107**, and small length of lead wire, **15/108**
16.1.	Distribution of clay textile artifacts across different levels of the Hypogeion
16.2.	Clay biconical and conical spindlewhorls from the Hypogeion: **16/1, 16/2, 16/3, 16/4, 16/5, 16/6, 16/7, 16/8, 16/9, 16/10, 16/11, 16/12, 16/13, 16/20, 16/22**
16.3.	Discoid, "doughnut," and flat spindlewhorls from the Hypogeion: **16/14, 16/15, 16/16, 16/17, 16/18, 16/19, 16/21, 16/23**
16.4.	Pyramidal and large loomweights (and miscellaneous) from the Hypogeion: **16/24, 16/25, 16/26, 16/27, 16/28, 16/29, 16/30, 16/31, 16/32, 16/33, 16/34**
16.5.	Clay "spools" from the Hypogeion: **16/35, 16/36, 16/37, 16/38, 16/39, 16/40**
16.6.	Hemispherical weights from the Hypogeion: **16/41, 16/42, 16/43, 16/44, 16/45, 16/46, 16/47, 16/48**
17.1.	The context of the catalogued cut sherd disks from the Hypogeion
17.2.	Selected cut sherd disks from the Hypogeion, obverse
17.3.	Selected cut sherd disks from the Hypogeion, reverse

Volume 2

18.1.	Aerial view of Building A and the agora and East Hill as exposed in 2014
18.2.	General plan of the agora of Methone; photogrammetric view of the Ephoreia excavations on the East Hill, generated by drone photography
18.3.	State plan of Building A, showing phases in color
18.4.	View of Building A from the west (2014); view of the 2014 cleaning operations to re-expose Building A
18.5.	Wall 8, Room 6, view from west
18.6.	Wall 18, east, view from northwest
18.7.	Wall 18, west, view from northwest; view from east-northeast of Building A with Wall 18 at the center of the frame
18.8.	Wall 18 and Wall 31, elevation
18.9.	Wall 30/31 cornerstone integrated into Wall 18
18.10.	Lifting boss on stylobate block of Wall 18, southern elevation
18.11.	Doorstep (threshold block) of Wall 18, view from east
18.12.	Doorstep and general threshold space of Wall 18, view from south
18.13.	Detail of Wall 18 with mud bricks in situ; details of mud-brick superstructure (collapsed) from Wall 18 taken at the time of excavation
18.14.	Wall 21, exterior, western elevation
18.15.	Wall 21, western elevation, drawn with phases indicated in color
18.16.	Wall 21, eastern elevation, showing mud-brick interior
18.17.	Wall 12, general view from the west

LIST OF ILLUSTRATIONS

18.18.	Wall 12, northern elevation as viewed from Room 4
18.19.	Wall 12, southern elevation viewed from Room 2
18.20.	Eastern termination of Wall 12, where it meets Wall 8, view from west-southwest
18.21.	The western portion of the main hall of Building A
18.22.	Eastern elevation of Wall 16
18.23.	Detail of Wall 17, view from west
18.24.	Detail of Wall 30, view from the south
18.25.	Wall 31, view from north
18.26.	Wall 8, polygonal section in Room 1, view from west
18.27.	The western elevations of Walls 8 and 9, view from west-northwest
18.28.	The western elevation of Wall 9, with Wall 8 behind, view from west; eastern elevation of Wall 9, view from east
18.29.	Walls 19 and 20, with Wall 18, general view from northwest
18.30.	Detail of the northeast corner of Wall 19, view from north
18.31.	Wall 19, northeast end, detail of transition between orthostate and stylobate, view from north
18.32.	Wall 19, threshold block and stylobate, view from north
18.33.	The western portion of Wall 19, view from north
18.34.	Wall 20, view from west
18.35.	Line of orthogonal stones between Wall 18 and Wall 19, with drain west of Wall 21, view from north
19.1.	Aerial view from west of the West Hill at Methone as uncovered in 2014; 2014 aerial of the West Hill, from south; plan of the building, kilns, and tombs excavated on the West Hill of Methone up to the end of the 2011 season
19.2.	West Hill (Plot 229), kiln 1
19.3.	West Hill (Plot 229), kiln 2
19.4.	Fragmentary locally made krater with Geometric ornament
19.5.	Part of the destruction layer on the West Hill in Sector B, Plot 229
19.6.	Drawing and four views of a Corinthian column krater
19.7.	Corinthian plate
19.8.	Drawing and three views of fragmentary Corinthian aryballos
19.9.	Fragmentary Corinthian alabastron
19.10.	Attic black-figure Siana cup by the Taras Painter
19.11.	Painted amphora from a workshop in the Chalkidike
20.1.	Physical map of northern Greece
20.2.	A young *P. sylvestris* growing out of shade at Sarakatsana, Pieria Mts.
20.3.	Mixed stand of young and mature *P. sylvestris* trees at Sarakatsana, Pieria Mts.
20.4.	Distribution map of Scots pine (*Pinus sylvestris*) in Europe
20.5.	Map of forest coverage of the Rhetine-Vrya forest, Pieria Mts.
20.6.	Map of forest coverage of Pieria Prefecture
21.1.	Chian amphora, **21/1**
21.2.	Chian hydria, **21/2**, and shoulder fr of Chian amphora, **21/3**
21.3.	Milesian amphora, **21/4**
21.4.	Milesian amphora, **21/5**
21.5.	Lesbian amphora, **21/6**
21.6.	Lesbian amphora, **21/7**
21.7.	Euboian(?) SOS amphora, **21/8**, and SOS amphora *à la brosse*, **21/9**
21.8.	Corinthian amphora, **21/10**
21.9.	Lakonian amphora, **21/11**
21.10.	Local amphora, **21/12**
21.11.	Local amphora, **21/13**
22.1.	Two grayware jugs, **22/1**, **22/2**
22.2.	Selection of grayware fragments of closed vessels, **22/3**, **22/4**, **22/5**, **22/6**

LIST OF ILLUSTRATIONS

22.3.	Selected grayware base fragments, **22/7, 22/8, 22/9**
22.4.	Selected grayware skyphoi/bowls, **22/10, 22/11, 22/12, 22/13**
22.5.	Grayware lekanis, **22/14**
22.6.	Grayware lekanides, **22/15, 22/16**
22.7.	Grayware open vessels, **22/17, 22/18**
22.8.	Grayware open vessels, **22/19, 22/20**
22.9.	Bucchero alabastron, **22/21**
22.10.	Distribution of north Ionian bird kotylai fragments across different levels of the Hypogeion; two north Ionian bird oinochoai from the Hypogeion; c) North Ionian bird kotyle from the agora at Methone
22.11.	The cup of Nestor from Pithekoussai
22.12.	North Ionian bird kotyle, **22/22**
22.13.	North Ionian bird kotyle, **22/23**
22.14.	North Ionian bird kotyle, **22/24**
22.15.	North Ionian bird kotylai, **22/25, 22/26**
22.16.	North Ionian bird kotylai, **22/27, 22/28**
22.17.	North Ionian bird kotylai, **22/29, 22/30, 22/31**
22.18.	Fragmentary North Ionian bird kotyle, **22/32**
22.19.	Fragmentary North Ionian bird kotylai, **22/33, 22/34**
22.20.	Fragments of North Ionian bird bowls, **22/35, 22/36**
22.21.	Early Chian chalice (πρωτο-κάλυκας) **22/37**
22.22.	Fragments of Chian chalices from the West Hill, **22/38, 22/39**
22.23.	Fragment of Milesian bowl ("fruit stand"), **22/40**
22.24.	Athenian banded cups, Class of Athens 1104, **22/41, 22/42**
22.25.	East Greek (South Ionian) kylikes/cups, **22/43, 22/44, 22/45**
22.26.	Athenian banded cup, Class of Athens 1104, **22/46**
22.27.	Large East Greek *Knickrandschale* **22/47**
22.28.	East Greek (South Ionian) kylikes/cups, **22/48, 22/49**
22.29.	East Greek (South Ionian) kylikes/cups, **22/50, 22/51**, and East-Greek style cup, perhaps of north Aegean manufacture, **22/52**.
22.30.	"Samian" lekythos, **22/53**
23.1.	Handle plate fragment, Attic black-figure column krater, **23/1**
23.2.	Body and rim fragments, Attic black-figure Siana cup, **23/2**
23.3.	Fragmentary Attic black-figure Little Master band cup, **23/3**
23.4.	Foot and tondo fragment, Attic black-figure stemless cup, **23/4**
23.5.	Fragmentary body, Attic black-figure kylix, **23/5**
23.6.	Body fragment, Attic black-figure closed pouring vessel (olpe?), **23/6**
23.7.	Fragmentary Attic black-figure skyphos, **23/7**
23.8.	Body fragment, Attic red-figure krater, **23/8**; base/tondo fragment, Attic red-figure stemless cup, **23/9**; body fragment, Attic red-figure uncertain, **23/10**
23.9.	Rim fragment, Attic red-figure calyx krater, **23/11**
23.10.	Spouted head fragment, Attic red-figure askos, **23/12**
23.11.	Fragmentary Attic red-figure bell krater, **23/13**
23.12.	Lid fragment, Attic red-figure lekanis, **23/14**
23.13.	Fragmentary Attic red-figure pelike, **23/15**
23.14.	Attic red-figure miniature squat lekythos, **23/16**
23.15.	Attic red-figure cup, **23/17**
23.16.	Attic red-figure cup, **23/17**
24.1.	Attic black-gloss lamps, Type 16 B, from the area of the agora, **24/1, 24/2, 24/3**
24.2.	Attic black-gloss lamps from the area of the agora, **24/4, 24/5**
24.3.	Attic black-gloss lamp from the area of the agora, **24/6**
24.4.	Additional fragments of Attic BG lamps from the area of the agora
24.5.	Non-Attic black-gloss lamp from the area of the agora, **24/7**

LIST OF ILLUSTRATIONS xxxi

24.6. Non-Attic black-gloss lamps from the area of the agora, **24/8**, **24/9**
24.7. Corinthian Type II lamp from the area of the agora, **24/10**
24.8. Corinthian Type II lamp from the area of the agora, **24/11**
24.9. Lamps made of semi-fine local fabric from the area of the agora, **24/12**, **24/13**
24.10. Lamp made of semi-fine local fabric from the area of the agora, **24/14**
24.11. Lamps from the area south of the East Hill, **24/15**, **24/16**
25.1. The agora area of Methone showing the findspots of aqua glass poppy beads and aqua glass rods
25.2. Pulling a mass of glass to make a twisted rod
25.3. Making the ribs on a poppy bead
25.4. Core-formed glass vessels from the Hypogeion, **25/1**, **25/2**
25.5. Glass eye beads from the Hypogeion, **25/3–25/8**
25.6. Plain glass beads from the Hypogeion, **25/9–25/11**
25.7. Core-formed glass vessels from the agora, **25/14–25/17**
25.8. Core-formed glass vessels from the agora, **25/18–25/25**
25.9. Core-formed glass vessels from the agora, **25/26–25/32**
25.10. Core-formed glass vessels from the agora, **25/33–25/38**
25.11. Core-formed glass vessels from the agora, **25/39–25/42**, **25/44–25/47**
25.12. Blown-glass vessels from the agora, **25/48–25/51**
25.13. Modern glass vessel, **25/52**, decorated glass poppy bead, **25/53**, and glass poppy beads, **25/54**, **25/55**, all from the agora
25.14. Glass poppy beads from the agora, **25/56–25/63**
25.15. Glass poppy beads from the agora, **25/64–25/71**
25.16. Glass poppy beads from the agora, **25/72–25/77**
25.17. Glass poppy beads from the agora, **25/78–25/85**
25.18. Glass poppy beads from the agora, **25/86–25/93**, **25/95**
25.19. Glass eye bead from the agora, **25/96**
25.20. Glass eye beads from the agora, **25/97–25/99**
25.21. Glass eye bead, **25/100**, decorated glass bead, **25/101**, plain glass beads, **25/102–25/104**, from the agora
25.22. Plain glass beads from the agora, **25/105–25/108**
25.23. Plain glass beads from the agora, **25/109–25/111**
25.24. Glass rods, **25/112–25/114**
25.25. Glass gem from the agora, **25/115**
25.26. Remnants of glass object from the agora, **25/117**
25.27. Core-formed glass vessels, **25/120**, **25/121**, glass poppy bead, **25/122**, plain glass bead, **25/123**
25.28. Plain glass beads from the acropolis, **25/124–25/128**
25.29. Faience objects from Methone, **25/129**, **25/130**, and rock crystal, **25/131**
25.30. Ternary diagram of Methone glass compared with bibliographical data
25.31. Methone samples against samples of contemporary glass (in general) and glass beads
25.32. 6th–2nd century B.C. glass in general; 8th–4th century B.C. glass from Methone; Pikrolimni natron
26.1. West Hill bronze pendant, **26/1**
26.2. West Hill bronze pendant, **26/2**
26.3. West Hill bronze fibulae, arched fibula **26/3**, "Phrygian" fibula **26/4**
26.4. West Hill bronze fibulae a navicella, **26/5**, **26/6**
26.5. West Hill bronze dress pins, *Rollenkopfnadeln*, **26/7**, **26/8**, fragmentary double pin **26/9**
26.6. West Hill bronze bead, **26/10**, bronze rings/*krikoi*, **26/1**), **26/12**
26.7. Various bronze implements from the West Hill: cheese grater **26/13**, needle(?) **26/14**, nail **26/15**

26.8.	West Hill bronze rods, strips, and wire, **26/16**, **26/17**, **26/18**, **26/19**
26.9.	West Hill bronze sheet, **26/20**, **26/21**
26.10.	West Hill bronze arrowheads, **26/22**, **26/23**, **26/24**, **26/25**; bronze cone, **26/26**
26.11.	West Hill iron knife, **26/27**; iron axe/adze/hoe, **26/28**
26.12.	West Hill iron chisels, **26/29**, **26/30**
26.13.	West Hill large iron nail, **26/31**, iron axe pendant, **26/32**
26.14.	West Hill fragmentary iron obelos, **26/33**
26.15.	West Hill lead fishnet weight, **26/34**; uncertain lead object, possible mending clamp/plug, **26/35**
26.16.	West Hill lead rod, **26/36**, lead disks, **26/37**, **26/38** (ΜΕΘ 4965)
26.17.	West Hill unidentified domed object, **26/39**; lead "branch" for the casting of lead sling bullets, **26/40**
26.18.	Acropolis east slope bronze pendants, **26/41**, **26/42**
26.19.	Acropolis east slope bronze fibulae: fragmentary spectacle fibula, **26/43**, arched fibula, **26/44**, "Phrygian" fibulae, **26/45**, **26/46**
26.20.	Acropolis east slope bronzes: tutulus/small boss, **26/47**; cheese grater, **26/48**; nails/tacks, **26/49**, **26/50**
26.21.	Acropolis east slope large iron nail, **26/51**
26.22.	Acropolis east slope lead objects: large mending clamp, **26/52**; mending plug/clamp, **26/53**; small bead, button, or weight, **26/54**
26.23.	Agora bronze fibulae, violin-bow fibula, **26/55**; pin and spring of large fibula, **26/56**
26.24.	Agora bronze "Phrygian" fibulae, **26/57**, **26/58**, **26/59**, **26/60**
26.25.	Agora bronze "Phrygian" fibulae, **26/61**, **26/62**, **26/63**, **26/64**
26.26.	Agora bronze "Phrygian" fibulae, **26/65**, **26/66**, **26/67**
26.27.	Agora bronze dress pins, *Rollenkopfnadeln*, **26/68**, **26/69**; knot-headed pins, **26/70**, **26/71**
26.28.	Agora bronze pins, ribbed-head pins, **26/72**, **26/73**; pin with beaded head, **26/74**
26.29.	Agora bronze pins, pin with flattened head, **26/75**, poppy- or pomegranate-headed pin, **26/76**
26.30.	Agora bronze double pins, **26/77**, **26/78**
26.31.	Agora bronze finials for pins, **26/79**, **26/80**; shafts of bronze pins (or needles), **26/81**, **26/82** (ΜΕΘ 2143)
26.32.	Agora bronze beads, **26/83**, **26/84**, **26/85**, **26/86**, **26/87**
26.33.	Agora bronze finger rings: plain finger rings, **26/88**, **26/89**; finger rings with bezels, **26/90**, **26/91**, **26/92**
26.34.	Agora bronze earrings/hairrings, **26/93**, **26/94**, **26/95**
26.35.	Agora bronze rings (*krikoi*), **26/96**), **26/97**, **26/98**, **26/99**
26.36.	Agora bronze bracelets, **26/100**, **26/101**, **26/102**, **26/103**
26.37.	Agora bronze tutuli, **26/104**, **26/105**, **26/106**
26.38.	Agora bronze musical instrument, bronze terminal for wind instrument, **26/107**; related, **26/108**
26.39.	Agora fragmentary bronze vessels: tripod stand with feline leg, **26/109**; rim fragment of small phiale, **26/110**; decorative roundel for vessel, **26/111**
26.40.	Agora, various bronze implements: cheese grater, **26/112**); ear spoons, **26/113**, **26/114**; spatulate implement/instrument **26/115**
26.41.	Agora bronze needles, **26/116**, **26/117**, **26/118**, **26/119**, **26/120**
26.42.	Agora bronze spindle hook, **26/121**; bronze cones, **26/122**; **26/123**; **26/124**; **26/125**; **26/126**
26.43.	Agora bronze fishhooks, **26/127**, **26/128**, **26/129**, **26/130**, **26/131**; bronze knife, **26/132**

LIST OF ILLUSTRATIONS

xxxiii

26.44. Agora bronze nails, **26/133**, **26/134**, **26/135**, **26/136**, **26/137**, **26/138**
26.45. Agora bronze nails and tacks, **26/139**, **26/140**, **26/141**, **26/142**, **26/143**, **26/144**; tacks, **26/145**, **26/146** (ΜΕΘ 1692)
26.46. Agora bronze T-staples, **26/147**, **26/148**, **26/149**; bronze bindings/sheaths, **26/150**, **26/151**, **26/152**
26.47. Agora bronze binding plates, **26/153**, **26/154**, **26/155**, **26/156**, **26/157**, **26/158**
26.48. Agora bronze disks, **26/159**, **26/160**, **26/161**; bronze sheet, **26/162**, **26/163**, **26/164**, **26/165**, **26/166**
26.49. Agora bronze rods and related, **26/167**, **26/168**, **26/169**
26.50. Agora bronze varia: hinged objects, **26/170**, **26/171**; wedge-shaped object, **26/172**; attachment (decorative rivet), **26/173**; folded sheet/small tube, **26/174**
26.51. Agora bronze arrowheads, **26/175**, **26/176**, **26/177**, **26/178**, **26/179**, **26/180**, **26/181**, **26/182**
26.52. Agora iron arrowheads, **26/183**, **26/184**, **26/185**, **26/186**, **26/187**
26.53. Agora iron spearheads, **26/188**, **26/189**; sauroter, **26/190**
26.54. Agora iron swords, **26/191**, **26/192**
26.55. Agora iron tools/implements: knife, **26/193**; large sickle/scythe, or pruning hook, **26/194**; tongs/poker fragment, **26/195**
26.56. Agora large iron scraper, **26/196**, and a modern tool of similar form and size, from the excavations at Pylos
26.57. Agora iron rings (*krikoi*) and related, **26/197**, **26/198**; iron nails, **26/199**, **26/200**, **26/201**, **26/202**
26.58. Agora iron cylinder/tube segment, **26/203**; iron attachment(?), **26/204**
26.59. Agora lead mending clamps, **26/205**, **26/206**, **26/207**, **26/208**, **26/209**, **26/210**), **26/211**
26.60. Agora lead weights, **26/212**, **26/213**, **26/214**; related, **26/215**
26.61. Agora lead wheel, **26/216**; lead sheet, **26/217**, **26/218**
26.62. Agora lead sheet (continued), **26/219**, **26/220**, **26/221**, **26/222**
26.63. Agora rods and strips of lead, **26/223**, **26/224**, **26/225**; globular piece of lead (ingot?), **26/226**
26.64. Agora lead filling, **26/227**; amorphous lead, **26/228**
26.65. Agora amorphous lead (continued), **26/229**, **26/230**
26.66. South harbor area, bronze fishhook, **26/231**; bronze triangular object, **26/232**; iron nail, **26/233**
27.1.   Stone mold ΤΣ 1080, made of micrite fossiliferous limestone
27.2.   ΤΣ 1080 showing the perimeter groove on all four vertical sides
27.3.   Primary surface of ΤΣ 1080
27.4.   ΤΣ 1080
27.5.   Details of the primary surface of ΤΣ 1080
27.6.   The secondary surface of the mold ΤΣ 1080
27.7.   Detail of the top right corner of the secondary surface of ΤΣ 1080
27.8.   Detail of the upper central portion of ΤΣ 1080
27.9.   Detail of the lower central portion of ΤΣ 1080
27.10. Two parallel incisions, running diagonally, visible on the vertical surface B of both halves of ΤΣ 1080
27.11. Detail of vertical face C of ΤΣ 1080
27.12. Detail of mark in the form of the letter "A" on side A of the lower block of ΤΣ 1080
27.13. Closer details of side A of ΤΣ 1080
27.14. Detail of the carved decoration on the primary surface of ΤΣ 1080.
27.15. Modern figure-of-eight-shaped fibula made from rubber copy of ΤΣ 1080

27.16.	Initial X-ray testing of ΤΣ 1080 in 2005
27.17.	Top-view scan of ΤΣ 1080 in 2019
27.18.	Scan of vertical face C showing the small depression *m*
27.19.	Vertical scan of ΤΣ 1080
27.20.	Vertical scan of ΤΣ 1080 showing perforation *k*
27.21.	Detail of the circlets of the decorative register of the large disk and in the depression at the center of the disk of ΤΣ 1080 showing traces of metal estimated to be silver oxides
27.22.	Detail showing traces of unidentified metal, on the perimeter of the tear-shaped depression on ΤΣ 1080
27.23.	Detail of ΤΣ 1080 showing grains of unidentified metal, in the depressions/funnel A2
27.24.	Two alternative methods of the use of the mold ΤΣ 1080
27.25.	Pyramidal stone mold ΤΣ 1081
27.26.	ΤΣ 1081
27.27.	One of the primary carved horizontal surfaces of ΤΣ 1081
27.28.	Some of the modern jewelry made on the basis of the stone mold ΤΣ 1081
27.29.	Additional modern jewelry made on the basis of ΤΣ 1081
27.30.	Two rectangular lateral surfaces of ΤΣ 1081 bearing discoid patterns
27.31.	Lateral view of ΤΣ 1081
27.32.	View and detail of one of the vertical triangular surfaces of ΤΣ 1081
27.33.	The other vertical triangular surface of ΤΣ 1081
27.34.	View of the primary surface of the stone mold ΤΣ 1082
27.35.	Mold ΤΣ 1082
27.36.	Modern pins made on the basis of the mold ΤΣ 1082
27.37.	The secondary surface of ΤΣ 1082
27.38.	Detail of assorted localized incisions
28.1.	Inscribed lead sling bullets: Μερ|να( )? *vel* Να|μερ( ), **28/1, 28/2, 28/3, 28/4, 28/5**
28.2.	Inscribed lead sling bullets: Μερ|να( )? *vel* Να|μερ( ), **28/6, 28/7, 28/8, 28/9, 28/10, 28/11**
28.3.	Inscribed lead sling bullets: Μερ|να( )? *vel* Να|μερ( ), **28/12, 28/13, 28/14, 28/15), 28/16**
28.4.	Inscribed lead sling bullets: Μερ|να( )? *vel* Να|μερ( ), **28/17, 28/18, 28/19, 28/20, 28/21**
28.5.	Inscribed lead sling bullets: Μερ|να( )? *vel* Να|μερ( ), **28/22, 28/23, 28/24, 28/25, 28/26**
28.6.	Inscribed lead sling bullets: Μερ|να( )? *vel* Να|μερ( ), **28/27, 28/28, 28/29, 28/30, 28/31**
28.7.	Inscribed lead sling bullets: Μερ|να( )? *vel* Να|μερ( ), **28/32, 28/33, 28/34, 28/35, 28/36**
28.8.	Inscribed lead sling bullets: Μικινα, **28/37, 28/38, 28/39 28/40, 28/41**
28.9.	Inscribed lead sling bullets: Μικινα, **28/42, 28/43, 28/44, 28/45**
28.10.	Inscribed lead sling bullets: Μικινα, **28/46, 28/47, 28/48, 28/49**
28.11.	Inscribed lead sling bullets: Μικινα, **28/50, 28/51, 28/52, 28/53**
28.12.	Inscribed lead sling bullets: Μικινα, **28/54, 28/55, 28/56, 28/57**
28.13.	Inscribed lead sling bullets: Κλεοβουλο̄, **28/58, 28/59, 28/60, 28/61**
28.14.	Cluster of inscribed lead sling bullets: Ευγενεος, **28/62**
28.15.	Inscribed lead sling bullets: Ευγενεος, **28/63, 28/64, 28/65**
28.16.	Originally uninscribed lead sling bullet with graffito, **28/66**
28.17.	Uninscribed lead sling bullets, **28/67, 28/68, 28/69, 28/70, 28/71, 28/72**
28.18.	Uninscribed lead sling bullets, **28/73, 28/74, 28/75, 28/76, 28/77, 28/78, 28/79**

28.19.	Uninscribed lead sling bullets, **28/80**, **28/81**, **28/82**, **28/83**, **28/84**, **28/85**, **28/86**
28.20.	Uninscribed lead sling bullets, **28/87**, **28/88**, **28/89**, **28/90**, **28/91**, **28/92**, **28/93**
28.21.	Uninscribed lead sling bullets, **28/94**, **28/95**, **28/96**, **28/97**, **28/98**, **28/99**
28.22.	Uninscribed lead sling bullets, **28/100**, **28/101**, **28/102**, **28/103**, **28/104**, **28/105**
28.23.	Inscribed bronze catapult bolt: ΦΙΛΙΠΠŌ, **28/106**
29.1.	Plan of the ancient agora of Methone
29.2.	Building A from west
29.3.	Building B from southwest
29.4.	BG bowl with incurving rim, **29/1**
29.5.	BG bowl with incurving rim, **29/2**
29.6.	BG bowl with incurving rim, **29/3**
29.7.	BG bowl with incurving rim (later and light), **29/4**
29.8.	BG bowl with incurving rim (later and light), **29/5**
29.9.	BG bowl with rounded rim, **29/6**
29.10.	BG bowl with incurving rim, **29/7**
29.11.	BG bowl with incurving rim, **29/8**
29.12.	BG bowl with incurving rim, **29/9**
29.13.	BG bowl with incurving rim (footed saltcellar), **29/10**
29.14.	BG bowl with incurving rim (footed saltcellar), **29/11**
29.15.	BG bowl with incurving rim (footed saltcellar), **29/12**
29.16.	BG bowl with outturned rim, **29/13**
29.17.	BG Attic-type skyphos, Type A, **29/14**
29.18.	BG Attic-type skyphos, Type A, **29/15**
29.19.	BG Attic-type skyphos, Type A, **29/16**
29.20.	BG plate with rolled rim, **29/17**
29.21.	Glazed plate with rolled rim, **29/18**
29.22.	BG plate with rilled rim, **29/19**
29.23.	BG fish plate, **29/20**
29.24.	BG fish plate, **29/21**
29.25.	BG one-handler, **29/22**
29.26.	BG one-handler, **29/23**
29.27.	Glazed one-handler, **29/24**
29.28.	BG saltcellar with concave wall, **29/25**
29.29.	BG saltcellar with concave wall, **29/26**
29.30.	BG saltcellar with concave wall, **29/27**
29.31.	BG saltcellar with concave wall, **29/28**
29.32.	BG saltcellar with concave wall, **29/29**
29.33.	BG bolsal, **29/30**
29.34.	BG bolsal, **29/31**
29.35.	BG bolsal, **29/32**
29.36.	RF askos, shallow type, **29/33**
29.37.	BG askos, shallow type, **29/34**
29.38.	Black painted lidded lekanis with ribbon handles, **29/35**
29.39.	BG lidded lekanis with horizontal handles, **29/36**
29.40.	BG lekanis lid, **29/37**
29.41.	Locally produced skyphos/bowl, **29/38**
29.42.	Locally produced skyphos/bowl, **29/39**
29.43.	Locally made stamnoid pyxis, **29/40**
29.44.	Plain ware oinochoe/jug, **29/41**
29.45.	Plain ware oinochoe/jug, **29/42**

29.46.	Plain ware oinochoe/jug, **29/43**
29.47.	Plain ware lekythos, **29/44**
29.48.	Plain ware lekythos, **29/45**
29.49.	Plain ware olpe, **29/46**
29.50.	Plain ware olpe, **29/47**
29.51.	Plain ware pelike, **29/48**
29.52.	Plain ware lekane, **29/49**
29.53.	Plain ware lekane, **29/50**
29.54.	Plain ware mortar, **29/51**
29.55.	Plain ware mortar, **29/52**
29.56.	Plain ware mortar, **29/53**
29.57.	Plain ware mortar, **29/54**
29.58.	Plain ware ladle, **29/55**
29.59.	Cooking ware two-handled lidded chytra, **29/56**
29.60.	Cooking ware two-handled lidded chytra, **29/57**
29.61.	Cooking ware one-handled lidless chytra, **29/58**
29.62.	Cooking ware one-handled lidless chytra, **29/59**
29.63.	Cooking ware one-handled lidless chytra, **29/60**
29.64.	Cooking ware one-handled lidless chytra, **29/61**
29.65.	Cooking ware one-handled lidless chytra, **29/62**
29.66.	Cooking ware one-handled lidless chytra, **29/63**
29.67.	Cooking ware one-handled lidless chytra, **29/64**
29.68.	Cooking ware lopas, Type 1, **29/65**
29.69.	Cooking ware lopas, Type 1, **29/66**
29.70.	Cooking ware lopas, Type 2, **29/67**
29.71.	Cooking ware lopas, Type 3, **29/68**
29.72.	Cooking ware lid, **29/69**
29.73.	Cooking ware lid, **29/70**
29.74.	Cooking ware lid, **29/71**
29.75.	Cooking ware lid, **29/72**
29.76.	Fragmentary partly glazed lamp, **29/73**
29.77.	Fragmentary partly glazed lamp, **29/74**
29.78.	Fragmentary BG lamp, **29/75**
29.79.	Fragmentary BG lamp, **29/76**
29.80.	Fragmentary partly glazed lamp, **29/77**
29.81.	Fragmentary BG lamp, **29/78**
29.82.	Fragmentary BG lamp, **29/79**
29.83.	Fragmentary BG lamp, **29/80**
29.84.	Fragmentary BG lamp, **29/81**
29.85.	Fragmentary BG lamp, **29/82**
29.86.	Lamp with curved closed body and groove on rim, **29/83**
29.87.	Fragmentary lamp with curved closed body and ridges on shoulder, **29/84**
29.88.	Fragmentary lamp with curved closed body and ridges on shoulder, **29/85**
29.89.	Fragmentary Rhodian amphora
29.90.	Mendaian amphora
29.91.	Mendaian amphora
29.92.	Mendaian amphora
29.93.	Northeast Aegean amphora
29.94.	Northeast Aegean amphora
29.95.	Chian amphora
29.96.	Phoenician amphora

LIST OF TABLES

Volume 1

6.1.	Results of AMS ^{14}C dating of bone and tooth samples
6.2.	Stable-isotope results for bone (collagen) and tooth (dentin) to assess quality
7.1.	Summary listing of the Early Iron Age pottery from the area of the agora of Methone (Plot 274)
9.1.	Context and phases of the catalogued pottery
9.2.	Concordance of catalogue numbers in this volume and figure numbers in *Methone Pierias* I (Bessios, Tzifopoulos, and Kotsonas 2012)
15.1.	The context of the Hypogeion metal objects and the phase to which they belong

Volume 2

20.1.	The forest species on the Pieria Mts.
22.1.	The Hypogeion contexts of the north Ionian bird kotylai
25.1.	Glass finds in Methone according to area and type
25.2.	Analyzed glass artifacts from Methone
26.1.	Summary listing of the context and type of the metal objects from the West Hill at Methone
26.2.	Summary listing of the context and type of the metal objects from the eastern slopes of the acropolis (West Hill) in Plot 245
26.3.	Summary listing of the context and type of the metal objects from the area of the agora of Methone (Plot 274) (this table was prepared with the collaboration of Athena Athanassiadou)
26.4.	Summary listing of the context and type of the metal objects from the area of the south harbor (Plot 278)

Introduction

INTRODUCTION

THE ANCIENT METHONE ARCHAEOLOGICAL PROJECT

John K. Papadopoulos and Sarah P. Morris
(with contributions by Antonis Kotsonas)

GEOGRAPHIC SETTING

Ancient Methone lies in northern Pieria at the delta of the Haliakmon River—the longest river to run entirely in Greece (297 km or 185 miles)—immediately north of Mt. Olympos, and was occupied from the Late Neolithic period (ca. 4000 B.C.) until its destruction by Philip II in 354 B.C. (Chapter 1; Fig. I.1).[1] The settlement enjoyed a strategic location throughout its long history, attracting traders, prospectors, colonists, and conquerors from various parts of the Greek world and the broader Mediterranean beyond. In Greek sources (Chapter 2), it figures as one of the earliest northern Greek colonies, traditionally settled by Eretrians expelled from Korkyra in ca. 733/2 B.C.[2] Its location on a coastal promontory and adjacent hills, near the mouth of the Haliakmon, made it a gateway to rich inland resources (especially timber and metals, see Chapters 12–15, 20, and 26), as well as a harbor protected from the south winds for ships from around the Aegean. By the 5th century B.C., Methone was part of the Athenian League and supplied timber to Athens, especially the finest wood for trireme (warship) oars. In 354 B.C. Methone was besieged by Philip II, who lost an eye in battle but destroyed the city (Chapter 2); survivors were expelled and Philip established a Macedonian garrison a short distance to the northwest (here referred to as Macedonian Methone) (Fig. I.2); this left no later remains at the site of ancient Methone, but provides archaeologists with two and a half millennia of buried layers, sealed by a valuable chronological fixed point.[3]

The prominence of Methone in the Bronze Age (Chapters 4–6), Early Iron Age (Chapters 7–9, 10–17), and Archaic to Classical periods (Chapters 18–29) is best appreciated from the Aster (Advanced Spaceborne Thermal Emissions and Reflection Radiometer) 30 m contour map (Fig. I.3) that shows the extent of the Thermaic Gulf in antiquity, before the extensive silting of the Axios, Haliakmon, Gallikos, and Loudias Rivers.[4] The siting of Methone on the westernmost rim of the gulf anchored its access to Aegean maritime traffic and to the interior, including western Macedonia, Epirus, and the Balkan peninsula north of Greece. In fact, Philip's destruction of Methone promoted the city of Pella, on the northern side of the same gulf, as the new industrial center, main harbor, and chief royal city, if not capital, of Macedon in the later 4th century B.C. Thus perched, between the Aegean and the vast inland of Macedonia and the Balkans beyond, Methone served as a conduit for the movement of commodities, peoples, and ideas across a relatively large area of the Greek world, with input from, among others, Mycenaeans, Euboians, Athenians, east and northern Greeks, and indigenous populations, as well as Phoenicians, in both the prehistoric and historic periods.

As for the rivers, the Loudias, through its lagoon, which bordered the southern edge of Pella, allowed the Macedonian navy access to the Thermaic Gulf and from there to the Aegean and

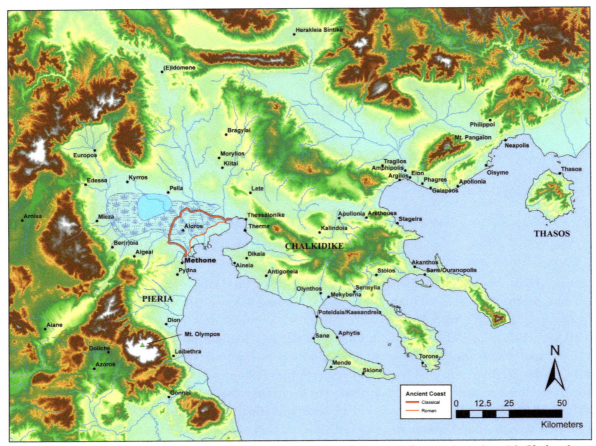

FIGURE I.1. Map of northern Greece showing Methone in relation to other ancient sites. M. Chykerda

Mediterranean seas. Although considerably longer today than in antiquity, the Loudias was a fully functioning and navigable river in antiquity. That the much larger Axios and Haliakmon Rivers were similarly navigable was illustrated with a journey, taken with two local fishermen, from Makrygialos, first to the current delta of the Haliakmon (see Fig. 3.15), and later a few kilometers up river, in the summer of 2012 (see Fig. 3.2 for the route taken by boat, and Fig. I.4). Farther west, just below the Monastery of St. John the Baptist (Fig. 3.7), and immediately off the modern road from Veroia to Vergina (ancient Aigai), the river widens to create the spectacular Haliakmon Gorge (Fig. I.5).[5] The similarity in material remains, both in the Bronze Age and in the historic period, between coastal sites like Methone and inland sites on the Haliakmon such as Aiani, reflects their close connections enabled by the navigability of rivers like the Haliakmon.

The existence of terms for "Pierians" and "Perrhaibians" (the latter perhaps in Thessaly and thus possibly hinting at other northern ethnic place names in the region) in Linear B (Mycenaean Greek) tablets from Pylos and Mycenae (Chapters 2, 6) points to possible palatial connections in this region before 1200 B.C. The memory of such connections may help support the identification of the Homeric kingdom of Philoktetes, including a city called Methone, within this region of Pieria.[6] Indeed, the memory or impression of early sites like Methone, encircled with renewable, mud-brick fortifications until the siege by Philip II, may have encouraged Greek legends such as "the curse of Agamemnon" (Chapters 2, 6).[7]

The city of Methone in the historical period was identified on the hilltop called Koryphi, north of the modern village of Methone and adjacent to Nea Agathoupolis, by Greek archaeologists in

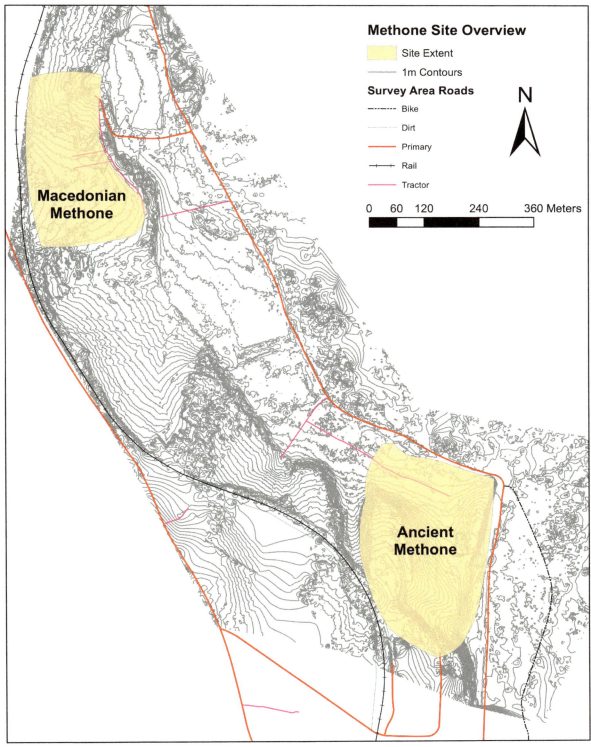

FIGURE I.2. Contour map of ancient Methone showing the extent of ancient (prehistoric through Classical) and Macedonian (Hellenistic and Roman) occupation. Prepared by M. Chykerda, based on the LiDAR contour map of the site prepared by R. Kayen and S. Corbett

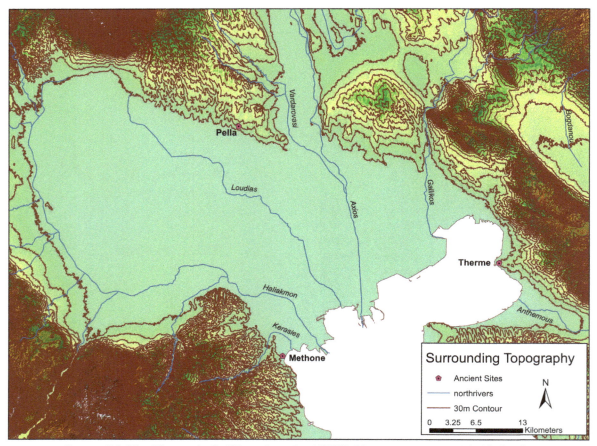

FIGURE I.3. The Thermaic Gulf based on the ASTER 30 m contour map. M. Chykerda

FIGURE I.4. Boat trip up the Haliakmon River in the summer of 2012. Photo I. Coyle

Figure I.5. The Haliakmon Gorge, taken from the Monastery of St. John the Baptist.
Photo J. Papadopoulos

1970 (Chapter 1).[8] Excavations were initiated by Manthos Bessios in 2003 and continued annually through 2011, with supplemental work in 2012 and 2013 (summarized in Chapter 1), but the site remained relatively unknown beyond preliminary Greek reports and brief chapters in a popular volume on Pieria, before the recent conferences, exhibits, and volumes devoted to the early inscriptions in Thessaloniki.[9]

INITIATING THE ANCIENT METHONE ARCHAEOLOGICAL PROJECT AND COLLABORATION

After a series of meetings at the site in 2011–2012, Bessios formally invited Papadopoulos and Morris to collaborate with his team on the publication of past finds and to initiate future archaeological investigations at Methone. The critical discussions to initiate the Ancient Methone Archaeological Project (AMAP) occurred during February of 2012 during a visit to the site by Papadopoulos and Brian Damiata, with Manthos Bessios, Yannis Tzifopoulos, Athena Athanassiadou, and Konstantinos Noulas at Methone, and in the archaeological storerooms and Ephoreia facilities at Makrygialos, at a time when the site and the beach of the Thermaic Gulf was covered with over 60 cm of snow (Figs. I.6a–d). This volume fulfills the first of these goals: to assemble a team of experts and technicians to record, study, and publish the material that was excavated prior to 2012, in a synthetic but selective volume on the site.[10]

The second aim, three seasons of fieldwork, which later blossomed into four, and included extensive geophysical and geoarchaeological survey of the site, a comprehensive LiDAR survey,[11]

FIGURE I.6. Ancient Methone in February 2012: a) the beach between modern Methone and Nea Agathoupolis, from south-southwest; b) view of ancient Methone from the bird tower (from the northeast), the West Hill in the background; c) Tzifopoulos, Bessios, and Papadopoulos on their way up to the West Hill; d) view from west of the East Hill with the open trench that uncovered the agora of Methone.
Photos B. Damiata

together with intensive surface survey and targeted excavations, was initiated as a multi-year collaboration (*synergasia*) between the former KZ´ Ephoreia of Prehistoric and Classical Antiquities (Pieria) and UCLA through the auspices of the American School of Classical Studies at Athens. A preliminary report of the fieldwork of 2014–2017 appeared in *Hesperia*,[12] with more comprehensive accounts of the recent excavations in progress. Consequently, excavations at ancient Methone by the Greek Ministry of Culture since 2003, and in collaboration with UCLA since 2014, have uncovered one of the most significant harbor and industrial sites of the north Aegean, an early version of a role later played by Thessaloniki.

MAJOR RESULTS OF THE 2003–2013 EXCAVATIONS[13]

An overall summary of the 2003–2013 excavations at Methone is provided in Chapter 1, together with more detailed reports of investigations in certain areas of the site in Chapters 8 (the excavation of the "Hypogeion") and 19 (which deals with the pottery workshops and Archaic pottery on the West Hill), with supplementary details provided in Chapters 18 (on the important early stoa, Building A, in the agora of Methone) and 29 (on the destruction deposit and pottery from the agora). In addition to the accounts of the early excavations, the volume also presents an introductory overview of Methone in ancient literary and epigraphical sources (Chapter 2), and a more detailed and nuanced account of the landscape on which the ancient settlement was established, at the water's edge (Chapter 3).

Major results of the 2003–2013 investigations include an early agora below the East Hill with public buildings (Chapters 1, 18, 29); an "acropolis" area on the West Hill with houses and workshops of the Archaic and Classical periods (Chapter 19) built near and over burials of the Bronze Age (Chapter 6), and Early Iron Age precolonial levels; earthen fortifications in various phases, including a series of tunnels dug by the Methonaians under siege, in order to supply the settlement with water and food and as sally ports for active defense, as well as the earth ramps constructed by Philip II to lay siege to the town (Chapter 1, Fig. 1.26). Smaller sondages at different points of the ancient city have established a sequence of human occupation from the Late Neolithic through various stages of the Bronze Age into the Early Iron Age, Archaic, and Classical periods. These discoveries include a prehistoric settlement on the East Hill (Chapters 4–5) that buried its dead on the West Hill (Chapter 6), and Early Iron Age occupation preceding the Eretrian colony (Chapter 7, see also Chapters 9 and 12). At the end of the Bronze Age, the site of Methone seems to have survived the demise of Mycenaean palatial civilization in central and southern Greece, according to burials post-palatial in date (Chapter 6). Such continuities suggest how the afterlife of Bronze Age culture in the north could have stimulated the rise of new interactive communities in the Early Iron Age and later periods.

Particularly important is the well-preserved destruction level of 354 B.C. in the agora (Chapter 29), together with the numerous lead sling bullets (Chapter 28) and bronze and iron weapons (Chapter 26) associated with the destruction of the city, providing something of a glimpse into the final days of Classical Methone. Perhaps the most spectacular discovery was the deep (over 11.5 m below surface), rectangular "Hypogeion" ("basement") sunk into the East Hill (Figs. 1.4, 1.5) and filled with fragments of hundreds of complete and semi-complete vessels (including transport amphoras), many of the later 8th and early 7th century B.C., from virtually every corner of the Aegean and beyond, including five Phoenician storage jars (Chapters 1, 8–9, 12). Most importantly, just under 200 of these storage vessels, together with drinking cups, were incised (graffiti) or painted (dipinti) with early letters, or potters' marks.[14] At least 25 of these inscriptions are in alphabetic Greek, particularly in Euboian and probably other local scripts and dialects, forming the largest and most diverse early corpus to date, with important implications for the formation of the early Greek alphabet in the Aegean (Chapter 11).[15]

Because of the unfinished state of the Hypogeion, and the effects of erosion, no final assumption as to its intended function was offered in the original publication in 2012. Following the publication of Μεθώνη Πιερίας 1,[16] two reviewers proposed different interpretations of the stratigraphy and purpose of the Hypogeion.[17] These interpretations misrepresent the excavation of Methone, propose selective and distorted understandings of the stratigraphic evidence, site formation processes, and fieldwork in general, and hypothesize different functions for the structure, without engaging sufficiently with the primary evidence. One hypothesis has the feature constructed to serve as a rubbish pit (or "dump"), a scenario that imagines the investment of countless human-hours in: a) cutting through over 11 m of bedrock, and additional meters of soil, using simple tools and manual labor to create a shaft of 181.44 m^3 at minimum (12 x 3.6 x 4.2 m); b) smoothing vertical walls for a space solely used for disposing of rubbish; c) hauling out the earth from a deep shaft (a huge challenge for the excavation team in the 21st century) and disposing of the quantities of soil and bedrock that were dug up. The end process and the expenditure of so much energy would have left the people of Methone with huge amounts of debris (largely soil) to dispose of, comparable to the quantity of debris they originally intended to bury. Hence, the investment would offer no practical gain. It would have been much easier for the inhabitants of Methone to dispose of the assumed rubbish a few meters to the east of the Hypogeion, downhill at the seashore that reached the east foot of the hill, a practice widely attested in ancient literature and also documented archaeologically.[18] Advocates of the idea of a rubbish pit failed to compare the Hypogeion to such pits elsewhere in the area of the Thermaic Gulf, or in the Euboian homeland of the colonists.[19] For example, Archaic rubbish pits found at Pydna are much shallower and round in shape, while those at Karabournaki, which date from the Early Iron Age to Archaic period, are much shallower and typically show irregular or rounded shapes.[20] The content of these contexts was also different, with Karabournaki Pit 1 being filled with ceramics, but producing few finds of any other sort, unlike the Hypogeion (for various finds from the Hypogeion, see Chapters 8–17). Finally, Methone itself features storage or rubbish pits of the type also attested at Pydna and Karabournaki in the Early Iron Age, but these are most unlike the Hypogeion (Chapter 1, Figs. 1.31–32).

Another idea put forward is that the Hypogeion was designed to serve as a well, to explain the relative care in the construction of the shaft. It is unlikely, however, that anyone would dig a deep well next to the seashore, given the likelihood of hitting seawater or, at the very least, brackish water. Besides, the rectangular plan and fairly large breadth and width of the feature find hardly any match in wells from the Aegean of the same period.[21] These features are closer to those of cisterns (especially those of later periods), yet there is no evidence whatsoever of waterproofing in the Hypogeion to support the interpretation of a cistern, though it is clear that the Hypogeion was never finished and thus never waterproofed. Moreover, why dig a well, or cistern, at the highest point of a hill, and not nearby, where the ground level was considerably lower? The subsequent discovery of Hypogeion 2 in the excavations of 2014–2017, a pit deeper but narrower than the first Hypogeion, and one in use for several centuries, showed conclusively that it could not have been a cistern.[22] Consequently, the excavators of Hypogeion 2 returned to the possibility that it functioned as a storage shaft, thus recalling the working hypothesis that Bessios presented for the first Hypogeion.[23]

Finally, there have also been a few misunderstandings of the stratigraphy and chronology of specific phases of the Hypogeion. It has been suggested that Phases I and II are basically one phase because there are pottery joins between them. This idea fails to appreciate the varied evidence for the stratigraphic division and the very different properties of the soils and their content, which are explained in detail by Bessios in Μεθώνη Πιερίας 1,[24] and in Chapter 8. Furthermore, it relies on a misunderstanding of the role of depositional processes in the formation of the archaeological record, and fails to appreciate the clear evidence that the (ceramic) material from Phases I and II does not form a primary deposit.[25] This material was originally dumped elsewhere, and was taken to the Hypogeion as debris for a secondary (or tertiary) deposit. What modern conservators mend together as one pot did not necessarily arrive as such at the Hypogeion sometime around 700 B.C.; moreover, it was not necessarily dumped or preserved as one unit in the primary deposit. The argument for the uniformity of Phases I and II is thus based on the unfounded, and highly questionable, assumption that each pot used in the filling of the Hypogeion was singled out and treated as such, at a particular moment in time. This said, it is worth repeating the argument of Bessios that Phases I and II must have been formed within a very short time span, perhaps within a few weeks.[26]

Such misunderstandings of stratigraphy are accompanied by some problematic suggestions on chronology. It was suggested, for example, that Phases I and II of the Hypogeion date not to 720–690 B.C., as originally proposed, but to the early 7th century, the reason being that in the original publication, some of the East Greek transport amphoras were compared to pieces dating to the late 7th century B.C. Several facts render this suggestion unnecessary: First, 690 B.C. already falls in the early 7th century B.C. Second, such a discussion of chronology overlooks the many dozens of locally produced and especially imported fine wares from Euboia, Attica, Corinth, and different parts of the East Aegean,[27] that consistently indicate a Late Geometric II stylistic date (traditionally assigned to 720–690 B.C.). Third, it is a well-known fact among ceramic experts that the sequence of many types of Greek transport amphoras is well documented only from the late 7th century, because of the paucity of published finds from closed contexts of earlier date (including the late 8th and early 7th century) reported in the older literature.[28] More recent publication of well-dated amphora finds from across the Mediterranean suggests an earlier date for different types, as noted in *Μεθώνη Πιερίας* 1,[29] but these finds are occasionally not given the attention they deserve. Accordingly, the citation of a few amphora comparanda from ca. 700 B.C. and the more numerous ones from the later 7th century B.C. represents the current state of research and provides no basis for downdating the amphora material in question. It is worth noting that amphora experts have accepted the proposed date of the finds from Methone, have highlighted the importance of the finds for the study of the earliest Aegean amphoras, and have drawn attention to the early comparanda.[30] With these remarks, we hope to clarify the excavated results of the first Hypogeion in response to inaccurate reviews.

PRIMARY CATEGORIES OF FINDS

As has been outlined above, Chapters 4–7, which constitute Part I of the volume, present the Neolithic, Bronze, and Early Iron Age pottery from various deposits in the excavations of the East Hill, as well as the Late Bronze Age cemetery on the West Hill, an area that was, in the prehistoric period, beyond the primary settlement that centered on the East Hill. These finds well illustrate the thriving character of the Late Neolithic through Early Iron Age settlement at Methone well before the arrival of colonists from Eretria. Indeed, the finds also establish that Methone as a settlement was not only well connected with regional networks in the north Aegean, the Balkans, and beyond, throughout its early history, but that it was at this location for a very long time, at least three millennia before the Eretrians ever ventured this far north. A corollary to this longevity may well lie in the very name of the site. While Plutarch credits an eponymous "Methon" as namesake of the Eretrian colony, the very name Methone could be prehellenic in formation (with a suffix -*ōnē* familiar in other Greek place names in northern Greece, such as Torone, Skione, or even in those originally in -*ānā* [*ānē*] such as Methana in southern Greece or Pallene in Chalkidike).[31] A pre-Greek etymology could indicate pre-Indo-European speakers in northern Greece and in Pieria, home to *Olympos*, a pre-Indo-European name common for "mountain," and to prehistoric settlement at Makrygialos (Agiasma) and Methone itself.[32] In contrast, a recent proposal derives the name of Methone from Greek μεθίημι, as a place of "release" or relief (from sailing), or a suitable name for a harbor site.[33] In either case, "Methone" would be an early site, and possibly one renowned for the shelter it offered to ships.

Part II of the volume, Chapters 8–17, deals with the excavation and material recovered from the Hypogeion. These contributions focus on the trade, industry, and lifeways of Early Iron Age Methone, especially in the Late Geometric period and earlier part of the 7th century B.C. Chapter 8 provides an account of the excavation of the Hypogeion and Chapter 9 presents select pottery from this remarkable context. Chapter 10, entitled "Lifeways and Foodways in Iron Age Methone: A Perishable Material Culture Approach," presents a preliminary overview of the floral, faunal, and marine molluskan finds from the Hypogeion, one of the first and most comprehensive accounts of such materials from a stratified Early Iron Age and early Archaic site in the Greek world. Chapter 11 summarizes inscriptions (graffiti and dipinti) and trademarks at Methone around 700 B.C., presented more fully in Greek in *Μεθώνη Πιερίας* 1, and Chapter 12, through an analysis of transport amphoras from the Hypogeion, asks why Methone was colonized. In so doing, the contribution clearly shows that trade was a major motive for the Eretrian settlement of Methone and, more broadly, for Greek colonization. The next three chapters deal with metallurgy and the metal finds from the Hypogeion. Chapter 13, undertaking to present the broad array of prehistoric stone tools from the site, shows that many of them were repurposed and reused for metallurgical activity in the Late Geometric period. Chapter 14 argues that goldworking was very important at Methone, in accordance with both the predominance of gold in the metalworking ceramics there, and with Strabo's testimony (*Geog.* 5.4.9) that the Euboians' source of wealth on Pithekoussai was agriculture and the production of gold jewelry (χρυσία); the contribution showcases the new evidence from Methone against the backdrop of goldworking in Eretria. Chapter 15 presents an overview of the primary categories of base metal—bronze, iron, and lead—objects from the Hypogeion (there were no Early Iron Age gold objects, only ingots, as outlined in Chapter 14). Chapters 16 and 17 present, respectively, a selection of clay tools from the Hypogeion, especially the spindlewhorls, loomweights, and related tools, and the latter chapter the cut sherd disks from the Hypogeion.

Part III of the volume deals with Methone in the Archaic and Classical periods, beginning with the important early stoa in the agora on the East Hill, dubbed Building A (Chapter 18). This is followed by an account of the pottery workshops on the acropolis, West Hill, at Methone, and an overview of the Archaic pottery from this quarter of the site (Chapter 19). Chapter 20 provides an overview of the literary evidence for the timber trade, together with its natural history, and is especially important for dealing with a resource that was critical to the economy of Methone, as it was to the economies of Macedon and Athens, a resource that often defies the archaeological record. The next four chapters deal with pottery: Chapter 21 summarizes some of the representative Archaic transport amphoras from the West Hill; Chapter 22 presents the primary categories of the imported East Greek pottery at Methone; Chapter 23 a small selection of Attic black-figure and red-figure pottery from various contexts across the site, and Chapter 24 a synthesis of imported (Attic and Corinthian) and locally produced or north Aegean terracotta lamps from the site (a few additional lamps are presented in the destruction deposit associated with the agora of Methone, Chapter 29).

Another important industrial category of objects, produced locally at Methone, is the early glass. The glass finds from various parts of the site—including the Hypogeion and the East and West Hills—comprising glass rods and glass production discards, add a significant component to a site that was a leading industrial center and harbor of the north Aegean. Chapter 26 publishes the metal objects from Methone of the Archaic and Classical period, recovered from the acropolis and its eastern slopes, the agora, and the south harbor area of Methone. The two final chapters deal with the large quantity of inscribed and uninscribed lead sling bullets from Methone (Chapter 28) and the pottery from the destruction deposit in the agora (Chapter 29). Although the lead sling bullets were among the very latest objects from the site (as were the many arrowheads in Chapter 26) and provide a poignant insight into the siege of the city by Philip II and the defense of the Methonaians, we end the volume with the remarkable destruction deposit in the agora of Methone, which constitutes an important sealed context of 354 B.C.

Although the present volume was intended to give as comprehensive a synthesis as possible of the excavations of 2003–2013 in English, it was not possible to include every category of material uncovered at Methone. The editors regret that Christos Gatzolis and Selene Psoma, who were invited to contribute a preview of the remarkable Classical coin hoard found in the agora of Methone, did not submit a paper for this volume; we look forward to the ultimate presentation of this significant material.[34] Another contribution that we had hoped to include was a report on the impressive array of Archaic Corinthian fine ware pottery imported to the site, undertaken by Konstantinos Noulas; his various commitments with the Ephoreia, together with pressures to work on his doctoral dissertation, prevented him from completing such a summary. A few of the more representative examples of Archaic Corinthian pottery are presented in this volume in a more preliminary way (Figs. 1.35, 19.6–19.9), while the earlier Late Geometric and early 7th-century Corinthian fine ware from the Hypogeion is presented more fully by Bessios (Chapter 9). In a similar vein, a study of one of the most important categories of material—broadly labeled "*ergastiriaka*," especially from the Hypogeion, was undertaken by Bessios. This is a large group, including tools and waste products (debitage) from a wide variety of materials, such as metals, glass, ivory and worked bone, horn, antler, and other products, both natural and human-made. Whereas some of these more specialized categories are included in the present volume (e.g., Chapters 13, 14, 25), others, such as the large number of stone and terracotta molds for metalworking, were not ready for publication. As with the Archaic Corinthian pottery, a selection of these molds is presented here to display their range and significance (Figs. 1.15, 1.16, 1.36, 14.3, 14.4), along with examples of ivory debitage and a worked ivory seal (Figs. 1.14, 1.37).

At the same time, we were able to include additional material collected at ancient Methone on the surface of the site in the 1980s, prior to the systematic excavations begun in 2003, and given to the Archaeological Museum of Thessaloniki by Stamatios Tsakos. In Chapter 27, Styliana Galiniki presents a close study of the three stone molds picked up by Tsakos at Methone that are now on display in the permanent exhibition "Macedonia from the 7th Century B.C. until Late Antiquity" in the Thessaloniki Museum.[35]

Other materials not presented in this volume include a study of the unfired clay basins, together with associated terracotta installations, such as hearths and ovens, from the Hypogeion; an initial study of this material was conducted by Dr. Sara Strack in 2013 (then research associate at the University of Leicester), but never completed or published. Finally, the considerable ecofacts collected since 2003, in particular the fauna, plant and charcoal remains from soil flotation, and mollusks, are still under study; this volume presents a synthetic preview of those recovered from the Hypogeion (Chapter 10), with a much fuller study in progress.

The 29 chapters published in this volume were written by more than 30 contributors, and present over 1,200 catalogued and illustrated objects from the site. The task of coordinating this many presentations, translating those papers submitted in Greek, and ensuring a consistent formatting for the text and illustrations, took longer than anticipated when the project was initiated in 2012, and was further delayed by the resumption of excavations in 2014.[36] The intervening time, however, brought several advantages, including the recent submission (June 2020) of Vaso Papathanasiou's M.A. thesis at the University of Thessaloniki, under the supervision of Sevi Triantaphyllou, on the bioarchaeology of the Bronze Age burials on the West Hill of Methone, and the opportunity for AMS ^{14}C dating and stable isotopic analysis of the skeletons (both developments have enriched Chapter 6).

While it appears long, we cannot stress enough that the present volume is largely a synthetic one, as the quantity and quality of the material from Methone, especially from the early excavations begun in 2003, demand additional years of conservation, study, and documentation. Almost all of the chapters, with the sole exception of Chapter 27, present only a selection of the material covered under each chapter heading. Given the number of contributors, the nature and quantity of the material at hand, and the various other commitments of those involved, what was included or not was left to individual contributors, with the agreement to present as representative a sample of the material as possible. Consequently, some contributions are longer than others, while some are more circumscribed: Chapters 4, 5, 7, 15, and 26, for example, offer a fairly substantial representation of the material from their respective deposits, while other chapters (e.g., 12, 13, and 21) are a prelude to more comprehensive publications of the material. Three categories—East Greek fine pottery, Athenian black- and red-figure, and terracotta lamps (Chapters 22, 23, 24)—represent only a minimal number of selected pieces. Each of these categories, together with many others, is newly enriched by a good deal of additional material recovered in the more recent excavations of 2014–2017, under preparation for publication.[37] The same holds true for additional inscriptions on pottery from the 2014–2017 seasons, including inscriptions in various Greek epichoric scripts and a few that may well not be Greek.

As a result, the present volume is not only synthetic but also uneven in coverage, and for this the editors bear full responsibility. Our hope, however, is to broaden the scope of the material from the site presented in full detail in *Μεθώνη Πιερίας* 1,[38] by including the material pre- and postdating the Hypogeion and its rich finds. Methone is a large and complex site, and despite the quantity of material already recovered, the excavations of 2003–2013 and 2014–2017 have only scratched the surface. As a deposit, the Hypogeion only covered a paltry area measuring 3.6 by 4.2 m at the bottom, but one containing 181.44 cubic m^3 at minimum (Chapter 8). A second Hypogeion, much narrower than that on the East Hill, but deeper, was excavated in 2014–2017. Almost square in plan, oriented northeast to southwest, it measured ca. 2.2 m (east–west) by 2.3 m (north–south) at the top, tapering to about 1.9 by 1.7 m at lower depths, with the faces of the shaft not strictly vertical. By the end of the 2017 season, excavation reached a depth of 9.4 m, where the lower walls showed collapse, but cores sunk in remaining fill reached deeper levels, at least 12.15 m below the modern surface, without ever reaching the bottom. The total fill recovered was estimated at 46 tons of material, or 33 m^3 in volume, with over 53,000 sherds collected, relatively little in comparison to the first Hypogeion. The collapse of the lower walls as reached made further excavation dangerous, and the decision was made by Bessios and Papadopoulos to suspend its excavation. As a second Hypogeion excavated at Methone, what was dubbed "pit 46" raises as many challenging questions on its purpose, history, and function as the one found on the East Hill, and a more meaningful interpretation of the function of both features should await the final publication of "pit 46."[39]

CULTURAL HERITAGE DEVELOPMENTS AND THE FUTURE POTENTIAL OF METHONE

Beyond the significant prehistoric remains and deposits of Early Iron Age and Archaic date, the importance of Methone lies in the fact that it was destroyed by Philip II in 354 B.C. To commemorate this event, the local inhabitants of modern Methone and Nea Agathoupolis erected a bronze statue of Philip II in 2010 (Fig. I.7). Philip's destruction was a watershed moment, both for the inhabitants of ancient Methone and for Classical archaeology.[40] With the establishment of a garrison at the site (dubbed Macedonian Methone), Philip ensured an unimaginable afterlife for the Classical and earlier settlement a short distance to the southeast. Subsequent erosion and plowing have largely eradicated vestiges of the Classical period, especially on the West Hill, even though significant deposits of the destruction are preserved. To scratch the surface of ancient Methone is to encounter significant horizons of Archaic and earlier date. Consequently, the site has much to offer future generations of archaeologists.

Our project also sought to honor more recent chapters in the cultural heritage of Greece, in particular in the community of Nea Agathoupolis, the modern locale of ancient Methone. One of a number of early 20th-century refugee settlements in northern Greece, once linked by rail to its coastal neighbors to the south and to the city of Thessaloniki, it lost this vital link with the displacement of the railway to a new line far west of the village, some decades ago. This left the abandoned station as a relic of past travel, an opportunity ripe for community engagement, which we undertook with a restoration of the multi-room building in 2015.[41] This project also gave us a chance to include the work of local artist and poet Nikolaos Semizidis, who designed and painted a new sign for the station.[42] Officially inaugurated by the village as a cultural center in 2016, when it opened with an exhibit of local nature photographs by AMAP conservator Alekos Tsiogkas, the structure is now managed by the local women's cultural organization, the Agathones of Nea Agathoupolis. Every Wednesday they host an open house coffee hour, and on special occasions they assemble to celebrate religious feast days, often in costume, with traditional dances, and always with refreshments.[43] This gives our project a link to the living community that has replaced the ancient settlement and hosted its exploration.

We end with a plea for the preservation of ancient Methone. Most of the archaeological site of ancient Methone, and all of Macedonian Methone, lie on private property. The excavations on the East Hill were only possible because the landowner of the relevant plot of land, Konstantinos Mamoukaris, allowed its excavation by the Ephoreia. The only plot of public land, Plot 229, which represents most of the summit of the West Hill, was excavated first by the former KZ´ Ephoreia, and later through the *synergasia* permit, in 2014–2017, because it was available without expropriation. Ironically, the vast wetlands of the Haliakmon Delta that skirt the north and northeast parts of the site (Fig. I.8a), including the bird tower (Fig. I.8b), built to promote bird-watching and ecotourism, are public, protected by the Natura 2000 program of the European Union.[44] Natura 2000 is a network of core breeding and resting sites for rare and threatened species, and some rare natural habitat types which are protected in their own right. Covering 18% of the land area of the European Union and almost 6% of its marine territory, Natura 2000 is the largest coordinated network of

FIGURE I.7. Bronze statue of Philip II erected at modern Methone and Nea Agathoupolis in 2010. Photo S. Morris

protected areas in the world. It extends across all 27 European Union countries, both on land and at sea, and ensures the long-term survival of those species and habitats that are most threatened, listed under both the "Birds Directive" and the "Habitats Directive."[45] It has been a long-standing dream of virtually all archaeologists ever involved with ancient Methone, beginning with Manthos Bessios, to expropriate the land that covers the ancient site and thus join the Natura 2000 zone with the archaeological site of Methone.

FIGURE I.8. a) Aerial view taken by drone from above the West Hill, showing the East Hill, with the wetlands of the Haliakmon Delta, including the bird tower (see Fig. I.8b) in the distance to the left, view from west. Photo H. Thomas; b) The bird tower immediately to the north-northeast of ancient Methone, built as part of the Natura 2000 program of the European Union. Photo J. Vanderpool

NOTES

1. The earliest material recovered at the site dates from the Late and Final Neolithic periods, in deposits and installations found on bedrock on the East Hill (see Chapters 1, 4). This makes Methone one of the nearest successors to the site of Makrygialos (Agiasma), one of the largest Neolithic settlements in Europe, which was abandoned in the 4th millennium B.C.: see Pappa and Bessios 1999. As an ancient literary topos, Methone in Pieria features prominently in Leake 1835, Vol. III, pp. 401, 429, 435, 447.
2. Plutarch, *Moralia* 293b.
3. For the destruction of Methone, see Bessios, Athanassiadou, and Noulas 2021a.
4. Between 1929 and 1936, large hydraulic projects installed drainage canals, land reclamation works, and embankments to create large areas for agriculture and livestock breeding while promoting agricultural activity through irrigation. The most important works involved the diversion of the Axios River bed and the draining of the Giannitsa lake. The Axios River was shifted from its natural flow to reduce the silting of the Thermaic Gulf in the bay of Thessaloniki and to keep its port open, while the Giannitsa lake was drained by a large artificial canal, named after the old river Loudias. Among other references, see Konstantinidis 1989; Poulos et al. 2000; Ghilardi et al. 2008b; see also https://axiosdelta.gr/en/national-park/protected-area/delta-creation/.
5. The Haliakmon today has been dammed at several points, and some segments of the riverbed intentionally flooded. The river was navigable in the Middle Ages, but the hydroelectric dam south of Veroia is now a barrier to river traffic. Among other sites, Neolithic Servia, first investigated by Alan Wace and later excavated by Walter Heurtley (1939, pp. 43–46) is today submerged beneath Lake Polyphytos, see Ridley and Wardle 1979; Ridley, Wardle, and Mould 2000.
6. For the kingdom of Philoktetes, see *Iliad* 2.716–719, which names a city called Methone, located by some scholars in this part of Pieria: see Helly 2006; Chapter 6.
7. Strabo VII fr. 20c Baladié, from Theopompus (discussed in Chapters 2, 6, and 20).
8. For an overview, see Bessios 2012a; see also Hammond 1972, p. 129; Hammond 1998; Hatzopoulos, Knoepfler, and Marigo-Papadopoulos 1990. It is clear in the Archives of of the ΙΣΤ΄ Ephoreia that the site of Ancient Methone was identified with the present location by Andreas Vavritsas and Mary Siganidou.
9. Bessios 2003, 2010; Bessios et al. 2004; for the volume introducing the site, with a focus on the early inscriptions from the Hypogeion, see Bessios, Tzifopoulos, and Kotsonas 2012; for the 2012 conference on these early inscriptions, see Strauss Clay, Malkin, and Tzifopoulos 2017b; for the exhibit at the Archaeological Museum of Thessaloniki, see Tzifopoulos 2013.
10. The publication of this volume was formalized as a collaboration between the members of the former KZ΄ (now Pieria) Ephoreia (Bessios, Athanassiadou, and Noulas) and UCLA (Papadopoulos and Morris), submitted by the American School of Classical Studies at Athens and approved by the Greek Ministry of Culture (study permit #1690, Katerini, 23/5/2012).
11. The term LiDAR, or LIDAR, was originally a portmanteau of "light and radar," but the acronym has been come to refer to either "Light Detection and Ranging" or "Laser Imaging, Detection, and Ranging."
12. Morris et al. 2020. For a full account of the pedestrian surface survey, see Chykerda and Kontonicolas forthcoming. A further aim of the project was aerial photography and photogrammetry, first performed by Hugh Thomas and Michael Rocchio in 2014, continued by Thomas and Robert Kayen in 2015–2017, and by Jeff Vanderpool in 2018 and 2019; for further discussion and bibliography, see Morris et al. 2020, pp. 675–677.
13. The account of the Hypogeion and its stratigraphy in this section was coauthored with Antonis Kotsonas.
14. Bessios, Tzifopoulos, and Kotsonas 2012; see further Papadopoulos 2016, 2017a; Strauss Clay, Malkin, and Tzifopoulos 2017b; for Early Iron Age potters' marks, see Papadopoulos 1994.
15. Although many of the inscriptions from the Hypogeion are in Eretrian or Euboian epichoric script, many of the most recent vessel inscriptions from the 2014–2017 excavations at the site of the later Geometric and Archaic periods, as well as some inscriptions of Classical date, are in a variety of local scripts, including a fragment that may well be non-Greek; see Morris et al. 2020, pp. 712–713, fig. 65.
16. Bessios, Tzifopoulos, and Kotsonas 2012.
17. See Gimatzidis 2013; Chavela 2013; for a more balanced response, which explains the misunderstandings of the other two reviews, see Perron 2015 (esp. pp. 687–696).
18. See, among others, Lindenlauf 2004, pp. 425–428.
19. For the rubbish pits of Eretria, all of which are circular or elliptical, or else irregular in shape, and considerably shallower than the Hypogeion at Methone, see *Eretria* XX, esp. pls. 3–4; *Eretria* XXII, pp. 37–63, pls. 3–4, 7–16.

20 For Pydna, see Vokotopoulou 1984, p. 219; for those at Karabournaki, see Pantermali and Trakosopoulou 1995: 97 pits, an unspecified number of which were for rubbish; Tsimpidou-Avloniti et al. 2006, pp. 271–273 (five rubbish pits and 13 more pits of unspecified or unclear function). Even the largest dump at Karabournaki, Pit 1, was deeper than 5 m, and much broader than the Hypogeion (ca. 8.35 x 5.2 m).
21 For wells and cisterns, see Klingborg 2017.
22 See Morris et al. 2020, pp. 702–712 (esp. p. 711), figs. 54–64.
23 Morris et al. 2020, pp. 711–712; see also Bessios et al. 2004, p. 368; Bessios 2012a, pp. 47–48. As the first Hypogeion was never finished, the completion of the excavation could not confirm the working hypothesis.
24 Bessios 2012a.
25 As explained in Bessios 2012a, pp. 57, 64, n. 13. See also Perron 2015, pp. 688–689, who defends the stratigraphic distinction drawn by Bessios.
26 Bessios 2012a, pp. 48, 52, 58.
27 See Chapters 9, 12 and 22, and Kotsonas 2012.
28 See especially Dupont 1998.
29 See, for example, Kotsonas 2012, pp. 198, 200, 208, 230.
30 See, for example, Lawall 2016a, pp. 220–223; Johnston 2016, p. 45; 2017; Lawall and Tzochev 2019–2020, p. 118. Also, Chapter 12.
31 We are grateful to Richard Janko for drawing our attention to the possible prehellenic formation of the name Methone.
32 On the arrival of Indo-European speakers in Greece by Early Helladic III, see Haley 1928 and Blegen 1928; and, most recently, Coleman 2000, who advocates for an earlier date.
33 Blanc 2018; see Chapter 2 for further discussion of the name and foundation of Methone.
34 The coin hoard, discovered in Building A in 2006, was reported in Bessios, Athanassiadou, and Noulas 2008, p. 243; Bessios 2012b, p. 16; for an oral presentation in Greek on these silver coins (15 Attic tetradrachms of the later 5th century B.C., and nine staters of Alexander I of Macedon), see Gatzolis and Psoma 2017.
35 The molds were first published, in a more circumscribed manner and with fewer illustrations, in Galiniki 2006. Galiniki was later invited to present a more detailed discussion of these molds, together with replicas of the jewelry made from their designs that she had commissioned to be made by the gold- and silversmith Nikos Xanthopoulos; for further details, see Chapter 27.
36 The first contribution submitted (in 2014) was Chapter 10; for the delay in publication of this volume, especially to those authors who submitted their chapters promptly, the editors apologize.
37 See Morris et al. 2020 for a preliminary overview.
38 Bessios, Tzifopoulos, and Kotsonas 2012.
39 For a preliminary report on the second Hypogeion, see Morris et al. 2020, pp. 702–712, figs. 54–64, which presents a very small selection of the material recovered from this feature.
40 For an overview of the destruction of Methone, see Bessios, Athanassiadou, and Noulas 2021a.
41 For a fuller illustrated overview of this restoration project see Morris et al. 2020, pp. 717–719, figs. 66a–c.
42 Morris et al. 2020, p. 718, fig. 66c.
43 Further details of the Ancient Methone Archaeological Project, including a fuller overview of the restoration of the old railway station and local community events, are available in Methone: the Movie, available at https://www.ascsa.edu.gr/news/newsDetails/webinar-the-ancient-methone-archaeological-project-the-movie.
44 For which see: https://ec.europa.eu/environment/nature/natura2000/index_en.htm. The lowermost stretch of the East Hill is just visible in the left frame of the photograph on Figure I.8a.
45 For the "Birds Directive" and the "Habitats Directive" see the following web sites: https://ec.europa.eu/environment/nature/legislation/birdsdirective/index_en.htm; https://ec.europa.eu/environment/nature/legislation/habitatsdirective/index_en.htm.

1

EXCAVATIONS AT METHONE (2003–2013)

Matthaios Bessios, Athena Athanassiadou, and Konstantinos Noulas

Excavations in the settlement of ancient Methone, a colony of the Eretrians in the historical period, only began in 2003, but have already yielded particularly rich results.[1] On account of the importance of this particular location for the colonization of the north Aegean area, the KZ´ Ephoreia of Prehistoric and Classical Antiquities (now the Ephoreia of Antiquities of Pieria) collaborated with the University of California, Los Angeles (UCLA, represented by Professors John K. Papadopoulos and Sarah P. Morris) through the auspices of the American School of Classical Studies at Athens.[2] This volume focuses on the original rescue excavations first conducted by the IΣT´ Ephoreia of Prehistoric and Classical Antiquities, and later the KZ´ Ephoreia of Prehistoric and Classical Antiquities, not only in the fortified settlement of Methone, but also in its immediate surroundings.

The settlement of Methone developed over time on two adjacent hills, together with the flatter ground north of them, which in antiquity reached the sea. Of the two hills, the eastern is lower and more gentle, while the West Hill is taller with steeper slopes. The trapezoidal shape of the peak of the West Hill indicates that it was once surrounded by a fortification wall, and it has rightly been considered as the acropolis of the settlement.

EXCAVATIONS ON THE EAST HILL AND THE AGORA OF METHONE

The eastern slope of the lower East Hill has clear traces of erosion by the action of the sea. The excavations in Plot 274 showed that there was continuous habitation here from the Late Neolithic period through 354 B.C. (for the various agricultural land plots, see Fig. 1.1). The erosion from the sea, however, significantly reduced the extent of the hill; even so, the western edge of the residential phases of the Late Neolithic and the Early Bronze Age was preserved (Fig. 1.2). Moreover, limited excavations in Plot 278, located on the eastern slope of the hill, showed that, at least from the Archaic period, the settlement had extended to this area as well. This is a clear indication that a coastal zone had already been created here that prevented waves from eroding the hill. We can also accept the high possibility of a secondary harbor here, but this was always exposed to the severe southern winds that often batter the coast of Pieria.

In contrast, the northern port of Methone was among the safest in the entire Thermaic Gulf, since it was not affected by either the southern or northern winds. This, coupled with the immediate proximity of the settlement to the north–south main road that provided access, gave the site a strategic significance that allowed contact with central and western Macedonia, as well as the interior of the Balkans beyond. Consequently, we can easily understand the importance of the settlement in its earlier phases, but especially in the Late Geometric and Archaic periods.

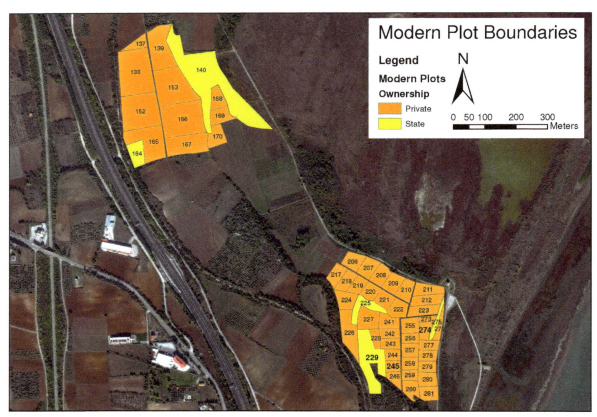

FIGURE 1.1. Google Earth view of the area of ancient and Macedonian Methone, showing the location of the various land holdings (plot numbers). Prepared by M. Chykerda

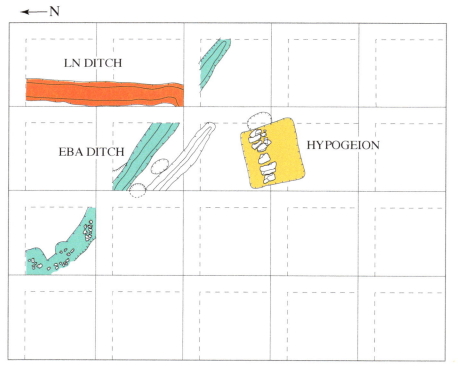

FIGURE 1.2. Plan of the northeast section of the East Hill as it survives today, showing the location of the prehistoric (Late Neolithic and Early Bronze) defensive ditches and the Hypogeion. Drawing I. Moschou

Our primary excavation activity was initially focused on Plot 274. At its peak, erosion, together with some likely subsequent interventions, eliminated most of the cultural deposits dating from the Late Neolithic period to 354 B.C. What survived included the lower portions of several prehistoric defensive ditches, as well as a unique underground feature (deep pit) of the Late Geometric period (Fig. 1.2). The latter, the so-called "Hypogeion" of Methone (Figs. 1.3–1.5),[3] with a depth of over 11.50 m, and measuring 4.20 m by 3.60 m, yielded an enormous amount of archaeological material, most of which can be attributed to the first phase of the colonization of Methone by the Eretrians in the late 8th and early 7th centuries B.C. (the colony was traditionally founded in 733 B.C.).[4]

FIGURE 1.3. General view of the Hypogeion, with wall no. 5, taken in 2003 during its excavation. Photo M. Christakou-Tolia

FIGURE 1.4. General view of the Hypogeion taken in 2006 during its excavation. Photo A. Athanassiadou

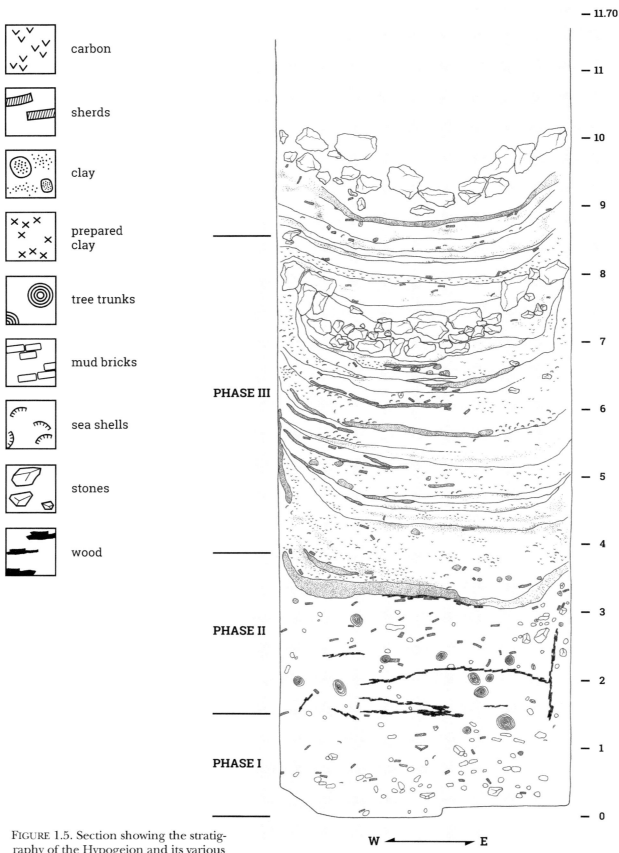

FIGURE 1.5. Section showing the stratigraphy of the Hypogeion and its various primary phases. Drawing I. Moschou

The ceramic corpus from this one deposit alone is surely the largest assemblage of the period in Macedonia and the north Aegean more generally. It includes large quantities of pottery that can be attributed to the local workshops of Methone and the broader region of the Thermaic Gulf, as well as imported pottery from the metropolis of Eretria and Euboia in general (Figs. 1.6–1.7). There is also a significant and varied sample of pottery from different production centers of the eastern (Fig. 1.8) and northeastern Aegean. In contrast, there are very few imports from the Cyclades. A remarkable assemblage of Corinthian pottery (Fig. 1.9), as well as Attic (Fig. 1.10), helps us with the chronology of the rest of the pottery. Indeed, almost all the major centers of the Aegean are represented, which makes this closed context unique to the entire ancient Greek world for studying the ceramics of the early colonial era of the historical period, beginning in the Late Geometric period and continuing well into the Archaic. Finally, there is pottery from the eastern Mediterranean, among which the five Phoenician amphoras stand out (two of which are illustrated in Figs. 1.11a–d).[5]

FIGURE 1.6. Spouted Euboian krater with pierced floor, serving as strainer, ΜΕΘ 1343. Photo I. Coyle

FIGURE 1.7. Skyphos of Euboian manufacture, ΜΕΘ 1321. Photo ΚΖ´ Ephoreia

FIGURE 1.8. East Greek "bird kotyle," ΜΕΘ 1591. Photo ΚΖ´ Ephoreia

FIGURE 1.9. Protocorinthian kotyle, ΜΕΘ 1319. Photo ΚΖ´ Ephoreia

FIGURE 1.10. Attic spouted krater, ΜΕΘ 2032, attributed to the Painter of Athens 897. Photo I. Coyle

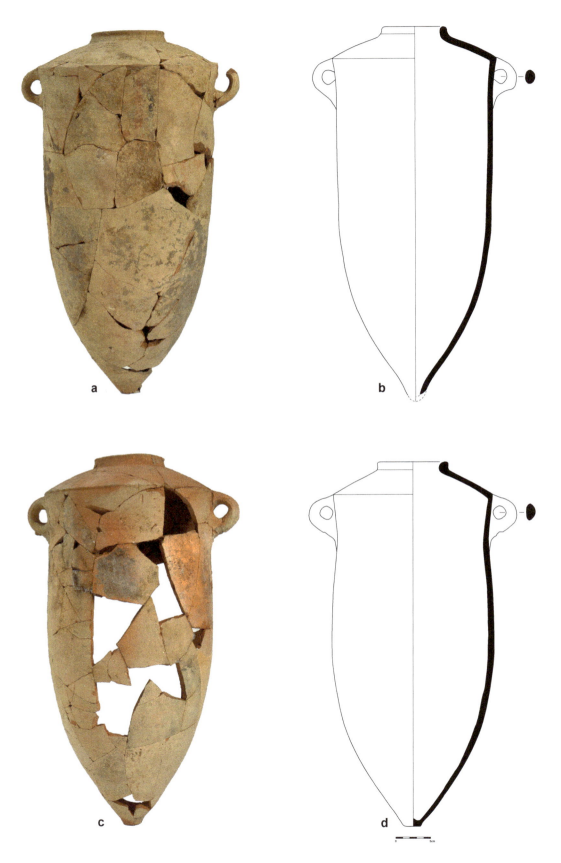

FIGURE 1.11. Phoenician amphoras from the Hypogeion: a)–b) ΜΕΘ 2033; c)–d) ΜΕΘ 2034. Photos I. Coyle, drawings I. Moschou and T. Ross

The large number of vessels with alphabetic inscriptions, single letters, trade-marks, and other symbols from the Hypogeion (e.g., Figs. 1.12–1.13), already published in *Methone* 1, should, therefore, come as no surprise.[6] It is the largest corpus of early alphabetic Greek in the Aegean, which, together with the plethora of imported pottery and other materials, establishes the port of Methone as one of the primary trade stations of the period. Among the various pieces made from imported materials is the well-preserved and magnificent ivory seal (Fig. 1.14).

FIGURE 1.12. Fragmentary Aiolian/Lesbian drinking cup with incised, post-firing inscription, ΜΕΘ 2249: Φιλίōνος ἐμί (retrograde). Photo KZ´ Ephoreia

FIGURE 1.13. Fragmentary Lesbian amphora with incised, post-firing inscription on the neck, ΜΕΘ 2237: Ἀντερύδεος. Photo KZ´ Ephoreia

FIGURE 1.14. Ivory seal, ΜΕΘ 507.
Photos J. Vanderpool, drawings T. Ross

But perhaps the most important discovery in the Hypogeion is the multitude of workshop waste: molds of terracotta (Fig. 1.15) and stone (Fig. 1.16a–d), crucibles, melting plates, and related objects (Figs. 1.17–1.19), bellows nozzles (Fig. 1.20), various tools, and remnants of materials in the course of being processed. All these finds indicate that Methone, apart from being a large trading center of the Aegean, was also a major industrial center, a place where a number of products of every available material of the period were manufactured.[7]

The Hypogeion sheds considerable light on the processes of propagation and prevalence of the early colonial era along the north Greek coasts. It demonstrates how an enterprising group of individuals who—if we are to believe the literary record, were both compatriots, and persecuted as enemies, of Eretria—established an *emporion* on the Thermaic Gulf, initiated technology and commerce, and managed to turn an indigenous settlement into a colony. It would not be an exaggeration to regard it as one of the most important archaeological discoveries of recent years in Macedonia.

To return to the excavation of Plot 274, the west slope of the East Hill brought to light evidence of large-scale earthworks, apparently intended to retain or stabilize the upper part of the hill. The initial earthworks were most likely begun at least in the Late Bronze Age, but on account of the great depth of deposits in the lower part of the slope, it was not possible to reach the earliest levels. What can be said, for the time being, is that in the upper and middle sections of the west slope of the East Hill sturdy walls were laid that functioned first for purposes of retention, creating terraces of sorts. Our first thoughts were that these walls were primarily for the fortification of the hill. They date to the Protogeometric, Late Geometric, and early Archaic periods. In particular, the Archaic Wall

FIGURE 1.15. Fragments of clay mold (upper fragment ΜΕΘ 5337, lower fragment ΜΕΘ 5335). Photo I. Coyle

7 gives the impression of a defensive circuit wall. Immediately to the west of this feature, part of the agora of ancient Methone was uncovered in the hollow created between the East and West Hills (Figs. 1.21–1.22). Erosion from the east, south, and west resulted in further deposits, which, particularly in the Archaic period, required continuous structural interventions to adapt the use of the buildings to the newly created levels of the settlement.

On account of subsequent erosion after the abandonment of the settlement in 354 B.C., a substantial dark-colored layer, up to 2.0 m thick, had collapsed over the agora, a process that significantly protected the underlying structures, after the initial damage to the buildings. We thus have, for the first time, well-preserved early monumental buildings, something previously unthinkable for northern Pieria given the lack of stone quarries in the wider area and constant stone-robbing of earlier structures. Above all, it should be stressed that for the first time in Lower Macedonia there are monumental buildings that can be characterized as public in function.

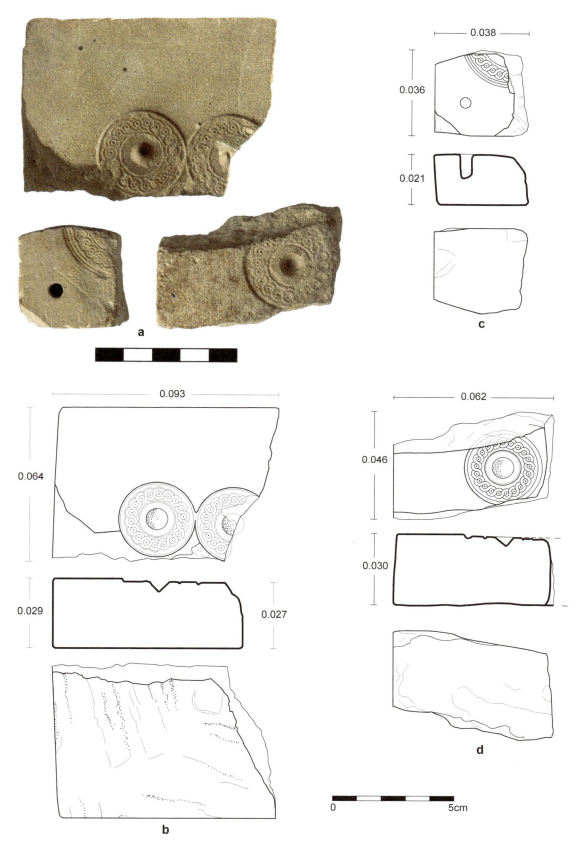

FIGURE 1.16. Stone molds for jewelry: a) ΜΕΘ 504 (top), ΜΕΘ 506 (bottom left), ΜΕΘ 4141 (bottom right); b) ΜΕΘ 504; c) ΜΕΘ 506; d) ΜΕΘ 4141. Photo J. Vanderpool, drawings A. Hooton

FIGURE 1.17. Clay crucible for bronzeworking, MEΘ 5344. Photo I. Coyle

FIGURE 1.18. Gold melting plate of clay, MEΘ 5331. Photo I. Coyle

FIGURE 1.19. Small clay crucible, MEΘ 515. Photo I. Coyle

FIGURE 1.20. Bellows nozzles, MEΘ 5329 and MEΘ 5330. Photos I. Coyle

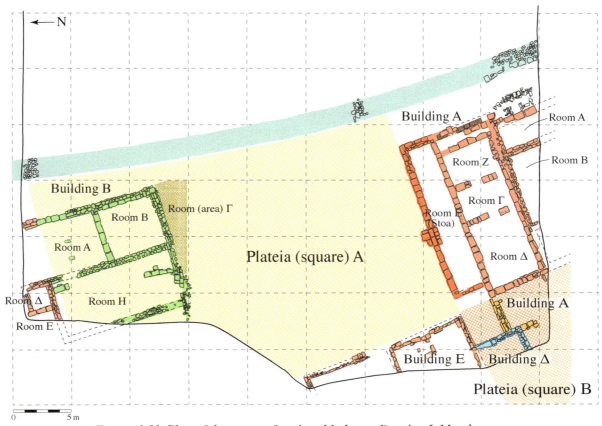

FIGURE 1.21. Plan of the agora of ancient Methone. Drawing I. Moschou

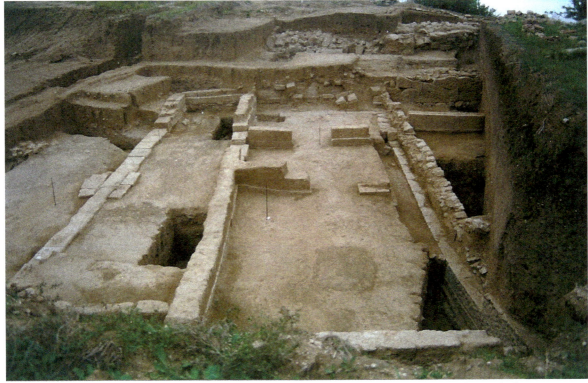

FIGURE 1.22. View of the agora from west, showing Building A. Photo A. Athanassiadou

In an initial phase of construction of these buildings, well-built polygonal walls were uncovered in Buildings A, B, and Δ that can be dated to the end of the 7th and the beginnings of the 6th century B.C. (Fig. 1.23). A major monumental phase with large well-cut ashlar blocks, and walls with a width of 0.80 m, was found in Building A and dates back to the first half of the 6th century B.C. At a higher level we have a more complete picture of a substantial building program dating back to the late 6th century B.C. The walls in this phase are 0.50 m thick, with well-cut stone socles, supporting upper walls of mud brick (Fig. 1.24). The roof was of Lakonian type.[8]

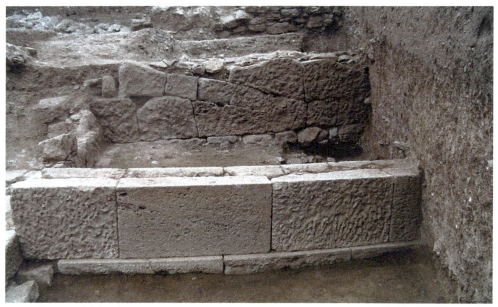

FIGURE 1.23. View from west of Building A in the agora, showing portion of a polygonal wall from the earliest phase of the building. Photo A. Athanassiadou

FIGURE 1.24. View from north of the later phases of Building A, showing mud-brick walls on a stone socle. Photo J. Papadopoulos

The interventions of the Classical era were at a smaller scale. In the 5th century B.C. the stoa (colonnade, porch) was built onto the north side of Building A opening onto Plateia A. In the northern part of the same square, there was also a rough extension of Building B, resulting in a space that only had access to the square, dating to the first half of the 4th century B.C. Substantial evidence for ironworking associated with the southern section of this building characterizes it as a blacksmith's workshop.

The fact that Buildings A, B, Δ, and E continue beyond Plot 274 onto adjacent parcels of unexcavated land does not allow a complete picture of their form and function. The information we have so far of these buildings and their associated squares and open areas shows that they were given over to industrial workshop activity of a commercial nature. It is no coincidence that Plateia A was covered by a thick black layer, the color of which was not due to the destruction of the area by the Macedonians, but to the operation of the workshops. Thanks to the destruction of Methone by Philip II in 354 B.C., we have a unique opportunity to study the form of one of the best-preserved Archaic agoras of the ancient Greek world.

The buildings of the agora in Plot 274 developed around two relatively small squares. A small portion of another monumental building (Building Γ) was investigated a little to the south, in Plot 278; it did not have access to these squares but faced east toward the sea. As noted above, there was possibly a secondary harbor located in this area. We thus have public buildings developing around contiguous small squares. It is even possible that there was a similar square farther north of Plot 274, toward the main port of Methone, which is located a short distance to the north. It is also worth considering the corresponding agora of the metropolis of Eretria, which was also located a short distance from its harbor. The direct relationship between the commercial market and its port is an obvious necessity.

In concluding this short presentation of the excavation of Plot 274, it is important to point out the collapse of the central and western parts of Building A and the relationship with its eastern part. It is certain that in this area there was a deep trench, which must be associated with the ancient excavations aimed at strengthening the East Hill that were mentioned earlier and which are to be placed chronologically before the Early Iron Age.

In all of the above buildings, the pottery collected from the destruction deposit (Fig. 1.25), together with a significant number of lead sling bullets and some bronze and iron arrowheads, provides an impression of the historical setting of the last days of the settlement of Methone.[9]

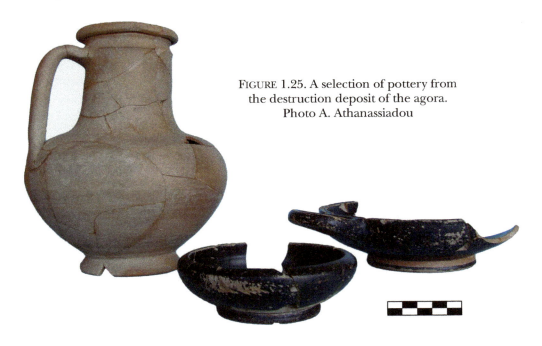

FIGURE 1.25. A selection of pottery from the destruction deposit of the agora. Photo A. Athanassiadou

EXCAVATIONS ON THE WEST HILL: THE ACROPOLIS OF METHONE

FIGURE 1.26. Underground tunnel dug by the Methonaians in the later Classical period as part of their defense system against the siege of Philip II in 354 B.C. (Plot 245, West Hill). Photo K. Noulas

The excavations of the West Hill, identified as the acropolis of the settlement, were located in Plots 229 and 245. Here, the soil morphology as well as the surface finds indicated the possible line of the south wall of the ancient fortifications of Methone. Unfortunately, here, too, the erosion of the cultural deposits of the settlement, already described for the East Hill, resulted in the loss of all the superstructures associated with the fortification system. However, in all of the excavation areas that have been investigated along the presumed course of the wall, underground tunnels have been identified that should be considered as defensive works of the Methonaians (Fig. 1.26).

Another interesting feature of the defense works of Methone on the south side is the observation that the hill outside the wall was dug away to a depth of many meters, thereby greatly enhancing the effectiveness of the fortifications. However, to the south of sector A in Plot 229, this trench had largely disappeared. A trial trench in this area was dug to a depth of 4.00 m, but bedrock was not reached. This showed that massive volumes of soil had been transferred to this area, the soil containing few sherds, although a number of lead sling bullets were collected.

It is a well-known siege practice of the period to bring large quantities of soil to create embankments in front of the walls, so as to enable the assailants to ascend to the level of the walls by means of ladders or siege engines. In this particular instance, the fill found on the neck of land to the south of the acropolis of Methone should be attributed to the siege of the city by Philip II in 354 B.C.

The excavations undertaken as part of the construction of the Nea Agathoupolis sewerage network (from 2013 to 2015) on the plateau south of the acropolis help us in particular to come to a better understanding of this siege.[10] Just a short distance south of the dilapidated trench dug by the Methonaians, and around 70 m from the line of the city wall, a large pit with a length of 16 m and a maximum depth of 2.70 m was found. It is likely that the quantities of soil that the Macedonians needed for the construction of the embankment came from here.

Sections of two other ditches, one running east–west and the other north–south, were located farther south. They can be attributed to the defensive trench that surrounded the Macedonian camp, according to the practice of ancient siege craft. The eastern trench is estimated to have a length of 300 m. Assuming that the camp was square, then the area enclosed would be about nine hectares (90 stremmata).

The northern ditch is some 140 m from the line of the Methone wall. This is not a great distance, and the likelihood that Philip II lost his right eye here is not due to "chance" (schol. Dem. *Olynth.* III. 43a), but to the skill of a Methonaian archer named Aster. The height differential between the upper ramparts of the wall and the most likely position of Philip, who as leader of the army would usually be at the forefront, is minimal. Aster, therefore, had a clear sightline to his goal and it is more likely that the orb of the arrow had a straight path rather than a curve. The phrase "by chance" should refer to the fact that the path of the arrow had avoided Philip's defensive equipment.[11]

Moreover, this particular section of the fortification of Methone, in front of the embankment, is mentioned in the well-known stratagem noted by Polyainos: "Philip was able to place on the walls of Methone many Macedonians by means of ladders, which were then removed and, thus having no hope of retreating, these Macedonians fought with greater stubbornness to prevail over the walls."[12]

The excavation of Plots 229 and 245 indicated that there may have been some sparse habitation at the top of the West Hill already from the Early Bronze Age. There were also a few simple pit graves of the same period, which only rarely contained pottery as grave goods. In contrast, the number of graves increased significantly in the Late Bronze Age, often with interesting grave goods (Fig. 1.27a–b).[13] Wheelmade and painted pottery is in the majority (Fig. 1.28a–d), resulting from contacts

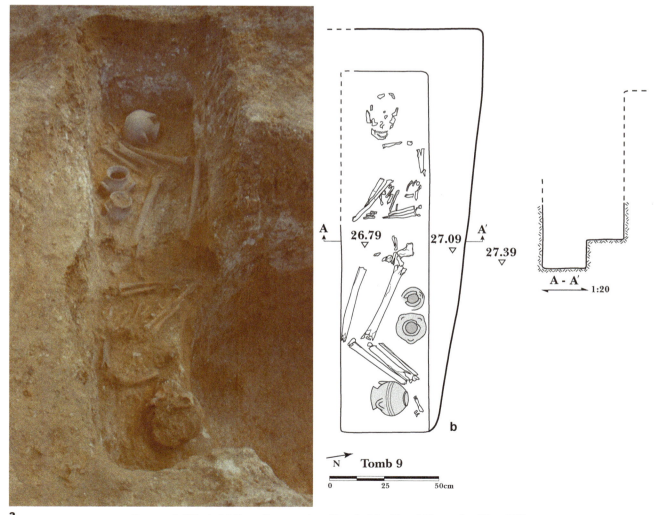

FIGURE 1.27. a)–b) Late Bronze Age Tomb 9 in Plot 245 on the West Hill.
Photo K. Noulas, drawing I. Moschou and T. Ross

with the Mycenaean world, but there is no dearth of local handmade pottery (Fig. 1.28e–f). The jewelry includes various ornaments made of gold, bronze, glass, terracotta, animal bone, amber, and semi-precious stone (Fig. 1.29). The tombs are almost exclusively inhumations in wooden coffins, or in pits with timber covers that rest on cut ledges. There is, however, a single cremation tomb where the cremated remains of the deceased were placed in a handmade pot (Fig. 1.30).

FIGURE 1.28. Selection of wheelmade and painted, as well as handmade, pottery deposited in Late Bronze Age tombs: a) ΜΕΘ 865; b) ΜΕΘ 861; c) ΜΕΘ 864; d) ΜΕΘ 860; e) ΜΕΘ 862; f) ΜΕΘ 866. Photos I. Coyle

FIGURE 1.29. The jewelry from Tomb 10 in Plot 229 on the West Hill, including ornaments made of gold, amber, semi-precious stone, animal bone, and terracotta. Photo I. Coyle

FIGURE 1.30. The solitary Late Bronze Age cremation, Tomb 8 in Plot 229, showing cinerary urn (ΜΕΘ 4068) and cremated remains. Photo I. Coyle

FIGURE 1.31. View from east of the Early Iron Age fortification trench in Plot 245. Photo K. Noulas

During the Early Iron Age, and specifically in the Protogeometric and Subprotogeometric periods, there is a clear increase in the size of the fortified settlement, which now includes the West Hill. In Plots 229 and 245, on the upper part of the eastern slope of the hill, a fortification trench was investigated, which had been cut in the Early Iron Age to extend the settlement to the south (Fig. 1.31). Adjacent to it was an apsidal building, as indicated by the arrangement of its postholes. Similarly, on the level summit of the hill, in all of the excavation squares of sector B, wherever bedrock was reached, were Early Iron Age buildings, as indicated by postholes, one

Figure 1.32. View of one of the Ephoreia trenches in Plot 229 excavated between 2008 and 2011, but photographed, after cleaning, in 2014, showing Early Iron Age postholes and refuse pits.
Photo J. Papadopoulos

of which preserved a portion of the apse of the building (Fig. 1.32). It should be noted that at the top of the West Hill we did not encounter a characteristic layer of the Late Geometric and Subgeometric period. We have only stray finds of these phases and it is possible that here in the early phase of the arrival of the Eretrians there was only sparse habitation.[14]

The primary deposits at the top of the hill are associated with the remains of at least three buildings with various additions and interventions (Fig. 1.33), belonging to the second half of the 7th and the first half of the 6th century B.C. An extensive layer of destruction by fire was noted across these buildings during the first half of the 6th century B.C. and has yielded rich finds, mainly pottery, not least commercial amphoras and imported fine-ware pottery (Figs. 1.34–1.35).

In most parts of the excavated area there are clear indications of metalworking and other small-scale craft workshops. The existence of two kilns in semi-open spaces (Figs. 1.33, 6.3a, 19.1c) allows us to attribute them to a ceramic workshop.[15] Among the various implements used in metalworking, we illustrate only two among several other fragments of stone molds (Fig. 1.36a–f). These were for producing not only jewelry and items of personal ornaments, but also for small implements, such as the fishhooks as seen on the mold ΜΕΘ 2977 (Fig. 1.36a–c). But among the most interesting and surprising finds were the many small fragments of elephant ivory, which represent debitage from the working of the ivory on the West Hill (Fig. 1.37). This is one of the very rare contexts in Archaic Greece where ivory-working has been documented. The general picture that emerges thus far is one of extensive industrial activity; this is the case in virtually every area of Methone where Archaic deposits have been reached. Methone can veritably be classified as an industrial city.

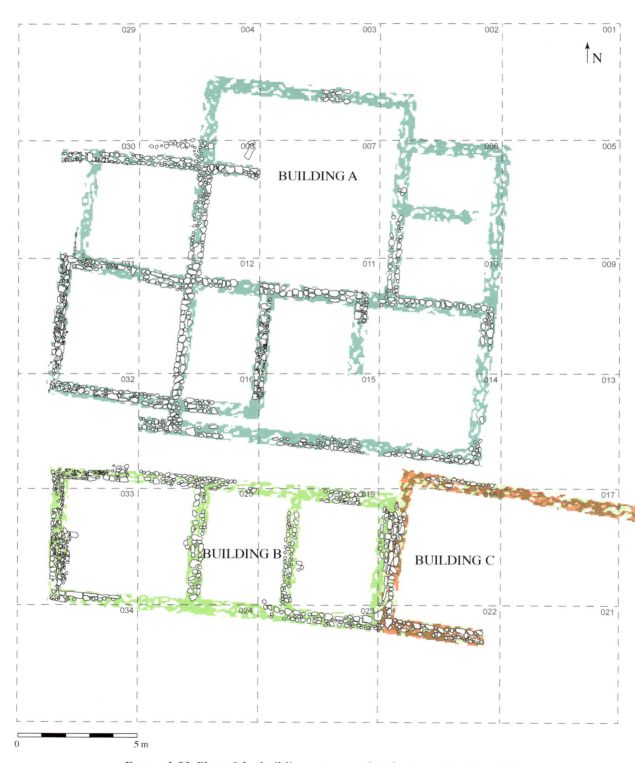

FIGURE 1.33. Plan of the buildings uncovered at the top of the West Hill.
Drawing I. Moschou

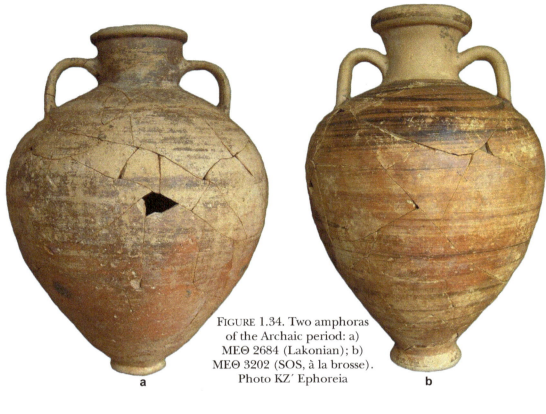

FIGURE 1.34. Two amphoras of the Archaic period: a) ΜΕΘ 2684 (Lakonian); b) ΜΕΘ 3202 (SOS, à la brosse). Photo ΚΖ´ Ephoreia

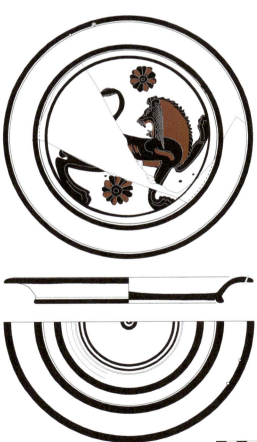

FIGURE 1.35. Archaic Corinthian plate, ΜΕΘ 2695. Photo I. Coyle, drawing A. Hooton

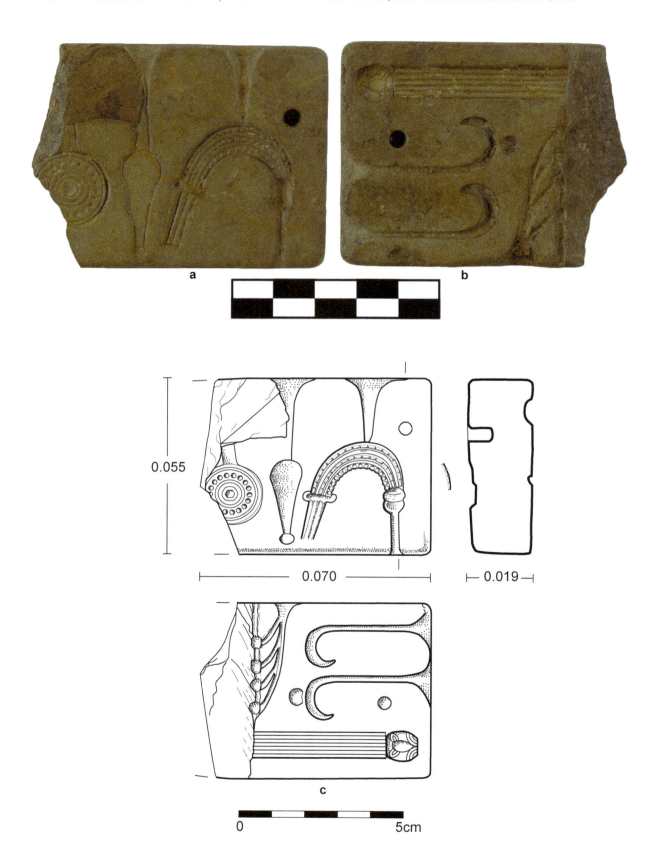

FIGURE 1.36. (on this and facing page) Two stone molds from the West Hill of Methone: a)–c) ΜΕΘ 2977; d)–f) ΜΕΘ 2976. Photos I. Coyle, drawings A. Hooton

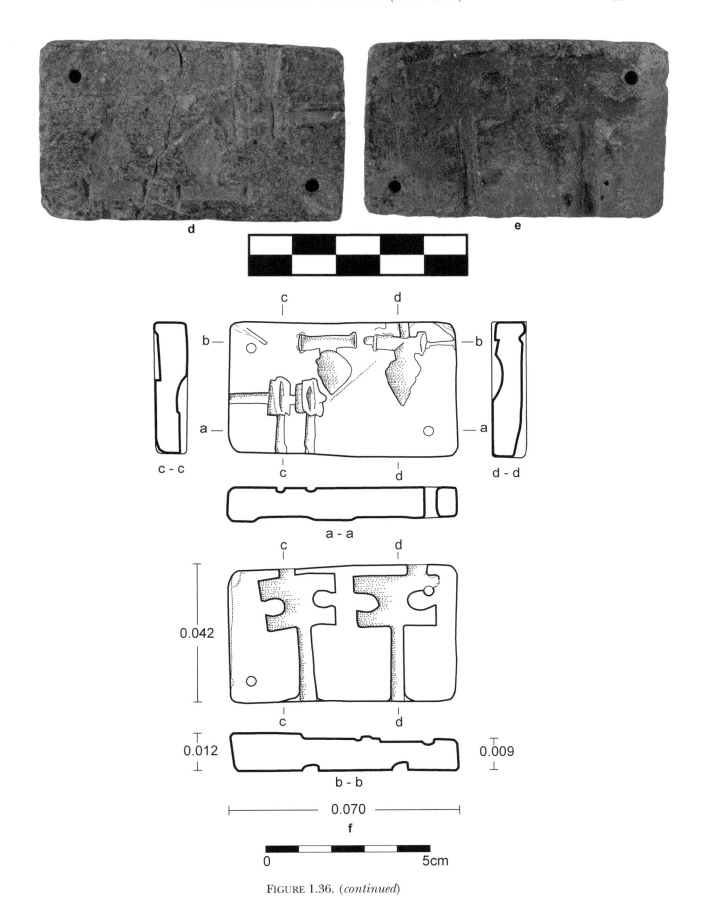

FIGURE 1.36. (*continued*)

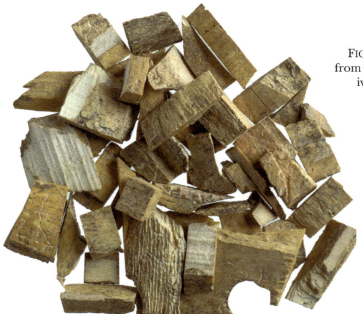

FIGURE 1.37. Elephant ivory debitage from the West Hill, showing that imported ivory was worked on the West Hill. Photo J. Vanderpool

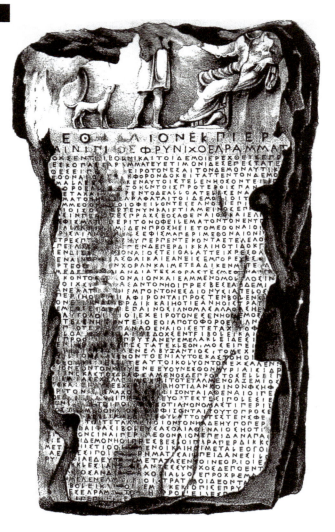

FIGURE 1.38. Inscription recording the alliance between Athens and Methone found in Athens (Theater of Dionysos) and now in the Acropolis Museum, formerly Athens, Epigraphical Museum EM 6596 (428/7–424/3 B.C.). Drawing after Pittakis 1838, pp. 96–98, inscription no. 45

The use of the West Hill continues into the second half of the 6th century B.C., but it is particularly fragmented due to the intense erosion of the upper part of the hill. The same reasons should account for the total loss of undisturbed deposits of the Classical period, at which time there are only isolated finds from the surface, disturbed by plowing, and some material deposited in underground installations. Only one Classical pit was identified in an area otherwise dominated by Archaic buildings, which was not investigated.

Most of the finds on the West Hill from the last phase of Methone were found in the four underground tunnels belonging to the fortification works of the Methonaians, which were abandoned after 354 B.C. Their density, of course, cannot be disassociated from the need to undermine the embankment built by Philip in this area, as well as to allow for active defense. The fortified settlement captured by Philip II in 354 B.C. is estimated at around 10 hectares, which, for the period, is not a particularly significant size.

Since 2013, the archaeological investigations and related work carried out as part of the installation of the sewerage network of Nea Agathoupolis, already noted, has provided a good deal of additional evidence for the diachronic use of a much larger area by the ancient Methonaians.[16] As noted above, due to the intense erosion of various parts of the site, the finds are fragmentary. However, we have evidence on the use of the site throughout the Bronze Age, for which at least ten pit graves of the Early Bronze Age stand out. The Early Iron Age habitation occupied a much larger area, and from the Archaic and Classical periods there are similar indications of habitation, as well as an infant burial in a pithos.

CONCLUDING REMARKS

Concluding the presentation of this summary overview of the excavations of Methone, it must be said that the period in which the settlement develops into something truly distinctive—the period in which it reaches its acme—is the early colonial era of the Late Geometric and Archaic periods.

After the Persian wars, Methone entered the sphere of Athenian influence and became a member of the Delian League. This was an alliance that constituted a lasting strategic and economic threat to the emerging power of the region, the Macedonian kingdom. At the same time, and immediately to the south, Pydna was developing as the primary harbor of the Macedonians. The location of the port of Pydna, exposed as it is to the south and north winds, cannot be compared to the natural advantages of the port of Methone. It is reasonable to conclude that Alexander I took certain measures to establish here, in the immediate vicinity of Methone, a rival Macedonian port.

In the 5th century B.C., the fate of Methone was intimately tied to the support of Athens, and this is most clearly seen by the special privileges that Methone enjoyed that were voted on by the Athenians and set in stone in an inscription found on the Athenian Acropolis and now on display in the Acropolis Museum (Fig. 1.38). Following the vicissitudes in the fate of Athens and Macedon in the 4th century B.C., the end of Methone was prescribed. In 354 B.C. Philip II besieged and captured the city, even though the Athenians had sent 3,000 hoplites to the defense of Methone. According to Diodorus Siculus, Philip expelled the Methonaians and distributed their land to the Macedonians. The excavation record leaves no doubt as to the complete abandonment of the settlement.[17] At the same time, Philip established a settlement of the Macedonians only a short distance northwest of ancient Methone, and still on what was at the time the west coast of the Thermaic Gulf (Fig. 1.39). This action by Philip II clearly conveyed

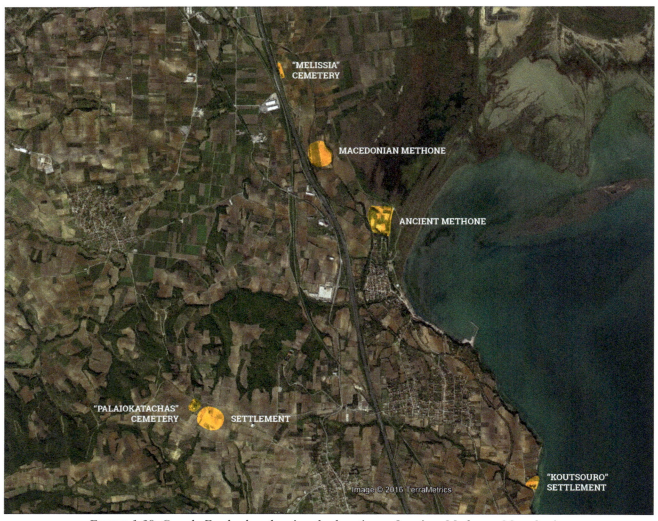

FIGURE 1.39. Google Earth plan showing the locations of ancient Methone, Macedonian Methone, the "Melissia" cemetery, and the settlement and cemetery at Palaiokatachas. Prepared by I. Moschou

strong symbolism, but it cannot be ruled out that the port of Methone had already begun to be silted up during this period, owing to the nearby rivers, not least the Haliakmon.

From the newly created settlement of Macedonian Methone, many fragments of architectural members have been gathered, mainly from doorjambs, as well as parts of pebble-mosaic floors destroyed by plowing. These remains provide clear evidence of the existence of a large building, although it is not known whether it was of a public character or the monumental residence of a local overlord, on the analogy of ancient Argilos.[18] The discovery of a large millstone a short distance from the building suggests that the latter option is perhaps more likely. Finally, part of a marble male statue picked up in the general vicinity, as well as a fragment of a stele, may suggest the location of a nearby sanctuary. Be that as it may, from surface finds it appears that Macedonian Methone was inhabited until the Early Christian period.

Another settlement of the Macedonians, about 3 km to the southwest, enjoyed a much longer life, at the location known as "Palaiokatachas," so named at least since Byzantine times (Fig. 1.39). This settlement was inhabited from the 4th century B.C. until the 19th century, when it was destroyed in one of the local uprisings against the Ottomans. In the area of both Macedonian Methone and Palaiokatachas, cemeteries were explored, which gave particularly rich finds.[19] These cemeteries belong to the time when the Macedonian kingdom was at its height, especially after the campaigns of Alexander the Great in the East, but also the generous land grants and privileges bestowed on the Macedonians by Philip II.

In the cemetery of the coastal village of Macedonian Methone, at the location of "Melissia" Aiginiou, there were also a few earlier tombs belonging to the early colonial period. Among these was a cist tomb of an Early Iron Age warrior replete with iron weapons and an Euboian Late Protogeometric oinochoe (Figs. 1.40–1.41). This tomb bolsters the evidence for early contact between Euboia and Methone, and there are related finds in the wider area of the Thermaic Gulf. When, exactly, an Eretrian *"emporion"* was established at Methone is, of course, difficult to determine. But from the period immediately before, and close in date to that of the foundation of the early colony, comes a body fragment of an Attic Middle Geometric amphora from the Hypogeion, 9/1 (Fig. 1.42). On its interior wall are traces of water damage, most likely from the action of the sea at the harbor beach, prior to deposition. Perhaps this Attic amphora with its contents was carried by a merchant from Eretria to the port of Methone? In whatever way, and by whose conveyance, this amphora made its way to Methone, on this one small fragment converge the three factors that determined and defined the fate of the colony at Methone: Eretria, Athens, and the sea.

FIGURE 1.40. Cist tomb at "Melissia" cemetery northwest of Methone containing Euboian Late Protogeometric oinochoe Πυ 1516.
Photo K. Noulas

FIGURE 1.41. Euboian Late Protogeometric oinochoe Πυ 1516.
Photo KZ´ Ephoreia, drawing A. Hooton

FIGURE 1.42. Body fragment, Attic Middle Geometric amphora, ΜΕΘ 3807. Photo I. Coyle

NOTES

1. For the excavations at ancient Methone, see Bessios 2003; Bessios et al. 2004; Bessios, Athanassiadou, and Noulas 2008, 2021b. This chapter was translated from the Greek by John Papadopoulos.
2. This new research program—the Ancient Methone Archaeological Project (AMAP)—covers the period 2014–2017 and includes, in addition to systematic excavations on the West Hill, a pedestrian surface survey of the settlement and its surrounding area, a geophysical survey, and a geomorphological program of coring in the area of the ancient harbor, as well as one of the first LiDAR (Light Detection and Ranging) surveys of an Archaic and Classical Greek city. The results of the collaboration between the Ephoreia of Antiquities of Pieria and UCLA in 2014–2017 are presented elsewhere in a preliminary report on all aspects of the fieldwork; see Morris et al. 2020.
3. Taken in 2006 during the excavation of the Hypogeion, Figure 1.4 best shows the size and great depth of this significant feature, and the difficulties of its excavation.
4. For a historical introduction to Methone, see Chapter 2.
5. For these, see Athanassiadou 2012; Kasseri 2012. A very similar Late Geometric II Phoenician amphora was found in tomb 483 at Pithekoussai, see *Pithekoussai* I, p. 487, pl. 144, no. 483-26 (inv. 167893).
6. Bessios, Tzifopoulos, and Kotsonas 2012. See also Strauss Clay, Malkin, and Tzifopoulos 2017b; Papadopoulos 2016.
7. See also Bessios 2013.
8. For a detailed study of the architecture of Building A by Samantha Martin, see Chapter 18.
9. For the pottery from the destruction deposit of Methone, as well as the lead sling bullets, see Chapters 29 and 28; the bronze and iron arrowheads are presented in Chapter 26 (John Papadopoulos).
10. Bessios et al. 2014.
11. For further details, together with the literary sources concerning Aster and Philip II, see Chapter 2.
12. The relevant section of Polyainos, *Strategemata* 4.2.15 (Wölffin and Melber ed.), reads: "Φίλιππος τοῖς Μεθωναίων τείχεσι κλίμακας προσήγαγεν καὶ δι' αὐτῶν πολλοὺς Μακεδόνας ἀνεβίβασε πολιορκητάς. ἐπεὶ δὲ ἀνέβησαν ἐπὶ τὰ τείχη, ἀφεῖλε τὰς κλίμακας, ὅπως ἐλπίδα τοῦ καταβῆναι μὴ ἔχοντες προθυμότερον τῶν τειχῶν κρατήσειαν."
13. See further Bessios 2010, pp. 61–62.
14. Well-stratified cultural deposits of the 8th and early 7th centuries B.C. were encountered in the more recent excavations on the West Hill in 2014–2017, see Morris et al. 2020, esp. pp. 693–699.
15. These kilns are discussed in more detail below, Chapter 19.
16. See Bessios et al. 2014.
17. For the consistency (or otherwise) between the literary and archaeological evidence in the case of ancient Methone, see Bessios, Athanassiadou, and Noulas 2021a.
18. For the building at Argilos, see Bonias and Perreault 1996, esp. pp. 672–675; Bonias and Perreault 1997; Perreault and Bonias 2017; Zampas et al. 2021.
19. See Bessios 2010, pp. 305–319.

2

METHONE IN ANCIENT SOURCES

Yannis Z. Tzifopoulos

The ancient sources for Methone, as for the rest of Macedonia, are quite fragmentary, and relate mainly short mythical and historical narratives, a few scattered comments on the toponym and geography, and only exceptionally historical events.[1]

The toponym Methone (Μεθώνη) and its suffix -ōnā/-ōnē, perhaps a variant of an original -ānā, may suggest a prehellenic stratum of similarly composed toponyms—like Dodona, Korone, Torone, Skione, Methana, Messana, Athenai, Mykenai, Pallene, Pellana, and many others—but its stem μεθ- points to the Greek verb μεθίημι.[2] In the sources, however, the mythical mind is at work in various ways:[3] 1) Methone was one of the seven Alkyonids, daughters of the giant Alkyoneus, whom Herakles with the help of Athena killed in Pallene of Chalkidike during the Gigantomachy;[4] 2) Methone was the name of a daughter of Linos and sister of Pieros, the oikist of Pieria, or, alternatively, the local nymph Methone was the wife of Pieros and mother of Oiagros;[5] 3) Methon, an ancestor of Orpheus and a mythical oikist or resident of the area, gave his name to the city;[6] 4) *methu* (μέθυ),[7] the Homeric intoxicating wine sometimes identified with pure, undiluted wine and sometimes with excessive drinking,[8] became the reason for naming the place Methone, because the many vineyards in the area produced large quantities of wine (πολύοινος).

The toponym Methone is not unique in the Greek world. Demetrios of Magnesia (ca. 1st century B.C.) knew four cities named Methone, while according to Stephanus of Byzantium (late 5th century A.D.) there were five: the one in Thrace/Macedonia,[9] another in Magnesia (one of the four cities under Philoktetes in the Trojan War),[10] a third in Lakonia/Messenia, a fourth in Persia, and a fifth in Euboia.

Moreover, according to Strabo, the name Methana of the peninsula between Epidauros and Troizen,[11] which is given as Methone in Thucydides' manuscripts (4.45),[12] caused confusion with the Macedonian Methone, where Philip II lost his eye during the siege. As the geographer explains, based on the testimony of Demetrios of Skepsis and Theopompos, this confusion between the two toponyms has misled some writers who relate that the curses of Agamemnon's naval recruiters (*nau(s) tologoi*), because the inhabitants of Methone refused to join the Trojan expedition, concerned the inhabitants of Methone in Argolis and not in Macedonia. According to Theopompos' argument, which is accepted by Strabo, the inhabitants of Methone in Argolis could not have denied their participation and must have heeded Agamemnon's request because of their immediate proximity to Mycenae. Consequently, the legend of the refusal to participate in the Trojan campaign should reasonably concern the inhabitants of Macedonian Methone.

This much is also repeated in a papyrus fragment, probably from the end of Strabo's seventh book and based on Theopompos, with two differences: it quotes verbatim the purported curse "may you never stop building walls," presumably echoing the excuse put forward by the inhabitants in order to refuse the request,[13] and also notes that Methone and its environs was a wooded area;

consequently it was only natural to be approached by Agamemnon's *nau(s)tologoi* for the repair of ships.[14] It is remarkable that this request concerns both the repair (ἐπισκευή, and perhaps even construction) of ships, one of the activities associated with Methone (as a source of nautical timber) in later times, which is not refused by the inhabitants, and the recruitment for the expedition, which is denied. The possibility that Agamemnon had reached Methone in Pieria seeking support for the fleet of the Trojan expedition may look far-fetched, but, as Bruno Helly has shown, Philoktetes' kingdom (Homer *Iliad* 2. 716–720) may very well have extended up to the river Haliakmon. Be that as it may, a relationship between Magnesia and Pieria seems to predate the destruction of Pierian Methone by Philip in 354 B.C. and the settlement of Magnesian Methone after ca. 350 B.C., as the curious entry in the Delphic *theorodokoi* list attests about the contribution of the Magnesian Methonaioi (*FdD* III 5.4 col. III, 39 = *CID* 2.5, col. II, 39), dated to 358 B.C.[15] After all, according to Hesiod (fr. 7 West and Merkelbach 1967), Magnes and Macedon are Zeus' children and inhabit the area around Pieria and Olympos with the northern boundary probably at the Haliakmon estuaries, while Philoktetes' archers and oarsmen, his Magnetes, are the northernmost allies of the Achaeans in the Trojan campaign.[16]

Methone's geographical location dominates north Pieria,[17] and it is the last city on the border with Emathia and Bottiaia.[18] According to Ps.-Skylax (*Periplous* 66), the coastal cities that one met sailing north of Magnesia and after the river Peneios in the territory of the Macedonians and the Thermaic Gulf were: Herakleion (modern Platamon), Dion, Pydna (πόλις Ἑλληνίς), Methone (πόλις Ἑλληνίς), the river Haliakmon, Aloros, the river Lydias (Loudias), and Pella, the capital of the kingdom reached by sailing up the Lydias (Loudias).[19] Pydna and Methone (as well as other cities in Chalkidike) termed "Greek cities," in contrast to the ones without designation, probably indicate that these existed as colonies of southern Greeks before the Macedonian kingdom.

The description of the geographer Strabo (7.20 and 22) offers more topographical details and makes clear that the river Peneios is the natural southern boundary between Thessaly-Magnesia and Macedonia, and Haliakmon the northern and eastern limit between Pieria and Bottiaia, while the Pieria and Olympos mountains designated the western boundary of Pieria.[20] Strabo records only three cities north of Dion, that is, Pydna, Methone, and Aloros, of which the last, on the banks of the Haliakmon, belongs to the region of Bottiaia, while Pydna is in Pieria. Although the boundary between the two Macedonian regions is determined by the Haliakmon, and Methone is closer to the river, it remains questionable whether Bottiaia and Pieria are geographical and/or political units. What is more, Strabo does not mention whether Methone was considered part of Pieria or Bottiaia, apparently because of the city's history. For the geographer, Methone is sometimes Macedonian and sometimes Thracian, when distinguishing it from Methone in Magnesia, but always the city that Philip II destroyed losing his right eye.[21]

This controversial state of the city is not at all accidental, as it is closely related to that of Pieria. This name is explained as that of either a Pieros, brother of Methone or son of Eleuther; or a nymph Pieria; or, according to Eustathios' commentary, the name of the land or one of Olympos' peaks; or, more likely, as derived from the word πίηρ/πίαρ (from the verb πίω or the adjectival noun πῖον, IE root *piH_1w-), that is, the moist and by extension rich and fertile land.[22] Curiously enough, the name *pi-we-ri-si* ("Pierian women") is attested in Linear B tablets from Pylos and Mycenae, and makes it highly probable that Pieria and Methone—if Agamemnon's curse above has any credence—were known to the Mycenaeans (see further Chapter 6). Already in Homer and Hesiod the region and the mountain are identified with the wild and dangerous Olympos to the south as the dwelling of the gods, while in the north-northwest the calm and more accessible ridges, later called the Pierian mountains, are the birthplace of the nine Pierian Muses, children of Zeus and Mnemosyne.

Moreover, according to Pausanias (9.29.1–4), the Boiotians themselves argued that the Macedonian Pieros, who named the mountain, also established the worship of the nine Muses in Helikon, whereas some sources remark that the nine Muses were Pieros' daughters.[23] Yet the nine Pierian Muses are not the only ones that, according to Boiotian tradition, were imported from Macedonia. Forty stades from Koronia, Pausanias mentions Mt. Libethron (Λιβήθριον) with statues of the Libethrian (Λιβηθρίων or Λιβηθρίδων) Muses and Nymphs and the springs Libethrias (Λιβηθριάς) and Petra (Πέτρα) in the form of female breasts from which water flows like milk.[24] Likewise, when describing Helikon and the surrounding area, Strabo (9.2.25) mentions the existence of the sanctuary of the Muses, Hippokrene, and the Cave of the Leibethrion Nymphs. On account of this, Strabo conjectures that the Thracian tribe Pieres may have consecrated this sanctuary, as they dedicated to the same goddesses Pieria, Leibethrion, and Pimpleia, where the Pieres once lived; but after they were displaced, the Macedonians occupied the area. This conjecture is based on a report that Thracians, Pelasgians, and other barbarians violently expelled the Boiotians and occupied the place in antiquity.[25]

This myth-historic narrative of Strabo and Pausanias acquires particular interest after the excavations of the Ephoreia of Paleoanthropology and Speleology in the Boiotian cave, during which inscribed clay figurines and vases were unearthed, dated to the end of the 6th and the beginning of the 5th century B.C. Not only the dedicatory inscriptions to the Nymphs Λειβεσθριάδες (Λειβηθριάδες in literature), but also a fragmentary inscription at the end of the Archaic period recording an offer of Pieres at Delphi, are noteworthy, even if problematic.[26] This identification of place- and cult-names indicates some kind of connection between the inhabitants of Pieria and Boiotia, which according to Strabo (10.3.17) is not limited to names alone but extends to poetry and its accompanying music (with Orpheus, Musaios, and Thamyris as prominent Thracian representatives), the melody, the rhythm, and the musical instruments, such as the Asian kithara, the Berekynthian or Phrygian aulos, the nabla, the sambyke, the barbitos, the magadis, etc.[27] The identical names of the places and of the Muses' cult, as well as the accompanying ritual music, are, according to Strabo, strong signs of one-time relations between Pieria and Boiotia, and of Thracian Pieres with Makedones and Boiotians.

These particular characteristics of Pieria are also celebrated in Euripides' *Bacchae* of 407 B.C., written after the tragedian, supposedly in self-exile from Athens, accepted Archelaos' invitation in 408 B.C. to move to Macedonia where he also became a member of Archelaos' *hetaireia*.[28] The conception and composition of this uniquely provocative tragedy may have been inspired in Macedonia, specifically in the area of Pieria between the river Axios, celebrated in the tragedy, and Olympos, an area whose topography, mythic associations, and legends had a strong effect on Euripides, as is suggested especially by lines 410–416 and 560–575.[29]

Fortunately for Methone in Pieria, an incident of its protohistory has survived as Plutarch's reply to the question: Who were the *aposphendonetoi* (Plutarch, *Quaest. Graec.*, 293a–b):[30]

> Men from Eretria used to inhabit the island of Korkyra. But Charikrates sailed there from Corinth with an army and defeated them in war; so the Eretrians embarked in their ships and sailed back home. Their fellow-citizens, however, having learned of the matter before their arrival, barred their return to the country and prevented them from disembarking by showering upon them missiles from slings. Since the exiles were unable either to persuade or to overcome their fellow-citizens, who were numerous and inexorable, they sailed to Thrace and occupied a territory in which, according to tradition, Methon, the ancestor of Orpheus, had formerly lived. So the Eretrians named their city Methone, but they were also named by their neighbors the "Men repulsed by slings" (trans. Babbitt 1936a).

In Strabo's narrative about the establishment of a Corinthian colony in Korkyra, the Eretrians are absent and only the Liburnians are mentioned as expelled by the Herakleid Chersikrates (not Plutarch's Charikrates) and part of the army, which the Corinthians had sent to Sicily under Archias for the foundation of Syracuse.[31] The founding of the Corinthian colony in Korkyra led by Charikrates (or Chersikrates) and the foundation of Taras by the Spartans, according to the chronology of Eusebius and Hieronymos, date back to ca. 709 B.C., during the reign of Perdikkas I in Macedonia.[32] Modern historians, however, date Methone's foundation one generation earlier, to around 733/2 B.C. or a few years later.[33] Even though Plutarch attributes the foundation of Methone to the newly arrived Eretrians, it is rather unlikely that the exiled Eretrians' voyage to the north and their settlement in the area happened incidentally. Obviously the area was known, perhaps as a trading station, but the arrival of the "repulsed by slings" Eretrian settlers gave a boost for remarkable growth.[34] Even so, the inhabitants and neighbors of the region, who named the newcomers "repulsed by slings" (ἀποσφενδόνητοι), are not mentioned by Plutarch, except as *prosoikoi*, although the Eretrians supposedly chose to name the place Methone in honor of the Thracian Methon, a local former inhabitant. According to Thucydides (2.99.3), when the Macedonians began their expansion in Pieria to the sea, the south, and the east, they expelled after a battle the Thracian tribe of Pieres who were living there and forced them to flee east of the river Strymon and settle in Phagres and the surrounding area on the foothills of Mt. Pangaion, whence the name Pierian Gulf.[35]

The appearance of Macedonians on the coast and the expulsion of the Thracian Pieres, dated from the mid-9th to the mid-8th century B.C., or to the middle of the 7th century B.C.,[36] and the foundation of Methone around 733 B.C., present interesting questions but also complicate the protohistory of Methone. Nicholas Hammond has tried in a masterful attempt to reconcile the conflicting pieces of the puzzle:[37]

> The tradition that the site of Methone had once been occupied by an ancestor of Orpheus (Plu. *GQ* 11) should be referred to a Thracian period of occupation, which in 730 B.C. was relatively remote (p. 430). When they (Argeadae Macedones) reached what we call northern Pieria, they were at last close to the great plain of coastal Macedonia and they came into contact with more civilized people in the Pieres of southern Pieria, the Eretrians of Methone who appeared c. 730 B.C., and the unnamed citizens of Vergina (p. 432). As a hill-people of northern Pieria the Macedones were unlikely to be of any importance, until they acquired the rich plain which runs from Methone to Katerini. This they seem to have done at some time before the foundation of the Eretrian colony at Methone c. 730 B.C. The dispossesed Thracians, the "Pieres," were thus confined to the narrow coastal plain south of Katerini and to the region of lower Olympos, and it was there that the scene of stories about Orpheus and the Thracians was usually set (p. 434).

If Hammond's proposal for the early history of the Macedonians is plausible, then the "repulsed by slings" Eretrians reached the southern estuaries of the Haliakmon in ca. 733 B.C., where they met not only Thracian Pieres, the alleged descendants of Methon and Orpheus, but also Macedonians and perhaps other tribes,[38] some of whom may have participated in the foundation and population of Methone.

During the 7th and 6th centuries B.C., ancient sources are silent on Methone and Pieria, as they do not appear to play a major role. Information, however, is not lacking but amply supplied in remarkable ways by the archaeological record, which proves that Methone's production activities and trade turned the city into a major player, as the contributions in this volume demonstrate. At the end of the 6th century (513–509 B.C.), Thrace and Macedonia appear incorporated into

Persian territory after Darius' campaign in Scythia and the operations of Megabazus. A few years later, in 492 B.C., the Persian expedition under Mardonius reached Macedonia, but the fleet was shipwrecked off Mt. Athos and the infantry fled during a night attack by the Thracian Bryges.[39] During Xerxes' passage through Thrace in 481/0 B.C., the Pieres in Phagres, Pergamon, and the surrounding countryside participated as subordinates in the infantry of the Persian king.[40] In Herodotos' prolific narrative, however, both the word *Pieria* and Thucydides' adjective *Pierikos* are absent, probably in order to avoid confusion with the original Pieria, the region south and west of the Haliakmon, where Methone is located. In Herodotos, the rivers Lydias (Loudias) and Haliakmon merge before flowing into the Thermaic Gulf and become the natural boundary between Macedonia (γῆν . . . Μακεδονίδα) and Bottiaia.[41] In this coastal region of Pieria all the way to Mt. Olympos (Μακεδονικὸν ὄρος), and in Bottiaia, divisions of the Persian army were forced to camp for several days while Xerxes' camp was in Therme. This forced delay was necessary because a third of the army was ordered to construct a road for safe passage of the entire Persian army from Macedonia to Thessaly,[42] which eventually took place inland, through the Skotina–Kallipeuki (Nezero)–Gonnoi pass in lower Olympos and the territory of Perrhaibia, rather than along the coast.[43]

After the battle at Plataia and the Persian retreat in 479 B.C., things changed for northern Pieria.[44] Although the fortunes of Methone are not known, the gradual expansion of the Macedonian kingdom to the Strymon River by Alexander I (495–454 B.C.) and, at the same time, the competing interests among Corinth, Athens, and Sparta for raw materials from the Thermaic Gulf to the river Hebros (Evros) (the area called τὰ ἐπὶ Θρᾴκης) involved, in one way or another, the two major ports of northern Pieria.[45] Excavations suggest that, during the 5th century B.C., the settlement of Pydna was expanding considerably and became the largest and most populous city in the north,[46] when most probably Pydna was chosen as the main port of the kingdom, a harbor competing with, if not antagonistic to, that of Methone. After all, it is from the harbor of Alexandros' Pydna that Themistokles, in ca. 469/8 B.C., sailed on board a cargo ship for Asia Minor, when, pursued by the Athenians and the Peloponnesians, he traveled from the Peloponnese to Korkyra and thence to the Molossian king Admetos in Epirus, and finally arrived at the Pydna of Alexandros.[47]

Even though clear-cut evidence is lacking, the different fate and treatment of the two harbor cities in Pieria throughout the events of the 5th century and until the destruction of Methone by Philip II in the mid-4th century B.C. suggest intense competition between them and between Athens and the kings of Macedonia.[48] Unlike Dion and Pydna, Methone appears in the Athenian Tribute List for the year 429/8 or 427/6 B.C. for the 300 drachmas *aparche*,[49] although it is not known whether Methone, as a former Eretrian colony, still, if it ever had, maintained commercial or other links with its metropolis or Athens: either an agreement was reached between Athens and Alexander I, whom the Athenians had honored as a *proxenos* and benefactor before the Persian campaign under Mardonius;[50] or Methone on the western coast of the Thermaic Gulf was registered as an Athenian ally, after Euboia's revolt from the Athenian Empire was suppressed by Pericles in 446/5 B.C.[51] The information is fragmentary, but Themistokles' escape on a cargo ship from Pydna to Asia Minor suggests that this port was in the control of Alexander I and therefore safer, whereas Methone was not. At any rate, both harbors were already important commercial stations for, among other things, the Macedonian kings' lucrative trade in pitch and shipbuilding timber,[52] undoubtedly one if not the major reason for the Athenian honors to Alexander I.

The revolt of Poteidaia, however, must have contributed decisively to Methone's formal attachment to the Athenian camp. The son of Alexander I, Perdikkas II, by becoming king of Macedonia in 454 B.C. had to face both internal problems with his brothers Philip and Alketas and his cousin Derdas, king of Elimeia, and also the inevitable presence of Athens in the Thermaic Gulf. With various clever maneuvers, allied sometimes with the Athenians and sometimes against them, he managed to keep Macedonia intact and remain king until his death in 413/2 B.C. The sequence of events leading to Poteidaia's defection from the Athenian Empire in 432/1 B.C. is not as clear. The Athenians' aim was probably to capture all coastal cities in Macedonia, hence the occupation of Therme and the siege of Pydna; in order to create a diversion from the western Thermaic Gulf, Perdikkas II may have instigated Poteidaia to revolt.[53] The urgent situation in Poteidaia, however, canceled the Athenian plans to capture Pydna, the neighbor of Methone, and forced Athens to make a hasty treaty with the king. The terms of this treaty are unknown, except for the withdrawal of the Athenians from Macedonia, whereas the 600 Macedonian cavalrymen under Philip and Pausanias who joined the Athenian force against Poteidaia were most probably Macedonian "rebels." In all likelihood, with this treaty Athens and Perdikkas II also decided upon the spheres of their dominance in the western Thermaic Gulf, that is, Pydna in the territory of Perdikkas II and Methone a member of the Athenian Empire.

Whatever the terms, the treaty was violated sooner rather than later. As a member of the Athenian Empire, Methone would survive in the future only thanks to the support of Athens, because it had been transformed into an Athenian enclave in the heart of the Macedonian kingdom and constituted a constant and serious risk of Athenian intervention in Macedonian affairs. Perdikkas II could not tolerate this situation and began to press Methone hard by hindering and blocking its commercial activities both by sea and in the mainland, and also by threatening military intervention.

The four decrees by the Athenian boule and demos dated to the decade of 430–420 B.C. are an eloquent witness to the difficult coexistence of Methone and, by extension, of Athens with Perdikkas II. After the preamble, which dates the publication of all four to 424/3 B.C., the first decree, dated to 430/429 or 427/6 B.C., occupies lines 3–32 of the inscription (trans. Stephen Lambert and P. J. Rhodes) (Fig. 2.1):[54]

Of the Methonaians from Pieria. Phainippos son of Phrynichos was secretary (424/3 B.C.).

The Council and the People decided. Erechtheis was in prytany. Skopas was secretary (430/429 or 427/6 B.C.). Timonides was chairman. [Diopeithes?] (l. 5) proposed: that the People shall vote immediately with regard to the Methonaians, whether it seems right that the People should assess their tribute immediately or that it should be sufficient for them to pay as much to the Goddess as resulted from the tribute which they were assessed at the previous Panathenaia to pay, and to be exempt from the remainder. Of the (l. 10) debts [being demanded?] which the Methonaians have been recorded as owing to the public treasury, if they are amenable to the Athenians as now and even better, the Athenians shall . . . concerning the exaction; and if there is any general decree about the debts recorded on the (l. 15) wooden tablets, nothing shall apply to the Methonaians unless there is a separate decree about the Methonaians. Three envoys over fifty years old shall be sent to Perdikkas, and say to Perdikkas that it seems right to allow the Methonaians to use the sea and that they should not (l. 20) be limited, and that he should allow them to enter his territory and trade as before, and that he should not wrong them or be wronged by them, nor send a military force through the territory of the Methonaians against the will of the Methonaians. And if the two parties agree let the envoys bring them to terms; if they do not, let each send a (l. 25) delegation to the Dionysia, with authority about the matters in dispute, to the Council and the People. And say to Perdikkas that if the soldiers in Poteidaia praise him the Athenians will hold a good opinion of him. The People voted that the Methonaians (l. 30) should pay as much to the Goddess as resulted from the tribute which they were assessed at the previous Panathenaia to pay, and be exempt from the remainder.

Figure 2.1. The four decrees of the Athenian boule and demos dated to the decade of 430–420 B.C. (*IG* I³ 61) recording the alliance between Athens and Methone, found in the Theater of Dionysos in Athens, and now in the Acropolis Museum (EM 6596). Photo courtesy Acropolis Museum

The second decree (lines 32–56) dated to 426/5 B.C. complements the previous one in specific issues of the alliance(?), but provides more substantial relief and accommodations for Methone as a member of the Empire. This fact underscores the failure of the first intervention of the Athenians, who sent at least two missions of envoys, and the ability of Perdikkas II to delay and postpone the solution of the Methone affair:

> The Council and the People decided. Hippothontis was in prytany. Megakleides was secretary (426/5 B.C.). [Niko-] was chairman. Kleonymos proposed: that the Methonaians (l. 35) shall be permitted to export grain from Byzantium up to — thousand medimnoi each year, and the guardians of the Hellespont shall not themselves prevent them from exporting or allow anybody else to prevent them, or else let them be fined ten thousand drachmas each. The Methonaians, having written to the guardians of the (l. 40) Hellespont, may export up to the limit fixed; and the ship exporting shall be exempt also. Whatever general decree about the allies the Athenians enact concerning going to support, or giving any other instruction to the cities either about the Athenians themselves or about the cities, whatever they enact mentioning the (l. 45) city of the Methonaians shall apply to them, but otherwise not; but if they guard their own territory they shall be doing their duty. As for the wrongs they say they have suffered from Perdikkas, the Athenians shall consider what may seem good to them concerning the Methonaians, when the envoys who have been with Perdikkas (l. 50) appear before the People, those who went with Pleistias and those with Leogoras. The other cities' business shall be dealt with when the second prytany has entered office, holding an Assembly immediately after the sessions in the dockyard: the Assemblies shall (l. 55) run continually until the business is completed, and no precedence shall be given over this to any other business, unless the generals ask for something.

The third decree (lines 56–60), dated probably between 425 and 424 B.C., is very fragmentary, whereas the fourth, dated to 424/3 B.C., is missing as the stele is broken below line 60:

> The Council and the People decided. Kekropis was in prytany... was secretary. Hierokleides was chairman... proposed: since... (l. 60) ... Athenia[...
>
> ...
>
> [The Council and the People decided. Akamantis was in prytany. Phainippos was secretary (424/3).]

The provisions of these successive decrees voted by the Athenians within a period of five to six years highlight the economic and political situation at Methone and reveal its difficult position from 429 B.C. onward, immediately after Poteidaia's occupation by Athens. The coordinated actions of Perdikkas II prevented Methone from engaging in any kind of activity, commercial or otherwise, by land and sea. This economic asphyxiation and malaise caused Methone's inability to pay the annual tax of three talents (or 18,000 drachmas). Athens therefore adjusted past debts to the treasury of the League favorably, by allowing Methone to pay only the portion of the total tax (the sixtieth) due to the goddess Athena,[55] provided Methone remained a faithful ally and useful for the interests of Athens in the region. On the political level, however, Athens also decided to send delegations to Perdikkas II to present the Athenian case as regarded the king's threats and economic blockade of Methone in an effort to reconcile their disputes, but at the same time to warn the king unmistakably that his behavior was being monitored by Athenian military presence in Poteidaia.

Obviously these economic and political arrangements proved ineffective, forcing the Athenians to vote even more favorable and drastic resolutions in the second decree of 426/5 B.C. Methone gains a particularly privileged if not unique relationship with Athens, distinct from that of all other allies in the League. Henceforth Athenian decisions concerning the allies are no longer valid for Methone, unless the Methonaians are named in them, so long as they protect their country according to the commitments undertaken toward Athens. But on the matter of the behavior of Perdikkas II, any resolution depended on the return of the two Athenian embassies from Macedonia. Thus, as Methone's economy and revenues dwindled and the previous tax relief was unavailing, the Athenians also allowed Methone to trade grain from Byzantium, tax-free up to a certain quantity, after their written request to the guardians of the Hellespont (the *Hellespontophylakes* being a kind of Athenian customs officers), whose obligation was to facilitate these grain exports, otherwise they would pay a serious fine.

These extraordinary and so far unprecedented measures and decisions for Methone are undoubtedly driven by the Peloponnesian War and its theaters in Macedonia and the north. Following upon the appeals of several cities in the north and the secret support of Perdikkas II for defection from Athens of her northern allies, the Spartan Brasidas, led by guides of Perrhaibia, a region under Thessalian influence at the time, arrived in 424 B.C. at Dion, a small town (πόλισμα) at the foot of Olympos, in the territory of the Macedonian kingdom.[56] Perdikkas II, in order to secure his northern interests, attempted unsuccessfully to drag Brasidas into his internal troubles with king Arrabaios of Lynkestis twice, in 424 and 423 B.C.[57] Brasidas' success, however, in winning over cities of Macedonia and Thrace caused an Athenian reaction. In 423 B.C. they sent reinforcements to Poteidaia and Poseidonion (modern Poseidi), among them 120 lightly armed Methonaians, for the recapture of Mende and Skione in the Pallene peninsula of Chalkidike.[58] The appearance of the Athenians in the Thermaic Gulf and the final breach of trust between Perdikkas II and Brasidas, on the occasion of the second campaign against Arrabaios, turned Perdikkas toward the Athenians. He signed a treaty (ὁμολογία and ξυμμαχία) offering the Athenians his support against the Spartans and their allies,[59] presumably until 421 B.C. when the two protagonists, the Athenian Kleon and the Spartan Brasidas, were killed in Amphipolis and the peace treaty of Nikias was concluded.[60]

The tensions in the volatile relation of Athens with Perdikkas II and the agitated internal struggles among the contenders to the throne of Macedonia certainly lie behind two fragmentary inscriptions, one of which is considered to be the very treaty of 423/2 B.C. between Perdikkas II and Athens mentioned by Thucydides.[61] In the fragmentary text, although the name of Perdikkas II leads as king, nevertheless the members of the royal house follow in the list of signatories on the Macedonian side by order of succession, that is, Perdikkas' brothers and children (among them the next king, Archelaos), other kings of Macedonia allied to Perdikkas, and Arrabaios of Lynkestis, all of whom sign the treaty under oath. Of particular interest is the stipulation of the treaty that the Macedonians agree not to export oars (κοπέας), except to Athens.[62] After the defection of Amphipolis from Athens while the war operations were prolonged, the needs of Athens for maintaining its fleet were dramatically increased and inevitably a recompense for the loss of Amphipolis had to be found;[63] hence the treaty's demand, among other provisions, that Macedonian oars be exported exclusively to Athens. The second fragmentary inscription pertains to an Athenian treaty with the Bottiaians dated between 422/1 and 416/5 B.C., by which the Athenians try again to ensure their uninterrupted presence in the Thermaic Gulf and the hinterland of Chalkidike, either as a result of the treaty with the Macedonians, as the Bottiaians occupied the area to the east of Macedonia, or because their treaty with Perdikkas II and the Makedones was already violated.[64]

In fact, the alliance between Perdikkas II and Athens did not last for long, because, as the Athenians claimed, Perdikkas began secret negotiations with Argos for a joint campaign against the cities of Chalkidike and Amphipolis. In the winter of 417/6 B.C. the Athenians retaliated by blocking entirely Macedonian access to the sea and therefore to imports and exports, a blockade in which the role of Methone must have been decisive, perhaps also that of Pydna, the only harbor in the Thermaic Gulf within the Macedonian kingdom.[65] A year later, in 416/5 B.C., a cavalry force of Athenians and Macedonian fugitives, who had probably found refuge in Athens, arrived again by sea at Methone, at the border of the Macedonian kingdom, in order to plunder the land of Perdikkas II.[66] The topographical detail of Thucydides leaves no doubt that, a few years before the death of Perdikkas II and the ascent of Archelaos to the throne in 413/2 B.C., Methone remains outside Macedonian territory and serves as the stronghold of Athenian operations in the western Thermaic Gulf.

Subsequently, Methone does not appear in the sources until the middle of the 4th century B.C., when Philip II decides to eliminate Athenian presence from the western Thermaic Gulf. Pydna, on the other hand, four kilometers to the south and the main harbor of the Macedonian kingdom, felt strong enough to secede from Macedonia in the winter of 411/10 B.C., just after Archelaos (413–399 B.C.) ascended to the throne and implemented extensive reforms. With the help of the Athenian fleet under Theramenes, Archelaos blockaded Pydna and after a long siege captured and punished it in exemplary fashion, forcing the inhabitants to move to an inland location 20 stades from the shore.[67] Athenian assistance to Archelaos was probably motivated by their urgent needs of timber for shipbuilding, after the fleet had been completely destroyed in Sicily. This is deduced from the testimony of the orator Andokides, who, because of his involvement in the affair of the Herms, lived in exile from Athens. In presenting his case before the Athenians for his return to the city, Andokides argues that during his exile he risked his life and property for the interests of Athens, when in 411 B.C. the regime of the Four Hundred seized power.[68] During this period, thanks to his family friendship with Archelaos, he secured from the king a license to cut timber and export oars to the Athenian fleet in Samos, which he sold at cost to the Athenians, while he imported grain and copper for the army's needs on the island.[69] The mutual interests of Athens and Archelaos are also evident in a fragmentary decree of 411/10 or 407/6 B.C., according to which the Athenians vote urgent measures to meet the immediate needs of the fleet with imports of ships which the shipbuilders will send from Macedonia.[70] Eventually this arrangement, as well as the earlier acquisition of timber and oars, probably contributed to Archelaos' and his descendants' honors as *proxenos* and benefactor of the Athenians.

The mutual understanding between Archelaos and Athens apparently pertained not only to the activities of Methone but also to those of Pydna. The significant revenues from the Macedonian timber trade also preoccupied Amyntas III (393–370/69 B.C.) as soon as he became king. In the treaty of the Macedonian king with the Chalkidic *koinon* dated to ca. 393/2 B.C. there is a clause, according to which the cities of the Chalkidic *koinon* are allowed to import timber for construction and shipbuilding and pitch (apparently from Pieria), but before exporting these raw materials the *koinon* is obliged to inform the Macedonian king.[71] The reign of Amyntas III, however, was hard pressed by the constant assaults of the Illyrians, during which the territory of the kingdom shrank probably to its limits at the time of Alexander I, namely Pieria and Emathia. During this time Methone's fortunes are not known, but the Illyrian attacks and the absence of the Athenians from the Thermaic Gulf probably forced Methone to join Amyntas III, as Pydna did, a semi-autonomous city at the time having also founded a sanctuary in honor of the king (Ἀμύντιον).[72] Perhaps this fact prompted Athens, in ca. 370 B.C., to conclude a treaty with Amyntas III,[73] as they had in the past with Perdikkas II and Archelaos, to secure the necessary imports of timber and other raw materials from the two harbors of Macedonia.

After the death of Amyntas III and the internal struggle for succession in Macedonia, in which sometimes the Thebans and at other times the Athenians intervened, Perdikkas III became king (365–359 B.C.). But when he renewed the Macedonian alliance with Thebes, Athens reacted immediately. The Athenian general Timotheos, with extensive military operations in 362/1 B.C., occupied Methone, Pydna, and Poteidaia, and later other cities in the north, all of which fell into the Athenian sphere of influence, perhaps also as members of the Second Athenian League, although there is no evidence that Athenian garrisons were stationed in these cities.[74] In 361/0 B.C. Kallistratos of Aphidnai, in exile from Athens and on his way to Thasos, stayed for some time in Methone, where he presumably proposed a raise in harbor dues (ἐλλιμένιον) of all ports in Macedonia, thus doubling the total sum from 20 to 40 talents and increasing considerably the income of the Macedonian king.[75] This semi-independent status of the harbor cities in Pieria is confirmed by the Epidaurian list of *theorodokoi* of the year 360/59 B.C. After Homolion of the Magnetes, the *theorodokoi* of cities in the Thermaic Gulf from south to north are identical to Ps.-Skylax's (66) list of cities he called "Greek": for Pydna, Damatrios; for Methone, Polyphantos; for Macedonia, King Perdikkas; for Aineia, Euboulos; for Dikaia, Nymphodoros; and for Poteidaia, Kallikrates. From this list, it is clear that the two harbor cities of Pieria retain a rather independent status from the Macedonian king, who nonetheless serves as *theorodokos* of the remaining cities of Pieria which, therefore, are included in his territory.[76]

This status quo, however, did not last long, as things changed dramatically in 359 B.C., when, in a battle with the Illyrians, Perdikkas III was killed and his brother Philip II ascended to the throne. As a new king he had to face his relatives as contenders for the throne, as well as the neighboring tribes, but managed, through coordinated diplomatic efforts and military action, to prevent the disintegration of Macedonia. The most pressing and immediate challenge was the Athenian support of the contender to the throne, Argaios, whom the Athenians sent to Methone with a contingent of 3,000 soldiers. The Athenian general Mantias decided to stay in Methone and send Argaios with an escort of mercenaries to Aigai in order to persuade the Macedonians to accept him as king instead of Philip II, who was in Pella. The Macedonians, however, did not respond and Argaios was forced to return back, but before he could reach Methone, Philip II, marching with his army from Pella, caught up with him and won an unexpectedly decisive victory; several mercenaries were killed and prisoners set free, after an agreement to surrender fugitives to Philip, perhaps among them his political opponents. This first military victory under the new king boosted the morale of the Macedonian army and predetermined the inevitable future plans of Philip II.[77]

While besieging Amphipolis in 357 B.C. and during the secret negotiations for a solution according to which Amphipolis was to be ceded to Athens and Pydna to Macedon, Philip II decided to capture Pydna after a brief siege and obviously with the support of some of its inhabitants.[78] Demosthenes, in narrating the siege of Olynthos, emphasized the harsh behavior of Philip II even toward those who surrendered their city to him by treason, recalling the examples of Amphipolis and Pydna. The ancient scholia explain this statement with a note that Philip behaved just as harshly against those residents who betrayed Pydna to him and who, in the hope of avoiding death, fled to the Amyntion, the sanctuary in honor of the father of Philip II.[79] These insinuations, however, are not corroborated by the excavations of graves and buildings of this period in Pydna.[80]

Even so, the fate of Methone was completely different from that of Pydna, and strategic, economic, and security reasons were not the only things that prompted such a drastic and extreme solution. The most crucial factor was that Methone, from its mythistoric foundation in ca. 733 B.C. by the "repulsed by slings" Eretrians, and throughout its history, was never fully integrated into the Macedonian kingdom, except for a short period in the reign of Amyntas III and under

Perdikkas III, until Timotheos' operations. Moreover, as the safest harbor in the western Thermaic Gulf, Methone boomed economically because of production and trading activities, and also because it served Athenian interests in the north. Methone's status therefore constituted a constant risk of interference in the Macedonian kingdom because this hostile stronghold lay in immediate proximity to the ancient capital at Aigai, a danger which became more than evident when the contender for the throne, Argaios, arrived at the port of Methone, escorted by the Athenian Mantias and 3,000 soldiers.[81]

Just three years after the capture of Pydna, Philip II decided, in 354 B.C., to eliminate the presence of the Athenian fleet in the Thermaic Gulf and thus ensure Macedonia's exclusive access to the sea. On the eve of the siege or at its beginning in 355–354 B.C., the Athenians honored Lachares(?) the son of Chares from Apollonia for his eagerness to serve the Athenian citizens and for sending someone of his own [family?] to Methone, most probably to help the Athenians there.[82] The siege of Methone was neither as short nor as easy as that of Pydna, as a stratagem of Philip II, recorded by Polyainos, suggests: when the soldiers would reach the top of the walls, Philip II would remove the ladders, so that with no hope of climbing down and no retreat for salvation, they had to fight even more willingly to capture the city.[83] Also, during the siege of Methone, an anecdotal incident happened that made the city famous, as several sources relate. A Methonaian soldier named Aster, after engraving on a spear or arrow or catapult (different sources mention different kinds of long-range weapons) the inscription "Aster launches a deadly arrow against Philip," launched it and managed to hit Philip's right eye, while Philip was inspecting the offensive and defensive siege machines. When the king recovered, he retaliated and launched a spear engraved with the text: "If Philip captures Aster, he will hang him," but he missed.[84]

Eventually, the residents of Methone were forced to hand over the city to Philip II, who allowed them to leave with a single piece of clothing, but he razed the city to the ground and forbade habitation of the area. After distributing the land to Macedonians, he founded another Macedonian settlement away from the sea to the north-northwest, and as Demosthenes categorically states, Methone along with 32 other cities captured by Philip II was never again inhabited.[85] The fate of the survivors is not known, but, as noted in a draft of a decree to honor Demosthenes for a series of benefits he made to Athens, Demosthenes had intervened for the release of many prisoners taken by Philip II in Pydna, Methone, and Olynthos.[86]

From its foundation around 733 B.C. by the "repulsed by slings" Eretrians to its destruction in 354 B.C. by Philip II, Methone was the most important—and safest—harbor in the western Thermaic Gulf, across periods of great prosperity and decline. Even Aristotle wrote a treatise on the Methonaian *politeia*, which certainly must have contained rich information and important details about Methone's status, but from which only two small excerpts have survived. One concerns the parasites (παράσιτοι) in Methone, two for each *archon* and one for each *polemarch*, who were responsible for collecting regular contributions from some others but mainly fish from the fishermen.[87] The other excerpt from Aristotle's treatise refers to the proverbial unmusicality of the Leibethrioi (ἀμουσότερος Λειβηθρίων), a tribe of Thracian Pieres, a proverb inspired by Orpheus' death in L(e)ibethra (Leivithra), a town at the foot of Olympos in south Pieria near modern Leptokarya.[88]

Whatever its accomplishments, Methone managed to remain in the memory of later generations only as Methone of Thrace on the border with Macedonia, in front of whose walls Philip II, son of Amyntas III, lost his right eye; not unlike the memory of Pydna, in front of whose valley the Romans fought Perseus in 148 B.C. and put an end to the kingdom of the Macedonians.[89]

These ancient sources illuminate only a few moments of Methone's historical course, from its foundation in the late 8th century until its annihilation in 354 B.C. by Philip II. The "repulsed by slings" Eretrian founders chose to settle in a place which they named not after their own oikist, but, as was their custom,⁹⁰ they used the local name which they heard from the *prosoikoi* of/to the site, no doubt suitable to the site's geomorphology. Their choice to settle in this region cannot have been accidental, as they must have known very well the rich resources near the estuaries of the Haliakmon, and especially the indispensable and unique timber reserves on the Olympos and Pieria mountains suitable in particular for shipbuilding and oars. After all, Eretria and Eretrians are "talking symbols" for the rowing city and its oarsmen citizens, the expert shipowners and merchants or eternal sailors (ἀειναῦται) of the time,⁹¹ who because of these activities developed skills in shipbuilding and shipping and expert knowledge of the best timber species in the Aegean and beyond.⁹² As Methone's subsequent course proves beyond doubt, its Eretrian founders managed to instruct the inhabitants of the new city and impart to them their expertise and specialized knowledge, and the Methonaians faithfully and successfully followed in their footsteps. Whatever the names Eretria and Eretrians meant, the Methonaians and later the Macedonian kings traded with it with unprecedented success. From Methone's harbor to the south of the Haliakmon estuaries they exported, among many other products, timber from the rich forests of Pieria and Olympos, suitable for shipbuilding but most notably oars, some of which presumably were manufactured in shipyards at Methone.

NOTES

1 What follows is an updated version of Tzifopoulos 2012a, pp. 15–40. I am most grateful to Stavros Frangoulidis, Niki Oikonomaki, and Angelos Boufalis for reading and commenting on drafts of this piece; to the editors of this volume, Sarah Morris and John Papadopoulos, for their unstinting effort; and to the anonymous reviewers for constructive suggestions and corrections.

2 See Haley 1928 and Blegen 1928, for which I am indebted to the anonymous reviewer; for its etymology, see further Blanc 2018, and n. 16.

3 Dimitsas 1874, vol. 2, pp. 48–51; see also pp. 51–67; Dimitsas 1896, vol. 2, pp. 160–169; see also pp. 114–161, 169–172; Becher 1932; van der Kolf 1932; Meyer 1932; Stählin 1932; Lenk 1932; Herzog-Hauser 1956a, 1956b; Hammond and Griffith 1979, pp. 3–54; Vassileva 2007; Mallios 2011; Blanc 2018.

4 Suda, s.v. Μεθώνη: ἡ πόλις. μία τῶν Ἀλκυονίδων. Δημοσθένης ἐν Φιλιππικοῖς λέγοι ἂν τὴν ἐν Θρᾴκη· ἣν πολιορκῶν Φίλιππος ἐξεκόπη τὸν δεξιὸν ὀφθαλμόν. τέσσαρας δὲ εἶναί φησι Μεθώνας Δημήτριος ὁ Μάγνης. Suda, s.v. Ἀλκυονίδες ἡμέραι· αἱ εὐδιειναί. περὶ τοῦ ἀριθμοῦ διαφέρονται. Σιμωνίδης γὰρ ἐν Πεντάθλοις ια΄ φησὶν αὐτὰς καὶ Ἀριστοτέλης ἐν τοῖς Περὶ ζῴων, Δημαγόρας δὲ ὁ Σάμιος ζ΄, καὶ Φιλόχορος θ΄. τὸν δὲ ἐπ' αὐταῖς μῦθον Ἡγήσανδρος ἐν τοῖς Περὶ ὑπομνημάτων λέγει οὕτως· Ἀλκυονέως τοῦ γίγαντος θυγατέρες ἦσαν, Φωσθονία, Ἄνθη, Μεθώνη, Ἀλκίππα, Παλλήνη, Δριμώ, Ἀστερίη. αὗται μετὰ τὴν τοῦ πατρὸς τελευτὴν ἀπὸ Καναστραίου, ὅ ἐστιν ἄκρον τῆς Πελλήνης, ἔρριψαν αὑτὰς εἰς τὴν θάλασσαν, Ἀμφιτρίτη δ' αὐτὰς ὄρνιθας ἐποίησε, καὶ ἀπὸ τοῦ πατρὸς Ἀλκυόνες ἐκλήθησαν. αἱ δὲ νήνεμοι καὶ γαλήνην ἔχουσαι ἡμέραι Ἀλκυονίδες καλοῦνται. καὶ Ἀλκυόνειος ἡμέρα. The name Φωσθονία (see the paremiographer Apostolios, *CPG* Centuria 2.20) is Φθονία in Eustathios (*Il.* 2, 810) and Χθονία in Photios (*Lexicon*, s.v.).

5 *Scholia in Hesiod's Works and Days*, lines 193–199 (Melisseus, *FGrH* 402 F1): καὶ πραγματικῶς μὲν Πιερία καὶ Ἑλικών, ὄρη καὶ πόλεις Βοιωτίας. καὶ ἡ μὲν Πιερία πρότερον ὑπὸ Πιέρου κτισθεῖσα τοῦ Μεθώνης ἀδελφοῦ, πατρὸς δὲ Λίνου, Πιερία ἐκέκλητο· ὕστερον δὲ Λύγκος ἐκλήθη, ἧς καὶ τὴν ἀρχὴν ἔσχεν Ἀέροπος, ὁ πρεσβύτατος τῶν Ἠμαθίωνος παίδων, καθὰ Μελισσεύς φησιν ὁ τὰ Δελφικὰ συνταξάμενος. *Certamen*, 44–50: ἔνιοι μὲν οὖν αὐτὸν προγενέστερον Ἡσιόδου φασὶν εἶναι, τινὲς δὲ νεώτερον καὶ συγγενῆ. γενεαλογοῦσι δὲ οὕτως· Ἀπόλλωνός φασι καὶ Θοώσης τῆς Ποσειδῶνος γενέσθαι Λίνον, Λίνου δὲ Πίερον, Πιέρου δὲ καὶ νύμφης Μεθώνης Οἴαγρον, Οἰάγρου δὲ καὶ Καλλιόπης Ὀρφέα, Ὀρφέως δὲ Ὄρτην, τοῦ δὲ Ἁρμονίδην, τοῦ δὲ Φιλοτέρπην, τοῦ δὲ Εὔφημον, τοῦ δὲ Ἐπιφράδην, τοῦ δὲ Μελάνωπον, τούτου δὲ Δῖον καὶ Ἀπέλλαιον, Δίου δὲ καὶ Πυκιμήδης τῆς Ἀπόλλωνος θυγατρὸς Ἡσίοδον καὶ Πέρσην· Πέρσου δὲ Μαίονα, Μαίονος δὲ θυγατρὸς καὶ Μέλητος τοῦ ποταμοῦ Ὅμηρον. Mallios 2011, pp. 81, 135–138.

6 Plut., *Quaest. Graec.* 293a–b: . . . χωρίον, ἐν ᾧ πρότερον οἰκῆσαι Μέθωνα τὸν Ὀρφέως πρόγονον ἱστοροῦσι, τὴν μὲν πόλιν ὠνόμασαν Μεθώνην. For Methon as a personal name in Tanagra, see Bechtel 1917, p. 506 and *LGPN* s.v. (https://www.lgpn.ox.ac.uk/); for Orpheus in Macedonia and Thrace, see also Gartziou-Tatti 1999; Mallios 2011, pp. 293–320; and nn. 30, 31, 37, 39, 89.

7   Steph. Byz., *Ethnica* 440–441: Μεθώνη, πόλις Θρᾴκης. Μαγνησίας, [ἣν] Ὅμηρος διὰ τοῦ η 'οἳ δ' ἄρα Μεθώνην καὶ Θαυμακίην ἐνέμοντο'. ὁ πολίτης Μεθωναῖος. ἔστι καὶ Μακεδονίας. ἐκλήθη ἀπὸ τοῦ μέθυ· πολύοινος γάρ ἐστι. καὶ τῆς Λακωνικῆς, ἧς τὸ ἐθνικὸν Μεθωναιεύς ὡς Κορωναιεύς. δ´ ἐν Περσίδι. ε´ Εὐβοίας. Cf. Eust., *Il*. 2, 506 lines 1–3, 507 lines 16–22, 763 lines 18–20. *Etym. Magn.*, s.v. Πιερία. Hammond (1972, p. 426 n. 1) rightly remarks that the confusion in the sources about a Methone in Macedonia and another one in Thrace is due to ancient authors calling the area north of the river Peneios sometimes Macedonia, but at other times Thrace.

8   It is not certain if the choice between οἶνος and μέθυ in the Homeric epics is dictated by the use of the metrical formula. Μέθυ appears three times in the *Iliad* (7.471; 9.469; 17.390) and 16 in the *Odyssey* (4.746; 7.179, 265; 9.9, 45, 162, 557; 10.184, 468, 477; 12.30, 362; 13.50; 14.194; 16.533; 17.240); in all these instances the use of μέθυ apparently does not imply a meaning different from οἶνος (Suda, Chantraine 1980, Beekes 2010, and Montanari 2013, s.v. μέθυ and οἶνος). Forms of the verb μεθύω 'I am drunk' occur twice: in a remarkable metaphor in *Il*. 17.390, and in *Od*. 18.240. The famous wine of Maron in *Odyssey* is: μέλας οἶνος ἡδὺς ἀκηράσιος, θεῖον ποτόν (9.196–197), οἶνος ἀκηράσιος, θεῖον ποτόν (9.204–205), οἶνος μελιηδὺς ἐρυθρός, ἓν δέπας ἐμπλήσας ὕδατος ἀνὰ εἴκοσι μέτρα (9.208–209), but in Euripides' *Cyclops*: πῶμα Διονύσου (139), ἄκρατον μέθυ (149), so strong ὥστ' εἰς ἄκρους γε τοὺς ὄνυχας ἀφίκετο (159). For the wine from Ismaros (also in Archilochos, fr. 2) and the unrealistic analogy of 1 to 20, see Kourakou-Dragona 2009. In Hesiod's works μέθυ does not appear. For ἄκρατον or κεκραμένον μέθυ and οἶνος, see Arist., fr. 102 (*Συμπόσιον ἢ περὶ μέθης*); Plut., *Mor*. 648e–f; Philo, *Περὶ φυτουργίας Νῶε τὸ δεύτερον* 139–174.

9   See also above nn. 4, 7, and below, n. 46.

10 Hom., *Il*. 2.716–720 (Kirk 1985, pp. 232–234): οἳ δ' ἄρα Μεθώνην καὶ Θαυμακίην ἐνέμοντο | καὶ Μελίβοιαν ἔχον καὶ Ὀλιζῶνα τρηχεῖαν, | τῶν δὲ Φιλοκτήτης ἦρχεν τόξων εὖ εἰδὼς | ἑπτὰ νεῶν· ἐρέται δ' ἐν ἑκάστῃ πεντήκοντα | ἐμβέβασαν τόξων εὖ εἰδότες ἶφι μάχεσθαι. The *Scholia* ad loc. mention three cities named Methone: Μεθῶναι δὲ τρεῖς, ἡ ἐν Μακεδονίᾳ, ἡ ὑπὸ Φιλοκτήτην καὶ ἡ περὶ Τροιζῆνα; cf. also Strabo 9.5.16; and Heiden 2008, p. 143. Blanc (2018) convincingly explains the epic long η (for ε) in Μηθώνη, and its etymology from Greek μεθίημι, i.e., cessation (from sailing), nautical halt; hence port, harbor.

11 Strabo 8.6.15 (Theopompos, *FGrH* 2b 115 F 384): μεταξὺ δὲ Τροιζῆνος καὶ Ἐπιδαύρου χωρίον ἦν ἐρυμνὸν Μέθανα καὶ χερρόνησος ὁμώνυμος τούτῳ· παρὰ Θουκυδίδῃ δὲ ἔν τισιν ἀντιγράφοις Μεθώνη φέρεται ὁμωνύμως τῇ Μακεδονικῇ, ἐν ᾗ Φίλιππος ἐξεκόπη τὸν ὀφθαλμὸν πολιορκῶν· διόπερ οἴεταί τινας ἐξαπατηθέντας ὁ Σκήψιος Δημήτριος τὴν ἐν τῇ Τροιζηνίᾳ Μεθώνην ὑπονοεῖν, καθ' ἧς ἀράσασθαι λέγεται τοὺς ὑπ' Ἀγαμέμνονος πεμφθέντας ναυτολόγους μηδέποτε παύσασθαι [τοῦ] τειχοδομεῖν, οὐ τούτων ἀλλὰ τῶν Μακεδόνων ἀνανευσάντων, ὥς φησι Θεόπομπος· τούτους δ' οὐκ εἰκὸς ἐγγὺς ὄντας ἀπειθῆσαι. Hatzopoulos, Knoepfler, and Marigo-Papadopoulos 1990, pp. 663–665; Helly 2006; and Blanc 2018.

12 Thuc. 4.45.2 (Alberti 1992, p. 143; Hornblower 1996, pp. 203–204): τῇ δ' ὑστεραίᾳ παραπλεύσαντες ἐς τὴν Ἐπιδαυρίαν πρῶτον καὶ ἀπόβασίν τινα ποιησάμενοι ἀφίκοντο ἐς Μεθάναν τὴν μεταξὺ Ἐπιδαύρου καὶ Τροζῆνος, καὶ ἀπολαβόντες τὸν τῆς χερσονήσου ἰσθμὸν ἐτείχισαν, ἐν ᾧ ἡ Μεθάνα ἐστί, καὶ φρούριον καταστησάμενοι ἐλῄστευον τὸν ἔπειτα χρόνον τήν τε Τροζηνίαν γῆν καὶ Ἁλιάδα καὶ Ἐπιδαυρίαν. ταῖς δὲ ναυσίν, ἐπειδὴ ἐξετείχισαν τὸ χωρίον, ἀπέπλευσαν ἐπ' οἴκου. The reading Μεθάνα (ἡ), a variant of the manuscripts' Μεθώνην, is a correction (Dittenberger 1907, pp. 542–545; in other editions the reading [τὰ Μέθανα], as also in Pausanias 2.34.1–5, which Dittenberger explains as a misunderstanding of the copyists), which Strabo had probably seen (see n. 11). Gomme (1956, pp. 494–495) does not comment on this but see Hornblower 1996, pp. 203–204, and Blanc 2018.

13 *P.Köln* 5861, Luppe 1994 (with previous bibliography): . . . ἡ δ' ἐ[στὶ]ν Μεθώ[νη, | ὡς Θεόπ]ομπός φησιν, [χώρα | τίς ποθ'] ὑλήεσσα, εἰς ἣν τῇ[ν | τῶν νεῶν ἐ]πισκευὴν κατὰ τὰς | [σπονδὰς ἔθ]εντο οἱ παρ' Ἀγαμέ|[μνονος] ναυστολόγοι κα|[λοῦντε]ς ἐπὶ τὴν στρατείαν· | οἱ δ' ἀπειθ]οῦντες κατηρνή|[σαντο δ]ύνασθαι. οἱ δ' ἐπεῖ[πον· εἴθ]ε μὴ παύσαισθε τ<ε>ι|[χοδομοῦντες. Πέλλα δ' ἐστὶ | ⌐μ⌐ ἐν κάτω Μακεδονί|ας . . . This fragment probably belongs after fr. 20 (in n. 21), while the similarities with 8.6.15 (text in n. 11) are obvious, unlike the restored σπονδὰς which may or may not refer to the oath of Tyndareos.

14 For the two words *nautologoi* and *naustologoi* see Montanari 2013, s.v.; perhaps the difference may indicate sailors and ships respectively.

15 Hatzopoulos, Knoepfler, and Marigo-Papadopoulos (1990, pp. 663–665) conclude that the Methone mentioned is the one in Magnesia and not in Thrace/Macedonia, that is, Pieria (p. 664). Helly 2006 discusses in detail the narrative of Theopompos and Strabo and suggests that Magnetes may very well have been dwelling in Pierian Methone since the Bronze Age, and after Philip's destruction they may have returned home, founding the Methone in Magnesia. This attractive hypothesis need not be perforce relegated to

the destruction of Pierian Methone in 354 B.C., and there is no reason to exclude the possibility of two cities with the same name, according to Ps.-Skylax, Περίπλους 65–66, dated by Shipley (2011, pp. 6–8) to 338–337 B.C., one in Magnesia and one in Pieria, both according to Blanc's (2018) etymology 'ports, harbors.' At present, secure evidence is lacking, but Magnesia and Pieria in the sources appear as mutually inclusive (see also n. 17; Morris, Chapter 6 and forthcoming, who revisits cogently Methone's Mycenaean past). For the northern borders during Mycenaean times see Eder 2008. Another baffling piece of information is, for example, the restoration of some form of Μηθώνη by West in POxy 3965, fr. 22, line 3 (= Sider 2001, p. 17, fr. 10; Rutherford 2001, p. 43, fr. 10 W²), a proem addressed to Achilles in the New Simonides (Plataea elegy). For Thessaly in the 4th century B.C. see Graninger 2010; Helly 2018; and n. 82.

16   Hes., fr. 7: ἣ δ' ὑποκυσαμένη Διὶ γείνατο τερπικεραύνωι | υἷε δύω, Μάγνητα Μακεδόνα θ' ἱππιοχάρμην, | οἳ περὶ Πιερίην καὶ Ὄλυμπον δώματ' ἔναιον. Also Hammond 1972, pp. 416–418.

17   For the geoarchaeology in northern Pieria and its sites see Hammond 1972, pp. 123–139; Papazoglou 1988, pp. 103–124; Girtzy 2001, pp. 81–106; Tiverios 2008, pp. 5–8, 17–21, 31–32; Krahtopoulou 2010, pp. 48–76 with earlier bibliography; and Morris et al. 2020.

18   Dimitsas 1874, vol. 2, pp. 44–67.

19   Ps.-Skylax, Περίπλους 66 (Shipley 2011, ad loc. and p. 141): Ἀπὸ δὲ Πηνειοῦ ποταμοῦ Μακεδόνες εἰσὶν ἔθνος, καὶ κόλπος Θερμαῖος. Πρώτη πόλις Μακεδονίας Ἡράκλειον· Δῖον, Πύδνα πόλις Ἑλληνίς, Μεθώνη πόλις Ἑλληνὶς καὶ Ἁλιάκμων ποταμός, Ἄλωρος πόλις καὶ ποταμὸς Λυδίας, Πέλλα πόλις καὶ βασίλειον ἐν αὐτῇ καὶ ἀνάπλους εἰς αὐτὴν ἀνὰ τὸν Λυδίαν; and n. 77. Cf. Plin., HN 4.32.1. According to Edson (1970, p. 24 with nn. 32, 35, 38), Pydna and Methone were Greek colonies, even though Pydna's metropolis remains unknown, which the weak Macedonian kingdom tolerated in the western Thermaic Gulf, whereas the region from Strepsa (Hatzopoulos and Loukopoulou 1987, pp. 21–60) to the Hellespont was under Athenian control, as also was Methone from 434 B.C. on. For Borza (1990, pp. 98–100), Pydna and Methone were frontiers of Greek colonization, and for Touratsoglou (2010, pp. 50–51) they were colonies of southern Greeks. Tiverios (2008, pp. 17–18 with n. 77 and p. 31 with n. 131) rightly argues that the absence of a metropolis for Pydna may be due to its colonization right after the Trojan War, during the so-called "first colonization period." See also Kalléris 1976, pp. 592–594 and 603 n. 3; Flensted-Jensen and Hansen 1996, p. 151; Hatzopoulos 1996, p. 473; Mari 2002, pp. 68–69 with n. 5; Mari 2007, pp. 32–33; Cohen 2013, pp. 360–377; Cohen 2015, pp. 263–264; Raynor 2016, pp. 229–234; Bessios 2010, pp. 94–95 and 132–133. For the cities in Pieria see Papazoglou 1988, pp. 103–124; Hatzopoulos and Paschidis 2004, pp. 795, 797, 800, 802–804, 806; for Herakleion in the Early Iron Age see Poulaki-Pantermali 2007.

20   The repetition of sentences in paragraphs 20 and 22 of Book 7 is due to the fact that parts of Strabo's work have survived in epitomes in various manuscripts. Strabo 7a.1.20: μετὰ δὲ τὸ Δῖον αἱ τοῦ Ἁλιάκμονος ἐκβολαί· εἶτα Πύδνα Μεθώνη Ἄλωρος καὶ ὁ Ἐρίγων ποταμὸς καὶ Λουδίας, ὁ μὲν ἐκ Τρικλάρων ῥέων δι' Ὀρεστῶν καὶ τῆς Πελαγονίας ἐν ἀριστερᾷ ἀφιεὶς τὴν πόλιν καὶ συμβάλλων τῷ Ἀξιῷ· ὁ δὲ Λουδίας εἰς Πέλλαν ἀνάπλουν ἔχων σταδίων ἑκατὸν καὶ εἴκοσι. μέση δ' οὖσα ἡ Μεθώνη τῆς μὲν Πύδνης ὅσον τετταράκοντα σταδίους ἀπέχει, τῆς Ἀλώρου δὲ ἑβδομήκοντα. ἔστι δ' ἡ Ἄλωρος τὸ μυχαίτατον τοῦ Θερμαίου κόλπου *** λέγεται δὲ Θεσσαλονίκεια διὰ τὴν ἐπιφάνειαν. τὴν μὲν οὖν Ἄλωρον Βοττιαϊκὴν νομίζουσι, τὴν δὲ Πύδναν Πιερικήν. Also Strabo 7a.1.22: ὅτι μετὰ τὸ Δῖον πόλιν ὁ Ἁλιάκμων ποταμὸς ἔστιν, ἐκβάλλων εἰς τὸν Θερμαῖον κόλπον· καὶ τὸ ἀπὸ τούτου ἡ πρὸς βορρᾶν τοῦ κόλπου παραλία Πιερία καλεῖται ἕως τοῦ Ἀξιοῦ ποταμοῦ, ἐν ᾗ καὶ πόλις Πύδνα, ἣ νῦν Κίτρον καλεῖται· εἶτα Μεθώνη καὶ Ἄλωρος πόλεις· εἶτα Ἐρίγων καὶ Λουδίας ποταμοί· ἀπὸ δὲ Λουδίου εἰς Πέλλαν πόλιν ἀνάπλους στάδια ἑκατὸν εἴκοσιν. ἀπέχει δ' ἡ Μεθώνη τῆς μὲν Πύδνης στάδια τετταράκοντα, τῆς Ἀλώρου δὲ ἑβδομήκοντα στάδια. ἡ μὲν οὖν Πύδνα Πιερική ἐστι πόλις, ἡ δὲ Ἄλωρος Βοττιαϊκή.

21   Strabo 8.6.15 (text in n. 11) and Strabo 9.5.16: ἑξῆς δ' αἱ ὑπὸ Φιλοκτήτῃ πόλεις καταλέγονται. ἡ μὲν οὖν Μηθώνη ἑτέρα ἐστὶ τῆς Θρᾳκίας Μεθώνης, ἣν κατέσκαψε Φίλιππος· ἐμνήσθημεν δὲ καὶ πρότερον τῆς τῶν ὀνομάτων τούτων καὶ τῶν ἐν Πελοποννήσῳ . . . τροπῆς. Hammond (1972, p. 426, with n. 1) notes that during the Classical period Methone was called Macedonian. Cf. Hatzopoulos, Knoepfler, and Marigo-Papadopoulos 1990, pp. 642–650.

22   Etym. Magn., s.v. Πιερία: ὄνομα τόπου, ἔνθα αἱ Μοῦσαι ἐγεννήθησαν. παρὰ τὸ πίηρ γέγονεν· ἢ ἀπὸ τοῦ Πιέρου ἀδελφοῦ τῆς Μεθώνης· ἢ ἀπὸ Πιερίας νύμφης. τὸ δὲ πίηρ, παρὰ τὸ πίω ῥῆμα· ἢ παρὰ τὸ πῖον, ὃ σημαίνει τὸ λιπαρόν· ἔστι δὲ ὄνομα κύριον. καὶ πίειρα, ἡ λιπαρά, παρὰ τὸ πῖον, Ἰλιάδος ς'. Eust., Il. 3.623: Πιερίαν δὲ οἱ μὲν ἀκρώρειάν τινα εἶπον Ὀλύμπου, οἱ δὲ χώραν ἀπὸ νύμφης ὁμωνύμου, ἢ ἀπὸ Πιέρος υἱοῦ Ἐλευθῆρος, οἱ δὲ πόλιν. For Thracians in Pieria, see Hammond 1972, pp. 416–418; and for Thrace and Macedonia, see Archibald 2010.

23 Paus. 9.29.1:... θῦσαι δὲ ἐν Ἑλικῶνι Μούσαις πρώτους καὶ ἐπονομάσαι τὸ ὄρος ἱερὸν εἶναι Μουσῶν Ἐφιάλτην καὶ Ὦτον λέγουσιν, οἰκίσαι δὲ αὐτοὺς καὶ Ἄσκρην· **(2)**... οἱ δὲ τοῦ Ἀλωέως παῖδες ἀριθμόν τε Μούσας ἐνόμισαν εἶναι τρεῖς καὶ ὀνόματα αὐταῖς ἔθεντο Μελέτην καὶ Μνήμην καὶ Ἀοιδήν. **(3)** χρόνῳ δὲ ὕστερόν φασι Πίερον Μακεδόνα, ἀφ᾽ οὗ καὶ Μακεδόσιν ὠνόμασται τὸ ὄρος, τοῦτον ἐλθόντα ἐς Θεσπιὰς ἐννέα τε Μούσας καταστήσασθαι καὶ τὰ ὀνόματα τὰ νῦν μεταθέσθαι σφίσι. ταῦτα δὲ ἐνόμιζεν οὕτως ὁ Πίερος ἢ σοφώτερά οἱ εἶναι φανέντα ἢ κατά τι μάντευμα ἢ παρά του διδαχθεὶς τῶν Θρᾳκῶν· δεξιώτερον γὰρ τά τε ἄλλα ἐδόκει τοῦ Μακεδονικοῦ τὸ ἔθνος εἶναι πάλαι τὸ Θρᾴκιον καὶ οὐχ ὁμοίως ἐς τὰ θεῖα ὀλίγωρον. **(4)** εἰσὶ δ᾽ οἳ καὶ αὐτῷ θυγατέρας ἐννέα Πιέρῳ γενέσθαι λέγουσι καὶ τὰ ὀνόματα ἅπερ ταῖς θεαῖς τεθῆναι καὶ ταύταις, καὶ ὅσοι Μουσῶν παῖδες ἐκλήθησαν ὑπὸ Ἑλλήνων, θυγατριδοῦς εἶναι σφᾶς Πιέρου. Also Hammond 1972, pp. 416–418; Mallios 2011, pp. 82–91.

24 Paus. 9.34.4: Κορωνείας δὲ σταδίους ὡς τεσσαράκοντα ὄρος ἀπέχει τὸ Λιβήθριον, ἀγάλματα δὲ ἐν αὐτῷ Μουσῶν τε καὶ νυμφῶν ἐπίκλησίν ἐστι Λιβηθρίων· καὶ πηγαί–τὴν μὲν Λιβηθριάδα ὀνομάζουσιν, ἡ δὲ ἑτέρα † Πέτρα–γυναικὸς μαστοῖς εἰσιν εἰκασμέναι, καὶ ὅμοιον γάλακτι ὕδωρ ἀπ᾽ αὐτῶν ἄνεισιν. For Livithra (Λ(ε)ίβηθρα) in Pieria and the Ephoreia excavations, see Poulaki-Pantermali 2008b.

25 Strabo 9.2.25: ὁ μὲν οὖν Ἑλικὼν οὐ πολὺ διεστηκὼς τοῦ Παρνασσοῦ ἐνάμιλλός ἐστιν ἐκείνῳ κατά τε ὕψος καὶ περίμετρον· ἄμφω γὰρ χιονόβολα τὰ ὄρη καὶ πετρώδη, περιγράφεται δ᾽ οὐ πολλῇ χώρᾳ. ἐνταῦθα δ᾽ ἐστὶ τό τε τῶν Μουσῶν ἱερὸν καὶ ἡ Ἵππου κρήνη καὶ τὸ τῶν Λειβηθρίδων νυμφῶν ἄντρον· ἐξ οὗ τεκμαίροιτ᾽ ἄν τις Θρᾷκας εἶναι τοὺς τὸν Ἑλικῶνα ταῖς Μούσαις καθιερώσαντας, οἳ καὶ τὴν Πιερίδα καὶ τὸ Λείβηθρον καὶ τὴν Πίμπλειαν ταῖς αὐταῖς θεαῖς ἀνέδειξαν· ἐκαλοῦντο δὲ Πίερες· ἐκλιπόντων δ᾽ ἐκείνων Μακεδόνες νῦν ἔχουσι τὰ χωρία ταῦτα. εἴρηται δ᾽ ὅτι τὴν Βοιωτίαν ταύτην ἐπῴκησάν ποτε Θρᾷκες βιασάμενοι τοὺς Βοιωτοὺς καὶ Πελασγοὶ καὶ ἄλλοι βάρβαροι.

26 I am indebted to Angelos Matthaiou for sending me his study of these remarkable inscriptions, for which see Vassilopoulou and Matthaiou 2013a and 2013b; Zampiti 2012; Zampiti and Vassilopoulou 2008; Vassilopoulou 2000. For another cult of Pan and the Nymphs in nearby Phokis, see Katsarou 2013. For the fragmentary inscription at Delphi dated ca. 500 B.C. (*CID* 1.1: [π]ελανὸν Πίερες [– –] | πεντεκαίδεκα δρα[χμὰς [– –]), see Mari 2002, pp. 29–31, and 2007, pp. 36–37; Mallios 2011, pp. 135–138.

27 Strabo 10.3.17: ἀπὸ δὲ τοῦ μέλους καὶ τοῦ ῥυθμοῦ καὶ τῶν ὀργάνων καὶ ἡ μουσικὴ πᾶσα Θρᾳκία καὶ Ἀσιᾶτις νενόμισται. δῆλον δ᾽ ἔκ τε τῶν τόπων ἐν οἷς αἱ Μοῦσαι τετίμηνται· Πιερία γὰρ καὶ Ὄλυμπος καὶ Πίμπλα καὶ Λείβηθρον τὸ παλαιὸν ἦν Θρᾴκια χωρία καὶ ὄρη, νῦν δὲ ἔχουσι Μακεδόνες· τόν τε Ἑλικῶνα καθιέρωσαν ταῖς Μούσαις Θρᾷκες οἱ τὴν Βοιωτίαν ἐποικήσαντες, οἵπερ καὶ τὸ τῶν Λειβηθριάδων νυμφῶν ἄντρον καθιέρωσαν. οἵ τ᾽ ἐπιμεληθέντες τῆς ἀρχαίας μουσικῆς Θρᾷκες λέγονται, Ὀρφεύς τε καὶ Μουσαῖος καὶ Θάμυρις, καὶ τῷ Εὐμόλπῳ δὲ τοὔνομα ἐνθένδε, καὶ οἱ τῷ Διονύσῳ τὴν Ἀσίαν ὅλην καθιερώσαντες μέχρι τῆς Ἰνδικῆς ἐκεῖθεν καὶ τὴν πολλὴν μουσικὴν μεταφέρουσι· καὶ ὁ μέν τίς φησιν 'κιθάραν Ἀσιᾶτιν ῥάσσων', ὁ δὲ τοὺς αὐλοὺς Βερεκυντίους καλεῖ καὶ Φρυγίους· καὶ τῶν ὀργάνων ἔνια βαρβάρως ὠνόμασται νάβλας καὶ σαμβύκη καὶ βάρβιτος καὶ μαγάδις καὶ ἄλλα πλείω. Also Hammond 1972, pp. 416–418; Bonanno-Aravantinou 1999.

28 According to the epigram of the Macedonian Adaios (*Anth. Pal.* 7.51): οὔ σε κυνῶν γένος εἷλ᾽, Εὐριπίδη, οὐδὲ γυναικὸς | οἶστρος, τὸν σκοτίης Κύπριδος ἀλλότριον, | ἀλλ᾽ Ἀίδης καὶ γῆρας· ὑπαὶ Μακέτῃ δ᾽ Ἀρεθούσῃ | κεῖσαι ἑταιρείῃ τίμιος Ἀρχελέῳ. | σὸν δ᾽ οὐ τοῦτον ἐγὼ τίθεμαι τάφον, ἀλλὰ τὰ Βάκχου | βήματα καὶ σκηνὰς ἐμβάδι πειθομένας. Euripides, whose burial place was purportedly in Macedonian Arethousa, also composed the lost *Archelaos* in honor of the king; see Edson 1970, pp. 39–41; Saatsoglou-Paliadeli 2007; but cf. Scullion 2003.

29 Eur., *Bacch.* 410–416: οὗ ἁ καλλιστευομένα | Πιερία, μούσειος ἕδρα, | σεμνὰ κλειτὺς Ὀλύμπου | ἐκεῖσ᾽ ἄγε με, Βρόμιε Βρόμιε, | πρόβακχ᾽ εὔιε δαῖμον. | ἐκεῖ Χάριτες, ἐκεῖ δὲ Πόθος, ἐκεῖ δὲ βάκ|χαις θέμις ὀργιάζειν; and lines 560–575: τάχα δ᾽ ἐν ταῖς πολυδένδροισιν Ὀλύμπου | θαλάμαις, ἔνθα ποτ᾽ Ὀρφεὺς κιθαρίζων | σύναγεν δένδρεα μούσαις, | σύναγεν θῆρας ἀγρώστας. | μάκαρ ὦ Πιερία, | σέβεταί σ᾽ Εὔιος, ἥξει | τε χορεύσων ἅμα βακχεύ|μασι, τόν τ᾽ ὠκυρόαν | διαβὰς Ἀξιὸν εἱλισ|σομένας μαινάδας ἄξει | Λυδίαν τε τὸν εὐδαιμονίας βροτοῖς | ὀλβοδόταν πατέρ᾽, ὃν ἔκλυον | εὔιππον χώραν ὕδασιν | καλλίστοισι λιπαίνειν.

30 Plut., *Quaest. Graec.* 293a–b: 'Τίνες οἱ ἀποσφενδόνητοι;' Κέρκυραν τὴν νῆσον Ἐρετριεῖς κατῴκουν· Χαρικράτους δὲ πλεύσαντος ἐκ Κορίνθου μετὰ δυνάμεως καὶ τῷ πολέμῳ κρατοῦντος ἐμβάντες εἰς τὰς ναῦς οἱ Ἐρετριεῖς ἀπέπλευσαν οἴκαδε. προαισθόμενοι δ᾽ οἱ πολῖται τῆς χώρας εἶργον αὐτοὺς καὶ ἀποβαίνειν ἐκώλυον σφενδονῶντες. μὴ δυνάμενοι δὲ μήτε πεῖσαι μήτε βιάσασθαι πολλοὺς καὶ ἀπαραιτήτους ὄντας ἐπὶ Θρᾴκης ἔπλευσαν καὶ κατασχόντες χωρίον, ἐν ᾧ πρότερον οἰκῆσαι Μέθωνα τὸν Ὀρφέως πρόγονον ἱστοροῦσι, τὴν μὲν πόλιν ὠνόμασαν Μεθώνην, ὑπὸ δὲ τῶν προσοίκων 'ἀποσφενδόνητοι' προσωνομάσθησαν. See Kontoleon 1963, pp. 2, 20; Hammond 1972, pp. 425–426, 430–441; Papazoglou 1988, pp. 105–106; Hatzopoulos, Knoepfler, and Marigo-Papadopoulos 1990, pp. 665–668; Pritchett (1991b, p. 27) notes Halliday's view (accepted by Hammond 1972, pp. 425–426) that the source of the question is Aristotle's *Constitution of the Methonaians* (nn. 88–89). Hammond (1998, p. 393, n.3) argues that Plutarch's ultimate source was probably Hekataios' Γῆς περίοδος in the later 6th century B.C. Hatzopoulos and Paschidis 2004, p. 804; Graham 2001, pp. 20–23; Tiverios 2008, pp. 5–8 and 17–19; Bessios 2010, pp. 94–95, 105, 306–315. It is noteworthy that

the inhabitants of Eretria, in order to prevent the disembarcation of their compatriots, use long-range weapons (as do Philoktetes' warriors, n. 10), in contradistinction to the close-range ones, for which see the characteristic fragment of Archilochos fr. 3 West: οὔτοι πόλλ' ἐπὶ τόξα τανύσσεται, οὐδὲ θαμειαὶ | σφενδόναι, εὖτ' ἂν δὴ μῶλον Ἄρης συνάγηι | ἐν πεδίωι· ξιφέων δὲ πολύστονον ἔσσεται ἔργον· | ταύτης γὰρ κεῖνοι δάμονές εἰσι μάχης | δεσπόται Εὐβοίης δουρικλυτοί; Kontoleon 1963, pp. 15–16; Donlan 1970; Tsantsanoglou 2000, 2003; cf. Chapter 28.

31 Strabo 6.2.4: πλέοντα δὲ τὸν Ἀρχίαν εἰς τὴν Σικελίαν καταλιπεῖν μετὰ μέρους τῆς στρατιᾶς τοῦ τῶν Ἡρακλειδῶν γένους Χερσικράτη συνοικιοῦντα τὴν νῦν Κέρκυραν καλουμένην, πρότερον δὲ Σχερίαν. ἐκεῖνον μὲν οὖν ἐκβαλόντα Λιβυρνοὺς κατέχοντας οἰκίσαι τὴν νῆσον, τὸν δ' Ἀρχίαν κατασχόντα πρὸς τὸ Ζεφύριον τῶν Δωριέων εὑρόντα τινὰς δεῦρο ἀφιγμένους ἐκ τῆς Σικελίας παρὰ τῶν τὰ Μέγαρα κτισάντων ἀναλαβεῖν αὐτούς, καὶ κοινῇ μετ' αὐτῶν κτίσαι τὰς Συρακούσσας. Hammond 1967, pp. 414–424.

32 Eusebius, *Chron.* (Fotheringham 1923, pp. 158–159): *hi qui Partheniae vocabantur Tarenum condiderunt et Corinthii Corcyram.*

33 Hammond 1972, pp. 424–427; Hatzopoulos, Knoepfler, and Marigo-Papadopoulos 1990, pp. 661–668; Borza 1990, p. 75; Hammond 1998, pp. 393–395; Graham 2001, pp. 20–23. Tiverios (2006, p. 76; 2008, p. 127) argues that the Euboians were attracted to the region of the Thermaic Gulf by the gold of the river Echedoros, the rich ores, the forests, the agricultural, livestock, and fishing products, and the human resources; of all these, especially as regards the Eretrians (see Kontoleon 1963), the timber of the forests suitable for shipbuilding and oars must have been an added incentive. For Eretria's expertise in navigation and its tools see esp. Verdan 2006; van Wees 2010; Chapter 20.

34 For Euboian colonies in the north see Strabo 10.1.8: αἱ δ' οὖν πόλεις αὗται διαφερόντως αὐξηθεῖσαι καὶ ἀποικίας ἔστειλαν ἀξιολόγους εἰς Μακεδονίαν· Ἐρέτρια μὲν γὰρ συνῴκισε τὰς περὶ Παλλήνην καὶ τὸν Ἄθω πόλεις, ἡ δὲ Χαλκὶς τὰς ὑπὸ Ὀλύνθῳ, ἃς Φίλιππος διελυμήνατο. καὶ τῆς Ἰταλίας δὲ καὶ Σικελίας πολλὰ χωρία Χαλκιδέων ἐστίν· ἐστάλησαν δὲ αἱ ἀποικίαι αὗται, καθάπερ εἴρηκεν Ἀριστοτέλης, ἡνίκα ἡ τῶν Ἱπποβοτῶν καλουμένη ἐπεκράτει πολιτεία· προέστησαν γὰρ αὐτῆς ἀπὸ τιμημάτων ἄνδρες ἀριστοκρατικῶς ἄρχοντες. See also Kontoleon 1963; Forrest 1982; Papadopoulos 1996; Hornblower 1997; Papadopoulos 1997; Graham 2001; Papadopoulos 2005, pp, 571–595; Tiverios 2008, pp. 1–17; Papadopoulos 2011; Kotsonas 2012; Zahrnt 2012; Tiverios 2013a; Kotsonas 2020; Chapter 12.

35 Thuc. 2.99.3 (Gomme 1956, p. 247; Hornblower 1991, pp. 374–375): τὴν δὲ παρὰ θάλασσαν νῦν Μακεδονίαν Ἀλέξανδρος ὁ Περδίκκου πατὴρ καὶ οἱ πρόγονοι αὐτοῦ, Τημενίδαι τὸ ἀρχαῖον ὄντες ἐξ Ἄργους, πρῶτοι ἐκτήσαντο καὶ ἐβασίλευσαν ἀναστήσαντες μάχῃ ἐκ μὲν Πιερίας Πίερας, οἳ ὕστερον ὑπὸ τὸ Πάγγαιον πέραν Στρυμόνος ᾤκησαν Φάγρητα καὶ ἄλλα χωρία (καὶ ἔτι καὶ νῦν Πιερικὸς κόλπος καλεῖται ἡ ὑπὸ τῷ Παγγαίῳ πρὸς θάλασσαν γῆ), ἐκ δὲ τῆς Βοττίας καλουμένης Βοττιαίους, οἳ νῦν ὅμοροι Χαλκιδέων οἰκοῦσιν. Also Hammond and Griffith 1979, pp. 3–54; Borza 1982; Hammond 1989, pp. 7–8, 82–83.

36 For an early date see Dimitsas 1874, vol. 2, pp. 3–4; Casson 1919–1921, p. 30; Casson 1926, p. 161; Pritchett 1961, p. 373; Vokotopoulou 1988; and as a possibility Tiverios 2019a. For a later date, Hammond 1972, pp. 416–418, 430–441 (but on pp. 433–434: ca. 650 B.C. the Macedonians displaced the Bottiaians); Borza 1990, pp. 62–65, 84–87; Hatzopoulos, Knoepfler, and Marigo-Papadopoulos 1990, pp. 661–668; Hatzopoulos and Loukopoulou 1992, pp. 15–25; Pikoulas 2001, pp. 22, 39; Graham 2001, pp. 20–22; Tiverios 2008, p. 18 with n. 81; Zahrnt 2011, pp. 614–615. Edson (1970, pp. 20–21) dates the descent of Macedonians from Orestis and Pindos to Pieria and the sea ca. 700 B.C. Saripanidi (2017, pp. 117–124) detects an unmistakable Macedonian "idiom" in her study of funerary practices from ca. 570 B.C. onward. For migrations see Papadopoulos 2005, pp. 580–588; Rose 2008; Parker 2008; Aydıngün 2015; Manoledakis 2016; Mac Sweeney 2017. For the Dorian descent and their expansion in Greece, see Andronikos 1954; Borza 1990, pp. 65–66; the contributions in Malkin 2001 (particularly David Konstan, Jeremy McInerney, Rosalind Thomas, Catherine Morgan, Carla Antonaccio, and Jonathan Hall); Sakellariou 2009, pp. 351–368 (the historicity of the descent), pp. 89–350 (Dorians), pp. 329–344 (Dorians in Phthiotis, Ossa and Olympos, Pindos, and in Doris), pp. 238–242 (Dorians in Macedonia); Mallios 2011, pp. 115–122. For the "second colonization" see also Graham 1982; Cook 1982; Hammond 1982; Forrest 1982; Chapter 12.

37 Hammond 1972, pp. 430–434.

38 See nn. 26, 28, and 31; Hammond 1995a; Hammond 1998, pp. 393–395; Thomas 2008; Hatzopoulos 2011a; Sprawski 2010; Mari 2011; Betcher 2012. For borders and identities in Upper Macedonia, see Xydopoulos 2012, whose arguments *mutatis mutandis* are also applicable to "borderline" Methone; also Muller 2012. Soueref (2007) convincingly argues that in the Archaic period the colonies of the southern Greeks coexist with local settlements in the Thermaic Gulf and throughout the Mediterranean for the sake of trading activities; for this rather peaceful coexistence see also Tiverios 2008, pp. 18, 124–129, esp. pp. 126–127; Tiverios 2019b.

39 Hdt. 4.143–144; 5.1–27; 6.44–48; the Pieres, however, are not mentioned during the operations of Darius and Megabazus in the area between 513 and 509 B.C., when Thrace and Macedonia become Persian satrapies (Hdt. 5.1–27). Hammond and Griffith 1979, pp. 55–60; for Macedonians in Herodotos, see Xydopoulos 2007; for the Athenian presence in Thrace and their naval power before Themistokles and the Peloponnesian War, see Haas 1985; Strauss 2000; van Wees 2010; Davies 2013; Aperghis 2013; O'Halloran 2019.

40 Hdt. 7.112 (How and Wells 1928, vol. 2, p. 168): παραμειψάμενος δὲ ὁ Ξέρξης τὴν εἰρημένην δεύτερα τούτων παραμείβετο τείχεα τὰ Πιέρων, τῶν ἑνὶ Φάγρης ἐστὶ οὔνομα καὶ ἑτέρῳ Πέργαμος. ταύτῃ μὲν δὴ παρ' αὐτὰ τὰ τείχεα τὴν ὁδὸν ἐποιέετο, ἐκ δεξιῆς χειρὸς τὸ Πάγγαιον ὄρος ἀπέργων, ἐὸν μέγα τε καὶ ὑψηλόν, ἐν τῷ χρύσεά τε καὶ ἀργύρεα ἔνι μέταλλα, τὰ νέμονται Πιέρες τε καὶ Ὀδόμαντοι καὶ μάλιστα Σάτραι. Hdt. 7.185 (How and Wells 1928, vol. 2, p. 213): πεζοῦ δὲ τὸν Θρήικες παρείχοντο καὶ Παίονες καὶ Ἐορδοὶ καὶ Βοττιαῖοι καὶ τὸ Χαλκιδικὸν γένος καὶ Βρύγοι καὶ Πίερες καὶ Μακεδόνες καὶ Περραιβοὶ καὶ Ἐνιῆνες καὶ Δόλοπες καὶ Μάγνητες καὶ Ἀχαιοὶ καὶ ὅσοι τῆς Θρηίκης τὴν παραλίην νέμονται, τούτων τῶν ἐθνέων τριήκοντα μυριάδας δοκέω γενέσθαι. Also Pikoulas 2001, pp. 21–24, 39–41, 174–203; Hammond and Griffith 1979, pp. 55–60.

41 Hdt. 7.127 (How and Wells 1928, vol. 2, p. 274): ὡς δὲ ἐς τὴν Θέρμην ἀπίκετο ὁ Ξέρξης, ἵδρυσε αὐτοῦ τὴν στρατιήν. ἐπέσχε δὲ ὁ στρατὸς αὐτοῦ στρατοπεδευόμενος τὴν παρὰ θάλασσαν χώρην τοσήνδε, ἀρξάμενος ἀπὸ Θέρμης πόλιος καὶ τῆς Μυγδονίης μέχρι Λυδίεω τε ποταμοῦ καὶ Ἁλιάκμονος, οἳ οὐρίζουσι γῆν τὴν Βοττιαιίδα τε καὶ Μακεδονίδα, ἐς τὠυτὸ ῥέεθρον τὸ ὕδωρ συμμίσγοντες. ἐστρατοπεδεύοντο μὲν δὴ ἐν τούτοισι τοῖσι χωρίοισι οἱ βάρβαροι, τῶν δὲ καταλεχθέντων τούτων ποταμῶν ἐκ Κρηστωναίων ῥέων Χείδωρος μοῦνος οὐκ ἀντέχρησε τῇ στρατιῇ πινόμενος ἀλλ' ἐπέλιπε. This topographical reference, especially the identification of Pieria south of the river Haliakmon with Macedonia (Μακεδονὶς γῆ), known from the name of its previous inhabitants the Pieres, has been variously commented upon: see Edson 1970, p. 21, with n. 16; Hammond 1972, pp. 430–431, 433–434; Hammond and Griffith 1979, pp. 60–62; Poulaki-Pantermali 1987; Borza 1990, pp. 105–108, 290–291; Xydopoulos 2006, pp. 50–51, with nn. 77–80, with extensive bibliography; Mallios 2011, pp. 105–138.

42 Hdt. 7.131 (How and Wells 1928, vol. 2, pp. 176–177): ὁ μὲν δὴ περὶ Πιερίην διέτριβε ἡμέρας συχνάς· τὸ γὰρ δὴ ὄρος τὸ Μακεδονικὸν ἔκειρε τῆς στρατιῆς τριτημορίς, ἵνα ταύτῃ διεξίῃ ἅπασα ἡ στρατιὴ ἐς Περραιβούς. The identification by How and Wells of Herodotos' Μακεδονικὸν ὄρος with the Pieria mountains is deduced from the fact that Herodotos calls the entire area south of the river Haliakmon Pieria; but in Book 4 (4.195.2: ἐν Ζακύνθῳ ἐκ λίμνης καὶ ὕδατος πίσσαν ἀναφερομένην αὐτὸς ἐγὼ ὥρων . . . ὀδμὴν μὲν ἔχουσαν ἀσφάλτου, τὰ δ' ἄλλα τῆς Πιερικῆς πίσσης ἀμείνω), How and Wells (1928, vol. 1, p. 368) state that this pitch was manufactured from the forests of Olympos and not Pieria. Pliny's statement that in Greece they particularly valued Pierian pitch (*HN* 14.128: ... *picem ... maxime probat, Graecia Piericam*) refers naturally to the mixing of pitch/resin with wine and/or its use for waterproofing in large storage vessels and of course in ships; see also Vassileiadou 2011, pp. 67–98, and 2019; and nn. 40–42.

43 Hdt. 7.173 (How and Wells 1928, vol. 2, p. 206): οἱ δὲ Ἕλληνες πρὸς ταῦτα ἐβουλεύσαντο ἐς Θεσσαλίην πέμπειν κατὰ θάλασσαν πεζὸν στρατὸν φυλάξοντα τὴν ἐσβολήν· ὡς δὲ συνελέχθη ὁ στρατός, ἔπλεε δι' Εὐρίπου. ἀπικόμενος δὲ τῆς Ἀχαιίης ἐς Ἄλον, ἀποβὰς ἐπορεύετο ἐς Θεσσαλίην, τὰς νέας αὐτοῦ καταλιπών, καὶ ἀπίκετο ἐς τὰ Τέμπεα ἐς τὴν ἐσβολὴν ἥ περ ἀπὸ Μακεδονίης τῆς κάτω ἐς Θεσσαλίην φέρει παρὰ ποταμὸν Πηνειόν, μεταξὺ δὲ Ὀλύμπου τε ὄρεος [ἐόντα] καὶ τῆς Ὄσσης. ἐνθαῦτα ἐστρατοπεδεύοντο τῶν Ἑλλήνων κατὰ μυρίους ὁπλίτας συλλεγέντες, καί σφι προσῆν ἡ Θεσσαλῶν ἵππος· ἐστρατήγεε δὲ Λακεδαιμονίων μὲν Εὐαίνετος ὁ Καρήνου ἐκ τῶν πολεμάρχων ἀραιρημένος, γένεος μέντοι ἐὼν οὐ τοῦ βασιληίου, Ἀθηναίων δὲ Θεμιστοκλέης ὁ Νεοκλέος. ἔμειναν δὲ ὀλίγας ἡμέρας ἐνθαῦτα· ἀπικόμενοι γὰρ ἄγγελοι παρὰ Ἀλεξάνδρου τοῦ Ἀμύντεω ἀνδρὸς Μακεδόνος συνεβούλευόν σφι ἀπαλλάσσεσθαι μηδὲ μένοντας ἐν τῇ ἐσβολῇ καταπατηθῆναι ὑπὸ τοῦ στρατοῦ τοῦ ἐπιόντος, σημαίνοντες τὸ πλῆθός τε τῆς στρατιῆς καὶ τὰς νέας. ὡς δὲ οὗτοί σφι ταῦτα συνεβούλευον (χρηστὰ γὰρ ἐδόκεον συμβουλεύειν, καί σφι εὔνοος ἐφαίνετο ἐὼν ὁ Μακεδών), ἐπείθοντο. δοκέειν δέ μοι, ἀρρωδίη ἦν τὸ πεῖθον, ὡς ἐπύθοντο καὶ ἄλλην ἐοῦσαν ἐσβολὴν ἐς Θεσσαλοὺς κατὰ τὴν ἄνω Μακεδονίην διὰ Περραιβῶν κατὰ Γόννον πόλιν, τῇ περ δὴ καὶ ἐσέβαλε ἡ στρατιὴ ἡ Ξέρξεω. καταβάντες δὲ οἱ Ἕλληνες ἐπὶ τὰς νέας ὀπίσω ἐπορεύοντο ἐς τὸν Ἰσθμόν. For bypassing Thessalian Tempe via Upper Macedonia and Perrhaibia (the pass Karavida from Skotina–Kallipeuke–Gonnoi or the pass of the ancient river Sys from Leptokarya–Karya–the Konispoli plateau), see Pritchett 1961; 1980, pp. 347–369; 1991a, pp. 129–136; 1993, pp. 290–292, with earlier bibliography; Pikoulas 2010 and 2022; there was no need that would also demand several days for opening a road through the known passes—that is, the pass through Tempe valley (as Heinrichs 2017, pp. 91–94) or the narrows of Petra (as Vasilev 2015, pp. 190–194) or the even more distant pass of Volustana; undoubtedly, small contingents used these passes, if only for strategic purposes.

44 Hammond and Griffth 1979, pp. 55–69; Roisman 2010.

45 Thucydides' expression τὰ ἐπὶ Θράκης is understood either specifically, Thracians and their kingdom east of the river Strymon, or more generally, the area east of Macedonia with the rivers Haliakmon or Axios as boundaries; see Gomme 1945, pp. 203–208; Hornblower 1991, pp. 101–102; Zahrnt 2011, pp. 613–638; Xydopoulos 2016. For Thracians in Herodotos, see Xydopoulos 2007; for Macedonians in literary and epigraphical sources, Xydopoulos 2006, pp. 47–114; Rhodes 2010; and for Macedonian "ethnicity" see Hall 2001; Asirvatham 2008; Engels 2010; and esp. Hatzopoulos 2011a, 2011b.

46 Bessios 2010, p. 132.

47 Thuc. 1.136.1–2 (Gomme 1945, pp. 394–409, 438–440; Hornblower 1991, pp. 220–222): ὁ δὲ Θεμιστοκλῆς προαισθόμενος φεύγει ἐκ Πελοποννήσου ἐς Κέρκυραν, ὢν αὐτῶν εὐεργέτης . . . ἀναγκάζεται κατά τι ἄπορον παρὰ Ἄδμητον τὸν Μολοσσῶν βασιλέα ὄντα αὐτῷ οὐ φίλον καταλῦσαι. (1.137.1–2) . . . καὶ ὕστερον οὐ πολλῷ τοῖς τε Λακεδαιμονίοις καὶ Ἀθηναίοις ἐλθοῦσι καὶ πολλὰ εἰποῦσιν οὐκ ἐκδίδωσιν, ἀλλ' ἀποστέλλει βουλόμενον ὡς βασιλέα πορευθῆναι ἐπὶ τὴν ἑτέραν θάλασσαν πεζῇ ἐς Πύδναν τὴν Ἀλεξάνδρου. (2) ἐν ᾗ ὁλκάδος τυχὼν ἀναγομένης ἐπ' Ἰωνίας καὶ ἐπιβὰς καταφέρεται χειμῶνι ἐς τὸ Ἀθηναίων στρατόπεδον, ὃ ἐπολιόρκει Νάξον. For Alexander I, see Hammond and Griffth 1979, pp. 98–104; Tripodi 2007.

48 Gomme's (1945, p. 202) opinion that Athens respected Macedonian domination of and influence on the cities of the Thermaic Gulf colonized by southern Greeks is too general to be of any help.

49 IG I³ 282A col. II, line 53. For an early date see IG I³; GHI 61 (Meiggs and Lewis 1988, no. 65); Meritt 1944, pp. 215–217; 1980; Edson 1947; Gomme 1945, pp. 213–215; 1956, p. 620; Gomme, Andrewes, and Dover 1970, pp. 222–223; Hammond 1989, pp. 83–85; Borza 1990, pp. 148–150 with n. 45; Hatzopoulos, Knoepfler, and Marigo-Papadopoulos 1990, p. 661. For a later date, see Mattingly 1961; 1996b, pp. 525–527.

50 Hdt. 8.136 (How and Wells 1928, vol. 2, pp. 281–282): Μαρδόνιος δὲ ἐπιλεξάμενος ὅ τι δὴ λέγοντα ἦν τὰ χρηστήρια, μετὰ ταῦτα ἔπεμψε ἄγγελον ἐς Ἀθήνας Ἀλέξανδρον τὸν Ἀμύντεω ἄνδρα Μακεδόνα, ἅμα μὲν ὅτι οἱ προσκηδέες οἱ Πέρσαι ἦσαν (Ἀλεξάνδρου γὰρ ἀδελφεὴν Γυγαίην, Ἀμύντεω δὲ θυγατέρα, Βουβάρης ἀνὴρ Πέρσης ἔσχε, ἐκ τῆς οἱ ἐγεγόνεε Ἀμύντης ὁ ἐν τῇ Ἀσίῃ, ἔχων [τὸ] οὔνομα τὸ τοῦ μητροπάτορος, τῷ δὴ ἐκ βασιλέος τῆς Φρυγίης ἐδόθη Ἀλάβαστρα πόλις μεγάλη νέμεσθαι), ἅμα δὲ ὁ Μαρδόνιος πυθόμενος ὅτι πρόξεινός τε εἴη <ἐκεῖ> καὶ εὐεργέτης ὁ Ἀλέξανδρος ἔπεμπε. Also Gomme 1945, pp. 201–202; Walbank 1978, no. 1.

51 Thuc. 1.114 (Gomme 1945, pp. 340–347; Hornblower 1991, pp. 184–186) notes that the Athenians displaced all the inhabitants of Histiaia; Theopompos adds (FGrH 115 fr. 387: Θεόπομπος δέ φησί Περικλέους χειρουμένου Εὔβοιαν τοὺς Ἱστιαιεῖς καθ' ὁμολογίας εἰς Μακεδονίαν μεταστῆναι) that the inhabitants of Histiaia migrated to Macedonia, just as earlier (478 B.C.), after Argos destroyed Mycenae, more than half of Mycenae's population took refuge with Alexander I in Macedonia, as also Pausanias mentions (7.25.6: τοῦ δήμου δὲ πλέον μὲν ἥμισυ ἐς Μακεδονίαν καταφεύγουσι παρὰ Ἀλέξανδρον, ᾧ Μαρδόνιος ὁ Γωβρύου τὴν ἀγγελίαν ἐπίστευσεν ἐς Ἀθηναίους ἀπαγγεῖλαι). See also Edson 1970, p. 38.

52 For timber and particular species in Macedonia see: Theophr., Hist. Pl. 1.9.2–3; 3.3.1, 4, 8; 3.2.5; 3.4.1; 3.5.4; 3.8.7; 3.9.2, 6; 3.10.2; 3.12.2; 3.15.3, 5; 4.5.4–5; 5.2.1; 7.1–3; 8.4.5; 8.9.1; 9.2.3; 9.3.1–3; and esp. 5.1.5–5.2.1; Thuc. 4.108.1; Xen., Hell. 6.1.11; [Ps.] Xen., Ath. Pol. 2.11–12; Dem. 19 (Περὶ τῆς παραπρεσβείας), 265; 49 (Πρὸς Τιμόθεον), 26 and 36; Diod. Sic. 20.46.4; Plut., Demetr. 10.1; GHI 91 (Meiggs and Lewis 1988, no. 91); 111 (Rhodes and Osborne 2003, no. 12), 129 (nn. 69–70 and 72); IG XI.2.199, side A.1 line 57; CID 2, side B, col. II, lines 7–14; Psoma 2015; Vassileiadou 2011, pp. 99–113; Karathanasis 2019, pp. 714–720; Chapter 20.

53 Thuc. 1.61.1–4 (Gomme 1945, pp. 199–219; Hornblower 1991, pp. 104–105): ἦλθε δὲ καὶ τοῖς Ἀθηναίοις εὐθὺς ἡ ἀγγελία τῶν πόλεων ὅτι ἀφεστᾶσι, καὶ πέμπουσιν, ὡς ᾔσθοντο καὶ τοὺς μετ' Ἀριστέως ἐπιπαριόντας, δισχιλίους ἑαυτῶν ὁπλίτας καὶ τεσσαράκοντα ναῦς πρὸς τὰ ἀφεστῶτα, καὶ Καλλίαν τὸν Καλλιάδου πέμπτον αὐτὸν στρατηγόν, οἳ ἀφικόμενοι ἐς Μακεδονίαν πρῶτον καταλαμβάνουσι τοὺς προτέρους χιλίους Θέρμην ἄρτι ᾑρηκότας καὶ Πύδναν πολιορκοῦντας. προσκαθεζόμενοι δὲ καὶ αὐτοὶ τὴν Πύδναν ἐπολιόρκησαν μέν, ἔπειτα δὲ ξύμβασιν ποιησάμενοι καὶ ξυμμαχίαν ἀναγκαίαν πρὸς τὸν Περδίκκαν, ὡς αὐτοὺς κατήπειγεν ἡ Ποτείδαια καὶ ὁ Ἀριστεὺς παρεληλυθώς, ἀπανίστανται ἐκ τῆς Μακεδονίας, καὶ ἀφικόμενοι ἐς Βέροιαν κἀκεῖθεν ἐπὶ Στρέψαν καὶ πειράσαντες πρῶτον τοῦ χωρίου καὶ οὐχ ἑλόντες ἐπορεύοντο κατὰ γῆν πρὸς τὴν Ποτείδαιαν, τρισχιλίοις μὲν ὁπλίταις ἑαυτῶν, χωρὶς δὲ τῶν ξυμμάχων πολλοῖς, ἱππεῦσι δὲ ἑξακοσίοις Μακεδόνων τοῖς μετὰ Φιλίππου καὶ Παυσανίου· ἅμα δὲ νῆες παρέπλεον ἑβδομήκοντα. For Pydna see Papazoglou 1988, pp. 106–110; Bessios and Pappa 1995; Hatzopoulos and Paschidis 2004, p. 806; Tiverios 2008, pp. 19–21. For Perdikkas II see Gomme 1945, pp. 200–202; 1956, pp. 621–622; Hammond and Griffth 1979, pp. 115–136; Chambers 1986; Heskel 1997, p. 31; Roisman 2010, pp. 146–154; Psoma 2011, pp. 113–119; Psoma 2015, pp. 4–5; Ruffing 2017; Karathanasis 2019. According to Borza (1990, p. 149), Pydna's siege would make no sense if Methone was a member of the Athenian League and consequently it must have been under the rule of Perdikkas II for some time; cf., however, Hornblower 1991, pp. 104–105, Hatzopoulos 2021, and Chapter 20.

54 *IG* I³ 61; *GHI* 61 (Meiggs and Lewis 1988, no. 65); the earlier bibliography in n. 48; Lambert in https://www.atticinscriptions.com/inscription/IGI3/61. The decrees are inscribed stoichedon (41 letters) on a large stele of Pentelic marble, broken at top and bottom; it was found in the Theater of Dionysos and today is exhibited in the Acropolis Museum. At the top there is a relief scene of a seated Athena extending her right hand (in *dexiosis*) to a standing figure with a short chiton accompanied by a hound (Artemis?), for which see Lawton 1995, pp. 27, 36, 42–43, 47, 67, 73, 81–82 no. 2.

Μεθοναίον ἐκ Πιερ[ίας]·

[Φ]αίνιππος Φρυνίχο ἐγραμμάτ[ευε]·   424/3
[ἔδ]οχσεν τῆι βολῆι καὶ τῶι δέμοι· Ἐρεχθεῒς ἐπρ[υτάν]-   430/429 or 428/7 (1st decree)
[ευε], Σκόπας ἐγραμμάτευε, Τιμονίδες ἐπεστάτε, Δ[ιοπ]-
[εί]θες εἶπε· δι[α]χειροτονέσαι τὸν δέμον αὐτίκ[α πρὸ]-   5
[ς Μ]εθοναίος εἴτε φόρον δοκεῖ τάττεν τὸν δέμο[ν αὐτ]-
[ίκ]α μάλα ἒ ἐχ[σ]αρκέν αὐτοῖς τελέν hόσον τῆι θε[ῶι ἀπ]-
[ὸ τ]ō φόρο ἐγίγνετο, hὸν τοῖς προτέροις Παν[αθ]ε[ναίο]-
[ις] ἐτετάχατο φέρεν, τὸ δὲ ἄλλο ἀτελὲς ἔνα[ι· τὸν δὲ ὀφ]-
[ει]λεμάτον hὰ γεγράφαται τῶι δεμοσίοι τ[ôι τôν Ἀθε]-   10
[να]<ί>ομ Μεθοναῖοι ὀφείλοντες, ἐὰν ὄσι ἐπιτ[έδειοι Ἀ]-
[θε]ναίοις ὄσπερ τε νῦν καὶ ἔτι ἀμείνος, ἐπι[χορέν ἀπ]-
[ότ]αχσιν περὶ τές πράχσεος Ἀθεναίος, καὶ ἐὰν [κοινὸ]-
[ν] φσέφισμά τι περὶ τôν ὀφειλεμάτον τôν ἐν τε̄[ισι σα]-
[νί]σι γίγνεται μεδὲν προσhεκέτο Μεθοναίο[ις, ἐὰμ μ]-   15
[ὲ χ]ορὶς γίγνεται φσέφισμα περὶ Μεθοναίον· π[ρέσβε]-
[ς δ]ὲ τρές πέμφσαι hυπὲρ πεντέκοντα ἔτε γεγον[ότας]
[hο]ς Περδίκκα[ν], εἰπὲν δὲ Περδίκκαι hότι δοκε[ῖ δίκα]-
[ιο]ν ἔναι ἐὰν Μεθοναίος τῆι θαλάττει χρέσθα[ι μεδὲ]
[ἐχσ]ἔναι hορίσασθαι, καὶ ἐὰν εἰσεμπορεύεσθ[αι καθ]-   20
[άπε]ρ τέος ἐ[ς] τὲν χόραν καὶ μέτε ἀδικέν μ[έ]τε [ἀ]δ[ικέσ]-
[θαι] μεδὲ στρα[τ]ιὰν διὰ τές χόρας τές Μεθ[ο]ναίον [διά]-
[γεν ἀ]κόντομ [Με]θοναίον, καὶ ἐὰμ μὲν ὁμολ[ο]γōσιν [hεκ]-
[άτερ]οι χσυ[μβι]βασάντον hοι πρέσβες, ἐὰν δὲ μέ, [πρεσ]-
[βεί]αν ἑκάτ[ερ]ο[ι] πεμπόντον ἐς Διονύσια, τέλος [ἔχον]-   25
[τας] περὶ hôν ἂν διαφ<έ>ρονται, πρὸς τὲν βολὲν κα[ὶ τὸν]
[δε̄μ]ον· ε[ἰ]πὲν δὲ [Π]ερδίκκαι hότι ἐὰν hοι στρατι[ōται]
[hοι] ἐμ Ποτειδ[ά]αι ἐπαινôσι γνόμας ἀγαθὰς hέ[χσοσι]
[περὶ] αὐτὸ Ἀθε[ν]αῖοι. ἐχειροτόνεσεν hο δε̄μος [Μεθον]-
[αίο]ς τελέν h[όσο]ν τῆι θεῶι ἀπὸ τō φόρο ἐγίγνε[το hὸν]   30
[τοῖ]ς προτέρο[ις] Παναθεναίοις ἐτετάχατο φ[έρεν, τὸ]
[δὲ ἄ]λλο ἀτελὲς ἒ̄ναι. ν ἔδοχσεν τε̄ι βολε̄ι καὶ [τôι δέμ]-   426/5 (2nd decree)
[οι· h]ιπποθο[ντὶς ἐ]πρυτάνευε, Μεγακλείδες [ἐγραμμά]-
[τευ]ε, Νι[κ]ο[. .5. . ἐ]πεστάτε, Κλεόνυμος εἶπε· Μ[εθοναί]-
[οις] εἶν[αι ἐχ]σα[γο]γὲν ἐγ Βυζαντίο σίτο μέχ[ρι . . . . α]-   35
[κισχ]ιλίον μεδίμνον τὸ ἐνιαυτō ἑκάστο, hοι [δὲ ἑλλε]-
[σπ]οντοφύλακες μέτε αὐτοὶ κολυόντον ἐχσάγεν μ[έτ]-
[ε ἄλ]λον ἐόντον κολύεν, ἒ εὐθυνέσθον μυρίαισι δρ[αχ]-
[μει̃σ]ιν ἕκαστος· γραφσαμένος δὲ πρὸς τὸς ἑλλεσπ[ον]-
[το]φύλακας ἐχσάγε[ν] μέχρι τō τεταγμένο· ἀζέμιος [δὲ]   40
[ἔσ]το καὶ ἐ ναῦς ἐ ἐχσάγοσα· hοι τι δ᾽ ἂν κοινὸν φσήφ[ισμ]-
[α π]ερὶ τôν χσυμμάχο[ν] φσεφίζονται Ἀθεναῖοι πε[ρὶ β]-
[οε]θείας ἒ ἄ[λ]λο τι προ[σ]τάττο[ν]τες τέσι πόλεσι ἒ [περ]-
[ὶ σ]φôν [ἒ] περὶ τôν πόλεον, hό τι ἂν ὀνομαστὶ περὶ τ[ές π]-
[όλε]ος τε̄[ς] Μεθοναίον φσεφίζονται τοῦτο προσέ[κεν]   45
[αὐτοῖ]ς, τ[ὰ] δὲ ἄλλα μέ, ἀλλὰ φυλάττοντες τὲν σφετ[έρα]-
[ν αὐτôν ἐ]ν τôι τεταγμένοι ὄντον· hὰ δὲ hυπὸ Περδ[ίκκ]-
[ο ἀδικε̄σ]θαί φασι βουλεύσασθαι Ἀθεναίος hό τι ἂ[ν δο]-
[κ]ει̃ [ἀγαθ]ὸν εἶναι περὶ Μεθοναίον, ἐπειδὰν ἀπαν[τέσ]-   49

[ο]σι ἐ[ς τὸ]ν δέμον hοι πρέσβες [h]οι παρὰ Περδίκκο [hοι τ]- 50
ε μετ[ὰ Πλ]ειστίο οἰ[χ]όμενοι καὶ hοι μετὰ Λεογό[ρο· τê]-
[σ]ι δὲ [ἄλλ]εσι πόλε[σι χ]ρηματίσαι, ἐπειδὰν ἐσέλ[θει ἑ]
[π]ρυ[ταν]εία ἑ δευτ[έρα] μετὰ τὰς ἐν τôι νεορίοι ἕ[δρας]
[ε]ὐθ[ὺς] ἐκκλεσίαν [πο]έσαντες· συν[ε]χὸς δὲ ποêν τ[ὰς ἐκ]-
[ε]ῖ ἕ[δρα]ς ἕος ἂν δι[απρ]αχθêι, ἄλλο δὲ προχρεμα[τίσαι] 55
[το]ύ[το]ν μεδὲν ἐὰμ μέ τι οἱ στρατε[γ]οὶ δέοντα[ι. ν ἔδοχ]-   425–424 (3rd decree)
[σεν τêι] βολêι καὶ τôι δέμοι· Κεκροπὶς ἐπρυ[τάνευε, .]
[. .6. . .]ες ἐγραμμάτε[υ]ε, h[ι]εροκλείδες ἐ[πεστάτε, . .]
[. .6. . .] εἶπε· ἐπειδὲ ε[. . . . . .24. . . . .]-
[ι hοπόσα]ι Ἀθεναι[. . . . . .29. . . . .] 60
lacuna
[ἔδοχσεν τêι βολêι καὶ τôι δέμοι· Ἀκαμαντὶς ἐπρυτά]-   424/3 (4th decree)
[νευε, Φαίνιππος ἐγραμμάτευε, ...17. . . . .]
[. . . . . .41. . . . .].

Interestingly, some of these provisions were also voted for the Chalkidic city of Aphytis, according to a fragmentary inscription dated 426/5 B.C. or a little later, where instead of repeating all the provisions for Methone, in the decree for Aphytis the expression καθάπερ Μεθωναίοις is inscribed (*IG* I³ 62 and *Agora* 16, no. 15, lines 4–5 [restoration certain] and line 7; *SEG* 10.67, 13.7, 24.6, 28.7, 30.10). A second decree for Aphytis (*IG* I³ 63) outlines even further Athenian action to ease the city's problems.

55 *IG* I³ 281, lines 31–35, dated to 430/29 B.C. (text restored from *IG* I³ 282), and *IG* I³ 282, face A front. col. II, lines 51–53, dated to 429/8 B.C.: [haί]δε τὸν π[ό]λε[ο]ν [a]ὐτὲ[ν] | τὲν ἀπα[ρ]χὲν ἀπέγαγον | ΗΗΗ Μεθον[α]ῖοι κ.λπ.

56 Thuc. 4.78.6 (Gomme 1956, pp. 545–546; Hornblower 1996, pp. 261–262, where also a note on the meaning of πόλισμα): οἱ δὲ Περραιβοὶ αὐτόν, ὑπήκοοι ὄντες Θεσσαλῶν, κατέστησαν ἐς Δῖον τῆς Περδίκκου ἀρχῆς, ὃ ὑπὸ τῷ Ὀλύμπῳ Μακεδονίας πρὸς Θεσσαλοὺς πόλισμα κεῖται. Thucydides narrates Brasidas' expedition to the north in Book 4 (78–88, 102–116, 120–132, 135) and Book 5 (2, 6–11).

57 Thuc. 4.83 and 4.124–128 respectively (Gomme 1956, pp. 550–551, 612–619; Hornblower 1996, pp. 273–274, 390–402).

58 Thuc. 4.129.2–4 (Gomme 1956, p. 620; Hornblower 1996, pp. 402–405): ὑπὸ γὰρ τὸν αὐτὸν χρόνον τοῖς ἐν τῇ Λύγκῳ ἐξέπλευσαν ἐπί τε τὴν Μένδην καὶ τὴν Σκιώνην οἱ Ἀθηναῖοι, ὥσπερ παρεσκευάζοντο, ναυσὶ μὲν πεντήκοντα, ὧν ἦσαν δέκα Χῖαι, ὁπλίταις δὲ χιλίοις ἑαυτῶν καὶ τοξόταις ἑξακοσίοις καὶ Θραξὶ μισθωτοῖς χιλίοις καὶ ἄλλοις τῶν αὐτόθεν ξυμμάχων πελτασταῖς· ἐστρατήγει δὲ Νικίας ὁ Νικηράτου καὶ Νικόστρατος ὁ Διειτρέφους. ἄραντες δὲ ἐκ Ποτειδαίας ταῖς ναυσὶ καὶ σχόντες κατὰ τὸ Ποσειδώνιον ἐχώρουν ἐς τοὺς Μενδαίους . . . καὶ αὐτοῖς Νικίας μὲν Μεθωναίους τε ἔχων εἴκοσι καὶ ἑκατὸν ψιλοὺς καὶ λογάδας τῶν Ἀθηναίων ὁπλιτῶν ἑξήκοντα καὶ τοὺς τοξότας ἅπαντας κατὰ ἀτραπόν τινα τοῦ λόφου πειρώμενος προσβῆναι καὶ τραυματιζόμενος ὑπ' αὐτῶν οὐκ ἐδυνήθη βιάσασθαι. For slingers and sling bullets see Chapter 28.

59 Thuc. 4.132.1 (Gomme 1956, pp. 621–622; Hornblower 1996, pp. 407–408): περιτειχιζομένης δὲ τῆς Σκιώνης Περδίκκας τοῖς τῶν Ἀθηναίων στρατηγοῖς ἐπικηρυκευσάμενος ὁμολογίαν ποιεῖται πρὸς τοὺς Ἀθηναίους διὰ τὴν τοῦ Βρασίδου ἔχθραν περὶ τῆς ἐκ τῆς Λύγκου ἀναχωρήσεως, εὐθὺς τότε ἀρξάμενος πράσσειν. 5.6.1–2 (Gomme 1956, pp. 635–636; Hornblower 1996, pp. 436–437): ὁ δὲ Κλέων ὡς ἀπὸ τῆς Τορώνης τότε περιέπλευσεν ἐπὶ τὴν Ἀμφίπολιν, ὁρμώμενος ἐκ τῆς Ἠιόνος Σταγίρῳ μὲν προσβάλλει Ἀνδρίων ἀποικίᾳ καὶ οὐχ εἷλε, Γαληψὸν δὲ τὴν Θασίων ἀποικίαν λαμβάνει κατὰ κράτος. (2) καὶ πέμψας ὡς Περδίκκαν πρέσβεις, ὅπως παραγένοιτο στρατιᾷ κατὰ τὸ ξυμμαχικόν, καὶ ἐς τὴν Θρᾴκην ἄλλους παρὰ Πολλῆν τὸν Ὀδομάντων βασιλέα, ἄξοντας μισθοῦ Θρᾷκας ὡς πλείστους, αὐτὸς ἡσύχαζε περιμένων ἐν τῇ Ἠιόνι.

60 Thuc. 5.2 and 5.6–11 (Gomme 1956, pp. 635–657; Hornblower 1996, pp. 424–457).

61 *IG* I³ 89, with uncertain date, and thus the period between 417 and 413 B.C. has also been proposed; see also n. 54.

62 *IG* I³ 89 line 31: [καὶ οὐδένα κο]πέας ἐχσάγεν ἔασο ἐὰμ μὲ Ἀθε[ναίο]. The export of oars exclusively to Athens may seem strange, but as Borza (1987, p. 34; 1990, pp. 55–56) has calculated, following Meiggs' (1982, pp. 126–127, 131) figures, the needs of the Athenian triremes were immense: each trireme with a life expectancy of ca. 20 years had 170 oars and 30 replacements; consequently, a fleet of 200 triremes demanded 40,000 oars, while every year approximately 20 new triremes were constructed to replace those lost at sea or old ships; see also Billows 1995, p. 6; Psoma 2015, pp. 2–7; Ruffing 2017; Karathanasis 2019, pp. 709–714; Chapter 20. For the order of the signatories of the treaty, see esp. Psoma 2012.

63 Thuc. 4.108.1 (Gomme 1956, pp. 580–581; Hornblower 1996, pp. 340–342): ἐχομένης δὲ τῆς Ἀμφιπόλεως οἱ Ἀθηναῖοι ἐς μέγα δέος κατέστησαν, ἄλλως τε καὶ ὅτι ἡ πόλις αὐτοῖς ἦν ὠφέλιμος ξύλων τε ναυπηγησίμων πομπῇ καὶ χρημάτων προσόδῳ, καὶ ὅτι μέχρι μὲν τοῦ Στρυμόνος ἦν πάροδος Θεσσαλῶν διαγόντων ἐπὶ τοὺς ξυμμάχους σφῶν τοῖς Λακεδαιμονίοις, τῆς δὲ γεφύρας μὴ κρατούντων, ἄνωθεν μὲν μεγάλης οὔσης ἐπὶ πολὺ λίμνης τοῦ ποταμοῦ, τὰ δὲ πρὸς Ἠιόνα τριήρεσι τηρουμένων, οὐκ ἂν δύνασθαι προελθεῖν· τότε δὲ ῥᾴδια ἤδη ἐνόμιζεν γεγενῆσθαι. καὶ τοὺς ξυμμάχους ἐφοβοῦντο μὴ ἀποστῶσιν.

64 *IG* I³ 76; *GHI* 68; Gomme 1945, p. 207; Hammond and Griffith 1979, pp. 115–136; Hornblower 1991, pp. 99–101.

65 Thuc. 5.83.4: κατέκλῃσαν δὲ τοῦ αὐτοῦ χειμῶνος καὶ Μακεδονίας Ἀθηναῖοι Περδίκκαν, ἐπικαλοῦντες τήν τε πρὸς Ἀργείους καὶ Λακεδαιμονίους γενομένην ξυνωμοσίαν, καὶ ὅτι παρασκευασαμένων αὐτῶν στρατιὰν ἄγειν ἐπὶ Χαλκιδέας τοὺς ἐπὶ Θρᾴκης καὶ Ἀμφίπολιν Νικίου τοῦ Νικηράτου στρατηγοῦντος ἔψευστο τὴν ξυμμαχίαν καὶ ἡ στρατεία μάλιστα διελύθη ἐκείνου †ἀπάραντος†· πολέμιος οὖν ἦν. καὶ ὁ χειμὼν ἐτελεύτα οὗτος, καὶ πέμπτον καὶ δέκατον ἔτος τῷ πολέμῳ ἐτελεύτα. Gomme, Andrewes, and Dover (1970, pp. 153–154) and Alberti (1992, p. 299) accept the following correction to the manuscript: καὶ Μακεδόνας Ἀθηναῖοι, Περδίκκᾳ κτλ., because of the meaning of the verb κατακλῄω/-είω in Thucydides, and also because they believed that a complete blockade of Macedonia from the sea, even though in this period the coastline of the kingdom was very small, could not have been as effective as a blockade by sea of an island or a Greek city in the south. For the participle †ἀπάραντος† Gomme, Andrewes, and Dover suggest reading: ἀποστάντος *vel sim.*, and Alberti (1992, p. 299) ἐπάραντος, because ἀπαίρω in Thucydides is always used for the departure of the fleet; see also Hammond and Griffith 1979, p. 132; Hornblower 2008, pp. 214–215. For the syntax and meaning of ἀπαίρω see LSJ⁹, s.v. II, and Montanari 2013, s.v. The Macedonian king could have withdrawn either a contingent of Macedonians or even ships from the common operation with Athenians. Moreover, the complete blockade of Macedonia may have been just as effective, since Macedonian access to the sea relied exclusively on the harbor city of Pydna immediately to the south of Methone; the blockade by sea, therefore, actually meant blockading the western Thermaic Gulf, especially Pydna, whose territory may have also been plundered in the following year (see n. 67). Inter-Macedonian conflicts for succession may have emboldened Pydna, which, a few years after Archelaos became king, felt strong enough to secede, unsuccessfully, from the Macedonian kingdom.

66 Thuc. 6.7.3–4 (Gomme, Andrewes, and Dover 1970, pp. 222–223; Hornblower 2008, p. 311): καὶ ἐς Μεθώνην τὴν ὅμορον Μακεδονίᾳ ἱππέας κατὰ θάλασσαν κομίσαντες Ἀθηναῖοι σφῶν τε αὐτῶν καὶ Μακεδόνων τοὺς παρὰ σφίσι φυγάδας ἐκακούργουν τὴν Περδίκκου. Λακεδαιμόνιοι δὲ πέμψαντες παρὰ Χαλκιδέας τοὺς ἐπὶ Θρᾴκης, ἄγοντας πρὸς Ἀθηναίους δεχημέρους σπονδάς, ξυμπολεμεῖν ἐκέλευον Περδίκκᾳ· οἱ δ' οὐκ ἤθελον. καὶ ὁ χειμὼν ἐτελεύτα, καὶ ἕκτον καὶ δέκατον ἔτος ἐτελεύτα τῷ πολέμῳ τῷδε ὃν Θουκυδίδης ξυνέγραψεν.

67 Diod. Sic. 13.49.1–2: Ἀρχέλαος δ' ὁ τῶν Μακεδόνων βασιλεύς, τῶν Πυδναίων ἀπειθούντων, πολλῇ δυνάμει τὴν πόλιν περιεστρατοπέδευσεν. παρεβοήθησε δ' αὐτῷ καὶ Θηραμένης ἔχων στόλον· ὃς χρονιζούσης τῆς πολιορκίας ἀπέπλευσεν εἰς Θρᾴκην πρὸς Θρασύβουλον τὸν ἀφηγούμενον τοῦ στόλου παντός. ὁ μὲν οὖν Ἀρχέλαος φιλοτιμότερον πολιορκήσας τὴν Πύδναν καὶ κρατήσας μετῴκισεν αὐτὴν ἀπὸ θαλάττης ὡς εἴκοσι στάδια. See also Bessios 2010, p. 134; for Diodoros and Macedonian history see Chamoux 1983; for Archelaos see Gomme, Andrewes, and Dover 1981, p. 33; Hammond and Griffith 1979, pp. 137–141; Borza 1990, pp. 162–163 and n. 9, with a brief note about the probability of shipyards in northern Pieria, either in Pydna or Methone or both; Mikrogiannakis 2007; Hornblower 2008, pp. 758–759; Roisman, 2010, pp. 154–158; Psoma 2011, pp. 120–124; Psoma 2015, pp. 2–7. The relocation site of Pydna has been identified with Kitros (Bessios 2010, pp. 134, 260).

68 Athens' dramatic situation in 411 B.C. is also emphasized in Ar. *Lys.* 420–423: the Proboulos cannot get the money needed to buy oars from the treasury (τοιαῦτ' ἀπήντηκ' ἐς τοιαυτὶ πράγματα, | ὅτε γ' ἂν ἐγὼ πρόβουλος, ἐκπορίσας ὅπως | κωπῆς ἔσονται, τἀργυρίου νυνὶ δέον, | ὑπὸ τῶν γυναικῶν ἀποκέκλημαι ταῖς πύλαις).

69 Andokides 2.11 (*Περὶ τῆς ἑαυτοῦ καθόδου*; Gagarin and MacDowell 1998, p. 141): ἐκ δὲ τούτου οὐ πώποτε οὔτε τοῦ σώματος οὔτε τῶν ὄντων ἐμοὶ ἐφεισάμην, ὅπου ἔδει παρακινδυνεύειν· ἀλλ' αὐτίκα μὲν τότε εἰσήγαγον εἰς <τὴν> στρατιὰν ὑμῶν οὖσαν ἐν Σάμῳ κωπέας, τῶν τετρακοσίων ἤδη τὰ πράγματα ἐνθάδε κατειληφότων, ὄντος μοι Ἀρχελάου ξένου πατρικοῦ καὶ διδόντος τέμνεσθαί τε καὶ ἐξάγεσθαι ὁπόσους ἐβουλόμην. τούτους τε εἰσήγαγον τοὺς κωπέας, καὶ παρόν μοι πέντε δραχμῶν τὴν τιμὴν αὐτῶν δέξασθαι οὐκ ἠθέλησα πράξασθαι πλέον ἢ ὅσου ἐμοὶ κατέστησαν, εἰσήγαγον δὲ σῖτόν τε καὶ χαλκόν.

70 *IG* I³ 117 (*GHI* 91; Meiggs and Lewis 1988, no. 91; Walbank 1978, no. 90), lines 15–38 heavily restored: [τὲς δ]ὲ κομιδὲς τὸν νε[ο͂]ν, hὰς ἂν hοι ναυπεγοὶ] ἐγ Μακεδονίας στ|[έλλοσι, τὲν βολὲν ἐπιμ]ελ[εθ]ε͂ναι, hόπος | [ἂν σταλδο͂σιν hος τάχισ]τα Ἀθέναζε καὶ π|[λεροθο͂σι καὶ ἐπὶ Ἰονί]αν κομίζεται hε | [στρατιὰ φυλάχσοσα φυ]λακὲν τὲν ἀρίστ|[εν· ἐὰν δέ τις μὲ ποέσει] κατὰ ταῦτα, ὀφέλ|[εν μυρίας δραχμὰς αὐτὸ]ν hιερὰς τε͂ι Ἀθ|[εναίαι· το͂ι δὲ πρότοι ἐλθ]όντι καὶ κομ[ι|σ]αμένοι ναῦν δο͂ναι δορεὰν κ]αθάπ[ερ ἔδ|ο]χσεν το͂ι δέμοι· ἐπειδὲ δὲ Ἀρχέλας καὶ | νῦν καὶ ἐν το͂ι

πρόσθεν χρ]όνοι ἐσ[τὶν ἀν|ὲρ ἀγαθὸς περὶ Ἀθεναί]ος τός τε ἐκπ[λεύ|σαντας Ἀθεναίον ἀνέλ]αβεν καὶ ἐς τὸ [ἐπ|ὶ Πύδνει στρατόπεδον] ἀπέπεμφσεν κα[ὶ | εὖ ἐπόεσεν Ἀθεναίον τ]ὸ στρατόπεδον κ|[αὶ ἔδοκεν αὐτοῖς χσύλ]α καὶ κοπέας καὶ | [ἄλλα hόσον ἐδέοντο παρ'] αὐτὸ ἀγαθά, ἐπα|[ινέσαι Ἀρχέλαι hος ὄν]τι ἀνδρὶ ἀγαθδι | [καὶ προθύμοι ποιὲν hό τ]ι δύναται ἀγαθ|[όν, καὶ ἀνθ' ὃν εὐεργέτεκ]εν τέν τε πόλιν | [καὶ τὸν δεμον τὸν Ἀθεναί]ον ἀναγράφσα|[ι αὐτὸν καὶ παῖδας προχσένο]ς καὶ ε[ὐερ]|[γέτας ἐμ πόλει ἐστέλεν λιθίνε]ν κ[αὶ ἐπι|μελε͂σθαι αὐτὸν – –]. Although fragmentary, the dramatic condition is rather evident, after the loss of the fleet in Sicily as narrated by Thuc. 8.1.2–3 and 8.4 (Gomme, Andrewes, and Dover 1981, pp. 6, 10–11; Hornblower 2008, pp. 751–752, 758–759): ἅμα δὲ ναῦς οὐχ ὁρῶντες ἐν τοῖς νεωσοίκοις ἱκανὰς οὐδὲ χρήματα ἐν τῷ κοινῷ οὐδ' ὑπηρεσίας ταῖς ναυσὶν ἀνέλπιστοι ἦσαν ἐν τῷ παρόντι σωθήσεσθαι . . . (3) ὅμως δὲ ὡς ἐκ τῶν ὑπαρχόντων ἐδόκει χρῆναι μὴ ἐνδιδόναι, ἀλλὰ παρασκευάζεσθαι καὶ ναυτικόν, ὅθεν ἂν δύνωνται ξύλα ξυμπορισαμένους, καὶ χρήματα, καὶ τὰ τῶν ξυμμάχων ἐς ἀσφάλειαν ποιεῖσθαι, καὶ μάλιστα τὴν Εὔβοιαν, τῶν τε κατὰ τὴν πόλιν τι ἐς εὐτέλειαν σωφρονίσαι, καὶ ἀρχήν τινα πρεσβυτέρων ἀνδρῶν ἑλέσθαι, οἵτινες περὶ τῶν παρόντων ὡς ἂν καιρὸς ᾖ προβουλεύσουσιν. (8.4.1) παρεσκευάζοντο δὲ καὶ Ἀθηναῖοι, ὥσπερ διενοήθησαν, ἐν τῷ αὐτῷ χειμῶνι τούτῳ τήν τε ναυπηγίαν, ξύλα ξυμπορισάμενοι, καὶ Σούνιον τειχίσαντες, ὅπως αὐτοῖς ἀσφάλεια ταῖς σιταγωγοῖς ναυσὶν εἴη τοῦ περίπλου, καὶ τό τε ἐν τῇ Λακωνικῇ τείχισμα ἐκλιπόντες ὃ ἐνῳκοδόμησαν παραπλέοντες ἐς Σικελίαν, καὶ τἆλλα, εἴ πού τι ἐδόκει ἀχρεῖον ἀναλίσκεσθαι, ξυστελλόμενοι ἐς εὐτέλειαν, μάλιστα δὲ τὰ τῶν ξυμμάχων διασκοποῦντες ὅπως μὴ σφῶν ἀποστήσονται. For the crucial issue of importing shipbuilding timber for the Athenian fleet after Sicily, as well as for Athens' antagonists Sparta and Thebes until the ascension of Philip II to the throne, see Borza 1987, 44–52; Hatzopoulos 1985; Psoma 2015; Chapter 20.

71 *GHI* 111 (Rhodes and Osborne 2003, no. 12); Hatzopoulos 1996, vol. 2, pp. 19–20, no. 1, side B, lines 1–10: ἐσαγωγὴ δ' ἔστω καὶ πίσσης καὶ ξύλων, | οἰκοδομιστηρίωμ πάντων, ναυπηγη|σίμων δὲ πλὴν ἐλατίνων. ὅ τι ἄμ μὴ τὸ | κοινὸν δέηται, τῶι δὲ κοινῶι καὶ τούτων | εἶν ἐξαγωγῆς, εἰπόντας Ἀμύνται πρὶν ἐξ|άγειν, τελέοντας τὰ τέλεα τὰ γεγραμμέν[α]. | καὶ τῶν ἄλλων ἐξαγωγὴν δὲ εἶν καὶ δια|<α>γωγήν, τελέουσιν τέλεα καὶ Χαλκιδεῦ|σι ἐκγ Μακεδονίης καὶ Μακεδόσιν ἐκ | Χαλκιδέων. Hatzopoulos argues that in line 1 the original engraving ἐξαγωγή corrected by the cutter to εἰσαγωγή makes better sense; see Chapter 20. But ἐσαγωγὴ denotes imports from Macedonia to the Chalkidic *koinon* of every kind of timber, except fir trees, for construction or shipbuilding, which the *koinon* may export (lines 4–10) provided Amyntas III is notified and dues are paid. For Amyntas III see Hammond and Griffith 1979, pp. 172–180; Hammond 1989, pp. 79–80; Borza 1990, pp. 182–183; Zahrnt 2007; Consolo Langher 2007; Roisman 2010, 158–161; Psoma 2011, pp. 124–132; Lane Fox 2011b.

72 For this sanctuary see n. 80. For Illyrians and Macedonians see Dell 1970; Greenwalt 2010; Howe 2017.

73 *IG* II² 102; *GHI* 129. For the dates of the proxeny decrees in Oropos in honor of Amyntas III son of Perdikkas II and Amyntas son of Antiochus see Petrakos 1997, nos. 1 and 2; for Amyntas' descent in Trophonios' cave (*IG* VII 3055), see Ellis 1970.

74 Dem. 4 (*Κατὰ Φιλίππου Α*).4; Din., *Κατὰ Δημοσθένους* 14 (Worthington, Cooper, and Harris 2001). Also Hammond 1989, pp. 88–89; and cf. Heskel 1997, pp. 31–34, 51–52, 116–117; Buckler 2003, pp. 369–371; Roisman 2010, pp. 161–164; and Psoma 2015, pp. 4–6.

75 Dem. 50 (*Πρὸς Πολυκλέα*) 46, 48–49, 52; Arist., [*Oec.*] 1350a. Also Hammond and Griffith 1979, pp. 187–188; Hammond 1989, pp. 94–95; Psoma 2011, pp. 131–132; Funke 2018.

76 *IG* IV² 1.94, fr. B, col. I, lines 6–12: Ὁμόλιον· Δωριεύς, | Πύδνα· Δαμάτριος, | Μεθώνα· Πολύφαντος, | Μακεδονία· Περδίκκας, | Αἴνεια· Εὔβουλος, | Δίκαια· Νυμφόδωρος, | Ποτείδαια· Καλλικράτης; and cf. Ps.-Scylax's text in n. 20. Also Hammond and Griffith 1979, pp. 193–195; Perlman 2000, pp. 68–74, 275, no. 254; cf. Raynor 2016. For Macedonian presence in sanctuaries see Mari 2007. For the fluctuating borders in Macedonia until Philip II see Hatzopoulos 1995; Ma 2018.

77 Diod. Sic. 16.2.1–6: ὁμοίως δὲ καὶ Ἀθηναῖοι πρὸς Φίλιππον ἀλλοτρίως ἔχοντες κατῆγον ἐπὶ τὴν βασιλείαν Ἀργαῖον καὶ στρατηγὸν ἀπεστάλκεισαν Μαντίαν ἔχοντα τρισχιλίους μὲν ὁπλίτας, ναυτικὴν δὲ δύναμιν ἀξιόλογον. (16.3.5–6) Μαντίας δ' ὁ τῶν Ἀθηναίων στρατηγὸς καταπλεύσας εἰς Μεθώνην αὐτὸς μὲν ἐνταῦθα κατέμεινε, τὸν Ἀργαῖον δὲ μετὰ τῶν μισθοφόρων ἐπὶ τὰς Αἰγὰς ἀπέστειλεν. οὗτος δὲ προσελθὼν τῇ πόλει παρεκάλει τοὺς ἐν ταῖς Αἰγαῖς προσδέξασθαι τὴν κάθοδον καὶ γενέσθαι τῆς αὐτοῦ βασιλείας ἀρχηγούς. οὐδενὸς δ' αὐτῷ προσέχοντος ὁ μὲν ἀνέκαμπτεν εἰς τὴν Μεθώνην, ὁ δὲ Φίλιππος ἐπιφανεὶς μετὰ στρατιωτῶν καὶ συνάψας μάχην πολλοὺς μὲν ἀνεῖλε τῶν μισθοφόρων, τοὺς δὲ λοιποὺς εἴς τινα λόφον καταφυγόντας ὑποσπόνδους ἀφῆκεν, λαβὼν παρ' αὐτῶν ἐκδότους τοὺς φυγάδας. Φίλιππος μὲν οὖν ταύτην πρώτην μάχην νικήσας εὐθαρσεστέρους ἐποίησε τοὺς Μακεδόνας πρὸς τοὺς ἐφεξῆς ἀγῶνας. Cf. Just. 7.6.6–16 (Seel 1935); Hammond and Griffith 1979, pp. 203–212; Hammond 1989, p. 138; Worthington 2008, pp. 19–25; and Psoma 2015, pp. 4–6.

78 Diod. Sic. 16.8.3: ἡ δὲ πόλις αὕτη κειμένη κατὰ τῆς Θρᾴκης καὶ τῶν σύνεγγυς τόπων εὐφυῶς πολλὰ συνεβάλετο τῷ Φιλίππῳ πρὸς αὔξησιν. εὐθὺ γὰρ τὴν μὲν Πύδναν ἐχειρώσατο, πρὸς δὲ Ὀλυνθίους συμμαχίαν ἔθετο καὶ Ποτίδαιαν ὡμολόγησε περιποιήσειν αὐτοῖς, ὑπὲρ ἧς Ὀλύνθιοι πολλὴν σπουδὴν ἔσχον κυριεῦσαι τῆς πόλεως. For the secret

negotiations, see Theopompos, *FGrH* 115 fr. 30ab; Dem. 20 (Πρὸς Λεπτίνην), 63; *Scholia in Olynthiaca* II, 50; Aelius Aristides, *Or.* 38 (Συμμαχικός Α), p. 480. Clement of Alexandria, *Protrepticus* (Προτρεπτικὸς πρὸς Ἕλληνας) 54.5 (Herrero de Jauregui 2008, pp. 79, 183–184); Libanius, *Progymnasmata* 9.3.8. Also Hammond and Griffith 1979, pp. 238–244, 356–357; Hammond 1989, p. 110; Hatzopoulos 1996, vol. 1, pp. 179–181; Hornblower 2008, pp. 27–28; Worthington 2008, pp. 41–42.

79 Dem. 1 (Ὀλυνθιακός Α), 5: δῆλον γάρ ἐστι τοῖς Ὀλυνθίοις ὅτι νῦν οὐ περὶ δόξης οὐδ᾽ ὑπὲρ μέρους χώρας πολεμοῦσιν, ἀλλ᾽ ἀναστάσεως καὶ ἀνδραποδισμοῦ τῆς πατρίδος, καὶ ἴσασιν ἅ τ᾽ Ἀμφιπολιτῶν ἐποίησε τοὺς παραδόντας αὐτῷ τὴν πόλιν καὶ Πυδναίων τοὺς ὑποδεξαμένους· καὶ ὅλως ἄπιστον, οἶμαι, ταῖς πολιτείαις ἡ τυραννίς, ἄλλως τε κἂν ὅμορον χώραν ἔχωσι. *Scholia in Olynthiaca* I, 41, s.v. καὶ Πυδναίων τοὺς ὑποδεξαμένους: Πύδνα πόλις Μακεδονίας. αὕτη ἀπέστη τοῦ ὑπακούειν Φιλίππῳ, καὶ ἐστράτευσε κατ᾽ αὐτῆς καὶ περὶ ταύτην τοιοῦτόν τι συνέβη· ὡς γὰρ κἀκεῖ τινες προδεδώκασιν, εἶθ᾽ ὕστερον γνόντες ὅτι οὐκ ἂν αὐτῶν φείσαιτο, ἔφυγον ἐπὶ τὸ Ἀμύντιον ἱερὸν τοῦ πατρὸς αὐτοῦ· κολακεύοντες γὰρ αὐτοῦ τὸν πατέρα πρώην οἱ Πυδναῖοι ἱερὸν αὐτοῦ ἐποίησαν· ὅμως οὐδ᾽ ἐκεῖσε καταφυγόντων ἐφείσατο, ἀλλ᾽ ἀναστήσας αὐτοὺς ὅρκοις ἐπὶ τῷ μηδὲν ποιῆσαι ἐξελθόντας ἀνεῖλε. F1S. See also n. 73; Bessios 2010, pp. 114–115; Habicht 1970, pp. 11–12. For Philip II see Müller 2010; Lane Fox 2011c; and Psoma 2011, pp. 132–135; for Philip II in Athenian orators see Alexiou 2015; for Philip II and Demosthenes, in particular, see Harris 2018.

80 There is an extraordinary, albeit elusive as to its historical context, find of a mass burial in Pydna's Classical cemetery, for which see Triantaphyllou and Bessios 2005; Bessios 2010, p. 115.

81 Diod. Sic., 16.31.6: ἅμα δὲ τούτοις πραττομένοις Φίλιππος ὁ τῶν Μακεδόνων βασιλεὺς Μεθώνην μὲν ἐκπολιορκήσας καὶ διαρπάσας κατέσκαψε, Παγασὰς δὲ χειρωσάμενος ἠνάγκασεν ὑποταγῆναι. (16.34.4–5) Φίλιππος δ᾽ ὁρῶν τοὺς Μεθωναίους ὁρμητήριον παρεχομένους τὴν πόλιν τοῖς πολεμίοις ἑαυτοῦ πολιορκίαν συνεστήσατο. καὶ μέχρι μέν τινος οἱ Μεθωναῖοι διεκαρτέρουν, ἔπειτα κατισχυόμενοι συνηναγκάσθησαν παραδοῦναι τὴν πόλιν τῷ βασιλεῖ ὥστε ἀπελθεῖν τοὺς πολίτας ἐκ τῆς Μεθώνης ἔχοντας ἓν ἱμάτιον ἕκαστον. ὁ δὲ Φίλιππος τὴν μὲν πόλιν κατέσκαψε, τὴν δὲ χώραν διένειμε τοῖς Μακεδόσιν. ἐν δὲ τῇ πολιορκίᾳ ταύτῃ συνέβη τὸν Φίλιππον εἰς τὸν ὀφθαλμὸν πληγέντα τοξεύματι διαφθαρῆναι τὴν ὅρασιν. Interestingly, in Diodoros' narrative, Methone follows Pagasai in Magnesia and its forced subjection (above, n. 16). See also Chapter 28; Hammond and Griffith 1979, pp. 254–258, 361–362; Hammond 1989, pp. 156–157; Boehm 2011, pp. 31–34. Errington (2007) emphasizes Philip's different treatment of the cities he would conquer; also Worthington 2008, pp. 47–49.

82 *IGLPalermo* 128 (= *IG* II² 130; *SEG* 24.85) lines 8–14: ἐπαινέ[σ]|[αι Λαχάρ- *vel* Σωχάρη]ν Χάρητος Ἀπολλωνιάτη[ν] | [...8....]ον ὅτι πρόθυμος ἦν τ[οῖς π]|[ολίταις ὑ]πηρετεῖν καὶ ἔπεμψ[εν ..] | [...7...]ον ἑαυτοῦ εἰς Μεθώνη[ν κ]α[ὶ] | [εἶναι αὐ]τὸν πρόξενον τοῦ δήμου τ[ο]|[ῦ Ἀθηναί]ων κ.λπ. This decree is crucial for the date of the siege of Methone, for which see Buckler 1989, pp. 176–186; Buckler 2003, pp. 413–415; Chapters 20 and 28.

83 Polyainos, *Strat.* 4.2.15: Φίλιππος τοῖς Μεθωναίων τείχεσι κλίμακας προσήγαγεν καὶ δι᾽ αὐτῶν πολλοὺς Μακεδόνας ἀνεβίβασε πολιορκητάς. ἐπεὶ δὲ ἀνέβησαν ἐπὶ τὰ τείχη, ἀφεῖλε τὰς κλίμακας, ὅπως ἐλπίδα τοῦ καταβῆναι μὴ ἔχοντες προθυμότερον τῶν τειχῶν κρατήσειαν. Also Hatzopoulos, Knoepfler, and Marigo-Papadopoulos 1990, pp. 665–668.

84 *Scholia in Olynthiaca* III, 43a, Φίλιππος ἀσθενῶν: ἐπικινδύνως ἀσθενῆσαί φασι Φίλιππον ὅτε τὴν Μεθώνην ἐπολιόρκει, Ἀστέρος τινὸς στρατιώτου Μεθωναίου ἀπὸ τοῦ τείχους ἐπιγράψαντος τῷ δόρατι 'Ἀστὴρ Φιλίππῳ θανάσιμον [ἐπι] πέμπει βέλος', εἶτα πέμψαντος καὶ κατὰ τύχην τινὰ ἐπιτυχόντος κατὰ τοῦ ὀφθαλμοῦ. λέγεται δὲ ὅτι καὶ ὁ Φίλιππος ἀντέγραψε πρὸς αὐτὸν καὶ ἀντηκόντισεν, ὅμως οὐκ ἐπέτυχεν αὐτός, 'Ἀστέρα Φίλιππος ἢν λάβῃ κρεμήσεται'. *Scholia in De corona*, 124: τὸν ὀφθαλμὸν] ἤδη ἔγνωμεν ὅτι τὸν ὀφθαλμὸν ἐπλήγη ὁ Φίλιππος ἐν τῇ Μεθώνῃ, τὴν δὲ κλεῖν ἐν Ἰλλυριοῖς, τὸ δὲ σκέλος καὶ τὴν χεῖρα ἐν Σκύθαις. According to Plutarch, who probably is using Kallisthenes' Μακεδονικά, this incident happened during the siege of Olynthos (Συναγωγὴ ἱστοριῶν παραλλήλων ἑλληνικῶν καὶ ῥωμαϊκῶν 307d = Stobaios, 3.7.67): Φίλιππος Μεθώνην καὶ Ὄλυνθον βουλόμενος πορθῆσαι καὶ βιαζόμενος ἐπὶ τῷ Σανδάνῳ ποταμῷ διαβῆναι πέραν ὑπό τινος τῶν Ὀλυνθίων Ἀστέρος ὀνόματι ἐτοξεύθη τὸν ὀφθαλμόν, εἰπόντος· 'Ἀστὴρ Φιλίππῳ θανάσιμον πέμπει βέλος'· ὁ δ᾽ ὀπίσω διανηξάμενος πρὸς τοὺς οἰκείους σῴζεται ἀπολέσας τὸν ὀφθαλμόν· ὡς Καλλισθένης ἐν τρίτῳ Μακεδονικῶν. In the Demosthenic Scholia attributed to Didymos (Pearson and Stephens 1983, *P.Berol.* 9780, col. 12, 40–50), sources for the incident are listed as Theopompos (*FGrH* 115 fr. 384), Marsyas (*FGrH* 135 fr. 16), and Douris (*FGrH* 76 fr. 36), the last of whom (prone to teratology) mentions the name of the spearman: περὶ ὧν ἔσχε τραυμάτων ὁ Φίλιππ[ος ε]ἴρηται μ(ὲν) ἡμῖν ἐντελῶς· κ(αὶ) νυνὶ δ᾽ εἰς βραχὺ ὑπομνηστέον. περὶ μ(ὲν) γ(ὰρ) τὴν Μεθώνης πολιορκίαν τὸν δεξιὸν ὀφθαλ[μὸ]ν ἐξεκόπη τοξεύματι πληγείς, ἐ[ν] ᾧι τὰ μηχανώματα κ(αὶ) τὰς χωστρίδας [λ]εγομ(έν)ας ἐφεώρα, καθάπερ ἐν τῆι Δ τῶν περὶ αὐτὸν ἱστοριῶν ἀφηγεῖται Θεόπομπος, οἷς κ(αὶ) Μαρσύας ὁ Μακεδὼν ὁμολογεῖ. ὁ δ(ὲ) Δοῦρις, ἔδει γ(ὰρ) αὐτὸν κ(αὶ) ἐνταῦθα τερατ[ε]ύσε[σ]θαι, Ἀ]στέρα φησὶ (εἶναι) τοὔνομα τοῦ τὸ ἀκ[όντιον καιρίως] ἐπ᾽ αὐτὸν ἀφέντος, [τ]ῶν [συνεστρα]τευκότων αὐτῶι σχε[δ]ὸν [πάν]των τοξεύμα[τ]ι λεγόντων [α]ὐτὸ[ν] τετρῶσθαι. See also Diod. Sic. 16.34.5 (text in n. 82); Strabo 8.6.15 (text

in n. 11); Harp., s.v. Μεθώνη; Themistios 284c; Ael., *NA* 9.7; *Suda*, s.v. Κάρανος; also Hatzopoulos, Knoepfler, and Marigo-Papadopoulos 1990, pp. 661–663; and esp. Riginos 1994, pp. 106–114, who convincingly separates fact from fiction. For the possibility of urban combat inside the walls, see Bessios, Athanassiadou, and Noulas 2021a; Chapters 1 and 29.

85   Dem. 9 (*Κατὰ Φιλίππου Γ*), 26: Ὄλυνθον μὲν δὴ καὶ Μεθώνην καὶ Ἀπολλωνίαν καὶ δύο καὶ τριάκοντα πόλεις ἐπὶ Θρᾴκης ἑῶ, ἃς ἁπάσας οὕτως ὠμῶς ἀνῄρηκεν ὥστε μηδ' εἰ πώποτ' ᾠκήθησαν προσελθόντ' εἶναι ῥᾴδιον εἰπεῖν. Also Hammond and Griffith 1979, pp. 254–258, 361–362. The excavated graves at the site of Palaiokatachas and modern Aiginio belong to the new Macedonian settlements, which, according to Hatzopoulos, Knoepfler, and Marigo-Papadopoulos (1990, pp. 667–668 with n. 91), were incorporated into Pydna's territory; cf. Papazoglou 1988, pp. 105–106; Chapters 1 and 3.

86   [Plut.], *X orat.* 851a: καὶ λυτρωσαμένῳ πολλοὺς τῶν ἁλόντων ἐν Πύδνῃ καὶ Μεθώνῃ καὶ Ὀλύνθῳ ὑπὸ Φιλίππου. Hatzopoulos, Knoepfler, and Marigo-Papadopoulos (1990, pp. 665–668) suggest that some may have been transported to Athens and some even to Eretria; Morris (2015) argues that craftsmen and other specialists may have relocated to Pella.

87   Arist., fr. 551 (Rose) (Athenaios, *The Learned Banquet* 6.27): Ἀριστοτέλης δὲ ἐν τῇ Μεθωναίων πολιτείᾳ 'παράσιτοι, φησί, τοῖς μὲν ἄρχουσι δύο καθ' ἕκαστον ἦσαν, τοῖς δὲ πολεμάρχοις εἷς. τεταγμένα δ' ἐλάμβανον παρ' ἄλλων τέ τινων καὶ τῶν ἁλιέων ὄψον'. The parasites were appointed as personnel of a city's sanctuaries for the organization of the established common prayers in honor of a god, a fact which indicates that the political organization of Methone followed Athenian standards. For παράσιτοι and παρασίτιον see Athenaios, *The Learned Banquet* 6.26; *Agora* XVI, no. 153; *SEG* 34:157; Peek 1969, no. 338 (*SEG* 11.440a Addenda et Corrigenda); Ziehen 1949.

88   Aristotle, fr. 552 (Rose) (*CPG* I, Zenobios 1, 79, s.v. ἀμουσότερος Λειβηθρίων): Λειβήθριοι ἔθνος ἐστὶ Πιερικόν, οὗ καὶ Ἀριστοτέλης μέμνηται ἐν τῇ Μεθωναίων πολιτείᾳ. λέγονται δὲ ἀμουσότατοι εἶναι οἱ Λειβήθριοι, ἐπειδὴ παρ' αὐτοῖς ἐγένετο ὁ τοῦ Ὀρφέως θάνατος (also *CPG* I, Diogenianos 2, 26 and 7, 14; *CPG* II, Diogenianos 1, 37; Apostolios 2, 67 and 10, 50, s.v. ἀμουσότερος Λειβηθρίων: ἐπὶ τῶν ἀμούσων καὶ ἀπαιδεύτων. Λειβήθριοι γὰρ ἔθνος Πιερικόν ἐστιν οὔτε μέλους ἁπλῶς οὔτε ποιήματος ἔννοιαν λαμβάνον. λέγονται δὲ ἀμουσότατοι εἶναι, ἐπειδὴ παρ' αὐτοῖς ὁ τοῦ Ὀρφέως ἐγένετο θάνατος). For this proverb, see Romero 2011. For the site of Leivithra (Λ(ε)ίβηθρα), see Poulaki-Pantermali 2008b.

89   Strabo 7a.1.22: ἐν μὲν οὖν τῷ πρὸ τῆς Πύδνης πεδίῳ Ῥωμαῖοι Περσέα καταπολεμήσαντες καθεῖλον τὴν τῶν Μακεδόνων βασιλείαν, ἐν δὲ τῷ πρὸ τῆς Μεθώνης πεδίῳ γενέσθαι συνέβη Φιλίππῳ τῷ Ἀμύντου τὴν ἐκκοπὴν τοῦ δεξιοῦ ὀφθαλμοῦ καταπελτικῷ βέλει κατὰ τὴν πολιορκίαν τῆς πόλεως.

90   Kontoleon 1963, p. 25; Chapter 12.

91   Kontoleon 1963, pp. 6–26, esp. 11 and 24; also n. 34.

92   Theophr., *Hist. Pl.* 5.2.1: διαιροῦσι γάρ τινες κατὰ τὰς χώρας, καί φασιν ἀρίστην μὲν εἶναι τῆς ὕλης πρὸς τὴν τεκτονικὴν χρείαν τῆς εἰς τὴν Ἑλλάδα παραγινομένης τὴν Μακεδονικήν· λεία τε γάρ ἐστι καὶ ἀστραβὴς καὶ ἔχουσα θυῖον. δευτέραν δὲ τὴν Ποντικήν, τρίτην δὲ τὴν ἀπὸ τοῦ Ῥυνδάκου, τετάρτην δὲ τὴν Αἰνιανικήν· χειρίστην δὲ τήν τε Παρνασιακὴν καὶ τὴν Εὐβοϊκήν· καὶ γὰρ ὀζώδεις καὶ τραχείας καὶ ταχὺ σήπεσθαι. περὶ δὲ τῆς Ἀρκαδικῆς σκεπτέον; and for the difficulties in making good oars 5.1.5–8. See further Chapter 20.

3

AT THE WATER'S EDGE

Samantha L. Martin

PROSPECTS

From at least the medieval period, one of the most important navigational aids used by mariners was the coastal profile, a hand-drawn representation of a shore or coastline. These "coasting prospects" enabled a navigator or helmsman to discern and recognize important landfalls and seamarks from the water.[1] Such marks commonly included not only natural features like cliffs, promontories, inlets, and even prominent trees, but also human-made landmarks, such as harbor buildings and moles, shrines, and funerary monuments that punctuated the coast.[2]

Given the exceptionally long history of ancient Methone, it would be inappropriate to look for evidence of tangible drawings used by the earliest seafarers on the Thermaic Gulf. Nonetheless, a discussion of the coastal profile as a type of wayfinding document is an apposite and instructive starting point for our study of the landscape and territory of Methone. While all visitors to the site now arrive by road, Methone was first and foremost a place viewed and approached from the water. This perspective is easily overlooked by the 21st-century eye. Thus, the cornerstone of this investigation is a single premise: that in antiquity, the wealth and strength of Methone was largely contingent on how the city was perceived from the watery expanses of the gulf.[3]

In a most straightforward and explicit manner, a coastal profile provides a boat's-eye view of shorelines and landfalls. Yet beyond this it also implicitly underscores the value of assiduously reading a maritime environment. Anyone who embarks on the task of creating such a record will ultimately gain an insightful and exhaustive understanding of a terrestrial as well as a marine landscape—a total topography.[4] As such, a settlement at the edge of the sea should be seen as something integral to the land and the water in equal measure. This frame of reference is especially relevant to the study of Methone, a city that stood not only at the shore of the Thermaic Gulf, but also by the edge of the Haliakmon River and in close proximity to the mouths of two other substantial rivers, the Axios and Loudias.

SITE READING

What follows in this chapter is an explanation and overview of the preliminary analysis of the extensive terrain surrounding ancient Methone in the region of Pieria that took place in August and September of 2012. It should be noted that the principal objective of this analysis was description: a comprehensive register of the given landscape in its current form. The majority of the observations discussed here were recorded during six "site walks" that took place over a period of several days around the site and the adjacent modern seaside village of Nea Agathoupolis. Most of these walks occurred during the morning; one was conducted in the evening and focused on the present archaeological site of Methone itself. The method for the site walks was very straightforward: The routes traced all the human-made tracks (trails, foot and cycle paths, and dirt access roads) leading through and past the archaeological site. Another path followed the present-day shoreline from Nea Agathoupolis and then proceeded past Methone in a northeasterly direction (Fig. 3.1). On each walk photographs were taken at intervals of approximately 50–80 m. These images captured views in several directions, not just toward Methone itself. For example, extended vistas both north and south along the shoreline were included, as were views toward distant mountain ranges. At certain points in the walks, such as hilltops, panoramic movies were also recorded. Extensive written notes that described the views were made in tandem with the photographs. These included references to terrain, vegetation, and quality or character of light with respect to the time of day. Besides the site walks, there was one extended excursion by boat up the Haliakmon Delta (see Fig. I.4). Finally, the photographs of all these excursions were digitally catalogued and their routes were mapped.

While the site walks and boat trip demanded large amounts of time and patience, they were important for several reasons. In a very basic way, this catalog of images and field notes is a record, a straightforward account of the site of Methone and its surroundings in the present day. Methone—especially its agora and acropolis—is always the primary focus of the analysis, but the process of data collection was deliberately extensive and worked on the assumption that some observations, such as far-reaching sightlines, may ultimately prove to be immensely significant further along in the investigation. In other words, what might seem to be incidental at the beginning of this descriptive process could emerge as a salient feature in the final analysis and explanation of the wider landscape of Methone. Thus, the method as well as the immersive experience of this exercise are key. They acknowledge that it may take time to perceive and understand details and relationships in the landscape as a whole.

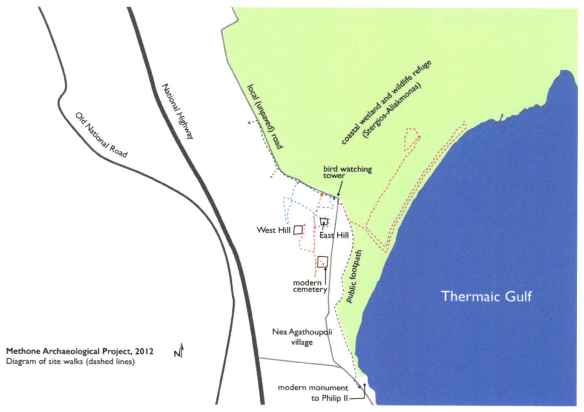

FIGURE 3.1. Map of "site walks" in and around Methone. Prepared by S. Martin

The remainder of the material presented in this contribution is organized according to three broad themes, subjects that convey the extensive scope of the initial study without confining the material to one particular methodology. This approach simultaneously outlines trajectories of further research and fieldwork. Ultimately, this investigation will not only address how the ancient city of Methone engaged with its surrounding territory, but it will also contend that this polyvalent terrain is still very much a living landscape; that is, a habitus in which deep-rooted, everyday patterns of human behavior and activity continue to endure.

CONTINUITY AND CHANGE

In August of 2012, a small group of members of the Ancient Methone Archaeological Project traveled by fishing boat from the town of Makrygialos into the Haliakmon River Delta (Fig. 3.2). This field trip enabled the group, for the first time, to view and approach Methone in a manner similar to that experienced by ancient inhabitants and visitors. It allowed for clear, unobstructed views of the site and its surroundings from a considerable distance at sea (Figs. 3.3a–b, 3.4, and I.4). Although the course of the Haliakmon as well as the shoreline of the Thermaic Gulf have changed dramatically, and are indeed still shifting, certain natural elements of the landscape of Methone can be understood as landmarks, features that have endured since antiquity and that continue to demarcate the terrain in the present day. Two of these, the so-called West and East Hills of the ancient city, can easily be identified from the current shoreline as well as from the Thermaic Gulf itself, depending on the weather.

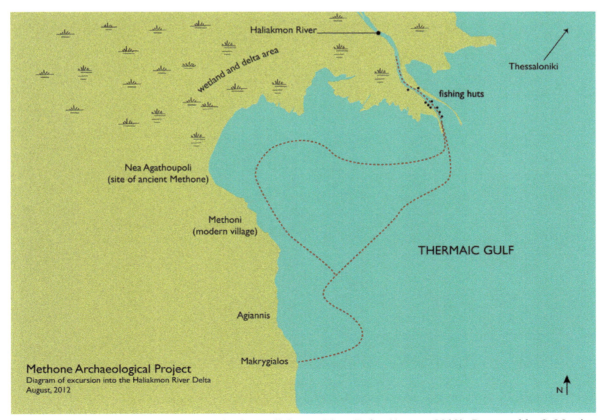

FIGURE 3.2. Map of excursion by boat in the Haliakmon River Delta (August 2012). Prepared by S. Martin

FIGURE 3.3. a) Boat's-eye view from east-northeast toward Nea Agathoupolis in the present day (August 2012); b) Boat's-eye view from east toward the site of Methone (August 2012). Photos I. Coyle

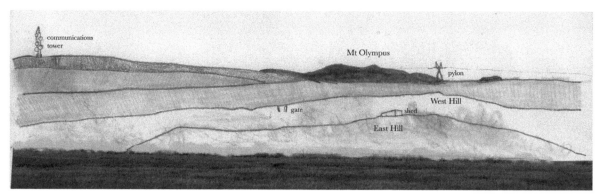

FIGURE 3.4. Profile sketch of Methone.
Prepared by S. Martin

The West and East Hills and their associated sites, the acropolis and agora, are the linchpins of this present study, yet their presence certainly does not preclude the possibility that other human-made features, now lost, once marked the original settlement. Given that Methone enjoyed a continuous span of human occupation from the Neolithic period through the 4th century B.C., it is reasonable to hypothesize that architectural monuments contributed to the prospect of the city from the water. One important avenue of further consideration in this respect would be the role played by the Mycenaean cemetery atop the West Hill (Chapter 6). Whether or not it was visible in the Bronze Age in some form from the shoreline or open water remains an unresolved, yet nonetheless enticing, question. There are other parallels, both material and literary, which may help shape this aspect of the study.[5] Another crucial facet of this investigation is the city's Archaic harbor. Any visualizations of the site, such as panoramic reconstructions or virtual reality (VR) models, will need to take into account and note the possible locations, as well as approaches, for this port.

At the earliest phase of any project it can seem logical to delimit firm boundaries around the subject matter; to focus closely on a set of known details and nuances of a particular site in order to gain purchase on it. Yet one can argue that it is often equally important to consider the widest possible contexts of a place even while a study is still in an inchoate stage. As we shall see, the immediate landscape to the north and east of Methone has been transformed immensely over millennia, but at the same time the hills and mountains on the horizon of the city have remained relatively unchanged. At one level, pointing out such aspects of the natural topography may seem overly simple, even superfluous. However, we must be mindful of how these features were more than mere backdrops to ancient Methone. Crucially, as stable elements, the contours of prominent mountains served as navigational aids and geographic reference points for seafarers.[6]

There are three main sets of hills and mountain ridges to consider in relation to Methone. First and foremost, a low-lying ridge of hills borders the ancient settlement at the west and northwest. This ridge is easily distinguishable from the modern shoreline (Fig. 3.5). When examining a contour map of this area it becomes immediately apparent that the ridge belongs to the easternmost foothills of the Pieria Mountains. Seen in relief, these foothills are clearly recognizable as a foreland that juts into the expansive agricultural plains north of Methone. Overall, this topographical feature resembles a promontory, and notably, in antiquity it most likely would have been surrounded by running water rather than dry land (Fig. 3.6). The present-day course of the Haliakmon River skirts around the north edge of this foreland and it is worth pointing out that besides ancient Methone, several other settlements, both ancient and modern, are sited at the edge of these same foothills. Vergina (ancient Aigai) is a key example (Fig. 3.7).

FIGURE 3.5. Pierian ridge from present-day shoreline east of Methone.
Photo S. Martin

Due north of Methone, across the flat plains, rises Mt. Paiko (1,650 m), another mountain that can easily been seen from Methone during clear weather (Fig. 3.8a–b).[7] Importantly, Mt. Paiko is situated just north of ancient Pella, once the seat of Philip II and the largest city or putative capital of the kingdom of Macedon in his day. Now landlocked, Pella was in antiquity a powerful port city located on one of the other regional rivers, the Loudias. It was also, crucially, a city that only really emerged once Methone was destroyed. During the Macedonian period it would have been possible to view the approximate location of Pella from Methone itself. As such, any discussion and hypothesis about Methone's maritime approaches must consider the prospects not only from the east, but also from Pella in the north. It is also worthwhile noting that farther southeast of Pella and Thessaloniki rises Mt. Chortiatis (1,201 m), another peak that can be seen from Methone on a bright day (Fig. 3.9). Known in antiquity as Kissos, this mountain forms the eastern edge of the Thermaic Gulf, towering above ancient Therme and Thessalonike. Thus, a ring of imposing mountain ranges forms a clear and easily distinguishable termination of the entire view north from Methone.

The other major mountain to consider is Mt. Olympos (2,919 m). It can be easy to overlook the significance of this peak because it cannot be seen from the site of the agora of Methone. It is, however, clearly viewable from the acropolis on the West Hill. More importantly, Mt. Olympos serves as a background setting for the entire site when observed from the northeast, that is, from the sea (Fig. 3.10). At this time, it is not possible to explain the precise significance of this sightline in antiquity, but it nonetheless raises an important question. It allows us to start thinking about how ancient inhabitants and visitors to Methone grasped and conceptualized the spatial conditions of the world around them.

As for Mt. Chortiatis, it dominates the view from Methone looking to the east and northeast (Fig. 3.9). This mountain is thus visible across the expanse of the Thermaic Gulf today. Situated as it is

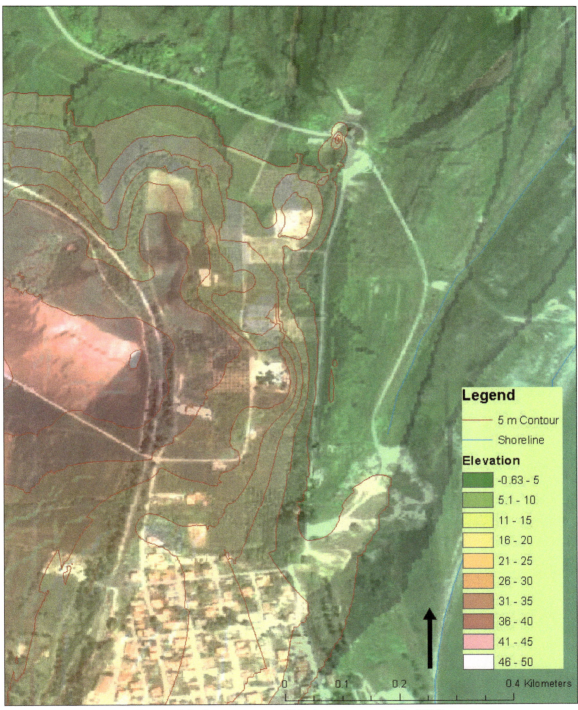

FIGURE 3.6. Contour map of Methone, prepared in 2012.
Prepared by E. McNicholas

behind modern Thessaloniki, Mt. Chortiatis also served as a convenient marker for all the ancient settlements in this part of the gulf, not least Therme, Karabournaki, and ancient Thessalonike. Sailing in the opposite direction, from, say, the ancient settlement at the site of Karabournaki toward Methone, Mt. Olympos would have loomed large either directly behind Methone or a little to the south, depending on the precise route taken across the Thermaic Gulf.

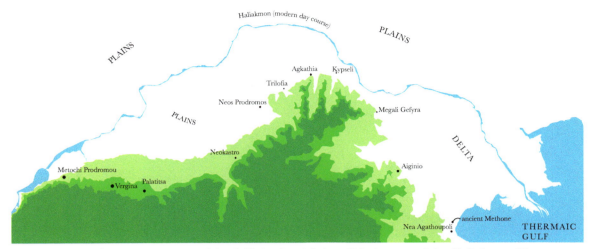

FIGURE 3.7. Map of towns and foothills in the vicinity of Methone and the Haliakmon River. Prepared by S. Martin

In dramatic contrast to these fixed landmarks, there is also a highly changeable and expansive riverine landscape connected to Methone. The three rivers associated with the site, in combination with their tributaries, are the most important agents of geomorphological change in the area. Although these waterways are themselves ancient and enduring features in the landscape, the expansive delta region of the Thermaic Gulf is testimony to their size, their strength, and in particular their fluctuating character.[8] The Haliakmon is especially notable for its changing course and unpredictability, yet at the same time it played a pivotal role in the ascendency of Methone.[9] Even with modern interventions, most specifically the process of damming the river in the 20th century, the Haliakmon remains today the site of constant flux.[10] This is most readily apparent in the ever-widening shoreline in the areas adjacent to the delta of the river (Fig. 3.11). Methone was once situated near the mouth of the Haliakmon and the tip of a much larger and more extensive Thermaic Gulf. Today, Methone still stands at the edge of the Gulf, but the river has migrated northward and, through this process, it has transformed a substantial body of water into sweeping, fertile plains. Pella now stands 28 km from the sea, although originally it was much closer to the coast.

Eventually, through further geomorphological and geospatial analysis, it will be possible to describe the changes of the Haliakmon River with greater specificity. How to read and represent this transformation within a visually accessible format is a separate challenge. One possible solution is the development of a three-dimensional, time-lapse model. This multifaceted approach to illustrating terrain can highlight changes in the landscape that may not be immediately apparent in stationary or two-dimensional formats. A model that shows changes over time can thereby provide opportunities for raising more pointed, nuanced questions.

Overall, it is worthwhile pointing out that sailing toward and approaching Methone would have presented a complex set of challenges for the ancient mariner. Whereas the mountainous topography of the mainland offered steady, fixed viewpoints, anyone sailing the Thermaic Gulf would not only have to contend with its changeable waters but also understand and negotiate the patterns of wind speed and direction. An examination of wind rose diagrams in the Gulf demonstrates that during the day throughout the year, the prevailing winds primarily blow from the north-northwest (Fig. 3.12). This is especially the case for the autumn and winter months. Notably, this presents a real challenge for travelers sailing toward Methone from southern Greece, such as from Euboia, Athens, and Corinth. This kind of information is useful insofar as it may influence our interpretation of trade and transport routes between Methone and other cities.

Figure 3.8. Two views toward the Voras mountain range and Mt. Paiko:
a) drone photography by J. Vanderpool; b) view from the West Hill of Methone.
Photo J. Papadopoulos

Figure 3.9. Mt. Chortiatis from the coast between Methone and Makrygialos at sunrise. Photo J. Vanderpool

MOVEMENT AND COMMUNICATION

We instinctively think of gulfs and the harbors or moorages at their edges as places of movement. They are sites that unambiguously denote and even sometimes symbolize both the departure and arrival of cargo. The Thermaic Gulf is a prime example of this, for it allowed, and continues to facilitate in the present day, the movement of goods and people.

In the end, the rich finds at Methone are testament to innumerable transactions, passages, and exchanges. In a very basic and straightforward way, these finds, particularly the transport amphoras, testify to the movement and systematic distribution of valuable commodities and bulk goods, such as wine and oil, among other commodities.[11] Yet it is equally important to acknowledge that such vessels, especially those which bear inscriptions, potters' marks, or graffiti, also transferred and disseminated something that is neither easily measured nor quantified: knowledge.[12] The alphabetic inscriptions that have been identified on pottery from Methone demonstrate how the city was an axis of communication in the Thermaic Gulf, the Aegean, and the wider Greek world. As such, Methone could be understood as a channel for the transmission and acquisition of language.

FIGURE 3.10. Mt. Olympos: drone aerial view from the West Hill of Methone looking south, Nea Agathoupolis in the center left. Photo J. Vanderpool

Two key focal points in this web of communication were Methone's harbor and agora, the latter of which has been located in the immediate vicinity of the East Hill. Much of this civic center has yet to be uncovered, but it is important to remember that the Greek agora was also a marketplace. The center of Methone should therefore be seen as both a political and a mercantile hub. Future work on the agora will hopefully clarify the identity and purpose of several structures, especially Building A, which has been tentatively identified as a stoa.[13] This type of structure was the most common form of public architecture in the Greek world and it was calculatedly versatile; that is, it could accommodate any number of activities, often simultaneously.

The discovery of Building A was immensely important for a number of reasons. Notably, its existence allows us to start developing some hypotheses about how Methone's architecture and urban order embodied its role as an early and important center of trade in the ancient Greek world. Although the study of this building and the agora as a whole is still in an early phase, it is worthwhile considering how the architecture could have provided space for the extensive mercantile activities of the city. Given the wide array of ceramic finds that have been found at Methone, it is possible that Building A played a central role in commercial transactions, namely the storage and

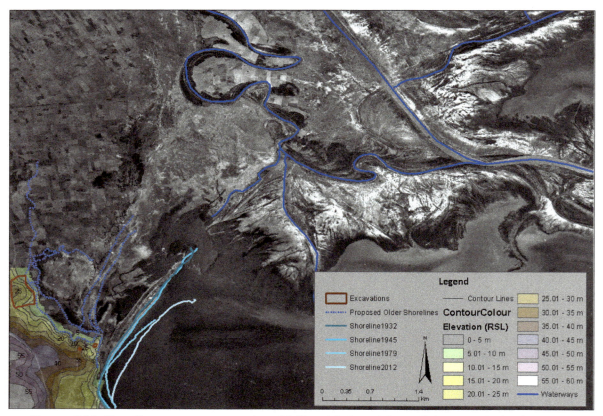

Figure 3.11. Shoreline movement over time. 1945 aerial view of the Haliakmon Delta by the Greek and U.S. Air Force, with modern shorelines indicated. Prepared by E. McNicholas

sale of goods. These considerations remain speculative, and yet they are absolutely crucial because they naturally lead us to think about how the agora, and in particular Building A, related to the surrounding landscape as well as seascape of Methone.

The initial excavations at Methone uncovered the full footprint of Building A and a small portion of adjacent structures. While the precise relationship between these buildings remains an open question, it is nonetheless possible to put forward some general observations about the wider topographical situation of the agora. In particular, given that we know the orientation of Building A, it is tempting to surmise how it could have communicated with both the roads or pathways used within Methone and perhaps also with the harbor itself.

Whether they are freestanding or appended to another structure, stoas typically demarcate the edge of an open space. It is very rare to see them positioned in the middle of an agora or sanctuary, and in these exceptional cases they are usually found to be delimiting a second area marked off from the principal one. An extension of this condition is that stoas are usually perceived very clearly from the entrance of an architectural square. They almost always face paths and roadways and in general provide a formal backdrop and boundary to an open space. Therefore, even though the function and even meaning of any given stoa may change over time, this type of building adheres to a reliable pattern with regard to how it is sited.

Although it is too early to make any firm conclusions, it appears as though Building A follows some of the basic criteria of a stoa. Firstly, besides having a rectangular plan, it is oriented toward an open space, which likely is the center of the agora. Beyond this, it also arguably faces the saddle in the land between the West and East hills of Methone. To put it a different way: The view from

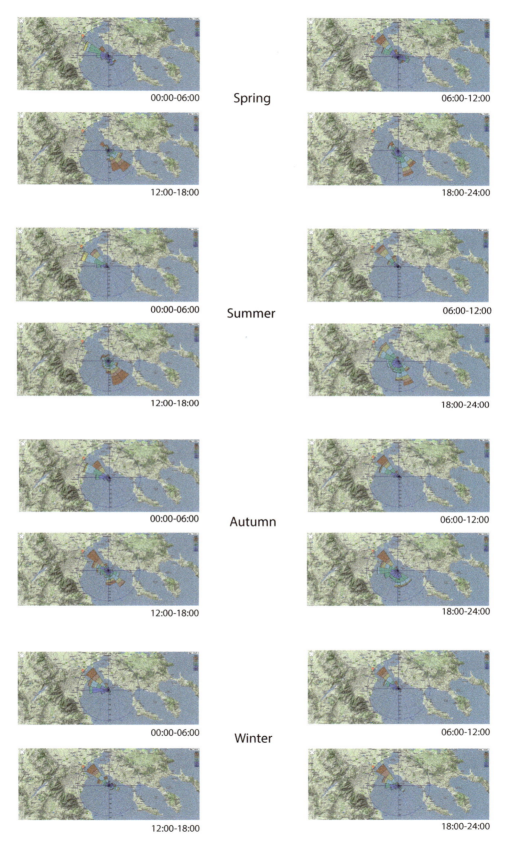

FIGURE 3.12. Wind rose diagrams showing the prevailing wind direction and strength throughout the year. Prepared by T. Martin

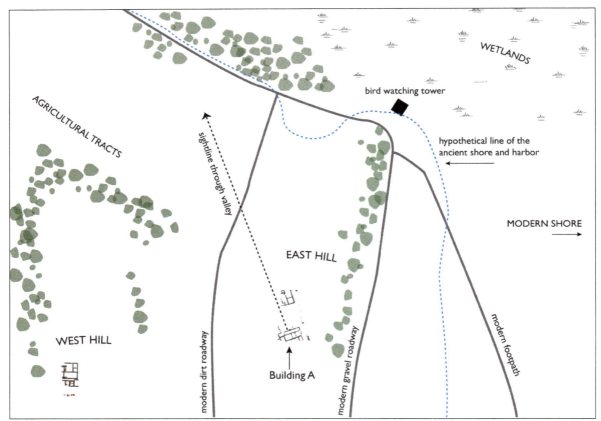

FIGURE 3.13. Sightline from the agora of Methone and Building A, toward the ancient shoreline and harbor of Methone. Prepared by S. Martin

Building A offers a clear perspective northwest, straight between the two hills that make up the site of Methone (Fig. 3.13). In the present day there is a dirt track that leads between these two knolls, and while it is impossible to confirm at this time whether a road existed there in antiquity, it is a logical place for one in the given landscape. Perhaps also it is coincidence that the perspective afforded by Building A happens to face this saddle. However, it deserves to be mentioned that the sightline from this building terminates in what is today a flat agricultural tract that has been singled out as a possible location of the Archaic harbor of Methone.

EDGE AND CONVERGENCE

There is yet another way of understanding Methone as a place of communication. The city stood on the edge of the Thermaic Gulf, thereby linking land, river, and sea. The East Hill was likely once part a significant promontory that reached into the gulf, but it is also useful to think about how the settlement as a whole was an in-between setting. Put categorically: The given topographic conditions of the site of Methone facilitated the exchange and intersection of many passages and routes, both terrestrial and seaborne.

Methone should not necessarily be understood first and foremost as a place that delimited the mainland. Rather, it may be more productive to describe it as a site where three distinct yet related regions—landscape, riverscape, and seascape—converged (Fig. 3.14). The city did not exclusively belong to dry land, the Haliakmon River, or the Aegean Sea; instead, it was claimed by all three at

FIGURE 3.14. Aerial view of Methone in 2014 showing excavations on the West Hill (foreground), East Hill (in the center distance), with the present shoreline looking toward the delta of the Haliakmon River. Photo H. Thomas

once. It is tempting to use the term "liminal" to describe this kind of situation. Certainly, Methone can be seen as a kind of threshold, yet liminality often embodies a binary edge—an oppositional relationship between two distinct places or states—as well as one principal sense of direction.[14] Ancient Methone, however, was multidirectional, oriented toward and connecting with many roads and seaways. We are only just beginning to understand how it was the nodal point of an exceptionally rich network, a fulcrum of the Aegean.[15] As such, in the future, a map of Methone that illustrates its connectivity, including its many trade and navigational routes, political alliances, and economic activities, may ultimately resemble one of the modern route maps of a major airline: a principal hub with many radiating spokes.

Even when the importance of maritime interconnectivity is acknowledged within the study of port cities, there is still a tendency to perceive the sea in a general sense as being a separate entity or a boundary of sorts—something "out there."[16] Yet this was not always the perception in antiquity. Homer's use of the phrase ὑγρὰ κέλευθα (*hygra keleutha*: "watery paths") suggests that the highways crisscrossing water are relative and indeed comparable to those on terra firma.[17] The sea, while liquid and highly changeable, is "not a void but rather a lesser solidity" that nonetheless exists as a daily and therefore typical experience in the lives of fishermen and seafarers.[18] Other modern authors contend that the sea and land in Greek antiquity were understood as a continuum, as if they were but varying textured surfaces or reliefs of a single vast province.[19]

The sea was once regarded as a watery hinterland, and certainly not only by Homer. Remarkably, this kind of perspective survived well into the modern period. Pierre Belon, the 16th-century explorer and polymath, wrote of sailing from the Hellespont "et entrés en pleine champagne de mer

Égée."[20] Belon's metaphor of the Aegean being a yawning countryside was productively extended in the 20th century by Fernand Braudel in his monumental study of the Mediterranean. For Braudel, the very heart of the Mediterranean was the open expanse of the water, "the liquid plains of the sea."[21] Describing the sea as a productive landscape or fertile grassland may seem imaginative and highly poetic, but these comparisons are informative insofar as they underscore the degree to which our impressions of the wider Mediterranean—and indeed most large bodies of water—have utterly transformed since the mid-20th century. With the advent of air travel and satellite imagery, open expanses of water have become more readily abstracted and easily accessible to an exceptionally wide audience. The highly privileged views offered by air and space flight have not only physically distanced us from the sea, but they arguably also have detached us from the water in a cognitive sense. Ironically, although we now may conceptualize the Aegean and Mediterranean in their totality and observe them as a coherent, unified whole in the blink of an eye, we do not really experience them. Yet for millennia the waters that converged at the city of Methone were quite literally a vehicle of mediation between other urban centers, territories, and even whole cultures. Moreover, these waters were also inhabited. It is toward this twofold observation that we now turn as a way of conclusion.

We know that ancient geographers compiled *periploi* ("sailings around"), navigational guides for seafarers that named and described coastlines.[22] At the heart of this kind of account is enumeration—of landfalls, anchorages, coastal enclaves, and their respective distances. Yet far from being a mere log or itinerary, the *periplous* was arguably an "influential expression of geographical coherence" that ultimately gave rise to the first cartographic charts and maps of the sea.[23] What is important here, and what can be easily discerned when looking at our earliest extant nautical maps, is the priority of the sea view, that is, the boat's-eye perspective of the seaboard. In portolan charts, the water is always what is most familiar, the place from which the known world is understood. The sea is central, both as a focus of communication and as a way of perceiving and interpreting geography.[24] This kind of orientation is what led D. H. Trump to assert that the Mediterranean is a "peninsula in reverse," whereby the sea is considered to be the heartland—the major field of activity—and the dry land represents uncharted depths.[25] Horden and Purcell further honed this expression by giving close attention to the particular conditions of coastal cities: "Distance is, in effect, inverted: places linked by the sea are always 'close,' while neighbours on land may, in terms of interaction, be quite 'distant.'"[26] When this interpretation is applied to ancient Methone, the primacy of its maritime approaches and coastal passages become ever more clear. The city likely served as an important gateway to inland routes, and it perhaps controlled access to one or more navigable rivers. Through further study it also may be possible to ascertain whether and how Methone was connected with far-flung cities via long-distance sea lanes that spanned the Aegean and beyond. What should not be underestimated, however, is the importance of the small-scale passages that hemmed and skirted the coastline of the Thermaic Gulf. It is possible that these shorter, local, and more routine journeys were paramount to the identity of ancient Methone.[27] It is beyond our reach to determine the precise courses of these innumerable byways during antiquity, but to some degree we can still experience them because they effectively live on in the numerous channels used by fishermen off the coasts of Pieria in the present day.

Visitors to Methone today will likely glance east toward the water and notice a vast and uniform expanse of sea. Closer observation from the shore that is adjacent to the archaeological site also reveals, depending on the weather, distant landfalls, namely the coast of Thessaloniki toward the northeast and bluffs that protrude from the mainland south of Nea Agathoupolis. But for those who reside along the shore, and especially for the fishermen who ply the coastal waters, a mirrored landscape is also manifest. Rising below the surface of the Thermaic Gulf is a terrain configured by innumerable peaks, valleys, basins, shoals, and straits. Anyone with an in-depth familiarity and knowledge of these waters will see in them many particularities. The surface reveals a diversity of textures and colors—clues to the presence of flotsam, banks, traversable narrows, and fluctuating currents. Just as the farmer on dry land intuitively knows the limits and precise contours of his fields, the families who farm shellfish off the coast of ancient Methone possess a detailed mental map of their productive seabed.[28] These maritime farmers travel throughout the gulf with such regularity and frequency that they could be said to inhabit the sea.[29]

Deep within the Haliakmon River delta sits a community that is visible and accessible only to fishermen. A series of huts, built inexpensively of timber, sheet metal, corrugated plastic, and other found materials, populates the edges of one of the main channels of the delta (Fig. 3.15). These are highly informal vernacular shelters and yet they are replete with the trappings of domestic life: a porch, chairs, tables, sofas, the occasional generator, and sometimes even a resident pack of cats. Although jerrybuilt, these fishing huts are clearly well worn and regularly occupied. That is to say, they are dwellings. It is conceivable that the fishermen who maintain them effectively understand this watery environment as a kind of home even while they formally reside in a village on dry land. The huts are fixed markers—scaled-up buoys—for a community that is almost exclusively characterized by movement, passage, and transience. This community cultivates and harvests seafood that can be consumed locally but which also is exported to distant markets. From this perspective it is possible to contend that these goods connect the modern fishermen who live in villages along the coast of Pieria with cities much farther afield. But it is much more likely that the sense of identity of this maritime community stems from regional patterns. Gradual yet steady, deliberate but routine, the tracing of pathways over the Thermaic Gulf has created a veritable scaffold onto which locals have fastened their knowledge and customs.

FIGURE 3.15. Fishing hut in the Haliakmon River Delta.
Photo I. Coyle (2012)

NOTES

1. In contemporary scholarship, the term "coastal profile" almost exclusively refers to shoreline management and planning in a broad sense and includes such measures as the control of erosion and implementation of artificial beaches. It maintains only a tenuous link to the medieval and early modern graphic representation of a coastline from open water. For descriptions of the earliest historical sources relating to the coastal profile, see Sloan 2007, pp. 98–99; Schilder and van Egmond 1987, pp. 1384–1432, esp. p. 1387. These early views of the coast often accompanied written texts or sailing manuals (rutters, *routier*, *Seebuch*), for which see Waters 1967.

    The author wishes to thank Elizabeth McNicholas for her assistance compiling maps, and Teresa Martin for her generous help in documenting various aspects of the landscape at Methone, including its weather patterns and topography. For a seminal study of the geoarchaeology of northern Pieria, see Krahtopoulou 2010.

2. Parker 2001, esp. pp. 37–39, and Hunter 1994, pp. 261–264. In his discussion of the symbolism embodied by the sea and its reciprocity with the coast (pp. 263–264), Hunter describes how "Beowulf's cenotaph was built in a prominent position that made it visible from far out at sea."

3. Indeed, this is how many important maritime cities were understood; see Horden and Purcell 2000, p. 126.

4. As such, it may be possible to describe Methone as a "maritime landscape" or "maritime cultural landscape"; see Parker 2001 and Westerdahl 1992.

5. Parker 2001, pp. 37–39; Bradley 2000, pp. 3–17, 97–114.

6. Waters 1967, p. 32. The earliest coastal profiles were crude but easily decipherable. The intent "was not to depict detail but to impress outlines on the mariner's retina, and was prompted by his personal experience of how the seaman first sees an unfamiliar coast, as often as not looming up suddenly over a darkening sea, or frowning over spume-swept waters through the gloom of leaden skies." It is also worthwhile noting that the earliest surviving printed sea chart, a woodcut from 1541 by G. A. Vavassore, clearly prioritizes important landfalls and prominent mountains, presumably peaks that can be seen from the shore. Vavassore's chart depicts the eastern Mediterranean—including the Aegean and Thermaic Gulf—and includes a single mountain at the eastern shore of Macedonia. Given that this peak is shown northwest of "Platamona" on the chart it is likely that it represents Mt. Olympos. Royal Maritime Museum, Greenwich, G235:1/3.

7. Mt. Paiko is part of the extensive Voras mountain range that straddles the border of Greece and the Republic of North Macedonia.

8. Hammond 1995b.

9. During the Ottoman period, and during modern times, the river was variously known as Lolopotamos, and also as the Delí.

10. The Haliakmon was dammed in the mid-20th century; see Thomas 2011. The disagreement, in both ancient and early modern sources, with regard to the courses and toponyms of the rivers running into the Thermaic Gulf likely testifies to the highly changeable nature of this landscape.

11. See Chapters 12 (Kotsonas) and 21 (Kasseri); see also Kotsonas 2012.

12. See Bessios, Tzifopoulos, and Kotsonas 2012, pp. 220–227; see also Chapter 11 (Tzifopoulos).

13. Bessios 2010, pp. 106–107; see below, Chapter 18.

14. Van Gennep 1961; also Turner 1969, p. 94.

15. For "nodal points," see Parker 2001, p. 23; see also Westerdahl 1994, pp. 265–270.

16. Fentress and Fentress (2001, p. 204), in their review of *The Corrupting Sea* (Horden and Purcell 2000), go as far as to describe the Mediterranean Sea as a "no man's land." Even the doyen of Mediterranean studies, Fernand Braudel (1992, p. 65), has unhelpfully characterized the sea as "empty as the Sahara." Surely, both modern Mediterranean and Saharan scholars alike would challenge this description. It should be emphasized that the ancient Greek perception of the sea was nuanced insofar as there were marked variations between the surface of the water and its invisible depths, both vertical and horizontal. The former, especially water in view of the coast, is a plane well traveled, but the latter may be a place where things were disposed of "once and for all." For a literary and archaeological discussion of the sea being an enormous waste disposal site, see Lindenlauf 2004. For the idea of the sea being a boundary in ancient Greek thought, see Romm 1992, pp. 9–34; Purves 2006.

17. *Odyssey*, III.71; *Iliad*, I.312.

18. Güthenke 2006, version 1.1,13.

19. For the idea of land and sea as a continuum, see Crielaard 2010, p. 138. It is interesting to note that "surface mail" in the present day denotes the transport of goods both overland and by sea in contrast to airmail.

20 Belon 2001, p. 114.
21 Braudel 1992, p. 65. See also Broodbank 2013.
22 Methone, in fact, is named in the *periplous* of Pseudo-Scylax (66); see Shipley 2011. For the difference between *periplous* and *periegesis*, see Kish 1978, pp. 21–26.
23 Horden and Purcell 2000, p. 11.
24 Even up until the 18th century, important maps of Ireland could be oriented west–east, rather than north–south, in order to emphasize the maritime approaches; see Andrews 1977, p. 57.
25 Trump 1980, p. 3. Malkin (1998, p. 14) discusses the Greek priority of colonizing and establishing cities along the coast.
26 Horden and Purcell 2000, p. 133.
27 Güthenke 2006, p. 10; Horden and Purcell 2000, p. 140.
28 Parker 2001, p. 33.
29 Nicholas Purcell (2003, p. 18) convincingly argues for an interpretation of the Mediterranean as a place of inhabitation. For a broader discussion of how seafarers and fishermen may be said to live on and across the open water, see Cooney 2003, pp. 323–324.

PART I

Methone Before Eretria:
The Late Neolithic Through Early Iron Age Settlement

4

THE NEOLITHIC AND EARLY BRONZE AGE SETTLEMENT AND POTTERY

Marianna Nikolaidou

INTRODUCTION

The prehistoric pottery presented in this chapter[1] constitutes important evidence for the earliest habitation periods on the East Hill coastal promontory of ancient Methone, spanning the Late Neolithic, Final Neolithic, and Early Bronze Age (early 5th to late 3rd–early 2nd millennium B.C.).[2] The later prehistoric horizons, Middle to Late Bronze Age and Early Iron Age, are presented by Trevor Van Damme and John K. Papadopoulos, respectively, in Chapters 5 and 7.

A small but significant component of early material was retrieved within and near the fragmentary remains of three ditches and four pits, which were excavated on the top of the East Hill by the KZ´ Ephoreia of Prehistoric and Classical Antiquities—northeast sector of the excavation grid, Trenches 001, 011, 021, 002, 012, 022, 003 (Figs. 4.1–4.3).[3] These features were part of external (western) boundaries or else intrasite divisions of the prehistoric settlements, and they would have originally extended northward and eastward, to a now eroded part of the promontory.[4] The preserved sections of the ditches run in two different directions, suggesting changes in spatial configuration from the Late Neolithic to the Final Neolithic and Early Bronze Age (see below). It must be noted that very little post–Early Bronze Age material was identified among the modest quantities of handmade pottery retrieved from these excavated units, in primary or secondary deposition.[5]

The rest of the prehistoric settlement has been lost to natural erosion and millennia of subsequent occupation,[6] with most of the pottery dispersed and redeposited amid the debris of Late Bronze–Early Iron Age construction works and under buildings dating to the Archaic and Classical periods.[7] Of these later horizons we sampled promising units across the excavated area of the East Hill, including the so-called Hypogeion on the top (Trenches 022, 032) and sectors of the slope to the northeast (Trenches 004, 005), east (Trenches 053, 054), and southeast (Trenches 084, 085) of the agora and its precinct wall (Fig. 4.2). Each of these units yielded diagnostic material spanning a long sequence from the Neolithic to the Late Bronze Age, and ranging in density from isolated finds to sizable clusters. The spatial distribution of the Neolithic and Early Bronze Age sherds, in particular, although well explicable as material fallen down the slopes of the hill, may nevertheless also indicate that the early settlements covered a wider area of the promontory than the limited space represented by the habitation remnants on the top. The same possibility is suggested by the recovery pattern of Neolithic and Early Bronze Age pottery from the Ancient Methone Archaeological Survey (2014): small groups of sherds or isolated pieces were collected over an extensive area to the north, northeast, and northwest of the East Hill.[8]

Figure 4.1. Methone, East Hill, #274. Aerial view of the Ephoreia excavations on the East Hill, from above west, after re-exposing the architectural remains in 2014. Photo H. Thomas

Taphonomic processes largely account for the fragmentary and often weathered condition of the pottery presented here. The relatively small size of the sample and, in most cases, the lack of primary contextual association further hamper the study of form and function. Despite such limitations, the material is diagnostic enough to be compared with well-understood corpora from other sites in the region and beyond, thus making possible a relative dating to the respective phases of the Macedonian Late Neolithic, Final Neolithic, Early Bronze Age, and transition to the Middle Bronze Age.[9]

All pottery is handmade and comes in a variety of shapes and wares, from storage and cooking containers to vessels of consumption and symbolic forms. Different methods and steps of manufacture have left discernible traces on imperfectly produced or worn and damaged sherds: unsmoothed building coils, wall-layering, and joints between vessel parts; excess clay folds; fingerprints from pinching and pulling; marks of shaping, scraping, smoothing, and burnishing; asymmetric contours and/or walls of uneven thickness; poorly applied or cracked slips; imprints from woven surfaces (basket trays or disks) used to support the pot during shaping or drying; hollows left from carbonized vegetal material mixed in the clay body; firing clouds and core.[10] Macroscopic examination has allowed the tentative distinction of ten different fabrics, some specific to one period and others persisting longer. These observations were not tested by petrographic analysis—the assemblage being too limited for a profitable application of that method. Had the sherds been examined petrographically, further diversification of fabrics and complexity in ceramic recipes might have been revealed, as the instructive example of Late Neolithic pottery from nearby Makrygialos II demonstrates.[11] The non-plastic inclusions, as far as they could be identified with the naked eye, appear compatible with the geology of northern Pieria:[12]

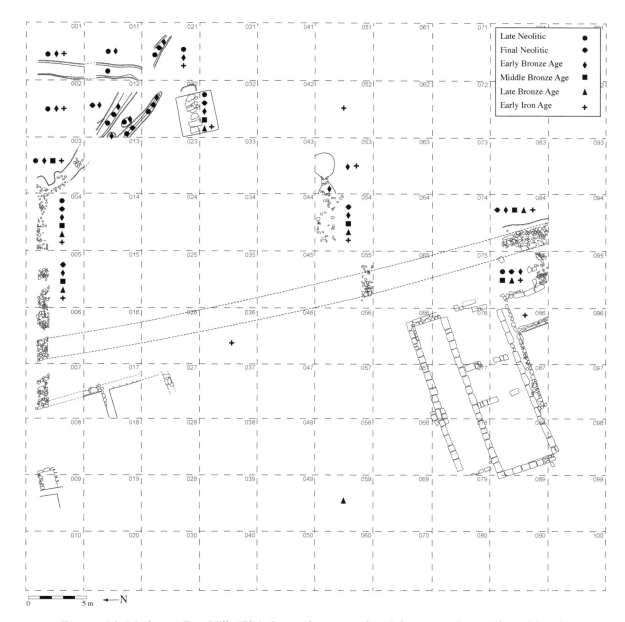

FIGURE 4.2. Methone, East Hill, #274. General topography of the excavations with prehistoric pottery plotted on the areas of recovery. Plan KZ´ Ephoreia of Prehistoric and Classical Antiquities, modified by M. Nikolaidou and T. Ross

pebbles, sand, silicate, limestone or marble (?),[13] as well as seashells. It is likely that potting clays were mined locally or regionally, from different coastal and inland geological beds.[14] Although fragmentary and disparate, the sample nevertheless points to important ceramic traditions and informs about a spectrum of practices involving pottery, in the prehistoric communities residing at this key site on the coast of northern Pieria.

The pottery is presented in chronological order, together with period-specific summaries of stratigraphy, archaeological context, and regional comparisons. Detailed comparanda are listed in the appended comprehensive catalogue of inventoried sherds. A few other inventoried ceramic artifacts from the same contexts are also reported, including two in the catalogue.

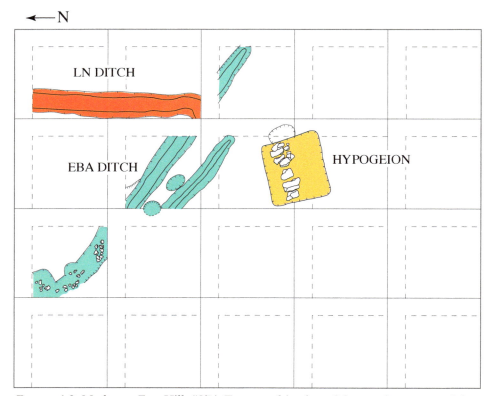

FIGURE 4.3. Methone, East Hill, #274. Topographic plan of the northeast area of the excavation, with the prehistoric ditches and the Hypogeion. Bessios 2012a, p. 46, fig. 3. Plan legends correspond to descriptions in this chapter as follows: LN Ditch: Late Neolithic Ditch (Τάφρος 1); EBA Ditch: Early Bronze Age Ditch (includes Τάφροι 2 and 3, Late Final Neolithic–Early Bronze Age). Plan I. Moschou

1. THE LATE NEOLITHIC (LN) SETTLEMENT

FEATURES AND CONTEXTS (FIGS 4.2–4.3)

Diagnostic pottery places the beginning of occupation to the LN I (5400/5300–4800 B.C.), with possibly long duration through the LN II (4800–4500 B.C.).[15]

a. Τάφρος [Ditch] 1: Τετράγωνα [Trenches] 001, 011; passes 001003, 001005, 001006, 00107, 011003, 011005
A small segment of a ditch with posthole, uncovered at the northeast corner of the excavation grid (Fig. 4.3), is the only architectural remnant from the earliest settlement on the promontory. Revealed down to its floor, the ditch is U-shaped in section (slightly narrower at the bottom), measuring 1.12–1.38 m in width, and preserved to 0.36–0.48 m of its original depth and about 9 m of its length.[16] The surviving portion runs in a north–south direction. This feature seems to have extended farther northward into unexcavated ground, as either an external or an intrasite boundary. In form and size it resembles ditches excavated at Makrygialos, Phases I and II.[17] The better-preserved system of Makrygialos I (LN I) consists of two parallel arch-shaped enclosures and a small segment of ditch running within the settlement. Both the outermost boundary arch and the intrasite divider are narrow, and V-shaped; they are thus very similar to the Methone feature.

A likely LN I date for Τάφρος 1 is indicated by the recovery on its floor (pass 011005, stratum 3) of **4/1** (ΜΕΘ 2009), a black-burnished biconical pot with tall neck ("amphoriskos"). Preserved to its full height and in about half of its circumference, it was the best surviving piece among the highly fragmented contents of the ditch. The shape and ware are distinctive of the period in Macedonia and beyond.[18] Shattered and heavily worn on the surface, this vessel was apparently discarded in the Τάφρος after considerable use—a well-documented practice, especially visible in the rich ceramic contents of the ditches and pits at Makrygialos I.[19]

From the surface layers of Trench 1 comes an additional piece datable to LN I: **4/7** (ΜΕΘ 4880), a black-polished corner fragment from a model, lid, or stand.

Other diagnostic, albeit poorly preserved, sherds collected from the fill of Τάφρος 1 also point to a general date in the LN, or early FN at the latest: carinated bodies, including a black-polished piece with small perforated handle; one "black-topped"(?) rim; and black-burnished fragments, among which are a couple of rims from larger vessels.[20] It should be noted that very little, if any, post-Neolithic pottery was retrieved from these units.[21]

The few non-ceramic finds include tools of chipped, ground, and polished stone (ΜΕ 19; ΜΕΘ 211, 232, 1586, 1890, 1891), as well as a perforated valve of cockle shell (ΜΕ 25); all could be of Neolithic date.

b. Features with redeposited material: Τάφροι [Ditches] 2 and 3, and Hypogeion; Τετράγωνα [Trenches] 012, 021, 022, 032, 003

The Late Neolithic settlement was repeatedly disturbed by later features, which yielded small amounts of diagnostic redeposited pottery.

Τάφρος [Ditch] 2 and associated Λάκκοι [Pits] 1, 2 (late FN–EBA early)

- **4/3** (ΜΕΘ 4253) Incised fragment from an elevated vessel. #274/021007 [4] (fill on floor of Τάφρος)
- **4/5** (ΜΕΘ 4301) Incised corner fragment from an elevated (?) vessel. #274/012003 [2] (fill)
- **4/13** (ΜΕΘ 4220) Reused sherd in Neolithic fabric; burnisher (?). #274/012003 [2]

Other, not inventoried Neolithic pottery from these layers consists mainly of dark-burnished rim and body fragments from fine and medium-fine bowls and cups of conical, biconical, or rounded profile. Also present are a few protomed and carinated forms (including one with relief ridge at the carination), notched rims, and fragments with small relief knobs. Incised and/or dotted decoration with white infill appears occasionally, along with a couple of possible white-painted examples. In addition, there are several burnished fragments from large vessels in coarser fabrics, including a heavy, burnished base from cookware (?), of profile and fabric comparable to the Neolithic cooking pot (χύτρα, **4/11** [ΜΕΘ 4221], see below). All the above categories compare closely to the inventoried pieces described in the catalogue.

Τάφρος [Ditch] 3 and associated Λάκκοι [Pits] 3, 4 (late FN–EBA early)

- **4/11** (ΜΕΘ 4221) Open cooking pot with handle. #274/012009 [5] (Pit 4)

The rest of the identified Neolithic sherds belong to the usual range of black-burnished or black-polished wares and features: carinated and incurving profiles, notched rims, small mastoi attached to bodies, and a protomed fragment from a lamp (?).

Fill around, and likely associated with, Τάφροι 2 and 3: Τετράγωνα [Trenches] 002, 021, 022, 003

More of the same material, but no inventoried pieces.

The Hypogeion

Located directly to the south of the prehistoric remains, this large subterranean structure of Late Geometric date was dug deep though earlier strata and bedrock, resulting in redeposition of pottery from all previous periods among its fill; sherds of different date were often found in the same stratigraphic context (Figs. 1.4–1.5; Figs. 4.4–4.5).[22] The LN material includes the following inventoried pieces, all very fragmentary and quite worn:

- **4/8** (ΜΕΘ 4954) Body fragment in dark fabric; incised spiral (?) decoration. #274/032012 [4]
- **4/9** (ΜΕΘ 4956) Small rim fragment to black-burnished open vessel; incised linear decoration. #274/032070 [7]
- **4/10** (ΜΕΘ 4959) Carinated fragment to closed vessel in dark fabric; incised spiral decoration. #274/022, depth 8.86–8.23 m

FIGURE 4.4. Prehistoric incised sherds from the "Hypogeion" (various depths). Date range: LN, late FN–EBA, LBA–EIA. Photo I. Coyle

FIGURE 4.5. LN polished sherd from the Hypogeion; (a) exterior, (b) interior.
Photos I. Coyle

c. Other redeposited material
Additional small quantities of Neolithic pottery, of the same types as those summarized above, were identified in the following areas:

Trench 004 on the northwest slope, immediately west of the prehistoric ditches, including:
- **4/4** (ΜΕΘ 4257) Rim to carinated (?) open vessel; incised decoration, red paint. #274/004002 [1]
- **4/12** (ΜΕΘ 4316) Leg of a cooking vessel in burnished fabric. #274/004018 [7]

Fill of Trench 85, outside the southeast wall of the agora Building A, includes:
- **4/2** (ΜΕΘ 5626) Dark-polished collar fragment to open vessel. #274/085, erosion layer [στρώμα διάβρωσης]

d. Comparative material from the Ancient Methone Archaeological Survey (2014)
Three Neolithic (LN–FN) sherds were collected, all from survey unit 90 to the northwest of the East Hill. Two of these were inventoried for publication in the survey report:[23]

- ΜΕΘ 5723 Carinated body fragment of a fine open vessel; dark gray fabric, buff-polished surface
- ΜΕΘ 5725 Burnished base to cooking pot; comparable to **4/11** (ΜΕΘ 4221)

LATE NEOLITHIC CERAMIC FABRICS AND WARES
The corpus consists primarily of the dark-burnished and dark-polished wares typical of the Late Neolithic period.[24] Fabrics range from very fine to medium-coarse, well fired to oxidized or reduced ceramic; surfaces are as a rule monochrome, in uniform hues of dark gray, brown, or black—an indication of intentional reduced firing.[25] A few chromatic variations include the dark-burnished rim, **4/4** (ΜΕΘ 4257), with traces of added red, a highly polished sherd from the Hypogeion with differently colored exterior and interior (Fig. 4.5), and one worn rim which may have been "black-topped" (a distinctive bichrome category of contrasting dark upper and red lower body).[26] Decoration, when present, is incised (rarely also excised) and/or dotted, usually white-filled, and consists of simple linear or curvilinear elements. Most fragments belong to

common shapes of small to medium-sized tableware: bowls and cups of rounded, flaring, or carinated profile, and the occasional wide-mouthed jar. More limited is the presence of elevated or angular forms (stands, models, or "lamps"), cookware, and large storage or transport containers. Although fragmentary, the East Hill assemblage nevertheless exemplifies the innovative ceramic technologies (possibly associated with aesthetic and cultural shifts) that mark the onset of the Late Neolithic in Macedonia and beyond, with a strong developing taste for dark-colored vessels versus the red and lighter-colored surfaces favored in earlier periods.[27]

Three fabrics have been distinguished macroscopically:

*Fabric 1 (Fig. 4.6a). Sandy, medium-fine, black-burnished (**4/1** [MEΘ 2009], **4/3** [MEΘ 4253], **4/10** [MEΘ 4959], **4/13** [MEΘ 4220]), and Fabric 1a, finer variation (**4/4** [MEΘ 4257], **4/5** [4301], **4/7** [MEΘ 4880], **4/8** [MEΘ 4954])*

The clay is fine-grained and gritty, with small quantities of sand, mica, silicate, white inclusions, and shell fragments. Varied in size and randomly distributed, these non-plastics probably represent common impurities or, in the case of shell, fossils embedded in the clay source, rather than ingredients added to the ceramic paste.[28] Clays of such consistency could be found, for instance, along dried-up or buried shorelines that formed part of the geology of the region.[29] Fabrics of similar composition are common in Macedonia,[30] most notably documented at Makrygialos.[31]

Vessels in Fabric 1 are thin-walled and carefully fired, the surfaces burnished or polished in dark gray, black, or brown, and the decoration consisting of simple incised or excised motifs. Shapes include small biconical jars **4/1** and **4/10** (MEΘ 2009, MEΘ 4959), a carinated bowl (?) **4/4** (MEΘ 4257), a "fruit stand" (?) **4/3** (MEΘ 4253), and two corner fragments from other elevated or figurative forms **4/5** and **4/7** (MEΘ 4301, MEΘ 4880). **4/13** (MEΘ 4220) is a flat sherd from a now unrecognizable shape that seems to have been repurposed as a scraper/burnisher—likely used in pot manufacture—to judge from the apparently intentional wear and polish on the surface and around the edges.

*Fabric 2 (Fig. 4.6b). Fine, micaceous, dark-burnished (**4/2** [MEΘ 5626], **4/6** [MEΘ 4328], **4/9** [MEΘ 4956])*

Finely levigated clay, with scant and tiny inclusions (silicates[?], limestone[?]). The fabric is compact, thoroughly fired to reduced gray. Surface finish is excellent, highly burnished or polished to a lustrous dark gray or black, often shiny with mica; a two-color variation is seen on the sherd from the Hypogeion, with brown exterior and black interior surfaces (Fig. 4.5; the shape is unidentifiable).[32] The shapes that can be inferred from the small surviving sherds include a closed cup with dotted decoration **4/6** (MEΘ 4328) and two collared bowls, one monochrome **4/2** (MEΘ 5626) and one incised **4/9** (MEΘ 4956).

This fabric can be attributed to the broad category formerly known as Larissa ware, a generic term for the fine-burnished dark pottery that had originally been associated with the post-Dimini (Larissa) phases of the Thessalian Neolithic.[33] Far from being confined to that regional stylistic sub-phase, however, such wares represent a robust ceramic tradition with wide geographical distribution in the Aegean and the Balkans, a long life spanning the late 6th to 4th millennia, and further echoes in the late FN and EBA (see below, Fabrics 2a, 2b).

*Fabric 3 (Fig. 4.6c). Cooking fabric (**4/11** [MEΘ 4221], **4/12** [MEΘ 4316])*

A sandy, gray-colored, medium fabric, rich in non-plastics with refractory and heat-conductive qualities: mica and silicate, along with larger pebbles and organic matter (now carbonized). Each of the two preserved fragments can be compared to a well-documented type of boiling pot (χύτρα) at LN I Makrygialos:[34] **4/11** (MEΘ 4221) has a deep and open conical shape, suitable for thick

FIGURE 4.6. LN ceramic fabrics (macroscopic close-ups): (a) Fabric 1, (b) Fabric 2, (c) Fabric 3. Photos M. Nikolaidou

soups, porridges, or vegetable stews; the leg **4/12** (ΜΕΘ 4316) probably belonged to an elevated cooker, likewise fit for slow, low-temperature boiling.[35] In the "stew pot" we see the careful finish and burnish which were systematically pursued by the makers of cookware, with the intent to produce a strong, impermeable and wear-resistant surface, thus ensuring food hygiene. The careful modeling of the leg is a standard feature of elevated vessels, the joints of which were carefully smoothed and slipped to avoid cracks from use wear, and to achieve maximum useful surface and form efficiency.[36]

In fabric composition and form finish, the two cookware fragments from Methone share features with both Fabric 1 and Fabric 2. Such overlap is common in the Neolithic; elaborate fine ceramics could be used in cooking and, reversely, cookware was manufactured according to the same ceramic recipe as fine tableware. Indeed, any fabric seems to have qualified for a cooking function, as long as it was rich enough in minerals that would guarantee the necessary heat-conductive properties.[37] Particularly interesting is the interchangeability of fabric and function between elaborate elevated vessels—fine tableware, stands, and plastic vessels—and tripod cookers. Following the suggestion by Marina Sofronidou and Zoi Tsirtsoni that the very concept of elevation could carry symbolisms and connotations of value across wares,[38] it is worth comparing the fabric and surface finish of **4/3** (ΜΕΘ 4253, an elevated vessel) and **4/12** (ΜΕΘ 4316, the tripod leg). In a cross-cultural assessment of the prestige symbolisms of early pottery, Brian Hayden has argued for a special significance attached to time-consuming cooking methods (such as the slow boiling carried out in Neolithic χύτραι) and to the foods prepared in such ways.[39]

Established habits of cooking and cuisine in Neolithic Macedonia are attested by a rich archaeobotanical, archaeofaunal, and archaeomalacological record.[40] They are also reflected in the variety and structured presence of thermal installations,[41] and in significant pottery assemblages, such as a large number of cooking utensils at Paliambela[42] and sets of vessels for cooking and storage or serving and eating/drinking at Dikili Tash[43] and Makrygialos.[44]

BEYOND THE SITE

The Late Neolithic settlement at Methone existed and produced its material culture within a connected geographical and social landscape. Prominently situated at the western curve of the Thermaic Gulf, near the confluence of four major rivers (Haliakmon, Axios, Loudias, and Gallikos), backed by the rolling hills of the Pieria mountains to the west and northwest, and with access to the coastal plain of Pieria and the Olympos mountain range to the south and southeast,[45] the site participated in local, regional, and interregional networks.

Around the prehistoric Thermaic Gulf—its west and north shorelines now largely submerged under subsequent alluviation—habitation is well documented through the Neolithic, starting already in the 7th millennium B.C.[46] During the LN, a substantial number of new settlements developed alongside older ones in the Giannitsa plain and the Langadas basin, and along the western coast of Chalkidike. Some of the better-known sites include (from west to east) Aravissos, Axos A and B, Giannitsa A and B, Archontiko, Mesimeriani Toumba, Stavroupolis, Therme, Vassilika, and Olynthos.[47] Beyond the gulf, the sea offered access to Chalkidike, east Macedonia, Thrace, the Aegean islands, and shores farther east. Across the diverse Pierian landscape, the long-lasting Neolithic period is documented by a few settlements situated along the coast (Makrygialos, Methone, possibly Koutsouro, Platamon), several others established in the fertile, well-watered lowlands and foothills (Kolindros-Paliambela, Kitros–Hassan Vrysi,[48] Korinos-Revenia, Korinos-Krania, Sevasti–Toumba Pappa, Olympos–Pigi Athinas), and some placed higher up the mountains (Sevasti, Sfendami, Ritini–Agios Nikolaos).[49] A system of navigable rivers, valleys, terrestrial passes, and harbors led farther south to Thessaly, west and northwest to the Macedonian hinterland, Epirus, the southwest Balkans, and the Adriatic.[50] Geographical features constituted both barriers and pathways to intersecting trajectories of connectivity, which at Neolithic Methone are reflected in site organization and ceramic styles.

The settlement on the East Hill belongs to the flat, extended type distinctive in Pieria and the Thermaic Gulf area (as opposed to tell sites elsewhere);[51] as discussed above, it likely occupied a larger area beyond the present East Hill. The location on a coastal promontory has been noted as exceptional in the region,[52] although another such settlement may have existed on the now eroded promontory of Koutsouro just a few kilometers to the south, as indicated by diagnostic LN pottery collected there;[53] farther south, Makrygialos-Agiasma was also very close to the sea. The surviving evidence does not allow any assessment of the scale and character of occupation on the East Hill and Koutsouro(?) promontories versus the substantial settlement at Makrygialos. Nevertheless, the close proximity of these three, roughly contemporary, localities along the northern stretch of the Pierian coast invites questions regarding the regional organization of the physical and social space. One possible explanation would be along the lines of horizontal expansion; namely, that shifts in habitation and permeability of boundaries, such as have been documented at Makrygialos I–II,[54] were practiced not only on the site level, but had validity among settlements as well.

The surviving ditch, Τάφρος 1, fits well within the range of Neolithic enclosures and intrasite dividers (single or multiple ditches, palisades, and walls), which are typical of the north Aegean and Balkan Neolithic.[55] First seen in west Macedonia in the Early Neolithic at Nea Nikomedeia,[56] they became distinctive features in the Middle and especially the Late Neolithic periods.[57] The construction and upkeep of these features was a demanding process; for example, the large boundary ditch at Makrygialos I (very wide and deep) was initially formed as a chain of pits, then partially filled and redug as a V-shaped trench.[58] At Ritini, on the Pieria mountains, a large pit of the MN period was filled in and replaced by a ditch in the LN.[59] At Trilofos-Kolimpakos, on the foothills of Mt. Vermion, a long apsidal ditch apparently defined an area within the settlement, and was associated with a system of pits and a hearth[60]—possibly in a manner similar to the divider trench of Makrygialos II. These different configurations underline the considerable scale of communal effort and resources invested in prehistoric enclosures, works of multi-purpose utility and polysemous value, as territorial markers and boundaries, protective devices against natural hazards, predators, and invaders, grounds for burial and refuse, organizers of living and/or working space, clay mining areas, or even water reservoirs.[61]

Systems of ditches and pits are often found containing assortments of artifacts, including black-burnished pottery.[62] At Methone, there is no way of knowing whether ΜΕΘ 2009 and the few other fragmented objects recovered within and around Τάφρος 1 represent ordinary detritus, or were the result of intentional fragmentation and deposition. Structured, ritualized deposition—not necessarily incompatible with productive activities or refuse habits[63]—has been documented in a number of sites, by a spectrum of practices associated with ditches and pits: burials (some furnished with high-quality pottery, shell and gold ornaments), selective burial of artifacts and ecofacts, apparently purposeful breakage, and feasting.[64]

The local and more distant affinities of the Methone pottery have been outlined above and are detailed in the catalogue. Remarkable cross-regional similarities in fabrics, shapes, and decorative modes constitute evidence for widely shared cultural practices involving pottery production and consumption.[65] At the same time, strong local traditions (possibly signaling identities tied to place of origin and a shared craft) can be detected in preferences for certain fabrics or forms or aesthetics by the potters in one site or region[66]—Makrygialos being a notable example,[67] and the closest one to Methone. The investment in ceramic technology by the Neolithic communities in Macedonia is additionally highlighted by the operation of kilns, which have come to light at Limenaria on Thasos (MN),[68] Kryoneri near Serres (LN I),[69] and (more dubiously) at Olynthos.[70]

2. THE FINAL NEOLITHIC (FN) SETTLEMENT

Features and Contexts (Figs. 4.2–4.3)

Diagnostic pottery associated with two parallel ditches and four pits, as well as additional redeposited sherds, provide evidence of occupation sometime around or after the mid-4th millennium B.C., at the transition from the late Final Neolithic (FN II) to the EBA. Conversely, pottery attributable to earlier phases of the FN (FN I or Chalcolithic, late 5th to early 4th millennium) gives some indication for a longer duration of the FN settlement—perhaps in unbroken continuation from the LN.

a. The late FN–early EBA occupation

There seems to have been repeated construction and reconfiguration of the earthworks on the hilltop. As mentioned already with regard to the LN ditch (Τάφρος 1), it is unclear whether these features constituted an exterior boundary or internal division of the settlement.

Τάφρος [Ditch] 2 with Λάκκοι [Pits] 1, 2: Τετράγωνα [Trenches] 003, 012, 021; passes 003003, 012002, 012003, 012004, 012005, 012012, 021003, 021004, 021005, 021007

Excavated down to its floor, where large quantities of structural clay were recovered, Τάφρος 2 is U-shaped in section and narrower toward the bottom. It measures 0.62–1.25 m in width, and is preserved to 0.8–1.1 m in depth and about 15.5 m in length. Running in a southeast–northwest direction from the hilltop down to the western slope, it would originally have cut across the LN Τάφρος 1 (somewhere in Trench 011 [see Figs. 4.1–4.2]); an indication of spatial rearrangement over time. Τάφρος 2 also cut through and disturbed the outline of Λάκκοι [pits] 1, 2 (in Trench 003), which thus seem to predate it—although it is not clear by how long: they could be Neolithic, early FN, or simply date to an earlier building episode in the advanced FN–EBA.[71] Τάφρος 2 itself was disturbed by two later walls (Τοίχος 1 and 2, in Trench 003).

Τάφρος [Ditch] 3 and associated Λάκκοι [Pits] 3, 4: Τετράγωνα [Trenches] 012, 022; passes 012006, 012007, 012008, 012009, 022029

Excavated down to its floor, this ditch is roughly V-shaped in section. It measures about 1 m at its widest, with a preserved maximum depth of 0.5 m and length of 5.4 m. Oriented on a southeast–northwest course from the hilltop down to the western slope, it runs parallel and slightly to the south of Τάφρος 2. The close proximity and co-alignment of these two features, as well as the fact that they contained the same range of pottery (LN–FN and EBA), supports their dating to the same period. The more modest dimensions of Τάφρος 3 in comparison to Τάφρος 2 suggest that the former was opened as reinforcement to the latter, although there is no knowing whether they operated together from the start or coexisted only part of the time. Pits 3 and 4, measuring 0.5–1 m in diameter, were dug in contact with the northern bank of Τάφρος 3. Although preserved only in their lowest portion, their original depth was estimated to about 1 m, on the comparative basis of the smaller but deep pits at Kitros–Hassan Vrysi.[72] In contrast, wider but shallower pits (0.70–1.40 m in diameter, up to 0.5 m deep) were found at the late FN site (Plot 617 [henceforth abbreviated as Αποχέτευση Μεθώνης]) that recently came to light during the course of the Methone-Agathoupolis Sewerage Project (Αποχέτευση Μεθώνης-Αγαθούπολης), in the vicinity of modern Methone.[73]

Mixed Neolithic–EBA pottery made up the main fill of the pits and the Τάφροι, all of which contained very little post–EBA pottery. Indeed, much of the material belonged to disturbed LN–early FN deposits,[74] or included coarser sherds in shell-rich fabrics that could be dated to either the FN or the EBA. On the basis of the available stratigraphic and ceramic evidence (admittedly rather limited), the most likely date we can propose for these features is the transitional late FN–early EBA I; their operation possibly continued into the EBA (see below).

Some chronological indicators were found in Τάφρος 2, which contained a few diagnostic FN ceramics in a relatively good state of preservation, in addition to very fragmentary fill material. The most important piece is **4/14** (ΜΕΘ 2010): a deep bowl with incurving rim, in shell-rich fabric, with burnished and mottled surface. It was found, more than half of it preserved, on the floor of the Τάφρος (pass 021004, stratum 3). The form, fabric, and surface finish of this vessel closely resemble late FN–early EBA I wares in the immediate region and beyond, in particular the finds from Αποχέτευση Μεθώνης and Kitros–Hassan Vrysi (although the shape and mottled firing are also well attested in later, EBA contexts). It must be noted that **4/14** (ΜΕΘ 2010) was the best preserved among the ceramic finds of Τάφρος 2. With one more exception (**4/15**, ΜΕΘ 4222), all pottery from the pits and Τάφροι 2, 3 was very fragmentary.

Two other ceramics from the fill of Τάφρος 2 were inventoried:

- **4/15** (ΜΕΘ 4222) Small crusted (?) bowl, full profile fragment. FN I–II. #274/012012 [6]
- **4/18** (ΜΕΘ 4300) Rim fragment to open vessel. FN I–II. #274/012003 [2][75]

Other diagnostic pottery collected from within and around the Τάφροι and pits consists mostly of fragments to bowls of incurving or S-profile and small jars, monochrome-burnished/polished or mottled in red, black, or brown (some with differently colored interior and exterior); a few bear incised decoration. Τάφρος 3 produced an additional red-crusted (?) fragment of carinated shape, with incised decoration (pass 022029, stratum 9; not inventoried). A "cheese pot"—a distinct late FN shape—may be represented by a fragment collected from Trench 11, just to the east of the Τάφροι.

With the exception of one bone tool (ME 35), the few other non-ceramic artifacts are tools of chipped and ground stone (including ME 30, 31, 33, 34). The inventoried finds from Τάφρος 2 are a beautifully worked blade of brown flint from the fill above the floor of the Τάφρος (ΜΕΘ 603, pass 021007)[76] and a small grinder (ΜΕΘ 251, #274/003, Pit 1). A few pieces of quartz, probably worked,[77] were also collected from Τάφρος 2 (including ΜΕ 34 in Pit 1 and a large piece from pass 012005, stratum 2). The inventoried finds from Τάφρος 3 are an adze (ΜΕΘ 235) and a fragment from a large quern (ΜΕΘ 268), both from the same unit (pass 012007), and a small grinder (ΜΕΘ 548). All of these tools would be in place in a Neolithic or FN context—with the exception, perhaps, of the heavy quern fragment ΜΕΘ 268, which may be associated with the subsequent EBA horizon.[78]

b. Redeposited material from the Hypogeion: Τετράγωνα [Trenches] 022, 032

- **4/26** (ΜΕΘ 4955) Rim fragment to open vessel; incised decoration. Late FN. #274/032012 [4]
- **4/27** (ΜΕΘ 4957) Small body fragment of an open (?) vessel; incised decoration. #274/022066 [14]
- **4/30** (ΜΕΘ 4967) Coarse body fragment to jar or urn; incised decoration. #274/032050 [7]

c. Redeposited material from the slopes

The thick layers accumulated on the slopes of the East Hill produced more finds than the shallow deposits associated with the prehistoric features on the hilltop.

The western slope: Τετράγωνα [Trenches] 004, 005

Located directly below the western preserved end of Τάφρος 2 (in Trench 003), Trench 004 and, to a lesser degree, Trench 005 contained several FN sherds, including the following inventoried:

- **4/16** (ΜΕΘ 4254) Collar and rim fragment to open vessel; mottled. #274/004006 [4]
- **4/17** (ΜΕΘ 4258) Partial profile to carinated conical bowl. #274/004002 [1]
- **4/19** (ΜΕΘ 4324) Partial S-profile, open vessel; mottled. #274/004023 [10]
- **4/29** (ΜΕΘ 4290) Perforated body fragment ("strainer"). #274/004019 [7]
- **4/20** (ΜΕΘ 4334) Partial profile to conical bowl. Late FN. #274/004006 [4]
- **4/21** (ΜΕΘ 4996) Partial profile to open vessel with lug. #274/005013 [5]

The area of the later pottery kiln: Τετράγωνο [Trench] 054, surface layer

- **4/22** (ΜΕΘ 5022) Partial profile to open vessel. Late FN(?). #274/054009 [1]
- **4/31** (ΜΕΘ 5091) Partial profile to coarse jar. Late FN–EBA I. #274/054012 [1]

Several other fragments of red- and dark-burnished bowls of incurving or everted profile, as well as jars, were collected from these and other passes. They likely date to the late FN.

The southeast area of the agora proper: Τετράγωνα [Trenches] 084, 085

Trench 084 contains the southeastern segment of the retaining wall of the agora, and surrounding debris layers mostly outside of the agora proper. Trench 085 contains an area of the agora directly inside of the retaining wall, including the southeastern excavated portion of the Stoa Building A. Fragmentary remains of an EIA floor, disturbed by the walls of that building, were uncovered in the northwest corner of the trench.

Several diagnostic FN sherds came from these thick deposits, including the following inventoried:

- **4/23** (ΜΕΘ 5638) Partial S-profile with ridge lug. #274/085, Στρώμα διάβρωσης [erosion layer]
- **4/24** (ΜΕΘ 5639) Partial profile to open vessel with lug. #274/084, Στρώμα διάβρωσης [erosion layer]
- **4/25** (ΜΕΘ 5641) Partial profile to large bowl with lug. #274/085, ΒΔ γωνία [northwest corner of trench]
- **4/32** (ΜΕΘ 5618) Complete profile, baking (?) pan or tray. #274/085, Κέντρο τετραγώνου [center of trench]
- **4/33** (ΜΕΘ 5628) Ovoid large bead, button, or spindlewhorl; its mottled and burnished fabric points to a FN date. From the same pass as **4/32** (ΜΕΘ 5618)

CERAMIC FABRICS AND WARES

The small sample of FN monochrome and decorated wares from the East Hill exhibits distinctive features of the ceramic traditions of the period, as known from published assemblages across the Aegean and the mainland.[79] Regarding northern Greece, in particular, reference works for the early FN/Chalcolithic pottery (late fifth to early fourth millennium) include the publications of Kitrini Limni–Megalo Nisi Galanis Phase II, Dikili Tash Phase II, and Sitagroi Phase III,[80] as well as preliminary reports from Mandalo Phases Ib–II, Polyplatanos, Kryoneri, and Promachon-Topolniča Phase IV.[81] In Thessaly the type sites are Rachmani Phase III and Pefkakia, *Rachmanistratum*.[82] These assemblages can be compared to a wide range of regional developments in the Aegean and the southern Balkans.[83] The later FN (FN II) spans a good part of the fourth millennium, including the FN–EBA I transition. In northern Greece, this phase has been identified at Doliana in Epirus, Petromagoula and Mikrothives in Magnesia, and Farangi Messianis near Kozani.[84] To the same period probably belong also the earliest horizons at Kritsana (I–II) and Agios Mamas (pits D 33d, E 33d) in Chalkidike;[85] in addition, Sitagroi IV and Agios Ioannis on Thasos have produced diagnostic ceramics and radiocarbon dates around the mid-fourth millennium.[86] These sequences are broadly parallel to the pre-Troy I horizons in the northern Aegean and coastal Anatolia (Kum Tepe, Çukuriçi Höyük VII–Vb, Poliochni Black, Emporio VII–VI, Late Chalcolithic Heraion and Tigani on Samos),[87] the successive Attica-Kephala and Acropolis North Slope cultures in the southern Aegean and mainland, the Maliq IIIa horizons in Albania, and the Baden culture in the Balkans and central Europe.[88]

In northern Pieria, the end of the Final Neolithic period is documented at two recently excavated locations, already mentioned above: Kitros–Hassan Vrysi, in the Pieria hills;[89] and Methone Plot 617 (Αποχέτευση Μεθώνης), situated at a short distance from the coast of modern Methone and just a few kilometers southeast of ancient Methone, which was investigated as part of the Methone-Agathoupolis Sewerage Project.[90] The pottery from both sites is still under study; however, preliminary reports and personal examination of some of the material (by courtesy of the excavators) indicate close similarities of form and fabric with the finds from the East Hill—thus supporting a date of the latter to the late FN. In addition to these two sites, evidence for FN habitation has been identified in the course of salvage work at several other locales in the wider area of Methone–Nea Agathoupolis (M. Bessios, pers. comm., 2015).

As happens elsewhere, the FN pottery from ancient Methone is indebted to earlier Neolithic traditions, yet features many innovative aspects, too. The fine, dark-burnished and dark-polished wares characteristic of the LN are now largely replaced by monochrome burnished and mottled surfaces, in a spectrum of colors ranging from light brown to bright red. There are also one or two possible examples of crusted ware, a distinctive FN product,[91] including **4/15** (ΜΕΘ 4222). The fabrics are heavier than before, resulting from new recipes for clay sourcing and/or preparing and firing.

Representative shapes in the finer categories include medium to large bowls of incurved or S-profile with large appendages (lugs, handles), and bowls/jars of carinated profile. Coarse wares are represented by heavy jars and by utility forms related to cooking or craft, including a pan and a "strainer." This repertory reflects well-documented shifts in the technological choices of the potters, as well as in the needs and tastes of the consumers, during this period.[92] In contrast, the occasional black-burnished surfaces and the incised, white-filled motifs of decoration recall the styles of previous times.

Two main fabrics have been identified, each with finer and/or coarser variations.

*Fabric 4 (Fig. 4.7a). Medium-fine with mineral and organic inclusions; unevenly fired, mottled and burnished (**4/17** [ΜΕΘ 4258], **4/19** [ΜΕΘ 4324], **4/21** [ΜΕΘ 4996], **4/23** [ΜΕΘ 5638], **4/25** [ΜΕΘ 5641], **4/28** [ΜΕΘ 5061], **4/33** [ΜΕΘ 5628])*

Rather loose fabric, consisting of fine-grained clay mixed with various non-plastics: minerals (limestone, silicate, feldspar), plant material (now carbonized), small and larger pebbles, and shell fragments. Oxidized, uneven firing results in light-colored fabric of brown or red, with extensive gray core, carbonized specks, and large pores indicative of vegetal matter mixed in the clay. Surfaces are generally well burnished, often lustrous, but unevenly fired to a mottled effect. There is often a thick, creamy slip, well burnished and fired in hues of red, brown, buff, or dark gray, with clouds of different color that often create a pleasing contrast to the background, and may well have been intentional.[93]

The main shapes are medium- to large-sized bowls of conical, incurving, or sinuous profile, almost all of them monochrome/mottled. Forms are strong and carefully built, but finish can be cursory; modeling and/or burnishing marks are still occasionally visible (for example, on **4/23–4/25** [ΜΕΘ 5638, ΜΕΘ 5639, ΜΕΘ 5641]). Large appendages are characteristic: triangular handles, elongated ridges, shelf- or tongue-shaped lugs, perforated mastoids. These features have good parallels among the monochrome burnished, utilitarian pottery (*Gebrauchskeramik*) at Pefkakia, which spans the long duration of the FN,[94] and in the repertory of FN I monochrome burnished bowls at Kitrini Limni–Megalo Nisi Galanis.[95] They can also be compared to the (somewhat later?) "Varnished" or "Tartar" ware at Servia: a vegetal-tempered, thickly slipped and burnished type of monochrome bowl, which was distinctive of the earliest EBA phases and associated foremost with the large V-ditch that bounded the settlement of the time.[96] Similar fabrics have been reported, for example, from the LN/FN layers at Emporio and Agio Gala on Chios,[97] from the Athenian Agora,[98] and from Franchthi Cave, Phase 5.[99]

The only decorated sherd in this group, **4/28** (ΜΕΘ 5061), likewise belonged to an open shape, of angular profile. It combines the traditional decoration of incised and white-filled linear motifs with the novel fashion of bright-colored mottling. The same surface treatment and decorative mode are seen elsewhere, on shapes as diverse as the so-called scoops—peculiar handled containers of probable ritual function[100]—and the "Bratislava bowls or lids"—a *fossil directeur* of the late FN, with mottled fabrics and occasionally angular motifs of decoration.[101] In west Macedonia, examples of "Bratislava bowls" have been reported from Farangi Messianis near Kozani[102] and from the Αποχέτευση Μεθώνης site.[103]

This fabric was versatile and long-lived, with both finer and coarse variations:[104]

*Fabric 4a, finer variation (**4/16** [ΜΕΘ 4254], **4/18** [ΜΕΘ 4300], **4/24** [ΜΕΘ 5639])*

More compact, with few non-plastics, more evenly fired (almost without core). Shape and surface features are same as in the standard version. This finer fabric is represented by three rim fragments: a small bowl or cup (**4/18** [ΜΕΘ 4300]) and two wide-mouthed jars or bowls of sinuous profile (**4/16** [ΜΕΘ 4254], **4/24** [ΜΕΘ 5639]).

*Fabric 4b, finer variation, late FN (**4/2** [ΜΕΘ 5022], **4/26** [ΜΕΘ 4955])*
Low-fired with distinctive very dark core, it features a thickly slipped and burnished surface. This variation is recognized in two fragments of open vessels: **4/22** (ΜΕΘ 5022) and **4/26** (ΜΕΘ 4955), which find parallels among late FN assemblages at Doliana, Mikrothives, Emporio, Kephala, Heraion on Samos, and, locally, at Kitros–Hassan Vrysi and Αποχέτευση Μεθώνης (see catalogue for references).

*Fabric 4c, coarse variation (Fig. 4.7b) (**4/29** [ΜΕΘ 4290], **4/30** [ΜΕΘ 4967], **4/31** [ΜΕΘ 5091], **4/32** [ΜΕΘ 5618]).*
The fabric is unevenly fired, with extensive gray core indicative of a substantial vegetal component, and heavy in non-plastics, including shell fragments and large pebbles visible through the surface.[105] The interior is thickly coated and burnished, although barely enough to cover the larger inclusions; the exterior can be burnished, too.

The four fragments in this group represent an interesting range of shapes which exemplify the technological and functional innovations in pottery production during the FN.[106] The perforated sherd **4/29** (ΜΕΘ 4290) belongs to a diverse group of pierced-wall vessels that are often described collectively as strainers or (more tentatively) as "cheese pots."[107] The dairy-making use of such containers was first proposed for Balkan finds in the context of the "secondary products revolution," presumably well in place already in the FN[108]—although not a uniform process in the Aegean, as the evidence indicates.[109] Conversely, Alexandra Kalogirou has persuasively argued that many LN and early FN perforated pots from the Aegean (including those from Macedonia) were rather used for the no-boil processing of vegetable or other non-solid foods, such as honey.[110] A wide range of domesticated and wild fruits, pulses, cereals, nuts, and grasses is indeed attested in the paleobotanical record of the Neolithic and the Early Bronze Age in Macedonia;[111] these could have been made palatable in many different ways, by straining, drying, sprouting, toasting, and parching. **4/32** (ΜΕΘ 5618), a profile portion of a pan with strong marks of burning, may have been put to similar uses.[112] Close local parallels for both shapes are present among the rich corpus from Αποχέτευση Μεθώνης,[113] and "baking pans" are also reported from the settlement at Kato Agios Ioannis, on the Katerini plain.[114]

Vivid glimpses of the culinary tastes and technologies of the period are offered by the apparatus of excavated households at Dikili Tash (Phase II, FN I), where wild fruits were stored in baskets and shelved alongside ceramic containers and stands; grapes were processed for their juice and for wine(?); and a variety of fine tableware and cookware were kept together in rooms with ovens.[115] Ovens were also part of domestic equipment at Agios Ioannis on Thasos (late FN).[116] Miniatures and models of ovens further highlight the significance of such installations.[117]

4/30 (ΜΕΘ 4967) and **4/31** (ΜΕΘ 5091) are fragments from large coarse vessels, storage jars that became increasingly prominent from the FN onward. Functionally, these large containers materialize the onset of different practical and social processes for the management of food.[118] Technologically, they represent new challenges regarding the ceramic recipes, shaping methods, and firing techniques required to produce such capacious forms. The surface elaboration of many FN storage jars, including **4/30** (ΜΕΘ 4967), evokes a crafter's pride in their handiwork, and perhaps also a social value surrounding these containers—in their distinct way as socially meaningful as the fine decorated tableware of earlier periods.[119]

*Fabric 5 (Fig. 4.7c). Shell-tempered, very dark-fired; late FN (**4/14** [ΜΕΘ 2010], **4/20** [ΜΕΘ 4334])*
Compact, fine fabric, fired in alternating atmosphere to dark gray-red hues with mottling. Contains minimal amount of mineral inclusions, but is heavily tempered with shell fragments of relatively consistent size (small to medium) that are quite evenly distributed in the clay body, together with

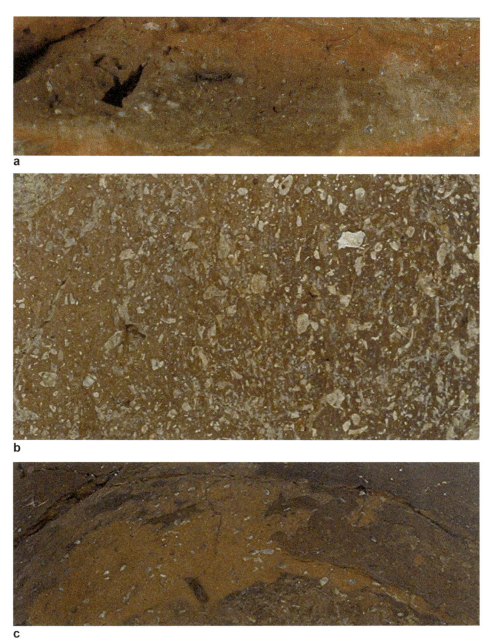

FIGURE 4.7. FN ceramic fabrics (macroscopic close-ups): (a) Fabric 4, (b) Fabric 4c, (c) Fabric 5. Photos M. Nikolaidou

much powdered shell. Surface is thinly slipped, burnished to a distinctive "waxy" texture; mottling creates strong color contrasts. The close resemblance of this fabric to the dark, shell-rich wares from Αποχέτευση Μεθώνης may point to a local recipe[120]—although similar fabrics are known elsewhere in the Aegean.[121] The deep conical bowl **4/14** (ΜΕΘ 2010), with incurving rim and burnished mottled surface, is a signature FN shape; rooted in earlier Neolithic forms, it would develop further during the EBA.

Two additional fabrics are represented by isolated pieces: **4/27** (ΜΕΘ 4957), of Fabric 2a, is a "sandier" variation of the LN dark-burnished Fabric 2 (see above); **4/15** (ΜΕΘ 4222) is an early example of Fabric 6a, which is seen primarily in the EBA (see below).

BEYOND THE SITE

In northern Greece, as elsewhere in the Aegean, occupation at many Neolithic sites continues—uninterrupted or with intermittent hiatuses—during the FN, and is documented by both relative and absolute chronologies.[122] In northern Pieria, such continuity is seen at Paliambela Kolindros,[123] Kitros–Hassan Vrysi,[124] and of course on the East Hill of ancient Methone, while the settlements at Αποχέτευση Μεθώνης and Agios Ioannis A date to the FN only.[125]

The latter part of the period (FN II), spanning the fourth millennium, for a long time remained more difficult to grasp than the earlier Chalcolithic phases, which show a smoother continuum from the preceding LN.[126] An apparent discrepancy between, on the one hand, uninterrupted stratigraphic sequences from the Neolithic to the EBA and, on the other hand, a lack of reliable radiocarbon dates to bridge the fifth and third millennia had created the impression of an "elusive" fourth millennium at many sites.[127] Recently, however, important answers have been forthcoming from sites with single-phase occupation and material culture distinctive of the late FN. Radiocarbon determinations place these horizons around the mid-fourth millennium or shortly after[128], at the cusp of the emerging EBA and in synchrony with broader Aegean developments.[129] Forthcoming radiocarbon dates from the undisturbed deposits at Αποχέτευση Μεθώνης are anticipated with particular interest for northern Pieria.[130]

The fragmentary remains of FN habitation on the East Hill of ancient Methone preserve enough indicators to connect the site with processes taking place within and beyond the region. The boundary ditches (Τάφροι 2, 3) with adjacent pits (Λάκκοι 1–2, and 3–4, respectively) trace their roots to much earlier local traditions, but also find a contemporary parallel in the two ditches and associated pits at Kato Agios Ioannis A, of which the larger (exterior boundary?) was reinforced by an additional stone wall.[131] A multitude of artifacts (pottery, stone tools, ornaments) and ecofacts (bone and shell) were deposited therein, several of them associated with three burials in the larger ditch.[132] Not only do these findings highlight the survival of strong Neolithic practices involving earthworks; they further suggest that the original contents of the East Hill Τάφροι 2 and 3 may also have been richer and more varied than the sparse surviving record. The pits associated with the Τάφροι possibly had a role in the spatial articulation of various onsite activities, in a manner comparable to the clusters of pits at Kitros–Hassan Vrysi and at Αποχέτευση Μεθώνης, which apparently served for storage and/or refuse as well as craftwork—most importantly, metallurgy and textile production.[133]

In terms of regional topography, special attention must be drawn to the apparent coexistence, toward the end of the late FN, of at least two settlements at a very short distance from each other, on the East Hill and at Αποχέτευση Μεθώνης. The latter occupied a low rise of fertile land bordered by a stream, just 200 meters away from the coast. It is tempting to consider these two loci—both of the flat type characteristic in the region—as different sectors of one larger territorial unit, which conceivably emerged as the original core settlement on the East Hill promontory expanded to include more favorable land on higher and drier grounds; safe from the advancing alluviation and progressive transformation of the coast into marshland,[134] and yet with easy access to both freshwater and the sea. Or, there may have been horizontal shifts in occupation (a regional practice going back at least to the Late Neolithic), representing different time phases during the FN. As noted earlier, several sherds from the East Hill can be dated to the FN I phase, while the pottery from the Αποχέτευση Μεθώνης site consistently belongs to the late stages of the period.[135] Small-scale salvage work in the area of modern Methone–Nea Agathoupolis has provided some evidence that the FN landscape may have included other locales in addition to these two sites, although the nature of such an occupation is not clear. It is also worth noting the lack of contemporary horizons at either Makrygialos or Koutsouro, where habitation seems to have resumed only in the EBA.[136] The abandonment of older sites in favor of new ones was common practice in the fourth millennium,[137] and a new interest in moving closer to the coast is indeed evident in Pieria at the cusp of the EBA.[138] Such trends could account for a double focus of habitation in the area of ancient Methone during the late FN, right at the coast (East Hill promontory) and a little higher and further inland (Αποχέτευση Μεθώνης).[139] A few kilometers farther to the southwest and higher on the Pieria hills, the settlement at Kitros–Hassan Vrysi also enjoyed an advantageous location: at a short distance from a lagoon that had formed on the coast around Korinos, it had easy access to, and command of, coast and marshland as well as a fertile hinterland.[140]

These three identified sites of the late FN in northern Pieria sit at nodal locations between the fertile plains of west/central Macedonia and the coasts and plains of Thessaly.[141] Their material culture[142] appears attuned to key developments of the time around the Aegean and beyond:[143] animal husbandry, production and use of metal objects including innovative bronze daggers,[144] cloth production, elaborate stamps/pintaderas (one was found at Αποχέτευση Μεθώνης), emphasis on storage in the form of pits and large containers, as well as quantities of distinct pottery wares ranging from burnished and incised vessels to cooking implements. Variations of these themes occur across regions, landscapes, and settlements of different size, format, and history; situated on mountains (Doliana), in river valleys (Farangi Messianis), in plains (long-lived tells such as Sitagroi, Rachmani, Sesklo), by lakes (Palioskala), on or near the coast (Dimini, Pefkakia, Petromagoula, Mikrothives, Agios Ioannis on Thasos), at the confluence of marine and estuarine zones (Tsepi Marathon, Çukuriçi Höyük), on island promontories (Plakari, Kephala, Aigina Kolonna, Strofilas, Emporio), and in caves (Skoteini, Agio Gala, Zas, Franchthi)—to name but a few. These widely shared material aspects—and their social and symbolic correlates[145]—give testimony to an outward-looking, enterprising spirit prevalent during the Final Neolithic, when ideas, goods, and people (among them, potters) were moving within and across regions over land (partly as pastoralists) and, ever more importantly, along sea routes.[146]

3. THE EARLY BRONZE AGE (EBA) SETTLEMENT

Features and Contexts (Figs. 4.2–4.3)

a. The hilltop: Τάφροι and Hypogeion
Diagnostic pottery indicates a long occupation spanning the entire duration of the Macedonian EBA, from the late fourth millennium (EBA I) to the EBA–MBA transition in the early second millennium.[147] The presence of EBA material in or around all three prehistoric ditches, Τάφροι 1–3, is evidence that the EBA settlement occupied the hilltop, as did its Neolithic and FN predecessors.

Τάφροι [Ditches] 2 and 3, with associated Λάκκοι [Pits] 1, 2, 3, 4: Τετράγωνα [Trenches] 003, 012, 021, 022; passes 003003, 012002, 012003, 012004, 012005, 012006, 012007, 012008, 012009, 012012, 021003, 021004, 021005, 021007, 022029
To judge from the presence of EBA pottery among their fill, the late FN ditches probably continued to be used during the EBA.[148] The range of diagnostic EBA pottery includes striated and/or burnished fragments of medium-to-coarse large vessels, monochrome-burnished and/or mottled bodies and bases to open vessels (of heavier fabric and coarser finish than their Neolithic counterparts), appendages such as large "buttons," mastoi, and plastic rope bands, coarse sherds in shell- and lithic-rich fabrics, and a rounded "anchor"(?) fragment.[149]

Other EBA material from the hilltop: Τετράγωνα [Trenches] 001, 011, 021, 002, 012, 022, 032
The entire investigated area on the hilltop, including the fill layers of the Neolithic Τάφρος 1 and the Early Iron Age Hypogeion, produced more pottery of the kind retrieved from Τάφροι 2 and 3. In addition, there were various diagnostic rims—mostly from jars and a few from coarse pithoi: straight, flat-lipped, thickened, incurving, notched or slashed, pierced, or equipped with attached lugs and strap handles. Dark-burnished fragments of S-profile pots and incurving bowls in finer fabrics, body fragments with lugs (simple or double) or with relief bands, and cylindrical and strap handles were also present. One whole vessel from the Hypogeion was inventoried:

- **4/43** (ΜΕΘ 1582) One-handled dipper cup. Transitional EBA–MBA. #274/022032 [10]

b. Redeposited material from the slopes
The western slope: Τετράγωνα [Trenches] 003, 004, 005
Larger quantities of EBA pottery had accumulated in the debris down the northwest slope. A range of fine to coarse wares is represented, including more examples of all the types listed above, as well as fragments of cookware. Trench 004 was especially productive, both in EBA and earlier (LN–FN) material, and of additional interest because of the discovery of EIA habitation levels: a "pebbly floor" at the bottom of stratum 7 (pass 004021), postholes dug in sterile soil in strata 10 (passes 004025, 026, 027) and 11 (pass 004037). Among the handmade pottery associated with these contexts, several sherds can be attributed to the EBA, including the following inventoried:

- **4/35** (ΜΕΘ 4332) Shoulder fragment to closed vessel; channeled decoration. #274/004029 [10]
- **4/36** (ΜΕΘ 4326) Body fragment to a bowl with tubular lug. EBA I–II. #274/004023 [10]
- **4/37** (ΜΕΘ 4886) Strongly incurved partial profile to large bowl. #274/004037 [11]
- **4/45** (ΜΕΘ 4287) Small cup/beaker or miniature, partial profile. #274/004016 [7]
- **4/50** (ΜΕΘ 4872) Partial profile to open jar/urn. #274/004030 [10]
- **4/59** (ΜΕΘ 4869) Leg/wall to a tripod cooker. LBA (?). #274/004030 [10]

Another interesting find in stratum 7 was two spherical mace heads of polished stone, ΜΕΘ 78 and ΜΕΘ 264 (passes 004017 and 004020, respectively). The type is well known in the Neolithic and EBA Macedonia and Balkans.[150]

The rest of the inventoried pottery from the northwest slope includes:

- **4/48** (ΜΕΘ 4183) Partial profile, "amphoriskos" or jug. #274/003003, fill around Τοίχος [Wall] 1
- **4/49** (ΜΕΘ 4272) Flaring rim and neck fragment to a jug. Late EBA–early MBA. #274/004009 [4]
- **4/55** (ΜΕΘ 2008) Dipper jug. Late or post-EBA. #274/005010 [5]

The area of the later pottery kiln: Τετράγωνα [Trenches] 053, 054
In Trench 053, the fill of Λάκκος [Pit] 5 included:

- **4/39** (ΜΕΘ 4991) Partial incurved profile to large shallow bowl, with mastos. #274/053006 [5]

In Trench 054, the surface layers contained interesting EBA material—much of it quite early—mixed with late FN, MBA, and handmade EIA pottery; three pieces were inventoried:

- **4/34** (ΜΕΘ 5021) Incised rim fragment to black-burnished bowl. EBA I–II. #274/054009 [1]
- **4/40** (ΜΕΘ 5047) T-rim and body with lug to large, shallow bowl. #274/054011 [1]

- **4/51** (ΜΕΘ 5023) Partial profile to jar with shelf lug. EBA I (?). #274/054009 [1][151]

Other diagnostic sherds from these and adjacent passes included flaring, incurving, and everted rims to open and closed shapes, mostly dark-burnished; flat rims and body fragments to large and smaller jars, many of them striated; medium to coarse body fragments with plastic ridges, rope bands, mastoi, and lugs; and a couple of legs to cooking tripods.

The southeast area of the agora proper: Τετράγωνα [Trenches] 084, 085

Fair amounts of EBA pottery were identified among the prehistoric material (FN–EIA) that was redeposited in the fill layers of this area. Of particular interest is the strong presence of EBA pottery in the floor stratum of an EIA structure that was excavated beneath the Stoa Building A, in the northwest corner of Trench 085 (excavated on May 29, 2006). Among the rich ceramic contents of this unit, quantities of sherds attributable to the EBA (albeit mostly coarse and thus not particularly diagnostic) suggest the existence of (undetected) EBA habitation underneath the excavated EIA strata.

All diagnostic EBA types are represented in this fill, including the following inventoried:

- **4/38** (ΜΕΘ 4887) Carinated partial profile to a large bowl, with mastos. #274/085, Στρώμα διάβρωσης [erosion layer]
- **4/41** (ΜΕΘ 5089) Flaring partial profile to deep bowl. Late EBA–early MBA. #274/084002 [2]
- **4/42** (ΜΕΘ 5090) Carinated partial profile to large, shallow bowl. EBA II–III. #274/084003 [2]
- **4/46** (ΜΕΘ 5612) Partial profile to miniature(?) cup/bowl. EBA I–II. #274/085, Κέντρο τετραγώνου [center of trench]
- **4/47** (ΜΕΘ 5622) Miniature kantharos, complete profile. Late EBA–early MBA. #274/085, Ανατολικός μάρτυρας [east balk]
- **4/52** (ΜΕΘ 5083) Body fragment with rope band(s), to a water jar (?). #274/084001 [1]
- **4/53** (ΜΕΘ 5613) Partial profile with rope band, to a water jar (?). #274/085023 [9]
- **4/54** (ΜΕΘ 5623) Rim/neck fragment to a jar/urn. #274/085, Ανατολικός μάρτυρας [east balk]
- **4/60** (ΜΕΘ 5652) Partial profile to a cooking(?) jar. #274/085, ΒΔ τμήμα [northwest quadrant]

c. Comparative material from the West Hill

Recent (2014–2017) excavations by the ΚΖ´ Ephoreia and the Cotsen Institute of Archaeology at UCLA on the West Hill of ancient Methone (Plots 229, 245) have revealed a fragmentary component of a pre-LBA cemetery, in close proximity to—and largely disturbed by—the substantial remains of LBA burials and EIA–Archaic horizons of habitation and industry. Contracted inhumations datable to the EBA or slightly later were identified close to the surface on the hilltop, in two sectors: in Sector Γ of the Ephoreia excavations, around the tunnels cut during the time of the Macedonian siege (Μακεδονική Σήραγγα);[152] and, immediately to the north, in Trench 5 of the UCLA excavation grid.[153]

In Sector Γ, a child's grave (Tomb #229/14) was furnished with two vessels datable to EBA–early MBA: a miniature beaker with handle (ΜΕΘ 7140), of EBA fabric, and a carinated cup with strap handle (ΜΕΘ 7141), of a type known from the advanced EBA phases at Armenochori, and now identified as well in an EBA tomb south of the West Hill.[154] In Trench 5, the early (EBA[?]) burials contained no grave goods; however, a small amount of pottery that seems diagnostic of the EBA (study of this material by the author is still in progress) came from Trench 5 and the adjacent Trenches 1 and 2, redeposited amid fill from later periods. The represented shapes include a large, burnished bowl with strongly incurving rim and raised handle (ΜΕΘ 7263), the profile of which can be compared with **4/38** (ΜΕΘ 4887) and with EBA handled types from elsewhere;[155] a bowl of incurving profile with relief ridge (ΜΕΘ 7437), in burnished fabric comparable to the East Hill Fabric 6 (see below); a funnel-shaped rim to a large dark-burnished open shape, the profile of which (if not the fabric) compares with **4/41** (ΜΕΘ 5089) and may thus be dated to the EBA–MBA transition; and a burnished base to a large vessel with elaborately striated interior (ΜΕΘ 7264).[156] An additional isolated burnt rim to an EBA(?) coarse jar or urn (ΜΕΘ 7107) was found amid Archaic fill in the northern slope of the West Hill; however, there were no other traces of EBA occupation in this area of the hill, despite the fact that excavation reached bedrock there.[157]

d. Comparative material from the Ancient Methone Regional Survey
Small quantities of sherds, mostly from coarse vessels, datable to the EBA were found widely distributed in the survey units north of the West and East Hills. The highest count came from SU047, immediately north of the East Hill excavation area, along with diagnostic pottery from the Middle Bronze and the Early Iron Age.[158]

Thus, settlement seems considerably expanded during the EBA, as compared to its LN and FN predecessors, although it remains unclear whether this expansion represents a single major episode or shifts across space and time.[159] In either case, the continued and even increased interest in this key location by the coast is unmistakable, and resonates with the overall importance of seaside habitation during the EBA. The establishment of a distinct cemetery alongside the settlement is another crucial development, in line with broader phenomena in Macedonia and the region of northern Pieria, in particular.[160]

CERAMIC FABRICS AND WARES

All phases of the Macedonian EBA (I–III) have been identified at ancient Methone, spanning a long sequence from the late FN–EBA I transition (late fourth millennium) to the late EBA–MBA threshold (early second millennium). A few handmade pieces of cookware (**4/56** [ΜΕΘ 4182], **4/57** [ΜΕΘ 4256], **4/59** [ΜΕΘ 4869]) are possibly later (Bronze Age or EIA), but nevertheless are included here because they echo EBA traditions of fabric and shape. Many of the EBA shapes and wares in common use around the north Aegean, and beyond, are seen on site. The closest parallels are found (as expected) in Macedonia, to a lesser degree in Thessaly; thus our comparative discussion focuses on these two regions, with occasional references elsewhere.

Walter Heurtley's pioneering synthesis of pottery-based chronological correlations and interregional comparisons for the EBA in Macedonia[161] was subsequently expanded and elaborated in the publications of Kastanas and Sitagroi,[162] updated and clarified at Sindos and Torone,[163] and recently reviewed anew.[164] Based on these works, the key Macedonian sites with material comparable to Methone can be grouped as follows:

Early Phases/EBA I:
Servia 8, Kastanas Level 28, Sindos (EBA I–II), Kritsana I–II, Agios Mamas Pits D33 and E33, Torone I, Pentapolis I, Dikili Tash IIIa, Sitagroi IV–Va, and Skala Sotiros I.

Middle Phases/EBA II:
Kastanas Levels 27–24, Axiochori Pits S33, SE33/34, I33, and Z39, Perivolaki/Saratsé Pits I33

and Z40, Sindos (EBA I–II), Agios Athanassios Thesssalonikis (advanced EBA II), Kritsana III–IV, Torone II, Agios Mamas Pits D29 and E31, Agios Mamas cemetery (advanced EBA II–early EBA III),[165] Pentapolis II, Dikili Tash IIIb, Sitagroi Va–Vb, and Skala Sotiros II.

Late Phases/EBA III:
Armenochori, Archontiko IV–III, Kastanas Levels 23–22b, Axiochori Pit S30, Kritsana V, Agios Mamas Level 18, Sitagroi Vb.

Transitional EBA–early MBA:
Cemeteries at Goules and Xeropigado Kozanis. Archontiko II, Kastanas Levels 22A–21, Kritsana VI, Agios Mamas Pits D27–25 and Levels 17–16, and Torone III.[166]

Both vessel shape and fabric are useful indicators of date. The chronological sequence is best seen in the typology of bowls, which range from early conical forms with incurving rims, in shell-rich fabrics reminiscent of late FN traditions (for example, **4/37**, **4/38** [MEΘ 4886, MEΘ 4887]), to large shallow phialai in medium-fine sandy fabric, with strongly carinated or T-rims typical of the more advanced stages of the EBA (**4/40**, **4/42** [MEΘ 5047, MEΘ 5090]), and a deeper form with flaring rim, in polished fine gray fabric typical of the EBA–MBA transition (**4/41** [MEΘ 5089]).

The potters of the period expanded the material, formal, technical, and functional possibilities of their craft, keeping pace with the novelties of the time while also observing time-honored traditions.[167] They experimented with clay recipes and firing methods to achieve both dark- and bright-colored fabrics and surfaces, produced a broad repertoire of forms suitable to serve many different needs, and shifted attention from surface decoration to mastery of raw material and size. Ceramic kilns dating to this period have been excavated at Sindos on the west Thermaic Gulf, and at Agios Mamas and Polychrono in Chalkidike.[168] A noteworthy abundance of coarse fragments from storage jars among the fill and on the floor of the kiln at Polychrono points to the functional priorities related to the potter's craft in this period (although it is not reported whether this particular installation served exclusively for the firing of storage ware).

The spectrum of shapes at ancient Methone (as everywhere else) encompasses small to medium-sized containers for liquid transport, serving, and drinking: cups, kantharoi, jugs, and jars; medium- to large-capacity bowls, suitable for collective food presentation and consumption; heavy cooking and/or industrial ware; and a variety of large storage jars and pithoi, including two fragments from specialized water containers(?). Such diverse ceramics accommodated the significantly varied repertory of foods and drinks—land- and sea-based, vegetal and animal—that were cooked and consumed by the EBA households: new species of cereals and oil-producing seeds, acorns, fruit, wine, milk and other dairy, stew meat from livestock and game, and many types of fish and shellfish.[169] Size gradation and stylistic variation can be seen not only among but also within shape categories, notably in the bowls and storage jars, which are best represented numerically. Formal variability is evident across both space and time, as is illustrated in the seriation of variously sized open and closed vessels at Kastanas and Agios Athanassios,[170] cups and bowls at Sitagroi,[171] and pithoi at Archontiko.[172] At the miniature end of the size spectrum, a couple of cups and kanthariskoi may have contained sparingly apportioned herbs, medicines, potions, and exotic foods;[173] and/or they served as symbolic representations of drink-related material culture and behaviors.[174]

Five different fabrics, fine to coarse, were in use, almost all rooted in earlier ceramic traditions. Some were interchangeable across formal and functional categories.

*Fabric 2b. Fine, dark-fired and dark-burnished (**4/34** [ΜΕΘ 5021], **4/36** [ΜΕΘ 4326])*
This fine, dark, and strong fabric echoes the LN–FN Fabrics 2 and 2a (see above), and is represented by two early bowls of EBA I-II date. Of these, **4/34** (ΜΕΘ 5021) is further indebted to earlier techniques for its black-polished surface and white-filled incised technique of decoration;[175] in contrast, the lattice decorative motif and its arrangement below the offset vessel rim belong to the EBA. **4/36** (ΜΕΘ 4326), a gray-burnished and mottled body fragment, clearly recalls FN techniques of surface treatment, but also finds EBA I parallels in gray-burnished wares from Torone I and Pentapolis I;[176] its tubular horizontal lug is likewise distinctive and widespread in the EBA.

*FN Fabric 5. Shell-rich, dark-fired (**4/37** [ΜΕΘ 4886], **4/45** [ΜΕΘ 4287], **4/46** [ΜΕΘ 5612])*
The dark, shell-rich fabric first seen in the late FN (see above) survives in two small/miniature cups (**4/45** [ΜΕΘ 4287], **4/46** [ΜΕΘ 5612]) and a large bowl with incurving rim (**4/37** [ΜΕΘ 4886]). All three can be dated early, to the EBA I or II, to judge from their well-documented comparanda (see catalogue).

*Fabric 6 (Fig. 4.8a). Sandy and micaceous, medium-fine, red-fired, and burnished (**4/35** [ΜΕΘ 4332], **4/39** [ΜΕΘ 4991], **4/40** [ΜΕΘ 5047], **4/42** [ΜΕΘ 5090], **4/43** [ΜΕΘ 1582]), and*
*Fabric 6a, fine variation with sharply layered ("sandwiched") core (**4/48** [ΜΕΘ 4183])*
The distinctive fine fabric of the EBA, in use throughout the period and across shapes, is of quite good quality—although somewhat heavier than earlier fine wares.[177] Its few non-plastic components (sand, mica, small pebbles, some thin shell fragments) may have been naturally mixed in the clay rather than added as temper, as was also previously the case with Neolithic Fabric 1 (see above). Oxidized firing was not always thorough, resulting in the occasional patchy core and clouds. The finer variation (Fabric 6a) features a "sandwiched" section with sharply layered oxidized mantle and grayish core, indicating a rapid cooling process.[178] Surfaces are well burnished, monochrome or mottled in a spectrum of bright to dark hues of buff, red-brown, gray, and black. Both open and closed shapes are represented, ranging from small to large: a cup (**4/43** [ΜΕΘ 1582]), an "amphoriskos" (**4/48** [ΜΕΘ 4183]), a jug or S-profile pot (**4/35** [ΜΕΘ 4332]), and an assortment of capacious bowls (**4/39** [ΜΕΘ 4991], **4/40** [ΜΕΘ 5047], **4/42** [ΜΕΘ 5090]).

*Fabric 7 (Fig. 4.8b). Fine, gray-fired, and burnished; late EBA–early MBA (**4/41** [ΜΕΘ 5089], **4/44** [ΜΕΘ 4251], **4/47** [ΜΕΘ 5622], **4/49** [ΜΕΘ 4272])*
This very fine, slightly micaceous fabric is well fired to dark or light gray, probably in reduced conditions; one example, **4/47** (ΜΕΘ 5622), has a "sandwiched" section of darker and lighter gray. The color range of the carefully burnished surfaces includes buff, light gray, and dark gray-brown. Shapes include a medium-sized deep bowl with large flaring rim (**4/41** [ΜΕΘ 5089]), a beveled-rim jug (**4/49** [ΜΕΘ 4272]), and two miniature(?) kantharoi (**4/44** [ΜΕΘ 4251], **4/47** [ΜΕΘ 5622]), all distinctive of the transitional EBA–MBA phase.

The latest in a long tradition of fine gray-/black-colored ceramics since the Neolithic, gray-burnished wares became widespread in the Aegean, the Balkans, and Anatolia during the later stages of the EBA and continued throughout the MBA, eventually leading to the wheelmade Gray Minyan ware characteristic of the latter period.[179] Handmade gray-burnished pottery of late EBA–early MBA date has been reported from Torone Phases III and IV,[180] Agios Mamas,[181] and Pefkakia,[182] as well as from the Early Helladic IIIC levels at Lerna IV, Nemea, Tiryns, Olympia, Pelikata, and possibly Lefkandi.[183]

Fabric 8 (Fig. 4.8c). "Amphora" fabric: Medium-fine, micaceous, with mineral and organic temper; striated (4/50 [ΜΕΘ 4872], 4/52 [ΜΕΘ 5083], 4/53 [ΜΕΘ 5613])

Strong and compact, this new fabric seems specifically meant for large storage containers. It contains a variety of small-sized lithic inclusions (temper?)—silicates, feldspar, limestone(?), other pebbles—as well as a little vegetal matter evident in the carbonized core. Surfaces are very carefully striated and slipped, and may have been burnished on the exterior but not inside. **4/50** (ΜΕΘ 4872) belongs to a bucket-shaped jar, suitable for keeping dry goods. **4/52** (ΜΕΘ 5083) and especially **4/53** (ΜΕΘ 5613) have features typical of water jars: hard-fired reddish fabric, fine and dense striations, restricted neck/mouth, and plastic rope bands at the shoulder/neck.[184]

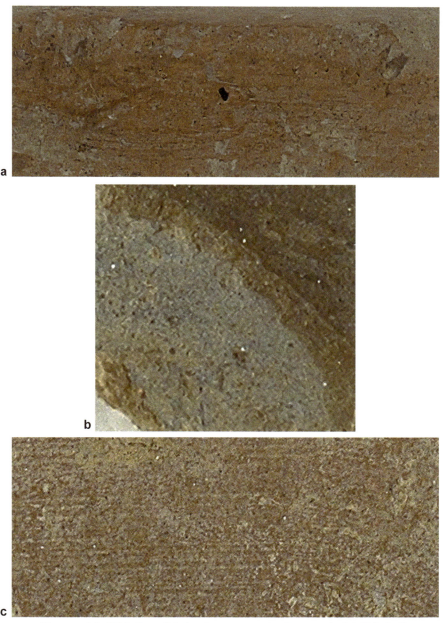

FIGURE 4.8. EBA finer fabrics (macroscopic close-ups): (a) Fabric 6, (b) Fabric 7, (c) Fabric 8. Photos M. Nikolaidou

*Fabric 9 (Fig. 4.9a, b). Medium–coarse with mineral, shell, and organic inclusions; dark-fired (**4/38** [MEΘ 4887], **4/51** [MEΘ 5023], **4/54** [MEΘ 5623], **4/59** [MEΘ 4869]).*

Heavy in sand, mica, miscellaneous pebbles, silicate, and shell, this fabric was prepared from a clay or clays (combined together) that were likely mined from coastal beds rich in such components, and possibly tempered with additional organic matter. The recipe seems similar to the ones used for the earlier or finer Fabrics 1, 4 and 6, but it has more abundant and heterogeneous non-plastics. **4/59** (MEΘ 4869, Fig. 4.9b) and **4/51** (MEΘ 5023), in particular, have a very high shell content, including even whole valves of tiny mussels (*Mytilus*) and limpets (identified macroscopically by Rena Veropoulidou). These "conglomerate" clays must have been challenging to shape and fire;[185] although the potters resorted to careful slipping and burnishing in order to ensure compactness and impermeability, the fabric remained rather loose and grainy, unevenly and insufficiently fired—as exemplified by the "muddy" texture of **4/38** (MEΘ 4887). Conversely, the crafters may have appreciated the relative accessibility of such "naturally tempered" raw material which they used throughout the period and possibly later, perhaps in order to expedite the production of various large containers. A heavy conical bowl (**4/38** [MEΘ 4887]), suitable for preparing and serving thick porridges and stews,[186] two jars (**4/51** [MEΘ 5023], **4/54** [MEΘ 5623]), and a leg from a tripod cooker (**4/59** [MEΘ 4869]) were inventoried; additional lugs, legs, bases, and body fragments of similar vessels also exist.

*Fabric 10 (Fig. 4.9c). Cooking fabric, coarse (**4/57** [MEΘ 4256], **4/58** [MEΘ 4264], **4/60** [MEΘ 5652]) and Fabric 10a, finer variation (**4/55** [MEΘ 2008], **4/56** [MEΘ 4182])*

Both coarse and fine variations of this fabric contain the array of heat-conductive and refractory non-plastics that are typical of cookware since the Neolithic: lots of mica and heavy lithic temper including silicate, calcite(?), igneous rocks, and miscellaneous pebbles. The bright red color of the fabric indicates strongly oxidized firing, possibly also subsequent refirings as a result of use. Deep carbon penetration of the walls, extensive soot, and overall wear attest to heavy-duty use around fire. This fabric was versatile and long-lived. It was used for vessels as diverse as large cooking jars (**4/58** [MEΘ 4264], **4/60** [MEΘ 5652]: the former is more enigmatic, perhaps some sort of heavy pan rather than a jar), a stand or pyraunos(?) (**4/57** [MEΘ 4256]), a rather large lekane (**4/56** [MEΘ 4182]), and a small dipper jug (**4/55** [MEΘ 2008]).[187] On the basis of comparative material (see catalogue), a middle to late EBA date is likely for the cooking jars and the jug, while the lekane and the stand/pyraunos(?) date to the onset of the MBA at the earliest, and possibly as late as the LBA.

In addition to the above identifiable cooking and storage pottery in Fabrics 9 and 10, a few other coarse fragments probably belonged to kitchen and/or industrial ware,[188] including pans[189] or "griddles"(?) with multiple depressions on one surface.[190] A couple of sherds with deeply scored interior recall dairy-making churns, examples of which have been identified at Torone and Mesimeriani Toumba.[191] There are also some thick, slab-like fragmentary objects with intentionally(?) rounded edges—possibly repurposed sherds from very large vessels (including MEΘ 4890 and 4980 [not catalogued])—which may have served as palettes or rubbers. A very modest sample, all in all, and yet diversified enough to echo a range of culinary habits and technologies, such as are attested by the rich record of ecofacts, cookware and other related artifacts, and kitchen installations at many sites across Macedonia.[192]

BEYOND THE SITE

Carrying on a long tradition of habitation at the favorable coastal promontory of the East Hill, and expanding farther inland with settlement and cemetery, the site at ancient Methone features prominently in the geographical and cultural landscape of EBA northern Pieria. Its topography, layout, and surviving material culture resonate (on however modest a scale) with trends of wider validity across Macedonia and beyond.[193]

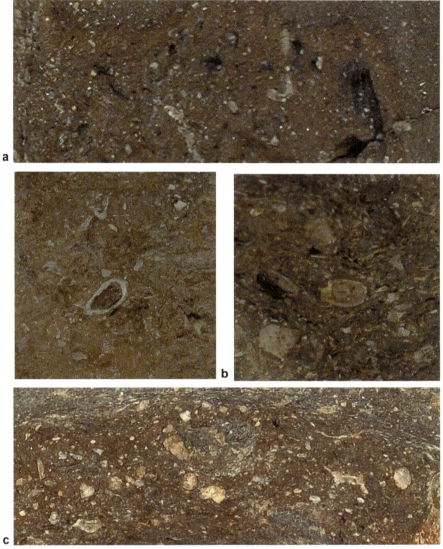

FIGURE 4.9. EBA coarser fabrics (macroscopic close-ups): (a) and (b) Fabric 9 (b showing details of two fragments of the same vessel), (c) Fabric 10. Photos M. Nikolaidou

Archaeological and geoarchaeological research in northern Pieria has documented a shift away from the Neolithic practice of flat extended sites, to more spatially restricted locales with long sequences of occupation during the Bronze Age and afterward.[194] EBA habitation at ancient Methone, Methone-Koutsouro, and Palaia Chrani A exemplify this trend—all three sites spanning the entire Bronze Age. Palaia Chrani was located upland on the Pieria mountains, as was also Sevasti, a shorter-lived site with only an EBA horizon. Kitros–Hassan Vrysi, another inland settlement with a relatively short life in the late FN/incipient EBA, was situated on the Pieria foothills but overlooking the lagoon of Korinos, as discussed above. In contrast, the coastal promontories at ancient Methone and Koutsouro (both heavily eroded as a result of their location) highlight the consistent choice—in place since the Neolithic—for seaside occupation, which took different forms: continuing residence on the old established locale of the East Hill at Methone, revisiting Koutsouro and Makrygialos-Agiasma after a long hiatus, or exploring new possibilities down the coast, such as Korinos Toumbes very close to the lagoon. EBA presence at Makrygialos and Korinos is attested by burial evidence only; an organized cemetery existed at Makrygialos and an additional single grave was dug within the LN I boundary ditch, while EBA burials were located within the MBA cemetery at Korinos. From the MBA onward, a network of settlements—some long-lived, others more ephemeral—crisscrossed the land of northern Pieria from mountains to coast. Outstanding among those is the LBA Pydna Toumba (now severely eroded), a few kilometers north of the ancient Macedonian city. Geoarchaeological[195] and archaeological evidence brings into focus the long prehistory and permanence, albeit with possible interruptions, of what became the two most important urban centers of ancient Pieria: the harbors of Methone[196] and Pydna.[197]

Although our current understanding of Bronze Age Pieria does not allow direct comparisons with the settlement "hierarchies" in central and east Macedonia, nodal locales such as ancient Methone and Pydna may nevertheless be compared to other important Bronze Age "emporia" established on the Macedonian coasts, which enjoyed long-lasting and thriving lives in antiquity. North of Methone, the double trapeza of Sindos/Nea Anchialos was situated on the west Thermaic Gulf and in proximity to the gold-bearing Gallikos river (ancient Εχέδωρος); its first horizons date to the LBA, but earlier evidence in its vicinity dates to the LN–EBA.[198] Toumba Thessalonikis was first settled at the end of the EBA at the hub of the Thermaic Gulf,[199] where the capital city of ancient Therme/Thessaloniki would later develop.[200] Prehistoric Torone was founded at the very beginning of the EBA on the coastal promontory of Lekythos in Sithonia.[201] In addition to such key locations of diachronic resilience, a host of other coastal or near-coastal sites emerged along the northern Greek shores from the start of the EBA on—some newly established but others building upon earlier settlements close by, with lives of either brief episodic existence or durable stability.[202] Those around the Thermaic Gulf, north and east of Methone, included Agios Athanassios Thessalonikis, Archontiko, Mesimeriani Toumba Trilofou, and Kritsana,[203] while more settlements dotted the shores of Chalkidike and east Macedonia.[204]

Excavated archaeofauna at both coastal and inland sites provide evidence for increasing reliance on marine resources by the Bronze Age populations, who fished on a more intense scale and for a greater variety of species than their Neolithic predecessors; they did so most actively at coastal sites close to river confluences or outlets.[205] We can plausibly assume that the inhabitants of EBA Methone, favorably situated as they were at the convergence of diverse aquatic environments, engaged in such profitable fishing and shellfishing, of which there is plenty of onsite evidence in later times (see Livarda et al., Chapter 10). It is also likely that they explored the opportunities open to them via sea routes and navigable rivers, as did many other neighbors and contemporaries around the north Aegean.

The engagement of Macedonian communities in sea- and land-traveled networks connecting the EBA Aegean, the Balkans, and Anatolia is not documented only by widely shared techniques and styles, both mainstream and those more specialized[206]—an example of the latter being the imported EH "sauceboats" and local imitations thereof at Torone.[207] Connectivity and interaction are further highlighted by a range of exotic or foreign-inspired artifacts, features, innovative substances, and technologies that have been unearthed in coastal and inland sites. New culinary habits are attested by plant species of northern origin, such as the *spelta* wheat and oil-rich *Lallemantia*, at Archontiko, Kastanas, and Mesimeriani Toumba,[208] and by dairy churns at Torone and Mesimeriani Toumba.[209] Strong fortifications and large anthropomorphic stelae appear at Skala Sotiros on Thasos.[210] Novel bronze tools are known from Mandalo, Petralona, and Sitagroi, along with evidence for metal circulation from and to Macedonia,[211] and recent indications for metallurgical installations and activity at Krania Platamon.[212] Faience beads, among the earliest in the Aegean, were found at Agios Mamas, including one piece from the settlement and a large group from a woman's tomb in the cemetery, the latter strung together with wild animal teeth and a gold bead into a valuable composite necklace.[213] Closer to Methone, a female burial from Korinos contained a marble Early Cycladic II bowl and a necklace of stone, gold, and silver beads.[214] On the East Hill itself, some traces of interregional movement or influence may be cautiously identified in the two stone mace heads (ΜΕΘ 78, 264; see contextual discussion above), parallels for which are widespread geographically but come in small numbers, suggesting a special (prestigious?) character.[215] Beyond the rather obvious "exotica" of limited presence in individual sites, compelling evidence can also be gained from the in-depth examination of handmade utilitarian pottery, a material category that has not often featured in the discussion of far-reaching interaction. The example of striated water jars from Sindos is instructive: although akin to containers from other central Macedonia sites (Axiochori, Perivolaki/Saratsé, Agios Mamas, Torone, and Pentapolis) in terms of fabric composition and technique of manufacture and firing, their shape and the type of their striations resemble more closely products from the northeastern Aegean (Troy, Poliochni).[216]

If the "exotic" and new aspects of life in EBA Methone remain elusive in the face of the available evidence, the *longue durée* components of its existence are tangible in the record of architecture and pottery that survived later successors. Indeed, Methone belongs to the host of Macedonian EBA settlements—many of them tells—with millennia-long sequence firmly rooted in the Neolithic, where spatial articulation and activity largely carried on according to the blueprints of tradition. Thus at Servia, a large boundary ditch defined the inhabited space in the beginning of the EBA.[217] At Mandalo, a substantial stone enclosure was founded in the FN and continued in use during two successive EBA phases.[218] At Sitagroi, a series of superimposed dwellings and communal installations, partly built upon even earlier Neolithic houses, spans the millennium from the late FN throughout the EBA.[219] Other important examples of long-lived habitation across Macedonia include (from west to east) Megalo Nisi Galanis–Kitrini Limni, Mesimeriani Toumba, Kryoneri, Orpheus Cave at Alistrati Serres, Dikili Tash, and Limenaria (Thasos).[220] More such sites are coming to light every year by the endeavors of Greek and international scholars.

The past must have been a powerful presence in those age-old places of choice. People not only held on to the land itself—populated by the living as much as by ancestral spirits, legends, and beliefs. Their ways of sustenance, habitation, craft, and society largely developed according to the venerable rhythms of tradition as well, which were respected enough to be shared widely among old and new settlements alike.[221] Change and innovation seem to have materialized against a background of familiarity and long cumulative experience. Such cultural dialectic found a durable manifestation in the thriving production of handmade ceramics, which embodied constancy and tradition while accommodating and enabling, perhaps even stimulating, novelty. Not only did the scope of the craft expand from its previous range to serve the ongoing needs of the living,[222] pottery was also instrumental for the implementation of new burial practices, in the organized cemeteries that constitute a hallmark of the period. Inhumations and cremations were often contained in large storage jars, and tableware featured frequently among the grave goods and furnishings.[223]

Long dismissed as the prime indicator of the assumed Macedonian backwardness ushered in during the EBA,[224] handmade pottery is, instead, more fruitfully assessed in terms of cultural resilience and regional diversity in the prehistoric Aegean.[225] The fragmentary but illustrative assemblage from the East Hill at ancient Methone, presented here in its contextual and cultural associations, contributes, albeit in a small way, to our understanding of prehistoric life at this important site and in the region of northern Pieria.

CATALOGUE

LATE NEOLITHIC

Monochrome Burnished/Polished

4/1. (ΜΕΘ 2009) "Amphoriskos." LN I(?)   Fig. 4.10

East Hill, #274/011005, floor of Τάφρος (Ditch) 1 [3].

H. 0.178; Diam. (rim) est. 0.15; Diam. (base) 0.046–0.05; Diam. (body) 0.139; Th. (max.) 0.0035.

Partially reconstructed from several frr, about half of vessel preserved; complete profile.

Well shaped; biconical body, almost flat (slightly concave) base, long neck, and wide mouth. The lower body is straight-walled, the upper slightly convex. Neck rises in continuous line with the body, flares gently to everted rim. Vertical angular handle, triangular in section and flattened at the root, spans the upper part of the body from carination to just below rim. A second symmetrical handle or more than two handles may have existed, but cannot be ascertained due to incomplete preservation.

Fabric 1: Sandy, medium-fine, with mica, some silicate and white inclusions. Thoroughly fired, yellowish red 5YR 5/6; no core or clouds.

Surfaces slipped and burnished, with shiny mica and some lithic particles visible through; fired dark gray 5YR 4/1. Poor surface preservation, heavy wear on the base; extensive encrustation.

Close parallels to the shape, size, fabric, and surface treatment are found around the Thermaic Gulf: at Makrygialos I (liquid containers, type K2: Urem-Kotsou 2006, pp. 118, 120–121, pl. 4.15:4 ["amphora"]), Therme (Elezi 2014, p. 97 [Type 5K.1.4, αμφορίσκοι με τροπίδωση], pl. 3:7), Stavroupolis, and Vassilika (Elezi 2014, p. 97). Monochrome-burnished and decorated variations of biconical jugs and "amphoras" are common from the LN I on, around the Aegean, Balkans, and Anatolia (Elezi 2014, p. 139, with references). In east Macedonia, the type is seen at Olynthos (Heurtley 1939, p. 154, no. 127 [red jug, plainware]; p. 161, no. 146; p. 162, no. 153), Dikili Tash I (carinated collared pots [type M2] in strong fabric with calcareous and silicate inclusions, including painted jugs in the "Akropotamos" style: Koukouli-Chrysanthaki 1996, p. 247, cat. no. 80; Tsirtsoni 2000a, pp. 27–28, fig. 3), and at Promachon-Topolniča Phase II (LN I) (bitumen-decorated "amphoras": Vajsov 2007, p. 92, fig. 8:a). The type continues into the Final Neolithic, well attested at Sitagroi Phase III ("amphora" variations: R.K. Evans 1986, figs. 12.5:1,12, 12.6, 12.14:3; pls. XIII:1 [monochrome], XVI.1 [graphite-painted, with small spout on belly], XLI.2:a–b [graphite-painted]), and

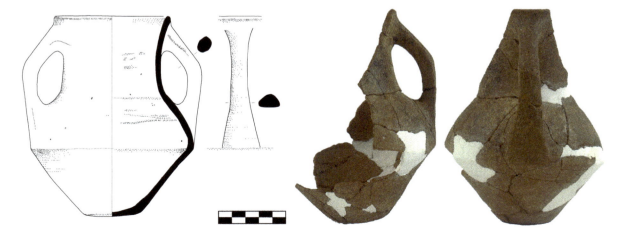

FIGURE 4.10. LN monochrome burnished/polished pottery: **4/1** (ΜΕΘ 2009). Drawing A. Hooton, photos I. Coyle

at Pefkakia, *unteres Rachmanistratum* (*Pevkakia* I, p. 34, pl. 11:3, 5 [closed shape of Type 91.1x, monochrome smoothed]). Compare also burnished biconical pots without handles or with small lugs at Dispilio Phase I (LN I; type BII.1: Voulgari 2011, p. 130, table 3.4), with a few examples attached on zoomorphic plastic vessels (Kotsakis 2010, p. 74, figs. 5–9). Vessels of this type were used as cremation receptacles, at Toumba Kremastis Koiladas (Chondroyianni-Metoki 2010, p. 217, fig. 5, T.16 [black-topped; also illustrated in Kotsakis 2010, p. 71, fig. 5-4]) and at Avgi Kastorias (Stratouli et al. 2009, fig. 14 [far right]).

4/2.   (ΜΕΘ 5626) Rim and Collar Fr, Open Shape. LN or Early FN   Fig. 4.11
East Hill, #274/085, Στρώμα διάβρωσης [erosion layer].
P.H. 0. 023; p.W. 0.033; Diam. (rim) est. 0.101; Th. (wall) 0.003–0.006.

Small fr preserving low collar and small portion of shoulder from a collared bowl or jar with nonrestricted rim. Open shape is inferred from interior burnish. Thin, shallow groove defines the smooth transition from shoulder to collar, which rises almost vertical toward gently flaring rim.

Fabric 2: very fine, almost pure clay with a fine dusting of mica. Excellently fired, dark grayish brown 2.5Y 4/2.

Surfaces very well smoothed, polished with fine horizontal strokes to a shiny dark luster. Decoration may have existed on the missing part of the body.

Use wear(?): strip of rough, thinly striated surface at the broken edge of the interior wall. Surface preservation is excellent otherwise.

Parallels include fine-burnished and/or decorated collared shapes of medium to small size, abundant in the region and elsewhere. Northern Pieria and Thermaic Gulf: Makrygialos I ("offering vessels with neck" of type A2: Urem-Kotsou 2006, pp. 97–98, table 4.6:2), Paliambela Kolindros (LN I) (wide-mouthed collared pot: Kotsakis and Halstead 2002, fig. 5), Therme (wide-mouthed vessels with neck, of continuous profile or with defined shoulder: Elezi 2014, pp. 101–103, pls. 3:9, 4E1:1, 4E2:1 [both upper row], 4E2:2 [second row, right]); Olympos and west Macedonia: Platamon Kastro (S-rim black-polished bowl, pre-Dimini phases: Poulaki-Pantermali 2013a, fig. on p. 39 [lower row, γ]), Servia (small-size bowls, gray- or black-polished and/or decorated: Heurtley 1939, pp. 141–144, esp. nos. 29–30, 39, 50–52, fig. 11, pl. VII no. 42), Kitrini Limni–Megalo Nisi Galanis Phase I (high-quality S-profile bowls and wide-mouthed pots, dark monochrome, blacktopped, or rippled: Kalogirou 1994, pp. 77–79, no. 83091, fig. 17:c); east Macedonia: Sitagroi, Phases I and II (Gray Lustre and fine black-burnished wares: Marriot Keighley 1986, figs. 11.2:16 [wide-mouthed jar], 11.3: 8, 11 [biconical bowl]).

Such vessels are further widespread in the Aegean and the Balkans (Kalogirou 1994, pp. 78–79 with references), including well-published material from Franchthi, Phases 3 and 4 (LN: *Franchthi* I. 3–5, p. 5, figs 3:a, 8:d, 26:c, 38:d). The type continues into the early FN.

Figure 4.11. LN monochrome burnished/polished pottery: **4/2** (ΜΕΘ 5626). Drawing T. Ross, photos I. Coyle

Decorated, Medium to Fine

4/3. (ΜΕΘ 4253) Flat Fr, Pedestaled(?) Vessel Fig. 4.12
East Hill #274/021007, Τάφρος [Ditch] 2 [4].
P.L. 0.086; p.W. 0.062; Th. (wall) 0.006–0.01.

Irregularly fractured, roughly rectangular flat sherd, possibly from the conical bowl of a "fruit stand" or (perhaps) from a foot/pedestal. Wall flares very slightly and opens toward one of the long broken edges; a thickening at the other long edge creates an obtuse angle to the profile, which suggests the area of joint between a receptacle and a foot. The breakage at this thickened portion reveals the forming of the wall by two or more superimposed layers of clay.

Fabric 1: Sandy, somewhat porous, medium-fine with various non-plastics—mica, silicate, white particles, tiny pebbles, and shell frr—some of them large. Fired somewhat unevenly, yellowish red 5YR 5/6 with some reddish firing clouds and light gray core.

Surface is almost completely worn, revealing the heavily encrusted clay body. Some faint traces of very dark gray paint 10YR 3/1 on the concave side suggest an originally dark surface.

Incised decoration on both sides: the concave exterior(?) preserves two large, parallel, and widely spaced "festoons" running across its entire width. The convex interior(?) preserves two antithetically arranged pairs of large vertical zigzags, also widely spaced. Traces of white infill(?) are visible on ext.

The inferred elevated form and large linear design find parallels among a range of pedestaled vessels and other high-standing forms, from different regions.

Most relevant and closest geographically are the locally produced fruit stands from Makrygialos Phase II (LN II), which feature conical bowls on tall fenestrated pedestals, dark-slipped and decorated on foot and/or body with large incised chevrons and zigzags; one example bears incised motifs on the bowl interior (Hitsiou 2003, pp. 81, 170–171, fig. 4:12, pls. 4:14–15). Other incised vessels from Makrygialos II—jars described as of "local" fabric but of "Balkan" inspiration—are also covered with large zigzags or chevrons (Hitsiou 2003, p. 80, pls. 4:12–13).

FIGURE 4.12. LN decorated, medium to fine pottery: **4/3** (ΜΕΘ 4253). Drawing T. Ross, photos I. Coyle

In west Macedonia, possible parallels for the shape and design concept (if not the decorative technique) are seen in the LN I fruit stands from Dispilio (Voulgari 2011, pls. 40–73) and Avgi (Katsikaridis 2021, pp. 143–146, figs 25, 63–64), richly painted inside and out with linear motifs including zigzags, wavy lines, and chevrons. In east Macedonia, LN I vessels are decorated in the distinctive "Akropotamos-Gradeznitza style" (the fabric description often resembles Fabric 1), several of which have been confirmed as lamps (Tsirtsoni and Bourguignon 2016). Examples have been found at Promachon-Topolniča ("ritual" vessels on cylindrical cutout bases: Koukouli-Chrysanthaki, Treuil, and Malamidou 1996, p. 508, fig. 12; Koukouli-Chrysanthaki et al. 2003, fig. 21), Limenaria on Thasos (bowls on four legs: Malamidou and Papadopoulos 1993, fig. 17), Dikili Tash (lamps: Tsirtsoni and Bourguignon 2016, figs. 1, 2, 8, 10), Sitagroi, Phases I and (mainly) II (pedestaled bowls in micaceous and slightly coarse fabrics: Marriot Keighley 1986, p. 360, figs. 11.10: 1–3, color pl. CIII:18), and Dimitra (wall frr of large vessels [one of them open-bottomed?] bearing wavy, zigzag, and straight incised lines with white infill: Grammenos 1997a, p. 42, pls. 24:370, 25:392,396). To the Late and early Final Neolithic date stands and plastic vessels with incised spiral and linear patterns from Sitagroi, Phases II and III (Elster 1986, figs. 10.1:4–6, 10.7, 10.8:1–3; pls. LXX, LXXI, LXXIV:1a–b [four-sided stands, various plastic forms]), and from Dikili Tash (Marangou 2004, pls. 108, XXIX [plastic vessels]; Tsirtsoni 2000b, p. 51, fig. 12 [cylindrical υποστατά]).

4/4. (ΜΕΘ 4257) Partial Profile, Open Vessel. LN I(?)   Fig. 4.13
East Hill #274/004002 [1].
P.H. 0.05; p.W. 0.0475; Th. (wall) 0.006–0.009.
Small, fractured piece preserving flaring upper wall and simple, tapered rim.
Traces of wide-angled carination are visible at the lower broken edge of the wall, indicating an articulated body profile.
Fabric 1a: Fine-grained and compact, with a small scatter of white inclusions (calcite?) and tiny pebbles, and a fine dusting of mica. Fired reddish brown, sharply layered in section with gray core, 5YR 4/3–5/1.
Exterior surface is well smoothed, thinly slipped, and dull-burnished, fired matt dark gray 10YR 4/1. The interior is shinier, fired a slightly darker gray 10R 3/1. Some wear on both surfaces, a few scratches (from digging tools or roots?). A peculiar long strip with slightly bent end, running almost vertically down the interior wall, may be an excised intentional mark or the result of use wear, rather than a post-depositional scar.
Decorative features: A wavy shallow groove on the exterior, at the line of the carination; a thin band of lustrous dark red 2.5YR 3/6 is painted on top of the burnish, around the rim and high up on the interior wall.

FIGURE 4.13. LN decorated, medium to fine pottery: **4/4** (ΜΕΘ 4257).
Drawing T. Ross, photos I. Coyle

Although the preserved fr does not allow a certain reconstruction of the original shape, a recently published LN I one-handled carinated bowl from Vassilika-Kyparissi may give an idea of what that form might have looked like: a shallow shape of articulated profile, with upper wall and rim closely comparable to the Methone fr, and conical lower body; double incised line forms large arches just above the carination (Pappa, Nanoglou, and Efthymiadou 2016, p. 268, fig. 13).

The additional red paint on the rim of **4/4** (ΜΕΘ 4257) is too poorly preserved for reliable comparisons, although it brings to mind the red-crusted decoration of LN II and FN vessels (for example, Papadopoulou et al. 2006, pp. 784–786; see also **4/15** [ΜΕΘ 4222], below).

4/5. (ΜΕΘ 4301) Corner Fr, Elevated/Figurative Vessel   Fig. 4.14
East Hill #274/012003, Τάφρος [Ditch] 2 [2].
P.H. 0.035; p.W. 0.04 (sides)–0.013 (upper surface); Th. (wall) 0.011.

Very small corner sherd, triangular in section, probably from a tripod "lamp" or a plastic vessel. Preserves two vertical sides and just the outer edge of the top, which has a flattened lip and trace of a central cavity. Heavily worn; many sections of the wall are broken off, one vertical side is almost effaced.

Fabric 1a: Fine-grained, sandy, with a few tiny inclusions of mica and limestone(?) as well as larger, angular shell frr. Fired dark gray brown 10YR 3/1–4/2, slightly underfired ("wet" and "muddy" in look and texture).

Surface is very worn, completely effaced at spots. Where preserved, it is carefully smoothed, with scant visible remains of gray-black slip.

Incised decoration: short diagonal lines form two antithetic V-elements, one on each vertical surface, which converge at the edge line of the corner. A small section of an additional line on the better-preserved surface probably belonged to another, parallel V-element.

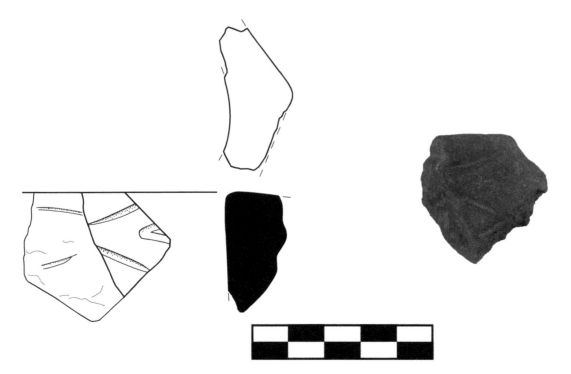

FIGURE 4.14. LN decorated, medium to fine pottery: **4/5** (ΜΕΘ 4301).
Drawing T. Ross, photo I. Coyle

This angular fr can be compared to a range of elevated and/or plastic forms, variously decorated: a rectangular cup from Makrygialos I, featuring incised elements and human protomes (Bessios 2010, p. 42; Urem-Kotsou 2006, 115, pl. 4.13:1); richly incised small tripods, variously known as lamps or altars and commonly found in Macedonia and the Balkans since the late MN—including many from Sitagroi (Elster 1986, pp. 307–312 with extensive comparanda, figs. 10.1–10.6, pls. LXVI–LXIX); a dark-burnished square "box" on a stand, decorated with white-filled chevrons, from Rachmani Phase I (MN: Wace and Thompson 1912, p. 27, fig. 5); zoomorphic vessels of different forms and designs from Dikili Tash (Marangou 2004, pls. 108.M1629, 109.M.1235 and M163, 110.M1278).

4/6. (ΜΕΘ 4328) Body Fr, Cup(?) Fig. 4.15
East Hill #274/004026 [10].
P.H. 0.033; p.W. 0.043; Th. (wall) 0.006–0.009.

Very small, thin-walled sherd from a closed cup(?). One fractured end is rounder and thicker, indicating an incurving or inclined profile.

Fabric 2: Clay body is fine-grained and compact, contains minimal inclusions of mica and white non-plastics, visible in section and on the surface. Fired brown 10Y 5/3; gray core, 7.5YR 4/1.

Exterior is smoothed, slipped, and burnished, fired dark gray 10YR 4/1. Interior is carefully smoothed but not burnished, fired in the color of the fabric.

Incised and dotted decoration, originally white-filled(?). Thin horizontal line runs just below the thickened part of the wall, possibly defining the transition from body to rim. The main part of the body preserves a small segment of two connected lines, one horizontal and the other diagonal(?), bordered by a double row of dots in elliptical(?) arrangement.

Two other, non-joining frr from the fill of Τάφρος 2 (passes 021003, 021004) belong to a comparable vessel: a carinated shape, black-polished, with two parallel rows of fine dots at the carination.

White-filled linear and dotted designs are common in LN fine wares (examples illustrated in Heurtley 1939; Korkuti 1995; *Pevkakia* I). The complete shape of the two fragmentary pieces from Methone is suggested by a cup from Makrygialos I, which has a gently carinated lower and inclined upper body, and is decorated with an arch-shaped dotted motif at the carination (Urem-Kotsou 2006, pl. 4.11:9). The rough and/or unslipped interiors of several cups from Makrygialos I (Urem-Kotsou 2006, pp. 106–115) also correspond to the inner surface of 4/6 (ΜΕΘ 4328).

FIGURE 4.15. LN decorated, medium to fine pottery: 4/6 (ΜΕΘ 4328).
Drawing A. Hooton, photo I. Coyle

4/7. (ΜΕΘ 4880) Corner Fr from a Lid, "Stand," or Model Fig. 4.16
East Hill #274/001002 [1].
P.L. 0.067; p.W. 0.024; H. 0.024.

Small sherd from a four-sided shape, horizontal on top and open underneath. Preserves one corner where two sides and the top meet. All surfaces are slightly concave, with rounded edges. The side walls open slightly from the top downward, suggesting a trapezoid (rather than rectangular) form.

Fabric 1a. Medium-fine, quite compact fabric contains angular shell frr, small and a few larger pebbles, and mica. Fired brown 10YR 5/3; slightly underfired core and a few clouds.

Exterior is smoothed, slipped, and burnished to shiny luster of which only few patches remain; fired black 7.5YR 2.5/0. The underside (much better preserved) is finely smoothed but not burnished, coated in thin black slip through which the non-plastics are visible. Some fine striations on underside may represent tooling marks (scraping? smoothing?) or wear.

Decoration on exterior: the perimeter of the top is bordered by two thin, white-filled lines, one inscribed into the other; the exterior line runs around the outer edge of the top surface, the interior one outlines the central area. The preserved section of another such line that runs down the perimeter of one vertical surface indicates that the sides of the vessel, too, were defined by similar borders.

FIGURE 4.16. LN decorated, medium to fine pottery: **4/7** (ΜΕΘ 4880).
Drawing A. Hooton, photos I. Coyle

A rectangular, incised fr of a lid is published from Servia (Heurtley 1939, p. 191, fig. 61e [possibly LN]). LN–FN stands of block- or box-like form are common in the Aegean and the Balkans, including many examples from Sitagroi, especially Phase III (Elster 1986, pp. 316–317 with comparanda, fig. 10.9:1–6, 9, pl. LXX:3). Rectangular models of tables, with flat or slightly convex top, are also found throughout the Neolithic (illustrated examples in Papathanassopoulos 1996, cat. nos. 268 [MN, from Achilleion], 269 [EN, from Sesklo]; the LN and FN corpus is collected in Marangou 1992, pp. 12–62, 162–166, 181). Although many models are coarse or carelessly made, more elaborate examples with polished and/or incised surfaces are also known, for example at Sitagroi Phases II and III (Nikolaidou 2003b, pp. 434–435, figs. 11.35–38). In Albania, models of rectangular tables, often bearing incised decoration, have been interpreted as ritual paraphernalia (*Kulttische*, "altars": Korkuti 1995, pls. LXVIII:1–6, 21:1–10 [from Kolsh, EN and MN], VII:2b [from Gradec, Chalcolithic], 94:18 [from Maliq II, Chalcolithic]).

4/8.   (MEΘ 4954) Body Fr, Shape Non-identifiable   Fig. 4.17
East Hill #274/032012, Hypogeion [4].
P.H. 0.014; p.W. 0.025; Th. (wall) 0.0015.

Tiny, slightly rounded fr from a thin-walled vessel, such as bowl or cup or small jar. Heavy surface wear does not allow identification of open or closed shape.

Fabric 1a: Fine and sandy, with a scant dusting of mica, white inclusions, and a few larger lithics. Well fired, dark gray 5YR 4/1; some reddish clouds.

Exterior is carefully finished, preserves faint traces of black burnish.

Decoration: deeply incised, white-filled segments of three concentric circles or semicircles, and a tiny section of a separate linear element.

The motif of incised concentric circles or semicircles finds parallels on pottery from Servia (a sherd of dark fabric is illustrated in Heurtley 1939, p. 146, fig. 13b–c), Dimitra (fine, unburnished closed shape: Grammenos 1997a, p. 42, pl. 23.357), and Stavroupolis (LN I: Grammenos, Kotsos, and Chatzoudi 1997, fig. 12).

FIGURE 4.17. LN decorated, medium to fine pottery: **4/8** (MEΘ 4954).
Drawing A. Hooton, photo I. Coyle

4/9. (MEΘ 4956) Body and Collar/Rim Fr, Open Vessel　　　　　　　　　　　　　　　　Fig. 4.18
East Hill #274/032070, Hypogeion [7].
P.H. 0.025; p.W. 0.018; Th. (wall) 0.005.

Very small sherd from a thin-walled, open vessel. Body inclines gently toward flaring rim or low collar, of which only the lower broken edge is preserved. Shallow, broad groove defines the transition from body to collar/rim.

Fabric 2: Very fine clay body contains a few scattered tiny pebbles, shell(?) frr, and a little mica visible on the surface. Thoroughly and hard fired, reddish black 10R 2.5/1.

Surfaces are well finished and polished, fired very dark gray 2.5YR 3/1.

Incised decoration: a linear motif. Deep thin incisions (originally white-filled[?]) create a vertical band consisting of a zigzag bordered by two straight lines, which runs down from the collar/rim groove. A repetitive design is indicated by traces of another strip and incised line that are preserved at one broken edge of the sherd.

The small surviving fr does not allow reliable inferences as to the complete shape, which might belong to any of the widely attested types of bowls or cups with defined rim.

FIGURE 4.18. LN decorated, medium to fine pottery: **4/9** (MEΘ 4956).
Drawing A. Hooton, photo I. Coyle

4/10. (MEΘ 4959) Carinated Body Fr, Closed Vessel. LN II(?) or Early FN　　　　　　Fig. 4.19
East Hill #274/022, Hypogeion. 8.86–8.23.
P.H. 0.032; p.W. 0.026; Th. (wall) 0.005–0.012.

Small sherd from a biconical jar(?), thin-walled and possibly small-sized. Body consists of two segments divided by sharp carination: the lower(?) is plain and has flat wall, the upper(?) is slightly convex and decorated. Each segment thickens progressively, from opposite directions, toward the carination.

Fabric 1: Medium-fine clay, sandy and "pebbly," rather loose in consistency due to various inclusions: tiny silicate and white mineral particles, angular flakes of shell, several larger pebbles, and shiny mica visible in section and on the surface. Thoroughly fired but somewhat brittle, very dark gray 2.5Y 3/1.

Surfaces well smoothed and strongly burnished, possibly in order to compact the clay body. Traces of shiny, dark gray slip 2.5Y 4/1 on the exterior, while the interior is left unslipped. Patches of wear.

Excised decoration was carved into the body wall by means of a sharp tool (cf. R. K. Evans 1986, p. 402), which produced a groove of somewhat irregular outline and width. The surviving decorative element is a spiral with long stem that starts at the line of the carination and rises at a gentle angle to form the coils in a continuous curve. Two short parallel lines run diagonally to the spiral stem and touch it at its lower end.

FIGURE 4.19. LN decorated, medium to fine pottery: **4/10**. (MEΘ 4959).
Drawing A. Hooton, photo I. Coyle

The inferred shape of biconical closed vessel and the decorative motif can be compared to a biconical pot from Dimini with tall neck, densely covered with incised lines and spirals (LN II: Papathanassopoulos 1996, cat. no. 115, with references). A good parallel to the decoration is seen on a deep globular bowl with large excised and white-filled spirals alternating with short vertical lines, from Sitagroi Phase III (Chalcolithic: *Sitagroi* 1, pl. XLIII:1). Other bowls and pyxides from Sitagroi bear complex spiral designs, mostly in the excised technique (R. K. Evans 1986, p. 402, fig. 12.11:5–6, pl. XCII [some with additional graphite decoration]), as do also bowls and dishes from Promachon-Topolniča Phase IV (Chalcolithic: Vajsov 2007, pp.102, 104, 106, 119, figs. 17, 28 [incised patterns, some with additional graphite decoration]). An LN incised sherd from Servia features a spiral very similar to that on **4/10** (MEΘ 4959) (Heurtley 1939, p. 140, fig. 9f), and incised spiral motifs appear in the repertory of the FN *mittleres Rachmanistratum* at Pefkakia (*Pevkakia* I, pl. 58:3).

Cooking Vessels

4/11.   (MEΘ 4221) Partial Profile, Open Shape. LN I(?)   Fig. 4.20
East Hill, #274/012009, Λάκκος [Pit] 4 [5].
P.H. 0.148; Diam. (base) est. 0.10 [25%]; Th. (wall–base) 0.011–0.034.

Two mended frr preserving the lower part of deep conical vessel with a thick horizontal handle or lug, of which only the elliptical root is preserved. Heavy wall opens up almost straight to the joint with the horizontal handle/lug, which would have provided a comfortable, safe grip. Round, flat base is considerably thicker than the body—apparently intended for heavy-duty use.

Fabric 3: Medium-fine, sandy in consistency, with a moderate amount of tiny silicate and white mineral inclusions, as well as some larger pebbles concentrated near the base. Fired very dark gray 10YR 4/1–10YR 3/1. Very extensive core indicates organic matter mixed with the clay, but also deep carbon penetration caused by repeated exposure to fire.

Surfaces are well smoothed and burnished, fired lustrous gray/dark gray 10YR 5/1–4/1; some lighter clouds.

Although **4/11** (MEΘ 4221) was completely covered with heavy encrustation when excavated, after conservation the burnish appeared quite well preserved on the exterior, but was heavily cracked in the lowest part of the interior and especially on the base. The latter has suffered heavy wear on its underside and around its edges (now rough and chipped), presumably through contact with rough surfaces and repeated thermal shock (cf. Sofronidou and Tsirtsoni 2007, p. 261). A couple of seed impressions on the underside, and marks of vegetal spikes(?) on the exterior body wall, were probably left from the shaping or drying process.

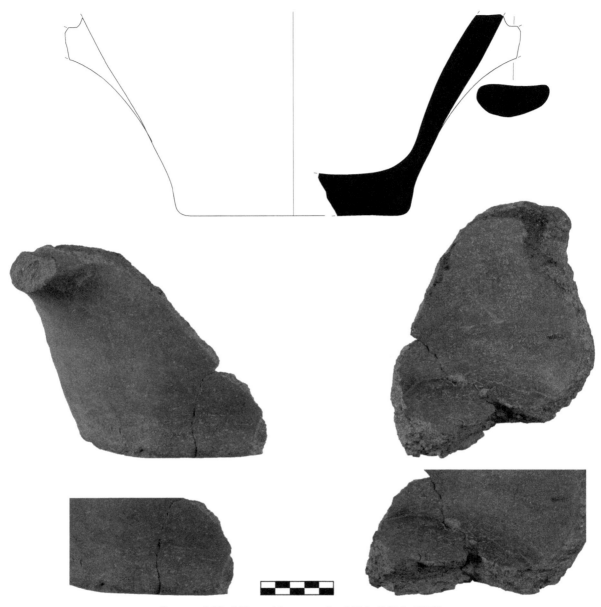

FIGURE 4.20. LN cooking vessels: **4/11** (MEΘ 4221).
Drawing A. Hooton and T. Ross, photos I. Coyle

The interior surface is shinier and slightly darker on and around the base, perhaps from the residue of a thick content—such as a porridge or thick soup—that gravitated toward the lower part of the vessel (cf. Urem-Kotsou 2006, p. 67).

Neolithic cooking wares from Macedonia have received extensive attention (for example, Sofronidou and Tsirtsoni 2007; Tsirtsoni 2001). In terms of shape, fabric, and surface finish and wear, MEΘ 4221 compares most closely to the deep, conical stewing bowls with lugs or horizontal handles from Makrygialos (χύτρες of type M3, the most common form of boiling vessel at the site [Urem-Kotsou 2006, pp. 76–77, 81, pl. 4.1:7, Graph 26; Urem-Kotsou and Kotsakis 2007, fig. 14.9:1). Residue analysis on the interior of such pots revealed fat of animal and vegetal origin (Urem-Kotsou 2006, pls. 6:5, 13–14).

4/12. (ΜΕΘ 4316) Leg to a Tripod Cooker Fig. 4.21
East Hill #274/004018 [7].
P.H. 0.056; p.W. (tip–base) 0.027–0.046; Th. (tip–base) 0.004–0.032.
Almost completely preserved, up to the fractured joint with the vessel body.
Tongue-shaped and plano-convex in section, with well-rounded edges, tapers progressively from broad upper base to narrow rounded tip. Slightly rounded exterior, flattened interior. Well built and massive enough to have supported a sizable tripod cooker or other elevated cooking shape.
Fabric 3: Clay is fine-grained, contains a little mica and tiny white non-plastics; additional organic inclusions are inferred from carbonized spots and large pores in the fabric. Fired pale brown 10YR 6/3; some gray core. Reddish clouds and carbonized areas likely resulted from exposure to fire during use, rather than from the original firing process. Fissures in the fabric could also have been caused by repeated thermal shocks during use.
Surface is carefully smoothed and burnished, fired dull grayish brown 2.5.Y 5/2. Vertical smoothing marks by tool or finger are visible on the exterior, and some more on the interior, near the base. Patches of wear, especially on the inside, breakage and chips and chipped all around.
Elevated vessels of probable cooking function, standing on tall or short legs and ranging in shape from deep bowls to shallow platters, are common in Northern Greece from the MN on:

FIGURE 4.21. LN cooking vessels: **4/12** (ΜΕΘ 4316).
Drawing T. Ross, photos I. Coyle

Sofronidou and Tsirtsoni (2007, figs. 15.2, 15.3) illustrate examples from Kryoneri, Paradimi, Dikili Tash, and Dispilio. More examples of shallow platters come from Sitagroi (Elster 1986, pp. 312–316, 318–319; table 10.1; figs. 10.8: 4, 8–9 [Phase III]; Marriot Keighley 1986, pp. 345–346, fig. 10.4: 2–4 and pl. LXXIX: bottom 2–4 [Phase I, Gray Lustre ware], fig. 11.18: 2–3 [Phase II, dark-burnished]). A LN coarse cooker from Olynthos is illustrated in Heurtley (1939, p. 162, no. 16). Deep open bowls on short conical legs come from the LN I phase at Makri, Evros (Urem-Kotsou and Efstratiou 1993, fig. 1). At Makrygialos, elevated cooking pots have been inferred by leg and base frr that bear traces of use on fire. Because their shape and clay composition do not differ from other types of raised forms, a specific cooking function cannot be certain (Urem-Kotsou 2006, p. 84, pls. 4.1:10; cf. Sofronidou and Tsirtsoni 2007). Non-cooking types of elevated shapes include a range of LN and FN plastic forms (anthropomorphic, zoomorphic, and other), standing on small or larger legs and feet. Examples have been published from Dispilio (Voulgari 2011, pp. 217–219, pl. 77:5–8), Sitagroi (Elster 1986, fig. 10.8: 21, pl. LXXI:13), Dikili Tash (Marangou 2004), and Tsangli (Wace and Thompson 1912, p. 108, fig. 58b).

MISCELLANEOUS

4/13. (ΜΕΘ 4220) Repurposed Sherd; Burnisher(?) Fig. 4.22

East Hill #274/012003, Τάφρος [Ditch] 2 [2].

L. 0.05; W. (max) 0.037; Th. 0.004.

Two frr mended into a trapezoidal, almost flat sherd with rounded edges; likely reworked as a scraping/burnishing tool suitable, among other uses, for pot finishing.

Fabric 1: micaceous, contains white mineral particles (calcite?) and angular shell frr. Clay core, where visible, close to dark gray 5YR 4/1; surfaces closer to reddish gray 5YR 5/2 and brown 7.5YR 5/2.

Dull polish and light striation on the surface, edges appear intentionally, rather than naturally, worn.

For the use of repurposed pottery sherds as scraping and burnishing tools for the surface finish of vessels, see recent experimental and use wear studies on ethnographic and European Neolithic ceramics (Crandell, Ionescu, and Mirea 2016, pp. 8, 12–13, figs. 11–12; Van Gijn and Lammers-Keijsers 2010, pp. 756–759, figs. 2, 3b). Compare also repurposed sherds with wear on the edges from LN Avgi (Katsikaridis 2021, fig. 107).

FIGURE 4.22. LN miscellaneous (burnisher [?]): **4/13** (ΜΕΘ 4220). Drawing A. Hooton, photos I. Coyle

FINAL NEOLITHIC

MONOCHROME/MOTTLED BURNISHED, OPEN VESSELS

4/14. (ΜΕΘ 2010) Bowl, Complete Profile. Late FN–EBA I   Fig. 4.23
East Hill #274/021004, floor of Τάφρος [ditch] 2 [3].
H. 0.159–0.162; Diam. (rim) 0.214; Diam. (max. body) 0.25; Diam. (base): 0.093; Th. (wall) 0.004.
Partially reconstructed from several frr; about one third missing.

Deep conical body, gently incurving rim with areas of sharper inclination, flat base. Thin-walled, carefully modeled overall, save minor irregularities in lower body and around rim. Some scraping or smoothing marks are visible through the surface finish, including fine horizontal striations under the rim on the exterior, fainter vertical ones running down from the rim wall on the interior. Four seed-like depressions on the base, and perhaps a few more, less distinct, may be the remnants of a smoothed-out mat impression, from a supporting basket or tray used during shaping or drying (cf. Koufovasilis 2016, vessel nos. K1767, K2789, A.T.146, A.T.148, A.T.174, A.T.295, A.T.1014 [from Marathon Tsepi]).

Fabric 5: Compact, medium-fine, contains substantial amounts of shell frr that seem to have been intentionally added as temper, and lithic inclusions. Thoroughly but unevenly fired in dark hues of red 7.5R 4/6–10R 5/8, with large clouds of very dusky red 2.5YR 2.5/2; no core.

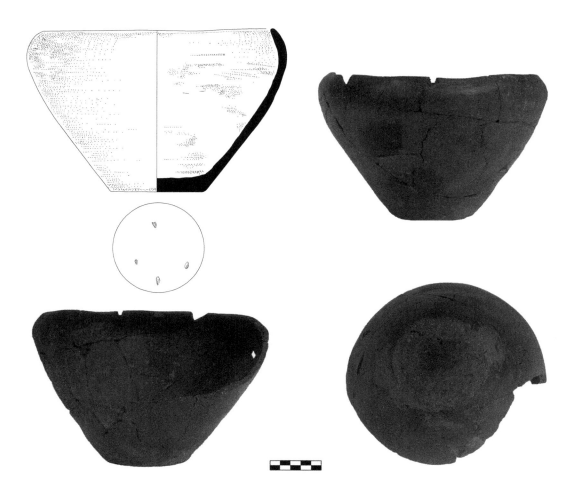

FIGURE 4.23. FN monochrome/mottled burnished, open vessels: **4/14** (ΜΕΘ 2010).
Drawing A. Hooton, photos I. Coyle

Surfaces are very well finished and burnished; the exterior is shinier and mottle-fired, reddish brown to very dusky red 5YR 4/4–2.5YR 2.5/2, while the interior is coated with thin slip of dark gray and burnished. The interior finish is chipped at spots but largely intact, while the exterior preserves strong indications of use-related and/or post-depositional wear: the burnish is only preserved around the rim, large flakes have been chipped off the lower body wall, and the base underside is rough and discolored.

Conical bowls of various sizes, with incurving rims and burnished mottled surface, are distinctive of the late FN period and the transition to the EBA, and developed further during the EBA (see **4/37** [ΜΕΘ 4886], below). They are indebted to LN and earlier FN traditions (cf. **4/17** [ΜΕΘ 4258], below). Late FN and transitional FN–EBA parallels include (from north to south) finds from Sitagroi Phase IV (Sherratt 1986, p. 435, fig. 13.6:7 [dated in the publication to the EBA I, but attributable to the late FN–EBA transition on the basis of ^{14}C dates for Phase IV]), Kritsana Settlements 1–2 (Heurtley 1939, p. 166, fig. 36a–c); Doliana (Douzougli 1996, p. 117, cat. nos. 92, 94; Douzougli and Zachos 2002, p. 127, figs 9:3–6, 10:3); Mikrothives (Adrimi-Sismani 2007, pl. XII:i); Emporio (bowls of type 7: Hood 1982, pp. 173–175, 253–255, 312–314; figs. 98, 122, 144; pl. 31 nos. 122, 113 [both with raised vertical lugs]); Kephala (Coleman 1977, pl. 29A); Plakari on Euboia (red-slipped and burnished: Cullen et al. 2013, pp. 28, 32, fig. 6:4, pl. 20); and Tsepi (fine-burnished deep bowls [σκύφοι, types 1 and 2] and conical bowls with raised strap lugs [αρύταινες]: Pantelidou-Gofa 2016, pp. 105–108, 171–205, pls. 42–43, 80–84). Important comparanda from northern Pieria come from Kitros–Hassan Vrysi (originally reported as early EBA, but with acknowledgment of Neolithic influences: Bessios et al. 2003, pp. 438–439; illustrated in Bessios 2010, pp. 68–69), and Αποχέτευση Μεθώνης (Tsiloyianni 2014, p. 225, fig. 4γ, and pers. comm. 2016). Pottery from both these local sites features distinctive, shell-rich fabrics similar to Fabric 5 (personal observation, courtesy Athanassiadou, Bessios, and Tsiloyianni). EBA developments range from fine-burnished bowls at Torone I (EBA I: Morris 2009–2010, p. 15, figs. 13 no. 90.149, 16 nos 89.1256, 90.1143, 1533) to heavy, mottled but unburnished containers from Sindos (EBA I–II: Andreou 1997, p. 79, cat. no. 30, fig. 7, pl. 26:b), and a large mottled-burnished vessel with lugs and horizontal handles from the cemetery at Agios Mamas (Pappa 2010, pp. 385–386 [cat. no. ΜΠ1556], 400, pl. 5:1–2); see further **4/37** (ΜΕΘ 4886, below).

4/15. (ΜΕΘ 4222) Miniature(?) Bowl, Complete Profile. Late FN(?)   Fig. 4.24
East Hill, #274/012012 [6].

H. 0.06; Diam. (rim) 0.10; Diam. (base) 0.03; Th. (wall) 0.003–0.06.

Single fr preserving about one-third of the vessel. Small, hemispherical form with flattened thick base and walls tapering progressively to simple, straight rim. Somewhat cursory, asymmetric modeling on the exterior, while the better-preserved interior is more carefully formed, with clearly defined contours. The greater attention given to the shaping of the interior may have been related to the use of the vessel, as a cup or container of special substances (see below).

Fabric 6a: Fine-grained and quite compact, contains medium amount of tiny inclusions—pebbles, limestone, shell(?)—visible in section and on the surface. Fired reddish brown 2.5YR 5/4, sharply layered with gray core 5YR 5/3.

Surfaces are smoothed, slipped, and burnished to a matt luster; fired dark gray 5YR 4/1. The burnish is almost completely eroded on the outside but quite well preserved inside.

Additional crusting(?): a layer of thick paint in red 2.5R 4/8, applied on top of the dark burnish, runs in a thin band (0.5 cm) around the rim and seems to have extended down the exterior wall. This paint was probably added post-firing, as indicated by its rather poor preservation.

Surface wear around the rim, patches of thick deposit on the exterior, stains of yellowish caked soil inside.

Figure 4.24. FN monochrome/mottled burnished, open vessels: **4/15** (ΜΕΘ 4222).
Drawing A. Hooton and T. Ross, photos I. Coyle

Vessels with diameter up to 10 cm, although typologically classifiable as miniatures (Tringham and Stefanovic 1990, p. 348), could very well have served "practical" functions too; for example, as containers for small (select[?]) quantities of food, drink, aromatics, and medicines, or as toys (Nikolaidou 2003b, pp. 436–437). The careful manufacture of the Methone bowl indeed points to "functional" utility; by contrast, many FN miniatures are of rather cursory make (examples in Marangou 1992). In addition, the size lies within the range of FN open shapes (cf. Papathanassopoulos 1996, diagram pp. 110–111). Comparanda include different types of small bowls, cups or "scoops," from Sitagroi Phase III (R. K. Evans 1986, p. 404, pls. LXXXIX: 13 [small bowl, dark-burnished], XCIII [bottom left: a "scoop" with raised plaque handle]) and Phase IV ("cups" or "dippers" with high strap handles: Sherratt 1986, p. 435, fig. 13.4: 6–12); Emporio Phase IV (early EBA I small bowls with raised horned handles: Hood 1982, pp. 364–366, fig. 165 no. 927, pl. 57); Maliq IIa (Korkuti 1995, pl. LXXX: 6 [with incised interior]); and Kitrini Limni–Megalo Nisi Galanis Phase II (bowls of "cup size", 0.12–0.3 l. capacity: Kalogirou 1994, p. 116, fig. 39). From Kitrini Limni also come dark-burnished bowls with rims and/or other parts crusted in red or in a combination of colors (Kalogirou 1994, pp. 119–125, fig. 43:b). Red-crusted ware, a distinctive FN feature (*Franchthi* I.3–5, pp. 68–69), is also prominent at Polyplatanos Imathias (Merousis 2002; Papadopoulou et al. 2006) and at Pefkakia (*Pastos-bemalte*: *Pevkakia* I)—to name only major examples from northern Greece.

Close similarities with the form and fabric of rounded bowls from Αποχέτευση Μεθώνης (Tsiloyianni 2014, and pers. comm. 2016) suggest a date to the late FN for the Methone fr.

4/16. (ΜΕΘ 4254) Rim and Collar/Neck Fr, Open Vessel Fig. 4.25
East Hill, #274/004006 [4].
P.H. 0.033; Diam. (rim) est. 0.15; Th. (wall) 0.005–0.008.

Small sherd preserving the whole height of low collar/neck, rim, and a tiny portion of the upper wall curvature from a wide-mouthed jar or S-profile bowl (cf. 4/19 [ΜΕΘ 4324], below). Slightly concave wall rises toward tapered rim, beveled in the interior.

Fabric 4a: Very fine-grained, pure clay; fired dark brown 10YR 4/3.

Surfaces are slipped and burnished, fired dark gray 10YR 4/1, mottled with brighter yellowish clouds. Slight wear and cracks.

Variations of collared vessels, in a range of fabrics, were common throughout the FN, including S-profile bowls with tall rim or collar, wide-mouthed jars, and beakers. Macedonian comparanda: Servia (LN: Heurtley 1939, p. 143, nos. 39, 43), Kitrini Limni–Megalo Nisi Galanis Phase II (small collared bowls, monochrome burnished: Kalogirou 1994, figs. 33e, 110–115), Sitagroi Phase III (R. K. Evans 1986, figs. 12.2.: 5 [graphite-panted], 12.13: 6 [smooth ware, rounded S-profile]). Other Aegean examples: Rachmani Phase III (collared amphoras and "amphoriskoi," found in the fill of a well and probably used to draw water: Toufexis, Karapanou, and Mangafa 2000, pp. 108–109, fig. 5); Franchthi Phase 5 (mottled, burnished pots: *Franchthi* I.3–5, fig. 69: a–b); Athenian Acropolis (collared jar, burnished inside: Papathanassopoulos 1996, cat. no. 128); Marathon Tsepi (αμφορίσκοι with tall conical neck and squat body: Pantelidou-Gofa 2016, pp. 73–86, pls. 18–23); Plakari and Kazara, on Euboia (late FN, unburnished: Cullen et al. 2013, pp. 32, 117, figs. 6:12, 1:.40, pl. 20); Agios Bartholomaios Cave on Lesbos ("pyxis," burnished inside: Papathanassopoulos 1996, cat. no. 154); Agio Gala and Emporio on Chios (Hood 1982, pp. 50–51, figs. 34–35, and pp. 272–274, figs. 130–131, respectively). Albanian parallels are illustrated in Korkuti 1995, from Burimas II (bowls and collared pots: pl. 88:1–15, 18, 20, 22 and pl. 89), Maliq II (pot and beaker: pl. 96:8–10), and Dajc (biconical bowl with collar: pl. 117:9).

FIGURE 4.25. FN monochrome/mottled burnished, open vessels: 4/16 (ΜΕΘ 4254). Drawing T. Ross, photos I. Coyle

4/17. (ΜΕΘ 4258) Partial Profile, Conical Bowl Fig. 4.26
East Hill #274/004002 [1].

P.H. 0.056; Diam. (rim) est. 0.24–0.26; Th. (wall) 0.004–0.008.

Single sherd preserving carinated upper wall and tiny portion of rim to a conical bowl, medium- to large-sized. Body wall opens up toward sharp carination that marks the transition to upright rim with rounded lip.

Fabric 4a: Quite fine, contains scant and tiny white inclusions and some organic matter (the latter indicated by the loose and porous consistency of the core). Unevenly fired, dark gray 5YR 4/1; reddish gray core 5YR 5/2.

Surfaces are carefully finished, coated with creamy slip, and well polished to a shiny effect; fine, regular tooling striations extend over the interior. Fired red/red brown 2.5YR 5/4–5/6, mottled with large clouds of dark brown 7.5YR 3/2 (especially prominent on the interior). Fairly well preserved, with only a few chips and encrusted spots.

Conical bowls with profiled rims, monochrome or decorated, are common since the late MN (Heurtley 1939; Korkuti 1995; pottery chapters in Papathanassopoulos 1996 and diagram pp. 110–111; Tsirtsoni 2001; Wace and Thompson 1912). Regional predecessors to the Methone piece may be seen in LN dark-polished examples from Makrygialos (Urem-Kotsou 2006, pl. 4.4: 1–2) and Kato Agios Ioannis (Karanika 2014, pl. 6). FN parallels (late) are found at Αποχέτευση Μεθώνης (Tsiloyianni 2014, p. 225, fig. 5:α, and Tsiloyianni, pers. comm. 2016).

The carinated-rim version of the conical bowl, with variously colored monochrome and/or mottled shiny surfaces, became distinctive of the FN repertory, as exemplified by the long Rachmani sequence at Pefkakia (*Pevkakia* I, p. 154, pls. 13:1, 100:e [type 18, red-slipped and polished, *unteres Rachmanistratum*]; p. 181, pls. 44.2, 103 [type 28, slipped and polished, mottled yellow-brown, *mittleres Rachmanistratum*]; pls. 73.17,19, 102 [types 26 and 27,

FIGURE 4.26. FN monochrome/mottled burnished, open vessels: **4/17** (ΜΕΘ 4258).
Drawing A. Hooton, photos I. Coyle

monochrome polished, *oberes Rachmanistratum*]). Macedonian parallels, FN: Mandalo Phases Ib–II (Nikolaidou et al. 2003, p. 321, fig. LXIV:c), Kitrini Limni–Megalo Nisi Galanis Phase II (Kalogirou 1994, pp. 110–155, figs. 28–29), Sitagroi Phase III (R. K. Evans 1986, figs. 12.2: 5), and Asprovalta (Adam-Veleni et al. 2002, fig. 6 [upper right]). Finds from elsewhere: Rachmani Phase III (Wace and Thompson 1912, pp. 29–30, fig. 7:a), Burimas II in Albania (Korkuti 1995, pls. 85:20,2, 86:14), Agio Gala and Emporio on Chios (bowl types 8, 9: Hood 1982, pp. 42–43, fig. 24 and pp. 255–256, fig. 122, respectively), and Plakari on Euboia (Cullen et al. 2013, p. 32, fig. 6:8, pl. 20).

4/18. (ΜΕΘ 4300) Rim Fr, Bowl or Cup   Fig. 4.27

East Hill #274/012003, Τάφρος [ditch] 2 [2].

P.H. 0.03; p.W. 0.028; Diam. (rim) est. 0.20 [4%]; Th. (wall) 0.004–0.007.

Small portion of straight rim from a conical or rounded bowl/cup, of slightly incurving profile.

Fabric 4a: Very fine and pure, thoroughly fired, dark red 2.5YR 3/4.

Surface slipped and polished; exterior is fired lustrous red 2.5YR 4/8. Interior is mottled with large yellowish brown cloud 10YR 5/8. Largely covered with encrustation inside.

Compare a range of burnished, monochrome or mottled small bowls, including incurved shapes, from Kitrini Limni–Megalo Nisi Galanis Phase II (Kalogirou 1994, pp. 110–115, fig. 33).

4/19. (ΜΕΘ 4324) Partial S-Profile, Open Vessel with Lug/Handle   Fig. 4.28

East Hill #274/004023 [10].

P.H. 0.071; p.W. 0.081; Diam. (rim) ext. 0.22; Th. (wall) 0.005–0.008; L. (lug) 0.021.

Two frr mended into a large sherd from a deep, S-profile bowl.

Wall rises in a continuous convex–concave line toward flaring rim. A large elliptical scar, located below the rim at the body's greatest width, is the sole remnant of an inferred strap handle or a shelf lug placed at an obtuse angle to the body. Well shaped.

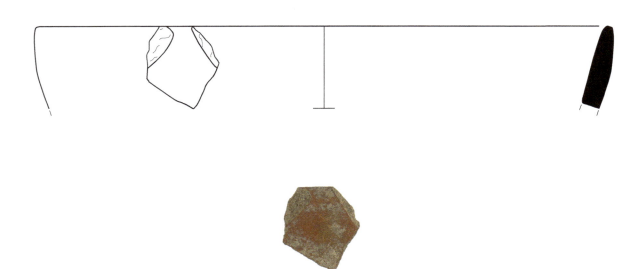

FIGURE 4.27. FN monochrome/mottled burnished, open vessels: **4/18** (ΜΕΘ 4300). Drawing T. Ross, photo I. Coyle

FIGURE 4.28. FN monochrome/mottled burnished, open vessels: **4/19** (MEΘ 4324). Drawing A. Hooton, photos I. Coyle

Fabric 4: Medium-fine, contains moderate quantities of tiny white inclusions (calcite and shell?), larger silicate frr, and angular gray pebbles. Large pores and carbonized remains in the core indicate a fair amount of organic additives. Unevenly fired, red 2.5YR 4/6, layered with extensive, loose-textured core of weaker red 2.5YR 4/2.

Surfaces are very well smoothed, slipped, and polished to a shiny effect; fired red brown 2.5YR 5/4, mottled with large black clouds 10YR 3/1, in a pleasing chromatic effect. Areas of encrustation and extensive wear on the exterior; interior is better preserved.

Parallels are seen at Pefkakia, *mittleres–oberes Rachmanistratum* (large monochrome bowls [various colors], of S-profile with triangular lugs: *Pevkakia* I, pls. 49:14–18; 50:1, 3, 6–17), Mandalo II (monochrome burnished S-profile bowls with large rounded handles: Nikolaidou et al. 2003, p. 321, pl. LXIVc), Asprovalta (Adam-Veleni et al. 2002, fig. 5), and sites in Albania (S-profile shapes in a range of fabrics and sizes: Korkuti 1995, pls. 92:5–6, 8–9 [Burimas II], 98:10 [Maliq II], 11.19 [Gradec I]).

4/20. (MEΘ 4334) Rim Fr, Conical Bowl. Late FN–EBA I   Fig. 4.29
East Hill, #274/004006 [4].
P.H. 0.050; p.W. 0.039; Th. (wall) 0.0025–0.004.
Small sherd preserving upper wall with trace of rim, from a conical bowl.
Wall rises almost vertical, incurving very slightly and tapering toward rim.
Fabric 5: Medium-fine and quite compact, tempered with tiny, almost powdered white inclusions (calcite?) and shell frr, with a few larger pebbles mixed in. Unevenly fired very dark gray 10YR 3/1 with light brown clouds 7.5YR 5/4.
Surfaces are carefully finished and burnished; exterior has a matt, waxlike finish and is fired black 10YR 2/1 to brown 7.5YR 4/5, while the interior is of a uniform, shinier black. Extensive surface wear.

FIGURE 4.29. FN monochrome/mottled burnished, open vessels: **4/20** (MEΘ 4334).
Drawing T. Ross, photos I. Coyle

The fabric composition and mottled surface compare with **4/14** (MEΘ 2010) (above) and, further, with material from Αποχέτευση Μεθώνης (Tsiloyianni 2014, and pers. comm. 2016). The complete profile of a conical bowl with slightly incurving rim, in similarly mottled fabric, from Kitros–Hassan Vrysi, is illustrated in Bessios 2010 (p. 69, lower row right). Other parallels include conical and rounded bowls from Doliana (Douzougli 1996, cat. no. 92 [burnished and mottled]), Petromagoula (Chatziangelakis 1984, fig. 3:1–5, 7), and Kephala (Coleman, 1977, p. 27, cat. no. 27, pls. 27, 74).

4/21. (MEΘ 4996) Partial Profile, Open(?)Vessel with Lug Fig. 4.30
East Hill, #274/005013 [1, 2].
P.H. 0.031; p.W. 0.030; Th. (lug). 0.021.

Small fr preserving upper wall, small trace of rim, and complete ridge lug with horizontal perforation. The interior wall is almost entirely missing, its broken surface and edges covered with thick encrustation.

The exterior inclines gently toward slightly tapered rim. The ridge lug, thick and trapezoidal in section, is placed almost horizontally and protrudes strongly from the body, the joint to which is still visible in the broken section. Slight asymmetries in modeling.

Fabric 4a: Quite fine and compact, contains scant and small white inclusions, tiny gray pebbles. Fired yellowish red 5YR 5/8; extensive gray core 5YR 4/1.

Exterior surface has careless finish, with unsmoothed joints and broad finishing marks, but is carefully burnished and lustrous; fired red 2.5YR 5/8, now is largely cracked and dulled. Traces of brown slip(?) on the interior.

Figure 4.30. FN monochrome/mottled burnished, open vessels: **4/21** (ΜΕΘ 4996). Drawing T. Ross, photos I. Coyle

Horizontal lugs are seen mostly on conical bowls, examples of which in Pieria include a piece with rounded upper body and angular lug from Kato Agios Ioannis (Bessios and Adaktylou 2008, fig. 7 [found in the fill of a FN ditch]), and more such finds from Αποχέτευση Μεθώνης (Tsiloyianni, pers. comm. 2016). A range of comparable late FN lekanai and lekanides has recently been published from Marathon Tsepi (Pantelidou-Gofa 2016, pp. 124–141, pls. 58–61, with comparanda), and a deep shape with the lugs placed low on the body comes from the Pan Cave in Attica (Papathanassopoulos 1996, p. 268, cat. no. 126).

4/22. (ΜΕΘ 5022) Partial Profile, Deep Open Vessel. Late FN(?)   Fig. 4.31
East Hill #274/054009 [1].
P.H. 0.043; p.W. 0.032; Diam. (rim) est. 0.120–0.170; Th. (wall) 0.004–0.007.
Small fr preserving upper wall and rim to a deep bowl.
Wall opens up almost vertical and thickens before turning outward toward strongly flaring rim with rounded lip.
Fabric 4b: Fine to medium, contains a few small white inclusions, mica, and gray angular frr (schist?); organic material must originally have been mixed in, as indicated by the extensive carbonized core of rather loose consistency and large pores left by burnt matter. Low-fired, strong brown 7.5YR 5/6; core of dark gray 10YR 4/1.
Surfaces are carefully finished, thickly slipped, and burnished in broad horizontal strokes; fired shiny red 2.5YR 5/6. Spots of cracked burnish, large flake on rim exterior.
The low-fired, dark fabric also compares with late FN wares from Αποχέτευση Μεθώνης (Tsiloyianni 2014, p. 225, figs. 4α, 5α, and pers. comm. 2016).

FIGURE 4.31. FN monochrome/mottled burnished, open vessels: **4/22** (MEΘ 5022). Drawing A. Hooton, photos I. Coyle

Bowls and open jars of bell or calyx form with flaring rims, burnished and often thickly slipped, are a signal and widespread FN shape. Examples come from Sideri Cave in Epirus (Douzougli 1996, cat. no. 89 [reddish brown]), Gradec I in Albania (*trichterförmig*: Korkuti 1995, pl. 112:9), Petromagoula in Thessaly (Chatziangelakis 1984, fig. 3 no. 9), Franchthi Cave Phase 5 (*Franchthi* I.3–5, fig. 67:f, j [red-burnished with dark gray core, and pattern-burnished, respectively]), Agio Gala (Upper Cave, lower levels: Hood 1982, pp. 30–33, figs. 16 nos. 56–59 [deep bowls], 17 nos. 70, 71, 75 [fine jars], pl. 9), Emporio (Periods VII–VI: Hood 1982, pp. 315–317, figs. 145–146, pl. 44 no. 564 [bowls type 10, shallow and deeper variations; many mottled or red-burnished]), Heraion on Samos (Kouka 2015, fig. 6:c [black-burnished with two small mastoids under rim]), Aigina Kolonna (City I, lower levels: Walter and Felten 1981, pp. 86–88, fig. 68, pls. 72, 77 [two pattern-burnished bowls: cat. nos. 8, 37]), and Marathon Tsepi (fine-burnished bowls, shallower variety: Pantelidou-Gofa 2016, pls. 90–91).

4/23. (MEΘ 5638) Partial S-Profile with Lug, Open Vessel Fig. 4.32
East Hill #274/085, Στρώμα διάβρωσης [erosion layer].
P.H. 0.063; p.W. 0.088; Diam. (rim) 0.036; Th. (wall): 0.008. Lug: 0.088 x 0.018 x 0.005–0. 017 (at apex).
Single sherd preserving rim, upper wall, and a complete ridge lug to a large, deep bowl of smooth sinuous profile. Small breakage at the tip of the lug.
The transition from upper body to collar and rim is accentuated by a prominent ridge, positioned at a slightly upward angle to the body and with its middle part pulled higher to create a triangular shelf lug. Two groups of short, nail-shaped lines, running horizontally and diagonally on the ridge and the lug, likely represent the fingermarks of the potter while pinching and pulling up the clay mass to shape. Well formed.

FIGURE 4.32. FN monochrome/mottled burnished, open vessels: **4/23** (ΜΕΘ 5638). Drawing T. Ross, photos I. Coyle

Fabric 4: Fine-grained clay, contains a little scattered mica, tiny pebbles and a few larger ones, and organic temper(?) indicated by the extensive carbonized core. Fired reddish brown 5YR 5/4; core of dark gray 5YR 4/1.

Surfaces are carefully smoothed and well burnished in broad strokes; fired shiny reddish brown 5YR 4/3. Multiple fine striations are probably tooling marks, whereas finer, irregular scratches on the interior seem like use-related and/or post-depositional wear. Areas of cracked and chipped burnish and wall; two elongated deep scars by modern digging tools on the interior.

The sinuous profile compares with **4/19** (ΜΕΘ 4324), above. Additional comparanda, with triangular and ridge lugs, come from Pefkakia, *unteres Rachmanistratum* (monochrome wares: *Pevkakia* I, pls. 19:13–14, 21:12–13,15,18, 25:1,10,11–12), Kitrini Limni–Megalo Nisi Galanis Phase II (rounded and incurving bowls with lugs and other appendages: Kalogirou 1994, figs. 36–37, esp. 37:c, g); Burimas II (incurving bowls: Korkuti 1995, pl. 87:19), and Franchthi (conical burnished bowl with downturned ridge-and-lug; upturned triangular lugs on burnished and unburnished vessels: *Franchthi* I.3–5, figs. 45:f–h, 47:a–b, 69:e).

4/24. (ΜΕΘ 5639) Partial Profile, Open Vessel with Lug Fig. 4.33

East Hill #274/084, Στρώμα διάβρωσης [erosion layer].

P.H. 0.047; p.W. 0.051, Diam. 0.12 (rim)–0.15 (max. body); Th. (wall) 0.003–0.006. Lug: 0.046 x 0.015 x 0.006.

Single sherd preserving rim, upper wall, and a complete lug to a globular bowl or wide-mouthed jar of articulated profile.

Upper wall inclines toward thickened, everted rim with its lip flattened and folded over the interior wall. Shaping marks are seen in a pronounced groove, at the transition between body and exterior rim curve, and in the line of the rim fold on the interior. A large shelf lug, roughly rectangular in section and formed from a separate piece of clay, runs just below the rim curve and is attached to the body at an acute upward angle, the joint still visible in section. The pronounced features of rim and lug create a strongly undulating form, which contrasts pleasingly with the simplicity of the dark, lustrous surface. Some asymmetries in modeling, careless finish.

FIGURE 4.33. FN monochrome/mottled burnished, open vessels: **4/24** (ΜΕΘ 5639).
Drawing T. Ross, photos I. Coyle

Fabric 4a: Fine and compact, contains a scant dusting of mica and tiny white (calcareous?) inclusions. Evenly and thoroughly fired, dark gray 5Y 4/1.

Surfaces smoothed, possibly slipped, and burnished; the exterior is fired shiny dark gray 5Y 4/1 with faint lighter clouds; the interior is of a duller and darker gray 5Y 3/1. Rather careless finish, with burnishing strokes and striations still visible. Very light wear and some encrustation, but well preserved overall.

Comparable black-burnished globular bowls and jars with appendages are seen at Pefkakia (Type 71.7x: *Bombentopf mit Griffzapfen*: *Pevkakia* I, pls. 40:2, 52:1,3, 55:12 [*mittleres Rachmanistratum*], 77 [shelf lugs, *oberes Rachmanistratum*], 110) and at Kitrini Limni–Megalo Nisi Galanis Phase II (Kalogirou 1994, figs. 36–37 [with various lugs]). Local, late FN parallels are seen at Αποχέτευση Μεθώνης (Tsiloyianni 2014, and pers. comm. 2016).

4/25. (ΜΕΘ 5641) Partial Profile, Conical Bowl with Lug   Fig. 4.34
East Hill #274/085, ΒΔ γωνία [NW corner].
P.H. 0.051; p.W. 0.075; Diam. (rim) est. 0.37; Th. (wall) 0.005–0.014. Lug: 0.042 x 0.018 x 0.022.
Single sherd preserving rim, upper wall, and complete lug to a large conical bowl with strongly incurving, slightly tapered rim.

The lug, tongue-shaped with undulating outer edge, is placed horizontally at the bend of the rim curve, creating a pronounced carinated profile. Shaping fingermarks include two very short and parallel nail incisions, almost perpendicular to the root, two or three small oval slashes a little farther up the ridge, and an additional pinching(?) impression under the ridge, where the clay mass was pulled to the desired shape. Well formed.

Fabric 4: Fine-medium and quite compact, lightly dusted with mica, contains a few white inclusions and grayish pebbles; additional organic matter is indicated by the extensive core. Unevenly fired, light red 2.5YR 6/6; gray core 5YR 5/1.

Surfaces are carefully smoothed, thinly slipped, and burnished in broad strokes; the exterior is a shiny light reddish brown 5YR 6/4, the interior is a duller pale brown 10YR 6/3. Groups of fine horizontal scratches that may represent use wear are concentrated on the upper wall and just below the lug. Burnish is extensively worn; there is some breakage around the rim and lug edges and spots of encrustation.

Figure 4.34. FN monochrome/mottled burnished, open vessels: **4/25** (ΜΕΘ 5641). Drawing T. Ross, photos I. Coyle

Horizontal lugs are common on FN bowls of various forms and sizes, including Macedonian examples from Kritsana (Heurtley 1939, p. 160 no. 143), Kitrini Limni–Megalo Nisi Galanis (Kalogirou 1994, figs. 36–37), and Αποχέτευση Μεθώνης (Tsiloyianni 2014, and pers. comm. 2016). Compare also **4/23** and **4/24** (ΜΕΘ 5638 and ΜΕΘ 5639), above. A painted conical bowl with slightly rounded rim from Rachmani has small mastoid lugs under the rim (Papathanassopoulos 1996, p. 264, cat. no. 118).

Incised, Medium to Fine

4/26. (ΜΕΘ 4955) Rim Fr, Open Vessel. Late FN Fig. 4.35
East Hill #274/032012, Hypogeion [4].
P.H. 0.022; P.W. 0.0275; Diam. (rim) est. 0.155; Th. (wall) 0.004–0.005.
Very small sherd preserving rim and uppermost wall to a medium-sized bowl or small jar.
Body wall inclines gently to short (less than 1 cm high) vertical rim, slightly everted; thin horizontal groove marks the transition from body to rim. Somewhat cursory modeling, slightly asymmetric around rim.
Fabric 4b: Medium-fine, contains mica, tiny white inclusions, angular shell frr, and quantities of organic matter evident in the extensive, loosely textured core. Low-fired, reddish yellow 7.5YR 7/6; "ashy," dark gray core 10Y 4/1.
Surfaces are smoothed, coated in a thin slip—barely enough to cover the non-plastics, especially on the interior—and seem to have been lightly burnished; fired dull brown 7.5YR 4/2. Rather cursory finish, now extensively worn.
Linear decoration consists of thin, deep incisions, including the rim groove that preserves traces of white infill. From this groove down radiate three parallel, slightly diagonal lines in vertical arrangement; next to them, two more strokes at an upside-down acute angle; and, a little further apart, an oblique line with curved, outturned end. All lines are spaced closely and at a more or less equal distance to each other, and they probably all belonged to the same motif.
Small, wide-mouthed jars of comparable rim profile and incised decoration are found at Kephala (Coleman 1977, p. 15, pls. 31:P–Q, 32:A–B,G, 77:AA, AS); medium-sized bowls with globular or inclined body and short everted rims come from Mikrothives (Adrimi-Sismani 2007, pl. XII:f–h).

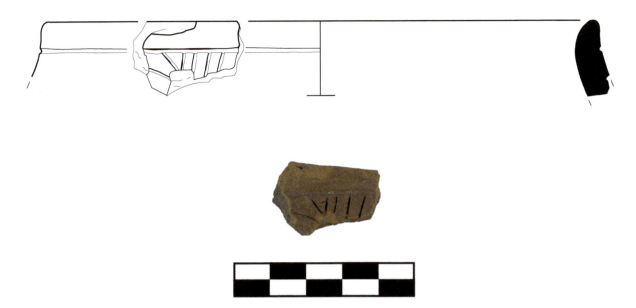

FIGURE 4.35. FN incised, medium to fine pottery: **4/26** (ΜΕΘ 4955).
Drawing A. Hooton, photo I. Coyle

The fabric, surface finish, and decorative elements of the Methone fr compare closely to local bowls with incised rims from Hassan Vrysi (unpublished; personal observation, courtesy M. Bessios and A. Athanassiadou).

4/27. (ΜΕΘ 4957) Body Fr, Open(?) Vessel. Late FN(?)   Fig. 4.36
East Hill #274/022066, Hypogeion [14].
P.H. 0.034; p.W. 0.033; Th. (wall) 0.004.
Very small sherd from a thin-walled vessel, probably small- to medium-sized; possibly an open shape, although the very worn interior does not allow positive identification.
The preserved fr is flat, but offers no further indications of the original form.
Fabric 2a (late variation): Fine-grained, sandy clay contains a fair amount of mica and tiny pebbles. Thoroughly and hard fired, black 10YR 2/1.
Surface is preserved only on the exterior, which is very well finished, thinly slipped(?), and polished; fired very dark gray 5Y 3/1, shiny with mica.
Decoration: linear-and-dotted motif with white infill. Two groups of parallel lines intersect at an angle, creating a triangular field filled with dots.
A late FN date for the Methone sherd is suggested by the similarity of its fabric and decoration to fine wares from Αποχέτευση Μεθώνης (Tsiloyianni 2014, and pers. comm. 2016). Black-burnished wares with incised and dotted decoration, common in the FN, continue a long LN tradition (compare **4/6** [ΜΕΘ 4328], above). The FN repertoire of motifs includes hatched and pointillé triangles on rounded and carinated bowls, examples of which are found at Kitrini Limni–Megalo Nisi Galanis Phase II (Kalogirou 1994, pp. 116–118, figs. 40:a–b, e, 41); Pefkakia (*Pevkakia* I, pls. 29 [*unteres Rachmanistratum* designs, including dot-filled triangles], 57:13–18 [*mittleres Rachmanistratum*]); Petromagoula (late FN: Chatziangelakis 1984, pls. 10–11); Phthiotic Thebes (*Pevkakia* I, pls. 88–89); and the Albanian sites of Burimas II, Maliq II, and Kamnik II (Korkuti 1995, pls. LXXV: 5. 11 and LXXVI:6–7, LXXX and 97, 100: 1–6, respectively).

Figure 4.36. FN incised, medium to fine pottery: **4/27** (MEΘ 4957). Drawing A. Hooton, photo I. Coyle

4/28. (MEΘ 5061) Carinated Body Fr, Open Vessel. Late FN(?)   Fig. 4.37
East Hill #274, surface collection.
P.H. 0.051; p.W. 0.043; Th. (wall) 0.007–0.009.

Single sherd from an open vessel of gently angular profile, medium- to large-sized, as can be inferred from the wall thickness and the very wide angle of the carination.

Possible shapes include bowls of conical, carinated (as suggested in the drawing, fig. 4.37), biconical, or sharply sinuous profiles, and biconical hole-mouthed jars. The carination divides the wall into two unequally preserved sections: the larger and slightly thicker one has very slight curvature, while the smaller section is flat and tapers from the carination onward. It is difficult to visualize from the preserved fr which section belongs to the upper and which to the lower body. Carefully shaped, but some unevenness in wall thickness.

Fabric 4: Medium-fine, quite compact, with white and angular gray inclusions, shell frr, and organic matter evident in the extensive core. Unevenly and rather low-fired, brown 7.5YR 5/4; dark gray core 7.5YR 3/0.

Exterior surface is well smoothed and burnished, fired shiny reddish brown 2.5YR 5/4 with some thin clouds of dark gray, while the interior has a rougher finish (smoothing marks are visible) and is fired a dull reddish brown 5YR 4/3. Minimal surface wear, a few cracks, and some spots of encrustation.

Linear decoration on the exterior is executed in deep incisions, with traces of white infill. The larger body surface preserves a hatched triangular segment from a diamond(?) motif, which is placed sideways at an acute angle to the carination, apparently opening up and extending above it. On the other side of the carination, the lower corner of another angular shape such as a triangle or rectangle/diamond is visible, spaced apart but seemingly running parallel to the hatched triangle.

Late FN comparanda include local bowls with angular upper body and hatched motifs at the shoulder, from Hassan Vrysi and Αποχέτευση Μεθώνης (unpublished; personal observation, courtesy Athanassiadou, Bessios, and Tsiloyianni); and incised triangular motifs on pottery from Mikrothives (Adrimi-Sismani 2007, p. 76, pl. XIIIe). FN comparanda for shape and decorative syntax: concave body fr of a deep bowl with inclined wall, decorated with incised and white-filled chevrons and hatching, from Kitrini Limni–Megalo Nisi Galanis Phase II (Kalogirou 1994, fig. 41:f; compare also fig. 40:d [rounded bowl with juxtaposed curvilinear elements and a lozenge, all hatched]); carinated bowls with arrangements of hatched and dotted triangles, from Burimas II and Kamnik II in Albania (Korkuti 1995, pls. 86 and 100:1–6, respectively). A biconical hole-mouthed pot from Kastritsa Cave, Ioannina (Douzougli 1996, cat. no. 90) offers a possible shape parallel, but is not decorated. Other comparanda for the surface treatment and decorative syntax include a FN "scoop" from Sesklo (Papathanassopoulos 1996, cat no. 116, with references), and an elevated vessel (published as cup) with handle, from Rachmani II (LN: Wace and Thompson 1912, pp. 29–31, fig. 9 [right]).

Figure 4.37. FN incised, medium to fine pottery: **4/28** (ΜΕΘ 5061).
Drawing T. Ross, photo I. Coyle

The decorative concept of large, deeply incised, and white-filled motifs, arranged on burnished mottled surfaces, finds additional parallels in the distinctive "Bratislava bowls," some of which feature angular elements besides the more typical spiral patterns (Coleman 2011, figs. 5–7; Tsirtsoni 2010, fig. 7:1). West Macedonian examples of "Bratislava bowls" come from Farangi Messianis near Kozani (Chondroyianni-Metoki 1997, 32, fig.1), and from Αποχέτευση Μεθώνης (Tsiloyianni 2014, p. 226, fig. 6)—an important local reference.

Utility Forms, Medium to Coarse

4/29. (ΜΕΘ 4290) Perforated Body/Base Fr, "Strainer"   Fig. 4.38

East Hill #274/004019 [7].

P.H. 0.054; p.W. 0.098; Th (wall) 0.009–0.012; Diam. (perforations) 0.007–0.011.

Two sherds mended into a curved and multiply perforated wall or base fr, slightly tapering toward one fractured end.

The wall curvature and thickness indicate a large, deep container, probably of rounded form. Thirteen perforations are preserved, four of them complete, the others in different degrees of fragmentation. They are spaced quite closely (0.005–0.02 apart), in seemingly irregular arrangement, and come in two slightly different sizes. All are carefully pierced and well finished around their edge, evidence that they were opened before firing.

Fabric 4: Medium-fine, contains moderate amount of tiny- to medium-sized white and silicate inclusions visible in section and on the surface, and possibly organic matter as well. Unevenly fired, reddish brown 5YR 5/4; dark reddish gray core 2.5YR 4/1.

Surface is carefully smoothed, well burnished in broad strokes; the exterior is fired shiny red 2.5YR 5/4, the interior is reddish brown 5YR 4/4. Burnish damage around the perforations and on the lower(?) part of the exterior suggests use-related wear; the interior is extensively cracked, chipped, and encrusted.

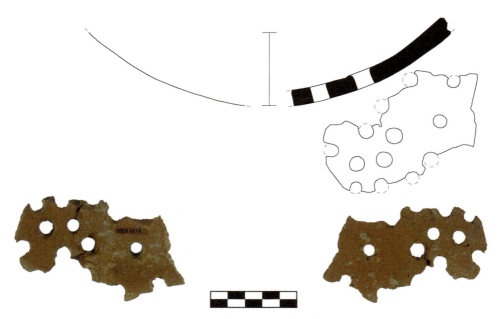

FIGURE 4.38. FN utility forms, medium to coarse: **4/29** (ΜΕΘ 4290).
Drawing T. Ross, photos I. Coyle

Perforated pots of various forms and fabrics, commonly described as sieves or strainers, are found in the southern Balkans and the Aegean since the Middle and Late Neolithic (Kalogirou 1994, pp. 154–155, with references). Some enigmatic examples from Sitagroi Phases I and II (Marriot Keighley 1986, p. 350, figs. 11.8: 7, 11.10: 15, pl. LXXVII [bottom: 3 and 6]) and from Paradimi (Bakalakis and Sakellariou 1981, pls. 21:a [nos. 1–2], 70 [nos. 7–8]) do not have bottoms. Perforated shapes became widespread and further diversified during the FN. In Macedonia, an example from Sitagroi Phase III has a deep cylindrical/conical shape, and its entire wall is pierced with closely spaced perforations in slightly varying sizes (R. K. Evans 1986, pl. XCIII [top left], an arrangement that looks similar to that of ΜΕΘ 4290), while a piece of very similar shape from Dikili Tash also preserves a base with additional perforations on it (Demoule 2004, pls. 18:1, XIV:8). Both sites produced several other perforated frr (Dikili Tash: Demoule 2004, p. 78, pls. XIV:9–10, XXI:5 [conical open shapes], Sitagroi Phase III: R. K. Evans 1986, fig. 12.10: 6a [small bowl with all-over perforations], Elster 2003b, p. 424, fig. 11:4 [a curved fr with four rows of holes]; Phase IV: Elster 2003b, p. 424, fig. 11.3; Sherratt 1986, pl. CI:7 ["shoe-shaped," with a solid flat surface and a concave perforated one]). Other examples are known from Kitrini Limni–Megalo Nisi Galanis Phase II, including deep bowls, collared pots, and many thick concave body frr (Kalogirou 1994, pp. 154–161, figs. 70–71). Late FN comparanda include, locally, many frr from Αποχέτευση Μεθώνης (Tsiloyianni 2014, p. 225, and pers. comm. 2015); further east, finds from the cave at Katarraktes Sidirokastrou on the Strymon River (transitional FN–EBA: Poulaki-Pantermali et al. 2004, p. 68).

Perforated vessels have often been associated with dairy-making (the distinctive FN vessels conventionally known as cheese pots, namely, coarse ware bowls or trays with perforated rim and/or wall, are discussed below in connection with the pan **4/32** (ΜΕΘ 5618), in the context of the "secondary products revolution" (Bogucki 1984). In contrast, Kalogirou (1994, pp. 154–161) drew attention to the variety of these perforated shapes, and accordingly proposed a range of different uses in the preservation and preparation of vegetable foods, such as straining, sprouting, or drying. Other industrial and craft-related functions of perforated vessels, as fire boxes or lamps or bee-keeping devices, are suggested by two LN I sherds with beeswax residue in their interior, from Limenaria on Thasos and Dikili Tash (Decavallas 2007). Onsite, note also the two Early Iron Age examples **7/52** and **7/53** (ΜΕΘ 4885 and ΜΕΘ 4323).

4/30. (ΜΕΘ 4967) Body Fr, Jar or Urn   Fig. 4.39
  East Hill #274/032050, Hypogeion [7].
  P.H. 0.102; p.W. 0.093; Th. (wall) 0.011.
  Two sherds mended into a curved wall fr from a large container.
  Fabric 4c: Coarse and heavy, loose in consistency due to many non-plastics, some of them large-sized: angular frr of limestone(?) and silicate, pebbles, and carbonized pieces of organic matter. Brittle and "muddy" in texture, low-fired in uneven conditions, reddish brown 2.5YR 4/4; red-gray firing clouds and extensive dark gray core 10YR 4/1.
  Exterior surface is smoothed and lightly burnished, fired brown 7.5YR 5/4. The interior is smoothed, coated with thick slip that barely covers the pebbly inclusions, and carefully burnished in an additional attempt to compact the loose clay body; fired brick red 2.5YR 5/6. Fairly good preservation.
  Incised decoration on the exterior: a large, vertical double chevron and an unconnected diagonal line (from another such motif?) are spaced widely apart from each other.
  Large utilitarian vessels with incised decoration are common in the LN and especially the FN, including finds from Kitrini Limni–Megalo Nisi Galanis Phase II (Kalogirou 1994, pp. 126–133, fig. 52:b [jar with incised chevrons on neck]); Pefkakia (*mittleres Rachmanistratum*: *Pevkakia* I, pls. 58:2 [jar], 69); and Tzani Magoula (*Pevkakia* I, pl. 95 [jar with incised spirals]). Of special interest are the finely decorated, incised pithoi from the Chalcolithic layers at Dikili Tash (Koukouli-Chrysanthaki, Treuil, and Malamidou 1996, fig. 20) and Sitagroi (R. K. Evans 1986, p. 403, pls. XIII: 2, XCIV [Middle]:1–5), as well as a coarse burnished jar from Emporio (Period VIII) which is decorated with a combination of diagonal incisions and red crusting (Hood 1982, p. 295, fig. 140, pl. 37).

FIGURE 4.39. FN utility forms, medium to coarse: **4/30** (ΜΕΘ 4967).
Drawing T. Ross, photos I. Coyle

Late FN parallels: jars and pithoi from Rachmani IV (Wace and Thompson 1912, p. 6, fig. 15 [with spiral decoration]); Kephala (Coleman 1977, pls. 80, 81 [incised chevrons]); Agio Gala (Hood 1982, pp. 60–61, fig. 42 [dot-filled chevrons]); Plakari (Cullen et al. 2013, p. 33, fig. 8, pl. 21 [incised slashes on rim]); and the Athenian Agora (*Agora* XIII p. 14). Local comparanda to the fabric are seen at Αποχέτευση Μεθώνης (Tsiloyianni 2014, and pers. comm. 2016), while a more distant parallel is a coarse pedestal fr from the Samian Heraion (Kouka 2015, fig. 6:b).

Other types of surface elaboration on FN large utility containers include paint (deep bowls with "raspberry red" slip at Pefkakia, *oberes Rachmanistratum*: *Pevkakia* I, pl. 78.8,11), various relief applications (examples from Kitrini Limni–Megalo Nisi Galanis [Kalogirou 1994 fig. 52c], Mikrothives [Adrimi-Sismani 2007, pl. XII.a], Agio Gala [Hood 1982, p. 60, fig. 142], Emporio [Hood 1982, p. 277, fig. 133], and Sfakovouni in Arcadia [Papathanassopoulos 1996: cat. no. 140]); and large "buttons" (for example, a late FN jar from Kitros–Hassan Vrysi [Bessios 2010, p. 69]).

4/31. (ΜΕΘ 5091) Partial Profile, Wide-mouthed Jar. Late FN–EBA I   Fig. 4.40
East Hill #274/054012 [1].
P.H. 0.108; p.W. 0.125; Diam. (rim) est. 0.45; Th. (wall) 0.009–0.011.

Two large sherds mended into a fr preserving the rim, collar, and upper wall to a large, wide-mouthed container of continuous profile.

Wall rises in a very slight curvature toward low collar and flaring thick rim with flattened lip. Modeling is cursory and asymmetric around the rim, where excess layers of clay have been left unpared and carelessly smoothed.

Fabric 4c: Coarse-grained, sand and micaceous, heavy with angular shell frr, small and large pebbles, and vegetal material that has left imprints on the surface and an extensive burnt core. Fabric is rather loose and brittle, unevenly fired, pale brown 10YR 6/3; core and large clouds of dark gray 5YR 4/1.

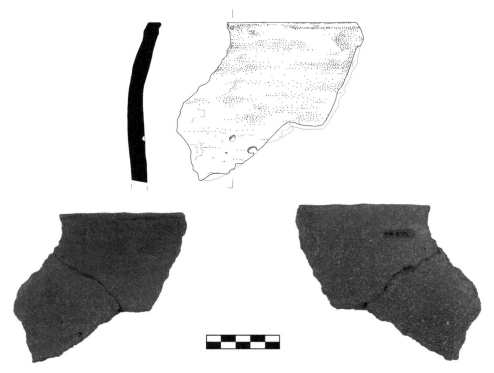

FIGURE 4.40. FN utility forms, medium to coarse: **4/31** (ΜΕΘ 5091).
Drawing A. Hooton, photos I. Coyle

Exterior surface is carefully smoothed, slipped(?), and lightly burnished but now largely worn off; fired reddish brown 2.5YR 5/4. Two small, roughly circular depressions that are diagonally aligned close to lower broken edge may have been decorative, or else they were left by pebbles that fell off the clay body. The interior is burnished but barely covering the rough shell-studded fabric underneath, fired brown 7.5YR 4/2 with some pale red clouds.

Late FN parallels include wide-mouthed jars with a series of impressed dots on the rim, from Αποχέτευση Μεθώνης (Veropoulidou et. al. forthcoming), Agios Ioannis on Thasos (Papadopoulos 2007, fig. 6), and Petromagoula (Chatziangelakis 1984, pl. 4).

4/32. (ΜΕΘ 5618) Complete Profile, Baking(?) Pan or Tray   Fig. 4.41

East Hill #274/085, Κέντρο τετραγώνου [center of trench].

P.H. (outer rim–outer base) 0.055; p.W. 0.068; Th. (rim–lower body) 0.018–0.024.

Single, small fr with almost complete profile to a shallow cooking or industrial shape; broken at the juncture of body to base.

Rectangular(?) form: flat base, thick body wall opens up slightly and tapers toward rim with broad, flattened lip. Roughly modeled and asymmetric on the exterior but better shaped on the inside.

Fabric 4c: Medium-coarse, micaceous, contains various non-plastics including white minerals, silicate, and dark red lithics (some quite large). Rather brittle and unevenly fired, strong brown 7.5YR 5/6; dark gray core 10YR 3/1, extensively carbonized walls.

Surfaces are carefully smoothed, slipped, and burnished; fired red to yellowish red 2.5YR 5/6–4/6. Heavy wear on the exterior and the underside of base, including cracks and fissures of the wall. In contrast, the interior is completely blackened (10YR 3/2) and shiny (vitrified[?]), with imprints from large pebbles and burnt grass. Microscopic examination proved inconclusive as to the consistency of this black interior layer, but further analysis was not undertaken.

FIGURE 4.41. FN utility forms, medium to coarse: **4/32** (ΜΕΘ 5618).
Drawing T. Ross, photos I. Coyle

Fabric, surface treatment, and wear all indicate heavy-duty function around fire. The large quantity of non-plastics in the clay, combined with the careful surface finish, would ensure resistance to thermal shock; the carbonized walls, the worn and sooty exterior, and the heavily cracked base point to contact with hot and/or rough surfaces; the blackened interior may represent accumulated residue from an overheated or burnt content. It is worth noting that heavily carbonized walls are seen in LN baking pans from Vinča (Vukovič 2013, esp. figs 1, 3a–b, 5a–b). The thick, burnished walls suggest a sturdy container, although the open and flat-based form may not have been suitable for direct contact with a flame, by way of a boiling pot.

If this utensil was indeed used for cooking, its flat-based shape would have lent itself to a number of non-boiling methods for processing grains, pulses, fruits, and nuts, for example, by soaking, toasting, parching, or fermenting (Kalogirou 1994, pp. 154–156). Or it could have been used for slow ember-roasting and baking of both meat and non-meat foods. Long horizontal scratches on the lip and the upper interior wall may have been caused by friction with a spoon or tong(?).

The closest parallels to the fabric of the Methone pan are the late FN coarse wares from Αποχέτευση Μεθώνης (Tsiloyianni 2014, p. 225, figs. 3:α–β, and pers. comm. 2016). Another local parallel, albeit of later date in the EBA I–II, is a tray from Sindos with profile very similar to the Methone piece, also in very coarse fabric, rough on the exterior but burnished inside (Andreou 1997, p. 83, cat. no. 51, fig. 9).

Rectangular baking pans in coarse fabrics are published from Pefkakia (*Pevkakia* I, pl. 62:8 [*mittleres Rachmanistratum*, smoothed, fired with dark gray core]) and Maliq II (featuring depressions on the base interior [griddles?]: Korkuti 1995, pl. 96:13; compare also MN to LN predecessors, from Duvanec I–II [Korkuti 1995, pls. 37.11–12, 47.13–14]). Hood (1982, pp. 247–248, 309) reports a coarse "baking pan ware" from Emporio, Periods X–VI: large shallow bowls and trays, in straw-rich fabric, with rough-finished exteriors but often burnished interiors. In contrast, the LN cooking pans from Makrygialos were constructed with thin bases and rough surfaces, to facilitate heat conduction (Urem-Kotsou 2006, p. 71).

These diagnostic FN shapes, at Emporio and elsewhere, feature a row of perforations under the rim (Hood 1982, pp. 247–248 with references; figs. 119, 141, pls. 30, 38). Although such vessels are conventionally known as cheese pots (overview in Cullen et al. 2013, pp. 70–71, figs 9:24, 33:182, pls. 21, 22:B, 3:9A), their uses in dairy-making are far from certain; conversely, the coarse fabric would have made them suitable for baking purposes (Alram-Stern 2014, pp. 314–315). The pan with perforated rim is also the standard type during the EBA, including examples from Torone (Morris 2009–2010, fig. 29, 90.823), Kastanas and Axiochori (Aslanis 1985, pp. 173–174, fig. 92, pl. 92, 11, respectively), and Argissa (House B, "*Sommerküche*": *Argissa-Magoula* III, pls. VI.4, 44.6). If the Methone pan had a perforated rim, it has not been preserved; however, unperforated examples are also known, for instance at Kephala (Coleman 1977, pl. 84:O–Q).

Miscellaneous

4/33. (ΜΕΘ 5628) Spindlewhorl, Bead, or Button   Fig. 4.42
East Hill #274/085, Κέντρο τετραγώνου [center of trench].
H. 0.045; p.W. 0.032; Diam. (perforation) 0.011.
About half preserved; broken lengthwise.
Ovoid shape, slightly asymmetric but well formed, with ends flattened around the perforation.
Fabric 4. Fired red 2.5YR 4/6, with large cloud of dark gray 5YR 4/1.
Exterior surface is carefully smoothed and preserves traces of burnish; fired reddish brown 5YR 4/3.

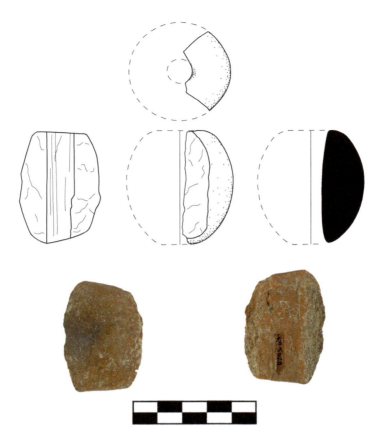

Figure 4.42. FN miscellaneous (spindlewhorl, bead, or button): **4/33** (MEΘ 5628). Drawing T. Ross, photos I. Coyle

Both ends of the perforation preserve traces of burnish, largely worn as a result of use(?). "Threading" wear, in the form of thin parallel striations, runs along the entire length of the perforation. Heurtley had described as spindlewhorls, beads, or buttons small perforated artifacts of EBA date and rather cursory make, including ovoid pieces from Kritsana (1939, pp. 87, 203, fig. 67:o–p). The range of possible uses for such prehistoric artifacts is discussed by Nikolaidou (2003a, pp. 344–345 [Neolithic–EBA]) and J. K. Papadopoulos (2005, pp. 553–555).

EARLY BRONZE AGE

Decorated, Fine

4/34. (MEΘ 5021) Incised Rim Fr, Open Vessel. EBA I–II Fig. 4.43
East Hill #274/054009 [1].
P.H. 0.021; p.W. 0.033; Diam. (rim) est. 0.17; Th. (wall) 0.005.
Tiny section from the rim and upper body of medium-sized, rounded(?) bowl.
Wall opens up gently to straight rim, separated from the body by a shallow groove that runs 1.1. cm below the lip line.
Fabric 2b: Fine-grained and compact clay, almost without inclusions. Hard-fired, very dark gray 10YR 3/1.

Figure 4.43. EBA decorated fine pottery: **4/34** (MEΘ 5021).
Drawing A. Hooton, photo I. Coyle

Surfaces are polished, fired dark gray to black 10YR 3/1–2/1, with faint clouds.

Incised decoration, originally white-filled(?), preserves the upper end of a horizontal lattice band which starts directly below the rim groove. Incised lattice and hatched patterns are typical on dark-burnished or dark-polished bowls of various profiles, dating to the Macedonian EBA I–II. Axios area: Axiochori, Settlement 3, Pit S33 (Aslanis 1985, pl. 84:9). Chalkidike: Agios Mamas, Pits E 33, D23/24 (Aslanis 1985, pls. 116:2, 117:1; Heurtley 1939, p. 172, cat. nos. 181–182, fig. 46b); Kritsana (Heurtley 1939, p. 167, cat. no. 167); Torone II (Cambitoglou and Papadopoulos 1989, fig. 16 [black-burnished rim with lattice pattern]; also published in Morris 2009–2010, p. 23, fig. 21). East Macedonia: Sitagroi, phases IV–Va (Sherratt 1986, pp. 435, 437, figs. 13.11:1–3,5 and 13.13:2,9,11, pl. XCVII:2–7, 9 [fine-burnished bowls of sinuous profile]; compare also fig. 13.12.2 [hatched patterns on and around the rim of large conical bowls]); Dikili Tash IIIb (Séferiadès 1983, figs. 64 [deep bowl with hatched diamonds and lozenges], 65); Skala Sotiros, Thasos, Phase I (Koukouli-Chrysanthaki 1987, p. 394, figs. 17–18; 1988, p. 424, fig. 13); Limenaria, Thasos, EBA II (S. Papadopoulos 2007, fig. 8 [especially third sherd on the right, top row]; Papadopoulos and Bechtsi 2003, fig. 7 [open black pot in coarser fabric, white-filled zigzag on rim and antithetical bands of hatched triangles on shoulder]).

4/35. (MEΘ 4332) Channeled Shoulder Fr, Closed Vessel Fig. 4.44
East Hill #274/004029 [10].
P.H. 0.0027; p.W. 0.047; Th. (wall) 0.004–0.006.

Small fr, preserving shoulder wall and traces of collar/neck or rim to a small- or medium-sized vessel with lentoid(?) body, such as a squat jug or bowl with restricted rim.

The preserved part of the shoulder is slightly convex, slopes gently upward to a thin shallow groove, which would have marked the transition to a (now missing) neck or collar.

Fabric 6: Fine-grained, contains tiny lumps of clay in different coloration, medium amounts of mica, white inclusions, and small and larger pebbles. Well fired, red 10R 4/6; no core or clouds.

Exterior is smoothed, slipped, and burnished to dull shine; fired dark reddish gray 10R 3/1 with large black cloud. Interior is smoothed, unslipped but carefully burnished, fired in the fabric color with faint dark clouds. Patches of encrustation on both surfaces.

Channeled decoration on exterior: broad, shallow grooves run diagonally on shoulder, following the wall curvature.

FIGURE 4.44. EBA decorated fine pottery: **4/35** (ΜΕΘ 4332). Drawing A. Hooton, photos I. Coyle

The closest parallel to shape and decoration is a fine, black-polished small bowl of sharp S-profile and squat conical body from Perivolaki/Saratsé, Pit Z40, EBA II in date (Aslanis 1985, pl. 127:13; Heurtley 1939, p. 183, fig. 56 i); compare also a fine, dark-burnished collared bowl from Lete (Heurtley 1939, p. 155, fig. 21b). Another possible shape parallel is a dark-burnished vessel with spherical body, conical neck, and vertical lugs, but no channeling, from the cemetery at Agios Mamas (Pappa 2010, pl. 8:4–5). Late FN–EBA I predecessors to channeled/rippled decoration—with densely arranged, thinner grooves—are known from the "Orpheus Cave" at Alistrati, Serres (Kontaxi, Giannopoulos, and Kaznesi 2004, fig. 4); Agios Ioannis, Thasos (S. Papadopoulos 2007, p. 322, fig. 7); and Sitagroi, Phase IV (Sherratt 1986, figs. 13.4:1–2,4–5 and 13.6:2,5,8 [especially no. 2 on fig. 13.6: S-profile bowl with channeling on shoulder]). Neolithic examples of channeled decoration are illustrated in Heurtley 1939 (fig. 11.1 and cat. no. 34 [bowls from Servia, LN]) and Korkuti 1995 (various Albanian sites, MN–LN).

Monochrome

Bowls, medium- to large-sized

4/36. (ΜΕΘ 4326) Body Fr with Tubular Lug, Open Vessel. EBA I–II   Fig. 4.45

East Hill, #274/004023 [10].

P.H. 0.046; p.W. 0.05; Th. (wall) 0.0055; Diam. (upper wall) est. 0.23. Lug: 0.03–0.043 x 0.021 x 0.019, Diam. (perforation) 0.005–0.007.

Small sherd from the upper body of a medium-sized, rounded shape.

Wall opens up in a gentle curve. Perforated tubular lug, half-elliptical in section, slightly concave in the middle. Some asymmetries in lug shaping and in wall thickness.

Fabric 2b: Very fine-grained and compact, lightly dusted with mica and calcite(?). Unevenly fired, gray 10YR 5/1 with yellowish clouds; no core.

FIGURE 4.45. EBA monochrome bowls, medium to large sized: **4/36** (MEΘ 4326). Drawing A. Hooton, photo I. Coyle

Exterior surface is carefully smoothed and burnished; fired matt dark gray mottled with grayish brown clouds, 5YR 4/1–10YR 5/2. The interior is less carefully smoothed and burnished, with some tooling marks still visible; fired a matt very dark gray 2.5Y 3/1.

Examples of tubular ("trumpet") lugs at or below the rim of dark-burnished bowls of various profiles are known from Servia (Heurtley 1939, p. 191, fig. 62f) in the West. Axios area: Axiochori, Pit SE 33 (Aslanis 1985, pl. 92:3 [medium-fine sandy fabric, gray-polished]); Prochoma (Aslanis 1985, fig. 113a); Perivolaki/Saratsé, Pits H30 and I37 (Aslanis 1985, pls. 125:3, 126:4, respectively; the latter also illustrated in Heurtley 1939, p. 183, cat. no. 252, fig. 56d); and Kastanas, Levels 25 through 22–21 (rounded bowls [*kalottenformige Schalen*], Type 3: Aslanis 1985, pp. 93, 131, figs. 32, 45). Chalkidike/east Macedonia: very early examples from Pentapolis I (Grammenos 1981, figs. 26:488 [lug below carinated rim], 29:563 [brown-burnished, lug below incurving rim], 31:614 [dark-gray-burnished]); Torone I (fine, gray sandy fabric, dark-burnished, incurving or S-profile rims [Morris 2009–2010, p. 14, figs. 13–14, especially no. 90.300 on fig. 14]); Dimitra (Grammenos 1997a, pl. 13.178); long sequence at Sitagroi, Phases IV through Vb (conical bowls with incurved or carinated rims, various lug sizes: Sherratt 1986, p. 439, figs. 13.9:3–5, 13.26:13–16,18–20, pls. XCVI:9–11, XCIX:5, 7). Coarser variations of raised lugs on carinated-rim bowls are seen at Sindos (Andreou 1997, p. 76, cat. nos. 1, 3, fig. 4, pl. 25a–b).

4/37. (MEΘ 4886) Partial Profile, Incurved-rim Bowl. EBA I–II Fig. 4.46
East Hill, #274/004037 [11].
P.H. 0.050; p.W. 0.235; Diam. (rim) 0.343; Diam. (body) max. 0.41; Th. (wall) 0.005–0.010.
Small fr to a large shallow bowl, probably of conical form.
Upper wall opens up almost straight, turning at a sharp angle to form a pronounced rounded rim that curves inward over the body wall. Well shaped.

Figure 4.46. EBA monochrome bowls, medium to large sized: **4/37** (MEΘ 4886). Drawing A. Hooton, photos I. Coyle

Fabric 5: Clay body is fine-grained and compact, tempered with small amounts of mica, silicate, and white (calcareous?) inclusions. Hard-fired, very dark gray 7.5YR 3/1; large cloud in yellowish brown 10YR 5/4 extends below rim.

Surfaces are very well smoothed, coated with rather fugitive slip, and burnished to "waxy" luster; the exterior is fired dark red 7.5R 3/6, the interior red 10R 4/6. Very extensive surface wear, patches of dark gray encrustation cover much of the surviving red burnish.

Local late FN predecessors to both form and fabric include the dark-fired, shell-rich bodies of **4/14** (MEΘ 2010) and **4/20** (MEΘ 4334), and the fugitive purplish red slip on vessels from Hassan Vrysi (illustrated in Bessios 2010, pp. 68–69)—which, in turn, recalls the "raspberry red" coating (*himbeerroter Überzug*) on monochrome wares at Pefkakia (*Pevkakia* I). Comparanda dating to the early EBA phases include shallow bowls with incurving rims (often with lugs) from Tsani Magoula (Wace and Thompson 1912, p. 144 [monochrome category Γ3, fig. 86c–d; reported as of excellent quality and usually highly burnished]), Argissa (*Argissa-Magoula* III, pls. 1:4, 5.12 [from Graben 2/3]; also pls. 14:14–15, 22:3,6 [from Graben 5, later EBA]), and Beşik Tepe (*Argissa-Magoula* III, pl. 54A:3,7,9) in Thessaly; and burnished bowls from Pentapolis I (Grammenos 1981, p. 198, fig. 31:607). The strongly incurving rim became a widespread and distinctive feature of EBA styles throughout the period. In Macedonia, the type progression (EBA I through EBA III) is best seen at Kastanas, in a long sequence of large incurving and shallow bowls of Type 5.2 (*Schale mit einbeziehendem Oberteil*) and Type 6.2 (*Flachschalen*) (Aslanis 1985, p. 93, fig. 37:3–4, pls. 2:3 [Schicht 27], 4:15 and 5:1–2,8–9 [Schicht 26], 8:17–18 [Schicht 25], 10:1,10 and 14:1,4,9 [Schicht 24], 29:1,8 [Schicht 23b], 55:3 [Schicht 22b]). Parallel developments occur at Agios Mamas (Aslanis 1985, pls. 107:1 and 117:4 [Pits D33 and E33, respectively], 108:11 and 110:3 [Pit D29], 112:7,10 and 116:3 [Pits D27 and D23/24, respectively]); and at Kritsana (Aslanis 1985, pls. 96:15, 97:16, 99:6–8,10,12 [Settlements III, III/IV and IV, respectively; also published in Heurtley 1939, p. 178, cat. no. 216, figs. 36d–e], 103:5 and 106:1–2 [Settlements V and VI, respectively]). To the middle and later phases of the EBA date examples from Perivolaki/Saratsé, Pits I33 and Z39 (Aslanis 1985, pls. 126:1 and 127:5, respectively), Axiochori and Prochoma (Aslanis 1985, fig. 113); Sitagroi, Bin Complex of Phase Vb (Sherratt 1986, fig. 13.26:1); and Kitrini Limni (correlated with Sitagroi Vb: Fotiadis and Chondroyianni-Metoki 1993, p. 24, fig. 4:θ–κ).

FIGURE 4.47. EBA monochrome bowls, medium to large sized: **4/38** (MEΘ 4887).
Drawing A. Hooton, photos I. Coyle

4/38. (MEΘ 4887) Partial Profile, Carinated Bowl. EBA II(?)   Fig. 4.47
East Hill, #274/085, Στρώμα διάβρωσης [erosion layer].
P.H. 0.054; p.W. 0.10; Diam. (rim) est. 0.338; Diam. (body) max. 0.362; Th. (wall) 0.008–0.012.
Two sherds mended into a fr of rim and upper wall with mastos to a large, thick-walled conical bowl.
Body opens up gradually toward sharply inclined, tapered rim. Small button-like mastos at the carination. Carefully shaped.

Fabric 9: Medium-grained and heavy, "muddy" in texture, with significant quantities of carbonized organics, thin shell frr, mica, small- to medium-sized silicate and limestone(?) inclusions, pebbles, and some vegetal matter. Unevenly and slightly under-fired, dark brown 7.5YR 3/2; thin reddish clouds and carbonized core.

Surfaces are carefully smoothed, slipped, and burnished—but large non-plastics are still visible through, and there is a small imprint from pebble or grain at the carination; fired matt dark reddish brown 5YR 3/3. Burnish has worn off extensively, especially on the interior, thus exposing the dull coating of slip and the core underneath. The exterior bears many thin irregular scratches (probably use wear) and several deeper scars (from digging tools?). Three parallel lines, slightly arched, on one side of the mastos may have been decorative rather than caused by damage.

Bowls with carinated rims—a variation of the basic incurving-rim type, such as **4/37** (MEΘ 4886)—occur mainly in the EBA II, although earlier and later examples also exist. At Kastanas, the large bowl of Type 5.2 (*Schale mit einbeziehendem Oberteil, Profilvariant* 4) spans a large part of the local EBA (Aslanis 1985, p. 92, fig. 37:4, pls. 5:2–4,7 [Schicht 26], 13:9, 14:5,7, and 15:1 [Schicht 24], 25:14 [Schicht 24–23b], 28:10 and 29:1 [Schicht 23b], 42:6 [Schicht 23a]). Comparable long sequences are seen at Axiochori (Aslanis 1985, pls. 91:1,3 [Pit SE33/34], 85:1,13 [Settlement 3], 93:5,10 [the former with lug, Settlement 5], 89:11,14 [Pit S30], 90:1 [Settlement 7]); Kritsana (Aslanis 1985, pls. 95:1 [Settlement I/II], 95:14 [with lug handle, Settlement III], 100:2 [Settlement IV; also illustrated in Heurtley 1939, fig. 36f], 102:6,11 and 103:7 [Settlement V], 105.1 [Settlement VI]); and Agios Mamas (Aslanis 1985, pls. 108:7, 110:5 [Pit D29, the latter with mastos], 117:11 [Pit E30], 111:3 [Pit D28], 111:2 and 112.3,8 [Pit D27]). Other Macedonian parallels, east to west: Sitagroi, Burnt House of Phase Va (Sherratt 1986, figs. 13.11:4, 13.17:1, pl. CV:4 [large conical bowl with rough burnish]) and Bin Complex of Phase Vb, (Sherratt 1986, fig. 13:26.2); Pentapolis II (Grammenos

1981, p. 198, figs. 29:552, 562, 26:488 [with pierced lugs]); Torone, especially the heavy-fabric bowls of Phase II (Morris 2009–2010, p. 23 with extensive comparanda, fig. 18); Langadas basin (Aslanis 1985, figs. 113:3–4 [Prochoma], 113:2 [Aspros]); in the west Thermaic, Sindos, EBA I–II (finer and coarser variations, with or without lugs: Andreou 1997, pp. 76, 79, cat. nos. 1–4, 6, 30, figs. 4, 7, pls. 25–26) and Agios Athanassios Thessalonikis, advanced EBA II (Mavroeidi 2012, especially pp. 179–180, 209–210, pls. 25–27; Mavroeidi, Andreou, and Pappa 2006, pp. 480–482, fig. 2α, pl. 2 [very common local shape for food preparation, offering, and consumption]). Thessaly: Argissa (*Argissa-Magoula* III, pls. 17–18 [Graben 2/3], 15:1–9 [Graben 5], 49:2 [Graben 1 or 5], VI.6 [burnt layer outside houses]); Beşik Tepe (*Argissa-Magoula* III, pl. 54A:3,7,9); Pefkakia (*Rachmanifläche*: *Argissa-Magoula* III, pl. 64A:1–3); and Tsani Magoula (Wace and Thompson 1912, fig. 86c–d).

4/39. (ΜΕΘ 4991) Partial Profile, Incurving-rim Bowl. EBA II (?)   Fig. 4.48
East Hill #274/053006 [5], Λάκκος [Pit] 5.
P.H. 0.036; p.W. 0.052; Diam. (rim) est. 0.29 [6%]; Th. (wall) 0.004–0.017 (with mastos).
Small fr preserving rim and upper wall with mastos to a large, rather shallow bowl.

Curved upper wall opens up gradually to slightly incurved, thickened rim with tapered lip. Exterior profile of body and rim form one continuous curve, while the interior rim wall curves at a very shallow angle to the body and rises almost vertical. Small, low mastos is placed below rim, at the thickest portion of the wall. Carefully formed. Well preserved.

Fabric 6: Clay is fine-grained and compact, with a slight scatter of little pebbles and mica. Fired somewhat unevenly, brown 7.5YR 4/4 with patchy core of very dark grayish brown 10YR 3/2.

Surface is well finished, burnished to lustrous matt exterior but duller interior; fired dark grayish brown 10YR 4/2. Interior is heavy encrusted, the exterior less so but has small chips and scattered scratches (probably post-depositional wear). Traces of use wear (?) on and around the mastos, where burnish is completely effaced and two groups of very thin, short diagonal scratches run across the vessel wall.

FIGURE 4.48. EBA monochrome bowls, medium to large sized: **4/39** (ΜΕΘ 4991).
Drawing T. Ross, photo I. Coyle

The shape is common throughout the EBA (compare **4/37** [MEΘ 4886] and **4/38** [MEΘ 4887]), including a long sequence at Kritsana, Settlements I–II and IV (Aslanis 1985, pl. 106:3 [with mastos]; Heurtley 1939, fig. 36c;). EBA I–II: Torone, Phases I–II (bowls with mastoi, including brown-burnished: Morris 2009–2010, p. 23, figs. 16, 18); Sitagroi, Burnt House of Phase Va (Sherratt 1986, fig. 13.11:3, pl. CV:1). EBA II and later: Kastanas (large bowl of Type 5.2 [*Schale mit einbeziehendem Oberteil, Profilvariant* 1], mainly from Levels 24–23a: Aslanis 1985, pp. 74, 92, fig. 37:1, pls. 25:3, 25 [with mastos], 27:3, 43:2); Argissa (bowls with small mastoid: *Argissa-Magoula* III, 1976, pls. 16.23 [Graben 5], 24.1, 2 [Graben 5B]).

4/40. (MEΘ 5047) Partial Profile, T-rim Bowl. EBA II or Later   Fig. 4.49
East Hill #274/054011 [1] (5-9-2003, 8-9-2003).
P.H. 0.035; p.W. 0.035; Diam. (rim) est. 0.260; Th. (wall–max. rim) 0.005–0.015.

Small segment preserving rim and upper wall with lug to a large, shallow bowl of rounded profile.

Wall curves up gradually, then turns almost vertically toward a T-rim of pronounced curvy shape, rolled over both sides of the body wall and sloping slightly inward—to prevent spillage (?). Small triangular lug is partly preserved just below rim. Graceful form; good state of preservation.

Fabric 6: Clay is fine-grained and compact, with a fine dusting of mica and a few small mineral inclusions visible in section and on the surface. Thoroughly and hard fired, very dark grayish brown 2.5Y 4/2.

Surface is well smoothed and slipped, the exterior burnished and fired shiny dark grayish brown 10YR 4/2, the interior unburnished and fired brown 10YR 5/3. Thin parallel striations around the top of the lip may represent finishing/burnishing marks. Localized damage, likely use wear, on the exterior: narrow strip of chipped burnish immediately below rim, similar around the edges of the lug. A few scattered patches of encrustation inside.

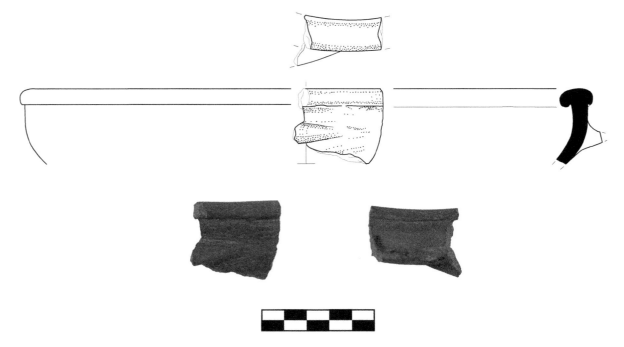

FIGURE 4.49. EBA monochrome bowls, medium to large sized: **4/40** (MEΘ 5047).
Drawing A. Hooton, photos I. Coyle

The form can be compared to large T-rimmed shallow bowls of Type 6.2 (*Flachschalen*/λοπάδες) and rounded bowls (*kalottenförmige Schalen*) at Kastanas (Aslanis 1985, p. 93, pls. 1:13 [Schicht 27], 10:1,10 [Schichten 25–24]). Similar rims are seen at Agios Mamas, Pit E31 (Aslanis 1985, pl. 117:2); Kritsana, Settlement 5 (Heurtley 1939, fig. 36:k); Kitrini Limni (Fotiadis and Chondroyianni-Metoki 1993, p. 24, fig. 4:ζ–η [correlated with Sitagroi Vb]); Argissa, ditches [Graben] 5 and 5b (*Argissa-Magoula* III, pls. 16:20, 23; 23:1, 8, 11, 19; 24:1, 2, 9 [some with mastoi]). Except for one earlier piece from Level 27 at Kastanas, most comparanda date to the middle and late EBA phases.

4/41. (ΜΕΘ 5089) Partial Profile, Funnel-rim Bowl or Jar. Late EBA–Early MBA Fig. 4.50
East Hill, #274/084002 [2].
P.H. 0.051; p.W. 0.05; Diam. (rim) est. 0.18 [10%]; Th. (wall) 0.006–0.010.
Large fr from a deep bowl or open-mouth jar with funnel-shaped, widely flaring rim.
Somewhat cursory finish, asymmetric around the rim, with coiling or pulling marks still visible on the exterior wall.
Fabric 7. Fine and compact, with a slight dusting of mica. Well fired, very dark gray 10YR 3/1; no core.
Surfaces are well burnished, fired in lustrous hues of very dark gray to yellowish brown 10YR 3/1–3/4. Slightly chipped off and encrusted.
The form can be compared to the deep conical or S-profile bowls with tall, everted rims (*Trichterrand*, types 2.1, 3.1, 3.2) from Kastanas Levels 22a–21 (Aslanis 1985, pp. 73, 92, figs 34:1, 35:1, pls. 1:6,11, 69:1,5). Contemporary is an S-profile bowl with large rim from Perivolaki/Saratsé, Pit D24 (Aslanis 1985, pl. 122:12).

FIGURE 4.50. EBA monochrome bowls, medium to large sized: **4/41** (ΜΕΘ 5089).
Drawing T. Ross, photos I. Coyle

4/42. (ΜΕΘ 5090) Partial Profile, Carinated Bowl. EBA II–III Fig. 4.51
East Hill #274/084003 [2].
P.H. 0.036; p.W. 0.079; Diam. (rim) 0.36; Th. (wall) 0.0055–0.011.
Two sherds mended into a fr of rim and upper wall to a large, very shallow bowl of angular/sinuous profile.
Slightly rounded wall opens up gently to carination, then rises vertically and thickens toward a slightly curved rim with flattened lip. Some asymmetries in modeling. Fairly well preserved.
Fabric 6: Clay is fine-grained and very compact, with just a little mica visible on the interior. Hard-fired, red 2.5YR 4/4; a few patches of gray core.
Exterior surface and rim are smoothed, slipped, and burnished; fired lustrous reddish brown 5YR 5/4, mottled with dark gray 10YR 4/1. The interior is smoothed and striated with horizontal strokes in low relief, but left unslipped and unburnished except for a thin burnished band running around the inside of the rim; fired dull light red 2.5YR 6/8. Slight wear and patches of encrustation on the interior, while the exterior is heavily worn and chipped off.
Use wear: a thin horizontal strip (about 0.5 cm wide) of fine, parallel scratches runs a little below rim on the outside; no corresponding marks are seen on the inside.
Comparanda include rounded and shallow bowls with carinated rims from Kastanas (*kalottenförmige Schalen*, Types 1.1, 1.2, and *Flachschalen*/λοπάδες, Types 6.1, 6.2, medium- to large-sized: Aslanis 1985, p. 92, pls. 27:10 and 30:3 [Schicht 23b], 43:7,9 [Schicht 23a]); Agios Mamas, Pit E31 (with mottled surface and double mastos lug: Aslanis 1985, pl. 117:2); and Perivolaki/Saratsé, Pit G29 (with inclined profile and spout under rim: Aslanis 1985, pl. 123:2). All date to the middle and late phases of the EBA.

Figure 4.51. EBA monochrome bowls, medium to large sized: **4/42** (ΜΕΘ 5090). Drawing A. Hooton, photos I. Coyle

Small open vessels

4/43. (ΜΕΘ 1582) One-handled Dipper Cup. Late EBA–Early MBA Fig. 4.52

East Hill #274/022032 [10], Hypogeion (NW area).

H. 0.068; Diam. (rim) 0.110; Diam. (base) 0.055.

Fully preserved and in good condition.

Conical body opens up smoothly toward simple, flattened rim; thick, arch-shaped perforated handle rises directly from the rim, in alignment with the body profile; rounded base, rather unevenly modeled. Some asymmetries in wall thickness and rim contour.

Fabric 6: Clay body is fine-grained and compact, tempered with a small amount of (mostly tiny) white inclusions—calcite (?). Fired reddish yellow 5YR 6/6, with large firing clouds in dark gray 10YR 4/1.

Surfaces are smoothed and well burnished, with broad, finger-applied (?) striations running around the interior wall and creating a shiny textured effect; fired yellowish red 5YR 4/6. The burnish is mainly preserved on the interior, but is much patchier on the exterior and on the handle, which also bear heavier encrustation. Short, shallow scratches (tooling marks?) are visible on the exterior wall, where burnish has worn off.

A late date is suggested by almost identical cups from the late EBA–early MBA cemeteries at Xeropigado and Goules, in the area of Kitrini Limni (Ziota 2007, figs 5:6 and 10:5, respectively); and a cup of the same form, but with differently formed handle, from Kastanas Level 22b (Aslanis 1985, pl. 57:14). Other examples of the same form and of EBA date (although without closer chronological definition) come from Mandalo III (Papaefthymiou-Papanthimou and Pilali-Papasteriou 1988, fig. 3 [left]), as well as from Sedes and Kalindria/Kilindir in the Langadas plain (Heurtley 1939, p. 187, cat. no. 280 [good fabric, smooth red surface] and p. 181, cat. no. 243 [with different handle], respectively). Compare also a conical "kalathos" with two arch-shaped handles from Toumba Episkopis in Imathia (Merousis 2004, pl. 1b).

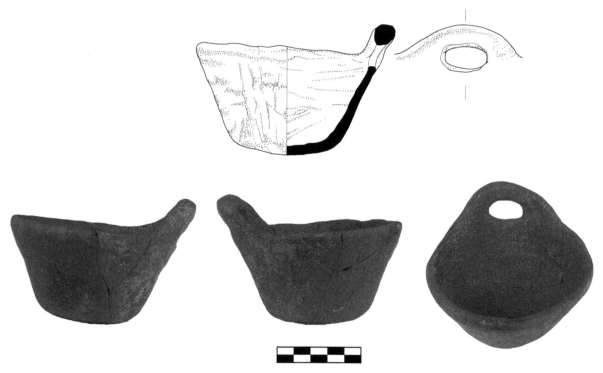

FIGURE 4.52. EBA small open vessels: **4/43** (ΜΕΘ 1582).
Drawing A. Hooton, photos I. Coyle

4/44. (ΜΕΘ 4251) Partial Profile, Miniature(?) Kantharos or Mug. Late EBA–Early MBA Fig. 4.53
East Hill, #274/003003, Τοίχος 1 (fill around wall).
P.H. 0.039; p.W. 0.075; Diam. (rim) est. 0.100; Th. (wall) 0.005–0.007.
Single fr preserving large part of sharply carinated body with root of large strap handle.
Wall is straight below the carination, convex above it. The handle, rectangular in the root section, joins the body at the carination; a second, symmetrically placed handle may have existed. Well shaped; good state of preservation.
Fabric 7: Clay is very fine and compact, without visible non-plastics but with a fine dusting of mica visible on the surface. Evenly fired, gray 10YR 5/1; gray core.
Exterior is carefully smoothed and slipped, fired matt yellowish brown 10YR 5/4; interior is burnished, fired lustrous grayish brown 2.5Y 5/2. Groups of short fine striations, possibly finger or tool marks, run along the line of the carination on the inside; a few short scratches may represent either use-related or post-depositional wear.
Surface color compares with MBA cups from Palaia Chrani in Pieria (illustrated in Bessios 2010, p. 75) and from Molyvopyrgos in Chalkidike (buff exterior/gray interior, polished: Heurtley 1939, p. 209, cat. no. 393). Carinated kantharoi and mugs with strap handles are common in Macedonia; among them, a large and distinctive late EBA group (including some very small examples) from Armenochori (Heurtley 1939, pp. 192–194), transitional EBA–MBA pieces (some with burnished interiors) from the cemetery at Xeropigado Koiladas in Kitrini Limni (Ziota 2007, pp. 239–241, fig. 3:1,12), and examples in dark-burnished gray fabrics from the MBA levels at Toumba Thessalonikis (Andreou and Psaraki 2007, pp. 405–406, figs. 4.KA1929, 5). At Pefkakia in Thessaly, handmade monochrome kantharoi and small cups are likewise prominent in the transitional EBA–MBA levels, and continue well into the MBA alongside wheelmade "Gray Minyan" wares (*Pevkakia* III, p. 117, Beil. 2, cat. nos. 21–22, pls. 4:4, 5:2, 16:12–13 [early MBA kantharoi]; p. 127 [cups, *Tasse Typ* 2C1]); compare also handmade kantharoi/cups in local Gray Minyan fabrics from Middle Helladic I–II levels at Aspis, Argos (Philippa-Touchais and Touchais 2011, pp. 211–212, fig. 13:32–33).

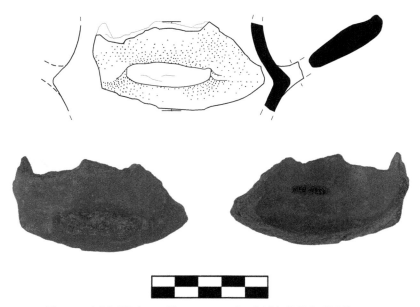

FIGURE 4.53. EBA small open vessels: **4/44** (ΜΕΘ 4251).
Drawing A. Hooton, photos I. Coyle

The kantharos is a distinctive shape in the Gray Minyan repertory, as well as in its ancestral Early Helladic III fine-burnished gray wares of southern Greece. In Early Helladic III assemblages, handmade kantharoi occur either alongside the predominant wheelmade examples (at Lerna IV, Nemea, and Tiryns) or on their own (at Olympia, Pelikata, and, possibly, at Lefkandi [Rutter 1983, pp. 336–342, tables 2–3]).

4/45. (ΜΕΘ 4287) Partial Profile, Cup/Beaker or Miniature. EBA I–II (?)   Fig. 4.54
East Hill #274/004016 [7].
P.H. 0.049; p.W. 0.051; Diam. (rim) 0.069; Diam. (max. body) 0.062; Th. (wall) 0.004–0.006.
About one-third preserved.
Sinuous profile; globular body rises to rather tall, cylindrical neck and flaring rim. Large elliptical scar from a lug or strap handle is placed at maximum body width, just below the neck; a slight thickening and breakage at the corresponding portion of the rim indicates where such a handle would have been attached. Carefully shaped and proportioned.
Fabric 5: Clay is fine-grained, mixed with a fair amount of shell temper, also some mica and pebbles. Fired very dark gray 10YR 3/1.
Surfaces are carefully smoothed, slipped, and burnished; fired matt brown 10YR 5/3. Fabric inclusions are visible through the burnish, and finishing marks are seen on the interior lower body. Burnish is best preserved on the exterior upper neck and rim, but is patchier on the inside of the rim and hardly survives elsewhere. Slip and burnish are almost effaced—use-worn(?)—below the handle/lug root.

FIGURE 4.54. EBA small open vessels: **4/45** (ΜΕΘ 4287).
Drawing A. Hooton, photos I. Coyle

The shell-rich dark fabric and buff-brown surface echo local wares of the late FN–EBA I, including pieces found onsite (**4/14** [MEΘ 2010] and **4/20** [MEΘ 4334]) and others from Kitros–Hassan Vrysi (brown-burnished; illustrated in Bessios 2010, pp. 68–69). Form and dimensions compare with fine beakers and cups at Kastanas, mainly from the early levels but also some late examples (Aslanis 1985: p. 154, pls. 2:5,7 [Schicht 27], 5:2 [Schicht 26], 80:7 [Schicht 20]). In the west Thermaic area, a comparable range of S-profile burnished beakers and one-handled cups, of advanced EBA II date, comes from Agios Athanassios Thessalonikis (Mavroeidi 2012, pp. 132–134, pl. 1 [open vessels of Type A I1–3]; Mavroeidi, Andreou, and Pappa 2006, p. 481, fig. 3:β–δ). Comparanda among miniature shapes include one-handled cups from Skala Sotiros, Phase I (EBA I: S. Papadopoulos, Papalazarou, and Tsoutsoumpei-Lioliou 2007, p. 430, pl. 9); a jug from the "Orpheus Cave" at Alistrati (late FN–EBA I: Kontaxi, Giannopoulos, and Kaznesi 2004, pl. 5); and jars with handles or lugs from Thermi on Lesvos and the Samian Heraion (Marangou 1992, p. 76, cat. no. 89, fig. 38, and p. 117, fig. 41g, respectively).

4/46. (MEΘ 5612) Partial Profile, Minature (?) Cup or Bowl. EBA I–II Fig. 4.55
East Hill #274/085, Κέντρο τετραγώνου [center of trench].
P.H. 0.05; Diam. (rim) est. ca. 0.070; Th. (rim–base) 0.002–0.008.
About half preserved; almost complete profile, but base is missing.
Small dimensions suggest a miniature shape. Angular/sinuous profile, with soft carination, placed on the lower one-third of the body, creating an asymmetric biconical wall; flaring rim. Carefully modeled.

FIGURE 4.55. EBA small open vessels: **4/46** (MEΘ 5612).
Drawing T. Ross, photos I. Coyle

Fabric 5: Fine-grained and compact, lightly dusted with mica and calcite (?) visible in section and on surface. Evenly fired, very dark grayish brown 10YR 3/2.

Surfaces are carefully smoothed, finely striated with dense diagonal strokes, thinly slipped but left unburnished; fired in the color of the fabric. Extensively worn and encrusted.

Dark fabric and surface recall local late FN wares (compare **4/45** [ΜΕΘ 4287]). The shape finds parallels in EBA I carinated cups (not miniatures) from Kritsana, Settlement I (illustrated in *Argissa-Magoula* III, pl. 70.2–3), and Pentapolis I (Grammenos 1981, figs. 28:532, 31:603 [with raised handle]). Later (advanced EBA II) examples from Agios Athanassios Thessalonikis are very small, comparable in size to the Methone piece (Mavroeidi, Andreou, and Pappa 2006, p. 481, fig. 3:β–δ). For the EBA I–II date see also small, sinuous bowls from Sitagroi, Phases IV–Va (Sherratt 1986, figs. 13:10, 13:11), and from Pentapolis I–II (Grammenos 1981, figs. 12:175, 28:543).

4/47. (ΜΕΘ 5622) Complete Profile, Miniature Kantharos. Late EBA–Early MBA Fig. 4.56
East Hill, #274/085, Ανατολικός μάρτυρας [East balk].
P.H. 0.036; p.W. 0.045; Diam. (rim) 0.060; Th. (rim–max. body) 0.004–0.008.
Single fr preserving large portion of the body, small part of the rim, and trace of the base.
Sharply carinated form; biconical body, flaring rim with flattened and beveled lip, large elliptical scar from a strap handle is preserved at carination. Well shaped, but slightly asymmetric around rim. Broken all around the edges.

FIGURE 4.56. EBA small open vessels: **4/47** (ΜΕΘ 5622).
Drawing T. Ross, photos I. Coyle

Fabric 7: Very fine and compact, with a slight dusting of mica and tiny white (calcareous?) inclusions; fired gray 5Y 5/1, sharply layered with extensive core of lighter gray 5Y 6/1.

Exterior surface is smoothed and burnished to a matt luster, finished with broad strokes that are still visible; the interior is well smoothed but not burnished. Surfaces are fired to the color of the fabric.

Form and fabric compare with **4/44** (MEΘ 4251). Parallels include carinated kantharoi/cups with high strap handles in burnished gray fabrics from the MBA levels at Toumba Thessalonikis (Andreou and Psaraki 2007, pp. 405–406, figs. 4:KA1929, 5); handmade kantharoi in light gray, imitation Minyan ware from Pefkakia IV (early MBA: *Pevkakia* III, p. 117, Beil. 1, cat. nos. 2, 12–13, pls. 3:14, 4:4, 6:13); and small handmade kantharoi/cups in local Gray Minyan at Aspis, Argos (MH I–II: Philippa-Touchais and Touchais 2011, pp. 211–212, fig. 13:32–33).

Closed vessels, fine to medium

4/48. (MEΘ 4183) Partial Profile, "Amphoriskos" or Jug. Late EBA–Early MBA   Fig. 4.57
East Hill, #274/003003, Τοίχος 1 (fill around wall).

P.H. 0.098; Diam. (rim) est. 0.087; Diam. (body) max. 0.11; Th. (rim–max. body) 0.003–0.008; handle scar: 0.034 x 0.008.

About one-third preserved. Almost complete profile, but base is missing; handle is broken, parts of the rim are chipped off.

FIGURE 4.57. EBA closed vessels, fine to medium: **4/48** (MEΘ 4183).
Drawing A. Hooton, photos I. Coyle

Small, S-profile shape. Globular body with evenly thick walls, funnel-shaped neck offset by shallow groove at its base, flaring tapered rim. Elliptical scar and root from strap handle, rectangular in section, located at the upper body, a little below shoulder; another handle may have originally existed. Careful modeling.

Fabric 6a: Clay is fine-grained, contains small amounts of mica, white (calcite?) specks, and thin shell frr; unevenly fired, reddish brown 5YR 4/4–5/2, sharply layered in section with extensive reddish gray core.

Surface is carefully smoothed, coated with thick slip, and burnished, with smoothing/burnishing strokes still visible; fired very dark gray 10YR 3/1, lustrous on the outside but duller on the inside; faint reddish firing cloud below handle. The exterior is very well preserved, but the interior surface has flaked off and is heavily encrusted.

Long sequences of fine "amphoriskoi" and jugs are seen at Kastanas Levels 26 through 22b, increasing in frequency toward the later EBA (*Gießgefässe, zweihenklige Gefässe*: Aslanis 1985, p. 154, pls. 11:11, 65:7); compare also middle to late EBA examples from Perivolaki/Saratsé, Pits G31 and I37, and from Agios Mamas, Pit D27 (Aslanis 1985, pls. 123:6, 126:13, and 113:9, respectively). Small jugs from the late EBA–early MBA cemetery at Xeropigado (Ziota 2007, p. 243, fig. 4.2–7) have shape and surface treatment similar to the Methone piece. The flaring, funnel-shaped neck and the thick, shiny slip can also be compared to **4/49** (MEΘ 4272), below.

4/49. (MEΘ 4272) Rim and Neck Fr, Jug. Late EBA–Early MBA Fig. 4.58
East Hill #274/004009 [4].
P.H. 0.070; Diam. (rim) est. 0.090; Th. 0.003 (wall)–0.008 (lip).

Tall cylindrical neck is preserved in its entire height; slightly concave, it thickens progressively toward flaring rim with beveled interior. Some asymmetries in contours; traces of building coils are visible on the exterior.

Fabric 7: Very fine and compact, with a light dusting of mica; evenly fired, dark gray 10YR 4/1.

Surface is carefully smoothed, coated with thick slip, and burnished; fired lustrous dark gray with grayish brown clouds 10YR 4/1–4/2, shinier on the exterior, matt on the interior. Very well preserved; only few spots of encrustation inside.

FIGURE 4.58. EBA closed vessels, fine to medium: **4/49** (MEΘ 4272).
Drawing A. Hooton, photos I. Coyle

Pouring vessels with cylindrical or funnel-shaped necks are seen from the EB II through the late EBA and during the EBA–MBA transition; for example, at Torone, Phases II and III (Morris 2009–2010, figs. 23 nos 93.1515 and 90.1312, respectively); Kritsana, Settlement III (Aslanis 1985, pl. 97:2–4,14); Axiochori, Settlements 4 and 5 (Aslanis 1985, pls. 87:8–9 [Pit S32], 93:7 [Pit S30]); Archontiko, late EBA (Merousis 2004, p. 1292, pl. 4c [right]); and from the MBA levels at Toumba Thessalonikis (Andreou and Psaraki 2007, pp. 405–406, fig. 4.KA1617 [dark-burnished gray fabric]). Beveled rims, fine gray fabrics, and lustrous surfaces are all ancestral features of the distinctive gray wares—both handmade and wheelmade—of the subsequent MBA period in Macedonia and beyond (Aslanis 2009; Heurtley 1939, figs. 80–81; Horejs 2007a, pp. 211–217; Pavúk 2014).

Storage containers, medium-fine to coarse

4/50. (ΜΕΘ 4872) Partial Profile, Open Jar or Urn   Fig. 4.59
East Hill #274/004030 [10].
P.H. 0.088; p.W. 0.100; Diam. (rim) est. 0.255–0.27; Th. (wall–rim) 0.008–0.012.
Two sherds mended into a large fr preserving rim and upper wall to a deep, wide-mouthed vessel.
Thick, slightly rounded wall rises almost vertically and inclines gently toward straight rim with flattened lip. Semicircular scar at the lower broken edge of the body indicates the existence of cylindrical handle or large "button." Somewhat careless, asymmetric modeling; excess clay left unpared and unsmoothed around rim and on lip.
Fabric 8: Medium-fine and quite compact, tempered with small quantities of pebbles, powdered calcite (?), and mica, visible in section and on the surface. Unevenly fired, brown 7.5YR 5/4; core of dark gray 10YR 4/1.

FIGURE 4.59. EBA storage containers, medium-fine to coarse: **4/50** (ΜΕΘ 4872).
Drawing A. Hooton, photos I. Coyle

Surfaces are well smoothed, densely striated with fine horizontal strokes (more carefully applied on the inside), and slipped; fired grayish brown 10YR 5/2, with large cloud of dark gray 2.5Y 4/2 on the exterior. Good state of preservation, but a few patches of encrustation inside.

Very early examples of open storage containers are known from Pentapolis I (Grammenos 1981, p. 149, fig. 30:574) and Kastanas Level 28 (Aslanis 1985, pl.1:4). At Kastanas, such bucket-shaped vessels (*eimerförmiges Vorratsgefäss, Typ* 3) continue in use until the late EBA (Aslanis 1985, pp. 79–81, fig. 42, pls. 22–23 [Schicht 24], 132:7 [Schicht 22b, with loop handles]). To the EBA II belong jars from Torone II (straight-walled and equipped with lugs or handles: Morris 2009–2010, fig. 24, esp. no. 90.1318), and large coarse urns from Sitagroi Phase Vb (Sherratt 1986, fig. 13.22:4 and pl. XXII:3 [from the Bin Complex], fig. 13.23:5 [with slightly incurving upper body, similar to **4/50** (MEΘ 4872)]). Large open-mouthed vessels for the storage of dry goods are also commonly found at Agios Athanassios Thessalonikis, dating to the advanced EBA II or later (Mavroeidi 2012, pp. 167–172, pl. 2 [type AVI2]; Mavroeidi, Andreou, and Pappa 2006, pp. 480–482, 488, fig. 1:γ [vertical walls], pl. 2); examples of similar shape and date also come from Perivolaki/Saratsé, Pit G31 (Aslanis 1985, pl. 123:10). Additional comparanda from Kritsana, without phase specification, were reported in Heurtley 1939 (p. 174, cat. nos. 203–205 and especially cat. no. 206, red-baked with firing clouds, illustrated in pl. XIII).

4/51. (MEΘ 5023) Partial Profile, Wide-mouthed Jar. EBA I (?)   Fig. 4.60
East Hill #274/054009 [1], Β Επιφανειακό [surface level].
P.H. 0.074; p.W. 0.120; Diam. (rim) est. 0.30; Th. (wall) 0.008–0.012.
Two sherds mended into a fr preserving rim, collar, and shoulder wall with shelf lug to a large collared vessel of S-profile.

FIGURE 4.60. EBA storage containers, medium-fine to coarse: **4/51** (MEΘ 5023).
Drawing A. Hooton, photos I. Coyle

Inclined upper wall, cylindrical collar of slightly curved profile, gently flaring rim; narrow, flat ridge separates collar from body, creating a small dent in an otherwise continuous wall line. Horizontal shelf lug, small and very flat, is placed just below the rim flare. Well shaped.

Fabric 9: Clay is medium-grained, "sandy" in consistency, with substantial amounts of angular shell frr (some of them burnt), pebbles, and mica visible in section and on the surface; very dark core indicates organic inclusions as well. The fabric is somewhat loose because of the many non-plastics. Fired reddish brown 5YR 5/3; core of very dark gray 10YR 3/1.

Surfaces are smoothed, carefully finished with fine horizontal striations; exterior may have originally been slipped and/or burnished, while the interior is slipped but has rougher texture, due to the many non-plastics that are barely covered by the surface coating. Exterior is fired a dull black 10YR 2/1, with some reddish brown clouds; the interior is dull yellowish brown 10YR 5/4 with thin gray cloud on rim.

The shell-rich fabric echoes the local traditions of the late FN (compare **4/38** [MEΘ 4887]), to which period also date forerunners of the small shelf lug (for example, at Kephala [Coleman 1977, pl. 81.AL] or Katundas IV in Albania [Korkuti 1995, pl. 103:18]). The shape is seen throughout the EBA, in the successive phases at Kastanas (*S-Profil Vorratsgefäss, Typ* 4: Aslanis 1985, pp. 81–82, 166, fig. 42:4, pls. 3:6, 6:12 [early examples, Schichten 27–26]); at Kritsana Settlement III/IV of the EBA II (Aslanis 1985, pl. 98.9 [with rope band on shoulder and lugs]); and at Agios Mamas Pit D27, dating to late EBA–early MBA (Aslanis 1985, pl. 111:6 [with double mastos]).

4/52. (MEΘ 5083) Striated Body Fr with Rope Band(s), Water Jar (?)   Fig. 4.61
East Hill #274/084001 [1].
P.H. 0.042; p.W. 0.062; Th. 0.016.

Small flat fr from the shoulder of a jar or amphora. Broken around the edges, with large portions of the interior wall missing.

Thick relief band of the slashed-rope type runs horizontally, bordered by thin shallow grooves above and below. Traces of another such band, parallel to the former.

Fabric 8. Clay is fine-grained, contains small amounts of mica, scattered tiny pebbles and a few large ones; carbonized spots, small pores and oval depressions (from grains?) in the clay body indicate additional vegetal inclusions. Well fired, brown 7.5YR 4/2, with thin strips of dark grayish brown core 10YR 3/2.

Exterior surface is carefully smoothed and finely striated, slipped, and burnished; fired brown 7.5YR 5/4. The burnish is preserved only on the relief band(s), while the rest of the wall is covered by a thin film and some thicker patches of encrustation. The interior is largely encrusted, but was originally finely striated, although unburnished.

EBA water jars feature relatively fine fabrics and distinctive dense striation, as a means to decrease porosity and increase cooling properties (Aslanis 1985, p. 173; Andreou 1997, p. 73; Morris 2009–2010, p. 25). Such liquid containers, often decorated with plastic bands, are well documented in the sequences at Kastanas (Aslanis 1985, pls. 4:10, 133:6, 38:1 [Schichten 27, 24, 23b, respectively]); Axiochori (Aslanis 1985, pl. 92:2 [Pit SE 33/34]); Kritsana (Aslanis 1985, pls. 98:9, 104:16 [Settlement III/IV and Settlement V, respectively; the latter with rope band at neck basis, also illustrated in *Argissa-Magoula* III, pl. 73:7; Heurtley 1939, figs. 42c, 53]); and Torone (phases I–III: Morris 2009–2010, p. 25, fig. 27). They are likewise represented at Sindos (EBA II: Andreou 1997, pp. 65, 70, 73, 83, cat. nos. 34–35, 43, fig. 8, pl. 28β–γ). Compare also the large burial jars with heavy striation and rope bands from the cemetery at Agios Mamas (Pappa 2010, pls. 2:4–6, 5:3,5, 6:4–5 [with slashed band at neck], 10:3–5). Cf. also **4/53** (MEΘ 5613), below.

FIGURE 4.61. EBA storage containers, medium-fine to coarse: **4/52** (MEΘ 5083). Drawing T. Ross, photos I. Coyle

4/53. (MEΘ 5613) Striated Partial Profile with Rope Band, Water Jar (?)   Fig. 4.62
East Hill #274/085023 [9].
P.H. 0.070; p.W. 0.050; Th. (wall) 0.001–0.013.

Small fr preserving rim, neck, and upper body to a thick-walled amphora or similar liquid container. Broken all around the rim edge, but otherwise in good condition.

Slightly curved upper wall inclines toward high, funnel-shaped neck that opens up at a shallow angle to the body and tapers toward rim. A relief rope band (0.010 wide) articulates neck and body, and thus reinforces the vulnerable area of joint—indicated by a horizontal crack at neck base on the inside—between these two parts.

Fabric 8: Clay is fine-grained and compact, contains a little mica and tiny frr of white and gray minerals, visible in core and on the surface; hard-fired, light reddish brown 2.5YR 6/4 with gray core 5YR 5/1.

Surfaces are well smoothed, slipped (?), fired light reddish brown 2.5YR 6/4. Both exterior and interior are densely covered with fine parallel striations, differently arranged on the body and neck—probably reflecting the changing movements of the potter's hands and a finishing tool around the thick wall of this large vessel (cf. the patterned striations on the amphoras from Sindos, all of which were finished with the paddle-and-anvil technique: bunches of dense fine grooves, slightly curved, running in up–down or diagonal directions, and often intersecting. Andreou [1997, p. 65, pl. 28β] points to their possible decorative purpose, and further observes that an appearance of slip may be created by the density and technique of execution of striations). The body, including the relief band, bears fine horizontal lines inside and outside; on the neck, groups of striations run down vertically on the exterior, horizontally and down-bent on the interior. Slight wear and encrustation.

The fabric quality and composition, the articulated shape, the careful striation, and the strong firing all compare well with the distinct categories of amphoras/water jars of the EBA. These vessels were purposefully shaped and finished, and fired to ensure impermeability and good cooling properties (discussion and comparanda in Aslanis 1985, p. 173; Andreou 1997, pp. 65, 73; Morris 2009–2010, p. 25). Throughout the long sequence at Kastanas, amphoras are typically narrow-mouthed with funnel-shaped or flaring necks, of fine to medium hard-fired fabric (often red), treated with fine striations (*Besenstriche*) and finger-impressed bands at the shoulder or lower neck base (Aslanis 1985, p. 173, pls. 4:10–11 [Schicht 27], 11.4 and 24:3–4 [Schicht 24], 37:6 and 38:4,6 [Schicht 23b], 39:7 [Schicht 23a–b], 48:6 [Schicht 23a]). Such distinct wares are also reported from two adjacent sites on the West Thermaic sites, Sindos (EBA II: Andreou 1997, pp. 65, 70, 73, 83, cat. nos. 34–35, 43, fig. 8, pl. 28β–γ) and Agios Athanassios Thessalonikis (late EBA II: Mavroeidi, Andreou, and Pappa 2006, pp. 482, 488, fig. 5β); from Torone (specifically made of non-calcareous clays, to reduce porosity: Morris 2009–2010, p. 25, fig. 27); and from the cemetery at Agios Mamas (where they had been used as burial containers: Pappa 2010, pls. 4:4–6, 5:3,5, 6:4–5, 10:3–5). From the late EBA levels at Archontiko comes a series of standardized amphoras and other striated liquid containers (Deliopoulos, Papadias, and Papaefthymiou-Papanthimou 2014, pp. 565–568, fig. 3); compare also a jar with funnel-shaped neck from Armenochori (Heurtley 1939, p. 195, cat. no. 352). Cf. also **4/52** (MEΘ 5083).

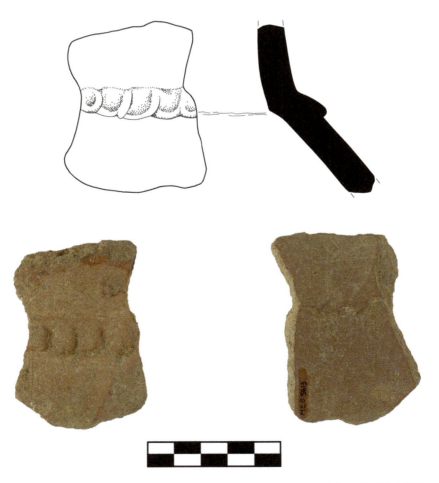

FIGURE 4.62. EBA storage containers, medium-fine to coarse: **4/53** (MEΘ 5613). Drawing T. Ross, photos I. Coyle

4/54. (ΜΕΘ 5623) Rim and Neck Fr with Rope Band, Jar or Urn. EBA I–II (?)   Fig. 4.63
East Hill #274/085, Ανατολικός μάρτυρας [East balk].
P.H. 0.051; p.W. 0.063; Diam. (rim) est. 0.28; Th. (wall–rim) 0.009–0.0105.

Small fr preserving flaring neck and rim, and a tiny trace of upper wall curvature of a large, wide-mouthed jar or urn.

The neck opens up gently toward a flattened rim with broad, finger-impressed band (W: 0.015), attached on its exterior. Slight asymmetries in modeling.

Fabric 9: Medium-coarse, rather loose in consistency, rich in mica, white (calcareous?) inclusions, pebbles of various sizes (some very large), and small angular frr of shell(?). Evenly fired, very dark grayish brown 10YR3/2; some black core.

Surfaces are roughly smoothed, burnished in broad strokes (visible on exterior); fired matt dark gray 5YR 4/1. Fairly well preserved. Some use wear(?) on the interior is concentrated around the lower fractured end, where the neck would have joined the body.

Both fabric and rope decoration have late FN forerunners in the region and beyond. For the fabric, compare **4/38** (ΜΕΘ 4887), **4/51** (ΜΕΘ 5023), and **4/31** ΜΕΘ 5091); rope-decorated vessels are discussed by Douzougli and Zachos (2002, p. 127, figs. 5–6 [from Doliana, with comparanda]). Parallels dating to EBA I through late EBA II include S-profile jars at Kastanas (Aslanis 1985, pp. 81–82, fig. 42:4, pls. 6:4,14 [Schicht 26]) and Agios Mamas, Pit 29/30 (Aslanis 1985, pl. 109:1); large coarse urns with rope decoration on rim from Sitagroi Vb (Sherratt 1986, figs. 13.22:5 [from the Bin Complex], 13.23: 6, pl. C [Top: 1–8]) and Torone II (Morris 2009–2010, fig. 25); a large group of capacious containers for dry goods, bell-shaped and wide-mouthed with ropes on rim, at Agios Athanassios Thessalonikis (Mavroeidi 2012, pp. 162–167, 171–173, pl. 2 [type AVI1]; Mavroeidi, Andreou, and Pappa 2006, pp. 480–482, 488, fig. 1:a [shallow S-profile and flaring rim, smoothed and burnished], pl. 2); additional comparanda from Perivolaki/Saratsé (Heurtley 1939, p. 185, fig. 58) and Pefkakia, *Rachmanifläche* (*Argissa-Magoula* III, pl. 65:1).

FIGURE 4.63. EBA storage containers, medium-fine to coarse: **4/54** (ΜΕΘ 5623).
Drawing T. Ross, photos I. Coyle

Cooking/utility forms

4/55. (ΜΕΘ 2008) Dipper Jug. Late or Post-EBA   Fig. 4.64
East Hill, #274/005010 [5].
H. 0.115; Diam. (rim) 0.090; Diam. (base) 0.050–0070; Diam. (body) max. 0.133; Th. (wall) 0.04.
Partially reconstructed from several frr; complete profile.

Globular body rises in a continuous curve toward low collar/neck and wide-mouthed, slightly flaring rim with flattened lip. Thick, semicircular "spur" handle—rectangular in section, grooved along its length, and flattened at both ends—is attached from upper wall directly to the rim, with horn-shaped protuberance (broken on top) rising almost vertically above rim level. Base is flattened, slightly concave. Roughly modeled, asymmetric in contours and wall thickness.

Fabric and surface features indicate fire- or cooking-related use. Fabric 10a: fine, micaceous clay with white mineral inclusions (calcite?) is common among cookwares (cf. **4/11** [ΜΕΘ 4221] and **4/12** [ΜΕΘ 4316]). Reddish brown 2.5YR 5/4, hard-fired but somewhat brittle, possibly as a result of repeated thermal shocks. At Sindos, coarse clays containing large calcite pieces were used for large bowls, jars, and shallow trays which have been tentatively identified as cookware, because of the heat-resistant qualities that the calcareous and many other non-plastics lent to the fabric (Andreou 1997, pp. 73–74).

FIGURE 4.64. EBA/Bronze Age cooking/utility forms: **4/55** (ΜΕΘ 2008).
Drawing A. Hooton, photos I. Coyle

Surfaces are carefully smoothed and finely striated, fired dark gray 5YR 4/1; now covered with large patches of encrustation.

Extensive use wear on the exterior: the surface finish has eroded, leaving a porous and "raw" texture with sporadic lustrous (vitrified?) patches; some exploded white minerals and shiny specks of mica are visible through; the wall is cracked and chipped in several parts, especially on the base where firing core is revealed. Such damage points to heavy friction, repeated immersion in hot substances, and/or direct contact with fire (perhaps to boil small quantities of food).

The vessel form and the spur handle have parallels in the various types of jugs from Agios Mamas (Heurtley 1939, p. 172, cat. nos. 183, pp. 185–287). To the author's knowledge, no information on small cookware (of a finer variety) is available for EBA Macedonia; the reported assemblages from Archontiko (Deliopoulos, Papadias, and Papaefthymiou-Papanthimou 2014) and Sindos (Andreou 1997) consist mainly of large, coarse shapes. Nevertheless, the qualities of the fabric (if not the shape) of **4/55** (MEΘ 2008) find parallels in the cookware from the LBA, especially at Kastanas and Agios Mamas (Horejs 2005, with references).

4/56. (MEΘ 4182) Partial Profile, Cooking Bowl (Χύτρα). Transitional EBA–MBA or Later   Fig. 4.65
East Hill, #274/004010 [5].
P.H. 0.128; Diam. (rim) 0.200; Diam. (body) max. 0.24; Th. (wall) 0.004–0.008.

Many sherds mended into large section of rim, upper body, and one complete handle to a deep vessel of sinuous profile.

Bulbous upper wall rises to short, upright collar which tapers to slightly everted rim. Cylindrical, slightly flattened handle is attached horizontally at the maximum body diameter, upturned at an obtuse angle to the wall. Well built, symmetric, and thin-walled.

Fabric 10a: Clay is fine-grained but rich in the mineral non-plastics typical for cooking fabrics: mica, white (calcareous?) inclusions, angular silicate frr, and large pebbles. Many lithic inclusions are visible on the surface, some of them exploded by fire. Unevenly fired, red 2.5YR 4/8 with extensive carbonized core 2.5YR 5/1. The fabric is brittle, probably as a result of repeated thermal shock.

Interior surface is carefully smoothed, striated, and slipped; fired red 2.5YR 5/6, but now covered with extensive film of encrustation and spots of dark soot. The exterior seems to have been similar originally, but is now largely covered by clouds of very dark gray soot(?) 2.5YR 3/1, especially on the lower body, and the handle is completely blackened. The surface, where visible, has lost its slip, is porous and "soapy" with shiny (vitrified?) patches. Large chips on the body wall expose core. Thick layer of encrustation covers much of the exterior wall.

Parallels span a good part of the second millennium, from the EBA–MBA transition to the advanced LBA. Transitional EBA–MBA and MBA: Levels 22a–21 at Kastanas (Aslanis 1985, pls. 74:1, 75:4 [deep bowls with upturned handles]); Pits E29–28/Settlements 6–7 at Axiochori (Aslanis 1985, pl. 94:8,10); Kitrini Limni (Fotiadis and Chondroyianni-Metoki 1993, p. 24, fig. 4:λ); Kallipetra Imathias (L. Stefani 2000, pp. 546–547, fig. 9 [χυτροειδή αγγεία]); the cemeteries at Xeropigado and Goules Kozanis (Ziota 2007, fig. 6:2; 2010, fig. 1:στ [deep lekanai, used as burial receptacles]); and Argissa, MBA *Bauhorizont, Haus* 3 (*Argissa-Magoula* III, pl. 54:7). LBA: at Agios Mamas, S-profile open pots (*Töpfe*), long-lived from the late MBA throughout the LBA (Horejs 2005, pp. 73–70, fig. 2); at Kastanas, deep bowls of Type 5b (*Schüsseln mit bauchständigen Querhenkeln und gedrungen breitem Körper*), which are long-lived and include thin-walled and hard-fired examples (Hochstetter 1984, p. 112, pls. 3:2–3 [Schicht 19], 43:4–5 [*Antenhau*s, Schicht 14b]).

Figure 4.65. EBA/Bronze Age cooking/utility forms: **4/56** (ΜΕΘ 4182). Drawing A. Hooton, photos I. Coyle.

4/57. (MEΘ 4256) Leg/Base and Wall Fr, Tripod Cooker or Pyraunos (?). Post-EBA   Fig. 4.66
East Hill #274/004001 [1].

P.H. 0.058; p.W. 0.083; Diam. (inner bowl) est. 0.27; max. Diam. (exterior profile) est. 0.308; Th. (leg) 0.007; Th. (base–body joint): 0.028.

Small fr preserving the upper end of a leg or base with joined lower body wall; irregularly fractured around the edges.

The leg/base portion is flattened and rectangular in section; it rises vertically and fuses with the lower part of a receptacle, the interior of which is concave while its exterior wall inclines slightly and tapers upward, where the main body curvature would have continued.

Fabric 10: Coarse, heavy with non-plastics typical of cookware: pebbles of various sizes, angular silicate frr, and white (limestone?) inclusions. Fired red 10R 4/8; strips of dark gray core 5YR 4/1 are probably the result of carbon penetration during use.

Surfaces are carefully smoothed, covered with thin slip (barely sufficient to cover the larger non-plastics), but left unburnished; fired weak red 10R 4/4, with extensive clouds of gray to pale red 2.5YR 6/0–6/2 (possibly soot). Patches of wear and encrustation on the exterior, while the interior is almost completely covered with thick encrustation that has also spilled over the broken edges. The visible surface underneath is cracked and worn—an additional indication of repeated thermal shocks (cf. **4/55** [MEΘ 2008], and **4/11** [MEΘ 4221]).

Decorative (?) shallow grooves, cursorily drawn with the finger or a blunt instrument over the wet clay surface, run vertical on the exterior. Although the preserved fr is too small and damaged to give any conclusive information as to the original form, comparative material of Macedonian cookware suggests a tripod cooker (see **4/59** [MEΘ 4869], below), or a pyraunos: a cooking pot fused with a tall, "skirt"-like base of straight or curved profile, which facilitated the use of the cooker over fire (Horejs 2005, pp. 79–81, figs. 5–6). A distinct, northern Greek and Balkan alternative to the tripod cookers known from the southern Aegean, pyraunoi are reported from the Middle throughout the Late Bronze Age, at Torone, Agios Mamas, Kastanas, Angelochori, Archontiko, and Nea Zoi and Apsalos Almopias (discussion and comparanda in Horejs 2005, pp. 79–82, fig. 7; Morris 2009–2010, p. 52, fig. 41; Georgiadou and Lagoudi 2014, pp. 285–286; Chapter 7).

FIGURE 4.66. EBA/Bronze Age cooking/utility forms: **4/57** (MEΘ 4256).
Drawing A. Hooton, photo I. Coyle

4/58. (MEΘ 4264) Striated Rim and Body Fr, Cooking Jar (?)   Fig. 4.67
East Hill #274/004001 [1].
P.H. 0.081; p.W. 0.085; Th. 0.015 (body wall), 0.018 (rim).

Thick-walled, coarse fr of a large vessel of collared or sinuous profile, flaring up toward thickened rim with flattened lip.

Undulating rim interior, with a narrow ledge running 0.015 below lip line—possibly intended for the fitting of a lid. The face of the ledge is broken, as is also a large part of the wall, thus the original form is unclear. Poor preservation, breakages around edges.

Fabric 10: Coarse, contains lots of mica and various lithics, including silicate and igneous (?) frr and some very large pebbles. Hard-fired, bricklike, red 10R 4/8 with some reddish gray clouds 10YR 5/; possibly over-fired.

FIGURE 4.67. EBA/Bronze Age cooking/utility forms: **4/58** (MEΘ 4264).
Drawing T. Ross, photos I. Coyle

Surfaces are smoothed, striated, and coated with thick slip in order to compact the heavily tempered clay body; fired lighter red 10YR 5/6. Dense striations of different shapes and arrangements cover the entire surface: shallow diagonal ridges on the exterior, dense horizontal lines on the interior, and a decorative (?) "fishbone" pattern on the flattened lip. Surface is largely effaced, possibly as a result of use wear; thickly encrusted on broken edges and lip.

Possible parallels to shape include S-profile jars at Kastanas, many of which are large and heavy, with flattened rims and striations (Aslanis 1985, fig. 42, pls. 7:3, 38:9 [Schichten 26, 23b, respectively]); and thick, decorated pithoi rims from Rachmani IV (Wace and Thompson 1912, pp. 34–35, fig. 15 [one with incised festoons]). Important comparanda for a possible cooking function are the cooking pithoi from Archontiko (Deliopoulos, Papadias, and Papaefthymiou-Papanthimou 2014, p. 567, fig. 4); cf. also **4/60** (MEΘ 5652).

4/59. (MEΘ 4869) Leg/Wall to a Tripod Cooker. LBA (?)   Fig. 4.68
East Hill #274/004030 [10].
P.H. 0.072; p.W. 0.063; Th. (leg, tip–base) 0.013–0.033; Th. (body) 0.034.

Complete leg attached to the wall of a rounded receptacle, of which only the lower curvature is preserved.

The leg is tongue-shaped, flattened, and approximately elliptical in section, massive at its juncture with the vessel and progressively tapering toward its tip. Large finger impression runs down the middle of the inner surface. Roughly finished contours.

FIGURE 4.68. EBA cooking/utility forms: **4/59** (MEΘ 4869).
Drawing T. Ross, photos I. Coyle

Fabric 9: Medium-coarse and heavy, rather loose, contains great quantities of seashells—among which whole valves of tiny mussels (*Mytilus*) and limpets were identified macroscopically by the archaeomalacologist Rena Veropoulidou—some pebbles, and organic material which left carbonized patches, pores, and fissures in the clay body. Unevenly fired, dark gray 5YR 4/1; fabric is brittle as a result of its composition and use-related thermal stress.

Surface is roughly smoothed, coated with dull slip; fired pink 5YR 7/3–7/4 with gray clouds 5YR 5/1 (soot?). If burnish existed, it has not been preserved. Heavy wear, possibly use-related, has exposed large areas of the core on both the leg and the vessel interior, which is also largely encrusted.

Although tripod cookers were used in Neolithic Macedonia (**4/12** [ΜΕΘ 4316] being one such example), the type is not attested during the EBA and MBA, when pyraunoi were preferred instead (see **4/57** [ΜΕΘ 4256]). The tripod cooker resurfaces—even if rarely—in the LBA, as a result of influences from the southern Aegean, where tripods were in use in the interim periods (Horejs 2005, pp. 82–86). Two frr from Agios Mamas represent two different tripod shapes (Horejs 2005, p. 83, fig. 8.3–4): a leg, of profile similar to the Methone piece, belonged to what is reconstructed as a vat-like shape—its fabric familiar to other local wares, as it also happens at Methone; the lower wall of a rounded pot preserved the root of a flat (?) leg, attached at a wide angle to the body.

Other (not inventoried) pieces of cookware(?) at Methone, including a leg and base and body frr in fabric comparable to **4/59** (ΜΕΘ 4869), were excavated in the same floor stratum [10] and in other units of Trenches 004 and 005.

4/60. (ΜΕΘ 5652) Partial Profile with Lunate Band, Cooking (?) Jar Fig. 4.69
East Hill #274/085, ΒΔ τμήμα [NW Quadrant].
P.H. 0.048; p.W. 0.100; Diam. (rim) est. 0.360; Th. (rim–wall) 0.007–0.011; relief band: W. 0.010; Th. 0.032.

Two sherds mended into a fr of rim and upper wall from a large, wide-mouthed jar/pithos.

Upper wall rises slightly inclined, then opens toward everted rim with rounded lip. A thick, finger-impressed lunate lug (*Ohrengriff*) below the rim would have provided a comfortable grip. A mass of untrimmed excess clay runs in an irregular arch within the inner curve of the lug. Breakages on lug and adjacent wall, wear on rim.

Fabric 10: Clay is coarse-grained, heavy and rather loose in consistency, mixed with large quantities of mica, medium- to large-sized silicate and white (calcareous?) inclusions, and pebbles. Unevenly fired, light red 2.5YR 6/8, with some gray core; rather brittle, possibly over-fired as result of use.

Surfaces are carefully smoothed and thickly slipped; fired dark gray 5YR 4/1. Finishing strokes are visible, as well as traces of dull burnish (which would have helped to compact the loose clay body).

Heavy, localized wear is visible on the rim exterior and on the lug, where the surface is completely destroyed and the core revealed; this damage was probably caused by repeated contact with heat and fire, possibly also by friction with cooking or serving utensils. By contrast, the interior is quite well preserved, except for some thin encrustation; it may have been more carefully finished in order to seal the fabric and render it safe for food-related use.

At Kastanas, large containers of inclined or S-profile, with *Ohrengriffe* and rope bands (*Vorratsgefässe mit einbiegendem Oberteil, Typ* 1, *S-Profil Vorratsgefässe, Typ* 4), occur from early on, but are more frequent in the middle and late levels (Aslanis 1985, pp. 81–82, fig. 42:1,4, pls. 1:9 [Schicht 28], 6:2,5 [Schicht 26], 15:5–6,8–16 and 16:1–5 [Schicht 24], 25:11 [Schicht 24–23b], 31:2,4, 32:7,9, and 36:6 [Schicht 23.b], 59:1–7,11 [Schicht 22b], 75:11 and 76:1–3 [Schicht 21]). Comparable forms are seen at Axiochori, Settlement 4 (Aslanis 1985, pl. 87:2–3); Perivolaki/Saratsé, Pits G32, H32, I 37 (Aslanis 1985, pls. 122:15, 124:3, 126:3 [the latter with lunate lug]); Pentapolis II (Grammenos 1981, fig. 24 no. 449 [oxidized firing]); Kritsana, Settlement IV (Aslanis 1985, pl. 101:15;

more frr with wavy relief bands are illustrated in Heurtley 1939, p. 170, fig. 42c,f); Agios Mamas, late levels from Pit 27 (Aslanis 1985, pl. 111:7), and Pefkakia, *Rachmanifläche* (*Argissa-Magoula* III, pl. 65:3 [S-profile jar]). At Torone, ovoid jars with *Ohrengriffe* are present in Phases II (EBA II) through IV (MBA), and have been interpreted as cooking and serving containers for liquids and stews (Morris 2009–2010, p. 25, fig. 25 no. 88.340). In the late EBA levels at Archontiko, pithoi constituted the principal category of identifiable cooking vessels, although their form is similar to other pithoi types (Deliopoulos, Papadias, and Papaefthymiou-Papanthimou 2014, p. 567, fig. 4).

FIGURE 4.69. EBA/Bronze Age cooking/utility forms: **4/60** (MEΘ 5652). Drawing T. Ross, photos I. Coyle

NOTES

1 I am very grateful to Sarah Morris and John Papadopoulos for the opportunity to study the material presented here. The prehistoric pottery from the East Hill was sampled and analyzed during the seasons 2012–2015 at the Makrygialos Archaeological Apotheke, in collaboration with Sarah Morris and Trevor Van Damme, whose input and collegiality were instrumental and much appreciated. I am grateful to Manthos Bessios for sharing his unparalleled knowledge of the site and region and for offering access to unpublished comparative material. Special thanks to Athena Athanassiadou, who made available all archival material of her excavations on the East Hill and facilitated the study of the pottery in every way. Kostas Noulas was generous with information on his excavations of Bronze Age graves on the West Hill. Myles Chykerda and MaryAnn Kontonicolas kindly provided data from their 2014 intensive survey of ancient Methone. Maria Karanika and Panagiota Tsiloyianni, then at the KZ´ Ephoreia, graciously showed me pottery from their respective projects at Kato Agios Ioannis and the Methone-Agathoupolis Drainage Project, and shared manuscripts of forthcoming reports. The macroscopic examination of ceramic fabrics owes a lot to the insights of Rena Veropoulidou, the project archaeomalacologist. Vanessa Muros and her team of conservators were unfailingly generous with their skills and time, no matter how short the notice. I am thankful to Anne Hooton and Tina Ross for the drawings, to Ian Coyle and Jeff Vanderpool for the photographs. This study further benefited from discussions with Christos Batzelas, Anastasia Dimoula, Gazmend Elezi, Nikos Merousis, John Papadopoulos, Jeremy Rutter, Liana Stefani, and Konstantinos Zachos. All omissions and errors remain mine.

2 Periodization and chronology follow Andreou 2014, p. 143, table 1; Andreou, Fotiadis, and Kotsakis 2001, table 1; Aslanis 2010.

3   The information summarized here was culled from the excavation notebooks (field seasons 2003–2005, 2008, 2013). Reports have previously been published in Bessios 2010, 2012a; Bessios et al. 2004.
4   Bessios 2012a, pp. 45–48, fig. 3.
5   Wheelmade pottery (Geometric or later) from these same units was likewise scarce.
6   Cf. Krahtopoulou 2010.
7   Bessios, Athanassiadou, and Noulas 2008, pp. 242–243.
8   Chykerda and Kontonicolas forthcoming; summary in Morris et al. 2020, pp. 671–675, figs. 14–16.
9   The seminal synthesis by Andreou, Fotiadis, and Kotsakis (2001) remains a key reference. More recently, see contributions in Adam-Veleni and Tzanavari 2009; Papadimitriou and Tsirtsoni 2010; Stefani, Merousis, and Dimoula 2014; see also Merousis 2004, Morris 2009–2010.
10 Compare Andreou 1997, pp. 62–67 (Sindos); Sheppard 1965, pp. 54–69, 181–193.
11 Hitsiou 2003, pp. 113–168. Petrographic analysis identified nine main fabric groups and several subgroups, which the Makrygialos potters produced by using different clays or mixing them differently in distinct recipes.
12 Krahtopoulou 2010, pp. 9–13, figs 2.1, 2.3.
13 Because no sherds were tested for calcium carbonate, the abundant white inclusions seen across most fabrics could not be positively identified as calcareous.
14 Compare Neolithic Makrygialos, where both "local" and "imported" fabrics have been identified in Phase II, but the former account for the large majority of the assemblage (Hitsiou 2003, pp. 162–167, 174). Of particular note at that site is the long-term and extensive exploitation of a local marly clay source, rich in shell and of a consistency comparable to the matrix of many sherds from Methone. At the Early Bronze Age site of Agios Athanassios Thessalonikis, not very far northeast of Methone, petrographic analysis likewise revealed the origin of potting clays from regional geological beds along the Thermaic coast (Mavroeidi 2012, Appendix 2). It is also worth mentioning two clay-mining ditches (albeit of unclear purpose) dating to the Early and Late Bronze Age, respectively, which were excavated at Palaia Chrani, in the inland of northern Pieria (Bessios 2010, p. 73).
15 Chronological periods are henceforth abbreviated as follows: EN (Early Neolithic), MN (Middle Neolithic) LN (Late Neolithic), FN (Final Neolithic), EBA (Early Bronze Age), MBA (Middle Bronze Age), LBA (Late Bronze Age), EIA (Early Iron Age).
16 The deposits on the hilltop were generally shallow due to severe erosion and reoccupation, which have resulted in an estimated elevation loss of at least one meter (Bessios 2012a, p. 45).
17 Pappa and Bessios 1999, pp. 181–183, 185, figs. 3–5, 8.
18 Elezi 2014, p. 97 (Type 5K.1.4), and p. 139, with references.
19 Urem-Kotsou 2006, pp. 148–182, Plan 2.2.
20 Cf. Koukouli-Chrysanthaki 1996; Kotsakis 2010.
21 Only two sherds were identified as possibly EBA in date, although they could also be placed in FN: a worn rim to an open vessel in red, shell-rich fabric (from pass 001006) and an incurved rim with lug to a jar (from pass 001007).
22 Bessios 2012a, p. 59.
23 Chykerda and Kontonicolas forthcoming.
24 Comparable material in west Macedonia and the Thermaic Gulf area includes the rich and well-published corpora from Dispilio (Voulgari 2011) and Avgi (Katsikaridis 2021) in Kastoria; Kitrini Limni–Megalo Nisi Galanis, Kozani (Kalogirou 1994); Makrygialos (Hitsiou 2003; Urem-Kotsou 2006); Kato Agios Ioannis Pierias (Karanika 2014); and Therme (Elezi 2014).
25 Sheppard (1965, pp. 371–372) warns against the assumption that all dark pottery is fired in a reducing atmosphere. However, chemical analyses of the LN dark wares in Macedonia have produced evidence for such firing conditions (Kotsakis 2010, p. 70).
26 For Neolithic bichrome pottery see Kalogirou 1994, pp. 74, 86–89; Katsikaridis 2021, pp. 75–78, 109–111; Kotsakis 2010, p. 71; Papadopoulou et al. 2006, pp. 784–786.
27 Korkuti 1995; Kotsakis 2010; *Pevkakia* I.
28 Cf. Sheppard 1965, pp. 18–19. Shell fragments, in particular, range from tiny to quite large, whereas shell temper is usually crushed and powdered and mixed in more uniformly (Rena Veropoulidou, pers. comm. 2013; cf. Sheppard 1965, pp. 26–27). In their respective syntheses of ceramic technologies in EN Thessaly and in LN Dimini and the west Thermaic Gulf, Dimoula (2014, especially pp. 279–286) and Hitsiou (2003, especially pp. 113–167) have documented in detail various techniques of preparing clays, such as reliance on residual non-plastics or use of tempering recipes by the prehistoric potters.
29 Krahtopoulou 2010; Krahtopoulou and Veropoulidou 2014.

30 Elezi 2014, graph 3.32 (upper row, middle).
31 At Makrygialos, the potters of both Phases I and II manufactured the majority of their wares in a variety of "shelly" fabrics (coarse to fine), according to site-specific recipes for mixing a fossiliferous marl of local extraction with "sandy" clays (Hitsiou 2003, pp. 144–150, 167, 174; cf. Urem-Kotsou 2006, p. 51).
32 Similar fabrics are reported from Dikili Tash: fine clay pastes, rich in natural inclusions of mica and quartz, were the potters' choice for black-topped and dark-polished wares (Courtois 2004, p. 4).
33 Gallis 1987.
34 Urem-Kotsou 2006, pp. 77–91 (types M3 and M6, respectively); Urem-Kotsou and Kotsakis 2007.
35 Another such leg, possibly also Neolithic, was found in the fill of Τάφρος 1 (pass 011003, stratum 2, not inventoried).
36 Sofronidou and Tsirtsoni 2007, p. 261.
37 Tsirtsoni 2000a, 2001; Urem-Kotsou 2006, pp. 88–90.
38 Sofronidou and Tsirtsoni 2007, pp. 264–265, fig. 15:1a–d.
39 Hayden 1995, pp. 260–261. Residue analysis on boiling pots from Makrygialos I indicates their use for the cooking of both animal and vegetal foods (Urem-Kotsou 2006, pp. 220–222).
40 Pappa et al. 2013 (Makrygialos); see various contributions to the section "Παλαιοπεριβάλλον–Αρχαιοβοτανική–Ζωοαρχαιολογία/Φυσική Ανθρωπολογία," in Stefani, Merousis, and Dimoula 2014, pp. 401–488.
41 Kalogiropoulou 2014.
42 Kotsakis and Halstead 2002, p. 412.
43 Tsirtsoni 2000b.
44 Pappa et al. 2013, p. 81; Urem-Kotsou and Kotsakis 2007.
45 Krahtopoulou 2010, pp. 25–52; cf. Chapter 3.
46 Kotsakis 2014, with references.
47 *Olynthus* I; Grammenos and Skourtopoulou 1992; Pan. Chrysostomou 1996; Grammenos 1997b; Pappa 2007; Kotsos 2014; Pappa, Nanoglou, and Efthymiadou 2016.
48 Although this site is best known for its late FN–EBA occupation, Dimini-style pottery was also collected there (Bessios et al. 2003, p. 438, n. 1).
49 Krahtopoulou 2010, pp. 50–52, fig. 3.11; Poulaki-Pantermali 2013a, pp. 28–30.
50 Andreou, Fotiadis, and Kotsakis 2001; Kottaridi 2000.
51 Pappa 2007.
52 Krahtopoulou 2010, p. 52.
53 Although Koutsouro has been reported as an EBA site (Krahtopoulou 2010, fig. 3.12), fragments of fine black-burnished pottery seem well placed in the regional LN sequence (personal examination, courtesy M. Bessios; see also Bessios et al. 2014, p. 229).
54 Pappa and Bessios 1999.
55 Aslanis 1990; Kokkinidou and Nikolaidou 1999.
56 Rodden and Wardle 1996, p. 52, fig. 3.3.
57 Overview in Chondroyianni-Metoki 2009, pp. 511–527.
58 Pappa and Bessios 1999, pp. 181–184, figs. 5–6.
59 Bessios 2010, p. 35; Intze 2011, pp. 19–20.
60 Graikos 2006, p. 800, plan 3.
61 Andreou, Fotiadis, and Kotsakis 2001, pp. 294–295; Chatzitoulousis et al. 2014; Chondroyianni-Metoki 2009, pp. 526–537; Pappa and Bessios 1999.
62 Examples include the sites of Servia (Ridley, Wardle, and Mould 2000, pp. 97, 104); Avgi Kastorias (Stratouli 2005, plan 1, figs. 1–2); Kleitos I (Ziota 2014) and Kremasti Koilada near Kozani (Chondroyianni-Metoki 2009, pp. 624–627); Giannitsa B, LN phase (P. Chrysostomou and Pan. Chrysostomou 1990, p. 176, figs. 5, 7); Stavroupolis (Kotsos 2014); Paliambela Kolindros, MN and LN phases (Kotsakis and Halstead 2002, pp. 410–11, plan 2); Promachon-Topolniča, MN–LN (Koukouli-Chrysanthaki et al. 2014).
63 Cf. Brück 1999; Chapman 2000.
64 Kato Agio Ioannis, Pieria (Bessios and Adaktylou 2008); Makrygialos (Pappa et al. 2004; Pappa and Veropoulidou 2011; Triantaphyllou 1999b); Avgi, Kastoria (Stratouli et al. 2009, 2014); Kremasti Koilada (Chondroyianni-Metoki 2009, pp. 607–624; 2010); Aravissos, Pella (Pan. Chrysostomou 2001, p. 493).
65 Cf. Dimoula 2014; *Franchthi* I.1–2, p. 216; Perlès and Vitelli 1999.
66 For example, Courtois 2004, pp. 4–5; Katsikaridis 2021; Vajsov 2007; Voulgari 2011.
67 Hitsiou 2003.

68 S. Papadopoulos and Malamidou 2000, p. 26.
69 Malamidou 2007, p. 301.
70 *Olynthus* I, figs. 11–18; *contra* J. K. Papadopoulos 2005, p. 550; S. Papadopoulos and Malamidou 2000, p. 26.
71 Coexisting and overlapping pits and ditches are common structuring features of earlier Neolithic and FN settlements (overview in Aslanis 2010, with references). Although the excavation notebooks clearly mention that Τάφρος 2 cut through Pits 1 and 2 (which must, therefore, be earlier), all four pits on the hilltop were originally dated to the EBA (Bessios 2012a, pp. 45–47, n. 6), on the basis of similar well-preserved features at the site of Kitros–Hassan Vrysi, likewise ascribed to the EBA (Bessios 2010, pp. 57–59). These dates must now be revised, on the recent evidence of a closely comparable, undisturbed late FN horizon at the Methone-Agathoupolis Sewerage Project (Αποχέτευση Μεθώνης-Αγαθούπολης: Tsiloyianni 2014).
72 Bessios 2010, pp. 67–69; 2012a, pp. 46–47.
73 Tsiloyianni 2014, pp. 222–224, figs. 1–2; Veropoulidou et al. forthcoming.
74 For example, the LN cooking pot **4/11** (ΜΕΘ 4221) was found in the lowest layer of Pit 4.
75 From the same pass comes also a worn polychrome(?) rim.
76 For the use of brown flint in the Neolithic and FN industries see, for example, Tringham 2003, pp. 84–88, 124.
77 Quartz was used to manufacture a significant percentage of the chipped stone tools found at FN Αποχέτευση Μεθώνης (Veropoulidou et al. forthcoming). Likewise, local quartz and rock crystal were integral in the chipped stone industries of coastal east Macedonia, for example at Sitagroi Phase I, dating to the MN (Tringham 2003, pp. 83–84), and at the FN settlement at Agios Ioannis on Thasos (S. Papadopoulos et al. 2018, pp. 357–361).
78 A significant increase in the use of large querns during the EBA has been observed at Sitagroi Phases IV–V, where it has been associated with a stronger reliance on processed grains during these same phases (Biskowski 2003; Elster 2003a, pp. 186–187).
79 Overviews in Cullen et al. 2013, pp. 68–71; Pantelidou-Gofa 2016; Tsirtsoni 2010.
80 Kitrini Limni: Kalogirou 1994, 1997; Dikili Tash: Demoule 2004; Sitagroi: R. K. Evans 1986.
81 Mandalo: Merousis and Nikolaidou 1997; Nikolaidou et al. 2003; Pilali-Papasteriou et al. 1986. Polyplatanos: Merousis 2002; Papadopoulou et al. 2006. Kryoneri: Malamidou 2007; Malamidou et al. 2006. Promachon: Vajsov 2007.
82 Rachmani: Toufexis, Karapanou, and Mangafa 2000; Wace and Thompson 1912, pp. 31–34. Pefkakia: *Pevkakia* I.
83 Extensive overview in Demoule 2004, pp. 102–182.
84 Doliana: Douzougli and Zachos 2002; Petromagoula: Chatziangelakis 1984; Mikrothives: Adrimi-Sismani 2007; Farangi Mesianis: Chondroyianni-Metoki 1997.
85 Morris 2009–2010, pp. 13–14.
86 Sherratt (1986, pp. 442–448, fig. 13.3a–b, table 13.2) had synchronized Phase IV at Sitagroi with the middle–late fourth millennium horizons Baden, Ezero, Kum Tepe, and Early Helladic I, which (according to the evidence and terminology of the time) he ascribed to the onset of the EBA—although pointing out the transitional nature of the period. The more recently investigated mid-fourth millennium site of Agios Ioannis has been recognized as late FN (S. Papadopoulos et al. 2001; S. Papadopoulos 2007).
87 See recently Horejs 2017; Kouka 2015, with references.
88 Overviews in Coleman 2011; Maran 1998, pp. 7–160, pls. 80–81; Pantelidou-Gofa 2016, pp. 261–272.
89 Reported in Bessios 2010, pp. 57–59; Bessios et al. 2003, p. 438.
90 Tsiloyianni 2014; Veropoulidou et al. forthcoming.
91 For example, *Franchthi* I.3–5, pp. 68–69.
92 S. Papadopoulos 2002, 2007.
93 Cf. Hood 1982, pp. 242, 301 (FN "Mottled Ware").
94 *Pevkakia* I.
95 Kalogirou 1994, p. 111, figs. 36–37.
96 Ridley, Wardle, and Mould 2000, pp. 54–55.
97 Hood 1982, pp. 29, 301.
98 *Agora* XIII, pp. 4–5.
99 *Franchthi* I.3–5, pp 64–65.
100 For example, Papathanassopoulos 1996, p. 263, cat. no. 116 (from Sesklo), with references.
101 Coleman 2011, especially figs. 5–7; Tsirtsoni 2010, fig. 7:1.
102 Chondroyianni-Metoki 1997, fig. 1.
103 Tsiloyianni 2014, p. 226, fig. 6.

104 Compare the "main" ware at FN Franchthi, which exhibits such variability of clay bodies that, in Karen Vitelli's words, "they seem to have been prepared almost randomly" (*Franchthi* I.3–5, p. 64). According to Vitelli, the potters dug their clays from beds of different purity; the clay recipes varied with the potter, the occasion, and, perhaps, each particular pot.

105 Kouka (2015, p. 226, fig. 6b) illustrates a coarse pedestal fragment in very similar fabric from the Heraion in Samos.

106 Cf. Kalogirou 1997; *Franchthi* I.3–5.

107 There is indeed a distinctive type of rounded coarse bowl with pierced rim (but not body) which is conventionally known as cheese pot, frequent at fourth-millennium sites around the Aegean (Cullen et al. 2013, p. 70, with references); a striated rim fragment to such a shape was collected among the fill of Τάφρος 3, as mentioned above. Apart from the uncertainty surrounding the function of this particular type, its form and fabric are very different from the burnished perforated shapes, such as **4/29** (ΜΕΘ 4290).

108 Bogucki 1984.

109 In their study of the faunal record from Kitrini Limni, Greenfield et al. (2005, pp. 111–112) have argued for a gradual implementation of the "secondary products revolution"—including cheese-making—in Greece, starting only in the FN. Although dairy practices are known earlier in other areas of the world, in the Aegean they seem more safely associated with the pastoralist economies that emerged toward the very end of the late FN and during the EBA (Morris 2014). Even at the late FN site of Αποχέτευση Μεθώνης, ovicaprids and cattle were raised mainly for their meat and only to a smaller extent for milk exploitation (Veropoulidou et al. forthcoming). In eastern Macedonia, the focus on primary or secondary animal products seems to vary among different sites during the LN–EBA (S. Papadopoulos et al. 2018, p. 364).

110 Kalogirou 1994, pp. 154–161.

111 Valamoti 2007a, 2007b.

112 Cf. Hood (1982, pp. 172–174) for a comprehensive discussion of a distinct "baking pan ware": a coarse, tray-like form with a row of perforations under the rim, which spans the Neolithic and EBA in the Aegean and Anatolia.

113 Tsiloyianni 2014, and pers. comm., 2016.

114 Bessios and Adaktylou 2008, p. 238.

115 Darcque et al. 2007, pp. 252–254, fig. 7.

116 S. Papadopoulos et al. 2001, pp. 56–58, plan 1.

117 For example, Marangou 1996, cat. no. 267 (Dikili Tash); Nikolaidou 2003b, p. 439, pl. 11.28 (Sitagroi).

118 Touloumis 1994.

119 Kalogirou 1997.

120 Tsiloyianni 2014, p. 225, and pers. comm., 2016.

121 For example, Coleman 1977 (Kephala); Cullen et al. 2013, pp. 70–71 (southern Euboia).

122 Andreou, Fotiadis, and Kotsakis 2001; Aslanis 2010, with references.

123 Krahtopoulou 2010, p. 51, fig. 3.11.

124 Bessios et al. 2003, p. 438, n. 1.

125 Bessios and Adaktylou 2008; Tsiloyianni 2014.

126 Aslanis 1993.

127 Andreou, Fotiadis, and Kotsakis 2001, p. 565; Demoule 2004, pp. 184–185; S. Papadopoulos 2002. A notable example is Mandalo, where EBA houses were built directly on FN I strata—the two phases dated in both absolute and relative terms (Kotsakis et al. 1989). A transitional FN–EBA horizon at that site is suggested by stratified deposits featuring mixed pottery akin to both periods (Merousis and Nikolaidou 1997; Papaefthymiou-Papanthimou and Pilali-Papasteriou 1988).

128 Sites include Doliana in Epirus (Douzougli and Zachos 2002), Agios Ioannis on Thasos (S. Papadopoulos 2007, p. 323, figs. 6–7), Mikrothives in Thessaly (Adrimi-Sismani 2007, p. 74), and the FN Pit 96 at Tsepi Marathon (Pantelidou-Gofa 2016).

129 Overviews in Alram-Stern 2014; Coleman 2011; Horejs 2017; Tsirtsoni 2010.

130 Tsiloyianni 2014, and pers. comm., 2016.

131 Substantial stone *periboloi* are a distinct presence in FN mainland and island sites, for example, at Mandalo in northwest Macedonia, Sesklo, Dimini, and Palioskala in Thessaly, and Strofilas on Andros (Aslanis 2010, with references).

132 Bessios and Adaktylou 2008.

133 Bessios 2010, p. 67; Tsiloyianni 2014, pp. 223–224, 226–227, fig. 7 (metal); Veropoulidou et al. forthcoming. An interesting Thessalian parallel is seen in a concentration of water wells at Rachmani, which were filled in successive episodes of domestic deposition, including a remarkable assemblage of 13 almost intact vessels near the bottom of one well (Toufexis, Karapanou, and Mangafa 2000, especially figs. 2–5, Plans 3–4).
134 Krahtopoulou 2010, fig. 3.9a–b.
135 Tsiloyianni 2014, p. 228.
136 Krahtopoulou 2010, pp. 52–53, fig. 3.12.
137 Coleman 2011; Tsirtsoni 2010.
138 Bessios 2010. Similar relocations are seen in Chalkidike (Morris 2009–2010, p. 14).
139 Likewise, in coastal Thessaly, the site of Petromagoula was first settled in the late FN—habitation possibly shifted there from the older center of Dimini—and coexisted in close proximity with the long-established site of Pefkakia (Chatziangelakis 1984, pp. 84–85).
140 Bessios 2010, p. 67. Similar advantageous locations, at convergence points between terrestrial and aquatic ecozones, were chosen for other late FN sites, such as Tsepi Marathon (Gotsinas 2016, p. 368), Teichos Dymaion in northwest Achaia (Gazis 2017), Franchthi (*Franchthi* II), and Çukuriçi Höyük near Ephesos (Horejs 2017).
141 Cf. Kottaridi 2000.
142 Bessios 2010; Tsiloyianni 2014; Veropoulidou et al. forthcoming.
143 Overviews in Alram-Stern 2014; Coleman 2011; Maran 1998, pp. 161–305.
144 Zachos 2010; Zachos and Douzougli 1999; cf. Tsiloyianni 2014, p. 226, fig. 7 (Αποχέτευση Μεθώνης).
145 Important aspects of life are evoked by the rich material record of the ritual Αποθέτης 39 in the Tsepi cemetery at Marathon. Large numbers of vessels were deposited therein during successive ceremonies, together with obsidian and other stone tools (including two stone molds for metal artifacts), an unidentified metal object, a few ornaments, a figurine, and a seal, as well as animal and human bones (Pantelidou-Gofa 2016).
146 Cf. *Franchthi* I.3–5, pp. 102–105.
147 Overviews in Merousis 2004; Morris 2009–2010; Psaraki and Mavroeidi 2013.
148 Such practice is known at Mandalo, where a double stone enclosure was founded in the FN and remained functional through the EBA (Merousis 2004, pp. 1289–1290, with references). V-shaped ditches (their function not entirely clear) were also a feature of the EBA settlement at Servia (Phase 8), located mainly in the central area of the site (Ridley, Wardle, and Mould 2000, pp. 97, 104).
149 Clay anchor-shaped artifacts (hooks?) are diagnostic of the EBA (Weisshaar 1980).
150 Elster 2003a (Sitagroi, with comparanda); Papaefthymiou-Papanthimou and Pilali-Papasteriou 1997, fig. 57 (Mandalo, EBA).
151 From the same unit comes a slashed rim of a FN–EBA jar (not inventoried).
152 Bessios, Athanassiadou, and Noulas 2021b and forthcoming.
153 Morris et al. 2020, pp. 680–683, figs. 22–25.
154 Heurtley 1939, p. 132; for a shape identical to ΜΕΘ 7141, from Tomb 3 in Plot 53 at Nea Agathoupolis, see Bessios et al. 2014, p. 231, fig. 5.
155 Heurtley 1939, figs. 38:e (Kritsana Settlement V), 45:a (Agios Mamas); Morris 2009–2010, fig. 19, no. 86.596, 822, fig. 30 no. 90.575 (Torone).
156 Some additional concentrations of very coarse EBA body sherds, mixed in with later handmade and wheelmade pottery, seem to have been repurposed as construction material (floor packing?) by the occupants of the EIA and/or Archaic periods.
157 It should be noted that a small-scale excavation by the KZ´ Ephoreia in the outskirts of the modern town of Nea Agathoupolis near the village church brought to light some remains of EBA presence (M. Bessios, pers. comm. 2014)—perhaps to be associated with the cemetery on the West Hill and the settlement on the East Hill.
158 Chykerda and Kontonicolas forthcoming.
159 Cf. Andreou 2014, p. 144.
160 Andreou, Fotiadis, and Kotsakis 2001; Bessios 2010; Pappa 2010.
161 Heurtley 1939, pp. 79–86.
162 Aslanis 1985 (Kastanas); Sherratt 1986, esp. fig. 13.3a–b, table 13.2 (Sitagroi).
163 Andreou 1997 (Sindos); Morris 2009–2010 (Torone).
164 Andreou 2014, pp. 142–144, table 1; Psaraki and Mavroeidi 2013.

165 Pappa 2010.
166 Torone III probably dates to the MBA rather than the original proposed date of EBA III, according to comparative analysis by Aslanis 2017, pp. 502–504, 529–530, fig. 194.
167 Merousis 2004; S. Papadopoulos 2002; Psaraki and Mavroeidi 2013.
168 Sindos: Andreou 1997; Agios Mamas: Heurtley 1939, pp. 5–7; Polychrono: Pappa 1990, pp. 389–391, fig. 5.
169 Morris 2014; Nikolaidou, Elster, and Renfrew 2013; Theodoropoulou 2007a, 2014; Valamoti 2007b; Valamoti, Papanthimou, and Pilali 2003; Veropoulidou 2011a, pp. 425–443, 2014.
170 Aslanis 1985 and Mavroeidi 2012, respectively.
171 Sherratt 1986.
172 Deliopoulos, Papadias, and Papaefthymiou-Papanthimou 2014.
173 Cf. Valamoti 2007a, 2007b.
174 Cf. Marangou 1992, pp. 234–235; Nikolaidou 2003b, p. 441.
175 Cf. Morris 2009-2010, p. 23; Sherratt 1986, pp. 434–438.
176 Grammenos 1981, fig. 31 no. 614 (Pentapolis [dark gray–burnished]); Morris 2009-2010, 14, figs 13–14 (Torone).
177 A fine gritty fabric, distinctive of large black-burnished bowls, has been reported from EBA Servia (Ridley, Wardle, and Mould 2000, p. 65).
178 Andreou 1997, p. 67; Kalogirou 1994, p. 114.
179 Pavúk 2014. **5/10** [ΜΕΘ 5075] is a local post-EBA example of this survival (see Chapter 5).
180 Morris 2009–2010, pp. 39–43.
181 Aslanis 2009; Horejs 2007a, pp. 211–217.
182 *Pevkakia* III, pp. 112, 127.
183 Rutter 1983.
184 Andreou 1997, pp. 65, 73; Aslanis 1985, p. 173; Morris 2009–2010, p. 25.
185 It would be worth testing experimentally the workability of such clays.
186 Cf. large conical bowls from Torone (Morris 2009–2010, p. 23) and, especially, Agios Athanassios Thessalonikis, where such vessels show a high concentration around the hearths (Mavroeidi 2012, especially pp. 179–180, 209–210, pls. 25–27; Mavroeidi, Andreou, and Pappa 2006, pp. 487–489, fig. 2a).
187 Compare Agios Athanassios Thessalonikis, where a sizable group of cookware comes in a range of shapes, sizes, fabrics, and surface treatment (Mavroeidi 2012, pp. 162–172).
188 These were selected amid the contents of the pottery bags specific to each excavated pass, but not inventoried.
189 The typical EBA baking pans are coarsely made and bear perforations around the rim. Many were found at Agios Athanassios Thessalonikis, associated with a cluster of hearths (Mavroeidi 2012, pp. 160–161, pl. 23 [type AV3]; Mavroeidi, Andreou, and Pappa 2006, pp. 481–482, fig. 5:γ;); other examples come from Torone (Morris 2009–2010, fig. 29, 90.823), Kastanas and Axiochori (Aslanis 1985, pp. 173–174, fig. 92 and pl. 92.11, respectively), and Argissa, House B ("*Sommerküche*": *Argissa-Magoula* III, pls. VI:4, 44:6).
190 Cf. Morris 2009–2010, p. 26, fig. 29 (Torone).
191 Morris 2009–2010, pp. 25–26; 2014, with extensive comparanda.
192 Key sites include Archontiko (Papaefthymiou-Papanthimou and Papadopoulou 2014; Valamoti, Papanthimou, and Pilali 2003), Agios Athanassios Thessalonikis (Mavroeidi 2012, pp. 75–77, 162–172; Mavroeidi, Andreou, and Pappa 2006), Sitagroi (Elster 1997; Nikolaidou, Elster, and Renfrew 2013; J. M. Renfrew 2003), and Torone (Morris 2009–2010, 2014).
193 Andreou 2014; Andreou, Fotiadis, and Kotsakis 2001.
194 Bessios 2010; Bessios and Krahtopoulou 2001; Krahtopoulou 2010, 52–54, fig. 3.12.
195 Krahtopoulou 2010, p. 54.
196 Tzifopoulos 2012a; Tzifopoulos (Chapter 2, this volume).
197 Bessios and Pappa 1995; see also Tzifopoulos (Chapter 2) for the historical trajectory of Pydna.
198 Andreou 1997; Tiverios 2009a.
199 Andreou and Kotsakis 1996; Andreou and Psaraki 2007.
200 Adam-Veleni 1985.
201 *Torone* I; Morris 2009–2010.
202 Andreou 2014.
203 Veropoulidou 2014, fig. 1.
204 Morris 2009–2010, fig. 1.
205 Theodoropoulou 2014.

206 Comprehensive discussions in Aslanis 1985; Morris 2009–2010; Pappa 2010; Sherratt 1986.
207 Morris 2009–2010, pp. 23–24, fig. 21.
208 Valamoti 2007b; Valamoti, Papanthimou, and Pilali 2003.
209 Morris 2014.
210 Koukouli-Chrysanthaki 1987, 1988. Note also the prehistoric fortifications of Torone, which were probably first constructed in the EBA, and were continuously rebuilt through the EIA, see J. K. Papadopoulos et al. 1999.
211 Andreou 2014, with references; Merousis 2004, pl. 3 (axe from Mandalo).
212 Poulaki-Pantermali 2013a, pp. 31–32.
213 Pappa 2010, pp. 387–388, 401–402, pl. 7.
214 Bessios 2010, pp. 70–71.
215 Elster 2003a.
216 Kessisoglou, Mirtsou, and Stratis 1985; Morris 2009–2010, p. 25, fig. 27.
217 Ridley, Wardle, and Mould 2000.
218 Merousis 2004, pp. 1289–1290; Papaefthymiou-Papanthimou and Pilali-Papasteriou 1988.
219 C. Renfrew 1986.
220 Kitrini Limni: Fotiadis and Chondroyianni-Metoki 1993; Mesimeriani Toumba: Grammenos and Kotsos 1996; Kryoneri: Malamidou 2007; Orpheus Cave: Kontaxi, Giannopoulos, and Kaznesi 2004; Dikili Tash: Séfériadès 1983; Treuil 1992; Limenaria: Malamidou and Papadopoulos 1993, 1997.
221 Cf. Andreou 2014; Mavroeidi 2014.
222 For example, Merousis and Nikolaidou 1997; Sherratt 1986.
223 For example, Asouchidou 2009 (Kriaritsi, Sithonia); Pappa 2010 (Agios Mamas); Ziota 2007 (Goules and Xeropigado, Kozani).
224 For example, Sherratt 1986, pp. 448–449. Heurtley's authority had set the tone for many decades to come (cf. Fotiadis 2001). In concluding his seminal synthesis of prehistoric Macedonia, he commented: "The habits of the Macedonian folk underwent little change during the two thousand and odd years covered by this study. . . . if they [the Bronze Age people] were in advance of the Neolithic population in material things, aesthetically they were on a lower level . . . The lack of receptivity of the Bronze Age people . . . is shown by the fact that though the wheel was known they made practically no use of it, and the technically excellent Minyan and Mycenaean pottery made no impression on the local, which remained curiously impervious to external influences, retaining its provincial individuality from first to last. . . . Thus the cultural level of Macedonia was evidently never very high. We get the impression of a race of stolid peasants, largely self-contained. . . . and unconsciously beginning to fulfil their traditional role of a screen between Hellenism and barbarism" (Heurtley 1939, pp. 131–132). Eight decades and numerous excavations later, the image of prehistoric Macedonia has been profoundly transformed by the richness and complexity of the data, as well as by the depth and nuance of the archaeological narratives (for example, Andreou, Fotiadis, and Kotsakis 2001; contributions in Stefani, Merousis, and Dimoula 2014).
225 Cf. Andreou and Psaraki 2007; Kiriatzi et al. 1997.

5

THE MIDDLE AND LATE BRONZE AGE POTTERY

Trevor Van Damme

Excavations since 2003 have demonstrated the presence of a Middle and Late Bronze Age occupational phase at the site of ancient Methone.[1] The primary locus of settlement activity was in the area of the East Hill, which at the time would have formed an elongated peninsula jutting out into the Thermaic Gulf, forming sheltered natural anchorages to both the north and the south (see Chapters 1, 3). Unfortunately, much of the settlement proper has been destroyed, whether by natural processes, including the steady erosion of the Bronze Age promontory by wave activity, or later building activities, such as the monumental terracing and excavation activities that preceded the organization of the "agora" and the construction of the "Hypogeion." Despite these damaging effects, a small but significant body of Middle and Late Bronze Age pottery has been identified among the archaeological material excavated in secondary deposition within fills across the East Hill, testifying to the continued occupation of the site, even in the absence of any architectural remains.

This chapter presents for the first time a representative selection of the Middle and Late Bronze Age shapes and pottery groups/wares found in the 2003–2011 excavations and places them within a tentative interpretative framework. As this pottery comes entirely from secondary contexts, there is often a certain amount of ambiguity regarding the date of individual pieces. This is particularly true of the local matt-painted and handmade wares, which endured with little morphological development across the Late Bronze and Early Iron Age transition and are highly regional stylistically, preventing ready comparison between sites outside of the immediate region. In the catalogue that follows, I have tried to indicate wherever such uncertainty exists.

THE MIDDLE BRONZE AGE SETTLEMENT

While the last two decades have seen a great deal of attention paid to the archaeology of northern Greece,[2] and prehistory in particular,[3] much remains to be learned about the Middle Bronze Age occupation. In 2001, John Papadopoulos noted that "the most poorly understood of all periods in Macedonian prehistory is the Middle Bronze Age, so much so that it has led some scholars to conclude that an easily distinguished Middle Bronze Age phase does not really exist in Macedonia."[4] The situation 20 years later shows that as far as we have come, there is still a ways to go. While recent excavation of sites such as Kastanas, Toumba Thessalonikis, Archontiko, Torone, and Agios Mamas have revealed important new stratified Middle Bronze Age sequences, the final publications of these finds, including entire assemblages, have only recently begun to appear in print.[5] As preliminary reports inevitably prioritize the publication of southern Greek imports, which provide the basis for relative chronologies, considerably less attention has thus far been paid to the local handmade sequence. Ioannis Aslanis' recent volume on the stratified Middle Bronze Age sequence from Agios Mamas is particularly cautionary: throughout the Middle Bronze Age, wheelmade pottery never forms more than 50% of the total fine ware assemblage, even at a port site with abundant international contacts.[6]

Because of the conservative nature of handmade potting traditions in northern Greece, much of what can be said about Middle Bronze Age ceramic assemblages, especially those in secondary deposition, such as the Methone material discussed here, relies primarily on the identification of southern Greek imports or local imitations of these wares. In the present work, I have divided the Middle Bronze Age and initial Late Bronze Age material into four categories: wheelmade Minyan[7] and their handmade imitations, other local handmade wares, wheelmade Mycenaean style, and matt-painted and bichrome handmade. No further subcategorization of the Minyan pottery has been made on account of the limited range of the material. Concerning the local handmade material, only vessels for which there are well-dated comparanda from other sites in the region of northern Greece have been included. It is unfortunate, but probable, however, that these wares represent only a small fraction of the total Middle Bronze Age assemblage.

The Middle Bronze Age material from ancient Methone presented here, consists almost exclusively of wheelmade pottery in the Minyan tradition, or local handmade imitations of such vessels. The Minyan assemblage comprises mostly drinking and pouring vessels, a pattern of ceramic consumption that reoccurs in the Late Bronze Age material, and it is tempting to see the adoption of new ceramic tableware as the attempt of a limited group of elite members of the community to distinguish themselves by the adoption of new ceramic styles or new consumption habits or etiquette.[8] The fact that such Minyan imitations reach their peak popularity around the transition to the Late Bronze Age at the site of Agios Mamas,[9] at a time when Mycenaean lustrous decorated ceramics first appear in the north,[10] suggests that as these ceramics became embraced by, and accessible to, an increasing number of individuals, restricted groups—most likely a small group of elite individuals—turned to new foreign styles to set themselves apart once more. Although the Methone assemblage represents a fairly small sample of vessels, the current study supports the hypothesis that these styles only formed a restricted portion of the ceramic assemblage and, thus, their consumption or popularity was limited to a restricted number of households.

As far as the limited material of this period is concerned, most vessels find their closest parallels with the Mature and Late phases of southern Minyan development, with open shapes, such as the goblet (**5/11**, **5/13**, **5/15**, **5/16**), the kantharos (**5/9**), the kantharos bowl (**5/18**), and the cup (**5/8**), predominating, alongside the presence of small closed shapes such as the jar (**5/4**) and amphoriskos (**5/3**).[11] While a number of pieces are made on the wheel, or carefully finished so as to be almost indistinguishable from wheelmade pieces, others are clearly handmade imitations of wheelmade Minyan. There seems little reason to doubt that the handmade pieces are the product of potters trained in local techniques replicating the wheelmade Minyan style with an incomplete knowledge of southern production techniques. A good example of this is **5/16**, which has a squared rim and angular body that closely adheres to the characteristics of the wheelmade Minyan goblet, but is rather uneven in its execution, even considering the origin of this sherd near the handle attachment. Minyan bowls are also represented, of which one example (**5/14**) seems to be wheelmade Minyan, with a T-rim and slightly incurving wall, while two other specimens are handmade with imitation wheel grooves on the upper shoulder (**5/9**, **5/17**). Closed vessels are almost exclusively small in size. Most distinct is the Gray Minyan amphoriskos base (**5/7**). Many of the other sherds presented here represent small handmade closed shapes, either jugs, jars, or amphoriskoi (**5/1**, **5/2**, **5/3**, **5/4**, **5/5**, **5/6**). These are frequently decorated with bands of grooves meant to replicate similar ridges or grooves present on wheelmade Minyan.

A few handmade sherds find parallels with Middle Bronze Age to Late Bronze Age finds from other northern sites and are included here to give a sense of the range of the material. The majority of these shapes were part of a long-lasting local potting tradition, rather distinct from the imported wares and techniques from the south. Most diagnostic among these is the bowl with wishbone handle (**5/24, 5/25, 5/29**), a shape that becomes widely popular in the Middle Bronze Age across northern and central Greece. A sherd from a hemispherical bowl (**5/26**) may be Middle or Late Bronze Age in date.

THE LATE BRONZE AGE SETTLEMENT

The Late Bronze Age settlement was also situated on the East Hill, probably continuing without interruption from the Middle Bronze Age settlement. The presence of a significant Late Bronze Age cemetery on the West Hill provides a reliable boundary for the settlement in that direction. While a significant number of burials have already been identified in this cemetery (see Chapter 6), it is unlikely that the site of ancient Methone was particularly large during the Late Bronze Age—an observation that is reflected in the ceramic material of the settlement. For although the site shows some early connections with southern Greece, including the presence of an Aiginetan import in the early Mycenaean period (**5/40** [ΜΕΘ 4288]: LH I–LH IIIA), this gives way to an extended period with sparse evidence for imported pottery or interconnections with the south. It is only around the time of the palatial collapse in the southern Aegean (LH IIIB2) that the local production of Mycenaean pottery seems to take off, along with an awareness of ceramic developments in southern Greece.

It is noteworthy that no early Mycenaean lustrous decorated pottery has been discovered at Methone up until now. This pattern is somewhat striking when viewed in light of the quantity and quality of Mycenaean imports from southern Greece identified at the contemporaneous port settlement of Torone.[12] Indeed, it is all the more puzzling that such imported material would be absent from Methone, the gatekeeper of the Thermaic Gulf, when sites located up the Haliakmon River have produced imported and local material from the palatial period (LH IIIA2–B) in some quantity.[13] Perhaps the relevant material from Methone was lost when the better part of the settlement fell into the sea, or perhaps the small size of the community simply made it less attractive to merchant ships passing by on their way up to the rivers feeding into the Thermaic Gulf, or, indeed, the relevant material may yet remain to be identified in deeper deposits underlying the agora area. Alternatively, the large rivers may not have been the conduit of these wares at all, and instead an inland route through the passes of central Greece might be posited, bringing wares from Thessaly into the heart of Macedonia, bypassing the coast altogether (this said, the early Mycenaean pottery at Torone clearly arrived there by sea).[14] Whatever the case, based on the present evidence one might conclude that the inhabitants of Methone were slower to adopt the new techniques and decorative schemes associated with the Mycenaean style in contrast to neighboring settlements.

When Mycenaean forms do first appear at Methone (perhaps as early as LH IIIA: see Chapter 6 on the finds from the cemetery), the pottery is almost exclusively of a locally or regionally made character, a pattern observed elsewhere at small inland sites in northern Greece.[15] Thus the impetus for this style is likely to have come from much closer to home, rather than due to any direct connection with southern Greece. A likely source of inspiration was the area of southern Pieria, which exhibits a strong local Mycenaean potting tradition by LH II, or Thessaly, even farther south, where the sites of Kastro Palaia (Volos), Pefkakia, and Dimini bear witness to a full-fledged Mycenaean palatial state.[16] This is borne out by a close analysis of the technique of manufacture—several pieces seem likely to have been handmade and only turned, or carefully finished, to achieve a wheelmade effect. It is possible, therefore, that the production techniques involved in the production of Mycenaean style pottery were acquired second-hand. This fact makes the dating of Mycenaean ceramics in the north particularly challenging on stylistic grounds, since much of the decoration during the latter part of the Mycenaean sequence is of a highly regional character.[17] The publication of local wheelmade ceramics from Kastanas,[18] Toumba Thessalonikis,[19] Agios Mamas,[20] and elsewhere by Walter Heurtley,[21] has to a certain degree alleviated this problem, but some ambiguity necessarily remains.

The Late Bronze Age finds have been made in the same contexts as the Middle Bronze Age finds discussed previously. Although many of these appear to have been redeposited during slope erosion, a number of finds also come from the Hypogeion, some of which may have some significance when viewed within their larger archaeological context. These include two Mycenaean-style kylix stems from the first filling phase (**5/34**, **5/35**), one with evidence for reworking. Although battered and each comprising a single sherd, given the large number of fine ware closed shapes discarded in the Hypogeion, it seems possible, and even probable, that they were reused as convenient bottle stoppers, perhaps hundreds of years after they had first broken.[22] A handmade matt-painted kantharos (**5/52**) preserving several joining and non-joining fragments, comprising a near-complete profile, also discovered within the first filling phase of the Hypogeion is perfectly acceptable as a Late Bronze Age vessel, but given its position in the fill of the Hypogeion and near complete profile, an Early Iron Age date is equally, if not more, plausible (for the character of the first filling phase, see Chapter 8). Notably, this piece has a distinct fabric that was identified during the analysis as a possible import. While this may be true, it is also possible that the Early Iron Age handmade recipe was slightly different from its LBA predecessor and that this too is a local product separated from its LBA counterparts in time, not space.

Excluding this one piece as an Early Iron Age kantharos based on context, all of the remaining Late Bronze Age ceramics were found in redeposited fills. As such, the range of shapes presented here is once again heavily biased toward wheelmade and painted ceramics that stood out among the Early Iron Age and Archaic ceramics with which they were intermixed. The material presented here therefore cannot be assumed to represent the overall character of the settlement, in which only a small percentage of the total Late Bronze Age pottery would have been wheelmade and decorated.[23] Further problems in relative chronology arise from the long duration of ceramic styles in northern Greece. It is apparent from Agios Mamas that the Minyan style remains popular perhaps as late as LH II in the chronology of the south Greek mainland and, therefore, some of the pieces presented within that category above are likely to be early Late Bronze Age in date.[24] In addition, it is well known that the matt-painted style remained popular in northern Greece from the Late Bronze Age into the Early Iron Age.[25] On the basis of sherd evidence, therefore, distinguishing between the various periods can be difficult. Despite these caveats, a small number of handmade sherds can be placed with some confidence in the Late Bronze Age because of their diagnostic shape and decoration.

The Late Bronze Age assemblage offers some evidence for consumption practices within the settlement, contemporaneous with the burials on the West Hill, and therefore represents an important contribution toward our understanding of the otherwise invisible Late Bronze Age settlement. The most striking contrast observed in ceramics from the settlement versus those from the cemetery is the relative frequency of open versus closed shapes. This not only emphasizes the (rather obvious) functional difference between the two areas, but also the restriction of Mycenaean-style pottery to a fairly limited range of activities in both instances. While small closed shapes (i.e., containers for liquids or fats) such as alabastra and amphoriskoi form the vast majority of Mycenaean ceramics deposited in the Late Bronze Age cemetery (see Chapter 6), within the settlement it is open shapes used as tableware for drinking and dining that predominate.

Kylikes and deep bowls represent the two most common shapes. With the exception of **5/34**, which is marked out by its fabric, shape, and decoration as a probable LH IIIB import, possibly from Thessaly,[26] all kylikes are locally-made examples of the conical, FS 275, variety with monochrome interiors and exterior decoration consisting mainly of simple banding (**5/33, 5/35, 5/37**), sometimes in the form of a continuous spiral around the stem (**5/34, 5/38**). The best-preserved example (**5/36**) consists of two joining fragments and features a monochrome interior, and exterior decoration consisting of a monochrome stem with a thick wavy band between the handles. One kylix (**5/35**) is unique in having a distinct "blob" decoration between its handles. This type of decoration is likely intended to produce monochrome kylikes as seen on numerous kylikes from the Mycenaean Fountain on the North Slope of the Acropolis at Athens.[27] With the exception of **5/34**, all the kylikes are decorated with matt paint often fired to a reddish brown color. Deep bowls (FS 284/285) feature linear decoration on both the exterior and interior (**5/44**), linear decoration on the exterior with monochrome decoration on the interior (**5/45**), or a lip band and wavy band/horn/antithetic streamer on the exterior with monochrome decoration on the interior (**5/43**). This last bowl is rather large, suggesting it may have been used functionally as a mixing rather than serving vessel.

Other open shapes are represented by only one or two examples. These include the earliest Late Bronze Age material: a red painted krater of Aiginetan manufacture (**5/40**) and a highly burnished brown goblet (**5/39**), probably a local imitation of early Mycenaean goblets from southern Greece. A spouted krater (**5/42**) with a raised plastic spur on the rim represents a local peculiarity, possibly of Early Iron Age date, although the shape is common enough in Late Bronze Age deposits from Kastanas to warrant its inclusion here. In addition, the linear basin with monochrome interior is present (**5/41**), a typical serving vessel of the advanced stages of the Late Bronze Age, although appearing as early as the LH IIIB1 period in the southern mainland.[28]

In addition to the wide array of open vessels, a few sherds from the settlement also testify to the presence of small closed shapes, such as alabastra and piriform jars or amphoriskoi. These, rather than forming part of the dining assemblage, are more likely related to the function they served in funerary assemblages as containers of unguents, perfumes, or oils.[29] A larger closed shape (**5/30**) must be a local version of the amphoriskos (FS 59) or piriform jar (FS 48) with a flat rim and ridged shoulder from the crude addition of the neck to the shoulder. Two shoulder fragments represent the straight-sided (**5/32**) and rounded alabastron (**5/31**) respectively.

In addition to Mycenaean-style pottery, matt-painted pottery is present in small quantities. Although it is difficult to place this material chronologically, due to the difficulties presented above, the sherds are grouped together here for the sake of convenience. The most abundant types represented are again the open shapes, suggesting an overlapping function with the Minyan and Mycenaean assemblages already discussed. Indeed, Alix Hochstetter has argued as much with regard to the virtual absence of matt-painted pottery contemporary with the period of greatest use of Mycenaean-style pottery at the very end of the Late Bronze Age.[30] This seems to be corroborated by a similar dropoff in matt-painted pottery at Toumba Thessalonikis correlated with increased use of Mycenaean-style wheelmade pottery.[31] The material published here, therefore, is likely to either predate or postdate the vast majority of the Mycenaean material. While this would seem plausible, the longevity of certain decorative syntaxes and motifs clouds the precise dating of redeposited sherd material. The suggested dates presented in this catalogue are based on the most diagnostic pieces, but the possibility remains that some pieces may date to the Early Iron Age.[32]

The most popular vessels among the matt-painted pottery are the kantharos and the bowl. Among the kantharoi published here, two present short everted rims with vertical strap handles (**5/52, 5/53**). A third (**5/55**) is only a fragment of a handle, and thus it is unclear what exact form the rim of the vessel might have taken. It is worth noting here, however, the morphological distinction that can be made in the treatment of the kantharoi rims from Methone, and the Early Iron Age examples published from Vitsa, Liatovouni, and Marmariani, which are remarkably consistent in being vertical or near-vertical and lipless, giving the shape an almost collared appearance.[33] The short everted examples from Methone are rather quite similar to the Late Bronze Age examples from Aiani and Kastanas, suggesting that this is a chronological distinction and not merely local variation. Furthermore, the Early Iron Age examples are frequently much more geometric in their decoration, presumably on account of the emergent use of Protogeometric motifs on wheelmade pottery. The decoration of the matt-painted ware from Methone, however, remains for the most part curvilinear. This is best exemplified by the matt-painted bowls (**5/51, 5/54**), both of which feature a distinct decorative scheme consisting of joining semicircles and linear banding precisely paralleled by Late Bronze Age bowls from Agios Mamas.

The matt-painted closed shapes are dominated by a standard shape of amphora with tapering neck, sometimes flaring out at the rim (**5/46, 5/47, 5/48, 5/50**). These are decorated with linear bands, frequently with the addition of pendant fringe (German "Fransenband"), similar to the decorative syntax of such shapes at Agios Mamas.[34] A smaller variant of this shape, here termed a jar (**5/49**), is stylistically and morphologically closely related. One sherd from a large krater (**5/56**) is likely to be closely related to the mainland polychrome/bichrome tradition of southern and central Greece. The remaining vessels are difficult to place with any degree of certainty; no exact parallels exist for the decoration, which is likely to be regional. Indeed, the form of the handmade amphora is remarkably stable from the Late Bronze Age through the Early Iron Age. It seems prudent, therefore, not to attempt a more refined dating of these vessels here.

Among the remaining material likely to be of Late Bronze Age or Early Iron Age date, there is an eclectic mix of open and closed shapes. These have been primarily identified in the sherd material on account of their distinct morphological characteristics. A large undecorated closed shape (**5/21**) appears similar in form to the matt-painted examples just discussed. As noted, such amphoras are common in the latter part of the Late Bronze Age and the Early Iron Age. Likewise, a feeding bottle/jug/cup spout (**5/22**) rendered in similar fabric and almost certainly handmade, to judge by details of fabric and surface finish, clearly imitates the common Mycenaean funerary shape (found in a Methone tomb: **6/27** [ΜΕΘ 868]) and could likewise date to either period, as EIA examples are known from Vergina. In contrast, the rim of an ovoid jar should, based on parallels from Kastanas and Torone, date to the Late Bronze Age. Meanwhile two bowls (**5/26, 5/28**) are characteristic examples of a known Late Bronze Age type featuring a slight carination where the rim meets the shoulder and a beveled rim. A final class of local decorated ware, incised with added white pigment, is represented by two sherds, one rim from a small jar or amphoriskos (**5/20**) and a handle from an unknown shape (**5/19**).

Overall, the pottery from the Middle and Late Bronze Age settlement fits well with pottery found at contemporary settlements in the region of eastern Macedonia, especially those ringing the Thermaic Gulf or up the Haliakmon River, as well as at sites such as Agios Mamas and Torone in the Chalkidike, where the closest parallels can be found. Based on the common repertoire of shapes represented, the mechanism driving the acquisition of Minyan, matt-painted, and Mycenaean pottery is likely to have centered on the social acts of drinking and dining. Although the physical contexts of these events are nonexistent at the site of Methone, due to the lack of associated architectural remains, the fact that these vessels were largely for use exclusively by the living, rather than being deposited in the contemporaneous cemetery, at least in the Late Bronze Age, highlights the role they played in the everyday lives of the ancient inhabitants. The adoption of new drinking practices, or perhaps innovative forms of cuisine along with the new styles of tableware, suggests further opportunities for social differentiation and future grounds for research.[35] Furthermore, this assemblage highlights the need for additional work on refining the chronological and geographic distribution of the ceramic styles mentioned above in order to facilitate a better understanding of the important social developments that took place in northern Greece during the latter half of the third and the second millennium.

CATALOGUE

MBA–LBA—WHEELMADE MINYAN AND HANDMADE IMITATIONS

5/1. (ΜΕΘ 4879) Handmade Closed Shape Fig. 5.1
East Hill. #274/085. Erosion layer (NW quarter). 2004.
P.H. 0.036; p.W. 0.042.
Single fr of handmade shape apparently imitating Yellow Minyan.
Dark gray interior may suggest a closed shape, however, **5/39** (ΜΕΘ 4953) demonstrates that this could be the result of stacking as well. Sherd preserves three incised grooves in imitation of wheel marks/grooving on true Minyan.
Semi-coarse fabric rich in mica and grit fired to brown color 5YR 7/6–7.5YR 7/6.
Surface burnished yellow and smoothed; once glossy.
Although it is difficult to pinpoint the shape of the present example, the surface decoration is paralleled by MBA material from Agios Mamas and Torone. See also **5/2** (ΜΕΘ 5062) and **5/5** (ΜΕΘ 5238). Heurtley 1939, p. 208, fig. 74a; p. 210, fig. 76h; p. 212, nos. 400–401; Papadopoulos 2001, fig. 48, no. 3.21; Morris 2009–2010, p. 49, fig. 38, no. 90.1290; *Orchomenos* IV, p. 353, pl. 51, no. 4; p. 413, Phototafel 2, no. 5.

FIGURE 5.1. MBA Minyan/Imitation Minyan, a) closed vessels: **5/1** (ΜΕΘ 4879), **5/2** (ΜΕΘ 5062). Drawings T. Ross, photos I. Coyle

5/2. (ΜΕΘ 5062) Handmade Closed Shape   Fig. 5.1

    East Hill. #274/054014 [5]. 09/09/2003.

    P.H. 0.043; p.W. 0.031.

    Single fr of handmade imitation of Gray Minyan closed vessel.

    Sherd preserves three horizontal grooves in imitation of wheel marks on true Minyan.

    Fine fabric rich in mica fired gray throughout.

    Surface burnished(?) and smoothed. Now worn, but probably originally glossy.

    Other than firing conditions, this piece is very similar to the previous example, **5/1**, and **5/5** (ΜΕΘ 4879 and ΜΕΘ 5238). Heurtley 1939, p. 208, fig. 74a; p. 210, fig. 76h; p. 212, no. 400–401; Papadopoulos 2001, fig. 48, no. 3.21; Morris 2009–2010, p. 49, fig. 38, no. 90.1290; *Orchomenos* IV, p. 353, pl. 51, no. 4; p. 413, Phototafel 2, no. 5.

5/3. (ΜΕΘ 5097) Red Minyan Amphoriskos   Fig. 5.2

    East Hill. #274/084005 [3]. 21/07/2003 and 22/07/2003.

    P.H. 0.031; p.W. 0.059; Diam. (rim) est. 0.140.

    Single fr rim and upper wall of a red Minyan amphoriskos.

    Medium, everted rim with flat lip features a shallow central groove; three wheel grooves (or imitations) inside rim. An imitation rivet appears on the exterior of the rim, with corresponding hole for pushing out rivet on interior. While illogically placed for a real rivet, this appears to be a case of style trumping practicality as there is no obvious need for a firing hole in the rim to aid in the drying or firing process.

    Fine fabric features a few small dark brown and white inclusions. Fired to a deep red color 10YR 6/8–2.5YR 6/8.

    The vessel is unpainted, but highly burnished red on both interior and exterior surfaces of preserved fr.

    Although only a small fr, distinct features, such as interior wheel(?) marks and imitation rivet, clearly denote this a Minyan imitation. Probably wheelmade, although it cannot be excluded that it is an exceptionally fine handmade imitation. Parallels from Torone and Agios Mamas suggest the shape was common to the region ringing the Thermaic Gulf. The closest parallel, from Agios Mamas, comes from a Late Bronze Age context, but similar sherds from Torone were found in secure Middle Bronze Age contexts, thus a date MH–LH should be assigned to the present piece. See Papadopoulos 2001, fig. 48, no. 3.16; Horejs 2007a, pl. 72, no. 8760; Morris 2009–2010, fig. 39, no. 88.344. For imitation rivets as a characteristic of this period, Heurtley 1939, p. 210, fig. 76c; fig. 76i.

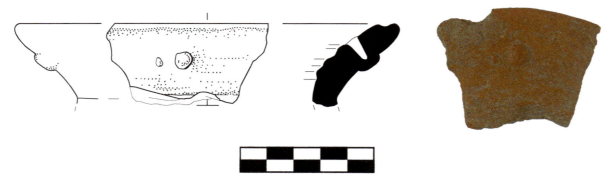

FIGURE 5.2. MBA Minyan/Imitation Minyan, a) closed vessels: **5/3** (ΜΕΘ 5097).
Drawing A. Hooton, photo I. Coyle

5/4. (MEΘ 5117) Gray Minyan Jar(?) Fig. 5.3
East Hill. #274/084012. 04/08/2003.
P.H. 0.050; p.W. 0.041; Diam. (neck) est. 0.070.

Single fr of neck and almost rim from a Gray Minyan wheelmade closed shape, broken at join to shoulder. Wheel marks visible inside.

Fine fabric with fine mica inclusions fired brownish gray 10YR 5/3 with a pure gray core 5Y 5/1. Surface originally carefully smoothed and burnished gray. Glossiness worn off over most of surface.

Best parallels for this piece are the cutaway jugs published by Heurtley from Agios Mamas. It is possible that this piece, like **5/6** (MEΘ 5610), is an Early Iron Age product. See Heurtley 1939, p. 210, fig. 76g; p. 210, no. 395.

5/5. (MEΘ 5238) Handmade Jug Fig. 5.3
East Hill. #274/084003. Layer 2. 21/7/2003.
P.H. 0.045; p.W. 0.042.

Biconical fr from a small closed vessel, preserving wall of a piriform body with shoulder and just the beginning of base.

Soft carination defines the transition from body to shoulder. Low ovoid mastos, probably decorative, on the carination, next to it the broken root of the handle or another plastic decoration.

Clay body is very fine, without visible inclusions. Evenly fired gray 10YR 5/1.

Exterior is slipped and burnished, fired to matt yellowish brown 10YR 5/8, with some faint mottling. Interior is also slipped, fired light gray 10YR 6/1, with textured surface created by intersecting groups of fine lines and broader shallow grooves. See also **5/1** and **5/2** (MEΘ 4879 and MEΘ 5062). Heurtley 1939, p. 208, fig. 74a; p. 210, fig. 76h; p. 212, nos. 400–401; Papadopoulos 2001, fig. 48, no. 3.21; Morris 2009–2010, p. 49, fig. 38, no. 90.1290; *Orchomenos* IV, p. 353, pl. 51, no. 4; p. 413, Phototafel 2, no. 5.

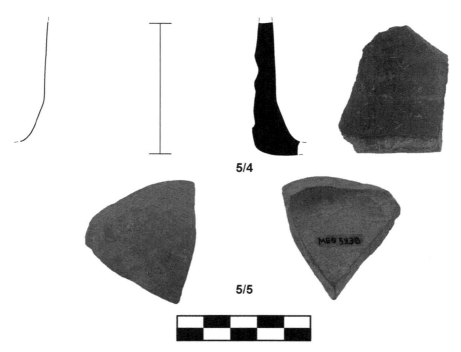

FIGURE 5.3. MBA Minyan/Imitation Minyan, a) closed vessels: **5/4** (MEΘ 5117), **5/5** (MEΘ 5238). Drawing T. Ross, photos I. Coyle

5/6. (ΜΕΘ 5610) Handmade Amphoriskos/Jar Fig. 5.4

East Hill. #274/085. Brownish red layer. 07/08/2004.

P.H. 0.038: p.W. 0.047: Diam. (rim) est. 0.100.

Single fr from wheelmade rim with grooves on exterior belonging to a small amphora or jar.

Fine micaceous fabric. Fired dark gray-brown on the surface 10YR 5/3 with a pure gray core 5Y 5/1.

Surface dark gray with no traces of burnish. Interior surface heavily worn, exposing brownish fabric in places.

This piece resembles other Minyan pieces in technique and fabric, except for the lack of burnishing on the exterior. A parallel piece from Agios Mamas is a handmade amphora with fake wheel marks on the exterior of the rim, considered by the author to be a Minyan imitation. A similar grayware piece from Kastanas, Schicht 11, suggests an EIA date. Because this piece was found in secondary deposition, an EIA date cannot be ruled out, since such graywares are common in northern Greece and Anatolia throughout this period. See also **5/4** (ΜΕΘ 5117), which has a similar fabric to this piece. See Jung 2002, pl. 66, no. 539; Horejs 2007a, pl. 28, no. 8762.

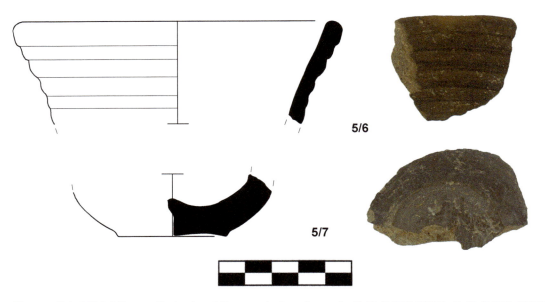

FIGURE 5.4. MBA Minyan/Imitation Minyan, a) closed vessels: **5/6** (ΜΕΘ 5610), **5/7** (ΜΕΘ 5632). Drawings T. Ross, photos I. Coyle

5/7. (ΜΕΘ 5632) Gray Minyan Amphoriskos Fig. 5.4

East Hill. #274/085023 [9]. 01/09/2003 and 02/09/2003.

P.H. 0.020; p.W. 0.058; Diam. (base) 0.040.

Single fr from partially concave base of a small closed shape with very thick lower walls and base.

Very fine clay with a few mica and white inclusions visible to naked eye. Fired hard, to a light gray color 5Y 6/1.

Exterior surface carefully burnished and smoothed, producing a dark gray finish. Interior unburnished.

The size and thickness of this base make it likely that it belongs to a small amphoriskos, of the type commonly found in Gray Minyan elsewhere in Greece. This is a relatively late-occurring shape and should likely date to very early LH I. See Mylonas 1973, Pin. 44b.2–4; Pin. 133g; *Pevkakia* III, pl. 123, no. 8; pl. 123, no. 12; pl. 123, no. 14; *Orchomenos* IV, p. 261, pl. 11, nos. 2, 6.

5/8. (ΜΕΘ 4891) Handmade One-handled Cup Fig. 5.5
East Hill. #274/005005 [3]. 23/06/2003.
H. 0.053; p.W. 0.072; Diam. (rim) 0.070.

Single fr from a handmade cup preserving nearly complete profile, excluding the handle.

Fr preserves a slightly flaring rim with rounded shoulder, giving a collared impression. The preserved portion of the base is flat.

Fine, well-levigated fabric with no inclusions visible to the naked eye fired to a pale gray throughout.

Exterior surface is slipped and carefully smoothed and burnished to a dark gray color, giving almost a wheelmade impression; 10YR 4/1. Uneven firing has resulted in brownish gray splotches 5YR 5/6. The interior is not smoothed, but only roughly burnished, perhaps due to the difficulty of reaching inside the vessel.

The cup shape became popular in the late phase of Minyan development. At Pefkakia-Magoula, such cups are documented as early as Phase 6 *Mitte*, and at Eutresis in LH I deposits. The present piece can therefore be placed sometime between MH III–LH I. See Goldman 1931, p. 163, fig. 226, no. 1; *Pevkakia* III, pl. XVII, nos. 5–6; pl. 83, no. 15; pl. 98, no. 4; pl. 123, no. 13; pl. 124, no. 1.

FIGURE 5.5. MBA Minyan/Imitation Minyan, b) open vessels: **5/8** (ΜΕΘ 4891).
Drawing A. Hooton, photo I. Coyle

5/9. (ΜΕΘ 5074) Handmade Bowl/Kantharos Fig. 5.6
East Hill. #274/032045. Hypogeion, Phase I. 2004 and 2006.
P.H. 0.032; p.W. 0.042; Diam. (rim) est. 0.200.

Single rim fr from a handmade bowl, kantharos, or comparable open shape with S-profile, flaring rim, and roughly squared lip. Three imitation wheel grooves are preserved on the exterior of the fr, just below attachment of lip to body.

Fine dense fabric with few visible inclusions fired to a brownish gray with dark gray core.

Surface burnished and roughly smoothed, but uneven; mottled gray, brown, and red from uneven firing.

Similar handmade bowls and other open shapes, decorated with grooves on the upper shoulder, are found in MBA–early LBA contexts of northern Greece. Likely an imitation of the Gray Minyan tradition. Horejs 2007a, pl. 29, no. 8818; pl. 31, no. 8820; Morris 2009–2010, p. 47, fig. 36, no. 89.1271; p. 48, fig. 37, no. 90.965; *Orchomenos* IV, p. 319, pl. 34, nos. 3–5. See also **5/17** (ΜΕΘ 5617).

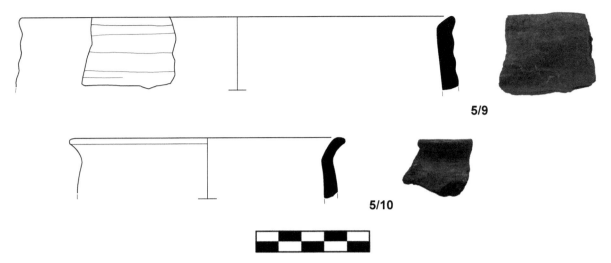

FIGURE 5.6. MBA Minyan/Imitation Minyan, b) open vessels: **5/9** (MEΘ 5074), **5/10** (MEΘ 5075). Drawings T. Ross, photos I. Coyle

5/10. (MEΘ 5075) Handmade Bowl/Kantharos Fig. 5.6
East Hill, #274/032082. Hypogeion. Layer 10. 20/10/2006.
P.H. 0.025; p.W. 0.029; Diam. (rim) est. 0.120.
Very small fr preserving rim and upper body of small, fine vessel of rounded form.
Body rises gently inclined toward everted, beveled rim. Slightly chipped around rim.
Clay body is very fine-grained and compact, with a little mica. Well fired to dark gray 10YR 4/1.
Slipped on both exterior and interior. Well burnished, fired to yellowish red 5YR 5/6 with some gray clouds 10YR 5/1. Patches of wear.
This piece most closely resembles vessels imitating the form of kantharoi from Torone Phases IV and V and Agios Mamas, levels 12–13. This suggests a transitional MBA–LBA date for the present piece. See Horejs 2007a, pp. 211–217, fig. 134C; pl. 24, nos. 8788 and 8830; Morris 2009–2010, p. 48, fig. 37, nos. 89.617, 89.1218, and 90.965.

5/11. (MEΘ 5088) Gray Minyan Goblet Fig. 5.7
East Hill. #274/084002 [2]. 17/07/2003 and 18/07/2003.
P.H. 0.033; p.W. 0.049; Diam. (rim) est. 0.180.
Single fr from the rim of a Gray Minyan goblet with carinated upper body.
Fine fabric with sparse mica inclusions, fired gray throughout.
Finely burnished and smoothed on exterior; however, only a light burnish is preserved on the interior.
In form and manufacture, this seems to be standard Gray Minyan, common to both northern and southern Greece in the Middle Bronze Age. Comparable examples include Mylonas 1973, Pin. 26a; Pin. 26b; *Pevkakia* III, pl. 69, no. 1; Horejs 2007a, pl. 121, no. M 1171_17; Morris 2009–2010, p. 44, fig. 33, no. 88.171; *Orchomenos* IV, p. 301, pl. 26, nos. 1–2.

5/12. (MEΘ 5092) Handmade Kantharos Fig. 5.7
East Hill. #274/054-009 [1] = [2d] surface layer. 14/07/2003.
P.H. 0.026; Diam. (base) est. 0.060–0.070 (oval).
Two frr (broken in field) of a very worn handmade red Minyan kantharos(?) with half of floor preserved.

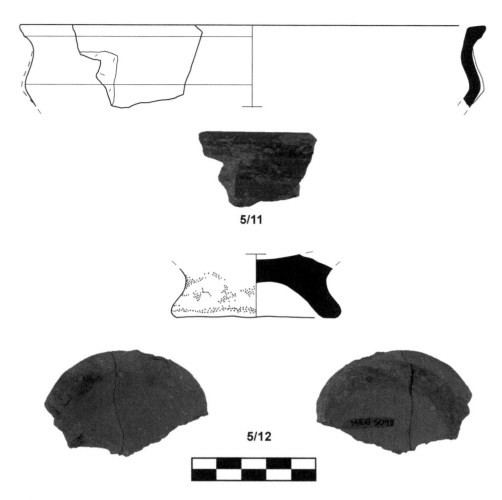

FIGURE 5.7. MBA Minyan/Imitation Minyan, b) open vessels: **5/11** (MEΘ 5088), **5/12** (MEΘ 5092). Drawings T. Ross and A. Hooton, photos I. Coyle

    Raised ring foot, flaring out in convex curve with raised dome on underside.
    Fine hard fabric with few visible inclusions and dark gray core; surface red, dull 10YR 6/6.
    Carefully burnished and unevenly smoothed. Likely only glossy, but now surface mostly worn through.
    Similar bases are published from Agios Mamas and Torone: Horejs 2007a, pl. 15, no. 8894; Morris 2009–2010, p. 47, fig. 36, no. 89.765; p. 48, fig. 37, nos. 89.1056, 1272.

5/13. (MEΘ 5094) Gray Minyan Goblet   Fig. 5.8
    East Hill. #274/084008 [4]. 22/07/2003.
    P.H. 0.029; p.W. 0.079; Diam. (rim) est. 0.300+.
    Single rim fr from wheelmade goblet.
    Short everted rim with squared, sloping lip. Strong carination on upper body of goblet also preserved.
    Fine, hard fabric with few inclusions fired to a dark gray 7.5YR 5/2–4/2.
    Finely burnished and smoothed. Two dark shallow grooves on exterior below rim either produced by burnishing or wheel grooves partially obscured by burnishing. Very glossy.
    Gray Minyan goblet of high technical quality. Sharply everted rim and carination are best paralleled by examples from Pefkakia-Magoula and Agios Mamas. *Pevkakia* III, pl. 141, no. 12; Horejs 2007a, pl. 120, no. M 729_6.

5/14. (MEΘ 5103) Gray Minyan Bowl Fig. 5.8
East Hill. #274/084009 [4]. 23/07/2003.
P.H. 0.031; p.W. 0.057; Diam. (rim) est. 0.180–0.190.
Single rim fr from a Gray Minyan bowl with T-rim, wall curving in below.
Fine fabric with some fine mica inclusions visible fired gray throughout, 7.5YR 5/1.
The closest comparable rims are frr of MBA bowls from Pefkakia-Magoula, Torone, and Orchomenos. See *Pevkakia* III, pl. 29, no. 7; Morris 2009–2010, p. 44, fig. 33, no. 89.474; *Orchomenos* IV, p. 349, pl. 49, nos. 5–6.

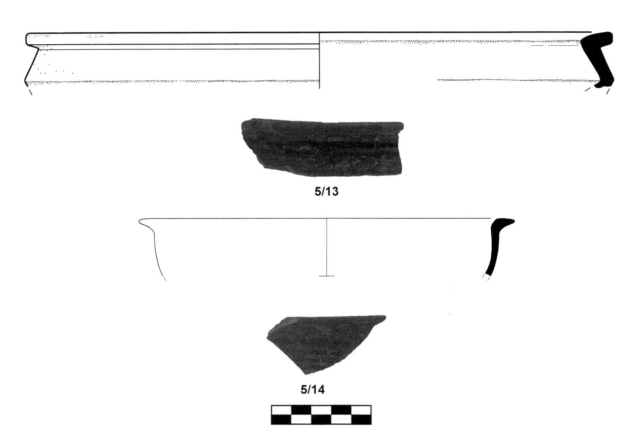

FIGURE 5.8. MBA Minyan/Imitation Minyan, b) open vessels: **5/13** (MEΘ 5094), **5/14** (MEΘ 5103). Drawing A. Hooton and T. Ross, photos I. Coyle

5/15. (MEΘ 5155) Gray Minyan Goblet Fig. 5.9
East Hill. #274/084. Erosion layer. 01/07/2004.
P.H. 0.037; p.W. 0.080; Diam. (rim) est. 0.210.
Two frr (modern break) from a Gray Minyan goblet rim.
Flat(?) rim curves in and under, then out to convex wall, then in to lower wall forming a rounded carination on the upper body.
Fine clay with few mica inclusions. Fired dark gray and hard.
Surface highly burnished and carefully smoothed. Once glossy, but use wear has left a series of parallel vertical striations on lip of rim and upper body carination, which suggests repeated scraping against a rough surface, although it seems rather large to be filled regularly in this fashion.

Similar examples with "softer" profiles than goblets, such as **5/11** (ΜΕΘ 5088), have been published by Mylonas (1973, Pin. 51g–d) and Morris (2009–2010, p. 44, fig. 33, no. 86.98). For a similar, flattened rim profile, see Horejs 2007a, pl. 127, no. B 1182_1. A date in late MBA is likely, but early LBA cannot be ruled out.

5/16. (ΜΕΘ 5600) Handmade Goblet Fig. 5.9

East Hill. #274/085. East balk. 01/09/2005.

P.H. 0.042; p.W. 0.069; Diam. (rim) est. 0.180–0.200.

Single fr of an irregularly shaped everted rim with squared lip and carinated upper body. Probably a handmade imitation of a Gray Minyan goblet. Possible thickening of rim for basket handle attachment.

Fabric fine with few visible inclusions. Fired grayish brown on surface 10YR 6/3 and gray in core 7.5YR 5/0.

Highly burnished and smoothed on exterior with traces of fire clouds. Interior surface also burnished, but more casually than exterior, or perhaps just not smoothed(?); feels chalky.

It seems probable that this is a local imitation of the canonical Gray Minyan goblet. For instance, Gauss and Smetana 2007, p. 74, fig. 6, nos. XXXV-4 and XXXV-5; Horejs 2007a, pl. 120, no. M 953_11; pl. 121, no. M 1171_17; *Orchomenos* IV, p. 301, pl. 26, no. 1. Closest parallels suggest a date in MH III.

FIGURE 5.9. MBA Minyan/Imitation Minyan, b) open vessels: **5/15** (ΜΕΘ 5155), **5/16** (ΜΕΘ 5600). Drawings A. Hooton and T. Ross, photos I. Coyle

5/17. (ΜΕΘ 5617) Handmade Bowl   Fig. 5.10

East Hill. #274/085. Erosion layer. NW corner. 02/08/2004.

P.H. 0.046; p.W. 0.044; Diam. (rim) est. 0.150–0.160.

Single fr with angular, almost carinated, S-profile and double groove at attachment of rim to body. Rim is everted with rounded lip.

Fabric fine with a few visible inclusions consisting of mica and white flecks. Fired light brown 7.5YR 6/4 with light gray firing core 10YR 7/1.

Highly burnished and smoothed on exterior and lightly burnished and smoothed on interior. Grooving from burnishing, or partially obscured by burnishing(?), present on upper shoulder in imitation of wheel marks.

Similar Minyan imitations occur in MBA–LBA contexts at Agios Mamas and Torone. Heurtley 1939, p. 208, no. 383, fig. 74e ("mug"); Horejs 2007a, pl. 26, no. 1684; pl. 29, no. 8818; Morris 2009–2010, p. 51, fig. 40, no. 88.422; *Orchomenos* IV, p. 319, pl. 34, nos. 3–5. See also **5/9** (ΜΕΘ 5074).

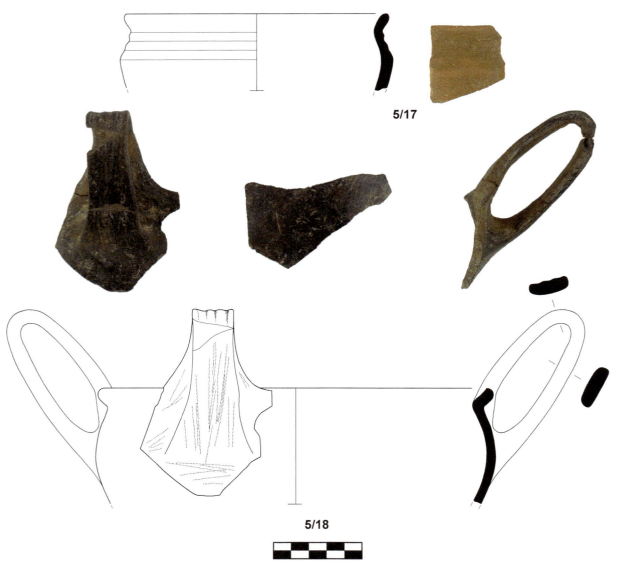

FIGURE 5.10. MBA Minyan/Imitation Minyan, b) open vessels: **5/17** (ΜΕΘ 5617), **5/18** (ΜΕΘ 5642). Drawings T. Ross, photos I. Coyle

5/18.   (ΜΕΘ 5642) Handmade Kantharos   Fig. 5.10
        East Hill. #274/085. NW corner. 29/05/2006.
        P.H. 0.125; p.W. 0.073; Diam. (rim) est. 0.200+.
        Three frr (one fresh break; one ancient) comprising the rim and handle of a kantharos bowl.
        Short everted rim with rounded lip. Vertical strap handle preserves three or four shallow grooves
            on upper surface.
        Medium fine fabric contains sandy inclusions and fine mica fired to a dark gray 7.5YR 5/0–4/0.
        Surface black burnished on exterior and interior surfaces with brown firing clouds preserved on
            interior and on handle. Long, fine burnishing marks preserved on all surfaces; no evidence for
            smoothing.
        Kantharoi with grooved vertical strap handles and rounded shoulders occur in Phases 4 and 5 at
            Pefkakia-Magoula and Phase G on Aigina, although normally with noticeably elongated lips. While
            this may simply be a product of wheelmade versus handmade traditions, two kantharos bowls, with-
            out grooved handles, but with a strikingly similar profile (high swung handles, a short, everted rim,
            and a globular body) have been found at Pefkakia-Magoula in Phase 6 deposits. Perhaps closest to
            the present piece in form is a local Red Minyan (*schwarzminysch*) kantharos bowl from the sixth
            house horizon at Argissa Magoula. A date in the first half of the MBA or slightly later seems likely.
            Compare *Argissa-Magoula* IV, p. 66, pl 105, 5; *Pevkakia* III, pl. 41, nos. 15, 17 (grooved handles);
            pl. 58, nos. 8, 12 (grooved handles); pl. 93, no. 9 (high handles, short everted lip); pl. 109, no.
            4 (high handles, short everted lip); Gauss and Smetana 2007, p. 71, fig. 3, no. XXXVII-1; Morris
            2009–2010, p. 47, fig. 36, no. 86.335.

MBA–LBA, HANDMADE LOCAL WARES

5/19.   (ΜΕΘ 4875) Incised Handle to Closed(?) Shape   Fig. 5.11
        East Hill. #274/059005. Layer 1. 22/05/2006.
        P.L. 0.027; p.W. 0.035.
        Small but well-preserved fr from a thin handle, rectangular in section, with slightly convex exterior
            surface.
        Clay body is fine-grained, with a few scattered calcareous inclusions and coarse sand. Fired dark gray
            to dark grayish brown 10YR 4/1–4/2.
        Surfaces are slipped and burnished, fired to glossy reddish brown 5YR 5/4. There is incised, white-filled
            decoration on the exterior face: a group of three parallel lines borders each long edge, creating
            a central zone bearing two small motifs—an inverted V-shaped band and a tiny diamond—both
            outlined and dot-filled. In terms of decoration, execution, and dating this piece is similar to **5/20**
            (ΜΕΘ 4881). Since this ware is dominated by small closed shapes, this handle is likely from an am-
            phoriskos/kantharos jar (*Kantharostöpfe*). Closest parallels are Hochstetter 1984, pl. 1, no. 11, 13.

5/20.   (ΜΕΘ 4881) Incised Amphoriskos/Jar   Fig. 5.11
        East Hill. #274/085. Erosion layer. 02/08/2004.
        P.H. 0.052; p.W. 0.034; Diam. (rim) 0.062.
        Small but well preserved fr from a small, narrow-mouthed amphoriskos or jar.
        Upper body/neck wall rises flat and strongly inclined toward broad, flaring rim with rounded lip.
            Slight curvature at the lower broken edge suggests a piriform body.
        Clay body is fine-grained and pure, contains very little mica (visible in section and on the surface).
            Well fired to hard, brown fabric 7.5YR 5/4, no core or clouds.

Surface is carefully finished and slipped. Burnish is visible on the exterior and interior of rim and uppermost portion of body/neck; the rest has a rougher finish. Fired to shiny brown 7.5YR 4/4, with spots of dark purple paint on exterior of rim. Rim worn in places. Incised, white-filled decoration of lines and dots on the exterior: a horizontal band consisting of two thin parallel lines bordering a row of dots defines the transition from upper body to rim. Another such band, at a right angle to the former, runs down the body and borders a panel(?), only a small corner of which is preserved with sections of a diagonal and a vertical line.

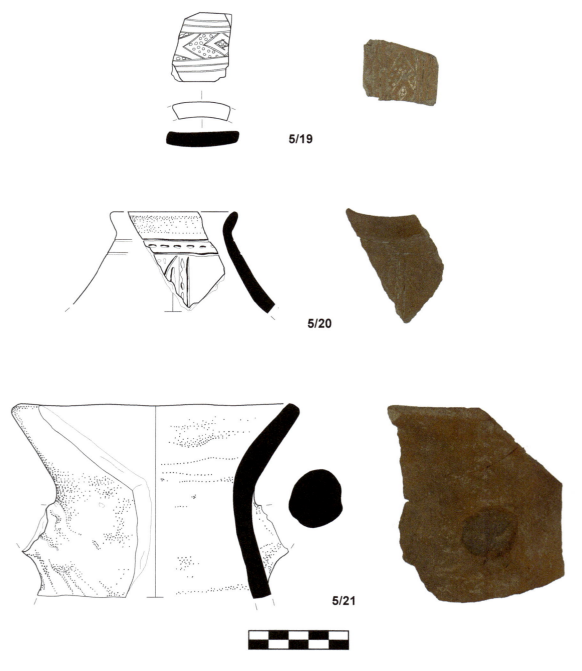

FIGURE 5.11. MBA–LBA, handmade, a) closed vessels: **5/19** (ΜΕΘ 4875), **5/20** (ΜΕΘ 4881), **5/21** (ΜΕΘ 5115). Drawings A. Hooton and T. Ross, photos I. Coyle

The closest parallels are the fine incised wares, especially amphoriskoi, from Archontiko Phase A, dating to the very early LBA. Deliopoulos describes in detail the careful manufacture of these vessels, in fine, well-fired micaceous fabric, with brown-burnished surfaces, and rich individualized designs; their well-sealed, impermeable surfaces can be associated with their function as containers for aromatics. Similar patterns on small, closed shapes are, however, also found in Schicht 14b–15 at Kastanas. A Late Bronze Age date is therefore likely for the present piece as well. See Hochstetter 1984, pl. 31, no. 10; pl. 40, nos. 3, 5–6, 8–10; Deliopoulos 2010, Drawing 3; fig. 2; Stefani and Merousis 2003; Valla 2007, pp. 368–369, fig. 12.

5/21.   (MEΘ 5115) Amphora   Fig. 5.11

East Hill. #274/084. Erosion layer. 01/07/2004.

P.H. 0.097; p.W. 0.085; Diam. (rim) est. 0.140.

Single fr consisting of an amphora rim, neck, and handle stub (broken in excavation).

Neck flares out to sloping, square rim. Horizontal(?) handle round in section (Diam. 0.030).

Fine, hard clay with few visible inclusions. Surface fired unevenly red with brown and black patches. Core fired to dark gray.

Unpainted, but heavily and roughly burnished with visible burnishing strokes remaining on interior and exterior of extant fr.

Narrow neck amphoras make their first appearance in the LBA and continue well into the EIA. Because this fr is from a disturbed erosion layer no more specific date can be assigned. Comparable examples include Heurtley 1939, p. 214, no. 408 (general shape, but handles placed on belly); Hochstetter 1984, pl. 105, no. 2; Vokotopoulou 1986, σχ. 39a–b; Horejs 2007a, pl. 38, no. 4015; pl. 38, no. 4020.

5/22.   (MEΘ 5616) Feeding Bottle/Cup   Fig. 5.12

East Hill. #274/085. East balk. 01/09/2005.

P.H. 0.039; p.W. 0.018; Diam. (spout) 0.015.

Single fr consisting of a short tubular spout from a feeding bottle or cutaway jug with side spout.

Hard fabric with few inclusions fired to a brown color 5YR 6/6.

Unpainted. Fr is heavily burnished with traces of rough strokes remaining.

This piece is a local imitation of a Mycenaean closed shape, occurring frequently in tomb assemblages from LH IIIA onward. Because the present fr is a handmade variant, its dating is difficult. Parallels from Vergina demonstrate that the shape remains popular into the EIA. Based on other settlement and tomb evidence, a date in LH IIIC–EIA is likely. See *Vergina* I, p. 198, fig. 41, no. Φ29 (handmade); p. 177, fig. 26, nos. P2 and AZ3 (wheelmade and painted); Mountjoy 1986, p. 144, fig. 179, no. 1; p. 188, fig. 246, no. 1; p. 199, fig. 266, no. 1; for a handmade cup with side spout in an LBA context, see Karamitrou-Mentesidi 2003, p. 187, fig. 13.

FIGURE 5.12. MBA–LBA, handmade, a) closed vessels: **5/22** (MEΘ 5616). Drawing T. Ross, photos I. Coyle

5/23. (ΜΕΘ 5631) Ovoid Jar Fig. 5.13

East Hill. #274/085. Northwest corner. 09/09/2013.

P.H. 0.045; p.W. 0.062; Diam. (rim) est. 0.180–0.190.

Single fr from a flat, incurving rim with rounded lip from a closed jar.

Slightly sandy fabric with fine mica inclusions visible, fired brown 7.5YR 6/4–5/4 with gray core 10YR 4/1.

Surface highly burnished and smoothed on exterior to an even brown color. Interior surface is more lightly burnished, but equally well smoothed.

Closest parallels come from LBA levels at Torone and Schicht 15 at Kastanas. The present piece should therefore date to the LBA. Hochstetter 1984, pl. 34, no. 9; Morris 2009–2010, p. 66, fig. 54, no. 86.616; fig. 54, no. 90.1123.

FIGURE 5.13. MBA–LBA, handmade, a) closed vessels: **5/23** (ΜΕΘ 5631).
Drawing T. Ross, photo I. Coyle

5/24. (ΜΕΘ 5096) Bowl with Wishbone(?) Handle Fig. 5.14

East Hill. #274/084005 [3]. 21/07/2003 and 22/07/2003.

P.H. 0.056; p.W. 0.079; Diam. (rim) est. 0.160–170.

Single fr from a skyphos-like bowl with short everted rim preserving part of an angular wishbone(?) handle.

Fabric is fine with a few mica and white inclusions visible. Fired to a pale brown 7.5YR 6/4 on exterior side of wall and dark gray 7.5YR 5/0–4/0 in core and interior wall (due to stacking of vessels in kiln?).

Both interior and exterior burnished and smoothed. Interior unpainted, but exterior preserves a thin brown paint.

This form has a wide distribution throughout the Middle Bronze Age of Greece with parallels extending as far south as Pefkakia-Magoula in Thessaly. There appears to be a general trend toward a shorter everted rim later in the Middle Bronze Age. Thus, the closest parallel to the example here comes from transitional MBA–LBA levels at Kastanas. See Heurtley 1939, p. 209, nos. 385–388; Hochstetter 1984, pl. 3, nos. 2–3; *Pevkakia* III, pl. 60, no. 2; pl. 56, no. 9; pl. 95, no. 12; Adrimi-Sismani 2010, p. 311, fig. 4, p. 312, fig. 6. See also **5/29** (ΜΕΘ 5630).

5/25. (ΜΕΘ 5601) Bowl with Wishbone Handle Fig. 5.14
East Hill. #274/085. East balk. 5/9/2005.
P.H. 0.080; p.W. 0.070; Diam. (rim) est. 0.170–0.190.
Single fr preserving small portion of rim and upper body, and a complete handle.
Slightly incurving upper body, featuring a thickened rim (almost triangular in profile) with flat lip. Perforated handle, roughly modeled in angular shape and elliptical in section, attached from upper wall directly to the rim, rises almost vertically high above rim level.
Clay is fine, evenly fired to reddish yellow 5YR 6/6; no firing core.
Carefully smoothed and burnished on interior and exterior with thick strokes, fired to the same reddish yellow as the fabric. Tooling marks run horizontally on rim interior, and almost vertically on interior face of handle, and around the upper section of the handle perforation.
The bowl with wishbone handle is a very long-lasting shape (Hochstetter 1984, 96–98, fig. 25). The handle of this piece is most closely paralleled in Schichten 14–17 at Kastanas, spanning the last half of the Late Bronze Age, and Schichten 3–4 at Agios Mamas, which likewise fall in the last half of the Late Bronze Age. Hochstetter 1984, pl. 14, nos. 1–3; pl. 29, no. 1; pl. 30, no. 1; pl. 49, nos. 1–3; pl. 57, no. 3; Horejs 2007a, pl. 83, no. 929; pl. 94, no. 395; pl. 97, no. 5540.

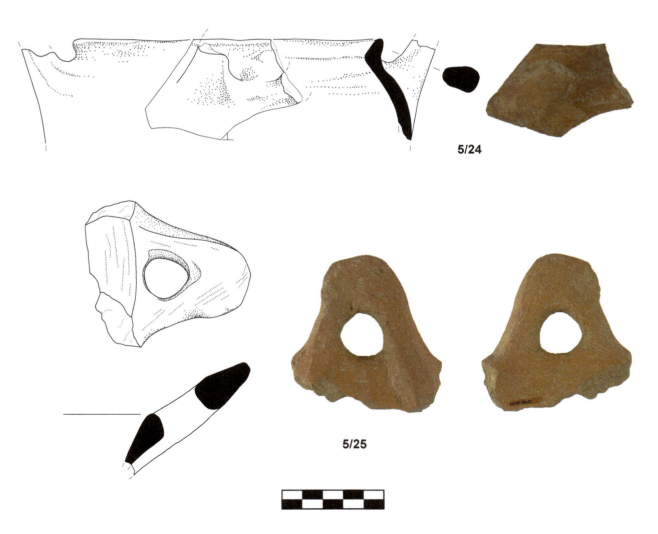

FIGURE 5.14. MBA–LBA, handmade, a) open vessels: **5/24** (ΜΕΘ 5096), **5/25** (ΜΕΘ 5601). Drawings A. Hooton and T. Ross, photos I. Coyle

5/26. (ΜΕΘ 5606) Bowl Fig. 5.15

   East Hill. #274/085. Erosion layer. 14/07/2004 and 15/07/2004.

   P.H. 0.043; p.W. 0.046; Diam. (rim) est. 0.080–0.090.

   Single fr from a handmade bowl with slight shoulder carination and a short flaring rim with slightly beveled exterior lip. Use wear indicates use as scoop.

   Sandy clay with mica inclusions fired brown 7.5YR 5/4 with light, grayish brown core 7.5YR 6/2.

   Highly burnished and carefully smoothed to a light brown color on both exterior and interior surfaces.

   This shape is presented by Morris as an imitation of Minyan hemispherical bowls and dated to the MBA. Horejs publishes an example from early in LBA levels of Agios Mamas. A date in late MBA–early LBA is preferred here. Horejs 2007a, pl. 7, no. 1784; Morris 2009–2010, p. 54, fig. 42, no. 88.426.

5/27. (ΜΕΘ 5608) Cup/Bowl Fig. 5.15

   East Hill. #274/085. Northwest corner. 4/11/2005.

   P.H. 0.063; Diam. (rim) est. 0.110.

   Large fr, preserving about half of a rounded cup or small incurving bowl.

   Concave body wall rises toward lipless, slightly incurving rim. Carefully shaped, but somewhat cursorily finished, with modeling marks visible on exterior and slight asymmetries around rim.

   Clay body is iron-rich and micaceous, fine-grained and compact. Overall few visible inclusions, but there is a rather dense concentration of calcareous inclusions on the lower body. Fired light red 2.5YR 5/6.

   Smoothed, slipped, and burnished with vertical broad strokes on both exterior and interior surfaces. Burnish patchily preserved on exterior, but seems to have been very carefully applied around the rim where a strip approximately 1 cm wide is furnished with regular horizontal burnishing strokes from lip down to body; the corresponding area on interior bears smoothing strokes similarly oriented. Fired reddish brown 2.5YR 5/4 with visible mica on all surfaces. The lower body bears an extensive zone of very dark gray 2.5YR N3/0 (possibly related to use? or else firing clouds from stacking?).

FIGURE 5.15. MBA–LBA, handmade, a) open vessels: **5/26** (ΜΕΘ 5606), **5/27** (ΜΕΘ 5608). Drawings T. Ross, photos I. Coyle

The interior is very worn, almost certainly from use. Wear marks on interior are scattered below rim and in lower body and of two types: fine, short striations arranged in groups of two or more, and deeper, somewhat longer scratches irregularly placed over a larger area.

There are a fair number of probable parallels from Kastanas and Agios Mamas, spanning the mid-Late Bronze Age through Early Iron Age. The profile alone is not sufficient to determine the shape, nor is the diameter. The use wear on the interior, however, may suggest a more likely identity as a bowl. Hochstetter 1984, pl. 42, nos. 4, 6; pl. 61, no. 4; pl. 70, nos. 3–4; pl. 118, no. 5; pl. 166, no. 2; pl. 269, nos. 2, 8; Horejs 2007a, pl. 56, no. 1071.

5/28. (ΜΕΘ 5627) Bowl   Fig. 5.16

East Hill. #274/085. Erosion layer. 13/07/2004, 14/07/2004, and 15/07/2004.

P.H. 0.038; p.W. 0.063; Diam. (rim) est. 0.100.

Single fr from a bowl with distinct carination where rim joins body and short flaring rim with slightly beveled exterior lip.

Hard fabric with small white inclusions fired grayish brown 7.5YR 6/2 with near black core 7.5YR 3/0.

Highly burnished on both interior and exterior surfaces. Wear on exterior surface of rim and carination may be the result of use wear, such as for use of vessel in scooping.

Close parallels include an example from Agios Mamas, Schicht 13, and Kastanas, Schicht 14a, but the shape may have a long history as two examples with a strikingly similar profile come from Schicht 3 at Pefkakia-Magoula. Therefore, while a date in the LBA is probable, lacking context, the present piece should be dated MBA–LBA. *Pevkakia* III, pl. 21, no. 20; pl. 35, no. 23; Hochstetter 1984, pl. 57, no. 8; Horejs 2007a, pl. 5, no. 1191.

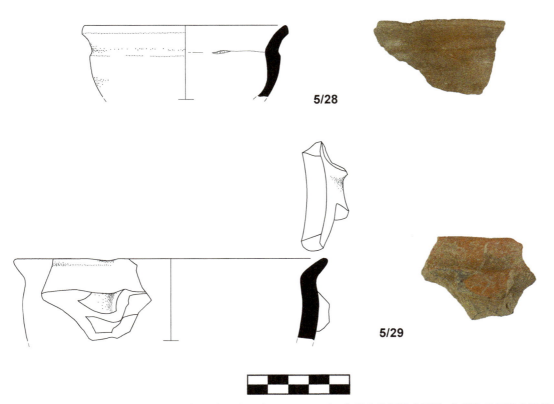

FIGURE 5.16. MBA–LBA, handmade, a) open vessels: **5/28** (ΜΕΘ 5627), **5/29** (ΜΕΘ 5630). Drawings T. Ross, photos I. Coyle

5/29. (ΜΕΘ 5630) Bowl with Wishbone(?) Handle　　　　　　　　　　　　　　　　　　　　Fig. 5.16
　　　East Hill. #274/085. East balk. 05/09/2005.
　　　P.H. 0.035; p.W. 0.055; Diam. (rim) est. 0.220.
　　　Single fr from rim of a bowl with angular wishbone(?) handle scar preserved.
　　　Short, everted rim with slightly rounded lip.
　　　Fabric has a few visible inclusions including mica and white flecks. Fired pinkish brown 5YR 6/6 with dark gray core 10YR 3/1.
　　　Surface burnished light pinkish brown, but not smoothed, burnishing marks remain visible.
　　　This vessel is typologically similar to 5/24 (ΜΕΘ 5096), even if their surface treatments differ. As noted above, this form of bowl is very popular in MBA contexts across northern Greece. This piece is also likely to be late in the sequence, due to its short, everted rim, a characteristic of transitional MBA–LBA Pieces. See Heurtley 1939, p. 209, nos. 385–388; Hochstetter 1984, pl. 3, nos. 2–3; *Pevkakia* III, pl. 60, no. 2; pl. 56, no. 9; pl. 95, no. 12.

LBA—MYCENAEAN AND OTHER WHEELMADE WARES

5/30. (ΜΕΘ 4982) Amphoriskos/Piriform Jar　　　　　　　　　　　　　　　　　　　　Fig. 5.17
　　　East Hill. #274/005 balk. 09/07/2003.
　　　P.H. 0.044; p.W. 0.086; Diam. (rim) est. 0.100.
　　　Single rim fr preserving neck and upper shoulder of amphoriskos or small piriform jar.
　　　Slight ridge at junction of neck and shoulder shows the neck and rim were added separately—perhaps coil construction with wheel finish. Flat rim unusual among comparable examples, but perhaps a local feature. FS 59/48.
　　　Fine fabric rich in mica and occasional fine white flecks fired to a buff brown 7.5YR 6/4.
　　　Paint fired unevenly to a reddish brown to brown hue; well preserved. A thick exterior lip band extends partway down neck. The lower neck and shoulder are decorated with narrow horizontal bands. A medium band, approximately equal in width to the exterior band, decorates the interior of lip and neck.
　　　Mountjoy (1999, p. 846, fig. 341.90) has published an LH IIIB example of a small piriform jar from Thessaly that shows a similar decorative scheme, albeit with a different rim profile. This suggests a terminus post quem for the present piece. Within the north, the best published examples come from LH IIIC Early–Middle contexts at Toumba Thessalonikis; see Andreou 2009, p. 35, fig. 10, nos. 3, 5.

5/31. (ΜΕΘ 5624) Alabastron　　　　　　　　　　　　　　　　　　　　　　　　　　　Fig. 5.17
　　　East Hill. #274/085. East balk. 07/09/2005.
　　　P.H. 0.040; p.W. 0.063.
　　　Single fr from the upper shoulder with preserved handle securely identifying the vessel as an alabastron/piriform jar (FS 85/39).
　　　Generally fine fabric with a few white inclusions visible to the naked eye. Fabric fired brown 10YR 6/4 on surface with gray core beginning immediately below 5Y 6/1.
　　　Paint fired to a dark brown color. Exterior decoration consists of a horizontal band running just below handle. The shoulder above is decorated with a band of net fill (FM 28) extending between the handles. Just preserved above the net fill is a row of joining semicircles (FM 42). Interior is unpainted.

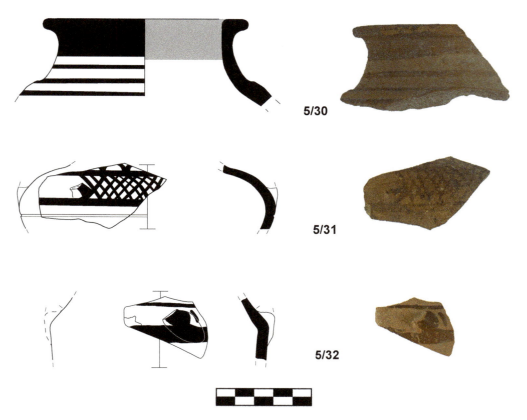

FIGURE 5.17. LBA Mycenaean, a) closed vessels: **5/30** (MEΘ 4982), **5/31** (MEΘ 5624), **5/32** (MEΘ 5607). Drawings T. Ross and F. Skyvalida, photos I. Coyle

Net fill is common on alabastra and piriform jars in Thessaly from the LH IIIB period onward; see Mountjoy 1999, p. 846, fig. 341, nos. 87, 88–89, 91. Published examples with net band fill from Kastanas testify to its persistence into LH IIIC Middle in the north: Jung 2002, pl. 13, no. 140; pl. 18, no. 207. The use of joining semicircles as a framing motif is common from LH IIIC Early onward (Mountjoy 1986, pp. 136–137). A date from LH IIIC Early to Middle is therefore most likely.

5/32. (MEΘ 5607) Alabastron, Straight-sided   Fig. 5.17

East Hill. #274/085. East balk. 05/09/2005.

P.H. 0.034; p.W. 0.041.

Single fr of upper shoulder with preserved handle root from a straight-sided alabastron.

Angle of wall and shoulder fairly obtuse, perhaps suggestive of an advanced date (FS 94/96).

Fine fabric with no visible inclusions fired to a buff brown 7.5YR 6/4.

Paint fired to a dark brown color; well preserved. Exterior decoration consists of a medium band running just below handle attachment and thin band running just above the maximum height of the handle. The first paint stroke of a foliate band (FM 64) between the handles, located in the space defined by the two bands, is preserved to the right of the preserved handle. The preserved portion of the handle suggests it was painted with a single, solid swath of paint.

Straight-sided alabastra with foliate band can be found as early as LH IIIB in Thessaly: Mountjoy 1999, p. 846, fig. 341, no. 99. Good comparanda to the present piece include a LH IIIC Early piece from Kastanas, Jung 2002, pl. 8, no. 88, and a LH IIIC Middle example from Thessaly, Mountjoy 1999, p. 850, fig. 344, no. 115 (although this has a quirk band rather than foliate band).

5/33. (ΜΕΘ 4986) Conical Kylix Figs. 5.18, 5.19
East Hill #274/005007 [5]. 25/06/2003.
P.H. 0.039; W. 0.058.
Single fr from lower bowl preserving the root of a vertical handle, oval in section. FS 275.
Fabric fine with few visible inclusions, fired to a pale red 2.5YR 6/8.
Exterior decoration consists of thin horizontal bands near juncture with (missing) stem and at least one vertical element. Paint darker red and dull, now very faded. Interior of bowl is monochrome in preserved fr.
The conical kylix with monochrome interior is a feature of the LH IIIC period. The addition of a vertical element may suggest a LH IIIC Middle (or later) date for this piece. Comparable examples include Mountjoy 1986, p. 172, fig. 222, nos. 1–2; Popham, Schofield, and Sherratt 2006, p. 185, fig. 2.17, nos. 6–7; p. 186, fig. 2.18, nos. 1, 5. See also **5/35** and **5/37** (ΜΕΘ 4993 and ΜΕΘ 5620).

FIGURE 5.18. LBA Mycenaean kylikes. Top row (left to right): **5/33**, **5/36**; middle row: **5/36**, **5/34**, **5/35**; bottom row: not catalogued, **5/38**, **5/37**.
Photo I. Coyle

5/34. (ΜΕΘ 4992) Kylix, Probable Import Figs. 5.18, 5.19
East Hill #274/032079 [9]. Hypogeion Phase I. 04/10/2006.
P.H. 0.060; Diam. (stem) 0.025.
Single fr preserving the lowest portion of the bowl and the upper half of the stem.
Possibly reused as stopper(?). FS 258/274(?).
Fine pale chalky clay with a few orange-brown inclusions (grog?), fired to a pale yellow 2.5Y 8/4/10YR 8/4.
Painted with a thick paint, fired to a dark brown color. Paint has mostly flaked off, but probably originally lustrous. Preserved decoration consists of two horizontal bands of medium width at juncture of stem and lower bowl; a continuous band spirals down the stem from the lower band (presumably all the way to the foot).
The quality of the paint and fabric both suggest that this piece is likely an import from farther south, although potentially as close as Thessaly, where calcareous fabrics and lustrous paint are produced (Buxeda I Garrigós et al. 2003). The shape suggests a piece intermediate between the rounded bowl of FS 258 and conical bowl of FS 274. Due to the limited amount of preserved bowl, however, the exact form remains open to question. Decorated kylikes with monochrome interiors from the destruction horizon at Dimini should date to LH IIIB2, as does a recently found specimen from ancient Eleon (pers. obs.), perhaps suggesting a central and northern Greek tradition of painted kylikes in LH IIIB2 unattested in the Argolid (see Jung 2002, p. 143, fig. 53 for other examples). A date in LH IIIB2 is possible for the present fr, although a later one cannot be excluded. See Mountjoy 1986, p. 89, fig. 107, nos. 2, 13; p. 114, fig. 141, no. 12; Adrimi-Sismani 2012, p. 174, nos. BE 46745, BE 46746.

5/35. (ΜΕΘ 4993) Conical Kylix Figs. 5.18, 5.19
East Hill #274/032046 [5]. Hypogeion Phase I. 30/06/2004.
P.H. 0.047; Diam. (stem) 0.025.
Single fr consisting of the upper portion of a kylix stem, including interior surface of bowl. FS 295.
Fine fabric with a few visible white and micaceous inclusions, fired to a deep red 5YR 6/6. Core is gray 5YR 6/1.
Decoration consists of three thin bands at the junction of the bowl and stem. Swath of paint, likely marking the base of the handle, interrupts horizontal bands on either side. Monochrome interior. All paint is dull red, with evidence of fading and flaking.
Comparable to **5/33** and **5/37** (ΜΕΘ 4986 and ΜΕΘ 5620). The decoration appears to be an attempt to create a monochrome kylix by painting both the front and back sides, resulting in an unpainted zone below the handles. Comparable kylikes have been found in the Mycenaean Fountain in Athens and should date to an advanced stage of LH IIIC Middle, which agrees well with the other material discussed here. See Broneer 1939, p. 376, fig. 57f–g.

5/36. (ΜΕΘ 5615 + 5619) Conical Kylix Figs. 5.18, 5.20
East Hill. #274/085. East balk. 05/09/2005 and #274/085. Erosion layer. 14/07/2004–15/07/2004.
P.H. 0.075; Diam. (stem) 0.029.
Two joining frr from two contexts forming the upper part of a kylix stem and the lower bowl with handle scar visible (FS 274/275).
Fabric fine with a few white and micaceous inclusions fired to a reddish buff color on exterior 5YR 7/6. Gray firing core begins immediately below surface 5Y 5/1.
Stem monochrome with dull red faded paint. Two bands are preserved above the monochrome stem where the lower bowl joins the stem. Traces above this may indicate a wavy band (?) between handles. The interior of the bowl is a dull monochrome red.

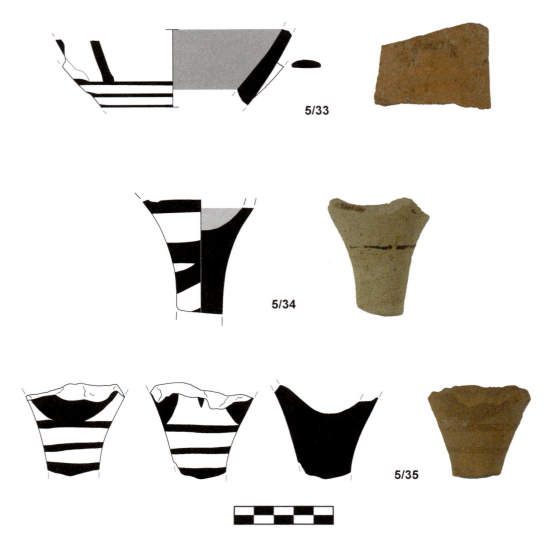

FIGURE 5.19. LBA Mycenaean, b) kylikes: **5/33** (ΜΕΘ 4986), **5/34** (ΜΕΘ 4992), **5/35** (ΜΕΘ 4993). Drawings A. Hooton, T. Ross, and F. Skyvalida, photos I. Coyle

In form, decoration, and manufacture, this example is similar to other local examples. The monochrome stem is notable among the preserved examples and it is tempting to see this as a LH IIIC Early feature; however, if the presence of a wavy band is taken into account, a date from LH IIIC Late seems more probable (Mountjoy 1986, p. 190). Cf. Mountjoy 1986, p. 191, fig. 252, no. 2.

5/37. (ΜΕΘ 5620) Conical Kylix Figs. 5.18, 5.20
East Hill. #274/085. Center of square. 25/05/2006.
P.H. 0.058; p.W. 0.047; Diam. (stem) 0.024.
Single fr consisting of the upper half of a kylix stem with the lower part of bowl preserved (FS 275). Fabric fine with few visible inclusions fired to a slightly pink buff brown 5YR 6/6.
Painted decoration all in a dull red, partially faded/poorly fired. Exterior of stem decorated with relatively thin bands. Interior of bowl monochrome.
Forms a cohesive group with **5/33** and **5/35** (ΜΕΘ 4986 and ΜΕΘ 4993). A date in LH IIIC Middle–Late is probable. See Mountjoy 1986, p. 172, fig. 222, nos. 1–2.

Figure 5.20. LBA Mycenaean, b) kylikes: **5/36** (ΜΕΘ 5615 + 5619), **5/37** (ΜΕΘ 5620), **5/38** (ΜΕΘ 5621). Drawings T. Ross, photos I. Coyle

5/38. (ΜΕΘ 5621) Conical Kylix Figs. 5.18, 5.20

East Hill. #274/085. Erosion layer. 14/07/2004–15/07/2004.

P.H. 0.040; p.W. 0.028; Diam. (stem) 0.021.

Single fr consisting of the lower half of a narrow kylix stem with top of dome in base preserved.

Slender proportions suggest an advanced shape (FS 275/276).

Fine fabric with few visible inclusions, fired to a pinkish buff color 5YR 7/6. Slightly darkened firing core visible 7.5YR 6/4.

The stem is decorated with fine dull red banding produced in a single continuous, spiraling stroke. The exterior surface of the foot may have been monochrome dull red or decorated with thicker bands.

The fine banding of the stem and the slender proportions of the kylix suggest an advanced date. While few parallels from northern Greece have been published, similarly proportioned and decorated examples exist in Thessaly during LH IIIC Late: Mountjoy 1999, p. 853, fig. 346, nos. 129–130. Mountjoy (1999, p. 236) dates the continuous spiral and FS 275 to LH IIIC Middle to Late.

5/39. (ΜΕΘ 4953) Goblet Fig. 5.21

East Hill. #274/032009 [3]. 04/08/2003.

P.H. 0.080; p.W. 0.050; Diam. (rim) est. 0.150.

Single rim fr with short everted lip from a small goblet.

Fine hard clay with dark gray core and light brown surface layers 7.5YR 6/4. Micaceous inclusions throughout. Interior of bowl fired dark gray-brown inside (stacked in firing, reduced?) 5Y 6/1.

Surface heavily burnished to a dark brown color on exterior. Interior also heavily burnished, but gray-brown. Unpainted.

The technique of manufacture is consistent with other local vessels. The shape strongly resembles early Mycenaean goblets from southern Greece. An early Mycenaean date is likely (LH II–IIIA). See *Orchomenos* V, p. 37, fig. 13, nos. 267–269; Morris 2009–2010, p. 55, fig. 43, no. 90.216; Romano and Voyatzis 2014, p. 593, nos. 10–12.

5/40. (ΜΕΘ 4288) Aiginetan Krater/Goblet Fig. 5.21
East Hill. #274/004017 [7]. 04/06/2003.
P.H. 0.056; p.W. 0.053; Diam. (rim) est. 0.190.
Single fr from a probable red-slipped and burnished Aiginetan krater or goblet.
Short everted rim with narrow rounded lip and interior groove. Additional groove on exterior below rim.
Fabric dense and with silver and gold micas and dark gray core 7.5YR 5/0.
Surface smoothed and burnished on interior and exterior. Coated with a thick red paint or slip, flaked off along edges. 10R 4/8–5/8.
Technical details, such as lip groove and distinct red coating and burnish, suggest an early Aiginetan import, probably LH I or II (Bartek Lis, pers. comm.), rather than a local imitation of an Aiginetan product. For a close parallel, see Lindblom 2007, p. 128, fig. 11.

5/41. (ΜΕΘ 4989) Basin Fig. 5.22
East Hill. #274/005015 [4]. 14/07/2003.
P.H. 0.035; p.W. 0.090; Diam. (rim) N/R.
One fr consisting of a rim with horizontal strap handle from a (spouted) basin (FS 294/295).
Fine clay, rich in mica and white grit, fired to a buff brown color 7.5YR 6/4.
Surface smoothed and decorated with dull reddish brown streaky paint. Exterior decoration consists of linear band on exterior lip and extending over horizontal handle. Interior monochrome.
Linear basins with monochrome interiors appear frequently in Mycenaean settlement contexts from LH IIIB1–LH IIIC Early. Comparison can be made with Mountjoy 1986, p. 132, fig. 163, nos. 1–3; Wardle 1993, p. 132, fig. 7.7; Jung 2002, pl. 9, no. 104.

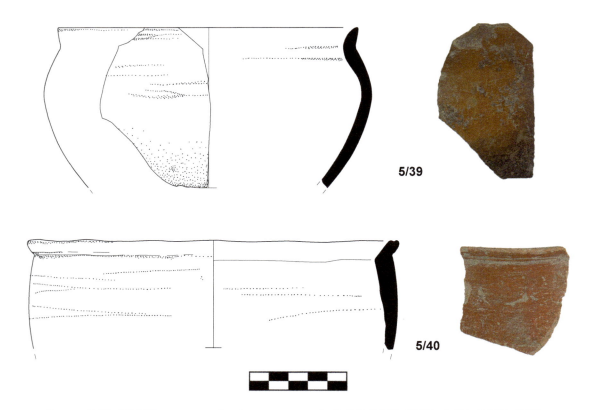

FIGURE 5.21. LBA Mycenaean, c) other open vessels: **5/39** (ΜΕΘ 4953), **5/40** (ΜΕΘ 4288).
Drawings A. Hooton, photos T. Ross

5/42. (ΜΕΘ 4990) Spouted Krater Fig. 5.22
East Hill. #274/005015 [4]. 14/07/2003.
P.H. 0.080; p.W. 0.060; Diam. (rim) N/R.
Single fr of a spouted krater, including rim and spout hole with spout broken away.
Sloping upper wall, exterior of rim rounded. A triangular spur projects up and out from rim above spout. Scar of spout visible on exterior (FS 298).
Hard clay with scattered angular white and micaceous inclusions fired to a buff brown 7.5YR 6/4.
Partially encrusted with heavy clay, but painted red decoration visible. Exterior medium lip band with medium band outlining attachment point of spout. Interior monochrome red.
The spouted krater is a common feature of late Mycenaean (and even Early Iron Age) assemblages in the north. An example from Agios Mamas may even be as early as LH IIIA. The stub above the spout is unusual, but perhaps reflective of local taste for protomes and spurs within the handmade assemblage. This example is likely to date from LH IIIC Middle–EIA. See Heurtley 1939, p. 226, fig. 96u; Mountjoy 1999, p. 855, fig. 347, no. 149 (LH IIIC late); Jung 2002, pl. 25, no. 281; pl. 43, no. 403; Hänsel and Aslanis 2010, p. 334, fig. 10, no. 11.

5/43. (ΜΕΘ 5024) Deep Bowl Fig. 5.23
East Hill. #274/0005015 [4]. 14/7/2003.
P.H. 0.055; Diam. (rim) est. 0.290.
Two joining frr of a local Mycenaean deep bowl with slightly flaring rim with rounded lip.
Upper body slopes inward slightly from widest point (FS 284).
Fabric fine with scattered micaceous, white, and brown inclusions. Fired to a buff brown color 7.5YR 6/4.
Painted decoration consists of a streaky brown paint, well preserved. Fairly narrow lip band on exterior below lip, with the upper arc of wavy band, horn, or antithetic streamer just preserved. Interior monochrome in surviving fr.

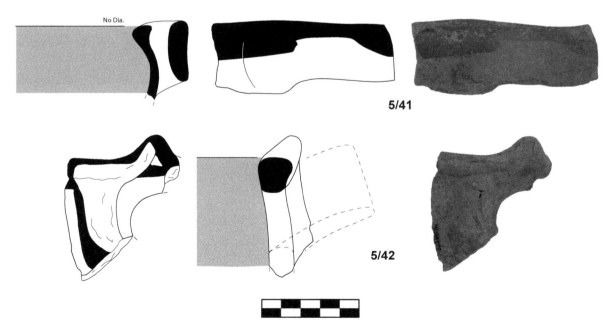

FIGURE 5.22. LBA Mycenaean, c) other open vessels: **5/41** (ΜΕΘ 4989), **5/42** (ΜΕΘ 4990).
Drawings T. Ross, photos I. Coyle

Painted decoration and form are echoed in deep bowls published from Kastanas and Toumba Thessalonikis. The diameter of the present example is large, and it likely functioned more in line with a krater than as a serving bowl. A date in LH IIIC Middle–Late fits well with other published examples. See Jung 2002, pl. 21, no. 229; pl. 22, no. 246; pl. 24, no. 268; Andreou 2009, p. 34, fig. 9, no. 5; p. 36, fig. 11, no. 3; Morris 2009–2010, p. 63, fig. 51, no. 89.1166.

5/44. (ΜΕΘ 5625) Deep Bowl Fig. 5.23

East Hill. #274/085. Center of the square. 26/05/2006.

P.H. 0.071; p.W. 0.091.

Large fr of Mycenaean deep bowl, broken in three, with full handle preserved.

Tip of rim has been chipped off, so exact diameter and shape are unknown (FS 284/285).

Fabric very fine with very minute visible inclusions in dark brown. Fired to a buff brown 7.5YR 6/4.

Paint fired to a red hue and well preserved. Exterior decoration consists of a medium(?) lip band and double band running just beneath handle. Handle tri-splashed. Interior decoration consists of two extant bands in red about halfway down wall.

In the south, linear banded deep bowls with linear interiors begin in LH IIIB2 contexts, but continue into LH IIIC. Comparable examples from Kastanas and Torone in LH IIIC feature near identical banding schemes, but always feature a wavy band or other motif between the handles. It is possible that such a feature is absent or simply not preserved on the Methone example. An example from Agios Mamas with linear banding on the interior and exterior comes from Schicht 3, which straddles the LH IIIB–C divide. See Jung 2002, pl. 5, no. 48; pl. 6, no. 66; pl. 6, no. 68; pl. 7, no. 69; Morris 2009–2010, p. 63, fig. 52, no. 90.290; Hänsel and Aslanis 2010, p. 335, fig. 11, no. 15.

5/45. (ΜΕΘ 5629) Deep Bowl Fig. 5.23

East Hill. #274/085. East balk. 01/09/2005.

P.H. 0.040; p.W. 0.053; Diam. (rim) est. 0.150.

Single fr from a slightly flaring Mycenaean deep bowl rim with a thickened and rounded lip.

Upper body slopes inward slightly from widest point (FS 284).

Fine fabric with few visible inclusions fired to a buff brown color 7.5YR 6/4.

Paint fired to a dull red color. Decoration consists of a medium lip band on exterior and a monochrome interior.

Simple linear banded deep bowls with monochrome interiors are characteristic of southern Mycenaean pottery from the LH IIIB2 period onward. The shape of this vessel, with inward sloping upper body, seems typical of more advanced examples in the north. Characteristic examples include Jung 2002, pl. 14, no. 148 (shape); pl. 15, no. 173 (decoration).

LBA–EIA MATT-PAINTED AND BICHROME

5/46. (ΜΕΘ 4950) Amphora Fig. 5.24

East Hill. #274/022042 [10]. Hypogeion.

P.H. 0.073; p.W. 0.058.

Two joining frr of flaring narrow neck and (almost) rim of a matt-painted amphora.

Fabric generally fine, with a few small, white inclusions visible to the naked eye, fired to a buff brown 7.5YR 7/6.

Surface burnished and smoothed unevenly. Painted with dark brown flaky paint, now heavily worn. Exterior decoration consists of medium horizontal bands where rim joins neck, as well as on lower neck. Pendant fringe hangs from the upper band. Interior undecorated.

THE MIDDLE AND LATE BRONZE AGE POTTERY

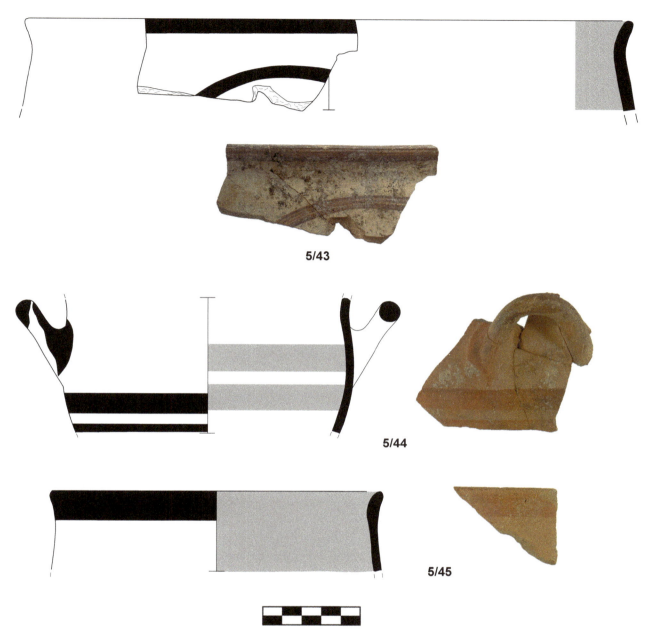

Figure 5.23. LBA Mycenaean, c) other open vessels: **5/43** (MEΘ 5024), **5/44** (MEΘ 5625), **5/45** (MEΘ 5629). Drawings T. Ross and F. Skyvalida, photos I. Coyle

Stylistically, this vase finds its closest parallel with a piece from Toumba Thessalonikis Phase 5, which dates approximately to the Mycenaean palatial period (Andreou 2003, p. 209, fig. 10, no. KA 991). Similar amphoras are published in LBA deposits from Kastanas and Agios Mamas: see Hochstetter 1984, pl. 6, no. 1; pl. 11, no. 5; pl. 93, no. 5; Horejs 2007a, pl. 70, no. 9180; pl. 79, no. 9237; Heurtley 1939, p. 229, fig. 94c. Fringed banding is likewise observed in LBA levels at Torone: Morris 2009–2010, p. 65, fig. 53, no. 89.818. It is important to note that this form endures well into the EIA at northern sites such as Vitsa and Liatovouni, where similar amphoras occur in clear 9th-century contexts: see Vokotopoulou 1986, sc. 32; Douzougli and Papadopoulos 2010, p. 44, fig. 17a–b. A tentative date for the present piece is LBA–EIA.

FIGURE 5.24. LBA–EIA matt-painted, a) closed vessels: **5/46** (ΜΕΘ 4950), **5/47** (ΜΕΘ 5602). Drawings A. Hooton and T. Ross, photos I. Coyle

5/47. (ΜΕΘ 5602) Amphora Fig. 5.24
East Hill. #274/085. Erosion layer B. 02/07/2004.
P.H. 0.026; p.W. 0.048.
Single body fr from a medium-large amphora.
Fine fabric with small white inclusions throughout fired pale pinkish brown 5YR 5/4 with gray core 5Y 5/1.
Preserved part of sherd carefully burnished and smoothed on exterior. A horizontal band, likely at juncture of rim and body or neck and body, with pendant, triangular-shaped fringe is rendered in dark brown paint. The interior is undecorated.
Original vessel was likely similar to **5/46** (ΜΕΘ 4950). See Hochstetter 1984, pl. 6, no. 1; pl. 11, no. 5; pl. 93, no. 5; Horejs 2007a, pl. 70, no. 9180; pl. 79, no. 9237; Heurtley 1939, p. 229, fig. 94c. This piece should likewise be placed LBA–EIA.

5/48. (ΜΕΘ 5603) Amphora Fig. 5.25
East Hill. #274/085. NW corner. 29/05/2006.
P.H. 0.049; p.W. 0.076; Diam. (rim) est. 0.110.
Single fr from a short, flaring, and rounded rim of medium to large amphora.
Fabric medium-fine with small, semi-rounded, white inclusions throughout. Fired pale pinkish brown 5YR 5/4 with gray core 5Y 5/1.
Surface is carefully burnished and smoothed. Painted decoration consists of exterior band of pendant triangular fringe situated at the juncture of the rim and neck in a dark brown paint. The interior is undecorated.
Similar to **5/50** (ΜΕΘ 5614). See Horejs 2007a, pl. 70, no. 9166. Although the parallel cited here is LBA, the continuity of this form elsewhere in the north suggests the present piece may be as late as EIA. See also **5/46** (ΜΕΘ 4950).

5/49. (ΜΕΘ 5604) Jar(?)   Fig. 5.25

East Hill. #274/085. Erosion layer (NW corner). 02/08/2004.

P.H. 0.038; p.L. 0.031; Diam. (rim) est. < 0.100.

Single rim fr from matt-painted jar with slightly flaring squared and sloping rim.

Generally fine fabric with small white visible inclusions, fired to a buff brown 7.5YR 7/6.

Carefully burnished and smoothed. Decoration painted in dark brown, flaky paint. Traces of decoration on lip of rim, but heavily worn. Exterior decoration consists of a medium band at juncture of rim with long, thin, and uneven pendant fringe. Interior undecorated.

In shape and decoration, this should represent a diminutive version of **5/46** (ΜΕΘ 4950), which suggests a similar dating in the LBA. Cf. Andreou 2003, p. 209, fig. 10, no. KA 991; Horejs 2007a, pl. 68, 9178; pl. 70, no. 9180; pl. 88, no. 9077; Heurtley 1939, p. 226, fig. 95g; p. 229, fig. 94c.

5/50. (ΜΕΘ 5614) Amphora   Fig. 5.25

East Hill. #274/085. East balk. 15/09/2005.

P.H. 0.043; p.L. 0.093; Diam. (rim) est. 0.140.

Single fr matt-painted flaring rim with rounded lip of medium-large narrow-necked amphora.

Very fine fabric with few visible inclusions fired to a pinkish brown 5YR 6/6.

Surface burnished and roughly smoothed. Paint is thick and dark brown, but flaky, and thus some of the decoration has become worn. Two uneven, roughly horizontal bands encircle the juncture of lip and neck. Possible traces of additional decoration below.

Probably very similar to **5/48** (ΜΕΘ 5603). Closest parallel for the present piece is Horejs 2007a, pl. 70, no. 9166. For the likelihood that this form continues into the EIA, see **5/46** (ΜΕΘ 4950).

FIGURE 5.25. LBA–EIA matt-painted, a) closed vessels: **5/48** (ΜΕΘ 5603), **5/49** (ΜΕΘ 5604), **5/50** (ΜΕΘ 5614). Drawings T. Ross, photos I. Coyle

5/51. (ΜΕΘ 4870) Small Bowl   Fig. 5.26

East Hill. #274/004031 [10]. 13/06/2003.

P.H. 0.027; p.W. 0.035; Diam. (rim) est. 0.070.

Single fr short everted rim of small hemispherical bowl.

Fine fabric with few visible inclusions fired light brown 7.5YR 7/6.

Vessel is finely burnished and carefully smoothed. Paint is dark brown and heavily worn in places. The lip has been painted with a narrow band. A medium band is placed just below the junction of the rim and body. On the shoulder there are traces of a wavy band/joining semicircles and a second narrow band (?).

The decoration and profile of this fr recall the better preserved **5/54** (ΜΕΘ 5073). The present piece should therefore date comfortably to the last half of the LBA. See Horejs 2007a, pl. 50, no. 9412; pl. 52, no. 9437; pl. 71, no. 9419; Hochstetter 1984, pl. 71, no. 4. See below for further discussion of date.

5/52. (ΜΕΘ 4951) Kantharos   Fig. 5.26

East Hill. #274/022065 [13] and 032073 [7]. Hypogeion.

P.H. 0.075; p.L. 0.098; Diam. (rim) est. 0.110.

Two joining frr from a matt-painted kantharos with a short flaring rim and rounded lip.

Medium-fine fabric with sandy, rounded visible inclusions. Fired to an orange color 5YR 6/6.

Entire vessel burnished and smoothed prior to painting. Paint dark brown and thick. Interior lip decorated with a fine wavy band. Exterior decoration consists of a medium horizontal band placed at the junction of the lip and neck, as well as two narrower horizontal bands placed immediately beneath the handle attachment. Panels of vertical lines, zigzags, and joining semicircles are positioned in the panel formed by these bands and the vertical strap handles. The handles themselves are decorated with horizontal bars, framed on either side.

Although it is difficult to find precise decorative parallels for such a regional style as the matt-painted wares of the north Aegean, especially for the most prized vessel—the kantharos—this piece finds close parallels in its shape and general decorative scheme with published examples excavated at Kastanas (Schicht 14a), Agios Mamas, and Toumba Thessalonikis (Phase 5). See Hochstetter 1984, pl. 56, no. 1; Heurtley 1939, p. 225, fig. 94k; Andreou 2003, p. 209, fig. 10, no. KA 1714. While the kantharos is another shape that endures into the EIA in the north, the EIA kantharoi from Vitsa (in Epirus), Liatovouni (in Epirus), and Marmariani (in Thessaly) have morphological characteristics that set them apart from the LBA parallels cited, including a lipless vertical or near-vertical rim, giving them a collared appearance: see Vokotopoulou 1986, σχ. 6; Douzougli and Papadopoulos 2010, p. 44, fig. 17e–f; Heurtley and Skeat 1930–1931, p. 28, fig. 12. This emphasizes the regional nature of handmade traditions and cautions against placing too much emphasis on distant comparanda. The completeness of this vessel and its position in the earliest filling phase of the Hypogeion suggest that an Early Iron Age date may be more appropriate.

5/53. (ΜΕΘ 4952) Kantharos   Fig. 5.26

East Hill. #274/022051 [11]. Hypogeion.

P.H. 0.038; p.L. 0.059; Diam. (rim) est. 0.170–180.

Single fr from a kantharos with short, sharply everted rim with flattened lip.

Sharp upper body carination preserved, giving the vessel a very angular and squat appearance. Lower root of vertical strap handle preserved, rising from shoulder carination.

Generally fine fabric with a few small white visible inclusions fired to a buff brown 7.5YR 7/6.

Carefully burnished and smoothed. Painted with a dark brown, thick paint. Exterior decoration consists of a horizontal band of brown paint where rim and body join, as well as along carination. Between the two bands, on shoulder, a wavy band/messy zigzag fills the area between the handles. Interior is undecorated as preserved, with exception of accidental paint stroke on inner lip of rim.

THE MIDDLE AND LATE BRONZE AGE POTTERY

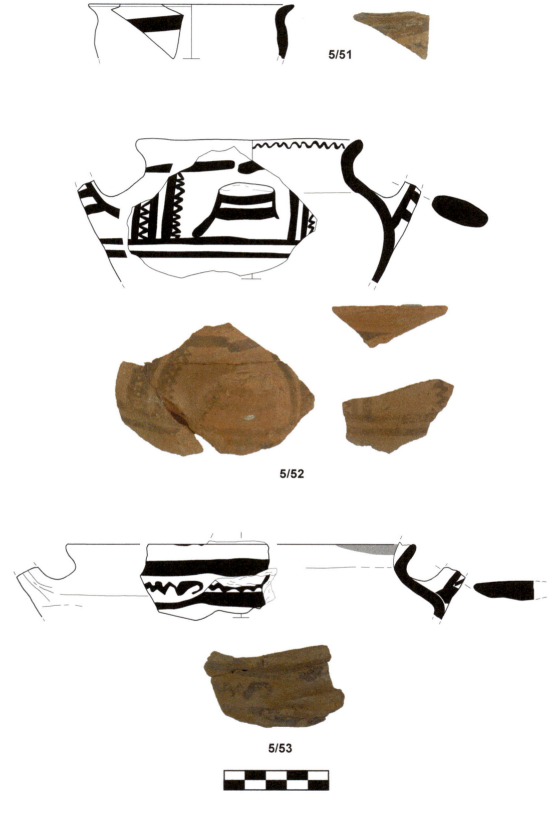

FIGURE 5.26. LBA–EIA matt-painted, b) open vessels: **5/51** (ΜΕΘ 4870), **5/52** (ΜΕΘ 4951), **5/53** (ΜΕΘ 4952). Drawings A. Hooton and T. Ross, photos I. Coyle

Published examples of comparable kantharoi suggest that the sharp profile of this piece may be slightly earlier than **5/52** (MEΘ 4951), which has a much more rounded shoulder. A suggested date in the LBA seems appropriate based on parallels from Kastanas (Schicht 18) and Toumba Thessalonikis (Phase 5): Hochstetter 1984, pl. 6, no. 4; pl. 29, no. 12; Andreou 2003, p. 209, fig. 10, no. 756. For a refutation of an EIA date, see **5/52** (MEΘ 4951). It is worth pointing out that the EIA examples always have rounded shoulders, never carinated ones like the present example.

5/54. (MEΘ 5073) Bowl Fig. 5.27
East Hill. #274/032005. Hypogeion.
P.H. 0.040; p.L. 0.052; Diam. (rim) est. 0.180–0.220.
Single fr from a rounded bowl with short, thin everted rim.
Traces of a slight carination just before sherd breaks off, possibly just uneven burnishing.
Generally fine fabric with a few dark brown inclusions fired orange-brown 5YR 5/8.

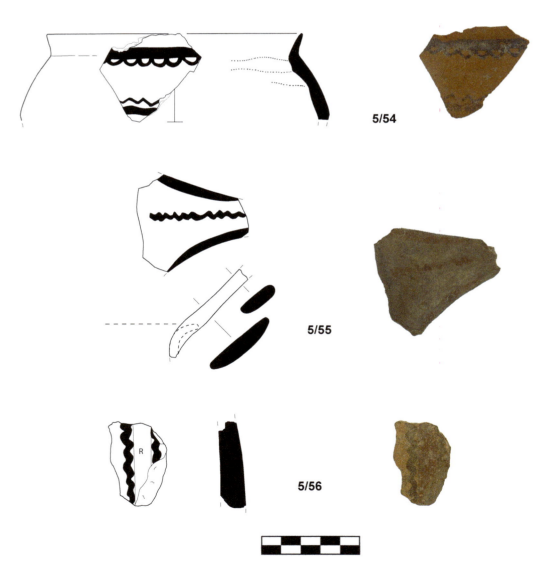

FIGURE 5.27. LBA–EIA matt-painted, b) open vessels: **5/54** (MEΘ 5073), **5/55** (MEΘ 5113), **5/56** (MEΘ 5605). Drawings A. Hooton and T. Ross, photos I. Coyle

Vessel carefully burnished and smoother on interior and exterior. Decoration applied with thick, dark brown paint; well preserved. Interior decoration consists of a fine lip band with pendant joining semicircles (not shown on drawing). Exterior decoration features a horizontal band at the juncture of rim and body with pendant semicircles, and another mid-body (at widest point) with a fine squiggly band/degenerate line of joining semicircles immediately above.

Similar bowls, with similar decorative schemes consisting of bands and joining semicircles, are relatively common among the matt-painted repertoire of Agios Mamas, especially in Schichten 6–7, and is found in Schicht 13 at Kastanas. The present piece should therefore date comfortably to the last half of the LBA. See Horejs 2007a, pl. 50, no. 9412; pl. 52, no. 9437; pl. 71, no. 9419; Hochstetter 1984, pl. 71, no. 4.

5/55. (ΜΕΘ 5113) Globular Kantharos Fig. 5.27
East Hill. #274/084. Erosion layer. 30/06/2004.
P.H. 0.055; p.W. 0.053; Diam. (rim) N/R.
Single handle fr from kantharoid shape, tapering inward as it extends from rim.
Fabric fine with a few visible inclusions, including mica, fired gray.
Dark brown worn paint outlines handle with squiggly line down center on upper surface. Lower surface undecorated, but traces of paint outlining attachment to rim.
Closest parallel is a globular kantharos handle from Agios Mamas, which is unfortunately from a disturbed context; see Horejs 2007a, pl. 119, no. 9446. Another close, but inexact, parallel from Kastanas comes from Schicht 14b, and thus dates to the LBA: Hochstetter 1984, pl. 46, no. 7. The present piece is also likely to be LBA in date, although an EIA date cannot be ruled out due to the small size of the fr.

5/56. (ΜΕΘ 5605) Krater Fig. 5.27
East Hill. #274/085. East balk. 07/09/2005.
P.H. 0.044; p.L. 0.029.
Single fr from a large open shape. Likely a krater.
Medium fine fabric with sandy, rounded inclusions fired to a buff brown color 7.5YR 6/4.
Carefully burnished and smoothed on exterior. Painted with thick, well-preserved paint. Exterior decoration consists of a vertical purple-red band framed by vertical, dark brown wavy bands on either side. Interior undecorated, but burnished and smoothed.
Comparable kraters with bichrome decoration are well attested in southern and central Greece. These examples suggest a date contemporary with MH III–LH II. See *Orchomenos* IV, p. 331, pl. 40, nos. 1–2, 4.

NOTES

1 I would like to thank Bartek Lis for his thoughts on various sherds, as well as for reading a draft of the manuscript. Many thanks also to Jerry Rutter, for looking over the material with me during a visit to Methone in 2015 and encouraging me to think more about the technical aspects of manufacture. The writing of the manuscript took place while I was the Emily Vermeule Fellow at the American School of Classical Studies at Athens.
2 Adam-Veleni and Tzanavari 2009.
3 Andreou, Fotiadis, and Kotsakis 2001 (with bibliography up to 2001); *Torone* I, pp. 273–291; Jung 2002; Pilali-Papasteriou and Papaefthymiou-Papanthimou 2002; Horejs 2007a; Becker and Kroll 2008; Andreou 2009; Morris 2009–2010; Hänsel and Aslanis 2010; Aslanis 2017; Andreou 2020.

4   Papadopoulos 2001, p. 278.
5   For Toumba Thessalonikis, see Andreou 2003, 2009; for Torone, see Morris 2009–2010, 43–52; for Kastanas, see Hochstetter 1984; Jung 2002; for Agios Mamas, see Horejs 2007a; Aslanis 2017. At all these sites the relevant pottery is divided among a number of individual scholars, increasing the length of time until the entire assemblage is represented and published.
6   Aslanis 2017, pp. 401–422.
7   Hale 2016 uses the more technical term "gray burnished ware" for this class. I use the term Minyan for the familiarity of the reader, but include under the appellation all categories of wheelmade burnished fine wares regardless of their firing color (gray, yellow, red).
8   Cf. Hayden 1995; Maran 2007, pp. 175–176; Valamoti 2016, p. 56; Lis 2017.
9   Horejs 2007a, pp. 183–211.
10 See Cambitoglou and Papadopoulos 1993; Papadopoulos 2001, pp. 280–281; Morris 2009–2010, p. 53, figs. 43–47.
11 Dickinson 1977, pp. 19–23, fig. 2.4; fig. 3; Hale 2016, esp. pp. 282–284.
12 Cambitoglou and Papadopoulos 1993; Morris 2009–2010, p. 53, figs. 43–47.
13 Karamitrou-Mentesidi 2003; Chatzitoulousis et al. 2014, p. 377, fig. 7 (Dispilio).
14 Eder 2009; I thank Jeremy Rutter for raising the possibility with me during a visit to the Aiani Museum in 2015.
15 Cf. Wardle 1993; Jung 2002; Buxeda I Garrigós et al. 2003, 265–268; Kiriatzi 2000, pp. 197–230.
16 For southern Pieria, see Koulidou 2007, 2015, 2021; Poulaki-Pantermali 2013a; Koulidou et al. 2012, 2014. For Thessaly, see Skafida, Karnava, and Olivier 2012; Adrimi-Sismani and Godart 2005; Adrimi-Sismani 2012, 2013, 2014; Batziou-Efstathiou 2015.
17 See Mountjoy 1986, p. 135.
18 Jung 2002.
19 Andreou 2003; Andreou and Psaraki 2007; Andreou 2009.
20 Hänsel and Aslanis 2010, pp. 334–337.
21 Heurtley 1939.
22 For an extended discussion of reworked sherds used for sealing vessels, including a discussion of reworked kylix stems, see Van Damme 2019.
23 See Hochstetter 1984, p. 197, fig. 53.
24 Horejs 2007b.
25 See Heurtley 1939; Hochstetter 1984, pp. 181–188.
26 Buxeda I Garrigós et al. 2003, p. 280.
27 See Broneer 1939, p. 376, fig. 57f–g.
28 Thomas 1992, pp. 72–73.
29 Valamoti and Jones 2010; Andreou et al. 2013.
30 Hochstetter 1984, pp. 187–188, fig. 49.
31 Andreou 2003.
32 I have attempted to make this ambiguity and the rationale for an early date clear in the catalogue.
33 For Vitsa, see Vokotopoulou 1986; for Liatovouni, see Douzougli and Papadopoulos 2010; for Marmariani, see Heurtley and Skeat 1930–1931.
34 Horejs 2007a, pp. 236–237.
35 Andreou 2001, pp. 166, 168; Jung 2002; Andreou and Psaraki 2007; Andreou et al. 2013; Valamoti 2016.

6

THE LATE BRONZE AGE CEMETERY

Sarah P. Morris, Sevi Triantaphyllou, and Vaso Papathanasiou
With contributions by John K. Papadopoulos (metal objects)
and Vanessa Muros (glass)

APPENDIX: AMS RADIOCARBON DATING OF SKELETAL REMAINS
by Brian Damiata and John Southon

Excavations at Methone on the West Hill or "acropolis" area uncovered 28 pit graves of the Late Bronze Age cut into sterile soil, in two areas: Plots 229 (Tombs 229/1–10) and 245 (Tombs 245/1–18), which probably belong to the same burial ground (Fig. 6.1).[1] During Early Iron Age reoccupation, over 80 domestic and industrial pits cut deeply into the level of the burials, disturbing their contents, as did several deep ditches and many postholes from a densely occupied hilltop of the early first millennium B.C. (Fig. 6.2). Later disruptions, such as the steps cut in bedrock through the mud-brick fortifications for the defensive "σήραγγες" [tunnels] during the siege of Methone in 357–354 B.C., further damaged the Bronze Age burials, cutting into Tombs 245/1, 2, and 3, for example.[2] All of the graves are single inhumations, primarily adult but several associated with infants or children, sometimes accompanying or added to adult burials (e.g., Tombs 246/16, 17; 229/1); most were provided with grave offerings (although those found disturbed held no *kterismata*). Despite these circumstances, which left few prehistoric burials intact, surviving evidence offers valuable information about the physical and cultural dimensions of the population of Methone at the end of the second millennium B.C.

The earliest prehistoric settlement at Methone survives on the natural ridge in the northeast corner of Plot 274 (Figs. 1.1, 6.1), in two ditches of the Late Neolithic and Early Bronze Age (Chapters 1, 4, Figs. 1.2, 4.3), with traces of Middle and Late Bronze Age (Chapter 5) and Early Iron Age (Chapter 7) occupation from the entire East Hill redeposited in the fill of monumental terraces and buildings of the Archaic through Classical periods. On the West Hill, burials of the Early Bronze Age have turned up south of the excavated area in salvage work in 2013, and on the southeast slopes of the West Hill (Tomb 229/14: ΜΕΘ 7140, 7141, in Chapter 4), in 2014;[3] moreover, Tomb 229/1 contained one of the earliest dated skeletons (its AMS ^{14}C dates range from the 18th to 16th centuries B.C.: Appendix, below) as well as one found in a highly contracted position (see Fig. 6.30), typical of third- or earlier second-millennium practices. This makes the West Hill, to the south and west of the prehistoric settlement on the East Hill (Chapter 4), the primary locale for burial outside habitation since the earliest occupation at Methone. This agrees closely with the pattern in this region, where Bronze Age burials were largely placed at a distance from human settlements.[4] The cluster of late second-millennium tombs presented in this chapter thus represents the northernmost extent to date (no tombs were found in 2014–2017 in the area north of the Ephoreia excavations: Fig. 6.1) of an older burying ground, now amplified by earlier graves immediately to the south (including Tomb 229/15, with a Mycenaean-style LH IIIA1 piriform jar, ΜΕΘ 7138) and complemented by Bronze Age graves at Pydna. The burials on the West Hill at

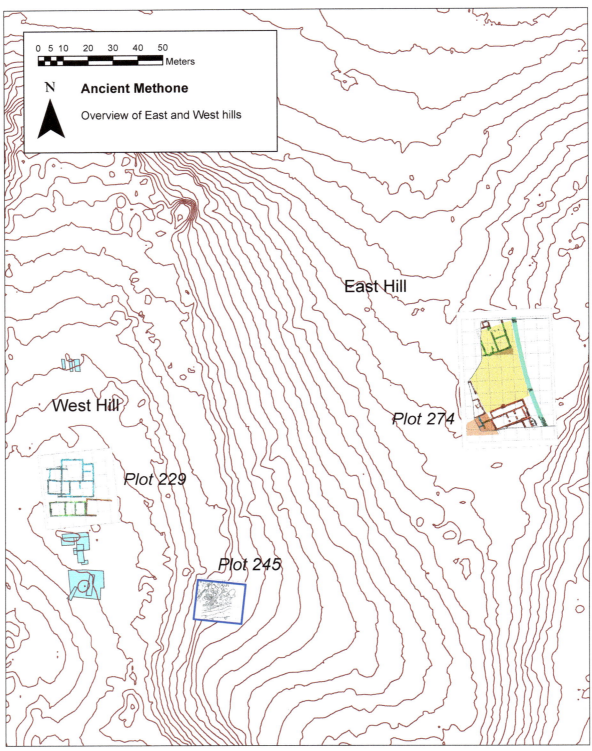

FIGURE 6.1. Ancient Methone: The acropolis area (Plots 229 and 245, locale of Bronze Age tombs) at left; agora area (Plot 274: prehistoric settlement and later remains) at upper right. Plan prepared by M. Chykerda using the LiDAR model of R. Kayen.

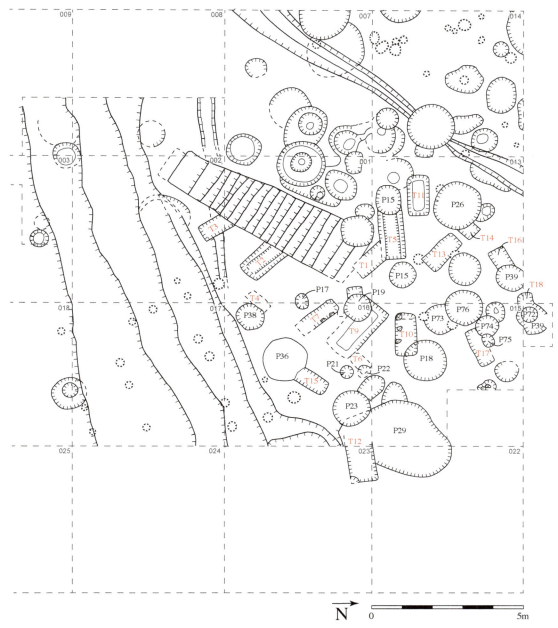

Figure 6.2. Methone Plot 245: Tombs 1–18 (under Early Iron Age pits, postholes, and Classical fortifications). Drawing I. Moschou and T. Ross

Methone add to a growing corpus of Bronze Age cemeteries in Pieria, excavated along its coastline and around Mt. Olympos, indicating a significant increase in evidence for those who lived (or died) here, especially from 1800 to 1200 B.C.[5]

BURIAL CUSTOMS

The Bronze Age cemetery at Methone followed practices common throughout Pieria: a rectangular pit was cut into the soft clay-rich limestone bedrock of the local environment to fit the dimensions of an extended or slightly contracted inhumation. Some pits included a narrow, rectangular central cavity with a surrounding ledge for a wooden lid, such as the cover of a coffin, to be fitted over the burial (with unworked stones set on the ledge to hold the lid in place), or for a deeper setting for the skeletal remains (e.g., Tombs 245/5, 229/4). Few burials were found intact enough at the ancient surface level to indicate evidence of cover slabs or tomb markers, neither likely in an area poor in stone, although prehistoric burials elsewhere in western Macedonia (near Kozani) and at Agios Mamas in Chalkidike held such surface markers.[6] Such pit graves dominate in northern Pieria, for example at Pydna, Kitros ("Louloudies"), Korinos ("Toumbes"), and Palaia Chrani.[7] Farther south among the many cemeteries on the western and northern slopes of Mt. Olympos, an area with more abundant stone, more elaborate cist graves survive, lined and covered with stone slabs, then sealed with a thick clay cover, some under an earth mound (tumulus) and/or stone circle, in some cases placed later than the burials.[8]

Elsewhere in northern Greece, a "striking transformation" was once noted from single inhumations in the Early Bronze Age to multiple and/or secondary burials in the Late Bronze and Early Iron Ages.[9] At Spathes on the slopes of Mt. Olympos, for example, three of 15 graves held from two to five individuals, as if in small kin groups, but Korinos had only one double burial (out of 30 graves). Double burials seem reserved for young adults, at least at Korinos and Spathes.[10] At Methone, the present sample may be too small and incomplete, with too many disturbed graves, to detect the original number and placement of individuals accurately and evaluate the wider distribution of this practice. So far only a few of the graves (6 of 28?) held more than a single inhumation, but almost all such additional burials were found as loose bones in tomb fill, often of infants, rather than as clearly defined primary or secondary inhumations.

A slightly contracted burial position (arms close to torso, legs drawn up at knees) is adopted in most of the Methone graves (in some examples the lower body is not preserved and its position not visible). Most skeletons were found supine with arms crossed over chest or abdomen, and legs slightly contracted to one side or fallen over since original placement (e.g., Tombs 245/9, 229/4). Grave goods were either worn by the deceased as jewelry (including bronze pins, gold earrings, and necklaces and bracelets of stone, bronze, glass, bone, clay, and amber beads) or placed as offerings near the head, hands, and feet, in the case of clay vessels and bronze knives. As mentioned above, the reopening of burials for the placement of additional individuals (common in southern Greek chamber tombs of the period, and in some cases in northern Greece) could not be confirmed, beyond a few disturbed contexts with additional bones.[11]

Cremation (once common in earlier periods, from the Neolithic) is rare in the Late Bronze Age Aegean, and Methone offers a single cremated adult(?), whose remains were collected in a local handmade jar, along with a fire-affected spindlewhorl (Tomb 229/8).[12]

GRAVE OFFERINGS

At Methone, the dead were buried in the Bronze Age with one or more clay vessels placed in the tomb, without exception all products of local workshops, many under the influence of southern Greek, Mycenaean shapes. The most frequent type of offering was a local version of the Mycenaean alabastron (both rounded, FS 85–86, and straight-sided, FS 91–98) that finds close parallels nearby in Pieria at Palaia Chrani and at Korinos ("Toumbes," part of the Pydna cemeteries).[13] Farther south, on the slopes of Mt. Olympos, the wheelmade alabastron is the most common grave offering at Leivithra, Spathes–Agios Dimitrios, and Platamon.[14] It is also found in Bronze Age burials farther west, up the Haliakmon River at Aiani.[15] In northern Greece, the shape can be traced well into the post-palatial Mycenaean period (alongside the amphoriskos) and evidently outlasted its southern

Greek counterparts, often in the form of local imitations.[16] These include handmade versions in local fabric at Methone (**6/55**, ΜΕΘ 4072, in Tomb 229/10), also found in graves at Palaia Chrani (Πυ 6484, 6485), at Vergina, and in west-central Macedonia at Almopia, suggesting how deeply and closely the wheelmade traditions of the Mycenaean heartland had penetrated the handmade techniques and tastes of the northern Aegean.[17]

In general, the Mycenaean stirrup jar dwindles in number in northern Greece (beginning with Thessaly), where there is also sparse evidence for olive cultivation in the Bronze Age.[18] Instead, the alabastron/amphoriskos dominates, possibly supplemented in function by local containers and products (see below). As alabastra are widely found in burial contexts (and less common in settlements) of Late Bronze Age Greece, it suggests that they were used for anointing the dead with aromatic oils, in the preparation of the corpse for burial or final treatment before sealing the tomb.[19] In an open jar, such perfumed fats might be in solid form (unlike liquid perfumed oil, commonly stored in sealed stirrup jars) and applied with a small bone pin as spatula (below), as in Classical times.[20] A residue analysis study of such vessels from northern Greece may reveal regional patterns in perfume use and its containers.[21]

Some burials also held local descendants of the small handleless jar (FS 77, a variant of the alabastron common in southern Greece in LH IIIA:1), found at Methone with both banded (**6/53**, ΜΕΘ 4073) and solid or semi-glazed (**6/51–6/52**, ΜΕΘ 4070, 4071) decoration. Handmade versions of this shape are common in Late Bronze Age burials on Mt. Olympos as the most characteristic and abundant local offering, where they are designated as perfume containers (μυροδοχεία).[22] So far, however, Methone has produced few examples of the handmade kantharoid amphoriskoi found in central Macedonia and identified via residue analysis as containers for oil made from plant seeds.[23] This may be a function of context, rather than perfume use, as most of the examples from central Macedonia derive from settlements, not from graves as at Methone.[24] Moreover, these local shapes may be replaced over time by alabastra (as at Toumba Thessalonikis)[25] by the LH IIIC period, the date of most burials at Methone.

Local handmade vases (kantharos, one-handled cup, and *thelastron* or feeder) that accompany imitations of southern Greek alabastra contextualize imported tastes within local traditions, in shapes also common at other sites in Pieria (for example, in the case of the footed kantharos, at Palaia Chrani). A single matt-painted biconical jar (**6/4** [ΜΕΘ 897]) appears in one of the earliest tombs (Tomb 245/1, with LH IIIA vessels) and, along with a few matt-painted sherds in the fill of Tomb 229/10, represents a local ceramic tradition otherwise found at Methone largely in redeposited sherds from the East Hill settlement, and which drops off elsewhere in northern Greece with an increasing taste for the Mycenaean style (see Chapter 5). Finally, a lone cremation burial was placed inside a tall handmade closed shape (jug or amphora), found in a pit within a balk: its date remains somewhat uncertain, but if not interred in the latest Bronze Age, it would belong to the Early Iron Age, as implied by close parallels from Palaio Gynaikokastro (ca. 1000 B.C.).[26] The convergence of a handmade utilitarian vessel with a burial custom eccentric to the dominant practice of inhumation may reflect local preferences in both burials and vessels, or could indicate the intrusion of a later, fully Early Iron Age burial.

As often noted in the study of pottery from northern Greece, local handmade vessels of the Bronze and Iron Age frequently exhibit a quality of manufacture and decoration superior to wheelmade imitations or even to imports of southern types.[27] Thus the elegant handmade, burnished jug with cutaway spout and spirally fluted handle in Tomb 229/10 (**6/56** [ΜΕΘ 4069]) outshines its wheelmade companions in the same tomb, and signals the high quality of northern Greek ceramic traditions (compare the rough, handmade imitation of a Mycenaean shape in the same tomb, **6/55** [ΜΕΘ 4072]). While the best parallels for this jug are found in Early Iron Age contexts (at Kastanas, Palaio Gynaikokastro, and Vergina), some aspects of the wheelmade Mycenaeanizing vessels (handleless jars, rosette motif) argue for an earlier date.[28]

A few of the burials (and in particular those of young females [Tomb 245/5]) were more richly furnished with bronze pins and other ornaments, necklaces of glass, stone, and amber beads, and in a single instance (Tomb 229/10), gold (spiral coil spacer beads, wire earrings) and amber jewelry. While the amber beads are familiar types common in the Mycenaean world, their co-occurrence with gold in the same set of ornaments recalls the "magic" power of amber argued for the Early Mycenaean and post-palatial periods.[29] Three graves (two adult males, one infant) held bronze knives (two with riveted handles are distinctly prehistoric in type), but nothing makes them weapons rather than tools and implements, nor do they indicate "warriors" (elsewhere in Greece, they are often found in female burials). Likewise, modest offerings such as clay spindlewhorls are frequently found near the hand or arm and probably worn or strung as beads (Tombs 245/5, 245/12, 229/10) with females and infants, but in other regions can be found in male burials.[30]

Of particular interest are the bone pins that were often found inside or near alabastra (as in Tomb 245/3: three pins in one alabastron; 245/9: one pin inside an alabastron; 229/4, the latter found under an alabastron; 229/10: two bone pins found inside an alabastron). These contexts suggest that the pins were used as applicators for perfumed ointment inside the Mycenaean alabastron, in one commonly accepted explanation of these vessels (see above). The Methone burials support this suggestion, and further indicate that these alabastra may have been distributed for their contents and function, rather than for their presumed status as a wheelmade vessel decorated in Mycenaean style. In addition, a piriform jar (ΜΕΘ 7138, from Tomb 229/15, excavated by the Pieria Ephoreia in 2014), a shape elsewhere identified with aromatics, also contained a bone pin, found in cleaning out its soil contents.[31] It remains unclear whether alabastra were covered with a cloth tied to the handles or left open, in which case one could imagine that the container could also continue to perfume (fumigate?) the tomb after burial.[32] Complex ointments associated with embalming purposes have been identified in Aegean burial contexts since the Early Helladic period (e.g., at Kalamaki, Achaia), according to residue analysis.[33] Other explanations for the Mycenaean alabastron (as a container for honey used in ritual libations for the dead) have not been confirmed by residue analysis, but few containers of this kind have been sampled for residue analysis.[34]

RELATIVE AND ABSOLUTE CHRONOLOGY

According to the late date of the Mycenaean-style vessels placed in nearly every grave, as well as aspects of the local handmade ones, many of these interments took place in a distinctly post-palatial age or during LH IIIC in terms of southern Greek stylistic and chronological sequences, several well after 1200 B.C. and perhaps even later. Within the sequence of burials, only one grave cut into another indicates relative dates: Tomb 245/5 (LH IIIB/C, 1261–1126 B.C., in ^{14}C dates) bisected Tomb 245/1 (also earlier in ceramic terms, LH II–III, confirmed by ^{14}C dates of 1501–1415 B.C.). Otherwise, most of the graves can only be roughly grouped, in terms of ceramic styles and/or ^{14}C dates (Appendix: Table 6.1, Fig, 6.45), from a few earlier burials (Tomb 245/1, 229/10), dating roughly to LH IIIA–B (1500–1300 B.C.), to a larger aggregate of about a dozen dating to LH IIIB or C, or 1300/1250 B.C. to 1200 and later. Most problematic for absolute dates and their relative relationship to the rock-cut graves are the remains of infants, some found in tomb fill, others found in pits with handmade vessels, in disturbed contexts which could well make them earlier, or later, than the rock-cut tombs: at least two (245/6 and 7) predate 1400 B.C., in ^{14}C terms, while Tomb

245/8 was disturbed by, and ended up inside, rock-cut Tomb 245/7. In Plot 229, Tomb 229/1 at the south end of the West Hill was heavily disturbed by an Iron Age pit, but its contracted position and initial ^{14}C date could agree in making this an early (EBA or MBA?) burial.

Throughout these vessels, the juxtaposition of southern types with northern favorites offers some interesting challenges for understanding the Late Bronze Age in northern Greece. For example, in the wealthiest burial of all and the last one to be excavated in this cemetery in 2011 (Tomb 229/10), four wheelmade, banded alabastra/amphoriskoi are accompanied by a roughly handmade version, as well as an elegant jug with cutaway neck and spirally fluted handle (**6/56** [MEΘ 4069], Fig. 6.39:a–d). The latter finds close parallels in northern Greece in well-dated tombs and domestic contexts of the Early Iron Age (1000–800 B.C., if not later, at Kastanas, Vergina, Torone, and Assiros).[35] Yet accompanying vessels in Mycenaean style represent ceramic types of the LH IIIA or pre-palatial age, suggesting a moment when new imported types met local handmade pottery traditions (whose artists promptly imitate wheelmade shapes).[36] And those handmade shapes continue to accompany the dead in later graves, sometimes next to wheelmade vessels (e.g., in Tombs 245/1, 5, 16). Meanwhile, in northern Pieria, the Mycenaean palatial influence represented by the bronze swords and sealstones (see below) that appear in graves closer to Mt. Olympos, Thessaly, and the inland route north is absent, at least in contexts excavated thus far.

METHONE: THE LATE BRONZE AGE SKELETAL POPULATION

Human remains in these burials were in general poorly preserved, many truncated by later pits that removed major skeletal elements, making it difficult to analyze a single complete skeleton. Preserved bone was often found crushed or disintegrated and heavily fragmented, missing extremities or even half an individual. Nevertheless, representative teeth and bones allowed some minimal identifications as to age, sex, and physical health (see Catalogue), prior to fuller analysis by Sevi Triantaphyllou and Vaso Papathanasiou. Moreover, human bones and teeth sampled for AMS ^{14}C dating and stable isotope analysis have provided initial absolute dates (Appendix), supported by preliminary C_4 isotopic values from the same samples that indicate consumption of millet (also identified by soil flotation in Bronze Age tombs excavated after 2014), rather than marine diet effect, which would have affected (by lowering) absolute dates from ^{14}C analysis.

GENERAL CONCLUSIONS

In many features, including tomb type (pit graves) and grave offerings (gold and amber jewelry, etc.), the graves uncovered at Methone compare closely to those of the Late Bronze Age found nearby in northern Pieria (Pydna area) as well as farther south near the slopes of Olympos (Spathes–Agios Dimitrios, Voulkani–Leivithra).[37] Important chance finds, in particular two swords and two spearheads in the Vergina museum, signal wealthy burials of the Late Bronze Age extending farther west toward the Haliakmon valley.[38] Collectively, they extend the northern borders of the Mycenaean world north of Thessaly and even far west up the Haliakmon River, as one scholar noted in tracking the distribution of Mycenaean seals around Mt. Olympos.[39] In its tomb types, Pieria featured cist and pit graves in the Late Bronze Age, but rarely built chamber tombs or tholos tombs with tumuli, which cease north of Thessaly.[40] The Peneios River valley may have formed an important watershed between northern and southern Greece in the Bronze Age, but the Haliakmon River proved a strong artery for the distribution of prestige goods to its burials (at Ano Komi, Kolitsaki,

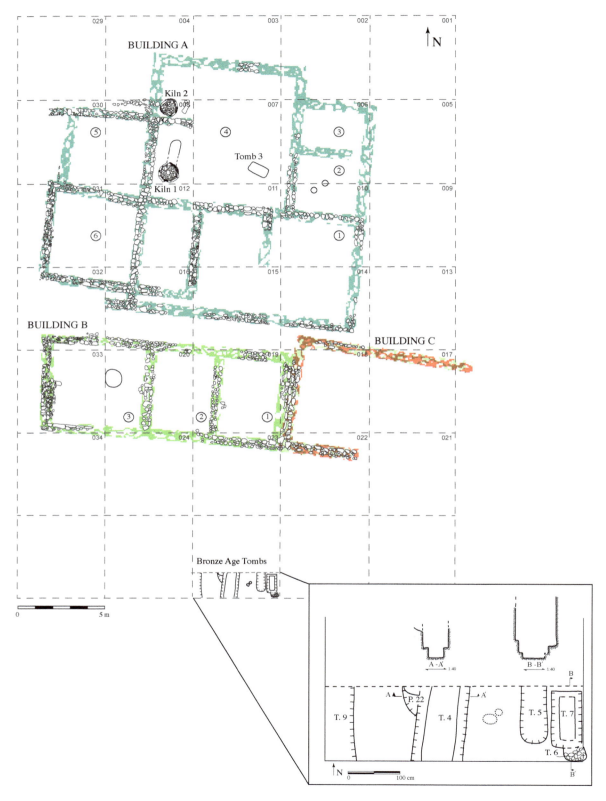

FIGURE 6.3. Methone West Hill (acropolis): Plot 229, Tomb 3 (under Building A), with inset of Tombs 4–9 (south end, at the bottom of plan). Drawing I. Moschou and T. Ross

and Aiani), and even distant Kastoria, where Late Helladic pottery has been found at Dispilio, was not isolated from contact with the Mycenaean world and its material culture.[41]

As such archaeological discoveries continue to push the "northern frontier" of the Mycenaean world farther north and west, so may philology. References to "Pierians" in Mycenaean Greek, in Linear B tablets from Mycenae and Pylos, could indicate personal names associated with this northern Greek locale (albeit the name indicates any "rich," fertile region, as in a Pylos place name: PY Aa 1182). "Pierian" women receive oil distributions at Mycenae (MY Fo 101, *pi-we-ri-[si?]*: dative plural?), where the term also appears in the name of a female recipient of wool, in the dative singular, *pi-we-ri-di* (MY Oe 103), and as a smith's name at Pylos (/*Piwerijātās*/: PY Jn 389.3).[42] Meanwhile, mythological memory and epic poetry could likewise expand the heroic world beyond Mt. Olympos, if the kingdom of Philoktetes in Homer (*Iliad* 2. 716–719, a domain of four cities including a Methone) reached Pieria as far as the Haliakmon River.[43]

A related legend has Agamemnon curse the Methonaians, for refusing him a safe harbor and naval repair station for the Achaian fleet, or for recruiting for the expedition, on the way to Troy (Strabo VII, fr. 20c, Baladié, citing Theopompos).[44] The story presumes the existence or memory of a Bronze Age predecessor for the port city later famous for offering Athens an ally, harbor, and source of valuable timber for its fleet. If as an imagined predecessor, this legend could simply reflect creative historicizing to fabricate an epic pedigree for a historical relationship between southern Greek naval powers and northern Greek natural resources. But it is the curse of Agamemnon that makes the whole story more intriguing: in response to Methone's refusal, his naval commanders (ναυστολόγοι) cursed the Methonaians by condemning them to perpetual wall-building (εἴθε μὴ παύσαισθε τ(ε)ι[χοδομοῦν]τες). This colorful curse could in fact reflect the long-term condition of a coastal city whose successive settlements eventually fell prey to erosion by the sea, and whose fortifications consisted of ditches cut into bedrock and bulwarks built of mud brick. Thus, in a very real sense, the Methonaians did keep rebuilding their walls, originally against erosion in an environment poor in stone, and finally, yet in vain, to protect the city against its last siege by Philip II. And while none of this can support the historicity of the anecdote of Agamemnon except in a circular way, like the legend of the Eretrian colonists who defended themselves with slings that complements the many sling bullets found at the site, what Theopompos reports finds resonance in both the early history and the mud-brick ramparts of Methone.

In conclusion, the emerging prehistory of Methone, whose recent archaeological record demonstrates a lengthy Bronze Age occupation, deserves fresh comparison to some of the intriguing ancient testimonia to its role in the epic imagination.

CATALOGUE OF TOMBS AND FINDS (MYCENAEAN TOMBS, 2005–2011)

PLOT 245

Tomb 245/1.	#245/001020 [2]. Notebook pp. 7–10. 26/8/2005.	Fig. 6.4a–b
Location:	#245/013002 [extension to north: most of grave in Sq. 13]	
Discovery, description:	Τομή Δ [Sector 4]: 26.66 below northeast corner (0.700 below surface); human bones; tomb continues into Square 13.	
24/8/2005:	#245/001019 = cutting for tomb cleared, trench extended	
25/8/2005:	#245/001020 + 013002 = Tomb 1; cut into bedrock north, east (but not disturbed by cutting of classical steps).	
Fill:	reddish brown earth, many limestone inclusions.	

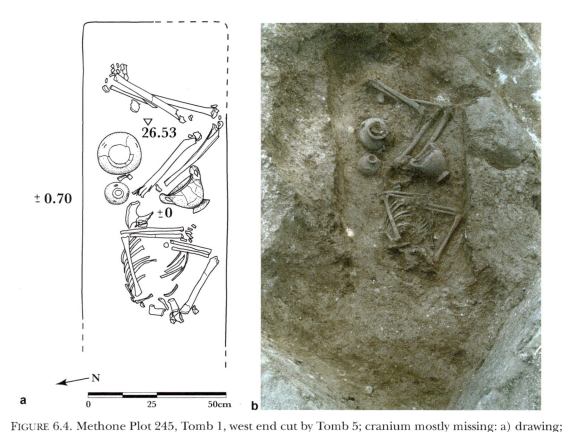

FIGURE 6.4. Methone Plot 245, Tomb 1, west end cut by Tomb 5; cranium mostly missing: a) drawing; b) view from west. Drawing I. Moschou and T. Ross, photo KZ´ Ephoreia

Sherds:	unglazed WM, a few HM; two glazed.
Dimensions:	P.L. 1.30 x W. 0.55–0.60.
Orientation:	Northwest–southeast.
Relative chronology:	Cut into by Tomb 5.
Absolute chronology:	AMS ^{14}C: 1501–1415 calBC (95.4%).
Skeleton:	Found at depth of 26.53 m, head to northwest; contracted position, on right side, arms crossed across lower abdomen. Cranium incomplete, only mandible preserved in good condition; post-cranial elements relatively well preserved.
Length:	1.05 m; max. W. at elbows 0.35 m.
Identification (2013):	Age 14–15 years; male?

GRAVE GOODS

Ceramics, wheelmade

6/1. (ΜΕΘ 860) Wheelmade Alabastron Fig. 6.5a–b
 #245/001020 [2]. 25/8/2005. Vase 12. Found at left side near pelvis.
 H. 0.085; Diam. (max, above base) 0.11; Diam. (at handle attachments) 0.090; Diam. (rim) 0.050; Diam. (neck) 0.035; handles: W. (at roots) 0.040, H. 0.015; Diam. 0.055.
 Complete.
 Wheelmade alabastron, three handles. FS 93–94 (LH IIIA–B). Sloping wall rising from rounded underside (no flat resting surface) to widest point of diameter, just above base, then sloping in to shoulder and handle attachments. Shoulder slopes in to narrow neck, articulated at join to shoulder by rounded (ring) molding. Narrow concave neck curves out to everted rim, sloping lip. Three horizontal ring handles set vertically at base of shoulder, rising to pointed arc (triangle).

Decoration: Mycenaean banded alabastron; net pattern (FM 57). Exterior base and body banded below shoulder and handles (six bands), banded shoulder (three bands). Molding reserved, neck painted solid with reserved line at narrowest point, rim very worn but probably glazed solid inside and out with reserved lip. Handle zone decorated with net pattern (cross-hatched lines), handles painted solid red outside.

Fabric: Fine clay, gold mica, white grit, many small hollows (lime spalling?). Surface very smooth, dull; inside of rim and top (lip) rough. Light red clay (2.5YR 6/6), fired dark red on one side of vase.

Published: Bessios 2010, p. 62 (lower row, right).

LH IIIA2: Mountjoy 1999, pp. 706–707, fig. 271, #45–47 (Euboia); pp. 803–804, fig. 320, #33 (Agios Ilias, Aitoloakarnania); pp. 845–847, fig. 341, #97 (Thessaly: LH IIIB).

6/2. (MEΘ 861) Wheelmade Straight-sided Alabastron   Fig. 6.5c–d

#245/001020 [2]; #245/013. Vase 13. Found at left side near pelvis, behind femur.

P.H 0.115; Diam. (neck) 0.083–0.087 (oval circumference); Diam. (max) 0.016; Diam. (rim) 0.100; Diam. (base) 0.150(?); Th. (rim) 0.011; handles: W. (at roots) 0.060; H. 0.030; Diam. 0.010.

Broken in many pieces (base cannot be restored).

Shape: Mycenaean alabastron, straight-sided, three handles. FS 93–94 (LH IIIA1/2–LH IIIB); wheelmade, missing base. Vertical wall rising to sloping shoulder, vertical neck flaring to flat rim with projecting lip.

Decoration: Rim glazed inside and out; banded body (three narrow bands) below handles at join of body to shoulder, around neck; broader bands define base, and handle zone. Net pattern (cross-hatched lines) on shoulder between handles. Handles painted with multi-splash pattern across top, at right angle to length of handle.

Fabric: Fine reddish clay, gold mica (2.5YR 6/6, "light red"); surface smoothed, dull, painted (streaky red glaze).

Published: Bessios 2010, p. 62 (lower row, center).

LH IIIA1: Mountjoy 1986, pp. 57–58, fig. 65, p. 73, fig. 84; 1999, pp. 750–751, fig. 289, #24 (Phokis); Mitrou: Vitale 2011, p. 335, fig. 2.11; Koulidou et al. 2014, p. 167, fig. 4 (A-17), n. 11 (LH IIIA2–B1). The shape lasts into LH IIIC (FS 96): Mountjoy 1986, pp. 140–141, fig. 173; Mountjoy 1999, pp. 557–558, fig. 203, #273 (Athens); *Lefkandi* IV, p. 206, fig. 2.27; Iolkos, Thessaly (Adrimi-Sismani 2014, p. 545, BE 35628).

Ceramics, handmade

6/3. (MEΘ 862) Handmade Footed Kantharos   Fig. 6.5e–f

#245/001020 [2] #245/013 25/08/2005. Vase 14. Found on right side of skeleton, near femur.

Restored from frr.

H. 0.163; Diam. (base) 0.075; H. (foot) 0.020; Diam. (max) 0.170; Diam. (rim) 0.125–135 (oval); handles: H. 0.065, W. (at base) 0.040; Th. 0.014; W. (at top) 0.015.

Shape: Handmade kantharos, footed; high-swung spur handles. Low conical foot, wall flaring to broadest point of maximum diameter and lower handle attachments, then in to broad open rim; squared strap handles rise above rim with squared spur inside rim. Flaring rim, narrows to lip. Handles squared in section, set at angle to wall and rim with spur at top, shallow channel inside along vertical axis of handle; attachment of handles to rim shaped circumference into slight oval.

Fabric: Fine red clay (2.5YR 6/6); surface once smoothed, burnished, now worn and flaked.

Published: Bessios 2010, p. 62 (lower row, left).

Cf. matt-painted version, Angelochori (Veroia Museum: Π 8326); Stefani 2011, p. 157, #63; Kastanas: Hochstetter 1987, pls. 27.5, 56.1; Agios Mamas: Horejs 2007a, pl. 51, #9433. Footed version of **6/37**? (MEΘ 874, Tomb 245/16).

FIGURE 6.5. Plot 245, Tomb 1: a)–b) **6/1** (MEΘ 860), alabastron; c)–d) **6/2** (MEΘ 861), alabastron, straight-sided; e)–f) **6/3** (MEΘ 862), handmade footed kantharos. Drawings A. Hooton, photos I. Coyle

6/4. (ΜΕΘ 897) Handmade Vessel Fig. 6.6a–b
#245/001020 [2]. Τομή Δ [Sector 4]. Vase 12. Not in Notebook (restored from frr from grave fill).
P.H. 0.170; Diam. (max) 0.180; Diam. (lip) 0.090; Diam. (max, rim) 0.095; lug: H. 0.010; W. 0.015.
Shape: Handmade biconical jar, matt-painted; missing base. Small biconical shape, lower wall flares out then in to narrow neck, everted rim with squared lip; small mastos (squarish lug) placed just above midpoint and below painted band.
Decoration: Matt-painted: solid red exterior rim and lip, red bands above and below midpoint and mastos; concentric circle motif in mastos zone? (only visible on drawing).
Fabric: Gray core, brown-gray surface; semicoarse fabric, much gold mica; 10YR 5/2 "grayish brown" [mottled]. Red paint: dark red? (very worn), patchy; 10R 4/6?
Cf. Albania: Lofkënd P168 (Papadopoulos et al. 2014, pp. 237, 291, figs. 9.25, 9.60, 9/220, from tumulus fill).

Small finds

6/5. (ΜΕΘ 878) Bronze Pin with Poppy or Vase Head Fig. 6.6c–d
#245/001020, #245/013, 2. 25/8/2005. Tomb 1. ME 115. Found at right shoulder.
L. 0.185; Diam. (head, max) 0.010; Diam. (head, top) 0.009; Diam. (shaft, at juncture with head) 0.006; Wt. 19.2 g.
Intact. Condition good.
Thick shaft, circular in section, tapering toward point. Well-formed head, resembling poppy head or vase, composed of biconical bead surmounted by shaft and ending with a flat disk finial.
Cf. Iolkos, Thessaly (Adrimi-Sismani 2014, pp. 754, 758, BE 44398: LH IIIC Early).

6/6. ΜΕΘ 884 (ME 116) is a collection of beads found near the right wrist, probably a small bracelet made of various different beads, as follows: **6/6α** large bone bead; **6/6β** small glass bead; **6/6γ** numerous minuscule bronze beads; **6/6δ** small bronze continuous spiral (coil) bead.

6/6α. (ΜΕΘ 884α) Bone Bead Fig. 6.6e–f
#245/00120, #245/013, 2. 25/8/2005. Tomb 1. ME 116.
Diam. 0.024; H. 0.010; Wt. 2.7 g.
Intact; somewhat chipped on one side.
Made of single piece of bone (of an unidentified mammal).
Dome-shaped bead, polished on top, with the porous structure of the bone visible on the underside. There is a neatly cut/drilled cavity at the center of the bottom and a continuous hole that goes through the cavity, as shown.

6/6β. (ΜΕΘ 884β) Glass Bead Fig. 6.6e
#245/00120, #245/013, 2. 25/8/2005. Tomb 1. ME 116.
Largest fr: p.L. x p.W. 0.007 x 0.006; Diam. (est) ca. 0.010; Wt. 0.2 g.
Five small frr, all of which probably join, preserving about one-half of bead.
As preserved, white opaque glass, with a greenish tinge (bead has corroded to a white color but has traces of green-blue colored glass).
Small circular/spherical bead, with small central hole.
Cf. glass beads from Lofkënd, Albania (Papadopoulos et al. 2014, Chapter 10).

6/6γ. (ΜΕΘ 884γ) 23 Small/Minuscule Bronze Beads Fig. 6.6e
#245/00120, #245/013, 2. 25/8/2005. Tomb 1. ME 116.
Average dimensions: H. 0.004; Diam: 0.005; Wt. 0.2 g; total Wt. (all pieces) 2.8 g.
A total of 23 complete and fragmentary beads; several of the frr join.
The average bead is minuscule, formed of a thin bronze band, defining a small closed ring. Some are plano-convex in section, but one or two approach biconical. At least one of the beads forms a small spiral, not unlike **6/6δ** (ΜΕΘ 884δ), but not the same.

6/6δ. (ΜΕΘ 884δ) Small Continuous Bronze Spiral Bead Fig. 6.6e, g
#245/00120, #245/013, 2. 25/8/2005. Tomb 1. ME 116.
L. (all frr laid in line) 0.106; Diam. 0.004–0.005; Wt. 4.2 g.
Ten frr, many, if not all, probably joining.
Continuous small coiled spiral.

6/7. (ΜΕΘ 886) Small Continuous Bronze Spiral Bead Fig. 6.6e, h
#245/013. 25/8/2005. ME 118. Found near jaw of skeleton; possibly part of necklace.
Diam. 0.003–0.005; p.L. (at least). 0.036; Wt. 1.4 g.
Continuous small coiled spiral bead (χαλκ. σύριγγα).
Cf. ΜΕΘ 884δ, 885γ.

Tomb 245/2.	#274/001 [2]. Τομή Δ [Sector 4]. Notebook pp. 10–12, 25-8-2005. Figs. 6.7a–b.
Description, discovery:	Cutting 0.55 from south and 0.50 from east side of square, at boundaries of Τομή Δ and E [Sectors 4 and 5].
Dimensions:	P.L. 1.60; W. 0.900; preserved depth 0.700 (once 1 m?).
Orientation:	Northwest–southeast (northwest corner cut by Classical stairs).
Fill:	#274/001024: soil reddish brown, fairly soft and loose, many limestone inclusions; several fieldstones in center of tomb, at 26.56 m and 26.3 m depth. Sherds: 3 unglazed, WM, 2 glazed.
Coffin:	Remains of wooden sarcophagus found at 26.38 m depth, along north–south side.
Absolute chronology:	AMS ^{14}C: 1219–1150 calBC (95.4%): LH IIIC?
Skeleton:	Inhumation, extended burial position, found at 26.21 m depth, 0.100–0.150 m below level of debris of wood coffin. Supine, head to northwest; pelvis bones fairly well preserved, also forearms, leg bones; cranium disturbed by cutting for stairs. P.L. 1.27 m.
Identification (2013):	Adult; male.
Study (2019):	Pathology: Musculo-skeletal markers: 1) Left femur: strongly marked linea aspera.

GRAVE GOODS

6/8. (ΜΕΘ 877) Bronze Knife Fig. 6.7c
#245/0010, 2. 2005. Tomb 2. ME 117.
Found at right side near forearm.
L. 0.163; L. (hilt) 0.039; W. (max, at juncture of blade and hilt) 0.019; Th. (blade back, max) 0.006; Wt: 37.0 g. Rivets: L: 0.012; Diam. (head) 0.007.
Intact. Condition very good.

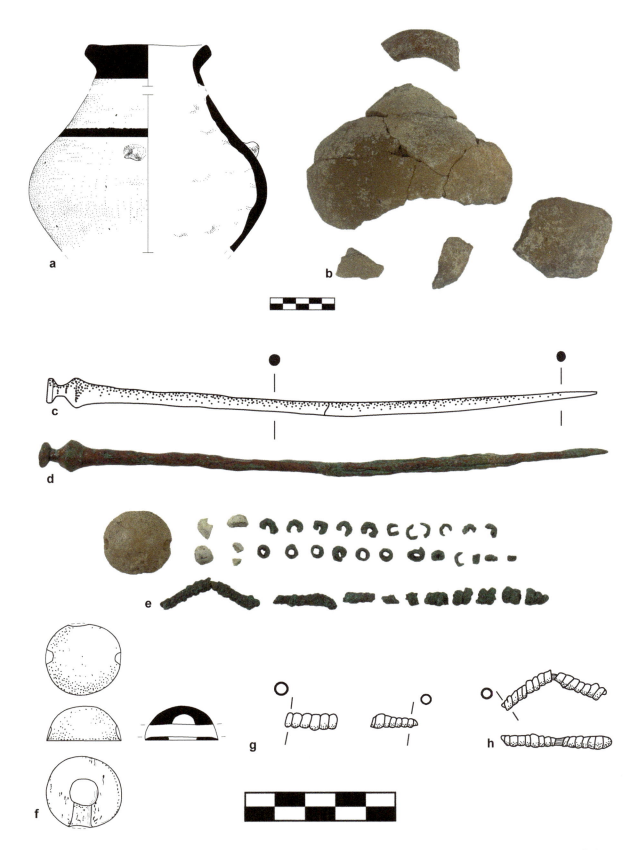

FIGURE 6.6. Plot 245, Tomb 1: a)–b) **6/4** (ΜΕΘ 897), handmade matt painted jar; c)–d) **6/5** (ΜΕΘ 878), bronze pin; e) **6/6α** (ΜΕΘ 884α), **6/7** (ΜΕΘ 886), beads of bone, glass, and bronze; f) **6/6δ** (ΜΕΘ 884δ); g) **6/6δ** (ΜΕΘ 884δ); h) **6/7** (ΜΕΘ 886). Drawings A. Hooton and F. Skyvalida, photos I. Coyle

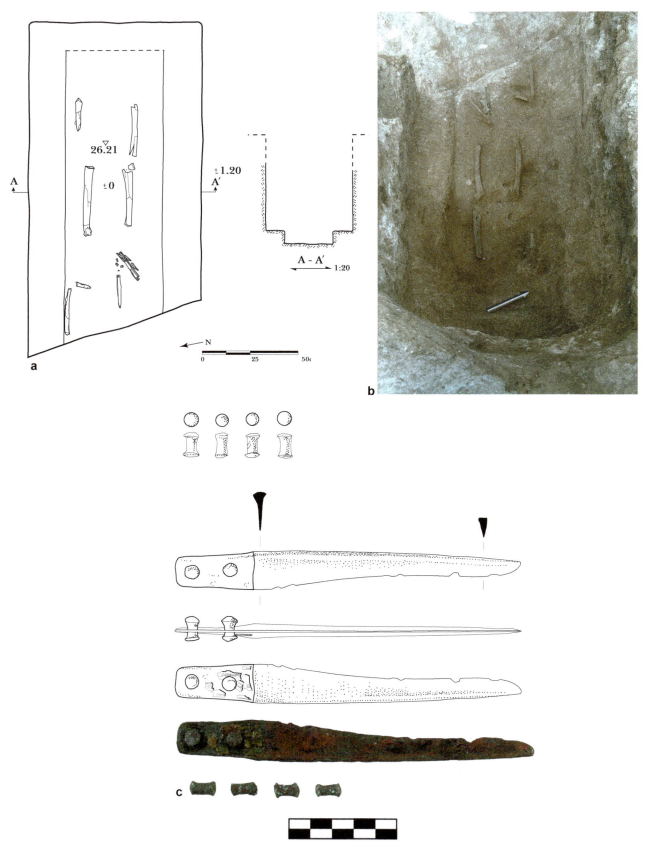

FIGURE 6.7. Methone Plot 245, Tomb 2, west end cut by Classical stairs; a) drawing I. Moschou and T. Ross; b) view from east, photo KZ´ Ephoreia; c) 6/8 (ΜΕΘ 877), bronze knife. Drawing A. Hooton, photo I. Coyle

Straight-sided knife, with distinct blade and hilt. Blade with substantial back along straight side, with a sharp cutting edge on the slightly concave side. Thickest point of back and widest point of knife at juncture of blade and hilt. Point rounded. Hilt more or less rectangular, with terminal slightly rounded off. Hilt bears substantial remains of wood on one side, kept in place by two rivets. The juncture of the blade with the backing is marked by an incised line.

Date: Late Bronze Age (LH IIIC): cf. Leivithra: Poulaki-Pantermali 2013b, pp. 47–48; *Lefkandi* IV, pp. 282–283, fig. 5.10, 5, pl. 89.3, 16.10.2a (iron).

Found together with MEΘ 877 were four additional bronze rivets of the same type as those on the knife (L. 0.012; Diam. [head] 0.007–0.008; Wt. [altogether] 8.4 g [2.0–2.2 g individually]), fig. 6.7c, upper left (on drawing).

Tomb 245/3. #245/002035. Notebook p. 13. 26/8/2005
Location: Southwest of Tomb 2, north edge of trench; 2.5 from east side of trench. Figs. 6.8a–b.
Dimensions: P.L. 1.55, p.W. 0.55; cut at northwest by Classical stairs.
Fill: #274/002034: Loose reddish brown earth, fair number of limestones; a few unglazed sherds and one glazed.
Absolute chronology: AMS ^{14}C: 1395–1333 calBC (37.4%), 1327–1223 calBC (58.0%).
Skeleton: No bones found at all in trench; probably infant? teeth found in water sieve, along with two HM sherds, one (bone?) bead.
Identification (2013): Infant (5.5–6 years); sex unknown.
Stable isotope sample: Deciduous maxillary canine.

Grave Goods
Ceramics, wheelmade

6/9.   (MEΘ 863) Straight-sided Alabastron   Fig. 6.8c–d
#245/002035. Vase 16.

Preserved whole, chip broken off rim (modern break), missing one handle; surface pitted, flaked. Neck broken (mended).

H. 0.095; Diam. (max) 0.110; Diam. (rim) 0.07; Diam. (neck) 0.055; Th. (rim) 0.004; handles: W. (at attachment) 0.045; H. 0.020; Th./Diam. 0.006.

Shape: Mycenaean alabastron, straight-sided; three handles; banded. FS 95–96: LH IIIB/C? Small alabastron, squat shape: vertical walls swelling slightly past maximum diameter to handles, shoulder sloping in to narrow neck. Underside flat but slightly domed (no horizontal resting surface), with small nipple inside center of floor. Three small handles set in triangle position, at 45° angle to shoulder.

Decoration: Exterior neck, rim, and inside rim glazed solid, three horizontal bands at join of neck and shoulder; two bands below handles. Handles glazed outside and across attachments. Glaze: bands fired light red to dark brown.

Fabric: Light red clay (5YR 7/6) throughout, fine white grit, dark inclusions; no mica?

Mountjoy 1999, p. 569, fig. 209 #328 (Athens, LH IIIC Early); pp. 709–710, fig. 272, #57 (Chalkis, Euboea: LH IIIB); pp. 730–731, fig. 282, #26–29 (Skyros: LH IIIC Early); pp. 845–847, fig. 341, #95, 99 (Thessaly: LH IIIB).

6/10α.   (MEΘ 894α) Bone Pin   Fig. 6.8e, h
#245/002. 26/8/2005. Tomb 3.

P.L. (main frr) 0.163; L. (together with tip) 0.178; L. x W. (head) 0.007 x 0.005; Wt. (after restoration): 5.8 g.

Three frr in all preserving complete pin, two frr joining, preserving great part of pin shaft, and one other fr, barely joining, preserving tip.

Upper shaft toward head rectangular in section, lower shaft circular, tapering to a sharp point. Head original. Original surfaces, wherever preserved, nicely polished smooth.

Perhaps tibia or metapodial bone, but difficult to determine.

Cf. Lofkënd, Albania: Papadopoulos and Kurti 2014, pp. 347–359.

6/10β. (ΜΕΘ 894β) Bone Pin Fig. 6.8f, h
#245/002. 26/08/2005. Tomb 3.
P.L: 0.093; L. x W. (head) max. 0.035 x 0.004; Wt. (after restoration): 1.4 g.
Single fr preserving greater part of pin, except for the head, which looks to be broken.
Upper shaft square to rectangular in section, lower shaft circular in section, tapering toward a sharp point. Original surfaces, wherever preserved, nicely polished smooth.
Type of bone difficult to determine.

6/10γ. (ΜΕΘ 894γ) Bone Pin Fig. 6.8g–h
#254/002. 26/08/2005. Tomb 3.
P.L. 0.111; Diam. (max); 0.004; Wt: 1.2 g.
Three joining frr preserving greater part of pin except for the head. The fact that this pin and **6/10β** (ΜΕΘ 894β) do not have intact heads may indicate that they were placed in the tomb as virtually complete objects, but with their heads damaged/chipped during use in life, during the funeral, or when tomb disturbed or damaged.
Thin shaft, circular in section, tapering to sharp point. Original surfaces, wherever preserved, nicely polished, but not as well finished as the other pins from the same tomb.
Type of bone difficult to determine.

6/11. (ΜΕΘ 5318) Glass/Faience Bead Fig. 6.8i
#245/002. Tomb 3 (found in sieve).
Diam. 0.004: H. 0.0025; Diam. (hole) 0.002; Wt: < 0.1 g.
Completely corroded (now white); glass.
Pierced circular bead, white.

Tomb 245/4.	#274/001027 + 016029. Notebook; drawing.	Fig. 6.9.
Location:	Cut by Pit 38 [grave cut?]; no finds.	
Skeleton:	1 bag: #245/001027 [4]. 26-8-2005.	
	1 bag: #274/016029 [23]. 19-10-2005.	
	Right femur (midshaft), various fragmentary post-cranial elements, no cranial bones, teeth. Probably supine, northwest–southeast, head to northwest.	
Identification:	Child (6–12 years, from bone morphology); sex unknown.	
Stable isotope sample	One unsided rib fr.	
Absolute chronology	AMS ^{14}C: 1265–1109 calBC (94.4%), 1099–1088 calBC (1.0%).	

GRAVE GOODS
None.

Tomb 245/5.	#245/013012 [3]. Notebook pp. 21ff.; 13-9-05.	Fig. 6.10a–c.
Published:	Bessios 2010, p. 61, right (photograph of grave).	
Type:	Pit grave with wooden sarcophagus; inhumation.	
Location:	Northeast corner of cutting disturbed by cutting for Tomb 1; west end cut by Pit 15 (missing extremities), missing edge of tomb cut.	

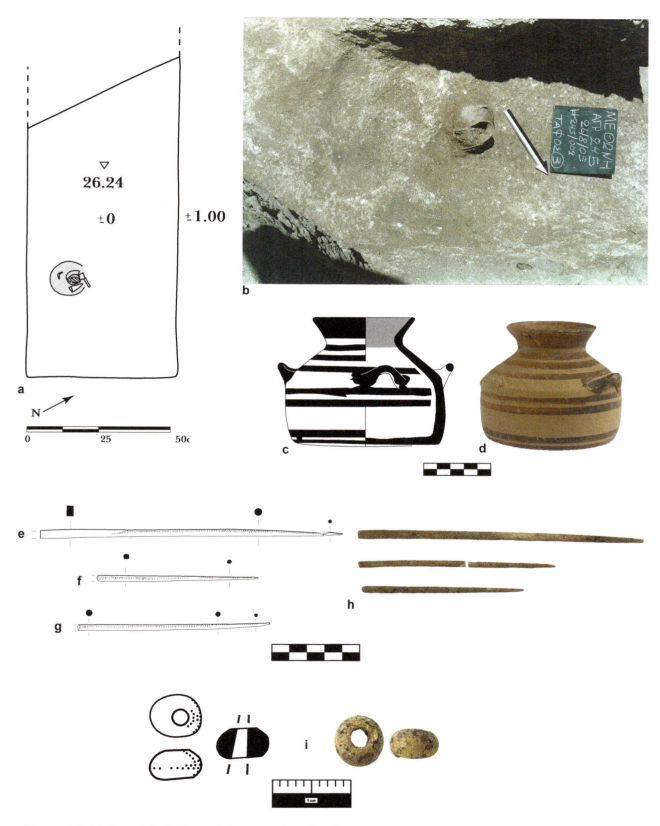

FIGURE 6.8. Methone Plot 245, Tomb 3, west end cut by Classical stairs: a) drawing I. Moschou and T. Ross; b) view from above east, photo KZ´ Ephoreia; c)–d) **6/9** (ΜΕΘ 863), straight-sided alabastron; bone pins: e) **6/10α** (ΜΕΘ 894α); f) **6/10β** (ΜΕΘ 894β); g) **6/10γ** (ΜΕΘ 894γ); h) **6/10α–6/10γ**; i) **6/11** (ΜΕΘ 5318). Drawings A. Hooton, photos I. Coyle and J. Vanderpool

FIGURE 6.9. Methone Plot 245, Tomb 4.
View from southwest. Photo KZ´ Ephoreia

Fill:	#274/013010: Loose soil, reddish brown with many limestone inclusions, no stones; 24 sherds, some Bronze Age (including from alabastra); handmade handle, Yellow (Minyan?) jar (rim, neck), Archaic wheelmade (Corinthian, painted, etc.), coarse body sherds. Human bone fragments #013007: 1) cranial fragments, 2) fragment of L humerus (infant)—Human bone fragments #013010: 1) unidentified long bone fragments 2) Note: one of the fragments joins with the distal third of the right femur from the primary skeleton.
Animal bones:	Yes.
Pit 24—#013017:	1) cranial fragments (vault and occipital (inion < female), 2) distal hand phalanx, 3) coronoid process (left scapula), 4) pelvic fragments, one fragment joins with the left acetabulum from the primary skeleton.
#274/013008:	West part of fill: different soil composition, softer and darker with traces of organic materials; fair number of clay lumps and coarse sherds (pithos), all characteristic finds from fill of pit (= Pit 5). Unglazed pottery, handmade, primarily Early Iron Age.
Dimensions:	L 1.57 x W 0.55; 27.55 deep; with low ledge (H. 0.20; W 0.20), cut on north and south sides (27.24 deep) for sarcophagus.
Orientation:	East–west.
Relative chronology:	Cuts Tomb 1 (LH IIIA1).
Absolute chronology:	AMS ^{14}C: 1261–1126 calBC (95.4%).
Skeleton:	Well preserved to tibia (feet missing, disturbed by Pit 5). Adult, supine, head to east, turned to right shoulder; right femur turned (fallen inward: contracted position). P.L. 1.15; depth 27.80–27.02.

Stature:	155.864 3.72 (L femur).
Study (2015):	Juvenile (16–19 years); female.
Additional:	bones of perinate found in fill (right humerus).
Study (2019):	Pathology: Right distal femur-stress lesion at the attachment site of gastrocnemius muscle.
Bronze discoloration:	Four left proximal hand phalanges, three left metacarpals.
Sampled for isotopes:	1) middle hand phalanx, 2) one unidentified bone fragment.

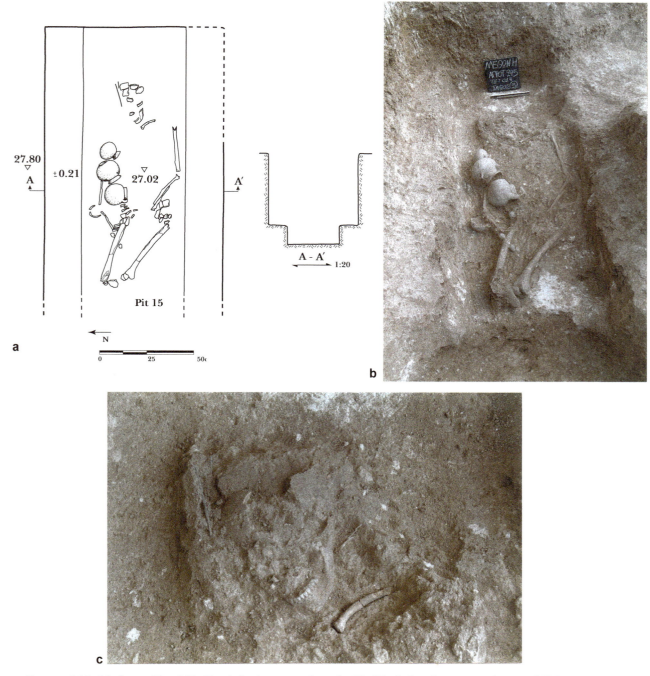

FIGURE 6.10. Methone Plot 245, Tomb 5: a) west end cut by Pit 15: a) drawing I. Moschou and T. Ross; b) view from west; c) detail of cranium with bronze pins, glass and stone beads. Photos KZ´ Ephoreia

GRAVE GOODS

Right arm and side: four vessels (2 Mycenaean alabastra).

Right femur: clay beads, fallen in shape of arc.

Fingers of left hand: bronze rings.

Right of skull: bronze pins.

Chest, neck and skull: glass, amber beads (necklace).

Found in water sieve: many amber, glass beads.

Found with human bone: bone? bead(s) (not inventoried).

Ceramics

6/12. (ΜΕΘ 864) Rounded Alabastron Fig. 6.11a–b

#245/013012 [3] 13-09-05. Vase 17. Found near right hand/arm.

Preserved whole, no breaks or chips; inside rim pitted, flaked.

H. 0.070; Th. (rim) 0.004; Diam. (rim) 0.060; Diam. (neck 0.053); Diam. (max) 0.085; handles: H. 0.020; W. 0.050; Diam. 0.006.

Shape: Small rounded alabastron, banded; three handles. FS 85 (LH IIIB/C). Rounded underside and biconical profile, wall shows continuous curve, maximum diameter at vertical midpoint, no neck, splaying rim.

Decoration: Two painted bands below handles at midpoint, single band on shoulder, band at join of shoulder to neck; rim glazed inside and out.

Fabric: Fine, light red-yellow, much gold mica/sand; 5YR 7/6.

Surface: Smoothed but not lustrous, paint light to dark brown.

Published: Bessios 2010, p. 62 (top row, center).

Cf. Mountjoy 1999, pp. 567–569, fig. 209, #326–327 (Perati); pp. 845–846, fig. 341, #92–93 (Thessaly: LH IIIB).

6/13. (ΜΕΘ 865) Amphoriskos Fig. 6.11c–d

#245/013012 [3] 19-09-05. Vase 18. Found near right hand/arm.

Completely preserved (neck broken in excavation, mended).

H. 0.110; Diam. (rim) 0.080; Diam. (max) 0.120; Diam. (base) 0.040; Th. (rim) 0.005; handles: H. 0.020; W. 0.040; Diam. 0.005.

Shape: Mycenaean amphoriskos; banded. Vertical slashes painted in handle zone. FS 59–61 (LH IIIB/C). Medium size, spherical profile with maximum diameter at vertical midpoint (well below handles), set on flat base with slightly raised underside; splayed rim, rounded lip. Ring handles set horizontally at irregular intervals (two close together, others far apart or in between).

Decoration: Rim glazed inside and out, vertical slashes painted between handles (in groups of 5, 9, and 11 strokes, determined by interval between handles: possibly FM 64, foliate band?

Fabric: Pale yellow-red clay (5YR 6/6, "reddish yellow"), fine gold mica; streaky pale red glaze, darker (browner) inside rim and over handle.

Published: Bessios 2010, p. 62 (top row, right).

Cf. Perati: Mountjoy 1986, p. 138, fig. 168; 1999, pp. 565–567, fig. 208, #312–315; pp. 581–584, fig. 215, #404; *Lefkandi* IV, pp. 203–204, fig. 2.31.

6/14. (ΜΕΘ 867) Amphoriskos Fig. 6.11e–f

Found near right forearm (smashed in many frr, mended). Vase 20.

H. 0.080; Diam. (rim) 0.060; Diam. (base) 0.040; Diam. (neck) 0.050; Th. rim 0.0045.

Shape: Mycenaean amphoriskos (small) rounded; banded. FS 59–61 (LH IIIB-C). Small wheelmade amphoriskos, spherical/globular shape, rising from flat disk base to sloping shoulder curving in to short everted rim, squared lip. Three ring handles set horizontally, rising nearly vertically to narrowest point.

Decoration: Lower body reserved, three bands below handles, two on shoulder; neck and lip articulated by single painted band, tops of handles painted.

Fabric: Very fine, gray core, light brown surface (7.5YR 7/4), fine gold mica.

Surface: Smoothed but not glossy, painted bands dark brown, streaky paint.

Cf. parallels for **6/13** (MEΘ 865).

6/15. (MEΘ 866) Handmade Jar   Fig. 6.11g–h

Found near right hand and side. Vase 19.

H. (with handles) 0.110; Diam. (max) 0.120; Diam. (rim) 0.085 (0.080 at handles: oval opening); Diam. (base) 0.050; handles: W. 0.015; H. 0.050; Th. 0.010.

Shape: Handmade jar, two-handled; nipple on both sides. Small, squat handmade jar, resembling kantharos; spherical body curving in from flat underside to short vertical neck, ending in squared lip. Two vertical strap handles, square in section, attached to shoulder and rising slightly above rim. Flat nipple (mastos/lug) applied on both sides at point of maximum diameter, midway between handles.

Fabric: Semicoarse, much gold mica; dark inclusions, blowouts; mottled gray-red-brown (5YR 6/4–6/6).

Surface: Once burnished (strokes near handles), now dull.

Published: Bessios 2010, p. 62 (top row, left).

Small finds: Metal

6/16. (MEΘ 879α) Bronze Pin (*Rollenkopfnadel*)   Fig. 6.12a–b

#245/023012, 3. Tomb 5 (right of cranium). ME 124α.

P.L. 0.182; Th. (shaft, max) 0.006; Th. (min) 0.002; Diam. (head) 0.010; Wt: 13.7 g.

Two joining frr preserving complete pin, except for very tip of point. Condition otherwise good.

Long shaft, circular in section, tapering toward point. Opposite end hammered flat and rolled to form the characteristic head.

Cf. an example from earlier burials of the Late Bronze Age, at Pigi Athenas (Platamon, Pieria): Poulaki-Pantermali 2013b, p. 47; Iolkos (Adrimi-Sismani 2014, pp. 754–757, BE 44453).

6/17. (MEΘ 879β) Bronze Pin (or Needle) with Eyelet   Fig. 6.12b

#245/023012, 3. Tomb 5 (right of cranium). ME 124β.

P.L. 0.101; Th. (head, max) 0.004; Wt: 2.6 g.

Three joining frr preserving greater part of pin, except for the tip. Condition quite good.

Relatively thin shaft, circular in section, tapering toward point, not preserved. Opposite end lightly hammered and formed into a long, pierced eyelet.

6/18α–β. (MEΘ 882α–β) Bronze Spiral Rings   Fig. 6.12c–d

#245/023012, 3. 2005. Tomb 5 (rings worn on the left hand). ME 125.

6/18α: Five joining frr, plus two small spirals.

H. (band) 0.008; Diam. 0.210 (misformed); Diam. (each small spiral) 0.009; Wt: 1.5 g.

6/18β: Three or four joining frr preserving greater part of ring and the less well-preserved spirals.

H. (band) 0.007–0.008; Diam. ca. 0.017; L. (spiral bezel) 0.012–0.013; Wt: 1.1 g.

Both rings are of the same type, made of a thin bronze band, hammered flat. The band is open-ended; one terminal tapers slightly and is nicely rounded. At the opposite terminal the band narrows and becomes one with the double spectacle spiral, which is set on a bezel. The form of the rings is clearest on **6/18β** (MEΘ 882β).

FIGURE 6.11. Plot 245, Tomb 5: a)–b) **6/12** (ΜΕΘ 864), rounded alabastron; c)–d) **6/13** (ΜΕΘ 865), rounded alabastron; e)–f) **6/14** (ΜΕΘ 867), rounded alabastron; g)–h) **6/15** (ΜΕΘ 866), handmade jar. Drawings A. Hooton and I. Moschou, photos I. Coyle

Small finds: Non-metal

6/19α–γ. (ΜΕΘ 891α,β,γ) Clay Spindlewhorl, Bead, or Buttons (3) Fig. 6.12e–f

Three conical and biconical clay beads or spindlewhorls. Found near right wrist and thigh (worn as bracelet?). ME 126.

6/19α: Conical bead, perforated vertically.

H. 0.023; Diam. (top) 0.013; Diam. (bottom) 0.030; Wt. 17.6 g.

Fine gray fabric, gold mica; surface dark gray to black, once burnished.

6/19β: Biconical (asymmetrical) spindlewhorl, bead, or button:

H. 0.031–0.032; Diam. (max) 0.025 (above midpoint); Diam. (top) 0.013; Diam. (bottom) 0.007; Diam. (perforation) 0.005; Wt. 16.5 g.

Worn: Upper and lower ends no longer parallel.

Fine dark yellow fabric (10YR 5/4), gold mica, white grit

6/19γ: Biconical spindlewhorl, bead, or button; lower body long and convex, upper body (neck) short and concave.

H. 0.0285; Diam. (max) 0.025; Diam. (top and bottom) 0.0075; Diam. (perforation) 0.005; Wt. 11.8 g.

Fabric: As **6/19β** (ΜΕΘ 891β).

6/20α–β. (ΜΕΘ 888α,β) Amber Beads (2) Fig. 6.13a–h

Frr; found to left of skull. ME 123.

One large bead (**6/20α**), flattened oval in section, pierced through length.

L. 0.025; W. (midpoint) 0.020; W. (ends) 0.018; H 0.011; Wt. 3.8 g.

One anchor-shaped bead (**6/20β**): L 0.016; W. 0.012; Th. 0.030–0.060.

Additional (10?) bead frr (powdered), total W. 2.6 g.

6/21. (ΜΕΘ 889) Necklace (Glass and Stone Beads) Fig. 6.13a

Found to left of skull. ME 123.

(21 spherical, six cogwheel); one carnelian bead.

Carnelian bead: H. 0.016; W. 0.0053; Wt. < 0.1 g.

Relatively flat disk, not polished or smooth (rough surface).

Six faience cogwheel (ribbed "melon") beads; four have six ribs, two have seven ribs.

Dimension averages: H. 0.045–0.060; W. 0.0057–0.0075; Wt. (all six) 1.3 g.

27? glass beads (total Wt. 3.7 g); 20 beads relatively whole (some joined from frr, others have some damaged areas); seven non-joining frr (one or several beads).

Very corroded to a white or yellow-white color, some with white weathered layer on the surface; a few beads (ca. seven) preserve light blue-green color, one is a dark blue or black color, others appear to be a light yellow-green color.

Cf. Uluburun wreck (ca. 1320 ± 15 B.C.): Ingram 2005, pp. 28–31, 101–102, 156–165, tables B3–B4, figs. 3.4, B11–16.

Additional seven(?) beads found in the water sieve.

One faience bead. Flat disk: appears white, some remnants of blue-surface glaze.

H. 0.0014; W. 0.0056; Wt. < 0.1 g.

Four glass beads: all appear white due to deterioration and corrosion; Total Wt. ca. 0.1 g.

6/22. (ΜΕΘ 890) Glass Beads (13); Carnelian Bead (1) Fig. 6.13i–j

From chest area.

Carnelian bead: H .0.031, W. 0.005, Wt. < 1.0 g.

One fr of copper alloy (tip of pin?).

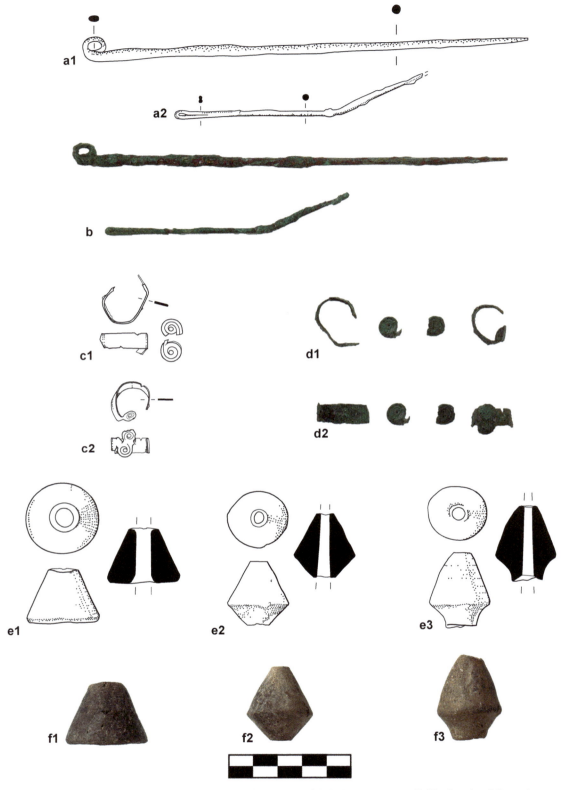

FIGURE 6.12. Plot 245, Tomb 5: a) **6/16** (ΜΕΘ 879α), bronze pin (*Rollenkopfnadel*) and **6/17** (ΜΕΘ 879β), bronze pin/needle; b) **6/16** and **6/17** (ΜΕΘ 879β), bronze needle/pin; c)–d) **6/18α** and **6/18β** (ΜΕΘ 882α–β), bronze spiral rings; e1, f1) **6/19α** (ΜΕΘ 891α), e2, f2) **6/19β** (ΜΕΘ 891β), e3, f3) **6/19γ** (ΜΕΘ 891γ), spindlewhorls, beads, or buttons. Drawings A. Hooton and F. Skyvalida, photos I. Coyle and J. Vanderpool

13? glass beads (total Wt 1.4 g); four intact beads, five beads in frr but join or part of the same bead, four non-joining frr. Most beads corroded (white) with little glass preserved, but two in better condition to see original glass color (one yellow-green, one dark blue or black with iridescence on the surface).

6/23. (ΜΕΘ 4164) Additional Glass Beads — Fig. 6.13i

From end of feet (now strung together).

One copper alloy bead: H. 0.0043–0.0048; W. 0.0085; Wt. 0.2 g.

Two glass beads: one spherical glass bead (H. 0.0043–0.0048; W. 0.0085, Wt. 0.2 g), appears white due to corrosion on the surface; one biconical glass bead (H. 0.0047; W. 0.0035–0.0052; Wt. < 0.1 g), appears white to yellow-white in areas due to corrosion, no visible glass preserved.

46 bone beads (flat disks); some beads cemented together by soil and burial deposits. Total Wt. 1.9 g. Dimensions vary: H. ca. 0.005–0.015; W. 0.0045–0.0055.

Five faience beads:

One white faience disk bead: H. 0.014; W. 0.044–0.048; Wt. < 0.1 g; disk appears white but under magnification has glassy material in surface; could be original color or lost blue glaze? Surface appears somewhat rough.

Four blue faience disk beads: total Wt. 0.1 g; vary in size and dimensions from H. ca. 0.01–0.0112. W. 0.005–0.0058. One bead lighter and whiter (surface glaze damaged and lost, or originally lighter?).

Two faience (or deteriorated glass) beads: dark in color, appear black; both are flat disk beads but vary in size. Smaller bead: H. 0.014; W. 0.0042; larger bead: H. 0.0021; W. 0.0048–0.0055; both weigh less than 0.1 g.

Two bags associated with strung beads, in same bag as ΜΕΘ 4164:

One bag contains scraps of copper alloy: two flat squarish pieces and three tiny flakes, Wt. 0.2 g; dark piece of stone: drop shaped (rounded end and tapers), with a white stripe, Wt. 0.2 g.

Another bag contains disk beads:

Five bone disk beads (non-joining frr); Wt. < 0.1 g.

One shell (?) bead (similar in color to bone beads but different surface appearance and texture, spiral striations: shell?).

Faience beads (small disk beads).

One faience bead appears white (similar to the one that is strung originally white, or light blue, suffered loss of glaze?).

H. 0.0014; Diam. 0.0043.

7 blue faience bead frr (disk beads), joining as 4–5 beads; total Wt. < 0.1 g; all roughly same H. (ca. 0.01) but not clear if all the same Diam.; some flat in section (both surfaces flat); others one flat side and one slightly rounded side.

Additional beads (2 small bone disks) found in cleaning skeletal remains.

Other

ΜΕΘ 4162 (ME 122)   Stone tool (?): red quartz flake (from fill in center of tomb).
   #245/013010 [3] 13-9-2005.

Tomb 245/6.   #245/016 [2]. Notebook p. 24. 15-9-2005.

Type: Shallow pit-shaped burial; cutting not clear; disturbed by Pit 22? (possible tomb cut?) For location, see Fig. 6.2.

Orientation: Northeast–southwest.

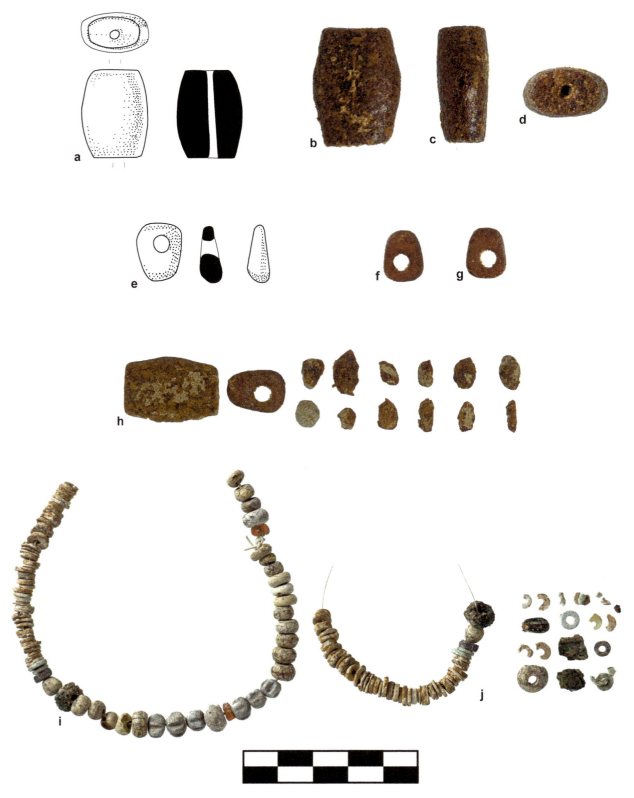

FIGURE 6.13. Plot 245, Tomb 5: a)–d) **6/20α** (ΜΕΘ 888α), amber bead; e)–g) **6/20β** (ΜΕΘ 888β), amber bead; h) **6/20α** and **6/20β** (ΜΕΘ 888α–β), amber beads, together with additional fragments of amber; i) **6/21** (ΜΕΘ 889 + ΜΕΘ 4164), necklace of glass and stone beads; j) showing additional beads and fragments. Drawings A. Hooton, photos J. Vanderpool

Skeleton:	Infant burial, head to southwest; very few post-cranial.
Identification (2013):	Infant (3–4 years).
Study (2015):	Infant (1 year–18 months).
Animal bones:	Yes.
Absolute chronology:	AMS ^{14}C: 1496–1471 calBC (11.7%), 1465–1396 calBC (83.7%).

GRAVE GOODS

Ceramics

6/24. (ΜΕΘ 898) Handmade Vessel Fig. 6.14
 #245/016 [2]. 15-9-2005. Vase 21.

 Mended from many frr, about one-third of vessel restored but missing rim, most of base.

 P.H. 0.050; Diam. (max) 0.060; Th. (rim and wall) 0.005.

 Small handleless open cup or jar, spherical lower body curves in to narrow neck, everted lip with rounded lip (rim broken).

 Fabric: Semicoarse, light brown core (5YR 7/6), fine gold mica, grayish surface (covered with incrustations).

FIGURE 6.14. Plot 245, Tomb 6: **6/24** (ΜΕΘ 898), small handmade cup or jar. Drawing A. Hooton, photo I. Coyle

Tomb 245/7.	#245/016003 [3]. Notebook p. 27; 30-9-2005.	Fig. 6.15a–b.
Type:	Pit grave (partially stone-lined), infant burial; wooden coffin?	
Location:	Boundary of Squares 001 and 016, 1.70 from North side of Square 16.	
Dimensions:	L. x W. 1.0 x 0.70; depth 27.14 m.	
Orientation:	East–west.	
Fill:	Loose reddish brown soil, limestone inclusions; scattered frr of human bones; two handmade sherds.	
	Human bones from the fill: right femur matches with the primary skeleton.	
	Three large stones; to stabilize coffin?	
Skeleton:	Small child, supine, head to northwest; teeth collected.	
	Cranium, tibia preserved. P.L. of burial 0.500.	
Study (2015):	Neonate (9 months); rib frr, teeth.	
Sampled for isotopes:	One unidentified bone fr.	
Absolute chronology:	AMS ^{14}C: 1261–1126 calBC (95.4%).	

Grave Goods

Small finds

6/25α–β. (ΜΕΘ 883α–β) Bronze Spiral Rings   Fig. 6.15c–f

    #245/016003, 3. 2005. Tomb 7. ME 114. Found with finger bones. Perhaps from two rings, rather than one, of which **6/25α** (ΜΕΘ 883α) is the better preserved.

    6/25α) H. 0.010; Diam. 0.021; Wt. 2.3 g.

    6/25β) Diam. (innermost ring) 0.013; Diam. (outermost ring): 0.020; Wt. 1.4 g.

    6/25α (ΜΕΘ 883α) is a ring of thin bronze band, plano-convex in section, formed into a spiral of at least three turns. **6/25β** (ΜΕΘ 883β) is composed of six frr, though it is not clear that they all join (the broader frr may belong with **6/25α**). **6/25β** preserves at least two turns.

    There are small associated frr and splinters of human fingers.

6/26. (ΜΕΘ 895) Fragmentary Bone Pin   Fig. 6.15g–h

    #245/016003. 30/9/2005. Tomb 7 (right side). ME 139.

    P.L. (largest joining frr) 0.057; p.L. (smaller fr) 0.022; Diam. (max) 0.004; Wt. (total): 1.2 g.

    Three frr in all, two joining, the other non-joining, plus a bone chip that may belong.

    Pin shaft circular in section, tapering toward point, itself not preserved. Original surfaces, wherever preserved, nicely polished smooth.

    Type of bone difficult to determine.

Tomb 245/8.	#245/016004 [4]. Notebook p. 28; 30-9-2005.	Fig. 6.16a–b.
Type:	Pit grave, inhumation.	
Location:	Immediately north of Tomb 7 (bones found 0.150 m higher than level of Tomb 7 skeleton). Cut by Pit 19 to north.	
Dimensions:	Max. depth 27.27.	
Orientation:	Northeast–southwest.	
Skeleton:	Human bone fragments found in fill of Tomb 7. Supine, head to northeast. P.L. 0.350 m. Infant (3 years); very few post-cranial (upper limbs mostly); good representation of teeth.	
Additional bones:	1) Right temporal mastoid process is missing (post-mortem broken) (adult), 2) Mandible with teeth, right clavicle (acromial end) and left clavicle (complete max length): infant (2 years).	
Isotopes:	1) unsided rib fr; 2) left unidentified bone fr.	
Animal bones:	Yes.	
Absolute chronology:	AMS ^{14}C: 1368–1364 (0.5%), 1286–1157 calBC (88.2%), 1146–1128 calBC (6.7%).	

Grave Goods

6/27. (ΜΕΘ 868) Small Handmade *Thelastron*   Fig. 6.16c–d

    Small handmade vessel with feeding spout.

    Found near legs (ὑφος σκελῶν) of child's skeleton during excavation of Tomb 7. Vase 22.

    H. 0.065; Diam. (max) 0.070 (with spout at its base); Diam. (rim) 0.040; Th. (rim) 0.004; Wt. 165 g.

    Small handmade baby feeder (θήλαστρον), missing spout (broken off at wall). Biconical profile on flat base, with spout attached to pierced wall just above midpoint of vessel. Slightly raised underside; upper wall slopes to narrow neck, everted rim. Entire profile without spout, rim heavily worn, vessel cracked on side (damaged in excavation?); underside pitted and flaked.

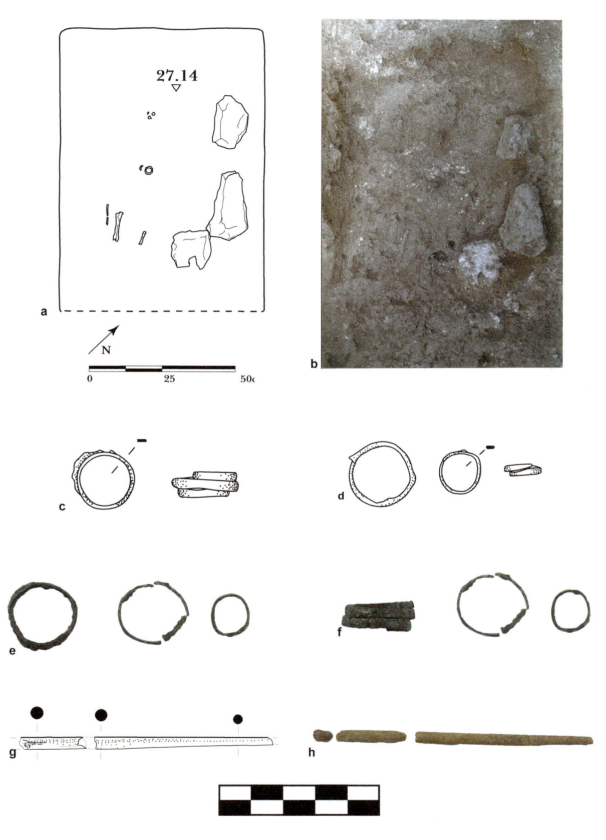

FIGURE 6.15. Methone Plot 245, Tomb 7: a) drawing I. Moschou and T. Ross; b) view from east, photo KZ´ Ephoreia; c)–f) **6/25α**–β (ΜΕΘ 883α–β), bronze spiral rings; g)–h) **6/26** (ΜΕΘ 895), bone pin. Drawings A. Hooton and F. Skyvalida, photos I. Coyle

Fabric: Semicoarse fabric, dark red (5YR 6/6), fine gold mica, dark inclusions; surface rough.

Cf. ΜΕΘ 5616 (tubular spout of feeder, found in east balk of Plot 274/Square 85, 05/09/2005: Chapter 5, **5/22**). Cf. Pella, Early Bronze Age cemetery, I. Akamatis 2011, p. 37; Perati: Iakovidis 1969, vol. 2, pp. 241–242, fig. 101, no. 101; Pomadère 2006. Cf. further wheelmade decorated Mycenaean types (FS 161–162): Mountjoy 1986, pp. 105–106, fig. 126; p. 144, fig. 179; p. 188, fig. 246; p. 199, fig. 266.

Stylistically Late Bronze Age or even Early Iron Age, but the AMS ^{14}C analysis shows it to be Late Bronze Age.

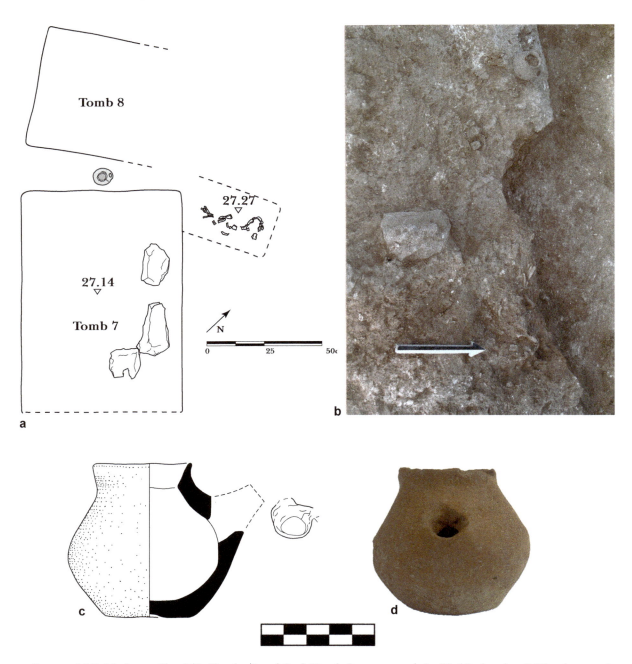

FIGURE 6.16. Methone Plot 245, Tombs 7 and 8: a) Tomb 8 cut at north by Pit 19, drawing I. Moschou and T. Ross; b) Tomb 8, view from east, photo ΚΖ´ Ephoreia; c)–d) **6/27** (ΜΕΘ 868), small handmade vessel with feeding spout (*thelastron*). Drawing A. Hooton and I. Moschou, photo I. Coyle

Tomb 245/9.	#245/015+016010 [9]. Notebook p. 30; 3/10/2005.	Fig. 6.17a–b.
	Bessios, Athanassiadou, and Noulas 2008, p. 246, Figs. 11 (grave), 12 (vases); Bessios 2010, p. 61, left (photograph of grave).	
Type:	Pit grave with wooden lid; inhumation.	
Location:	Directly east of Pit 19; half of west side and northwest corner cut by Pit 19.	
Orientation:	Northwest–southeast.	
Dimensions:	P.L. 1.650 x p.W. 0.400; depth 27.31 (upper)–26.79 (lower); ledge cut into west [and north?] side, 0.200 (tapers to 0.050–0.025 at east end), 27.04 m deep.	
Fill:	#245/016009 [9]: reddish brown earth, loose soil; few sherds.	
Skeleton:	Adult, head to northwest; legs slightly contracted, fallen to right. Well preserved: right side of torso; ribs missing. Left arm folded across abdomen, right drawn up higher, almost to chin. P.L. 1.50 m.	
Study (2015):	Adult (25–35 yrs., according to Brothwell tooth wear); male (based on bone morphology and robusticity).	
Dental pathologies:	Slight calculus, moderate caries.	
Skeletal pathologies:	Osteoarthritis: 1) Left and right carpals: slight lipping, 2) Left second, third, and fifth metacarpal: slight lipping, 3) Right third and fourth metacarpals: slight lipping. Musculo-skeletal markers: 1) hand phalanges: marked interosseous ligaments, 3) Left femur: marked gluteus maximus and vastus intermedius.	
Sampled for isotopes:	1) One proximal hand phalanx, 2) Right zygomatic process, 3) Left unidentified bone fr.	
Absolute chronology:	AMS ^{14}C: 1388–1339 calBC (16.7%), 1316–1194 calBC (77.9%), 1141–1134 calBC (0.9%).	

Grave Goods
Ceramics

6/28. (ΜΕΘ 869) Wheelmade Amphoriskos   Fig. 6.17c–d.

Placed right of and inside angle of feet and lower legs; vessel found lying on side, base facing feet of skeleton. Vase 23.

H. 0.140; Diam. (max) 0.150; Diam. (base) 0.065; Diam. (rim) 0.095; Diam. (neck) 0.075; Th. (rim at lip) 0.006; handles: H. 0.040; W. 0.065; Diam. 0.010.

Shape: Wheelmade spherical amphoriskos, three handles; FS 61–62. LH IIIC? Globular body rising from flat disk base (slightly raised underside) to maximum diameter at approximate midpoint of vertical height. Upper wall curves in to neck, out to tall everted rim with flat, sloping lip. Three horizontal ring handles attached above midpoint, nearly vertical profile.

Decoration: Painted band outside foot, three bands at/below midpoint, three bands on upper shoulder; rim glazed solid inside and out. Top and ends of handles glazed. Drop of paint splashed on lower body above foot.

Fabric: Light red-brown, brown core (7.5YR 6/6), pale surface (7.5YR 7/4).

Cf. parallels for **6/13** (ΜΕΘ 865).

6/29. (ΜΕΘ 870) Wheelmade Alabastron   Fig. 6.17e–g

Found on left side of body, next to contracted legs (near left femur), in upright position. Vase 24.

H. 0.120; Diam. (max) 0.130; Diam. (base) 0.050; Diam. (neck) 0.070; Diam. (rim) 0.080; Th. (rim) 0.005; handles: H. 0.040; Diam. 0.013; W. (at base) 0.060–0.070.

Shape: Large alabastron in local fabric: FS 86 (LH IIIC). Heavy globular shape with narrow base and thick lower body, slightly biconical in profile, sloping in to narrowest point at neck and up to short offset rim, rounded lip. Three large ring handles attached on shoulder, rising nearly vertically.

Decoration: Narrow band (0.013) above base, single broad band (0.020 wide) below midpoint and handles, broad red band between handles and neck; top of lip and inside rim glazed solid. Three broad arcs (single splashes) between handles.

Fabric: Semicoarse, white grit, dark inclusions, fine gold mica. Core 2.5YR 6/6, light red, with paler surface (5YR 6/6).

Surface smoothed, much grit visible, some spalling.

6/30. (ΜΕΘ 871) Wheelmade Alabastron   Fig. 6.18a–b

Found on left side of body, next to contracted legs (near left femur), in upright position. Vase 25.

H. 0.105; Diam. (max) 0.115; Diam. (rim) 0.080; Th. (rim) 0.006; handles: H. 0.030; W. 0.060; Diam. 0.006.

Shape: Rounded alabastron, three handles: FS 86 (LH IIIC). Small globular wheelmade alabastron; rounded underside with small resting surface. Globular body with maximum diameter below vertical midpoint, sloping shoulder rising to narrow neck, everted rim and rounded lip. Three ring handles attached horizontally above midpoint. Entire profile preserved, two large frr missing from opposite sides of rim; inside rim flaked, outside (top) of lip very worn.

Decoration: Two uneven bands at midpoint (maximum diameter) below handles, two bands above handles and below neck, outside rim and inside solidly glazed. Handles painted solid across top and attachments.

Fabric: Fine light-red clay (2.5YR 5/6), with fine white grit, some mica; surface pale (5YR 7/6), smoothed but now dull, some blowouts.

Cf. parallels for **6/12** (ΜΕΘ 864).

Small finds

6/31. (ΜΕΘ 896) Bone Pin   Fig. 6.18c–d

#245/016010. 3/10/2005. Tomb 9 (found inside **6/28**). ME 151.

P.L. (main joining frr) 0.109; p.L. (smaller joining fr) 0.015; L. (at least) 0.124; Diam. (max, at preserved end): 0.005; Wt. 1.7 g.

Three joining frr preserving greater part of pin, plus small non-joining fr preserving tip of pin. The pin may well be virtually complete, especially if the head, as preserved, is the original head, which is likely, rather than a broken edge.

Comparatively long pin shaft, circular section, tapering toward sharp tip. Original surfaces, wherever better preserved, nicely polished smooth.

Type of bone difficult to determine.

Tomb 245/10	#245/015004 [4]. Notebook p. 29; 3-10-2005.	Fig. 6.19a–b.
Type:	Pit grave (partially stone-lined), wooden sarcophagus; infant burial (inhumation).	
Location:	1 m from south side, 0.20 from east side of Square 15; cut by Pit 18.	
Orientation:	East–west.	
Dimensions:	L. 1.25 x W. 0.55; depth 27.33 (top), 27.03 m (bottom).	
Fill:	#245/013002 [2]: Reddish brown soil, loose with limestone inclusions; upper part of fill mixed with dark brown soil from Pit 18. Similar composition in fill E of Tomb 245/10: many ceramics, primarily handmade; bones, shell. Three small fieldstones along south side, irregular in size, placement; used to stabilize coffin?	
Skeleton:	Supine, head to west. Bones poorly preserved: only a few cranial and post-cranial bones.	
Study (2015):	Neonate, 9 months—1 year.	
Samples for isotopes:	1) one rib fr, 2) one (two?) unsided long bone frr.	
Absolute chronology:	AMS ^{14}C: 1374–1357 calBC (3.5%), 1300–1191 calBC (87.3%), 1178–1163 calBC (1.9%), 1144–1131 calBC (2.7%).	

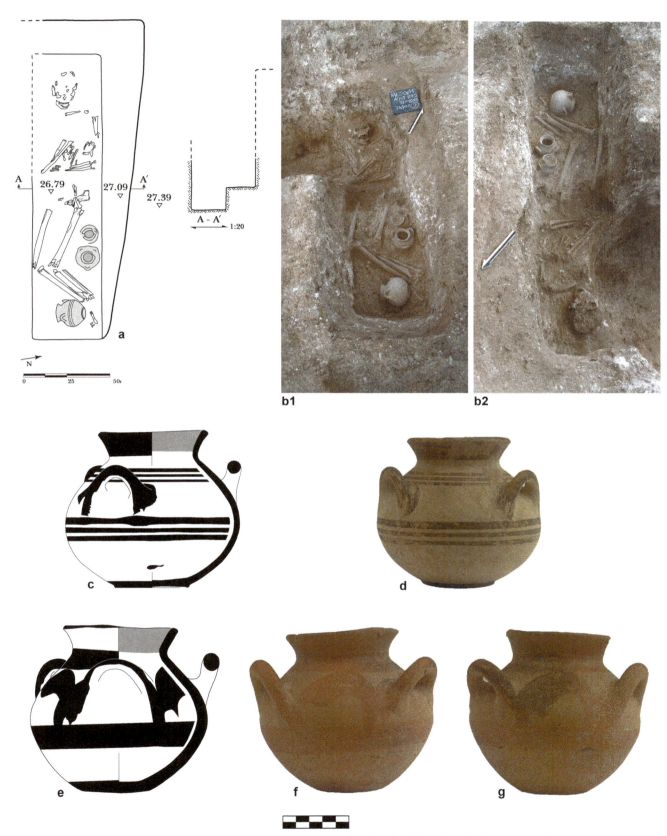

FIGURE 6.17. Methone Plot 245, Tomb 9, cut at northwest by Pit 19; a) drawing I. Moschou and T. Ross; b) two views, from east and from west, photos KZ´ Ephoreia; c)–d) **6/28** (ΜΕΘ 869), amphoriskos; e)–g) **6/29** (ΜΕΘ 870), alabastron. Drawings A. Hooton and I. Moschou, photo I. Coyle

FIGURE 6.18. Methone Plot 245, Tomb 9: a)–b) **6/30** (ΜΕΘ 871), rounded alabastron; **6/31** (ΜΕΘ 896), bone pin. Drawings A. Hooton, photos I. Coyle

GRAVE GOODS
None.

Tomb 245/11.	#245/013015 + 016 [5]. Notebook p. 31; 4-10-2005.	Fig. 6.20a–b.
Type:	Pit grave, wooden lid (?); inhumation.	
Location:	Directly northeast of Pit 61 and Tomb 245/5.	
Dimensions:	L. 1.40 x W. 0.50 m; raised ledge cut around perimeter of tomb, W. 0.25; 27.35 m deep, for support of wooden lid (?). Depth: 28.30 (upper), 27.30 m (lower).	
Orientation:	East–west.	
Fill:	#245/013015: loose, reddish brown soil, much lime; no stones. Sherds: a few, unglazed.	
Skeleton:	Supine, head to east; only cranial, left and right clavicle, part of tibia and femur. P.L. 0.65.	
Study (2015):	Infant (3–3.5 years), sex unknown.	
Sampled for isotopes:	1) Right clavicle, 2) deciduous maxillary second incisor.	
Animal bones:	Yes.	
Absolute chronology:	AMS ^{14}C: 1385–1341 calBC (12.9%), 1309–1192 calBC (79.6%), 1175–1165 calBC (1.0%), 1143–1132 calBC (1.8%).	

GRAVE GOODS
Small finds: Metal

6/32.   (ΜΕΘ 4163) Bronze Ring Frr (Earring?)   Fig. 6.20c

   #245/013015, 5. Tomb 11. Επίχωση νότια πλευρά, λίγο ψηλότερα άπο το σκελετό (found "in fill on south side, slightly above skeleton"). ME 144.

   Diam. 0.016; H./Th. 0.002; Wt. 0.4 g.

   Two frr, preserving greater part of ring.

   Ring formed of bronze wire, circular in section.

FIGURE 6.19. Methone Plot 245, Tomb 10, disturbed at northeast end by Pit 18:
a) drawing I. Moschou and T. Ross; b) view from east, photo KZ´ Ephoreia

Tomb 245/12.	#245/016019 [15]. Notebook p. 35; 7–10, 10-10-2005.	Fig. 6.21a–b.

Human bones found 26.16 m deep, also large stone, in Pit 23 (cut into tomb). No drawing (except for Pit 23).

Location: Northeast corner of Square 16 (extends into Square 23, unexcavated).
Dimensions (cutting): P.L. 0.95 (north–south axis).
Fill: Reddish brown soil, loose with many limestone chips.
Skeleton: Cranium, clavicle bones collected; rest of skeleton in unexcavated Square 23. Skull placed 0.60 m from north side of square, 25.29 m deep.

Rest of Tomb 12 (excavation completed in 2006)   #245/022004 [4]. 22-11-2006.

Dimensions: Northeast corner preserved, parts of north (1.65), east (0.40) and south (1.55) sides; depth 26.45 m. Drawing with Pit 23.
Depth: 26.48 (upper), 25.75 m (lower).
Fill: Loose gray-brown earth, lime; a few handmade sherds (Pit 29?).
Skeleton: Poorly preserved, most of upper body missing (west part of tomb disturbed by Pit 29); cranium (collected in 2005).
Contracted burial, turned on left side, legs bent at knees. Arms folded across abdomen. Bones fairly brittle.

Study (2015):	Adult (25–35 years, based on molar wear); female.
Dental pathology:	Slight calculus, large caries, enamel hypoplasia.
Skeletal pathology:	Musculo-skeletal markers: 1) Hand phalanges: marked interosseous ligaments, 2) Left humerus: small bony projection at brachialis muscle, 3) Right tibia: strongly marked popliteus muscle. Periostitis: 1) Right tibia: mid 1/3, medial aspect: active striated bone formation (non-specific infection).
Samples for isotopes:	Three cranial frr.
Absolute chronology:	AMS ^{14}C: 1375–1356 calBC (3.6%), 1301–1156 calBC (85.6%), 1147–1128 (6.2%) calBC.

FIGURE 6.20. Methone Plot 245, Tomb 11: a) drawing I. Moschou and T. Ross; b) view from west, photo KZ´ Ephoreia; c) **6/32** (ΜΕΘ 4163), bronze ring (earring?), photo I. Coyle

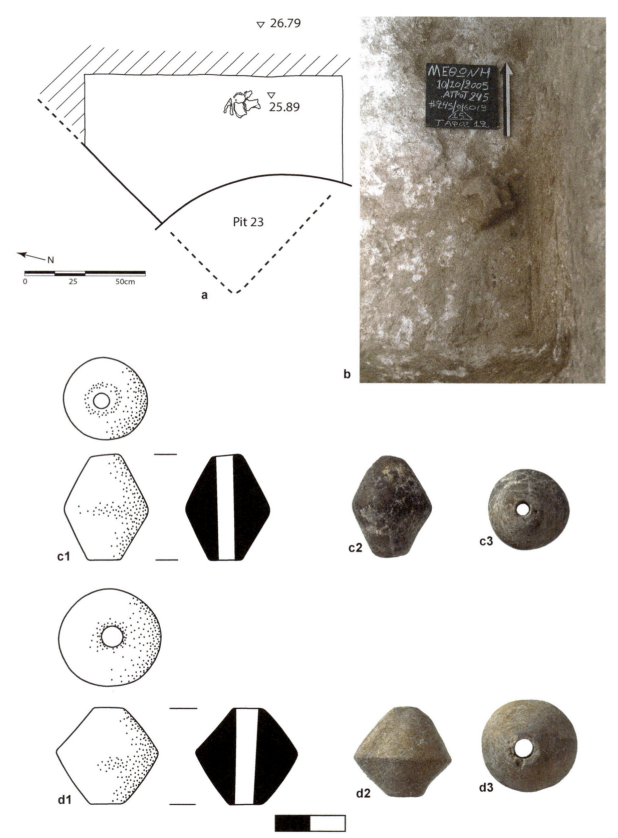

FIGURE 6.21. Methone Plot 245, Tomb 12, cut by Pits 23 and 29 at west: a) drawing I. Moschou and T. Ross; b) view from south, photo KZ´ Ephoreia; c) **6/33** (ΜΕΘ 4160); d) **6/34** (ΜΕΘ 4161), two spindlewhorls, beads, or buttons. Drawings F. Skyvalida, photos J. Vanderpool

Grave Goods
Small finds

6/33. (ΜΕΘ 4160) Spindlewhorl, Bead, or Button   Fig 6.21c
#245/022004 [4]. 22-11-2006. ME 324. Found near skeleton, at level of right shoulder.
H. 0.031; Diam. (max, midpoint) 0.023; Diam. (top/bottom) 0.009–0.010; Diam. (perforation) 0.0035–0.0045; Wt. 13 g.
Tall narrow biconical spindlewhorl, bead, or button; chipped around one perforation hole.
Fabric: Dark gray (10YR 4/2), fine mica, surface "sandy."

6/34. (ΜΕΘ 4161) Spindlewhorl, Bead, or Button   Fig. 6.21d
#245/022004 [4]. 22-11-2006. Found near finger bones. ME 325.
H. 0.027; Diam. (max) 0.029; Diam. (top/bottom) 0.010; Diam. perforation 0.005.
Biconical spindlewhorl, bead, or button.
Fabric: Fine, pale yellow-brown (10YR 7/4), surface smooth, mottled gray-yellow; once burnished?

Other

#245/022004 [4]. 22-11-2006
From the water sieve: two sherds (one banded: alabastron? one wheelmade, gray).

Tomb 245/13.	#245/013020-021. Notebook pp. 37–38; 10-10-2005. Fig. 6.22a–b.
Type:	Pit grave, inhumation (child).
Location:	Directly southeast of Pit 26 (northwest end of tomb not found, due to disturbance by Pit 26, directly to west).
Fill (directly east of Pit 26):	#245/013020: Fairly hard/compacted soil, many limestone inclusions; reddish brown soil. Sherds: A few Early Iron Age (handmade, wheelmade vessels); upper levels held stone lid for pithos (ME 166).
Dimensions:	L. 1.30 x W 0.60, 27.62 m deep (fill = 0.35 m deep).
Orientation:	Northwest–southeast.
Skeleton:	#245/013021: Neonate, supine, head to southeast; poorly preserved (cranial fragments, some extremities). P.L. 0.65.
Study (2015):	Neonate (9 months–1 year); very few post-cranial bones.
Sample for isotopes:	Left tibia fr (mid 1/3).
Absolute chronology:	AMS ^{14}C: 1273–1127 calBC (95.4%).

Grave Goods
Ceramics, wheelmade

6/35. (ΜΕΘ 872) Wheelmade One-handled Cup   Fig. 6.22c–e
#245/013021 [9]. 12-10-2005. Vase 27; found at tibia.
H. 0.080; Diam. (base) 0.040; Diam. (rim) 0.100; Th. (rim 0.005); handle: H. 0.060; W. 0.015; Th. 0.008.
Shape: One-handled cup, local Mycenaean fabric. Convex "teacup" shape (FS 215, etc.) on flat ring base with slightly raised underside (LH IIIC type?); single strap handle, rectangular in section, attached vertically on lower body, rises just above rim.
Decoration: Lip-band type (broad band/zone of paint covers exterior nearly down to midpoint); monochrome interior. Top/outside of handles painted with three horizontal slashes/bars.
Fabric: Fine light red clay (5YR 7/6), gold mica; dull red paint, streaky.
Surface: Much pitted inside (upper wall).

Mountjoy 1986, p. 146, fig. 183; Thessaly, Elasson (K2792): Mountjoy 1999, pp. 848–849, fig. 343; Iolkos: Adrimi-Sismani 2014, p. 526, BE 25693; Phokis: Mountjoy 1999, pp. 776–777, fig. 304, #187–188 (Delphi); pp. 814–815, fig. 324, #26 (Kalapodi); Perati: Iakovidis 1969, vol. 3, pl. 130, no. 896: *Lefkandi* IV, pp. 181–182, fig. 2.15.

Date: LH IIIC, or later.

FIGURE 6.22. Methone Plot 245, Tomb 13, damaged at northwest end by Pit 26: a) drawing I. Moschou and T. Ross; b) view from north, photo KZ´ Ephoreia; c)–e) **6/35** (ΜΕΘ 872), one-handled cup, drawing A. Hooton and I. Moschou, photos I. Coyle

Tomb 245/14.	#245/013023 [10]. Notebook p. 39; 13-10-2005.	Fig. 6.23a–b.
Type:	Pit grave; inhumation.	
Location:	Directly northeast of Pit 26 (cut by pit), contiguous with wall of pit; part of tomb cutting uncovered (full dimensions unclear). 0.70 from north, 2.40 from east side of Square 13.	
Orientation:	Southwest–northeast.	
Dimensions:	P.L. 0.60; p.W. 0.60.	
Fill:	Loose reddish brown soil, mixed in places with dark gray patches. Sherds: few handmade, one painted.	
Skeleton:	Only lower limbs preserved (tibia, left and right foot bones); possibly contracted on right side?	
Study (2015):	Adult, male? (due to bone morphology and robusticity); lower limbs only.	
Skeletal pathology:	Osteoarthritis: 1) Left and right metatarsals, base: slight marginal lipping, 2) Left and right talus: slight marginal lipping, 3) Left and right calcaneus: slight marginal lipping. Musculo-skeletal markers: 1) Left calcaneus: marked Achilles tendon.	
Sampled for isotopes:	1) foot phalanx, 2) femoral fr (prox 1/3).	
Absolute chronology:	AMS ^{14}C: 1411–1284 calBC (95.4%)	

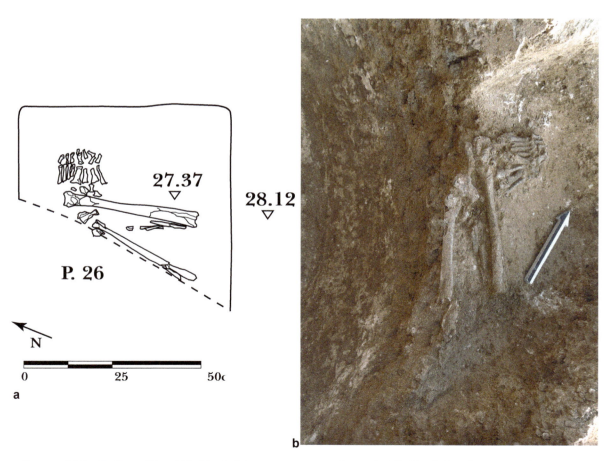

FIGURE 6.23. Methone Plot 245, Tomb 14, cut away at northwest by Pit 26; a) drawing I. Moschou and T. Ross; b) view from south, photo KZ´ Ephoreia

GRAVE GOODS
None.

Tomb 245/15.	#245/016025 [20]. Notebook p. 43; 17-10-2005.	Fig. 6.24a–b.
Orientation:	Northeast–southwest.	
Fill (cutting):	#245/016024: gray soil, full of ceramics, primarily handmade Early Iron Age.	
Fill (tomb):	#245/016025: lower strata of fill = yellow-brown soil, loose, many lime chips.	
Skeleton:	Supine? Head to southwest; few bone fragments preserved (cranium).	
Study (2015):	Early infant (1 year–18 months); cranium only and teeth.	
Skeletal pathology:	1) Vault fr with moderate small and large scattered foramina (active porotic hyperostosis).	
Absolute chronology:	AMS ^{14}C: 1226–1052 calBC (95.4%).	

GRAVE GOODS
Ceramics, wheelmade

6/36. (ΜΕΘ 873) Wheelmade Amphoriskos   Fig. 6.24c–d
#245/016025 [2]. 17-10-2005. Vase 28 (found at feet).
H. 0.080; Diam. (rim) 0.060; Diam. (max) 0.090; Diam. (base) 0.052; Diam. (neck) 0.040; Th. (rim) 0.005; handles: H. 0.025; W. (at root) 0.050; Diam. 0.008.
Shape: Mycenaean amphoriskos. FS 59 (LH IIIC Early?). Small spherical amphoriskos, with three handles. Biconical body rising from flat disk base (slightly domed underside) in continuous curve, past maximum diameter at vertical midpoint, below handles, then curving in to narrow neck and curving out to everted rim, squared lip. Three ring handles attached horizontally to shoulder, forming triangles in frontal view, and set at angle to sloping wall of vessel.
Decoration: Three horizontal bands at and below midpoint, three bands between handles and neck (two outer ones thick and uneven, central one narrow). Band painted around base.
Outside rim and inside painted solid.
Fabric: Pale red clay (5YR 6/6), paler surface. Very fine clay, gold mica, some dark inclusions, surface pitted with blowouts. Surface paint 5YR 5/6, light to dark brown.
Lefkandi IV, p. 204, fig. 2.31, nos. 1, 5.

Tomb 245/16.	#245/013028 [15]. Notebook p. 46; 20-10-2005.	Fig. 6.25a–c.
Type:	Pit grave, probably with wooden coffin (stones as wedges on narrow west side of cutting: not visible in drawing?).	
Location:	Northeast section of Square 013, 1.50 from east., 0.80 m from north. Tomb cut in half by Pit 39.	
Dimensions:	P.L. 0.75; p.W. 0.65; depth 0.45 (upper level 27.48, lower 27.03 m).	
Orientation:	Southwest–northeast.	
Fill:	Reddish brown, loose soil with limestone inclusions; a few sherds, various periods.	
Skeleton:	Upper half only, preserved above pelvis. Adult (upper body supine, lower/legs missing); arms folded over abdomen.	
Identification (2013):	1) Adult (17–20 years), male; caries, some metabolic disorder (perhaps in teeth).	
Study (2015):	Juvenile (16–17 years), male? (skull and pelvis morphology).	
Bronze discoloration:	1) Right third and fourth metacarpals, right and left ulna, left rib.	
Dental pathologies:	1) Large caries, 2) Slight calculus, 3) Enamel hypoplasia.	

FIGURE 6.24. Methone Plot 245, Tomb 15: a) drawing I. Moschou and T. Ross; b) view from north, photo KZ´ Ephoreia; c)–d) **6/36** (MEΘ 873), amphoriskos, drawing A. Hooton and I. Moschou, photo I. Coyle

Skeletal pathologies:	Porotic hyperostosis (healed): parietal and occipital, cribra orbitalia (active): right orbit, Musculo-skeletal markers: left and right humeri: marked deltoid, enthesophyte at pectoralis major muscle.
Additional bones:	1) Post-cranial: two fragmentary tibiae, left rib fragment (perinate; sex unknown).
Samples for isotopes:	1) left tibia (almost complete), 2) right tibia (fr from middle third) from perinate.
Absolute chronology:	AMS ^{14}C: 1284–1111 calBC (95.4%) (cf. Tombs 4, 5, 7, 8).

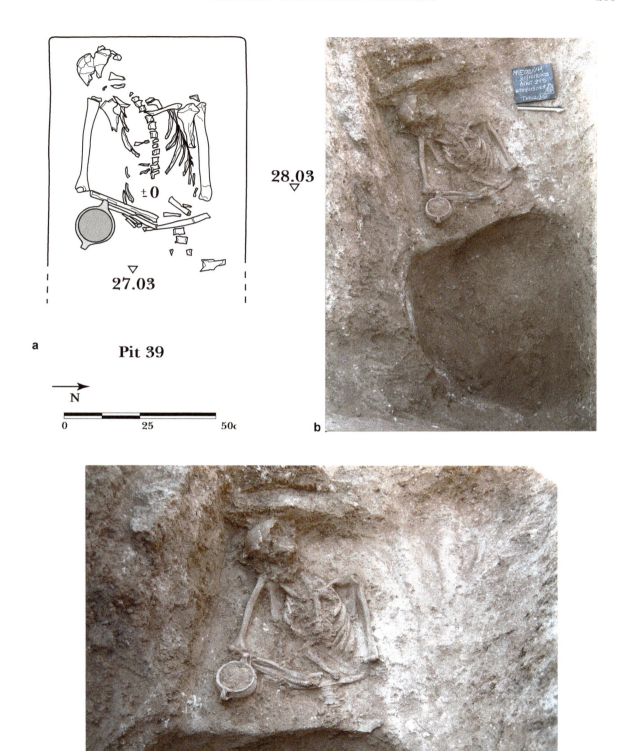

FIGURE 6.25. Methone Plot 245, Tomb 16, cut in half at northeast by Pit 39; a) drawing I. Moschou and T. Ross; b) view from east; c) detail of west end. Photos KZ′ Ephoreia

Grave Goods

Ceramics, handmade

6/37. (ΜΕΘ 874) Handmade Kantharos   Fig. 6.26a–b

#245/013028 [15]. Vase 29. Found at right forearm.

H. 0.070; Diam. (rim, inside handles) 0.100; 0.110; Diam. (rim, outside handles) 0.110; Diam. (max, at base of handles) 0.120.

Shape: Handmade kantharos. Low open kantharoid vessel, rounded underside (no flat resting surface), wide shallow bowl with short rim, slightly everted, ending in narrow lip. Two vertical strap handles, squarish in section with vertical central channel outside and shallow rounded notch on each side, attached to midpoint of body and flaring out to rise at angle above rim, with slight spur inside top of handle.

Fabric: Fine clay, with gold mica, quartz; mottled light red-gray with darker streaks.

Surface: Smoothed, dull, uneven with many "dimples."

Cf. Palaia Chrani (Πυ 10751, Πυ 10754).

Small finds

The following beads from Tomb 16 were found on the right arm of the deceased and were therefore worn as a bracelet on the right wrist. The beads were composed of: a) dark blue glass bead; a) opaque white glass bead; g) small bronze coil bead.

6/38α. (ΜΕΘ 885α) Blue Glass Bead   Fig. 6.26c–d

#245/013028, 15. 2005 Tomb 16 (δεξιός πήχης). ΜΕ 190α.

H. 0.011; Diam. 0.009; Diam. (hole) 0.002; Wt. 0.5 g.

Intact.

Elliptical-shaped bead (perhaps originally a white bead that had discolored?).

6/38β. (ΜΕΘ 885β) Opaque White Glass Bead   Fig. 6.26c, e

#245/013028, 15. 2005 Tomb 16 (δεξιός πήχης). ΜΕ 190β.

H. 0.006; Diam. 0.009–0.010; Wt. 0.2 g.

Three joining frr preserving greater part of bead.

Small, roughly spherical bead, flattened at both ends. Diam. (hole): 0.003–0.004.

One piece of the small spiral coil, ΜΕΘ 885γ, was found fused into the glass bead; hence, both beads were part of a bracelet formed of the continuous bronze spiral.

6/38γ. (ΜΕΘ 885γ) Small Continuous Bronze Spiral   Fig. 6.26c, f

#245/013028, 15. 2005 Tomb 16 (δεξιός πήχης). ΜΕ 190γ.

Diam. 0.003–0.005; Wt. 2.6 g. Too poorly preserved to determine accurate L.

29 frr, all probably joining, plus the piece within the glass bead **6/38β** (ΜΕΘ 885β).

Continuous bronze coiled spiral.

Cf. **6/6δ** (ΜΕΘ 884δ).

6/39. (ΜΕΘ 887) Fr Bronze Knife   Fig. 6.26g–h

#245/013028, 15. 20/10/2005. Tomb 16. Found near right forearm. ΜΕ 191.

P.L. 0.049; W. (max) 0.015; Wt. 5.6 g.

Single fr preserving portion of blade and hilt.

As preserved, straight-sided blade, with widest point at juncture with hilt. Hilt preserves two holes for rivets (Diam. 0.002), which do not survive.

Cf. **6/8** (ΜΕΘ 877), and **6/47** (ΜΕΘ 4149).

FIGURE 6.26. Plot 245, Tomb 16: a)–b) **6/37** (ΜΕΘ 874), handmade kantharos with spur handles; c) **6/38α** (ΜΕΘ 885α), blue glass bead; **6/38β** (ΜΕΘ 885β), opaque white bead; **6/38γ** (ΜΕΘ 885γ), small bronze spiral; d) (ΜΕΘ 885α), blue glass bead; e) **6/38β** (ΜΕΘ 885β), opaque white bead; f) **6/38γ** (ΜΕΘ 885γ), small bronze spiral; g)–h) **6/39** (ΜΕΘ 887), bronze knife fragment. Drawings A. Hooton and F. Skyvalida, photos I. Coyle

Tomb 245/17. #245/015014 [13]. Notebook p. 72; 09-10-2005. Fig. 6.27a–b.
Type: Pit grave, inhumation; cut away at northeast end by Pits 74, 75.
Location: Center of cut 2.50 m from N, 1.50 m from W side of Square 15.
Orientation: Southwest–northeast.
Dimensions: L. 1.24; p.W. 0.50; floor 0.85 x 0.45; 0.30 m deep.
Fill: Fairly loose light red-brown soil, many limestone inclusions. Shallow depth (0.30).
Skeleton: 26.77 m deep, poorly preserved bones (cranial fragments, clavicle, arms, fingers); head to southwest.
Study (2015): Adult; unknown sex. Feet only.
Skeletal pathology: Arthritis: 1) Left and right MTs: slight marginal lipping, 2) Left navicular, cuboid, and lateral cuneiform: moderate lipping, 3) Right navicular and medial cuneiform: slight lipping.
Samples for isotopes: 1) Left third metatarsal, 2) one rib fr.
Additional bones: 1) Cranial bones, ribs, right femur, unidentified long bones: Infant 3.5–4 yrs (from bone morphology).
Absolute chronology: AMS ^{14}C: 1492–1481 calBC (1.6%), 1454–1297 calBC (93.8%).

Grave Goods
Ceramics, wheelmade

6/40. (MEΘ 875) Small Wheelmade Handleless Jar Fig. 6.27c–d
#245/015014 [13] 22-11-2005. Vase 34. Found near infant bones (cranium), on south side of cutting.
H. 0.070; Diam. (max) 0.070; Diam. (foot) 0.030; Diam. (neck) 0.040; Diam. (rim) 0.055; Th. (rim) 0.003.
Shape: Small handleless jar, banded: FS 77 (LH IIIA1). Small wheelmade handleless jar, spherical body on flat disk base (slightly domed underside) curving in to narrow neck, curving out to rounded lip. Complete profile preserved, missing frr on one side, including from neck, rim.
Decoration: Upper body down to (below) midpoint of maximum diameter covered with painted bands; ext. neck and inside rim completely glazed with narrow reserved line below ext. lip.
Fabric: Fine light red clay (5YR 7/6), pale red bands carelessly painted (run together in places).
Mountjoy 1986, p. 56, fig. 63; Mountjoy 1999, pp. 750–751, fig. 289 #20 (Phokis); p. 837, fig. 336 (Thessaly) (all LH IIIA1); cf. south Pieria (Spathes–Agios Dimitrios): Poulaki-Pantermali 2013b, pp. 55–57, ζ–η (monochrome), 59β (handmade); Platamon (Rema Xydias): Koulidou et al. 2014, p. 167, fig. 4, A-18.

Tomb 245/18. #245/015015. Notebook pp. 73–75; 9-11-2005. Fig. 6.28a–b
Type: Pit grave; inhumation.
Location: Tomb encountered in northwest corner of Square 15, directly east of Pit 39, which cut tomb in half; trench extended 1 m north and 1.5 m east into balk in adjacent (not numbered) squares. East side of cutting not found, probably disturbed by some later installation (pit?). Small section of tomb cutting continued to west in Square 13, while large part of it found in area directly north (outside grid squares of excavation in Plot 245).
General remarks: Upper fill layer (0.55 thick): dark gray to reddish brown soil, fairly loose, with fair amount of limestone inclusions, a few small fieldstones. Many small fragments of roof tiles. Sherds: a fair number of unglazed sherds, worn, of various periods, especially wheelmade vessels (two sherds with painted Geometric decoration, one banded rim); a few open black-gloss shapes [Pit 39?]. ME 229: fragment of bronze foil.

FIGURE 6.27. Methone Plot 245, Tomb 17, cut away at north by Pits 74, 75: a) drawing I. Moschou and T. Ross; b) view from west, photo KZ´ Ephoreia; c)–d) **6/40** (MEΘ 875), small handleless jar. Drawing A. Hooton and I. Moschou, photo I. Coyle

Lower fill (below surface layer):	Reddish brown soil, fairly compact/hard, containing many limestone inclusions. No fieldstones, a few fragments of roof tiles. Early Iron Age sherds, unglazed, wheelmade and handmade.
	#245/105109: one wheelmade banded rim, Archaic (from bones).
	Shell, animal bones observed in both levels of fill.
Orientation:	Northeast–southwest.
	Excavation completed 29-11-2005.
Skeleton:	Disturbed by Pit 72 (fill: loose red-brown soil, limestone inclusions). Upper half of body preserved (cranium, torso, arms); arms crossed on chest; head to southwest. P.L. 0.50; p.W. 0.32; depth 26.49 m.

FIGURE 6.28. Methone Plot 245, Tomb 18, cut into at east end by Pit 39: a) drawing I. Moschou and T. Ross; b) view from south, photo KZ´ Ephoreia; c)–d) **6/41** (MEΘ 876), small handleless jar. Drawing A. Hooton and I. Moschou, photo I. Coyle

Pit 72: 1) Right second metatarsal, 2) Four unsided metatarsals (adult).
Study (2015): Adult (25–35, based on molar wear); female.
Dental pathology: 1) Large caries, 2) Slight calculus, 3) Heavy wear.
Skeletal pathology: Musculo-skeletal markers: 1) Left and right humerus: strongly marked pectoralis major and brachioradialis muscle, 2) Left and right ulna: strongly marked supinator crest.
Bronze discoloration: 1) Unsided parietal.

GRAVE GOODS
Ceramics, wheelmade

6/41.   (MEΘ 876) Small Wheelmade Handleless Jar   Fig. 6.28c–d
#245/015015 [14]. 29-11-2005. Found at left humerus. Vase 35.
H. 0.070; Diam. (max) 0.075; Diam. (foot) 0.035, Diam. (rim) 0.055.
Shape: Small Mycenaean wheelmade handleless jar (cf. **6/40**). Spherical (globular) body, set on ring foot with raised underside.

Decoration: Surface completely flaked off, probably once banded around foot, belly, and neck (small traces of paint).

Fabric: Semicoarse, brick red (2.5YR 5/8), gold mica.

Small finds: Metal

6/42. (ΜΕΘ 880 + 881) Bronze Pin (Needle) with Eyelet 16.25   Fig. 6.29a–b
#245/015015, 14. 29/11/2005. Tomb 18. ΜΕ 230 + ΜΕ 232.

P.L. 0.156; Diam. (shaft, average) 0.002; Diam. (shaft, central portion, where thickest) 0.003–0.004; Wt. 3.4 g.

Two joining frr preserving most of pin, including point, but not the top of the head. ΜΕΘ 880 and ΜΕΘ 881 were originally considered as two separate pins in the field, until it was clear that they joined.

Type as **6/17** (ΜΕΘ 879β). Mostly thin shaft, circular in section, with central portion thicker, almost certainly the result of bronze disease (according to Muros). Shaft tapers to a good, sharp point. Opposite end formed into an eyelet, only the lower part of which is preserved.

Cf. **6/17** (ΜΕΘ 879β).

Small finds: Clay

6/43α–γ. (ΜΕΘ 892α–γ) Spindlewhorls, Beads, or Buttons (3)   Fig. 6.29c–e
245/015015 [14]. 28-11-2005. ΜΕ 203.

Three large clay beads found near right arm, along south side of tomb cutting. All heavily encrusted, worn around string hole.

6/43α. (ΜΕΘ 892α) Biconical Spindlewhorl, Bead, or Button   Fig. 6.29c

H. 0.040; Diam. (max) 0.040 (at point 0.022 above one end, 0.018 from other end); Diam. (top/bottom) 0.014; Diam. (perforation) 0.007; Wt. 39.7 g.

Sharply articulated profile; maximum diameter above or below midpoint. Worn around both perforation (string?) holes.

Fabric: Fine, light red (2.5YR 6/6), gold mica.

6/43β. (ΜΕΘ 892β) Rounded Biconical Spindlewhorl, Bead, or Button   Fig. 6.29d

H. 0.029; Diam. (max) 0.032; Diam. (top/bottom) 0.015; Diam. (perforation) 0.006–0.0065; Wt. 29.6 g.

Surface heavily encrusted with whitish root marks. Both ends very worn, not parallel to each other (lopsided profile).

Fabric: Dark brown with lighter patches (5YR 5/4).

6/43γ. (ΜΕΘ 892γ) Rounded Biconical Spindlewhorl, Bead, or Button   Fig. 6.29e

H. 0.024; Diam. (max) 0.032; Diam. (top/bottom) 0.012; Diam. (perforation) 0.045; Wt. 21.9 g.

Flattened sphere in profile. Surface covered with root marks, etc.

Fabric: Dark yellow-brown (one end 5YR 6/4, other end 5YR 5/1).

6/44. (ΜΕΘ 893) Biconical Clay Spindlewhorl, Bead, or Button   Fig. 6.29f
#245/015015. 25/11/05. ΜΕ 231. Found near left hand.

H. 0.029; Diam. (max) 0.030; Diam. (top/bottom) 0.014–0.015; Diam. (perforation) 0.0055; Wt. 20.8 g.

Fabric: Semicoarse, dark yellow (7.5YR 6/4).

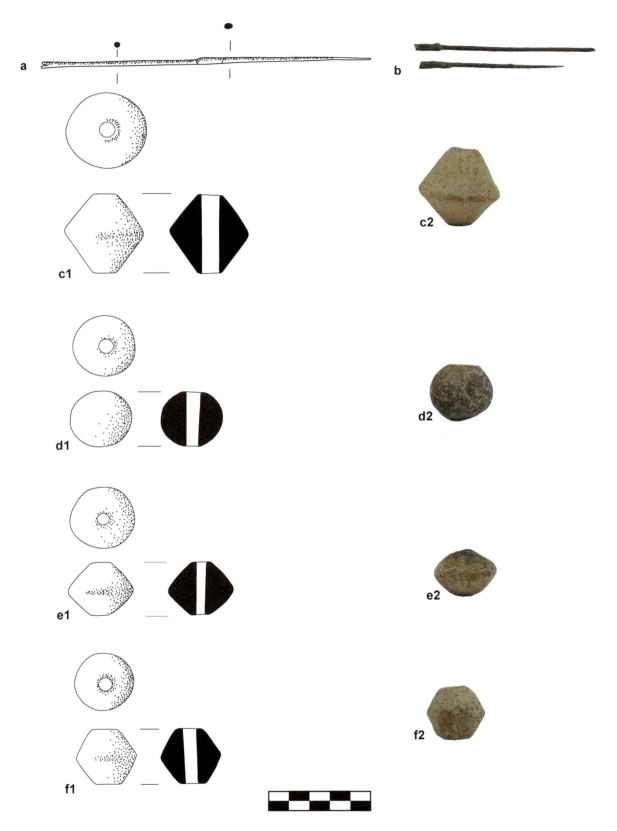

FIGURE 6.29. Methone Plot 245, Tomb 18: a)–b) **6/42** (ΜΕΘ 880 + 881), bronze pin frr; c) **6/43α** (ΜΕΘ 892α); d) **6/43β** (ΜΕΘ 892β); e) **6/43γ** (ΜΕΘ 892γ); f) **6/44** (ΜΕΘ 893), clay spindlewhorls, beads, or buttons. Drawings F. Skyvalida, photos I. Coyle

PLOT 229. NOTEBOOK 2007, P. 12 (K. NOULAS)

Note:	Grid squares added later, to Τομή Α, Β, Γ [Sector 1, 2, 3].
General remarks (2007):	Human bone [cranium, Tomb 1?) found immediately below surface, also artifacts (gold foil pendant: **6/69** = ΜΕΘ 2011); also close to bedrock (slopes away at southeast, toward Plot 245 and other tombs).

Tomb 229/1.   Τομή Γ [Sector 3], North Area, Square 007.
Notebook p. 12, 20-8-2007.   Fig. 6.30a–b.

Type:	Pit grave; inhumation.
Location:	ca. 4 m north of "μεγάλο σκάμμα"; part of skeleton (cranium) emerged during opening of trench; cut by Pit 2.
Orientation:	East–west.
Skeleton:	Adult, oriented east–west with cranium to west. Contracted position, lying on left side with legs drawn up. Preserved: back of skull, left arm, both femurs, part of tibia, toes; rest of skeleton disturbed and cut away by Pit 2, as well as by a second cutting to east [Tomb 229/2?], in debris of which were found fragments of tiles and Classical pottery. P.L. ca. 1.00 m.
Study (2015):	Adult (17–21, based on molar wear, active fusion distal epiphysis of ulnae); female.
Dental pathology:	1) Antemortem tooth loss (AMTL), 2) Large caries, 3) Slight calculus, 4) Periodontitis.

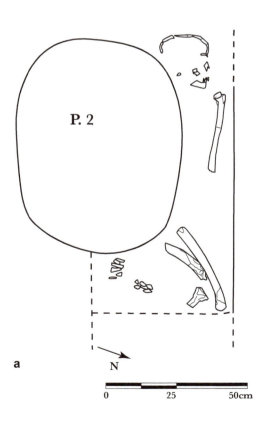

FIGURE 6.30. Methone Plot 229, Tomb 1, includes remains of Tomb 2; both cut by Pit 2: a) drawing I. Moschou and T. Ross; b) view from east, photo KZ´ Ephoreia

Skeletal pathology:	Musculo-skeletal markers: 1) Left and right humerus: marked brachioradialis muscle 2) Right third metacarpal: marked interosseous ligaments and transverse head of adductor pollicis, 3) Right femur: marked gluteus maximus and adductor longus; porotic hyperostosis: small foramina at frontal; cribra orbitalia: small foramina at left orbit.
Samples for isotopes:	1) unsided fibular fr; 2) maxillary right second molar (2021)
Absolute chronology:	1) AMS ^{14}C [IntCal13]: 1738–1714 calBC (5.6%), 1696–1608 calBC (86.1%), 1582–1560 calBC (3.7%)
2) AMS ^{14}C [IntCal20]:	1743–1623 calBC
Fill:	Sherds (found on skeleton).
Pit 2:	loose gray-brown soil, limestone inclusions, no fieldstones; a few Iron Age sherds, one black-gloss, some shells and human bone (from Tomb 1?).
Pit 2:	Cranial fragments, left and right scapula, fragments from humerus and femur, teeth (adult, female).
Samples for isotopes (Pit 2):	1) maxillary right second molar (no wear), 2) 1 unidentified bone fr.
Absolute chronology (bone):	2) AMS ^{14}C (2014) [IntCal13]: 1115–971 calBC (87.7%), 961–935 calBC (7.7%); 2021 [IntCal20]: 1117-967 (85%), 961-931 (9.7%).

GRAVE GOODS
None found.

Tomb 229/2.	#229/007. Τομή Γ [Sector 3], North Area (Notebook p. 12). 20-8-2007. Fig. 6.30a–b.
Skeleton:	Fragments of white bone found near extremities (toes) of skeleton [in Tomb 1?], probably from infant skull (thin bones); no signs of orientation, position. Disturbed by Pit 2.
Identification (2013):	Perinate; sex unknown. Cranial bones: 1 neural arch, vertebra.

GRAVE GOODS
None found.

Tomb 229/3.	#229/007016 [16]. Τομή Β [Sector 2]. 27-5-2008. Figs. 6.3 a–b, 6.31a–b.
Type:	Pit grave with raised ledge around perimeter; inhumation.
Location:	Tomb cutting was identified in bedrock in Square 7, 1.85 below surface, along with Pit 10, which cut into it.
Orientation:	East–west (slightly southeast–northwest).
Dimensions:	P.L. 1.10; p.W. 0.85; central pit: W. (floor) 0.35; W. (ledge) 0.15; depth 1.85–2.80 below surface (0.95: floor of pit; depth of pit: 0.28 m). Northwest corner cut away by Pit 10.
Fill:	#229/007016 (27-5-2008) + #229/007027 (23-6-2008). Fill of Pit 10 (extended into east part of Square 7). Red-brown soil mixed with dark brown soil (fill of Pit 10). Fairly loose, with limestone admixtures; burnt clay, sherds (handmade, Early Iron Age); a few bones with copper oxide, a few shells.
ME 312:	Iron pin/fibula, collected from bones in fill (EIA? not from tomb?). Three fragments, heavy corrosion. From Pit 10?
Skeleton:	No bones found.
Study (2009):	Five pit graves cut into fairly compact white clayey soil (bedrock), found as "pits" in 2009; aligned north–south in an east–west row. See Fig. 6.3b.

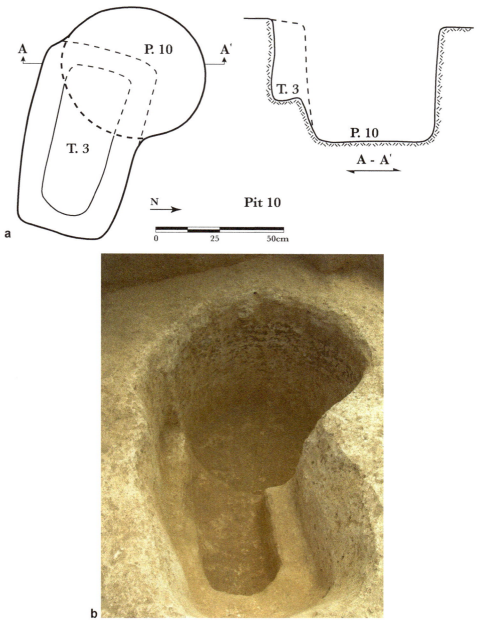

FIGURE 6.31. Methone Plot 229, Tomb 3, cut by Pit 10): a) drawing I. Moschou and T. Ross; b) view from east, after removal of remains, photo KZ´ Ephoreia

Tomb 229/4.	#229/027006 [6]. 4-8-2009.	Fig. 6.32.
Type:	Pit grave with raised ledge (for wooden lid?); inhumation.	
Location:	Tomb cut on northwest by Pit 22; north and south ends in unexcavated areas; 2.60–3.05 m deep.	
Dimensions:	1.82 deep (upper part of tomb); narrow pit just held skeleton (hence lid only, no sarcophagus): L. 1.60 x W. 0.45; 0.45 deep; ledge (on east and west sides) 0.25 x 0.28.	
Orientation:	North–south (slightly northeast–southwest), head to north.	
Fill:	Light red-brown soil, organic remains; a few sherds.	

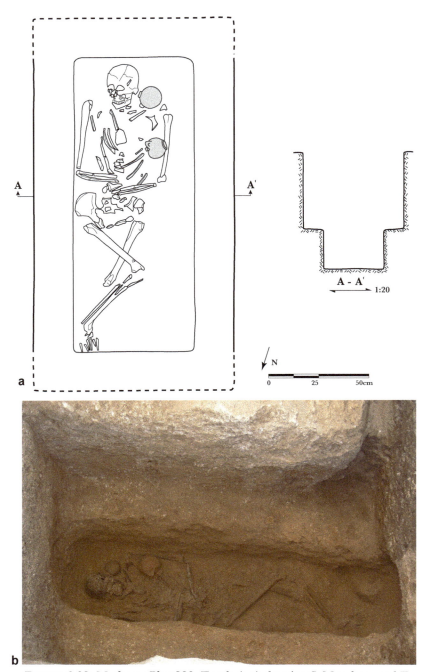

FIGURE 6.32. Methone Plot 229, Tomb 4: a) drawing I. Moschou and T. Ross; b) view from east, photo KZ´ Ephoreia

Skeleton:	Adult, extremely well preserved, including teeth; bones discolored (dark brown) because of decomposition of organic materials (wooden coffin or lid?). Supine, lower body contracted (legs tightly contracted at knees, right leg above left), lower arms folded over abdomen (left arm above right). L. 1.57; W. 0.40 (femur L: 0.47).
Identification (2013):	Adult; male. Extremely strong muscular attachments; calculus; enamel hypoplasia.
Bronze discoloration:	Four proximal hand phalanges, left third metacarpal, two rib frr, one vertebral body.
Study (2015):	Adult (30–35 based on cranial sutures, molar wear); male.

Dental pathology: 1) Small caries, 2) Slight calculus, 3) Enamel hypoplasia.
Skeletal pathology: Osteoarthritis: 1) Right tarsals, first metatarsal and femur: slight marginal lipping, 2) Left and right ulna: slight lipping, 3) Axis (A1) and atlas (A2): slight lipping, 4) Sternum (middle sternal notches): moderate lipping, MSM: 1) Proximal phalanx of great toe: strongly marked extensor hallucis brevis, 2) Right navicular: strongly marked tibialis posterior, 3) Right fibula: strongly marked peroneus tertius and interosseous ligament, 4) Right femur: strongly marked iliofemoral ligament and gluteus maximus muscle, 5) Left and right ulna, radius: marked supinator, 6) Left and right humerus: marked deltoid, extensor carpi radialis longus, brachioradialis and pectoralis major muscle.
Stature estimation: 180–184 cm (right humerus: 183.794 ± 4.05, right fibula: 180.856 ± 3.29 cm).
Samples for isotopes: Proximal hand phalanx; unsided rib fragment.
Absolute chronology: AMS ^{14}C: 1397–1259 calBC (94.5%), 1241–1236 calBC (0.9%).

Grave Goods
Ceramics

6/45. (MEΘ 3042) Wheelmade Rounded Alabastron   Fig. 6.33a–b

Found near left shoulder, close to cranium; mouth of vessel faced toward vertebral column. Vase 77.

Entire profile preserved, but broken at neck (half of rim circumference missing). Surface worn and pitted, much of paint and surface flaked off.

H. 0.085; Diam. (max) 0.105; Diam. (neck) 0.050; Th. (rim) 0.004; handles: W. 0.005; H. 0.020; Diam. 0.0075.

Shape: Mycenaean rounded alabastron, rounded, three handles; banded: FS 86 (LH IIIC). Small (nearly "squat"), flattened sphere in profile, maximum diameter below midpoint, rounded underside with small resting surface.

Decoration: Top of neck and rim entirely glazed inside and out; banded (two bands above handles on neck, three bands below handles and above point of maximum diameter). Handles painted with single dark band covering outer/upper surface and across attachments on to body.

Fabric: Dark gray core, surface light gray (reduced: firing accident?), 7.5YR 7/1; painted bands dark gray/black, dull.

6/46. (MEΘ 3043) Wheelmade Amphoriskos   Fig. 6.33c–e

Found near left arm, at side of body. Vase 76.

Smashed in trench but complete, mended; missing chips.

H. 0.126; Diam. (max) 0.133; Diam. (neck) 0.072; Diam. (rim) 0.090; Diam. (base) 0.053; Th. (rim) 0.0055; handles: L. (at attachments) 0.0053–0.0054, H. 0.030 (attachment to top of handle); Diam. 0.009.

Shape: Mycenaean amphoriskos, banded; three handles. FS 59–61 (LH IIIC). Spherical body on flat disk base, slightly raised underside. Three ring handles set horizontally at vertical angle to body, just above midpoint/maximum diameter. Wide flaring neck, rounded lip at rim.

Decoration: Upper neck and rim glazed solid, inside and out. Four bands on shoulder above handles, three bands below handles at midpoint/maximum diameter. Scroll motifs (FM 48) between handles; handles tri-splashed.

Fabric: Dark red clay, pale white surface (self-slipped?), dark red paint, streaking to brown. Core: 2.5YR 5/6 ("red").

Surface: 7.5YR 7/6 ("reddish yellow").

Mountjoy 1986, p. 138, fig. 168 (Perati); *Lefkandi* IV, p. 204, fig. 2.31, nos. 1, 2, 5.

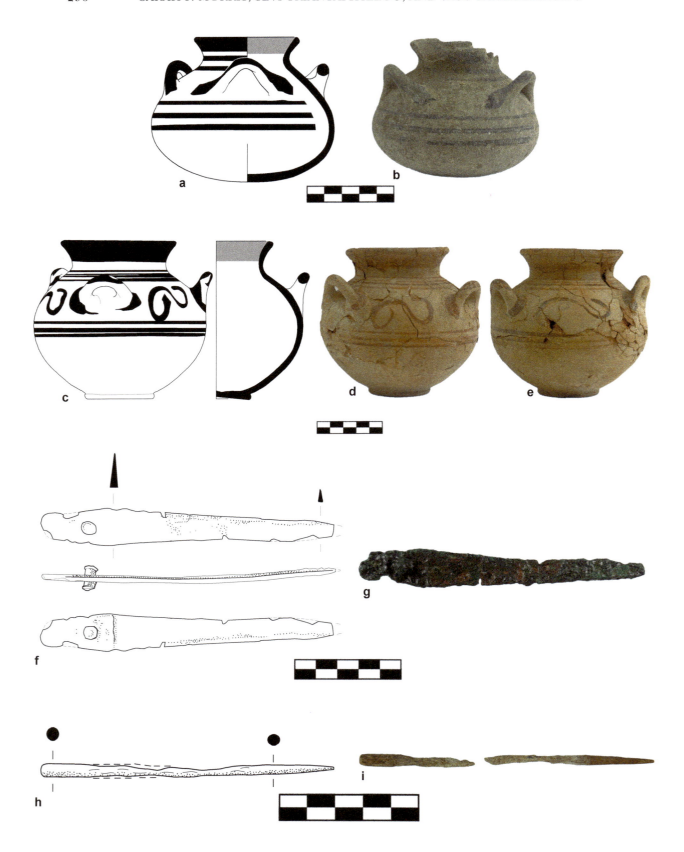

Figure 6.33. Methone Plot 229, Tomb 4: a)–b) **6/45** (ΜΕΘ 3042), rounded alabastron; c)–e) **6/46** (ΜΕΘ 3043), amphoriskos; f)–g) **6/47** (ΜΕΘ 4149), bronze knife; h)–i) **6/48** (ΜΕΘ 5347), bone pin. Drawings A. Hooton and F. Skyvalida, photos I. Coyle

Small finds

6/47. (ΜΕΘ 4149) Bronze Knife   Fig. 6.33f–g

#229/027006 [6]. 4/8/2009. Tomb 4 (near left hand). ME 637.

P.L. 0.134; W. (max, hilt) 0.019; Th. (blade, max.) 0.004; Wt. 16.5 g.

Three joining frr preserving almost complete knife; point not preserved and end of hilt chipped. Condition otherwise good.

Straight-sided blade, with cutting edge on the slightly concave side; opposite edge thicker. Hilt of uniform thickness on both sides, with single rivet (L. 0.012; Diam. [head] 0.007).

Cf. examples from Platamon (Tomb 2) and a looted tomb (LH IIIC?) at Voulkani, Leivithra: Poulaki-Pantermali 2013b, pp. 48, 50.

6/48. (ΜΕΘ 5347) Bone Pin   Fig. 6.33h–i

#229/027006 [6]. 4/8/2009. Found under **6/46** (ΜΕΘ 3043) (once inside?). ME 636.

Two frr, barely joining but preserving entire pin. Badly worn at center of pin along a 0.025 portion of upper shaft, as if habitually held and used at this position.

H./L. 0.103; Diam. (head) 0.005; Diam. (point) 0.002; Wt. 1.0 g.

Shaft tapers from rounded head to thick point; round in section. Plain head, thicker than the rest of the shaft and clearly intact. Original surfaces nicely polished smooth and patinated, as opposed to the broken center.

Type: As **6/57** (ΜΕΘ 4094), with shaft circular in section, tapering to a sharp point.

Tomb 229/5.	#229/027. 5-6-2009.	Figs. 6.3a–b, 6.34a
Type:	Pit grave (pit cut into sterile earth), inhumation.	
Location:	Directly west of Tomb 7, ca. 1.20 east of Tomb 4, same depth; north end of tomb in unexcavated area. Two pits [in tomb fill?]: 4 and 5: Pits 23 (#229/027008), 24 (#229/027009)	
Orientation:	North–south.	
Dimensions:	P.L. 0.085 (north–south), W. 0.60 (east–west); depth of pit 0.70; depth: 1.82 to 2.53 m below surface.	
Fill:	Yellow-brown earth, lime, few charcoal bits, some organic; at depth of 2.10 below surface, fill is dark brown mixed with upper fill of tomb (disturbed by pits).	
Skeleton:	No skeleton survives; frr of two bones reported in trench (not collected? not found in analysis).	

GRAVE GOODS
None.

Tomb 229/6.	#229/027011 [11]. 17-8-2009.	Figs. 6.3a–b, 6.34a–b.
Type:	Pit grave, floor paved with pebbles; infant (inhumation).	
Location:	South-southeast of Tomb 5; cut by Tomb 7; over half of tomb to south in balk (under excavation in 2014 and later); patch of pebble-paved floor preserved.	
Orientation:	North–south (slightly northwest–southeast?).	
Dimensions:	W. 0.35; p.L. 0.35; 1.95 below surface (pit 0.16 m deep, pebble [size?] ca. 0.090).	
Skeleton:	Supine, arms across abdomen. A few infant bones (right, left tibia) reported in notebook: not found in analysis.	

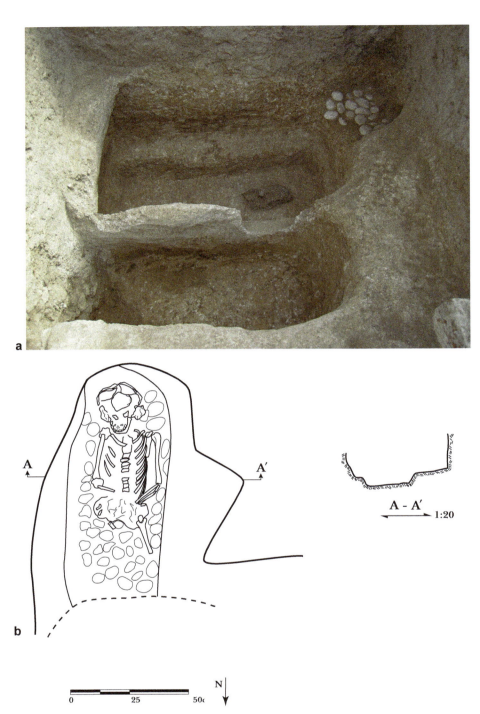

FIGURE 6.34. Methone Plot 229, Tombs 5, 6 and 7: a) overall view from west, photo KZ´ Ephoreia; b) Plot 229, Tomb 6 (2015), drawing T. Ross

2015
(excavation completed): #229 Trench 1: infant skeleton, pelvis and higher (no lower limbs preserved) identified, photographed, and drawn.
Study (2019): Upper skeleton survives better, few bones from lower skeleton because of disturbance by tomb 7.
Age: Child 7–8 years. Sex: Indeterminate.

Grave Goods
None.

Tomb 229/7. #229/027008 [8] + 027012 [12]. 2009. Figs. 6.3a–b, 6.35a.
Type: Pit grave with raised ledge around perimeter.
Location: Directly east of Tomb 5 and parallel to it; cuts into Tomb 6 at southeast corner (separated from it by thin strip of earth: see Section). North of it: probably another cutting for tomb or pit?
Orientation: North–south (head to south?).
Dimensions: Top of cutting: L. 1.15 (north–south axis), W. 0.60 (east–west), W. (ledge) 0.13; 1.82–2.40 below surface (upper edge: 1.89 below surface, floor of tomb/pit 2.40 below surface); ledge: 2.22 below surface). Pit: L. 1.05, W. 0.34 m.
Fill: Red-yellow soil, lime, fairly compact (hard); a few handmade (Iron Age?) sherds.
Skeleton: Cranium fragments at south end, ca. 0.12 from south wall of pit; thoracic fragments.
Study (2015): Human bones from fill? Early infant (18 mos.); sex unknown.
Samples for isotopes: One unidentified long bone fr.
Additional bones: 1) fragment from right tibia, posterior splinter (child?; belongs to the child of Tomb 6).

Grave Goods
None found.

Tomb 229/8. #229/028015 (east end of trench). Notebook pp. 6–7. 26-7-2011.
Figs. 1.30 (showing cremated remains), 6.3b, 6.35a.
Tomb 8 = Pit 28: Cremation burial in handmade cinerary urn (found in balk, below stones and in loose earth, identified initially as Pit 28).
Location: North balk of Square 28.
Dimensions (Pit 28): Depth 1.15–0.30, W. 1.10 (east–west, at south), W. 1.20 (east–west at north).
Fill: #229/02816 + 17 [7] = fill of Pit 28.
Skeleton: 1 bag, cremated remains (Fig. 1.30); weight 1.063 kg.
Study (2015): Age: Adult, Sex: Male? (porotic hyperostosis).

Grave Goods

6/49. (ΜΕΘ 4068) Handmade Jar (Cinerary Urn) Figs. 1.30, 6.35b–c
Found half in balk, in Pit 28; 1.0 m from west side of Square 28, in north balk of Sector 10. Vase 87. Broken in many frr, missing edge pieces below break.
P.H. 0.255 (original H. at least 0.30?); Diam. (base) 0.120–0.150 (rounded underside, no clear base); Diam. (max) body 0.250; Diam. (at break below neck) 0.089; handle: W. 0.037; Th. 0.009; H. 0.075; Th. (body) 0.0075.
Shape: Handmade jar (amphora?), broken at neck and missing rim; oval "baggy" profile, base flattened as resting surface. Two vertical strap handles attached above midpoint/maximum diameter of body. Two small horizontal lugs (resembling mastoid) added midway between handles, slightly above level of interior attachment of strap handles. Vertical scratches or striations (?) visible on one side, below handles and set at slight angle (slanting upper left to lower right), between strap and lug handles.
Fabric and surface: Fine, hard-fired reddish brown/yellow fabric (5YR 6/6), gray core; semicoarse (small dark inclusions). Surface hand smoothed, faint burnish marks visible but rough and uneven.
Cf. Kastanas, Schicht 14b (Hochstetter 1984, pl. 45.8, pl. 50, 1–2, pl. 265; LH IIIC); Palaio Gynaikokastro (Kilkis Museum 752, 754), Early Iron Age.

FIGURE 6.35. Methone Plot 229, Tomb 8 (= Pit 29): a) view from south, photo KZ´ Ephoreia; b)–c) **6/49** (ΜΕΘ 4068), handmade jar or amphora; d) **6/50** (ΜΕΘ 4175), clay spindlewhorl, bead, or button. Drawings A. Hooton, photos I. Coyle

6/50. (ΜΕΘ 4175) Spindlewhorl, Bead, or Button Fig. 6.35d
Found inside urn. ME 762.
Fire-affected, heavily cracked, but unbroken.
H. 0.031; Diam. 0.029–0.031; Diam. (hole) 0.004; Wt. 19 g.
Biconical spindlewhorl. Slightly oval in shape. Light striations around perforations (worn by use on string?).
Dark brown fabric, reddish in color (10R 4/6).

Tomb 229/9.	#229/027. Τομή I [Sector 10]; Notebook p. 19. 1-8-11.	Fig. 6.3
Type:	Pit grave cut into bedrock.	
Location:	Cut by Pits 25, 29 on south and west sides; most of east and north sides preserved	
Dimensions:	P.L. 0.89, p.W. 0.535; depth (at east end) 0.10–0.70.	
Fill:	#229/028018, 020 [7] = Pit 25, infill of Tomb 9. 8/27, 28-2011. Dark soil, full of clay, traces of burning; large number of shells.	
ME 766:	Spindlewhorl, dark fabric (not inventoried, intrusive?).	
Skeleton:	No remains found.	

GRAVE GOODS
None found.

Tomb 229/10.	#229/028: Notebook (Demosthenes Kehayias). 2011.	Figs. 6.36a–d.
Type:	Pit grave in bedrock; inhumation, probably in wooden sarcophagus.	
Location: 1-5/8/2011.	Τομή I (Sector 10), Square 028: west part of trench. #229/028032 [6].	
Orientation:	North–south (head to south).	
Dimensions:	L. 2.27; W. (at south end 0.69); W. (at north end) 0.61; W. (cutting, at south end) 1.11; W. (cutting, at north end) 1.14); ledge: 0.24 from floor of pit at SE, 0.20 from floor of pit at NW.	
Fill:	#229/028030-34 (depth: 2.35–2.68; 1.18 m above bedrock). Sherds: few, handmade.	
Water sieve:	teeth, bone fragments (skeleton), charcoal, very fine sherds (shattered from small vessels: Vase 93, 96?).	
ME 772:	Fragment of bronze sheet (west side of Tomb 10).	
Skeleton:	Poorly preserved, some bones completely disintegrated; cranium completely crushed, fragmented (preserved: sinciput, maxilla [jaw, teeth]; no bones of thorax, ribs). Upper arms (left), some of right arm preserved; both femurs and tibias. Found at 1.35 depth. Extended, supine, head slightly to west; slightly contracted along left side, left arm crossed over abdomen, palms cradling pelvis; lower legs contracted at right angle. Missing feet: no tarsals, metatarsals, or phalanges preserved.	
Study (2014):	Additional teeth, fragments of bone: found in water sieve.	
	Adult; female(?) (based on skeletal and tooth size and morphology).	
Skeletal pathology:	1) Vertebral body fragment, anterior aspect, active new bone formation.	
Bronze discoloration:	On rib, finger bone.	
Study (2015):	Left humerus (Perinate c. 0–38 weeks).	
Animal bones:	Yes (burnt).	

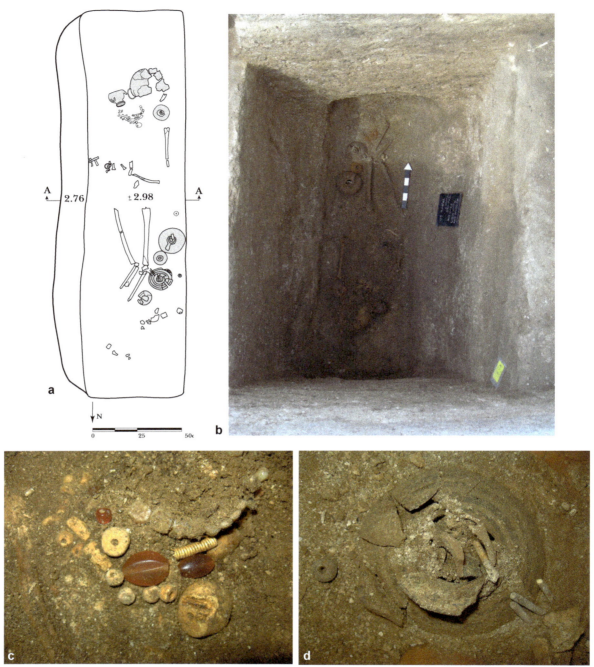

FIGURE 6.36. Methone Plot 229, Tomb 10: a) drawing I. Moschou and T. Ross; b) view (as shown) from above north; c) detail of some of the jewelry as found; d) detail of alabastron and bone pins.
Photos KZ´ Ephoreia

GRAVE GOODS

Fig. 6.37a (group photo of all the pottery), Fig. 6.39e (group photo of pottery and jewelry).

Ceramics, wheelmade

6/51. (ΜΕΘ 4070) Wheelmade Handleless Jar   Fig. 6.37b–c
      Vase 90.
        H. 0.082; Diam. (max) 0.090; Diam. (neck) 0.030; Diam. (rim) 0.047; Th. (rim) 0.004.

Shape: Mycenaean handleless jar. FS 77 (LH IIIA). Rounded shape, spherical body, narrow neck flares out to rounded rim. Cf. **6/40–6/41, 6/53**.

Decoration: Completely glazed (solid, in streaked bands) above midpoint and inside neck.

Glaze: Light-dark red, streaked; once glossy?, now dull.

Fabric: Fine pale red clay (5YR 6/6: reddish yellow), fine gold mica, fine white and black grit.

Surface: Smoothed, dull; some hollows (lime spalling?).

6/52. (MEΘ 4071) Wheelmade Handleless Jar Fig. 6.37d–e

Vase 92.

H. 0.067; Diam. (max) 0.083; Diam. (neck) 0.033; Diam. (rim) 0.040; Th. (rim/neck) 0.003.

Shape: Mycenaean handleless jar. FS 77 (LH IIIA). Rounded shape, biconical/ovoid, rounded underside (no flat resting surface).

Decoration: Completely glazed, including part of underside; dark red.

Surface: Badly flaked, neck and rim worn, broken below rim.

Fabric: 5YR 5/6, fine gold mica, white grit; surface red (3.5YR 4/8), completely glazed.

6/53. (MEΘ 4073) Wheelmade Handleless Jar Fig. 6.37f–g

#229/028032 [6]. West part of trench, at 2.68 depth. Vase 106.

Mended from sherds found dispersed throughout tomb cutting, during clearing of skeleton and after removal of other *kterismata*. Ca. 2/3 of original shape restored; neck mostly broken, but complete profile preserved.

H. 0.075, Diam. max. 0.085, Diam. neck 0.035, Th. rim 0.035.

Shape: Mycenaean handleless jar, banded. FS 77 (LH IIIA). Rounded body with maximum diameter below midpoint (pear-shaped); rounded underside (no flat resting surface).

Decoration: Banded at midpoint and on upper body up to narrowest point of neck; upper neck (rim) completely glazed inside and out down to midpoint of neck. Lower body unpainted.

Fabric: Fine, hard-fired, light gray-brown with fine mica, grit. 10YR 6/3, "pale brown"; darker core (10YR 4/3).

6/54. (MEΘ 4093) Rounded Alabastron Fig. 6.38a–c

Vase 91.

Complete (missing one handle), mended from sherds found scattered in tomb (modern breaks).

H. 0.110; Diam. (max) 0.130; Diam (neck) 0.050; Diam. (rim) 0.075; Th. (rim) 0.0045.

Shape: Mycenaean rounded alabastron; banded, dot rosettes. FS 85 (LH IIIA–B?).

Decoration: Banded shoulder and lower body, multi-splashed handles. Dot rosettes (three): single dot inside circle of six, eight, or nine dots, placed midway between handles. Underside: Painted spiral decoration, in uneven bands, rings.

Fabric: Fine brown clay, gray core (7.5YR 4/4), fine white grit, gold mica.

Surface: Smoothed, pale gray-brown (7.5YR 6/2, "pinkish gray").

Glaze: Dull brown, streaky in bands, solid areas (7.5YR 4/1, dark gray).

Cf. Mountjoy 1986, p. 73, fig. 83; p. 99, fig. 118.

Note: The lower shaft/point of two bone pins **6/57** (MEΘ 4094) and **6/58** (MEΘ 4095) found inside alabastron; upper/thick end of shafts of both pins found directly outside vessel and in direct contact with it.

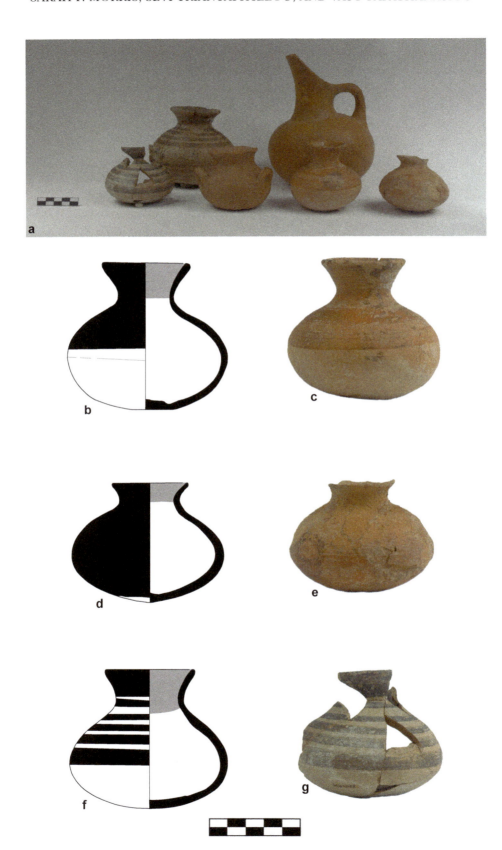

FIGURE 6.37. Methone Plot 229, Tomb 10: a) group shot of pottery; b)–c) **6/51** (ΜΕΘ 4070), small handleless jar; d)–e) **6/52** (ΜΕΘ 4071), small handleless jar; f)–g) **6/53** (ΜΕΘ 4073), small banded handleless jar. Photos I. Coyle, drawings A. Hooton

Ceramics, handmade

6/55. (MEΘ 4072) Handmade Alabastron   Fig. 6.38d–e

    #229/028; found in west part of Sector 10 (0.50 from west side of Tomb 10, 0.30 m from south side of Sector 10); depth: 2.85 m. Vase 95.

    H. ca. 0.075 (rim irregular); Diam. (rim) 0.060; Diam. (max) 0.085; Th. (rim) 0.045; Diam. (neck) 0.050; Wt. 237.2 g; handles: W. (root) 0.035; H. 0.020; Diam./Th. 0.008–0.010.

    Shape: Handmade alabastron, heavy red fabric; three horizontal ring handles. Handmade imitation of Mycenaean wheelmade shape.

    Fabric: Heavy, red, unglazed; surface roughly smoothed, lumpy. Fine white chips, dark inclusions, gold mica sparkles; visible lime spalls.

6/56. (MEΘ 4069) Handmade Jug with Cutaway Neck   Fig. 6.39a–d

    #229/028032 [6], at depth of 2.82 m; 0.42 from north side of Sector 10; 0.35 m from west side of Tomb 10. Vase 89.

    H. 0.193; Diam. (max) 0.157; Diam. (base) 0.085; Diam. (neck) 0.055; Diam. (handle) 0.0135–0.0185.

    Shape: Handmade jug with cutaway neck. Flattened base, spherical body below neck; maximum diameter at vertical midpoint of round body. Vertical neck with concave profile, flaring out to tall spout, cut away steeply to join horizontal top of vertical handle, forming right-angle arch as it joins shoulder. Handle rectangular in section (squared), made of single cylinder diagonally fluted/ribbed; round in section at base where it joins shoulder. Handle joins directly and smoothly to back of spout. Spout: Cut off smoothly at top (flat rim on top and sides), U-shaped in back view.

    Fabric: Even reddish brown (7.5YR 5/6, "strong brown"); fine clay, fine gold mica, fine white grit, many small hollows (lime?).

    Surface: Smoothed, stroke-burnished (visible tool marks).

    This is the most common vessel in Early Iron Age tombs at Dion-Olympos (Poulaki-Pantermali 2013a, pp. 79–81: Late PG–Sub PG) and Torone (Papadopoulos 2005, pp. 469–470); cf. Assiros, Phase I (Wardle and Wardle 2000, p. 660, fig. 3; p. 661, fig. 4; p. 665, fig. 7; p. 673, fig. 5): late 8th–early 7th century B.C. Early Iron Age: Kastanas (Hochstetter 1987, p. 53, fig. 12, pls. 141.5, 149.3, 267); Palaio Gynaikokastro (Kilkis Museum, MK 629): Savvopoulou 1987, p. 310, fig. 5; Savvopoulou 2001, p. 175, fig. 13; Nea Philadelphia: Misailidou-Despotidou 2013, p. 226, fig. 1 (MΘ 20274): 7th century B.C.? However, the shape has a long ancestry in Macedonia and Thessaly since the second millennium.

Additional pottery in tomb fill (not catalogued)

Vase 93 (not inventoried):	Mycenaean alabastron (neck, friated body frr of miniature vessel, Diam. [neck] ca. 0.048–0.050); found 0.050 from north side of Sector 10, 0.43 m from west side of Tomb 10.
Vase 96 (not inventoried):	Two small horizontal ring handles, broken from wall of miniature vessel (open shape?); many shattered body frr; found 0.40 m from west side of tomb, 0.10 from north side of tomb, in west part of trench, at depth of 2.90 m. Frr of similar small vessels found in water sieve: two miniature vessels, one banded, five miscellaneous handmade and wheelmade.
MEΘ 5353:	#229/028. Sector 10. 08-08-2011. West part of trench (from fill of Tomb 10, in south portion).
Matt-painted fr:	shoulder of closed vessel. W. (max) 0.067; H. (max) 0.0475; Th. (top) 0.005; Th. (bottom) 0.0075. Fine hard clay, rough interior surface (hand-smoothed).

FIGURE 6.38. Methone Plot 229, Tomb 10: a)–c) **6/54** (ΜΕΘ 4093), rounded alabastron; d)–e) **6/55** (ΜΕΘ 4072), local handmade alabastron. Drawings A. Hooton, photos I. Coyle

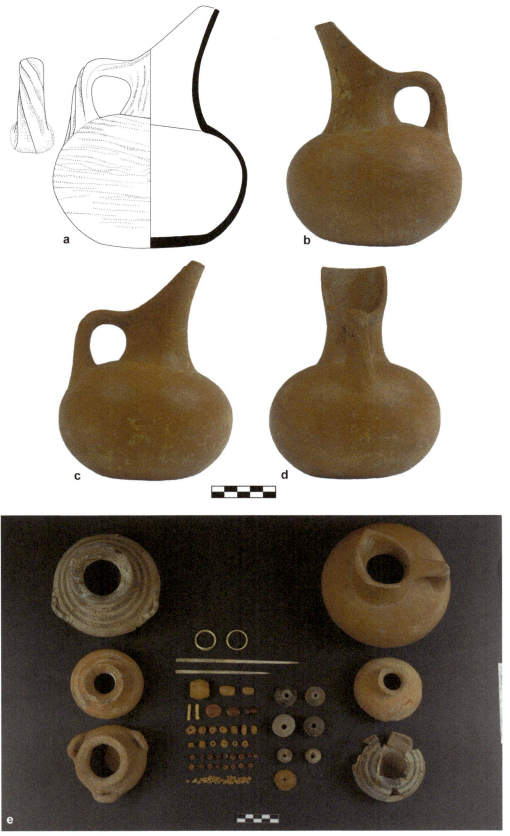

FIGURE 6.39. Methone Plot 229, Tomb 10: a)–d) **6/56** (ΜΕΘ 4069), north Aegean handmade jug with cutaway neck; e) group shot of ceramics, small finds. Drawing A. Hooton, photos I. Coyle

Fabric: Dark red throughout, white chips (visible on surface).

Decoration: Matt brown paint, vertical (or diagonal? position of sherd not certain) bands, one pair with chevrons.

Small finds

See Fig. 6.39e (group shot of ceramics with small finds).

*Two bone pins (found inside alabastron **6/54** [MEΘ 4093]).*

6/57. (MEΘ 4094) Bone Pin Fig. 6.40a–b

Tomb 10. Found inside alabastron **6/54** (MEΘ 4093). ME 778.

L. 0.118; Diam. (head, max) 0.005; Wt: 2.8 g.

Two joining frr preserving complete pin. The larger fr (head) was found inside Vase 91, the smaller fr (point) outside the vessel, 0.26 m from the north side of Sector 10, at a depth of 2.88 m; 0.404 m from the west side of the tomb.

Pin shaft circular in section, tapering to sharp point. Plain head (intact). Original surfaces nicely polished smooth.

Probably from a long bone (but not rib).

6/58. (MEΘ 4095) Bone Pin Fig. 6.40c–d

Tomb 10. Found inside alabastron **6/54** (MEΘ 4093). ME 779.

L. 0.153; Diam. (head, max) 0.004–0.005; Wt. 3.5 g.

Two joining frr preserving complete pin (tip found inside vessel, lower shaft outside and near vessel).

Pin shaft circular in section, tapering toward point, itself not preserved. Plain head, evidently intact, but looks to be slightly chipped. Original surfaces, wherever preserved, nicely polished smooth.

Probable long bone (but not rib).

Clay spindlewhorls, beads, or buttons Fig. 6.40e–l

Cf. Iolkos, Thessaly (Adrimi-Sismani 2014, pp. 772–781, 786–790: LH IIIB2–IIIC).

6/59. (MEΘ 4096) Spindlewhorl, Bead, or Button Fig. 6.40e–f

#229/028032 [6]. Depth: -2.68 m. 4-8-2011. Found 0.20 m from north side of Sector 10 (at -2.92 m); 0.21 m from west side of Tomb 10. ME 780.

H. 0.0185; Diam. 0.018; Diam. (hole) 0.001–0.0038; Wt. 4.7 g.

Spherical clay bead, slightly elongated along vertical axis, and perforated; worn at both ends of perforation.

Dark brown clay (5YR 5/6, "yellowish red").

Surface worn, grayish white; crusted, patchy.

6/60. (MEΘ 4099) Spindlewhorl, Bead, or Button Fig. 6.40g–h

#229/028032 [6]. 4-8-2011. Found 0.17 from north side of Sector 10, depth of 3.02, 0.37 m from west side of Tomb 10, under Vase 91. ME 786.

H. 0.017: Diam. 0.0185; Diam. hole 0.0033; Wt. 4.9 g.

Spherical clay bead, perforated vertically; chipped around top hole.

Dark brown clay (5YR 5/6), fine white grit, mica.

Surface worn, dull; light gray-brown, rough.

6/61. (MEΘ 4097) Spindlewhorl, Bead, or Button   Fig. 6.40i–j

#229/028032 [6] at depth of 2.68 m. 4-8-2011. Found 0.01 from north side of Sector 10, 0.25 from west side of Sector 10 (depth of 2.91). ME 781.

H. 0.029; Diam. 0.027; Wt. 15.2 g.

Biconical spindlewhorl, vertically pierced; not perfectly symmetrical around horizontal axis.

Pale gray clay (surface), dark yellow-gray core (7.5YR 5/6, "strong brown").

6/62. (MEΘ 4101) Spindlewhorl, Bead, or Button   Fig. 6.40k–l

#229/028032 [6]. 4-8-2011

Found 0.06 from north side of Sector 10, at depth of 3.06 m, 0.21 from west side of Tomb 10. ME 788.

H. 0.0238; Diam. 0.026; Diam. (hole) 0.0057–0.0058; Wt. 11.8 g.

Biconical spindlewhorl, vertically pierced, very worn around perforation. Surface dull.

Dark gray clay (5Y 3/1), fine gold mica.

6/63. (MEΘ 4098) Spindlewhorl, Bead, or Button   Fig. 6.40m–n

#229/028032 [6]. 4-8-2011. Found 0.20 from west side of Tomb 10, 0.53 from south side of Sector 1, at 2.94 m depth. ME 783.

Very worn, chipped around both ends of perforation.

H. 0.017; Diam. (top) 0.0095; Diam. (bottom) 0.0249; Diam. (hole) 0.0039–0.0049; Wt. 7.8 g.

Conical spindlewhorl, vertically pierced; truncated cone in profile.

Gray clay (5Y 4/1), surface dull and very worn.

6/64. (MEΘ 4100) Spindlewhorl, Bead, or Button   Fig. 6.40o–p

#229/028032 [6] at depth of 2.68 m. 4-8-2011. Found 0.40 from west side of Tomb 10 at 3.05 depth, 0.10 from north side of trench. ME 787.

Worn, chipped around top.

H. 0.023; Diam. (top) 0.0118; Diam. (bottom) 0.028; Diam. (hole) 0.005; Wt. 12.9 g.

Conical spindlewhorl, vertically pierced; top and bottom parallel.

Dark gray-brown fabric (10YR 3/1 to 5Y 3/1).

Jewelry (bronze, gold, amber)[45]

6/65. (MEΘ 4103) Bronze Finger Ring (Spiral Ring?)   Fig. 6.40q–r

West Hill #229/028032, 6. Tomb 10 (0.50 m from the west side and 0.68 m from the south). ME 785.

Nine frr preserving either one spiral ring, or parts of several rings (probably the former). Much corroded, especially the thinner frr.

Diam. (of one complete band) 0.022; H. (individual band, max) 0.005; Wt. (all frr) 2.3 g.

If one ring of spiral type (as **6/25** [MEΘ 883α–β]), then one portion of the ring is a thicker band, plano-convex in section, tapering to very thin ring composed of bronze wire circular in section (Diam. 0.001).

If a spiral ring, **6/65** (MEΘ 4103) maintains a consistent diameter throughout, unlike **6/25** (MEΘ 883α–β), which becomes progressively narrower.

6/66. (MEΘ 4102) Amber Bead   Fig. 6.41a–c

#229/028032 [6] at depth of 2.68–3.05.

Surface cracked on all sides, crumbled; dark orange-brown. Original surface condition, texture, and color no longer visible.

H. 0.009; Diam. (max) (bottom) 0.0275; Diam. (hole) 0.001; Wt. 3.3 g.

Amber bead, pierced: flat, disk-shaped, with slightly domed profile; perforated as shown.

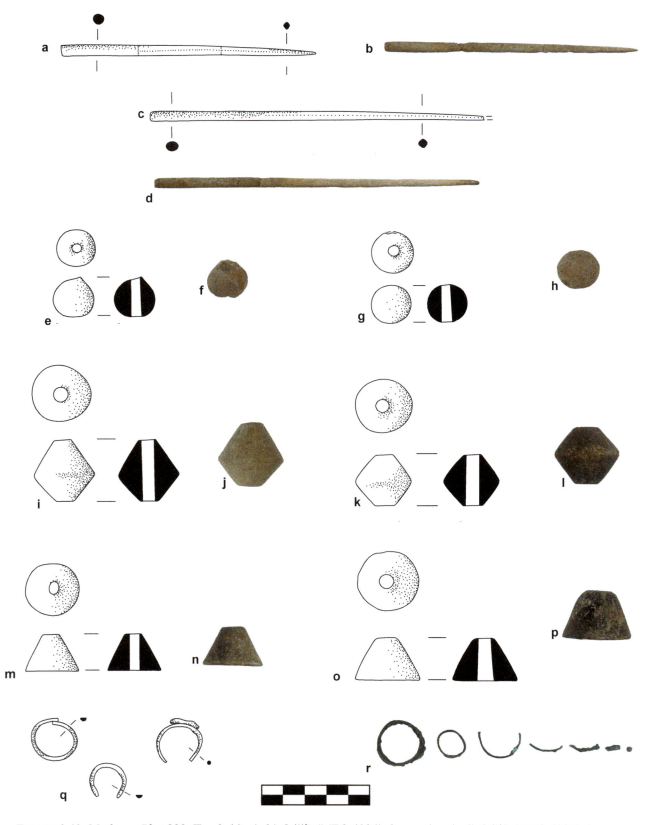

FIGURE 6.40. Methone Plot 229, Tomb 10: a)–b) **6/57** (ΜΕΘ 4094), bone pin; c)–d) **6/58** (ΜΕΘ 4095), bone pin; clay spindlewhorls, beads, or buttons: e)–f) **6/59** (ΜΕΘ 4096); g)–h) **6/60** (ΜΕΘ 4099); (i)–(j) **6/61** (ΜΕΘ 4097); (k)–(l) **6/62** (ΜΕΘ 4101); (m)–(n) **6/63** (ΜΕΘ 4098); (o)–(p) **6/64** (ΜΕΘ 4100); (q)–(r) **6/65** (ΜΕΘ 4103), bronze spiral ring. Drawings F. Skyvalida, photos I. Coyle

6/67α–θ. (ΜΕΘ 3961) Necklace (Gold, Amber, Semi-precious Stones) Figs. 6.41–6.42
#229/028. Sector 10, west part of trench. Found 0.35 from west side of Tomb 10, 0.44 from south side of Sector 10, at depth of 2.90 m below surface. ME 784.

6/67α. (ΜΕΘ 3961α) Gold Coiled Wire Bead Fig. 6.41d–e
L. 0.0195; Diam. (coils) 0.005–0.0055; Th. (wire) 0.005 mm; Wt. 2.5 g.
Gold wire coiled into continuous spiral (17 loops), one end of wire thin and flattened ("working" end, or last coil, cut point?).

6/67β. (ΜΕΘ 3961β) Gold Coiled Wire Bead Fig. 6.41f–g
L. 0.0195; Diam. 0.0045; Th. (wire) 0.006; Wt. 2.2 g.
Gold wire coiled into continuous spiral (17 loops), one end tapers to thin point; other end twisted or cut off? (These two coils could once have belonged to same object.)
Cf. Thrace (Ovčarci, SE Bulgaria), ca. 1500 B.C. (hair ornaments?): Alexandrov 2017, fig. 2.2; p. 172, nos. 45–55; see also Alexandrov 2009.

6/67γ, δ, ε. (ΜΕΘ 3961γ, δ, ε) Three Sardonyx/Carnelian Beads Fig. 6.41h–o
Three sardonyx or carnelian beads, flattened oval in shape (amygdaloid), ends flat; pierced through long axis; three sizes (large, medium, small).
Cf. Troy Level VI (*Troy* III, no. 35-531, fig. 298).
6/67γ (large): L. 0.023; W. 0.016; Th./H. 0.0075; Wt. 3.2 g.
6/67δ (medium): L. 0.017; W. 0.013; Th./H. 0.0074; Diam. (hole) 0.0015; Wt. 2.4 g.
6/67ε (small): L. 0.016; W. 0.011; Th./H. 0.006; Diam. (hole) 0.015; Wt. 1.4 g.
Additional: 17 small sardonyx/carnelian beads, ranging in size from 0.008 x 0.006 to 0.0045 x 0.0045. Fig. 6.42a.

6/67ζ, η, θ. (ΜΕΘ 3961ζ, η, θ) Three Amber Beads Fig. 6.42b–j
Three amber beads; **6/67ζ** is the largest and roughly biconical, as shown; **6/67η** and **6/67θ** are both cylindrical and flattened, one smaller than the other.
6/67ζ: L./H. 0.024: Diam. 0.026–0.027; Wt. 7.0 g.
6/67η: L./H. 0.020; W. 0.012; Th. 0.006–0.007; Wt. 1.2 g.
6/67θ: L./H. 0.015; W. 0.010; Th. 0.005; Wt. 0.4 g.
Not inventoried individually: 14 additional amber beads, flat disk shape, ranging from 0.0127 x 0.055 to 0.0068 x 0.0036 in size; ca. 40 small crumbs of amber (Fig. 6.42a, top two rows and bottom row).

6/68α–β. (ΜΕΘ 3960α, β) Pair of Gold Wire Earrings Fig. 6.43
#229/028032. Found in west part of Sector 10, 0.23 from south side of trench, 0.44 from west side of Tomb 10, at depth of 2.92 m. ME 789.
Two identical gold earrings (spirals of gold wire), found to right of cranium: gold wire coiled into 2 loops (2 full loops, ends overlapping by 0.010 m).
6/68α (ΜΕΘ 3960α): Diam. (max) 0.0265; H. (max) 0.007; Th. wire 0.0015–0.0017, Wt. 7.5 g.
Ends of wire overlap by 0.0012, one end of wire "squared," other end cut on sharp diagonal, with [sharp?] edge uncut, folded over?
6/68β (ΜΕΘ 3960β): Diam. (max) 0.0267; H. (max) 0.008; Th. (wire) 0.002; Wt. 8.4 g.
Ends of wire squared in section, cut at angle; main body of wire smoothly rounded (hammered?).
Konstantinidi 2001, p. 26, fig. 7b, NM 6220 (Tiryns treasure).

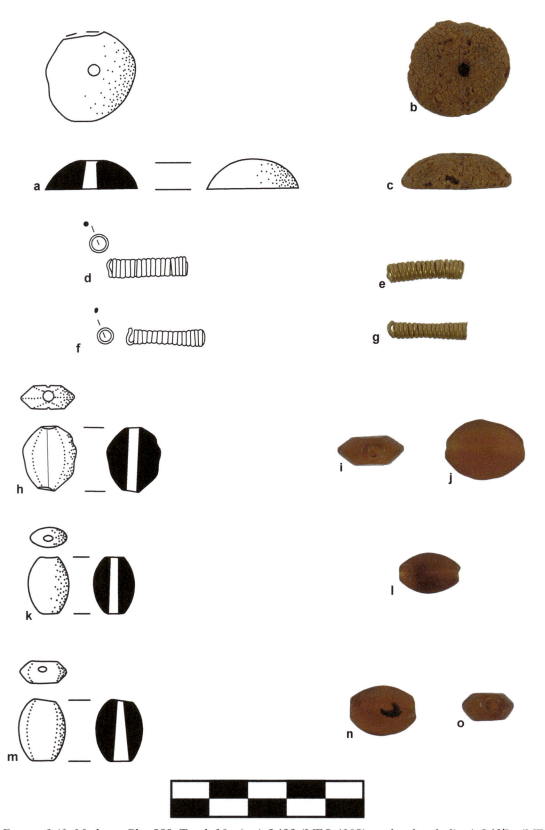

FIGURE 6.41. Methone Plot 229, Tomb 10: a)–c) **6/66** (ΜΕΘ 4102), amber bead; d)–e) **6/67α** (ΜΕΘ 3961α), gold coiled wire bead; f)–g) **6/67β** (ΜΕΘ 3961β), gold coiled wire bead; h)–j) **6/67γ** (ΜΕΘ 3961γ), sardonyx/carnelian bead; k)–l) **6/67δ** (ΜΕΘ 3961δ), sardonyx/carnelian bead; m)–o) **6/67ε** (ΜΕΘ 3961ε), sardonyx/carnelian bead. Drawings F. Skyvalida, photos I. Coyle

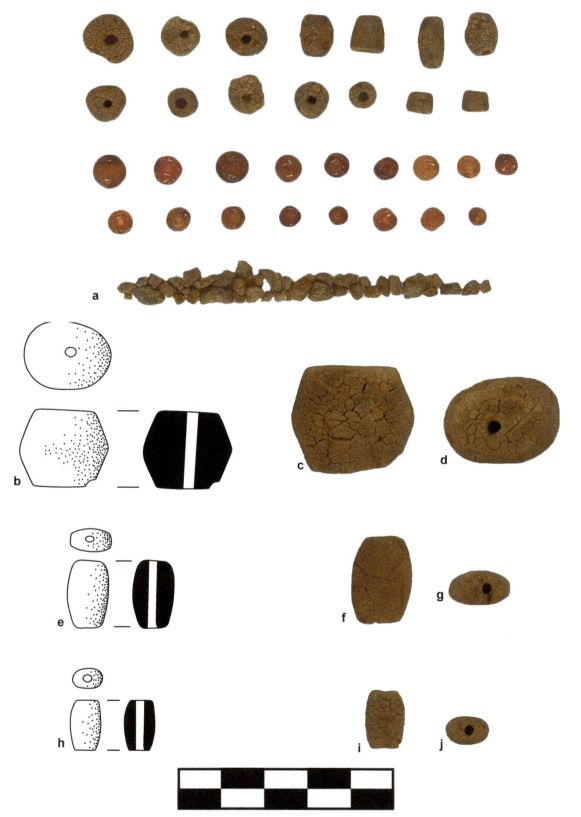

FIGURE 6.42. Methone Plot 229, Tomb 10: a) amber beads (top two rows), small sardonyx/carnelian beads (third and fourth rows), ca. 40 small crumbs of amber from disintegrated beads (bottom row); b)–d) **6/67ζ** (ΜΕΘ 3961ζ), amber bead; e)–g) **6/67η** (ΜΕΘ 3961η), amber bead; h)–j) **6/67θ** (ΜΕΘ 3961θ), amber bead. Photos I. Coyle, drawings F. Skyvalida

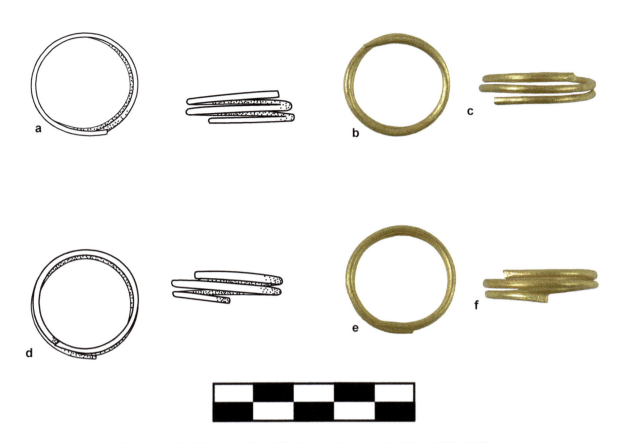

FIGURE 6.43. Methone Plot 229, Tomb 10: a)–c) **6/68α** (ΜΕΘ 3960α); d)–f) **6/68β** (ΜΕΘ 3960β), pair of gold wire earrings. Drawings A. Hooton and F. Skyvalida, photos I. Coyle

PLOT 229: OTHER FINDS (POSSIBLY FROM BRONZE AGE TOMBS)

Sector A (2011)
Found out of tomb context

6/69. (ΜΕΘ 2011) Gold Leaf Ornament Fig. 6.44a–b
#229, Τομή A (βόρειο πέρας), στρώμα 2 (depth 0.60) [Sector 1, north area, level 2], gray earth (gray-brown, fairly loose, with limestone chips); ceramics collected (handmade, Early Iron Age). Notebook p. 10 (17-8-2011): bedrock reached 0.70 below surface, in east part of trench. ME 33. L. 0.0385; W. 0.0215; Th. 0.003; H. (with bosses) 0.0048; Wt. 4.6 g.
Gold leaf ornament pointed at lower end, flat edge at top (folded over?); pierced with two (suspension?) holes at both ends (perforations punched through from front to back); three raised round bosses along vertical axis, shaped or punched from underside (central boss projects more than the others).
Probably from disturbed Bronze Age tomb?
Cf. *Lefkandi* IV, pp. 283–284, fig. 5.9, no. 12 (LH IIIC); bronze.

6/70. (ΜΕΘ 5634 = 8461) Sardonyx or Carnelian Bead Fig. 6.44c–d
#229, Τομή A [Sector 1] Unit 2.2; 13-08-2014. SF 21. Found in topsoil level, in west part of trench directly east of balk and south of Tombs 4–7. ME 1083.
L. (max) 0.023; W. (max) 0.015; Th./H. (max) 0.009; Diam. (perforation) 0.003; Wt. 4.7 g.
Truncated oval bead of sardonyx or carnelian, pierced horizontally for suspension. Flattened hexagon in section. Worn, slightly chipped around perforation.
Color: Dark orange-red with darker veins of color.
Cf. **6/67** (ΜΕΘ 3961γ, Tomb 229/10), Fig. 6.41h–j, with Troy Level VI parallel.
Possibly to be associated with Tomb 6, or Tomb 26?

FIGURE 6.44. Methone, West Hill (unstratified): a)–b) **6/69** (ΜΕΘ 2011), gold pendant ornament; c)–d) **6/70** (ΜΕΘ 5634), sardonyx/carnelian bead. Drawings T. Ross and F. Skyvalida, photos I. Coyle

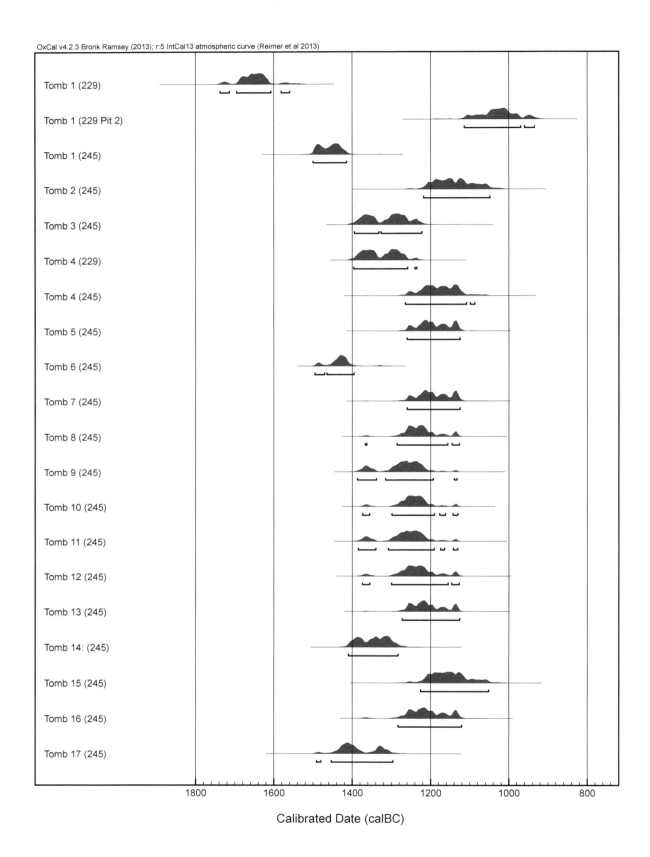

FIGURE 6.45. Chronological distribution of calibrated dates indicating absolute chronology (underlying brackets indicate 95.4% HPD range). Prepared by B. Damiata and J. Southon

ACCELERATOR MASS SPECTROMETRY (AMS) RADIOCARBON DATING OF SKELETAL REMAINS

Brian N. Damiata and John Southon[46]

Twenty samples were submitted for analysis. The procedure to convert raw samples into graphite targets for AMS dating involved several steps including removal of macroscopic contaminants, chemical cleaning (gelatinization and freeze-drying to isolate collagen), combustion, and graphitization. All samples were treated at the Keck–Carbon Cycle AMS facility, University of California, Irvine.

A Dremel drill and dental tools were used initially to scrape off macroscopic contaminants. The extraction of collagen was then performed using the modified Longin method.[47] The raw samples (~ 200 mg) were crushed and initially decalcified by application of 1 N HCl, which was applied at 1 mL/50 mg of raw sample for 24 to 36 hours. The supernatant was removed and the samples were neutralized with MilliQ water. The samples were then gelatinized by using 5 mL of 0.01 N HCl for approximately 12 hours at 60º C, followed by ultrafiltration (> 30 kD filter)/centrifugation for 20 minutes. To help reduce the chloride content, the filtrate was diluted with MilliQ water, followed by two more applications of ultrafiltration/centrifugation. The remaining filtrate (approximately 1 mL) was then frozen with liquid nitrogen and allowed to freeze dry under a vacuum centrifuge for at least 12 hours.

After chemical treatment, approximately 2 mg of individually dried sample were then placed in a quartz tube along with cupric oxide to provide an oxygen source, plus silver wire to "getter" any impurities that may adversely affect the graphitization process. The tube was sealed under vacuum using a gas torch and then combusted at 900º C for three hours to generate CO_2 gas. The tube was then placed on a vacuum line and the gaseous sample was cryogenically purified and then transferred to a vial containing an iron-powder catalyst. The gaseous sample was converted into graphite via the hydrogen-reduction method by heating to 525º C for three hours. The graphite was then packed into aluminum sample pellet and analyzed by the AMS spectrometer. The conventional radiocarbon age was corrected for fractionation using the $\delta^{13}C$ value from the AMS spectrometer (not reported). Aliquots of the dried collagen were analyzed separately for C and N stable isotopes using a Fisons NA-1500NC elemental analyzer equipped with a Delta-Plus IRMS stable-isotope mass spectrometer (reported value).

The results of the AMS dating and stable-isotope analysis are summarized in Tables 6.1 and 6.2. The identification of the sample includes its uniquely designated UCIAMS lab number. The output from AMS dating is given in terms of a conventional radiocarbon age, which is an uncalibrated age. This age was converted to a calibrated (calendrical) date using OxCal 4.3.2,[48] which incorporates the IntCal13 atmospheric curve.[49] This date(s) is reported in terms of the 95.4%

probability of the Highest Probability Density (HPD) range. Table 6.1 summarizes graphically the results of calibration. The stable-isotope data are reported in the conventional δ-notations that are referenced to the PDB standard for C[50] and the AIR standard for N.[51] The reported $\delta^{13}C$ and $\delta^{15}N$ values were measured to a precision of < 0.1‰ and < 0.2‰, respectively.

The purity of extracted collagen for a given sample was evaluated using three criteria: the C/N atomic ratio, the collagen yield, and the weight percent (wt %) concentrations of C and N.[52] The most widely used criterion for identifying contamination and/or diagenetic alteration is the C/N ratio. Modern collagen has an atomic ratio of 3.21. Values within an empirically derived range of 2.9 to 3.6 are commonly accepted for archaeological studies,[53] although Hedges restricts the range to 2.8 to 3.3.[54] Values above 3.4 may indicate contamination with carbon-rich substances such as humic acid.[55] The measured values reported herein are between 3.14 and 3.37 upon conversion from wt % ratio to the more commonly reported atomic ratio (see footnote in Table 6.2).

The second criterion is the collagen yield. Modern defatted bone can yield as much as 25% by weight but well-preserved archaeological samples are typically between 0.8 and 3.5%. The measured yields reported herein are between 1.3 and 8.3%.

The third criterion is the wt % concentrations of C and N. Modern collagen is over 43% C and 16% N by weight. The measured values reported herein are 39.9 to 46.1% for the former and 14.0 to 16.9% for the latter. Thus, by all of the established criteria, the extracted collagen for these samples was of high quality with no appreciable degradation or contamination.

There has been no correction in the AMS dating for marine component of diet. Variations in the reported values for $\delta^{13}C$ and $\delta^{15}N$ have been tentatively attributed to a mixed C_3 and C_4 diet with the latter from consumption of millet, in preliminary analysis by Sevi Triantaphyllou. If there was a marine component to diet, then the reported ages (dates) are older than their true age (date).

TABLE 6.1. Results of AMS ^{14}C dating of bone and tooth samples[56]

Tomb (Plot)	UCIAMS #	Type[57]	Modern Fraction	D^{14}C (‰)	^{14}C Age (BP)	Calibrated Date[58] (calAD/calBC) [IntCal13]
1 (229)	151749	B	0.6586 ± 0.0019	-341.4 ± 1.9	3355 ± 25	1738–1714 (5.6%) 1696–1608 (86.1%) 1582–1560 (3.7%)
1 Pit 2 (229)	151750	B	0.7004 ± 0.0019	-299.6 ± 1.9	2860 ± 25	1115–971 (87.7%) 961–935 (7.7%)
4 (229)	151754	B	0.6837 ± 0.0016	-316.3 ± 1.6	3055 ± 20	1397–1259 (94.5%) 1241–1236 (0.9%)
1 (245)	151751	B	0.6731 ± 0.0019	-326.9 ± 1.9	3180 ± 25	1501–1415 (95.4%)
2 (245)	151752	B	0.6939 ± 0.0019	-306.1 ± 1.9	2935 ± 25	1219–1049 (95.4%)
3 (245)	151753	T	0.6845 ± 0.0019	-315.5 ± 1.9	3045 ± 25	1395–1333 (37.4%) 1327–1223 (58.0%)
4 (245)	151755	B	0.6913 ± 0.0018	-308.7 ± 1.8	2965 ± 25	1265–1109 (94.4%) 1099–1088 (1.0%)
5 (245)	151756	B	0.6905 ± 0.0016	-309.5 ± 1.6	2975 ± 20	1261–1126 (95.4%)
6 (245)	151757	B	0.6752 ± 0.0015	-324.8 ± 1.5	3155 ± 20	1496–1471 (11.7%) 1465–1396 (83.7%)
7 (245)	151758	B	0.6906 ± 0.0017	-309.4 ± 1.7	2975 ± 20	1261–1126 (95.4%)
8 (245)	151759	B	0.6887 ± 0.0015	-311.3 ± 1.5	2995 ± 20	1368–1364 (0.5%) 1286–1157 (88.2%) 1146–1128 (6.7%)
9 (245)	151760	B	0.6865 ± 0.0018	-313.5 ± 1.8	3020 ± 25	1388–1339 (16.7%) 1316–1194 (77.9%) 1141–1134 (0.9%)
10 (245)	151761	B	0.6877 ± 0.0015	-312.3 ± 1.5	3005 ± 20	1374–1357 (3.5%) 1300–1191 (87.3%) 1178–1163 (1.9%) 1144–1131 (2.7%)
11 (245)	151762	B	0.6870 ± 0.0019	-313.0 ± 1.9	3015 ± 25	1385–1341 (12.9%) 1309–1192 (79.6%) 1175–1165 (1.0%) 1143–1132 (1.8%)
12 (245)	151763	B	0.6884 ± 0.0019	-311.6 ± 1.9	3000 ± 25	1375–1356 (3.6%) 1301–1156 (85.6%) 1147–1128 (6.2%)
13 (245)	151764	B	0.6895 ± 0.0017	-310.5 ± 1.7	2985 ± 20	1273–1127 (95.4%)
14 (245)	151765	B	0.6817 ± 0.0016	-318.3 ± 1.6	3080 ± 20	1411–1284 (95.4%)
15 (245)	151766	B	0.6932 ± 0.0021	-306.8 ± 2.1	2945 ± 25	1226–1052 (95.4%)
16 (245)	151767	B	0.6896 ± 0.0018	-310.4 ± 1.8	2985 ± 25	1284–1122 (95.4%)
17 (245)	151768	B	0.6778 ± 0.0022	-322.2 ± 2.2	3125 ± 30	1492–1481 (1.6%) 1454–1297 (93.8%)

TABLE 6.2. Stable-isotope results for bone (collagen) and tooth (dentin) to assess quality.[59]
Analysis of bone element, sex, and age by S. Triantaphyllou and V. Papathanasiou.

Tomb (Plot)	Element	Sex	Age	Collagen Yield (%)	δ¹³C (‰)	δ¹⁵N (‰)	N (wt %)	C (wt %)	C/N[1] (atomic)
1 (229)	Fibular Fragment		17–25 yr	3.3	-20.0	8.5	14.0	40.4	3.37
1 Pit 2 (229)	Unidentified Fragment	?	?	7.5	-19.9	3.9	16.8	45.6	3.16
4 (229)	Hand Phalanx Fragment		30–35 yr	4.8	-17.6	10.0	15.2	41.1	3.16
1 (245)	Lt. Clavicle Fragment	?	14–15 yr	6.8	-19.4	7.9	16.3	44.2	3.16
2 (245)	Radius Fragment		Adult	1.3	-17.1	10.8	14.3	39.9	3.26
3 (245)	Tooth [Deciduous Maxillar]	?	5–6 yr	5.2	-15.0	10.9	16.3	44.1	3.14
4 (245)	Rib Fragment	?	6–12 yr	4.9	-18.8	8.4	16.6	44.9	3.16
5 (245)	Unidentified Fragment		16–19 yr	1.7	-16.3	10.0	15.3	43.2	3.29
6 (245)	Unidentified Fragment	?	1–1.5 yr	6.0	-18.9	10.3	16.4	45.0	3.21
7 (245)	Unidentified Fragment	?	9 months	8.0	-15.6	12.3	16.1	44.2	3.21
8 (245)	Rib Fragment	?	3 yr	6.9	-16.6	11.3	16.2	44.2	3.19
9 (245)	Cranial Fragment		25–35 yr	5.5	-18.3	10.2	16.5	45.0	3.19
10 (245)	Long Bone Fragment	?	9 months–1 yr	4.7	-18.7	10.7	16.3	44.7	3.19
11 (245)	Rt. Clavicle Fragment	?	3.–3.5 yr	7.4	-15.6	12.7	16.4	45.0	3.20
12 (245)	Cranial Fragment		20–35 yr	4.4	-16.7	9.8	14.4	41.3	3.35
13 (245)	Lt. Tibia Fragment	?	9 months–1 yr	6.6	-17.2	11.0	16.3	44.8	3.21
14 (245)	Femoral Fragment	?	Adult	6.0	-19.1	8.0	16.2	44.1	3.18
15 (245)	Cranial Fragment	?	1 yr–18 months	3.0	-18.2	10.4	15.2	42.7	3.27
16 (245)	Lt. Tibia Fragment	?	17–20 yr	2.3	-15.6	10.4	15.7	43.4	3.21
17 (245)	Rib Fragment	?	Adult	8.3	-19.4	7.1	16.9	46.1	3.18

NOTES

1 For preliminary reports, see Bessios 2010, pp. 61–62; Bessios, Athanassiadou, and Noulas 2008, p. 246, figs. 11–12; Bessios 2012b, pp. 16–17, 19, fig. 18; Archibald 2011–2012, p. 100.

2 Bessios, Athanassiadou, and Noulas 2008, pp. 245–246, fig. 10.

3 Bessios et al. 2014, p. 231, figs. 4–5.

4 Triantaphyllou 2003, pp. 220–221; see also Triantaphyllou 2001; Kontonicolas 2018, p. 63. In central Macedonia, intramural burial is still practiced in the Early Bronze Age (Archontiko) and Late Bronze Age (at Toumba Thessalonikis): Chavela 2018; Triantaphyllou and Andreou 2020, p. 175.

5 Eder 2009; Bessios 2010; Poulaki-Pantermali 2013b, pp. 45–60; Koulidou 2007, 2015; Koulidou et al. 2012, 2014; Pappa 2017, pp. 147–149, figs. 258–259, 261–262; Papathanasiou 2020, pp. 20–26.

6 In 2016, a possible earth mound was noted in the section above Tomb 17 in Plot 229, and may represent a practice of marking tombs at the surface (Morris et al. 2020, fig. 23); furthermore, few of the Bronze Age tombs excavated in 2014–2017 cut into each other, implying the existence of some form of visible grave mound or marker at the surface.

7 Methone: Bessios 2010, pp. 61–62; Pydna: Bessios 2010, p. 65: Makrygialos, Plot 480; "Louloudies," Kitros: Bessios 2010, p. 66; Korinos: Bessios 2010, p. 71; Palaia Chrani: Bessios et al. 2003, pp. 452–453; Bessios 2010, p. 73.

8 Poulaki-Pantermali 1993; 2013b, pp. 45–60; Koulidou et al. 2014. A few cemeteries (Korinos and Rhymnio) may have been covered with tumuli, according to the radial placement of burials (at Rhymnio) and other surviving features: Triantaphyllou 2003, p. 221; Karamitrou-Mentessidi 1990; at Valtos-Leptokarya and Pigi Artemidos, earth mound and stone circle are added later: Triantaphyllou and Andreou 2020, pp. 176–178.

9 Triantaphyllou 1999a; 2003, p. 221.

10 Triantaphyllou 1998 p. 153; 1999a, pp. 56, 111 (Korinos).

11 Poulaki-Pantermali 2013b, pp. 55–57, for reuse of tombs at Spathes–Agios Dimitrios.

12 For a discussion of cremation in northern Greece, see Kontonicolas 2018; Chemsseddoha 2019, pp. 111, 119–121, 160–174. For cremations in Neolithic Thessaly, see Gallis 1982. On spindlewhorls as Bronze Age grave goods, see Vakirtzi 2018.

13 Bessios 2010, p. 74 (Πυ 12573, 6491, 6982, 6485, 6473, 6492, 6480, 6483).

14 Leivithra (Vakouphika-Palaiometocho): Poulaki-Pantermali 2013b, p. 51; Agios Dimitrios (Spathes): Poulaki-Pantermali 2013b, p. 57, figs. αστ, p. 58, fig. γ, p. 59, fig. α (Dion Museum 2586, 2568); Platamon: Poulaki-Pantermali 2013b, p. 49, figs. α, γ; Platamon Stop/Tribina 2: Koulidou et al. 2012, figs. 1, 7; Rema Xydias: Koulidou et al. 2014, figs. 4, 6–8.

15 Karamitrou-Mentessidi 2011a, pp. 162–163, #69–71; 2013, pp. 103118.

16 Jung 2002, pp. 160–164, fig. 59; Kountouri 2011, pp. 63–66 (in Thessaly, an LPG or Sub-PG amphora with concentric circles is found in the same burial as a straight-sided Mycenaean-style alabastron: Phiki, Trikala: Grave B: Mountjoy 1999, p. 857, fig. 348). For the purposes of this chapter, the amphoriskos is defined by its raised disk base; the alabastron has no separate base.

17 Almopia: A. Chrysostomou 1994, pp. 38–39, fig. 1; Vergina, Tumulus N (20): *Vergina* I, pl. 44:20; Kountouri 2011, pp. 65–66, cat. no. 12, fig. 47; cf. fig. 46, cat. nos. 8–11.

18 Thessaly: Mountjoy 1999, pp. 33, 825; absence of olive in north Aegean (Valamoti 2009) and of stirrup jars, including transport containers (Andreou et al. 2013, p. 174; for a recent study, see Pratt 2016a; 2021).

19 Cavanaugh 1998, p. 106; Boyd 2014, p. 197.

20 Amyx 1958, pp. 213–216.

21 Initiated in 2010: Andreou et al. 2013, p. 181, n. 72.

22 Poulaki-Pantermali 2013b, pp. 56, 59, fig. β; Koulidou et al. 2014, p. 167, fig. 4, A-18.

23 Andreou et al. 2013, but see Chapter 7, **7/50** (ΜΕΘ 4882), **7/51** (ΜΕΘ 4878). An exception may be an infant burial (Tomb 229/27) identified in 2016, associated with the lower half of a similar vessel (ΜΕΘ 7616): Morris et al. 2020, fig. 33a–b; Papathanasiou 2020 has now identified the remains of at least two more individuals in this burial.

24 For example, at Agios Mamas: Horejs 2007a.

25 As implied at Toumba Thessalonikis: Andreou et al. 2013, p. 179, table 1.

26 Savvopoulou 2004, p. 313, fig. 10 (described as a two-handled kantharoid vessel); see also Savvopoulou 1987, 1988, 2004.

27 Poulaki-Pantermali 2013b, pp. 79–83; Aiani: Karamitrou-Mentessidi 2013, pp. 93–97, 103–118.

28 Hochstetter 1987, p. 304; Jung 2002, p. 163; below, n. 35.
29 Hughes-Brock 2005; Maran 2013; Pieniążek 2016.
30 Vakirtzi 2018.
31 Andreou et al. 2013, pp. 173–174, 175, fig. 1a, pp. 178–179, 181.
32 Cloth cover: Mountjoy 1993, p. 127; Unruh 2007, pp. 171–172.
33 Tzedakis, Martlew, and Jones 2008, EUM 1117; Vassilogamvrou 2008.
34 Honey: Konsolaki 2001, pp. 215, 217.
35 Palaio Gynaikokastro: Savvopoulou 2001, p. 175, figs. 11, 13 (Kilkis Museum 629); Vergina, Tumulus Δ, VII: *Vergina* I, p. 17, pls. 33:5, 34:13, 83; further references to Assiros and Torone below (under **6/56**).
36 In tombs of this phase at Spathes–Agios Dimitrios on the slopes of Olympos, handmade and wheelmade vessels are found in equal proportions: Poulaki-Pantermali 2013b, p. 55.
37 For a recent summary of evidence from southern Pieria, see Triantaphyllou and Andreou 2020.
38 Kountouri 2011, pp. 59–63; Poulaki-Pantermali 2013b, pp. 52–60.
39 Eder 2007.
40 See, however, the incidence of rock-cut chamber tombs in the Early Iron Age (at Pydna: Makrygialos Tomb 11: Bessios 2010, pp. 78–82), and of tumuli in southern Pieria since the Middle Bronze Age (Pigi Artemidos, Pigi Athenas, Valtos Topolianis: Poulaki-Pantermali 2013b, pp. 35–44; Tritsaroli 2017) through the Early Iron Age (Poulaki-Pantermali 2013b, pp. 69–70).
41 Stavridopoulos and Sianos 2009, pp. 58–60, fig. 7; Chatzitoulousis et al. 2014, p. 377, fig. 7. Our thanks to Kostas Kotsakis for drawing our attention to these important finds.
42 Landau 1958, pp. 107, 183, 221; Leukart 1994, p. 184; Ventris and Chadwick 1973, p. 218; Nakassis 2013, p. 345. I am grateful to Dimitris Nakassis and Richard Janko for their advice on these references, which I will explore more fully in Morris (forthcoming). As Janko points out, other Linear B names may be northern in origin, if /*Perraig^{w}oi*/ (PY Ma 193, *pe-ra₃-qo*) are "Perrhaibians" (from Thessaly).
43 Helly 2006, esp. pp. 117, 119–122, fig. 1; Morris forthcoming.
44 P. Colon. 5861: Krebber 1972; Luppe 1994. While Strabo (VII. Frg. 20c) lists Methone before Pella, thus locating it clearly in Pieria rather than the Pagasitic Gulf, it is not certain which city Theopompos describes, and the Iolkos/Pelion area was also famous for shipbuilding (the Argo) in poetic memory.
45 ME 777 (not inventoried). Two frr of a bronze sheet (#229/028032 [6]).
46 Brian Damiata is an affiliate of the Cotsen Institute of Archaeology, UCLA; John Southon is the cofounder of the Keck–Carbon Cycle Accelerator Mass Spectrometry Facility, Earth System Science Department, at the University of California, Irvine.
47 Longin 1971; Brown et al. 1988.
48 Bronk Ramsey 2001, 2009; Bronk Ramsey and Lee, 2013.
49 Reimer et al. 2013.
50 Craig 1957.
51 Mariotti 1983.
52 Ambrose 1990; Ambrose and Norr 1992.
53 DeNiro 1985.
54 Hedges 2000.
55 Kennedy 1988.
56 Radiocarbon concentrations are given as fractions of modern standard, D^{14}C, and conventional radiocarbon age, following the conventions of Stuiver and Polach (1977, p. 355). Sample preparation backgrounds (combustion/graphitization) have been subtracted based on measurements of ^{14}C-free bone. All results have been corrected for isotopic fractionation according to Stuiver and Polach (1977) with δ^{13}C values measured on prepared graphite using the AMS spectrometer.
57 B—collagen from bone, T—dentin from tooth.
58 The OxCal 4.3.2 results are given as the 95.4% HPD range.
59 The δ^{13}C and δ^{15}N values are from aliquots of dried ultrafiltered (> 30kD) collagen (bone) or dentin (tooth) measured to a precision of < 0.1‰ and < 0.2‰ respectively, using a Thermo Finnigan Delta Plus stable-isotope mass spectrometer (IRMS).

7

THE EARLY IRON AGE SETTLEMENT AND POTTERY: AN OVERVIEW

John K. Papadopoulos

Most of the pottery published in this chapter derives from the prehistoric and early historic material that was redeposited in the area of the East Hill, above the stoa and associated buildings and open area of the Archaic and Classical agora of Methone. The context of this material is the same as that of the Bronze Age, discussed above by Marianna Nikolaidou (Chapter 4) and Trevor Van Damme (Chapter 5). Many of the fragments derive from the collapsed erosion deposits (στρώμα διάβρωσης) primarily to the east, on the higher ground. This earlier material, originally stratified, thus overlay the later Archaic and Classical material, including the destruction deposit of 354 B.C. The Early Iron Age pottery from the Hypogeion is published separately by Manthos Bessios (Chapter 9). A few of the pieces presented in this chapter derive from preexisting Early Iron Age deposits in the area of the East Hill; a few fragments were found in surface levels, and one (**7/50**) was from scarp cleaning and is thus of undetermined context; all of these pieces are noted in the catalogue below and in Table 7.1. In selecting the material for presentation in this volume I have strived to provide as representative a sample as possible of the various types of wares present, both wheelmade and painted, and handmade. Many of the more diagnostic Early Iron Age fragments from the deposits are presented below.

All of the material is fragmentary; it is presented according to categories, beginning with wheelmade and painted pottery—closed vessels, then open forms—followed by the finer handmade pottery, again with closed vessel forms first, followed by the open. I have, however, separated a number of classes of coarser handmade pottery, including cooking wares and pithoi; this is explained in more detail below. Given the eclectic character of the material, I list comparanda and notes on the chronology of each piece in the catalogue entry, rather than as categories. I do, however, provide more general comments on the material in the introductory sections.

From a brief glimpse of the material presented in this chapter, especially the wheelmade and painted pottery, one can quickly glean that the most diagnostic feature of the redeposited Early Iron Age material from the East Hill is the decoration that consists of mechanically drawn concentric circles and semicircles.[1] Surprisingly, the characteristic and diagnostic features of the decoration of the wheelmade and painted pottery of the second half of the 8th and the earlier 7th century B.C., seen on the pottery from the Hypogeion presented in Chapter 9, is all but absent from the largely redeposited material on the East Hill. It is important to stress that all of the material was collected, washed, sorted, and subsequently stored.[2] Consequently, the selection of the material to be presented in this chapter is far more comprehensive than that of the so-called "stray finds" or *Einzelfunde* of the Athenian Kerameikos, where the most numerous of the Early Iron Age shapes that were collected

TABLE 7.1. Summary listing of the Early Iron Age pottery from the area of the agora of Methone (Plot 274). The "date" column lists the contextual date of each piece (DD= destruction deposit).

Cat. no.	MEΘ	Context	Object	Date
7/1	4277	#274/004011 [5]	Rim WM amphora, North Aegean	Collapsed fill above DD
7/2	4325	#274/004023 [10]	Rim fr large WM amphora, North Aegean	Early Iron Age
7/3	4266	#274/004016 [7]	Fr WM NH amphora, North Aegean/local	Collapsed fill above DD
7/4	4210	#274/004012 [5]	Base WM amphora, North Aegean	Collapsed fill above DD
7/5	4919	#274/005008 [5]	Fr NH amphora, North Aegean	Collapsed fill above DD
7/6	4920	#274/005009 [5]	Fr amphora, North Aegean	Collapsed fill above DD
7/7	4211	#274/004012 [5]	Fr WM amphora, North Aegean	Collapsed fill above DD
7/8	4317	#274/004020 [7]	Shoulder WM amphora, North Aegean	Collapsed fill above DD
7/9	4199	#274/004001 [1]	Shoulder WM amphora, North Aegean	Surface find
7/10	4313	#274/004018 [7]	Body WM closed vessel, North Aegean	Collapsed fill above DD
7/11	4318	#274/004021-022	Fr WM amphora, North Aegean	Collapsed fill above DD
7/12	4212	#274/004012 [5]	Fr medium closed vessel, Euboian	Collapsed fill above DD
7/13	4877	#274/004035 [11]	Body PSC skyphos, probably Euboian	Early Iron Age
7/14	4889	#274/004036 [11]	Rim fr PSC skyphos, Euboian	Early Iron Age
7/15	4213	#274/004012 [5]	Body PSC skyphos, North Aegean	Collapsed fill above DD
7/16	4868	#274/004034 [10]	Rim PSC skyphos, North Aegean	Early Iron Age
7/17	4921	#274/005009 [5]	Fr PSC skyphos, North Aegean/local	Collapsed fill above DD
7/18	5019	#274/054009 [1]	Rim & body fr WM one-handled cup	Surface find
7/19	4331	#274/004028 [10]	Base WM skyphos or cup, North Aegean	Early Iron Age
7/20	4874	#274/004036 [11]	Rim fr WM krater, North Aegean/local	Early Iron Age
7/21	5108	#274/005010 [5]	Body frr WM lekanis, North Aegean	Collapsed fill above DD
7/22	4207	#274/004011 [5]	Rim & neck fr HM jar	Collapsed fill above DD
7/23	4279	#274/004013 [5]	Rim & upper body fr HM jar	Collapsed fill above DD
7/24	4271	#274/004009 [4]	Rim & upper body fr small HM jar	Collapsed fill above DD
7/25	4280	#274/004013 [5]	Rim & upper body fr large HM jar	Collapsed fill above DD
7/26	4329	#274/004028 [10]	Body & neck fr large HM jar	Early Iron Age
7/27	4208	#274/004011 [5]	Base fr HM closed vessel (jar)	Collapsed fill above DD
7/28	4209	#274/004011 [5]	Base & body fr HM closed vessel (jar)	Collapsed fill above DD
7/29	4201	#274/004011 [5]	Rim & handle fr HM kantharos	Collapsed fill above DD
7/30	5085	#274/005013	Rim & handle fr HM kantharos	Surface find

Cat. no.	ΜΕΘ	Context	Object	Date
7/31	4203	#274/004011 [5]	Rim & handle fr HM kantharos	Collapsed fill above DD
7/32	4202	#274/004011 [5]	Rim, body, & handle fr HM kantharos	Collapsed fill above DD
7/33	4205	#274/004011 [5]	Rim, body, & handle fr HM kantharos	Collapsed fill above DD
7/34	4204	#274/004011 [5]	Rim, body, & handle fr HM kantharos	Collapsed fill above DD
7/35	4884	#274/004036 [11]	Rim & handle fr HM kantharos	Early Iron Age
7/36	4284	#274/004014 [6]	Rim & handle fr HM kantharos	Collapsed fill above DD
7/37	4988	#274/005013	Rim & handle fr HM kantharos	Surface find
7/38	4214	#274/004011 [5]	Handle fr HM vessel	Collapsed fill above DD
7/39	4269	#274/004008 [4]	Rim & handle fr HM bowl	Collapsed fill above DD
7/40	4330	#274/004028 [10]	Rim & handle fr HM bowl	Early Iron Age
7/41	5633	#274/085 East balk	Rim, upper body, & handle fr HM bowl	Collapsed fill above DD
7/42	4237	#274/004011 [5] & #274/004013 [5]	Rim & handle fr HM bowl	Collapsed fill above DD
7/43	4275	#274/004011 [5]	Rim & handle fr HM bowl	Collapsed fill above DD
7/44	4276	#274/004011 [5]	Rim & handle fr HM bowl	Collapsed fill above DD
7/45	4322	#274/004021-022	Rim & handle fr HM bowl	Collapsed fill above DD
7/46	5637	#274/085	Rim, body, & handle fr HM open vessel	Collapsed fill above DD
7/47	5020	#274/054009 [1]	Fragmentary HM handle (ladle?)	Surface find
7/48	4315	#274/004021 [7]	Fragmentary HM handle	Collapsed fill above DD
7/49	4871	#274/004032 [10]	Handle fr unidentified HM form	Early Iron Age
7/50	4882	#274/084	Handle HM amphoriskos, incised decoration	Scarp cleaning
7/51	4878	#274/085. East balk	Body fr HM shape, incised decoration	Collapsed fill above DD
7/52	4885	#274/004036 [11]	Frr HM strainer/sieve	Early Iron Age
7/53	4323	#274/004021-022	Fr HM strainer/sieve	Collapsed fill above DD
7/54	4873	#274/004035 [11]	Clay burnisher	Early Iron Age
7/55	4273	#274/004009 [4]	Rim & handle fr large HM cooking pot	Collapsed fill above DD
7/56	4278	#274/004012 [5]	Rim & handle fr small HM cooking pot	Collapsed fill above DD
7/57	4883	#274/004036 [11]	Tripod leg HM tripod cooking pot	Early Iron Age
7/58	4270	#274/004008 [4]	Tripod leg HM tripod cooking pot	Collapsed fill above DD
7/59	4274	# 274/004009 [4]	Rim fr pithos	Collapsed fill above DD
7/60	4333	#274/004029 [10]	Body fr pithos	Early Iron Age

by the excavators were those that were most heavily decorated.³ The high proportion of diagnostic handmade pottery of the Early Iron Age provides testimony to the careful curation of the material.

Our knowledge of the Early Iron Age period at Methone is, therefore, characterized by two large assemblages: the late 8th- and early 7th-century material from the Hypogeion, and the material from the East Hill that is presented here. The latter includes material dating to the late 8th and earlier 7th centuries B.C., but most of the material is earlier, going back to the Protogeometric and the period of transition between the Late Bronze and Early Iron Age. In one part of the East Hill, along the northern section of Plot 274 (Fig. 4.2), Bessios opened a narrow and deep exploratory trench to test for the nature of the stratified deposits predating the destruction horizon of the agora in 354 B.C. The earliest material from this test trench in situ was said to be Protogeometric, but the area was small, and the depth of the trench, together with the instability of the overlying deposits, was such that further excavations were deemed unsafe and were thus abandoned. As a consequence, the excavations of 2003–2013 did not provide a stratified sequence on the East Hill. In other areas of Methone, the excavations on the West Hill in 2003–2013 brought to light some Early Iron Age material from pits and postholes, as well as residual material encountered in the Archaic workshop deposits that characterized the upper levels of the acropolis. The more recent excavations on the West Hill in 2014–2017 have brought to light stratified deposits extending from the transition from the Bronze Age to the Early Iron Age, through the Protogeometric and Geometric periods, and well into the Archaic period, particularly in the northern trenches, as well as in the area of the Early Iron Age posthole structure in the southern sector of the West Hill.⁴

To press the comparison—and contrast—between the material presented here and that from the Hypogeion a little further, the latter shows an aspect of the material culture of Methone after the arrival of the Eretrian colonists, the former shows what the Methone ceramic assemblage prior to Euboian colonization may have been like.⁵ To be sure, there are many points of continuity; for example, there is some Euboian pottery among the material presented below, but not in the same quantities, or style, as that in the Hypogeion. But it is perhaps in the area of the handmade pottery from Methone that the contrast between the two contexts is most stark. Among the pottery presented here, the handmade comprises a significant percentage of the total ceramic assemblage; in the published and unpublished material from the Hypogeion, it does not; there is some handmade pottery in the Hypogeion, but not in the same quantity as that largely deriving from the collapsed erosion layer. To what extent one can write a "history" of Methone on the basis of this material alone is moot, but in the absence of literary texts, the material record is all we have. However one characterizes Early Iron Age Methone, one thing is clear: it enjoyed a robust and long-lived existence before and after the arrival of the "repulsed by slings" Eretrians (Chapter 2).

CATALOGUE

WHEELMADE AND PAINTED POTTERY (LOCAL AND IMPORTED)

Closed Vessels

Amphoras are one of the most common shapes in the north Aegean and, ironically, one of the least understood. This may seem a controversial statement, but much of the problem as I see it has been the fixation on neck-handled amphoras, especially the widely traded commodity containers (see Kotsonas, Chapter 12), to the neglect of other amphora types. Here I wish to make a very simple point: not all Early Iron Age amphoras in the north Aegean are neck-handled, though even a cursory overview of the literature might suggest otherwise.⁶

In Walter Heurtley's seminal 1939 *Prehistoric Macedonia*, there is only one published fragmentary closed vessel, from Saré Omér (sometimes Sariomer), on the west bank of the Gallikos River, due north of Anchialos/Sindos, that is demonstrably an amphora, and it is clearly neck-handled.[7] Much earlier, in 1894, and on the other side of the Aegean at Troy—more often regarded as an "Anatolian" site rather than one of the north Aegean[8]—Alfred Brückner, one of the first ceramic experts to deal with the transition from Troy VII to VIII, illustrated a neck-handled amphora with mechanically drawn circles.[9] Whether Protogeometric (highly unlikely), Subprotogeometric, or Subgeometric, this amphora complements that from Saré Omér, which is either late SPG or Subgeometric. In a more recent attempt to deal with the same transition at Troy, in 1998, Dirk Lenz and his collaborators published the "Protogeometric" pottery of Troy.[10] In dealing with this material, the authors clearly state: "Since the resumption of excavations in 1988, a sizable number of diagnostic fragments of Protogeometric and Subprotogeometric vessels have been found at Troia, and it was our hope that a systematic study would put both the pottery and the issue of settlement continuity on a firmer basis. Unfortunately, the majority of pieces were discovered in mixed contexts, and the stratigraphy is not especially helpful in most cases in pinpointing a date."[11] Elsewhere they state: "Most of the Protogeometric sherds were discovered in stratified Hellenistic or Roman layers."[12]

Despite this poor stratigraphy, the authors create four "groups" and from there they neatly date the "Protogeometric" pottery from Troy. But the lack of stratigraphy is not the only issue. Another equally serious problem is that their "Protogeometric" pottery is, almost exclusively, made up of neck-handled amphoras.[13] A glimpse at a fully published Early Iron Age cemetery site in the north Aegean, Torone in Chalkidike, not only shows that the amphora is the most popular shape, but that there are, among 134 tombs, seven neck-handled amphoras, 12 belly-handled amphoras, one shoulder-handled amphora, 11 belly-and-shoulder-handled amphoras, and 53 amphoras of uncertain type.[14] The popularity of the amphora at the Early Iron Age cemetery at Torone is, in part, due to the fact that amphoras were ideal containers for cremated remains (of the 134 tombs at Torone, only 16 were inhumations), a phenomenon also seen in Early Iron Age Athens, where amphoras of different types were standard as cinerary urns.[15] In contrast, at a fully published settlement site in the north Aegean, Kastanas on the Axios River, amphoras are not as numerous; they are, however, found as various types, mostly in the closing stages of the Late Bronze Age and the Early Iron Age levels, including belly-handled and neck-handled, in addition to hydriai (in fragmentary form, the latter are often difficult to distinguish from belly-handled amphoras).[16]

One more feature of amphoras found in the north Aegean has loomed large in various discussions of Early Iron Age ceramics. In the late 1940s and early 1950s, Vincent Desborough argued that mechanically drawn circles and semicircles on Protogeometric pottery first appeared in Athens.[17] By arguing for the priority of Athens over other regions, Desborough issued a challenge that was to acquire a life of its own, as the field was now open to similar arguments, promoting the priority of one region over others in the "invention" of the Protogeometric style.[18] It is, however, important to note that the very first attempt—together with the most recent—to link the creation of the Protogeometric style to a particular region was in the north Aegean, specifically Macedonia. In 1934 Theodore Cressy Skeat, in his *The Dorians in Archaeology*, discussed the appearance of "compass-drawn" concentric circles on the pottery of Macedonia against the backdrop of northern, Danubian invaders. Building on the work of John Myres, Skeat concluded: "The foregoing argument leaves only one alternative open, and the inference is now inevitable that the concentric-circle style originated in Macedonia itself. How exactly it come to be invented is another matter."[19] The most recent challenge has come from central Macedonia and the site of Assiros Toumba, where a robust ^{14}C program, together with a fragmentary amphora with mechanically drawn concentric circles, suggests a higher date for the end of the Bronze Age in Greece, a conclusion that has already met with some resistance.[20] The validity of this chronology needs to be assessed, but this is not the place to embark on such a project.[21] It is, however, only fitting that I begin with amphoras, north Aegean in the main, decorated with mechanically drawn concentric circles and semicircles.

7/1. (ΜΕΘ 4277) Rim Fr, Large WM Amphora. North Aegean (Perhaps Chalkidic) Fig. 7.1
East Hill #274/004011 [5]. 30/5/2003.
P.H. 0.036; Diam. (rim) est. 0.250.
Single fr preserving small portion of rim and uppermost body.
Comparatively tall vertical upper neck; sharply everted or outturned rim, almost flat on top. Rim form commensurate with horizontal-handled, usually belly-handled, amphoras.
Fabric with small white and light-colored inclusions and quite a bit of mica, including some medium-sized golden flakes. Clay core and reserved surfaces fired closest to very pale brown 10YR 7/4.
Paint dull, fairly thickly applied and well adhering, fired black to very dark brown. Preserved exterior, including outer edge of rim, painted solid, with paint extending onto outer edge of rim top. Remainder of rim top reserved and decorated with one group of seven vertical or slightly diagonal bars.
The fabric is very similar to that of the larger wheelmade vessels from Torone, and this piece could well be a Chalkidic import. The shape is exactly that of the large WM belly-and-shoulder-handled jars (amphoras) of Early Iron Age Torone, though the closest Toronaian parallels have a rim diameter of 0.200; cf. Papadopoulos 2005, p. 819, fig. 112a, T56-1; p. 838, fig. 137a, T81-1; even closer in shape, but of smaller diameter, is p. 777, fig. 54, no. 4 (see also pp. 63–64, 782, fig. 59, no. 49, which is an imported belly-handled amphora rim, probably Euboian; cf. also *Lefkandi* I, pl. 107, Skoubris Tomb 56, no. 1 [belly-handled amphora]); cf. p. 840, fig. 138:a, T82-1, with a rim Diam. of 0.140. Related vessels from Kastanas include Jung 2002, pp. 402–403, pl. 37, no. 359 (rim Diam. ca. 0.150), Schicht 12 (which corresponds to LH IIIC, but dated by Jung to Early Protogeometric (FPG ["Übergang zur/Beginn der protogeometrischen Phase"]) (for a summary of the stratigraphical levels at Kastanas, see Hänsel 1989, esp. pp. 328–346); for a well-preserved belly-handled amphora from Toumba Thessalonikis, see Andreou and Kotsakis 1996, p. 372, fig. 3, no. TKA 641/707; Andreou 2009, p. 38, no. 10 (Phase 2B, equivalent to LH IIIC Late-Submycenaean; for the synchronization of Kastanas and Toumba Thessalonikis, see Jung, Andreou, and Weninger 2009); see also Kedrou and Andreou 2012, p. 433, fig. 4, KA2960; related rims from Sindos belong to the later Phase 8, equated with SPG (Gimatzidis 2010, p. 405, pl. 12, esp. no. 102, although Gimatzidis often conflates neck- and belly-handled amphoras); for well-preserved belly-handled amphoras and hydriai from Iolkos, see Sipsie-Eschbach 1991, pl. 14, no. 1; pl. 19, no. 1.

7/2. (ΜΕΘ 4325) Rim Fr, WM Amphora, Probably North Aegean/Local Fig. 7.1
East Hill #274/004023 [10]. 10/6/2003.
P.H. 0.035; p.W. 0.062; Diam. (rim) est. 0.170.
Single fr preserving small portion of upper neck and rim.
Upper neck vertical; flaring rim, thickened toward exterior, with rim top pointed.
Pale colored fabric, fine and dense, with few visible impurities and only a light dusting of fine mica. Misfired and not of a clearly determined workshop (though probably north Aegean/local). Clay core and reserved surfaces fired closest to pale brown 10YR 6/3.
Faint traces of paint on exterior, evidently fired black, but mostly flaked off. Too little survives of the paint to determine decoration.
In southern Greece, rims such as this tend to be associated with vertical-handled, usually neck-handled, amphoras (e.g., *Agora* XXXVI, pp. 694–604, figs. 6.1–6.2, 6.4), so, too, in the north Aegean (e.g., Papadopoulos 2005, p. 817, fig. 108a, T52-1; pp. 830–831, figs. 129a, 130, T73-1, T74-1; p.

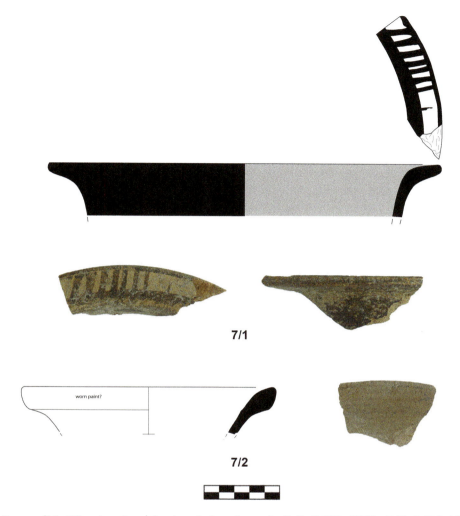

FIGURE 7.1. Wheelmade and painted closed vessels: **7/1** (ΜΕΘ 4277), **7/2** (ΜΕΘ 4325). Drawings T. Ross and F. Skyvalida, photos I. Coyle

835, fig. 133, T77-1; Gimatzidis 2010, pp. 389–390k, pl. 3, no. 24; p. 393, pl. 6, no. 46); often, there is a slight concavity on the rim interior (e.g., Papadopoulos 2005, p. 884, fig. 180a, T124-1; Gimatzidis 2010, p. 386, pl. 1, no. 8), not found on **7/2** (ΜΕΘ 4325). Unfortunately, the poorly preserved decoration on **7/2** does not assist in determining the rim type. Occasionally, the rim of a horizontal-handled vessel can come close (e.g., Papadopoulos 2005, p. 858, fig. 160, T104-1; and cf. p. 824, fig. 123, T67-1), though the closest comparanda are neck-handled amphoras; for north Aegean comparanda, see, among others, Kedrou and Andreou 2012, p. 436, fig. 6, ΑΠ 279.

7/3. (ΜΕΘ 4286) Neck and Handle Fr, WM Neck-handled Amphora. North Aegean/Local   Fig. 7.2
East Hill #274/004016 [7]. 4/6/2003.
P.H. 0.065; p.W. 0.069.
Single fr preserving small portion of neck and upper handle attachment.
Neck-handled amphora; vertical neck with prominent wheelmarks on interior; large vertical handle, with double concavity on upper face, attached immediately below rim, which is not preserved. Painted decoration establishes that the rim is near.

Fabric relatively fine and dense, with a few small white and light-colored inclusions and quite some mica, including medium to large flakes. Fabric north Aegean, and perhaps even Chalkidic. Clay core wherever visible fired close to light brown 7.5YR 6/4; reserved surfaces paler, fired closer to very pale brown 10YR 7/3.

Paint thickly applied and well adhering, fired black. Preserved upper neck above handle attachment painted solid, with paint extending down on neck on either side of handle. Two vertical stripes on upper face of handle follow the double concavity. Uppermost neck on interior painted.

Although handles of this type, with a double concavity on upper face, are standard on the north Aegean transport amphoras first distinguished by Catling (1996, 1998), and reanalyzed by numerous others (e.g., Kotsonas in Bessios, Tzifopoulos, and Kotsonas 2012, pp. 413–418, nos. 78–81; p. 419, no. 83 [one of the published examples from Methone has handles that are round in section: pp. 411–413, no. 77]; Gimatzidis 2010, esp. pls. 43–46, numerous examples, mostly Phase 7, Late Geometric; see also Pratt 2015, esp. pp. 217–220), they are also the standard for earlier (PG and early SPG) table amphoras from many northern sites, not least Torone, for which see, among others, Papadopoulos 2005, p. 777, fig. 54, no. 8; p. 807, fig. 97, T41-1; p. 817, fig. 108, T52-1; pp. 830–832, figs. 129–130, T73-1, T74-1; p. 884, fig. 180, T124-1; pp. 1078–1088, figs. 259–265. The decoration of **7/3** (ΜΕΘ 4286) indicates that it is later than the main series of Toronaian neck-handled amphoras.

7/4. (ΜΕΘ 4210) Base Fr, Large WM Amphora. North Aegean/Local   Fig. 7.2
East Hill #274/004012 [5]. 2/6/2003.
P.H. 0.069; Diam. (base) 0.124.
Single fr preserving portion of base and lower body.

Flat disk base, articulated from lower wall on exterior as shown; lower wall rising steeply. Wheelmarks prominent on interior.

Fabric contains some small to medium white inclusions and fine silvery mica; a few small blowouts, but generally fairly dense fabric. Core mostly fired gray, close to gray 7.5YR 6/1; reserved surfaces fired closer to light brown 7.5YR 6/4.

Dull black paint, thickly applied and well adhering. Thick band below a series of thinner bands at upper break (at least three).

Although the form of the base is common for earlier belly-and neck-handled amphoras (e.g., Papadopoulos 2005, among belly-handled amphoras, see esp. p. 858, fig. 160a, T104-1; p. 849, fig. 151a, T95-1; cf. also p. 796, fig. 76a, T20-1; p. 815, fig. 107a, T51-1; p. 821, fig. 116a, T60-1; p. 871, fig. 170a, T114-1; for neck-handled, see p. 817, fig. 108a, T52-1; p. 830, fig. 129a, T73-1), the combination of shape and decoration, especially the thicker band below thinner bands, is more common among neck-handled amphoras.

7/5. (ΜΕΘ 4919) Body and Shoulder Fr, Neck-handled Amphora. North Aegean   Fig. 7.3
East Hill #274/005008 [5]. 26/6/2003.
P.H. 0.126; p.W. 0.133.
Three joining frr, broken on all sides, preserving portion of shoulder and body.

Lower preserved body at break rising vertically; shoulder curving in. On the basis of the decoration, the form must be a neck-handled amphora.

North Aegean, perhaps Chalkidic. Clay with many small to relatively large white and light-colored inclusions and much mica, including larger flakes; some prominent blowouts. Clay body and reserved surfaces on interior fired closest to light reddish brown 7.5YR 6/4.

Paint thickly applied and mostly well adhering, fired red, shading to dark reddish brown

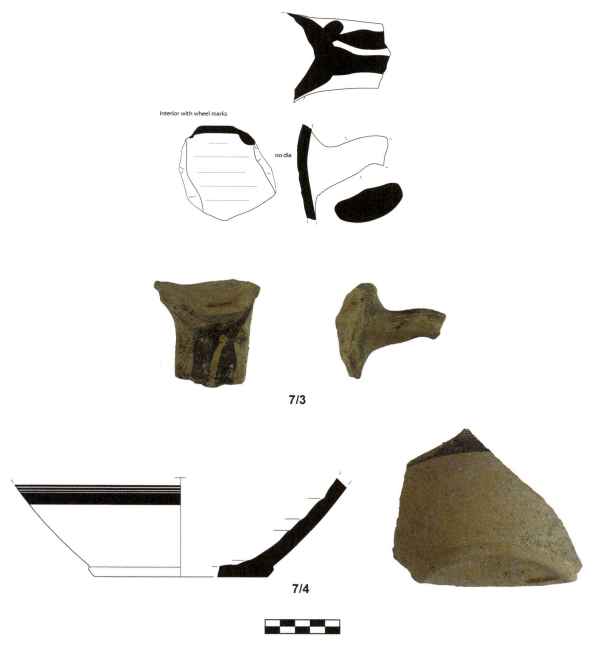

FIGURE 7.2. Wheelmade and painted closed vessels: **7/3** (ΜΕΘ 4286), **7/4** (ΜΕΘ 4210). Drawings A. Hooton and T. Ross, photos I. Coyle

approaching black at a few points. Three thin bands near midpoint, above point of max Diam.; thick band above, from which spring portions of two preserved upright sets of mechanically drawn concentric semicircles; the better-preserved right set comprising eight semicircles with small dot at center.

For similar decoration, cf., among others, Papadopoulos 2005, pp. 1078–1088, various neck-handled amphoras, esp. pp. 777, 1085, figs. 54, 262, no. 8. The decoration would preclude normal belly-and-shoulder-handled amphoras; cf., among others, Dakoronia 2003, p. 42, fig. 5, bottom left (Kynos).

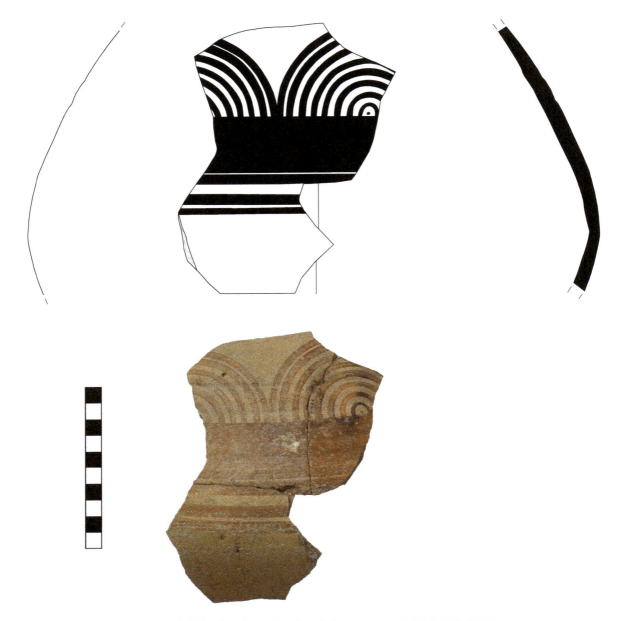

FIGURE 7.3. Wheelmade and painted closed vessel: **7/5** (ΜΕΘ 4919).
Drawing F. Skyvalida, photo I. Coyle

7/6. (ΜΕΘ 4920) Shoulder and Neck Fr, WM Amphora. North Aegean Fig. 7.4
East Hill #274/005009 [5]. 26-27/6/2003.
P.H. 0.037; p.W. 0.082.
Single fr, broken on all sides, preserving small portion of upper shoulder and lower neck.
Shoulder sloping in to neck, which is becoming vertical; juncture of shoulder and neck marked by a prominent ridge on exterior.
North Aegean/local, perhaps Chalkidic fabric. Clay contains small to medium white and light-colored inclusions and quite a bit of mica, including large golden flakes. Clay core and preserved surfaces on interior fired close to reddish yellow 5YR 6/6. Reserved and slipped surfaces on exterior paler, closer to pink 7.5YR 7/3.

Paint thickly applied and mostly well adhering, fired various shades of reddish brown and brown. Portion of one preserved set of mechanically drawn concentric circles on upper shoulder, extending over ridge onto band on lower neck; set consists of at least four or five circles and clearly originally more. Thick band on lower neck above ridge. Lower portion of vertical/diagonal stroke on neck above band and extending onto it.

Cf., among others, Sipsie-Eschbach 1991, pl. 28, no. 6. The prominent ridge at the juncture of shoulder and neck is a standard feature of most amphora types in the north Aegean; for neck-handled amphoras, see Papadopoulos 2005, p. 777, fig. 54, no. 8; p. 807, fig. 97a, T41-1; p. 817, fig. 108a, T52-1; pp. 830–831, figs. 129a, 130, T73-1, T74-1; p. 835, fig. 133a, T77-1; cf. Jung 2002, pp. 417–418, pl. 45, no. 417 (neck-handled amphora or hydria); for belly-handled amphoras, see Papadopoulos 2005, p. 798, fig. 80a, T24-1; p. 815, fig. 107a, T51-1; p. 821, fig. 116a, T60-1; p. 833, fig. 131a, T75-1; p. 871, fig. 170a, T114-1; p. 873, fig. 171a, T115-1; p. 890, fig. 190, T134-1; cf. Jung 2002, p. 398, pl. 33, no. 342 (Schicht 12); pp. 399–400, pl. 36, no. 346 (Schicht 12); for belly-and-shoulder-handled amphoras (jars), see Papadopoulos 2005, p. 800, fig. 82a, T26-1; p. 824, fig. 123a, T67-1; p. 836, fig. 134, T78-1; pp. 842–843, figs. 139a, 140a, T83-1, T84-1; p. 845, fig. 142a, T86-1; p. 881, fig. 178a, T122-1; pp. 434–437, 1100–1113, figs. 276–287. Such ridges are also found on smaller amphoriskoi, e.g., Papadopoulos 2005, p. 864, fig. 163a, T107-1 (neck-handled). Some early amphoras do not have this ridge, see, among others, Papadopoulos 2005, p. 858, fig. 160a, T104-1 (belly-handled). The vast majority of belly-handled amphoras and belly-and-shoulder-handled amphoras have necks painted solid, so the decoration of **7/6** would suggest a neck-handled amphora. It is worth noting that many later north Aegean transport/commodity amphoras lack this ridge, see, among others, Bessios, Tzifopoulos, and Kotsonas 2012, pp. 411–420; Gimatzidis 2010, pls. 43–46, though a few do, e.g., pl. 4, no. 382.

7/7. (ΜΕΘ 4211) Shoulder Fr, Large WM Painted Amphora. North Aegean/Local (Thermaic Gulf)   Fig. 7.4
East Hill #274/004012 [5]. 2/6/2003.
P.H. 0.075; p.W. 0.100.
Single fr, broken on all sides, preserving small portion of shoulder.
Fr from large, thick-walled vessel; wall rising steeply.
North Aegean/Thermaic Gulf fabric, very micaceous, with predominantly silver mica. Clay relatively dense, with some small white and dark inclusions and some minuscule blowouts. Clay body fired closest to light reddish brown 5YR 6/4. Reserved slipped surface on exterior closer to pink 5YR 7/4.
Paint fairly thickly applied and well adhering, fired various shades of red. Thick band or area painted solid at lower break. Preserved shoulder decorated with one preserved set of mechanically drawn circles (rather than semicircles); preserved set comprises at least six (and originally more) circles.
Too little survives of this amphora to determine the type; for similar decoration on neck-handled amphoras, see Papadopoulos 2005, esp. p. 807, fig. 97a, T41-1; cf. also Cambitoglou and Papadopoulos 1991, p. 153, fig. 8; Bessios, Tzifopoulos, and Kotsonas 2012, pp. 411–420, nos. 77–85; Gimatzidis 2010, pls. 43–44; for belly-handled amphoras, see Papadopoulos 2005, esp. p. 815, fig. 107a, T51-1; for belly-and-shoulder-handled amphoras (jars), Papadopoulos 2005, p. 843, fig. 140a, T84-1. The overall decoration, together with the fabric and feel, would suggest a developed date in the Early Iron Age, SPG or Geometric.

7/8. (ΜΕΘ 4317) Shoulder Fr, WM Amphora. North Aegean/Local   Fig. 7.4
East Hill #274/004020 [7]. 5/6/2003.
P.H. 0.065; p.W. 0.091.
Single fr, broken on all sides, preserving small portion of shoulder.

Shoulder curving in to neck.

Fabric dense, with a few white and dark-colored inclusions and quite a bit of mica, including large flakes of silver mica. Pale fabric, with clay core and reserved surfaces consistently fired close to light gray and very pale brown 10YR 7/2–7/3 and light gray and pale yellow 2.5Y 7/2–7/3. Fabric north Aegean.

Paint tending to flake; fired brown as preserved, probably originally black. Portions of two large sets of mechanically drawn concentric circles on shoulder; the better-preserved set comprises at least five circles.

Cf., among others, Poulaki-Pantermali 2008b, p. 32, Geometric pottery (middle right and lower right) (Leivithra).

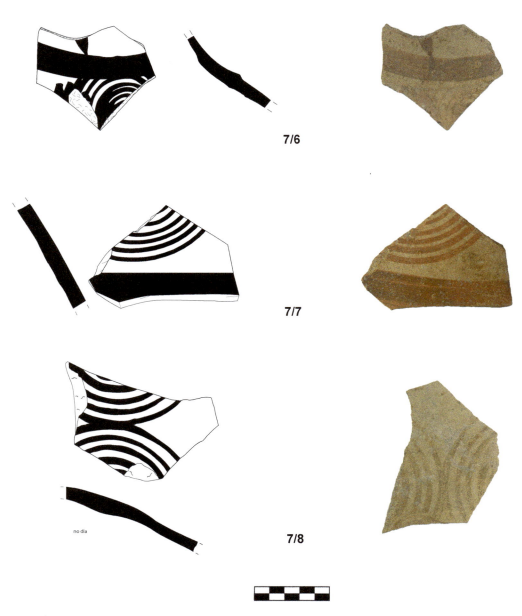

FIGURE 7.4. Wheelmade and painted closed vessels: **7/6** (ΜΕΘ 4920), **7/7** (ΜΕΘ 4211), **7/8** (ΜΕΘ 4317). Drawings A. Hooton, T. Ross, and F. Skyvalida, photos I. Coyle

7/9. (ΜΕΘ 4199) Shoulder Fr, Large WM Amphora. North Aegean/Local   Fig. 7.5
East Hill #274/004001 [1]. 21/5/2003.
P.H. 0.042; p.W. 0.074.
Single fr, broken on all sides, preserving small portion of shoulder.
Shoulder curving in.

FIGURE 7.5. Wheelmade and painted closed vessels: **7/9** (ΜΕΘ 4199), **7/10** (ΜΕΘ 4313). Drawings A. Hooton and T. Ross, photos I. Coyle

Fabric with quite a few white and some dark-colored inclusions, plus flakes of silver mica. Clean breaks, rather grainy. Clay core and reserved surfaces fired close to very pale brown 10YR 7/3, approaching pale yellow 2.5YR 7/3.

Paint thickly applied, though flaked, fired black as preserved. Preserved shoulder decorated with portion of one set of mechanically drawn circles, set consists of four circles with small dot at center.

Although north Aegean, the fabric is different from that of many other large WM painted vessels.

The decoration is standard for north Aegean belly- and neck-handled amphoras, as well as the belly- and-shoulder-handled amphoras or jars of Early Iron Age Torone, see Papadopoulos 2005, pp. 426–437. Cf., among others, Cambitoglou and Papadopoulos 1988, p. 26, ill. 38 (Torone, settlement); Poulaki-Pantermali 2008, p. 32, Geometric pottery (bottom left) (Leivithra); Dakoronia 2003, p. 44, fig. 14, top left (Kynos).

7/10. (MEΘ 4313) Body Frr, Large WM Closed Vessel. North Aegean/Local   Fig. 7.5
East Hill #274/004018 [7]. 4/6/2003.
P.H. 0.105; p.W. 0.132.

Two joining frr, broken on all sides, preserving small portion of body of large closed vessel.

Lower preserved body near break rising vertically, upper body curving in. Probably a belly-handled amphora or hydria on account of decoration.

Fabric dense, with some small white and light-colored inclusions and quite a bit of mica. Clay core and reserved surfaces fired closest to pink 5YR 7/3.

Paint well adhering, mostly fired reddish brown to brown, approaching black. Four horizontal bands near lower break. Three horizontal bands on upper fr, as preserved, which should be part of the shoulder. The belly-zone, thus defined, is decorated with two parallel diagonal lines, conceivably wavy lines.

The decoration is especially close to a series of belly-handled amphoras (or hydriai) from Schicht 12 at Kastanas, which corresponds to LH IIIC in southern Greece; see Jung 2002, pls. 33–36, esp. p. 398, pl. 33, no. 342; pp. 399–400, pl. 36, no. 346 (for an overview of Kastanas Schicht 12 and its synchronisms, see Hänsel 1989, pp. 336–337). This fragmentary vessel may be among the earliest in the collapsed deposit on the East Hill.

7/11. (MEΘ 4318) Shoulder and Neck Fr, WM Amphora. North Aegean/Local   Fig. 7.6
East Hill #274/004021-022.
P.H. 0.035; p.W. 0.047.

Single fr, broken on all sides, preserving small portion of upper shoulder and lower neck.

Shape as **7/6** (MEΘ 4920), but with less prominent ridge and clearly from a smaller vessel.

Fabric as **7/6** (MEΘ 4920). Clay core and reserved surface on interior fired close to light red 2.5YR 6/6 and reddish yellow 5YR 6/6; reserved and slipped surface on exterior fired closer to pink 5YR 7/3.

Paint thickly applied and well adhering, fired red. Portion of circular or curvilinear motif, painted solid as preserved, on shoulder at break; thickish band on lower neck, above ridge.

The thickish curvilinear decoration on the upper shoulder immediately below the band at juncture with the neck is reminiscent of some of the amphoras with tassel pattern from Schichten 12 and 11 at Kastanas, see esp. Jung 2002, pls. 34–35, nos. 344–345 (Schicht 12); pl. 47, nos. 423 (and cf. no. 422) (Schicht 11).

7/12. (MEΘ 4212) Shoulder Fr, Medium-size Closed Vessel, Euboian   Fig. 7.6
East Hill #274/004012 [5]. 2/6/2003.
P.H. 0.017; p.W. 0.045.

FIGURE 7.6. Wheelmade and painted closed vessels: **7/11** (MEΘ 4318), **7/12** (MEΘ 4212). Drawings A. Hooton and T. Ross, photos I. Coyle

Single fr, broken on all sides, preserving small portion of shoulder and lower neck.

Upper wall almost flat, curving in to neck, only the lower portion of which is preserved. Juncture of shoulder and neck articulated as shown.

Fabric fine and dense, with few visible impurities, some small white inclusions and a dusting of fine mica. Clay body and reserved surfaces fired closest to light reddish brown 5YR 6/4.

Paint thickly applied and well adhering, with a slight luster; fired black, thinning to dark reddish brown where more dilute. Portion of one set of preserved mechanically drawn circles on shoulder; preserved set comprises at least six circles and clearly originally more. Lower neck painted solid (the outermost of the circles merges with the paint on lower neck).

The closest comparanda, particularly in terms of the decoration where the concentric circles merge with the painted decoration immediately above, are a series of medium-sized oinochoai, round-mouth jugs, and small neck-handled amphoras from Lefkandi, see, among others, *Lefkandi* I, pl. 107, Skoubris Tomb 56, no. 1; pl. 126, Palaia Perivolia (PP) Tomb 3, nos. 2–3 (oinochoe and jug); pl. 135, PP Tomb 19, no. 1 (oinochoe); pl. 140, PP Tomb 22, no. 6 (oinochoe); pl. 141, PP Tomb 23, no. 4 (small amphora); the earliest comparandum may be the MPG small neck-handled amphora from the fill of the Toumba building, *Lefkandi* II.1, p. 124, pls. 37, 71, no. 353. The few commensurate frr from Eretria, all amphoras, differ in that the concentric circles are at some distance from the solidly painted decoration above, see, for example, *Eretria* XXII, vol. 2, p. 8, pl. 61, nos. 26–27; p. 11, pl. 70, no. 102.

OPEN VESSELS

I begin the catalogue of the wheelmade and painted open vessels with the familiar pendent semicircle skyphos (henceforth PSC skyphos), first those pieces thought to be Euboian imports (**7/13–7/14**), followed by the locally produced examples (**7/15–7/17**). I continue with the fragmentary one-handled cups (**7/18–7/19**), the solitary fragment of a krater (**7/20**), and a good example of a relatively neglected north Aegean Early Iron Age vessel form, the lekanis (**7/21**).

The PSC skyphos is the hallmark of an oft-cited, and arguably overemphasized, regional *koine* comprising Euboia, Thessaly, the northern Cyclades, and Skyros during the later stages of Protogeometric and in the course of Subprotogeometric.[22] On the basis of context, PSC skyphoi—variously classified as skyphoi and "krater-bowls," the latter an unhappy and inaccurate term—are attested as early as Middle Protogeometric in the Toumba building at Lefkandi.[23] The PSC skyphos enjoys a wide distribution in the Aegean and eastern Mediterranean.[24] It is, moreover, conspicuous in many parts of Macedonia from both cemetery and settlement sites, where it is among the most common wheelmade shapes during the Early Iron Age.[25] What is interesting about the fragmentary PSC skyphoi from Methone is that all can be reasonably assigned to LPG and various phases of SPG, and thus predate the arrival of Eretrian colonists in the later 8th century B.C. by several, if not many, generations, and that they include both imported and locally produced examples.

In contrast, the other fragmentary wheelmade open vessels are not as numerous as the PSC skyphoi. There are two one-handled cups (**7/18–7/19**), one very small fragment of a krater from just below the rim (**7/20**), and the distinctive shape that I refer to as the "lekanis," as opposed to "shallow bowl," largely for reasons of personal preference and to distinguish the shape from Late Bronze Age shallow bowls (**7/21**). Although many sites in the north and central Aegean have brought to light kraters, much of the material is fragmentary as it derives from settlement sites. The site of Sindos is a classic case in point, and the proposed typology put forward by Stephanos Gimatzidis is incomplete, as it is largely based on Middle Geometric and later kraters.[26] It is, moreover, a typology that is largely derivative, based on kraters from central and southern Greece, beginning with Jean Davison's seminal *Attic Geometric Workshops*, and not from the north Aegean.[27] Consequently, Gimatzidis's "Grundtypen und Varianten der eisenzeitliche Kratere" only includes tall-footed kraters.[28] For the earlier stages of the Early Iron Age, from ca. 1200 to 850 B.C., only the Early Iron Age cemetery at Torone has produced any number of complete or near-complete kraters from which a robust sequence could be traced from a flat-based or low-footed early type, through a transitional type characterized by a foot of medium height, to the later tall-footed kraters of the Middle and Late Geometric periods.[29]

The lekanis is distinguished from the krater by a considerably smaller and more shallow body, and is further characterized by a short horizontal or everted rim and two horizontal ribbon handles attached immediately below. A few examples of the lekanis from Torone are equipped with a spout.[30] The largest number of complete or near-complete lekanides currently known from the north Aegean were found in the Early Iron Age cemetery at Torone, on the basis of which two types could be distinguished: Type 1, with tall conical or flaring foot, and Type 2, with a low ring base. In Macedonia the shape is rare during the Early Iron Age on the basis of what is currently published. Among examples associated with Torone Type 1, there are at least two examples at Vergina,[31] another from Toumba Thessalonikis,[32] and a very likely local Mycenaean antecedent of the shape at Kastanas and Assiros Toumba,[33] with more recently published lekanides (referred to as *Schalen*) from Kastanas by Reinhard Jung.[34] Outside Macedonia, the basic form appears to be confined to Thessaly and Euboia,[35] although a comparable tall-footed variety is known on Cyprus,[36] and a spouted example, very similar to Torone T51-3, is known from Kos, Serraglio Tomb B.[37] Among several varieties of the "shallow bowl" at Lefkandi, the closest to the Toronaian are two Middle Protogeometric vessels, as well as an import, perhaps even Toronaian, assigned to SPG;[38] related examples from Thessaly are illustrated by Nikolaos Verdelis.[39] As a group, these Thessalian and Euboian examples are considered by Desborough to represent a probable local shape with no apparent antecedents, either in LH III or in Submycenaean.[40] A likely Mycenaean antecedent is the shallow bowl, FS 295;[41] an example of the shape was found in the Granary Class and also in the Bronze Age levels at Lefkandi (and note the examples from Kastanas and Assiros already cited).[42] The shape is very well represented in Late Bronze Age Cyprus,[43] but is virtually absent in Early Iron Age Athens, although there is an example of similar form from the Erechtheion Street cemetery dating to the period of transition from Submycenaean to Early Protogeometric.[44]

As for comparanda for the Torone Type 2 lekanides, these are clearly later: there is a near identical parallel to Torone T81-2 from the Sanctuary of Dionysos and the Nymphs at Aphytis in Chalkidike, a site that was in use from the 8th century B.C. into the Classical period, from a context that is clearly post-Protogeometric,[45] and a similar lekanis from Vergina.[46] A related, but not identical, shape is known at Lefkandi, confined almost exclusively to the Xeropolis settlement and dating to SPG.[47] A similar "bowl" is also known from Nea Anchialos.[48] At Torone, as in Chalkidike generally, the shape enjoys a long history, both as lekanis and as larger lekane, well into the Archaic and Classical periods;[49] the shape is represented in the pre-Persian debris at Olynthos.[50] There is also a related series of bowls from Chios, dating to the 8th–7th centuries B.C., and a related vessel form from southern Anatolia.[51]

7/13. (ΜΕΘ 4877) Body Fr, PSC Skyphos, Probably Euboian Fig. 7.7
East Hill #274/004035 [11]. 15/7/2003.
P.H. 0.043; p.W. 0.055.
Single fr, broken on all sides, preserving small portion of body.
Body rising steeply.
Dense fabric, with few visible impurities and no mica to speak of. Reserved surfaces fired close to light reddish brown 5YR 6/4.
Paint looks and feels Euboian, well applied and well adhering, mostly fired a dark reddish brown approaching black, with streaks of red here and there. Lower body at break painted solid. Upper body decorated with one partially preserved set of mechanically drawn pendent semicircles, preserved set comprises six arcs.
While this could be a Euboian circles skyphos (e.g., *Lefkandi* II.1, pl. 11, nos. 121–154; *Lefkandi* III, pl. 81, nos. 5, 49; pl. 82, nos. 1, 3–4, 6–8), a PSC seems more likely (cf. *Lefkandi* II.1, pl. 12, nos. 155–161) on account of the space between the semicircles and the band or area painted solid below, for which see, among others, *Vergina* I, p. 169, fig. 23, P 1 and ΑΓ 24; p. 170, fig. 24, no. T 1; cf. also p. 174, fig. 25, no. N 36; Misailidou-Despotidou 1998, p. 267, fig. 6, top left; Allamani-Souri 2008, p. 355, fig. 6 (Souroti, Thessaloniki); Kearsley 1989, pl. 1c–d (Delphi and Marmariani); *Lefkandi* II.1, pls. 12 and 49, no. 157; pls. 15 and 52, no. 294; *Lefkandi* I, pl. 30, no. 12; pl. 31, nos. 5–6; pl. 102, Skoubris Tomb 33-2; pl. 136, PP T21-10; pl. 143, PP T27-2; pl. 146, PP T39B-5; *Lefkandi* III, pl. 49D; pl. 63, no. 1 (Tomb 55); pl. 100, no. 57.1. Such a broad space is rarely found on Euboian circles skyphoi.

7/14. (ΜΕΘ 4889) Rim and Upper Body Frr, PSC Skyphos. Euboian Fig. 7.7
East Hill #274/004036 [11]. 16/7/2003.
P.H. 0.035; p.W. 0.046; Diam. (rim) est. 0.140.
Four joining frr preserving small portion of rim and upper body.
Upper preserved wall curving up vertically; sharp offset between upper body and rim; gently flaring rim, with plain rounded lip.
Fabric Euboian, fine and dense, with few visible impurities, primarily small white inclusions, and no mica, but with several small pinprick blowouts visible on interior and exterior. Clay core and reserved surfaces fired close to pink 5YR 7/4 and 7.5YR 7/4.
Paint thickly applied and well adhering, uniformly fired red, dull. Rim exterior and uppermost wall painted solid (a streak at upper rim resembles a thin reserved band, but this is probably nothing more than a streak). Preserved upper body decorated with one partially preserved set of mechanically drawn concentric pendent semicircles; preserved set appears to comprise 11 semicircles with small dot at center. All of these arcs, except for the innermost two or three, are overlapped by a neighboring set of pendent semicircles from a set to the right. Interior painted solid except for thin reserved band at rim.
For tightly overlapping pendent semicircles, as here, with broad reserved circle at center, cf., among others, Misailidou-Despotidou 1998, p. 267, fig. 6, bottom left (Nea Philadelphia); Kearsley 1989, p. 40, figs. 21a–b (Knossos); pl. 3b–d (all Thessalian); pl. 4b (Kapakli); pl. 8d (Delos); Gimatzidis 2010, pls. 8–9, nos. 61, 64, 72; pl. 14, no. 118; pl. 98, no. 709; *Lefkandi* I, pl. 31, nos. 6–7; pl. 105, Skoubris T45-2; pl. 107, Skoubris T56-3; pl. 108, Skoubris T59-2; pl. 109, Skoubris T 59a-3 and T59a-4; *Lefkandi* III, pl. 86, nos. 3, 10, 12, and top left; pl. 992, Pyre 34, no. 1; pl. 100, nos. 80.10–11, Pyre 14.1, 59.1; pl. 111c; *Eretria* XX, pl. 6, no. 15; Mazarakis Ainian 1998, p. 183, fig. 5, no. 2; see also Sipsie-Eschbach 1991, pl. 3, no. 6; pl. 6, nos. 1–2; pl. 32, nos. 16–18 (Iolkos).

7/15. (MEΘ 4213) Body Fr, PSC Skyphos. North Aegean/Local   Fig. 7.7
East Hill #274/004012 [5]. 2/6/2003.
P.H. 0.057; p.W. 0.052.

Single fr, broken on all sides, preserving portion of upper body and very small portion of lower rim (lip not preserved).

Preserved lower wall rising steeply; upper body rising vertically; lower rim beginning to flare.

Fabric not unlike **7/7** (MEΘ 4211), clearly north Aegean/Thermaic Gulf, but trying to be Euboian. Micaceous, but with few other visible impurities. Clay body fired closest to light reddish brown 5YR 6/4–6/3; reserved surfaces closer to pink 5YR 7/4.

Paint as **7/7** (MEΘ 4211), thickly applied and well adhering, but dull and matt. Mostly fired dark reddish brown shading almost to black at rim. Thin band above thicker band or area painted solid at lower break on exterior. Preserved lower rim painted solid. Upper body decorated with sets of mechanically drawn pendent semicircles, hanging pendent from band at rim; preserved set comprises six semicircles, and clearly originally more. Preserved interior painted solid.

A north Aegean version of a PSC skyphos like **7/13** (MEΘ 4877), but with little or no space between the semicircles and the band or area painted solid below; cf., among others, *Vergina* I, p. 169, fig. 23, Δ 15, P 21, AZ 16; Kearsley 1989, pl. 2a–b, c (Tsaoutsitsa and Marmariani); pl. 5 (various examples from Kapakli and Nea Ionia); pl. 7d (Kapakli); cf., among Euboian versions of the shape, *Lefkandi* I, pl. 31, no. 4; pl. 125, PP T2-1; *Lefkandi* III, pl. 50, no. 26; pl. 82, nos. 9–12; *Eretria* XX, pl. 24, no. 94; *Eretria* XXII, pl. 72, no. 121; cf. also Kearsley 1989, pl. 2c (Marmariani). For pendent semicircle skyphoi from tombs in tumuli on the slopes of Mt. Olympos, see Poulaki-Pantermali 2013a; see also Poulaki-Pantermali 2008b, p. 32, Geometric pottery from Leivithra (top row, middle); for PSC skyphoi from tombs in the north cemetery of Pydna and other parts of northern Pieria, see Bessios 2010, p. 84, lower left (Makrygialos); p. 91, top (Alykes Kitrou, "Toumba"); for an early locally made PSC skyphos at Torone, see Papadopoulos 2005, p. 840, fig. 138, T82-2.

7/16. (MEΘ 4868) Body and Lower Rim Fr, PSC Skyphos. North Aegean/Local   Fig. 7.7
East Hill #274/004034 [10]. 17/6/2003.
P.H. 0.027; p.W. 0.045.

Single fr, broken on all sides, preserving small portion of upper body and lower rim.

Upper wall curving in; rim flaring; juncture between wall and rim marked by a shallow groove creating a slight ridge.

Local fabric containing small white inclusions and a little fine mica. Clay core fired close to gray 5YR 5/1; reserved surfaces fired closer to light reddish brown 5YR 6/4 and light brown 7.5YR 6/4.

Dull paint, well applied and well adhering, fired red on exterior, dark reddish brown on interior. Preserved lower rim painted solid; preserved upper body decorated with one partially preserved set of mechanically drawn concentric pendent semicircles; preserved set comprising at least four semicircles. Preserved interior painted solid except for a possible reserved band toward upper break, which may be little more than a streak.

Clearly from a large skyphos. The form of the rim of **7/16** is close to that of some of the PSC skyphoi from Sindos, see Gimatzidis 2010, pls. 8–9 (various examples) and pl. 14, no. 118; note also the large PSC skyphos from the north cemetery at Pydna, Bessios 2010, p. 80 (Makrygialos); cf., among others, Kearsley 1989, p. 34, fig. 15, no. 84 from Kalamaria, Thessaloniki (= Heurtley 1939, p. 238, no. 497); p. 66, fig. 31, no. 223 (Volos); *Vergina* I, p. 174, fig. 25, N 36; *Lefkandi* II.1, pl. 5:i; pl. 12, no. 157; pls. 15 and 51, nos. 293–294.

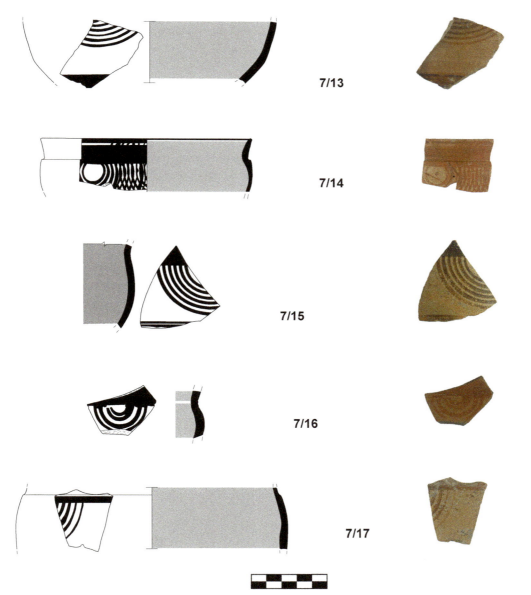

FIGURE 7.7. Wheelmade and painted open vessels: **7/13** (MEΘ 4877), **7/14** (MEΘ 4889), **7/15** (MEΘ 4213), **7/16** (MEΘ 4868), **7/17** (MEΘ 4921). Drawings A. Hooton, T. Ross, and F. Skyvalida, photos I. Coyle

7/17. (MEΘ 4921) Upper Body and Lower Rim Fr, PSC Skyphos. North Aegean/Local   Fig. 7.7
East Hill #274/005009 [5]. 26–27/6/2003.
P.H. 0.040; p.W. 0.039.
Single fr preserving small portion of upper body and lowermost rim.
Shape as **7/14** (MEΘ 4889), but with nothing of the lip preserved.
Fabric local/north Aegean, fine and dense, with few visible impurities, but replete with mica. Reserved surfaces fired closest to light brown 7.5YR 6/4; clay body closer to brown 7.5YR 5/4.
Paint fairly thickly applied, especially on interior, and well adhering, fired red to reddish brown. Uppermost body and lower rim painted solid, from which hangs pendent one partially preserved set of mechanically drawn concentric semicircles; preserved set comprises at least five arcs and clearly originally more. Preserved interior painted solid.

Cf. **7/13–7/16**, but what is interesting here is that part of the rim is clearly reserved, a feature that is generally rare for PSC skyphoi, see, for example, *Lefkandi* II.1, pl. 52, no. 294 (which is early: MPG).

7/18. (ΜΕΘ 5019) Rim and Body Fr, WM One-handled Cup Fig. 7.8
East Hill #274/054009 [1]. 14/7/2003.
P.H. 0.040; p.W. 0.052; Diam. (rim) est. 0.070.
Single fr preserving small portion of rim and body.
Small, almost miniature cup, with rounded body and gently flaring rim, with plain rounded lip.
Fabric with a few small white inclusions, but no mica to speak of; probably imported, but not clearly identifiable (perhaps Euboian, but not certainly so). Clay core fired closest to light reddish brown 2.5YR 6/3–6/4 and 5YR 6/3–6/4.
Paint fairly thickly applied, flaked and pitted in parts, fired dark brown approaching black. Monochrome decoration, with preserved interior and exterior painted solid.
Most of the Euboian one-handled monochrome cups tend to be more upright and with gently flaring rims. A few, however, have a more prominently flaring rim, like *Lefkandi* II.1, pl. 45, no. 16 (MPG). Shape and decoration are not unlike a "gray ware" cup from Kastanas, Jung 2002, p. 451, pl. 68, no. 550 (Schicht 11, which corresponds, chronologically, in southern Greek terms, from the end of LH IIIC, through "Submycenaean," and into Protogeometric), but classified as gray ware.

7/19. (ΜΕΘ 4331) Base Fr, Low-footed Skyphos or Cup. North Aegean/Local Fig. 7.8
East Hill #274/004028 [10]. 11/6/2003.
P.H. 0.020; Diam. (base) 0.048–0.050.
Single fr preserving complete base but only small portion of lower body.
Flat disk base, very slightly pushed up on underside; lower wall rising steeply.
Fabric fairly dense, with few visible impurities and quite a bit of mica. Clay core fired close to yellowish red 5YR 5/6.

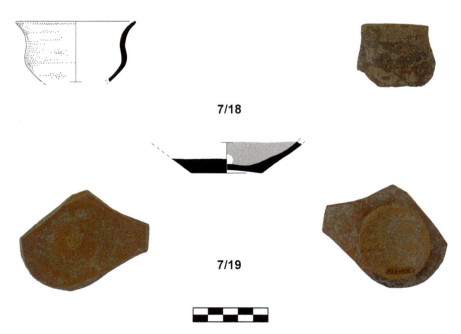

FIGURE 7.8. Wheelmade and painted open vessels: **7/18** (ΜΕΘ 5019), **7/19** (ΜΕΘ 4331). Drawings A. Hooton and T. Ross, photos I. Coyle

Paint thickly applied and well adhering, fired red, except for small area on exterior shading to black. Underside reserved; exterior painted solid except for small and partial reserved band on lowermost wall at juncture with body. Interior painted solid except for small and rather irregular dot at center of floor.

In Attica, low-footed one-handled cups first appear in Late Protogeometric and continue, with increasing quantities, throughout the Geometric period, see *Agora* XXXVI, pp. 814–819, fig. 6.33; in terms of shape and proportions, **7/19** is especially close to examples such as *Agora* XXXVI, p. 815, fig. 6.33, T16-3 and KA10 (Early Geometric), T15-26 (Early Geometric II), and T20-10 (Middle Geometric I); for similar Late Geometric one-handled cups, see *Agora* VIII, pp. 52–54, pl. 10, esp. nos. 177–180. If **7/19** is a skyphos, then the closest comparanda are vessels that range in date from EG II right through to the end of Late Geometric, see Coldstream 1968, pls. 2, 15; *Agora* VIII, pp. 46–48, pl. 8, esp. nos. 125–131. For related one-handled cups from Alykes Kitrou ("Toumba"), see Bessios 2010, p. 91, bottom left and right; for a similar cup from Leivithra, see Poulaki-Pantermali 2008b, p. 29, bottom row, right.

Other decorated frr open vessels not catalogued:
ΜΕΘ 4983. East Hill #274/005. 24/6/2003. LG skyphos rim fr. Local Euboian-style.
ΜΕΘ 4327a. East Hill #274/004025 [10]. 11/6/2003. Skyphos rim fr. Local.
ΜΕΘ 4327b. East Hill #274/004025, 029 [10]. 11–12/6/2003. Skyphos/cup fr. Local Euboian-style.

7/20. (ΜΕΘ 4874) Rim and Upper Body Fr, WM Painted Krater. North Aegean/Local   Fig. 7.9
East Hill #274/004036 [11].
P.H. 0.032; p.W. 0.030.
Single fr, broken on all sides, preserving very small portion of upper body and lower rim.
Vertical upper body; flaring rim, with the juncture of body and rim marked by a prominent ridge on exterior, corresponding to an offset on interior.
Fabric dense, with few visible impurities and quite a bit of mica, including small to medium flakes; occasional blowouts. Clay body and reserved surfaces fired close to pink 7.5YR 7/4.
Paint dull, thickly applied and well adhering, mostly fired red on exterior and lower preserved interior, dark reddish brown on upper preserved interior. Upper body as preserved decorated with one partially preserved set of mechanically drawn pendent semicircles; preserved set clearly preserves three arcs and traces of a fourth, with small dot at center.
One of the best assemblages of Early Iron Age kraters from the north Aegean comes from Torone, where a clear chronological development could be traced from a low-footed Type 1, through a transitional type, and on to the later Type 2, characterized by a tall foot: see Papadopoulos 2005, pp. 450–454. The fragmentary state of **7/20** is such that its type cannot be gleaned, but Chalkidic kraters with pendent semicircles are not uncommon, cf. Papadopoulos 2005, p. 812, fig. 104, T48-1; p. 856, fig. 158a, T102-1 (the latter is Type 1, whereas T48-1 belongs to the transitional type). In terms of shape, Torone T48-1 is closer to **7/20** (ΜΕΘ 4874) than T102-1. For the form of the rim and the strengthening ridge below, see, among others, Sipsie-Eschbach 1991, pl. 37, nos. 10–11.

7/21. (ΜΕΘ 5108) Body Frr, WM Painted Lekanis   Fig. 7.9
East Hill #274/005010 [5]. 27/6/2003.
P.H. 0.070; p.W. 0.082; Diam. (uppermost body, as preserved) ca. 0.170.
Four joining frr preserving small portion of body and lower rim.
Shallow lower wall; vertical, slightly incurved, upper wall; flaring lower rim, as preserved. Frr from a lekanis with ribbon handles rather than skyphos.

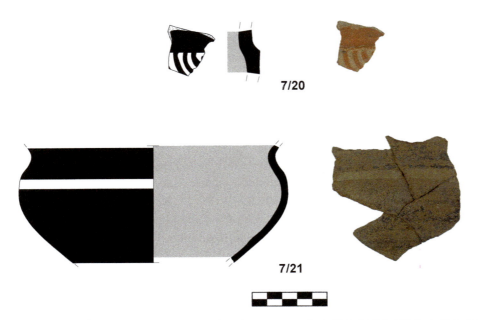

Figure 7.9. Wheelmade and painted open vessels: **7/20** (MEΘ 4874), **7/21** (MEΘ 5108). Drawings T. Ross and F. Skyvalida, photos I. Coyle

North Aegean fabric, full of mica and occasional white and some darker inclusions. Clay body fired close to brown/pale brown 10YR 5/3–6/3; reserved and slipped surfaces paler, fired closer to light gray/very pale brown 10YR 7/2–7/3.

Paint rather thickly applied, but much peeled on exterior, better adhering on interior, fired black. Exterior painted solid except for reserved band on uppermost body, just below juncture with rim; preserved interior painted solid.

For a typology of the shape from Torone, with comparanda from other sites, see Papadopoulos 2005, pp. 447–450; among others, cf. esp. p. 865, fig. 164g, T108-7, which must be fairly early in the period of the use of the cemetery; for an import from the north Aegean to Lefkandi, probably misdated by the excavators, see *Lefkandi* I, pp. 181, 353, pl. 181, T24-1 (dated SPG II, but it should be earlier, LPG-SPG I).

A NOTE ON HANDMADE MATT-PAINTED POTTERY

The quantity of bona fide handmade matt-painted vessels at Methone in comparison to other wares, wheelmade and handmade, is not great, unlike in parts of western Thessaly, western Macedonia, Epirus, and Illyria. Most of the preserved fragments should be Late Bronze and some are Early Iron Age in date, to judge from comparanda. Among the more than 50 pieces from the Hypogeion alone—most of which are fragmentary and many residual—some are early, perhaps as early as the Middle Bronze Age, but the majority should date to the Late Bronze and Early Iron Age. Distinguishing between Late Bronze Age and Early Iron Age matt-painted pottery on the basis of style alone is not straightforward in the current state of knowledge. Consequently, it was decided that all the matt-painted handmade pottery would be presented together by Trevor Van Damme in Chapter 5.

HANDMADE BURNISHED POTTERY (NORTH AEGEAN/LOCAL)

The handmade pottery of Early Iron Age Methone—like the handmade wares of any site in the north Aegean—is perhaps the most distinctive aspect of the local potters' craft and includes some of the finest products of the local ceramic tradition. The strong local—north Aegean—character of this material is its most enduring feature, but however closely the local handmade ware of Methone adheres to a Macedonian tradition, there are certain noteworthy differences between it and the wares of other northern sites. This is hardly surprising as Macedonia covers a large and diverse geographical area, and the influences and trends current at a coastal site near the deltas of several major rivers—the Haliakmon, Loudias, Axios—would naturally be different from those of mounds in central and western Macedonia.[52] This aspect is not peculiar to Methone. As Ken Wardle has noted, few of the pots from Assiros have exact parallels in both shape and decoration to those from sites farther north or east.[53] Indeed, comparisons of material from Assiros in the Langadas Basin and Kastanas on the Axios River have yielded some important differences.[54] Perhaps the most striking feature of Methone is the strong influence from central and southern Greece that continues from the Bronze Age into the Protogeometric period, with the result that both wheelmade and handmade wares are common. As already noted, quantifying this on the basis of the excavations of 2003–2013 is not currently possible, though the more recent excavations on the West Hill (2014–2017) will go a long way in shedding light on this issue. The quantitative study of the pottery from the Kastanas settlement revealed that 64% of the total at that site was handmade, though in certain periods in the Early Iron Age it was as high as 88%.[55] In the Vergina tombs, only 58 wheelmade vessels were encountered among the 544 excavated by Manolis Andronikos, or about 90% handmade,[56] while at the settlement of Assiros, as Wardle states, "no Protogeometric imports or imitations or any other wheelmade ware was found in this level (Early Iron Age Phase 2), apart from the Mycenaean survivals."[57]

A detailed study of trends, developments, connections, and influences in the various parts of Macedonia is presented by Alix Hochstetter in a meticulous study of the handmade pottery of Kastanas. Hochstetter notes similar basic lines in the development of handmade wares in central Macedonia, as well as in eastern Macedonia and Thrace, whereas the situation in western Macedonia appears to reveal closer links with Epirus and northwest Greece, with similar connections also noted for northern Thessaly during the Early Iron Age.[58]

Against such a backdrop, the local situation at Methone is interesting: the distinctive burnishing of the handmade pottery, especially that on the open shapes, together with differences in details of shape of individual vessel forms from those of other Macedonia sites, are noted accordingly. Certain shapes well represented all over Macedonia are conspicuously absent in the redeposited material on the East Hill. Here, the dearth of handmade jugs with cutaway necks, a prominent vessel form in Early Iron Age Macedonia, is noteworthy. At nearby Vergina—no more than 30 km to the west—the jug with cutaway neck is the most common and most characteristic vessel form of the Early Iron Age, accounting for 236 of the 544 vases excavated by Andronikos (just over 43% of the total).[59] To what extent this impression at Methone is determined by redeposited material is difficult at present to evaluate, but more recent excavations at the site have only complicated the issue. There is, for example, a magnificent intact handmade jug with cutaway neck from one of the tombs of the Late Bronze Age on the West Hill, **6/56** (ΜΕΘ 4069) in Tomb 10 (see Chapter 6), together with Mycenaean-style pots. Had this jug been found by itself in a tomb, I would have no hesitation in assigning it to the Early Iron Age, but here it is, in a full-fledged Late Bronze Age context. Similarly, the Early Iron Age levels in the 2014–2017 excavations on the West Hill confirm that handmade jugs with cutaway necks are rare indeed.

Incised decoration, frequent elsewhere in the north during the Late Bronze and Early Iron Ages, is rare at Methone, as are various grooved, channeled, and relief wares that once dominated discussions of early Macedonia and conjured up notions of northern invaders.[60] As both Wardle and Bernhard Hänsel have noted, many of the new traits of decoration belong to a broad spectrum of pottery groups encountered over a wide area, from the middle Danube to the Black Sea, and from the Troad to Macedonia, which develop at the end of the Bronze Age.[61] Among other types of decoration, the channeled "Lausitz" pottery inspired Walter Heurtley to see an influence on Macedonian ceramics, by way of direct invaders, an idea that Wardle and others have laid to rest.[62]

However notable these differences and variations may appear, it is clear, nevertheless, that the Early Iron Age handmade pottery of Methone owes a great deal to the Macedonian Bronze Age tradition, especially in the matter of overall shapes, which is perhaps best seen when comparing ceramic assemblages from Macedonian sites with those of areas beyond.[63] At Assiros, Wardle noted certain links with the lower Danube and Bulgaria, as well as similarities and differences with other Macedonian sites; he emphasizes, however, that these are influences only, which modified rather than supplanted existing pottery types, and he concluded that the Early Iron Age potters of Assiros were descended from Macedonian Bronze Age ancestors.[64] At Kastanas, certain links with sites in the former southern Yugoslavia are attested in the Early Iron Age on the basis of the distribution of certain shapes, with the Axios River usually considered as the primary means of communication,[65] but direct links with other neighboring regions, including the former southwest Yugoslavia, Albania, Bulgaria, and Romania, were limited.[66] At both sites, contacts with central and southern Greece in the Early Iron Age were far less pronounced than those of coastal sites like Methone or Torone.[67] But however strong the influences from the south were at Methone, the local handmade tradition maintained a vigorous and independent trajectory.

At other sites in the north Aegean, direct contacts with settlements in the region are attested by the presence of imported handmade vessels. This is true for both inland sites, like Assiros, and coastal sites like Torone.[68] The fabric of the handmade pottery of Methone presented below is not all standard, and differences are noted in the catalogue below. It remains difficult, however, on the basis of visual inspection alone, to isolate elements diagnostic enough to establish more precisely from which quarter of the north their origin derives. This is especially exacerbated at Methone by the fragmentary nature of the material, with the result that similarities and differences in overall shape and proportions with similar vessel forms from other sites are more difficult to ascertain. The very few examples of handmade jugs with cutaway neck, already noted, may well be imports. In the case of Methone, influences and imports could both arrive overland, via the several large rivers that empty out into the Thermaic Gulf and form veritable corridors for the movement of commodities, people, and ideas, or by sea from various parts of the Aegean and the Mediterranean beyond.

CLOSED SHAPES

Among the handmade burnished closed shapes, only one vessel form is easily distinguished, the handmade jar, which comes in various sizes. Although these jars of Early Iron Age Methone show affinities with examples from, among other sites, Vergina, Kastanas, Torone, Koukos, and, to a lesser extent, Assiros, their fragmentary nature impedes a more detailed comparison.[69] The Methone jars also recall a few of the earlier, Bronze Age, jars (*Töpfe*) of Agios Mamas, and in the catalogue below I refer to a few of these.[70] One site with which the differences are stark is nearby Sindos/Anchialos. There, handmade jars are rare, and the few examples are of quite different forms; to what extent this is a result of diachronic differences—the Sindos material being largely later—is difficult to establish, as the Methone pieces are not only fragmentary, but many cannot be dated more precisely than Early Iron Age.[71] Comparisons with those sites already named, however, clearly show that the Methone examples are, in the main, earlier than those from Sindos.

7/22. (ΜΕΘ 4207) Rim and Neck Fr, HM Jar Fig. 7.10
East Hill #274/004011 [5]. 30/5/2003.
P.H. 0.054; p.W. 0.061; Diam. (rim) est. ca. 0.130.
Single fr preserving small portion of rim and neck.
Vertical neck; flaring rim, terminating in plain rounded lip, slightly flat on top.
Fabric comparatively fine and dense, with few visible impurities, except for quite a dusting of fine mica. Clay core and most of interior surface fired gray, closest to reddish gray 2.5YR 5/1; part of exterior surface closer to reddish brown 5YR 5/3–5/4.
Surfaces nicely burnished, with tooling marks much more prominent on interior, mostly horizontal; tooling marks more vertical, but smoothed on exterior.
Cf., among others, *Vergina* I, p. 205, fig. 44, E 9; Hochstetter 1984, pl. 119, no. 12 (Schicht 10, PG); pl. 120, nos. 2, 10, 12 (all Schicht 10); pl. 122, no. 4 (Schicht 10); pl. 142, no. 1 (Schicht 9, equivalent to the Geometric period in central or southern Greece); shape reminiscent of some of the Early Iron Age handmade jars at Torone, Papadopoulos 2005, p. 810, fig. 102a, T46-1; p. 828, fig. 126a, T70-1; p. 887, fig. 184a, T128-1. Cf. also Horejs 2007a, pl. 108, no. 3915 (Schicht 1+0 = still containing some material of the latest stages of LH IIIC), though the neck of **7/22** is not as tall.

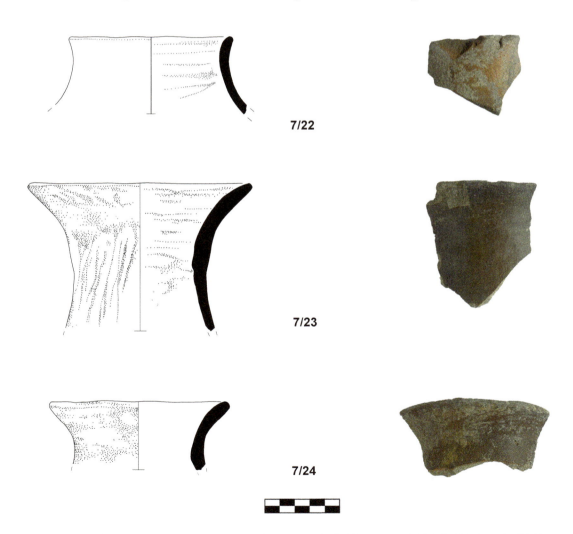

FIGURE 7.10. Handmade burnished closed vessels: **7/22** (ΜΕΘ 4207), **7/23** (ΜΕΘ 4279), **7/24** (ΜΕΘ 4271). Drawings A. Hooton, photos I. Coyle

7/23. (ΜΕΘ 4279) Rim and Upper Body Fr, HM Jar Fig. 7.10
East Hill #274/004013 [5]. 3/6/2003.
P.H. 0.100; Diam. (rim) ca. 0.140.
Single fr preserving small portion of rim and upper body.
Uppermost wall sloping in to vertical neck and gently flaring rim, tapering toward rim, which is cut and flat on top.
Clay coarser than for the open vessels, with small and occasional larger white inclusions and a dusting of fine mica. Clay core and surfaces mostly fired close to reddish yellow 5YR 6/6 on interior; ranging between reddish brown 5YR 5/4 and dark reddish brown 5YR 4/2 on exterior.
Surfaces burnished, with tooling marks running mainly horizontally on interior, vertically for most of exterior.
Cf. Hochstetter 1984, pl. 109, no. 4 (Kastanas, Schicht 11, LH IIIC into PG); pl. 119, no. 13 (Schicht 10, PG); pl. 130, no. 8 (Schicht [9]–10); the proportions of the neck and rim are not unlike the hydria, *Vergina* I, p. 210, fig. 49, E 24; Papadopoulos 2005, p. 818, fig. 109b, T53-2; not unlike Wardle 1980, p. 258, fig. 17, no. 45 from Assiros, but with a more flaring rim. Although **7/23** resembles some of the jars of Agios Mamas Schicht 13 (the closing stages of the Middle Bronze Age), such as Horejs 2007a, pl. 1, no. 4103 (cf. also *Argissa-Magoula* IV, pl. 78, no. 5; pl. 109, no. 7), **7/23** does not have a neck as tall; its proportions, together with the flaring of the rim, are closer to examples from Agios Mamas Schicht 1+0 (which still contains the latest of the LH IIIC pottery), e.g., Horejs 2007a, pl. 108, no. 4039. A date, therefore, at the very end of the Bronze Age or during the transition to the Early Iron Age is likely.

7/24. (ΜΕΘ 4271) Rim and Upper Body Fr, Small HM Jar Fig. 7.10
East Hill #274/004009 [4]. 30/5/2003.
P.H. 0.047; p.W. 0.098; Diam. (rim) est. 0.120.
Single fr preserving small portion of rim and upper body.
Shape as **7/23** (ΜΕΘ 4279).
Clay as **7/23** (ΜΕΘ 4279), but with clay core fired gray 7.5YR 6/1; outer core closer to light red 2.5YR 6/6 and reddish yellow 5YR 6/6; surfaces mostly fired close to dark reddish gray 5YR 4/2.
Surfaces burnished, with visible tooling marks mainly horizontal on interior and exterior.
Cf. Hochstetter 1984, pl. 109, no. 5 (Kastanas, Schicht 11, LH IIIC into PG); pl. 142, no. 2 (Schicht 9, equivalent to the Geometric period in central or southern Greece); also pl. 167, no. 6 (Schicht 8, equivalent to Late Geometric in central and southern Greek terms); cf. also *Vergina* I, p. 192, fig. 38, A 13.

7/25. (ΜΕΘ 4280) Rim and Upper Body Fr, Large HM Jar Fig. 7.11
East Hill #274/004013 [5]. 3/6/2003.
P.H. 0.057; p.W. 0.139; Diam. (rim) est. 0.310.
Single fr preserving small portion of rim.
Upper neck as preserved vertical; flaring rim, with lip cut flat on top.
Fabric as **7/23** (ΜΕΘ 4279); surfaces mainly fired close to reddish gray 5YR 5/2.
Surfaces burnished, with tooling marks running mainly horizontally on interior; vertically on exterior.
Cf., among others, Hochstetter 1984, pl. 120, no. 1 (Schicht 10, PG); pl. 130, no. 9 (Schicht 10–[11]); pl. 131, no. 6 (Schicht 10–[11]); and esp. pl. 142, no. 7 (Schicht 9, equivalent to the Geometric period in central or southern Greece); pl. 144, no. 1 (Schicht 9); cf. also pl. 213, no. 4 (Schicht 5, which spans the period from the end of the Geometric into the Classical era); particularly close is the jar from Torone, Papadopoulos 2005, p. 805, fig. 94:a, T38-1; cf. also p. 822, fig. 119a, T63-1; p. 888, fig. 186, T130-1; p. 890, fig. 189, T133-1.

FIGURE 7.11. Handmade burnished closed vessels: **7/25** (MEΘ 4280), **7/26** (MEΘ 4329). Drawings A. Hooton, photos I. Coyle

7/26. (MEΘ 4329) Body and Neck Fr, Large HM Jar   Fig. 7.11
East Hill #274/004028 [10]. 11/6/2003.
P.H. 0.077; p.W. 0.104.

Single fr, broken on all sides, preserving portion of upper body, including one complete mastos, and small portion of lower neck.

Upper body curving in, neck becoming vertical, with the juncture of the two marked by an offset inside and out. Prominent mastos, as shown, on upper wall just below juncture with neck.

Clay relatively fine, with a few dark and some light-colored inclusions and some blowouts; only a fine dusting of mica, which is consistent over the vessel. Clay core fired closest to red 2.5YR 5/6; surfaces on interior close to light reddish brown 2.5YR 6/3 and 5YR 6/3; exterior closer to weak red and reddish brown 2.5YR 5/2–5/3.

Surfaces on exterior very nicely burnished, with tooling marks mainly running horizontally and converging around the mastos, where they are primarily diagonal. The contrast between well-burnished exterior and unburnished interior is perhaps clearer on this fr than on any other.

Mastoi on the upper shoulder of jars (amphoras) from Vergina are relatively common, see *Vergina* I, p. 205, fig. 44, E 9, A 16; p. 206, fig. 45, no. A 24 (= Radt 1974, p. 35, nos. 28–31); also the mastos on the jar with incised decoration, p. 192, fig. 38, A 13; cf. also from Vergina, Petsas 1961–1962, pl. 103α, left (III Λ 83); pl. 149β–γ. The shape, including the mastos, though less so the fabric, is close to Toronaian handmade jars, see especially Papadopoulos 2005, p. 853, fig. 156a, T100-1, though the mastos is not as high on the shoulder; for a handmade hydria/jar with mastoi on the upper shoulder from the north cemetery at Pydna, see Bessios 2010, p. 90, top (Makrygialos); see also the handmade hydria with a mastos high on the shoulder in *Vergina* I, p. 210, fig. 49, E 24; Radt 1974, pl. 36, nos. 12, 14.

7/27. (ΜΕΘ 4208) Base Fr, HM Closed Vessel (Jar) Fig. 7.12
East Hill #274/004011 [5]. 30/5/2003.
P.H. 0.059; p.L. (max): 0.113; Diam. (base) est. 0.080.
Five joining frr preserving small portion of base and lower body.
Base flat; lower wall rising at angle of about 45º.
Fabric comparatively fine and dense, with few visible impurities, except for occasional small white inclusions and quite a dusting of fine mica. Clay body fired darker gray, close to dark reddish gray 2.5YR 3/1–4/1; surfaces lighter, closer to reddish gray 2.5YR 5/1.
Exterior surfaces burnished; visible tooling marks on lower wall running vertically and diagonally; not clearly visible on underside. Interior not burnished.

FIGURE 7.12. Handmade burnished closed vessels: **7/27** (ΜΕΘ 4208), **7/28** (ΜΕΘ 4209).
Drawings A. Hooton and T. Ross, photos I. Coyle

For the form of the base, cf. esp. *Vergina* I, p. 205, fig. 44, E 4. Cf., among others from Torone, Papadopoulos 2005, p. 853, fig. 156a, T100-1; p. 890, fig. 189, T133-1; the form of the base is closer to some of the handmade jugs with cutaway neck from Torone, though as a group, the lower walls of the Torone jugs tend to rise more steeply, cf., among others, Papadopoulos 2005, p. 800, fig. 82c, T26-3; p. 826, fig. 124b, T68-2; p. 828, fig. 126b, T70-2; p. 830, fig. 129b, T73-2; p. 832, fig. 130c, T74-2. Unfortunately, relatively few bases are preserved among the more fragmentary settlement material from Kastanas.

7/28. (ΜΕΘ 4209) Base and Lower Body Fr, HM Closed Vessel (Jar)   Fig. 7.12
East Hill #274/004011 [5]. 30/5/2003.
P.H. 0.039; p.L. (max): 0.080; Diam. (base) est. 0.080–0.090.
Single fr, broken on all sides, preserving small portion of base and lower body.
Shape as **7/27** (ΜΕΘ 4208).
Fabric as **7/27**, but oxidized (red), with a light maroon tinge, not unlike pale red 10R 6/3.
Underside and lower body burnished smooth; interior not burnished.
The form of the base is not unlike the handmade hydria, *Vergina* I, p. 210, fig. 49, E 24; cf. also, from Torone, Papadopoulos 2005, p. 795, figs. 74–75, T18-1, T19-1; p. 810, fig. 102a, T46-1; p. 851, fig. 153, T97-1; p. 878, fig. 174a, T118-1; cf. also the coarse ware wheelmade jar, p. 794, fig. 73, T17-1.

OPEN SHAPES

One of the most characteristic shapes of the local handmade repertoire is the kantharos with vertical handles surmounted by disk knobs (**7/29–7/37**, and cf. **7/38**). The form is well represented in Early Iron Age tombs in Pieria since the Protogeometric period. An example of such a kantharos was found in Tomb 216 in the north cemetery of Pydna, in association with a Euboian pendent semicircle skyphos, and another was found in an Early Iron Age tomb at Leivithra.[72] At nearby Vergina, this type of kantharos is the second most popular after the jug with cutaway neck, with 99 examples among the tombs excavated by Andronikos (a little over 18% of all pottery); Andronikos refers to vessels of this type as "δίωτα μὲ δισκόμορφον ἀπόληξιν λαβῶν."[73] Numerous additional examples from Vergina were published by Photios Petsas.[74] At Torone there is a solitary example of a two-handled kantharos, and an identical vessel but with only one handle (referred to as a cup/kyathos).[75] Both of the Torone examples are early, with the kantharos among the earliest vessels encountered in the cemetery, Final Mycenaean or Submycenaean on account of the stratigraphical interrelations of tombs 6 and 7. One- and two-handled versions of the shape are also found at Koukos, Sykia.[76] The Torone examples differ from those at Vergina in that the latter, together with the examples from Methone presented below, invariably have offset rims, some of which are quite tall (the rims on the Torone examples are incurved, thickened, and obliquely cut). Elsewhere in Macedonia, verifiable two-handled versions of the shape are occasionally found: a few examples from Konstantia Almopias and the cemetery at Stavroupolis northwest of Thessaloniki may be cited; a more fragmentary example from Arnissa in western Macedonia could be from a one- or two-handled version of the shape.[77] There are also several two-handled bowls that date to the very latest stages of the Early Iron Age, and some dating after 700 B.C.[78] This handle type does not appear to predate the onset of the Early Iron Age, although a possible Bronze Age candidate, heavily decorated with incision and dating to the 16th century B.C., is offered by a single fragment from Kastanas.[79]

The one-handled version of the shape appears to have a somewhat wider distribution in Macedonia than its two-handled counterpart (although many examples are fragmentary and it is thus impossible to determine whether they derive from one- or two-handled versions) and, as already noted, is largely confined to the Early Iron Age. At Kastanas there is a related type that is common in levels 13 through 4—that is, ca. 1190 to shortly after 700 B.C.—represented by some 34 examples, with additional examples from Tsaoutsitsa, Perivolaki/Saratsé, Olynthos, and elsewhere.[80] It is interesting to note that at Vergina, while the two-handled version is well represented, the one-handled version is rare, with only one example, as far as I know, from the tombs excavated by Andronikos, although some partially preserved examples might also be one-handled.[81]

As for the date of the Methone kantharoi, this is difficult to establish as the material is largely redeposited. Dating the majority of the Vergina examples of the form is also difficult, given the small quantity of contemporary wheelmade and painted vessels, especially imports. The Torone examples cited above are probably the earliest we have, and the example cited from the north cemetery at Pydna is best accommodated in the earlier stages of Subprotogeometric. What is interesting chronologically is that the other open vessel forms of various types at Methone are, on the whole, later, and it is possible that this kantharos was the primary open vessel form at the site before the later stages of SPG, Late Geometric, and Subgeometric.

One other feature clearly seen on the kantharoi, and more noticeable on the open shapes than the closed vessel forms as a whole at Methone, is the distinctive burnishing, with prominent tooling marks visible, particularly on the exterior surfaces. These, together with the various other types of handles and rims found on open vessels, have a very "wooden" appearance, as if they were carved, and I wonder whether these are not ceramic skeuomorphs of vessels carved out of timber? If any place on the Greek mainland had wooden vessels, Pieria, with its heavily timbered landscape (see Boufalis, Chapter 20), certainly stands out.

Given the standard nature of the shape and burnishing of the kantharoi, and the plethora of cited examples from Vergina, Kastanas, Torone, and other sites, I have not included individual comparanda for the kantharoi entries presented below (**7/29–7/37**). I have also avoided presenting the Methone handmade open vessels forms according to a typology, as the material is simply too fragmentary to warrant such an undertaking.

The remaining open vessels are essentially bowls, what Andronikos classified as "φιαλόσχημα ἀγγεῖα." Among some 44 vessels of this type at Vergina, Andronikos distinguished two broad subtypes: τὰ ἄωτα, of which there are 32 examples, and τὰ δίωτα, with a total of 12.[82] Some of the Methone examples follow some of the details of those from Vergina, while others do not. At Methone, only one clear type can be discerned. Some, like **7/39** and **7/40**, appear to have a vertical or very slightly incurved rim, with two horizontal handles, oval or plano-convex in section (**7/39–7/40**), but such a profile only occurs at the handle attachment. The Methone examples are characterized by a thickened, almost triangular, rim, noticeably incurved on the interior, but continuing the line of the upper wall on the exterior (especially **7/41–7/45**), equipped with a ledge-lug handle or handles that can be perforated (**7/39–7/44**) or unperforated (**7/45**); the ledge-lug of one (**7/41**) is further elaborated with small "horns" on either side of the perforation. Some of the Vergina examples can have four ledge-lug handles.[83] At Perivolaki/Saratsé, examples of such bowls have incised decoration.[84] In addition to Vergina, there are a good number of parallels to the Methone bowls at Kastanas, which are noted in the catalogue entries below. At Kastanas, similar bowls with ledge-lug handles are not really attested much before Schicht 8 (contemporary with advanced or Late Geometric), and the type continues into Schicht 4 (7th to 5th centuries B.C.) if not later.[85]

Another bowl type at Methone, typified by **7/46**, is far less common, at least to judge from the preserved material. The vessel is a comparatively deep bowl, which rises vertically to a thickened rim, slightly incurved on the interior. The flat rim top is decorated with prominent broad diagonal grooves. The vessel has at least one broad horizontal handle, rectangular in section, that rises steeply from the rim. The closest parallels are two similar bowls from Kastanas Schicht 8, which is contemporary to Late Geometric in central and southern Greece; the distinctive decoration is referred to by Andronikos as φιαλόσχημον μὲ "ραβδωτὸν" περιχείλωμα.[86]

THE EARLY IRON AGE SETTLEMENT AND POTTERY: AN OVERVIEW   353

The open vessels are followed by three rather idiosyncratic handle fragments, none of which preserve any trace of the rim, thus making it difficult to determine the shapes from which they derive. They can, however, be reasonably assigned to the Early Iron Age on the basis of their fabric and burnishing, but pinpointing their date within the period remains impossible. The long and slender forms of **7/47** and **7/48** indicate that they must derive from some sort of ladle with a long handle, a shape not commonly attested in Early Iron Age deposits in the north Aegean, though a number of comparanda from Kastanas and Sindos are given in the catalogue entry. The shape should be related to both the Mycenaean ladle or scoop and the brazier, though the form of **7/47** fits better with the ladle or scoop.[87] Determining the shape of **7/49** remains a challenge, and it is not absolutely clear whether the handle belongs on an open or closed vessel form, though such "trigger" handles, as they are called by Heurtley, are more common on open rather than closed shapes, even though there are closed vessels with similar handles.[88]

Kantharoi with vertical handles surmounted by disk knobs

7/29.   (ΜΕΘ 4201) HM Kantharos, Rim and Handle Fr   Fig. 7.13
East Hill #274/004011 [5]. 30/5/2003.
P.H. (including handle) 0.082; p.W. 0.090.
Single fr preserving small portion of rim and upper body and one complete handle.
Preserved lower wall curving up to vertical, slightly incurved, upper wall; gently flaring rim. Vertical handle, thin and strap in section, surmounted by disked knob with concave upper face, attached from upper wall directly to rim, but rising substantially above the level of the rim. Rim and body marked off by articulation inside and out.
Clay relatively fine, with few visible impurities outside of a dusting of fine golden/silvery mica. Clay core and reserved surfaces fired closest to light reddish brown 2.5YR 6/3.
Surfaces inside and out nicely burnished, with tool marks mainly running horizontally on body and rim, vertically on outside face of handle.

7/30.   (ΜΕΘ 5085) Rim, Body, and Handle Frr, HM Kantharos   Fig. 7.13
East Hill #274/005013. 11/7/2003.
Rim fr: p.H. (including handle) 0.091; p.W. 0.165; Diam. (rim) est. ca. 0.200.
Five joining frr preserving about one-quarter to one-third of rim and upper body, including one complete handle. Two additional joining frr, non-joining with the main group, preserve small portion of lower body that may or may not be from the same vessel.
Shape as **7/29** (ΜΕΘ 4201).
Fabric as **7/29** (ΜΕΘ 4201), with clay core and surfaces fired closest to reddish brown 2.5YR 5/4.
Surfaces nicely burnished inside and out, as **7/29** (ΜΕΘ 4201), with preserved tooling marks on exterior mainly running horizontally.

7/31.   (ΜΕΘ 4203) Rim and Handle Fr, HM Kantharos   Fig. 7.14
East Hill #274/004011 [5]. 30/5/2003.
P.H. 0.081; p.W. 0.063.
Single fr preserving small portion of body and rim, but complete handle.
Shape as **7/29** (ΜΕΘ 4201).
Clay body and reserved surfaces fired closest to reddish brown 5YR 5/4. Fabric otherwise similar to **7/29**, but not from the same vessel.
Surfaces as **7/29**.

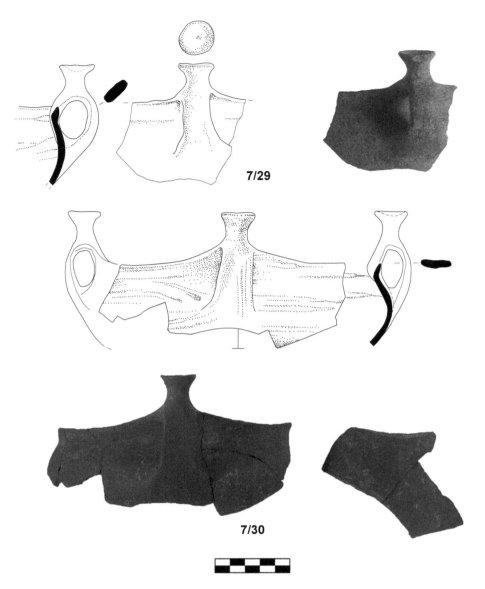

FIGURE 7.13. Handmade burnished open vessels: **7/29** (MEΘ 4201), **7/30** (MEΘ 5085). Drawings A. Hooton, photos I. Coyle

7/32. (MEΘ 4202) Rim, Body, and Handle Fr, HM Kantharos   Fig. 7.14
East Hill #274/004011 [5]. 30/5/2003.
P.H. 0.077; p.W. 0.085.
Two joining frr preserving portion of body, rim, and one entire handle.
Shape similar to **7/29** (MEΘ 4201), but with outside profile of rim less flaring and a little more vertical, with the result that the inner rim face appears more beveled. Handle and disk knob as **7/29** (MEΘ 4201).
Fabric as other HM kantharoi, but with white and dark inclusions erupting onto surface, and a little more mica. Much of the clay body, all of interior surfaces, and upper part of exterior fired/discolored gray, close to dark reddish gray 5YR 4/2. Lower preserved body on exterior fired closer to reddish brown and red 2.5YR 5/4–5/6.
Surfaces as **7/29** (MEΘ 4201), but a little less well finished.

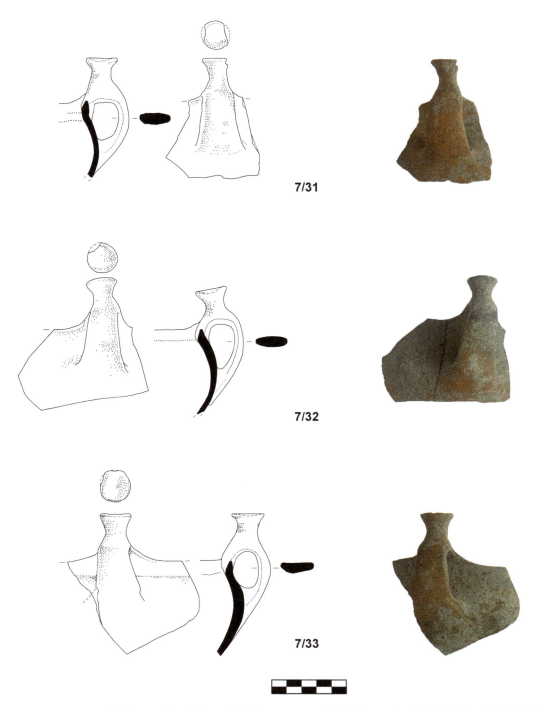

FIGURE 7.14. Handmade burnished open vessels: **7/31** (ΜΕΘ 4203), **7/32** (ΜΕΘ 4202), **7/33** (ΜΕΘ 4205). Drawings A. Hooton, photos I. Coyle

7/33. (ΜΕΘ 4205) Rim, Body, and Handle Fr, HM Kantharos   Fig. 7.14
East Hill #274/004011 [5]. 30/5/2003.
P.H. 0.096; p.W. 0.094.
Single fr preserving portion of body, rim, and one entire handle.
Shape as **7/29** (ΜΕΘ 4201).

Fabric as **7/29** (MEΘ 4201), with a dusting of mica, but no other visible impurities. Clay surfaces mostly fired close to reddish brown 5YR 5/3–5/4; clay core, where visible, a little lighter, closer to light reddish brown 5YR 6/3–6/4; interior surface somewhat more gray, closest to pinkish gray 5YR 6/2.

Surfaces as **7/29** (MEΘ 4201).

7/34. (MEΘ 4204) Rim, Body, and Handle Fr, HM Kantharos   Fig. 7.15
East Hill #274/004011 [5]. 30/5/2003.
P.H. 0.096; p.W. 0.074.
Single fr, preserving small portion of upper body, rim, and one entire handle.
Shape as **7/29** (MEΘ 4201).
Fabric as **7/29** (MEΘ 4201), clay core and surfaces mostly fired closest to reddish brown 2.5YR 5/4.
Surfaces as **7/29** (MEΘ 4201).

7/35. (MEΘ 4884) Rim and Handle Fr, HM Kantharos   Fig. 7.15
East Hill #274/004036 [11]. 16/7/2003.
P.H. 0.082; p.W. 0.052; Diam. (knob) 0.035.
Single fr preserving entire handle, but only a small portion of the corresponding rim and upper body.
Shape as **7/29** (MEΘ 4201).
Fabric as **7/29** (MEΘ 4201), but with clay core fired closer to reddish gray 2.5YR 6/1; surfaces closer to weak red 2.5YR 5/2 and reddish gray 5YR 5/2.
Surfaces as **7/29** (MEΘ 4201).

7/36. (MEΘ 4284) Rim and Handle Fr, HM Kantharos   Fig. 7.15
East Hill #274/004014 [6]. 3/6/2003.
P.H. 0.087; p.W. 0.051; Diam. (knob) 0.021–0.022.
Single fr preserving entire handle but only small portion of corresponding rim and upper body.
Shape as **7/35** (MEΘ 4884), but smaller, with less thick handle and knob.
Fabric as **7/35** (MEΘ 4884), with clay core and surfaces closer to reddish gray 5YR 5.2.
Surfaces as **7/29** (MEΘ 4201) and **7/35** (MEΘ 4884).

7/37. (MEΘ 4988) Rim and Handle Fr, HM Kantharos   Fig. 7.16
East Hill #274/005013. 11/7/2003.
P.H. 0.091; p.W. 0.106; Diam. (rim): N/R.
Three joining frr preserving portion of rim and upper body, and one complete handle.
Shape as **7/29** (MEΘ 4201).
Fabric as **7/29** (MEΘ 4201), but with clay core fired very close to red 2.5YR 5/6; surfaces, where not blackened on upper part of exterior and interior, fired close to reddish brown 2.5YR 5/4.
Surfaces burnished as **7/29** (MEΘ 4201).

Similar handle not catalogued:
MEΘ 4314

Related

The following handle, although related to those of **7/29–7/37**, is clearly not from a kantharos, but a different type of open vessel.

FIGURE 7.15. Handmade burnished open vessels: **7/34** (MEΘ 4204), **7/35** (MEΘ 4884), **7/36** (MEΘ 4284). Drawings A. Hooton, photos I. Coyle

7/38. (MEΘ 4214) Handle Fr, HM Vessel   Fig. 7.16
East Hill #274/004011 [5]. 30/5/2003.
P.H. 0.066 p.W. 0.058.
Single fr preserving almost entire handle, but nothing of the rim and body.
Wishbone handle, surmounted by disk knob; handle struts more solid and more widely spaced than **7/29** (MEΘ 4201), **7/31** (MEΘ 4203), etc., and clearly not from a kantharos, but a different type of vessel.
Fabric closely related to **7/29** (MEΘ 4201) and **7/31** (MEΘ 4203), but a little coarser, with small white and occasional darker inclusions erupting onto the surface. Clay body fired closest to reddish brown 5YR 5/4; surfaces a little lighter, closer to light reddish brown 5YR 6/4. Very slight gray discoloration at points.

Surfaces burnished, but rather more crudely than on **7/29** and **7/31** (MEΘ 4201 and 4203). Tooling marks mainly running vertically on handle struts.

Fr clearly from a larger and not as finely finished vessel as the kantharoi.

Cf. Chrysostomou 2016, p. 20, fig. 17 (bottom left). Although not unlike some of the deeper bowls with a handle or handles surmounted by a disk knob, found both in the Late Bronze and Early Iron Age, e.g., Wardle 1980, p. 245, fig. 9, no. 1 (Bronze Age); p. 257, fig. 16, no. 38 (Early Iron Age); Hochstetter 1984, pl. 63, no. 1 (Schicht 13, contemporary with LH IIIC), **7/38** is different as the handle struts, and the handle opening, are more rounded, instead of triangular. Cf. Hochstetter 1984, pl. 211, no. 2 (Schicht 6–[7]), which is post-Geometric.

FIGURE 7.16. Handmade burnished open vessels: **7/37** (MEΘ 4988), **7/38** (MEΘ 4214). Drawings A. Hooton and T. Ross, photos I. Coyle

Bowls

7/39. (ΜΕΘ 4269) Rim and Handle Fr, HM Bowl Fig. 7.17
East Hill #274/004008 [4]. 29–30/5/2003.
P.H. 0.048; p.W. 0.099; Diam. (rim) est. 0.280.
Single fr preserving entire handle, but only small portion of rim and upper body.
Upper wall rising steeply; rim thickened substantially, except where connected with handle, almost triangular in section, flat on top. Horizontal handle, quite thick, plano-convex in section, attached directly to rim, with rim top and handle top continuous.

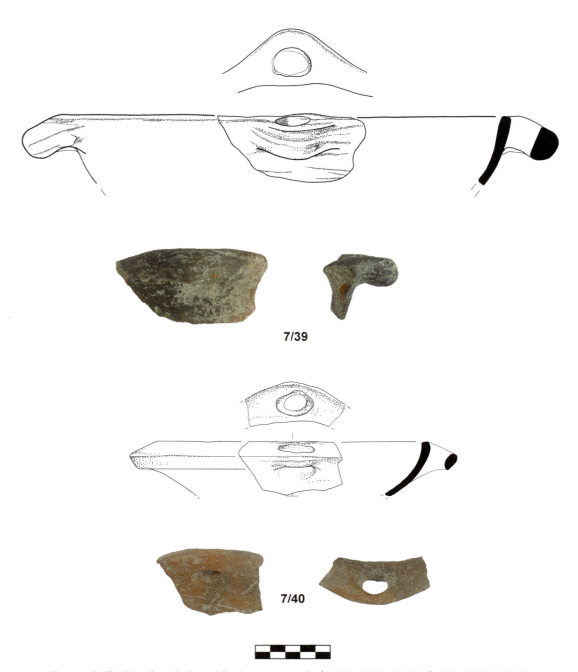

FIGURE 7.17. Handmade burnished open vessels: **7/39** (ΜΕΘ 4269), **7/40** (ΜΕΘ 4330).
Drawings A. Hooton, photos I. Coyle

Fabric semi-fine, with small inclusions of various colors, but only a dusting of fine mica. Clay core where visible fired closest to red 2.5YR 4/6. Surfaces mainly fired close to weak red 2.5YR 4/2 and dark reddish gray 5YR 4/2, shading in places to red 2.5YR 5/6.

Interior and exterior surfaces burnished, with tooling marks mainly running horizontally.

Cf., among others, *Vergina* I, p. 207, fig. 46, pl. 33, esp. Δ 6, and cf. also p. 207, fig. 46, pl. 40, K 5; cf. also pl. 38, Z 4; pl. 44, N 19; Petsas 1961–1962, pl. 94β, left; cf. also the rounded ledge-lug on Hochstetter 1984, pl. 163, no. 3 (Schicht 8); cf. further Hochstetter 1984, pl. 201, no. 1 (Schicht 6).

7/40. (ΜΕΘ 4330) Rim and Handle Fr, HM Bowl Fig. 7.17
East Hill #274/004028 [10]. 11/6/2003.
P.H. 0.043; p.W. 0.065; Diam. (rim) N/R.
Single fr preserving small portion of rim and upper wall, together with handle.
Shape as **7/39** (ΜΕΘ 4269); handle section more ovoid.
Fabric dense, with few visible impurities and quite a bit of mica. Clay core in parts fired gray, close to dark reddish gray 2.5YR 4/1; elsewhere clay core and surfaces more consistently fired close to red 2.5YR 5/6.
Surfaces inside and out, together with rim top, burnished, with visible tooling marks mainly running horizontally.
Cf., among others, *Vergina* I, pl. 38, Z 15; cf. also some of the Vergina bowls cited under **7/39**; Petsas 1961–1962, pl. 151α, middle; Apostolou 1991, p. 37, fig. 2 (middle front) from Kypseli.

7/41. (ΜΕΘ 5633) Rim, Upper Body, and Handle Fr, HM Bowl Fig. 7.18
East Hill #274/085. 5/9/2005. East balk.
P.H. 0.034; Diam. (rim) est. 0.210.
Single fr preserving only a very small portion of rim and upper body, including one complete handle. Condition good.
Preserved uppermost body curving up to vertical, thickened rim, flat on top. Pierced horizontal handle framed by two spurs or horns.
Clay relatively fine and quite dense, with few visible impurities; a little fine mica. Clay core and surfaces evenly fired close to light brown and light reddish brown 7.5YR 6/4 and 5YR 6/4.
Surfaces on interior, exterior, and rim top nicely burnished, with tooling marks mainly running horizontally on interior and exterior; smooth on rim top; area between the horns burnished.
Cf. the "horns" on the finial of the ladle handle **7/48** (ΜΕΘ 4315). For related, but not identical, "horns" on Early Iron Age vessels, see Hochstetter 1984, pl. 108, no. 2 (Schicht 11, LH IIIC into PG).

7/42. (ΜΕΘ 4237) Rim and Handle Fr, HM Bowl Fig. 7.18
East Hill #274/004011 [5] and #274/004013 [5]. 2–3/6/2005.
P.H. 0.049; Diam. (rim) 0.220.
Two joining frr preserving about one-quarter of rim and upper body, plus one complete handle.
Upper wall rising steeply; rim thickened substantially, almost triangular in section, flat on top. Rim at handle thickened even more and pierced vertically to create handle.
Fabric dense, with few visible impurities and quite a bit of mica. Clay core and reserved surfaces fired closest to red 2.5YR 5/6 and yellowish red 5YR 5/6.
Surfaces on exterior burnished, with visible, but not prominent, tooling marks running horizontally. Interior burnished smooth.
Cf. *Vergina* I, pl. 33, Δ 1; pl. 36, E 3; Hochstetter 1984, pl. 163, no. 3 (Schicht 8).

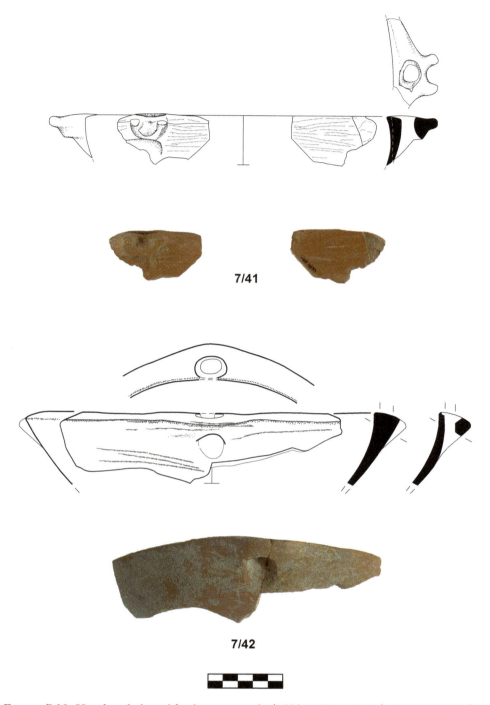

FIGURE 7.18. Handmade burnished open vessels: **7/41** (ΜΕΘ 5633), **7/42** (ΜΕΘ 4237). Drawings A. Hooton and T. Ross, photos I. Coyle

7/43. (ΜΕΘ 4275) Rim and Handle Fr, HM Bowl   Fig. 7.19
East Hill #274/004011 [5]. 30/5/2003.
P.H. 0.021; p.W. 0.055.
Single fr preserving handle, but only small portion of rim and upper wall.
Shape as **7/42** (ΜΕΘ 4237) and **7/44** (ΜΕΘ 4276).

Fabric as **7/42** (MEΘ 4237), with occasional white and some darker inclusions, quite some mica, and blowouts. Clay core fired close to weak red 2.5YR 4/2, surfaces closer to light reddish brown 2.5YR 6/4.

Too little survives of the interior and exterior surfaces to determine the nature of the burnishing, but characteristic burnishing tooling marks are visible on the rim top.

Cf., among others, *Vergina* I, pl. 36, E 3; pl. 75, AΘ 2; Petsas 1961–1962, pl. 119δ, middle. The form of the ledge-lug on **7/43** is not unlike Hochstetter 1984, pl. 204, no. 8, which also has crudely incised decoration (Schicht 6), as well as nos. 6–7 from the same level, without incised decoration.

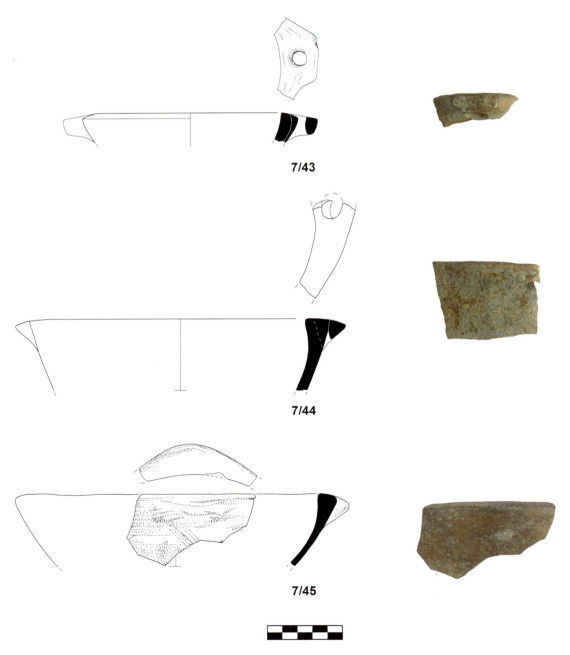

FIGURE 7.19. Handmade burnished open vessels: **7/43** (MEΘ 4275), **7/44** (MEΘ 4276), **7/45** (MEΘ 4322). Drawings A. Hooton and T. Ross, photos I. Coyle

7/44. (ΜΕΘ 4276) Rim and Handle Fr, HM Bowl Fig. 7.19
East Hill #274/004011 [5]. 30/5/2003.
P.H. 0.052; p.W. 0.070; Diam. (rim) N/R.
Single fr preserving portion of rim, upper body, and about one-half of handle.
Shape as **7/42** (ΜΕΘ 4237) and **7/43** (ΜΕΘ 4275).
Fabric as **7/42** (ΜΕΘ 4237), with clay fired closest to reddish brown 5YR 5/4; surfaces closer to light reddish brown 5YR 6/4.
Surfaces as **7/42** (ΜΕΘ 4237).
For the shape, cf. esp. **7/43** (ΜΕΘ 4275) and the parallels cited there.

7/45. (ΜΕΘ 4322) Rim and Handle Fr, HM Bowl Fig. 7.19
East Hill #274/004021-022.
P.H. 0.051; p.W. 0.092; Diam. (rim) N/R.
Single fr preserving small portion of rim and upper wall, together with handle.
Shape as **7/42** (ΜΕΘ 4237) and cf. **7/40** (ΜΕΘ 4330), but with an unperforated ledge-lug handle.
Fabric as **7/42** (ΜΕΘ 4237), with a few white inclusions erupting onto the surface. Most of clay core and surfaces fired close to reddish brown 5YR 5/3.
Surfaces burnished, with tooling marks running horizontally on interior and mostly horizontally on exterior, except under the ledge-lug, where they are running diagonally.
For bowls of this type without perforated ledge-lugs, see *Vergina* I, pl. 74, AH 16; cf. also pl. 41, K 25; pl. 61, AB 20; pl. 71, AE 35.

FIGURE 7.20. Handmade burnished open vessel: **7/46** (ΜΕΘ 5637).
Drawing T. Ross, photos I. Coyle

7/46. (ΜΕΘ 5637) Rim, Upper Body, and Handle Fr, Large HM Open Vessel   Fig. 7.20
East Hill #274/085. Στρώμα διάβρωσης (erosion layer). 14–15/7/2004.
P.H. (including handle): 0.096; Diam. (rim) est. 0.230.
Single fr preserving small portion of rim, upper body and even smaller portion of one handle.
Upper wall rising vertically to thickened rim, slightly incurving on interior, rounded on exterior. Rim flat on top and decorated with prominent broad diagonal grooves. Broad horizontal handle, rectangular in section, rising steeply directly from rim vertically. The shape is a relatively deep bowl.
Clay coarse, with small to large inclusions, primarily white, but relatively little mica. Clay core variegated, ranging from dark brown/black to red, close to red 2.5YR 5/6. Interior surface and most of rim top fired gray, close to weak red 2.5YR 5/2; exterior surface closer to reddish brown 2.5YR 5/4.
Surface nicely burnished to produce a sealed surface with a slight sheen. Tooling marks on interior mainly horizontal and diagonal; running in various directions on exterior.
The closest parallels are two similar bowls (*Schalen*), from Kastanas Schicht 8, which corresponds to Late Geometric in central and southern Greek terms, see Hochstetter 1984, pl. 154, nos. 3–4; cf. also the slightly earlier examples from Schicht 9, pl. 135, nos. 2–3, and Schicht 8, pl. 157, no. 9; and for a related bowl from the somewhat later Schicht 6, see pl. 196, no. 3; see also pl. 170, no. 4 (Schicht 7); as well as a similar bowl from Vergina, referred to as a φιαλόσχημον μὲ "ραβδωτὸν" περιχείλωμα, see *Vergina* I, p. 188, fig. 36, Φ 25.

Various handle fragments

7/47. (ΜΕΘ 5020) Fragmentary HM Handle (Ladle?)   Fig. 7.21
East Hill #274/054009 [1]. 11, 14–15/7/2003.
P.L. 0.064; W. (max) 0.037; Th. 0.012.
Single fr preserving portion of handle, including pierced terminal.
Flat strap handle, widening toward terminal, where it is pierced with a single hole (D: 0.008–0.013).
Semi-fine clay, with few visible impurities and much mica. Clay core fired closest to reddish gray 5YR 5/2; surfaces closer to reddish brown 5YR 5/3.
Surfaces as **7/48** (ΜΕΘ 4315).
Cf. **7/48** (ΜΕΘ 4315). The closest parallel is perhaps from Anchialos/Sindos, see Tiverios 1998, p. 249, fig. 9, bottom left: there is also from the same site a longer, thinner, and somewhat differently shaped handle, referred to as a "Kelle" (ladle), which looks later than **7/47**, see Gimatzidis 2010, p. 491, pl. 65, no. 535 (assigned to Phase 4, dating to the end of the Early Iron Age). There is a close parallel from Late Bronze Age Iolkos: Adrimi-Sismani 2014, p. 448, "σέσουλα" (ladle), with reference to Blegen and Rawson 1966, pp. 411–412; Tournavitou 1992, p. 209, fig. 6, FS 311 (ladle or scoop); Moore and Taylour 1999, p. 42, fig. 16 (68-1436, brazier). For an idiosyncratic handle with a large round perforation, rising steeply from the rim of a vessel classified among the bowls (*Schalen*), see Hochstetter 1984, pl. 130, no. 2 (Schicht [9]–10; Schicht 10 corresponds to PG, Schicht 9 to the Geometric period); although referred to as a bowl, the vessel seems smaller and deeper than most of the Kastanas *Schalen*, more in line with a ladle; an even closer parallel, but with a large hole, is pl. 205, no. 3 (Schicht 6); cf. also an earlier example from Kastanas, Hochstetter 1984, pl. 82, no. 8 (Schicht 12, contemporary with LH IIIC); there is also a significantly later handle, though perhaps not as long as **7/47**, from Schicht 6, Hochstetter 1984, pl. 197, no. 4.

7/48. (ΜΕΘ 4315) Fragmentary HM Handle   Fig. 7.21
East Hill #274/004021 [7]. 5/6/2003.
L. (handle) 0.102; W. 0.031.
Single fr preserving complete handle, but only very small portion of articulation toward rim or whatever it is attached to.

Flat, strap handle, terminating with two "horns."

Semi-fine fabric, with small white inclusions and some mica. Clay core and surfaces fired closest to dark reddish gray 5YR 4/2 and brown 7.5YR 4/2.

Surfaces burnished, with prominent tooling marks running the length of the handle on both sides; area between the "horns" not burnished.

Cf. **7/47** (ΜΕΘ 5020). Occasionally, handles can have horned finials, e.g., Hochstetter 1984, pl. 78, no. 6 (Schicht 12, contemporary with LH IIIC); pl. 108, no. 2 (Schicht 11, LH IIIC into PG); pl. 205, no. 11 (Schicht 6, as late as the Archaic period or later), but these are handles with a top and bottom attachment, or else quite different from **7/48**.

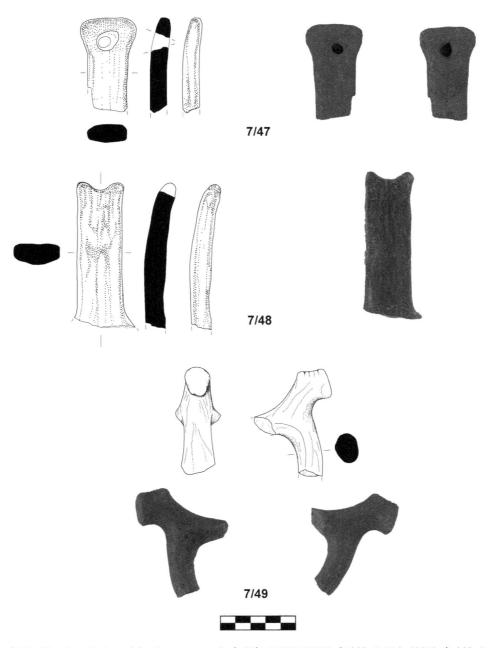

FIGURE 7.21. Handmade burnished open vessels: **7/47** (ΜΕΘ 5020), **7/48** (ΜΕΘ 4315), **7/49** (ΜΕΘ 4871). Drawings A. Hooton and T. Ross, photos I. Coyle

7/49. (ΜΕΘ 4871) Handle Fr, Unidentified HM Form   Fig. 7.21
East Hill #274/004032 [10]. 17/6/2003.
P.H. 0.073; Diam. (knob) 0.021.

Single fr preserving much of upper handle, but nothing of the body or rim.

Shape of vessel difficult to determine, particularly as this is a unique handle type that could conceivably belong to an open or closed vessel form. The handle itself is trigger-shaped. Vertical part of handle ovoid in section, rising toward knob; outer face lightly grooved. Horizontal element splays out on side opposite knob toward rim, which is not preserved. Outer face of knob circular/ovoid; upper part decorated with four or five shallow grooves.

Typical Macedonian HM fabric of the later Bronze and Early Iron Age. Semi-fine, with a few white and light-colored inclusions and much mica, including medium to large flakes. Clay core and surfaces consistently fired throughout close to reddish brown 5YR 5/4 and brown 7.5YR 5/4.

All surfaces of the handle nicely burnished, with outer face of vertical element grooved and tooling marks on adjacent edges running vertically; tooling marks essentially follow the contours of the handle and its constituent elements.

Related handles are found at Kastanas from as early as Schicht 11 (LH IIIC into PG) and continuing into periods postdating 700 B.C., see Hochstetter 1984, pl. 99, no. 1 (Schicht 11); pl. 102, no. 3 (Schicht 11); pl. 117, no. 8 (Schicht 10); pl. 147, nos. 1, 4 (Schichten 9–10); pl. 156, no. 10 (Schicht 8); pl. 169, no. 12 (Schicht 8); pl. 183, nos. 4–5, 11 (Schicht 7); pl. 228, no. 5 (Schicht 4); also pl. 253, nos. 3–4. A close parallel is the closed vessel with trigger handle from Toumba Thessalonikis dated to the later stages of the Late Bronze Age, see Andreou et al. 2013, p. 177, fig. 2b; Andreou and Eukleidou 2008, p. 326, fig. 1, bottom right (KA 2713); Morris 2009–2010, p. 66, fig. 54, 89.1113 (Torone, latest phase of the Late Bronze Age).

FRAGMENTS WITH INCISED DECORATION

As noted above, Early Iron Age pottery with incised decoration was rare at Methone. Only two pieces have been selected for presentation, and, as they were all redeposited, there is no secure stratigraphy to determine their date. Consequently, both are best regarded as "problem pieces" that could be either Late Bronze Age or Early Iron Age. The first, **7/50**, is a small fragment preserving part of a handle; the other, **7/51**, is a similarly small body fragment of an undetermined closed vessel form. Although **7/50** resembles the Late Bronze Age incised and paste-filled kantharoid amphoriskoi of the north Aegean, there is no trace of any paste in the incised decoration, and related incised decoration is found on a variety of shapes throughout the course of the Early Iron Age (comparanda are given in the catalogue entry).[89]

The small size of the sherd, together with the poor state of preservation of **7/51**, does not inspire confidence, and although I do not know of an identical parallel from the north Aegean, the fragment can be compared to a few sherds from Kastanas, dating to the period of transition from the Late Bronze Age into the Early Iron Age, and to more developed phases of the Early Iron Age (see entry below). The fragment can also, however, be compared, in a general sense, with the Attic Fine Handmade Incised Ware, common in Athens during Late Protogeometric and Early Geometric I and II.[90] Although the fabric of **7/51** is clearly not Attic, the combination of linear and circular motifs recalls the distinctive decoration of the vessels found in Athens.

7/50. (ΜΕΘ 4882) Handle Fr, HM Kantharoid Amphoriskos, Incised Decoration   Fig. 7.22
East Hill #274/084. Ξύσιμο παριών (scarp cleaning). 18/7/2005.
P.H. 0.032; p.L. 0.064.

Single fr preserving portion of handle and its attachment to rim.

Handle circular to plano-convex in section, flatter side toward the top, attached directly to rim. Probably a kantharoid amphoriskos rather than a kantharos (cf. **7/51** [MEΘ 4878]).

Fabric semi-fine, with many small to medium white inclusions erupting onto the surface and quite a bit of mica. Clay core fired gray, close to reddish gray 2.5YR 6/1, with streaks of red toward outer core, something like reddish brown 2.5YR 5/3–5/4. Exterior surfaces close to dark reddish gray 2.5YR 4/1 and dark gray 5YR 4/1.

Surfaces smoothed. Incised decoration, as preserved, confined to upper face of handle: cross-hatched connected triangles (the bottom triangle may be a lozenge); base of triangle toward rim framed by five horizontal lines.

For similar Late Bronze Age kantharoid amphoriskoi, cf. Grammenos 1979, p. 32, fig. 1, no. 9; p. 35, fig. 3, no. 1; Hochstetter 1984, pl. 47, nos. 1–3; pls. 258–259; Wardle 1980, p. 247, fig. 11, nos. 18–19, pl. 21a–b, d–e; Andreou et al. 2013, p. 175, figs. 1b–c; p. 177, fig. 2a. Cross-hatched triangles appear early on the lug handles of open vessels, together with a variety of other shapes; among others, see Hochstetter 1984, pl. 6, no. 10 (Schicht 18, transition from the Middle to the early stages of the Late Bronze Age); pl. 93, no. 3 (Schicht 12, advanced LH IIIC); pl. 114, no. 3 (Schicht 10, primarily Protogeometric); cf. also pl. 157, no. 4 (Schicht 8, corresponding to Late Geometric). Cross-hatched triangles are also common on the bodies of handmade vessels in the later Geometric and historic period levels at Kastanas, e.g., Hochstetter 1984, pl. 165, no. 9 (Schicht 8); pl. 198, nos. 3–4 (Schicht 6); pl. 226, no. 1 (Schicht 4).

7/51. (MEΘ 4878) Body Fr, Undetermined HM Shape, Incised Decoration   Fig. 7.22
East Hill #274/085. East balk. 1/9/2005.
P.H. 0.038; p.W. 0.044.

Single fr, broken on all sides, preserving small portion of body.

Too little survives to determine shape with absolute conviction, but the clearly rounded body of the fr as preserved and the less well finished interior suggest a small closed vessel.

Semi-fine fabric, with a lot of mica, predominantly small to medium flakes. Interior blackened; exterior fired closest to reddish brown 5YR 5/3.

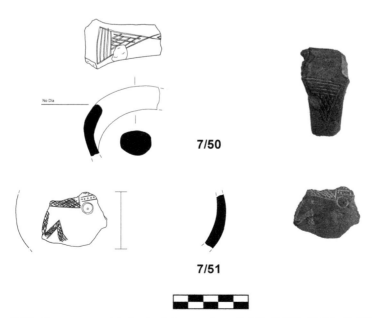

FIGURE 7.22. Fragments with incised decoration: **7/50** (MEΘ 4882), **7/51** (MEΘ 4878).
Drawings T. Ross, photos I. Coyle

Exterior surface burnished smooth and decorated with incised motifs, filled with a white substance (calcium). On lower portion of fr as preserved, zigzag defined by two parallel lines, its interior cross-hatched. Upper fr, to left, rectangle, only partially preserved, also cross-hatched. To right two parallel horizontal lines, with small dots, above a small circle with small dot at center, as if to indicate that it was incised with a small compass. Interior less well finished.

Cf., among others, Hochstetter 1984, pl. 110, no. 13 (Schichten 11–12, LH IIIC into Protogeometric); pl. 147, no. 7 (Schichten 9–10, equated with PG and Geometric).

MISCELLANEOUS

Only two types of terracotta objects are presented here: strainers or sieves (*Siebgefässe*) (**7/52**–**7/53**), and a worn and worked sherd that could have been used for burnishing pottery (**7/54**). Regarding the first category, although not common, handmade strainers/sieves are found in settlement contexts at a number of sites in the north Aegean, including Agios Mamas (later stages of the Bronze Age), and Kastanas (in various Early Iron Age levels).[91] It is worth stressing that **7/52** is very similar to **4/29** (MEΘ 4290), which is assigned to the Final Neolithic period, and it is possible that **7/52** may be an earlier, residual fragment. At Methone in the Early Iron Age, sieves are not limited to just handmade vessels, but also include large wheelmade and painted vessels, such as the Late Geometric Euboian or Euboian-inspired krater found in the Hypogeion, the floor of which was repurposed to serve as a strainer/sieve (see **9/83** [MEΘ 1343]). Strainer/sieves are long-lived, as there are very similar examples, often wheelmade, of the Classical and later periods known from houses and farmsteads in Macedonia.[92]

Of the second category, I had originally selected two terracotta sherds that I believed were repurposed sherds used as burnishers, **7/54** and **4/13** (MEΘ 4220); the latter was subsequently claimed by Marianna Nikolaidou, who showed that its context on the East Hill should be Late Neolithic (see Chapter 4). Not much has been written about terracotta burnishers made from broken pottery sherds. I know of a few unpublished examples from the non-funerary deposits in the Athenian Agora, and **7/54** is presented here in the hope that additional examples may be noted and discussed. The fragment, polished smooth all around, is unlike the cut sherds presented elsewhere in this volume (Chapter 17), and their context, in an essentially industrial district, especially in the Early Iron Age and Archaic period, is potentially telling. It is worth noting that similar objects were more recently found in the 2014–2017 excavations on the West Hill, where at least three Archaic kilns have been excavated to date.[93]

7/52. (MEΘ 4885) Frr of HM Strainer/Sieve   Fig. 7.23
East Hill #274/004036 [11]. 16/7/2003.
P.L. x p.W. 0.099 x 0.057; Th. 0.008–0.010.
Two joining frr preserving undetermined portion of object.
Body curved, clearly not flat, with two complete holes and portions of six more (Diam. of holes 0.012–0.014).
Semi-fine clay, with some small predominantly white and light-colored inclusions and much fine mica. Clay core fired gray, close to gray and dark gray 5YR 5/1–4/1; exterior surface closer to reddish brown 5YR 5/4; interior surface reddish brown 2.5YR 5/4.
Exterior burnished, with faint tooling marks visible here and there; interior smoothed.
Cf. **7/53** (MEΘ 4323). Of the cited Late Bronze Age examples from Agios Mamas, the closest is Horejs 2007a, pl. 49, no. 8710, though the holes of **7/52** are larger still. For strainers/sieves with holes closer to the size of **7/52**, see Hochstetter 1984, pl. 144, no. 3 (Schicht 9), though this was a heavier, flat-based small basin.

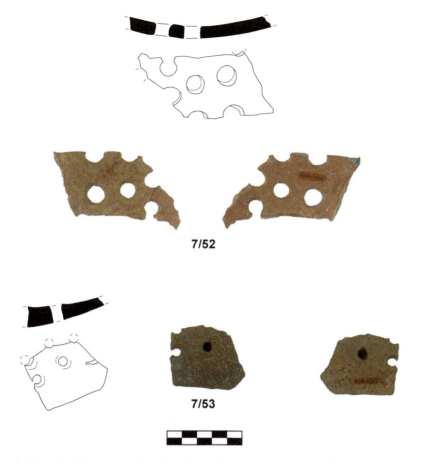

FIGURE 7.23. Miscellaneous, sieves/strainers: **7/52** (MEΘ 4885), **7/53** (MEΘ 4323). Drawings T. Ross, photos I. Coyle

7/53. (MEΘ 4323) Fr of HM Strainer/Sieve Fig. 7.23
East Hill #274/004021-022.
P.L. x p.W. 0.055 x 0.050; Th. 0.007–0.014.
Single fr, broken on all sides, preserving undetermined portion of object. Fr preserves one complete hole and portions of at least three more, perhaps four.
Form as **7/52** (MEΘ 4885), clearly handmade, but with smaller holes (Diam. of holes 0.006).
Fabric as **7/52** (MEΘ 4885); clay core and exterior surfaces fired close to gray 5YR 5/1; interior surface fired closer to reddish gray 5YR 5/2 and weak red 2.5YR 5/2.
Interior and exterior surfaces burnished, with tooling marks visible on both sides.
Cf. **7/52** (MEΘ 4885).

7/54. (MEΘ 4873) Clay Burnisher (Λειαντήρας)? Fig. 7.24
East Hill #274/994035 [11]. 15/7/2003.
P.L. x p.W. 0.056 x 0.038; Th. 0.008.
Single fr preserving portion of intentionally (rather than naturally) polished sherd.
Preserved edges and all surfaces clearly polished smooth and rounded; original vessel difficult to determine.
Local micaceous fabric; clay core fired closest to red 2.5YR 5/6.
Cf. **4/13** (MEΘ 4220), which is Late Neolithic.

Figure 7.24. Miscellaneous, terracotta burnisher: **7/54** (MEΘ 4873). Drawing T. Ross, photos I. Coyle

Cooking Pots

I have separated the cooking pots from the rest of the handmade vessels on account of their practical use for cooking, as opposed to storage, pouring, eating, or drinking. Unlike other handmade vessels, they are specifically designed to be placed on or in a fire; they are also, as a group, made of a coarser fabric than the other handmade vessels. Two broad types have been distinguished among the redeposited material on the East Hill, the first, typified by **7/55** and **7/56**, more closely resembles central and southern Greek types as opposed to the more standard Macedonian pyraunoi and other cooking vessels of the Bronze and Early Iron Age.[94] The second type, of which **7/57** and **7/58** are good examples, comprises the tripod cooking pots that are standard for Early Iron Age sites in Chalkidike—and, as we shall see, for much of the Minoan and Mycenaean worlds, especially in central and southern Greece.

The first type of cooking pot is a fairly standard handmade type found over various regions of Greece, including the central and south Aegean. Of the two selected examples, **7/55** is larger; although the drawing is reconstructed with two handles, this could be a one- or two-handled pot, both of which are common in Early Iron Age Athens.[95] In contrast, **7/56** should be a one-handled cooking pot. Unlike the north Aegean, what is interesting about Athens is that, in the course of the final stages of the LH IIIC period and the transition to the Early Iron Age, handmade cooking pots replace the wheelmade versions that were prevalent in the Bronze Age.[96] Handmade cooking pots, usually with rounded bases, are well represented in the closing stages of the Late Bronze Age and throughout the Early Iron Age in the north Aegean.[97] In the catalogue entries below I have provided parallels for **7/55** from Athens, Iolkos, Kynos, Elateia, and Kalapodi; and, for **7/56**, from Toumba Thessalonikis, Iolkos, Kalapodi, Kynos, and Elateia. At least one cooking ware vessel, not unlike **7/55**, was found among the collapsed pottery in the Early Iron Age kiln at Torone dating to Late Geometric.[98]

Although fragmentary, each preserving only one leg and nothing of the actual body, **7/57** and **7/58** are clearly legs from tripod cooking pots. The tripod cauldron, both as coarse ware cooking vessel and as a finer wheelmade and painted form, is well known in Minoan and Mycenaean ceramic history, and there are many coarse ware tripods from Mycenaean Athens.[99] The shape, in both fine and coarse ware varieties, continues to be found at a number of sites during the Protogeometric and Geometric periods,[100] and in its monumentalized form in bronze is well known at Olympia, Delphi, and elsewhere, and even earlier in the Minoan and Mycenaean world.[101] But whatever ubiquity the shape enjoys in Greece, it is conspicuously absent in the local Macedonian repertoire, with the exception of Early Iron Age sites in Chalkidike, particularly on Sithonia, and especially at the site of Torone.[102] In 1939 there were almost none known to Heurtley and, since that time, the excavations at Kastanas, Assiros, and Vergina have yielded no certain examples.[103] Hochstetter discusses a number of legged vessels preserved only as fragments; some are from vessels that are anthropomorphic or zoomorphic, while others are from vessels that bear no resemblance to the tripods of Chalkidike.[104] Against this backdrop, the 25 mostly fragmentary tripod cooking pots recovered from tombs and various contexts in the Early Iron Age cemetery at Torone, together with a single fragment from the 1975 excavations at the Gate Area of Torone, stand out.[105] In addition to Torone, only Koukos near Sykia in southern Sithonia, a few kilometers from Torone, and the Early Iron Age settlement at Lagomandra, near Nikiti, at the northern end of the Sithonia peninsula, have yielded numerous tripod cauldrons.[106] There are fragments of tripod legs at Thasos postdating those of Torone and Koukos (7th century B.C.),[107] but beyond these the rarity of the shape in the north Aegean is noteworthy, and it is within this broader context that the two fragments from Methone should be seen.

7/55. (MEΘ 4273) Rim, Upper Body, and Handle Fr, Large HM Cooking Pot　　　　Fig. 7.25
East Hill #274/004009 [4]. 30/5/2003.
P.H. 0.129; Diam. (rim) est. 0.210.
Single fr preserving small portion of upper body, rim, and one complete handle.
Upper wall curving in to vertical neck and gently flaring rim, cut flat on top. Thickish handle, ovoid in section and thinner/less wide at lower attachment than at upper, attached from uppermost body directly to rim.
Fabric quite coarse in comparison to the HM burnished jars, with numerous small, medium, and occasional larger inclusions, primarily white, and a fine dusting of mica. Clay core and surfaces consistently fired close to red 2.5YR 5/6.
Surfaces inside and out roughly smoothed, but not burnished.
Cf., among others, *Agora* XXXVI, p. 266, fig. 2.173, T28-4 (EPG–MPG); p. 371, fig. 2.258, T53-2 (LPG); p. 885, fig. 6.52, T28-4 and T53-2 (both one-handled); also p. 889, fig. 6.53, T47-1 (PG), T74-1 (MPG–LPG), T54-1 (LPG); Sipsie-Eschbach 1991, pl. 46, no. 6 (Iolkos); Dakoronia 2003, p. 44, figs. 12–13 (Kynos); Deger-Jalkotzy 2009, p. 116, fig. 15, various examples (Elateia); Jacob-Felsch 1996, pl. 19, various examples (Kalapodi); for the stratigraphy of Kalapodi, see *Kalapodi* II.

7/56. (MEΘ 4278) Rim, Upper Body, and Handle Fr, Small HM Cooking Pot　　　　Fig. 7.25
East Hill: #274/004012 [5]. 2/6/2003.
P.H. 0.093; p.W. 0.070; Diam. (rim) N/R.
Single fr preserving small portion of upper body, rim, and one complete handle.
Shape as **7/55** (MEΘ 4273), but smaller, and with lower handle attachment of the same width as the rest of the handle; upper handle attachment rising slightly above the level of the rim.
Coarse fabric, a little coarser than **7/55** (MEΘ 4273), with small, medium, and large inclusions of various colors, but a little less mica. Clay core and surfaces fired close to reddish brown 5YR 4/3 and brown 7.5YR 4/3.
Surfaces as **7/55**.
Cf., among others, Andreou, Eukleidou, and Triantaphyllou 2010, p. 361, fig. 3, bottom (Toumba Thessalonikis); Sipsie-Eschbach 1991, pl. 62, no. 1 (Iolkos); Jacob-Felsch 1996, p. 134, pl. 29, no. 121 ("Kochtopf") (Kalapodi); Dakoronia and Kounouklas 2009, p. 75, fig. 20 (Kynos); Deger-Jalkotzy 2009, p. 116, fig. 15, esp. some of the one-handled jugs (Elateia).

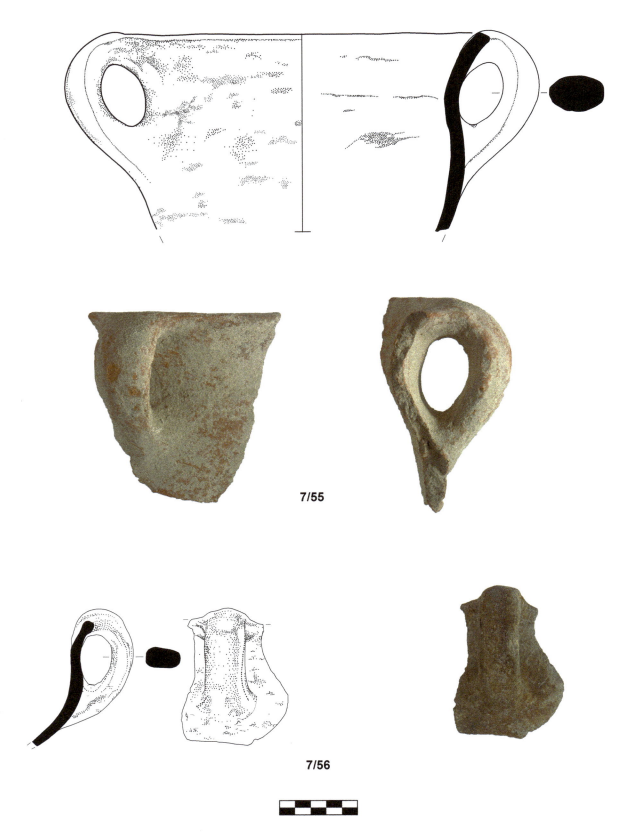

FIGURE 7.25. Cooking pottery: **7/55** (ΜΕΘ 4273), **7/56** (ΜΕΘ 4278).
Drawings A. Hooton, photos I. Coyle

7/57. (ΜΕΘ 4883) Tripod Leg, HM Tripod Cooking Pot Fig. 7.26
East Hill #274/004036 [11]. 16/7/2003.
P.H. 0.124; W. (max) 0.061.

Single fr preserving most of tripod leg and portion of scar of attachment to body at upper break.

Large leg, comparatively thin and rectangular/strap in section, rectangular in plan, but tapering slightly toward the resting surface at bottom.

Semi-coarse fabric, with white and various-colored inclusions, mostly small, some larger, and much mica. Clay core in parts fired close to reddish brown 2.5YR 4/4; remainder of core and surfaces closer to reddish brown 2.5YR 5/3.

Exterior surface burnished with prominent tooling marks mainly running vertically; inside face more roughly smoothed.

Cf. many of the tripod cooking pots from Torone, Papadopoulos 2005, p. 779, fig. 6, nos. 20, 23; p. 789, fig. 67d, T7-4; p. 811, fig. 103d, T47-4; p. 828, fig. 126c, T70-3; p. 852, fig. 155c, T99-3; p. 879, fig. 174k, T118-11; pp. 882–883, figs. 179b, c, T123-2, T123-3; p. 1203, pl. 386, T123-3; p. 1204, pls. 387–388, T99-3, T123-2; p. 1206, pl. 391, T7-4; p. 1218, pl. 408, no. 23. For much earlier, Neolithic, legs of πυξίδες or τράπεζες from eastern Macedonia, see Grammenos 1975, pp. 211, 213, fig. 4, nos. 1–4.

7/58. (ΜΕΘ 4270) Tripod Leg, HM Tripod Cooking Pot Fig. 7.26
East Hill #274/004008 [4]. 29–30/5/2003.
P.L. (= L. of leg) 0.042; W. (leg, max) 0.018; W. (max, at juncture with body) 0.019.

Single fr preserving all of leg, but nothing of the body except for the articulation toward the body.

Small leg, from a vessel considerably smaller than 7/57 (ΜΕΘ 4883), ovoid in section, with a slight concavity on outer face; leg tapering toward bottom.

FIGURE 7.26. Cooking pottery, tripod legs: **7/57** (ΜΕΘ 4883), **7/58** (ΜΕΘ 4270).
Drawings A. Hooton and T. Ross, photos I. Coyle

Clay as **7/57** (ΜΕΘ 4883), but with comparatively little mica. Clay body and surfaces mostly blackened due to use.

Surfaces are not burnished as **7/57** (ΜΕΘ 4883), but only roughly smoothed.

Cf. Papadopoulos 2005, p. 779, fig. 56, no. 20; p. 786, fig. 64, no. 88; p. 788, fig. 66c, T6-3; p. 855, fig. 157k, T101-11 (with a more rectangular section); p. 870, fig. 169q, T113-17; p. 872, fig. 170g, T114-7; p. 876, fig. 172f, T116-4; p. 1226, pl. 428, T101-11.

PITHOS FRAGMENTS

The history of the Early Iron Age pithos in the Greek world remains to be written. The storage container is fairly well represented in Macedonia from the Neolithic period through the Bronze Age and into the Early Iron Age, but few pithoi are adequately published with drawings and photographs.[108] Complete pithoi are notoriously difficult and time-consuming to mend and to store. Occasionally, a complete or near-complete pithos is illustrated, but these are usually of the vessel in situ.[109] For the north Aegean, the most systematic study of pithoi to date is that by Hochstetter, dealing with the settlement material from Kastanas, but this is largely a typology based on disconnected pithos rims and bases, and one that is chronologically limited to the Late Bronze and Early Iron Age.[110] The Early Iron Age settlement on the Lekythos (Promontory 1) at Torone has also brought to light a number of near-complete pithoi, and the Late Geometric potter's kiln on Terrace V had, as part of its collapsed kiln load, one almost complete and several more fragmentary pithoi.[111] Judging from the better preserved of the Torone pithoi, there appear to be two broad categories of pithos represented at that site: one with a wide neck and mouth, and another where the upper body curves in rather noticeably to a narrower neck and mouth.[112] The almost complete pithos from Koukos illustrated in situ is of this second type.[113] A similar division into two broad categories of pithos was noted for the fragmentary Protogeometric pithoi at Asine in the Argolid, and at Kastanas the 12 distinguished rim types were all of the narrow-necked variety of pithos.[114] As for the base, most would have been either very narrow and flat-based, or else pointed, consistent with the two basic types of base found on Mycenaean pithoi.[115]

Incised or impressed decoration, usually applied to a band or cord of clay, is found on **7/60**, and this appears to be relatively common, not only in Macedonia. A simple raised cord decorated with incised strokes or notches (rope pattern) is found at the juncture of body and neck on the well-preserved Late Bronze Age pithos from Limnotopos (Vardino, Várdina) and on two pithoi from Torone.[116] There is a raised band of clay on the body of a pithos from Vergina decorated with incised triangles, which are hatched, and another from Torone that is undecorated.[117] One of the body fragments from Torone has a thin raised band of clay with two roughly parallel rows of impressed circles, a type of decoration common on Early Iron Age Crete and elsewhere.[118] The impressed decoration on **7/60** is closest to some of the pithos fragments of the early, but unpublished, non-funerary deposits from the Athenian Agora (Final Mycenaean, Submycenaean, Early Protogeometric).

In terms of size, this remains difficult to determine given the dearth of complete pithoi from the north that are fully published. The preserved height of two of the better-preserved pithoi from Torone were 0.598 and 0.567 respectively, and both would have been considerably larger in their original state; another fragment would have had an original height exceeding 1.0 m, and the near-complete pithos from the Late Geometric kiln at Torone stood to a height of 0.720 m.[119] The complete pithos from Late Bronze Age Vardino was 1.2 m tall.[120] A pithos preserved from the base to the upper shoulder from the settlement on Promontory 1 at Torone would have stood, originally, to a height of about 2.0 m.[121] The more recent excavations on the West Hill at Methone uncovered an Early Iron Age pithos preserved to a height of about 1.0 m, but originally considerably taller.[122]

What this brief survey of pithoi in the north Aegean brings to the fore is how little we know about the shape, one of the most common in any Greek house from the Neolithic period to the 20th—if not the 21st—century A.D. In publishing Protogeometric Asine, Berit Wells remarked that pithoi were poorly represented in contexts of the Protogeometric period, but the pieces published from central and southern Greece preserve features very similar to the two fragments from Methone.[123]

7/59.   (ΜΕΘ 4274) Rim Fr, Pithos   Fig. 7.27
East Hill # 274.004009 [4]. 30/5/2003.
P.H. 0.045; p.W. 0.108; Diam. (rim) N/R.
Single fr preserving small portion of rim.
The little that survives of the preserved upper wall is vertical. Thickened, horizontal rim, flat on top.
Fabric coarse, but not as coarse as **7/60** (ΜΕΘ 4333), with far fewer, primarily small white inclusions and a dusting of fine mica. Clay core and surfaces fired close to reddish brown 2.5YR 5/3–5/4, 4/3–4/4.
Preserved surfaces smoothed, especially on rim top.
Cf., among others, Papadopoulos 2005, p. 793, fig. 71b, T12-1 (rim), but with outer face grooved; cf. also the projecting, though not horizontal, rims of the pithoi from the Late Geometric kiln at Torone, Papadopoulos 1989, pp. 29, 36–37, ills. 12–14, KP-1, KP-2. For a related pithos rim, with incised decoration on the outer face, see Sipsie-Eschbach 1991, pl. 46, no. 3 (Iolkos). For a pithos in situ at Early Iron Age Koukos, which appears to have a horizontal rim, see Carington Smith and Vokotopoulou 1992, p. 501, fig. 4.

FIGURE 7.27. Pithos fragments: **7/59** (ΜΕΘ 4274), **7/60** (ΜΕΘ 4333).
Drawings A. Hooton and T. Ross, photos I. Coyle

7/60. (ΜΕΘ 4333) Body Fr, Pithos Fig. 7.27
East Hill #274/004029 [10]. 12/6/2003.
P.H. 0.069; p.W. 0.128.
Single fr preserving small portion of body and applied band with incised decoration.
Shoulder sloping in toward rim, which is not preserved. Applied band, about 0.010 thick and 0.038 wide, decorated with incised motifs: at least two stamped circles (Diam. 0.018), that to the left framed on either side by diagonal.
Coarse pithos fabric, with numerous medium to large inclusions of various colors, but only a relatively small dusting of mica. Clay core and surfaces fired close to red 2.5YR 5/6–5/8.
Exterior surface somewhat better smoothed than interior.
For impressed circles on a slightly raised band on a pithos fr from Torone, see Papadopoulos 2005, p. 800, fig. 83b; p. 1201, fig. 382, T27-2; for an undecorated raised band, see p. 810, pl. 102b, T46-2. For decorated and undecorated applied bands, cf., among others, those in *Agora* XXXVI, pp. 48–49, fig. 2.7, T1-3; pp. 304–305, fig. 2.208, T41-2; pp. 436–437, fig. 2.323, T67-1; pp. 891–894, with fig. 6.55, including one with impressions made by a short comb-like implement with rectangular tines, which forms a design of stacked chevrons set vertically (W. 0.040; Th. 0.006). For applied bands with incised decoration in the north Aegean, see esp. *Vergina* I, pl. 134, middle row left, and bottom. For incised, rouletted, and stamped decoration on pithoi from Kalapodi, see Jacob-Felsch 1996, pls. 21–22, 29, 38–39, 41, 44–46, various examples; for pithos frr with incised decoration from Euboian Kyme, see Sapouna-Sakellarakis 1998, p. 98, fig. 38:1–2; for the pithoi from Argos with applied bands and incised decoration, see Courbin 1974, pl. 51, T190, T191; Hägg 1974, p. 103, fig. 15; p. 139, fig. 38.

NOTES

1 For the pivoted multiple brush that made these mechanically drawn circles and semicircles, see Papadopoulos, Vedder, and Schreiber 1998. I am grateful to my colleagues Manthos Bessios, Sarah Morris, Athena Athanassiadou, Antonis Kotsonas, Trevor Van Damme, Marianna Nikolaidou, and Stamatia (Matoula) Kordanouli for assistance with various aspects of this chapter.

2 The only exception was the roof tiles of Archaic and Classical date. Although a representative sample was kept, the majority of roof tiles was stored in discrete stacks on site.

3 See *Kerameikos* XIII; Bohen 2017.

4 See Morris et. al. 2020, pp. 693–699, figs. 42–49.

5 Ceramics aside, an important point suggested by the preliminary study of the archaeobotanical remains at Methone, as reported in Morris et al. 2020, pp. 715–716, is that there was no obvious change in the range of the basic food plants that were at the core of subsistence strategies before and after the arrival of the Eretrians. For the botanical and archaeological dimensions of colonial encounters in the Mediterranean, see further Buxó 2009; for a synthetic overview of Bronze Age foods, see Tzedakis and Martlew 1999.

6 In Gimatzidis 2010, pp. 252–274, for example, there are only two amphora types discussed, neck-handled amphoras, and those with belly-and-shoulder handles, even though a number of the published fragments could belong to belly-handled amphoras.

7 Heurtley 1939, p. 236, no. 485. Some of the fragments illustrated on pp. 233, 234, 238, figs. 107, 108, 111, may be from amphoras, but this could not be determined. On Gimatzidis's (2010, p. 53, fig. 1) map, Saré Omér is shown due north of Inglis (Anchialos) and "Antike Sindos."

8   For which see Papadopoulos forthcoming. For Anchialos/Sindos, see further Tiverios 2009a.

9   Conveniently illustrated and discussed in Lenz et al. 1998, pp. 190–191, fig. 1 (with references).

10 Lenz et al. 1998; see also Catling 1998; for "PG" amphoras from Troy, see, most recently, Aslan 2019, pp. 213–215, 313–315, pls. 31–33, nos. 212–224 (all from mixed contexts, many "LBA/PG/G/Hell," i.e., deposits from the Late Bronze Age into the Hellenistic period); for the chronology of the "PG" phase at Troy, see pp. 250–258.

11 Lenz et al. 1998, p. 194.

12 Lenz et al. 1998, p. 197.

13 In Group I there are 68 entries divided between Groups IA, IB, IC, all of which are considered neck-handled amphoras. There are 30 entries in Group II, all neck-handled amphoras; Group III comprises 21 pieces, all considered "amphoras of uncertain type." Only Group IV, with a paltry five sherds, has vessels other than amphoras: three pendent semicircle skyphoi and two closed shapes, one an amphora or jug. A "Protogeometric" assemblage that consists largely of neck-handled amphoras, other possible amphora types, and three skyphoi is not only highly unusual but in need of explanation, which the authors do not offer.

14 Papadopoulos 2005, pp. 418–437.

15 See, for example, *Kerameikos* I; *Kerameikos* IV; *Agora* XXXVI.

16 Jung 2002, pp. 173–181. I hope to be able to deal with this issue more fully elsewhere.

17 Desborough 1948, 1952.

18 See Papadopoulos, Damiata, and Marston 2011; *Agora* XXXVI, pp. 26–28. For further discussion, see Verdelis 1958, esp. pp. 49–60; see also pp. 40–48, 100–102; Desborough 1960; 1964, pp. 261–263. For Theocharis's thoughts, see Orlandos 1960, p. 59; Orlandos 1961, pp. 58–59; and see further Sipsie-Eschbach 1991; see also Jacob-Felsch 1988, esp. p. 198; Jacob-Felsch 1996; Marinatos 1932, p. 37; Wells 1983a; Zapheiropoulos 1960, pp. 330–332, 338–340, pl. 276α. See also Starr 1961, pp. 96–97; and esp. Frizell 1986, pp. 85–86.

19 Skeat 1934, p. 8; cf. Myres 1930, esp. pp. 450–454.

20 See Newton, Wardle, and Kuniholm 2003 (*contra*: Weninger and Jung 2009, pp. 374–380); and, most recently, Wardle 2011; Wardle, Higham, and Kromer 2014.

21 See, in the meantime, Toffolo et al. 2013; also Fantalkin 2001, 2006; Mazar and Bronk Ramsey 2008; Finkelstein and Piasetzky 2009; Fantalkin, Finkelstein, and Piasetzky 2015.

22 For PSC skyphoi, see Desborough 1952, pp. 127–179; 1972, pp. 185–220; Coldstream 1968, pp. 148–157; *Lefkandi* I, pp. 291–292, 297–302; Descoeudres and Kearsley 1983, pp. 41–53; Kearsley 1989. The idea of a Euboian *koine* was first aired by Desborough (1976) and perhaps too zealously promoted by scholars like I.S. Lemos (1986, 1998, 2002, pp. 212–217); see also various papers in Bats and d'Agostino 1998. As I have stated elsewhere, such a "*koine* is another colossus with feet of clay, for it is ceramic, not political. An Early Iron Age Euboian *koine* is about as edifying as an Athenian [red-figure] *koine* in the Classical period" (see Papadopoulos 2011, pp. 127–128). The PSC skyphos is prominent in the Xeropolis settlement of Lefkandi during LPG and SPG (e.g., *Lefkandi* I, pls. 13, 15, 18, 24–25, 30–31, 33, various examples), but does not continue into the Late Geometric deposits (see *Lefkandi* I, pp. 57–66).

23 *Lefkandi* II.1, pp. 22–23, pls. 12, 48–49, and see also pls. 5:i, 15, 52. The difference in shape and decoration between the skyphoi and so-called "krater-bowls" is so minor as to seem pedantic. The fact that examples of the same shape have been classified as two different forms has obscured, rather than clarified, the study of this vessel type, see further Papadopoulos 1998, and, for the inadequacy of the term "krater-bowl," see Papadopoulos 2015. It is worth adding that Kopcke (2002) has questioned the MPG date of the Toumba building, but with little conclusive evidence; see, further, Popham, Touloupa, and Sackett 1982b.

24 Descoeudres and Kearsley 1983, pp. 44, 47; Kearsley 1989, pp. 126–132; Kearsley 1995, pp. 67–69; see further *Délos* XV, pl. XXVI; Desborough 1952, pp. 180–194; Desborough 1963, 1979; Hanfmann 1956, pp. 173–175; Boardman 1957, pp. 2–10; Coldstream 1968, pp. 148–157; Riis 1970, pp. 126–175; Ridgway and Dickinson 1973, pp. 191–192; Ploug 1973, pp. 11–14; Gjerstad et al. 1977, p. 24, pl. I:4–14, pl. II:1; pp. 61–62, pl. L:3–5; Gjerstad 1979, pl. VII:7 (no. 106); *Lefkandi* I, pp. 297–302; Coldstream 1981, pp. 17–18, pl. 16, nos. 2–3 (900–850 B.C.).

25 Desborough's (1952, p. 190) list of sites (cf. also Skeat 1934, p. 7, n. 2) is now supplemented by Kearsley 1989, pp. 72–73; see further Chrysostomou and Chrysostomou 1995, p. 82, fig. 9; Misailidou-Despotidou 1998, p. 267, pl. 6; with further examples from Aphytis and the vicinity of Dion/Mt. Olympos (Poulaki-Pantermali 2013a; see also Poulaki-Pantermali 2008b, p. 32, Geometric pottery from Leivithra [top row, middle]). The paucity of the shape at Torone is noteworthy, but is largely on account of the earlier date of the Early Iron Age cemetery, which ends around 850 B.C.; see Papadopoulos 2005, pp. 445–446, 487, 840, fig. 138:b (local skyphos); p. 836, fig. 133:c (Euboian import).

26 Gimatzidis 2010, pp. 191–196.

27 Davison 1961; see Gimatzidis 2010, p. 191.

28 Gimatzidis 2010, p. 192, fig. 50.

29 Papadopoulos 2005, pp. 450–454; this is further elaborated in the catalogue entry for **7/20**.

30 Papadopoulos 2005, pp. 415, 447–450.

31 *Vergina* I, pp. 181–182, fig. 32, pl. 75, AΘ 1, referred to as a "βραχύπους κύλιξ"; Petsas 1961–1962, pl. 150γ, left (Π 61).

32 Andreou and Kotsakis 1996, p. 372, fig. 3, no. TKA 1114 (Phase 2).

33 For Kastanas, see Podzuweit 1979, p. 213, fig. 21, no. 9; for Assiros, Wardle 1980, pp. 250–252, fig. 14, no. 31.

34 Jung 2002, esp. pl. 44, nos. 407–409 (Schicht 11 bis 12); see also pl. 29, nos. 297–306 (Schicht 12); pl. 52, no. 452 (Schicht 11); pl. 53, nos. 453–455 (Schicht 11).

35 *Lefkandi* I, p. 303, nn. 152–154; cf. *Lefkandi* II.1, pp. 31–32.

36 Pieridou 1973, pl. 42, no. K38; pl. 16, nos. K34, K36.

37 Morricone 1978, p. 392, fig. 875, inv. 889.

38 *Lefkandi* I, p. 302, fig. 9B, pls. 97, 106, nos. S18-1, S51-4 (both from the Skoubris Cemetery); cf. *Lefkandi* II.1, pp. 31–32, 104–105, nos. 181–198. The likely Toronaian import is *Lefkandi* I, p. 353, pl. 181. Unfortunately, the latter was found in a tomb with no other pottery, and it appears to have been dated by the excavators on the basis of style; consequently, an earlier date, commensurate with comparanda from Torone, is not only possible, but highly likely.

39 Verdelis 1958, pp. 37–38, pl. 12, nos. 139–141.

40 In *Lefkandi* I, p. 303.

41 Cf. Mountjoy 1986, p. 153, fig. 197, Type A.

42 For the Granary Class, see Wace 1921–1923, p. 33, fig. 9:c; for examples from the Bronze Age levels at Lefkandi, see Popham and Milburn 1971, p. 347, fig. 8, no. 1; from Methone, Tomb 229/21, see Morris et al. 2020, pp. 687–689, fig. 36:a (LH IIIC).

43 Karageorghis 1974, pls. 57–61, 73–79; cf. Yon 1971, pl. 37, no. 141; see also Karageorghis 1963, pl. 32, no. 6.

44 Brouskari 1980, pp. 25–28, pl. 5:a, no. 26 (EPK 555); for a related vessel form with handles set vertically on the rim, see Papadopoulos 2005, p. 504, n. 32.

45 Polygyros Museum, inv. 270, see Giouri 1971.

46 Petsas 1961–1962, pl. 150γ, no. Π61.

47 *Lefkandi* I, p. 303, fig. 9:c, type B, and see pls. 15, 18, 25, 28, 273, esp. nos. 324, 844–847; cf. *Lefkandi* II.1, pp. 31–32, which are earlier and somewhat different.

48 Sakellariou 1965, p. 421, pl. 471:b.
49 Paspalas 1995; *Torone* I, pp. 477–483.
50 *Olynthus* XIII, p. 49, pl. 4, no. P4; *Olynthus* V, pl. 25, P28A–B.
51 For Chios, see Boardman 1967, pp. 115–117; for southern Anatolia, see Mellaart 1955, p. 131, pl. 1, nos. 7, 9.
52 See, for example, Wardle 1980, p. 262.
53 Wardle 1980, p. 263.
54 Hänsel 1979, pp. 167–207; Wardle 1980, pp. 261–265; Hochstetter 1984, pp. 290–293.
55 Hochstetter 1984, p. 12, fig. 1. The levels contemporary with the Early Iron Age at Methone include Kastanas levels (Schichten) 13 through 8 (i.e., K periods V, VI, and the early part of VII). In Schicht 13, 88% of the total is handmade, the proportion falling to its lowest in Schicht 11 (slightly more than 50%), while in Schicht 9 handmade pottery accounts for 75% of the total and in Schicht 8 back to 88%.
56 *Vergina* I, pp. 193–194; Radt 1974, p. 116; Desborough 1972, p. 217.
57 Wardle 1980, p. 260.
58 For central Macedonia, see Hochstetter 1984, pp. 277–309 (the overview is based on a careful analysis of settlement sites, including Axiochorion [Vardaroftsa], Limnotopos [Vardino], Tsaoutsitsa, Kalindria [Kilindir], Assiros, Perivolaki [Saratsé], Gona, Agios Mamas, and Molyvopyrgos), as well as cemetery sites, such as Vergina and Tsaoutsitsa. For eastern Macedonia and Thrace, see Hochstetter 1984, pp. 309–319 (based on the settlement sites of Angista and Dikili Tash, together with cemetery sites at Exochi, Potami, Amphipolis, Mesembria [Dikella], and Thasos; Theocharis 1971, map fig. 5; Koukouli-Chrysanthaki 1970, 1971, 1973–1974, 1980, 1992; Grammenos and Fotiadis 1980; for Dikili Tash see, most recently, Koukouli-Chrysanthaki et al. 2008. For western Macedonia, see Hochstetter 1984, pp. 319–325 (largely based on Platania [Boubousti] and Agios Panteleimon [Pateli], among other sites; cf. Wardle 1980, pp. 263–264; Schachermeyr (1980, pp. 271–300) distinguishes between "der Kreis um Boubousti und der Kreis um Vergina und Vardaroftsa." For Epirus (including Kastritsa, Dodona, and Vitsa Zagoriou) see Hochstetter 1984, pp. 325–329 and, more recently, Douzougli and Papadopoulos 2010. For Thessaly, see Hochstetter 1984, pp. 329–337. For handmade wares in Thessaly, see further Tsountas 1899b, pp. 101–102; Tsountas 1908, esp. for the earlier material; Wace and Droop 1906–1907; Wace and Thompson 1912, pp. 206–216; Heurtley and Skeat 1930–1931; Hansen 1933, pp. 117–122; Desborough 1952, pp. 135–153; Verdelis 1958, pp. 62–63; Theochari 1960, 1962, 1966; Kilian 1975b; see further Theocharis 1961–1962. Contrast, however, the situation at Ktouri and Palaiokastro, Béquignon 1932. For the earlier Bronze Age material in Thessaly the most comprehensive study is that of Hanschmann and Milojčić (*Argissa-Magoula* III).
59 *Vergina* I, pp. 194–201, figs. 39–41. Similar jugs are also found at nearby Sindos, though not in the quantities found at Vergina, see Gimatzidis 2010, pl. 37, nos. 310–311; pl. 41 (various examples); pl. 42, no. 346.
60 For incised decoration on Macedonian Early Iron Age handmade pottery, see Heurtley 1939, p. 232, fig. 105; p. 236, fig. 110; *Vergina* I, pp. 191–193; Radt 1974, pl. 34; Wardle 1980, p. 257, fig. 16; p. 260, fig. 19; Hochstetter 1984, various examples, pls. 62–151, and cf. Schicht 8 (early 9th century B.C.). For discussion of the various grooved, channeled, and relief wares, including "turban," "pie-crust," and other decoration, see *Vergina* I, pp. 185–190; Wardle 1980, pp. 253–265; Hochstetter 1984, pp. 188–194 (cf. Heurtley 1939, pp. 98–99, 103–104; see also Heurtley 1925).
61 Wardle 1980, p. 263; Hänsel 1976, pp. 88–117; cf. Bouzek 1969, pp. 41–45; Bouzek 1983.
62 See Heurtley 1939, p. 103; Wardle 1980, p. 230; and esp. Behrends 1982.
63 A survey of handmade wares from regions north and south of Macedonia, as well as connections with Troy, is presented in Hochstetter 1984, pp. 325–375 (with full references). The chapters by Dumitrescu, Bolomey, and Mogoşanu (1982), and Garašanin (1982a, 1982b, 1982c, 1982d), and Prendi (1982) in the *Cambridge Ancient History* vol. 3.1, and by Hammond (1982) for the Early Iron Age are particularly useful for their syntheses, references to the earlier literature, maps, and representative assemblages.

Despite its early date, Childe 1929 remains useful; see also Alexander 1962; Snodgrass 1962; Gimbutas 1965, pp. 113–159. For the handmade wares of central and southern Greece see generally Bouzek 1985, pp. 183–201, and, among others, *Kerameikos* I, p. 74, pls. 25, 75; *Kerameikos* IV, pls. 28–31; *Corinth* VII.1, pp. 7–8, pl. 2, nos. 13–19; p. 15, pls. 8–9, nos. 50–53; p. 29, pl. 13, nos. 81–82; pp. 30–31, pl. 14, nos. 86–97; Courbin 1954, p. 178, fig. 37; Verdelis 1963, Beil. 12, no. 6; Beil. 21, no. 2; Desborough 1954, 1955, 1956, 1965, 1973; Charitonidis 1955, p. 125, pl. 39, no. 1; Smithson 1961, p. 176, pl. 31; Courbin 1966, pp. 29–38, 70–74, 235–251, 467–468; *Zagora* 1, pp. 52–57; Cambitoglou et al. 1981, pp. 35–44; Hägg 1971; Dekoulakou 1973; Despoinis 1979; *Lefkandi* I, pp. 342–343; Wells 1983a, pp. 69–79, 85–88, 99–100, 113–116; Coulson 1985, p. 63. Interestingly, the so-called Handmade Burnished Ware encountered at several southern Greek sites during the Late Bronze Age appears to be unrelated to the mainstream of Macedonian handmade wares: see Hochstetter 1984, pp. 339–343; also Rutter 1975, 1979; Deger-Jalkotzy 1977, 1983; French and Rutter 1977; Catling and Catling 1981; Kilian 1981; cf. Wardle 1973; Walberg 1976; Hüttel 1980. More recent overviews include Reber 1991; Eder 1998; Strack 2007. See also Small 1990, 1997; Rutter 1990; Bankoff, Meyer, and Stefanovich 1996; Genz 1997.

64 Wardle 1980, pp. 261–265; see also Wardle 1983, pp. 291–305.
65 Hochstetter 1984, pp. 345–358, 378, 380, figs. 59–60.
66 Hochstetter 1984, pp. 358–375; cf. Snodgrass 1965.
67 For Torone, see Papadopoulos 2005.
68 The quantity of handmade imports to Early Iron Age Torone was not great, but they stand apart from the local handmade in details of shape, the manner of burnishing, and in fabric and feel; see Papadopoulos 2005, pp. 490–493. At Assiros, there was a distinction between "local," "provincial," and "imported" classes of pottery, for which see, esp., Jones 1986, pp. 108–110, 494.
69 See *Vergina* I, pp. 204–207, referred to as "amphoras"; for Kastanas, see Hochstetter 1984, pp. 38–48, referred to as "amphoras," as well as pp. 115–142, referred to as "Töpfe," a name applied to a broad variety of shapes; for Torone, see Papadopoulos 2005, pp. 467–469, referred to as "two-handled jars (amphoras)," though I avoided the term "amphoras" since the two-handled jars of Torone came in belly-handled (Type 1) and neck-handled (Type 2) versions, and there was also a solitary wheelmade version (T17-1); for Koukos (only published in preliminary reports), see Carington Smith and Vokotopoulou 1990, p. 449, fig. 2; for Assiros, see Wardle 1980, pp. 257–258, figs. 16–17, nos. 43–44, 45–46.
70 For the handmade jars of Bronze Age Agios Mamas, see Horejs 2007a, pp. 126–145; for the relative and absolute chronology of the site, and the different architectural phases, see Hänsel and Aslanis 2010; for the Early Bronze Age see Pappa 1992, 2010; for the Middle Bronze Age, see Aslanis and Hänsel 1999; Aslanis 2017.
71 See Gimatzidis 2010, esp. p. 447, pl. 37, no. 312 (referred to as a neck-handled amphora); cf. p. 452, pl. 40, no. 339 (referred to as a "pithoid amphora"). The smaller jars with horizontal handles rising at an angle of 45º or more on the shoulder, and with a relatively short everted or flaring rim, such as Gimatzidis 2010, p. 452, pl. 40, no. 338, and the larger but spouted example on p. 452, pl. 40, no. 337 (both curiously labeled "pithos"), are very different from the jars of Methone.
72 Bessios 2010, p. 84; for Leivithra, see Poulaki-Pantermali 2008b, p. 29, bottom row, second from left.
73 *Vergina* I, pp. 202–204, figs. 42–43; Radt 1974, pl. 35, nos. 23–27, where they are referred to as "Gefässe mit Scheibenknopfhenkeln."
74 Petsas 1961–1962, pl. 102β, right; pl. 103α–β, both right; pl. 150δ, left; pl. 151γ, left; pl. 151ε, left; pl. 153δ, middle.
75 Papadopoulos 2005, pp. 474–476, 789, 792, figs. 67b, 69e, pls. 374, 377.
76 For examples from Koukos, see Carington Smith and Vokotopoulou 1989, p. 437, fig. 9, right (two-handled); Carington Smith and Vokotopoulou 1990, p. 452, fig. 7 (one-handled); see also Carington Smith 1991, p. 347, fig. 3 (for the two-handled version).

77 Chrysostomou 1995; Lioutas and Gkioura 1997, p. 326, fig. 8, far left. For the example from Arnissa, see Chrysostomou 2016, p. 26, fig. 23 (lower right).

78 Cf. Heurtley 1939, p. 239, no. 499 from Olynthos (= *Olynthus* V, pl. 23, P 25), which differs from the examples at Methone and Vergina in that, instead of a handle top that is concave, the handle finial is a small cone; see also Hochstetter 1984, pl. 240, no. 1 (Schicht 3), which postdates 700 B.C. and which has a concave handle top.

79 Hochstetter 1984, pl. 1, no. 10 (Schicht 19). Andronikos (in *Vergina* I, p. 202, nn. 4–5) cites the Late Neolithic jug (from Olynthos): Heurtley 1939, p. 162, no. 157 (= *Olynthus* I, p. 30, and fig. 48) as a forerunner, as well as Italian parallels dating to the first half of the 2nd millennium B.C.; both seem somewhat remote as immediate predecessors.

80 See Hochstetter 1984, pp. 74–75, fig. 18, type 6b (I stress that this is a related type, not identical to those of Methone, Vergina, and Torone); cf. Heurtley 1939, p. 235, nos. 476–477 (Tsaoutsitsa); p. 236, nos. 486–487 (Perivolaki/Saratsé); p. 239, no. 500 (Olynthos = *Olynthus* V, pl. 24, P 26b); Forsdyke 1925, p. 17, pl. III, A78; see further Casson 1919–1921, p. 20, fig. 13; Casson 1923–1925, p. 10, fig. 3:g, i, j; Casson 1926, p. 138, fig. 47.

81 *Vergina* I, pl. 65, ΑΓ 44.

82 *Vergina* I, pp. 207–209, figs. 46–48.

83 E.g., *Vergina* I, pl. 34, Δ 20; pl. 61, ΑΒ 6, ΑΒ 17, ΑΒ 19; cf. Petsas 1961–1962, pl. 150δ, Χ 132 (left).

84 See Heurtley 1939, p. 236, fig. 110:c, h.

85 One of the earliest is Hochstetter 1984, p. 163, no. 3. Occasionally, related bowls not unlike these can appear earlier (e.g., Hochstetter 1984, p. 83, no. 1, Schicht 12, developed or advanced LH IIIC), but are not identical. For a related example from Schicht 4, see pl. 225, no. 2; there is an even slightly later example from Schicht (2)–3, pl. 241, no. 5.

86 See Hochstetter 1984, pl. 154, nos. 3–4; *Vergina* I, p. 188, fig. 36, Φ 25.

87 Cf. esp. Blegen and Rawson 1966, pp. 411–412, shape 66 (= FS 311): ladle or scoop (coarse), and shape 67 (= FS 312): brazier (coarse); see also Tournavitou 1992, p. 209, fig. 6, FS 311.

88 See Heurtley 1939, p. 104. As applied to a variety of shapes, the term can be confusing, like the so-called "wish-bone handle"; for discussion, see Papadopoulos 2005, p. 507, n. 56. For a Late Bronze Age closed vessel with a related handle, see Andreou et al. 2013, p. 177, fig. 2b.

89 For the incised and paste-filled kantharoi of Macedonia, see, among others, Hochstetter 1984, pl. 47, nos. 1–3 (Schicht 14b, contemporary with the end of LH IIIB); pls. 258–259, various examples (Kastanas); Wardle 1980, p. 247, fig. 11, nos. 18–19, pl. 21a–b, d–e (Assiros); Andreou et al. 2013, p. 175, fig. 1b–c; p. 177, fig. 2a.

90 See *Agora* XXXVI, pp. 863–875; for earlier studies see esp. Bouzek 1974a; Smithson 1968.

91 For the strainers/sieves (*Siebgefässe*) from Agios Mamas, see Horejs 2007a, pl. 49, nos. 8706, 8709, 8710 (Schicht 7+0); pl. 111, no. 8691 (Schicht 1+0), the latter with smaller holes (all dating to the later stages of the Bronze Age). For examples from Kastanas (all dating to various stages of the Early Iron Age), see Hochstetter 1984, pl. 122, no. 2 (*Siebplatte*, Schicht 10); pl. 144, no. 3 (*Siebgefäss*, Schicht 9); pl. 158, no. 2 (with much smaller holes).

92 Adam-Veleni, Poulaki, and Tzanavari 2003, p. 183, nos. 48–49; p. 200, no. 111; pp. 231–232, nos. 282, 292 (all Classical and later).

93 For the two kilns excavated during 2003–2013, see Chapter 19; for the third kiln encountered in the excavations of 2014–2017, see Morris et al. 2020, pp. 702–703, figs. 53:a–c (the kiln will be published by Dr. Debby Sneed).

94 One standard type of cooking vessel elsewhere in Macedonia in the course of the Bronze and Early Iron Age was the pyraunos (Chapter 4, **4/57**), for which see Hochstetter 1984, pp. 155–164 (Kastanas), where the form is popular from Schicht 19 to Schicht 1, peaking in Schicht 7; Wardle

1980, p. 249, fig. 13 (Assiros); for a well-preserved Middle Bronze Age pyraunos from Torone, see Morris 2008, p. 438, fig. 7; Morris 2009–2010, p. 52, fig. 41, 89.704. There is also a curious variety of cauldron stand with two broad legs from Vergina that is somewhat later, see Petsas 1961–1962, pls. 146γ, 147β; for related stands in Italy, see Scheffer 1981.

95 *Agora* XXXVI, pp. 884–887, with fig. 6.52 for the one-handled version; pp. 887–890, with fig. 6.53 for the two-handled version.

96 For discussion, see *Agora* XXXVI, pp. 881–884. The exception to wheelmade Bronze Age cooking wares are Aiginetan cooking pots, which appear to have been made by hand throughout the Bronze Age. These pots, commonly of globular shape with a flat base, or with a rounded base and three sturdy feet, are widespread throughout the Bronze Age Aegean (e.g., Lindblom 2001, pp. 37–38). In fact, Agora deposits O 7:14 and P 8:9 (*Agora* XIII, pp. 248–251, Late Helladic IIIA–B) largely contain Aiginetan cooking ware, while the presumably locally made ware is only sparsely represented. The only other exception is the handmade tripod cooking pot of Mycenaean Athens and Attica, for which see pp. 370-374. Handmade cooking ware of non-Aiginetan, and presumably local, provenance first occurs in the Klepsydra Court cuttings (deposit T 26–27:2, provisionally dated to Late Helladic IIIC Late; *Agora* XIII, pp. 261–262; Smithson 1982). In the slightly later well U 26:4 in the Athenian Agora (from the very end of Late Helladic IIIC), handmade cooking pots outnumber wheelmade ones, and in wells H 12:10 and O 8:5 (both provisionally dated to Submycenaean or the very latest Mycenaean), wheelmade cooking ware has all but disappeared.

97 See, for example, Heurtley 1939, p. 234, nos. 472 and 473 (Axiochorion [Vardaroftsa]).

98 Papadopoulos 1989, pp. 34, 42, ills. 38–39, KP-13.

99 The tripod enjoys a long history in Crete from Early Minoan through Subminoan, see, among others, Popham and Sackett 1984, pl. 86f, g, h; pl. 162, nos. 9–11; p. 174, n. 125; Betancourt 1985, figs. 29E, 31, 68, 86, 116; for further references, see Papadopoulos 2005, p. 508, n. 62; for the Mycenaean version, see Furumark 1972, FS 320; Lacy 1967, p. 185, Shape 7; p. 184, fig. 72b; for further references, see Papadopoulos 2005, p. 508, n. 63. For tripods of Mycenaean date in Athens and Attica, see Broneer 1933, pp. 371–372, fig. 45; Broneer 1939, pp. 398–400, Shape 27, fig. 81a–b; Hansen 1937, pp. 562–564, fig. 17f–k; Stubbings 1947, p. 54, fig. 23B; *Agora* XIII, p. 140, pl. 61, no. 441; Benzi 1975, p. 225, pl. 7, no. 174; Mountjoy 1981, p. 22, fig. 6, pl. 5b, no. 25; cf. also the wheelmade and painted "τριποδικὰ ἀλαβαστροειδῆ" in Iakovidis 1969–1970, vol. 2, pp. 209–212, with fig. 81.

100 *CVA* Athens 1, pl. 6, nos. 13–14; Benton 1934–1935, pp. 101–102; *Kerameikos* I, pl. 63, inv. 554; pl. 64, inv. 555; *Kerameikos* V.1, p. 156, inv. 782; *Perachora* I, pl. 14, no. 6; Vokotopoulou 1969, pp. 84–85, no. 36; pl. 30a–b; Hägg and Hägg 1978, pp. 86–87, figs. 75, 77, nos. 146–151. Cf. related shapes in *Lefkandi* I, pl. 284, no. 9; Popham, Touloupa, and Sackett 1982a, pl. 15, no. 13; *Nichoria* III, p. 95; p. 137, fig. 3-21, nos. P408, P860, P833; p. 178, fig. 3-62, no. P1313; Wells 1983a, pp. 77, 88, 100, 115. For coarse ware tripods from Early Iron Age Kos, see Morricone 1978, p. 291, fig. 621; p. 293, fig. 625; p. 306, fig. 652; for painted examples, see pp. 206–207, figs. 403–404. See also Desborough 1952, pl. 30:c (Kos); Brock 1957, pp. 49, 51, 167, Tomb X, nos. 483, 515 (Fortetsa, Crete); Rocchetti 1967–1968, p. 206, fig. 48 (Phaistos); Rocchetti 1974–1975, pp. 186–187, figs. 23, 25; p. 220, fig. 72; p. 278, 157 (Phaistos); for Cyprus, see Yon 1971, pl. 19, no. 55; Pieridou 1973, p. 107, Shape 23, pl. 7, nos. 10–12.

101 For bronze tripods at Olympia, see *OlForsch* III; Schweitzer 1971, ch. 7; Coldstream 1977, pp. 333–339; Maass 1977, 1981; Heilmeyer 1982, pp. 39–45, figs. 29–32; for Delphi, see *FdD* V.1, pp. 59–72; *FdD* V.5; *FdD* V.3; for elsewhere, see Benton 1934–1935; Touloupa 1972; Maass 1977. For Minoan and Mycenaean bronze tripods, see Matthäus 1980; cf. Onassoglou 1995, fig. 56:2, pls. 1, 10b, 11; and for Cyprus, see Catling 1964, pp. 169–170, 190–223.

102 For the Torone tripod cooking pots, see Papadopoulos 2005, pp. 479–481.

103 The only legged vessels mentioned by Heurtley are Neolithic: see Heurtley 1939, p. 150, no. 91 (four-legged); p. 161, no. 148 (three-legged "table" = *Olynthus* I, figs. 62b, 63, pl. 2) and p. 162, no. 161 (= *Olynthus* I, fig. 22, 1–2).

104 See discussion in Hochstetter 1984, pp. 179–180; for the legged fragment very different from those of Chalkidike, see pl. 280, no. 3 (Schicht 8).

105 For the tripods from the Early Iron Age cemetery, see Papadopoulos 2005, pp. 479–481; the examples found extend in time throughout most of the period of use of the cemetery, from Final Mycenaean/Submycenaean through Protogeometric; the latest of the Torone tripods are perhaps those from Tomb 123. For the fragment from the Gate Area, see *Torone* I, pp. 293–308.

106 For the tripod cooking pots from Koukos, see Carington Smith and Vokotopoulou 1989, p. 437, fig. 6, right; Carington Smith and Vokotopoulou 1990, p. 450, fig. 4; and esp. Carington Smith 2000, pp. 219–225, fig. 1, pls. 1–3; for the excavations at Koukos, see also Carington Smith and Vokotopoulou 1988. What is arguably one of the most important Early Iron Age settlement sites in the north Aegean, at Lagomandra, is largely unpublished; for the nearby cemetery at Ai Yanni, Nikiti, see Trakosopoulou-Salakidou 1988.

107 Bernard 1964, pp. 134–136, figs. 46–48.

108 Casson 1926, p. 134, figs. 42–43; Heurtley 1939, pp. 33, 38, 64, 98, 100, and esp. p. 218, pl. 20, no. 420; *Vergina* I, pp. 221–222, pls. 134–135; Cambitoglou and Papadopoulos 1994, pl. 21:5; for a remarkable painted pithos decorated with sets of concentric circles executed with a pivoted multiple brush, see Petsas 1964, pp. 255–258. Margomenou, Andreou, and Kotsakis 2005 (Late Bronze Age, Toumba Thessalonikis).

109 See, e.g., Petsas 1961–1962, pl. 132α–β; pl. 133β, ε; pl. 134α, γ; pl. 136γ; pl. 137β–γ; pl. 140β–γ; Cambitoglou and Papadopoulos 1991, pp. 150–152, figs. 3–5, pl. 21:3–5; Cambitoglou and Papadopoulos 1994, pp. 150–151, figs. 2, 4, 8, pl. 21:4; Carington Smith and Vokotopoulou 1992, p. 501, fig. 4; Morris 2009–2010, pp. 12–13, figs. 10–11.

110 Hochstetter 1984, pp. 142–155.

111 For the Torone kiln, see Papadopoulos 1989, pp. 29, 36–37, ills. 12–14, esp. the better preserved KP-1 and KP-2; for pithoi in situ on Promontory 1 at Torone, see Morris 2009–2010, pp. 12–13, figs. 10–11.

112 Papadopoulos 1989, pp. 36–37, ills. 12–15, KP-1, KP-2, KP-3; Papadopoulos 2005, pp. 476–478.

113 Carington Smith and Vokotopoulou 1992, p. 501, fig. 4.

114 Wells 1983a, p. 69; Hochstetter 1984, pp. 142–155, esp. p. 147, fig. 39.

115 Cf. Hochstetter 1984, p. 152, fig. 40; for Mycenaean pithos types, see Furumark 1972, p. 74; for a pithos with pointed base from Euboian Kyme, see Sapouna-Sakellarakis 1998, p. 72, fig. 26.

116 See Heurtley 1939, pp. 218, 251, pl. 20, no. 420; Papadopoulos 2005, p. 780, fig. 57, no. 30; p. 789, fig. 67a, T7-1; the latter also has lightly incised diagonal strokes around the outside chamfered edge of the rim (this pithos neck is very similar to one from Oropos, see Mazarakis Ainian 1998, p. 209, fig. 30); cf. also *Vergina* I, pl. 135, middle row, right.

117 *Vergina* I, pl. 134, middle left and bottom; Papadopoulos 2005, p. 810, fig. 102b, T46-2.

118 Papadopoulos 2005, p. 800, fig. 83b, T27-2; for similarly decorated coarse ware vessels from Karphi, see Seiradaki 1960, p. 29, pl. 12a; cf. the stamped concentric circles on pithos fragments from a Geometric well at Knossos, Coldstream 1960, p. 170, pl. 47d, nos. 120–124; for other parts of Greece, see Heurtley and Lorimer 1932–1933, p. 53, fig. 31, nos. 98–99 (Ithaka); Young 1939, p. 189, fig. 138m no. C164 (Athens); *Nichoria* III, pls. 3-113, 3-114; Jacob-Felsch 1996, pls. 21–22, 29, 38–39, 41, 44–46, various examples, including circles (nos. 128, 130); rouletting (nos. 262, 288, 335, 400, 414, 416, 425, 426, 427, 434); hatched triangles, alternating upright and pendent (no. 129) (Kalapodi); impressed (nos. 263, 415); Sapouna-Sakellarakis 1998, p. 98, fig. 38:2, top left (Euboian Kyme).

119 Papadopoulos 2005, p. 477; p. 787, fig. 65a, T1-1; p. 789, fig. 67a, T7-1; p. 793, fig. 12a, T12-1; for the kiln pithos KP-1, see Papadopoulos 1989.

120 Heurtley 1939, p. 218, pl. 20, no. 420.
121 Cambitoglou and Papadopoulos 1994, pl. 21:5; the pithos from Euboian Kyme may have been of comparable height, Sapouna-Sakellaris 1998, p. 72, fig. 26.
122 See Morris et al. 2020, pp. 693–696, figs. 43:a–b.
123 Wells 1983a, p. 69; and see further Wells 1983a, pp. 69–70, 85, 99, 113–114; for contemporary material from the Argolid, see Wells 1983b, pp. 213–214, figs. 156–159; p. 233, fig. 176; p. 253, fig. 191, nos. 705–708; p. 275, fig. 207, nos. 911–913; also Hägg and Hägg 1978, pp. 85–86, figs. 75–76, nos. 127–130; Brouskari 1980, p. 21, pl. 5e, no. 7; *Lefkandi* I, p. 36, pl. 17, nos. 248–249; *Lefkandi* II.1, pp. 62–63.

Part II

Trade, Industry, and Lifeways in Early Iron Age Methone:
The Hypogeion

8

THE EXCAVATION OF THE HYPOGEION

Matthaios Bessios

INTRODUCTION

The settlement of ancient Methone, its location on the western coast of the Thermaic Gulf, immediately north of the modern village of Nea Agathoupolis, is noted in Chapter 1, with supplementary notes in Chapter 3.[1] The silting of the rivers Axios, Loudias, and especially the Haliakmon has significantly altered the landscape, so that today the ancient settlement is located at a distance of some 500 m from the sea. In antiquity, however, the Thermaic Gulf washed upon the east side of the settlement and reached deeply onto the north side as well, while anchorage was possible on both sides. The main harbor must be placed on the north side, which was protected both from the southerly winds—which put particular strain on the coast of Pieria at various times of the year—and from the northerly winds. As a result, the northern harbor of Methone was among the safest around the Thermaic Gulf (Figs. 8.1, 8.2). The protected nature of the harbor at Methone, coupled with the direct proximity of the site to the principal north–south road axis in antiquity, gave Methone a special geostrategic significance, as it afforded the possibility of contacts both by sea with the Aegean and the Mediterranean beyond, and by land, to central and western Macedonia, and the Balkans more generally.

Excavations at ancient Methone since 2003 have shown that the site was continuously inhabited from the Late Neolithic period until 354 B.C., and its harbor a hub of Aegean trade already since the early phases of the Bronze Age.[2] Indeed, there is strong evidence for interactions with southern Greek centers in the Late Bronze Age.[3] It is notable that the ancient literary tradition, however scant, refers to Methone as the earliest colony on the north Aegean shores. Plutarch (*Aetia* 239a–b)[4] described Methone as a Euboian colony, dated by later scholars to the later 8th century B.C., and his testimony finds considerable support in the archaeological record, which further documents that connections between the site and Euboia go back to the Protogeometric period. The wealth of finds from the relatively limited investigations at Methone has clearly demonstrated the diachronic prosperity of the settlement from the Late Neolithic period to 354 B.C.

Archaeological fieldwork at Methone since 2003 has already identified the Archaic and Classical agora, the commercial and political center of the city, on the saddle between two low hills (the East and West Hills), which have also been partly explored (Figs. 1.21–1.22). Fieldwork on the top of the East Hill revealed a context that is particularly important for the archaeology of the Aegean Early Iron Age, and for colonization in particular. This context was conventionally called the "Hypogeion" (referred to as "Ypogeio" in *Methone Pierias* I). The construction of this subterranean structure

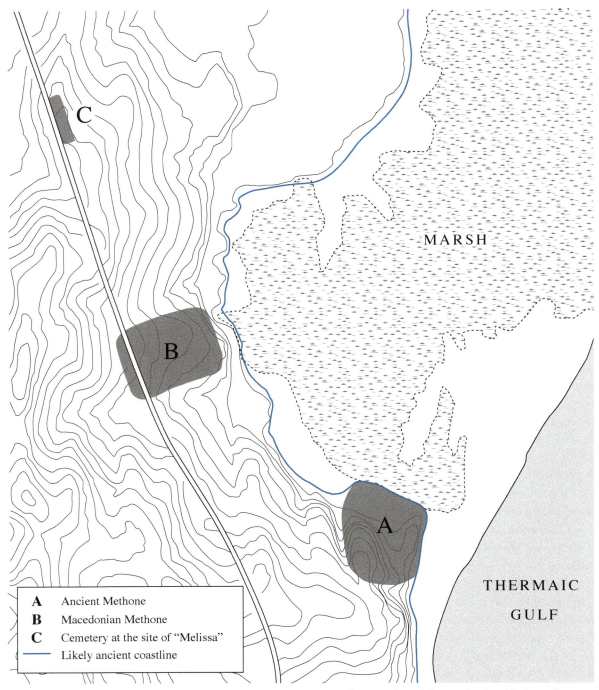

FIGURE 8.1. Map showing the settlements of ancient Methone (A) and "Macedonian Methone" (B, after 354 B.C.). Prepared by T. Ross (after Bessios 2012a, p. 44, fig. 1)

can be dated to the end of the Geometric period, that is, to the period of the initial foundation of the colony by the Eretrians at the site of a preexisting settlement. The abundance of finds from this area confirms the extensive contacts between Methone and a large number of centers in the Aegean and the eastern Mediterranean. The finds from the Hypogeion also show that workshops were established for the manufacture of items in a large variety of materials, including gold, bronze, iron, clay, glass, ivory, antler, and bone, since the period of the early foundation of the colony.

FIGURE 8.2. The site of ancient Methone from the northwest (Bessios 2010, p. 104).
Photo M. Bessios

INVESTIGATIONS ON THE SUMMIT OF THE EAST HILL

The excavation of Plot 274, as already noted, revealed that the summit of the East Hill had been inhabited since the Late Neolithic period. The sea, which has risen precipitously since the initial stages of the Holocene, eroded the largest part of the hill, where a settlement existed during the Neolithic and Early Bronze Age. The only extant remnant of these early phases is a small part of the western boundary of the settlement, defined by a series of ditches (Figs. 1.2, 8.3).[5]

The notable rise in sea level after the initial phase of the Holocene led to the erosion of the east part of the hill, which was once coastal. Erosion was also identified on the hilltop, which was explored in a number of trenches. Only a thin layer of plow soil was overlying the bedrock in this area and only Late Neolithic and Early Bronze Age features were preserved. These features include the lower surface of one Late Neolithic and one Early Bronze Age ditch, and several Early Bronze Age storage pits. Close comparisons for storage pits, which can be commonly found at prehistoric sites in the surrounding region of Pieria, are typically no more than 1.5 m deep.[6] This indicates that erosion on the hilltop washed away not only the layers dating from the Middle Bronze Age onward (which must have existed at such a strategic location, and are confirmed by redeposited second-millennium finds in the agora below: Chapter 5), but also the earlier layers (Chapter 4) and an additional 1 m of bedrock. Accordingly, the Hypogeion, with a preserved depth of 11.5 m, must have been originally deeper than 12 m. One cannot exclude the possibility that the hilltop was leveled for the purposes of a major building project. However, the thick (> 2 m) dark layers identified on the western slopes of the hill suggest the gradual erosion of the hilltop after the destruction and abandonment of the site in 354 B.C. In conclusion, erosion has taken a heavy toll here, leaving the Hypogeion as the only substantial constructed feature postdating the Early Bronze Age that remains on the hilltop of the East Hill.

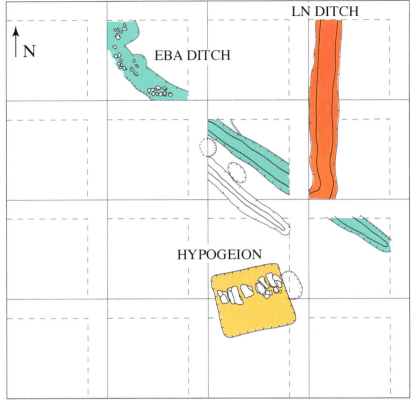

FIGURE 8.3. Plan of the summit of the East Hill (Plot 274), showing the Late Neolithic and Early Bronze Age ditches, Early Bronze Age pits, and the Hypogeion. Drawing I. Moschou

The only survivor from the later operations of the historical periods is the Hypogeion pit, which was dug in the end of the Geometric period (Fig. 8.3). No above-ground structure remains on the summit of the hill, which partly hampers the interpretation of the Hypogeion itself; had excavation been limited to this area, the picture of the settlement at Methone would have appeared very fragmentary indeed. Nevertheless, it seems that the Hypogeion served as the basement for some building, as the pit itself must have had some superstructure above ground, including a roof, but this has disappeared completely, making the identification of the structure particularly challenging.[7]

THE HYPOGEION: ITS LOCATION AND STRATIGRAPHY

The Hypogeion is a very deep, fairly broad, roughly rectangular rock-cut shaft found on top of the East Hill of Methone (Plot 274), east of the Archaic and Classical agora, and immediately south of the probable area of the ancient harbor of Methone, which is now buried under silt. The shaft has a depth of at least 11.5 m (but was originally deeper; see above), and measures 3.6 m by 4.2 m at the bottom. The excavation of the hilltop, and especially of the Hypogeion, began in 2003 and continued in 2004. The Hypogeion was then backfilled for safety reasons, and excavations were resumed in 2006–2007.[8]

Excavation was time-consuming due to the unique character of the feature, the density of finds, and especially the technical difficulties that were intensified by the unstable sides of the pit, which had to be continuously buttressed for the safety of the excavation crew.[9] As excavations progressed, the soft bedrock around the pit had to be dug out to form a wide sill around the pit itself, which not only afforded additional safety, but also facilitated access to the feature as it was being excavated, and the efficient removal of the excavated soil (Figs. 8.4a–b).

FIGURE 8.4. a) and b) The Hypogeion during excavation. Photos M. Bessios

At the conclusion of the 2004 season, a working hypothesis was proposed that this was an underground space that served as a kind of cool storage for some product, perhaps wine.[10] In order to fulfill such a function within its existing dimensions, the pit would have included stories of plank floors, reached by means of wooden ladders. This conclusion was based on the abundant traces of timber posts that were found, especially in the lower part of the Hypogeion (see below); in particular, the presence of continuous wooden traces in a uniform layer of greenish clay was interpreted as floor insulation (Fig. 8.5). In support of this view, the hollow space from an upright beam had been preserved in the northeast corner of the Hypogeion, at a depth of 7–10 m (Fig. 8.6); two additional small alcoves—likely the imprints of horizontal beams—were found in the area of the southeast corner, at 4.20 m above the floor.

FIGURE 8.5. The Hypogeion: traces of wooden beams in a layer of greenish clay.
Photo A. Athanassiadou

FIGURE 8.6. Hypogeion: beam imprint
in the northeast corner. Photo A. Athanassiadou

As it turned out, the completion of the excavations in the Hypogeion in 2006 and 2007 refuted the preliminary hypothesis and assessment. The western part of the floor of the pit was unevenly dug and extended deeper than the eastern part. In the southern area of the floor there was a depth difference of about 0.15 m between the western (lower) and the eastern (higher) sectors, while the levels evened out toward the northern boundary. In addition, the lowest section of the west scarp had not been cut vertically, as was the case with the other three sides of the pit (Figs. 8.7–8.8). Taken together, these are strong indications that the digging of the Hypogeion was never completed. The reason for the abandonment of the nearly finished feature remains unclear, but it can be understood on the basis of our own experience in excavating the structure. The use of the feature was abandoned by the excavators of the late 8th century B.C. because of the same problems

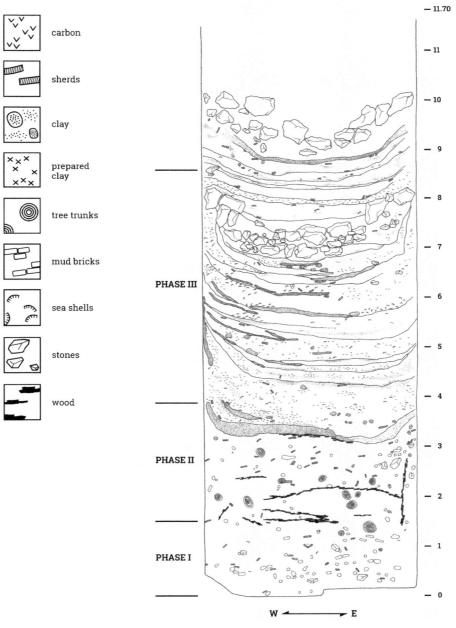

FIGURE 8.7. Stratigraphic section of the Hypogeion. Drawing I. Moschou

FIGURE 8.8. The Hypogeion floor. The western part was visibly dug deeper than the eastern part. In the eastern part are visible the discarded crude and unworked stones from the lower layers of the fill. Photo A. Athanassiadou

faced by the excavators of the early 21st century A.D., namely, the geological strata of the bedrock on the East Hill. These strata—that is, the strata of bedrock into which the Hypogeion was dug—mainly consist of alternating layers of clay and marl, and some lesser layers of sand or sandstone.[11] The layers of marl are stable, in contrast to those of clay, which separate into large blocks and thus weaken the stability of the pit. This problem was especially noteworthy in the upper levels, where soil humidity and temperature fluctuated in the different seasons of the year.

On the basis of the excavated data, we estimate that the filling-in of the Hypogeion began in haste. The lowest 1 m of the pit was filled with greenish raw clay, unbaked mud bricks, stones, timber, ceramics, and animal bones, including parts of the skeleton of a small animal. This homogeneous layer, which dominated the lower meter or so of the deposit, labeled as Phase I, must have been created very quickly (Figs. 8.9–8.10a–b). There were imprints of tree trunks or wooden beams, while fragments of a pithos were found, in addition to the skeletal parts of the small animal already noted which were found intermingled in the habitation debris that had been thrown in. This deposit must have formed within a very brief interval, when all the above materials were thrown in simultaneously from different sides of the pit (Fig. 8.11). The deposits of Phase I show that the Hypogeion never functioned as an underground space for whatever purpose, and no intermediate wooden floors were ever constructed.

The immediately overlying layer, Phase II, which was more than 2 m deep, was also completed in a very short time. Unlike the fill of Phase I, that in Phase II is characterized by planning, and by successive layers that were created with some care. Timber, in the form of both tree trunks and worked beams, was abundant in this phase as well, but the arrangement of this material was very different (Fig. 8.12).[12] Some of the numerous superimposed layers of wood run parallel to the faces of the shaft in an east–west or north–south direction. Originally, the timber would have been arranged horizontally, but was found sloping inward because of the gradual decomposition of the organic remains in the fill. Part of the timber found in the fill of Phase II may have served for the consolidation of the walls during the construction of the shaft—a wooden scaffolding of sorts—but there was also at least one massive trunk that was clearly dumped there during the backfilling that was not related to anything carefully constructed (Fig. 8.13).

FIGURE 8.9. Hypogeion, Phase I: Visible features include unbaked mud bricks, organic remains of wooden posts, and part of a pithos embedded in a greenish layer of decomposed mud brick. Photo A. Athanassiadou

A layer of clay marks the upper edge of Phase II, but probably belongs to Phase III, which is characterized by clay layers. The filling of Phase III is typical for rubbish pits found in the area of the Thermaic Gulf.[13] It is arranged in successive layers with varied material, including pottery, parts of clay basins, metal objects, animal bones, seashells, tools, workshop debris of various kinds, ashes, and charcoal (Chapter 10), in addition to quantities of decomposed organic materials, including decayed wood, only traces of which survived (Figs. 8.14–8.15). The decomposition of this material explains the characteristic brown color and loose texture of the soil in this phase, which was easy to excavate.

The primary concern of those involved with the deposition of the Phase III fill was to secure and stabilize, as much as possible, the area of the Hypogeion. Phases I–III can be grouped together as the first part of the fill of the Hypogeion, or "fill A."[14]

A fairly thick wall (0.90–1.00 m in width), Wall T.14 (originally dubbed T.14, T being from *Toichos* = wall), cut into the upper layers of the filling of Phase III, but does not belong to it (see Fig. 8.7). Functionally, Wall T.14 is not related to the Hypogeion because it: a) is not centrally located within the shaft; b) does not run parallel to the walls of the Hypogeion (the west end of the wall lies at a distance of 1 m from the northwest corner of the shaft, while the east end lies 1.5 m from the northeast corner) (Fig. 8.16); and c) has a well-cut north face made of large stones, but a south face that was probably not well prepared (the upper courses, which were heavily tilted

FIGURE 8.10. Hypogeion, Phase I: a) unworked stones in the southeast corner; b) unworked stones in the northwest corner. Photos A. Athanassiadou

outward, obstructed the study of this side of the wall), consisted of rough stones, a large pebble, and part of a large quern, and was probably intended to be invisible (Figs. 8.17a, 8.17b). The difference in the construction of the north and south faces of the wall (Fig. 8.17a–b) may well suggest a retaining wall, which represents a different phase of activity that postdates the original filling of the Hypogeion and was originally located above ground. As time passed, the deposits shrank and subsided on account of the large amount of organic materials enclosed therein. These processes must have been more rapid during the initial phase. It is especially noteworthy that Wall T.14, being a fairly dense and heavy structure, gave way faster and earlier than the total fill of the pit. It was because of this that the area of Wall T.14, part of which is stratigraphically mixed, represents the interstices of the upper end fill A.

FIGURE 8.11. Hypogeion stratigraphy of Phase I: The strata, consisting mainly of clay, intersect at different heights depending on which side the fill materials were thrown in from. Photo A. Athanassiadou

FIGURE 8.12. Hypogeion, Phase II: Horizontal imprints of wooden beams, and vertical imprints of round trunks. Photo A. Athanassiadou

On the evidence of the fragmentation and conservation of the pottery, the surface of the initial deposits of the Hypogeion fill—Phases I–III ("phase α" or "fill A")—was placed at least as high as 8.50 m from the floor of the pit. Wall T.14 was most likely built immediately after the filling of the Hypogeion. The compression and shrinkage of the discard materials of the fill, and the gradual subsidence of the surface of the pit (that is, the surface of the Phase III fill), necessitated the construction of another, similarly oriented wall, sometime in the mid-7th century B.C. This second Wall, T.5, was found at a higher level within the shaft, 1.6–1.8 m higher than T.14. Wall T.5 (see Fig. 8.7) resembled T.14 in: a) running along the same orientation as T.14; b) having a comparable width (1 m); c) having a well-cut north face made of large stones and a south face made of smaller rough stones (Fig. 8.18). Accordingly, T.5 seems to have replaced T.14 when the latter subsided into the shaft with the decomposition of organic remains, and functioned as a retaining wall.[15] A few highly diagnostic pieces from this fill favor a date in the 7th century B.C. (see **9/93–9/95**, Figs. 9.40–9.41).[16] Severe erosion on the summit of the East Hill erased the continuation of both Walls T.14 and T.5 and of their associated fills, east and west of the Hypogeion pit.

The phases overlying (and thus postdating) "phase α" or "fill A" require further study. Of particular importance is a stratum that lies above Wall T.5. This stratum, which constitutes a separate phase, is represented by a layer that was rich in pottery and clay from decomposed mud brick. This latest phase (here labeled "fill C")[17] was found overlying Wall T.5 and extended both

FIGURE 8.13. Hypogeion, Phase II. Imprint and remnants of an unworked tree trunk along the east scarp of the Hypogeion pit. Photo A. Athanassiadou

FIGURE 8.14. Hypogeion, Phase III: The deposits as they appeared on the west side, detail. Photo A. Athanassiadou

north and south. Indeed, some mud bricks located south of T.5 (and at a higher level) apparently remained in place, and had probably fallen from a wall that was clearly later than T.5 (Fig. 8.19). This phase yielded much diagnostic pottery, including Corinthian and Ionian imports from the last quarter of the 7th to the mid-6th century B.C. (see **9/96–9/98**, Figs. 9.42–9.43), but also an Attic red-figure sherd that dates from the end of the 6th century B.C.[18]

In conclusion, all the layers which overlie "phase α" ("fill A") do not make up a second phase of use, but represent layers which were once on the surface but sank within the Hypogeion as its original fill was compressed.

FIGURE 8.15. Hypogeion, Phase III: The deposits directly underneath Wall 14 (T.14), detail. Photo A. Athanassiadou

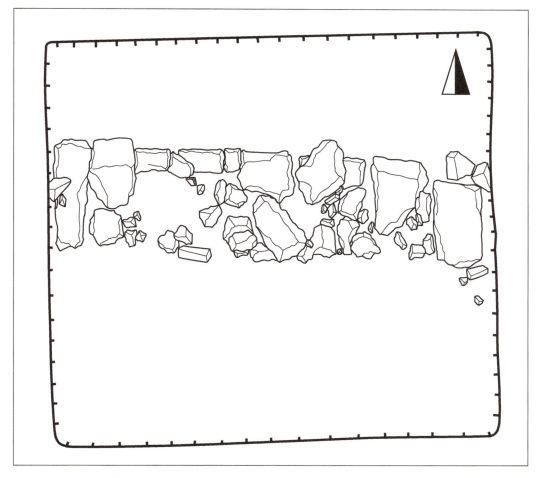

FIGURE 8.16. Plan of wall T.14, as found within the area of the Hypogeion. Drawing I. Moschou

FIGURE 8.17. a) Wall T.14 from the north side; b) wall T.14 from the south side.
Photos A. Athanassiadou

THE CHRONOLOGY OF THE HYPOGEION

What is clear from the stratigraphical sequence outlined above is that the filling of the Hypogeion pit occurred over a very short period of time. Construction materials featured prominently in the fill—unbaked mud bricks, unworked stone, and timber (both worked beams and in the form of tree trunks)—as well as a large volume of debris, both industrial and domestic. This refuse did not originate in some sanctuary or public building, but primarily derived from a quarter of pronounced industrial character. The fact that sherds from the same vessel were often found at different depths, highly fragmented, indicate that most of the debris had been transported from an original place of

FIGURE 8.18. Hypogeion, wall T.5 from the north side. Photo M. Tolia-Christakou

FIGURE 8.19. Hypogeion, detail, from the north, showing the habitation deposits above wall T.5, with visible layers of unbaked mud bricks. Photo M. Tolia-Christakou

discard. The deposits within the Hypogeion (Phases I–III or "fill A")—extraordinary rich in ceramics, small finds in a broad variety of materials, industrial waste, and more—can all be attributed to a narrow chronological horizon. It is precisely this that makes the assemblage so important and unique.

Any attempt to piece together the chronology of the depositional phases of the Hypogeion relies primarily on the pottery, which constitutes the single largest and most diagnostic category of material from the deposit. Mended vessels and a copious quantity of fragments belong to a broad array of vessel forms: kraters, skyphoi, kantharoi, kotylai, eggshell-ware cups, phialai, lekanides, plates, dinoi, pyxides, oinochoai, small lekythoi, olpai, amphoras, and hydriai (see Chapter 9).[19] Prominent among the ceramics are the transport amphoras, from various centers of the Greek world: Athens, Corinth, Samos, Chios, Aiolis, the broader Thermaic Gulf, and elsewhere (see Chapter 12, and for later trade amphoras, see Chapter 21). Noteworthy are the sherds from at least five Phoenician amphoras (see Chapter 1, Figs. 1.11a–d), as well as a few fragments from smaller Phoenician shapes.[20] There is also a significant quantity of cooking wares. A large number of the mended vessels and fragments are the products of local workshops, including those of Methone, the broader Thermaic Gulf region, and the Chalkidike, and others belong to the workshops of major centers in the Aegean and eastern Mediterranean (see Chapters 9, 12, 22).[21]

The filling of the Hypogeion (Phases I to III) includes pottery ranging from the end of the Stone Age to the later part of the Early Iron Age. More specifically, there is comparatively little Late Neolithic to Subprotogeometric material, which is highly fragmentary, includes few joining sherds, and is clearly residual.[22] A relatively small number of pieces can be dated to the third quarter of the 8th century B.C. (740–730 B.C.), including Corinthian fine wares and Thapsos class pottery. The stylistic study of the vast majority of the local and imported material, however, strongly indicates, or is consistent with, an LG IIb date (720–690 B.C.).

It is suggested that the filling (and also the construction) of the Hypogeion (Phases I to III ["fill A"]) took place in the LG II period and not earlier because of the following criteria: a) the stratigraphy indicates that the process of filling was speedy, and perhaps lasted only for some weeks; b) the many complete or well-preserved vessels must date from around the time of deposition and these are the most reliable indications for dating, and they are LG II; c) the quantity of specimens from specific vessel types suggests that these date from around the time of deposition and the ceramic types that are well represented in the fill favor the same date; d) the vessel types that are copiously represented are more likely to derive from local workshops; e) the farther the distance from the time of deposition, the more fragmentary the state of the pottery, coupled with significantly lower quantities. Indeed, it must be emphasized that the mending of individual vessels, and especially the percentage of mendability of each vessel, are key factors in addressing the chronology of the filling in of the Hypogeion.[23]

The LG II date proposed for the filling of the Hypogeion is grounded on the rich evidence of imported fine wares from regions with well-studied and finely dated ceramic sequences, especially Euboia, Attica, and Corinth (fully discussed in Chapter 9).[24] The best comparative evidence for the range of the material recovered from the Hypogeion comes from the *metropolis* of Methone, Eretria, and is represented by Pit 53 in the West Quarter (see Chapter 9).[25] Indeed, there are many direct correspondences between ceramic types recovered from the two contexts.[26]

The chronological range of the material from Phases I to III of the Hypogeion is confirmed by the Corinthian fine wares. This applies especially to a rich series of kotylai that can be dated to 720–705 B.C., and other pieces which are Corinthian Late Geometric or Early Protocorinthian (740–705 B.C.). Likewise, the fewer Attic imports, which include pieces by the Painter of Athens 897, suggest an Attic LG IIb date (730–700 B.C.). Locally produced copies of Euboian and Corinthian pottery also adhere to types of the last two decades of the 8th century B.C. Accordingly, the process of filling (and also constructing) the Hypogeion is placed late in the LG II period, that is, in 720–690 B.C. according to the conventional chronology.

As noted above, the material from the phases that postdate phases I–III ("fill A") was not documented in great detail in *Methone Pierias* I because of limitations of time and resources, and also because the vast majority of the inscribed material published there came from the Late Geometric fill (Phases I–III). The study of this material is still in progress, but the primary later phases have already been identified and discussed above.[27] A fuller and representative account of the pottery from Phases I–III, as well as selected pottery from the overlying levels of the Hypogeion, is presented in Chapter 9.

EPILOGUE

To reiterate, the deep empty shaft of the Hypogeion was filled very soon after its construction was abandoned, sometime around 720–690 B.C. It was cut through bedrock and soil to a depth of over 12 m using simple tools and manual labor to create a shaft of 181.44 m³ at minimum (12 x 3.6 x 4.2 m). As a massive pit over 12 m deep it was too dangerous to be left exposed. Moreover, this pit occupied a considerable area (3.6 m x 4.2 m at floor level) on the strategic location of a hilltop located by the coast and the economic heart of the site of ancient Methone. Filling would thus ensure that this space could be used for other purposes.

The initial filling of the Hypogeion (Phases I to III, or "fill A") would have reached up to the rim of the original shaft, but the subsequent decomposition of the rich organic remains, with the resulting subsidence, brought it to a much lower level, at least 8.5 m above the floor of the feature.

All layers lying above Phase III (including Walls T.5 and T.14) do not belong to the primary fill, but represent activity on the hilltop after the filling of the shaft. The subsidence of these surface layers into the area of the Hypogeion occurred as early as the 7th century B.C. The distinction between Phases I–III ("fill A"), on the one hand, and those located above, on the other, is also evident in the pottery. The material from the later levels is much less in quantity, considerably more fragmentary, with relatively few joins, and typically does not allow for the reconstruction of whole pots. The relatively complete vases from the uppermost phases remain few in number and are all particularly small. There is no comparison to the state of preservation of the pottery from the lower fill (Phases I–III ["fill A"]), which can be reconstructed by the mending of many sherds, often preserving complete or near-complete vessels.

The Hypogeion remains a unique structure with exceptionally rich epigraphic (Chapter 11) and ceramic finds (Chapters 9, 12), but also a wide variety of other material, including industrial debris (Chapters 13, 14), metals (Chapter 15), worked ivory, antler, and bone, and various clay objects (Chapters 16–17). As an assemblage it has already garnered considerable interest in the scholarly community.[28] What is presented in this volume is only a sampling of the material from this one context—the proverbial tip of an iceberg. The sheer quantity of the finds still requires conservation, study, and presentation. It is an assemblage that has a lot more to offer.

NOTES

1 The text is based on Bessios 2012a, but excludes the study and illustrated catalogue of the pottery (which is presented separately in Chapter 9) and is focused on the stratigraphy and interpretation of the excavated feature referred to as the Hypogeion. In the original text, there was an introduction to the location and importance of Methone, which now appears as Chapter 1, so this part has been slightly modified to avoid repetition. For the location of the site, see Hammond 1972, p. 129, who proposed to locate Methone north of Nea Agathoupolis. According to the archives of the former 16th Ephoreia of Prehistoric and Classical Antiquities, Andreas Vavritsas and Maria Siganidou identified the site as Methone in 1970, and it was included in the catalogue of archaeological sites of the Greek Ministry of Culture in 1989 (full details in Bessios 2012a, p. 63, n. 1: Ministerial decree ΥΠΠΟ/ΑΡΧ/Α1/Φ16/52381/2075/26.04.1989 [ΦΕΚ410/τ.Β/29.05.1989]). The location of Methone is also discussed in Bessios 1990, p. 83, and Hatzopoulos, Knoepfler, and Marigo-Papadopoulos 1990. The text was translated by Marianna Nikolaidou, Antonis Kotsonas, and John Papadopoulos.

2 For the excavations at the site since 2003, see Bessios 2003 and Chapter 1.

3   Pits graves dating to the end of the Late Bronze Age were excavated in Plots 229 and 245 (see Chapter 6). The pottery shows clear influences from Mycenaean ceramic styles (outlined in Chapter 6, and see Bessios 2010, pp. 61–62; Bessios, Athanassiadou, and Noulas 2008). During the construction of a side road off the Athens–Thessaloniki national highway, at the location "Melissia" northwest of ancient Methone (see Fig. 1.39), an Early Iron Age grave was uncovered in 1995, containing an imported Euboian oinochoe (see Figs. 1.40–1.41; and Bessios 2010, pp. 88–89). Excavations in Plots 274, 245, 225, and 229 also yielded significant numbers of sherds of various shapes with painted decoration of concentric circles or semicircles of Protogeometric and Subprotogeometric date.

4   For the literary references to Methone, see Tzifopoulos 2012a, pp. 19–21, and Chapter 2.

5   See Bessios 2003.

6   Part of an Early Bronze Age settlement was excavated in Plot 953 of the Kitros estate. A number of pits were investigated, some of which were large and shallow, whereas others had a smaller diameter but reached a depth of 1.00–1.50 m, see Bessios 2010, pp. 67–69.

7   The possibility of it serving as a rubbish pit or well/cistern is discussed in the Introduction of this volume and both of these interpretations are highly unlikely for reasons given there.

8   The excavation of the Hypogeion lasted many months because of the unique character of the context, the rich finds, and the challenges posed by the excavation of a deep shaft with unstable sides or faces. These faces were systematically reinforced with wooden planks that prevented the collapse of geological layers and ensured the safety of the excavation team; see Bessios 2012a, p. 47, figs. 3–4. The excavation of the Hypogeion lasted from May 29 to October 10, 2003 (supervision by Maria Tolia-Christakou); March 16 to September 28, 2004; July 26 to December 14, 2006; and May 3–8, 2007 (supervision by Athena Athanassiadou). The excavation staff included: Themistokles Avramidis, Ioannis Angathangelidis, Giorgos Vaidis, Andronikos Daniilidis, Ioannis Theodoridis, Nikolaos Kalaitzidis, Sotiris Kountourianos, Iordanis Mavridis, Panagiotis Meligkonis, Ioannis Moschos, Iordanis Poimenidis, Christos Prokopidis, Kyriakos Sanianos, Constantinos Tobris. The excavation drawings were made by Ioannis Moschou, while the huge task of the conservation of the pottery was carried out by Christos Avramidis, Charilaos Karanikas, Dimitra Makantasi, and Anastasia Bania.

9   Comparable challenges were noted with the excavation of Hypogeion 2 on the West Hill in 2014–2017, the sides of which required substantial reinforcement for the safety of the excavators, see Morris et al. 2020, pp. 702–712.

10 Bessios et al. 2004.

11 Geological map of Greece, Sheet Katerini/Tertiary/Neogene/Upper Miocene-Lower Pleiocene, where it is noted that the riverine and terrestrial deposits of Methone and Makrygialos consist of alternating joining clays, sandy clays, marly and clay sandstones, and sand in a pattern of cross-linked lenses. The intermediate layers of sand detach laterally or transition into binding sandstones and loose conglomerates with cobbles of tufa. Visible thickness 300 m.

12 The documentation of these layers was careful, but the level of detail was affected by limitations of time and financial resources. Although we were able to photograph many of the changes within Phase II, it was not possible to draw each subsequent level within the phase.

13 For disturbance of the upper layers of Phase III see pp. 395-396.

14 Cf. "phase α" in Kotsonas 2012, p. 123.

15 Cf. Kotsonas 2012, p. 123 ("phase β").

16 These vessels, all dating to the first half of the 7th century B.C., were originally published in Bessios 2012a, pp. 56, 63, n. 10, pp. 109–110, figs. 95–97.

17 Cf. Kotsonas 2012, p. 123 ("phase γ").

18 These vessels were originally published in Bessios 2012a, pp. 57, 58, 63 nn. 11–12, pp. 110–111, figs. 98–100.

19 See further Kotsonas 2012.
20 For the Phoenician amphoras from Methone, see Athanassiadou 2012; Kasseri 2012; Kotsonas 2012, pp. 237–239; Papadopoulos 2016, pp. 1245–1246, fig. 7.
21 See also Kotsonas 2012.
22 This is mostly handmade burnished pottery, including a few painted pieces, ranging from the Early Bronze Age to the Subprotogeometric period. Wheelmade painted material dates from the Late Bronze Age to the Subprotogeometric and Middle Geometric periods. The material is not related to the dating of the Hypogeion and most of it must have been found in among (or as part of the matrix of) the mud bricks that were common in Phase I. There was much less of this material in the overlying Phases II and III.
23 It is important to stress that the pottery was thrown into the Hypogeion in secondary deposition, since the material had already been discarded and hauled from elsewhere. It is, therefore, reasonable to assume that the older refuse exhibits a higher degree of fragmentation and scatter in the Hypogeion than in its original place of discard.
24 As well as Bessios 2012a, pp. 57–62.
25 See *Eretria* XX, pp. 60–64.
26 The only notable exception is the paucity of Protocorinthian kotylai in Eretria Pit 53, in contrast to their presence in the Hypogeion. This may be on account of a slight chronological discrepancy or because of different choices by consumers at the two sites.
27 Bessios 2012a, pp. 54–57; cf. Kotsonas 2012, p. 123.
28 Bessios, Tzifopoulos, and Kotsonas 2012; Tzifopoulos 2013; Strauss Clay, Malkin, and Tzifopoulos 2017b; Papadopoulos 2016.

9

CATALOGUE OF SELECT POTTERY FROM THE HYPOGEION

Matthaios Bessios

A version of this chapter originally appeared in Greek in 2012 in *Methone* I, and its original aim was to provide, through a selection of the most representative wheelmade and painted pieces, the pottery from the fill of the Hypogeion.[1] An even larger selection of pottery, including a variety of different wares, such as transport amphoras, with inscribed or painted markings, from the same context was published in the same volume (191 pieces in all).[2]

The sherds **9/1** and **9/2** (ΜΕΘ 3807, ΜΕΘ 3818; Figs. 1.42, 9.1) should be considered chance finds, related to the precolonial activity at the harbor of Methone; so too, the small fragments of Corinthian kotylai, **9/7** and **9/8** (ΜΕΘ 4054, ΜΕΘ 4051; Fig. 9.3). The earliest specimens of Euboian pottery, **9/3** and **9/4** (ΜΕΘ 3819, ΜΕΘ 3811; Figs. 9.1–9.2), datable to 740–730 B.C., must be associated with the time of the arrival of the Eretrian colonists, whereas the skyphoi **9/5** and **9/6** (ΜΕΘ 3606 and ΜΕΘ 2248; Fig. 9.2) are better placed in the decade 730–720 B.C. The Late Geometric period of Corinth is represented by a significant number of partially preserved vessels, hemispherical kotylai datable between 740 and 720 B.C. (**9/9–9/15**, and perhaps also **9/16, 9/17, 9/24**) (Figs. 9.3–9.5, 9.8). To the same period can also be placed the two unique examples of "Thapsos Class" skyphoi, similarly preserved as small fragments (**9/18–9/19**; Fig. 9.6).

The tall kotylai (**9/20–9/25**; Figs. 9.7–9.8) belong to the initial phase of the development of this type, as is indicated by the double lines along the contours of most preserved handles and by the oblique placement of the handles in relation to the body of the vessel. The resemblance of the schematized bird motif (wire-bird) between the tall and the hemispherical kotylai suggests a chronological overlap of the two types, which most likely dates between 725 and 715 B.C.

The next group of tall kotylai (**9/26–9/31**; Figs. 9.8–9.10) is characterized by further schematization of the bird motif; a thin reserved band, which in the previous group ran around the middle of the belly, has risen close to the group of bands that runs directly under the decorative register between the handles. One more thin, reserved band exists between the monochrome-painted belly and the ring base of the vessel. These features, as well as the fact that this is the best represented type in terms of quantity, degree of body preservation, and surface condition, point to a somewhat later date,[3] perhaps between 720 and 705 B.C., that is, in the initial phase of Early Protocorinthian pottery. This phase cannot be very distant from the previous one, and the two may have partly overlapped.

The other pieces of Corinthian pottery (**9/32–9/36**; Figs. 9.10–9.11) cannot be securely attributed to either the Late Geometric or the Early Protocorinthian period, because of their fragmentary condition and their decorative features. Since fragmentary preservation usually, although not always, indicates an earlier date, such vessels must fall within the chronological range defined by the aforementioned more representative examples; that is, between 740 and 705 B.C. To judge from this assemblage of Corinthian pottery, and also taking into account the use-life of the vessels—as attested, for example, by ancient mending holes—the filling of the Hypogeion must have taken place in the last years of the decade 710–700 B.C., or possibly during the following decade, 700–690 B.C.

To the same chronological conclusion point the few specimens of Athenian pottery, which were found in the Hypogeion and can be dated to the Late Geometric IIb period (730–700 B.C.): the largest part of an Attic krater by the Painter of Athens 897 with minimal use wear on the surface (**9/37**; Fig. 9.12);[4] fragments of another such krater (**9/38**; Fig. 9.13); and kraters of similar form and decorative subject (**9/39–9/40**; Figs. 9.14–9.15), which are considered imports of eastern Aegean manufacture because of their clay composition, and thus indicate the far-reaching influence of this Attic workshop. The maker of another krater (**9/41**; Fig. 9.16), which may also be assigned to the east Aegean workshop, was probably influenced by the Attic workshop of the Lion Painter.[5] To the beginning of the period (730–720 B.C.) must belong the sherd of a large painted amphora (**9/42**; Fig. 9.17), with a wall thickness comparable to the monumental vessels of the Athenian Kerameikos, the presence of which at Methone is telling; in contrast, the fragment of an oinochoe belongs to the end of Late Geometric IIb (**9/43**; Fig. 9.17). All these Athenian examples, together with the aforementioned Corinthian vessels, confirm that the Hypogeion was filled in during the decade 700–690 B.C. at the latest.

As noted in Chapter 8, in order to date the assemblage from the Hypogeion, it is particularly useful to examine this material together with the pottery of Pit 53 from the West Quarter at Eretria.[6] There is a remarkable similarity of shapes and decorative subjects between the Euboian-style pottery from the Hypogeion and the majority of vessels from Pit 53. The small sample illustrated here (**9/44–9/58**; Figs. 9.18–9.23) includes telling examples of the affinity between the finds from the Hypogeion at Methone and those from Pit 53 at Eretria. The only shapes in Pit 53 that are absent in the Hypogeion are the kotylai.[7] In contrast, the Hypogeion included a large number of kotylai that are confirmed imitations of Early Protocorinthian prototypes. The absence of kotylai imitations from the contents of Pit 53 in Eretria has been interpreted as a sign of delay—namely, "that they [the kotylai] appear somewhat later than their Corinthian prototypes"[8]—although this delay is not explained. However, misfired vessels from the Hypogeion, that is, wasters, document the existence of local potteries at the colony of Methone, which operated under the influence of both the metropolis and other production centers in the Aegean. In addition to kotyle imitations, the Hypogeion also contained a large number of open shapes with recognizable Euboian and Corinthian inspiration. The abundance of such vessels (see criterion d, Chapter 8) and the composition of their clay provide strong evidence that these were, for the most part, local products.[9] Included here are examples of different types attributable to the workshops of Methone or its broader region (**9/65–9/92**; Figs. 9.29–9.39). Among these, 9/83 and 9/84 (Figs. 9.35 and 9.36) are likely Euboian imports. The illustrated vessels from the Hypogeion, being imitations and thus later than their prototypes, must be dated to the phase closest in time to the filling-in of the pit; according to the aforementioned criteria,[10] this pottery should be synchronized with the last group of Corinthian vessels (**9/26–9/31**; Figs. 9.8–9.10), which fall within the chronological range of 720 and 705 B.C. If we consider the kotylai as imitations of Early Protocorinthian models, the terminus post quem for this particular local product can be set at 710 B.C. However, the kotyle **9/66** (ΜΕΘ 1577; Fig. 9.29) is modeled after the Corinthian hemispherical shape of Late Geometric date; to the same shape point also the short vertical strokes that adorn the handles of the local products which should also be assigned to the same chronology. Similarly, the skyphos **9/77** (ΜΕΘ 1354; Fig. 9.33) follows a type earlier than the Early Protocorinthian.[11] The influence of the Early Protocorinthian tall kotylai is clear on many of the Methone examples; therefore, the dating of the local assemblage in the decade 710–700 B.C. seems fairly secure. Apparently, toward the end of the 8th century B.C. the Methonaian workshops preserved shapes and decorative themes of Corinthian Late Geometric wares, which had long ceased to be produced in the workshops of Corinth itself. Accordingly, the lack of imitations of Early Protocorinthian kotylai among the pottery of Pit 53 in Eretria can be explained in two ways: either the pit contents belong to a horizon earlier than the decade 720–710 B.C., or this particular type of vessel was not produced in Eretria. The small quantities of Early Protocorinthian imitation kotylai, which have been found elsewhere in Eretria, in no way compare to the respective quantities from the Hypogeion;[12] it is even possible that the former were exports from the colony to its metropolis.

We should also consider the possibility that the shapes of presumably local origin—which also belong to the ceramic deposit of the Hypogeion—date to the Subgeometric period; that is, they are later than the lowest chronological limit of Euboian Late Geometric II. A large number of kotylai and skyphoi from the Hypogeion are decorated with schematized birds in panels. The skyphos with concentric circles around the rim—another local Methonaian product—is likewise represented by a large number of examples, which differ from the corresponding Euboian prototype in both the shape and the decoration of the panels.[13] Two other types of skyphoi that occur in large numbers must also be attributed to local workshops: one has the panels filled with multiple zigzags (**9/78–9/82**; Figs. 9.33–9.34), the other with a row of S-shaped motifs (**9/85–9/87**; Fig. 9.37). All these local wares of Methone were created under Euboian and Corinthian influences and thus must postdate their prototypes, although the chronological sequence still remains to be defined.

Taken together, the selected diagnostic examples from the voluminous and varied ceramic assemblage of the Hypogeion at Methone point to a date for this deposit between 710 and 690 B.C. This view is supported by two vessels with distinctive decorative themes of the Euboian Late Geometric II style: a) the large skyphos **9/59** (ΜΕΘ 3368; Fig. 9.24), which features around the rim and on the shoulder birds with outspread wings; examples of this motif have been found at Eretria,[14] Oropos (across the Euboian Gulf),[15] and Pithekoussai;[16] b) the krater **9/62** (ΜΕΘ 3823; Fig. 9.27), with double handles at the shoulder; the central area of the shoulder on both sides is decorated with the distinctive Euboian motif of a horse tethered at a stall. Since most fragments of the krater were found in the upper layers of the Hypogeion fill, this vessel provides indisputable evidence for the dating of the ceramic assemblage from the pit to the Late Geometric II period.

The time window between 710 and 690 B.C. must be considered a secure bracket for the filling of the Hypogeion, according to the aforementioned criteria a–e and the imports from Euboia, Corinth, and Attica (see Chapter 8). These chronological limits are strongly corroborated by the synchronicity of the Hypogeion pottery with the main bulk of ceramics from Pit 53 in the West Quarter at Eretria. Even if the two assemblages do not coincide exactly, they cannot be separated by more than a decade. The same conclusion is also indicated by the large groups of local products in the Hypogeion, which, however, are not represented in the material from the metropolis. This terminus ante quem indicates that the total ceramic assemblage from the Hypogeion belongs to one or two generations, and must be dated between 740 and 690 B.C.

The context of the pottery presented below, together with the stratigraphical phase to which each piece belongs, is presented in Table 9.1.

CATALOGUE

9/1. (ΜΕΘ 3807) Attic Amphora Fr Fig. 9.1
P.H. 0.090; p.L. 0.085; Th. 0.008.
Body fr, amphora.
Portion of one set of partially preserved mechanically drawn concentric circles, with reserved cross at center, flanked by a hatched meander to right, and multiple zigzag below, the various zones separated by multiple vertical and horizontal lines.
Middle Geometric II.

9/2. (ΜΕΘ 3818) Euboian Skyphos Fr Fig. 9.1
P.H. 0.022; p.L. 0.025; Th. 0.004.
Rim fr, skyphos. Row of chevrons, framed by two horizontal bands above, and three below. Off-white slip.
Late Geometric I.

9/3. (ΜΕΘ 3819) Euboian Skyphos Fr Fig. 9.1
P.H. 0.055; Diam. (rim) est. 0.110.
Rim and upper body frr, skyphos. Preserved lower body painted solid. Upper body decorated with a metope, consisting of row of wiggly lines set vertically above three horizontal bands, with row of vertical lines to right. Four horizontal bands on rim exterior; two similar bands on rim interior. On the lower body on the interior a broad reserved band. The preserved handle is decorated with a row of vertical lines. On account of use there is intense wear on the main part of the decoration. Off-white slip.
Late Geometric I.

9/4. (ΜΕΘ 3811) Euboian Skyphos Fr Fig. 9.2
P.H. 0.060; Diam. (rim) est. 0.110.
Rim and upper body frr, skyphos. Preserved lower body painted solid. Comparatively tall decorated zone (H. 0.028). Portion of preserved cross-hatched lozenge in metope, framed on either side by vertical lines (nine vertical lines on the right cluster). Three thin horizontal bands on rim exterior. Preserved handle decorated with vertical lines approaching dots. Interior painted solid. Off-white slip.
Cf. Descoeudres 1978 (*Eretria* IV), pl. 2.3.
Late Geometric I.

9/5. (ΜΕΘ 3606) Fragmentary Euboian Skyphos Fig. 9.2
H. 0.095; Diam. (rim) 0.140; Diam. (base) 0.060; H. (decorative zone) 0.025.
Painted skyphos. The central metope, framed by groups of ten vertical lines on either side, is decorated with a row of loose lozenges (or linked Xs); three horizontal bands below, below which the vessel is painted solid. Rim exterior decorated with two thin horizontal bands surmounted by a slightly thicker band. Preserved handle decorated with a horizontal band that extends over the two first vertical lines framing the metope. Off-white slip on the decorated zone. Interior painted solid except for a reserved band at rim.
Cf. Coldstream 1995, p. 259, fig. 3.84.
730–720 B.C.

CATALOGUE OF SELECT POTTERY FROM THE HYPOGEION

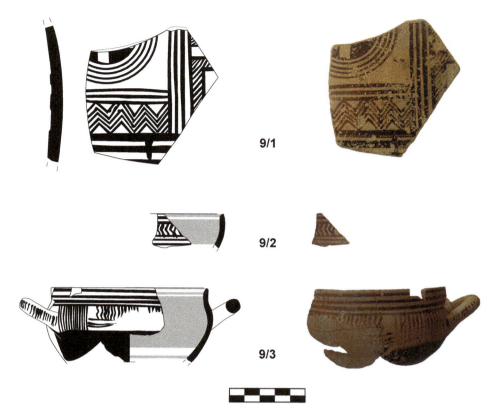

FIGURE 9.1. Attic MG II amphora body fr, **9/1** (ΜΕΘ 3807);
Euboian LG I skyphos rim fr, **9/2** (ΜΕΘ 3818); Euboian LG I skyphos, **9/3** (ΜΕΘ 3819).
Drawings A. Hooton, I. Moschou, and T. Ross, photos I. Coyle and KZ´ Ephoreia

9/6. (ΜΕΘ 2248) Fragmentary Euboian Skyphos Fig. 9.2
P.H. (of the two main frr) 0.082 and 0.065; Diam. (rim) est. 0.150.
The cup of Hakesandros (for the inscription, see Chapter 11).
Decoration similar to **9/5**, but with one horizontal band below decorative zone and three thin bands on rim; interior painted solid.
730–720 B.C. or later.

9/7. (ΜΕΘ 4054) Corinthian Kotyle Body Fr Fig. 9.3
P.H. 0.040; p.L. 0.028.
Small body fr of Corinthian kotyle, with relatively thick wall. Decorative zone on upper preserved body decorated with thin vertical lines (at least 12 preserved); lower preserved body painted solid. Interior painted solid.
Late Geometric.

9/8. (ΜΕΘ 4051) Rim Fr, Corinthian Kotyle Fig. 9.3
P.H. 0.030; p.L. 0.034; Diam. (rim) est. 0.160.
Small rim fr, relatively thick-walled, and decorated with thick lines. Preserved decorative zone on upper body decorated with five vertical lines, with portion of a sixth, to right of small portion of hatched meander. Horizontal band or area painted solid below; two bands on rim exterior. Interior painted solid.
Late Geometric.

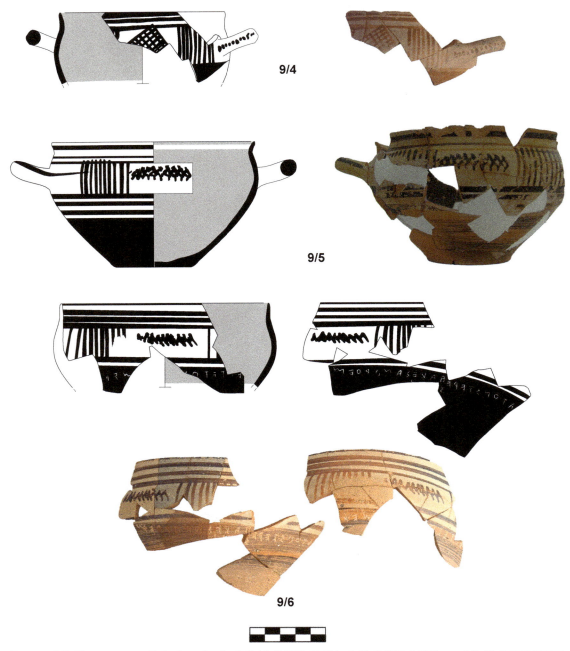

FIGURE 9.2. Fragmentary Euboian skyphoi, **9/4** (ΜΕΘ 3811), **9/5** (ΜΕΘ 3606), and **9/6** (ΜΕΘ 2248) (the cup of Hakesandros). Drawings I. Moschou and T. Ross, photos I. Coyle and KZ´ Ephoreia

9/9. (ΜΕΘ 4042) Rim and Upper Body Fr, Corinthian Kotyle   Fig. 9.3
P.H. 0.055; p.L. 0.078; Diam. (rim) est. 0.150.
Decorative metope on upper body decorated with row of Ss, framed by a zigzag below and one above. This is framed to one preserved side by panel of 12 vertical lines, solid double axe, and then at least seven preserved vertical lines. Ten thin horizontal bands on area below decorative zone, below which is an area painted solid. Two bands on rim. Interior painted solid, except for reserved band, much worn.
Late Geometric.

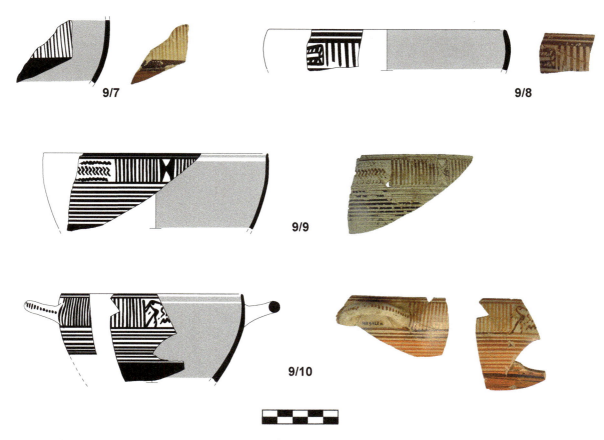

FIGURE 9.3. Fragmentary Corinthian kotylai, **9/7** (ΜΕΘ 4054), **9/8** (ΜΕΘ 4051), **9/9** (ΜΕΘ 4042), and **9/10** (ΜΕΘ 3413). Drawings I. Moschou and T. Ross, photos I. Coyle and KZ´ Ephoreia

9/10. (ΜΕΘ 3413) Rim and Upper Body Frr, Corinthian Kotyle Fig. 9.3
P.H. (max) 0.061; Diam. (rim) est. 0.120.

Two groups of non-joining frr, preserving portion of rim, body, and one handle of kotyle. The decorative zone on the preserved upper body consists of multiple thin vertical lines framing a central metope, decorated with a single bird (heron), facing right, and then row of Ss, only partially preserved, framed by single zigzag below and one above. Ten thin horizontal bands immediately below, above area painted solid; two thin bands on rim exterior. Exterior face of handle decorated with vertical strokes, becoming dots toward the handle attachment. Interior painted solid, except for reserved band at rim, below which is a thin band of added white.

Late Geometric.

9/11. (ΜΕΘ 3409) Fragmentary Corinthian Kotyle Fig. 9.4
H. 0.113; Diam. (base) 0.050; Diam. (rim) est. 0.150.

Large portion preserved of Corinthian kotyle, hastily made; complete profile preserved. Central metope on uppermost body decorated with a row of birds ("soldier birds"), seven preserved, together with small portion of an eighth, facing left. Immediately below the metope of birds, two thin horizontal bands. This is framed, on the preserved left side, by thin vertical lines (at least four preserved). Eight horizontal bands on body below, below which the vessel, to base, is painted solid. Two thin horizontal bands on rim. Interior painted solid, except for thin reserved band near rim.

Late Geometric.

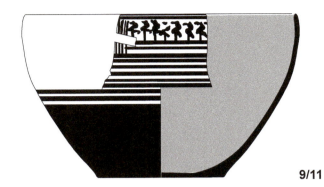

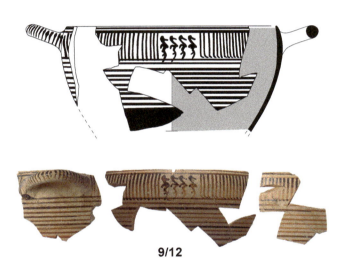
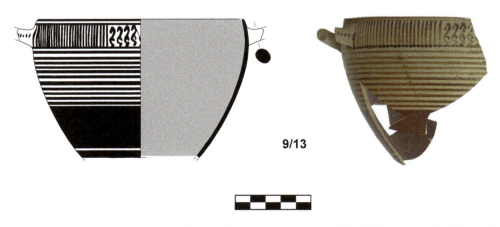

FIGURE 9.4. Fragmentary Corinthian kotylai, **9/11** (MEΘ 3409), **9/12** (MEΘ 3415), and **9/13** (MEΘ 3411). Drawings I. Moschou and T. Ross, photos I. Coyle and KZ´ Ephoreia

9/12. (ΜΕΘ 3415α, β, γ) Upper Body Frr, Corinthian Kotyle Fig. 9.4
P.H. (max) 0.073; Diam. (rim) est. 0.140.

Three non-joining groups of frr, preserving portion of rim, upper body, and one complete handle. Small metope, framed by multiple thin vertical lines on either side, decorated with four birds (wire-birds), facing right. Body below decorated with ten horizontal bands, above area painted solid. Two thin horizontal bands at rim. Preserved handle decorated with slightly curved vertical lines following the contour of the handle. Interior painted solid, except for reserved band at rim.
Late Geometric.

9/13. (ΜΕΘ 3411) Fragmentary Corinthian Kotyle Fig. 9.4
P.H. 0.097; Diam. (rim) est. 0.145.

Substantial portion of rim, body, and one handle of kotyle; base not preserved. Four preserved birds and portion of a fifth in the central metope, facing left, framed by multiple thin vertical lines (the metope on **9/14** [ΜΕΘ 4033] preserves a total of six birds almost identical to those on **9/13**). Twelve horizontal bands on body below, below which is an area painted solid, interrupted by a reserved band. Two thin horizontal bands at rim. Handle, as preserved, decorated with a row of dots. Interior painted solid, except for a thin reserved band at rim.
Late Geometric.

9/14. (ΜΕΘ 4033α, β) Frr of Corinthian Kotyle Fig. 9.5
P.H. 0.070; p.L. 0.099; Diam. (rim) 0.140.

Two groups of non-joining frr preserving portion of rim, upper body, and one handle. Decoration very similar to **9/13** (ΜΕΘ 3411), but with slightly smaller dimensions.
Late Geometric.

9/15. (ΜΕΘ 4035α, β, γ) Frr of Corinthian Kotyle Fig. 9.5
Diam. (rim) est. 0.150.

Three groups of non-joining frr preserving portion of rim, uppermost body, and one handle. Decorative metope preserves four birds (wire-birds), facing left, framed by multiple thin vertical lines. Horizontal bands below (at least six preserved). Two thin horizontal bands on rim. Exterior face of handle decorated with row of short vertical lines. Interior painted solid, except for reserved band at rim.
Late Geometric.

9/16. (ΜΕΘ 4035) Rim Fr, Corinthian Kotyle Fig. 9.5
P.H. 0.031.

Minuscule fr, preserving small portion of rim of kotyle. Surviving metope preserves three birds, facing left, framed by multiple thin vertical lines (only two preserved); at least three horizontal bands below; two thin bands on rim. Interior painted solid, except for reserved band at rim.
Late Geometric?

9/17. (ΜΕΘ 4053α, β, γ) Fragmentary Corinthian Kotyle Fig. 9.5
P.H. 0.078; Diam. (rim) est. 0.170.

Four groups of non-joining frr, preserving portion of rim and body of a kotyle, perhaps tall. Of the small portion that survives of the central metope, there is part of a bird, facing right, probably from an original set of four. The multiple thin vertical lines framing the metope are interrupted by a double axe, in the sections between the central metope and the handles (portions of two double

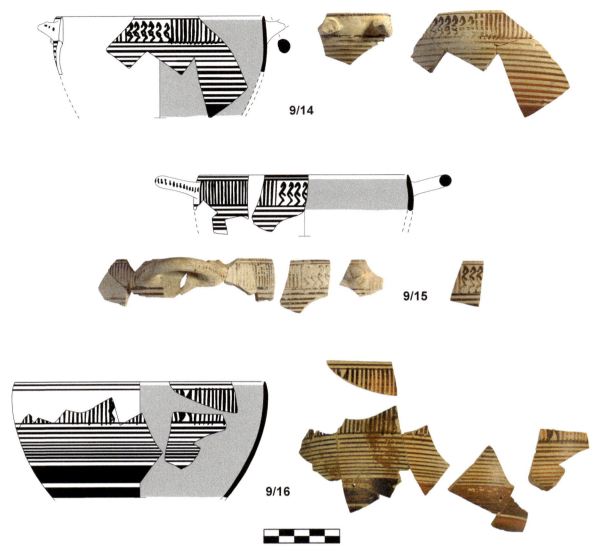

FIGURE 9.5. Fragmentary Corinthian kotylai, **9/14** (MEΘ 4033), **9/15** (MEΘ 4035), **9/16** (MEΘ 4035), and **9/17** (MEΘ 4053). Drawings I. Moschou and T. Ross, photos I. Coyle and KZ´ Ephoreia

axes preserved). Eleven horizontal bands on body below the decorative zone, below which is an area painted solid, interrupted by a reserved band; two thin horizontal bands on rim. Interior painted solid, except for reserved band at rim. For decorative idiom, cf. **9/20** (MEΘ 1319).

Mending holes indicate that the vessel was repaired in antiquity.

Late Geometric?

9/18. (MEΘ 3808) Skyphos Rim Fr, Thapsos Class   Fig. 9.6
P.H. 0.040; p.L. 0.084; Diam. (rim) est. 0.140.

Central metope, framed by sets of four vertical lines on either side, decorated with a row of five lozenges, each with a dot at center; this decorative zone is further framed by four horizontal bands. Above the decorative zone, on the rim, four horizontal bands, with a fifth on the lip top; at least four bands on body below decorative zone. Interior painted solid, except for a comparatively broad reserved band at rim.

730–720 B.C.

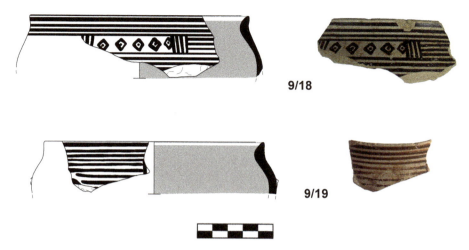

FIGURE 9.6. Fragments of Thapsos Class skyphoi, **9/18** MEΘ (3808) and **9/19** (MEΘ 4044). Drawings T. Ross, photos I. Coyle

9/19. (MEΘ 4044) Skyphos Rim Fr, Thapsos Class   Fig. 9.6

P.H. 0.034; p.L. 0.051; Diam. (rim) est. 0.120.

Only the upper left portion survives of one preserved side of the vessel, from the very edge of the metope to the handle. Only a small portion of one vertical line defining the edge of the metope is visible. Above the decorative metope, four horizontal bands at rim. There are at least four horizontal bands framing the metope, with portion of a fifth immediately below. Interior painted solid, except for a reserved band at rim.

Cf. Benton 1953, pp. 275, 277, fig. 8, no. 643.

730–720 B.C.

9/20. (MEΘ 1319) Tall Corinthian Kotyle   Fig. 9.7

H. 0.112; Diam. (base) 0.053; Diam. (rim) 0.140.

Complete, except for one missing handle and small parts of the body and rim. Six birds (wire-birds) in the central metope, facing right, framed on either side by multiple thin vertical lines, which are interrupted by a single solid double axe. Ten horizontal bands below, below which the vessel is painted solid down to the base, except for a thin reserved band. Two thin horizontal bands on rim. The exterior of the preserved handle is decorated with two parallel bands following the contour of the handle. Interior painted solid, except for two reserved bands at rim. Surface of the vessel worn probably on account of long-term use.

725–710 B.C. An early example of a tall, deep kotyle.

9/21. (MEΘ 3410) Rim and Handle Fr, Corinthian Kotyle   Fig. 9.7

P.H. 0.051; Diam. (rim) est. 0.160.

Portion preserved of the rim, upper body, and one handle. All that survives of the decorative zone are the multiple thin vertical lines, interrupted by a partially preserved double axe. Body immediately below decorated with at least eight horizontal bands, below which is a ninth (or the upper part of an area painted solid). Two thin horizontal bands on rim. The exterior of the preserved handle is decorated with two parallel bands following the contour of the handle. Interior painted solid, except for a thin reserved band at lip, and a band in added white below.

725–710 B.C. An early example of a tall, deep kotyle.

9/22. (ΜΕΘ 4045α, β, γ) Fragmentary Corinthian Kotyle   Fig. 9.7
H. 0.104; Diam. (rim) est. 0.140.

Three groups of non-joining frr preserving complete profile, including one handle. In the central preserved metope on one side of the vessel are four preserved birds facing right; the metope is framed by multiple thin vertical lines, only a small portion of which survives. Fourteen horizontal bands below, below which the vessel is painted solid down to the base, except for a thin reserved band. Two thin horizontal bands on rim. Exterior, upper face of preserved handle decorated with a band following the contour of the handle. Interior painted solid, except for comparatively thin reserved band at rim. Underside decorated as shown.

725–710 B.C. An early example of a tall, deep kotyle.

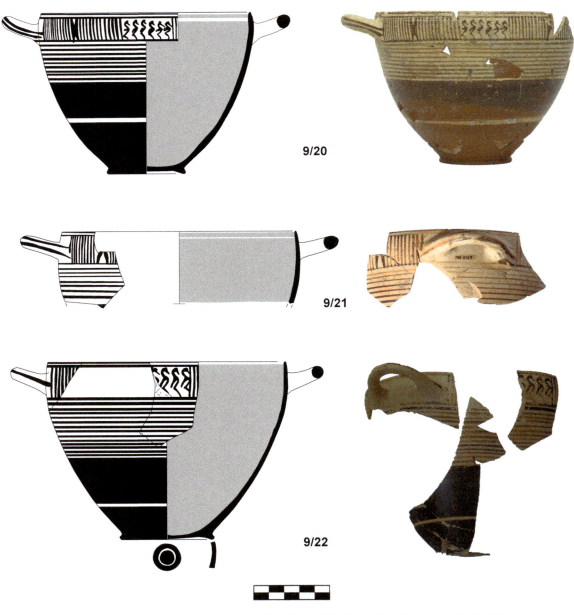

FIGURE 9.7. Fragmentary Corinthian kotylai, **9/20** (ΜΕΘ 1319), **9/21** (ΜΕΘ 3410), and **9/22** (ΜΕΘ 4045). Drawings I. Moschou and T. Ross, photos I. Coyle and KZ´ Ephoreia

9/23.   (MEΘ 3810) Body, Rim, and Handle Fr, Corinthian Kotyle   Fig. 9.8
P.H. 0.048; p.L. 0.067; Diam. (rim) est. 0.100.

Fr preserves much of the rim, body, and portion of one handle. The central metope is decorated with a row of four-bar sigmas, facing right, of which 12 are preserved, together with a tiny portion of a 13th, framed on one side by 12 vertical lines. Fifteen horizontal bands below, below which is the upper part of an area painted solid. Two horizontal bands on rim. Outer face of preserved handle decorated with two parallel bands following the contour of the handle. Interior painted solid, except for two thin reserved bands at rim.

725–710 B.C. An early example of a tall, deep kotyle.

9/24.   (MEΘ 4037) Rim and Body Fr, Corinthian Kotyle   Fig. 9.8
P.H. 0.069; p.L. 0.085; Diam. (rim) est. 0.150.

The fragmentary state and comparative wall thickness of the vessel is not unlike **9/17** (MEΘ 4053), clearly a kotyle, but uncertain as to whether or not it is of the tall type. The central metope is decorated with a row of four-bar sigmas, facing left (20 preserved, together with a small portion of a 21st), framed by multiple vertical lines. Body immediately below decorated with 13 horizontal bands, below which is an area painted solid. Two thin horizontal bands at rim. Interior painted solid, except for two reserved bands at rim.

Late Geometric?

9/25.   (MEΘ 3407) Rim and Body Fr, Corinthian Kotyle   Fig. 9.8
P.H. 0.076; Diam. (rim) est. 0.095.

Small and thin-walled kotyle (oval mouth). The central metope is decorated with eight birds (wire-birds) facing right, framed by multiple thin vertical lines on either side. Nine horizontal bands on body immediately below, below which is an area painted solid, interrupted by a reserved band. Two thin bands at rim. Interior painted solid, except for two thin reserved bands at rim.

725–710 B.C. An early example of a tall, deep kotyle.

9/26.   (MEΘ 1309) Corinthian Kotyle   Fig. 9.8
H. 0.087; Diam. (base) 0.038; Diam. (rim) 0.108.

Complete, except for minor missing frr. Central metope decorated with 13 birds facing right, framed by multiple thin vertical lines on either side. Body immediately below decorated with nine horizontal bands, the lowest being the thickest; lower body to base painted solid, except for reserved band on foot exterior. Three thin bands on rim. Outer face of handle decorated with band that follows the contour of the handle. Interior painted solid, except for two thin reserved bands at rim. Drilled holes indicate that the vessel had been repaired in antiquity.

720–705 B.C.

9/27.   (MEΘ 1308) Corinthian Kotyle   Fig. 9.9
H. 0.080; Diam. (base) 0.035; Diam. (rim) 0.105.

Almost complete, but missing one handle and associated part of upper body. Kotyle very similar to the previous but a little smaller, and with 12 birds facing right in the central metope, framed by multiple thin vertical lines on either side. Body immediately below decorated with nine horizontal bands, the lowest being the thickest; lower body to base painted solid, except for reserved band on foot exterior, which is not as prominent as that on **9/26** (MEΘ 1309). Two thin bands on rim. Outer face of preserved handle decorated with band that follows the contour of the handle. Interior painted solid, except for reserved band at rim.

720–705 B.C.

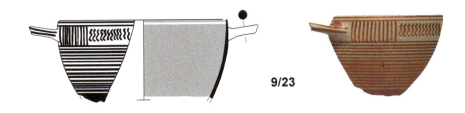
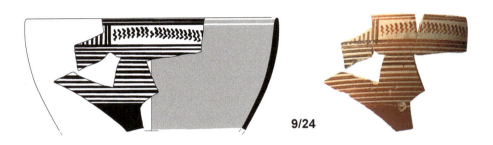

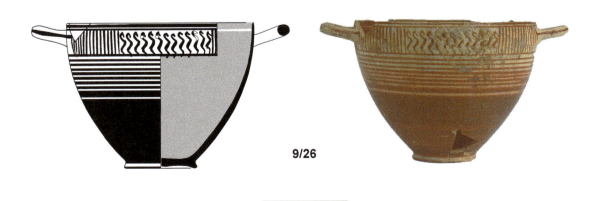

FIGURE 9.8. Complete and fragmentary Corinthian kotylai, **9/23** (MEΘ 3810), **9/24** (MEΘ 4037), **9/25** (MEΘ 3407), and **9/26** (MEΘ 1309). Drawings I. Moschou and T. Ross, photos I. Coyle and KZ´ Ephoreia

CATALOGUE OF SELECT POTTERY FROM THE HYPOGEION

9/28. (ΜΕΘ 3412) Fragmentary Corinthian Kotyle Fig. 9.9
P.H. 0.071; Diam. (rim) est. 0.105.
Form and decoration similar to **9/27** (ΜΕΘ 1308). A solitary preserved drilled hole indicates the vessel was mended in antiquity.
720–705 B.C.

9/29. (ΜΕΘ 3406) Fragmentary Corinthian Kotyle Fig. 9.9
P.H. 0.059; Diam. (rim) est. 0.110.
Fragmentary kotyle preserving portion of rim, upper body, and one handle. The little that survives of the central metope preserves only two birds, facing right, framed by multiple thin vertical lines. Body immediately below decorated with seven horizontal bands, the lowest being the thickest, below which the preserved fr is painted solid. Two thin bands on rim. Outer face of preserved handle decorated with band that follows the contour of the handle. Interior painted solid, except for two reserved bands at rim.
720–705 B.C.

9/30. (ΜΕΘ 3408) Fragmentary Corinthian Kotyle Fig. 9.9
P.H. 0.080; Diam. (base) 0.042; Diam. (rim) est. 0.115.
Much of base and parts of lower body preserved, but less so of upper body. The only part of the decorative zone that survives are the multiple lines that would have framed the metope, which is not preserved. The frr of this vessel may belong with those of **9/31** (ΜΕΘ 4043α, β), or the two are from separate vessels similarly decorated. Both have two thin bands at rim, and seven horizontal bands below, the lowest being the thickest. The interior of both kotylai is painted solid with two horizontal bands at rim. **9/30** also has a reserved band on the foot exterior, similar to **9/26** (ΜΕΘ 1309), and it belongs to the same class of tall kotylai as **9/26** (ΜΕΘ 1309), **9/27** (ΜΕΘ 1308), **9/28** (ΜΕΘ 3412), and **9/29** (ΜΕΘ 3406).
720–705 B.C.

9/31. (ΜΕΘ 4043α, β) Fragmentary Corinthian Kotyle Fig. 9.10
Diam. (rim) est. 0.115.
Two groups of non-joining frr, perhaps from the same vessel as **9/30** (ΜΕΘ 3408). Fr **9/31**α preserves portion of the central metope, decorated with a row of birds, facing right, framed by multiple vertical lines; fr β preserves one handle, decorated with a band following the contours of the upper and outer face of the handle.
720–705 B.C.

9/32. (ΜΕΘ 4060α, β) Rim Frr, Corinthian Kotyle Fig. 9.10
P.H. (max) 0.027.
Two small non-joining frr, probably from the same small and thin-walled kotyle. Fr α preserves portion of the central metope decorated with a row of cross-hatched triangles, whereas fr β preserves the greater part of a solid double axe framed by vertical lines. There are at least ten thin horizontal bands below the metope on fr α; three thin horizontal bands on the rim of both frr. Interior painted solid, except for two reserved bands at rim.
720–705 B.C.

9/33. (ΜΕΘ 4038α, β) Rim Frr, from Two Corinthian Kotylai Fig. 9.10
Fr α: p.H. 0.035; Diam. (rim) est. 0.150; fr β: p.H. 0.030.
Two frr, probably from two different kotylai, similarly decorated.

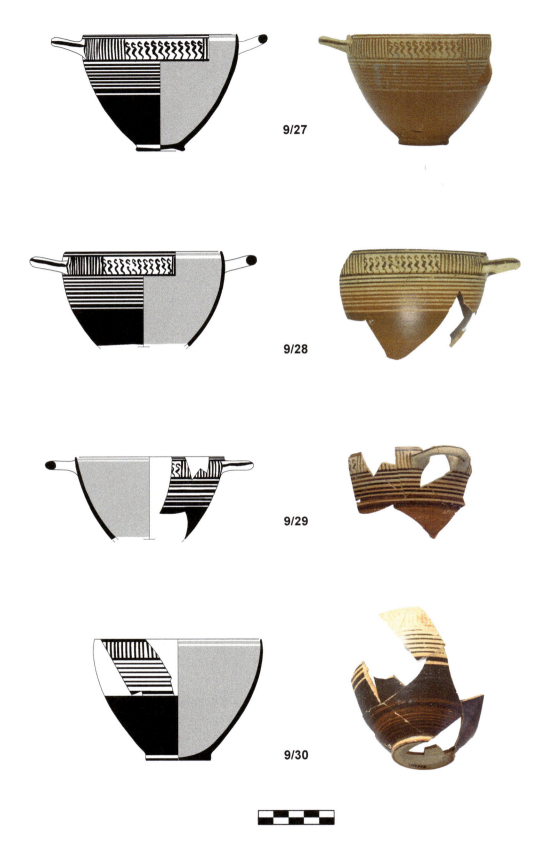

FIGURE 9.9. Fragmentary Corinthian kotylai, **9/27** (ΜΕΘ 1308), **9/28** (ΜΕΘ 3412), **9/29** (ΜΕΘ 3406), and **9/30** (ΜΕΘ 3408). Drawings I. Moschou and T. Ross, photos I. Coyle and KZ´ Ephoreia

FIGURE 9.10. Fragmentary Corinthian kotylai, **9/31** (MEΘ 4043), **9/32** (MEΘ 4060), and **9/33** (MEΘ 4038). Drawings T. Ross, photos I. Coyle and KZ´ Ephoreia

Fr α (right sherd): paint largely peeled, inside and out, painted solid on exterior, with two horizontal bands in added white, one at the level of the handle, itself not preserved, and another lower down, below the handle (0.026) from the rim.

Fr β (left sherd): probably from a slightly smaller kotyle, also painted solid on exterior. There is a thin horizontal band in added white on the rim exterior, barely visible, and another, clearly visible below the preserved stump of the handle (0.024) from the rim.

720–705 B.C.

9/34. (MEΘ 4041) Frr Corinthian Krater   Fig. 9.11

P.H. (fr with handle stump) 0.032.

Three non-joining body frr, one preserving portion of horizontal handle stump. In addition to the handle stump, what survives are very small portions of the decorated body in the handle zone, consisting of multiple vertical lines (framing the handle) and at least two parallel tremulous lines, with horizontal bands below. Preserved interior painted solid.

720–705 B.C.

9/35. (MEΘ 4040) Corinthian Lid Fr   Fig. 9.11

Diam. (lid rim) est. 0.190; H. (of articulated rim) 0.012; p.L. 0.045.

Single fr preserving small portion of lid. Five fine horizontal bands on the articulated, downturned portion of rim; eight slightly thicker bands on lid top. Toward the preserved center a thicker band or area painted solid.

720–705 B.C.

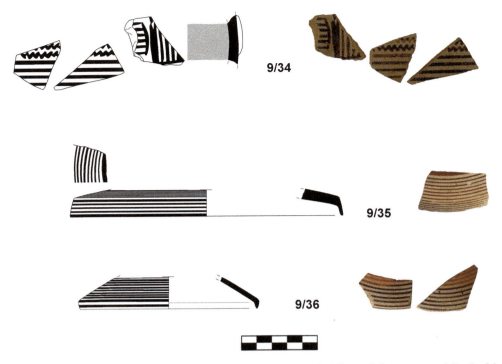

FIGURE 9.11. Fragmentary Corinthinan krater, **9/34** (MEΘ 4041), and fragments of Corinthian lids, **9/35** (MEΘ 4040) and **9/36** (MEΘ 4039). Drawings T. Ross, photos I. Coyle and KZ′ Ephoreia

9/36. (MEΘ 4039) Corinthian Lid Frr Fig. 9.11
Diam. (lid rim) est. 0.150; H. (of articulated rim) 0.005.
Two non-joining frr preserving small portion of lid. Two thin bands on articulated, downturned rim perimeter; at least nine on the flat lid top.
720–705 B.C.

9/37. (MEΘ 2032) Fragmentary Attic Krater Fig. 9.12
P.H. 0.195; Diam. (rim) 0.275–0.283; max p.D. (body) 0.316.
Fragmentary spouted krater attributed to the Painter of Athens 897. On the better preserved side, two dogs, running to the left, in a metope defined to the far left and right with sets of multiple vertical bands. Filling ornaments in this metope include birds, Ss (variously displaced), a double axe in outline, lozenge chains, and tremulous lines approaching zigzags; below the metope 12 horizontal bands, below which is an area painted solid, enlivened with two reserved bands. Two bands on rim exterior; rim tops decorated with groups of multiple lines, arranged in groups of 12. Off-white slip.
Late Geometric IIb.

9/38. (MEΘ 4059) Attic Krater Body Frr Fig. 9.13
Fr α (left on photo): p.H. 0.075; p.L. 0.060.
Fr β (right on photo): p.H. 0.040; p.L. 0.056.
Two non-joining frr of krater attributed to the Painter of Athens 897, stylistically similar to **9/37**. Portions preserved of two dogs running to right. The only surviving filling ornament is the tremulous line approaching zigzag on fr α. Below the decorated metope, at least seven horizontal bands are preserved. Off-white slip. Interior painted solid.
Late Geometric IIb.

FIGURE 9.12. Fragmentary Attic krater attributed to the Painter or Workshop of Athens 897, **9/37** (ΜΕΘ 2032). Drawings A. Hooton, photos I. Coyle

FIGURE 9.13. Fragments of an Attic krater, **9/38** (ΜΕΘ 4059), attributed to the Painter or Workshop of Athens 897. Drawings A. Hooton and T. Ross, photos J. Vanderpool

9/39.   (ΜΕΘ 2031) Fragmentary Krater   Fig. 9.14

H. 0.249–0.255; Diam. (base) 0.114; Diam. (rim) 0.304; max Diam. (body) 0.380.

The metope, defined by sets of ten vertical lines, is decorated with a scene strongly influenced by the Painter of Athens 897. To the right, a dog attacking a hare in the central portion of the metope; to the left a small part of a second dog attacking the same hare. Filling ornaments largely consist of rows of Ss of various sizes, facing right. Six horizontal bands below, below which the vessel is painted solid, except for a comparatively thick reserved band at the center of the lower body, and the lower outer face of the base, which is also reserved. Horizontal band on rim exterior. The upper surface of the rim is decorated with sets of small vertical lines, with reserved areas between the sets. Small diagonal bands decorate the preserved handle, placed between two parallel bands that follow the contour of the handle. Exterior decoration on off-white slip, which enhanced the entire decorative scheme. Interior painted solid. On the basis purely of the visual characteristics of the clay, the vessel was assigned to some workshop (as yet undetermined) of the eastern Aegean.

Late Geometric IIb.

9/40.   (ΜΕΘ 4058) Krater Frr   Fig. 9.15

Diam. (rim) est. 0.270.

Three main non-joining groups of frr preserving portions of the rim and body of the krater, plus a fourth fr preserving a handle stump. The metope is framed by a set of ten vertical lines; the body below the metope is decorated with seven or eight horizontal bands, below which is a broader area painted solid (the lowest preserved part of the body is too abraded to determine the nature of the painted decoration). Broad band on rim exterior. The upper surface of the rim is decorated with sets of small lines, as shown. The little that survives of the handle suggests that it was decorated in the same manner as **9/39** (ΜΕΘ 2031). On this particular krater, the metope has, on the right, a dog running left, toward another animal to left, only a small portion of which survives of its hindquarters, perhaps a deer or wild sheep or goat. Filling ornaments are primarily rows of Ss, of various sizes, as well as tremulous lines approaching zigzags. As with **9/39** (ΜΕΘ 2031), the decoration on an off-white slip on the exterior only serves to enhance the painted decoration. Interior painted solid.

Late Geometric IIb.

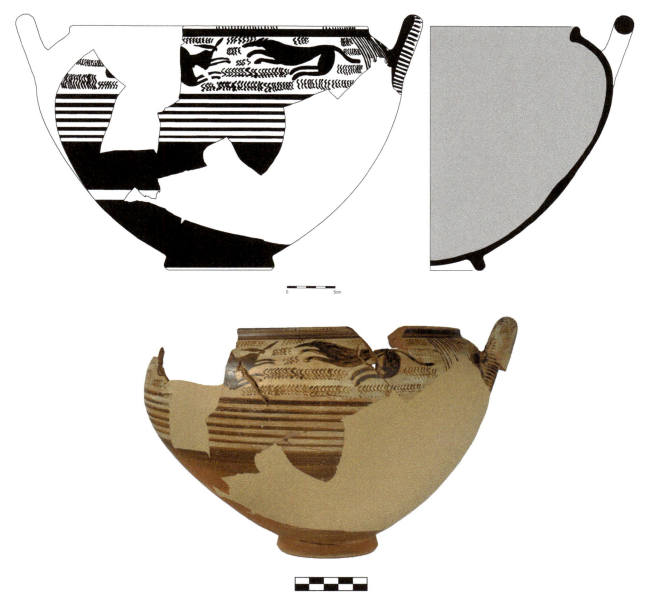

Figure 9.14. Fragmentary krater, **9/39** (ΜΕΘ 2031), stylistically related to the Workshop of the Painter of Athens 897. Drawing I. Moschou and T. Ross, photo I. Coyle

9/41. (ΜΕΘ 2021) Fragmentary Krater Fig. 9.16
H. 0.195; Diam. (rim) est. 0.300.

Small krater with tall rim. The reserved exterior, together with the upper reserved surface of the rim, bears an off-white slip. The tall rim is decorated with two menacing, heraldically opposed, roaring lions. This metope is framed, right and left, with hatched meanders (the preserved hatching all one direction), keyed in opposite directions. The metope is further framed by five horizontal bands below and at least three above. The upper surface of the rim is decorated with sets of seven vertical lines, each set separated from the other by reserved spaces. On the upper shoulder of the krater, directly below the lions on the rim, there appears to be a corresponding pair of lions, of which only the largest part of the right lion is preserved. To the right of the central metope on the shoulder is a smaller

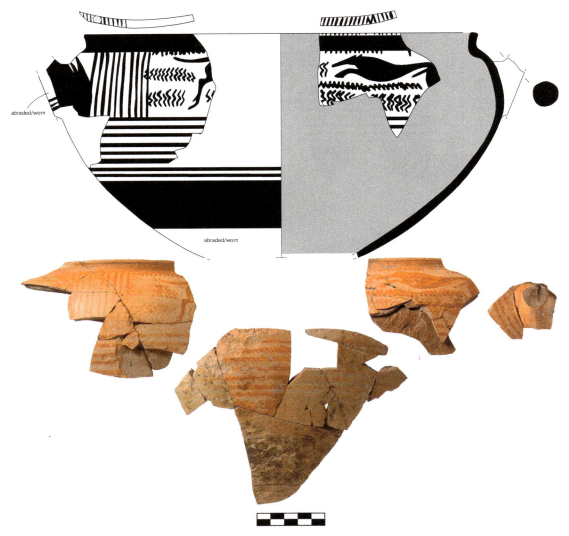

Figure 9.15. Fragments of krater, **9/40** (MEΘ 4058), stylistically related to the Workshop of the Painter of Athens 897. Drawing A. Hooton and T. Ross, photo J. Vanderpool

metope decorated with six horizontal tremulous lines approaching zigzags, framed by sets of seven vertical lines. Below this decorative band on the shoulder, a broad horizontal band, below which the lower body is decorated with numerous thin horizontal bands, as shown. The lowermost body and the ring-shaped base are painted solid. Interior painted solid. The clay contains much silver mica. Late Geometric IIb.

9/42. (MEΘ 4052) Body Fr, Attic Amphora Fig. 9.17
P.H. 0.100; p.L. 0.047.

The thickness of the body (0.013) indicates a size proportional to the monumental funerary vessels of the Athenian Kerameikos. The preserved body of the amphora is decorated with thin zones, each separated from the other by groups of three horizontal bands. The lower decorative zone has a horizontal tremulous line approaching zigzag; the other is decorated with a row of dotted triangles, the apex of each triangle surmounted by a vertical line, which reach to the horizontal band above. Above this is a third decorative zone that is too poorly preserved to determine. Off-white slip. Late Geometric IIb.

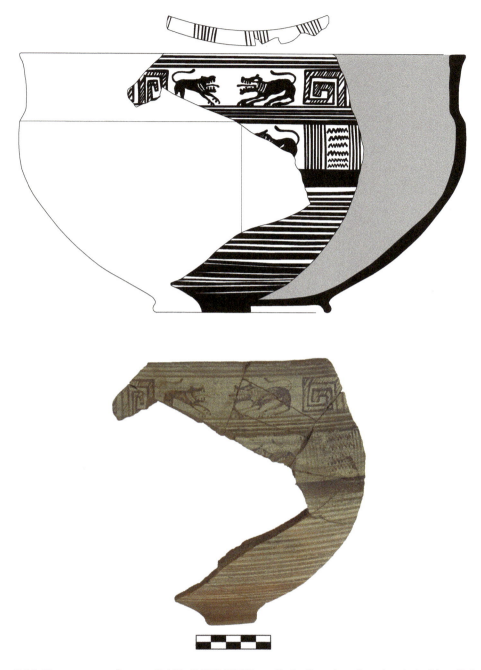

FIGURE 9.16. Fragmentary krater, **9/41** (ΜΕΘ 2021), stylistically related to the Attic Lion Painter. Drawing I. Moschou and T. Ross, photo ΚΖ´ Ephoreia

9/43. (ΜΕΘ 4034) Body Fr, Attic Oinochoe Fig. 9.17
P.H. 0.111.
Shoulder and upper body fr, oinochoe. As preserved, the decoration of the shoulder includes the lower legs of a deer or horse, to the right of which is portion of a lozenge star (for the motif, see Coldstream 1968, p. 396, pl. 11:g). Between the animal legs a vertical stack of four Ms. The remainder of the preserved body is decorated with numerous thin horizontal bands (over 20 preserved).
Late Geometric IIb

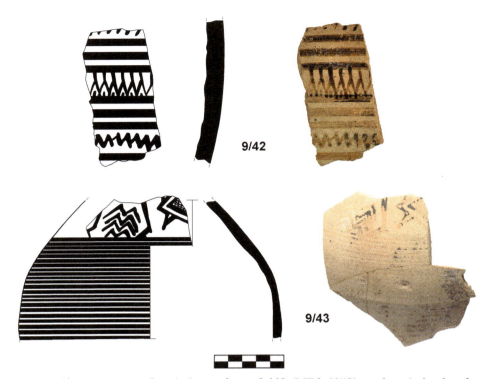

FIGURE 9.17. Fragments of an Attic amphora, **9/42** (MEΘ 4052), and an Attic oinochoe, **9/43** (MEΘ 4034). Drawings I. Moschou and T. Ross, photos I. Coyle

9/44. (MEΘ 3318) Local Euboian-style Fragmentary Cup   Fig. 9.18

P.H. 0.058; Diam. (rim) est. 0.080.

Portion of upper body, including handle, preserved, but nothing of the base. The body is decorated with clusters of eight lines set vertically; handle barred. Off-white slip.

Cf. *Eretria* XX, p. 130, pl. 64, no. 308 (Pit 53).

Late Geometric IIb.

9/45. (MEΘ 3816) Local Euboian-style Skyphos Body Fr   Fig. 9.18

P.H. 0.038; p.W. 0.046.

Small portion of body of skyphos. Of the decoration of the central metope all that survives is a mechanically drawn set of two concentric circles with large dot at center, framed by four preserved vertical lines. What survives of the lower body is painted solid. Preserved interior painted solid, except for a reserved band near lower break. Off-white slip.

Cf. *Eretria* XX, p. 130, pl. 64, no. 311, or p. 130, pl. 65, no. 316 (Pit 53).

Late Geometric IIb.

9/46. (MEΘ 1314) Local Euboian-style Fragmentary Skyphos   Fig. 9.18

H. 0.097; Diam. (base) 0.048; Diam. (rim) 0.135.

Paint mostly dark reddish brown on body and the side of the preserved handle, but not on the lower body and base. Two thin bands on lower rim on exterior, above which is a row of dots; thin band at rim top. Interior painted solid except for four reserved bands at rim, and a thicker reserved band on the lower central body. Off-white slip.

Cf. *Eretria* XX, p. 130, pl. 64, no. 312 (Pit 53).

Late Geometric IIb,

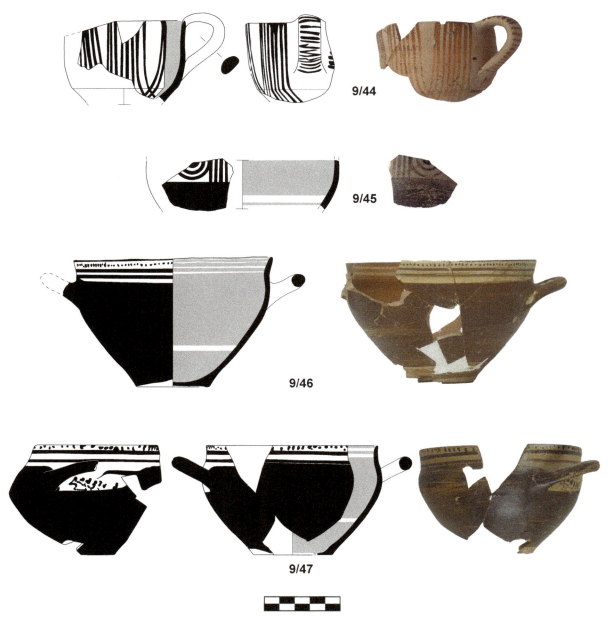

FIGURE 9.18. Euboian or Euboian-style open vessels, cup (**9/44** [ΜΕΘ 3318]) and skyphoi (**9/45** [ΜΕΘ 3816], **9/46** [ΜΕΘ 1314], **9/47** [ΜΕΘ 3582]). Drawings A. Hooton, I. Moschou, and T. Ross, photos I. Coyle and KZ´ Ephoreia

9/47. (ΜΕΘ 3582) Local Euboian-style Fragmentary Skyphos Fig. 9.18
H. 0.075; Diam. (base) est. 0.050; Diam. (rim) 0.115.

Skyphos similar in shape and decoration to **9/46** (ΜΕΘ 1314), but smaller. The black-brown paint covers the body, except for an irregular reserved band at base and area below and around handles. Reserved rim decorated with two horizontal bands and row of dots. Reserved area under preserved handle decorated with irregular lines, as shown. Interior painted solid except for two thin reserved bands at rim, and a slightly thicker reserved band on lower central body. Off-white slip.

Cf. **9/46** and *Eretria* XX, p. 130, pl. 64, no. 312 (Pit 53).

Late Geometric IIb.

9/48. (ΜΕΘ 1326) Local Euboian-style Skyphos   Fig. 9.19

H. (max) 0.088; Diam. (base) 0.047; Diam. (rim) 0.145.

The metope on the upper body of the vessel, defined on either side by a set of eight vertical lines, is decorated with a gentle wavy line, accompanied by a row of dots above and below; the lower body is painted solid, except for the slightly articulated base, which is reserved. The rim is decorated with three horizontal bands of varying thickness. There is a band along the outer faces of the handles, following their contours. The interior is painted solid, except for four reserved bands at the rim, and another lower down on the body. Off-white slip.

Cf. *Eretria* XX, p. 130, pl. 64, no. 313 (Pit 53).

Late Geometric II.

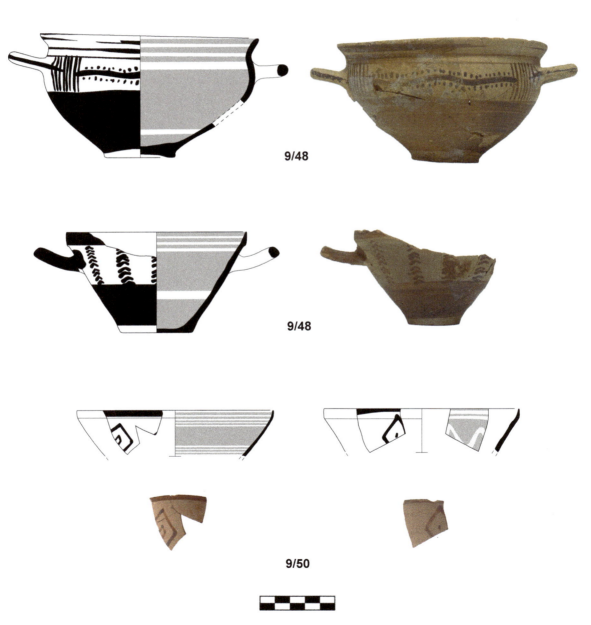

FIGURE 9.19. Euboian or Euboian-style skyphoi, including conical skyphoi, **9/48** (ΜΕΘ 1326), **9/49** (ΜΕΘ 1352), and **9/50** (ΜΕΘ 3814, ΜΕΘ 4061). Drawings A. Hooton, I. Moschou, and T. Ross, photos I. Coyle and KZ´ Ephoreia

9/49. (ΜΕΘ 1352) Local Euboian-style Fragmentary Conical Skyphos   Fig. 9.19
H. 0.067; Diam. (base) 0.035; Diam. (rim) est. 0.120.

Conical skyphos with articulated rim. The decoration is painted over an off-white slip that covers the entire vessel. In the comparatively high zone between the lower edge of the articulated rim and lower body of the vessel, four vertical rows of stacked chevrons. The lower body, except the lower part of the base, is painted solid; the rim and the outer and upper faces of the preserved handle are also painted solid. Interior painted solid except for four reserved bands at rim, and a broader reserved band lower down.

For the shape, cf. *Eretria* XX, p. 130, pl. 65, no. 315 (Pit 53).

Beginnings of Late Geometric II.

9/50. (ΜΕΘ 3814 and ΜΕΘ 4061) Rim Frr, Local Euboian-style Conical Skyphoi   Fig. 9.19
Fr α (ΜΕΘ 3814): p.H. 0.038; p.W. 0.038; Diam. (rim) est. 0.130.
Fr β (ΜΕΘ 4061): p.H. 0.032; p.W. 0.028; Diam. (rim) est. 0.130.

Fr α, which consists of three joining frr, preserves the greater part of a double-outlined lozenge in the decorative zone; the rim exterior is painted solid, and the interior is painted solid, except for four reserved bands at rim, and another analogous set of reserved bands lower down on the body, as shown.

The decorated zone of fr β (ΜΕΘ 4061) preserves a large portion of a lozenge with small dot at center; rim exterior painted solid. The interior is painted solid, except for two reserved bands at rim; below this, on top of the paint, a wavy line in added white. Off-white slip(?). The presence of silvery mica indicates that this is a product of a local workshop, rather than Euboian import (cf. the waster or production discard, **9/63** [ΜΕΘ 3809]).

For the shape, cf. *Eretria* XX, p. 130, pl. 65, no. 315 (Pit 53).

Beginnings of Late Geometric II.

9/51. (ΜΕΘ 3343) Rim, Upper Body, and Handle Fr, Local Euboian-style Conical Skyphos   Fig. 9.20
P.H. 0.044; Diam. (rim) est. 0.150.

Partially preserved conical skyphos, fire-affected. Rim decorated with three horizontal bands, above which is a row of dots. In the zone between the handles, double-outlined lozenges (one almost completely preserved, the other only partially), while outer face of the preserved handle is decorated with two bands following its contour, and extending onto the body as shown. Immediately below, but only partially preserved near the handle, a small portion of the solidly painted lower body. Interior painted solid, except for seven reserved bands of varying thickness at rim.

The shape is especially close to *Eretria* XX, p. 130, pl. 65, no. 315 (Pit 53).

Beginnings of Late Geometric II.

9/52. (ΜΕΘ 3344) Upper Body and Handle Fr, Local Euboian-style Conical Skyphos   Fig. 9.20
P.H. 0.046.

Fr clearly fire-affected. What survives of the lower portion of the articulated rim has two thin horizontal bands. The main handle zone is decorated with double-outlined lozenges (portion of one preserved), and a similar, but smaller, double lozenge below the preserved handle. The preserved handle is laddered, as shown. The preserved interior painted solid, except for six thin reserved bands at the height of the handle, above which is a wavy line in added white.

For the shape, see *Eretria* XX, p. 130, pl. 65, no. 315 (Pit 53).

Beginnings of Late Geometric II.

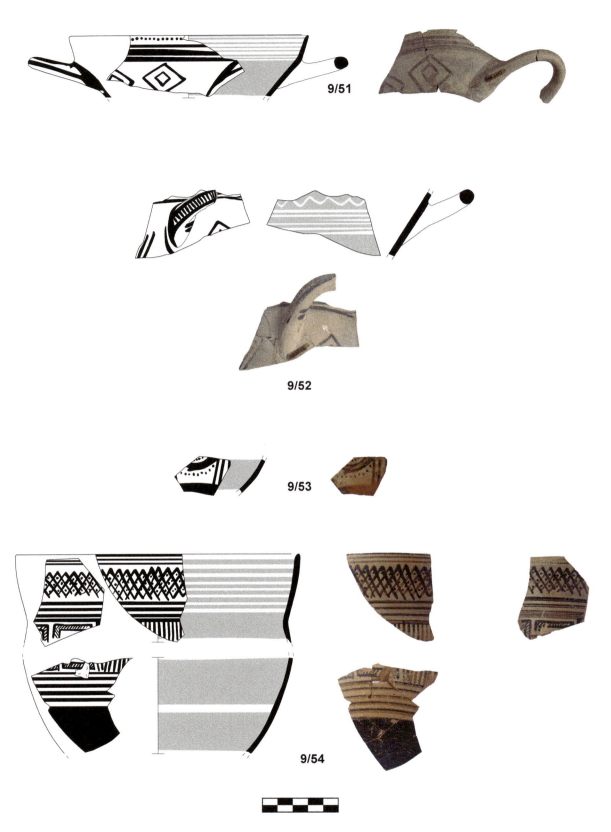

FIGURE 9.20. Euboian or Euboian-style skyphoi, including conical skyphoi, **9/51** (ΜΕΘ 3343), **9/52** (ΜΕΘ 3344), **9/53** (ΜΕΘ 3815), and **9/54** (ΜΕΘ 3812). Drawings A. Hooton and T. Ross, photos I. Coyle and KZ´ Ephoreia

9/53. (ΜΕΘ 3815) Local Euboian-style Body Fr, Skyphos Fig. 9.20
P.H. 0.026; p.W. 0.036.

Small fr, broken on all sides, preserving small portion of body. The preserved metope is decorated with a circle, painted with a thick line, only a small portion of which survives, which is framed on either side by a row of dots. To the right, portions of three vertical lines; the preserved lower body below is painted solid. Interior painted solid. Off-white slip.

For the decoration, cf. *Eretria* XX, p. 130, pl. 65, no. 318 (Pit 53), with dotted and spoked wheels in metopes.

Beginnings of Late Geometric II.

9/54. (ΜΕΘ 3812) Frr of Large Tall-rimmed Local Euboian-style Skyphos Fig. 9.20
Diam. (rim) est. 0.190.

Rim and body frr (three groups of non-joining frr). The central zone, below the rim, is decorated with metopes separated by sets of vertical lines enclosing hatched meanders, the hatching occasionally changing direction. Below the metopes, five horizontal bands, with the preserved lower body below painted solid. The tall rim has four thin horizontal bands immediately at the juncture with the body, and three at the top of the rim; the area between the bands is decorated with a three-tiered, dotted lozenge net (for the motif, see Coldstream 1968, p. 396). Interior painted solid, except for eight reserved bands on rim, and a slightly thicker band near the midpoint of the body. Off-white slip.

For a close parallel in terms of decoration and shape, cf. *Eretria* XX, p. 130, pl. 65, no. 319 (Pit 53).

Beginnings of Late Geometric II.

9/55. (ΜΕΘ 1355) Local Euboian-style Kotyle Fig. 9.21
H. 0.077; Diam. (base) est. 0.050; Diam. (rim) 0.103.

Kotyle decorated with reddish brown paint. Exterior painted solid, except for two reserved bands at rim, an analogous reserved band near the center of the body, and another two below at the juncture with the base. The body is further decorated with thin horizontal bands of added white: there are three immediately below the handle zone, and another two lower down on the body, above the reserved band near the midpoint. The central portion of the handle zone is decorated with two opposed arcs in added white, defining an "hourglass" of sorts. The interior is painted solid and is further decorated with horizontal bands of added white: two at the rim, and two further down, set quite apart. Off-white slip.

A drilled hole indicates that the vessel was repaired in antiquity.

For the shape and decoration, cf. *Eretria* XX, p. 130, pl. 66, nos. 323–324.

Late Geometric II.

9/56. (ΜΕΘ 3397) Local Euboian-style Fragmentary Krater Fig. 9.21
H. 0.240; Diam. (base) 0.110; Diam. (rim) 0.270.

Krater, perhaps originally spouted. The decoration in the handle zone on the better-preserved side is decorated by three metopes, each separated, on either side, by sets of vertical lines. The central metope is decorated by two superimposed crosses, a St. George's cross and a St. Andrew's cross, the former with perpendicular smaller lines at all four terminations (for the motifs, cf. Coldstream 1968, p. 395). The metope to the right is decorated with two rows of tremulous lines approaching zigzags, above and below which is a horizontal row of mostly four-bar sigmas. In contrast, the left metope is decorated with five superimposed tremulous lines approaching zigzags. The body below the handle zone is decorated with multiple horizontal bands, below which is an area painted solid, then three horizontal bands in a reserved zone, and another area painted solid. The outer face of the ring foot

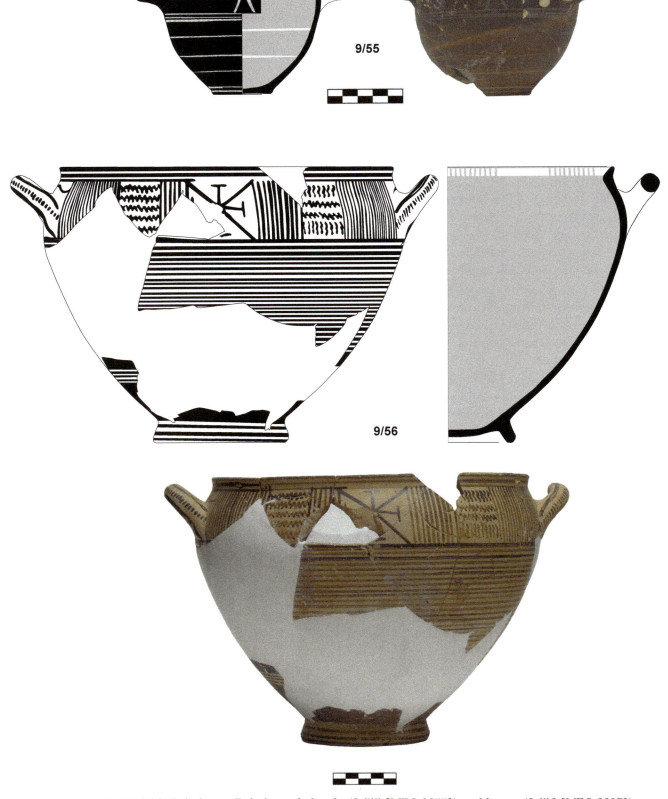

FIGURE 9.21. Euboian or Euboian-style kotyle (**9/55** [ΜΕΘ 1355]) and krater (**9/56** [ΜΕΘ 3397]). Drawings I. Moschou and T. Ross, photos I. Coyle and ΚΖ´ Ephoreia

is decorated with three additional horizontal bands. Three thin horizontal bands on rim exterior. The outer faces of the handles are decorated with two parallel lines enclosing a row of short strokes or bars. The interior is painted solid, except for a broad reserved band at the rim, which is further decorated with clusters of small vertical lines set apart. Off-white slip.

For the general form of the krater, especially in terms of shape, cf. *Eretria* XX, p. 130, pl. 67, no. 330 (Pit 53).

Late Geometric II.

9/57. (ΜΕΘ 3371) Local Euboian-style Fragmentary Spouted Krater   Fig. 9.22
P.H. 0.147.

Two non-joining frr of spouted krater, similar in type to **9/56** (ΜΕΘ 3397), but smaller. The metopes in the handle zone are defined by sets of vertical lines; one preserved metope is decorated with four stacked rows of tremulous lines approaching zigzags, while another two, much thinner, are each decorated with a vertical lozenge chain. Under the spout, which is painted solid, a bird (body cross-hatched), surrounded by filling ornaments: two lozenges, each with a superimposed cross, and a triangle. The body below the handle zone is decorated with multiple horizontal bands, below which is an area painted solid, with a wavy line in added white, below which are more horizontal bands and another area painted solid. The rim has two horizontal bands. Preserved interior painted solid, except for the rim, which is decorated with sets of vertical lines, as shown. Off-white slip.

For thin metopes on kraters decorated with vertical lozenge chain, cf. *Eretria* XX, pp. 130–131, pls. 67–69, nos. 330–334, 336 (Pit 53).

Late Geometric II.

9/58. (ΜΕΘ 3384) Local Euboian-style Fragmentary Krater   Fig. 9.23
P.H. 0.137.

Three non-joining groups of frr of krater similar to **9/56** (ΜΕΘ 3397) and of similar size. The handle zone is decorated with metopes, only small portions of which survive, separated by sets or clusters of vertical lines. Of what survives of the metopes, birds with open wings are partially preserved, as well as a vertical lozenge chain similar to those on **9/57** (ΜΕΘ 3371). The body below is decorated with multiple horizontal bands, an area painted solid with a wavy line in added white; more horizontal bands, and another area painted solid with a wavy line in added white. Off-white slip. Interior below rim painted solid.

Cf. the corresponding motifs on *Eretria* XX, p. 131, pl. 69, no. 336 (Pit 53).

Late Geometric II.

9/59. (ΜΕΘ 3368) Fragmentary Euboian or Euboian-style Large Skyphos   Fig. 9.24
H. 0.144; Diam. (base) 0.060; Diam. (rim), est. 0.200.

Large but fragmentary skyphos with tall rim. The tall rim, as well as the central metope in the handle zone, are decorated with birds with open wings. Filling ornaments in the central metope consist of hatched and cross-hatched triangles or partial triangles. Multiple horizontal bands on body below the handle zone, extending to the base, interspersed with two areas painted solid (as on **9/56** [ΜΕΘ 3397]). Four horizontal bands on lower rim frame the series of birds, and there are two bands above, near the lip. Preserved handle laddered. Interior painted solid, except for reserved rim decorated with nine horizontal bands, and another reserved band lower down on the body. Off-white slip.

For the decorative syntax, cf. *Eretria* XX, pp. 130–131, pls. 67–69, nos. 330–334, 336 (Pit 53); for the birds cf. especially the krater no. 336.

Late Geometric II.

Figure 9.22. Euboian or Euboian-style krater, **9/57** (ΜΕΘ 3371).
Drawing T. Ross, photo KZ´ Ephoreia

9/60. (ΜΕΘ 1599) Fragmentary Euboian Oinochoe Fig. 9.25

P.H. 0.221; Diam. (base) 0.078; Diam. (max, body) 0.159.

Likely trefoil oinochoe. Mostly black paint on preserved upper and lower neck, upper shoulder, and lower body; off-white slip. The central neck is decorated with a row of mechanically drawn concentric circles (each set comprising two circles with dot at center); two horizontal bands above and below. Uppermost neck painted solid; lower neck and shoulder also painted solid. Central portion of the body decorated with 16 horizontal bands; lower body painted solid. Product of a Euboian workshop.

Late Geometric II.

9/61. (ΜΕΘ 1344) Fragmentary Euboian Lid Fig. 9.26

P.H. 0.045; Diam. (max) 0.080.

Carefully worked, with good, off-white slip. The body is decorated with multiple thin horizontal bands, although toward the top there are two somewhat thicker bands. On the lower lid, near the rim, a quadruple checkerboard (for a similarly, though more complex, decorated rim, cf. the celebrated Cesnola krater in New York, Coldstream 1968, pl. 35).

Mending holes indicate that the vessel was mended in antiquity.

Late Geometric II.

Figure 9.23. Fragmentary Euboian or Euboian-style krater, **9/58** (MEΘ 3384).
Photo KZ´ Ephoreia

9/62. (MEΘ 3823) Fragmentary Euboian Krater Fig. 9.27
Diam. (rim) 0.295.

Euboian krater with tall rim and double handles on shoulder. The central metope in the handle zone on both sides is decorated with the popular Euboian horse motif, the horse tied, as shown; filling ornaments include lozenge stars, swastikas, and at least one bird. To the left and right sets of thin vertical lines, with thinner metopes decorated with vertical lozenge chain. Three thin horizontal bands below, below which are sets of sigmas (mostly three-barred), arranged in groups. The preserved body below is decorated with multiple horizontal bands, interspersed with two broader bands decorated with wavy lines in added white; there is a similarly decorated band with wavy line in added white at the uppermost shoulder, immediately below rim. The rim is decorated with two rows of sigmas, like those on the body, arranged in sets of eight, separated by horizontal bands, as shown. Rim top decorated with sets of eight short strokes. The outer faces of the handles decorated with two parallel lines following the contour of the handle, decorated with short vertical lines. The upper rim on the interior is painted as shown, whereas the lower rim and body below appear to be unpainted.

Late Geometric II.

9/63. (MEΘ 3809) Local Euboian-style Waster Frr Fig. 9.28
P.H. 0.040.

Two non-joining frr of a waster (production discard) of a conical skyphos, decorated with double-outlined lozenges (one complete and one partially preserved). Handle decorated as shown. Interior painted solid, except for reserved bands at rim. The characteristic Euboian shape and decoration of the vessel leave no doubt that similar vessels were also locally made at Methone.

For the Eretrian prototype of the shape and decoration, see Descoeudres 1976 (*Eretria* V), pl. 3, Eretria Museum inv. 432.

Late Geometric II.

FIGURE 9.24. Euboian or Euboian-style large skyphos, **9/59** (ΜΕΘ 3368).
Drawing T. Ross, photos I. Coyle

FIGURE 9.25. Euboian oinochoe, **9/60** (ΜΕΘ 1599).
Drawing I. Moschou and T. Ross, photo KZ´ Ephoreia

FIGURE 9.26. Fragmentary Euboian lid, **9/61** (ΜΕΘ 1344).
Drawing I. Moschou and T. Ross, photos I. Coyle

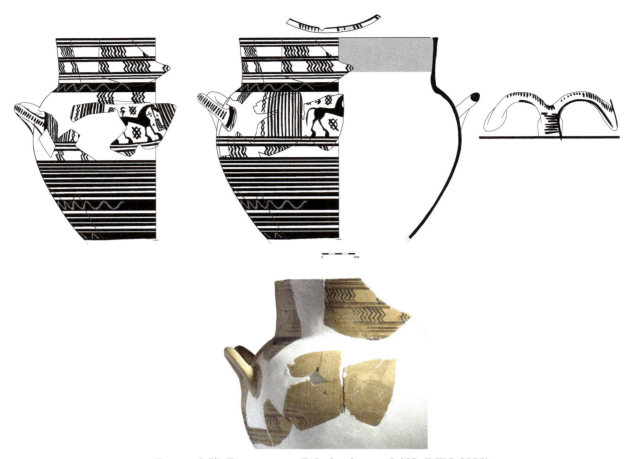

Figure 9.27. Fragmentary Euboian krater, **9/62** (ΜΕΘ 3823).
Drawing T. Ross, photo KZ´ Ephoreia

9/64. (ΜΕΘ 1337) Fragmentary Oinochoe (Production Discard) — Fig. 9.28

H. 0.264; Diam. (base) 0.094; Diam. (rim) 0.088; Diam. (max, body) 0.234.

Oinochoe with round mouth and horizontal rim. The body, neck, rim, and outer faces of the handle are painted solid, except for four reserved bands on neck, and three groups of five reserved bands on the body, as shown. As with **9/63** (ΜΕΘ 3809), this vessel is also a production discard and is thus locally made in Methone.

Late Geometric II.

9/65. (ΜΕΘ 1334) Local Kotyle — Fig. 9.29

H. 0.073; Diam. (base) 0.043; Diam. (rim) 0.103.

The decoration in the handle zone consists of a central metope with five schematic birds facing right; to the left and right, multiple vertical lines. The upper body immediately below is decorated with eight horizontal bands, below which the body is painted solid down to the base, and this area has three horizontal bands in added white, widely spaced. Two thin horizontal bands on rim, which have largely merged into one. Handles barred. Interior painted solid, with the addition of three horizontal bands in added white: one high, below the rim; another lower down below the level of the handles; a third lower still, just above the floor. Off-white slip.

For the shape and decoration, cf. **9/66** (ΜΕΘ 1577) and **9/71** (ΜΕΘ 1330).

Late Geometric IIb.

FIGURE 9.28. Local waster fragments, **9/63** (MEΘ 3809), and fragmentary local oinochoe (production discard), **9/64** (MEΘ 1337). Drawings A. Hooton, I. Moschou, and T. Ross, photos I. Coyle and KZ´ Ephoreia

9/66. (ΜΕΘ 1577) Local Kotyle Fig. 9.29
H. 0.079; Diam. (base) 0.041; Diam. (rim) 0.111.
The decoration in the handle zone consists of a central metope with five schematic birds facing right; to the left and right, multiple vertical lines. Body below painted solid. Two thin horizontal bands on rim. Handles barred. Interior originally painted solid, but little of the paint survives.
The birds are very similar to those of **9/65** (ΜΕΘ 1334) and **9/71** (ΜΕΘ 1330), and it is highly likely that all three were made in the same local workshop.
Late Geometric IIb.

9/67. (ΜΕΘ 1574) Fragmentary Local Kotyle Fig. 9.29
H. 0.107; Diam. (base) 0.047; Diam. (rim) 0.132.
The decoration in the handle zone consists of a central metope with ten schematic birds facing left; to the left and right, multiple vertical lines. Body immediately below decorated with multiple thin horizontal bands (19); lower body to base painted solid, and this area has three thin horizontal bands in added white widely spaced, and one on the ring base. Two thin horizontal bands on rim. Preserved handle barred, as shown. Interior painted solid, and with thin bands of added white: three at the rim, one near the midpoint of the interior, and another lower down. Off-white slip.
Cf. **9/69** (ΜΕΘ 1307) and **9/73** (ΜΕΘ 3646).
Late Geometric II.

9/68. (ΜΕΘ 2039) Fragmentary Local Kotyle Fig. 9.30
H. 0.104; Diam. (base) 0.050; Diam. (rim) 0.132.
The decoration in the handle zone consists of a central metope with at least five preserved schematic birds facing left; to the left and right, multiple vertical lines. Immediately below, five (or six) horizontal bands. Body below painted solid, except for the base exterior, and this solidly painted lower body has two bands in added white. Two thin horizontal bands on rim. Handles barred. Interior painted solid, but decorated with horizontal bands of added white: two just below the rim, one lower down, and another at the center of the floor. Off-white slip.
Late Geometric II.

9/69. (ΜΕΘ 1307) Small Local Kotyle Fig. 9.30
H. 0.075; Diam. (base) 0.035; Diam. (rim) 0.100.
The decoration in the handle zone consists of a central metope consisting of two tremulous lines approaching zigzags, flanked on either side by a row of five schematic birds facing left and then a row of vertical lines framing the handles. Body below decorated with multiple horizontal bands (at least 15), below which, down to the base, the lower body is painted solid in dilute paint, with at least two horizontal bands in added white. Two thin horizontal bands at rim. Handles, as preserved, barred. Interior painted solid and further decorated with horizontal bands in added white: three at the rim, one in the central portion of the vessel, and another lower down. Off-white slip.
The birds of the central metope are very close to those of **9/67** (ΜΕΘ 1574) and **9/73** (ΜΕΘ 3646) and, as such, all three may derive from the same local workshop.
Late Geometric II.

9/70. (ΜΕΘ 1335) Small Local Kotyle Fig. 9.30
H. 0.076; Diam. (base) 0.043; Diam. (rim) 0.102.
The central metope, which is flanked by multiple vertical lines on either side, is decorated with two superimposed horizontal rows of Λs which resemble a tremulous line approaching zigzag. Body

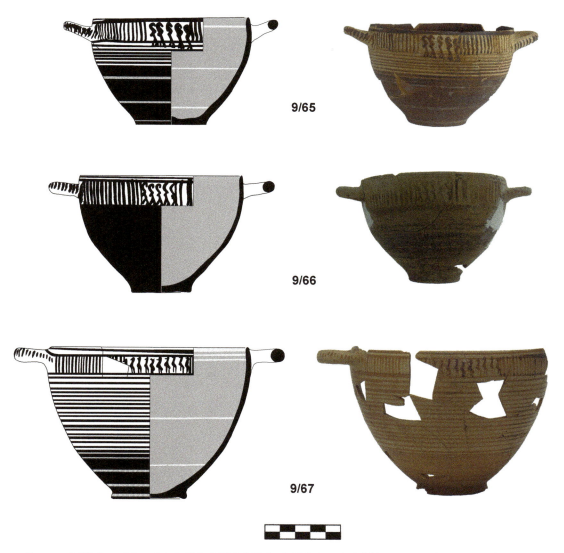

FIGURE 9.29. Local kotylai, **9/65** (MEΘ 1334), **9/66** (MEΘ 1577), and **9/67** (MEΘ 1574). Drawings I. Moschou and T. Ross, photos I. Coyle and KZ´ Ephoreia

below decorated with multiple horizontal bands (at least eight); two thin bands on rim. The lower body, down to the base, is painted solid and is decorated with three thin horizontal bands of added white. Handles barred. Interior painted solid, and further decorated with thin bands of added white: one at upper rim, one in the central portion of the vessel, and another lower down. Off-white slip. Late Geometric II.

9/71. (MEΘ 1330) Fragmentary Local Skyphos Fig. 9.31
H. 0.085; Diam. (base) 0.052; Diam. (rim) 0.130.

The decoration in the handle zone consists of a central metope with five schematic birds facing right; to the left and right, multiple vertical lines. Three thin horizontal bands above, on rim, and four on body below. Lower body to base painted solid. Preserved handle barred. Interior painted solid, except for two reserved bands at rim, and another, broader band, lower down. Off-white slip. Cf. **9/65** (MEΘ 1334) and **9/66** (MEΘ 1577).
Late Geometric II.

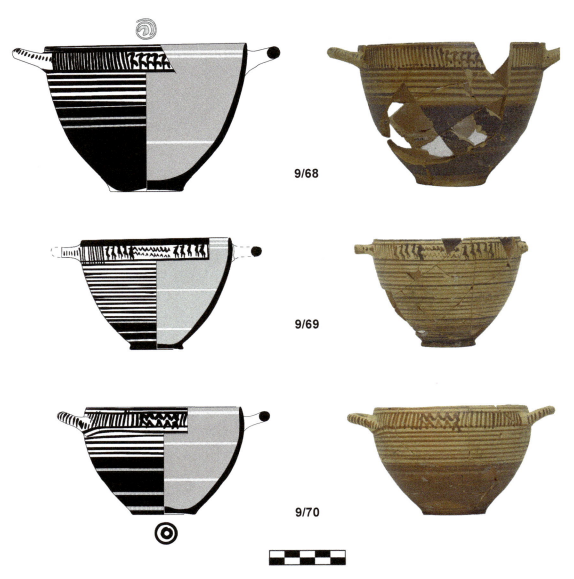

FIGURE 9.30. Local kotylai, **9/68** (MEΘ 2039), **9/69** (MEΘ 1307), and **9/70** (MEΘ 1335). Drawings I. Moschou and T. Ross, photos I. Coyle and KZ´ Ephoreia

9/72. (MEΘ 3569) Fragmentary Local Skyphos   Fig. 9.31
H. 0.095; Diam. (base) est. 0.050; Diam. (rim) est. 0.130.
The decoration in the handle zone consists of a central metope with five schematic birds facing right; to the left and right, multiple vertical lines. Six thin horizontal bands above, on rim, and three on body below. Lower body to base painted solid. Preserved handle barred. Interior painted solid, except for broad reserved band high on rim and a similar broad reserved band on the body below.
Late Geometric II.

9/73. (MEΘ 3646) Fragmentary Upper Body, Local Skyphos   Fig. 9.31
P.H. 0.056; Diam. (rim) est. 0.140.
Fragmentary upper body, rim, and one handle. The decoration in the handle zone consists of

a central metope with ten schematic birds facing left; to the left and right, multiple vertical δ lines. Five thin horizontal bands on rim above, and eight below, above an area painted solid (on similarly decorated vessels, this area painted solid is often decorated with horizontal bands of added white). Preserved handle barred. Interior painted solid, except for reserved band at rim, immediately below which are two thin horizontal bands of added white; another, but broader, reserved band lower down. Off-white slip.

Cf. **9/69** (MEΘ 1307).

Late Geometric IIb.

9/74. (MEΘ 3420) Fragmentary Local Skyphos   Fig. 9.32
H. 0.092; Diam. (base) 0.052; Diam. (rim) 0.148.

The decoration in the handle zone consists of a central metope with eleven schematic birds facing right; to the left and right, multiple vertical lines. Four thin horizontal bands on rim above, and three below; remainder of body, to base, painted solid. Handles barred. Interior painted solid, except for three reserved bands at rim, and a broader reserved band on body below. Off-white slip.

Late Geometric IIb.

9/75. (MEΘ 3579) Fragmentary Local Skyphos   Fig. 9.32
H. 0.131; Diam. (base) 0.062; Diam. (rim) est. 0.160.

Large skyphos. The decoration in the handle zone consists of a central metope with four schematic birds facing left; to the left and right, multiple vertical lines. Four thin horizontal bands on rim above, and six below; lower body painted solid, except for lower edge of base. Preserved handle barred, but with the bars becoming dots near the attachment of the handle to the body. Interior painted solid, except for broad reserved band near midpoint. Off-white slip.

Late Geometric IIb.

9/76. (MEΘ 3581) Rim and Body Fr, Local Tall-rimmed Skyphos   Fig. 9.32
P.H. 0.119; p.W. 0.145; Diam. (rim) est. 0.190.

Fr preserves portion of rim and upper body, including stump of one handle. The decoration in the handle zone consists of a central metope with 12 schematic birds facing right; to the left and right, multiple vertical lines. What survives of the lower body below is decorated with at least seven thin horizontal bands. Five horizontal bands above the metope, on lower rim, above which the preserved rim is decorated with a two-tiered, dotted lozenge net (for the motif, see Coldstream 1968, p. 396); three thin horizontal bands above. Interior painted solid, except for reserved bands on the upper rim (seven), and a broader reserved band below. Off-white slip.

Late Geometric II.

9/77. (MEΘ 1354) Local Skyphos   Fig. 9.33
H. 0.090; Diam. (base) 0.050; Diam. (rim) 0.130.

Skyphos decorated with black paint. Exterior painted solid, except for three reserved bands at rim; interior painted solid, except for two thin reserved bands at rim, and a broader reserved band below. Off-white slip.

Cf. Benton 1953, pp. 273, 278, fig. 7, no. 653 (Aetos, Ithaka); Vokotopoulou 1986, vol. 1, p. 279, no. 5419/T 175; vol. 2, pl. 201:α (right), fig. 67:δ (Vitsa Zagoriou, Epirus, skyphos considered Corinthian).

Late Geometric II.

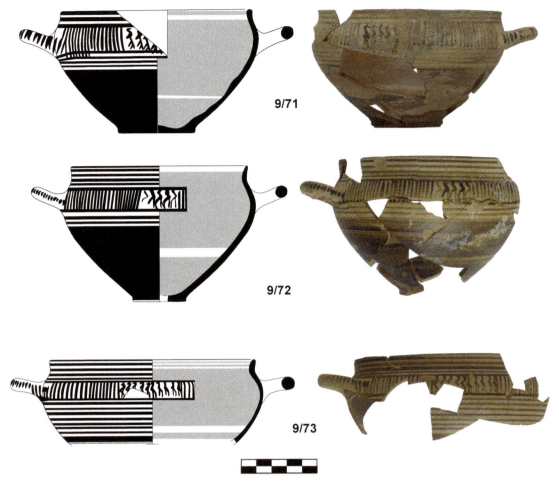

FIGURE 9.31. Fragmentary local skyphoi, **9/71** (ΜΕΘ 1330), **9/72** (ΜΕΘ 3569), and **9/73** (ΜΕΘ 3646). Drawings I. Moschou and T. Ross, photos I. Coyle and KZ´ Ephoreia

9/78. (ΜΕΘ 3578) Local Skyphos Fig. 9.33

H. 0.098; Diam. (base) 0.050; Diam. (rim) 0.130.

The decoration in the handle zone consists of a central metope with two horizontal tremulous lines approaching zigzags; to the left and right, multiple vertical lines. Five thin horizontal bands on rim above, and two on body below; remainder of body to base painted solid. Handles barred. Interior painted solid, except for reserved band at rim, and a somewhat broader reserved band on body, lower down. Off-white slip.

Late Geometric IIb.

9/79. (ΜΕΘ 1586) Local Skyphos Fig. 9.33

H. 0.103; Diam. (base) 0.051; Diam. (rim) 0.141.

The decoration in the handle zone consists of a central metope with three horizontal tremulous lines approaching zigzags; to the left and right, multiple vertical lines. Three thin horizontal bands on rim above, and four on body below; remainder of body painted solid, except for reserved outside edge of base. Handles barred. Interior painted solid, except for a broad reserved band on the lower body. Off-white slip.

Late Geometric IIb.

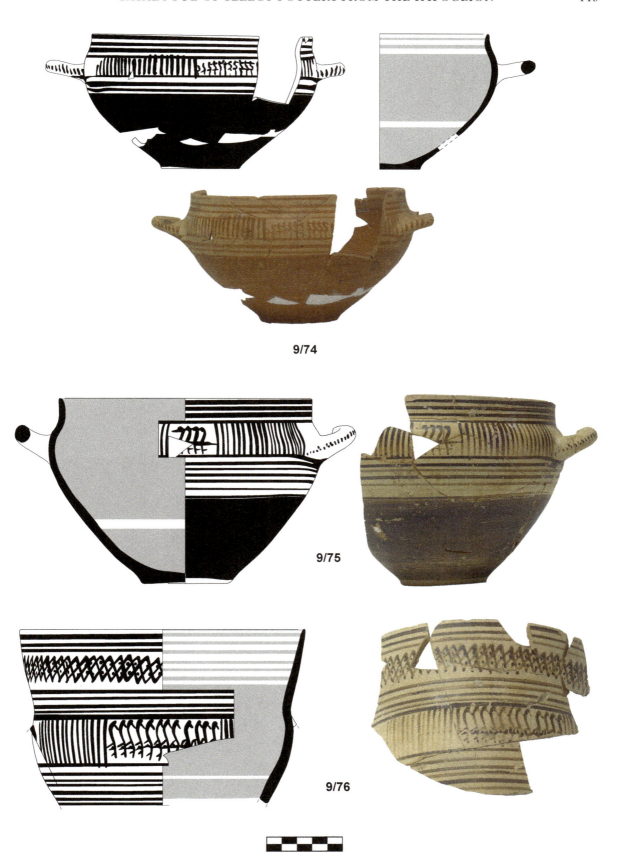

FIGURE 9.32. Fragmentary local skyphoi, **9/74** (ΜΕΘ 3420), **9/75** (ΜΕΘ 3579), and **9/76** (ΜΕΘ 3581). Drawings I. Moschou and T. Ross, photos I. Coyle and KZ´ Ephoreia

FIGURE 9.33. Local skyphoi, **9/77** (ΜΕΘ 1354), **9/78** (ΜΕΘ 3578), and **9/79** (ΜΕΘ 1586). Drawings I. Moschou and T. Ross, photos I. Coyle and KZ´ Ephoreia

9/80. (ΜΕΘ 1589) Fragmentary Local Skyphos Fig. 9.34

H. 0.090; Diam. (base) 0.049; Diam. (rim) 0.131.

The decoration in the handle zone consists of a central metope with four horizontal tremulous lines approaching zigzags; to the left and right, multiple vertical lines. Four thin horizontal bands on rim above, and three on body below; remainder of body painted solid, except for reserved outside edge of base. Handles barred. Interior painted solid, except for reserved band at top of rim, and a somewhat broader reserved band on the lower body below. Off-white slip.

Late Geometric IIb.

CATALOGUE OF SELECT POTTERY FROM THE HYPOGEION

9/81. (ΜΕΘ 3425) Fragmentary Local Skyphos   Fig. 9.34
P.H. 0.064; Diam. (rim) 0.100.

Small fragmentary skyphos, preserving rim, upper body, and both handles. The decoration in the handle zone consists of a central metope with two horizontal tremulous lines approaching zigzags; to the left and right, multiple vertical lines. Three horizontal bands of varying thickness on rim above; remainder of preserved body painted solid. Handles barred. Interior painted solid, except for a broad reserved band on body, as shown.

Late Geometric IIb.

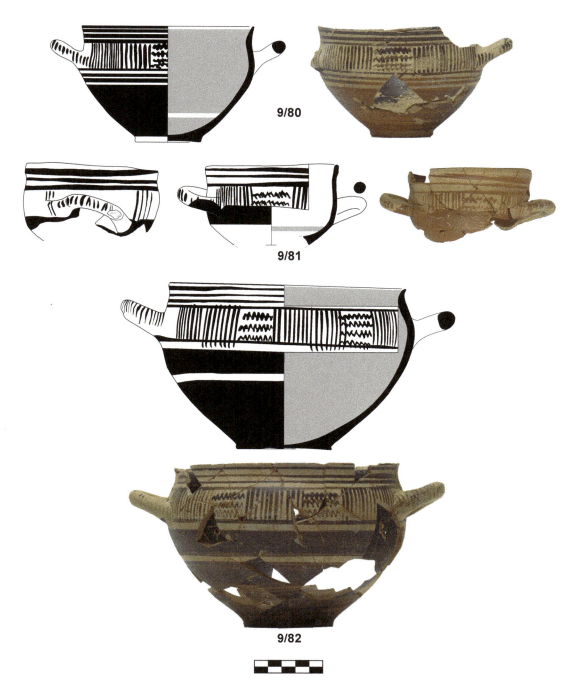

FIGURE 9.34. Fragmentary local skyphoi, **9/80** (ΜΕΘ 1589), **9/81** (ΜΕΘ 3425), and **9/82** (ΜΕΘ 3588). Drawings A. Hooton, I. Moschou, and T. Ross, photos I. Coyle and KZ´ Ephoreia

9/82. (ΜΕΘ 3588) Fragmentary Large Local Skyphos Fig. 9.34
H. 0.137; Diam. (base) 0.069; Diam. (rim) 0.179.

The decoration in the handle zone consists of three sets of vertical lines defining two metopes, each decorated with three horizontal tremulous lines approaching zigzags, although one has four. Four thin horizontal bands on rim above, one below; remainder of the body to base painted solid, except for reserved band, as shown. Handles barred. Interior painted solid, except for a reserved band at the rim. Off-white slip.

Late Geometric IIb.

9/83. (ΜΕΘ 1343) Spouted Krater, Perhaps Euboian Fig. 9.35
Max H. 0.210; Diam. (base) 0.110; Diam. (rim) 0.235.

Spouted krater with perforated base (the vessel thus functioned as a sieve/colander). The metope directly below the spout (which, itself, is painted solid) is decorated with two rows of tremulous lines, executed in such a way that the lower row in particular almost resembles a row of Xs, at least in part. Between the spout and the two handles, two more metopes, with similar decoration, but with four rows of tremulous lines, some executed in the same manner as those under the spout; these metopes are framed, on either side, by sets of vertical lines. On the opposite side of the vessel there are two similar metopes with analogous decoration. Two horizontal bands on the rim above, as shown. Below the decorated handle zone 14 horizontal bands; the remainder of the lower body, to the base, is painted solid, except for a broader reserved band, as shown. The outer faces of the spout and handles are painted solid. The interior is painted solid. Off-white slip.

A possible Euboian import.

Late Geometric II.

9/84. (ΜΕΘ 1575) Fragmentary Spouted Krater, Likely Euboian Fig. 9.36
H. 0.223; Diam. (base) 0.106; Diam. (rim) 0.240.

In the metope directly below the painted spout, a single tremulous line (drawn not unlike some of the tremulous lines on **9/83** [ΜΕΘ 1343]). Between the spout and the handles, two further metopes, framed on either side by sets of vertical lines, decorated with three rows of tremulous lines (some almost hastily drawn rows of Xs). On the opposite side of the vessels, two similar metopes with analogous decoration. Two horizontal bands on rim. The body below the decorated handle zone has ten horizontal bands; the remainder of the body to the base is painted solid, except for a broad reserved band; the lower outer edge of the foot is also reserved. The outer faces of the horizontal handles, together with the spout, are painted. Interior painted solid. Off-white slip.

Drilled holes indicate that the vessel was mended in antiquity.

Cf. **9/83** (ΜΕΘ 1343).

Late Geometric II.

9/85. (ΜΕΘ 1351) Small Local Skyphos Fig. 9.37
H. 0.072; Diam. (base) 0.040; Diam. (rim) 0.098.

The decoration in the handle zone consists of a central metope with a row of sigmas (three-bar); to the left and right, multiple vertical lines. Four thin horizontal bands on rim above, and three on body below; remainder of body painted solid. Handles barred. Interior painted solid, except for two thin reserved bands on the rim, and a broader reserved band on the lower body. Off-white slip.

Late Geometric IIb.

FIGURE 9.35. Spouted krater, perhaps Euboian, **9/83** (ΜΕΘ 1343). Drawing A. Hooton, photos I. Coyle

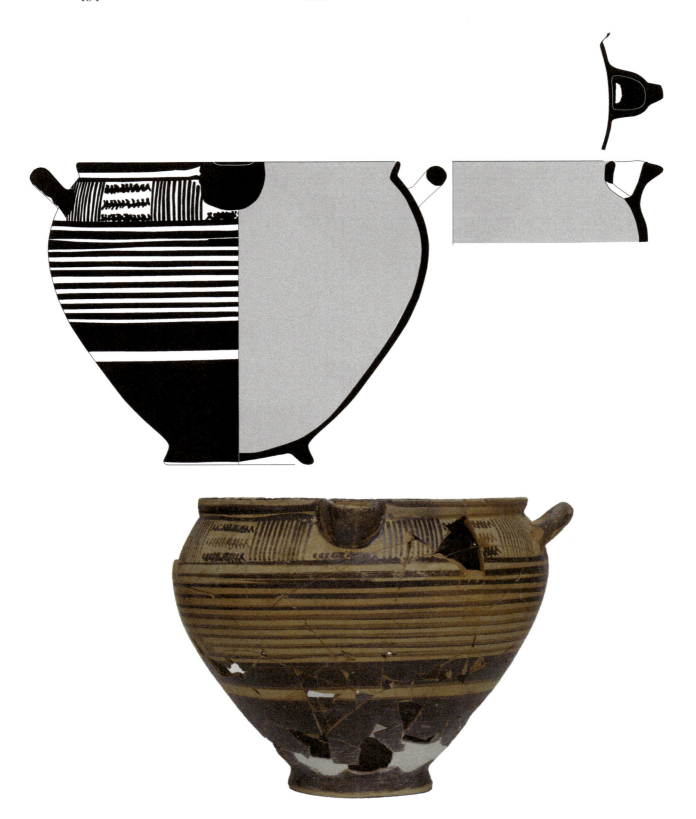

FIGURE 9.36. Fragmentary spouted krater, likely Euboian, **9/84** (ΜΕΘ 1575). Drawing I. Moschou and T. Ross, photo ΚΖ´ Ephoreia

9/86. (ΜΕΘ 3604) Fragmentary Local Skyphos Fig. 9.37
H. 0.100; Diam. (base) 0.051; Diam. (rim) est. 0.135.
The decoration in the handle zone consists of a central metope with a row of 18 sigmas (mostly four-bar, occasionally three-bar, but with one smaller central three-bar sigma facing the opposite direction); to the left and right, multiple vertical lines (14 to the left, 18 to the right). Six horizontal bands on rim above, and two on body below; remainder of body painted solid. Preserved handle barred. Interior painted solid, except for a rather broad reserved band on the lower body. Off-white slip.
Late Geometric IIb

9/87. (ΜΕΘ 3567) Fragmentary Local Skyphos Fig. 9.37
H. 0.094; Diam. (base) 0.055; Diam. (rim) est. 0.130.
The decoration in the handle zone consists of a central metope with a row of eight three-bar sigmas; to the left and right, multiple vertical lines (19 to the left, 16 to the right). Five horizontal bands on rim above, and five on body below; remainder of body to base painted solid. Handles barred. Interior painted solid, except for a very thin reserved band at rim, and a broader reserved band on body below. Off-white slip.
Late Geometric IIb

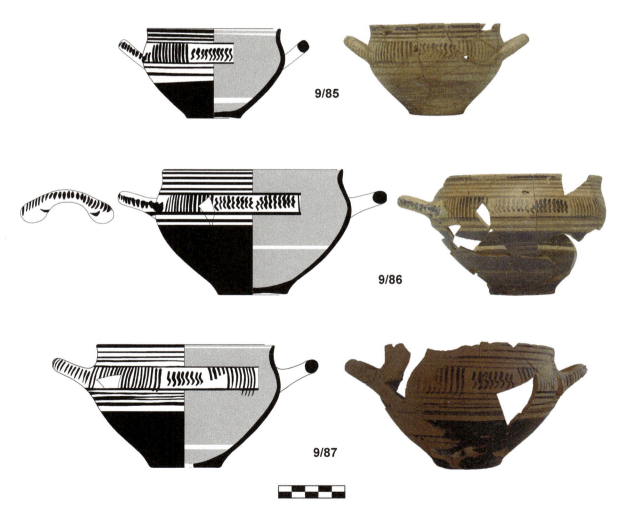

FIGURE 9.37. Local skyphoi, **9/85** (ΜΕΘ 1351), **9/86** (ΜΕΘ 3604), **9/87** (ΜΕΘ 3567). Drawings I. Moschou and T. Ross, photos I. Coyle and KZ´ Ephoreia.

9/88. (ΜΕΘ 1321) Local Skyphos with Tall Rim　　　　　　　　　　　　　　　　　　　　　　　Fig. 9.38
H. 0.100; Diam. (base) 0.063; Diam. (rim) 0.130.

Low, flat-based skyphos, with tall rim. The decoration in the handle zone consists of a central metope decorated with a row of eight originally (six clearly preserved) chevrons rather than sigmas, each with a dot approaching a short stroke above and below; this metope is framed by sets of vertical lines on either side. Body below, down to base, painted solid. Comparatively broad horizontal band above the decorated handle zone, near juncture of rim and body. The rim, thus defined, is decorated with a continuous row of mechanically drawn concentric circles; each set consists of four circles with small dot at center. Outer faces of handle painted solid, with the decoration extending onto body, as shown. Interior painted solid, except for two reserved bands at rim. Off-white slip.

For further examples of this type of skyphos from Methone, see Bessios, Tzifopoulos, and Kotsonas 2012, pp. 375–383, nos. 26–32 (referred to there as skyphoi of Euboian type from the Thermaic Gulf).

Late Geometric IIb.

9/89. (ΜΕΘ 1360) Local Skyphos with Tall Rim　　　　　　　　　　　　　　　　　　　　　　　Fig. 9.38
H. 0.098 (ranging between 0.094 and 0.101); Diam. (base) 0.062–0.064; Diam. (rim, max) 0.142; Diam. (rim, min) 0.127.

The decoration in the handle zone consists of a central metope decorated with a row of 11 (originally perhaps 12), pseudo-chevrons, some trying to be sigmas, each with a dot above and below; this metope is framed by sets of vertical lines on either side. Body below, down to base, painted solid. Two horizontal bands near juncture of body and the tall, but comparatively compressed, rim; single thin band at the very top of the rim. The rim, thus defined, is decorated with a continuous row of mechanically drawn concentric circles; each set consists of four circles with small dot at center. Outer faces of handle painted solid. Interior painted solid, except for two reserved bands at rim. Off-white slip.

For a dipinto painted before firing (potter's mark) below one handle, consisting of two small vertical lines, see Bessios, Tzifopoulos, and Kotsonas 2012, pp. 375–376, no. 26.

Cf. **9/88** (ΜΕΘ 1321), but less carefully made and decorated.

Late Geometric IIb.

9/90. (ΜΕΘ 2019) Fragmentary Local Skyphos with Tall Rim　　　　　　　　　　　　　　　　　Fig. 9.38
H. 0.098; Diam. (base) 0.059; Diam. (rim) 0.130.

Skyphos of the same type as **9/88** (ΜΕΘ 1321) and **9/89** (ΜΕΘ 1360), but with shorter, more compressed, decorated handle zone. The central metope in the handle zone, defined on either side by sets of numerous vertical lines, has two rows of what are best described as tremulous lines. Body below, down to base, painted solid. Three thin horizontal bands on lower rim, near juncture with body; one horizontal band near top of rim. The rim, thus defined, is decorated with a continuous row of mechanically drawn concentric circles; each set consists of two circles with small dot at center. Preserved handle barred. Interior painted solid, except for a comparatively broad band on lower body.

Late Geometric IIb.

9/91. (ΜΕΘ 3442) Fragmentary Local Skyphos　　　　　　　　　　　　　　　　　　　　　　　Fig. 9.39
P.H. 0.077; Diam. (rim) est. 0.140.

The decoration in the handle zone consists of two metopes alternating with three sets of eight vertical lines, each metope decorated with a row of eight chevrons, with row of eight strokes above and eight below in line with the chevrons. Three broad horizontal bands below, below which what survives of the lower body is painted solid. Two analogous broad bands on lower rim, and a thin band at rim top. Outer faces of preserved handle painted solid. Interior painted solid, but poorly preserved,

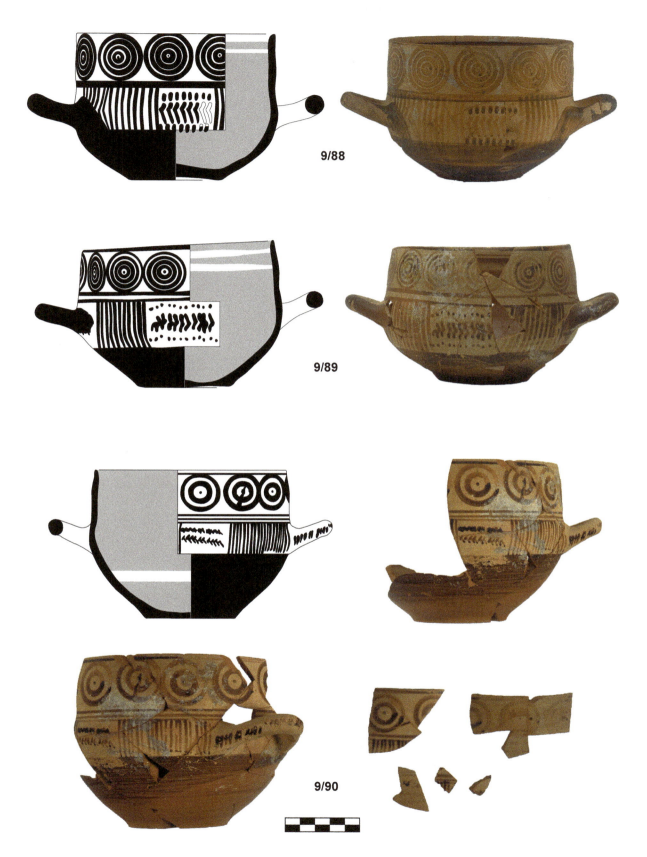

FIGURE 9.38. Local skyphoi with tall rims, **9/88** (ΜΕΘ 1321), **9/89** (ΜΕΘ 1360), and **9/90** (ΜΕΘ 2019). Drawings I. Moschou and T. Ross, photos I. Coyle and KZ´ Ephoreia

except traces of a reserved band, and probably two originally.

The decoration of the metopes is closely related to **9/88** (ΜΕΘ 1321) and this skyphos likely derives from the same workshop.

Late Geometric IIb.

9/92. (ΜΕΘ 1327) Fragmentary Local Skyphos Fig. 9.39
H. 0.074; Diam. (base) 0.060; Diam. (rim) 0.140.

The decoration in the handle zone consists of two metopes alternating with three sets of eight vertical lines (only two sets of which are preserved), each metope decorated with a row of eight chevrons, with row of eight strokes approaching dots above and eight below in line with the chevrons. Single horizontal band below, below which the lower body to base is painted solid. Three horizontal bands on rim. Outer faces of preserved handle painted solid. Interior painted solid, except for three reserved bands at rim, and a broader reserved band on body lower down.

Decoration analogous to **9/91** (ΜΕΘ 3442).

Late Geometric IIb.

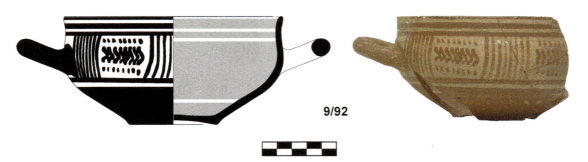

FIGURE 9.39. Fragmentary local skyphoi, **9/91** (ΜΕΘ 3442) and **9/92** (ΜΕΘ 1327).
Drawings T. Ross, photos I. Coyle and KZ´ Ephoreia

CATALOGUE OF SELECT POTTERY FROM THE HYPOGEION

9/93. (ΜΕΘ 3532) Fragmentary East Greek Oinochoe Fig. 9.40
P.H. 0.147; Diam. (max) est. 0.198.

Only portion of body survives of East Greek oinochoe related to the bird kotylai (see Chapter 22). Carinated body. Decorative zone has solid double axes alternating with sets of eight vertical lines. Four thin horizontal bands below and three above; preserved area above and below these bands painted solid. For further discussion, see Chapter 22.

First half of the 7th century B.C.

9/94. (ΜΕΘ 4046) Fragmentary East Greek Oinochoe Fig. 9.40
P.H. 0.122; Diam. (max) est. 0.159.

Various joining and non-joining frr preserving portion of body of East Greek oinochoe related to the bird kotylai. Carinated body. The decorative zone above the carination consists of two rows of decoration. The lower zone has solid double axes alternating with sets of eight vertical lines. Three thin horizontal bands below, below which the body to base is painted solid. Two thin horizontal bands above define the lower portion of the upper decorative zone. This upper zone also consists of metopes, here separated by sets of three vertical lines, decorated with characteristic motifs well known from north Ionian bird kotylai: cross-hatched and outlined lozenges; smaller cross-hatched triangles; larger multi-outlined triangles, their centers cross-hatched, from the apex of which extends a meander, the whole defining a "tree of life"; schematic birds. For further discussion, see Chapter 22.

First half of the 7th century B.C.

9/95. (ΜΕΘ 1953) Fragmentary Local Skyphos Fig. 9.41
Max H. 0.150; Diam. (base) 0.070; Diam. (rim) 0.190.

Large skyphos, the product of a local workshop, the fabric containing much silver mica. In the comparatively low decorative handle zone, two elongated metopes at the center of which is a row of six Ss, as shown. The metopes alternate with sets of six vertical lines. Four poorly drawn horizontal bands below, merging at points into three, below which is an area painted solid, then a reserved band with a single horizontal band; remainder of body to base painted solid, except for lowermost outside edge of foot. Three horizontal bands on rim. The outer parts of the handle where it is attached to the body are striped (the central portion reserved). Interior reserved, but decorated with three broad bands of paint, one at the rim, one at the center of the body, and another lower down covering the floor of the vessel.

First half of the 7th century B.C.

9/96. (ΜΕΘ 3821) Fragmentary Base, Corinthian Oinochoe Fig. 9.42
P.H. 0.065; Diam. (base) 0.170.

Likely trefoil oinochoe with broad base. On the preserved body of the vessel, a feeding wild goat alternating with two preserved felines stand on a ground line, of which the largest portion of the goat, facing right, survives, together with the front of one feline, and the rear of another, both facing left. Filling ornaments include rosettes and other floral ornaments, together with small dots. The anatomical details of the animals and the subsidiary ornaments are enlivened with the incision of black-figure, as well as added red for various parts of the bodies of the goat and felines. Below the figured zone, a row of rays emanating from a thin horizontal band. Thin horizontal band on outside edge of foot.

Later 6th century B.C.

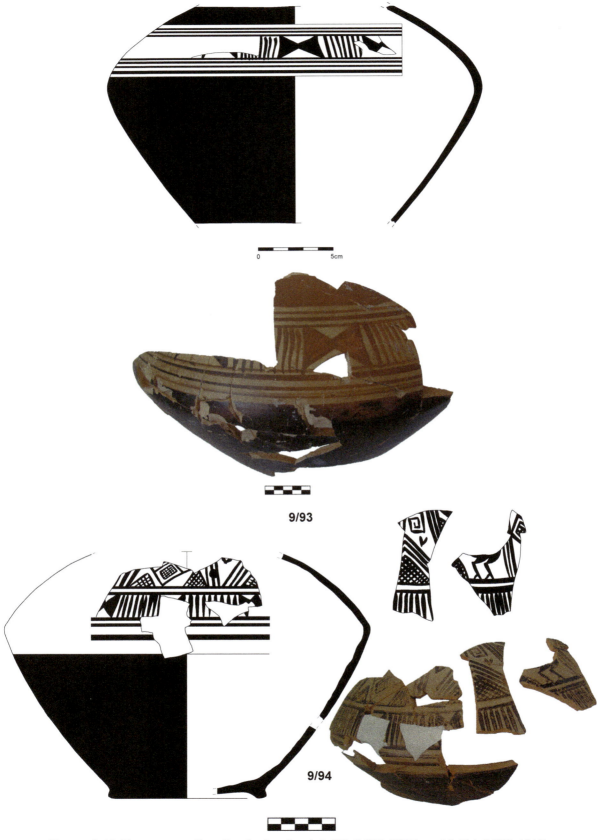

FIGURE 9.40. Fragmentary East Greek oinochoai, **9/93** (ΜΕΘ 3532) and **9/94** (ΜΕΘ 4046). Drawings T. Ross, photos I. Coyle and KZ´ Ephoreia

FIGURE 9.41. Fragmentary local skyphos, **9/95** (ΜΕΘ 1953).
Drawing I. Moschou and T. Ross, photo ΚΖ´ Ephoreia

9/97. (ΜΕΘ 2022) Fragmentary Ionian Cup Fig. 9.43

H. 0.072; Diam. (base) 0.054; Diam. (rim) 0.120 (originally perhaps as much as 0.130).

Ionian cup (the so-called *Knickrandschale*: see Chapter 22), with low conical foot and sharply everted flaring rim. Decoration as shown, with most of the body and base painted solid, except for lowermost outside edge of foot. Horizontal band on uppermost body, just below juncture with rim, thin horizontal band on rim. Outer faces of handle painted solid. Interior painted solid, except for thin reserved band at rim.

For the incised graffito (cross) on base, see Bessios, Tzifopoulos, and Kotsonas 2012, pp. 507–508, no. 191.

First half of the 6th century B.C.

9/98. (ΜΕΘ 3822) Base Fr, Corinthian Spherical Aryballos Fig. 9.43

P.Diam. 0.060.

Rounded base of spherical aryballos. Within the double concentric circles framing the base of the vessel, a whirligig with five elements/legs. The little that survives of the body of the vessel above preserves portion of the body, tail, and wing of a bird. The anatomical details are enlivened with the incision of black-figure.

Middle Corinthian period.

FIGURE 9.42. Fragmentary base, Corinthian oinochoe, **9/96** (ΜΕΘ 3821). Drawing I. Moschou and T. Ross, photo KZ´ Ephoreia

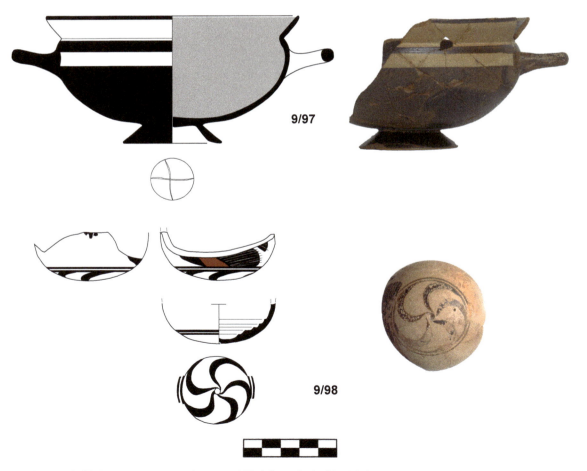

FIGURE 9.43. Fragmentary Ionian cup (*Knickrandschale*), **9/97** (ΜΕΘ 2022) and base fragment Corinthian spherical aryballos, **9/98** (ΜΕΘ 3822). Drawings T. Ross, photos I. Coyle and KZ´ Ephoreia

TABLE 9.1. Context and phases of the catalogued pottery (9/1–9/98)

Cat. and inv. no.	Context (East Hill)	Phase(s)
9/1 (ΜΕΘ 3807)	#274/022066 [14] (13-10-2006)	I
9/2 (ΜΕΘ 3818)	#274/022, 032	Unclear stratigraphy
9/3 (ΜΕΘ 3819)	#274/022, 032	Unclear stratigraphy
9/4 (ΜΕΘ 3811)	#274/022, 032	Unclear stratigraphy
9/5 (ΜΕΘ 3606)	#274/022048 [1], 022051 [1], 022052 [1], 022054 [1], 022055 [6], 022056 [1], 022058 [2], 032010 [2], 032027 [3], 032028 [1], 032030 [3], 032036 [1], 032037 [3], 032048 [2]	I–III
9/6 (ΜΕΘ 2248)	#274/022044 [2], 022045 [1], 022063 [1], 022 T.14, 032048 [11], 032049 [5]	I–II
9/7 (ΜΕΘ 4054)	#274/032072 [1]	I
9/8 (ΜΕΘ 4051)	#274/032073	I
9/9 (ΜΕΘ 4042)	#274/022044 [11]	II
9/10 (ΜΕΘ 3413)	Fr α: #274/032077 [1], 032079 [1], 032086 [4]; fr β: 022072 [1], 022064 [1], 032056 [2], 032060 [1]	I–II
9/11 (ΜΕΘ 3409)	#274/022031 [1], 022050 [1], 022051 [7], 022058 [2]	I–III
9/12 (ΜΕΘ 3415α, β, γ)	Fr α: #274/022042 [1], 032052 [2], 032065 [1]; fr β: 032053 [3]; fr γ: 022047 [1], 032043-051 [1], 032046 [1]	II–III
9/13 (ΜΕΘ 3411)	#274/022060 [2], 022065 [6], 022066 [7], 032079 [1], 032081 [4]	I
9/14 (ΜΕΘ 4033α, β)	Fr α: #274/032079 [1]; Fr β: 022070 [4], 032061 [1]	I
9/15 (ΜΕΘ 4035α, β, γ)	Fr α: #274/o22055 [1], 032029 [2], 032081 [1], 032086 [1], 032089 [1]; fr β: 032029 [1]; fr γ: 022063 [1], 022066 [1], 022070 [1]	I–II
9/16 (ΜΕΘ 4035)	# 022063 [1], 022066 [1], 022070 [1], 274/022055 [1], 032029 [1]; 032029 [2], 032081 [1], 032086 [1], 032089 [1]	I–II
9/17 (ΜΕΘ 4053α, β, γ)	Fr α: #274/022071 [2], 022073 [3], 032087 [1], 032089 [1]; fr β: 022071 [1], 032027 [1], 032085 [1]; fr γ: 022068 [1], 022072 [1]; fr δ: 032071 [1], 032072 [1]	I, III
9/18 (ΜΕΘ 3808)	#274/022052 [11]	II
9/19 (ΜΕΘ 4044)	#274	Unclear stratigraphy
9/20 (ΜΕΘ 1319)	#274/ 022049 [1], 022058 [1], 022059 [2], 022060 [3], 022061 [5], 022062 [21], 022063 [8], 022065 [1], 032059 [2], 032064 [5], 032070 [4], 032071 [6], 032072 [2], 032075 [1]	I–II
9/21 (ΜΕΘ 3410)	#274/022065 [1], 022066 [1], 032041 [3], 032061 [1], 032074 [1]	I–II
9/22 (ΜΕΘ 4045α, β, γ)	Fr α: #274/022050 [3], 022065 [1], 032064 [3], 032065 [1]; fr β: 032054 [2], 032067 [1]; Fr γ: 032061 [2]	I–II
9/23 (ΜΕΘ 3810)	#274/032056 [1], 032059 [1]	I
9/24 (ΜΕΘ 4037)	#274/022037 [5], 022038 [1], 022042 [1]	III & mixed levels immediately above
9/25 (ΜΕΘ 3407)	#274/022, ΖΒΠ [1], 022065 [7], 032075 [1]	I
9/26 (ΜΕΘ 1309)	#274/022008 [1], 022064 [3], 022065 [5], 032055 [1], 032059 [1], 032061 [1], 032074 [1], 032075 [2], 032077 [7]	I–III
9/27 (ΜΕΘ 1308)	#274/022051 [18], 022058 [3], 022059 [5], 022060 [1], 022061 [1], 032055 [6], 032056 [1], 032065 [1], 032070 [1]	I–II
9/28 (ΜΕΘ 3412)	#274/022045 [1], 022046 [2], 022047 [1], 022050 [1], 032027 [2], 032028 [1]	II–III

TABLE 9.1. Context and phases of the catalogued pottery (9/1–9/98) *(continued)*

Cat. and inv. no.	Context (East Hill)	Phase(s)
9/29 (ΜΕΘ 3406)	#274/032080 [3], 032086 [7]	I
9/30 (ΜΕΘ 3408)	#274/022060 [3], 022062 [2], 022063 [1], 022064 [2], 022065 [1], 032035 [1], 032058 [1]	I–II
9/31 (4043α, β)	Fr α: #274/022062 [1], 032071 [1]; fr β: 022059 [2], 032062 [4]	I
9/32 (ΜΕΘ 4060α, β)	Fr α: #274/032051 [1]; fr β: 032039 [1]	II–III & mixed immediately levels above
9/33 (ΜΕΘ 4038α, β)	Fr α: #274/022072 [2]; fr β: 022058 [1]	I
9/34 (ΜΕΘ 4041)	Fr α: #274/032085 [1], fr β: 022072 [1]; γ: 032084 [1]; fr δ: 032090 [1]	I
9/35 (ΜΕΘ 4040)	#274/022063	I
9/36 (ΜΕΘ 4039)	Fr α: #274/032084 [1]; fr β: 022069 [2]	I
9/37 (ΜΕΘ 2032)	#274/022058 [2], 022059 [4], 022060 [1], 022061 [4], 022062 [19], 022063 [2], 022064 [4], 032042 [3], 032056 [2], 032058 [1], 032059 [1], 032052-060 [1], 032065 [1], 032068 [1], 032069 [1], 032071 [1], 032072 [2]	I–II
9/38 (ΜΕΘ 4059)	Fr α: #274/022070 [2], 022074 [1]; fr β: 032086 [1]	I
9/39 (ΜΕΘ 2031)	#274/022057 [1], 022058 [3], 022061 [3], 022062 [2], 022063 [6], 022064 [10], 032057 [1], 032058 [2], 032060 [2], 032070 [1], 032073 [2], 032079 [1]	I–II
9/40 (ΜΕΘ 4058α-δ)	Fr α: #274/022062 [4], 032036 [1], -32-54 [1], 032055 [1], 032058 [1], fr β: 032060 [3]; fr γ: 022062 [2], 022063 [2], 022064 [1], 022066 [1], 032058 [1], 032059 [11], 032077 [2], 032071 [1]; fr δ: 022061 [1], 032060 [1]	I–II
9/41 (ΜΕΘ 2021)	#274/022048 [1], 022051 [1], 032037 [1], 032041 [1]. 032049 [4]	II
9/42 (ΜΕΘ 4052)	#274/022041 [1]	III
9/43 (ΜΕΘ 4034)	#274/022043 [1], 022045 [1], 022049 [1]	II–III
9/44 (ΜΕΘ 3318)	#274/032043-051 [1], 032059 [1], T.14 [1]	I, III & mixed levels immediately above
9/45 (ΜΕΘ 3816)	#274/022, 032	Unclear stratigraphy
9/46 (ΜΕΘ 1314)	#274/022045 [1], 022047 [1], 022059 [2], 022060 [5], 022061 [2], 022062 [2], 032029 [1], 032050 [1], 032055 [2], 032005 [1], 032057 [8], 032059 [1], 032071 [2]	I–II
9/47 (ΜΕΘ 3582)	#274/022070 [4], 032079 [5], 032086 [1]	I
9/48 (ΜΕΘ 1326)	#274/022048 [1], 022057 [1], 022059 [2], 022060 [4], 022061 [4], 022062 [2], 022064 [4], 032055 [1], 032701 [1]	I–II
9/49 (ΜΕΘ 1352)	#274/022, ΖΒΠ [5], 022065 [3], 022066 [2], 022070 [1], 022071 [1]	I
9/50α, β (ΜΕΘ 3814, ΜΕΘ 4061)	#274/022, 032	Unclear stratigraphy
9/51 (ΜΕΘ 3343)	#274/022046 [2], 032051 [3]	II
9/52 (ΜΕΘ 3344)	#274/032052 [3]	II
9/53 (ΜΕΘ 3815)	#274/022, 032	Unclear stratigraphy
9/54 (ΜΕΘ 3812)	#274/022, 032	Unclear stratigraphy
9/55 (ΜΕΘ 1355)	#274/022, ΖΒΠ [4], 022063 [1], 022065 [4], 022066 [3], 032074 [2], 032075 [3], 032081 [2]	I

CATALOGUE OF SELECT POTTERY FROM THE HYPOGEION

Cat. and inv. no.	Context (East Hill)	Phase(s)
9/56 (ΜΕΘ 3397)	#274/022044 [1], 022050 [2], 022051 [1], 033056 [1], 022058 [2], 032030 [1], 032045 [2], 032047 [1], 032049 [2], 032053 [2], 032054 [5], 032055 [2], 032065 [3], 032066 [5], 032067 [7]	I–III
9/57 (ΜΕΘ 3371)	Fr α: #274/022, ΖΒΠ [3], 022061 [4], 022064 [1], 032062 [3], 032063 [2]; fr β: 022011 [1], 022044 [2], 022045 [5], 022047 [3], 022052 [1], 022, Τ.14 [1], 032043-051 [1], 032048 [4]	I–III & mixed levels immediately above
9/58 (ΜΕΘ 3384)	#274/022, ΖΒΠ [1], 022066 [1], 022068 [1], 022070 [1], 022071 [1], 032062 [2], 032063 [3], 032078 [1], 032079 [2], 032080 [12], 032086 [6]	I
9/59 (ΜΕΘ 3368)	#274/022, 022046 [1], 022058 [1], 022059 [1], 022060 [4], 022061 [4], 022062 [4], 032052 [1], 032055 [1], 032056 [4], 032057 [5], 032059 [1], 032066 [1], 032071 [1]	I–II
9/60 (ΜΕΘ 1599)	#274/ 022065 [1], 022066 [3], 022067 [1], 022068 [1], 022070 [14], 032080 [1]	I
9/61 (ΜΕΘ 1344)	#274/022045 [4], 032052 [3]	II
9/62 (ΜΕΘ 3823)	#274/022044 [3], 022048 [1], 022049 [1], 033050 [1], 022052 [2], 022063 [2], 022064 [1], 022066 [2], 032017 [1], 032021 [1], 032025 [1], 032027 [53], 032033 [2], 032034 [1], 032035 [5], 032036 [10], 032038 [5], 032041 [1], 032047 [3], 032048 [10], 032049 [9], 032067 [4], 032081 [3]	I–III & mixed levels immediately above
9/63 (ΜΕΘ 3809)	#274/032050 [7], 032067 [7]	II
9/64 (ΜΕΘ 1337)	#274/022, ΖΒΠ [8], 022, ΖΑΠ [1], 022060 [1], 022062 [1], 022063 [1], 022064 [10], 022065 [22], 022066 [12], 022067 [1], 022068 [1], 022077 [1], 032060 [4], 032061 [10], 032066 [1], 032073 [9], 032074 [5], 032075 [1], 032077 [7], 032080 [1], 032081 [1]	I–II
9/65 (ΜΕΘ 1334)	#274/022063 [7], 032036 [2], 032037 [2], 032041 [3], 032042 [1], 032048 [1], 032074 [1]	I–II
9/66 (ΜΕΘ 1577)	#274/022057 [1], 022058 [1], 022060 [2], 022061 [1], 022062 [1], 022063 [3], 032037 [7], 032060 [1]	I–II
9/67 (ΜΕΘ 1574)	#274/022058 [6], 032018 [1], 032041 [2], 032042 [1], 032043-051 [1], 032048 [1], 032049 [5], 032052 [1], 032053 [8], 032054 [3]	I–III & mixed levels immediately above
9/68 (ΜΕΘ 2039)	#274/022032 [1], 022061 [3], 022062 [3], 022063 [3], 022064 [1], 022065 [2], 032029 [1], 032035 [4], 032044 [4], 032045 [3], 032053 [2]	I–III & mixed levels immediately above
9/69 (ΜΕΘ 1307)	#274/022058 [1], 032026 [1], 032029 [4], 032037 [3], 032041 [1], 032042 [5], 032048 [2], 032053 [2], 032055 [1], 032069 [10]	I–III & mixed levels immediately above
9/70 (ΜΕΘ 1335)	#274/022061 [2], 022062 [4], 022063 [8], 022064 [8]	III
9/71 (ΜΕΘ 1330)	#274/022061 [1], 022062 [1], 022064 [17], 022065 [2], 032075 [1]	I
9/72 (ΜΕΘ 3569)	#274/022031 [1], 022045 [1], 022047 [1], 032027 [3], 032036 [1], 032044 [5], 032046 [1], 032049 [1], 032067 [2]	II–III & mixed levels immediately above
9/73 (ΜΕΘ 3646)	#274/032065 [7]	II
9/74 (ΜΕΘ 3420)	#274/022, Τ.14 [2], 022046 [2], 022058 [3], 022059 [2], 022060 [3], 032044 [1], 032049 [1], 032052-060 [1], 032054 [3], 032055 [1], 032056 [2], 032065 [1]	I–III & mixed levels immediately above
9/75 (ΜΕΘ 3579)	#274/022056 [1], 022058 [2], 022059 [3], 032037 [1], 032054 [2], 032055 [1], 032056 [2], 032057 [2], 032069 [1]	I–II
9/76 (ΜΕΘ 3581)	#274/022058 [2], 022059 [2], 022060 [5], 032060 [1]	I
9/77 (ΜΕΘ 1354)	#274/022049 [1], 022051 [12], 032067 [3], 032066 [7]	II

TABLE 9.1. Context and phases of the catalogued pottery (9/1–9/98) *(continued)*

Cat. and inv. no.	Context (East Hill)	Phase(s)
9/78 (ΜΕΘ 3578)	#274/022055 [1], 022060 [1], 022062 [5], 032050 [1], 032050-060 [1], 032030 [2], 032052 [1], 032053 [1], 032054 [1], 032055 [1], 032056 [3], 032067 [1], 032070 [1], 032071 [4]	I–II
9/79 (ΜΕΘ 1586)	#274/022058 [4], 022059 [3], 022060 [2], 032028 [3], 032030 [5], 032037 [1], 032042 [1], 032055 [1], 032064 [1], 032067 [1], 032068 [1]	I–II
9/80 (ΜΕΘ 1589)	#274/022060 [1], 022061 [2], 022062 [8], 022063 [3], 032059 [1], 032071 [1]	I
9/81 (ΜΕΘ 3425)	#274/022044 [1], 022045 [3], 022047 [5], 032027 [1], 032043-051 [1], 032044 [1], 032046 [1], 032049 [3], 032050 [4], 032051 [2]	II–III & mixed levels immediately above
9/82 (ΜΕΘ 3588)	#274/022044 [1], 022046 [3], 022047 [3], 022050 [1], 022051 [1], 022052 [1], 022058 [3], 022059 [4], 022061 [7], 022062 [8], 032027 [1], 032050 [1], 032052-060 [2], 032054 [1], 032055 [1], 032056 [3], 032058 [5], 032070 [1], 032071 [1]	I–III
9/83 (ΜΕΘ 1343)	#274/022, ZBΠ [10], 022060 [3], 022061 [1], 022064 [5], 022065 [1], 032058 [6], 032061 [7], 032066 [2], 032069 [1], 032070 [1], 032071 [2], 032072 [1], 032073 [4], 032074 [11], 032075 [15], 032079 [2]	I–II
9/84 (ΜΕΘ 1575)	#275/022044 [1], 022053 [1], 022059 [3], 022060 [1], 022061 [7], 022062 [1], 022063 [1], 032028-030 [1], 032037 [4], 032041 [1], 032042 [10], 032043 [1], 032047 [1], 032049 [1], 032050 [3], 032052 [1], 032052-0.060 [7], 032054 [1], 032056 [1], 032057 [20], 032058 [9], 032059 [4], 032060 [1], 032061 [1], 032066 [1], 032067 [2], 032068 [1], 032069 [2], 032070 [5], 032071 [4], 032072 [1], 032073 [1]	I–III
9/85 (ΜΕΘ 1351)	#274/022044 [2], 022045 [1], 022049 [7], 022054 [1], 022058 [7], 022059 [3], 022060 [3], 032028-030 [1], 032067 [5]	I–II
9/86 (ΜΕΘ 3604)	#274/022051 [1], 022052 [1], 022054 [1], 022056 [3], 022058 [4], 032040 [1], 032042 [1], 032048 [1], 032053 [2], 032054 [1], 032066 [3], 032071 [1]	I–III & mixed levels immediately above
9/87 (ΜΕΘ 3567)	#274/022058 [1], 022059 [8], 022060 [4], 032027 [1], 032069 [1]	I, III
9/88 (ΜΕΘ 1321)	#274/022058 [5], 022061 [3], 022062 [7], 022064 [3], 022065 [1], 032058 [3], 032059 [2]	I
9/89 (ΜΕΘ 1360)	#274/022058 [2], 022059 [1], 022064 [1], 022065 [10], 032055 [1], 032056 [6], 032057 [1], 032060 [1], 032061 [6], 032066 [2], 032073 [16], 032074 [1], 032079 [1]	I–II
9/90 (ΜΕΘ 2019)	#274/022044 [1], 032027 [6], 032028 [9], 032032 [1], 032035 [1], 032049 [1]	II–III & mixed levels immediately above
9/91 (ΜΕΘ 3442)	#274/022060 [1], 022061 [6], 022062 [5], 022064 [2], 032058 [2]	I
9/92 (ΜΕΘ 1327)	#274/022052 [1], 032045 [2], 032047 [5], 032048 [2], 032049 [2], 032050 [7]	II–III
9/93 (ΜΕΘ 3532)	#274/022, T.5/7, 022025 [8], 022034 [4], 022039 [1], 032020 [1], 032022 [1], 032023 [1]	Mixed levels above III & occupation levels
9/94 (ΜΕ 4046α, β)	Fr α: #274/022023 [1], 022032 [1], 022034 [1], 022035 [1], 032043 [1], 032044 [1]; fr β:022038 [2]	Mixed levels above Phase III
9/95 (ΜΕΘ 1953)	#274/022, 032 T.5 [1], 032005 [3], 032015 [1], 032017 [1], 032019 [4], 032033 [7], 032034 [6]	Mixed levels above III & occupation levels
9/96 (ΜΕΘ 3821)	#274/022, 032	Unclear stratigraphy
9/97 (ΜΕΘ 2022)	#274/022008 [6], 022009 [21]	Above III to occupation levels
9/98 (ΜΕΘ 3822)	#274/022003 [3]	Occupation levels

TABLE 9.2. Concordance of catalogue numbers in this volume and figure numbers in *Methone Pierias* I (Bessios, Tzifopoulos, and Kotsonas 2012)

Catalogue no.	Fig. no. in *Methone* I	Catalogue no.	Fig. no. in *Methone* I	Catalogue no.	Fig. no. in *Methone* I	Catalogue no.	Fig. no. in *Methone* I
9/1	1	9/26	26	9/51	51	9/76	78
9/2	2	9/27	27	9/52	52	9/77	79
9/3	3	9/28	28	9/53	53	9/78	80
9/4	4	9/29	29	9/54	54	9/79	81
9/5	5	9/30	30	9/55	55	9/80	82
9/6	6	9/31	31	9/56	56	9/81	83
9/7	7	9/32	32	9/57	57	9/82	84
9/8	8	9/33	33	9/58	58	9/83	85
9/9	9	9/34	34	9/59	59	9/84	86
9/10	10	9/35	35	9/60	60	9/85	87
9/11	11	9/36	36	9/61	61	9/86	88
9/12	12	9/37	37	9/62	62–64	9/87	89
9/13	13	9/38	38	9/63	65	9/88	90
9/14	14	9/39	39	9/64	66	9/89	91
9/15	15	9/40	40	9/65	67	9/90	92
9/16	16	9/41	41	9/66	68	9/91	93
9/17	17	9/42	42	9/67	69	9/92	94
9/18	18	9/43	43	9/68	70	9/93	95
9/19	19	9/44	44	9/69	71	9/94	96
9/20	20	9/45	45	9/70	72	9/95	97
9/21	21	9/46	46	9/71	73	9/96	98
9/22	22	9/47	47	9/72	74	9/97	99
9/23	23	9/48	48	9/73	75	9/98	100
9/24	24	9/49	49	9/74	76		
9/25	25	9/50	50	9/75	77		

NOTES

1. Translator's note (John Papadopoulos). In the following catalogue, all pottery is wheelmade (WM) unless otherwise noted. This catalogue is a translation of the catalogue published in Greek in Bessios, Tzifopoulos, and Kotsonas 2012, pp. 65–111. It also incorporates the introduction to this pottery in Bessios, Tzifopoulos, and Kotsonas 2012, pp. 59–62 (translated by Marianna Nikolaidou). In certain places I have taken the liberty of adding a little detail for the sake of clarity in English. These additions were all approved by Bessios. I have also incorporated a few minor corrections of inventory numbers and measurements, again with the approval of my colleagues in the Pieria Ephoreia. In terms of illustrations, the original publication presented primarily photographs, with only two drawings; here we present both drawings and photographs for the majority of the pieces. In the original Greek publication of this pottery in Bessios, Tzifopoulos, and Kotsonas 2012, catalogue numbers were not provided so that there would be no confusion with the primary catalogue of the pottery with inscriptions (for which, see Bessios, Tzifopoulos, and Kotsonas 2012, pp. 331–508). Instead, each piece was identified with a figure number. In the case of one vessel (**9/62**, p. 439), three figure numbers were given. Consequently, the original figure numbers and the current catalogue numbers beginning with **9/63** do not correspond; in order to avoid confusion, I append a concordance at the end of this catalogue of the current catalogue numbers and the original figure numbers.

2. Bessios, Tzifopoulos, and Kotsonas 2012, pp. 331–508.

3. Cf. the criteria outlined in Chapter 8 (esp. criteria b and c).

4. For the Painter of Athens 897, see Cook 1947, pp. 144–146; Davison 1961, pp. 45–48, figs. 40–47; Coldstream 1968, pp. 77–81; Papadopoulos 2021a, with further references.

5. In the Greek text, Bessios referred to the Attic LG IIb potter as the Ζωγράφου των "βρυχόμενων λεόντων" (Painter of the "Roaring Lions"), who, in English, is known as the Lion Painter, see Kahane 1940, pp. 479–480, 482; Cook 1947, pp. 143–144, figs. 4:a–b; Davison 1961, p. 41; Coldstream 1968, pp. 73–74; several of the works of the Lion Painter are also illustrated and discussed in Brokaw 1963, Beil. 28:7, Beil. 29:1.

6. *Eretria* XX, pp. 60–64.

7. *Eretria* XX, pl. 66, nos. 325–329.

8. *Eretria* XX, p. 249.

9. With the foundation of the colony, Methone appears to have been transformed into a production center for the manufacture of items of every sort, especially in the areas of metallurgy and minor arts, which demand specialized knowledge and techniques. Pottery requires simpler techniques, and raw materials that abound throughout Greece. The misfired skyphos fragments **9/63** (ΜΕΘ 3809; Fig. 9.28; and cf. the oinochoe, **9/64**, ΜΕΘ 1337; Fig. 9.28) from the Hypogeion provide unequivocal evidence that the colonists established pottery workshops under the influence of the metropolis, mainly in order to satisfy local demand. In addition, the Hypogeion contained a significant number of triangular sherds with intentionally shaped sharp edges, which have been recognized as potters' tools, useful for modeling the pot on the wheel. A large portion of the pottery from the Hypogeion can be attributed to the workshops of Methone, based on the abundant examples of specific shape categories and the composition of the potting clay (see criterion d, Chapter 8). Apparently, Methone presented ideal conditions for interactions with various Aegean centers and for the mixing of influences; there was also larger flexibility in the choice and adoption of certain vessel types. For example, the type of skyphos with four concentric circles on the rim (see Kotsonas 2012, pp. 128–134) must have been created in such an environment of contacts and mutual impact, rather than under oppressive control of local production by metropolitan workshops. The large number of imitations of Early Protocorinthian kotylai was probably created locally at Methone, without interference or impact from Eretria, as is confirmed by similar products

from Pithekoussai. The distance of the colony from its metropolis must have allowed larger independence from the Eretrian workshops. Moreover, the presence of colonists from other regions, and the contacts with many production centers in the Aegean and the eastern and central Mediterranean (for example, Pithekoussai), were decisive for the greater variety and independence of the local workshops at Methone. It is not a coincidence that excavations at Eretria have revealed pottery of predominantly local character, versus a small portion of imported wares; it seems that access to the harbor of Eretria was mainly afforded to the fleet of the dominant sea power, that is, the Eretrians.

10 Especially criterion b and, mainly, c.
11 Neeft 1975, type β.
12 Andreiomenou 1975, pl. 54:γ; Andreiomenou 1982, pl. 23, nos. 25, 30–31; Boardman 1952, fig. 1, pl. 1:a.
13 See Kotsonas 2012, pp. 128–134.
14 Andreiomenou 1977, pls. 39:γ, 40:α–δ; Andreiomenou 1982, pl. 23, no. 28.
15 Mazarakis Ainian 1996, pl. 27.
16 Ridgway 1992, p. 88, fig. 22.

10

LIFEWAYS AND FOODWAYS IN IRON AGE METHONE: A PERISHABLE MATERIAL CULTURE APPROACH

*Alexandra Livarda, Rena Veropoulidou,
Anastasia Vasileiadou, and Llorenç Picornell-Gelabert*

One of the largest and most impressive assemblages of bioarchaeological finds in the Aegean dated to the Early Iron Age was collected during the excavation of the feature conventionally called the "Hypogeion" at Methone.[1] The ancient settlement of Methone is located at the western shore of the Thermaic Gulf and was conventionally founded in 733 B.C. by Eretrians expelled from the island of Kerkyra.[2] The Hypogeion is in reality a rectangular subterranean structure (pit) on top of the East Hill, east of the agora of Methone, the construction of which was never completed and which was instead filled with a variety of materials within a very short period of time.[3] Meticulous study of its stratigraphy and pottery suggested that the dating of its fill began at the end of the Early Iron Age, sometime between 720 and 690 B.C., which places the Hypogeion in the first phase of the life of the colony.[4] Among the plentiful ceramics, mud bricks, metals, and stones, a wealth of bioarchaeological remains was present. This perishable material culture provides an alternative means and a rare opportunity through which light can be shed on the history of the beginnings of the colony.

The systematic collection of all classes of bioarchaeological remains is still a rather uncommon practice in most excavations conducted by the Greek Archaeological Service. Larger specimens visible to the naked eye, such as long bones of animals and big pieces of charcoal from specific constructions, are recovered more often, but normally in a haphazard manner and outside a framework of a clearly defined sampling strategy. In contrast, the collection of soil samples and their processing with a flotation system usually depends on the input and personal contacts, requests, and determination of individual archaeobotanists or other bioarchaeologists. As Dr. Anaya Sarpaki has argued, this situation seems to be perpetuated largely by the lack of relevant legislation in Greece that explicitly enforces the collection of bioarchaeological remains as part of the archaeological process.[5] The excavation at the Hypogeion is one of the few examples where, thanks to the efforts of its director, Matthaios Bessios, of the former KZ´ Ephoreia of Prehistoric and Classical Antiquities, this situation was reversed. Along with the recovery of the plentiful artifacts, time and labor were invested for the collection of organic remains, including terrestrial and marine animal bones, molluskan remains, charcoal, seeds, and other macrofossils, which have been entrusted to the authors for their study.

In this chapter a first presentation of all bioarchaeological remains from this deposit is attempted in an integrated approach. The aim is to showcase their potential in illuminating aspects of the lifeways and foodways of the inhabitants and in shedding light on the social history of the ancient town. The study is based on the preliminary assessment of the bioarchaeological assemblage and highlights how all lines of this type of evidence can successfully contribute to disentangling a series of research questions. These include the reconstruction of the physical setting and how this was experienced, the development of food culture and "cuisine" of the Iron Age settlement, the interactions between people and their environment, and the establishment of fashions incorporated into the social life of the settlement's inhabitants.

MATERIAL AND METHODS

Two trenches were opened (in squares 022 and 032) during the excavation and all organic materials visible to the naked eye were recovered and stored in the premises of the KZ´ Ephoreia. Dry-sieving was also carried out for the majority of the excavated soil, which allowed higher recovery rates of all classes of material. Animal bones and shells were later washed for the removal of soil to allow their study. In addition, 92 soil samples were collected from areas with visible concentrations of charred material and were processed with flotation, using a modified version of the Ankara machine designed by David French.[6] A stack of two geological sieves with apertures of 1 mm and 0.3 mm were used for the collection of the light, floatable material (coarse and fine flot respectively), and a mesh with 1 mm aperture for the retention of the heavy fraction (residue) of the sample that sank in the lower part of the flotation tank. After processing, the material was dried, packed in labeled plastic bags, and stored alongside the hand-selected material.

Standard laboratory procedures were followed by each member of the team for the study of the bioarchaeological remains. The methodologies adopted for the full analyses of the material are briefly outlined here, as they form the basis that allows specific research lines to be followed and the validity of results to be assessed.

Based on macroscopic and low magnification examination, animal bones and shells were identified to taxon/species level, using modern reference collections and identification atlases.[7] The dimensions of a stratified random sample of intact shell specimens and of several selected fused bones were measured with Vernier calipers. The size of fused bones was measured with calipers, following methods recommended by Angela von den Driesch,[8] and has an accuracy to the nearest tenth of a millimeter. The degree and mode of fragmentation of each shell and bone specimen and any evidence of burning were recorded in order to understand both the taphonomic and cultural processes (e.g., cooking methods, trampling) that led to the formation of these classes of material. Similarly, processing marks were recorded, such as gnawing in the case of animal bones, butchery and incisions, cuts and surface treatment, as well as other human modifications (e.g., perforations) in the case of both animal bones and shells. With regard to the animal bones, a series of additional observations were made: identification of the body part, the side (left/right), whether proximal or distal axis, and where possible, documentation of the age at death and sex of the animal, and recording of any evidence of pathologies. For the shells, identification of the side of valves (right/left), recording of the diagnostic body parts (umbo for bivalves; apex/aperture/siphonal canal for gastropods) and all non-diagnostic fragmented material, and categorization of specimens as fresh or water/beach-worn were also carried out.

For the flotation material, all coarse flots were sieved in the laboratory, using a stack of brass sieves with apertures of 2 mm and 1 mm. Charcoal material was then sorted for analysis only from the 2 mm sieve in order to ensure the presence of large enough pieces with clear anatomical features to allow the detailed identification of taxa. All other plant macrofossils (seeds, chaff, stones, fruit/nut shells, etc.) were sorted from all fractions of the coarse flots and from the fine flots with the aid of a stereomicroscope with magnifications ranging from x 7 to x 45. These remains were classified into different plant parts and identified to the taxon/species level on the basis of their morphological characteristics, with the aid of modern reference collection material and identification manuals.[9] Notes on the preservation, distortion, and degree and mode of fragmentation of the different specimens were also taken. Recording of the fragmentation mode of this material allows monitoring, apart from taphonomic factors, of potential cooking practices that may have led to specific breakage patterns of certain ingredients[10]. For the identification of charcoal fragments, an optical microscope with reflected light and bright/dark fields (Olympus BX41) was used. Each charcoal fragment was manually fractured to obtain the three anatomical planes (transversal, longitudinal radial, and longitudinal tangential) and examine their cell structure. The characteristic wood anatomy in the form of presence/absence, shape, density, and distribution of diverse anatomical features, such as pores, rays, vessels, and perforation plates in the three planes, defined the identity of each species. A reference collection of Mediterranean woody plants and the atlas of wood anatomy of European and Mediterranean species were employed to aid the identification process.[11]

The heavy residue material was sorted with the naked eye for all classes of material.

Different quantification methods were employed for each bioarchaeological material type in order to account for their different levels of analyses. Animal bones were quantified following the methodology developed by Halstead to estimate the relative taxonomic and anatomic frequencies of the assemblage.[12] First, the total number of anatomical units was calculated on the basis of the Maximum Number of Anatomical Units (MaxAU). Then the Minimum Number of Anatomical Unit (MinAU) was introduced in order to estimate the relative frequency of units in each species' body part and avoid double counting (due to excessive fragmentation) that could lead to overrepresentation in the final assemblage.[13] Bones susceptible to excessive fragmentation are those from the trunk, the cranium, and the maxilla (including the maxillary teeth), and thus were not included in the quantification process. Overall, only those bones that could be safely classified according to their anatomical and taxonomic identity were included in the quantification and analysis.[14]

The quantification of the molluskan remains was based on the principles of the Number of Identified Specimens (NISP), the Number of Intact specimens (NI), the Number of Fragments (NF), and the Minimum Number of Individuals (MNI), considering the minimum number of diagnostic shell parts, such as right or left umbos for bivalves and apices or apertures for gastropods. Plant macrofossils other than charcoal were counted on the basis of the Minimum Number of Individuals (MNI), taking into account the minimum number of characteristic plant parts, such as the embryo ends in cereal grains. Charcoal quantification was conducted on the basis of Number of Fragments (NF) and Ubiquity (U), that is, the number of occurrences of each taxon in every unit of analysis (stratigraphic sample).

The assessment of the assemblage as a whole suggested that it is one of the largest and most impressive concentrations of such remains in the Iron Age Aegean. The shell assemblage from the Hypogeion in particular is about 330 kg and can thus be considered one of the largest so far in the Aegean, irrespective of period. Its examination indicated that the recovery during excavation was very thorough, as the material included mollusk remains of very small size as well as small fragments of shells. The archaeobotanical remains were equally substantial in both quantity and quality, providing one of the very few rich assemblages of late Early Iron Age contexts with such precise dating. The assessment of the animal bones presents a similar picture of a rich assemblage that also includes small bones, fragments of various sizes, and bones of small fauna. The preservation of all classes of bioarchaeological material was particularly good, allowing an increased level of detail in the identification of species and usage patterns.

The results outlined in the discussion that follows form part of the preliminary stage of the analysis of the abovementioned bioarchaeological remains.

LANDSCAPES, WATERSCAPES, AND ATTITUDES TOWARD SPACE

In order to explore the lifeways of Methone, its overall physical setting needs to be understood first. This is because the physical environment is culturally shaped, providing thus a unique framework within which a society operates. Past human environments are no longer seen as passive backdrops onto which humans mapped their activities, but as active and socially constructed, being created as they were experienced.[15] The physical environment can, in fact, be considered as the "mediatory influence" in the establishment of social conditions by individuals or groups.[16]

Standard zooarchaeological, archaeobotanical, and charcoal analyses as described in the previous section, in conjunction with information from a series of other datasets, such as geoarchaeological and climatic, and contextual approaches in various scales, have been employed here to provide an overview of the Iron Age "space" around Methone. Drawing upon the concepts of agency[17] and biography,[18] our chosen approach acknowledges the relationship between material culture (in this case the surrounding environment and its resources) and people as complex, context-specific, and dialectical.[19] The ultimate aim is to provide insights into the environment of ancient Methone and the particular human-environment interactions that were formed then and there.

To delineate first the basic setting, ancient Methone is located on the southwestern shore of the Thermaic Gulf. In the north there are extensive coastal lagoons and river deltas created by the activities of the Haliakmon and Loudias rivers, and in the east, the area is delimited by the marine environment of the Thermaic Gulf. The Pierian hills and Mt. Olympos in the west and south complete the rich and diverse land- and waterscape of the area (Fig. I.1; Chapter 3).

Palynological studies from several sites in Pieria and other sites in northern Greece and the Balkans have indicated the presence of coniferous and oak forests on the higher elevations of the area during the Iron Age, and the probable domination of an open deciduous forest of *Quercus* with *Tilia, Corylus, Ostrya-Carpinus orientalis*-type and *Fraxinus*, on the lowlands and hilly areas.[20] The presence of sun-loving taxa (e.g., *Pistacia, Fraxinus*) denotes the possibly relatively open character of the deciduous and evergreen forest.[21] The charcoal study from the Hypogeion is consistent with the palynological analyses, as *Quercus*, together with *Pinus* t. *sylvestris, Arbutus unedo, Celtis, Cornus*, and *Fraxinus*, among other taxa, have been identified in the assemblage. In addition, charcoal from trees and shrubs, as well as from species with a variety of ecological habitats, was recorded, which indicates that the inhabitants of Methone exploited different environmental niches in order to fulfill their energy (fuel) and other relevant demands. Notably, at the current stage of research, deciduous oak (*Quercus*) wood seems to have been of particular importance as a fuel resource, being the most recurrent taxon (higher NF) and present in all the analyzed units (high U level). It can be postulated that one of the reasons for the strategic importance of Methone was the accessibility to these woodlands for a series of reasons, such as timber, shipbuilding, and fuel supply. It may not be a coincidence that later on, in the Classical period, Methone was identified as possibly the main port of the Macedonian timber trade and the Pierian Mountains, near the only dominant stand of *Pinus sylvestris* in Macedonia that was used for shipbuilding and oars, as the possible source of the timber.[22]

Woodland use and management seem to have altered the landscape, as the exploitation of such resources would have had an impact on the forest ecosystems. This is supported by the palynological data, according to which, from the Early Iron Age (*c.* 2750 B.P.) onward, the coniferous and, to a lesser extent, the oak forests were seriously disturbed, and open-ground and cultivation/disturbance indicators increased considerably; these vegetation developments continued and intensified in the following years.[23] Such anthropogenic disturbance possibly triggered landscape destabilization and alluviation, as has been documented by alluvia deposited in stream valleys farther south.[24] The archaeobotanical and zooarchaeological evidence from the Hypogeion also points toward systematic landscape exploitation and seems to be suggestive of a possibly intensive, mixed agro-pastoral economy (see below), which is compatible with the results of current geoarchaeological work in the broader area.[25]

The coastal landscapes can be tentatively reconstructed on the basis of geoarchaeological and paleoenvironmental research from the broader area of northern Greece. Lithostratigraphic and malacological evidence from the northwest and the central part of the former Thermaic Gulf indicates that at about 10,000 B.P. the Pleistocene landscape was inundated by rapid sea level rise and, by the Early Bronze Age, a large shallow marine bay had formed on the actual plain of Thessaloniki.[26] Lower sea level rise rates were suggested for the last 4,000 years, when fluvial sedimentation to the west and the north of the gulf pushed the shoreline gradually to its present position. River deltas were gradually transformed into lagoons and brackish conditions were established around the margins of the bay.[27] In southern areas, lithostratigraphic, chronostratigraphic, and biostratigraphic analyses indicate that the coastal plain of Korinos,[28] as well as the entire coastal zone of Pieria farther south, must have experienced similar landscape modifications during the Holocene.[29]

Focusing on the landscape of Iron Age Methone, the Pierian hills formed a gently rolling terrain, dipping toward the east and south, and were traversed by a network of meandering streams draining into the ancient Thermaic Gulf. The narrow coastal plain included shallow-water zones, received low-energy waves, and was interrupted by small estuaries. In all likelihood, the shallow marine bay exhibited variability in aquatic conditions, due to the regular freshwater inputs from the large rivers and streams.[30] The substrate was sandy in shallow marine areas with fluctuating salinities, accommodating typical molluskan fauna, such as *Hexaplex trunculus, Ostrea edulis,* and *Cerithium vulgatum,* as also attested by the shell assemblage at Methone. The presence of monotonous euryhaline molluskan fauna, including *Cerastoderma glaucum* and *Tritia neritea,* in the Hypogeion further suggested that ancient inhabitants were visiting and exploiting the sandy-muddy substrates of estuaries and coastal lagoons in the area. As regards full marine conditions, the typical marine fauna were present, such as *Arca noae, Glycymeris* sp., and *Spondylus gaederopus.*[31] The data, therefore, allude to interactions with and usage of a variety of niches of the coastal environment at ancient Methone. A closer inspection of the molluskan remains, however, indicates that the inhabitants of the settlement focused principally on the exploitation of estuarine ecosystems for the bulk procurement of the readily available brackish-water species, which formed the vast majority of the shell assemblage.

The data thus far suggest a continuous and selective exploitation of local resources, which would have created an ideological relation among people, places, and time.[32] Despite the fact that it is very difficult to incorporate the physical environment into a historical narrative,[33] outlining the environment of ancient Methone has indicated the availability of diverse micro-ecologies in the area, while the study of the bioarchaeological evidence sketched the interactions of the inhabitants with this fragmented environment. On this basis it is argued here that the distinct identity of ancient Methone derived partly from the variable set of productive opportunities and the particular human responses to these. The following section investigates these issues in some more detail with particular reference to foodways.

FLAVORS OF SUBSISTENCE; TASTES OF CULTURE

Food, as Paul Freedman argues, "reflects the environment of a society, but is not completely determined by it."[34] There are several factors contributing to perceptions of what is edible or not and the development of particular tastes. The environment certainly provides a framework, and within this, social norms and economic relations interplay toward the development of a food culture. A food culture also presupposes a whole range of culturally determined "technologies" distinct for different places and times. These range from landscape manipulation for both wild and domesticate resources to food processing, cooking, and discard methods/practices. In other words, there is a whole *chaîne opératoire* that involves a series of choices and social acts. In this section the final stages of this operational sequence will be primarily discussed, to provide a background for the exploration of foodways at Methone.

The fill of the Hypogeion contained a wealth of bioarchaeological remains that attests to the availability of a rich dietary base for the inhabitants of the ancient town. Different lines of bioarchaeological evidence are normally treated separately in Aegean archaeology,[35] which often obscures the full picture of "cuisine." Here a synthesis of all this evidence together is attempted.

Bioarchaeological remains from the Hypogeion and their analysis suggested that people at the settlement regularly harvested the sea, the estuary, and the land. In doing so, they collected and utilized a range of domesticated and naturally occurring resources, with several of the latter potentially considered as "wild." Domesticated animals, cereals, legumes, fruits, oil-producing plants, fish, including cuttlefish, marine and brackish-water mollusks, wild animals, fruits, and other herbaceous and possibly tuberous plants were processed for consumption. This range of foodstuffs alludes to a partitioned engagement with the overall environment. Although many of the aforementioned products can be stored for relatively long periods, most of them would still need to be collected, killed, or harvested at certain seasons or time periods. By investigating the available resources from the Hypogeion, we can start sketching this temporally organized activity pattern alongside the dietary base and the "cuisine" of the settlement.

Food Tradition and Organization at Methone

A combination of domesticated animals, cereals, legumes, and brackish-water mollusks dominates the assemblage and seems to form the bulk of subsistence and the core of "cuisine" at Early Iron Age Methone, on current evidence.

In terms of the animals, ovicaprids (*Ovis aries/Capra hircus*), followed by pig (*Sus domesticus*), and then cattle (*Bos taurus*), were the most commonly encountered species. Analysis of the age of the cattle at death and the male to female sex ratio indicated that, possibly, mostly male animals were slaughtered for meat at an age when they would have gained enough weight to be attractive for consumption. The mortality pattern for ovicaprids (sheep and goat), following Payne's models,[36] suggests a rearing strategy focused mainly on meat production. The slaughter of the ovicaprids started when they reached an age of two months and most of them were killed by three years of age. Pigs were slaughtered at a younger overall age than the ruminants, but this was in all likelihood because they gain weight faster. In particular, at Methone most pigs were killed before the age of two years for meat consumption, and the main age of slaughter was between two and six months old. Only a small number of pigs, possibly sows, were kept up to an older age, probably reserved for breeding purposes. In traditional husbandry systems, sheep and pigs deliver one litter a year in early spring, and the latter, if the food is sufficient, have a second litter in late summer/early autumn.[37] Taking into account the age at death of these animals, it seems possible that killing was not concentrated at a particular season, but was taking place in a piecemeal fashion, possibly spread during the year, with pigs being killed in all likelihood mostly throughout the summer or winter.

Lamb, mutton, kid, chevon, pork, and to a lesser extent beef, were thus consumed at this Iron Age settlement. Mutton and chevon, which refer to the meat of the older sheep and goat respectively, are tougher and have a stronger flavor compared to the meat of the younger animals, and this difference may potentially attest to a greater variety of meat choices and diversity in recipes. Culinary preferences at Methone are also manifested in the consumption of marrow. The fragmentation on several cattle and ovicaprid bones suggests frequent marrow extraction for human consumption, a valued delicacy for some or perhaps a perceived healthy resource. Marrow, however, was not valued as a universal resource but was taken mostly from the ruminants. Pig bones exhibited very little fragmentation, suggesting limited and very occasional marrow extraction. This, in combination with fewer butchery marks on pig bones, could be explained by a possible preference for roasting either whole pigs or their individual complete meaty parts.

The range of the available staple food plants from the Hypogeion assemblage provides more insights into the cultural preferences of the inhabitants in relation to food, and reveals possible concerns for the spread of the cultivation season throughout the year. Einkorn (*Triticum monococcum*) and emmer (*Triticum dicoccum*) wheat, hulled barley (*Hordeum vulgare*), and broomcorn millet (*Panicum miliaceum*) were the most frequent cereal finds at Methone. Broomcorn millet has a very short life cycle of two to three months, and does very well in intense heat, drought, and poor soils.[38] It is usually a spring-sown crop and its cultivation can complement other frequently autumn-sown crops, such as wheat and barley. Several harvesting and crop processing seasons within one year can be advantageous, implying the spread of the labor force and improved food security, as there is a second crop if the first one fails. Furthermore, both millet and barley are quite hardy and can do better than wheat if the environmental conditions are not favorable.

Whatever the reason(s) behind this choice of cereals, a continuity in practices observed since the Bronze Age in northern Greece may be hypothesized. These are manifested mainly in the presence of einkorn wheat and broomcorn millet as important parts of the diet. The latter was introduced in Greece in the Bronze Age, during which it was present as a regular crop in its own right, almost exclusively in the north.[39] Similarly, einkorn, in both the Neolithic and Bronze Age periods, predominates in northern Greece and some areas of the Balkans, while it is rare in southern Greece.[40] This pattern has been interpreted as cultural traditionalism,[41] or part of certain regional cultural dietary preferences, possibly related to the identity of the population in the area.[42] Very few archaeobotanical studies exist for the Iron Age period in Greece and thus an overall pattern is difficult to establish.[43] So far, the only substantial evidence for the cultivation and consumption of broomcorn millet comes from Kastanas.[44] The status of einkorn is still not clear on the basis of the available evidence,[45] with some more substantial quantities deriving, once again, from northern Greece, this time from a 7th-century B.C. pit unearthed at the excavation of Karabournaki in Thessaloniki.[46] Further studies and the recovery of more Iron Age archaeobotanical assemblages will help establish whether the observed trends at Methone with regard to cereal consumption represent a wider regional pattern or not.

The range of cereals at Methone also implies a great variety of flavors, colors, and "dishes" available for the people at the settlement, from the bright yellow flour of einkorn, rich in protein and carotene,[47] to the darker brown barley, and from flat breads and rusks to gruels and bulgur among many potential recipes. A variety of pulses is also present that added to the culinary regime according to contextual evidence. The analysis so far has verified the presence of lentil (*Lens culinaris*), bitter vetch (*Vicia ervilia*), grass pea (*Lathyrus sativus*), and fava bean (*Vicia faba*). Legumes could be cultivated in garden plots or in rotation with the cereals, as their symbiotic relationship with the *Rhizobium* bacterium allows them to fix atmospheric nitrogen and hence replenish the fertility of soil. Soil fertility at Methone could have additionally or alternatively been improved through the application of manure. Analysis, for instance, of the cattle remains strongly suggests that, although some animals were killed after the age of 1.5 years, their population included mainly adult animals among which females were the prevalent sex. Furthermore, their mortality pattern showed no evidence of culling of young animals toward cattle exploitation for milk production. It can be therefore argued that cattle were being maintained in herds in the settlement in order to breed them, produce meat, and use their strength and manure in agricultural and other activities.

Pathological traces seem to support, tentatively, the use of cattle as a means of traction.[48] An integrated farming and agricultural regime, therefore, seems to emerge as an important part of the lifeways of Methone. Investigation of agricultural practices, through the analysis, for instance, of stable isotopes or of weedy species that can act as indirect indices for manuring, irrigation, and other husbandry practices, has good potential to add further insights into land and livestock management at the next stage of this research.

Keeping domesticates presupposes a whole range of other activities prior to and after the final slaughter of certain animals and the harvesting of cereals and pulses. Tending the animals, providing for their feed, stabling some of them, preparing the land, sowing, weeding, and protecting the seed from predators are all time-consuming activities, whether on a regular, daily, or seasonal basis. After harvesting, cereals and legumes also need to be processed by threshing, winnowing, and sieving. The final food product will then have to be prepared for storage. Cereal grains and pulses can be stored in dried form and last until the next harvest. The regular but relatively low presence of glume bases and spikelet forks in the Hypogeion refuse deposit points to the storage of the glume wheat (einkorn and emmer) within their husks and their piecemeal cleaning only prior to cooking. Dehusking, according to ethnographic studies,[49] is a very laborious task and therefore it would not normally be carried out if the product were destined for animal feed. However, experiments conducted by Soultana Valamoti and Michael Charles, and by Michael Wallace and Michael Charles, have shown that cereals enclosed in their glume bases and used as feed separate in the digestive system of the animal and the glume bases can survive in a recognizable form, albeit rarely, and often heavily damaged.[50] Valamoti's further experimental work indicates that digested glume bases exhibit a distinct "rugged" appearance which contrasts with the very smooth surface of undigested ones.[51] Macroscopic examination of the Methone assemblage at the current stage of research indicated a high occurrence of well-preserved glume bases with seemingly smooth surfaces, and it can therefore be suggested that the material with this patterning points to food processing activities.

Storage of glume wheats in their husks has many advantages, from spreading the labor throughout the year to protecting the crop from pests, such as insects and fungi, and the practice has been attested, for instance, in the Bronze Age burnt storage complex at Assiros in northern Greece.[52] Meat can be also kept for a longer period of time if dried, smoked, or salted. Evidence to suggest meat preservation methods is not easy to identify archaeologically, and it is only with the combination of different lines of evidence that some more insights in this direction may be gained. What is evident, however, is that meat consumption was taking place directly from the bone, regardless of the species (Fig. 10.1), according to the filleting marks present on bones of all species with similar frequencies. It can be hypothesized that possibly some of these meaty parts on the bone were cured to extend their consumption span.

Other resources have a limited "lifespan" after collection, and without appropriate means of preservation need to be consumed soon after their procurement. This seems to be the case of the common cockle (*Cerastoderma glaucum*), which made up more than 97% of the shell assemblage (Fig. 10.2). The large amount and the high density of cockle remains suggest a high scale of exploitation of estuarine environments for the bulk gathering of this mollusk for food consumption. Metrical data and the study of morphological characteristics of the cockles so far suggest that people collected mainly adult specimens with simple tools, such as their bare hands or rakes, possibly throughout the year. The presence of shells originating from healthy natural populations indicates that gatherers used tools that did not affect natural beds and larvae.[53] It also implies that the inhabitants in the area may have practiced some form of "semi-cultivation" of cockles, such as seasonal or spatial rotation of harvesting schemes and thinning of shell beds for larvae development, probably aiming at the preservation of natural stocks for future exploitation.[54]

FIGURE 10.1. Examples of cutmarks on ribs recovered from Trench 032 of the Hypogeion. Photo Ian Coyle

FIGURE 10.2. A concentration of *Cerastoderma glaucum* shells, the most commonly encountered mollusk species in the Hypogeion. Photo Rena Veropoulidou

This strong preference for the common cockle, despite the variety of the aquatic environments, was not an isolated phenomenon at Methone. In fact, across all communities in central Macedonia, whether coastal or semi-coastal, the common cockle appears to have been a favorite food resource. This preference seems to have endured through time, as in all settlements in the area, from the Early Neolithic until at least the Late Bronze Age and Early Iron Age, cockles were the most common molluskan foodstuff.[55] Early Iron Age mollusk assemblages are rare and an overall pattern is more difficult to discern.[56] On current evidence, however, molluskan food habits seem to have remained rather similar for a very long period of time (ca. 5,000 years), suggesting another possibly long tradition in the foodways of Methone. Gathering of mollusks thus appears to have been a successful and specialized economic activity in addition to agrarian practices and was embedded into the ways of life at the settlement.

ALTERNATIVE FOOD PROCUREMENT AND SOCIAL BONDS

Alongside the staples and the regular food procurement and consumption habits, several other activities contributed not only to the foodways of Methone but also to forging social bonds and identities among its inhabitants. Hunting and gathering are such activities for which there is evidence within the Hypogeion assemblage. These practices in the context of farming societies have received relatively little attention, mainly due to the dominance of paleoeconomic approaches to their study that see hunting and gathering as economic strategies integral to foraging societies, and thus, as remnants of a "backward" stage in the context of the superior way of life implied by farming and herding.[57] People in the past did not necessarily separate food into "wild" or "domesticated" but rather classified certain foodstuffs culturally as edible or not. Gathering and hunting in farming societies are thus complicated social phenomena that may be linked to perceptions of time and space, and the negotiation of gender, age, and social roles in a society.[58]

At Methone, hunting should have been relatively rare, as the percentages of wild animals were particularly low in comparison with the domesticated ones. Yet given the opportunity, some people were engaged in such activities, hunting red deer (*Cervus elaphus*), fallow deer (*Dama dama*), roe deer (*Capreolus capreolus*), boar (*Sus scrofa*), fox (*Vulpes vulpes*), and hare (*Lepus europaeus*), with red deer being the most common game. The contribution of wild animals to the dietary base of the settlement was very limited, a trend also observed in several other sites from the Late Bronze Age onward, such as Agios Mamas, Toumba Thessalonikis, and the cemetery in Torone, although not at Kastanas.[59] Deer hunting in the area also served other purposes, as attested by the various objects unearthed made from red and fallow deer antlers. The overall rarity of wild animal bones, however, as well as their differential presence and quantity in other sites, may point to a conscious choice at Methone for lesser use, potentially by certain people and/or for specific purposes and occasions, triggered by environmental or cultural concerns and impositions or a combination of the two.

Gathering of resources was taking place at Methone from both the land and the water. Apart from the common cockles, a variety of mollusks largely from marine and brackish waters were gathered, but in a less systematic manner than the former, suggesting a particular focus on the estuarine environment. On land, wild fruits and other potentially edible plants were collected but in equally low numbers, similarly to wild animals. Unlike wild animals, however, such plants have a taphonomic "disadvantage" compared to domesticates, and in particular to staples like cereals and legumes: they do not need to come into contact with fire to be prepared for consumption and thus charred specimens are most commonly end products of accidental burning. Their presence, therefore, can suggest usage but their low quantities may not necessarily indicate lesser importance. In areas where waterlogging preserves plant material, the significance of plant resources other than cereals and pulses, such as fruits, condiments, and vegetables, can be better appreciated.[60] In Greece, waterlogged conditions are the exception, and thus the consistent occurrence, even though in low numbers, across the Methone assemblage of plants such as *Rubus* berries may be a testimony to their regular consumption.

Whether from land or water, the social implications of gathering must have been quite important. Ethnobotanic studies in the Mediterranean, Greece, and Turkey indicate that gathering of wild plant resources is a well-established, common practice.[61] Plant gathering is strongly seasonal, with different plants collected at different times, spreading these activities throughout the year and thus adding seasonal variation to recipes and cuisine.[62] Füsun Ertuğ's study in the village of Kızılkaya in central Anatolia identified over 100 wild plant species that were considered to be edible by the locals, including mainly wild greens, followed by fruits, roots, and stems, collected and eaten regularly.[63] Gathering plants, according to Ertuğ, was mainly the task of women often accompanied by children, and was a welcome social opportunity to meet with peers and leave the house.[64] Similarly, ethnographic studies of mollusk gathering suggest that this is normally based on teamwork and is a social activity, conducted mainly by women, and often considered as time for recreation during which knowledge is shared and family or friendship bonds are tightened.[65] Although direct applications to the past cannot be made, it can be argued that whether small scale and irregular or a more common practice, collective activities for the selective procurement of animals, mollusks, and plants from the environment around Methone had a strong cultural element and were important agents in forging social identities and strengthening ties between certain groups of people. In the next section a different type of use in the settlement of some elements of such collected bioarchaeological remains is briefly explored.

FASHIONS IN THE COLONY

Animals and plants are sought after for a range of reasons beyond culinary ones. Aesthetic, spiritual, cultural, and economic motives, ranging from the simple olfactory and visual attraction of a flower to the handling of ecofacts given their plasticity toward making more or less durable objects, work together to contribute to the selection of certain raw materials that enter into various aspects of social life at a site. Here a first attempt is made to examine the bioarchaeological remains of such practices at Methone.

Shell ornaments and other artifacts made of shell are abundant in the prehistoric Aegean and more particularly in the northern Aegean.[66] Nevertheless, examples from the Early Iron Age are few and seem to be better represented in funerary contexts.[67] At ancient Methone, similarly, there are only a few perforated shells from various taxa, such as *Arca noae* and *Glycymeris* sp., among which the most common is the perforated cockle (*C. glaucum*, Fig. 10.3). Different types of wear (striations, incisions, polishing) on the periphery of holes suggest that they were suspended with threads, and therefore must have had an ornamental character. Interestingly, the cockle is also the preferred shell ornament in the broader area from the Early Neolithic to the Early Iron Age.[68] However, contrary to the existing tradition of recycling food debris to manufacture perforated shells and of avoiding using either beach-worn shells or naturally perforated specimens in the majority of the settlements in central Macedonia,[69] the inhabitants of ancient Methone, in addition to fresh specimens originating from food debris, also perforated beach-worn specimens and used naturally perforated shells. This practice suggests a shift in perception in regard to which shell is appropriate or not for the manufacture of ornaments that contrasts not only with earlier periods but also with contemporary sites.[70] Meanwhile, it points toward alternative stages in the biography of shell ornaments, as beach-worn and naturally perforated shells have not passed through the same series of social practices as the recycled food debris.[71]

FIGURE 10.3. Examples of *Cerastoderma glaucum* artifacts from the Hypogeion. The second and the third (from left) are fresh and bear human-made perforations, while the first and the fourth are beach-worn with natural holes. Photo Rena Veropoulidou

In terms of tools made of shell, there are only a few examples that represent expedient tools, namely thorny oysters (*Spondylus gaederopus*) with flaked and/or ground lip that might have been used in several tasks, such as scraping implements for soft and hard surfaces, treating hides, carving wood, and so on. Similar finds have been reported from prehistoric sites in the area and from other Early Iron Age sites.[72] The use of shells as spoons and vases has also been reported,[73] but the lack of systematic analysis and survey of such finds prevents any secure conclusion. Animal bones were also made into various artifacts at Methone and their analysis is currently in progress.

Small-scale skinning of animals and possibly textile production are attested, according to evidence from the zooarchaeological analysis and the presence of spindlewhorls and loomweights among the Hypogeion assemblage, thus suggesting a variety of household crafts at ancient Methone.[74]

No indications of the coloring of textiles, such as with purple dye manufactured from the Mediterranean purple-shells (*Hexaplex trunculus, Bolinus brandaris, Thais haemostoma*), have been traced so far at Methone. This is interesting considering that several Aegean sites have produced evidence for purple dye during the Early Iron Age, and in several of them, production waste and relevant finds were found in domestic contexts and/or inside the habitation space.[75] Whether or not purple dye was produced at ancient Methone, and whether or not its shells were disposed of in the Hypogeion or within the confines of the settlement, needs further investigation. The study of the whole range of artifacts and products made of organic material holds significant potential to shed light on socially and culturally specific preferences and practices at the settlement, and to contribute toward a better understanding of the negotiations of ancient people with their world.

CONCLUDING REMARKS

This chapter has reported on some of the most significant bioarchaeological finds recovered from the Hypogeion of Methone and has highlighted how a systematic and integrated study of such material can contribute to a less fragmented appreciation of Early Iron Age lifeways to ultimately weave together aspects of the social history of this ancient settlement. The colony was founded on a variable land- and waterscape, rich in resources that could support a seemingly prosperous population. A mixed farming system, using a variety of plants and animals, seemed to be in place at the settlement, complemented by the systematic exploitation of the nearby estuarine environments. People, however, interacted and negotiated with their broader environment in a more complex and multifaceted manner, selecting certain areas and their resources to be incorporated into their social living, following certain previous local traditions in particular cases. These choices left their impact, but not necessarily in a negative way. Exploitation of the trees and the natural vegetation contributed to changing and shaping their surrounding environment, while other activities, such as the employment of particular strategies for the collection of mollusks and the integration of a complementary set of plants and animals, demonstrate possible concerns for the long-term sustainability and maintenance of the capacity of their most valued resources. What we hope has ultimately become evident in this chapter is the great potential of employing all branches of bioarchaeological evidence together to understand aspects of life that, no matter how mundane, constitute part of the core of the sociocultural identities of a population and strongly dictate its place within its contemporary world.

NOTES

1. We are grateful to Matthaios Bessios for entrusting us with the study of this bioarchaeological assemblage, for the many discussions he shared with us, and for his open-mindedness and holistic approach to archaeology. Alexandra Livarda and Rena Veropoulidou would like to thank the Psychas Foundation, which generously funded part of the archaeobotanical and archaeomalacological study. The University of California, Los Angeles (through an NEH grant and the Steinmetz Chair in Classical Archaeology and Material Culture) funded the sorting of heavy residue, which was conducted by Anastasia Vasileiadou and Daphne Nikolaidou, as well as the washing of shells in 2012 by Stamatia Kordanouli. We would also like to thank Mila Andonova and Haris Karanikas for their help with the processing of the flotation samples. Many thanks are also due to Ala Marambagkidou and Yiannis Theodoridis for washing the shells, Nikos Valasiadis for processing the shell pictures, Rebecca Sgouros and Katie Tardio for processing part of the animal bone assemblage, and Professor Stelios Andreou and Associate Professor Sevasti Triantafyllou for giving us access to the Laboratory of Toumba Thessalonikis Excavations for part of the bioarchaeological study. Anastasia Vasileiadou would like also to thank Paul Halstead and Valasia Isaakidou for their help and supervision of the zooarchaeological study, and Stelios Andreou for his constant guidance.
2. Tzifopoulos 2012a, pp. 19–20.
3. See Chapter 8, and Bessios 2012a, pp. 48–51.
4. See Chapter 8, and Bessios 2012a, pp. 57–62.
5. Sarpaki 2012, p. 37.
6. French 1971.
7. For animal bones: Boessneck 1969; Halstead and Collins 1995; Lister 1996; Payne 1985; Prummel and Frisch 1986; Schmid 1972; Halstead, Collins, and Isaakidou 2002. For shells: Abbott 1989; Delamotte and Vardala-Theodorou 1994; Pfleger 1999; Poppe and Goto 1991, 1993.
8. Von den Driesch 1976.
9. Cappers, Bekker, and Jans 2006; Cappers, Neef, and Bekker 2009; Jacomet 2006.
10. E.g., Valamoti 2009.
11. Schweingruber 1990.
12. Halstead 1985, 2011.
13. Halstead 1985, 2011.
14. Following Halstead 2011.
15. Barry 1999; Evans 2003; Ingold 2000.
16. Evans 2003, p. 14.
17. Dobres and Robb 2000.
18. Kopytoff 1986.
19. See Dobres and Robb 2000, p. 161.
20. Bottema 1994; Filipovic, Allué, and Boric 2010; Marinova et al. 2013; Ntinou 2002; Willis 1994.
21. Bottema 1994; Filipovic, Allué, and Boric 2010; Marinova et al. 2013; Ntinou 2002; Willis 1994.
22. Boufalis, Chapter 20.
23. Krahtopoulou 2010, p. 246.
24. Krahtopoulou 2010, pp. 247–257.
25. Krahtopoulou 2010; Krahtopoulou et al. 2020, pp. 667–669.
26. Fouache et al. 2008; Ghilardi et al. 2008a; Ghilardi et al. 2008b.
27. Ghilardi et al. 2008a, p. 123.
28. Krahtopoulou and Veropoulidou 2014; Krahtopoulou and Veropoulidou 2017.
29. Bessios and Krahtopoulou 2001 [2003].

30   Krahtopoulou et al. 2020; Krahtopoulou 2010.
31   See also Veropoulidou 2011a, pp. 128–141.
32   See also Sillar 1997, p. 8.
33   See also Sillar 1997, p. 8.
34   Freedman 2007, p. 8.
35   But see, for example, Livarda et al. 2021.
36   Payne 1973.
37   Halstead and Isaakidou 2011, p. 166; Lentacker, Ervynck, and Van Neer 2004, p. 84.
38   Zohary and Hopf 2000, p. 83.
39   Livarda and Kotzamani 2014, p. 11; Valamoti 2009, pp. 121–123.
40   Livarda and Kotzamani 2014, pp. 10–11; Megaloudi 2006, p. 34; Valamoti 2004, pp. 111–115; 2009, pp. 50–51.
41   Sarpaki 1995, p. 294.
42   Valamoti 2009, pp. 51–52.
43   See, for example, Livarda 2012; Megaloudi 2006.
44   Kroll 1983.
45   Livarda 2012; Megaloudi 2006, p. 78.
46   Valamoti and Gkatzogia 2010.
47   Valamoti 2009, pp. 60–61.
48   See, for example, Groot 2005, pp. 55–56; Isaakidou 2006, pp. 104–109.
49   For instance, D'Andrea and Mitiku 2002, pp. 186, 206–207.
50   Valamoti and Charles 2005; Wallace and Charles 2013.
51   Valamoti 2013.
52   Jones et al. 1986.
53   Veropoulidou 2011a, pp. 434–445.
54   See, for example, Caddy and Defeo 2003.
55   Tiverios et al. 2013; Veropoulidou 2011a; Veropoulidou 2014.
56   See, for example, Ruscillo 2005.
57   For hunting and gathering as integral strategies to foraging societies, see Bailey 1981, p. 3; for the connotation of a "backward" stage, see Zvelebil 1992, p. 8; for the implied superiority of farming and herding, see Pollard 1994, p. 170.
58   See, for instance, Hamilakis 2003.
59   Becker and Kroll 2008 (Agios Mamas); Nikolaidou 2010 and Vasileiadou 2009 (Toumba Thessalonikis); Bökönyi 2005 (Torone); Becker 1986, pp. 230–236 (Kastanas).
60   See, for example, Livarda 2008, 2011; Wiethold 2003, p. 270; Willerding 1971, 1991.
61   For the Mediterranean, see, for example, Hadjichambis et al. 2007; for Greece, see Skoula et al. 2010; for Turkey, see Ertuğ 2000.
62   Hadjichambis et al. 2007, p. 20.
63   Ertuğ 2000.
64   Ertuğ 2000, p. 175.
65   Claassen 1991, p. 285; Meehan 1982, p. 86.
66   For the Aegean generally, see, among others Karali 1999; Miller 1997; for central Macedonia more specifically, see Veropoulidou 2022.
67   See, for example, Ruscillo 2005; Theodoropoulou 2017.
68   Veropoulidou 2011a, pp. 410–415; Veropoulidou 2022.
69   Veropoulidou 2022; an exception worth noting is the Final Neolithic site at Methone Pieria, see Veropoulidou et al. 2022.

70 See, for example, the discussion of the material from Toumba Thessalonikis, Veropoulidou 2011a, pp. 410–415; Veropoulidou 2022.

71 Veropoulidou 2022.

72 For prehistoric sites, see Veropoulidou 2011a, pp. 410–415, 461–468; for Early Iron Age sites, see, e.g., Veropoulidou 2011b, pp. 198–204.

73 Theodoropoulou 2017, p. 90; Tiverios et al. 2013, p. 210.

74 For terracotta loomweights and spindlewhorls, and other objects related to textile production from the Hypogeion, see Chapter 16.

75 For evidence of purple dye in the Early Iron Age, see Reese 2000; Theodoropoulou 2011; Veropoulidou 2011a, pp. 399–408; Veropoulidou 2012; for evidence of purple dye manufacture in domestic contexts, see, for example, Lefkandi and Oropos: Theodoropoulou 2007b: 293–294. Toumba Thessalonikis: Veropoulidou 2011a, pp. 403–405; Mitrou Lokris: Veropoulidou 2011b, p. 202.

11

INSCRIPTIONS, GRAFFITI/DIPINTI, AND (TRADE)MARKS AT METHONE (CA. 700 B.C.)

Yannis Z. Tzifopoulos

The scanty and random references to Methone in the surviving literary and epigraphical sources (Chapter 2) offered only modest expectations for fieldwork, which, however, have been confounded by archaeological discoveries made since 2003. The excavations not only confirmed the tradition narrated by Plutarch of the arrival of the "repulsed by slings" Eretrians, but also confirmed the traditional date of 733 B.C. for their arrival.[1] Thus, Methone could be seen as the oldest southern Greek colony on the northern shores of the Aegean and, by the end of the 8th century B.C., a major trade and industrial center, as the arrival of the Eretrians invigorated the Methonaian economy.

Methone's epigraphical corpus so far comprises:[2] the Athenian decrees of the decade 430–420 B.C. (*IG* I³ 61; Figs. 1.38, 2.1; and Chapter 2); a number of inscriptions from rescue excavations; a great number of inscribed pottery sherds dated to a period that spans the lifetime of the historical settlement, from ca. 730 to 354 B.C., among them, those from the Hypogeion found between 2003 and 2007, and the ones from the 2014–2017 *synergasia* field project;[3] and a number of inscribed (molded) sling bullets and an arrowhead dated to the period of the siege of Methone by the Macedonian king Philip II (Chapter 28). Of the inscribed pottery, 191 pots and potsherds with inscriptions, graffiti, and (trade)marks were published in 2012, the majority of which date from 730 to 690 B.C.[4] while the rest date to the 7th and 6th centuries B.C.[5] All these pots and potsherds came from the excavations conducted between 2003 and 2007 in a rectangular pit, apparently used as an *apothetes* or dump on top of the East Hill of the site, together with a massive amount of stones, mud bricks, timber, and the remains of the industrial activities conducted in nearby workshops (Chapters 1, 8). A similar picture emerges from excavations in other areas of the site, as the preliminary study of the inscribed objects suggests, and complements *viva voce* the "silence" of the sources about Methone.

The inscribed pottery mostly includes transport amphoras and sympotic vessels, while pouring and storage vessels are clearly underrepresented. The great majority of the material, 166 pots and potsherds, bear non-alphabetic symbols,[6] marks, graffiti, and very few dipinti,[7] which are probably signs of ownership and/or trading. Of the remaining 25 amphoras and sympotic vessels, 18 bear alphabetic symbols, marks, and graffiti, which again probably denote ownership and/or trading activities.

However, the remaining seven, mostly drinking vessels, bear complete or fragmentary inscriptions. These are listed below in ascending chronological order, the latest first, according to their letter shapes (admittedly a subjective criterion):

11/1. (ΜΕΘ 2238) ca. 700 B.C., on an amphora of unknown provenance coated in black slip: *vacat* Θεο() *vacat*, a name abbreviated, whose circular letters were incised with a compass (Fig. 11.1; Bessios, Tzifopoulos, and Kotsonas 2012, pp. 347–349, no. 5; *SEG* 62.424).

11/2. (ΜΕΘ 2237) ca. 700 B.C., on an amphora from Lesbos: *vacat* Ἀντερύδεος *vacat* (Fig. 11.2; Bessios, Tzifopoulos, and Kotsonas 2012, pp. 345–347, no. 4; *SEG* 62.424).

11/3. (ΜΕΘ 2247) ca. 700 B.C., on a skyphos from the Thermaic Gulf, retrograde: *vacat* Σχενι() *vacat* (= <Xσ>ενι() = <Ξ>ενι()), an abbreviated name (Fig. 11.3; Bessios, Tzifopoulos, and Kotsonas 2012, pp. 369–370, no. 22; *SEG* 62.424).

11/4. (ΜΕΘ 2253) ca. 730–720 B.C., on a local drinking cup, retrograde: *vacat* Ἐπιγέ[νεος? ἐμί?] (Fig. 11.3; Bessios, Tzifopoulos, and Kotsonas 2012, pp. 343–344, no. 3; *SEG* 62.424).

11/5. (ΜΕΘ 2255) ca. 730–720 B.C., on a Euboian skyphos, retrograde: [-?]ō ἐμ[ί] (Fig. 11.3; Bessios, Tzifopoulos, and Kotsonas 2012, p. 350, no. 7; *SEG* 62.424).

11/6. (ΜΕΘ 2248) ca. 730–720 B.C., on a Euboian skyphos, retrograde: Ηακεσάνδρō ἐμ[ὶ - - - - -]ατον στερέ|σ[ετα]ι (Fig. 11.4; Bessios, Tzifopoulos, and Kotsonas 2012, pp. 339–343, no. 2; *SEG* 62.424).

11/7. (ΜΕΘ 2249) ca. 730 B.C., on a mug from Lesbos, retrograde: Φιλίōνος ἐμί (Fig. 11.5; Bessios, Tzifopoulos, and Kotsonas 2012, pp, 337–339, no. 1; *SEG* 62.424).

All seven texts, inscribed on sympotic pots and transport amphoras, stem from a context dated to ca. 730–690 B.C. It is generally assumed that the lifespan of small clay vessels is no more than one generation, whereas large ones may last longer. However, the dating of pottery cannot give precise answers about the date of inscriptions rendered post-firing, especially inscriptions on objects intended for private rather than public use. The date of production of an object is not always the same as the date of the inscription, unlike, for example, with public state decrees and laws, or potters' marks inscribed before the vessels were fired.[8] Moreover, in the case of Hakesandros, the date of the poetic composition inscribed need not be the same as that of the incision of the text on the cup. Consequently, in dating inscribed, especially portable, objects, chronological questions about provenance, manufacture, inscribing, and usage must perforce remain relative, and take into consideration the differing stages of each action.

The seven brief texts presented here, together with the remaining 18 alphabetic and 166 non-alphabetic marks on pots and potsherds, comprise a group which should be added to the chronologically comparable collections from Lefkandi, Eretria, and Zarakes in Euboia;[9] from Oropos and Thebes;[10] from Hymettos and Athens;[11] from Pithekoussai and Cumae (Kyme) in the Bay of Naples;[12] and, last but not least, from Kommos on Crete,[13] which is characterized by the variety in the provenance of the ceramics and the broad range of incised inscriptions, symbols, and (trade)marks.

Both the place of discovery of these inscribed vessels, Methone in Pieria, and the date, 730–690 B.C., are remarkable because excavations in the north Aegean have so far yielded

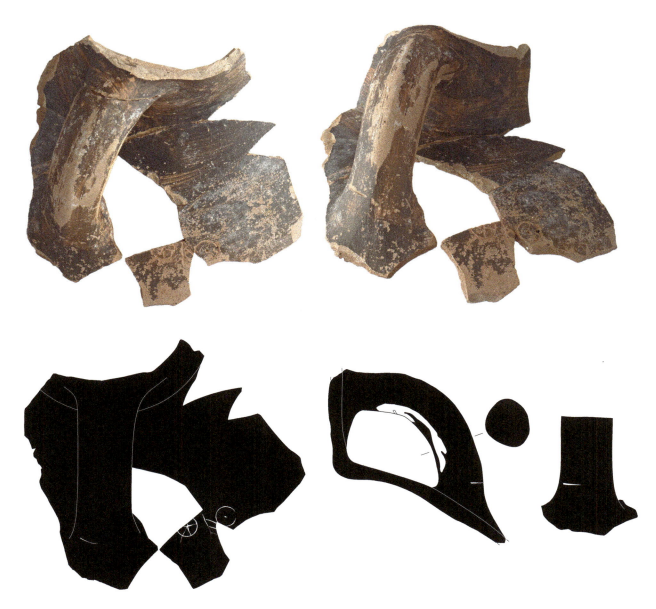

Figure 11.1. Amphora, unknown provenance, **11/1** (MEΘ 2238), ca. 700 B.C. Photos O. Kourakis and M. Chykerda, drawing I. Moschou

hardly any inscribed, incised, scratched, or painted finds of such an early date (with a few exceptions from Torone, Poseidi in Chalkidike, Karabournaki on the eastern Thermaic Gulf, and Krania/Platamon in southern Pieria)[14]. Most of the letters on pottery from Methone are scratched or incised after firing, but there are rare instances of marks made before firing.[15]

All seven texts from Methone, some "professionally" inscribed (**11/1, 11/4, 11/6, 11/7**) and others less so (**11/2, 11/3, 11/5**), are ownership tags using the familiar formula of the speaking object, "I belong to X," with the verb εἰμί inscribed or implied. Five are incised sinistrograde and two dextrograde, a fact that indicates that in certain areas of the Greek world both directions for the alphabet coexisted early on. Because of their brevity, the few letters of each text are not conclusive as to the script (local or imported) of the owner/trader or the engraver, except for the cup of Hakesandros, the script of which, like the pot itself, is Eretrian/Euboian. But even

FIGURE 11.2. Antekydes amphora, **11/2** (ΜΕΘ 2237), ca. 700 B.C.
Photos O. Kourakis and M. Chykerda, drawing I. Moschou

Figure 11.3. Scheni() drinking cup from the Thermaic Gulf, **11/3** (ΜΕΘ 2247), ca. 700 B.C.; Epige[nes] drinking cup, **11/4** (ΜΕΘ 2253), ca. 730–720; Euboian drinking cup, **11/5** (ΜΕΘ 2255), ca. 730–720 B.C. Photos O. Kourakis and M. Chykerda, drawings I. Moschou

this is of little help in identifying the origins of the anonymous composer, and perhaps even of the owner Hakesandros. The seven texts from Methone, however, do emphasize one crucial fact which is often overlooked in discussions of Archaic local scripts: although Methone was, according to Plutarch, an Eretrian colony and one would expect the Eretrian script to have been widely used at the site, as the majority of scholars claim,[16] the variety of letter shapes in these texts (Fig. 11.6) may attest that not all literate traders and residents at the site were using the Eretrian/Euboian script.[17] It seems that the concept "local script" cannot be applied to these few texts from Methone in the same way as it is to the local scripts of, for example, Corinth or Athens, or perhaps even to any texts incised on portable objects.

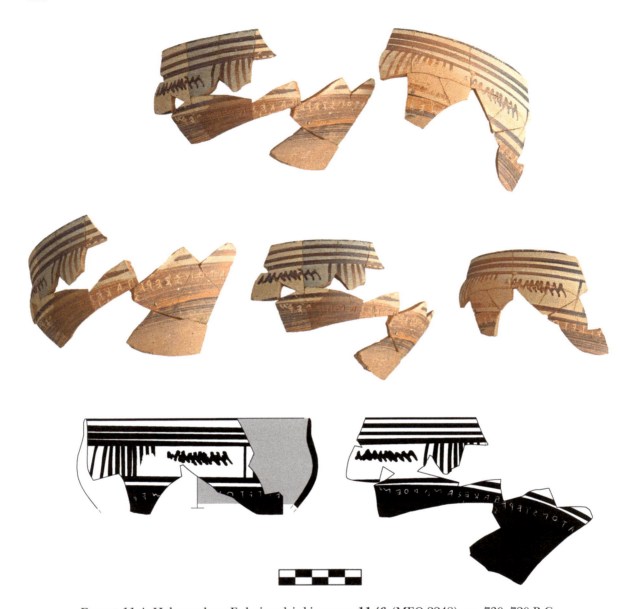

FIGURE 11.4. Hakesandros: Euboian drinking cup, **11/6** (MEΘ 2248), ca. 730–720 B.C.
Photos O. Kourakis and M. Chykerda, drawing I. Moschou

FIGURE 11.5. Philion mug from Lesbos, **11/7** (MEΘ 2249), ca. 730 B.C.
Photo O. Kourakis and M. Chykerda, drawing I. Moschou and T. Ross

FIGURE 11.6. Letter-shapes on all seven vessels, **11/1–11/7**.
Photos Y. Tzifopoulos, drawings T. Ross

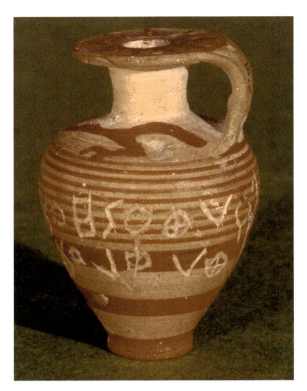

Figure 11.7. Tataie's lekythos from Cumae (Kyme). Protocorinthian aryballos/lekythos, British Museum 1885, 0613.1. Photo courtesy British Museum

More specifically, the fact of the matter remains that an Eretrian/Euboian alphabet and dialect unequivocally apply to only one text, that of Hakesandros (**11/6** and Figs. 11.4, 11.6), and perhaps also to two or three more fragments the provenance of which is Euboian (**11/5** and maybe **11/4**, Fig. 11.3). However, Philion's cup (**11/7**) and Antekydes' amphora (**11/2**) may equally be either Eretrian/Euboean or Aiolian,[18] while serious doubts for a Euboian provenance remain for **11/1** (Figs. 11.1–11.2, 11.5–11.6). Be that as it may, there is no way that **11/3** may be classified as Euboian, because the double consonant (SX = XS for xi) is in all probability foreign to Euboia, either Eretria or Chalkis,[19] but it is attested so far only in Attica, Boiotia, Paros/Thasos, and Rhodes.[20] At present, alphabetic and dialectic ascriptions must perforce remain open one way or another and must await further evidence, as both the Archaic alphabets and the Greek dialects are still far from clear-cut.[21] A more nuanced approach is required for sites at crossroads and/or major trading routes (e.g., Kommos and now Methone), where more than one script and more than one dialect would have inevitably been employed, which the residents would recognize as different but nonetheless could read. With reference to dialect, the texts from Methone, like the majority of early Greek inscriptions, employ the shapes of E for ε, η, ει, and O for ο, ω, ου. The brevity of the texts hinders the identification of the spoken dialect, although Ionic is the primary candidate.

FIGURE 11.8. The Dipylon oinochoe. Athens, National Museum 192 [2074].
Photo Deutsches Archäologisches Institut, Athens, NM 4700–4701 (photo Eva-Marie Czakó)

The 191 incised inscriptions, symbols, and (trade)marks from Methone belong to the epigraphical category of *fictilia* and *instrumenta domestica*, and thus are private inscriptions. However, as a number of them are inscribed on drinking vessels, they also have a semi-public aspect within sympotic and trading contexts. It cannot be a coincidence that most of the earliest Greek inscriptions belong to this category, suggesting that trade and the symposium played an important role in the introduction, but also the dissemination, of the alphabet and the art and techniques of writing. As private but at the same time on public display in a trading—and sympotic—context, these brief texts proclaimed or advertised the literacy of their owners.

Of the seven texts, the mug from Lesbos with the retrograde owner's inscription of Philion (**11/7**, Fig. 11.5) and the inscribed Euboian skyphos of Hakesandros (**11/6**, Fig. 11.4) stand out, not only for the professional engraving and their script, but most importantly, in the case of Hakesandros' cup, for the text incised on it. Although the text is fragmentary, its ending in an iambic rhythm (-]ατον στερήσ[ετα]ι = υ – υ – υ –) indicates that the inscription consisted of the ownership tag in prose in the beginning (Ηακεσάνδρο ἐμ[ὶ ποτέριον *vel sim.*), and of an iambic dimeter or trimeter, the oldest one attested. The secure restoration of the final word στερέ|σ[ετα]ι (the third singular future form of στεροῦμαι), and the probable restoration of ὀμμ]άτον or χρεμ]άτον "will be deprived of / lose his [money/eyes]" *vel sim.*), strongly suggest that this text, like other early inscriptions on sympotic pots, was also composed in a playful manner within a sympotic context. Hakesandros' text seems to be a forerunner of that on Tataie's lekythos from Cumae (Kyme), dated to the second quarter of the 7th century B.C. (Fig. 11.7):[22] Ταταίες ἐμὶ λ|έρυθος· hὸς δ' ἄν με κλέφσ|ει, θυφλὸς ἔσται. This text supplies the most probable meaning of the missing part of Hakesandros' text: "I belong to Hakesandros; [whoever steals me from him], will be deprived of / lose his [money/eyes]."

Hakesandros' poetic, but not hexametric, text brings to the fore once more the beginnings of literature in Greece. Trade facilitated the spread both of the alphabet quickly and widely, and also of engraving techniques and epigraphical habits within trading and sympotic contexts, that is, the beginnings of literacy. As soon as people learned the alphabet (or while they were learning it), they continued to compose small poems orally, but now they engraved some of them on sympotic pots which are otherwise everyday objects.

The few earliest Greek epigrams—that is, the first epigraphical examples of attempts at poetic composition from the Dipylon jug (Fig. 11.8) and Nestor's cup (Fig. 11.9, Fig. 22.11) to Hakesandros' cup (Fig. 11.4) and Tataie's lekythos (Fig. 11.7)—display impressive similarities and bespeak a playful tone expected within a sympotic context (notwithstanding different interpretations).[23] They constitute a distinct category of early poetic efforts with specific characteristics: 1) The archaeological context of the provenance—from an *apothetes* in Methone and from graves in Athens (Dipylon/Kerameikos), in Pithekoussai (Ischia) and in Cumae (Kyme) (Italy)—suggests that these four inscribed objects, however modest, had acquired in time some special, sentimental value for their owner or family member; hence three of them were chosen as grave goods. 2) All texts are inscribed on clay objects that are not luxury items; and yet, the texts on them declare otherwise in a pompous style, so much so that they attribute to them either excessive value or supernatural qualities as the threats, prompts, or promises indicate. 3) All four epigrams exhibit metrical peculiarities: either they combine prose and verse, as in the epigrams of Hakesandros and Tataie, where the owner's tag in prose is followed by iambic verse; or they combine different meters, such as in Nestor's epigram, where the first verse is an iambic trimeter (or in prose) and the next two are hexameters; or even the verse has more than the necessary syllables, as if to confound and outwit rhythmical and metrical perfection, as in the hexameter of the Dipylon epigram. 4) It is beyond doubt that the contradiction expressed between the value of the object and the value declared by the engraved text is a conscious choice of the anonymous versifiers and is not unprecedented. The "playful" manner, the mood, and the witty conception of these short, rhythmic compositions is identical to the iambic style of synthesis and to the *skolia* performed during a symposium as a kind of an *agon* among participants; or, as the Dipylon epigram suggests, on the occasion of an *agon* of a musical dance and song.

The epigram of Hakesandros, the oldest in iambic verse, and that of Tataie are two rare, early, written compositions, iambic in ideas, style, and conception, either improvised orally on the spur of the moment in a symposium, or widely circulated orally and at some time engraved or copied. Even if they are not Homeric/Hesiodic epics or high lyric poetry, they are lyric and sympotic poetry *in nascendi*, a genre which they presage and which emerges sooner rather than later with Archilochos of Paros and Kallinos of Ephesos.

The Methone inscriptions, graffiti, and (trade)marks are a test case of sorts and present evidence for:[24] trading and economic activities during the colonial period throughout the Mediterranean;[25] the early phase of the Greek alphabet with its local variations and the techniques of engraving;[26] the Greek language and dialects, including those of Methone's founder, Eretria;[27] competence in writing in commercial and sympotic contexts;[28] and, finally, literary beginnings in Greece, which emerged soon afterward. It is a kind of prelude to significant historical processes and developments that were to come in the following centuries and that culminated in the Athenian decree, "Of the Methonaians from Pieria (Fig. 2.1)," the copy of which in Methone apparently did not survive Philip's annihilation of the city in 354 B.C.

NOTES

1. What follows draws from Tzifopoulos 2012b, pp. 307–319. I am most grateful to Manthos Bessios, Athena Athanassiadou, and Konstantinos Noulas for the permit to study the material and for facilitating my countless visits; Orestis Kourakis for the photographs and Ioannis Moschou for the drawings; and especially to the editors of this volume, Sarah Morris and John Papadopoulos, for their unstinting effort, as well as to the anonymous reviewers for constructive suggestions and corrections.

2. The Epigraphy and Papyrology Laboratory (EREP) of the Classics Department at Aristotle University of Thessaloniki, in collaboration with the Ephorate of Pieria, has undertaken the task of compiling an archive of inscriptions of northern Pieria.

3. Bessios, Chapters 1 and 8; for a selection of the 2014–2017 finds, see Morris et al. 2020, pp. 712–713.

4. Bessios, Tzifopoulos, and Kotsonas 2012, pp. 303–484, nos. 1–161; *SEG* 62.424.

5. Bessios, Tzifopoulos, and Kotsonas 2012, pp. 484–503, nos. 162–191; *SEG* 62.424.

6. Bessios, Tzifopoulos, and Kotsonas 2012, pp. 362–364, no. 17; pp. 463–464, no. 130; pp. 475–476. no. 145; pp. 478–479, no. 149; pp. 489–490, no. 162.

7. Bessios, Tzifopoulos, and Kotsonas 2012, pp. 384–385, no. 34; pp. 433–434, no. 94.

8. For which see Papadopoulos 1994 and 2017a.

9. Jeffery 1980; Kenzelmann Pfyffer, Theurillat, and Verdan 2005; Matthaiou 2004–2009; Chatzidimitriou 2004–2009.

10. Mazarakis Ainian and Matthaiou 1999; Powell 1991, pp. 123–186; Aravantinos 2010, p. 149.

11. Langdon 1976, 2015, 2016; Powell 1991, pp. 123–186.

12. *Pithekoussai* I; Bartoněk and Buchner 1995; Powell 1991, pp. 123–186; Pavese 1996; Faraone 1996; Malkin 1998, pp. 156–177; cf. Cook 2000.

13. Csapo, Johnston, and Geagan 2000. For more early inscriptions scattered throughout the Aegean and Mediterranean, see Janko 2015 = 2017; Johnston 2017; Woodard 2017.

14. For the Argilos inscriptions see Boufalis, Oikonomaki, and Tzifopoulos 2021.

15. Bessios, Tzifopoulos, and Kotsonas 2012, pp. 362–364, no. 17.

16. The majority of scholars opt for an Eretrian/Euboian alphabet and dialect for all 25 fragmentary texts, obviously because a group of Eretrians led the way according to Plutarch, but also on account of letter forms: *BÉ* 2012, no. 244; Méndez Dosuna 2017; Panayotou-Triantaphyllopoulou 2017; Janko 2015, 2017; *BÉ* 2018, no. 264; Bourogiannis 2019, 158–163; and Tiverios 2019b, p. 39, n. 1. Cf. Papadopoulos 2016.

17. For Methone as a city characteristic of an *emporion*, see Chapters 12, 20.

18. The shapes of the letters mu and sigma are inconclusive, although Jeffery (1980, p. 92), correctly in my view, ascribed both shapes to Aiolis (the five-bar mu in Ionian Samos explained as an Aiolian loan, something that may be argued for the Methone inscriptions). As things stand, her suggestion is still valid, as it seems that an Aiolian letter form could very well have been used to convey a text in an Ionian dialect. Even so, the five-bar mu (Jeffery and Johnston 1990, p. 31, fig. 13) is attested in Attica (Immerwahr 1990, p. xii, no. M6), in the Doric alphabets of Crete, Melos, and Sikinos, and also in the West Semitic alphabet (Naveh 1982, p. 56, fig. 46; p. 58, fig. 49); in Euboia the five-bar mu is attested in Eretria, but apparently not in Chalkis where the mu was simplified (Jeffery and Johnston 1990, p. 90). This choice may be evidence for a political or commercial attempt of Eretria to differentiate and distinguish its letter shapes from its neighbor Chalkis, as has been cogently argued about local scripts and alphabets in general (Luraghi 2010), and as is the case among neighboring Cretan poleis during the Archaic period (Oikonomaki 2010). Likewise, the six-bar sigma, similar in both **11/7** and **11/3**, which caused confusion with an iota with more than three bars (Jeffery and Johnston 1990, p. 34, fig. 20, and p. 29, fig. 10; Jeffery 1982, p. 829), is attested in Lefkandi (five-bar, Jeffery 1980 and Jeffery

Johnston 1990, pp. 433–434, no. 24b, A), Boiotia (five- and four-bar in Mantiklos' inscription, Jeffery 1980; Jeffery and Johnston 1990, pp. 90–91, pl. 7, no. 1), Attica (Jeffery and Johnston 1990, p. 66, fig. 26 3, pl. 1, no. 2; Immerwahr 1990, p. xiii, no. 8), Sparta (five to eight bars, Jeffery and Johnston 1990, p. 183, fig. 39 2, pl. 35, no. 1), Smyrna (Jeffery and Johnston 1990, p. 325, fig. 46 4, 473, pl. 79, no. 8), Gordion (more than five bars, Young 1969, pp. 260–261, no. 30, fig. 2; pp. 284–286, no. 56, 58, fig. 9, pls. 73–74; pp. 289–291, nos. 71–73a, fig. 10, pls. 70, 72), and Kerkenes-Dağ (Brixhe and Summers 2007, 123–129, no. VI–VII, figs. 26–29).

19 For the double consonant, problematic in all local alphabets, see Jeffery and Johnston 1990, pp. 25–28, 32; Threatte 1980, pp. 20–21; Threatte 1996, p. 677; Immerwahr 1990, p. 62; Wachter 2001, pp. 230–231 §110; for the common inversion, see ΣΧ/ΧΣ Woodard 2017, pp. 205–206. Janko (2017) opts to overlook it and argues for a Euboian alphabet, and Méndez Dosuna (2017) reads it as the Euboian X = xi (Jeffery 1990, 79 ξ2) and a pleonastic sigma, a phenomenon attested elsewhere. For a similar case of a 6th-century B.C. Attic cup (ΜΕΘ 8103) in Methone see Morris et al. 2020, p. 712, figs. 58c, 64d; Boufalis 2020, pp. 130–131, no. ΜΕΘ-32.

20 Jeffery and Johnston 1990, 66, 89–90 ξ1, 289 ξ1, 345–346 respectively. See further Boufalis 2020, pp. 123–125, no. ΜΕΘ-23.

21 For dialectic or/and alphabetic oddities explained away as scribal mistakes, see especially Boufalis 2020, pp. 650–653.

22 *IG* XIV.865; Jeffery and Johnston 1990, pp. 236, 240, no. 3; p. 456; Friedländer and Hoffleit 1987 [1948], pp. 163–164, no. 177c; Day 2019, pp. 233–234.

23 Day (2019, p. 234) calls these epigrams "primordial," "neither dedicatory nor originally sepulchral (apparently, though some were deposited in graves)." In addition, there are one or two metrical inscriptions from Thera and a fragmentary inscription in three lines on a cup from Eretria, for which see Powell 1991, pp. 158–180; Johnston and Andreiomenou 1989; Wachter 2010. For the early dedicatory epigrams of Mantiklos from Thebes and Nikandre from Naxos, see Day 2010.

24 See Strauss Clay, Malkin, and Tzifopoulos 2017a.

25 Kotsonas et al. 2017; Kourou 2017; Papadopoulos 2017a; Verdan 2017; Johnston 2017; Kotsonas 2020.

26 Papadopoulos 2016; Janko 2017; Woodard 2017; Dell'Oro 2017; Oikonomaki 2017; Waal 2018; Bourogiannis 2018, 2019.

27 Méndez Dosuna 2017; Panayotou-Triantaphyllopoulou 2017; Janko 2017; Dell'Oro 2017; Skelton 2017.

28 Oikonomaki 2017; Pappas 2017; Węcowski 2017; Bourogiannis 2018 and 2019.

12

WHY WAS METHONE COLONIZED?
TRANSPORT AMPHORAS AND THE ECONOMICS OF GREEK COLONIZATION BETWEEN HISTORY AND ARCHAEOLOGY

Antonis Kotsonas

INTRODUCTION

Numerous current discourses pervade the study of ancient Greek and Mediterranean colonization.[1] One of the most prominent is over the actual use of the term, which conflates the homonymous European practice with the very different ancient phenomenon. Arguments for the abandonment of the term and for the establishment of alternative ones, such as migration or *apoikiazation*, have not been widely accepted.[2] Accordingly, I maintain the traditional terms "colony" and "colonization," despite their misleading connotations, while acknowledging that recent scholarship has increased awareness of the problem and has helped overcome certain aspects of it.[3] David Ridgway, co-excavator of Pithekoussai and leading expert on Greek colonization, systematically used a vintage poster (Fig. 12.1) in his teaching to address a wider range of problems and explain different misconceptions that pervade scholarship on Greek colonization. He especially challenged the notion that Greek colonization involved the dominance of people of culturally and economically advanced background over local populations who only had a passive and subordinate role in any interaction, including trade and exchange in containers and the commodities they contained.[4] This chapter builds on this approach in investigating the economic factors that pushed or pulled Greek populations to overseas locations.

"The question of the cause or causes of the great colonizing movement of the Archaic period is endlessly debated," wrote Alexander John Graham four decades ago.[5] The variety of answers this question continues to attract is suggestive of both its enduring relevance and the state of research on the topic.[6] In reviewing past and current approaches to the subject, I place particular emphasis on the site of Methone in the Thermaic Gulf, which is traditionally regarded as the earliest (late 8th century B.C.) Greek colony in the north Aegean. The case of Methone is particularly significant in revealing how a general consensus on the causes of colonization can be challenged on the basis of new finds and innovative research methodologies centered on transport amphoras and the goods they contained.

WHY DID THE GREEKS COLONIZE? ECONOMIC AND OTHER CONSIDERATIONS

During the last century, historians typically engaged with the question of the causes of Greek colonization on the basis of foundation stories, which emphasize that land hunger, occasionally

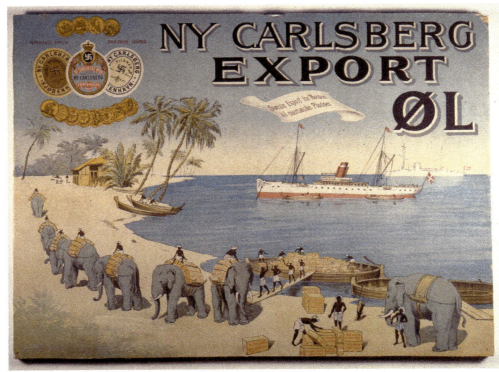

FIGURE 12.1. Vintage poster of Carlsberg beer.
Reproduced by permission of the Carlsberg Group

aggravated by overpopulation or drought and crop failure, was the catalyst for Greek colonization.[7] Indirect evidence in support of the centrality of land acquisition has been deduced from the names of the aristocratic classes in metropoleis and colonies, or from related references in (later) historical accounts.[8] Moreover, as Moses Finley has argued, the agrarian focus of Greek colonization is implicitly promoted by the etymology of the term (from the Latin verb *colere*, to cultivate, to farm) and the experience of comparable phenomena in world history of the last centuries.[9]

Historians of ancient Greece disagree on the importance of trade as a stimulus for Greek colonization. Some insist on its marginal significance,[10] but others have been more accommodating; for example, Graham argued: "But it was a rare colony in which trade was entirely negligible, and there were many where it was important, and a few where it was all-important."[11] Geoffrey de Ste. Croix proposed a certain historical scenario for such "atypical" colonies: "although there were trading colonies in the general sense, they were not founded *in the first place* by a deliberate act of state . . . but they grew originally *from below*."[12] According to this "bottom up" scenario, Greek merchants would first create an *emporion* and this would later attract more Greeks led by an oikist and would be transformed into a colony.

The position of de Ste. Croix, and of several other historians of the postwar period, depends on a broader approach to the ancient Greek economy, which has been termed substantivist/primitivist (as opposed to the formalist/modernist) and has been traced back to a work by Johannes Hasebroek published in 1928.[13] This approach emphasizes the agricultural basis and self-sufficiency of the ancient economy, and considers the role of interregional trade marginal. The assumed marginality of trade was founded on several factors: a) the similarity of climatic conditions across the Mediterranean basin, which meant that similar crops were grown across this vast region; and b) the high cost of transporting anything but luxury goods. Challenges to the substantivist/primitivist view are not lacking among historians of the postwar period, and a few scholars have argued specifically for the close connection between Greek trade and colonization (even if they also distance themselves from certain aspects of the formalist/modernist approach).[14] Over time, several basic tenets of the substantivist/primitivist position—and especially the romanticized contrast between ancient economies embedded in sociopolitical configurations and "disembedded" modern economies—were challenged.[15] Also, scholars increasingly understood that the paucity of references to trade in early Greek literature does not reflect ancient economic realities, but relates more closely to the aristocratic context of production and performance of this literature. Thus, several recent studies by historians emphasize the importance of trade for the Archaic Greek economy.[16]

Archaeologists overlooked the debate on the Greek economy for several decades and traditionally approached the relation between trade and colonization from an empirical perspective.[17] This perspective has a considerable history, but was canonized in Alan Blakeway's concept of "trade before the flag," which was centered on the notion that the foundation of Greek colonies was preceded by trade contacts with the areas to be settled.[18] Thomas Dunbabin stated that "the intentions of the colonists were both commercial and agricultural."[19] Dunbabin, together with other scholars, not least Georges Vallet, further developed the notion of "commerce colonial," which involved the privileged trading relations between a colony and a metropolis. The problematic character of this notion, including its dependence on the European colonial experience of the last few centuries, has recently been fully demonstrated.[20] Nevertheless, trade remains important for archaeological literature on colonization, as evidenced especially by the subtitle of (the various editions of) John Boardman's influential monograph on *The Greeks Overseas: Their Early Colonies and Trade*.[21] Boardman argued that "it would be idle to pretend that consideration of trade did not provide some part of the motive in founding many colonies, and the major part in a few . . . in the case of some of the earliest colonies trade rather than land was the dominant factor in choosing a site."[22] Significantly, Boardman also noted that Greek colonization was not uniform in several respects, including in its causes, which were determined by the varied conditions in each metropolis and the particular geographic and cultural context of each colony.[23] Indeed, one could hardly expect a similar cause or set of causes for the foundation of perhaps as many as 500 colonies spread across the Mediterranean and the Black Sea.[24] This deduction is particularly important in moving the relevant discourse from the level of generalizing accounts to that of site-specific, bottom-up assessments, like the one that is offered here with reference to the Eretrian colony of Methone in the Thermaic Gulf.[25]

Disciplinary strife between historians and archaeologists over the causes of Greek colonization has declined in recent years but is not absent altogether. For example, Franco De Angelis has argued that archaeology is unable to illuminate "the individual thoughts and intentions that crossed the minds of those making the decision to colonize."[26] One could, of course, turn this around and ask whether foundation stories can really shed light on the thoughts and intentions of all the Therans on board the two *penteconters* that sailed to Kyrenaika, or of the putative 200 Corinthians who settled Apollonia in Illyria.[27] And the issue is exacerbated if one follows Robin Osborne, who has argued—controversially—that Greek colonies were not established as state-sponsored enterprises, but emerged in the context of increased mobility of private individuals in search for profit in the Mediterranean of the Early Iron Age.[28]

The disciplinary divide over the causes of Greek colonization is increasingly being bridged in the last few decades.[29] Archaeologists have sought to document the historian's favorite causes of overpopulation and drought,[30] whereas historians have questioned the impact of these phenomena,[31] and increasingly discuss the relevance of trade to colonization, despite the conviction of most that the prime motivation was the search for land.[32] Most recently, the once sharp division between agrarian and commercial motives has faded.[33] Likewise, current approaches have eroded the notion of a polarity between Greek and Phoenician colonization. Long-held assumptions that the Phoenicians developed a "non-Greek model of expansion," with a very different economic agenda focused on the acquisition and trade of raw materials and manufactured goods, have recently been revisited.[34] Lastly, the development of new approaches to interregional interaction, including world systems analyses and network perspectives, and the interest in the entire Mediterranean as an analytical unit of research, promotes—directly or indirectly—the relevance of trade and exchange to colonization.[35] Nevertheless, Charles Reed has recently observed: "So currently discounted is a causal connection between archaic [Greek] trade and colonisation that recent works on colonisation neglect to mention trade, just as recent or forthcoming treatments of archaic trade or traders ignore colonization."[36] My purpose in this chapter is to explore this connection on the basis of historical and archaeological evidence, including early transport amphoras from Methone.

A SURPRISING CONSENSUS FOR THE COLONIZATION OF METHONE

Given the varying approaches to the causes of Greek colonization, and the division between historians and archaeologists sketched above, one may be surprised to find that scholarship has reached a widely shared consensus minimizing the role of trade in the foundation of the Euboian colony at Methone. The purpose of this paper is to expose the weak basis of this consensus, and to provide archaeological evidence confirming the close link between Greek colonization and trade in the late 8th century B.C.

Historians have typically approached the colonization of Methone on the basis of the foundation story preserved in Plutarch's *Moralia: Greek Questions* (293A–B), which is worth citing in full:

> Who are the "Men repulsed by slings"? Men from Eretria used to inhabit the island of Corcyra. But Charicrates sailed thither from Corinth with an army and defeated them in war; so the Eretrians embarked in their ships and sailed back home. Their fellow-citizens, however, having learned of the matter before their arrival, barred their return to the country and prevented them from disembarking by showering upon them missiles from slings. Since the exiles were unable either to persuade or to overcome their fellow-citizens, who were numerous and inexorable, they sailed to Thrace and occupied a territory in which, according to tradition, Methon, the ancestor of Orpheus, had formerly lived. So the Eretrians named their city Methonê, but they were also named by their neighbours the "Men repulsed by slings."[37]

In this story, Plutarch reports that the colony at Methone was founded by Eretrians who had previously settled Korkyra; were expelled from there by Corinthians; were prevented from returning to Eretria by their former compatriots; and thus settled a site at coastal Pieria which had an indigenous history of occupation represented by the shadowy figure of Methon.[38] The historicity of (the core of) this story, and the dating of the associated events to 733–732 B.C., has been accepted by most scholars.[39] Only a few have doubted the reliability of Plutarch on the foundation of a colony at Methone, or have expressed reservations concerning the part of the story that relates to Korkyra, which has yielded poor archaeological evidence in support of Euboian colonization.[40]

Plutarch does not provide any direct explanation of the reasons that attracted the Eretrians to Methone, but some scholars have been tempted to draw conclusions from the passage above. George Cawkwell has doubted that trade was of prime importance to the Eretrians who settled Korkyra and eventually Methone: "if the colony had been sent out for commercial reasons, one would hardly expect them to be treated as if their mother city wanted to have nothing more to do with them."[41] This argument, however, is founded on the concept of "commerce colonial," which was criticized above. Furthermore, it does not take full account of the broader significance of "the right to return," and adheres to the notion of a colony as a state-sponsored enterprise, which has been challenged in recent years.[42]

Other historians have drawn conclusions on the causes for the colonization of Methone by comparative examination of other foundation stories. For example, Irad Malkin has approached the story of the foundation of Methone in the light of another, less well-known passage of Plutarch (*Moralia: The Oracles at Delphi*, 401F–402A).

> I commend . . . and still more the inhabitants of Eretria and Magnesia who presented the god with the first fruits of their people, in the belief that he is the giver of crops, the god of their fathers, the author of their being and a friend of man.[43]

According to Malkin, this passage refers to the episode that led the inhabitants of Eretria to colonize Korkyra and Methone.[44] The link that Malkin draws between the two passages is not implausible,[45] especially since the *Moralia* involve recurring references to the history of Eretria, including the Lelantine and Persian wars.[46] If this link is accepted, the causes of the colonization of Methone could be illuminated by comparison to the story of Magnesia on the Maiander, which is mentioned in the second passage. As Malkin notes, different mythological accounts suggest that the Magnesians settled their land after being sent to Delphi as a tithe (*dekate*), which raises the possibility that the Eretrians of Korkyra and Methone had also been sent out as a tithe. Interestingly, the colonization of Rhegion by Euboian Chalkis, which is contemporary with the foundation of Methone,[47] is known to have involved the sending of a tithe of the population of Chalkis to Delphi in response to crop failure (Strabo 6.1.6). This set of associations could be taken to support the notion that the Eretrians who settled Methone left their hometown in search of land. Indeed, the name of the area they settled, Pieria (the region surrounding Methone), declares the richness and fertility of the land.[48]

A different approach to the foundation story of Methone has been pursued by de Ste. Croix, who has compared this story to the tradition for the establishment of the Theran colony at Kyrene. Based on the failed attempt of the colonists of the two sites to return to their metropoleis (on the Therans of Kyrene see Herodotus 4.156),[49] de Ste. Croix has deduced that the primary cause for the foundation of the two colonies must have been similar, namely the acquisition of land. Indeed, Herodotus (4.151, 158–159) notes that this was the motivation for the colonization of Kyrene. However, the (admittedly much later) 2nd-century B.C. author Menekles of Barka gives a different reason for the colonization of the city in Libya, namely civil strife.[50] Additionally, the archaeology of Kyrene suggests the importation of copious materials from overseas shortly after the establishment of the colony.[51] In any case, there is reason to question that the Therans of Kyrene and the Eretrians of Methone had the same motives in settling abroad. This is particularly so because the Therans settled a previously unoccupied site removed from the coast (Herodotus 4.158), whereas Methone was a preexisting coastal site with an excellent harbor. The existence of an earlier settlement at Methone, which is indicated by Plutarch and also by two mythological traditions that refer to different female characters eponymous to the site (Methone),[52] is also confirmed by archaeology. Bessios has established that habitation at Methone extends back to the Neolithic period and he has confirmed the persistence of aspects of the indigenous material culture after the arrival of the colonists.[53] This evidence does not encourage any assumption that the Eretrians expelled the local population to seize their fertile land, as ancient sources report for other Greek colonies, especially in Sicily.⁵⁴ Indeed, Methone grew in size after the reported establishment of the Eretrians, unlike other sites in its vicinity, which apparently either shrank, such as Pydna, or vanished, like the settlement at Koutsouro (whatever its ancient name), at the time.⁵⁵

Other historians have downplayed the significance of Methone for interregional interaction irrespective of foundation stories. On the one hand, Graham hypothesized that the most prominent colonies of the northwest Aegean were in Chalkidike.⁵⁶ On the other, Eugene Borza considered that the Eretrian colonies of Methone, Dikaia, and Mende "were probably founded as agricultural settlements, although in time commerce became paramount."⁵⁷

I suspect that this consensus among historians is influenced by traditional ideas on the conservative sociopolitical system and agro-pastoral economy of areas around the Thermaic Gulf in early Archaic times. This idea can be traced back to ancient sources, for example, to the narrative of Herodotus (8.137–138) on the establishment of the Argead dynasty in Macedonia.⁵⁸ Significantly, this story, which is one of the very few we have on the early myth-history of the region, has often been compared to foundation stories of Greek colonies.⁵⁹ The story in Herodotus, which has three brothers exiled from Argos serving as shepherds for the petty ruler of a city in Upper Macedonia—in addition to three related narratives that emphasize the role of goats in the establishment of the city of Aigai in Lower Macedonia⁶⁰—are fundamental to the historiographical trope of "the Macedonians as transhumant pastoralists."⁶¹ The same trope is found in the speech of Alexander III to his rebellious soldiers in Opis in 324 B.C. (Arrian 7.9.2–7), where he claims that before the reign of Philip II most Macedonians "were dressed in skins pasturing a few flocks."⁶² These stories stereotype the northwest Aegean as an isolated periphery with an inward-looking, agro-pastoral economy, and thus as a backwater in comparison to the developing economies farther south. The literary qualities of these passages have only come to be appreciated in the last few years, when the contrast between the stereotype of transhumant pastoralists and the archaeological record of the region is openly acknowledged.⁶³ Nonetheless, much remains to be done for the development of a different model for the early economy of the areas around the Thermaic Gulf.

The widely shared, text-based argument that trade was not a major concern for the colonization of Methone has found surprising support in archaeological discussions of colonization in the north Aegean. According to Boardman, who has otherwise been a major proponent of the link between trade and colonization: "For the Greek colonies on the northern shores of the Aegean, our evidence is mainly literary . . . the object was simply land, and there can have been little interest at first in trade,"⁶⁴ or in metallurgical resources.⁶⁵ Likewise, in his comprehensive overview of colonization in the north Aegean, Michalis Tiverios, the excavator of Sindos and Karabournaki and a leading authority on the archaeology of the Thermaic Gulf, argued that

> in the first phase (from the 8th to the first half of the 7th century B.C.), the metropoleis by and large had aristocratic régimes and the colonies established in this period were more agricultural in character. In the second phase (after 650 B.C.), when the aristocratic régimes were tottering, the colonies that were established were often also based on trade, since farming had ceased to be the Greeks' almost exclusive occupation. At this time, many of the earlier colonies too added trade to their agricultural activities.⁶⁶

Clearly, both Boardman and Tiverios agree with historians in considering that the main attraction for the earliest Greek colonies in the north was arable land, rather than trade. Their argument is, however, based on written sources and historical models for sociopolitical development in the Greek world, rather than on archaeological evidence. Archaeological evidence on trade in the Thermaic Gulf of the 8th century B.C. has received some attention in the last decade, especially through the work of Tiverios.[67] Indeed, Tiverios has noted the availability of metal resources (especially bronze and gold) in the area and has argued that these were an attraction to Euboians since the beginning of the Early Iron Age (see Chapter 14). Furthermore, he has proposed the identification of a Euboian *emporion* or trading station at Sindos in the 8th century B.C.[68] These arguments have promoted considerations on trade, but often retain a (nearly) exclusive focus on Euboian agency, and have occasionally generated questionable notions of economic and power relations, a case in point being the oversimplification that "the Euboians were bringing pots to Macedonia, which they exchanged for local gold."[69]

To a certain extent, this approach to trade can be explained by the delay in the intensification of archaeological fieldwork in the north Aegean and the persisting dearth of final publications of Early Iron Age archaeological material from this region. It is perhaps indicative that in the early 1970s, Nicholas Hammond could summarize all Early Iron Age southern Aegean imports to the northwest Aegean in five lines of text.[70] Despite the dearth of such evidence, and also despite his role in the development of the notion that pastoralism prevailed in the area in the early first millennium B.C.,[71] Hammond has been exceptional in envisaging an important economic role for Methone. Indeed, he argued that the foundation of the Eretrian colony at the site was a catalyst for the intensification of trade contacts between this area and the central and southern Aegean.[72] Hammond's ideas have found support in the excavations of Bessios, which commenced in 2003. As is increasingly appreciated, the discoveries at Methone have been particularly revealing about the role of trade in the colonization of the site, and, more broadly, of the north Aegean.[73]

TRADE, TRANSPORT AMPHORAS, AND COLONIZATION AT METHONE

Reflecting on the kind of evidence one could use to establish a causal link between trade and colonization, Graham has conceded that "to show that a colony was founded for trade one needs clear evidence, either of pre-colonization trade, or that the colony lived by trade from the first, or, preferably, both."[74] Methone has yielded rich material to satisfy Graham's criteria, and it is on this basis that one can start developing a site-specific approach to the causes of colonization, introducing further considerations as appropriate.

Excavations at Methone have produced rich evidence for wide-ranging imports and metalworking activities (molds, crucibles, and slag) dating back to the late 8th century B.C. (which is the traditional date for the foundation of the colony), and industrial facilities dating from the 6th century, on which basis Bessios has argued that the site emerged as a trading and industrial center at the time.[75] Additionally, Bessios has discussed the range of ceramic material, largely fine wares, which show that contacts between Methone and Euboia predate the alleged foundation date of the colony.[76]

Admittedly, the circulation of fine ware ceramics has long dominated discussion of "pre-colonization" and of trade and colonization,[77] but the weight of this evidence is increasingly questioned. This is especially because fine ware imports can also be found in considerable quantities at sites that were not colonized.[78] Indeed, the criticism has been leveled that "archaeologists can accumulate new evidence for archaic exchanges till doomsday without our necessarily comprehending its significance."[79] To compensate for the problems of the significance of the fine wares, and also of the poor recovery rate of many important products and goods, including metals, cereals, animal products, wood, slaves, and other "soft things,"[80] Jean-Paul Morel has recommended research on a different category of ceramic evidence, namely transport amphoras; his recommendation, published as early as 1984, is worth citing in full:

Commercial amphoras, the study of which for many years has remained a poor relation in respect to that of the "fine" pottery, should not be underestimated either in themselves (as products of the pottery worker) or, and especially, as containers and therefore an index of commerce in agricultural products, wine and oil principally... This is a vast area, and it is only partly explored, because still one must pass from the level of simple inventorying, a work often very incomplete, to interpretation in terms of production (at the point of departure), demand, absorption by the market, secondary circulation, influences (at the point of arrival), and exchange.[81]

Recent scholarship echoes Morel in treating transport amphoras as highly significant for the study of exchange systems and ancient economies and a far more reliable index of trade than fine ware ceramics.[82] Yet, until recently, fragments of such vessels were often discarded in bulk by excavators and remained unpublished.[83] Accordingly, John Davies has observed that although in theory the evidence of amphoras is "a godsend" for the study of the ancient economy, in practice it can be "at once a dream and a nightmare" because of the unsatisfactory state of primary research.[84] In the last few years Greek and Mediterranean transport amphoras have received extensive attention in three important studies which pursue a diachronic and cross-cultural perspective.[85] This recent work, along with Morel's comments, provides a framework for approaching a particularly large assemblage of transport amphoras from Methone,[86] which dates from the first decades after the establishment of the colony, and provides evidence for "trade from the first," *sensu* Graham.[87] The assemblage comes from the lower deposit of a rock-cut shaft, which was more than 11.5 m deep, measured 3.6 m by 4.2 m at the bottom, and was located on the top of a low coastal hill or promontory.[88] The shaft, conventionally called the "Hypogeion," was part of a structure of uncertain purpose that remained unfinished and was backfilled with all kinds of materials, including raw clay, mud bricks, stones, metal objects, animal bones, seashells, tools, workshop waste, large amounts of ceramics, and much timber and other organic material, extensive traces of which were identified during excavation. The backfilling occurred at around 700 B.C. or slightly later as evidenced by well-dated fine ware imports from Attica, Corinth, Euboia, and East Greece.[89] As the organic material decomposed, and the relevant layers were compressed, more recent layers originally lying on the surface subsided into the shaft. The original backfilling (Phases I–III) can, however, be clearly distinguished from three later phases on stratigraphic and ceramic grounds.[90] The deposit created by this backfilling is particularly interesting for the study of amphoras, and, more generally, of trade and colonization, as it largely corresponds to the criteria that David Peacock and David Williams have set for significant amphora deposits: "Homogeneous, relatively uncontaminated deposits can usually be recognized by examining the datable fine-ware assemblages, and it is these layers that should be selected for careful examination of the amphorae."[91]

Such an examination is currently underway for the assemblage from the Hypogeion in collaboration with colleagues at the Fitch Laboratory of the British School at Athens. In addition to studying the stratigraphy, style, and morphology of the amphoras from this context, we selected 75 samples for petrographic analysis with thin sections by Evangelia Kiriatzi and Xenia Charalambidou, and elemental analysis by Naomi Müller, while organic residue analysis using combined Gas Chromatography–Mass Spectrometry was conducted by Maria Roumpou on 45 samples.[92] Projects of such scope have hitherto not been conducted on Greek transport amphoras,[93] and the closest comparable research involves prehistoric Canaanite jars, Aegean stirrup jars, Phoenician transport amphoras, and Roman amphoras.[94] The interdisciplinary character of the Methone amphora project is improving the understanding of the date range, provenance, quantity, and likely contents of the amphoras, which is essential for any assessment of their economic significance.[95] Furthermore, this project promotes a more nuanced understanding of the role of trade shortly after the traditional date for the colonization of the site.

The early date and rich contents of this deposit (ca. 700 B.C.) are particularly significant for the appreciation of trade at Methone and, more broadly, in the Aegean and the Mediterranean of the Early Iron Age. For Mark Lawall, an authority on Greek amphoras, this amphora deposit is "a game changer" in providing "a view of a rich assemblage of diverse imports, the complexity and scale of which had not been seen elsewhere in the Aegean."[96] Likewise, Zosia Archibald has noted that that this deposit "gives an unexpected insight into the scale of maritime exchange before we have any narrative descriptions of such contacts."[97] Several other scholars have also highlighted the significance of the early date and the wide range of amphoras in the deposit in question.[98]

The early chronology of the deposit is particularly important. Scholars generally believe that the widespread production and distribution of Greek (especially east Greek) transport amphoras only began in the (late) 7th century B.C.,[99] with only few types dating earlier. This notion persists despite the publication of important (albeit mostly small) groups of finds from different Mediterranean areas, including Pithekoussai, Carthage, Toscanos in Spain, and Tell Qudadi in Israel, which suggest an earlier (late 8th century B.C.) date for several types, but have not been given the attention they deserve.[100] The large and diverse assemblage from the Hypogeion of Methone, which is dated by a wide variety of fine ware imports, has reaffirmed the early dates proposed for a range of amphora types, as well as the circulation of these vessels at considerable quantities and over long distances already in the late 8th century BCE. This revised chronology, which is increasingly acknowledged in studies of early amphora assemblages found within the Aegean,[101] can be taken to lend support to the view of some historians that bulk trade in foodstuffs had begun already in the late 8th century B.C.,[102] and it largely synchronizes the widespread circulation of Greek transport amphoras with the beginnings of Greek colonization.

The range in the type and provenance of the amphoras from the Hypogeion is surprisingly broad, which has considerable implications, as noted by Lawall. The inscribed transport amphoras (alone) from this context, which were published in 2012, are of different types: Thermaic, Corinthian, Attic and Euboian SOS, Cycladic, Samian, Milesian, Chian, and Lesbian.[103] Additionally, a dozen types of unknown provenance are poorly represented. The study of the much larger assemblage of the non-inscribed amphoras from the Hypogeion, which is ongoing, reveals many more specimens of the above-mentioned types, in addition to Phoenician amphoras, and a wider range of thinly represented types of unknown provenance. In the case of most amphora types represented in the Hypogeion, the petrographic and elemental analysis by Kiriatzi, Charalambidou, and Müller lent support to the assumptions on the provenance of these amphoras which were based on macroscopic examination. In specific cases, however, like that of amphoras from Lesbos, the petrographic analysis of Kiriatzi and Charalambidou offered a surprisingly high degree of resolution (see below). Working along these lines, we can develop a much finer understanding of patterns of exports, and trace back trade networks from the broad regional level to the level of the micro-region.

The quantification of the vessels among the different types is currently in progress, and the figures given below should be treated as preliminary. These figures rely on estimates of the Minimum Number of Individual vessels (MNI) of each type. The MNI method was preferred to the alternative method of Estimated Vessel Equivalent (EVE), which does not work well for amphora assemblages.[104] For the material from the Hypogeion, rims provide the most reliable basis for estimating the MNI, but bases, and even fabric characteristics, prove significant in the case of some types. All figures given below concern amphora material from the backfilling of Phases I–III, and not from the overlying layers, which yielded far less material. Notably, the material recovered from these three phases represents a minimum of over 200 amphoras. The large quantity and variety of the amphoras in this deposit strongly indicate patterns of trade rather than casual exchange.

The amphora type that is by far the best represented in the Hypogeion of Methone is the Thermaic type, with ca. 40 pieces (nearly one fifth of the overall total) (Figs. 12.2a–b).[105] This type was first identified by Tiverios, and was studied systematically by Richard Catling, which is why these amphoras are often identified as Catling's Type II amphoras.[106] Some scholars also call them north Aegean amphoras, a term that was originally intended to suggest that specimens belonging to related amphora types preceding Type II were produced in different parts of the region.[107] However, the expansive application of the term to different amphora types (including Catling's Type II) risks giving the dubious—if not misleading—impression that these vases were produced across the north Aegean and also that they form the only amphora type produced in this vast region at the time (cf. Chapter 7). Additionally, Greek scholarship uses as many as five more names for these vessels, which involve either the cultural designation "north Greek" or the art-historical term "Geometric," both of which I consider problematic.[108] I have explained elsewhere that this terminological profusion is exceptional for Aegean amphora studies, and involves names loaded with terminological and conceptual problems. Accordingly, I have argued that, in accordance with the long-standing practice in Aegean amphora studies, the type should be named after the core (but not necessarily exclusive) area of production, which is the Thermaic Gulf.[109] That the Thermaic Gulf was the core area of production has long been suggested by different scholars, including Tiverios and Catling, on the basis of copious finds from Mende and Sindos (and more recently from Methone), and of fewer specimens at numerous sites around the Gulf area which have received much less fieldwork and publication (Fig. 12.3a).[110] More recently, analytical research by Kiriatzi and her collaborators has shown the existence of at least four distinct fabrics of Thermaic amphoras, potentially associated with production locations around the Thermaic Gulf, across an area extending from the Kassandra peninsula in the Chalkidike to what is now the western edge of the Thessaloniki alluvial plain but was the northwest coastline of the Gulf in antiquity.[111]

FIGURE 12.2. Thermaic amphoras from the Hypogeion, ΜΕΘ 2186 and ΜΕΘ 2184.
Photo O. Kourakis

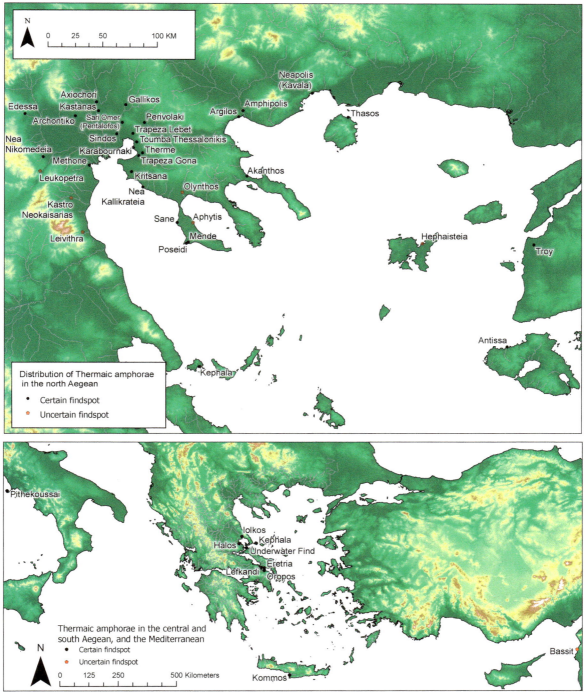

FIGURE 12.3. The distribution of a) Thermaic amphoras in the north Aegean; b) and in the Mediterranean. Maps created by M. Chykerda and V. Antoniadis (based on Kotsonas 2012, p. 160, maps 5 and 6)

The name "Thermaic (type) amphoras" has been treated favorably by amphora specialists and other experts in Aegean pottery of the period.[112] Individual scholars have expressed some concern over the possibility that additional production areas may be identified across other parts of the north Aegean in the future.[113] This point, however, fails to acknowledge that such a concern applies to all other amphora types that carry geographical designations. There are well-known cases in which the original area of production of an Aegean amphora type has been found to be broader than its name suggests, without this resulting in any terminological turmoil.[114] Others remain skeptical about this established practice in amphora studies and yet they consider the term "Chalkidian" better suited for these amphoras "since they were mainly distributed on the eastern coasts of the Thermaic Gulf."[115] But these coasts are surely part of the Gulf, and transport amphora types are typically named after areas of production, not areas of distribution. The possibility that Thermaic amphoras were produced in parts of the Chalkidike which lie beyond the Thermaic Gulf cannot be excluded, but the relevant argument remains unconvincing as long as it relies on unpublished specimens from a single site in Sithonia, and on the identification of kiln wasters of a fairly different, belly-and-shoulder-handled amphora type at Torone.[116]

Lastly, the assumption that Troy was a production center for the Thermaic amphoras, which is occasionally mentioned in the literature,[117] relies on dubious evidence. Three pieces of possibly Thermaic-type amphoras from Troy have been sampled for neutron activation analysis, but the results were not conclusive. As the relevant studies explain, two of the three samples may or may not belong to the amphoras in question,[118] while the third (which comes from the collection of Heinrich Schliemann and has no specific context) shows affiliation—but not a match—with an elemental group that characterizes Trojan ceramics.[119] I think more extensive and targeted research is needed, preferably including petrographic analysis which could anchor the fabrics into local geology,[120] before Troy can be identified as a major production center for these amphoras. It is also worth noting that although Troy is probably the most extensively excavated and published site in the north Aegean, the amphora type in question is not very common at the site, currently remains unattested elsewhere in the Troad and adjacent islands, and is thinly represented in the northeast Aegean (Fig. 12.3a).[121] This pattern, coupled with the fact that Troy in the Geometric period is apparently "without much pottery, architecture, or other small finds,"[122] raises questions over the assumed importance of Trojan production and export of these vessels. On these grounds, I think it is safer to assume that these vessels were primarily (though not necessarily exclusively) produced in the Thermaic Gulf and call them Thermaic amphoras, in accordance with established practice in Aegean amphora studies.

My emphasis on the Thermaic amphoras is because of their broader historical and especially economic significance and the evidence which they provide for local agency, which has been skewed by misunderstandings in the literature. Tiverios and his students have argued that these amphoras were produced at a Euboian trading station at Sindos, and were distributed by Euboian traders.[123] Indeed, it has been claimed that the attestation of these amphoras over an area occupied by diverse people and polities can best be attributed to a "mastermind," namely the Euboians.[124] An extreme but isolated version of this approach emphasizes the "Greekness" of these vessels.[125] I have argued against the Hellenocentric and Euboio-centric approach to these vessels.[126] I do not believe that the Euboio-centric economic model is applicable to the 8th century B.C. Aegean, especially since regional production of specific transport amphora types, cutting across political and other divisions and involving no "mastermind," is a well-known phenomenon.[127] I further find the Euboio-centric model to be tied to the paradigm of the Thermaic Gulf as a passive economic periphery, conforming to the widely shared tendency for attributing any evidence for overseas contacts of this area to foreign traders, especially the Euboians or—to a lesser extent—the Phoenicians.[128] Even when there is reason to think that people from the north Aegean may have traveled overseas, these people are identified only "as slaves or as spouses of colonists,"[129] and are thus denied any serious agency in accordance with antiquated colonial assumptions reminiscent of Figure 12.1. The only scholar who has entertained the possibility of local initiatives is John Papadopoulos, who, however, found little supporting evidence of this over 20 years ago.[130] The possibility of local initiatives begs for further consideration, especially on the basis of recent discoveries at Methone and elsewhere, and in the light of current postcolonial approaches which emphasize the cultural complexity of interactions in colonial landscapes and expose the long-downplayed aspect of local agency.[131]

Based on analytical and other evidence on the modes of production and distribution of this amphora type, and drawing from current postcolonial literature, I have challenged the assumed Euboian management of the distribution of these vessels.[132] The argument accepts some degree of Euboian involvement, but it emphasizes instead the initiative of "local"/"indigenous" people "from the Thermaic Gulf."[133] This interpretation relies on:

a) the decentralized pattern of production of these vessels, which has been revealed by the petrographic analysis of samples from several sites in the Thermaic Gulf by Kiriatzi and her collaborators.

b) the dense distribution pattern of the Thermaic amphoras within the gulf and, to a lesser extent, across the north Aegean (in contrast to their limited distribution farther afield) (Figs. 12.3a–b). This pattern finds no overlap with the distribution of Euboian ceramics. Also, leaving Eretria aside, no site in Euboia and no Euboian colony outside the Thermaic Gulf has revealed these vessels in any quantity.

c) the graffiti and other marks on Thermaic amphoras are unusually common but never alphabetic. This contrasts with the occurrence of Greek alphabetic writing on numerous other types of early transport amphoras produced in the Aegean.[134]

On this basis, I have argued that the production and distribution of Thermaic amphoras was not managed predominantly by Euboians, but rather by people from within the maritime small world of the Thermaic Gulf who had direct access to the manufacturers of these containers and to the producers of the commodities stored in the amphoras.[135] The argument received criticism by a few scholars who either insist on Euboian supremacy,[136] or prefer to substitute the traditional neglect of local agency with the tabooization of it.[137] Nevertheless, most scholars have resisted the powerful tropes that are embedded in the study of Greek and modern European colonization and that are so vividly illustrated on the poster of Figure 12.1, and they have accepted the new interpretative model on the Thermaic amphoras.[138] Indeed, this model has also informed the discussion of a comparable body of material found on Skiathos.[139] Even former critics quietly abandoned their earlier Hellenocentric and Euboio-centric approaches to these amphoras and accept the agency of local populations in their distribution.[140]

It is important to appreciate that the Thermaic amphora type was introduced in the early 8th century B.C. and thus predates the colonization of the north Aegean (as documented in our textual sources), and—more importantly—the beginning of amphora production in most parts of the Aegean. Because of their early date, decentralized production, and widespread distribution, the Thermaic amphoras openly challenge the assumptions of a backwater agro-pastoral economy around the Thermaic Gulf. It is worth contrasting the case of Sicily, where transport amphoras were largely imported from the Aegean, rather than locally produced, during the early Archaic period.[141]

The predominance of regionally produced amphoras (such as the Thermaic type) at a site in the same region (such as Methone) is widely attested in the Greek world from the Late Archaic period onward, when imports from long distances are less commonly represented.[142] The prevalence of Thermaic amphoras at Methone in the late 8th century B.C. perhaps presents the earliest known attestation of this phenomenon, but it is combined with an unusually broad range of amphora types from different parts of the Aegean and beyond.

The Hypogeion also yielded evidence for eight examples of an amphora type that is morphologically similar to the Thermaic amphoras, but is earlier in date and involves vessels made in much finer fabrics. These vessels, which are known as Catling's type I and I/II (transitional) amphoras or—again under several names—as north Aegean amphoras, or Protogeometric amphoras, were produced in different parts of the central and northern part of the Aegean, and date from the 11th to the 9th century B.C.[143] Significantly, the examples of the type found in the Hypogeion normally consist of small sherds that present no joins, unlike the much more numerous pieces from the later Thermaic amphoras (and of the other amphora types mentioned below), which can often be mended together in the dozens and make up nearly complete vessels. The pattern of fragmentation of the early amphoras in question is suggestive of residual material.

East Greek amphoras of different types are amply represented in the Hypogeion. Around 25 Lesbian amphoras belong to the gray series (Fig. 12.4), but some are light gray and others very dark gray.[144] Amphoras of this type were produced in different parts of Lesbos and probably on the adjacent coastal areas of Asia Minor,[145] but the petrographic analysis by Kiriatzi and Charalambidou established that the pieces from Methone come specifically from the central part of the island, the geology of which is characterized by volcanic rocks.[146] The ancient cities of Methymna and Arisbe fall within this geological zone, but Methymna is the more likely source of the amphoras because of its coastal location, its prominence in Archaic times, and its eventual destruction of Arisbe before the mid-5th century B.C.[147]

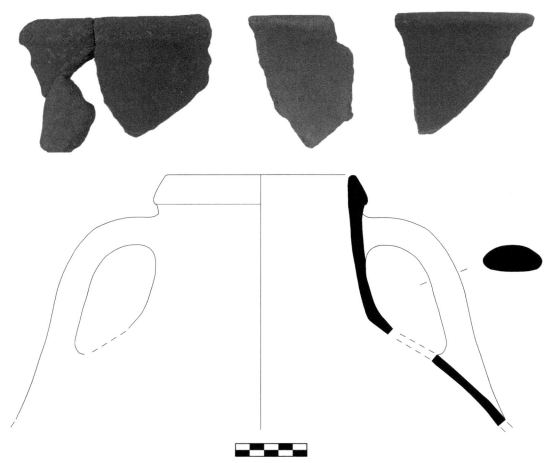

FIGURE 12.4. Lesbian amphoras from the Hypogeion: ΜΕΘ 5212, ΜΕΘ 5211, and ΜΕΘ 5213 (photo); drawing ΜΕΘ 5219. Photo I. Coyle, drawing F. Skyvalida

Samian amphoras (Fig. 12.5a–b) were slightly more abundant than Lesbian. Apparently, these vessels make up the most common amphora type imported to Methone from overseas, and comprise the type that carries the most numerous inscriptions and trademarks.[148] In contrast, there are only six Chian amphoras (Fig. 12.6), even though this type is considerably more common in later contexts at Methone.[149] Approximately 20 Milesian amphoras were identified and most belong to the banded Byblos type (Fig. 12.7), but two pieces are of a different undecorated type.[150] Interestingly, Archaic Milesian amphoras remain rare elsewhere in the north Aegean, but Samian and Lesbian types are more widespread, and Chian are even more common.[151]

FIGURE 12.5. Samian amphoras from the Hypogeion: ΜΕΘ 2028 and ΜΕΘ 2425.
Photo O. Kourakis

FIGURE 12.6. Chian amphoras from the Hypogeion: ΜΕΘ 5256 and ΜΕΘ 5308.
Photo I. Coyle, drawing F. Skyvalida

FIGURE 12.7. Milesian amphoras from the Hypogeion: ΜΕΘ 2240 and ΜΕΘ 5191.
Photo I. Coyle, drawing F. Skyvalida

FIGURE 12.8. Attic SOS amphora from the Hypogeion: ΜΕΘ 2206.
Photo O. Kourakis

Around 15 SOS amphoras are represented in the Hypogeion.[152] The macroscopic impression that nearly all pieces are Attic (Fig. 12.8) was endorsed by the petrographic and elemental analysis, which further confirmed the assumed Euboian provenance of one piece. A second piece, which was not sampled, is also considered Euboian (Fig. 12.9).[153] Attic SOS amphoras are fairly widespread in the north Aegean,[154] but their occurrence in Methone has been considered particularly significant for understanding trade networks (see below).

Corinthian and Phoenician amphoras are widely found in the central Mediterranean of the Archaic period, but they are thinly attested in the north Aegean in general and at Methone in particular. Indeed, Archaic Corinthian amphoras are known from only six other sites in the entire region,[155] whereas the Hypogeion yielded a minimum of three pieces (Fig. 12.10).[156] It is perhaps tempting to associate the paucity of Corinthian amphoras in this deposit with Plutarch's testimony for the aggression of the Corinthians against the Eretrian settlers at Korkyra who eventually colonized Methone. However, the limited distribution of Corinthian amphoras in the entire north Aegean and the high number of Corinthian fine ware imports at Methone[157] do not support this association.

Phoenician amphoras have not been attested in any north Aegean site other than Methone, and they are only known from very few sites in the rest of the Aegean (see Fig. 1.11a–d).[158] Indeed, the five Phoenician amphoras discovered in the Hypogeion make up the second largest assemblage of Phoenician amphoras anywhere in the Early Iron Age Aegean (after Kommos).[159] The discovery of Phoenician amphoras at Methone ties in with broader discussions of interregional

FIGURE 12.9. Euboian SOS amphora from the Hypogeion: ΜΕΘ 2207.
Photo O. Kourakis

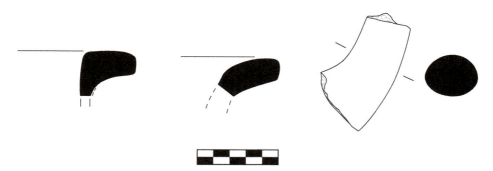

FIGURE 12.10. Corinthian amphoras from the Hypogeion: ΜΕΘ 5185, ΜΕΘ 5186, and ΜΕΘ 5187.
Drawings F. Skyvalida

trade. The finds from Methone—in addition to a small group of recently identified Phoenician and/or Cypriot pots from elsewhere in the north Aegean[160]—challenge the earlier impression of the paucity of Near Eastern material in the north Aegean. This paucity was the basis of the argument by Mervyn Popham that it was the Euboians, and not the Phoenicians, who held the key role in the importation of Near Eastern artifacts to Greece and the Aegean.[161] More recently, Catherine Pratt has approached the occurrence of both Phoenician and Attic SOS amphoras at Methone in the light of an earlier argument by Brian Shefton, which held that the SOS amphoras were traded by Phoenicians.[162] As originally formulated, however, Shefton's argument covered only the west Mediterranean, hence its extension to the Aegean on the basis of a single site is uncertain. It is perhaps worth noting that the only inscriptions rendered on SOS amphoras from Methone are in Greek.[163]

The Hypogeion yielded many more amphoras which cannot be attributed to established types, and/or are of unknown provenance, and are typically represented by one to three (and rarely more) pieces. Only a fraction of these amphoras is represented among the inscribed material that has hitherto been published.[164] These amphoras can be treated here only very sparingly, but their numbers are considerable and indicate that the number of amphora production sites active in the Aegean at around 700 B.C. was considerably higher than hitherto assumed, a finding which has some repercussions for our understanding of the early Greek economy.

The material of unknown provenance includes numerous pieces that exhibit surface decoration: A minimum of six coated amphoras is represented in the Hypogeion and several of them carry inscriptions or graffiti (Fig. 12.11).[165] Made in highly micaceous fabric, these amphoras are distinguished from the well-known Lakonian coated amphoras and may be associated with a group of vessels identified by Roald Docter at Carthage, Toscanos, and Bouthrotos (Butrint), and considered East Greek.[166] The Hypogeion also yielded a range of other amphoras with painted decoration, which must have been used as transport amphoras. This material includes some five pieces from Attica, one from the Cyclades, and about 20 from elsewhere.[167]

About 15 indeterminate types of amphoras are characterized by a plain surface: smoothed, polished, or burnished. The sole type that is adequately represented (although with fewer than ten pieces) involves amphoras characterized by a brown to gray surface and thick lip with undercutting (Fig. 12.12).[168] The analysis of the fabric of these vessels by Kiriatzi, Charalambidou, and Müller showed that the macroscopic variation observed in their fabric and morphology does not represent varied production centers, but left open the question of the specific area of production. Another type, which is represented by three pieces, recalls the purple ware amphoras that were identified in a late 7th-century B.C. context at Kommos.[169]

Transport amphoras were traded for their contents, which were largely foodstuffs. Traditionally, assumptions as to the contents of specific amphora types rely on patchy and often late references by Greek and Roman authors, or on epigraphic and iconographic evidence.[170] Analytical research on the contents of Greek amphoras remains rare,[171] forcing Michel Gras to conclude that "le débat sur le contenu des amphores archaïques a toujours été le 'tendon d'Achille' de la recherche sur ces récipients."[172] The organic residue analysis of amphoras from Methone by Roumpou offers a response to this state of the research.

Roumpou's analysis revealed traces of fatty acids, representing plant oil or animal fat, on different amphora types from the Hypogeion.[173] If these acids represent oil, as is often hypothesized with reference to the content of transport amphoras, this evidence for the import of olive oil could be explained by the climate of the northwest Aegean (excluding part of Chalkidike), which is not ideal for the cultivation of olive trees.[174] This possible evidence for the importation of olive oil

FIGURE 12.11. Coated amphoras of indeterminate provenance from the Hypogeion: MEΘ 5207, MEΘ 5205, MEΘ 5206, and MEΘ 5208. Photo I. Coyle

FIGURE 12.12. Amphoras of indeterminate provenance from the Hypogeion, with thick lip with undercutting: ΜΕΘ 2424, ΜΕΘ 2433. Photos O. Kourakis

to Methone recalls a recent study of olive stones and olive charcoal from across modern Greece, which concluded that olives were introduced to the north Aegean through Greek colonization.[175] In any case, the identification of fatty acids in Chian amphoras challenges the widespread treatment of these vessels as wine containers, which relies on literary and iconographic evidence.[176] Comparable challenges have been put forward by DNA analysis on a Classical Chian amphora, which identified oil and oregano.[177] These analytical results provide a warning against the widespread assumption that specific amphora types were used exclusively for particular products. Unfortunately, this assumption remains popular, despite relevant warnings raised by several scholars, and regardless of the probability of the reuse of the vessels, or the evidence of solid residue found in amphoras from shipwrecks of later date.[178]

Wine is difficult to identify with residue analysis, but Roumpou found several Lesbian amphoras from Methone to contain resinous substances which are usually interpreted as evidence for resinated wine, though this is not certain.[179] Lesbian wine was praised in Archaic and later literature, on which basis Lesbian amphoras are widely considered as wine vessels.[180] In contrast, historical sources make no reference to wine production around most of the Thermaic Gulf, except for a passage in Stephanus of Byzantium (*Ethnika*, 440–441) which mentions that Methone was named after a strong type of wine produced in the area.[181] However, relevant archaeobotanical remains are abundant at sites around the gulf, and neighboring Chalkidike was a source of some of the most celebrated wine in Classical antiquity.[182] It would not be surprising to find imported wines in Methone in the late 8th century B.C., especially as the contemporary epigraphic evidence on fine ware ceramics from the Hypogeion suggests the introduction of the sympotic lifestyle to the site.[183]

Roumpou's analysis further revealed beeswax on the interior of Attic SOS and Thermaic amphoras, which was probably used as a coating medium to enable better preservation of the content of these vessels, insulating the porous matrix.[184] This insulating technology was previously identified—also by Roumpou—in Late Bronze Age and Iron Age storage vessels from central Macedonia.[185] However, the vessels from Methone represent the first attestation of this technology on Aegean amphoras. The identification of beeswax in both Attic SOS and Thermaic amphoras is particularly interesting in the light of the morphological similarities between these two types,[186] and raises interesting questions on the origin and transfer of this technology, while establishing its use for transport containers already from the late 8th century B.C.

The early date, large quantity, and broad variety of transport amphoras found in the Hypogeion of Methone suggest complex patterns of economic interaction in the first decades after the traditional date for the foundation of the colony, or Graham's "trade from the first." This impression is corroborated by the numerous trademarks rendered on many of the amphoras.[187] The range of this evidence is best paralleled at Pithekoussai and Kommos, two sites that are widely conceived as major nodes in trade networks of the 8th and 7th centuries B.C.[188] In the light of these correspondences, I argue that the colonization of Methone cannot be dissociated from trade. This argument, however, does not diminish the probability that Methone (like Pithekoussai) presented further economic attractions. Indeed, the natural resources (including timber) and the metallurgical wealth of the site and the surrounding territory, which were mentioned above, receive detailed attention in different chapters of the present volume (see Chapters 14, 15, 26),[189] and will be elucidated further by the results of the *synergasia* between Manthos Bessios, John Papadopoulos, Sarah Morris, Athena Athanassiadou, and Kostas Noulas, and by forthcoming studies by different members of the Methone team.

CONCLUSIONS

It is essential to revisit the discourse on the causes and the economics of Greek colonization, which has long relied on generalizing models based on polarized ideas about the character of the Archaic Greek economy, or on empirical research on fine ware ceramics, and has been colored by serious disagreements between historians and archaeologists. I have argued that a different, bottom-up, micro-regional, and site-specific approach is much better suited to account for the varying socioeconomic conditions that prevailed in different parts of the Aegean and the Mediterranean, and for the complexity of colonial encounters.

This approach was developed above with reference to the case study of Methone in the Thermaic Gulf, which is widely agreed to have been settled for its fertile territory. This consensus was found to rely on a thin textual basis: a foundation story that makes no explicit reference to economics, and a questionable historiographical notion about the underdeveloped socioeconomic background of the area of the Thermaic Gulf. It is especially the stereotype of local populations as "transhumant pastoralists" that has misguided previous historical and archaeological approaches to the economy of the area and to the economic interaction between colonists and local populations. However, transport amphoras and a range of other archaeological evidence from Methone and elsewhere in the Thermaic Gulf suggest that by the 8th century B.C., this area was characterized by a mixed economy which involved trade and exchange on a scale that has not been appreciated before, and involved important economic initiatives developed by local populations. Thus, historical narratives and cognitive maps of the Aegean can no longer treat the Thermaic Gulf as a passive economic and cultural periphery.

NOTES

1 I am grateful to Manthos Bessios for entrusting me with the study of the amphoras from the "Hypogeion," and also for the invitation that he and Yannis Tzifopoulos extended to me to contribute to *Methone Pierias* I (Bessios, Tzifopoulos, and Kotsonas 2012). I thank John Papadopoulos and Sarah Morris for their generous advice and support, and Michalis Tiverios and Vivi Saripanidi for their feedback on a draft of this contribution. I also thank Carolyn Aslan for advising me on Troy and sharing her study of 2019. My work has benefited from the efforts of the staff of the Ephoreia of Antiquities of Pieria, especially Athena Athanassiadou and Kostas Noulas, and the expert advice of many colleagues (see the introduction in Bessios, Tzifopoulos, and Kotsonas 2012). The photographs of the Methone amphoras are by Orestis Kourakis and Ian Coyle, and the drawings by Fani Skyvalida. The original submission of this paper was in 2015, but more recent literature has been incorporated to the extent possible.

2 See Osborne 1998, p. 252; 2008; 2016 on the abandonment of the term. Van Dommelen 2012, and Osborne 2016, pp. 23–25 favor migration, while *apoikiazation* is promoted in De Angelis 2010, pp. 19–21. See also the contributions in the discussion forum in *Ancient West and East* volume 10, 2011.

3 Cf. Tsetskhladze 2006, pp. xxv–xxviii; Kotsonas 2015, p. 245; Malkin 2016, pp. 27–31; Kotsonas and Mokrisova 2020, pp. 219–221.

4 On Ridgway's research (which includes *Pithekoussai* I) and teaching, see Bell et al. 2012. I was privileged to attend Ridgway's lectures as a Ph.D. student at the University of Edinburgh.

5 Graham 1982, p. 157. The impression is shared by Asheri 1980, p. 103; Morel 1984, p. 124; Snodgrass 1994, p. 1; Treister 1996, p. 146; Osborne 1998, p. 251; Tsetskhladze 2006, p. xxviii; Wilson 2006, p. 25.

6 Indicative of persisting interest in the question is the attention it receives in a volume on *The Archaeology of Greek Colonisation* (see, especially, De Angelis 1994; Boardman 1994; Snodgrass 1994, pp. 1–2; Tsetskhladze 1994, pp. 123–126).

7 Gwynn 1918, pp. 88–98; Ste. Croix 2004 (based on a lecture delivered in 1959; see Reed 2004, p. 367); Lepore 1969; Graham 1982, pp. 157–159; Cawkwell 1992. Further references are collected in Bernstein 2004, p. 18, n. 21. Compare the emphasis on trade by prominent historians of the 19th century A.D. (Descoeudres 2008, pp. 293–296).

8 Asheri 1980, pp. 100–101; Zurbach 2008, pp. 91–95.

9 Finley 1976.

10 E.g., Gwynn 1918, p. 97; Cawkwell 1992, p. 297.

11 Graham 1982, p. 159.

12 Ste. Croix 2004, p. 365.

13 Hasebroek 1928. Summaries of the debate are provided in Cartledge 1983; Wilson 1997–1998, pp. 29–33 (with references); see also Lepore 1969; Asheri 1980, pp. 98–105. Bresson 2016, pp. 2–15 provides a broader overview.

14 Roebuck 1959; Humphreys 1965.

15 See, e.g., Feinman 2016.

16 E.g., Osborne 1996; Wilson 1997–1998; Foxhall 1998.

17 Notable exceptions include Snodgrass 1983.

18 Blakeway 1932–1933. For references to earlier and later works connecting trade and colonization see Bernstein 2004, p. 17, n. 17; see also Holloway 1981, pp. 133–154.
19 Dunbabin 1948, p. 211 (cf. pp. 3–36).
20 De Angelis 1998, pp. 545–547; Gras 1999, pp. 10–11.
21 Boardman 1999.
22 Boardman 1999, p. 162.
23 Boardman 1994, p. 147; cf. Asheri 1980, p. 105; Snodgrass 1994, p. 2; Tsetskhladze 1994, p. 124 (with a more skeptical approach to trade in Tsetskhladze 1998); cf. van Dommelen 2005, p. 122 on Phoenician colonization.
24 On the figure of 500 see Hansen and Nielsen 2004, pp. 53–54.
25 On Methone see especially Bessios, Tzifopoulos, and Kotsonas 2012. Also, Bessios 2003; Bessios et al. 2004; Bessios, Athanassiadou, and Noulas 2008; Bessios 2010, 2012a; Bessios and Noulas 2012.
26 De Angelis 1994, p. 105.
27 For Kyrene see Herodotus 4.153 and 4.156; for Apollonia see Stephanus of Byzantium, s.v. Apollonia. On questions of authenticity and the credibility of colonial foundation stories see especially Hall 2008; also, Yntema 2000; Mac Sweeney 2017.
28 Osborne 1998; cf. Morel 1984, pp. 145–150; and partly Morakis 2011. *Contra* Malkin 2009; 2011, pp. 23–24, 54–57; 2016; Figueira 2015, pp. 318–319.
29 Nonetheless, we still lack a holistic approach to the causes of Greek colonization of the kind currently available for Phoenician colonization (Aubet 1994, pp. 70–96).
30 Camp 1979; Snodgrass 1980, pp. 15–48 (esp. pp. 34–35); Zurbach 2008.
31 Figueira 2015, pp. 319–321.
32 Asheri 1980, pp. 98–105; Murray 1980, pp. 104–108; De Angelis 2002.
33 Horden and Purcell 2000, p. 349; De Angelis 2002, p. 299; Demetriou 2011, pp. 257–258, 261–263; De Angelis 2016, p. 49; Kotsonas and Mokrisova 2020, pp. 229–232.
34 For the traditional approach see Niemeyer 2006; cf. Aubet 1994, pp. 70–96. For revisionist approaches see van Dommelen 2005, pp. 120–122; Malkin 2011, p. 130; Pappa 2013; Hodos 2020, pp. 83–93; Kotsonas and Mokrisova 2020, pp. 231–232.
35 Sherratt and Sherratt 1992–1993; Horden and Purcell 2000; Morris 2003; Knappett 2011; Malkin 2011; Broodbank 2013, pp. 482–556; Bevan 2014.
36 Reed 2004, p. 368. But see, for example, Whitbread 1995, pp. 3–7.
37 Translation after Babbit 1936a, p. 184; cf. Chapter 2.
38 Precolonial habitation at the site is implicit in the argument of Bruno Helly (2007, pp. 197–200) that Pierian Methone is to be identified with the Homeric Methone in the kingdom of Philoktetes, on which see *Iliad* 2.716 and Strabo 8.6.15; Chapter 2.
39 Graham 1971, pp. 46–47; Hammond 1972, pp. 425–426; Graham 1982, pp. 113, 161; Hammond 1989, p. 8; Wilson 1997–1998, p. 52; Boardman 1999, p. 229. Further references are collected in Kotsonas 2012, pp. 298–299, n. 1513. On the narrative traditions of Euboian and other colonial foundations in the north Aegean see Kotsonas 2020.
40 The reliability of Plutarch's narrative is questioned in Cook 1946, pp. 70–71; Kahrstedt 1953, pp. 86–87; Bakhuizen 1976, p. 19. For doubts on the Korkyraian part of the story see: Morgan 1998, pp. 281–289, with extensive literature; also, Kotsonas 2012, p. 227; Šašel Kos 2015, pp. 7–9. I have explained my views on the Euboian colonization of Methone in Kotsonas 2012, pp. 227–239; 2015, pp. 253–256; 2020, pp. 307, 311, 315.
41 Cawkwell 1992, p. 297.
42 Malkin (2016) discusses both issues, but argues against Osborne's criticism of the concept of colonies as state-sponsored enterprises.

43 Translation after Babbit 1936b, p. 301.
44 Malkin 1987, pp. 31–41.
45 Cf. Kotsonas 2020, p. 313.
46 O'Neil 2004, p. 224.
47 The colonization of Rhegion is placed circa 730 B.C. (Dunbabin 1948, pp. 12–13; Graham 1982, p. 109; Malkin 1987, p. 31).
48 Mallios 2011, p. 136; Tzifopoulos 2012a, p. 17.
49 Ste. Croix 2004, pp. 350, 365. On the similarity of the two stories, see also Hammond 1972, pp. 416–418; Sakellariou 1979, pp. 31–32.
50 *FGH* 270 F6.
51 Boardman 1994, p. 143; cf. Murray 1980, p. 118.
52 Tzifopoulos 2012a, p. 15.
53 Bessios 2003, pp. 445–446, 448–449; 2010, pp. 78, 94, 105; 2012a, pp. 43, 58, 63, n. 3, p. 64, n. 4. 14; Bessios et al. 2004, pp. 369, 373–374; Bessios, Athanassiadou, and Noulas 2008, p. 241; Bessios and Noulas 2012, pp. 400, 404, 406. See Chapters 4–7.
54 For the settlement history of Methone and other sites in the area during the 8th and 7th centuries B.C. see Bessios, Athanassiadou, and Noulas 2008, p. 248; Bessios 2010, p. 76. For the seizing of land by Greek colonists, especially in Sicily, see Dunbabin 1948, pp. 43–47; Graham 1982, pp. 155–156.
55 Bessios 2010, pp. 76, 80, 86; cf. Bessios, Athanassiadou, and Noulas 2008, p. 248.
56 Graham 1971, pp. 46–47.
57 Borza 1990, p. 75.
58 On the story of Herodotus and related ancient references see Hammond and Griffith 1979, pp. 3–14; Borza 1990, pp. 80–84; Sprawski 2010, pp. 127–134; Mallios 2011, pp. 179–232.
59 Hammond and Griffith 1979, pp. 9–10; Dougherty 1993, pp. 47–48; Mallios 2011, pp. 194–195, 224–228. Tiverios (pers. comm.) doubts this comparison.
60 Diodorus Siculus, 7.16; Hyginus, *Fabulae*, 219; Euphorion fragment 35 in Lightfoot 2009, pp. 264–265. Also, Mallios 2011, pp. 224–232, 342, 346, with extensive bibliography.
61 Hammond 1989, pp. 1–8; followed by Borza 1995, pp. 44–45; Ruffing 2017, p. 127.
62 Ruffing 2017, pp. 125–126. On the disputed authenticity of the speech see Hammond and Griffith 1979, pp. 657–659.
63 Literary qualities: Mallios 2011, pp. 199–200, 206; Ruffing 2017, pp. 125–126. Archaeological record: Archibald 2013, pp. 182–183; Saripanidi 2017, pp. 112, 118, 122. Cf. Fotiadis 2001; Chapter 4.
64 Boardman 1999, p. 229.
65 Boardman 1999, p. 230; *contra*: Graham 1982, pp. 113, 115 (see also p. 505).
66 Tiverios 2008, p. 125.
67 See, e.g., Tiverios 2008, pp. 32, 125; Soueref 2011, pp. 276–277, 325–340.
68 On gold and bronze at Sindos, and on the early ventures of the Euboians in the Thermaic Gulf, see Tiverios 2008, pp. 4–17, 21 (references to further discussions by Tiverios are collected in Kotsonas 2012, pp. 229, 299, nn. 1533–1534). On Euboian colonization and gold in the Thermaic Gulf see Verdan and Heymans 2020; Cambitoglou and Papadopoulos 1993; Papadopoulos (1996, pp. 171–174; 2005, pp. 580–592; 2011, pp. 122–124; Papadopoulos 2021b, pp. 423, 429–430) favors an earlier date—certainly the Middle Bronze Age, if not already the Early Bronze Age—for the southern Aegean interest in the metals of the area and dissociates this interest from the Euboians (see further Morris 2009–2010). On Sindos as an *emporion* see Tiverios 2008, pp. 21, 24; I have expressed some skepticism on this suggestion (Kotsonas 2015, p. 249), but I appreciate Tiverios's discussion of *emporia* in the north Aegean (Tiverios 2008, pp. 32, 79, 86–87, 89–90, 121, 127; cf. Archibald 2013, pp. 252, 258–261).
69 Misailidou-Despotidou 2008, p. 60.

70 Hammond 1972, p. 424.

71 Hammond 1972, pp. 415–416, 439; Hammond and Griffith 1979, p. 28.

72 Hammond 1972, pp. 425–426; 1989, p. 8.

73 Kotsonas 2012, pp. 229–230; Ruffing 2017, p. 127; Tsiafaki 2020, pp. 412–413.

74 Graham 1982, pp. 158–159.

75 Bessios 2003, p. 449; 2010, pp. 80, 86; 2012a, p. 44; 2013; Bessios et al. 2004, pp. 369, 373, 375; Bessios and Noulas 2012, pp. 399–400; cf. Kotsonas 2015, pp. 255–256. On metalworking at Methone see: Bessios 2003, p. 449; 2010, p. 105; Bessios et al. 2004, p. 369; Verdan and Heymans 2020, pp. 281–287; Verdan (Chapter 14). Evidence for similar economic activities is not missing from other sites in the Thermaic Gulf and Chalkidike, but remains rarer.

76 Bessios 2003, p. 448; 2010, pp. 76, 86; 2012a, p. 63, n. 3; Chapters 7, 9. Imported pottery predating the late 8th century B.C. also appears at other sites in the area, not all of which were colonized (Papadopoulos 1996; Kotsonas 2012, pp. 132–133, 166–167; Charalambidou 2017, pp. 96–100; Kourou 2017, pp. 28, 32–34).

77 Blakeway 1932–1933; Dunbabin 1948; Boardman 1999.

78 Cartledge 1983, p. 12; Morel 1984, p. 142; Foxhall 1998, pp. 299, 302–304. The skepticism is increasingly shared by archaeologists, see, for example: Lawall 1998, p. 75; Papadopoulos 2005, pp. 493, 577–578; Dickinson 2006, pp. 199–202.

79 Reed 2004, pp. 368–369.

80 Graham 1982, pp. 158–159; Morel 1984, p. 142; Osborne 1996, p. 31; cf. Foxhall 1998, p. 299; Nantet 2010, pp. 97–102; Hodos 2020, pp. 95–146. On the role of metals in Greek colonization see Treister 1996, pp. 146–181. On the export of timber from Classical Methone see Boufalis (Chapter 20).

81 Morel 1984, p. 142.

82 See, e.g., Lawall 2011a, 2016b. For the terms "transport" and "commercial" amphoras and their use in different languages, see Kotsonas 2012, p. 184.

83 On the history of the study of transport amphoras see Peacock and Williams 1986, pp. 2–3; Gras 1985, pp. 272–278.

84 Davies 2001, p. 18.

85 Bevan 2014; Demesticha and Knapp 2016a; Knapp and Demesticha 2017.

86 On this assemblage see Bessios, Tzifopoulos, and Kotsonas 2012; see also Bessios 2003; Bessios et al. 2004; Bessios, Athanassiadou, and Noulas 2008; Kotsonas 2012; 2015, p. 256; Kotsonas et al. 2017.

87 Cf. Donnellan 2020 on the early amphoras that were produced locally at Pithekoussai.

88 Bessios 2012a, and Chapter 8.

89 Bessios 2012a, and Chapters 8, 9; Kotsonas 2012.

90 Bessios 2012a, pp. 48–57 (with emphasis on the characterization of Phases I–III of the backfilling), and with a shorter description of three more overlying phases. Also, Bessios (Chapter 8) and the Introduction to the present volume. The distinction drawn by Bessios between the two sets of phases finds support in the ongoing study of the fragmentation of the amphoras: fragments from Phases I–III present many joins, which occasionally allow for the reconstruction of complete profiles and the mending of nearly complete vessels. On the contrary, the amphora sherds from the three overlying phases are typically individual and, more rarely, join one or two more sherds. Cross-joins between the original backfilling and the overlying phases are extremely rare and can be explained by taphonomic processes and post-depositional disturbances, especially the decomposition of the rich organic remains (particularly timber) that were part of the backfilling of the Hypogeion. On the significance of different fragmentation patterns of amphoras in successive levels of a single part of a site, see Lawall 2002, p. 208.

91 Peacock and Williams 1986, p. 18.

92 A report on this project is published in Kotsonas et al. 2017. Preliminary notes are offered in Kotsonas 2012, *passim*; 2015, p. 256. The project was supported by funds from the European Union through the Greek Ministry of Education and the Centre for the Greek Language thanks to the unfailing efforts of Yannis Tzifopoulos.

93 However, integrated archaeological and archaeometric research on Greek—especially Late Archaic to Hellenistic—amphoras is flourishing in recent decades, e.g., Johnston and Jones 1978; Dupont 1982; Lawall 1995; Whitbread 1995; Dupont 1998; Lawall 2011a, 2011b. Further references are collected in Kotsonas 2012, p. 280, n. 1016.

94 Canaanite jars: Serpico et al. 2003; Smith et al. 2004. Aegean stirrup jars: Haskell et al. 2011; Day et al. 2011; see also Ben-Shlomo, Nodarou, and Rutter 2011; Kardamaki et al. 2016; Pratt 2016a. Phoenician amphoras: Ballard et al. 2002; Bettles 2003; Gilboa, Waiman-Barak, and Jones 2015; Madrigali and Zara 2018; Schmitt et al. 2018). Roman amphoras: Peacock and Williams 1986; Peña 2007. Also see the project at the University of Southampton "Roman Amphorae: A Digital Resource," http://archaeologydataservice.ac.uk/archives/view/amphora_ahrb_2005/.

95 Cf. Peacock and Williams 1986, pp. 9, 18.

96 Lawall 2016a, p. 221.

97 Archibald 2013, p. 251; cf. Bresson 2016, p. 346.

98 Bresson 2016, p. 346; Johnston 2017; Lawall and Tzochev 2019–2020, p. 118.

99 E.g., Sherratt and Sherratt 1992–1993, p. 371; Dupont 1998; Twede 2002, p. 98; Brun 2003, p. 166; Gras 2010; Denker and Oniz 2015; Demesticha and Knapp 2016b, p. 3. The idea of a (late) 7th-century B.C. introduction applies especially to East Greek transport amphoras, as is evident from their exclusion from Knapp and Demesticha 2017, pp. 132–147.

100 Kotsonas 2012, p. 230; Kotsonas et al. 2017, p. 10, with reference to *Pithekoussai* I; Docter 1997 (Carthage and Toscanos); Fantalkin and Tal 2010 (Israel). Also, an apsidal structure of the late 8th century at Krania in southern Pieria has yielded fine wares and transport amphoras of wide-ranging provenance known from preliminary reports (e.g., Poulaki 2012). I thank the excavator, Efi Poulaki, for permission to examine this material for comparative purposes (see my comments in Kotsonas 2012, pp. 132, 136, 169, 174, 177, 181, 200, 203, 270, n. 720, p. 277, n. 915, p. 278, n. 946, p. 288, n. 1195, with references).

101 Sezgin 2012, pp. 312, 318; Filis 2012a, pp. 266, 271, 273.

102 Bravo 1983; Osborne 1996, pp. 40–41; 1998, p. 258; De Angelis 2002, pp. 304–305.

103 Kotsonas 2012, pp. 150–162, 184–219.

104 Peacock and Williams 1986, pp. 18–19.

105 The reference to no more than five specimens of Thermaic amphoras at Methone in the distribution map in Pratt 2021, p. 236, Map 5.5 is incorrect. Nine specimens have previously been published and a quantity of unpublished material has been reported (Kotsonas 2012, pp. 154–162).

106 Tiverios 1996, pp. 416–417 (shorter references in earlier reports by Tiverios are collected in Kotsonas 2012, p. 262, n. 554); Catling 1998, pp. 166–172. My point that "it is doubtful that a uniform typology (like that of Catling) can cover adequately vessels deriving from different production centers" (Kotsonas 2012, p. 155) is not given due attention by Knapp and Demesticha (2017, p. 146), who note that "Catling (1998) and Kotsonas (2012) see a linear evolution of the north Aegean transport amphora shape."

107 Papadopoulos 2005, p. 576; Gimatzidis 2010, pp. 252–274; Pratt 2021, pp. 226–238.

108 As explained in Kotsonas 2012, pp. 154–155. This terminological profusion is overlooked by Martin Perron (2015, p. 691) when he complains that these amphoras already have a name, "amphores subprotogéométriques et géométriques nord-égéennes de type *Catling* II"; rather than an established convention, this name is his own fusion of four different designations used by different scholars (on which see Kotsonas 2012, pp. 154–155), it is perhaps the longest name applied to an Aegean amphora type, and it has proven unpopular.

109 Kotsonas 2012, pp. 154–159, with further discussion in which the possibility of additional manufacturing centers outside the gulf is not excluded; Kotsonas et al. 2017, pp. 16–18.

110 Catling 1998, pp. 167–171, 176; Tiverios 2012b, p. 180; 2013b, pp. 16–17. Previously Tiverios favored Sindos specifically, see, e.g., Tiverios and Gimatzidis 2000, p. 196; with further references collected in Kotsonas 2012, pp. 158, 261, n. 526.

111 Moschonissioti et al. 2005, pp. 250, 259–260, 264; Kiriatzi, Merousis, and Stefani 2014; Kotsonas et al. 2017, p. 17.

112 Lemos 2012, p. 178, n. 7; Tiverios 2013b, pp. 16–17, nn. 14 and 17; Lawall 2016a, pp. 221–222; Pratt 2016b, p. 198; 2021, pp. 229–230; Kourou 2017, p. 26; Mazarakis Ainian and Alexandridou 2015, p. 424; 2017, pp. 137–138; Knapp and Demesticha 2017, pp. 137–138, 147, 170; Alexandridou 2020, p. 269; Lawall 2021, p. 195.

113 E.g., Perron 2015, p. 691–692.

114 Cases in point include the Samian, Chian, and especially Lesbian type amphoras, which were probably also produced beyond these islands, on coastal western Anatolia (Kotsonas 2012, pp. 194, 201, 205, with references; on the Lesbian amphoras see also Sezgin 2012, pp. 204–207, 321). Among later amphora types, the Mendaian provide another case in point, see Papadopoulos and Paspalas 1999. This is actually why it is probably wiser to refer to, e.g., Samian-type amphoras, rather than Samian amphoras (Kotsonas et al. 2017, p. 9, n. 1).

115 Gimatzidis 2020, p. 251.

116 Gimatzidis (2020, pp. 251–252, n. 39) bases this argument on "the impressive concentration of" these amphoras in Sithonia and the discovery of kiln wasters at Torone, and cites for this Gimatzidis 2010, pp. 263–264, fig. 82, p. 273, fig. 85. However, according to the latter work, only one site in Sithonia has produced any specimens of these amphoras and these remain unpublished (Gimatzidis 2010, pp. 263–264 fig. 82, pp. 374–375). The same work notes that the wasters from Torone do not belong to Thermaic amphoras but to amphoras with belly and shoulder handles (Gimatzidis 2010, p. 273 fig. 85, p. 376). Papadopoulos (1989, pp. 24, 27, 30–31, no. KP-5, fig. 20–21; 2005, pp. 435–436), who published the material from Torone, provides a solid typological analysis of these amphoras with belly and shoulder handles and he does not identify them with the Thermaic amphoras, for good reasons.

117 E.g., Pratt 2021, pp. 229–230, Map 5.2. Others who once entertained this assumption (Gimatzidis 2010, p. 264) have lately abandoned it (Gimatzidis 2020, p. 251, n. 37).

118 Aslan, Kealhofer, and Grave 2014, pp. 286, 306, nos. 15–16: "Protogeometric or Geometric"; if the former, the vessels do not belong to the type in question.

119 This piece "is close to the local D-Troy [elemental] group" (Mommsen, Hertel, and Mountjoy 2001, pp. 195–196 (no. 118); on skepticism about the analytical results for this piece, see Gimatzidis 2010, p. 264; 2020, p. 251, n. 37; Kotsonas 2012, pp. 159, 261, n. 532.

120 Cf. the petrographic and elemental analysis by Kiriatzi and her collaborators on examples from around the Thermaic Gulf (Moschonissioti et al. 2005; Kiriatzi, Merousis, and Stefani 2014; Kotsonas et al. 2017, pp. 16–18).

121 References in Kotsonas 2012, p. 155. For a few new specimens from Troy and possibly from a few other sites in the Troad, see Aslan 2019, pp. 214–215, 255, 320, nos. 263–265. There is no published estimate of the minimum number of such amphoras found in Troy. The largest group of published specimens is the 30 sherds published in Lenz et al. 1998, pp. 204–206, not all of which represent individual vessels. Note that several hundred sherds from these amphoras have been found in the Hypogeion of Methone and in a single deposit at Iolkos, Thessaly (Catling 1998, 169), despite the fact that vessels of the type were not manufactured in either site. It is also worth noting that in Troy, Thermaic amphoras are much more uncommon than the earlier but related amphora types, of which nearly 200 specimens have been identified; Trojan production for these earlier types is much better grounded (Aslan, Kealhofer, and Grave 2014, esp. p. 285).

122 Aslan 2019, p. 258.
123 Tiverios and Gimatzidis 2000, p. 196; Chatzis 2010, p. 174; Gimatzidis 2010, pp. 268–269; 2011, p. 962; Tiverios 2012b, pp. 178–181; 2013b, pp. 16–17.
124 Tiverios 2013b, p. 17.
125 According to this approach, these vessels are "northern Greek wares" and "of north Greek origin," they circulated under "Greek auspices" (Gimatzidis 2011, p. 962), and they are "the earliest Greek amphorae" (Anagnostopoulou-Chatzipolychroni and Gimatzidis 2009, p. 373).
126 Kotsonas 2012, pp. 159–161, 232–237; 2013; 2020, pp. 304–305; cf. Dickinson 2006, pp. 207–208. On the notion of Euboiocentrism see Papadopoulos 2005, 252; Kotsonas 2013; 2020, pp. 301–305.
127 Lawall 2010; 2016a, pp. 217–218.
128 See, e.g., Heurtley 1939, p. 132; Hammond 1972, p. 132; Tiverios 1993, pp. 1488–1492; Chatzis 2010, pp. 184–185; Gimatzidis 2010, pp. 268–269; 2011, pp. 961–963; Soueref 2011, pp. 325–340.
129 Gimatzidis 2011, p. 962; cf. 2010, p. 269.
130 Papadopoulos 1996, p. 158; 2005, p. 577; 2021b, p. 429; cf. Dickinson 2006, pp. 207–208.
131 Van Dommelen 2005; Hodos 2006; Malkin 2009, p. 378; 2011; Dietler 2010; Broodbank 2013, pp. 482–495, 506–556; Donnellan 2016. More broadly, on postcolonialism, see Lyons and Papadopoulos 2002; Stein 2005a, 2005b.
132 Kotsonas 2012, pp. 159–161, 232–237; 2020, pp. 304–305; Kotsonas et al. 2017, pp. 16–18.
133 Kotsonas 2012, pp. 161, 234, 235; cf. 2020, pp. 304–305; Kotsonas et al. 2017, pp. 16–18.
134 As noted in Kotsonas 2012, pp. 161–162, 235–236, with references; on other aspects of the marks on these amphorae see Gimatzidis 2010, pp. 264–266; Pratt 2021, pp. 231-232. For early writing on amphoras see especially Johnston 2004. For the evidence from Methone see Bessios, Tzifopoulos, and Kotsonas 2012; Tzifopoulos 2012b.
135 Kotsonas 2012, pp. 159–161, 232–237; 2020, pp. 304–305; Kotsonas et al. 2017, pp. 16–18.
136 Tiverios (2013b, p. 16) has criticized me for "doubting the connection of these amphorae to the Euboians." However, my text actually reads: "I consider that these finds suggest the involvement of amphorae of this type in Euboian and other trade networks" (Kotsonas 2012, p. 159); and also: "The argument for the identification of the active role of indigenous people in trade in the Thermaic Gulf and more generally in Macedonia does not disregard the role of the Euboians" (Kotsonas 2012, p. 236).
137 As observed keenly in Saripanidi 2017, pp. 73, 87, n. 101.
138 Morgan 2013–2014, p. 35; Mazarakis Ainian and Alexandridou 2015, pp. 425–426; 2017, pp. 137–138; Alexandridou 2020, p. 271; Andreou 2020, pp. 924–926; Pratt 2021, pp. 241–242.
139 Mazarakis Ainian and Alexandridou 2015, pp. 425–426; 2017, pp. 137–138; Alexandridou 2020, p. 271.
140 See e.g. Gimatzidis (2020, p. 246), and compare his earlier statements cited in n. 125 above.
141 Klug 2013.
142 Lawall 2016b, pp. 269, 271.
143 Catling 1998, pp. 154–164, 171–177; Papadopoulos 2005, pp. 429–430; Gimatzidis 2010, pp. 253–258; Aslan 2019, pp. 213–215, 313–315, nos. 212–222; Knapp and Demesticha 2017, pp. 133–135; Pratt 2021, pp. 226–238.
144 Kotsonas 2012, pp. 205–209, with references; Kotsonas et al. 2017, pp. 13–15. The red series of Lesbian amphoras is not represented. For other recent studies of early Lesbian amphoras see *Histria* XV, pp. 25–35; Filis 2012b, pp. 314–316; Sezgin 2012, pp. 201–243.
145 Kotsonas 2012, pp. 205, with references; also, Sezgin 2012, pp. 204–207, 321.
146 Kotsonas et al. 2017, pp. 13–14.
147 Herodotus 1.151.2; cf. Spencer 1995a, p. 289.

148 Kotsonas 2012, pp. 194–199; for other recent studies of early Samian amphoras see *Histria* XV, pp. 145–162; Filis 2012a, pp. 272–273, 276; 2012b, p. 312; Sezgin 2012, pp. 177–199.

149 Kotsonas 2012, pp. 201–205, with references; Kotsonas et al. 2017, pp. 11–13. For other recent studies of early Chian amphoras see *Histria* XV, pp. 49–90; Filis 2012a, pp. 266–268, 276; 2012b, p. 310; Sezgin 2012, pp. 83–135. In the Hypogeion, Chian amphoras are the only type that is thinly represented in Phases I–III, but it becomes considerably more common in the overlying phases. For later Archaic Chian amphoras from elsewhere at Methone see Bessios and Noulas 2012, p. 402; Kasseri (Chapter 21).

150 One piece of the undecorated type is published in Kotsonas 2012, pp. 199–201, no. 126. For pieces of the Byblos type (on which see Bîrzescu 2009), see Kotsonas 2012, pp. 150–154; for other recent studies of early Milesian amphoras see *Histria* XV, pp. 127–143; Filis 2012a, pp. 273–274, 276; 2012b, p. 312; Sezgin 2012, pp. 139–173. On the basis of very preliminary analytical results (explicitly identified as such), these vessels were first ascribed to a Milesian type *possibly* manufactured locally at Methone, hence the term "Methonaian," with the quotation marks expressing uncertainty (see Kotsonas 2012, pp. 150–151). Actual Milesian production was established later in 2012 with further study of the petrographic thin sections (Kiriatzi et al. 2012; Kiriatzi et al. 2015; Kotsonas et al. 2017, p. 9, n. 1).

151 Kotsonas 2012, pp. 197–198, 200, 203, 208; Filis 2014, pp. 244–247.

152 Kotsonas 2012, pp. 201–205, with references; Kotsonas et al. 2017, pp. 15–16. On SOS amphoras see also Pratt 2015 (the reference to the discovery of ca. 30 SOS amphoras at Methone in Pratt 2015, pp. 222, 234 does not reflect the MNI of the pieces from the Hypogeion). Filis (2014, pp. 235–238) discusses finds from the north Aegean.

153 Kotsonas 2012, pp. 188–194 (no. 110 is Euboian). On the production of Euboian SOS amphoras in Chalkis see Charalambidou 2020, pp. 60–62. For such finds in the north Aegean see Kotsonas 2012, pp. 191–192; Filis 2014, p. 236, n. 15.

154 Kotsonas 2012, pp. 192–193.

155 Kotsonas 2012, p. 187; Filis 2012b, p. 316; Manakidou 2018, p. 189, n. 12. For recent studies of early Corinthian amphoras see *Histria* XV, 187–193; Knapp and Demesticha 2017, pp. 140–142. Filis (2014, pp. 238–240) discusses early finds from the north Aegean.

156 One piece is published in Kotsonas 2012, pp. 186–188, no. 103.

157 Bessios 2012, p. 59; for a selection of Corinthian fine wares from Methone, see Chapters 1, 9, 19.

158 Kotsonas 2012, pp. 232–239, with references; Tiverios 2012a, p. 70. On Phoenician amphoras see Bettles 2003; Waiman-Barak and Gilboa 2016.

159 On the pieces from Methone see Bessios 2003, p. 449; Athanassiadou 2012, p. 161, nos. 109–110; Kasseri 2012; Kotsonas 2012, p. 238. For Torone, see Fletcher 2008. On the amphoras from Kommos, see Bikai 2000; Gilboa, Waiman-Barak and Jones 2015.

160 For these identifications see Kotsonas 2012, p. 238; Tiverios 2012a.

161 Popham 1994, p. 30; cf. Dickinson 2006, p. 214. The Phoenician amphoras from Methone challenge the assertion that such vessels are conspicuously absent from the Greek mainland (Martin 2016, p. 123; Knapp and Demesticha 2017, p. 103).

162 Pratt 2015, pp. 231–232, referring to Shefton 1982. Cf. Pratt 2016b, p. 208.

163 Bessios, Tzifopoulos, and Kotsonas 2012, pp. 349–350, no. 6, pp. 371–372, no. 24 (the latter piece is of late 7th or early 6th century B.C. date); Kotsonas 2012, pp. 193–194 (which includes reference to an Attic SOS amphora from nearby Mende with a Cypriot syllabic inscription). On the uncertainties over the role(s) of the persons whose names are inscribed on SOS amphoras, see Tiverios 2000.

164 Kotsonas 2012, pp. 209–219.

165 Kotsonas 2012, pp. 200–213.

166	Docter 2000, pp. 70–72; Kotsonas 2012, pp. 210–212; Johnston 2017, p. 125. It would be worth exploring the relation of these amphoras with the late 7th and 6th century B.C. Ionian black-glazed amphoras from Belsk (ancient Gelonos?) in the Black Sea (Petropoulos 2005, p. 50, with references).
167	Kotsonas 2012, pp. 165–167, no. 89 (Attic); pp. 169–172, no. 90 (Cycladic).
168	Inscribed examples are discussed in Kotsonas 2012, pp. 214–216, nos. 15 and 149–153.
169	Johnston 1993, pp. 371–372.
170	For overviews of the range of evidence on amphora content see: Lawall 1995, pp. 1–2; 2011a, pp. 24–25; Whitbread 1995, pp. 37–38; Sourisseau 1997, pp. 268–270; Kotsonas 2012, pp. 85–86.
171	Lawall 1995, p. 1, n. 3. For a notable exception see Hansson and Foley 2008; Foley et al. 2012.
172	Gras 2010, p. 111.
173	Kotsonas et al. 2017.
174	Valamoti et al. 2018, pp. 275–276, 280–282; Valamoti, Gkatzogia, and Ntinou 2018. See also: Borza 1995, pp. 45–46; Millett 2010, pp. 482–483; Archibald 2013, pp. 285–287; Faklaris and Stamatopoulou 2021; Pratt 2021, pp. 36, 202.
175	Valamoti, Gkatzogia, and Ntinou 2018.
176	On Roumpou's analysis see Kotsonas et al. 2017, pp. 12–13. On Chian amphoras as wine containers see, e.g., Sourisseau 1997, pp. 133, 136; Dupont 1998, pp. 148, 151; Filis 2012b, p. 319. Further references in Kotsonas 2012, pp. 205, 293, n. 1341.
177	Hansson and Foley 2008; Foley et al. 2012, p. 391.
178	Whitbread 1995, p. 38; Lawall 2011a, pp. 23–25; 2011b, pp. 43–45; 2016b, p. 216; Kotsonas 2012, p. 186. On amphora reuse see especially: Peña 2007, pp. 61–192; Lawall 2011b; Abdelhamid 2013.
179	Kotsonas et al. 2017, pp. 14–15.
180	Clinkenbeard 1982, pp. 254–256. Further references in Kotsonas 2012, pp. 208–209, 295, n. 1409.
181	Possibly a false etymology, based on the Greek word for drink/drunkenness (μέθυ): Chapter 2, nn. 6–7 (for other possible origins of the name of Methone, see the Introduction).
182	On the archaeobotanical remains, see Valamoti et al. 2018, pp. 276–277. On the limited textual evidence for wine production in ancient Macedonia see Borza 1995, p. 46; Millett 2010, p. 483, n. 40; Vasileiadou 2011, pp. 128–130. On wine from Chalkidike see Papadopoulos and Paspalas 1999; Bresson 2016, pp. 370–371.
183	Bessios, Tzifopoulos, and Kotsonas 2012; Tzifopoulos 2012b; Murray 2016, p. 21; McInerney 2018, pp. 115–116.
184	Kotsonas et al. 2017, pp. 16–18.
185	Margomenou and Roumpou 2011.
186	Pratt 2015, pp. 217–218.
187	Bessios, Tzifopoulos, and Kotsonas 2012; Kotsonas 2012.
188	Pithekoussai: *Pithekoussai* I; Greco 1994; Bartoněk and Buchner 1995. Kommos: Callaghan and Johnston 2000; Csapo, Johnston, and Geagan 2000; Johnston 2005.
189	See also Vasileiadou 2011; Tsiafaki 2020, pp. 412–413.

13

METALLURGICAL ACTIVITY AT METHONE:
THE EVIDENCE OF THE STONE ARTIFACTS FROM THE HYPOGEION

Ioannis Manos and Ioannis Vlastaridis

Stone artifacts on archaeological sites are instrumental in understanding the exploitation of the environment by humans. They also play a central role in the domestic and industrial processes of commodities production. As vehicles of manufacture and use-related technology, these artifacts require artisans with specialized knowledge of both manufacture and use. Such knowledge and techniques signal technological homogeneity and inhomogeneity, continuities and discontinuities in space and time.[1]

STRATIGRAPHIC BACKGROUND

The present study included 86 stone macroartifacts from the Hypogeion at Methone, of which 18 are catalogued below. Several of these objects were manufactured with various methods of the carved stone technology; others were used in their natural form. The assemblage is distributed in archaeological deposits of up to 11.70 m in depth (Fig. 13.1a–b; see also Fig. 1.5). The large pit known as the Hypogeion—measuring 3.60 x 4.20 m at its floor—was dug by anthropogenic processes that took place at one time. According to the excavators, the construction dates from the end of the Geometric period (Chapters 8–9).[2]

Several phases have been distinguished for the filling-in of the Hypogeion.[3] The deposits of the earliest phase, collectively Phases I–III (fill A), date mainly from the first period of the colonization of Methone (720–700/690 B.C.). The fill of the first post–Phase III context, located between Walls T.14 and T.5, was deposited in the first half of the 7th century B.C. (fill B). However, the filling-in of this artificial pit and the buildup of the archaeological deposits feature an important peculiarity: on the one hand, the walls of the pit defined the surface of the horizontal scatter and limited depositional activity in these confines; on the other hand, the volume of accumulations and the depth of the pit created gravitational forces that contributed to the post-depositional alteration of the archaeological layers. In Phases I–III, together with the first post–Phase III level, the buildup of deposits and the disposal of archaeological finds took place, by necessity, within the defined and limited space of the pit. By contrast, depositional and taphonomic processes differ in the uppermost phases, when portions of above-ground debris shifted vertically into the pit due to natural processes. The finds in this fill were thus trapped in the pit, where they were excavated in closed space conditions. Consequently, the lithic assemblage associated with the upper phases belongs to the toolkit of activities that were taking place on utility floors above ground.

ARTIFACT DISTRIBUTION

The vertical distribution of artifacts within the Hypogeion was calculated by grouping and projecting the macro-artifacts onto conventional stratigraphic horizons of half-meter depth (Fig. 13.1a). The projection of the finds on the stratigraphic section verifies the excavators' observations regarding the differentiated filling in of the pit.

Five objects are distributed in the lowest context, Phase I, a uniform stratum that was filled within a very short time according to the excavators. Dominant in this stratum is a layer of greenish clay containing many bricks of unbaked clay and unworked stones; organic remains of timber beams and part of a pithos embedded in a greenish layer of dissolved clay bricks were also recorded (see further, Chapter 8).[4] All lithic finds were located at the 0.00–0.70 m excavation level (measured from the bottom of the pit), mainly in the earliest deposits. This group is stratigraphically distinct from the rest of the stone artifacts in the Hypogeion.

A two-meter-thick intermediate fill, devoid of stone macroartifacts, lies between the finds of Phase I and those of the subsequent Phase II. Two objects belong to Phase II. Approximately two meters thick, the Phase II stratum is characterized by very rapid deposition and by the strong presence of organic remains, predominantly wood. Phase II is sealed by a clay layer which clearly divides it from the superimposed stratigraphic Phase III. The excavators note that the clay layer possibly belonged to Phase III, an interpretation supported by the vertical distribution of the stone finds: six artifacts were directly associated with the clay layer and they all belong to Phase III.

Phase III, approximately four meters thick, includes a total of 43 objects—the most abundant lithic group in the Hypogeion. Stratigraphically, this phase differs significantly from the preceding Phase II; here, artifacts and organic materials were deposited in layers within the brown-hued soil of the fill. Phase III is stratigraphically homogenous, consisting mainly of successive clay layers of different thickness. There is a distinct uniformity in the vertical distribution of the macro-artifacts. Thirty-five out of 43 stone items were stratified with the same density,[5] across a fill thickness of about three meters. In addition, 11 out of the 12 igneous rocks (being the hardest and most percussion- and heat-resistant among the utilized lithic raw material) found in the Hypogeion were distributed evenly in the stratigraphy of Phase III.[6] The same phase (III) contains 11 out of the 18 macro-artifacts of sandstone (the raw material that lends itself well to grinding), which likewise exhibit a regular vertical distribution in the stratigraphy.[7]

The first of the post–Phase III deposits, approximately two meters thick, is enclosed between Walls T.14 and T.5 (fill B). These higher archaeological levels contained only eleven artifacts, the vertical distribution of which differs significantly from that of the preceding Phase III in terms of quantity and density. Firstly, there is a sharp decrease in quantity: whereas seven items were encountered in the half-meter horizon below Wall T.14, only three were present in the half-meter horizon directly above the same wall, and just one was found under Wall T.5. Secondly, there are no igneous rocks in this phase.

The uppermost of the deposits included 16 items (fill C). Of these, five come from the same stratigraphic horizon as Wall T.5. The other eleven are located at a level one meter above Wall T.5, within the fill that had shifted deep into the pit.

Ten artifacts in the assemblage bear clear traces of heat-induced stress and deterioration. Seven of these come from the deposits of Phase III, the other three from the occupation levels of the uppermost phase. The intensity of damage differs across the surface of an object; areas that were directly exposed to the source of heat have suffered heavier wear. According to macroscopic observation, heatproof objects dating to chronologically earlier cultural phases

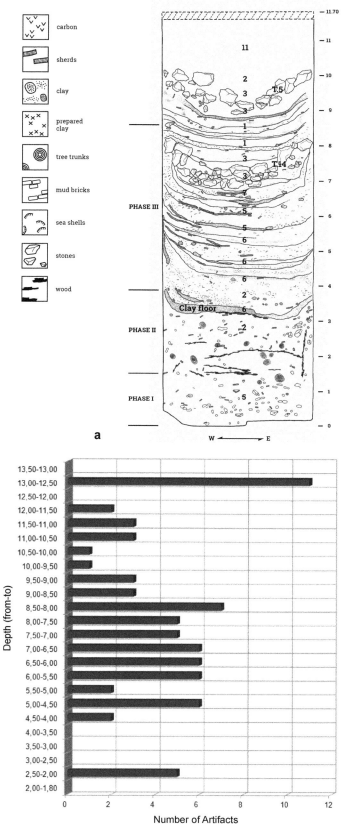

FIGURE 13.1. a) Stratigraphic projection of stone macroartifacts from the Hypogeion at Methone (numbers indicate the quantity of lithic macroartifacts in each successive level). Drawing: I. Moschou; b) histogram showing the number of macrolithic objects by depth. Prepared by I. Manos

(Neolithic and Bronze Age) that have been documented from the Hypogeion were intentionally used as building material in pyrotechnical installations (e.g., **13/1** [MEΘ 242], Fig. 13.2).[8] The damage on stone artifacts is caused not only by the intensity and duration of the heat but also by the mode of their application. Vitrified clay mass in the area of the pyrotechnical installations bears additional testimony to the high temperatures that developed therein.

RAW MATERIALS

Taking together all the stone objects from the Hypogeion, not just those catalogued here, the raw materials include igneous rocks; fine- and coarse-grained sedimentary rocks; metamorphic rocks, such as marble, serpentinite, and amphibolite; minerals including quartz; and undiagnostic materials. Twenty objects were used in their natural form as pebbles, without any ergonomic shaping. Half of these pebbles, ten in all, cluster in Phase III—especially from a depth of 4.70 m up to Wall T.14—while six others constitute the main morphological type in the occupation stratum of the uppermost phase. In contrast, the 27 artifacts in the shape of plaques are distributed over the entire depth of the Hypogeion.

The combined methods of techno-functional analysis of the worked-stone assemblage, macroscopic observation, and classification of wear-traces according to relative chronology point to the operation of a metallurgical and metalsmithing workshop in the area of the Hypogeion, one that heavily renewed and recycled the stone components of its tool arsenal.

THE TECHNOLOGY OF METALWORKING

The *chaîne opératoire* of metallurgical activity has two principal phases: a) metal extraction and b) metal processing, both of which have been analyzed and studied by many scholars.[9] Metal extraction involves voluminous and heavy raw material (ore), abundant fuel, and, depending on the metal, quantities of water. For these reasons, metal extraction usually takes place at a short distance from the metalliferous geological formation. In contrast, metal processing is usually directly related to political authority—in the case of weapons—or to a consumer market—in the case of utilitarian or ritual objects. As a result, metalwork takes place in controlled or accessible centers, according to the circumstances of production.[10]

Metal extraction can take the form of low-intensity activity, which involves the crumbling and smelting of small quantities of ore on site (**13/2** [MEΘ 257], Fig. 13.3). The processing phase includes a series of individual stages, such as hammering, annealing, grinding, smoothing, decoration, and dehumidification. The stages differ according to the metal or metal alloy, and they are repeated in relatively different sequences. Casting is one of the initial processing options (**13/3** [MEΘ 606], Fig. 13.4).

Hammering achieves better material uniformity and creates very thin objects. The necessary infrastructure is limited to an open pyrotechnical installation made of fireproof materials, and a hammering kit consisting of passive and active tools. The percussion surfaces of passive tools vary from convex (**13/4** [MEΘ 565], Fig. 13.5) to concave, flat, cylindrical (**13/5** [MEΘ 567], Fig. 13.6), or conical (**13/6** [MEΘ 589], **13/7** [MEΘ 590], Fig. 13.7). Raw materials can be as diverse as metal, stone, hard wood, or even earth and sand into which the desirable cavity is created, by way of a mold for the shaping of the metal (**13/5**, Fig. 13.6). Both unique items and multifunctional implements (with different surfaces and capabilities) are used as passive objects. Active tools likewise show great variety, with active surfaces of spherical (**13/8** [MEΘ 1110], Fig. 13.8), slightly convex (**13/9** [MEΘ 563], Fig. 13.9), or flat (**13/10** [MEΘ 2814], Fig. 13.10) shape.

The shaping of metal can also be achieved by applying indirect pressure on the surface under treatment, with the help of appropriate tools. During processing, the metal surface is repeatedly ground and smoothed, especially after every annealing, in order to remove the oxides that were released during heating and to even out the surface. Grinding and smoothing are done with stone tools, preferably of sandstone or andesite. The granulation of the stone determines the stage of the application of the tool: coarse-grained artifacts are employed at the initial stages (**13/11** [MEΘ 269], Fig. 13.11), while the fine-grained ones are used at the final stages of work (**13/12** [MEΘ 194], Fig. 13.12). Clay is also used for grinding and smoothing; pottery sherds possibly served this purpose, after they had been crumbled and pulverized with a stone pounder (such as **13/5** [MEΘ 567], Fig. 13.6). In addition, the abundance of clay molds (most likely associated with the lost-wax technique) points to the use of fine-grained and well-levigated clay, easily and quickly obtainable from pottery sherds,[11] as material for their manufacture. Clay further serves as intermediate material between a metal object and a stone grinder, and as an abrasive in the manufacture of active tools. For the latter task, clay is moistened and mixed with materials of equivalent granulation and hardness, such as ground quartz and marble. Marble pebbles were used as cores for the detachment of flakes and the production of chips. Eighteen unshaped quartz flakes, devoid of any tool-working traces, were found; they may have provided the raw material for the production of quartz chips by means of crushing. The mixture of clay and quartz or marble is rolled and shaped into a clay mass, then left to dry and harden (**13/13** [MEΘ 1117], Fig. 13.13). The grinding and smoothing of the metal object are usually carried out with the help of a liquid, which lubricates the two surfaces of friction and prevents rises in temperature. This liquid can be water that is either used intermittently to moisten the artifact or placed in a container or pit, in which the metal object or the stone grinder and polisher were immersed.

The final smoothing is followed by the decoration of the surface. Among the many different decorative techniques, repoussé and incision are especially distinctive, and they both involve an array of direct and indirect tools. The main tool for indirect- or direct-impact decoration is an elongated stone artifact, at the active extremity of which the head is pointed (**13/14** [MEΘ 210], Fig. 13.14), or edged and flat with central longitudinal groove (**13/15** [MEΘ 543], Fig. 13.14), or elliptical/hemispherical (**13/16** [MEΘ 2991], **13/17** [MEΘ 2521/1278], Fig. 13.14). The presence of metal cutters, awls, and knives with small active surfaces is inferred by the traces left by such implements on the stone tools that were used to sharpen them (**13/18** [MEΘ 529], Fig. 13.15).

Finally, the metal artifact is placed in a dehumidifying medium, such as wood chips, in order to shed the humidity that was accumulated during manufacture or repair.

The interpretation of the worked stone assemblage from the Hypogeion points to the toolkit of a workshop. These tools were mainly used for the tasks of percussion and grinding, which were practiced with marked intensity in Phase III (Late Geometric to ca. 690 B.C.).

CATALOGUE

13/1. (ΜΕΘ 242 [ΜΕ 106]) Axe   Fig. 13.2
East Hill #274/022008 [5].
L. 0.072; W. 0.044; Th. 0.028; Wt. 169 g.
Amphibolite.
Neolithic axe reused as building material in a pyrotechnical installation.

13/2. (ΜΕΘ 257 [ΜΕ 180]) Pebble   Fig. 13.3
East Hill #274/022009 [5].
L. 0.118; p.W. 0.075; p. Th. 0.064; Wt. 806 g.
Marble.
Pebble with percussion-induced cavities, repurposed to produce marble chips.

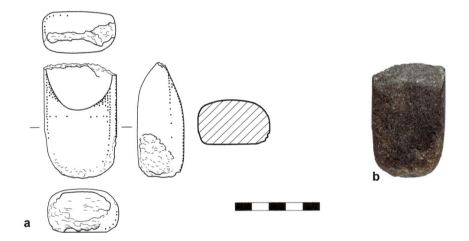

FIGURE 13.2. a) Drawing of Neolithic axe, **13/1** (ΜΕΘ 242); b) two views of **13/1**, made of amphibolite showing prominent traces of heat-induced substance deterioration and surface wear; used as building material in a pyrotechnical installation. Drawing A. Hooton, photo J. Vanderpool

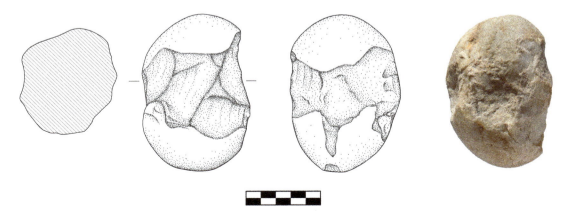

FIGURE 13.3. Marble pebble, **13/2** (ΜΕΘ 257) with percussion-induced cavities around the circumference, as a result of its use in the crumbling of ore. The pebble was repurposed to produce marble chips.
Drawing T. Ross, photo J. Vanderpool

13/3. (ΜΕΘ 606 [ME 755]) Funnel Fig. 13.4
East Hill #274/022044 [11].
L. 0.098; W. 0.075; Th. 0.063; Wt. 347 g.
Pyroclastic rock.
Stone, with funnel-shaped opening, with thermal traces on the funnel interior and around exit hole indicating the smelting of metal.

13/4. (ΜΕΘ 565 [ME 1108]) Hammering Tool Fig. 13.5
East Hill #274/022. Associated with Wall T.14.
L. 0.078; W. 0.038; Th. 0.022; Wt. 98 g.
Marble.
Passive hammering tool.
Cf., among others, Donnart 2007, p. 16, fig. 4, various examples.

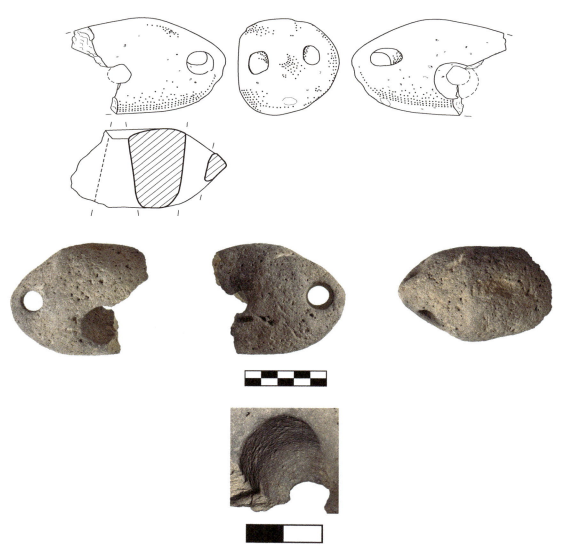

FIGURE 13.4. Stone object, **13/3** (ΜΕΘ 606), made from a pyroclastic rock, with perforation through one edge, and a large funnel-shaped opening in the body. Strong thermal traces on the funnel interior and around the exit hole indicate the smelting of metal. Drawing A. Hooton, photos J. Vanderpool

Figure 13.5. Passive hammering tool, **13/4** (MEΘ 565), made of marble, with convex surface.
Drawing T. Ross, photos J. Vanderpool

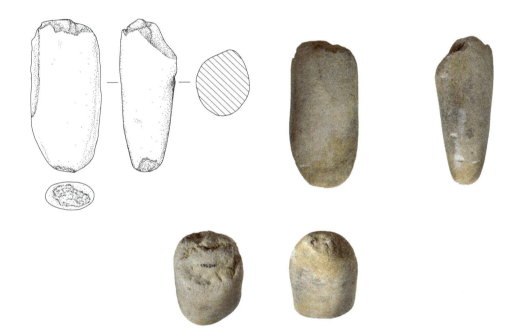

Figure 13.6. A multifunctional tool, **13/5** (MEΘ 567): marble pestle preserving remnants of compacted fine-grained clay and percussion spots on its lower, rounded end; percussion spots are also visible at the shaped edge of the upper end. This tool is applied to a two-step task: ceramic sherds or dried clay are first crumbled with the upper end of the tool, then pulverized with the lower end.
Drawing T. Ross, photos J. Vanderpool

13/5. (MEΘ 567 [ME 734]) Pestle/Percussion Tool Fig. 13.6
East Hill #274/022042 [10].
P.L. 0.105; W. 0.017; Th. 0.037; Wt. 283 g.
Marble.
Pestle, preserving remnants of compacted fine-grained clay and percussion spots. Used to crumble ceramic sherds or dried clay with the upper end, then to pulverize with the opposite end.
Cf. Donnart 2007, p. 13, fig. 3, no. 4; p. 19, fig. 5, various examples.

13/6. (ΜΕΘ 589 [ME 1512]) Hammering Tool Fig. 13.7
East Hill #274/032074 [7].
L. 0.087; Diam./W. (max) 0.043; Wt. 220 g.
Amphibolite.
Passive hammering tool.

13/7. (ΜΕΘ 590 [ME 1513]) Hammering Tool Fig. 13.7
East Hill #274/032074 [7].
L. 0.074; Diam./W. (max) 0.046; Wt. 173 g.
Amphibolite.
Passive hammering tool.

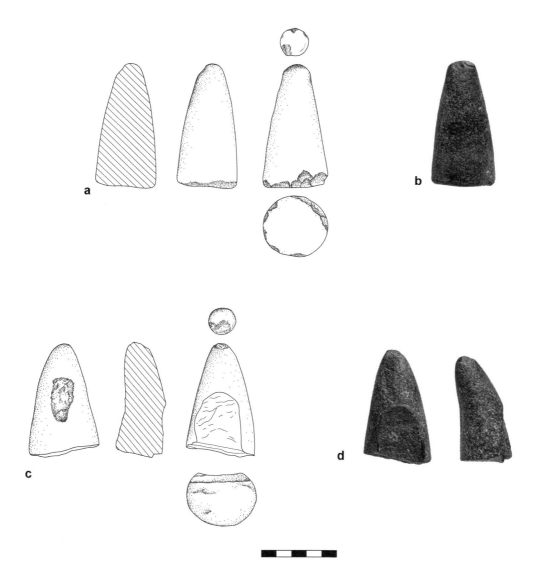

FIGURE 13.7. Passive hammering tools: a)–b) **13/6** (ΜΕΘ 589) and c)–d) **13/7** (ΜΕΘ 590), both made of amphibolite, with convex, flat, and conical surfaces. Drawings T. Ross, photos J. Vanderpool

13/8. (ΜΕΘ 1110 [ΜΕ 2970]) Percussion Tool Fig. 13.8
East Hill #274/022.
Diam. 0.069; Th. 0.029.
Marble.
With spherical active surfaces.

13/9. (ΜΕΘ 563 [ΜΕ 1276]) Percussion Tool Fig. 13.9
East Hill #274/022054 [12].
P.L. 0.032; W./p.W. 0.032; Th. 0.040; Wt. 79 g.
Amphibolite.
Prominent perforation, with slightly convex active surfaces.

13/10. (ΜΕΘ 2814 [ΜΕ 3545]) Percussion Tool Fig. 13.10
East Hill #274/032090 [10].
P.L. 0.057; p.W. 0.052; p.Th. 0.026; Wt. 180 g.
Amphibolite.
Prominent, but partially preserved, perforation, with flat active surfaces.

13/11. (ΜΕΘ 269 [ΜΕ 307]) Recycled Quern Fig. 13.11
East Hill #274/032008 [3].
L. 0.205; W. 0.124; Th. 0.030.
Diorite.
Form suggests a recycled Neolithic quern/millstone, reused for metalworking, with both the flat and convex surfaces used. One end (bottom as shown) shaped as a handle for hand-grip.

FIGURE 13.8. Marble percussion tool, **13/8** (ΜΕΘ 1110), with spherical active surfaces.
Drawing A. Hooton, photos J. Vanderpool

FIGURE 13.9. Amphibolite percussion tool, **13/9** (MEΘ 563) with slightly convex active surfaces. Drawing T. Ross, photos J. Vanderpool

FIGURE 13.10. Amphibolite percussion tool, **13/10** (MEΘ 2814) with flat active surfaces. Drawing T. Ross, photos J. Vanderpool

13/12. (MEΘ 194 [ME 194]) Polisher/Whetstone Fig. 13.12
East Hill #274/022018 [7].
P.L. 0.050; W. 0.030; Th. 0.017; Wt. 31 g.
Siltstone.
Traces of metal on the surface, suggesting use in the late stages of grinding/polishing.

13/13. (MEΘ 1117 [ME 3012]) Tool to Smooth Cylindrical Surfaces Fig. 13.13
East Hill #274/022058 [12].
P.L. 0.083; p.W. 0.051; Th. (max) 0.042; Wt. 177 g.
Clay mass.
The active surface is concave and semi-cylindrical, with clear traces of use wear. The tool was used to smooth cylindrical surfaces.

13/14. (MEΘ 210 [ME 302]) Tool for Decorating Metal Surfaces Fig. 13.14
East Hill #274/032008 [3].
L. 0.061; Th./Diam. 0.015.
Tuff (a light porous rock formed by consolidation of volcanic ash).
Tool used for the decoration of metal surfaces.

13/15. (MEΘ 543 [ME 1063]) Tool for Decorating Metal Surfaces Fig. 13.14
East Hill #274/032050 [7].
L./p.L. 0.072; W. 0.017; Th. 0.014; Wt. 38 g.
Undetermined stone.
Tool used for the decoration of metal surfaces.

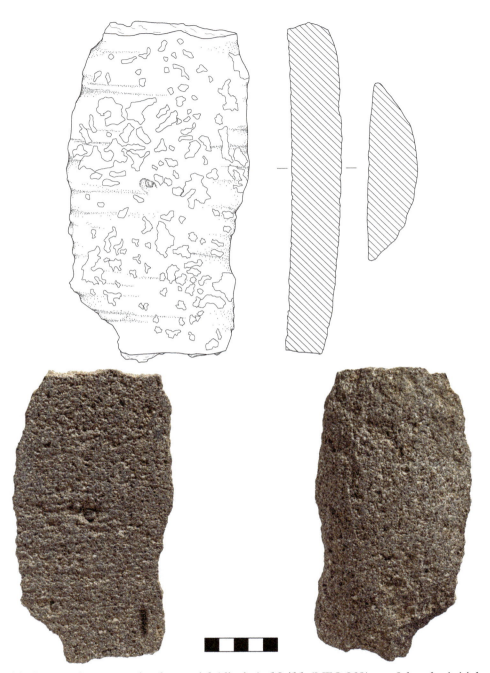

FIGURE 13.11. Quern of coarse-grained material (diorite), **13/11** (ΜΕΘ 269), useful at the initial stages of grinding. Its form points to a recycled Neolithic millstone; however, the tool was manufactured from the beginning for metal-grinding(?) purposes. Both the flat and the convex surfaces were used, depending on the needs of the surface to be ground. One end (visible in the lower part of the photograph) was shaped as a handle for hand-grip. Drawing T. Ross, photos J. Vanderpool

13/16. (ΜΕΘ 1080 [ΜΕ 2991]) Tool for Decorating Metal Surfaces   Fig. 13.14
    East Hill #274/022.
    L. 0.070; W, 0.014; Th. 0.012; Wt. 26 g.
    Sandstone.
    Partial perforation at one end, as shown. Tool used for the decoration of metal surfaces.

FIGURE 13.12. Polisher/whetstone **13/12** (ΜΕΘ 194) of fine-grained material (siltstone), useful at the late stages of grinding; traces of metal on the surface. Drawing T. Ross, photos J. Vanderpool

FIGURE 13.13. Clay mass formation containing inclusions of crushed quartz, **13/13** (ΜΕΘ 1117). The active surface is concave and semi-cylindrical, a solid triangular lug/handle rises at the convex ridge of the unworked exterior(?). The traces of use wear run parallel to the axis of the cavity and to the handle section/profile(?). Within the worked cavity, the silicate inclusions have been smoothed and reduced by grinding to the level of the clay surface. A sediment of fine-grained clay, remnant of the grinding process, is visible at the upper right side of the photograph. This synthetic tool was used to smooth cylindrical surfaces. Drawing A. Hooton, photos J. Vanderpool

13/17. (ΜΕΘ 532 [ΜΕ 1278]) Tool for Decorating Metal Surfaces Fig. 13.14
  East Hill #274/022/054 [12].
  L. 0.070; Th. 0.027; Th. 0.006.
  Schist.
  Tool used for the decoration of metal surfaces.

13/18. (ΜΕΘ 529 [ΜΕ 699]) Multi-purpose Tool Fig. 13.15
  East Hill #274/022.
  P.L. 0.090; W. 0.081; Th. (max) 0.022; Wt. 214 g.
  Fine-grained, undetermined stone.
  A passive multi-purpose tool, used as polisher, convex/concave mold for shaping metal, and whetstone for metal cutting tools. Both surfaces display traces of exposure to intense heat.

FIGURE 13.14. Tools used for the decoration of metal surfaces: **13/14** (MEΘ 210, made of tuff), **13/15** (MEΘ 543, undetermined stone), **13/16** (MEΘ 1080, sandstone), **13/17** (MEΘ 532, schist). Drawings A. Hooton and T. Ross, photos J. Vanderpool

FIGURE 13.15. Fine-grained raw material (of unknown stone), **13/18** (MEΘ 529). A passive multi-purpose tool: polisher, convex/concave mold for the shaping of metal, and whetstone for metal cutting tools. Both surfaces bear traces of exposure to intense heat. Drawing T. Ross, photos J. Vanderpool

NOTES

1. Ioannis Manos owes special thanks to the excavators Manthos Bessios and Athena Athanassiadou, for granting him the archaeological material and excavation data; and to Drs. Sarah Morris and John Papadopoulos, University of California, Los Angeles, for their hospitality and support during his study at the museum storeroom. The photographs are by Jeff Vanderpool, the drawings by Anne Hooton and Tina Ross. This chapter was translated from the Greek by Marianna Nikolaidou.
2. Bessios, Tzifopoulos, and Kotsonas 2012.
3. The stratigraphic distinctions and chronological definition of the filling phases are the result of collaboration with the excavators, Manthos Bessios and Athena Athanassiadou; cf. Chapter 8.
4. Bessios, Tzifopoulos, and Kotsonas 2012.
5. Five, six, or seven items per 0.50 m of deposit.
6. Two items per 0.50 m.
7. Two items per 0.50 m.
8. Bessios, Tzifopoulos, and Kotsonas 2012.
9. Among them Leroi-Gourhan 1971; Tylecote 1992; Pernot 1998.
10. Metalworking areas of the Archaic and Classical periods at Methone have been located in the agora (ironworking in Building B: Chapter 1, Fig. 1.21) and on the West Hill (Fig. 1.33; Chapter 19a; Morris et al. 2020, pp. 699–701, possibly placed for optimal ventilation).
11. Recycling practices may account for the wide stratigraphic scatter of fragmented pottery, as was observed during excavation. Having gone out of use, broken vessels were repurposed piecemeal and as occasion arose.

14

METALLURGICAL CERAMICS FROM THE HYPOGEION

Samuel Verdan

INTRODUCTION

Among a variety of other finds, the Hypogeion at Methone has yielded the remains of a range of metallurgical activities, in various forms: metal waste products, slag, and, especially, fragments of refractory ceramics. This material, the study of which is only in its early stages, is both abundant and of high quality. To the best of our knowledge, it is virtually unparalleled in Greece for the period in question (end of the 8th/beginning of the 7th century B.C.). It is of interest for two reasons: it provides us with information about the different types of craftsmanship (and industries) that complemented the trading activities well attested at the site, and it sheds new light on metalworking technologies at the beginning of the Archaic period, about some of which—most notably, goldworking—little is known. For these reasons the remains, which may seem modest in comparison with other types of material found at Methone, are worth discussing here and will be the subject of more extensive research in the future.

The present discussion is of a provisional nature, for a number of reasons. First of all, the material was surveyed in a very brief and summary manner.[1] As a result, attention was focused on one category of remains in particular, metallurgical ceramics. Other categories (metal waste products and slag) have not yet been examined. It has not been possible to engage in any systematic reassembly of this highly fragmentary material, which makes identification of the items difficult, with the result that only a few observations can be made about the specific technical features of the implements. More to the point, for the moment only a visual assessment has been undertaken, and at this preliminary stage of the study there has been no laboratory analysis. I am well aware that such analysis is indispensable when studying this kind of material, as there is no other way of achieving a detailed understanding of the metallurgical processes that were carried out.[2] With the knowledge we currently have, then, it is possible to list the main types of remains that have been discovered and to describe some of their characteristics. At best, it is also possible to link them with a particular metallurgical activity but, as regards their exact function, the most that can be done is to put forward hypotheses that will need to be tested at a later stage.

THE MATERIAL UNDER EXAMINATION: STATE OF PRESERVATION AND IDENTIFICATION

As noted above, the remains associated with metalworking did not receive an exhaustive examination. For the most part observations were confined to the metallurgical ceramics, of which the different categories (crucibles, furnaces, tuyères, melting plates) will be discussed below. The material considered here is what was previously sorted by the excavators. It consists of about a thousand artifacts in a highly variable state of preservation, from small fragments (of a few cm²) to objects that are almost completely intact, although there are not many examples of the latter. On average, the material has gone through a significant degree of fragmentation, which explains the number of remnants. Indeed, technical ceramics such as crucibles, tuyères, and molds do not benefit from even firing at a high temperature and are therefore more fragile than common pottery. If they are not deliberately smashed after being used,[3] they are particularly liable to being discarded, and thus at the mercy of various post-depositional processes.

The state of preservation of the material makes it difficult to identify individual items. Generally, the presence of metal (in the form of spills, prills, or globules) or signs of exposure to high temperatures (vitrification) make it possible to distinguish metallurgical ceramics from common pottery, but this is not always the case.[4] Often, the absence of distinctive morphological features means that it is impossible to determine whether an item was once part of a particular kind of implement.[5] Lengthy reassembly work and analysis will be required before a more precise identification can be achieved.

GENERAL OVERVIEW: WHICH METALS, IN WHICH PROPORTIONS?

Among the material under examination, it is possible to distinguish remains associated with the working of at least three "metals": iron, bronze,[6] and gold, in very uneven proportions. At this stage of the study, it is not possible to provide precise quantitative data, as no systematic reassembly work has been undertaken and no rigorous quantification method has been employed.[7] From a cursory estimate, however, a few figures can be extracted: although they remain very approximate, they are still meaningful. Of the almost 130 pieces that can be associated with a metal with relative certainty, only 6% relate to iron, 37% to bronze (and/or copper) and 57% to gold.[8] A second estimate completes the picture: of the just over 200 fragments (or groups of fragments) that have been documented, nine are pieces of slag of predominantly ferrous composition, ten are from tuyères (which cannot always be associated with a particular metal), 44 are from crucibles or furnace walls which relate mainly, but not exclusively, to bronze smelting, and 71 are fragments of melting plates for gold. So, among this material, the evidence for working of gold is most prevalent, directly followed by bronze. In terms of quantity, iron comes some way behind. Nevertheless, it would be advisable to refrain from drawing a definite conclusion about the relative predominance of these metals in the metallurgical activities carried out at Methone. The material examined so far largely consists of ceramics, and not all metalworking processes require recourse to clay materials to the same extent. Moreover, various factors, such as the location of work sites and deliberate sorting of waste products, could have determined what material was deposited (or not) in the Hypogeion. This material cannot be deemed a representative sample of all the metallurgical activities pursued at the site.

Although the great majority of the pieces that have been studied fall into the "technical ceramic" category, and it is not always possible to associate them with a particular metal, I have chosen to structure the discussion with reference to the metals that are known to have been worked at Methone. It will begin, therefore, with the material that relates to iron, then continue with bronze, and conclude with the material with links to goldworking.

IRON

Within the material under study, signs of ironworking are few and far between. They can be summed up as less than a dozen fragments of slag, most of which are small in size. For now, these pieces of slag cannot be assigned to a particular stage (smelting, primary smithing, or secondary smithing) of the iron production process.⁹ To say more would require pieces to be much better preserved, coupled with further analysis. The very scarcity of the remains may be a form of evidence in itself. Since ore processing generally produces more waste products (slag and furnace walls) than the other stages of the ironworking process, it is fair to assume that it was not carried out at the site and that our pieces of slag were the byproducts of either primary or secondary smithing. Indeed, one fragment is plano-convex in shape and has a "spongy" look, features that are typical of smithing hearth-bottom slag.¹⁰ Furthermore, it should be noted that smithing does not necessarily demand the use of technical ceramics, with the exception of bellow nozzles, and is a process for which there is a comparatively small chance of evidence being present in the material under examination. The best way of detecting it would be to find hearth sites along with high concentrations of hammerscales in the field.¹¹ At this point, it is worth recalling the inevitable limitations of a study of metallurgical activities that is based solely on material found in a context of secondary deposition, as is the case here. By way of a hypothesis, I suggest that ironworking at Methone was limited to smithing, for manufacturing and maintaining implements, possibly linked to other metallurgical activities.

BRONZE (AND COPPER?)

For bronzeworking we have the most reliable evidence possible in the form of indications of the final main stage of production (if cold working is excluded): clay and stone molds. These are well preserved and offer information of a specific kind about the items that were produced at the site: pendants and jewelry (see below). This is very fortunate, as these sorts of finds are rare. Stone molds were valuable implements which artisans sought to use for as long as possible. They are not found with other metallurgical waste products, except by accident. Lost-wax molds, in contrast, were smashed and thrown away after use, but the clay of which they were made was often imperfectly fired and can be very badly preserved, according to the conditions of deposition.¹² Consequently, the number of molds that have been recovered from the Hypogeion, and their quality, are worthy of note. It is tempting to base an argument on this material and link the other remains (crucibles, tuyères, and so on) to bronze casting, but it should not be forgotten that other stages of production (especially smelting) could have been undertaken at the site. In developing an interpretation of this material (which will remain in any case provisional until further analysis has been carried out), it is best to bear in mind all possibilities. In order to follow, to a certain extent, the order of the *chaîne opératoire*, I shall begin by discussing the crucibles and fragments of furnaces(?), then the tuyères, and finally the molds.

Crucibles and Furnaces

The fragments of refractory ceramic used in bronze melting (and smelting?) are well represented in the documented material (comprising 44 entries).¹³ They may come from either crucibles or furnaces. Initially I am allotting them to one single group, because the preserved fragments are often too small to allow identification with certainty. I will then show that different types of implements can be distinguished, with reference to their morphology and, especially, their size. By contrast, the fragmentary character of the material makes it impossible to reconstruct complete shapes.

The remains of crucibles and furnaces are relatively easy to recognize, as their fabric is coherent. They are made of quite fine clay, which is micaceous (silver mica) and most probably of local origin.¹⁴ No systematic addition of mineral tempers is discernible, contrary to what seems to be the case with local coarse ware.¹⁵ Limestone inclusions, of varying number and size, were probably naturally present in the clay and not added by metalworkers. Conversely, an organic, vegetal temper, which burned with the first use, left numerous clearly visible hollows or voids.[16] This is not at all unusual; several studies have previously shown that organic tempers are useful for this kind of technical ceramic. First, they make the item more resistant before firing; subsequently, their disappearance during firing makes the crucible and furnace walls porous, which improves the refractory properties of the ceramic.[17] The crucibles were probably not fired, at least not at a high temperature as vases were, before their first use, and the furnaces definitely were not. For this reason, they can display highly variable firing characteristics, according to the temperatures and atmospheres (oxidation or reduction) that they experienced. If metal melting or smelting was carried out with a constant supply of oxygen, most items would be of a reddish orange color, tending toward beige on the outside. Nevertheless, it is common to find small areas of a gray to black color. In both the crucibles and the furnaces, the main heat source was inside (see below). As a result, only the inner surface bears the marks of exposure to high temperatures, in the characteristic form of a vitrified layer, a mixture of melted clay, slag, and prills (Fig. 14.1). The thickness of this layer varies, but is generally no more than a few millimeters. Given that the refractory properties of the fabric limit the transfer of heat through the vessel wall, the external surface experiences a markedly lower temperature than the internal surface and retains its original look; often polishing marks can still be seen.

One crucible is sufficiently well preserved for its general morphology to be clear (Fig. 14.1).[18] It is hemispherical in shape and has a diameter of between 18 and 20 cm and a maximum depth of 6.5 cm (the total height of the bowl is 9 cm). Near the rim, its wall is about 1.5 cm thick; at the bottom, it is almost 3 cm thick. Lacking a foot or a base, it has a simple rounded underside. Its most important distinguishing feature is a ledge-handle that is more than 10 cm wide,[19] which projects at a slight angle at the point where the belly lengthens, and which protrudes over the top of the basin, above the level of the rim, by about 4 cm. It was clearly a device for gripping that made it possible to grasp the crucible with tongs during the casting process.[20] There must have been a pouring spout, placed either perpendicular to the handle or on the opposite side, but certainty is impossible as the item is only partly preserved.[21]

By referring to the profile, diameter, and thickness of the walls, it is possible to assign several fragments to crucibles similar to the one described above. In particular, there are two more rims with ledge-handles for gripping. If it is possible to make a judgment on the basis of this limited sample size, this kind of crucible does not seem to have been uncommon at Methone. It should also be noted that its morphology is such that it fits perfectly within the lengthy series of bronze melting crucibles used in the Mediterranean area during the Bronze Age and at the beginning of the Iron Age. It is one of the larger examples: limited as they were by technical constraints (which included handling difficulties, resistance to the weight of the metal, and the need for rapid casting), these crucibles generally have a diameter of less than 20 cm (and of 25 cm at most).[22] It can be estimated that our better-preserved crucible could contain about 0.5 liters, that is, almost 4.5 kg of metal. From this quantity, a significant number of items could have been manufactured in a single casting.

Some of the fragments are too thick or too large in diameter to belong to crucibles of the kind described above. They most probably come from one or several furnaces, the existence of which is indirectly attested by the presence of tuyères with a large diameter. Indeed, the latter were inserted through walls of an installation to blow air on the combustion zone (see below). This kind of cylindrical furnace, with a diameter of 30 cm or more, and which was several dozen cm in height, is well known.[23] It remains to be seen for which stage of production these were used at Methone. If the crucibles are compared with the other evidence for bronze casting, it can be assumed that there was a melting furnace at this site, which made it possible to work much more metal at one time than in a crucible. This sort of apparatus, which was stationary, would have been equipped with a metal-flow

Figure 14.1. Large crucible used for bronze melting and casting, MEΘ 5344 (ME 1928). Photo I. Coyle

system that was stoppered by a plug during the heating phase and released when casting began. This kind of furnace, however, tended to be used for copper smelting, which could also have been carried out on a small scale at the site at Methone.[24] Both solutions are plausible and further analysis is needed to obtain more information.

Tuyères (Bellows Nozzles)

Almost all the production stages in which ore or metal was worked at high temperatures (i.e., smelting, melting, and smithing) required an artificial air supply and therefore the use of tuyères: they were used not only in copper and bronze production but also in the working of iron and gold. Discussion of such tuyères is included in the section on bronze because the best-preserved examples seem to be linked to bronzeworking (or copperworking), but tuyères will also be mentioned in the discussion of goldworking.

Considering the fact that tuyères were frequently used implements, their limited number in the material at the Hypogeion is surprising, especially if this is compared with the total number of documented metallurgical remains. It is true, however, that these consist almost exclusively of those parts of metalworking ceramics which were placed in the hearth and which bear the marks of their exposure to high temperatures. It is probable that the backs of such objects, which were exposed to fire to a limited extent, or not at all, were not preserved, or that they were not identified in the first round of sorting because they lacked distinctive features.

In terms of their fabric, the tuyères can be compared with the crucibles: their clay predominantly contains vegetal tempers. The three best-preserved items are the extruding parts of three tuyères of a similar type (Fig. 14.2). Their cross sections are circular but slightly flattened on four sides (squared), and they have the same dimensions (an external diameter of 5.5 cm and an aperture diameter of 2 cm). In two of the items, it can be seen how they were inserted in the wall of a furnace, directed downward at an angle of about 45°. Only their extruding parts are vitrified: the remainder was protected from the heat by the furnace wall. In one, prills of bronze or copper were caught in the vitrified layer, which gives an initial indication of the type of work for

FIGURE 14.2. Tuyère ends: a) MEΘ 5329 (ME 1080); b–c) MEΘ 5330 (ME 2958).
Photos I. Coyle

which these tuyères were used. It is worth noting in passing that tuyères with an aperture of this diameter must have been used at the end of a bellow rather than a blowpipe.[25]

LOST-WAX MOLDS

The lost-wax molds, just like the stone molds,[26] are among the most important items of metallurgical material, not only because they offer evidence about the technologies used, but also because they provide detailed information about the objects produced at Methone. Indeed, many of them are sufficiently well preserved for it to be possible to discern the outline of the items they were used to make.

The fabric of these molds is notably homogeneous and can be clearly distinguished from that of other technical ceramics and common pottery: a special paste was mixed for this use. The clay, well fired prior to casting, is quite hard, which explains the good state of the preservation of these molds. In addition to the mica and some limestone inclusions, the paste contained fine mineral tempers that gave the material a rough texture easily recognizable to the touch. The clay was applied around the wax matrix in several successive layers (at least two, and sometimes perhaps four).[27] It seems that the outer layer contained some fine organic (vegetal) tempers. The colors change from the core to the surface. In the middle, the clay that came into contact with the molten metal took on a gray tinge. All around this a purplish area formed. Finally, the color of the outer layer varies between orange and beige.

The majority of the fragments come from molds that were used for casting a kind of pendant well known in northern Greece and generally described as a "jug stopper" or "bottle stopper." It consists of a seated figure, with its elbows resting on its knees and its hands close to its face, on top of a rod with vertical rows of knobs (Fig. 14.3).[28] The mold from Methone is illustrated (Fig. 14.3a), together with two pendants, one in the Ashmolean Museum, Oxford (Fig. 14.3b), the other in the Ny Carlsberg Glypothek, Copenhagen (Fig. 14.3c), that were produced in similar molds. The molds from the Hypogeion provide evidence for the production of a "naturalistic" type, as several scholars have defined it: the body appears to have a certain solidity, as does the head, which is rounded (rather than triangular, as with the more stylized versions). The figure is seated on a circular "platform" and the knobs are clearly distinct from each other.[29] It is generally thought that the more naturalistic types were succeeded by the more stylized types, but for the moment there are no fixed points of dating to which this hypothesis can be linked.[30]

This type of object was for a long time thought to be a jug stopper, a term that is still conventionally used, but it is actually a pendant, which has been found in a number of tombs, associated with other items of jewelry.[31] The geographical regions where these are most common are Macedonia and Chalkidike, as well as Thessaly (for example, the sanctuary of Artemis Enodia at Pherai).[32] On

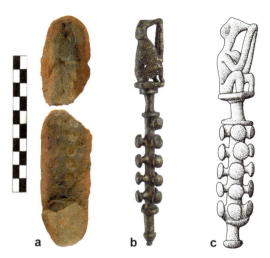

FIGURE 14.3. a) Lost-wax mold of a bronze pendant (so-called "jug stopper"), two non-joining fragments from Methone, upper fragment ΜΕΘ 5337, lower fragment ΜΕΘ 5335. Photo I. Coyle; b) bronze pendant ("jug-stopper") of unknown provenance, H. 10.5 cm, Ashmolean Museum, Oxford, inv. AN1938.365, photo courtesy Ashmolean Museum, University of Oxford; c) bronze pendant of unknown provenance, H. 11.3 cm, Ny Carlsberg Glyptotek, Copenhagen, after Kilian-Dirlmeier 1979, pl. 62, no. 1175

stylistic grounds, Imma Kilian-Dirlmeier has argued that production sites existed in each of these regions.[33] A detailed reconsideration of this issue would be worthwhile (cf. Chapter 26). In any case, Methone is, to my knowledge, the first site for which definite evidence exists for local production of these pendants, and this information is important for understanding how these items were distributed in northern Greece. Furthermore, it provides a new fixed point for the dating of these pendants. On account of the fact that only a small number of such objects have known, securely dated contexts, contradictory opinions have been put forward on the matter of chronology: some scholars have argued that they were produced principally in the 8th century, while others have reckoned that their production began only in the course of the 7th century.[34] Fragments of molds found in the deepest layers of the Hypogeion[35] make it possible to assert at least that the older type (if the notion of a stylistic evolution from a naturalistic to a stylized type is accepted, as was noted above) was already in existence between the end of the 8th century and the beginning of the 7th century.

Some of the fragments of molds are evidence for the manufacture of objects other than "jug stoppers" (pendants). In particular, the outline is discernible of a biconical bead, of a type widespread in northern Greece, which could easily have been found in a set of jewelry along with the pendants discussed above (Fig. 14.4).[36] There is also a conical molded item, which may be a pin head.

FIGURE 14.4. Lost-wax mold fragment for a biconical bead, ΜΕΘ 513 (ME 554). Photo I. Coyle

GOLD

Goldworking leaves very few traces (with the exception of the finished product). Extracting the metal does not require a smelting phase that produces a large amount of slag, as in the case of copper and iron. Generally, craftsmen only handle small quantities at a time, and thus large-scale infrastructure is not required. Moreover, the value of the metal is such that even the smallest remains (such as casting prills, offcuts, and filings) are carefully retrieved so they can be melted down again. As a result, we are familiar with the two endpoints of the production process—on the one hand, the areas delivering up the primary (ore) and placer deposits, and, on the other, the manufactured objects—but the intermediary stages of moving and working the metal remain, for the most part, obscure. In this respect, the Greek world is not exceptional. All discoveries are therefore of significance, and the material unearthed at Methone is especially so, in terms of its quantity and quality, although it is particularly informative about a very specific aspect of gold processing. Indeed, for the moment it has been possible to identify with certainty only one type of ceramic associated with goldworking, the melting plate (see below). Nevertheless, future analysis may reveal other types.

Melting Plates

This material, for which only a few parallels have been published,[37] is clearly less familiar than the crucibles and tuyères. It is, therefore, important to describe it here in detail and to explain precisely how it was used.

The melting plates are fragments of vases (or, possibly, other terracotta implements) reused for goldworking. Consequently, they are of irregular and variable shape. Their fabric also varies, because the sherds may have come from any one of the several different categories of locally made ware present at the site. Metalworkers generally preferred fragments of large coarse ware vessels with a thick wall, in particular pithoi, as this ensured solidity, but use of finer handmade pottery, with less thick walls, is also attested. Conversely, reuse of fine wheelmade pottery is not attested, as this type does not have the features necessary to withstand the thermal stresses produced by gold melting. Given the fragmentary state of the material, it is difficult to say if the sherds were recut in order to be reused. Either way, the few whole (or almost whole) examples (Figs. 14.5–14.6) are not regular in shape (see, for instance, Fig. 14.6). These pieces also supply information about the small dimensions of the melting plates: they vary from between ·10 and 16 cm in length, and 8.5 and 12 cm in width. Only one specimen, partially restored from a number of fragments, is larger (as its length is 20 cm). Although the shape of the sherds was not important, it seems that their curvature, by contrast, was a selection criterion. A shallow cavity was needed to collect the molten gold, but the metalworkers most often used fragments from the belly of a vase that were not especially concave, which gives an indication of the function of these plates (see below).

FIGURE 14.5. Gold melting plate, MEΘ 5331 (ME 1483). Photo I. Coyle

Figure 14.6. Gold melting plate, MEΘ 5332 (ME 1419). Photo I. Coyle

Since I am discussing reused ware here, I shall reserve for future study a detailed description of the fabrics for work that focuses on local/regional productions.[38] As noted earlier, most of the melting plates come from handmade coarse ware vessels, which contain a greater or lesser quantity of quartz. This feature deserves emphasis. A number of studies have shown that quartz makes ceramics better able to withstand mechanical stresses and thermal shocks.[39] These refractory properties, which were useful in the case of both large pithoi and cooking pots, might also have been put to good use in goldworking.[40] There is no doubt that the qualities of this ceramic, which contained a high level of quartz, were recognized by the craftsmen.

As on the crucibles, the upper side (i.e., the "inside") of the melting plates is partly covered by a vitrified and bubbly layer (Figs. 14.5–14.8). The vitrification is especially pronounced in the center of the objects and diminishes with distance from this area. At the edges, the clay has often kept its original look.[41] The vitrified layer principally consists of clay that melted when subjected to high temperatures. It is fine (rarely more than 1 mm thick), an indication that it was exposed to heat only for a short time.[42] Its color varies between gray and black, and parts of its surface sparkle. Within this layer the most important signs of goldworking can be seen: the globules and the location of the pellet produced by melting.

The globules of gold are found in highly variable quantities. On some plates, none can be seen with the naked eye, but others are studded with them (Fig. 14.7). The globules are spherical: the smallest visible ones have a diameter close to 100 microns (0.1 mm), but some are much bigger (up to 1 mm in diameter, if not more: Fig. 14.8). The globules are caught in the vitrified layer. They are tiny drops of liquid gold that were trapped in the layer, which during the melting process was of a viscous consistency, and which solidified in place. The globules are of obvious importance because they show which metal was melted on the plates. Moreover, it will be possible to analyze them in order to obtain valuable information about the composition, and consequently the provenance, of the gold (or types of gold) worked at Methone.[43]

Figure 14.7. Gold melting plate fragment, MEΘ 5340. Photo I. Coyle

Figure 14.8. Gold melting plate with large gold globule (Diam. 2 mm) and ingot impression, ΜΕΘ 5339 (ME 1924). Photo I. Coyle

In order to understand the stage of goldworking that involves the use of melting plates, another element is just as important as the globules, although it is less shiny and obvious: the "impressions" left by the molten metal in the vitrified layer (Figs. 14.5–14.8). So far, in the assemblages of material similar to ours (at Sardis and Eretria), it has not been possible to discern any marks of this kind.[44] At Methone, they are unmistakably visible on almost a dozen melting plates. On the best-preserved items, it can be seen that they are located approximately in the middle of the plate. They are more or less oval-shaped, and of variable size: the smallest measures 2 x 1.4 cm, the largest 5.5 x 5 cm (it appears to be atypical: Fig. 14.5). Their depth corresponds to the thickness of the vitrified layer (1–2 mm). It is easy to explain how these marks were formed. During melting, the molten gold formed a large drop in the lowest part of the plate (generally the center). The weight of this drop made it sink into the vitreous layer, which was then of a viscous consistency because of the high temperature. Once cooling had taken place, a pellet of metal remained caught in the vitrified layer; this had to be removed, and thus left the aforementioned outline.

The Melting Operation

Now that the melting plates have been described, it is appropriate to discuss in more general terms the process in which they played a role. Following this, the features of the goldworking carried out at Methone will be considered. The gold melting technique used here is clear. The metal, in a form that remains to be ascertained (see below) and in a quantity that varied (from a few grams to more than 100 g),[45] was placed on the plate and covered with charcoal: heat was supplied from above, as in the crucibles. On this subject, it should be mentioned that the charcoal needed to be fanned for the melting point of gold to be reached (1064° C). Considering the small scale and the speed of the process, as well as the care it demanded (especially if the gold was in the form of dust, and thus crucial not to scatter), it is not very likely that the necessary air was blown by bellows with large tuyères. More probably, the craftsmen made use of blowpipes with a small diameter, which allowed them to direct and control the airflow very precisely.[46] A fragment of fired clay may come from a nozzle that protected the end of these pipes. It contains vegetal tempers (like the crucibles and tuyères) and displays the marks of being exposed to the fire, and was molded on a perishable item with a diameter of 1.2 cm, which may have been a reed stem.[47]

FIGURE 14.9. Two pieces probably belonging to the same gold ingot, hammered and cut, ME 1345 and ME 1346. Photo I. Coyle

FIGURE 14.10. Lower surface of a large gold ingot (112 g, max. L. 6 cm) from the Geometric hoard found in Eretria, Eretria Museum inv. 14948. Photo courtesy École Suisse d'Archéologie en Grèce

Once the gold was liquid, it was very difficult to cast it in a mold with melting plates. These were too irregular in shape and had no fitting in the form of a channel or pouring spout that allowed this sort of operation to be carried out without wastage: with precious metal this is obviously essential. For this reason, the term "crucible" is not used when referring to these implements. The best solution was to let the gold cool on the melting plate and then to retrieve it, as I described above. Consequently, the "end product" of this operation was in the form of pellets of metal, of which two examples have been found at the site (Fig. 14.9);[48] the most striking examples, however, come from the gold hoard discovered at Eretria by Petros Themelis, which dates from the end of the Geometric period.[49] Indeed, this hoard contained many pieces of this kind, some of them whole, but most of them cut into small pieces. The spherical shape of the objects and the irregular look of their lower surface clearly show how they were produced (Fig. 14.10). In the following pages, these pellets will be termed "ingots," according to the common terminology. It should be noted, however, that this term could be misleading, if we have in mind the most common type of ingot nowadays, which is the result of metal casting in a mold. It has a set shape and weight, which allows for a certain level of standardization. Obviously, this does not apply to our ingots, which are of variable shape and size. But the principle, at least, is the same: in both instances the metal is in a form that facilitates its handling, transport, and use.

The melting plates were probably used several times, since it was possible to retrieve the gold without breaking them. Clearly, it was not difficult to obtain them, given that there was no lack of broken vessels, but the metalworkers were well advised to hold on to items with a proven ability to withstand thermal shocks. An indication of this repeated use has been discerned on the specimens from Sardis and Eretria: often the same plate held globules of different composition, a sign that different qualities of gold had been melted there.[50] In this way, one single plate could have served to transform a significant amount of metal.

What Sort of Goldworking at Methone?

Having described the material and melting operation, it makes sense to continue the inquiry by considering for what purposes gold was worked at the site. At this stage of the study, and with the material available, it is not possible to give a definite answer to this question.

The presence of stone molds indicates that jewels were cast, but it has not been determined yet whether they were used for bronze or gold, or for both. For the time being, evidence for bronze casting is plentiful, and absent for gold casting, since the melting plates were not fitted for the casting operation, and real crucibles for gold have not been retrieved as yet. One small-sized example could fit, but its surface shows no traces of the effects of the temperature needed to melt gold (Fig. 14.11). It might have been used for working lead, instead.

Consequently, the general picture that emerges from the data is relatively clear. It does not seem that the manufacture of gold objects was a priority at Methone, as for the moment the only activity for which there is secure evidence is the production of ingots. It is not inconceivable that recovered metal—goldsmithing waste or fragments of jewelry, as found in the Eretria hoard[51]—was melted to produce them, but more probably most of the metal transformed at the site was placer gold. The advantages of the process would have been obvious: from gold dust, which is difficult to handle, ingots were obtained which were easy to transport, weigh, assay, and exchange, and could be used immediately by a goldsmith (in cutting, hammering, stretching, drawing wire, and so on). In order to verify this hypothesis, it will be necessary to analyze the gold.

The example of the gold refinery at Sardis, where melting plates similar to those at Methone have been found, may suggest that gold refining was also practiced at our site.[52] Only analysis will make it possible to say for certain, but this scenario is not very likely. First, the situation at Methone was different from that at Sardis. In the Lydian capital, goldworking was associated with the minting of coins. Refining was genuinely useful for practical reasons: it made it possible to regulate gold composition (by separating it from silver) and so gain a better control of the alloy for electrum coin issues.[53] At Methone, and in Greece more generally before the advent of coinage, this was perhaps not a consideration. The quality of gold obviously mattered and might have been checked when it was used in transactions—probably with a touchstone[54]—but the natural variations in its composition were apparently not of crucial importance, especially if the quantities of metal in question were small.[55] The second point concerns what has been observed about the remains discovered at Sardis and Methone. At first sight, the gold-melting sherds (plates) are the same at both sites, with their globules caught in a vitrified layer. It is surprising, however, that no

FIGURE 14.11. Small crucible perhaps used for lead melting, ΜΕΘ 515.
Photo I. Coyle

outlines of ingots have been preserved on the Lydian specimens. This suggests that only very small quantities of gold were melted, as part of the refining process, in order to assay the metal with a touchstone.[56] At Methone, the size and weight of the ingots are much greater than what would have been necessary for an assay: their production was an end in itself. Finally, it should be noted that at Methone, remains of ceramics that could have been used for refining—specifically, parting vessels used for the cementation process[57]—have not been identified, for the time being.

To sum up, I am of the opinion that goldworking at Methone mainly consisted of the transformation of placer gold gathered in the region into a form that could be transported and traded easily. In geographical terms, the site was well placed for the collection of gold. There is no need here to emphasize the number of gold deposits in Macedonia and Thrace; I merely stress that Methone is not far from the mouths of three rivers that were most certainly exploited for their gold in antiquity—the Haliakmon, Axios, and Echedoros/Gallikos).[58] The site, linked as it was to maritime trade networks, was also a good base for the distribution of gold in Greece and the Aegean basin.

THE EUBOIAN *CHRUSIA*?

It is now possible to explore several lines of inquiry that are opening up as a result of the finds at Methone, although their study is only in its infancy. First of all, there is the question of gold circulation in the Greek world during the Early Iron Age and the early Archaic period, about which little is known.

I begin with the origin—or rather, the several possible origins—of the gold used in Greece in this period. Given that data to help advance our knowledge of this complex issue is very scarce, simple hypotheses have been favored: some, for example, think that Egypt was the principal source, while others assume that the supply came by way of the Phoenicians.[59] As this shows, closer sources, including those in northern Greece, are generally overlooked.[60] It is true that neither the geologically attested presence of gold nor the existence of texts that provide evidence for the ancient exploitation of this metal can prove that a region was productive during the Early Iron Age. Archaeological remains must be found, and datable ones at that. This is one of the reasons why the finds from Methone are so important. They strongly suggest that Macedonian gold was extensively exploited at the end of the 8th and in the 7th century, as it already was in the Bronze Age.[61] Of course, it is impossible to estimate how much was extracted in this region and what proportion it represented of the total quantity of gold in circulation in the Greek world. Once again, other areas in the eastern Mediterranean were much richer in gold than northern Greece. What was collected in the north Aegean, however, may have been enough to feed a significant "market" during the period in question.

An emerging body of evidence suggests that the Euboians played a not insignificant role in this precious-metal "market." A starting point is provided by archaeological data: it is hard to attribute to chance alone the finds made at Methone and Eretria, two sites whose history in the 8th century was linked.[62] It is not a question of gold alone, for it was shown earlier that there is a genuine correlation between the metallurgical material in the northern "colony" and the form of the metal in the hoard discovered in the Euboian *metropolis* ("mother-city"). For the time being, there is no proof that the Eretrian gold came from northern Greece. Nevertheless, although it may not make it possible to say for certain, analysis should at least provide information about the plausibility of this hypothesis. Two further arguments are relevant: Strabo's reference to Euboian *chrusia,* and the importance of the Euboian weight system in Greece. In a passage about the Euboian foundation of Pithekoussai, the author of the *Geography* mentions the *chrusia* that contributed to the prosperity of the Chalcidians and Eretrians.[63] The reading and the interpretation of this term have been disputed,[64] and the text does not make clear whether these *chrusia* relate to Pithekoussai in particular or to Euboian activities in general. Either way, in Strabo's account, the Euboians are unambiguously associated with goldworking. The second argument concerns the importance of the Euboian mass standard in Greece.[65] This standard was adopted by the Athenians and Corinthians for their coinage, and was also used to measure the gold tribute paid by each nation (*ethnos*) to the Persian king Darius, according to Herodotus.[66] This may seem implausible, but if the Greek historian was willing to transmit the information it must have had at least an element of truth. It should be emphasized that the passage makes a specific link between the Euboian weight system and gold. This surely means that at one time the Euboians played a special role in the circulation of this precious metal in Greece, and possibly beyond. Moreover, the form taken by the Eretrian gold hoard, comparable to that of many silver hoards discovered in the east, suggests that the metal could be used in "monetary" transactions.[67] This may provide another perspective on the finds at Methone, as they could indicate a starting point in a network in which gold in its raw state was used as a medium of exchange and hoarding, as well as a standard of value. In conclusion, I should stress that the term "Euboian" refers to practices common in the eastern Mediterranean (the system of weights and the "monetary" usage of metal)[68] and most probably the active participation of Levantine trading partners, who may even have been preeminent in taking the initiative. The fact remains that the archaeological evidence and literary sources are in agreement in suggesting that the Euboians were involved.[69]

CONCLUSION

The metallurgical remains from the Hypogeion at Methone are rich and varied, and give valuable information on two issues. First of all, they shed light on metalworking in Greece between the end of the Geometric period and the beginning of the Archaic period, a topic about which relatively little is known even today, and, secondly, they suggest the factors that drew people to the site of Methone at this point in history.

It is already certain that ironworking, bronzeworking, and goldworking were carried out here, but further analysis will be needed to determine precisely which stages of the sequence of operations are concerned, and to make better use of the information of a technological nature. It is worth recalling, too, that all the material was discovered in a context of secondary deposition. Ideally, we should relate these finds to remains on the ground, so as to have a more complete picture of the metallurgical activities carried out at the site and, crucially, of the scale on which this happened: was it a case of casual manufacturing work or, conversely, "industrial" production? Moreover, between these two extremes lies a whole range of possible intermediate solutions.

Fortunately, the material makes it possible to see that at least two categories of objects were produced at the site: bronze pendants and gold ingots. It is possible to trace the spread of the former through northern Greece (although not all the specimens that have been found were manufactured at Methone!), while the latter seem to have been circulated on a large scale, on routes taken by the Euboians and well beyond. These two scenarios show that the site occupied an advantageous position on both maritime and land-based trading networks, and was a point of contact between the Macedonian hinterland, Thrace, and the Aegean.

NOTES

1. I had occasion to study the material during a period of three days, in the archaeological storerooms at Makrygialos, in September 2013. I take this opportunity to thank Manthos Bessios, John Papadopoulos, and Sarah Morris for their invitation and their warm welcome, and the archaeologists from the Ephoreia, Athena Athanassiadou and Kostas Noulas, as well as the museum guards, for the exceptional working conditions at Makrygialos. I also pay tribute to the very substantial sorting work previously carried out, with great care, by the excavators, which made my task much easier. I also would like to thank Elon Heymans for his valuable comments, and Katie Low for the English translation.

2. The direction taken by archaeometallurgical research in the last three decades is a perfect demonstration of this, see esp. Rehren and Pernicka 2008.

3. This is especially the case with lost-wax molds, which need to be smashed so that the cast object can be retrieved. In the material under examination, fragments of molds make up about one-third of the remains.

4. Some items classified as metallurgical remains are probably just cooking ware, the results of unsuccessful firing in a potter's kiln, or other terracotta implements with no connection to metalworking. Conversely, it is likely that a large number of fragments of refractory ceramics remain classified as pottery, primarily as coarse wares, or as weights (for example, Chapter 16, MEΘ 2794, Fig. 16.4, top row, far right, from Phase I of the Hypogeion).

5. For example, distinguishing between fragments of crucibles and furnaces is highly problematic.

6. The term "bronze" is used here for convenience. In the absence of any analysis, however, it would be more correct to use the more neutral expression "copper-base alloys." Moreover, if bronze casting is securely attested by the presence of crucibles and molds, it is also not inconceivable that the copper was worked at the site (at the stage of the smelting process). This possibility will be discussed in the section on bronze, pp. 547-549.

7. For material of this kind, selecting a quantification method (counting the total number of remains, weighing them, or estimating the minimum number of individual items) is in any case difficult.

8. It is important to make clear that the remains of molds are excluded from these figures, as their high rate of fragmentation means they are present in large numbers, and would skew the percentages.

9. On the sequence of operations involved in the iron production process, and the different forms of slag produced, see Tylecote 1987, pp. 151–178, 248–280, 310–321; Craddock 1995, pp. 241–254; Serneels 1993, pp. 43–48; Fluzin, Ploquin, and Serneels 2000; Fluzin et al. 2001, pp. 114–115; Bachmann 1982, pp. 30–33.

10. Tylecote 1987, pp. 318–319; Fluzin, Ploquin, and Serneels 2000, p. 109 (and fig. 42.2); Bachmann 1982, pp. 30–33. For a possible ironsmithing hearth uncovered on the West Hill at Methone in 2014, see Morris et al. 2020, p. 701, fig. 52.

11. For a Greek case contemporary to the finds at Methone, see the example from the excavations at Oropos (Doonan and Mazarakis Ainian 2007).

12. Zimmer 1990, p. 133 (on molds, see pp. 133–139).

13. It should be recalled, however, that no systematic mending has been carried out yet. Several fragments can belong to the same piece, and this is particularly true of furnaces, which could be of large size.

14. On local pottery production, see Kotsonas 2012, especially pp. 126–127.

15. Kotsonas 2012, p. 163; see also pp. 552-554 on melting plates for gold.

16. From the appearance of these marks, the temper must have been chopped straw.

17. This porosity increases the insulating effect of the clay and so limits possible heat loss through the walls (crucibles and furnaces were heated from the inside): see Hein, Kilikoglou, and Kassianidou 2007; Hein et al. 2013.

18 More than half of the piece has been reconstructed from a number of fragments (ΜΕΘ 5344 [ΜΕ 1928]).

19 On account of damage, it is not possible to ascertain its exact dimensions.

20 For a useful parallel on Crete, see Evely, Hein, and Nodarou 2012, p. 1824, fig. 3e.

21 For a pouring spout on the opposite side of the handle, see Evely, Hein, and Nodarou 2012, p. 1824; for a pouring spout placed perpendicular to the handle, see Tylecote 1987, fig. 6.7, 1.

22 Verdan 2007, pp. 354–355 (appendix by W. Fasnacht). Cretan examples from the Late Bronze Age include Evely, Hein, and Nodarou 2012, p. 1822. Hemispherical crucibles there have a diameter of between 10 and 20 cm (and most often between 16 and 18 cm); their internal height is slightly less than the radius, and their volume varies from 250 to 4000 cm^3 (the larger number seems very high, and it probably refers to the total volume of the crucible rather than the volume of metal melted inside).

23 Tylecote 1982, pp. 89–92; 1987, pp. 109–115, 124–125, 182–183; Hein, Kilikoglou, and Kassianidou 2007, p. 143 (Cyprus).

24 To support this scenario, it would be advisable to seek other forms of evidence, in particular pieces of slag. The existence of this production stage was also dependent on the proximity of a source of ore (for the location of copper-mineral deposits in northern Greece, see Pernicka 1987, p. 620, fig. 5).

25 Rehder 1994.

26 For some of the stone molds, see Chapter 1, Figs. 1.16, 1.36; for surface finds, see Chapter 27.

27 For comparison, see Zimmer 1990, pp. 134–135; Hemingway 1996, p. 237.

28 Jantzen 1953; Bouzek 1974b, pp. 76–86; Vickers 1977; Kilian-Dirlmeier 1979, pp. 194–208, pls. 61–73. For further discussion of this type, see Chapter 26.

29 Kilian-Dirlmeier 1979, pp. 194–197, pls. 61–64, nos. 1164–1197.

30 Kilian-Dirlmeier 1979, pp. 206–208.

31 Vickers 1977, pp. 18–19; Kilian-Dirlmeier 1979, pp. 205–206. For two "jug stoppers" associated with other pendants and bracelets in a 7th-century female(?) grave from Axioupolis (in the Axios valley), see Descamps-Lequime 2011, pp. 89–92. For recent discoveries (some in the Haliakmon valley, not far from Methone), see references in Misailidou-Despotidou 2011, p. 57, n. 328.

32 Kilian-Dirlmeier 1979, pl. 107.

33 Kilian-Dirlmeier 1979, p. 208.

34 Vickers 1977, pp. 30–31; Kilian-Dirlmeier 1979, pp. 206–207.

35 It is clear that many fragments belong to lots attributed to the first phase.

36 Bouzek 1974b, pp. 105–117 (figs. 32–33); Vickers 1977, fig. III; Bouzek 1987, pp. 91–100 (see distribution maps figs. 8–9).

37 See *Sardis* 11, pp. 90, 100, 102–117, 126–127, 160–161, 207 (Sardis); *Eretria* XXII, pp. 148–149, pl. 114; Meeks and Craddock 2013, pp. 271–273 (Eretria).

38 A pilot analytical program has been undertaken by the Fitch Laboratory (British School at Athens) on coarse wares found in Methone, aiming to define characteristics of local products. Preliminary results indicate the presence of a number of potentially local fabrics for pithoi, but also of imported pottery from neighboring areas (pers. comm. E. Kiriatzi and X. Charalambidou).

39 Kilikoglou, Vekinis, and Maniatis 1995; Kilikoglou et al.1998.

40 It should be noted that at Sardis, in the gold refinery complex from the Archaic period, the ceramic used to make gold-melting sherds also contains quartz (*Sardis* 11, pp. 158–159).

41 When this happens, it becomes very difficult, if not impossible, to discern with the naked eye fragments of melting plates among the coarse wares.

42 See *Sardis* 11, pp. 126–127, 160–161; Meeks and Craddock 2013, pp. 271–272.

43 For examples of globule analysis, see *Sardis* 11, pp. 102–117 (and table 5.1); Meeks and Craddock 2013, p. 273, table 1.

44 At Sardis (*Sardis* 11, pp. 127, 207), the quantities of molten gold may have been too small to leave visible marks on the plates. At Eretria (*Eretria* XXII, pl. 114, cat. nos. 526–529), the material is fragmentary and items consistently lack a central section.

45 The only pellet/ingot discovered so far at Methone (Fig. 14.9) weighs 10 g (cut into two "halves" weighing 3 and 7 g respectively). In the largest cupule preserved on a melting plate (5.5 x 5 cm) was an ingot at least as big as the largest item in the gold hoard discovered at Eretria, which weighs 112 g (Fig. 14.10).

46 Craddock 1995, p. 177. Blowpipes used in metallurgical activities are depicted on Egyptian tombs (Craddock 1995, p. 178, fig. 5.17; Scheel 1989; Davey and Edwards 2008, figs. 1, 3 [relief in the Old Kingdom Tomb of Mereruka at Saqqara]).

47 It is worth noting that this diameter is itself too great to make an effective blowpipe (see Rehder 1994, pp. 348–349).

48 Most probably two halves of the same piece; note that the flat surface is the result of hammering.

49 Themelis 1981, 1983.

50 *Sardis* 11, p. 109 (sherd 45670U), pp. 116–117 (sherd 45681Z.IV, sherd 45684T), p. 126; Meeks and Craddock 2013, p. 272. The question remains, however, were the different types of gold melted one after the other, or at the same time?

51 Themelis 1983, pp. 162–164.

52 This hypothesis was also advanced with reference to the finds from the sanctuary of Apollo at Eretria, but the results of analysis of the gold disproved it, see Verdan 2007, pp. 348–349; *Eretria* XXII, p. 149; Meeks and Craddock 2013, pp. 271–272.

53 *Sardis* 11, pp. 169–173, 212–213; Craddock, Cowell, and Guerra 2005. On early Lydian electrum coinage, see also Le Rider 2001, pp. 85–100; Keyser and Clark 2001, pp. 115–117.

54 *Sardis* 11, pp. 247–249; Le Rider 2001, pp. 89–90.

55 On the variations in the composition of gold in its natural state, see, for instance, Boyle 1979, pp. 197–207; Chapman, Leake, and Styles 2002. The Eretrian hoard is a perfect case to tackle the issue, since it contains pieces that seem to be of very different composition, according to their color (Themelis uses the term "electrum" for some pieces, see Themelis 1983, pp. 160–161). This point certainly deserves further investigation.

56 This is the interpretation favored by the authors, see *Sardis* 11, pp. 127, 207, 210. Another hypothesis is possible: that the melting plates were used to make blanks to be struck. This method would not have been very productive but would have made it possible to calibrate the weight of the coinage accurately, by preliminary weighing of the quantity of metal to be melted, which is not possible when carrying out casting in multi-cavity molds (for experiments and discussion on this matter, see Faucher et al. 2009, pp. 53–61).

57 *Sardis* 11, pp. 122–124, 127–128, 159–160, 166, 202–208.

58 Mack 1964; Pernicka 1987, pp. 676–677; Vavelidis 2004; Vavelidis and Andreou 2008 (with further references). Placer gold is found in the Haliakmon, Axios, and Gallikos. As yet, its exploitation in antiquity is only attested for the Gallikos, called *Echedôros*, "having gifts," by ancient Greeks (already in Herodotus 7.124 and 7.127; see also *Etymologicum Magnum*, s.v. Ἐχέδωρος). See now the Ada Tepe gold mine in Thrace, in use since the Bronze Age: Haag et al. 2017.

59 See, most recently, Le Rider and Verdan 2002, pp. 147–148; Descoeudres 2008, pp. 306–307.

60 See, for instance, Bakhuizen 1976, p. 85, where he states: "There is no reason to assume that gold was mined (sic) in any of the places occupied by the Euboeans." *Contra*, Tiverios 1998, pp. 249–250; Tiverios 2008, p. 21; Tiverios 2013a, p. 101.

61 Vavelidis and Andreou 2008.

62 Plutarch *Quaest. Graec.* 11, *Mor.* 293A (whether or not the etiological tale of the *aposphendonetoi* is to be believed: Chapter 2). See Hammond 1998, pp. 393–395; Tzifopoulos 2012, pp. 19–21; see also Chapter 28.

63 Strabo 5.4.9.

64 I retain here the reading *chrusia* (χρυσία "gold objects") rather than *chruseia* (χρυσεῖα "gold mines," which definitely did not exist at Pithekoussai), which follows the suggestion of Giorgio Buchner (1979, pp. 136–137) and David Ridgway (1992, pp. 34–35, with further references); more recently, see Lane Fox 2008, p. 135 (in which the author argues that the gold possessed by the Euboians came from northern Greece). In fact, the *chrusia* mentioned by Strabo could refer not to gold artifacts produced in Pithekoussai (as proposed by Buchner and Ridgway), but rather to traded metal (see, first, Bakhuizen 1976, p. 85); *contra*, Radt 2007, pp. 127–128, who dismisses both the translation of *chruseia* by "goldsmiths' workshops" (Mureddu 1972) and the *chrusia* reading. It is worth adding that all of the accepted manuscripts of Strabo 5.4.9 have χρυσία; the variant χρυσεῖα is only in MS Par. Gr. 1408, dating to the 15th century and usually considered an emendation.

65 Kroll 2001, pp. 81–82; 2008a (44, where it is noted "the most influential weight standard of Archaic and later Greece").

66 Herodotus 3.89. The tribute paid in silver, however, was measured in Babylonian talents.

67 Furtwängler 1986, p. 156; Kroll 2001; Le Rider and Verdan 2002; Vargyas 2002. See also Kroll 2008b, and more recently Verdan and Heymans 2020; Heymans 2021 (especially pp. 205–207). On what happened in the east, see especially Balmuth 2001; Le Rider 2001, pp. 1–39; Thompson 2003; Kletter 2003; Heymans 2018a, 2018b, 2021.

68 For the eastern origin of the Euboian weight system, see Kroll 2001, pp. 80–82; Kroll 2008a, pp. 44–46.

69 More on this issue in Verdan and Heymans 2020; Heymans 2021, pp. 203–212.

15

METAL FINDS FROM THE HYPOGEION

John K. Papadopoulos

INTRODUCTION

The aim of this chapter is to publish a representative sample of the base metal objects—bronze, iron, lead—from the Hypogeion, the majority of which date to the late 8th and early 7th century B.C.[1] Although there was quantitatively more evidence of goldworking in the Hypogeion than there was evidence for the working of other metals, the number of finished gold objects was minimal indeed, with the two pieces that probably belong to the same gold "ingot" (Fig. 14.9) being the most noteworthy.[2] These were not finished products of personal ornament, but a raw commodity aimed at the market.

In addition to the material presented below, there were copious quantities of slag, as well as fragments of sheet bronze and fragments or pieces of iron (metalworking waste, broken objects, and scrap or recycled metal).[3] The full story of the working of metal at Methone is a work in progress, and it does not necessarily begin suddenly in the Geometric period, but may well have a venerable prehistory, extending back to the Late Bronze Age with the various metal finds deposited in tombs, or even earlier in the Bronze Age.[4] It would be interesting, for example, in future studies of this material to compare the composition of the Mycenaean-era bronzes of Methone with those of the Early Iron Age and Archaic periods.[5]

It is also worth noting here that the material from the Hypogeion is only one context at Methone where sizable quantities of metal objects have come to light. In Chapter 26, I present an even more cursory summary overview of the metal objects from other parts of the site excavated between 2003 and 2011, especially those from the agora of Methone on the slopes of the East Hill and in the saddle between the East and West Hills. This material includes objects from the destruction deposit of the settlement in 354 B.C. at the hands of Philip II—an important closed context—as well as from earlier contexts predating the agora. Then there is the material immediately south of the agora, in Plot 278, in the area where there was a possible second harbor of Methone. There are also the metal finds from the West Hill, the acropolis of Methone (Plot 229), as well as that from the acropolis east slopes (especially in Plot 245).

The material catalogued below is presented by metal, beginning with the bronzes, followed by the iron and lead objects; with each metal I begin with jewelry, including pendants, fibulae, dress pins, rings, and other items of personal ornament, then tools and implements, as well as weapons.

CONTEXT

Metal objects were encountered in all the phases of the Hypogeion, from the bottom to the top. The material is listed below in Table 15.1, with the various phases color-coded. Among the bronze objects catalogued or mentioned below, 23 were found in Phase I, 31 in Phase II, and 18 in Phase III; the context of an additional four objects was uncertain. The diagnostic iron objects, relatively fewer in comparison to bronze, were primarily from Phases I (a total of 12) and II (ten in all), with only six recorded from Phase III, and two from unclear contexts. There were only five inventoried lead objects from the Hypogeion, four from Phase I, one from Phase III. There were only 18 metal objects recovered from the post-Phase III contexts. Consequently, the majority of the material presented in this chapter dates to the later 8th and early 7th century B.C., while the post-Phase III objects dates mainly to the Archaic period.

Objects of Bronze
Jewelry and other items of personal ornament
Pendant

A solitary pendant from the Hypogeion, the fragmentary **15/1** (ΜΕΘ 1473) from the lowest deposit (Phase I) corresponds in type to what Imma Kilian-Dirlmeier refers to as "geschlossene Bommeln mit einfacher Öse und Stiel, ohne unteren Fortsatz,"[6] and is closest to the biconical variety of the type ("doppelkonisch"; rather than the spherical ["kugelig"] or ovoid [= Kilian-Dirlmeier's "Oblong"]).[7] Kilian-Dirlmeier lists six examples of the biconical type, including two from the Artemis Enodia sanctuary at Pherai, and one each from Thermon, Ithaka, Olympia, and Perachora.[8] The context of all six is uninformative as to date and, as such, the context of the Methone example is a welcome addition to the corpus, providing as it does a well-dated late 8th- or early 7th-century example. The closest parallels to **15/1** have a ring at the juncture of the biconical beaded terminal and the main shaft of the pendant; the example from Ithaka has no ring at the offset, but the beaded terminal of the pendant is larger, more rounded, and less biconical.

15/1. (ΜΕΘ 1473 [ME 3000]) Fragmentary Pendant Fig. 15.1
East Hill #274/022058 [12]. 22/8/2006. Phase I.
P.L. 0.055; Diam. (beaded terminal) 0.014; Wt. 10.9 g.
Single fr preserving beaded terminal and significant portion of shaft, but not the suspension ring; corroded.
Shaft rectangular in section, with heavy biconical beaded terminal at one end. At opposite there is a semicircle near the break that should be the eyelet from which the object was suspended.
Cf., among others, Kilian-Dirlmeier 1979, p. 57, pl. 21, nos. 348–353, esp. nos. 348–349 (Pherai); cf. Kilian 1975a, pl. 80, nos. 5–10; *Perachora* I, p. 182, pl. 66, no. 17.

FIGURE 15.1. Bronze pendant, **15/1** (ΜΕΘ 1473). Drawing F. Skyvalida, photo I. Coyle

TABLE 15.1. The context of the Hypogeion metal objects and the phase to which they belong.
Phase I = yellow; Phase II = green; Phase III = blue; Post Phase III = orange

	Phase	MEΘ	Metal	Context	Object
15/1	I	MEΘ 1473	Bronze	#274/022058 [12]	Pendant
15/2	I	MEΘ 1391	Bronze	#274/032057 [7]	Spectacle fibula
15/3	II	MEΘ 1480	Bronze	#274/032049 [5]	Spectacle fibula
15/4	II	MEΘ 1479	Bronze	#274/032048 [5]	Spectacle fibula
15/5	III	MEΘ 1478	Bronze	#274/032043 [5]	Spectacle fibula
15/6	II	MEΘ 1390	Bronze	#274/032055 [7]	Violin-bow fibula
15/7	Post-III	MEΘ 1387	Bronze	#274/032014 [3]	Violin-bow fibula
15/8	I	MEΘ 1393	Bronze	#274/032063 [9]	Fibula
15/9	I	MEΘ 1394	Bronze	#274/032086 [9]	Fibula
15/10	III	MEΘ 1388	Bronze	#274/032043 [5]	Beaded fibula
15/11	I	MEΘ 1385	Bronze	#274/022064 [13]	Fibula
15/12	III	MEΘ 1384	Bronze	#274/022036 [10]	Fibula
15/13	I	MEΘ 1499	Bronze	#274/032060 [7]	"Phrygian" fibula
15/14	I	MEΘ 1392	Bronze	#274/032061 [7]	"Phrygian" fibula
15/15	Post-III	MEΘ 1382	Bronze	#274/022007 [5]	"Phrygian" fibula
15/16	Post-III	MEΘ 1510	Bronze	#274/032011 [3]	Fibula a navicella
15/17	I	MEΘ 1519	Bronze	#274/032086 [9]	Fibula catchplate
15/18	II–III	MEΘ 1418	Bronze	#274/022 Fill below Wall 14	*Rollenkopfnadel*
15/19	II	MEΘ 1403	Bronze	#274/022052 [11]	*Rollenkopfnadel*
15/20	II	MEΘ 1434	Bronze	#274/032054 [7]	*Rollenkopfnadel*
15/21	Post-III	MEΘ 1395	Bronze	#274/022003 [2]	Dress pin
15/22	I	MEΘ 1459	Bronze	#274/032061-063 Backfill	Decorated pin shaft
Cf. 15/22	I	MEΘ 1450	Bronze	#274/032077 [7]	Decorated pin shaft
15/23	I	MEΘ 1491	Bronze	#274/032056 [7]	Dress pin or stylus
15/24	I	MEΘ 1410	Bronze	#274/022066 [14]	Small pin
15/25	Post-III	MEΘ 4137	Bronze	#274/032005 [3]	Dress pin
15/26	II–III	MEΘ 1417	Bronze	#274/022 Cleaning of Wall 14	Dress pin fr
15/27	II	MEΘ 1512	Bronze	#274/032037 [6]	Dress pin fr
15/28	II	MEΘ 1474	Bronze	#274/032054 [7]	Bead
15/29	II	MEΘ 1472	Bronze	#274/022054 [12]	Fish-shaped bead
15/30	Post-III	MEΘ 1524	Bronze	#274/032032 [5]	Fragmentary ring
15/31	II	MEΘ 4130	Bronze	#274/032051 [7]	Ring
15/32	Post-III	MEΘ 1475	Bronze	#274/032006 [3]	Spiral ring
Cf. 15/32	Post-III	MEΘ 1495	Bronze	#274/022009 [5]	Spiral ring
15/33	II	MEΘ 1496	Bronze	#274/022054 [12]	*Krikos*
15/34	I	MEΘ 1498	Bronze	#274/032057 [7]	*Krikos*
15/35	II	MEΘ 1386	Bronze	#274/022047-051	Spiral ornament
15/36	II	MEΘ 1493	Bronze	#274/032042 [6]	Button/tutulus
15/37	II	MEΘ 1487	Bronze	#274/032053 [7]	Button/tutulus

TABLE 15.1. The context of the Hypogeion metal objects and the phase to which they belong.
Phase I = yellow; Phase II = green; Phase III = blue; Post Phase III = orange *(continued)*

	Phase	ΜΕΘ	Metal	Context	Object
15/38	No context	ΜΕΘ 1484	Bronze	#274/032 Balk scraping	Button/tutulus
15/39	II	ΜΕΘ 1483	Bronze	#274/022 Fill below Wall 14	Button/tutulus
15/40	II	ΜΕΘ 1494	Bronze	#274/032050 [7]	Button/tutulus
15/41	II	ΜΕΘ 4117	Bronze	#274/032048 [5]	Button/tutulus
15/42	Post-III	ΜΕΘ 1523	Bronze	#274/032008 [3]	Button/tutulus
15/43	III	ΜΕΘ 1489	Bronze	#274/022042 [10]	Button or boss/tutulus
15/44	I	ΜΕΘ 1501	Bronze	#274/022058 [12]	Uncertain, tutulus?
15/45	II	ΜΕΘ 1467	Bronze	#274/022051 [11]	Needle/pin
15/46	II	ΜΕΘ 1468	Bronze	#274/022052 [11]	Needle/pin
15/47	I	ΜΕΘ 1409	Bronze	#274/022066 [14]	Small needle?
15/48	I	ΜΕΘ 4124	Bronze	#274/022070 [14]	Possible needle?
15/49	Backfill	ΜΕΘ 1521	Bronze	#274/032 Backfill	Perforated disk
15/50	II	ΜΕΘ 1476	Bronze	#274/022044 [11]	Fragmentary chain
15/51	III	ΜΕΘ 1497	Bronze	#274/032043 [5]	Chain link
15/52	II	ΜΕΘ 1508	Bronze	#274/022 fill below Wall 14	Miniature double axe
15/53	I	ΜΕΘ 1502	Bronze	#274/032063 [9]	Cube (weight/ingot?)
15/54	II	ΜΕΘ 1505	Bronze	#274/022050 [11]	Knife
15/55	II	ΜΕΘ 1504	Bronze	#274/022049 [11]	Cone (arrowhead)?
15/56	PostIII	ΜΕΘ 1522	Bronze	#274/022 Fill assoc. with Wall 5	Clamp/binding sheaths
15/57	II	ΜΕΘ 1486	Bronze	#274/032050 [7]	Nail head
15/58	III	ΜΕΘ 4118	Bronze	#274/032046 [5]	Nail shaft
15/59	Post-III	ΜΕΘ 4140	Bronze	#274/022034 [10]	Pin from hinged object
15/60	I	ΜΕΘ 1500	Bronze	#274/032062 [9]	Hooked object
15/61	II–III	ΜΕΘ 4135	Bronze	#274/032043-051	Wire
15/62	II	ΜΕΘ 4136	Bronze	#274/032054 [7]	Awl
15/63	II	ΜΕΘ 1516	Bronze	#274/032065 [7]	Possible awl
15/64	II–III	ΜΕΘ 4121	Bronze	#274/022 Cleaning of Wall 14	Fragmentary rod
15/65	I	ΜΕΘ 1490	Bronze	#274/022059 [12]	Spatula-shaped object
15/66	I	ΜΕΘ 1520	Bronze	#274/032086 [9]	Spatula-shaped object
15/67	I	ΜΕΘ 4120	Bronze	#274/032060 [7]	Small rod (L-staple)
15/68	II	ΜΕΘ 1517	Bronze	#274/032067 [7]	Narrow strip
15/69	Post-III	ΜΕΘ 5304	Bronze	#274/032010 [3]	Thin strip
15/70	I	ΜΕΘ 4110	Bronze	#274/022058 [12]	Perforated sheet
15/71	II	ΜΕΘ 4115	Bronze	#274/032049 [5]	Small perforated sheet
15/72	II	ΜΕΘ 4106	Bronze	#274/022045 [11]	Sheet attachment fr
15/73	I	ΜΕΘ 4113	Bronze	#274/032063 [9]	Sheet fr

TABLE 15.1. The context of the Hypogeion metal objects and the phase to which they belong.
Phase I = yellow; Phase II = green; Phase III = blue; Post Phase III = orange *(continued)*

	Phase	ΜΕΘ	Metal	Context	Object
15/74	II	ΜΕΘ 1503	Bronze	#274/022048 [11]	Leaf-shaped object
15/75	I	ΜΕΘ 1533	Iron	#274/032056 [7]	Spearhead
15/76	II	ΜΕΘ 1532	Iron	#274/022056 [12]	Spearhead socket fr
15/77	I	ΜΕΘ 5327	Iron	#274/022058 [12]	Spearhead socket fr
15/78	Post-III	ΜΕΘ 1566	Iron	#274/032011 [3]	Arrowhead
15/79	I	ΜΕΘ 1538	Iron	#274/022065 [13]	Fragmentary blade
15/80	Post-III	ΜΕΘ 1564	Iron	#274/032015 [4]	Blade fragment
15/81	I	ΜΕΘ 1537	Iron	#274/022064 [13]	Fragmentary blade
15/82	I	ΜΕΘ 1539	Iron	#274/032058 [7]	Blade fragment
15/83	II	ΜΕΘ 1540	Iron	#274/032067 [7]	Blade fragment
15/84	Backfill	ΜΕΘ 1534	Iron	#274/022047-051 Backfill	Knife
15/85	II	ΜΕΘ 5321	Iron	#274/032067 [7]	Knife fragment
15/86	I	ΜΕΘ 1545	Iron	#274/022061 [13]	Knife
15/87	Post-III	ΜΕΘ 1563	Iron	#274/032014 [3]	Small narrow knife
15/88	I	ΜΕΘ 1546	Iron	#274/022061 [13]	Small narrow knife
15/89	I	ΜΕΘ 1556	Iron	#274/032077 [7]	Axe/adze head
15/90	Post-III	ΜΕΘ 1565	Iron	#274/022024 [8]	Small axe/adze head
15/91	II	ΜΕΘ 1551	Iron	#274/022 Fill below Wall 14	Axe or hammer head
15/92	II	ΜΕΘ 1553	Iron	#274/032052 [7]	Hammer head fr?
15/93	I	ΜΕΘ 1554	Iron	#274/032056 [7]	Large pointed chisel
15/94	III	ΜΕΘ 1531	Iron	#274/032046 [5]	Pointed chisel
15/95	Post-III	ΜΕΘ 1530	Iron	#274/022 Cleaning of Wall 5	Likely pointed chisel
15/96	II	ΜΕΘ 1555	Iron	#274/032064 [7]	Likely pointed chisel
15/97	II	ΜΕΘ 1550	Iron	#274/022 Fill below Wall 14	Rod (possible chisel?)
Cf. 15/97	I	ΜΕΘ 1549	Iron	#274/022071 [15]	Rod (pointed chisel?)
15/98	I	ΜΕΘ 1544	Iron	#274/0220660 [12]	Metalworkers' tongs
15/99	I	ΜΕΘ 1548	Iron	#274/022070 [14]	Metalworkers' tongs
15/100	II	ΜΕΘ 5319	Iron	#274/032041 [6]	Tack
15/101	Backfill	ΜΕΘ 1558	Iron	#274/032 Backfill	Fr iron wire (spiral/ring)
15/102	II	ΜΕΘ 5323	Iron	#274/022 Fill below Wall 14	Fr iron wire (ring)
15/103	II	ΜΕΘ 1552	Iron	#274/032037 [6]	Fish-shaped attachment?
15/104	I	ΜΕΘ 1527	Lead	#274/022062 [13]	Fishnet weight
15/105	I	ΜΕΘ 1525	Lead	#274/032082 [10]	Fishnet weight
15/106	I	ΜΕΘ 1528	Lead	#274//032071 [7]	Fishnet weight
15/107	Post-III	ΜΕΘ 4369	Lead	#274/022004 [3]	Mending clamp
15/108	I	ΜΕΘ 1529	Lead	#274/032086 [9]	Fr lead wire (coiled)

Fibulae

What is immediately striking about the fibulae from the Hypogeion at Methone, especially for a relatively small number of examples, is their remarkable array of types. Spectacle fibulae (**15/2–15/5**) and "Phrygian" fibulae (**15/13–15/15**) are common, both in the Hypogeion and elsewhere on the site, but there are many others, including at least two distinct types of violin-bow fibulae (**15/6–15/7**), arched (**15/8–15/9**) and beaded (**15/10**) fibulae, together with the island fibula, characterized by a single, prominent bead (**15/11**). There are also fibulae with decorative elements on their arches (**15/12**) and even the popular Italian a navicella or boat fibula (**15/16**), not to mention a fragmentary catchplate of a fibula type common in the central Balkans and in Bulgaria (**15/17**). Such a broad variety of fibulae would not be surprising at a Panhellenic sanctuary like Olympia,[9] or at prominent regional sanctuaries such as Perachora or Lindos,[10] but the Methone fibulae do not derive from a sanctuary, nor are these fibulae from tombs. In the context of the abundant evidence for metalworking at Methone (see Chapters 1 and 14, see also Chapter 13), it is almost as if local bronze jewelry makers had assembled fibulae from neighboring and more distant regions in order to emulate them.

Spectacle fibulae (Blinkenberg Type XIV; Sapouna-Sakellarakis Type X)
I begin the overview of the fibulae from the Hypogeion with the so-called spectacle fibulae, because they have been classified as a northern type, or of northern—Hallstatt—origin, imported into southern Greece.[11] Designated Type XIV ("Agrafes en spirales") by Christian Blinkenberg and conventionally referred to as "Brillenfibeln," "Spiralplattenfibeln," or "Plattenfibeln" in German, as the "ὀκτώσχημος πόρπη" in Greek,[12] and as "spectacle fibulae" in English, the type is well represented in many parts of Europe, especially in central, eastern, and southeastern Europe.[13] The two better preserved fibulae from the Hypogeion, **15/2** (ΜΕΘ 1391) and **15/3** (ΜΕΘ 1480), have figure-of-eight single-coiled connecting spirals, which are particularly common in Greece,[14] and ubiquitous throughout various parts of Europe;[15] they correspond to John Alexander's Type Ia–d.[16]

As for their chronology, spectacle fibulae similar to those from Methone first appear shortly before 1000 B.C. and continue into the 5th century, with a few subtypes extending through the 4th century B.C., though most of the varieties do not extend much after 500 B.C.[17] Within the Hypogeion, spectacle fibulae were found in all three phases, though most belong to Phases I and II, late 8th and 7th century B.C. For Greece, Sylvia Benton, on the basis of stratigraphy and synchronisms with Early Iron Age and Protocorinthian pottery, and other small finds, placed the chronology of spectacle fibulae on a more secure footing; the fibulae from the five sites discussed by Benton all dated to the Early Iron Age into the Archaic period.[18] At the Illyrian burial tumulus of Lofkënd in Albania, where the tombs ranged in date from the 14th century to about 800 B.C., the bronze spectacle fibula was the most popular type, with examples ranging in date from Lofkënd Phase III (11th–10th century B.C., one example) to Phase Va (two examples, 9th to earlier 8th century B.C.). There were none in the earlier Lofkënd Phases I and II, or in the later Phase Vb.[19] The few examples of spectacle fibulae from the sanctuary of Athena Itonia near Philia in Thessaly are dated by Kilian-Dirlmeier from Late Geometric into the earlier Archaic period, which corresponds nicely to the examples from Methone.[20] At nearby Vergina there were no fewer than 104 spectacle fibulae in bronze and one in iron from the tombs excavated by Manolis Andronikos, all similar to those from Methone.[21]

15/2. (ΜΕΘ 1391 [ΜΕ 1198]) Small Spectable Fibula   Fig. 15.2
East Hill #274/032057 [7]. 12/8/2004. Phase I.
L. 0.053; H. 0.0 22; Wt. 6.0 g.

Almost complete but heavily corroded; preserved in two main joining frr.

Small spectacle fibula made of continuous bronze wire, circular in section, with single figure-of-eight connecting loop.

Cf. **15/3–15/5** (ΜΕΘ 1480, ΜΕΘ 1479, ΜΕΘ 1478). Heurtley 1939, p. 240, fig. 112:o. A good parallel in terms of shape and size is the small spectacle fibula from the Aphaia temple on Aigina, Maass and Kilian-Dirlmeier 1998, pp. 69-70, fig. 11, no. 12, and one from Tomb 292.f31 at Knossos, see Coldstream and Catling 1996, vol. 2, p. 553; vol. 3, fig. 171, f31; vol. 4, pl. 286. The contexts of the three spectacle fibulae from the north cemetery at Knossos range from PG B to Early Orientalizing, a date that accords nicely with the Methone examples. Cf. also Felsch 2007, pp. 290–291, pls. 31–32, esp. nos. 503 (LG I), 504 (contemporary with Early Protocorinthian), 506 (6th century B.C.), and 508 (also 6th century B.C.). For two contemporary (second half of the 8th–beginning of the 7th century B.C.) spectacle fibulae from the cemetery at Akanthos, see Stefani, Tsagkaraki, and Arvanitaki 2019, pp. 166–167, nos. 60–61; cf. also Makridis 1937, pl. IV:α, β; Chrysostomou 2016, p. 15, fig. 10; p. 23, fig. 19 (middle); p. 27, fig. 25.

15/3. (ΜΕΘ 1480 [ΜΕ 1026]) Small Spectacle Fibula   Fig. 15.2
East Hill #274/032049 [5]. 19/7/2004. Phase II.
L. (as reconstructed on drawing) 0.053; Diam. (better preserved spiral) 0.021; Wt: 5.0 g.
Reconstructed from several joining frr preserving one almost complete and one partial spiral coil, plus portion of the loop that connects them, but nothing of the pin.
Thin bronze wire, circular in section, coiled to form two separate spirals, with a single figure-of-eight loop connecting the two. In the center of one of the spiral coils, what appears to be the upturned wire that forms the catchplate.
Cf. **15/2, 15/4–15/5** (ΜΕΘ 1391, ΜΕΘ 1479, ΜΕΘ 1478). Cf. also Vokotopoulou 1986, fig. 109α, β, ια, ιβ; Gadolou 2008, p. 207, fig. 160, no. 99.

15/4. (ΜΕΘ 1479 [ΜΕ 1017]) Spectacle Fibula Frr   Fig. Fig. 15.2
East Hill #274/032048 [5]. 15/7/2004. Phase II.
Diam./p.Diam. 0.027; Th. (wire) 0.003; Wt: 5.3 g.
Single fr preserving about one-half of fibula, i.e., most of one spiral coil, plus two frr preserving small portion of connecting loop and possible part of pin.
Form as **15/5** (ΜΕΘ 1478), but with no traces of catchplate.

15/5. (ΜΕΘ 1478 [ΜΕ 820]) Spectacle Fibule Frr   Fig. 15.2
East Hill #274/032043 [5]. 24/6/2004. Phase III.
P.L./Diam. 0.028; Wt: 5.4 g.
Two frr preserving about one-half of fibula, including most of one spiral coil.
Bronze wire, circular in section, coiled to form a spiral. Small upturned terminal near center of one side is almost certainly what survives of the catchplate.
Cf. **15/4** (ΜΕΘ 1479).

Fragments of other spectacle fibulae:
ΜΕΘ 1481. Phase II

Violin-bow fibulae (Blinkenberg Type I; Sapouna-Sakellarakis Type I)
There are only two examples of the violin-bow fibula—"Violinbogelfibel" in German, often referred to as φυλλόσχημοι πόρπαι/πόρπες in Greek[22]—from the Hypogeion, one dating to Phase II (**15/6** [ΜΕΘ 1390]) (Late Geometric or early Archaic), the other (**15/7** [ΜΕΘ 1387]) to post–Phase III

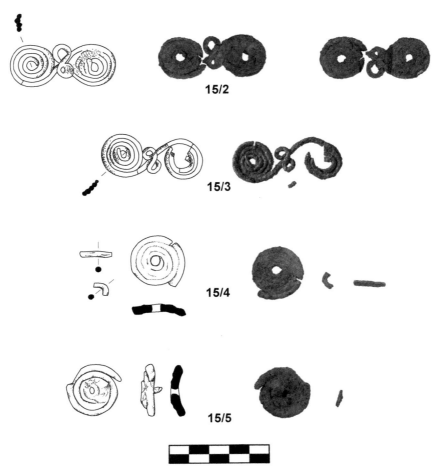

FIGURE 15.2. Bronze spectacle fibulae, **15/2** (MEΘ 1391), **15/3** (MEΘ 1480), **15/4** (MEΘ 1479), **15/5** (MEΘ 1478). Drawings T. Ross and F. Skyvalida, photos I. Coyle and J. Vanderpool

and, as such, could extend into the Archaic period. This basic type of fibula, simply designated "en archet" by Blinkenberg, enjoys a Mycenaean pedigree.[23] The basic form is classified by Effie Sapouna-Sakellarakis as her Type I, and there are at least eight varieties (Ia–Ih) outlined by her.[24] Unfortunately, both of the Methone examples are fragmentary and difficult to assign typologically with any precision.

The widened arch of **15/6** (MEΘ 1390), which has been hammered flat and which bears no incised decoration, accords with Blinkenberg's Type I 7, referred to as "l'arc a été élargi et aplati par le martelage; pas de décoration."[25] Of the five examples presented by Blinkenberg—from Therapnai near Sparta, Kephallenia, Vrokastro, Agia Anna near Thebes, and Delphi—all are assigned to LH or LM III, or else Submycenaean; the example from Vardino in Macedonia published by Heurtley is presented with the Late Bronze Age material (see catalogue entry). Although there is some earlier Bronze Age residual material in the Hypogeion (see Chapters 4–5), I doubt that **15/6** (MEΘ 1390) is Late Bronze Age. Although not common, the type is attested in Greece, the Balkans more generally, and the Italian peninsula during the Early Iron Age. Crete has produced two examples from Karphi which are clearly Early Iron Age, both dated as "Submycenaean" by Sapouna-Sakellarakis.[26] A number of related decorated and undecorated fibulae are referred to by Klaus Kilian as "Blattbügelfibeln"; of these, two from Pherai are dated by Kilian, one on the basis of comparanda to the 9th–8th century, the other to the 7th century B.C.[27] In the cemeteries of Vitsa Zagoriou there is at least one bronze fibula, decorated with incision on the arch, and over half a dozen undecorated iron examples that are all dated by Ioulia Vokotopoulou to the 8th century B.C., some as early as the first quarter or first half of the century, and several ca. 750 B.C.[28] Moreover, the distribution of the type in Greece, the Balkans, and the Italian peninsula in the 8th and 7th century B.C. has been mapped out by Kilian.[29]

The concave form of the arch of **15/7** (ΜΕΘ 1387) resembles some of Blinkenberg's "fibules hautes par devant," especially I 11 where "le profil de l'arc est concave."[30] It is of the same size and similar shape to an example from Kavousi, which should be of Early Iron Age date; a number of related examples similar to Blinkenberg's I 10–12 are assembled by Sapouna-Sakellarakis under her Type Ig ("Asymmetrische Violinbogenfibeln mit Blattbügel oder mit Bügel rundem Querschnitt"), which are found on Crete and Euboia from the end of the 12th century B.C. on.[31] The Methone fibula differs from these in two respects: it has a much more elaborate, spiral coil at or near the connection with the spring proper, and a swelling, rather than a bead, on the midpoint of the arch. The general form of **15/7** finds parallels in the central Balkans, where some examples have elaborate twisted decoration connected with the spring.[32]

15/6. (ΜΕΘ 1390 [ΜΕ 1177]) Violin-bow Fibula Fig. 15.3
East Hill #274/032055 [7]. 10/8/2004. Phase II.
P.L. 0.063; p.H. 0.018; Wt: 2.4 g.

Two main joining frr, plus small chips and flakes, preserving all of arch and much of the spring and catchplate, but nothing of the pin.

Violin-bow-shaped, with proportionately long arch, hammered flat and roughly lozenge-shaped. Catchplate set perpendicular to arch, also hammered flat and spreading toward the bottom to accommodate the pin, nothing of which survives. Spring two turns and probably originally more.

For a related violin-bow fibula from the agora at Methone, see **26/55** (ΜΕΘ 4196); for another from the more recent excavation at Methone, see Morris et al. 2020, p. 689, fig. 36:b (ΜΕΘ 7888) from the Late Bronze Age tomb 21; see also Heurtley 1939, p. 231, fig. 104:aa. Cf. esp. Blinkenberg 1926, pp. 50–51, I 7a and 7d (mostly Late Bronze Age); Sapouna-Sakellarakis 1978, pp. 37–39, pl. 2, no. 28, from Karphi (assigned "Submycenaean"), which is about twice the size of **15/6** (ΜΕΘ 1390); for a fragmentary fibula of similar size to **15/6**, but with a slightly wider plain bow, see *Lefkandi* I, pp. 112, 238, pls. 94, 239:i, S 10,10 (assigned EPG); Vokotopoulou 1986, fig. 114, no. κστ; cf. also Kilian 1975a, p. 19, pl. 1, no. 6; Aslan 2019, p. 285, pl. 2, no. 7 (Troy, from a mixed context, but thought to be Late Bronze Age or Submycenaean). For the same basic form and size, though without the incised decoration, cf. the fragmentary fibula from Francavilla Marittima in southern Italy, Papadopoulos 2003a, pp. 84–85, fig. 104, no. 231; for the range of this type in Italy, where it is referred to as "fibule ad arco di violino," see von Eles Masi 1986, pp. 1–13, pls. 1–3.

15/7. (ΜΕΘ 1387 [ΜΕ 343]) Bronze Violin-bow Fibula Fig. 15.3
East Hill #274/032014 [5]. 7/8/2003. Post–Phase III.
L. (as reconstructed): 0.088; H. 0.030 (or less); Wt. 8.3 g.

Five frr preserving most of arch, including catchplate, greater portion of pin, part of the connection from arch to pin, including a small portion of the spring.

Violin-bow fibula, with arch mostly circular in section, rectangular toward the edges, with swelling, rather than bead, at midpoint. Top of arch concave, with catchplate end hammered flat and bent to accommodate pin. At opposite end spiral coil that forms part of the spring or, more accurately, the connection to spring. As preserved, simple spring, with probably only one turn. Pin thin, circular in section, tapering toward well-preserved point.

Cf. Blinkenberg 1926, p. 55, I 11:b, from Kavousi (= Sapouna-Sakellarakis 1978, p. 40, pl. 2, no. 44). Cf. also Vasić 1999, various examples from the central Balkans on pl. 2.

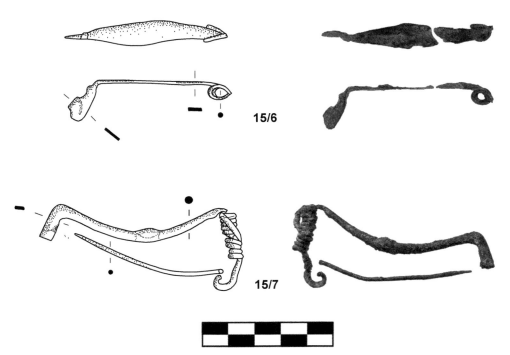

FIGURE 15.3. Bronze violin-bow fibulae, **15/6** (MEΘ 1390), **15/7** (MEΘ 1387).
Drawings F. Skyvalida, photos I. Coyle and J. Vanderpool

Arched or bow fibulae (Blinkenberg Type II; Sapouna-Sakellarakis Type II)
There are only two fragmentary examples of the arched fibula, what Blinkenberg simply referred to as "la fibule arquée" (soit la "fibule à arc simple"), often called bow fibulae in English, which corresponds to the classic "Bogenfibeln" in German, "τοξωταί πόρπαι" in Greek, and "fibule ad arco semplice" in Italian.[33] Both fragments were encountered in Phase I of the Hypogeion, and can therefore be dated to the late 8th or early 7th century B.C. As with the violin-bow fibulae, Sapouna-Sakellarakis distinguished eight types, labeled IIa–IIh, which began in Late Helladic IIIC, became popular during the Protogemetric period, and continued well into the Archaic period.[34] This is one of the most popular fibula types in the Aegean.[35] It is the most common fibula type in the Early Iron Age tombs at Lefkandi, and prominent among the Late Geometric and Archaic votive offerings at the sanctuary of Athena Itonia near Philia in Thessaly, as it is throughout Thessaly.[36] Farther afield, the basic type is well documented on the Italian peninsula, throughout the Balkans and the Danube region, the Caucasus and Asia Minor, but is exceedingly rare elsewhere in the Near East.[37] Closer to home, bronze τοξωταί πόρπαι are the second most popular fibula after the spectacle fibulae in the tombs of Vergina; Andronikos distinguished four types: 1) symmetrical with two beads on the arch; 2) with twisted arch or bow; 3) plain; and 4) with an arch of broad sheet bronze (τὰς ἐχούσας τόξον ἐκ πλατέος ἐλάσματος).[38] Among the fibulae of this type at Vergina there were only two iron examples, which are consistent with Type 2 fibulae from the Athenian Agora—asymmetrical bow fibulae with beaded moldings—found in both bronze and iron, common during the Protogeometric and Early Geometric periods.[39]

It is unfortunate that both **15/8** and **15/9** are so fragmentary, especially since neither preserves the catchplate and it is difficult to determine whether the arched bow is symmetrical or asymmetrical, though in both cases the bow looks symmetrical on the basis of what survives. As such, both examples can be classified under Blinkenberg's "fibules à arc symétrique," which he further divides into 14 subtypes, each with various examples.[40] **15/8** is a good example of a

Bogenfibel, with the arch ovoid in section and relatively thin, and a simple spring with at least one full turn. Although similar, **15/9** differs from **15/8** in two important respects: its bow is thicker and tapers more noticeably toward both ends, which also partly explains the weight difference between the two pieces, and it is decorated with three or four lightly incised fillets, barely visible in the corrosion, at the juncture of the arch and spring. Although the arched bow is thicker than that of **15/8**, **15/9** is not clearly an example of the "Bogenfibel mit geschwollenem Bügel," even though it is very close to some examples of the type.[41] If **15/9** is of the type with swollen arch, then it would correspond to Type IV of both Blinkenberg and Sapouna-Sakellarakis, though the latter does stress that Type IVa seems to be a continuation of Type II.[42] I assemble a few comparanda for both fibulae in the catalogue below.

15/8. (ΜΕΘ 1393 [ΜΕ 1477]) Small Arched Fibula Fig. 15.4
East Hill #274/032063 [9]. 23/8/2004. Phase I.
P.L. 0.031; p.W. 0.018; Wt. 0.9 g.
Two joining frr preserving greater part of arch and spring of fibula.
Arch ovoid in section and relatively thin. Spring at least one full turn.
Cf. **15/9** (ΜΕΘ 1394), but without the fillets; cf. also *Lefkandi* I, pl. 247, esp. nos. 2–5, all from the Skoubris cemetery (S 8,6; S 20,8, S 15B,5, S 10,8); also Skoubris Tomb 16, with at least 11 examples, mostly with the arch square or rhomboidal in section, see *Lefkandi* I, pl. 92. All of the Lefkandi comparanda are early, Submycenaean or EPG. For later LG and Archaic examples, cf., among others, Kilian-Dirlmeier 2002, pl. 15, esp. nos. 254, 256, 257, and also nos. 252–253, both with an elongated catchplate, and no. 260.

15/9. (ΜΕΘ 1394 [ΜΕ 3325]) Fragmentary Arched Fibula Fig. 15.4
East Hill #274/032086 [9]. 22/11/2006. Phase I.
P.L. 0.036; p.H. 0.020; Wt. 5.2 g.
Single fr, corroded, preserving most of arch and part of spring, but nothing of the catchplate or pin.
Plain arch, very slightly swollen near center, tapering toward both ends. Three or four fillets at terminal just before the spring. Spring at least one turn, probably originally more.
Cf. **15/8** (ΜΕΘ 1393), the surviving bow of which is not decorated. Although arched fibulae like **15/9** are common, examples with the incised decoration are less common; cf. among others, Kilian 1975a, pl. 1, nos. 13 (presumably from Pherai) and 21 (Pherai, but of silver); Gergova 1987, pl. 1, no. 16 (from Dolno Sahrane in Bulgaria); cf. also Sapouna-Sakellarakis 1978, pl. 18, no. 593 (from Hephaistia on Lemnos), which is significantly larger.

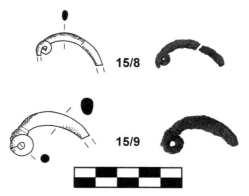

FIGURE 15.4. Bronze arched fibulae, **15/8** (ΜΕΘ 1393), **15/9** (ΜΕΘ 1394).
Drawings F. Skyvalida, photos I. Coyle and J. Vanderpool

Beaded fibula (Blinkenberg Type III; Sapouna-Sakellarakis Type III)

The solitary example of this fibula type from the Hypogeion corresponds to Sapouna-Sakellarakis' Type III, normally referred to as "Fibeln mit Kugelgliedern im Bügel," which she divides into six varieties, labeled Types IIIa–IIIf.[43] As she explains, Blinkenberg categorized various examples of the type rather inconsistently, either chronologically or regionally, to his Types III and IV. It remains true, however, that the vast majority of Sapouna-Sakellarakis' types correspond to Blinkenberg's Type III rather than Type IV, that Blinkenberg was fairly clear in his typology, and that examples of these two types tend to converge into one another.[44] **15/10** was encountered in Phase III of the fill of the Hypogeion, and the fibula can thus be placed from the later 8th century into the earlier 7th century B.C. Sapouna-Sakellarakis singles out an example of this type from Fortetsa as the earliest of the series, dating to Protogeometric, but notes that the type is common in the 8th–6th centuries B.C., which accords nicely with the date range of **15/10**.[45] It should be noted, however, that the Fortetsa fibula was found in Tomb II, which contained 18 burials inside and ten outside, ranging in date from Late Protogeometric to early Orientalizing with the majority being "Orientalizing."[46]

Although fragmentary, it is clear that **15/10** had only three beads, though the majority of Type III fibulae had considerably more. The three beads on the arch are comparatively large, the central bead the largest; the uppermost preserved portion of the catchplate was hammered flat, while the arch at the opposite end, circular in section, extended toward the spring, which was not preserved. It was here that at least three fillets, poorly preserved, were incised at the juncture of the arch, right up against the flanking bead, on the extension for the spring. As noted above, only a few examples of Type III fibulae had three beads and, ironically, the closest parallel for **15/10** is the Fortetsa fibula already mentioned. The sizes of the two fibulae are similar (the preserved length of **15/10** is 0.047, the length of Fortetsa 1106 0.045), as are the shapes of their respective catchplates and extensions for the springs, with the Fortetsa fibula having a spring with at least two turns. In the case of the latter, the lightly incised or poorly preserved fillets are on the catchplate, as opposed to the extension for the spring. Indeed, quite a few examples of Type IIIb fibulae are decorated with such fillets on one or both sides of the arch.[47] In addition to fibulae from Crete being close to **15/10**, several from Asia Minor also offer close parallels.[48]

15/10. (ΜΕΘ 1388 [ΜΕ 819]) Beaded Fibula   Fig. 15.5

   East Hill #274/032043 [5]. 24/6/2004. Phase III.

   P.L. 0.047; p.H. 0.024; Wt: 16.7 g.

   One primary fr, plus two small frr preserving most of arch and upper part of the catchplate, but nothing of the pin or spring. Heavily corroded.

   Beaded fibula, with three large beads on the arch, the central one the largest, flanked by two slightly smaller beads. Uppermost preserved portion of catchplate hammered flat. Arch at opposite end circular in section, extending toward the spring, which does not survive. Fillets, at least three and perhaps more, poorly preserved and barely visible at juncture of arch and extension for the spring.

   The closest parallel comes from Fortetsa Tomb II, see Brock 1957, pp. 84–88, 97, pls. 75, 167, no. 1106; Blinkenberg's (1926, p. 83, fig. 76) Type III 10 a ("arc composé d'une série de boutons") from Vrokastro, Crete, is also close (for which see further Mariaud 2011, p. 702, fig. 10b). Cf., among others, Boehlau 1898, p. 162, pl. 15, no. 10; Boehlau and Habich 1996, p. 15, Grab 36, no. 14; also an example from Troy, Aslan 2019, p. 286, pl. 2, no, 10. Cf. also some of the examples more recently published from Kythnos, Mazarakis Ainian 2010, pl. 22:2, esp. lower row, two on right; and Minoa Amorgos, Marangou 2002, p. 122, fig. 119α, bottom right; cf. Maass and Kilian-Dirlmeier 1998, pp. 72, 74, fig. 12, nos. 20, 21 (Aigina).

FIGURE 15.5. Beaded fibula, **15/10** (MEΘ 1388). Drawing F. Skyvalida, photo J. Vanderpool

(Island) fibula with one bead on arch (Blinkenberg Type IV 10; Sapouna-Sakellarakis Type V)
I follow Sapouna-Sakellarakis' nomenclature, who refers to these distinctive fibulae as "Inselfibeln mit einer Kugel im Bügel."[49] The type corresponds to Blinkenberg's IV 10 a–k.[50] Although classified as an island fibula by Sapouna-Sakellarakis, she did note the occurrence of the type at Ephesos, but also on the Greek mainland, in the Peloponnese (at the Argive Heraion and at the sanctuary of Artemis Orthia near Sparta), in Athens, and in Thessaly.[51] In his typically cogent manner, Blinkenberg noted that the examples of Type IV 10 that he put together came from the Troad, Caria, and Ephesos, together with examples from Athens, Thebes, Aigina, and Lindos.[52] Indeed, Ertuğrul Caner has shown the ubiquity of the type in coastal Asia Minor, with examples from Smyrna, Erythrai, Milas, Assarlik, Neandria, Ephesos, and Ainos, with additional examples said to be from Thymbra and the Troad.[53] Were I writing in German, I would prefer to call the type "Fibeln mit einer Kugel im Bügel" or "Fibeln mit Zierelementen auf dem Bügel."

As with the other fibula types from the Hypogeion at Methone, this too is fragmentary, though a good portion of the arch and much of the spring survives, but nothing of the catchplate and pin. The arch, circular in section, supports a single comparatively large bead, which was almost certainly originally spherical, but was misformed by corrosion. That part of the arch close to the spring was hammered and is rectangular in section, and decorated with four grooves halfway between the bead and the spring. In dealing with the distribution of the type in Greece, Sapouna-Sakellarakis wrote, "Diese Form ist im Westen und Norden unbekannt."[54] Consequently, the appearance of a single example from Methone, albeit fragmentary, is a welcome addition, especially as its context in Phase I of the Hypogeion fill fixes its chronology to the late 8th or early 7th century B.C.

Sapouna-Sakellarakis distinguishes two variants of this fibula, Types Va and Vb. The more common of the two, Type Va, is, indeed, common throughout the islands of the Aegean, and particularly so in the eastern Aegean. Rhodes has yielded the lion's share of the type, with examples primarily from Ialysos, but with smaller numbers from Lindos, Vroulia, and Kalymnos.[55] Type Va is also common on Samos; examples from Chios were found at the sanctuary of Apollo at Phana and at Emporio, both from the Temple of Athena on the acropolis and the so-called Harbor Sanctuary; and there is at least one example from the site of Klopede on Lesbos.[56] From the Cyclades there are a few examples from the Delion on Paros, and one from Thera; in the Saronic Gulf the Sanctuary of Aphaia on Aigina has yielded at least three examples; there is also at least one example from Kythnos.[57] To the south there is a solitary example from Arkades on Crete, and, noteworthy for a context in the north Aegean, at least three examples from the sanctuary of the Great Gods at Samothrace, two from the "Hall of the Votive Gifts."[58] In discussing the chronology of Type Va fibulae in the Aegean, Sapouna-Sakellarakis notes that the Aigina and Chios examples are Early Geometric to Archaic, the Kalymnos and Lesbos examples early Archaic, those from Paros date from the end of the 8th to the beginning of the 7th, those from Ialysos, Lindos, and Vroulia are Late Geometric to early Archaic, and those from Samos, Thera, Samothrace, and Crete are mostly Archaic.[59] In contrast, the Type Vb fibulae have a more circumscribed distribution, largely confined to Euboia (Lefkandi) and Skyros, and are earlier in the main, none securely dated after ca. 800 B.C.[60]

FIGURE 15.6. Island fibula with one bead on arch, **15/11** (MEΘ 1385).
Drawing F. Skyvalida, photo I. Coyle

15/11. (MEΘ 1385 [ME 3266]) Island Fibula with Single Large Bead   Fig. 15.6
East Hill #274/022064 [13]. 21/9/2006. Phase I.
P.L. (main fr) 0.031; p.H. 0.024; Wt. (all frr) 4.7 g.
One main fr preserving portion of arch, spring, and bead; one other non-joining fr may or may not belong (PL: 0.0110), plus three minuscule chips of corrosion.
Arch circular in section, supporting what is almost certainly a large single bead, spherical in the main, but misformed by corrosion. Portion of arch close to spring hammered flat, rectangular in section; spring at least two turns. Main arch decorated with four grooves halfway between bead and spring.
Among the various examples of Type Va fibulae, **15/11** is closest to a number of examples from Ialysos, esp. Sapouna-Sakellarakis 1978, pl. 32, no. 1073, cf. also nos. 1068–1072, and pl. 33, no. 1135; see also Caner 1983, pls. 6–7, nos. 95–107; Aslan 2019, p. 287, pl. 4, no. 15.

Fibula with decorative element on the arch (Blinkenberg Type VI; Sapouna-Sakellarakis Type VIIa) Versions of this fibula type have been variously classified in the literature, but their Thessalian pedigree was clearly noted by Blinkenberg early on under the general heading of his "types thessaliens."[61] Of the fibulae assembled by Blinkenberg, the closest to **15/12** correspond to his Types VI 8 and VI 15.[62] In his study of the fibulae from Thessaly, which provide the closest parallels for the solitary example of the type from Methone, **15/12**, Klaus Kilian gathered different fibula types under the broad heading "Bogenfibel, Bügel mit Ringwülsten, Kugeln und Kuben," which he placed under the broader heading of "Bogenfibeln mit kräftig geschwollenem (Sanguisugaförmigem) Bügel."[63] In her discussion of related fibulae from the sanctuary of Athena Itonia near Philia, Imma Kilian-Dirlmeier notes, "Bogelfibeln mit Sanguisuga-Bügel von rhombischen oder rundern Querschnitt; an den Bügelenden ein oder zwei Ringscheiben, auf dem Bügelscheitel kann ein Zierknopf sitzen; gestreckter Fuss mit Zierknopft auf dem hochgezogenen Ende," and she goes on to cite Kilian's analysis of the Pherai fibulae already noted.[64] In her analysis of the fibulae from the Aegean islands, Sapouna-Sakellarakis distinguished three variants under the broad heading of "Varianten der Typen II–IV mit Zierknöpfen auf dem Bügel," thereby conflating fibulae of very different types.[65] Of her three variants—Types VIIa, VIIb, and VIIc—the closest to **15/12** is VIIa, with the decorative element at the apex of the arch being a simple or slightly more elaborate button-like finial.[66] On the basis of the numerous examples of Type VIIa she amassed, Sapouna-Sakellarakis was able to date the type from ca. 750–600 B.C., which accords well with the date of **15/12**, found in Phase III of the fill of the Hypogeion.[67]

15/12. (MEΘ 1384 [ME 633]) Fragmentary Bronze Fibula   Fig. 15.7
East Hill #274/022036 [10]. 8/4/2004. Phase III.
P.L. 0.032; p.H. 0.022; Wt. 7.0 g.
Single piece preserving all of arch but little, if anything, of the spring or catchplate.
Swollen arch surmounted by a knob finial with small disk head. Substantial bead framing arch on either side. Below bead on one side, a circular extension, as preserved, conceivably, but not clearly, a

FIGURE 15.7. Fibula with decorative element on arch, **15/12** (MEΘ 1384).
Drawing A. Hooton, photo J. Vanderpool

double-spool pin connection, or else the upper part of the catchplate, which is more likely given the early date of the fibula. At the opposite end, a thin extension suggesting the beginning of the spring. A substantial portion of a textile pseudomorph appears to be preserved on one side.

The closest parallels for **15/12** are from Thessaly, cf., among others, Kilian 1975a, p. 34, pl. 7, nos. 240, 242, 244, 246, 248, 252–254 (all from Pherai); Kilian-Dirlmeier 2002, p. 22, pl. 16, nos. 267–270 (Athena Itonia sanctuary, Philia). Cf. also Maass and Kilian-Dirlmeier 1998, pp. 68, 70, fig. 11, no. 6 (Aigina); Blinkenberg 1926, p. 115, fig. 132, Type VI 8 b; p. 118, figs. 140–141, Type VI 15 a and b; Klebinder-Gauss 2007, pp. 27, 225, pl. 1, no. 11 (Ephesos, LG and 7th century B.C.).

"Phrygian" fibulae (Blinkenberg Type XII; Sapouna-Sakellarakis Type XII)
Perhaps the most surprising aspect of the fibulae from Methone is the ubiquity—the popularity—of the so-called "Phrygian" fibulae. Although there are only three examples from the Hypogeion, the Phrygian fibula type is the most common at Methone in contemporary and later contexts all over the site, including the finds from the agora area on the East Hill, as well as those from the most recent excavations (2014–2017). The popularity of the type at the site, the remarkable varieties of subtypes found there, coupled with the abundant evidence of bronze metalworking may even suggest that Methone was a place that produced this, and other fibula types, as well as various additional metal objects. What is interesting in this respect is that all of the fibulae at the nearby cemetery at Sindos, made of both gold and bronze, are of Phrygian type.[68]

The three examples from the Hypogeion derive from Phase I (**15/13** and **15/14**) and one from a post–Phase III (**15/15**) context; as such, the first two can be assigned to the late 8th and early 7th century, while **15/15** may be contemporary or a little later, extending into the Archaic period. What have come to be known as Phrygian fibulae were first classified by Blinkenberg as Type XII, under his heading of "Types d'Asie Mineure."[69] Blinkenberg distinguished 17 varieties or subtypes, and tabulated the provenance of the examples he was able to assemble, showing that the vast majority were indeed found in Asia Minor, with smaller quantities found in Syria and Palestine, the Aegean islands, the Peloponnese, and elsewhere on the Greek mainland, as well as in Albania and Bosnia.[70] This classification has been followed by later authors, with important corpora of the type published by Oscar White Muscarella from Gordion, Sapouna-Sakellarakis from the Aegean islands, and Caner from Asia Minor.[71]

Establishing the precise variety of **15/13** is difficult owing to its state of preservation, especially the corrosion of the arch, and the fact that only a small portion of the spring, but little of the catchplate and nothing of the pin, survives. I am fairly certain that the arch is not decorated, and the closest parallels include Blinkenberg's Type XII 7, Muscarella's Type XII 7 and 7A, Sapouna-Sakellaris's Type XII 7 (but also some of her XII 5–6, and Caner's Group A, especially Variant A 1,1 and A1,2 [see details in the catalogue entry below]). The smaller and more simple **15/14** accords primarily with examples of Blinkenberg's Type XII 12 and XII 13, particularly the latter, and finds especially close parallels from some of the Aegean islands and a few from Gordion (see entry below). Particularly interesting is a mold from Old Smyrna (Bayrakli), thought to date to the 7th century B.C., which is precisely of this type of fibula.[72] There is a very similar fibula from the West Hill of this same type (**26/4** [MEΘ 5285]). The one example of a "Phrygian" fibula from a post–Phase III context of the Hypogeion at Methone, **15/15**, is a solid fibula, with a beaded arch; rather than set continuously around the arch, the beads are arranged in five groups, each composed of five beads. The type corresponds to Blinkenberg's Type XII 14 (= Muscarella XII 14), although few of the fibulae illustrated by both Blinkenberg and Muscarella are close to **15/15**.[73] Close comparanda from Samos are published by Sapouna-Sakellarakis, and a few from Asia Minor can be compared (including examples from Gordion, Sardis, and Yazılıkaya), though very few of these have the beads, arranged in five groups, so close set as on **15/15** (see catalogue entry below).

Of the three examples from the Hypogeion, **15/13** is perhaps the only one that has any claim to be a Phrygian fibula proper, that is, one manufactured in Asia Minor. In contrast, **15/14** and **15/15** may be Greek fibulae derived from Type XII, 13 and 14.[74] As such, they are best classified as Type XII, 15–17. Most of the fibulae of the general Type XII from other areas of the site, including those from the summit of the West Hill (**26/4**) and the more numerous examples from the agora (**26/57–26/67**), are also of Type XII, 15–17, manufactured in the Aegean, perhaps even at Methone.

15/13. (MEΘ 1499 [ME 1248]) Large Phrygian Fibula   Fig. 15.8
   East Hill #274/032060 [7]. 19/8/2004. Phase I.
   P.L./L. 0.059; H. 0.046; Wt. 34.3 g.

   Three joining frr, all heavily corroded, preserving all of arch, small portion of spring, but little of the catchplate and nothing of the pin.

   Large and rather heavy fibula, with symmetrical, almost horseshoe-shaped arch, rectangular in section. Arch splays out very slightly toward terminal with catchplate, only the uppermost of which survives; rectangular as preserved and hammered flat. Opposite end extending to spring preserves two small projections, or ears, as shown, with terminal above the spring circular and framed by a band. Although poorly preserved, the spring is clear, with three turns and possibly more; spring made of bronze wire circular in section.

   Cf. Blinkenberg 1926, pp. 213–214, Type XII 7, and esp. the two illustrated examples under XII 7 f (both from Lindos); cf. also some examples of his Type XII 9, esp. pp. 214–217, XII 9 f, l–m, though it seems reasonably clear that there is no decoration on the arch, which would preclude Type VII 9; Muscarella 1967, pl. V, nos. 23–25 (all Type XII 7A); Sapouna-Sakellarakis 1978, p. 123, pl. 50, nos. 1614A–B (Lindos) and 1615 (Samos), and also some of her Type XII A c (pp. 122–123, pl. 50, esp. nos. 1611–163 (= Muscarella Type XII 5–6); Caner 1983, pp. 51–50, pls. 10–16, Type A 1,1–2, (= Muscarella Type XII 7, XII 7A), esp. nos. 161–167, 173–175, 184, among many others.

15/14. (MEΘ 1392 [ME 1254]) "Phrygian" Fibula   Fig. 15.8
   East Hill #274/032061 [7]. 20/8/2004. Phase I.
   L./p.L. 0.030; H: 0.025; Wt: 3.8 g.

   Single piece preserving all of fibula except for pin and spring. Catchplate, as preserved, folded over in a manner that is not original.

   Beaded fibula, with arch circular in section, with three beads, as shown. End with the catchplate hammered flat and bent up (before the post-depositional damage). Stem/shaft heading to spring is circular in section and, as preserved, tapers to a point.

   This type accords with Blinkenberg 1926, pp. 218–222, Type XII 12 and XII 13 (= Muscarella XII 12, 13, esp. the latter); esp. close are some examples in Sapouna-Sakellarakis 1978, p. 127, pl. 52, nos. 1657 (Samothrace) and 1659 (Chios); pl. 53, nos. 1661 (Chios), 1676–1677 (Ialysos); for related examples primarily, but not exclusively, from Gordion, see Caner 1983, pp. 86–87, pl. 37, Variante C 1,1, esp. nos. 479–482. About 50 examples of the type were encountered in the Harbor Sanctuary at Chios, a selection of which was published by Boardman (1967, pp. 209–210) as Type H, nos. 212–221; at Chios there appears to be no significant change in the form from Period II (680/670) to IV (620–600 B.C.). Cf. also *Sardis* 8, p. 114, pl. 43, no. 673 (dated to the 7th century B.C.); Boehlau 1898, p. 162, pl. 15, nos. 11–12; Boehlau and Habich 1996, p. 15, Grab 36, nos. 15–16; cf. also Bischop 1996, pp. 145–146, 161, fig. 2 no. 11 (= pl. 29, no. 4), classified as a "Phrygian" bronze fibula (stray find).

15/15. (MEΘ 1382 [ME 92]) "Phrygian" Fibula   Fig. 15.8

East Hill #274/022007 [3] or [5]. 6/6/2003. Post–Phase III.

L. 0.038; H. 0.033; Wt. 11.4 g.

Three joining frr preserving complete arch and catchplate, but nothing of the pin.

Solid fibula, with thick beaded arch, with some of the individual beads appearing square, others perhaps even rosette-shaped. Rather than set continuously around the arch, the beads appear to be arranged in groups, five groups completely preserved, each composed of five beads. Roughly triangular (rather than clover-shaped) connection to catchplate, hammered flat on side with projecting catchplate, with boss on the opposite side. Thin, rectangular catchplate, bent up to accommodate pin, which is not preserved. Small but broken projection of wire on side of arch opposite the pin would have formed the spring.

This fibula accords with Blinkenberg and Muscarella Type XII 14; esp. close are some examples from the Aegean, see Sapouna-Sakellarakis 1978, pp. 128–129, pls. 53–54, nos. 1681–1685, esp. nos. 1681, 1683, 1685–1686 (all from Samos); for examples of this and other Phrygian fibulae from Kythnos, see Mazarakis Ainian 2010, pl. 22:3; cf. also some Anatolian examples, Caner 1983, pp. 142–145, pls. 57–58, Variante J 11,1, esp. nos. 987 (Gordion), 989 (Sardis), 997 (Yazılıkaya). This appears to be a predecessor of later fibulae from the area of the agora on the East Hill, presented in Chapter 26.

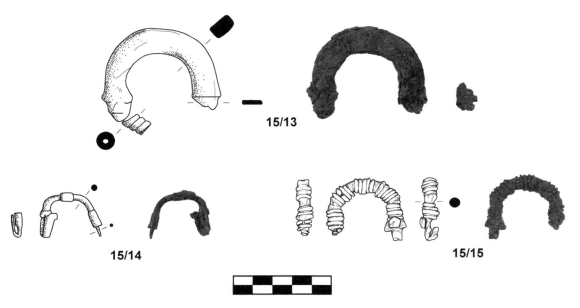

FIGURE 15.8. "Phrygian" fibulae, **15/13** (MEΘ 1499), **15/14** (MEΘ 1392), **15/15** (MEΘ 1382). Drawings T. Ross and F. Skyvalida, photos I. Coyle

Fibula a navicella (Blinkenberg Type XI 6–7; Sapouna-Sakellarakis Type XId)

Methone has produced several examples of this distinctive Italian type of fibula a navicella or "boat fibula," and most can be assigned an Archaic date. Two examples from the West Hill of the same general form as **15/16** (**26/5** and **26/6**), are mid-6th century B.C. or earlier, whereas **15/16** from the Hypogeion (post–Phase III), may be the earliest of the group, best assigned to the 7th century B.C., but perhaps as early as the late 8th century.[75] In his seminal publication of the earliest Italian fibulae, Johannes Sundwall classified various a navicella fibulae with the "kurzfüssige Sanguisugafibeln" of his Group F and with the "langfüssige Sanguisugafibeln" of his Group G.[76] One of the fullest corpora of boat fibulae from northern Italy was assembled by Patrizia von Eles Masi, who distinguished no fewer than 51 variants of the broad category; the earliest varieties can be assigned to the 8th century B.C., with most dating to the 7th and 6th centuries B.C., and only a few extending into the earliest 5th century.[77] The basic type corresponds to Blinkenberg's Type XI 6–7, though he did not actually illustrate any examples, and with Sapouna-Sakellarakis's Type XId, who illustrates examples from Lindos and Exochi on Rhodes, as well as from Samos, Emporio, and Aigina.[78] Although all of the latter are of the same broad type, the range in terms of variants, size, and decoration is noteworthy. Elsewhere in Greece, fibulae of this broad type were found at the sanctuaries of Zeus at Olympia, Hera Akraia and Limena at Perachora, and Artemis Orthia at Sparta.[79] Thessaly has yielded an impressive number of fibulae a navicella, especially from Pherai, again with a noteworthy range of sizes and varieties, mostly decorated.[80]

Enough of **15/16** survives to establish that the hollow, boat-like arch has a small protruding knob on either side at the point of the greatest width and the arch is defined by a set of three fillets on either side, one at the juncture of the arch and spring (the latter does not survive), the other at the juncture of the arch and catchplate. The latter is hammered flat, and several small non-joining fragments may well be from the pin (see Fig. 15.9). Although broken and corroded, it is clear that the arch did not have incised decoration. **15/16** is a good example of a boat fibula with lateral projections ("fibula a navicella con bottoni laterali"). It finds parallels in two related fibulae from Francavilla Marittima in southern Italy, one from tomb 59 at the Macchiabate necropolis, the other on the Timpone della Motta.[81] Among the almost bewildering array of varieties from north Italy, a few are close to **15/16**, though most lack the fillets framing the arch, while many others have incised decoration (see catalogue entry below).

15/16. (ΜΕΘ 1510 [ME 331]) Bronze Fibula a Navicella   Fig. 15.9

    East Hill #274/032011 [3]. 6/8/2003. Post–Phase III.

    P.L. 0.047; W. (arch) 0.019; Wt. 6.6 g.

    Recomposed from several joining frr preserving all of arch, portions of catchplate, but nothing of the spring; a few non-joining frr may be from the pin.

    Classic Italian a navicella or boat fibula, with distinctive boat-shaped arch, which is hollow, and with two knobs, one on either side at the point of greatest width. Band of fillets (three) at juncture of arch to spring and another at juncture of arch and catchplate. The area that is to become the catchplate is hammered flat.

    Cf. Lo Schiavo 1983–1984a, pp. 112–113, fig. 37, no. 7; Lo Schiavo 1983–1984b, pp. 130–131, fig. 45, no. 10 (both from Francavilla Marittima); von Eles Masi 1986, esp. pl. 107, nos. 1261, 1265–1266; pl. 108, various examples; pl. 109, esp. nos. 1289–1290 (with fillets on either side of the arch), but cf. also nos. 1288, 1296–1297, 1303; pl. 110, nos. 1307–1308 (among others); Kilian 1975a, pl. 31, no. 843 and esp. pl. 32, no. 869; an example from the acropolis of Lindos (see Blinkenberg 1931, p. 87, pl. 8, no. 104 = Sapouna-Sakellarakis 1978, p. 118, pl. 49, no. 184) is not unlike **15/16**, though it does not have the fillets on either side of the arch. Of the examples from Olympia, the closest is *OlForsch* XIII, pp. 292–293, pls. 20, 65, no. 1065 (though it has incised decoration).

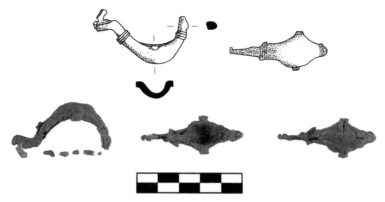

FIGURE 15.9. Bronze fibula a navicella, **15/16** (ΜΕΘ 1510).
Drawing F. Skyvalida, photos I. Coyle

Catchplate of a Gergova Type B II 1 fibula
This small bronze fragment was for a while a problem piece, until it was clear that it was a good example of a "Bogenfibeln mit hoher sanduhrförmiger Fussplate," also referred to as a "zweischleifige," or two-looped fibula, as well as a "zweischleifige Bogenfibel mit Schildfuss."[82] Whether classified as an hourglass or shield catchplate—in my original notes I had it down as "anthropomorphic"—is descriptively moot, but its form, and the fibula type from which it derives, is clear enough. The lower edge of the catchplate of **15/17** is straight, with projecting elements on either side; the longer vertical sides are concave, with two projecting "arms" and a "neck" above. The latter forms into a looped connection to the main arch of the fibula, which is not preserved. There is a central rib on the outer convex side that terminates just above the lower edge. The opposite, inner, side is concave, with the bottom edge curved up to accommodate the pin, nothing of which survives. This type of catchplate belongs to a variety of fibula types from various parts of the Balkans. In Bulgaria, Diana Gergova classifies related catchplates under the broad heading of "Bogenfibeln mit hoher sanduhrförmiger Fussplate," which she divides into seven variants, labeled α–η.[83] In a similar vein, Rastko Vasić classified fibulae with similar catchplates as "Zweischleifige Bogenfibeln mit sanduhrförmiger Fussplate," with six variants, and as "Zweischleifige Bogenfibeln mit Schildfuss."[84] This type of fibula catchplate is especially popular in the Glasinac region of Bosnia-Herzegovina, where various types of fibulae with similar catchplates begin in Period IVb (750–625 B.C.), become very popular in Period IVc (625–500 B.C.), and peter out by Period Va (500–350 B.C.).[85] As nothing of **15/17** beyond the catchplate survives, it is impossible to place our piece within this array of variants, but I assemble, in the catalogue entry below, catchplates from various fibulae that are close.

As for their chronology, Gergova, in her discussion of Type B II 1 Variant α, writes: "Im bulgarische Schrifttum werden derartige Fibeln in das 7. und 6. Jh. v.Chr. und später datiert. Da die Variante a typologisch einen etwas älteren Eindruck als die übrigen Varianten dieses Typus macht, verbinden wir sie der Frühphase der Periode II und datieren sie vorläufig in das 8., spätestens an den Beginn des 7. Jh."[86] Similarly, Vasić dates the earliest examples of his fibulae to the second half of the 8th and first half of the 7th century B.C., while later types extend well into the 7th and 6th centuries.[87] The fact that **15/17** was encountered in a well-dated context to the later 8th and early 7th century B.C. in the north Aegean provides welcome confirmation for the chronology of the fibula farther north in the Balkans. In Greece proper, this type of fibula is rare, though an example dated to the 7th century B.C. was found at the Athena Itonia sanctuary near Philia in Thessaly, another was found at Perachora, and a third of similar date was found on Chios and referred to by John Boardman as a so-called "Illyrian" type.[88]

FIGURE 15.10. Catchplate of bronze fibula, **15/17** (MEΘ 1519).
Drawing A. Hooton, photos J. Vanderpool

15/17. (MEΘ 1519 [ME 3655]) Catchplate of Bronze Fibula   Fig. 15.10
East Hill #274/032986 [9]. 22/11/2006. Phase I.
P.L. 0.019; W. (max.) 0.015–0.016; Wt. 1.2 g.

Single fr preserving most of catchplate, but nothing else of the fibula except a small part of the connection strut to the main arch.

Anthropomorphic in plan, as shown. Lower edge straight-sided, projecting on either side; concave sides, with two projecting "arms" and a "neck" above. Central rib on outer convex side terminates just short of the lower edge; inner side concave, with bottom edge slightly folded up, as shown, to accommodate pin.

Among the Bulgarian comparanda, the catchplates of Gergova's Type B II 1 Variant α and β are considerably larger than **15/17**, as are most of the other variants; closer are examples of Type B II 2 Variants α and β, and esp. γ, cf., among others, Gergova 1987, pls. 14–15, nos. 183, 187, 189, 195, and esp. pls. 16–17, nos. 197–199, 201–202, 208, 210, 212, 216–218 (with additional incised circles), and no. 220. Cf. also Vasić 1999, pl. 29, nos. 346–347; pl. 33, esp. no. 438; pls. 34–37, nos. 440–445, 449, 451–452, 454, 457–459, 468–469, 471–475, 477–479, 483, 485, 487, 489, 491, 495, 497, 500, 503, 505, 507–509, 511, 514, 517–520; pl. 38, nos. 521–525. Of the Glasinac examples, see, in particular, Benac and Čović 1957, pl. XXI, no. 6; pl. XXII, no. 3, also nos. 1–2. Cf. also Bouzek 1974b, p. 131, fig. 42, no. 2 (from Trilophon-Messimeri); Makridis 1937, pl. IV:θ; Maier 1956, p. 65, fig. 1, no. 1.

Similar to the above, but smaller and without the central rib:
MEΘ 4144. East Hill #274/032048 [5]. 15/7/2004. Phase II. P.L. 0.015; W. (max.) 0.012; Th. 0.003; Wt. (main fr) 0.7 g.

Dress pins

In comparison to the fibulae catalogued above, the dress pins from the various levels of the fill of the Hypogeion may seem, at first sight, a motley array, fragmentary in the main, and perhaps not as broad in terms of variety as the fibulae, but as an assemblage they are as interesting and idiosyncratic as the fibulae. A critical problem, which has plagued the appearance of the dress pin in the Aegean, has been the long-standing belief that dress pins essentially appear in the period of transition from the Bronze Age to the Iron Age. Indeed, a good deal of the literature on the dress pin in the Early Iron Age has been fixated on the origin and use of dress pins, and especially the evident change in fashion, as it is assumed to have accompanied the introduction of the peplos.[89] Much of the evidence, however, cited in favor of this view seems rather strained.[90] A number of scholars have argued that pins were introduced from either central Europe or northern Italy, or else from the east.[91] Other scholars prefer to see a more local development—and therefore continuity—from the metal and bone/ivory pins of the Late Bronze Age.[92] More to the point, both Erwin Bielefeld and Imma Kilian-Dirlmeier argued authoritatively against the introduction of pins by invaders from the north.[93]

The irony is that, as various scholars have established, fibulae first appear in Europe in the course of the later second millennium B.C., and it is generally accepted that they derived from pins, specifically from the so-called "eyelet" pins that were secured with thongs or threads of organic material.[94] Ingvald Undset was the first to suggest, as early as 1889, that the substitution in the eyelet pins of bronze for the organic material led to the development of fibulae.[95]

As for the Greek world, the antiquity of the use of dress pins in the Aegean needs to be emphasized, for pins interpreted as dress pins by Christos Tsountas at Chalandriani are Early Cycladic in date (3rd millennium B.C.).[96] There are Middle Helladic dress pins in tombs at Corinth, and similar Middle and Late Bronze Age examples in tombs at Eleusis.[97] Minoan Bronze Age examples are listed by Sinclair Hood, and there are large and elaborate pins from the Shaft Graves at Mycenae.[98] As we shall see, the *Rollenkopfnadel*, or rolled-head pin, goes back to the Chalcolithic period at various sites in the Aegean and continuing through the Early, Middle, and Late Bronze Age, and later. Consequently, Paul Jacobthal's statement that the "history of the Greek dress pin does not begin before the later twelfth century" no longer stands.[99]

Rollenkopfnadeln
I begin with one of the most common varieties of pins at Methone, the *Rollenkopfnadel* or *Rollennadel*. All three catalogued examples from the Hypogeion are from Phase II, and as such a late 8th- or early 7th-century B.C. date is clear enough. The basic form is straightforward and relatively easy to make: the shaft is circular in section, tapering to a point at one end, while the opposite end is hammered flat and rolled to form the characteristic head. This basic type of pin enjoys a venerable prehistory in Greece. The earliest published example, in almost pure copper, comes from Chalcolithic Sitagroi in the north Aegean.[100] There are similarly early examples from a number of Early Bronze Age contexts in Greece, including Lerna Phase IVB, the prehistoric settlement under the Heraion on Samos, three such pins from Early Bronze Age Thermi, and one from Phylakopi on Melos.[101] The type is well attested in the Late Bronze Age, becoming even more popular in the Early Iron Age (Submycenaean, Protogeometric, and Subprotogeometric).[102] During this period, and closer to home, an example of a *Rollenkopfnadel* was found at Vergina, and another at Kastanas, in Level 14b, which is transitional Late Bronze to Early Iron Age.[103] By the Geometric and Archaic period, which includes the examples from Methone, the type is found in many sites in Greece in both bronze and iron.[104] The pin with rolled head is very common in the central and northern Balkans,[105] including Albania,[106] as it is on the Italian peninsula,[107] as well as in central Europe north of the Alps,[108] and the type is also found in Georgia.[109] In his analysis of the *Rollenkopfnadeln* from the central Balkans, Rastko Vasić states: "Rollenkopfnadeln datieren von der frühen Bronzezeit bis zum Ende der Eisenzeit."[110]

There has been a good deal of discussion about the origin of this type of pin. Paul Jacobsthal, in his seminal study, concluded that these "pins originate in the Early Bronze Age in Europe and the Near East, and survive into the Early Iron Age."[111] Other scholars prefer an eastern origin,[112] and the type is found as far east as northern Bactria (modern Afghanistan).[113] An eastern origin was championed by Hector Catling, who concluded that they "are clearly of Near Eastern origin," citing examples from Byblos, Gezer, Megiddo, Tell Atchana, and Tarsus.[114] Catling also noted, as did John Boardman a few years later, that the form rarely appears in the Aegean.[115] The numerous examples cited above from Greece indicate that the type is not as rare in the Aegean as was once assumed. Indeed, the examples from Greece, the Balkans, the Italian peninsula, and central Europe, coupled with the fact that the type is found as early in Greece as it is in the east, if not earlier, does not give chronological priority to an eastern origin. I would, therefore, concur with Jacobsthal's judicious statement that this type of pin traces its origins to Europe and the Near East. Its simple form, easily made, may well argue for synchronous manufacture in more than one place.

15/18. (MEΘ 1418 [ME 2949]) Fragmentary *Rollenkopfnadel* Fig. 15.11
East Hill #274/022 fill below Wall 14. 10/8/2006. Phase II.
L. 0.102; Diam. (head) 0.008; Diam. (shaft) 0.005; Wt. 4.4 g.
Five frr preserving complete pin, heavily corroded.

Shaft circular in section, clearly tapering to a well-preserved point. Shaft at end of head hammered flat and rolled to form the characteristic head. Type as **15/19** (MEΘ 1403) and **15/20** (MEΘ 1434), but with proportionately smaller head. The shaft of this pin tapers quite quickly toward the point, which may suggest that the same holds true for **15/19** and **15/20**.

Cf., among others, Casson 1919–1921, pp. 15–16, fig. 11 (middle left). For a classic *Rollennadel* from a SPG II tomb, see *Lefkandi* I, pp. 149, 245, pls. 136, 242:f, P 21, 11. This type is common among the finds from the Greek levels at Troy; see Schalk 2008, p. 184, fig. 1, ε, f–g; p. 187, fig. 3, Type IXa–e; p. 225, fig. 35, nos. 266–303 ("Nadeln mit Rollenkopf").

15/19. (MEΘ 1403 [ME 1072]) *Rollenkopfnadel* Fig. 15.11
East Hill #274/022052 [11]. 27/7/2004. Phase II.
P.L. 0.076; Diam. (head) 0.011; Diam. (shaft) 0.004; Wt. 6.4 g.
Single fr preserving complete head and much of pin shaft.

Large pin, with shaft circular in section. Shaft at end of head hammered flat and rolled to form the characteristic head. The manner in which the head is hammered and rolled precludes this being the pin and spring of a fibula.

Cf. **15/18** (MEΘ 1418).

15/20. (MEΘ 1434 [ME 1155]) Fragmentary *Rollenkopfnadel* Fig. 15.11
East Hill #274/032054 [7]. 9/8/2004. Phase II.
P.L. 0.053; Diam. (head) 0.009; Diam. (shaft) 0.004; Wt. 2.5 g.
Two joining frr, plus many chips, preserving complete head and much of the upper and mid-shaft of pin; heavily corroded.

As **15/18** (MEΘ 1418) and **15/19** (MEΘ 1403), but slightly smaller.

Fragment of additional *Rollenkopfnadel*:

MEΘ 4116 (ME 4070). East Hill #274/022052 [11]. 27/7/2004. Phase II. Complete head, but no shaft: P.L. 0.013; Diam. (head) 0.010; Th. 0.008; Wt. 1.3 g.

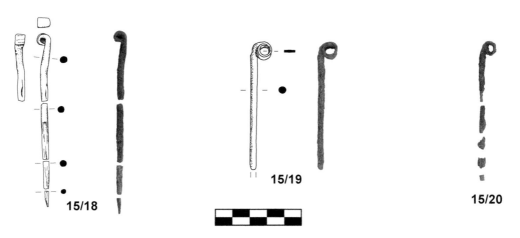

FIGURE 15.11. Bronze *Rollenkopfnadeln*, **15/18** (MEΘ 1418), **15/19** (MEΘ 1403), **15/20** (MEΘ 1434). Drawings T. Ross and F. Skyvalida, photos I. Coyle

Pin with coiled spiral head

There is only one example of a dress pin with a tightly coiled head, **15/21**, from a post–Phase III context of the Hypogeion and, as such, an Archaic date is assured. While it is related to the *Rollenkopfnadel*, this pin is smaller—although its overall original length remains unknown—and lighter, made of a thin shaft, circular in section, with the head formed by coiling the upper shaft onto itself to create the distinctive coiled spiral head. The resultant form resembles the Geometric T-headed pins, but **15/21** is different from the main series of such pins.[116] It resembles a pin from Troy, cited in the catalogue below, but in this case the coiling extends to the upper shaft of the pin. Related to both **15/21** and the example from Troy are the distinctive "loop pins" found in the Balkans and elsewhere in central Europe, but these are significantly larger, with the coiling extending well down onto the upper shaft, and much earlier, usually assigned to the Early or Middle Bronze Age, a date that cannot be maintained for **15/21**.[117] The latter is more closely related to the knot-headed pins ("Schlaufennadeln"), discussed more fully in Chapter 26 under **26/70** and **26/71** (both from the destruction deposit of 354 B.C. in the agora of Methone), which begin in the late 7th or early 6th centuries B.C. and continue through the Classical and Hellenistic periods into Late Roman times.[118]

15/21. (ΜΕΘ 1395) Dress Pin with Coiled Spiral Head   Fig. 15.12
  East Hill #274/022003 [2]. 3/6/2003. Post–Phase III.
  P.L. 0.054; Wt. 2.0 g.
  Single piece preserving all of head and much of the upper shaft, but not the pointed pin tip.
  Thin shaft, circular in section; head formed by coiling upper shaft on itself to create a coiled spiral head.
  Cf. Schalk 2008, p. 184, fig. 1, ε, e; p. 187, fig. 3, Type XVII; p. 195, fig. 21; p. 226, fig. 36, no. 336 (Schleifnadeln), but here the coiling extends to the upper shaft of the pin.

Keulenkopfnadeln with incised decoration

There are two examples of the dress pin with incised decoration that has entered the literature as *Keulenkopfnadeln*, or club-headed pin, **15/22** (ΜΕΘ 1459) and ΜΕΘ 1450. The former are both from Phase I and can be securely dated to the late 8th or early 7th century B.C. Both are fragmentary and heavily corroded, and it remains unclear whether the additional small fragment of bronze illustrated in the photo of **15/22** is from the same object or another. The shaft of the comparatively better preserved **15/22**, which is circular in section, widens fractionally toward the top, as well as the preserved bottom, though in the case of the latter this is probably corrosion. It also remains uncertain whether the top, as preserved, is the actual head, or whether the pin

FIGURE 15.12. Bronze pin with coiled spiral head, **15/21** (ΜΕΘ 1395).
Drawing F. Skyvalida, photo I. Coyle

continues, but the top does appear to be an original termination. This type of pin is not common on the Greek mainland, at least in southern and central Greece, and I know of no examples from the Peloponnese. The form, however, is quite common in the central Balkans—Voivodina, Serbia, Kosovo, and North Macedonia—where the type is referred to as "Keulenkopfnadeln, Variante mit verziertem Kopf," although with most of these the head is slightly wider than on **15/22**.[119] Examples of the type from the central Balkans closest to **15/22** are cited in the catalogue entry below. Related pins, earlier in the main, are also known from the Italian peninsula.[120] The decoration on the upper shaft consists of two groups of multiple grooves, which frame a very slightly raised band decorated with incised opposed diagonals.[121] The color and preservation of the bronze on **15/22** is somewhat different from the main series of bronzes from Methone, and I wonder whether this may be an imported pin.

15/22. (ΜΕΘ 1459 [ΜΕ 1640]) Fragmentary Pin with Incised Decoration Fig. 15.13
   East Hill #274/032061-063. 8/12/2004. Probably Phase I.
   P.L. (main fr) 0.038; Diam. (shaft) 0.003; P.W. (lower head?) 0.004; Wt: 2.3 g.
   Two frr, not clearly joining, preserving portion of shaft and what appears to be a widening of the shaft where there is considerable bronze disease. Remainder of bronze remarkably well preserved, with much of the original golden color preserved. It is not clear whether this is the widening of the lowest portion of the head, or a continuation of the main shaft.
   Type as ΜΕΘ 1450. Shaft circular in section, widening at one end. Shaft decorated with two groups of multiple grooves framing a slightly raised band decorated with incised opposed diagonals, as shown.
   Cf. ΜΕΘ 1450. Among various examples from the central Balkans, cf. esp. Vasić 2003, pl. 31, nos. 541, 545, 549, 556; pls. 32–33, nos. 561–562, 575, 591, 596, 598, 609, 612, 620; pl. 34, no. 625.

Fragment of additional fragmentary Keulenkopfnadel:
ΜΕΘ 1450. East Hill #274/032077 [7]. 11/9/2006. Phase I. Fragmentary, and highly corroded, but clearly of the same type as **15/22**. P.L. (largest fr) 0.075; P.L. (all frr lined up) ca. 0.120; Diam. (shaft, max.) 0.004; Wt. 4.1 g.

Pin with flattened head, variant of *Blattkopfnadel* (or spatula/stylus)?
Also from Phase I of the Hypogeion fill, **15/23** must be Geometric or early Archaic in date. As preserved, it appears to be complete or near-complete, and is clearly of small dimensions. The shaft, circular in section, tapers to a clear point at one end. The opposite end is hammered flat to create a slightly wider head, almost resembling a spatula. In shape and size, **15/23** resembles some of the bone pins from the Late Bronze Age tombs at Methone (see Chapter 6). It also resembles a stylus.[122] Given the early date of the writing habit at Methone, a small bronze stylus may not seem a far-fetched interpretation, but as tempting as such an interpretation may be, **15/23** does not

FIGURE 15.13. Bronze *Keulenkopfnadeln* with incised decoration, **15/22** (ΜΕΘ 1459). Drawing F. Skyvalida, photo I. Coyle

seem a convincing stylus, and if it were, it would be one of the earliest styli we have. I prefer to see it, at least for the time being, as a small dress pin. It is worth noting that a similar bone pin of the same size as **15/23** but with a square flat head found in the burial tumulus of Lofkënd in Albania clearly served as a dress pin; its context and date (14th–13th century) clearly preclude a stylus.[123]

In its form, it resembles some of the so-called Blattkopfnadeln of the Geometric period, though it is smaller than most.[124] The Blattkopfnadeln assembled by Kilian-Dirlmeier are more distinctly leaf-shaped, and a few also have incised decoration, whereas **15/23** is more spatula-shaped. A related form is known from Troy, one with a more square head, another with a flattened head, closer to **15/23** (MEΘ 1491), but a little broader.[125] There is also a related pin type in Italy, but with a more truncated, cone-shaped head, rather than one hammered flat.[126] In its overall form, **15/23** is not unlike a small *Rollennadel*, with the head hammered flat but not rolled; indeed, a few of the *Rollennadeln* from the central Balkans are very similar in shape and size to **15/23**, with their heads hammered flat, but only rolled over once to create the distinctive head.[127]

15/23. (MEΘ 1491) Small Pin Resembling Spatula/Stylus Fig. 15.14
East Hill # 274/032056 [7]. 11/8/2004. Phase I.
P.L. 0.058; W. (head) 0.005; Wt. 1.0 g.
Three joining frr preserving what may be the entire object.
Small pin resembling spatula, with thin shaft, circular in section, tapering toward point. Opposite end lightly hammered to create a slightly wider, but plain head.
Cf. Kilian-Dirlmeier 1984a, pp. 152–153, Geometrische Nadeln, Typengruppe XX (Blattkopfnadeln), Type XXA, pl. 63, nos. 1933–1948, esp. nos. 1933, 1938–1939. Bronze pins of related form are represented at Troy; one has a square rather than a slightly flattened top: Schalk 2008, p. 187, fig. 3, Type VII; p. 190, fig. 10, Type VII (Nadeln mit vierkantigem Kolbenkopf); the other has a flattened head, closer to **15/23** (MEΘ 1491), but broader: p. 187, fig. 3, Type XIII; p. 194, fig. 17; p. 226, fig. 36, no. 330 (Nadeln mit vertikalem Scheibenkopf).

Pin with small head (cf. Carancini's "Spilloni a capocchia minuscola"; cf. Kilian-Dirlmeier geometrische Nadeln Type I D4)
What survives of **15/24** is not enough to gauge even the overall size of the pin, although, as preserved, the fragment seems to come from a pin of modest size. Its context suggests a date in the later 8th or earlier 7th century B.C. Only the upper part of the shaft survives, which is square in section, surmounted by a small decorated head round in section comprising two minuscule beads, the lower a little larger than the upper. In its overall form, **15/24** is closest to a rare pin type in Italy, labeled by Gian Luigi Carancini as "Spillone a capocchia minuscola."[128] Carancini lists only two examples of the type, both from northern Italy, one from Bismantova in the Emilia-Romagna,

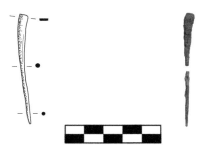

FIGURE 15.14. Variant of a *Blattkopfnadel*, **15/23** (MEΘ 1491).
Drawing F. Skyvalida, photo I. Coyle

FIGURE 15.15. Bronze pin with small head, **15/24** (MEΘ 1410).
Drawing A. Hooton, photo J. Vanderpool

the other from the San Vitale cemetery at Bologna. On the basis of their context, both are dated to the early stages of the local Early Iron Age. Closer to home, a number of bronze pins with simple heads are known from Eretria, at least one of which is surmounted by minuscule beads like **15/24**.[129] From the Peloponnese, there is a much larger pin type that appears to be related, classified by Kilian-Dirlmeier under her geometrische Nadeln, Type I D, variant 5 (I D5). Of the three examples closest to **15/24**, one is from the Argive Heraion, two from a tomb at Tiryns. These pins are larger, with heads of different types, but with the finial always surmounted by two or more minuscule beads.[130] The Argive pins are invariably larger, with a prominent bead or globe on the upper shaft, but well down from the head, their uppermost shafts are circular in section, but quickly become square in section. The type is Geometric, beginning in the Early Geometric period, although the examples close to **15/24** come from Late Geometric graves, a date that accords nicely with the context of **15/24**.

15/24. (MEΘ 1410 [ME 3261]) Small Pin Fig. 15.15
East Hill #274/022066 [14]. 13/10/2006. Phase I.
P.L. (largest fr) 0.035; L. (head) 0.005; Th. (shaft) 0.002; Wt. (both frr) 0.6 g.
Two joining frr preserving head and upper shaft of pin.
Upper shaft square in section, surmounted by small decorated head comprising two minuscule beads, the lower larger than the upper.
Cf. Carancini 1975, pl. 49, nos. 1529–1530; cf. also the much larger pins, Kilian-Dirlmier 1984a, pl. 26, nos. 607–609.

Pin with beaded head (cf. Kilian-Dirlmeier's geometrische Nadeln, Typengruppe XXI)
Although corroded, the basic outlines of **15/25** are clear enough. The head is beaded, with a flat plain circular top, with at least one larger almost biconical bead directly below and a smaller disk bead below that. The upper shaft is probably circular in section, but this is difficult to determine because of the corrosion. The fragments of **15/25** derive from the post–Phase III of the Hypogeion fill and, as such, an Archaic date is indicated. Comparanda closest to **15/25** come from Olympia and are dated to the Late Geometric or early Orientalizing period.[131]

I have referred to **15/25** as beaded, largely on account of its fragmentary state, but elsewhere in the literature, pins of related form are sometimes referred to as "vase-headed," or with a "pomegranate" head, and some as "poppy-headed."[132]

15/25. (MEΘ 4137 [ME 280]) Fragmentary Pin Fig. 15.16
East Hill #274/032005 [3]. 25/7/2003. Post–Phase III.
P.L. 0.052; Diam. (head) 0.009; Wt. 3.4 g.

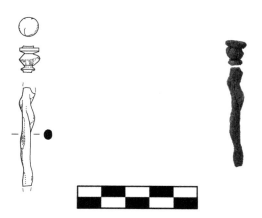

FIGURE 15.16. Bronze pin with beaded head, **15/25** (MEΘ 4137).
Drawing A. Hooton, photo J. Vanderpool

Two joining frr, heavily corroded, preserving head and upper shaft of dress pin; corroded.

Decorated head, beaded, perhaps in the form of a vase, pomegranate, or poppy flower, with plain flat circular top. Shaft evidently round in section, but difficult to determine on account of corrosion.

Cf., among others, *OlForsch* XIII, pp. 46, 48, pls. 27–28, nos. 38, 52 (= Kilian-Dirlmeier 1984a, p. 156, pl. 64, nos. 1977, 1979).

Pins of uncertain type

There are a number of fragments of pins of uncertain type from the Hypogeion, where only the shaft is preserved, with nothing of the head. Among these, I present only two, **15/26** and **15/27**. The shafts of both of the following are long and square in section. In the case of **15/26** the shaft tapers very slightly toward one end, though the tip is not preserved; a slight thickening at the opposite end may suggest proximity to the head. The shaft of **15/27** tapers to a fairly well-preserved point; the opposite end of the shaft is bent forward, but is clearly broken. Both were encountered in Phase II or III of the fill of the Hypogeion.

15/26. (MEΘ 1417 [ME 862]) Thin Rod Probably from Pin Fig. 15.17

East Hill #274/022. Cleaning of Wall 14. 1/7/2004. Phase II–III.

P.L. 0.108; L. x W. (shaft, max) 0.002 x 0.002–0.003; Wt. 2.3 g.

Single fr preserving substantial portion of a dress pin, rather than a rod.

Shaft thin, square in section, and appears to taper very slightly toward one end; tip not preserved. Slight thickening at opposite end suggests proximity to head.

Long thin bronze rods similar to **15/26** (MEΘ 1417) and **15/27** (MEΘ 1512) are classified under the pins at Troy as Nadelschäfte für Aufsteckköpfe: Schalk 2008, p. 187, fig. 3, Type XX; p. 197, fig. 24, no. 346.

15/27. (MEΘ 1512 [ME 622]) Long Pin Shaft Fig. 15.17

East Hill #274/032037 [6]. 8/4/2004. Phase II.

L./P.L. 0.243; Th. (max.) 0.002–0.003; Wt. 7.8 g.

Single piece preserving almost complete rod probably from a pin, except for the head.

Very long shaft, square in section, tapering toward a fairly well-preserved point. Head of shaft bent forward, but clearly broken.

Cf. **15/16** (MEΘ 1417).

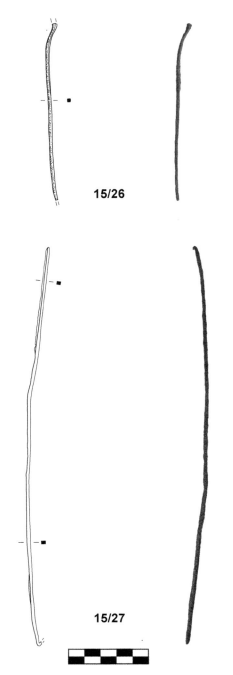

FIGURE 15.17. Bronze pins of uncertain type, **15/26** (MEΘ 1417), **15/27** (MEΘ 1512). Drawings A. Hooton and F. Skyvalida, photos I. Coyle and J. Vanderpool

Beads

Only two bronze beads were encountered in the Hypogeion, both from Phase II, and both can be assigned to the Late Geometric or earlier Archaic period. There are two types, one familiar, the other much less so. The first, **15/28**, is the standard biconical bronze bead that is common in the north Aegean and Balkans.[133] That this basic type of bead was manufactured at Methone is clear on account of the terracotta lost-wax mold, which was also found in the Hypogeion and is of contemporary date (see Fig. 14.4). A few examples from central and southern Greece are cited in the catalogue entry. The type is also common in Thessaly.[134]

In many ways, **15/29** is something of an oddity. One end terminates in a rounded point, resembling a fish head, the other splays out into two projections, resembling a fish tail. As a bead, it is solid, and the overall form, albeit unusual for a bead, resembles a bead in section. I know of no direct parallel in any material. The acropolis of Lindos on Rhodes has brought to light a number of small pendants ("pendeloques") made of animal bone in the form of a fish, at least one with incised decoration.[135] As a group, these differ from **15/29** not only in their material, but because all of them have a small drilled hole at the end of the fish head from which they were suspended as pendants. A small bronze pendant in the form of a fish was also found at Pherai, but of very different form.[136] The much larger and more centrally placed hole on **15/29** clearly makes it a bead rather than a pendant.

15/28. (ΜΕΘ 1474 [ΜΕ 1161]) Fragmentary Bronze Bead   Fig. 15.18
East Hill #274/032054 [7]. 9/8/2004. Phase II.
P.L. (main fr) 0.018; Diam. (terminal) 0.007–0.008; p.Diam. (max.) 0.015; Wt. 3.5 g.
Two joining frr preserving about one-half of bead; somewhat corroded.
Bead evidently biconical in form; rim very slightly flaring, with rounded, articulated lip, as shown.
Cf., among others, *Olympia* IV, pl. 24, no. 444; DeCou 1905, pl. 92, nos. 1547–1550 (Argive Heraion); Blinkenberg 1931, col. 95, pl. 10, no. 171 (Lindos); Kilian 1975a, pl. 76, esp. nos. 15, 20–25 (Pherai); Kilian-Dirlmeier 2002, p. 102, pl. 97, esp. nos. 1573–1575, and the larger nos. 1578–1979, which are of similar form (Philia); Felsch 2007, pl. 46, no. 1515 (Kalapodi); for a somewhat more elaborate bronze bead of the type from Macedonia, like **26/86** (ΜΕΘ 1649), see Casson 1919–1921, p. 15, pl. I (bottom).

15/29. (ΜΕΘ 1472 [ΜΕ 1275]) Fish-shaped Bead   Fig, 15.18
East Hill #274/022054 [12]. 27/8/2004. Phase II.
L./p.L. 0.037; H. 0.018; Wt. 9.9 g.
Single piece preserving most of bead; corroded.
Solid bead, with hole as shown (Diam. 0.004–0.005). One end terminates in a rounded point, the other splays out into two projections, resembling a fish tail.

FIGURE 15.18. Bronze beads, **15/28** (ΜΕΘ 1474), **15/29** (ΜΕΘ 1472).
Drawings F. Skyvalida, photos I. Coyle

Rings

Not all of the rings assembled under this heading are clearly jewelry. I have assembled them, however, as two groups, in order to distinguish the varieties present at Methone during the later Geometric into the Archaic period. They are presented below under the two overriding categories: jewelry (finger rings, hairrings, earrings) and *krikoi* of more utilitarian use.

Jewelry (finger rings, ear- or hairring)
In dealing with bronze finger rings of Early Iron Age Greece, Reynold Higgins noted their popularity and remarked that rings of the same general type were also made in iron.[137] For Athens and Attica, he listed several types, including rings with shield-shaped bezels (a type not represented at Methone), simple spirals, and plain hoops.[138] In his discussion of the bronze rings from the cemeteries at Lefkandi, Hector Catling distinguished three types: (1) a ring with shield-shaped bezels; (2) a closed ring, fairly solid, usually plano-convex in section; and (3) an open ring with overlapping terminals, usually made of a flat, hammered strip, coiled into a ring.[139] In dealing exclusively with Protogeometric finger rings, Irini Lemos, following Desborough and Higgins, makes the point that rings had been popular in Greece since the Mycenaean period and that they continued in use through Submycenaean into Protogemetric.[140] As Catling further noted, single rings found in the Athenian Kerameikos were just as likely to be in graves of men as of women, though female graves sometimes contained several rings.[141] For central and southern Greece, the five principal Early Iron Age varieties of finger rings are: 1) rings with shield-shaped bezels; 2) open rings, with overlapping terminals (usually made of a thin, hammered strip of bronze); 3) closed rings; 4) spiral rings; and 5) rings with double-spiral terminals (of "northern type" already noted).[142]

Among the rings from the Hypogeion that are likely jewelry, two were found in a post–Phase III context (**15/30** and **15/32**) and one in Phase II (**15/31**). Of these standard Early Iron Age and Archaic types, **15/30**, although fragmentary, should be an example of Type 2. The band that forms the ring is thin, rectangular to plano-convex in section. Despite the fact that it is classified as an open ring with overlapping terminals, neither of the actual terminals, if preserved, is clear due to corrosion. Rings of this type are fairly standard in Athens, well represented in the tombs of the Athenian Kerameikos, as well as from at least one tomb excavated during the construction of the Athens Metro.[143] There are nine rings of this type at Lefkandi, six of which are Submycenaean, two Early Protogeometric, and one, much smaller, dating to SPG I.[144] Elsewhere in the Aegean, rings of this type are common in, among other places, Aigina, the Argolid, Elis and elsewhere in the Peloponnese, central Greece, Thessaly, Macedonia, Epirus, Crete, and the Dodecanese.[145]

Although the closed ring of Type 3 is among the most common in Early Iron Age contexts in the Aegean,[146] the example from Methone, **15/31**, is a little unusual. The normal Early Iron Age type tends to be uniform in size and appearance, fairly solid, and usually plano-convex in section. In contrast, **15/31** is small, with a band circular and thicker in section, cast with seam clearly visible along the inner edge. The small bulge on one side is probably corrosion. The ring has a diameter of 0.018, which falls at the lower end of the average size for such rings (the 12 examples of closed rings from Lefkandi have diameters varying from 0.018 to 0.023 m).

The final example from Methone, **15/32**, is a spiral ring of Type 4. As preserved, the ring appears to be more or less complete, except perhaps for the terminals, which may be obscured by corrosion. The ring is formed with a small length of bronze wire, circular in section, forming a coil 0.015 m in diameter as preserved. The bronze clearly tapers toward a point at one end, and probably also at the other. Although the small size might suggest a hairring rather than an earring, the possibility of it being a finger ring for a child cannot be ruled out. Two similar spiral rings from the Athenian Agora were clearly finger rings associated with children (Agora T45-10 has a diameter of 0.016 m, which is almost precisely that of **15/32**, and Agora T70-10 was of similar size but was subsequently distorted to give a length, as preserved, of 0.020).[147] In both cases, context established them as finger rings, and this is important to note as many similar spirals, especially those dedicated in sanctuaries, or like **15/32** discarded as it was in the fill of the Hypogeion, cannot be decisively confirmed as being finger rings rather than hair spirals, earrings, or other forms of personal ornament since their contexts provide no clue as to their function.[148] Elsewhere in Greece, similar rings are well represented at a number of Early Iron Age and Archaic sites.[149]

15/30. (ΜΕΘ 1524 [ΜΕ 576]) Fragmentary Bronze Ring Fig. 15.19
East Hill #274/032032 [5]. 18/32004. Post–Phase III.
P.L. 0.018; W. (band) 0.005; Wt. 1.0 g.
Two joining frr preserving about three-quarters of ring.
Thin band, rectangular, where hammered flatter, to plano-convex in section. Almost certainly a finger ring, perhaps for a smaller adult individual.
Cf., among others, *Kerameikos* I, p. 85, fig. 3, esp. far left and far right; *Lefkandi* I, pl. 99, Skoubris Tomb 22, nos. 4, 6; pl. 131, Palia Perivolia Tomb 10, no. 21; *Lefkandi* III, pl. 39, Toumba Tomb 38, no. 5; Coldstream and Catling 1996, fig. 167, Tomb 219, f 21.

15/31. (ΜΕΘ 4130 [ΜΕ 4090]) Ring Fig. 15.19
East Hill #274/032051 [7]. 2/8/2004. Phase II.
Diam. 0.018; H./Th. (max.) 0.005; H./Th. (average) 0.003; Wt. 0.8 g.
Single fr preserving greater part of ring.
Small ring, with band circular in section; cast with seam clearly visible along inner edge.
Cf., among others, Coldstream and Catling 1996, vol. 3, fig. 169, Tomb 85, f 23; *Lefkandi* I, pl. 97, Skoubris Tomb 17, nos. 2–3; pl. 99, Skoubris Tomb 20, no. 20; pl. 100, Skoubris Tomb 31, no. 4; pl. 104, Skoubris Tomb 40, nos. 7–8, which are more plano-convex in section; cf. also Papadopoulos 2003a, p. 75, fig. 97:c–d; p. 105, fig. 132:b.

FIGURE 15.19. Bronze finger rings, ear- or hairrings, **15/30** (ΜΕΘ 1524), **15/31** (ΜΕΘ 4130), **15/32** (ΜΕΘ 1475). Drawings A. Hooton and T. Ross, photos I. Coyle and J. Vanderpool

15/32. (ΜΕΘ 1475 [ΜΕ 282]) Small Bronze Spiral, Possible Hairring   Fig. 15.19

    East Hill #274.032006 [3]. 28/7/2003. Post–Phase III.

    Diam./L. (as preserved) 0.015; H. 0.008; Wt. 1.0 g.

    Complete, except perhaps for terminals, which may be obscured by corrosion.

    Small length of bronze wire forming a coil. Shaft circular in section, clearly tapering toward a point at one end, and probably also at the other.

    Perhaps a hairring rather than an earring, although a finger ring for a child is also possible, see esp. *Agora* XXXVI, pp. 325, 328, fig. 2.227, T45-10; p. 450, fig. 2.336, T70-10; cf. among many others, Felsch 2007, pl. 37, no. 684, 686; *Lefkandi* I, pl. 105, Skoubris Tomb 45, 11 (gold); cf. also Papadopoulos 2003a, p. 75, fig. 97:e–l.

Similar to the above (**15/32**):

ΜΕΘ 1495 (ΜΕ 228). East Hill #274/022009 [5]. 11/6/2003. Post–Phase III. Six frr preserving a bronze coil similar to ΜΕΘ 1475. PL (largest fr): 0.014; Wt (total): 1.5 g.

Krikoi

Κρίκος—sometimes κίρκος—in Greek, as opposed to δακτύλιος (used specifically for finger ring or signet), refers to rings of various shapes and sizes that are not clearly items of personal ornament, and which functioned in a variety of ways. Greek literature from as early as Homer is full of references to κρίκοι, and their various functions. Bronze rings could have served as fasteners for a horse's breast band or to a carriage pole, as eyelet holes in sails, as curtain rings, nose rings, links in a chain, and so on.[150] The two examples from the Hypogeion at Methone presented below were found in Phases I and II of the fill. Similar rings that were clearly not finger rings, hair- or earrings were common dedications at sanctuaries throughout mainland and insular Greece, as well as in domestic contexts, and, less commonly, in tombs.[151] Identical rings are found in great numbers in southern Italy, Sicily, and beyond, both in colonial sanctuaries and in indigenous cemeteries.[152]

Despite their discovery in a number of different types of contexts, the high incidence of *krikoi* at sanctuary sites permits a further interpretation as to their function, or, at least, one of their functions. The Greek word σίγλος or σίκλος, from the Semitic *shekel*, could refer to a weight or a coin, and it could also refer to "earring," a critical point, since various items of jewelry, such as rings, bracelets, or anklets, could be used as "money" before coinage. Indeed, Phanouria Dakoronia has argued that bronze rings (*krikoi*) served as recognized values or weights in a premonetary system in Early Iron Age Greece.[153] In Amarna in Egypt in the 14th century B.C., a typical hoard of precious metal objects included gold and silver ingots, silver rings, wire, and other fragments found buried in a pot.[154] In late New Kingdom Egypt (ca. 1295–1069 B.C.) the standard weights were frequently mentioned in texts, particularly the *deben* (91 grams) and its tenth, the *kite*. Although the payment of amounts expressed in copper *deben* could have been in a variety of goods, it often assumed the form of copper rings or else silver rings and ingots.[155] Consequently, rings such as these could well have functioned as stores of value, in much the same way that bronze tripods did from the Late Bronze Age into the Archaic and Classical periods and beyond.[156]

15/33. (ΜΕΘ 1496 [ΜΕ 1277]) Large Ring   Fig. 15.20

    East Hill #274/022054 [12]. 27/8/2004. Phase II.

    Diam. (max.) 0.034; Th. 0.007–0.008; Wt. 18.9 g.

    Intact, but heavily corroded, with surface split at points.

    Large and heavy ring, circular in section.

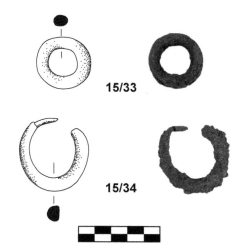

FIGURE 15.20. Bronze *krikoi*, **15/33** (MEΘ 1496), **15/34** (MEΘ 1498).
Drawings F. Skyvalida, photos I. Coyle

15/34. (MEΘ 1498 [ME 1201]) Large Ring?   Fig. 15.20
    East Hill #274/032057 [7]. 12/8/2004. Phase I.
    Diam. 0.044–0.049; W. (max.) 0.014; Wt. 18.2 g.
    Three joining frr, plus chips, preserving the greater part of what resembles a ring; heavily corroded.
    Thick and comparatively solid ring, plano-convex in section, thicker on one side than the other, and tapering toward one thin terminal, which appears to be preserved; it is not clear whether the terminal is articulated or this is the result of corrosion.
    A most unusual ring.

Spiral ornament

The unfortunate thing about **15/35** is that it has broken in a way that makes it difficult to reconstruct the original object with certainty. The piece is small, with a diameter of the spiral only 0.015 m. It may derive from a small spectacle fibula (see above), or a ring with double spiral already discussed, or one of any other type of spiral ornaments, such as a spiral or spectacle pendant,[157] or even a small dress pin with a spiral head.[158] Of these various possibilities, **15/35** is most likely to be a pendant or dress pin with spiral head. A range of such objects is cited in the catalogue entry below.[159]

15/35. (MEΘ 1386 [ME 1888]) Spiral Ornament   Fig. 15.21
    East Hill #274/022047-051. 27/5/2005. Phase II.
    P.L. 0.021–0.022; Diam. (spiral) 0.015; Wt. 1.2 g.
    Two joining frr preserving all of spiral, but unknown portion of shaft; corroded.
    Thin bronze wire, circular in section, coiled to form a spiral, with the shaft extending beyond the spiral.
    Cf., among others, the gold spectacle pendant suspended as part of an earring: *Lefkandi* I, pl. 173, Toumba T13, 16–17; similar spiral pendants can be suspended from necklaces (e.g., Gimbutas 1965, p. 109, fig. 71, nos. 1, 3), fibulae (e.g., Bartoloni et al. 1980, p. 175, pl. 67, no. 6; von Eles Masi 1986, pls. 24–25, nos. 397B and 401; pls. 26–27, nos. 405–406; pl. 63, no. 861; pl. 73, no. 966; pl. 84, no. 1043), headbands/diadems (e.g., Gimbutas 1965, pp. 598–599, fig. 420), or even directly to a textile. Cf. also: Felsch 2007, pp. 308–309, pl. 39, nos. 306–310 (finger rings with double or single spectacle spiral[s]); 291, pl. 32, no. 515 (with the insertion of a small fr of the pin; the Kalapodi example is clearly a fibula). For dress pins with spiral heads, see Carancini 1975, pls. 18–21, nos. 577–643, 648, 653; Vasić 2003, pls. 9–10, nos. 124–138.

FIGURE 15.21. Bronze spiral ornament, **15/35** (MEΘ 1386).
Drawing A. Hooton, photos I. Coyle

Tutuli/buttons

The eight "tutuli" from the Hypogeion at Methone were mostly found in Phase II of the fill (**15/36–15/37, 15/39–15/41**); one was found in Phase III (**15/43**), another in a post–Phase III context (**15/42**), and one (**15/38**) was encountered in scarp cleaning, and could not be dated more precisely. Consequently, most of the tutuli can be assigned to the Late Geometric or Archaic period.

There were numerous tutuli in the tombs of nearby Vergina, and they were the most common bronzes after the so-called σύριγγες (long spiral ornaments associated with some form of headdress), and the spectacle fibulae.[160] Despite the poor—almost nonexistent—state of the human remains at Vergina, Manolis Andronikos believed that these small bronzes were found in both female and male tombs. He distinguished three types of tutuli, which he referred to as: 1) large buttons ("μεγάλα κομβία"); 2) smaller shield-shaped buttons (κομβία ἀσπιδοειδῆ); 3) similarly small, or even minuscule, shield-shaped bosses with a thin shaft extending from their undersides, thus resembling small tacks or studs. It was this latter type, wrote Andronikos, that was usually referred to as tutuli in the literature.[161] Andronikos went on to note that the first type of tutulus was normally found associated with the head of the deceased, whereas the second type was usually found on the lower torso. The third type was also associated with the head, but these were usually found to the side(s) of the cranium. He was convinced that the numerous examples of the second type adorned belts worn by the dead, whereas the larger buttons of the first type were usually found with the σύριγγες, and normally above the latter, which led him to speculate that, together with the σύριγγες, they served as some form of a covering for the head of the deceased.[162] Consequently, he argued on the basis of the *kterismata* that the first type was primarily associated with women, the second type with male burials. The third type of tutulus, which resembled small tacks, and which were often very small, must have been associated with some form of dress, perhaps specifically with the arms of the deceased. Andronikos' astute comments about the latter were borne out by the discovery, many years later, of a breastplate or corselet made of organic material, almost certainly leather, adorned with decorated and undecorated tutuli and bosses, large and small, and with separate shoulder plates or pads on either side of the cranium of the deceased in Tomb 59 at the Molossian cemetery of Liatovouni. The shoulder plates each had two parallel rows of small tutuli precisely of this type.[163] The Liatovouni tomb, the earliest in the cemetery discovered by Angelika Douzougli, is Late Helladic IIIC and, as such, it is somewhat earlier than the Vergina tutuli. Andronikos also noted similar tutuli at the site of Lakkithras on Kephallenia, which he referred to as later Bronze Age, and perhaps also from the sanctuary at Olympia.[164]

In her study of the metal finds from the sanctuary of Athena Itonia near Philia in Thessaly, Kilian-Dirlmeier distinguished three types of bronze tutulus, which differ both in their manufacture and in their manner of attachment.[165] Her first type (nos. 2886–2888) were cast, and each had a triangular eyelet for attachment by sewing (she noted that most of the Vergina belts were covered with this type of tutulus).[166] The examples characterized by her nos. 2889–2890 were cut from thin sheet metal and hammered, their edges on two sides folded over for attachment and with pointed extensions on both sides between the folded-over edges. The profiled tutuli (nos. 2891–2893), at least one with repoussé dots, were probably hammered over a form, and were more clearly bosses, with no obvious attachment device. Unfortunately, the Philia tutuli derived from contexts that could not be dated stratigraphically. Kilian-Dirlmeier cited examples from the sanctuary of Demeter at Knossos dating to the 4th–3rd centuries B.C., as well as an example from Tomb B at Derveni (4th century B.C.), where the tutuli were interpreted as trimmings on a leather corselet, similar to that from Liatovouni already noted.[167] Given the chronology of the Vergina, Liatovouni, and now Methone examples, it seems clear that such small bronzes were manufactured from the Late Bronze Age, through the Early Iron Age, and well into the Archaic, Classical, and Hellenistic periods.

Similar bronze tutuli/buttons, normally referred to as "bottoncini emisferici di bronzo," with a small loop or eyelet on the concave side for attachment, are a characteristic feature of the Italian Early Iron Age. There are literally thousands of them: just one of the tombs in the Macchiabate cemetery at Francavilla Marittima in northern Calabria had 1,020 such bronzes, and related examples can be cited from all over south Italy and Sicily.[168] An evocative illustration of how such "bottoncini" were worn on indigenous dress is provided by a number of tombs from Tursi and Alianello—dating to the 8th and 7th centuries B.C.—reconstructed in the Museo Nazionale della Siritide at Policoro.[169] A solitary tutulus, described as a "stud" ("borchiette") was found in the LG I tomb 432 at Pithekoussai.[170] A number of related bosses without an eyelet or obvious form of attachment were also found in the Macchiabate cemetery, including small and large examples.[171] A variety of uses for such bosses is discussed by David Moore Robinson on the basis of numerous examples from Olynthos, mostly from non-funerary contexts.[172]

The majority of the Methone tutuli correspond to Andronikos' second type and Kilian-Dirlmeier's first type (nos. 2886–2888) (**15/36–15/40**). One tutulus, **15/41**, has broken in such a way that the arch of the connecting loop has partially looped onto itself. The larger **15/42** is most unusual because of the substantial form of its connecting loop; a related tutulus, a little larger, from Francavilla Marittima has a similarly large connecting loop or eyelet (cited in the entry below). In contrast, **15/43** was found together with various small fragments and chips of sheet bronze, though it remains unclear whether these were in fact part of the same object. As preserved, it resembles some of the tutuli with no obvious method of attachment, especially those from Francavilla, even though there is clearly something connected on the underside, which does not resemble the common eyelets found with many of the tutuli. It is worth noting that two of the cited examples from Francavilla Marittima were filled or partially filled on their undersides by a lead-tin solder, hence a pewter of sorts, 53% lead, 47% tin.[173]

15/36. (ΜΕΘ 1493 [ME 3679]) Small Bronze Tutulus/Button   Fig. 15.22
    East Hill #274/032042 [6]. 17/6/2004. Phase II.
    H. 0.006; Diam. 0.012; Wt. 0.6 g.
    Intact.
    Small domed head, a little more elliptical than circular, with small ring or loop on underside for attachment.
    Cf. *Vergina* I, pp. 236–238, fig. 76, from tombs ΑΙΧι and ΝVIβ; Vokotopoulou 1986, fig. 109:θ (Vitsa Zagoriou); Koukouli-Chrysanthaki 1992, p. 416, fig. 108 (Thasos); Kilian-Dirlmeier 2002, p. 167, pl. 171, nos. 2886–2888 (Philia); *Pithekoussai* I, p. 445, pl. 134, no. 432-7 (LG I; described as "borchiette").

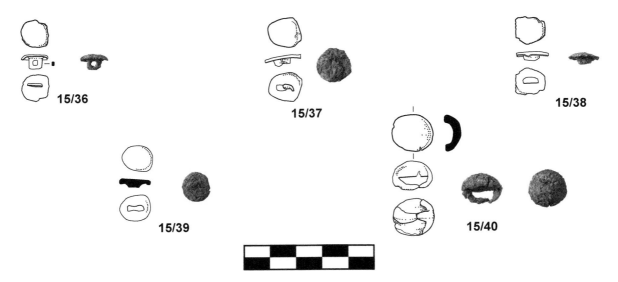

FIGURE 15.22. Bronze tutuli, **15/36** (MEΘ 1493), **15/37** (MEΘ 1487), **15/38** (MEΘ 1484), **15/39** (MEΘ 1483), **15/40** (MEΘ 1494). Drawings A. Hooton, photos J. Vanderpool

15/37. (MEΘ 1487 [ME 1139]) Small Tutulus/Button   Fig. 15.22

East Hill #274/032053 [7]/ 6/8/2004. Phase II.

Diam. (head) 0.014; p.H. (after cleaning) 0.005; L. x W. (loop) 0.007 x 0.003; Wt. 0.5 g.

Two joining frr originally preserving complete tutulus/button; heavily corroded. In the course of cleaning, the connecting loop disintegrated, so only the stumps now survive, but it was clearly a loop originally.

As **15/36** (MEΘ 1493) **15/38** (MEΘ 1484), but fractionally larger and with slightly flatter head.

15/38. (MEΘ 1484 [ME 642]) Small Tutulus/Button   Fig. 15.22

East Hill #274/032, scarp scraping. Phase undetermined.

H. 0.005; Diam. (head) 0.012; L. x W. (connecting loop) 0.005 x 0.003; Wt. 0.4 g.

Intact, but chipped; corroded.

Thin, round, slightly domed head; small connecting loop below (now largely covered by corrosion). Type as **15/36** (MEΘ 1493).

15/39. (MEΘ 1483 [ME 2977]) Small Tutulus/Button   Fig. 15.22

East Hill #274/022, fill under Wall 14. Phase II.

Diam. (head) 0.012; p.H. 0.004; Wt. 0.5 g.

Single fr preserving complete head, but nothing except the stumps of the loop; corroded.

Type as **15/36** (MEΘ 1493).

15/40. (MEΘ 1494 [ME 1046]) Small Tutulus/Button   Fig. 15.22

East Hill #274/032050 [7]. 23/7/2004. Phase II.

Diam. 0.016; H. 0.012; Wt. 2.7 g.

Single fr preserving complete or near-complete object. Corroded, with connecting loop broken through, but with no loss.

Domed head, comparatively thick. Connecting loop below, ovoid in section.

Type as **15/36** (MEΘ 1493).

15/41. (ΜΕΘ 4117 [ME 4047]) Tutulus/Button Fig. 15.23
East Hill #274/032048 [5]. 15/7/2004. Phase II.
Diam. (head) 0.012; H./p.H. 0.006; Wt. 0.4 g.
Single fr, corroded, preserving most of button.
Flat disk head, with connecting loop below, though it is unclear whether this is circular or rectangular in section. The piece has broken in such a way that the arch of the connecting loop has partially looped onto itself.
Cf. **15/36** (ΜΕΘ 1493).

15/42. (ΜΕΘ 1523 [ME 301]) Likely Tutulus/Button Fig. 15.23
East Hill #274/032008 [3]. 1/8/2003. Post–Phase III.
Diam. 0.017; H. 0.016; Wt. 3.8 g.
Two joining frr preserving complete but heavily corroded object.
Dome-shaped button, with a thick, substantial ring/connecting loop, circular in section, attached to bottom and sides of the dome. The ring appears to have a spur, which is too clear and too prominent to be corrosion alone.
Cf. Papadopoulos 2003a, p. 87, fig. 109, no. 245 (Francavilla Marittima).

15/43. (ΜΕΘ 1489 [ME 735]) Button or Boss/Tutulus Fig. 15.23
East Hill #274/922942 [10]. 27/5/2004. Phase III.
Diam. (head) 0.024; H. 0.007; Wt. (including all frr) 3.4 g; Wt. (primary piece) 2.9 g.
One primary piece preserving what appears to be most, if not all, of the head, plus five small flakes/chips, that may be part of the head or else the connecting loop, though they do not appear to be related; corroded.
Large round and domed head, made from thin sheet bronze. Form of the attachment on the underside, if there ever was an attachment, undetermined due to the corrosion.
It is possible that this is of the type with no obvious form of attachment; as preserved it most closely resembles Papadopoulos 2003a, pp. 87–88, fig. 110, nos. 246–248, and see also p. 207 (Francavilla Marittima), even though there is clearly something on the underside. Cf., among others, Boardman 1967, pp. 227, 229, fig. 149, nos. 429–430; cf. Felsch 2007, pp. 383–384, pl. 63, no. 2257, classified under "Nagel und Blechbuckel"; also Kilian-Dirlmeier 2002, pl. 170, nos. 2884–2885.

FIGURE 15.23. Bronze tutuli, **15/41** (ΜΕΘ 4117), **15/42** (ΜΕΘ 1523), **15/43** (ΜΕΘ 1489). Drawing A. Hooton and T. Ross, photos I. Coyle and J. Vanderpool

Related

15/44 is presented here as a problem piece. Made of thin sheet bronze, the object had not only collapsed onto itself, but was also heavily corroded. In form, it resembles a small bell or bell-shaped object. It was found together with a small eyelet or connecting loop, which does not clearly join, and which may have been part of another object, but does appear to be from the same object. As the two were found together, it is possible that this is an example of the larger tutuli such as those from Vergina discussed above.[174] Dating as it does to Phase I, a Late Geometric or early Archaic date is assured.

15/44. (ΜΕΘ 1501 [ΜΕ 3021]) Uncertain Object, Possible Tutulus Fig. 15.24
 East Hill #274/022058 [12]. 22/8/2006. Phase I.
 P.L. 0.040; p.H. 0.028; Wt. (both frr) 3.8 g.
 Two frr, heavily corroded, and not clearly joining, the larger preserving most of the bell-shaped object; the other a small button-like disk, only partially preserved, with connecting loop.
 Thin sheet bronze formed into a hollow bell shape, with an opening at the top and a small hole pierced through. It is unclear whether the button-like loop is part of the same object, though the two were found together. The hollow bell-like element has now collapsed onto itself.
 Cf. *Vergina* I, p. 237, fig. 75, from tomb ΝΧε.

Tools, implements, and weapons

Numerous bronzes, mostly small, were found in the fill of the Hypogeion that were not items of jewelry. The range of material is impressive, even if the majority of individual pieces are not glamorous: chains and chain links, a cube weight or ingot, needles, knives, a small hinged object, various nails, staples, and clamps, and a variety of bronze attachments, as well as small sheets and strips of bronze. What is lacking are bronze weapons, although several convincing weapons are found among the iron objects from the Hypogeion. The small bronze knives are all-purpose tools, not primarily offensive weapons, and the only possible bronze "weapon," a solitary small cone that may have served as something of an arrowhead, may well have served any number of functions. I begin the survey of bronze tools from the Hypogeion with the needles and chains, two classes of object that are often considered tools or implements, but which are sometimes items of jewelry or classified as such, as well as a small perforated disk, and a miniature double axe, which may or may not be an item of personal ornament.

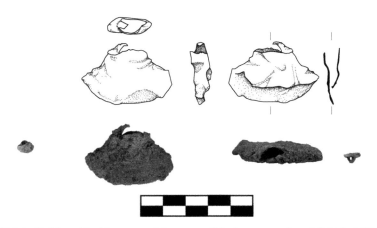

FIGURE 15.24. Unidentified bronze object, possible large tutulus, **15/44** (ΜΕΘ 1501).
Drawing T. Ross, photos I. Coyle

Needles

Distinguishing between a pin or a needle or just a rod can sometimes be challenging, particularly if pieces are broken, corroded, or worn. In dealing with the needles (Nähnadeln) from the Itonia sanctuary near Philia, Kilian-Dirlmeier notes that the bronze sewing needles from that site all have a flattened shaft with a round or slightly more elongated eyelet.[175] She goes on to cite 4th-century B.C. needles from Olynthos and the sanctuary of Demeter at Knossos, as well as examples from Corinth which range in date from the Roman Imperial period into Byzantine and post-Byzantine times.[176] Similarly, the needles from Isthmia—mostly of bronze, but including at least one of iron—are all of Classical date, or of uncertain date.[177] Dating to Phases I and II of the Hypogeion fill, all of the Methone needles presented below can be assigned to the Late Geometric or earlier Archaic period.

Given the level of industrial activity at Methone, including textile production from the Hypogeion indicated by spindlewhorls and loomweights (Chapter 16), and given their form and size, I think that all of the examples presented below are sewing needles as opposed to dress pins. Similar pins, also labeled "Nähnadeln," from the central Balkans date from the Early Bronze Age to the later stages of the Early Iron Age.[178] Related examples from the Greek levels at Troy are classified as pins.[179]

There are two types of needles from the Hypogeion at Methone. The first is represented by **15/45** and **15/46**. These are the classic sewing needles that can be found in bronze or bone throughout the Bronze Age and into modern times. The needle shaft is circular in section, with the slightly broader head hammered flat, with a perforation that can be very small (**15/45**) or slightly larger (**15/46**). The second type is represented by **15/47**, which is a small needle, with the shaft circular in section, tapering to a point. The head is hammered flat, and has a small circular projection on one side to accommodate the thread. I know of no parallel for this type of needle, but the manner of attaching the string is similar to that of fishhooks, some of which have eyelets, and many of which do not, having instead a broad circular or elliptical head hammered flat. I have listed **15/48** as related to **15/45** and **15/46**, but it is unusual in that the ovoid head is larger; it is articulated from the rest of the shaft or strip, with a small hole to take the thread and a pointed finial. As preserved, it appears to have been hammered flat, and this may suggest that it is a small attachment rather than a needle, but this could also be post-depositional damage. Its similarity to **15/45** and **15/46** warrants its inclusion here.

15/45. (ΜΕΘ 1467 [ΜΕ 899]) Fragmentary Needle/Pin   Fig. 15.25
    East Hill #274/022051 [11]. 12/07/2004. Phase II.
    P.L. 0.037; W. (head) 0.005; Diam. (shaft) 0.003; Wt. 0.8 g.
    Two joining frr preserving head and upper portion of shaft.
    Shaft circular in section (not enough survives of the shaft to see the taper toward the point). Slightly broader, roughly lozenge-shaped head hammered flat, with small hole near center.
    Cf. **15/46** (ΜΕΘ 1468); cf. also Schalk 2008, p. 187, fig. 3, Type XIa–c; p. 192, fig. 13, Type X (Nadel mit Drahtösenkopf); p. 193, fig. 15, Type XI (Nadeln mit geschlitztem Kopf). The Methone examples are closer to Troy Type XI, rather than Type X, which have the aperture formed simply by rolling over the top of the shaft.

15/46. (ΜΕΘ 1468 [M 1073]) Fragmentary Needle/Pin   Fig. 15.25
    East Hill #274/022052 [11]. 27/7/2004. Phase II.
    P.L. 0.047; W. (head) 0.007; Diam. (shaft) 0.004; Wt. 2.6 g.
    Four frr, all probably joining, though two are considerably corroded, preserving head and upper portion of shaft.

FIGURE 15.25. Bronze needles, **15/45** (ΜΕΘ 1467), **15/46** (ΜΕΘ 1468), **15/47** (ΜΕΘ 1409). Drawing T. Ross and F. Skyvalida, photos I. Coyle and J. Vanderpool

Large needle as **15/45** (ΜΕΘ 1467), but larger, and with more substantial perforation. Upper shaft square, lower and mid-shaft circular in section.

Cf. **15/45** (ΜΕΘ 1467); and cf. also *Nichoria* III, pp. 279, 301, 307, fig. 5-27, no. 42.

Fr of likely needle related to **15/45** (ΜΕΘ 1467) and **15/46** (ΜΕΘ 1468):
ΜΕΘ 1470 (ME 516) East Hill #274/032029 [4]. 9/10/2003. Three frr preserving portion of shaft, circular in section. P.L. 0.043; Diam. (shaft) 0.004; Wt. 1.0 g.

15/47. (ΜΕΘ 1409 [ME 3337]) Small Needle?   Fig. 15.25
East Hill #274/022066 [14]). 13/10/2006. Phase I.
L./p.L. 0.031; W. (head) 0.004; Wt. 0.6 g.
Single fr, probably preserving intact needle, except for the tip; heavily corroded.
Small needle, with shaft circular in section, tapering toward point. Head hammered flat, with a small circular projection on one side to accommodate string.
For a very closely related needle from the agora at Methone, see **26/119** (ΜΕΘ 2133 β).

Related

15/48. (ΜΕΘ 4124 [ME 3293]) Possible Needle?   Fig. 15.26
East Hill #274/022070 [14]. 15/11/2006. Phase I.
L./p.L. 0.036; W. (head) 0.007; Wt: 0.5 g.
Two joining frr preserving undetermined portion of shaft. Lower edge may be complete.
Thin strip of bronze, hammered flat. Ovoid head, articulated from the rest of the strip, and with small hole for attachment or threading. Pointed finial appears to be broken.
The fact that it is hammered flat may suggest that it is a small attachment rather than needle, but this could also be post-depositional damage?

FIGURE 15.26. Possible bronze needle rather than attachment, **15/48** (ΜΕΘ 4124). Drawing T. Ross, photo I. Coyle

FIGURE 15.27. Bronze disk (perhaps from pin), **15/49** (MEΘ 1521).
Drawing F. Skyvalida, photos J. Vanderpool

Disk

The small perforated disk **15/49** is perhaps better placed elsewhere, together with the cast or hammered bronze sheet and strips of bronze, but its resemblance to a distinctive type of disk associated with Geometric pins from the Peloponnese persuaded me to place it here instead.[180] Most of the Peloponnesian examples are a little larger than **15/49**, but some, including the decorated ones, are of similar size. Despite corrosion around its edges, **15/49** is clearly intact, and is not part of a different object.

15/49. (MEΘ 1521 [ME 680]) Small Perforated Disk   Fig. 15.27
 East Hill #274/032 (backfill). 3/5/2004. Phase undetermined.
 Diam. 0.020; Th 0.003; Wt. 2.5 g.
 Intact; corroded, especially around the edges.
 Thin circular disk, with small hole (Diam. 0.002) at center.
 Cf. Kilian-Dirlmeier 1984a, pp. 121–122, pl. 44, nos. 1282–1302.

Chains

There are two examples from the Hypogeion, **15/50**, a fairly well-preserved segment of a thin double-linked chain, and **15/51**, a very small segment made of larger and thicker single links, but as preserved a figure-of-eight shape due to corrosion. The former was encountered in Phase II, and is therefore Late Geometric or early Archaic, the latter in Phase III is contemporary. The closest comparanda for **15/50** are from southern Italy.[181] That most of these were associated with various items of jewelry is well established on account of their being worn by the deceased in a number of graves.[182] In this context, special mention should be made of the well-preserved necklace composed of a double-linked chain and a pendant with human figures from one of the Macchiabate tombs at Francavilla Marittima,[183] and there are numerous chains from the same cemetery associated with fibulae.[184] Examples of double-linked and single-linked chains from Greece, primarily sanctuary sites, are provided in the entries below.

15/50. (MEΘ 1476 [ME 750]) Bronze Chain   Fig. 15.28
 East Hill #274/022044 [11]. 4/6/2004. Phase II.
 Diam. (individual rings) 0.007; p.L. (of the surviving segments and rings) 0.033 + 0.029 + 0.018 + 0.016 + 0.015 + 0.007; Wt. (all frr) 9.4 g.
 Four primary segments, plus smaller frr of individual rings, preserving substantial length of chain.
 Chain composed of double rings, as illustrated.
 Cf., among others, the small segment of a double-ringed chain, *Eretria* XIV, vol. 2, p. 51, pl. 119, nos. O 50–O 51; *Eretria* XXII, vol. 2, p. 24, pl. 103, no. 400; Papadopoulos 2003a, p. 89, figs. 114a–d, nos. 256, 257 (double-linked chains of the Archaic period from Francavilla Marittima); cf. also the poorly preserved segment of a double-linked chain from Chios, Lamb 1934–1935, p. 149, pl. 32, no. 26.

FIGURE 15.28. Bronze chains and related, **15/50** (MEΘ 1476), **15/51** (MEΘ 1497).
Photos I. Coyle and J. Vanderpool, drawing A. Hooton

15/51. (MEΘ 1497 [ME 823]) Bronze Chain Segment   Fig. 15.28

East Hill #274/032043 [5]. 24/6/2004. Phase III.

P.L. 0.021; Diam. (ring shaft) 0.004; Diam. (individual rings) 0.011; Wt. 1.6 g.

Single fr, corroded, preserving two links of chain.

Chain composed of larger and thicker links. As preserved, figure-of-eight-shaped due to corrosion.

For single-link chains, see, among others, Dawkins 1929a, pl. LXXXVIII:a (Sparta, Artemis Orthia); Furtwängler 1906, pl. 117, no. 39 (Aigina); Brock and Mackworth Young 1949, pl. 11, no. 20 (Siphnos); Kilian 1975a, pp. 196–197, pl. 71, esp. nos. 36, 40, 42 (Pherai); Felsch 2007, p. 334, pl. 45, nos. 1471–1478 (Kalapodi); Amandry 1953, pl. XXVII, no. 184.

Additional ring bead, perhaps part of a chain (as **15/50**?):
MEΘ 4134 (ME 3546). East Hill #274/032090 [10]. Small ring bead. H. 0.002; Diam. 0.006; Wt. 0.1 g.

Miniature double axe

Although unprepossessing and heavily corroded, **15/52** is clearly in the form of a double axe, albeit schematic. It finds close parallels in a number of related bronzes from the sanctuary of Zeus at Olympia. In her discussion of the latter, Hanna Philipp distinguished two basic varieties, the first resembling what she refers to as a "böotischen Schild" (and what is sometimes referred to as a "Dipylon shield"), and the second of the same form as **15/52**.[185] The vast majority of these miniature double axes are perforated to receive the axe handle, but three from Olympia and at least two from Philia have no perforation and more closely resemble **15/52**.[186] After discussing the much larger multiple-double-axe pendants from Vergina and elsewere, Philipp provides a full list of comparanda for the smaller miniature double axes of both varieties, including examples from Sparta, Thermon, Elateia, Ithaka, Leukas, Kastritsa, Pherai, Philia, Karditsa, Amphipolis, Olynthos, Panteleimon/Pateli, Lindos, SemČinovo (Bulgaria), and Kuç i Zi (Albania).[187] Philipp also dutifully noted typological, chronological, and regional differentiation.[188] In her more recent study, Kilian-Dirlmeier dates the various miniature double axes on the basis of context from the Protogeometric into the Archaic period.[189] A Late Geometric to early Archaic date for **15/52** is assured.[190] Whether or not **15/52** is classified as jewelry is moot, as the type is found primarily, but not exclusively, as a votive offering in sanctuary sites.

15/52. (MEΘ 1508 [ME 3363]) Small Axe-shaped Object   Fig. 15.29

East Hill #274/022 fill below Wall 14. 8/8/2004. Phase II.

L. 0.020; W. (max.) 0.008; Th. 0.005; Wt. 1.1 g.

Figure 15.29. Miniature bronze double axe, **15/52** (MEΘ 1508). Drawing T. Ross, photo I. Coyle

Intact; corroded.

Small axe-shaped object, with concave long sides and slightly rounded short sides.

Cf. esp. Bouzek 1974b, p. 154, fig. 48, esp. no. 7; *OlForsch* XIII, p. 372, pl. 81, nos. 333–335; Boardman 1967, p. 227, fig. 149, no. 407; Kilian-Dirlmeier 2002, p. 66, pl. 64, nos. 993–994.

Weight/ingot

15/53 is one of the most interesting, idiosyncratic, and enigmatic objects recovered from the Hypogeion. Found in Phase I, its date is clearly Late Geometric or very early Archaic. It is a solid bronze cube, its surfaces appear to have been left intentionally rough, and its relatively small size is confounded by its great weight (270.2 g), so much so that the bronze must be heavily leaded. I know of no comparandum for this cube, which is dated second half of the 8th into the early 7th century B.C. Bronze cube-shaped weights, normally with an eyelet at the top, and sometimes with a ring for lifting, are known beginning in the 5th century B.C., especially from Olympia.[191] The largest is Kat. 1, inscribed "ΔΙΟΣ," measuring 0.155 x 0.153 x 0.115; it weighs 26.2 kg (with the ring), 25.5 kg (without), and is thus about ten times the weight of **15/53**.[192] Among the earliest are three bronze weights—more rectangular than cubed—from the Athenian Agora dated to about 500 B.C., each appropriately inscribed: "στατέρ" (stater), "τεταρτε(μόριον)" (one-fourth stater), and "ἡεμιτρίτον" (one-sixth stater), and all bearing the inscription "δεμόσιον Ἀθεναίον;" each has in relief at the top, respectively, an astragalos, an oval shield, and a sea turtle.[193] Lead square/rectangular weights (but not cubes) are also known from Sardis, including two thought to be Lydian and dated to the 6th century B.C.[194]

The possibility that **15/53** served as a weight or ingot of bronze already in the 8th century B.C. is speculative, but I cannot think what it might be if not a weight or ingot, its heftiness suggesting the former rather than the latter. The comparanda cited above from Olympia, the Athenian Agora, and Sardis are all considerably more developed than **15/53**, and about 200 years later.

15/53. (MEΘ 1502 [ME 1268]) Solid Bronze Cube, Weight/Ingot?   Fig. 15.30
East Hill #274/032063 [9]. 23/8/2004. Phase I.
L. x W. x Depth 0.035 x 0.035 x 0.034; Wt. 270.2 g.
Intact; surface corroded.
Heavy solid cube of bronze, which must be leaded. The surface, although corroded, appears to have been intentionally left rough, i.e., not smoothed.

Knife

The solitary bronze small blade or knife from the Hypogeion is best considered together with the iron knives and larger blades in the same context. Since the vast majority of Early Iron Age knives in Greece are of iron, I will discuss these together under the iron objects. Indeed, so rare are bronze knives in Early Iron Age Greece that most of the examples from the sanctuary at Kalapodi were considered Mycenaean, although a few may be Geometric or later in date.[195] Despite this, bronze knives are known in Early Iron Age contexts, although they are never very common.[196]

FIGURE 15.30. Solid bronze cube, possible weight or ingot, **15/53** (MEΘ 1502).
Drawing F. Skyvalida, photo I. Coyle

The context of **15/54** in Phase II of the Hypogeion fill is Late Geometric or early Archaic. The form of **15/54** is clearly a knife, straight-sided on one side, with the cutting edge on the convex side. The blade tapers toward a blunt point, and there is a short, roughly rectangular haft. As will be discussed below, such small blades are all-purpose implements rather than weapons, although they may have been used as weapons.

15/54. (MEΘ 1505 [ME 888]) Small Bronze Knife Fig. 15.31
   East Hill #274/022050 [11]. 8/7/2004. Phase II.
   L. 0.057; W. (max.) 0.016; Wt. 5.5 g.
   Intact, but heavily corroded.
   Knife straight-sided on one side, with the cutting edge on the convex side. Blade tapers toward a blunt point; short, roughly rectangular haft, as preserved, straight-sided.

Small cone (arrowhead?)
Made from a small sheet of bronze folded over to form a small cone, **15/55** would otherwise be unremarkable were it not for the fact that similar small bronze cones, made from thinner sheet bronze and more carefully manufactured, were found in the agora of Methone and on the West Hill, many associated with the siege of the city in 354 B.C. (Chapter 26).[197] The function of these small cones is not immediately clear, but their prominence among the bronzes from the siege of Methone renders their interpretation as arrowheads at least a possibility, albeit an unconvincing one. Whatever their function, **15/55** is the earliest example of this type of object from the site. I know of no comparanda.

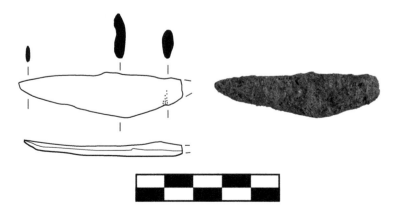

FIGURE 15.31. Bronze knife, **15/54** (MEΘ 1505).
Drawing A. Hooton, photo J. Vanderpool

FIGURE 15.32. Small bronze cone (arrowhead?), **15/55** (MEΘ 1504).
Drawing F. Skyvalida, photo I. Coyle

15/55. (MEΘ 1504 [ME 879]) Small Cone Fig. 15.32
East Hill #274/022049. 7/7/2004. Phase II.
L. 0.013–0.014; Diam. 0.006–0.007; Wt. 0.4 g.
Evidently complete, but slightly chipped/pitted and corroded.
Small sheet folded over to form a small cone, similar to those from the destruction level in the agora, but smaller and thicker.
This is among the earliest of these small bronze cones at Methone.

Clamp or binding sheaths

Encountered in a post–Phase III context of the Hypogeion fill, and associated with Wall 5, **15/56** is best assigned to the Archaic period. It is essentially a bronze version of the more standard lead clamp primarily used for mending pottery, but the bronze may have been used as a sheathing for wood, whether ornamental or non-decorative. Archaic comparanda are known from the Athenian Acropolis and at the sanctuary of Apollo at Bassai.[198] There are a number of closely related bronze reinforcements from Olynthos, and a few perhaps from the Argive Heraion.[199] At Isthmia, there is a related bronze reinforcement "plaque" for a bronze vessel of Archaic date, and several not unrelated iron objects from Isthmia are presented as clamps.[200] Bronze binding sheaths are also well known in Archaic southern Italy.[201]

15/56. (MEΘ 1522 [ME 702]) Bronze Clamp Fig. 15.33
East Hill #274/022, fill associated with Wall 5. 13/5/2004. Post–Phase III.
L. 0.038; H. 0.014; Th. (horizontal struts, max.) 0.011; Wt. 6.5 g.
Three joining frr preserving complete clamp.
Bronze version of the more standard lead clamp, made of two horizontal struts, hammered flat, rectangular in section, connected to each other by two shorter struts, ovoid to circular in section.

FIGURE 15.33. Bronze clamp/binding sheaths, **15/56** (MEΘ 1522).
Drawing F. Skyvalida, photo I. Coyle

Nails

Bronze nails of various forms and sizes are well known throughout Greece and neighboring lands. The two examples presented below from the Hypogeion were found in the fill of Phases II (**15/57**) and III (**15/58**) of the Hypogeion, and can thus be assigned a Geometric or very early Archaic date. The shafts of both are square or rectangular in section. **15/57** has a round, slightly domed head; the head of **15/58** is not preserved. Bronze nails of different sizes and associated with various types of objects from Isthmia derive from Classical, Hellenistic, and Roman contexts, and most of the nails from Philia are either Classical or of uncertain date.[202] Archaic bronze nails from Lindos, mostly 6th century B.C., are discussed by Blinkenberg, who cites comparanda from Olympia, the Argive Heraion, Aigina, and elsewhere.[203] Numerous Archaic bronze nails are published from the sanctuary of Artemis at Ephesos.[204] The importance of the Methone examples presented below lies in the fact that they can be assigned to the Late Geometric or early 7th-century B.C. period.

15/57. (ΜΕΘ 1486 [ΜΕ 1047]) Nail Head   Fig. 15.34
    East Hill #274/032050 [7]. 23/7/2004. Phase II.
    P.H. 0.009; Diam. (head) 0.013; L. x W. (shaft); 0.007 x 0.003; Wt. 1.2 g.
    Single fr preserving nail head and uppermost shaft; corroded.
    Round head, slightly domed; rectangular shaft.

15/58. (ΜΕΘ 4118 [ΜΕ 850]) Nail Shaft Fr   Fig. 15.34
    East Hill #274/032046 [5]. 30/6/2004. Phase III.
    P.L. 0.029; Wt. 1.4 g.
    Single fr preserving lower portion and tip of nail shaft.
    Shaft square in section, tapering toward point.

FIGURE 15.34. Bronze nails, **15/57** (ΜΕΘ 1486), **15/58** (ΜΕΘ 4118).
Drawings A. Hooton and T. Ross, photos I. Coyle and J. Vanderpool

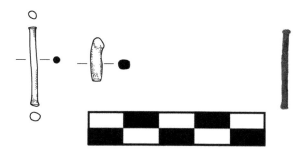

FIGURE 15.35. Small bronze pin associated with hinged object, **15/59** (ΜΕΘ 4140).
Drawing T. Ross, photo I. Coyle

Small pin associated with hinged object

The primary value of this small pin is its early date (Archaic) and its close resemblance to **26/170** (ΜΕΘ 4232) from the agora of Methone, which is later and is clearly associated with some form of hinged object. **15/59** is small, intact, its shaft circular in section, with both ends lightly hammered flat. Although small hinges from Archaic contexts in Greece and southern Italy are not uncommon, I know of no pin associated with such objects.[205]

15/59. (ΜΕΘ 4140 [ME 595]) Pin for Hinged Object   Fig. 15.35
    East Hill #274/022034 [10]. 5/4/2004. Post–Phase III.
    L. 0.023–0.024; Diam. (flattened ends) 0.003; Diam. (shaft) 0.002; Wt. 0.4 g.
    Intact.
    Small pin, with shaft circular in section, and both ends lightly hammered flat.
    Same type of pin as that associated with the hinged plate with pin **26/170** (ΜΕΘ 4232).

Hooked object other than fishhook

Little can be said about **15/60** especially because of its fragmentary and corroded state. Encountered in Phase I of the Hypogeion fill, the object can be securely dated to the Late Geometric or earlier Archaic period. The thickish and somewhat irregular shaft, which is circular in section, does not look or feel like the bow of a fibula, and the thinner hook, also circular in section, is a most unlikely spring or catchplate loop for a fibula. The triangular projection on the shaft may be corrosion, but it seems too regular to be a product of corrosion. Similarly, **15/60** does not resemble the small spindle hooks.[206] Small hooked implements are occasionally dedicated in sanctuaries.[207]

15/60. (ΜΕΘ 1500 [ME 1270]) Hooked Implement   Fig. 15.36
    East Hill #274/032062 [9]. 25/8/2004. Phase I.
    P.L. 0.027; Diam. (shaft) max. 0.005; Wt. 1.5 g.
    Single fr preserving undetermined portion of shaft and most of hook; corroded.
    Shaft, as preserved, thickish and a little irregular due to corrosion, circular in section; hook considerably thinner in section, also circular. There is a triangular projection off the main shaft, as shown; this may be corrosion, but it seems too regular to be a product of corrosion.

Wire

With its shaft mostly square in section, **15/61** preserves an undetermined length of bronze wire, bent and folded onto itself as shown. Its location within the Hypogeion fill is undetermined, but there is little doubt that the fragment is ancient. A few similar examples from Archaic southern Italy, and a few (undated) from Philia, are cited in the entry below.

FIGURE 15.36. Bronze hooked object other than fishhook, **15/60** (MEΘ 1500).
Drawing T. Ross, photo I. Coyle

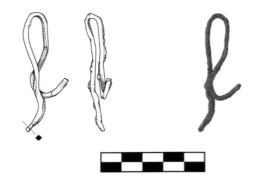

FIGURE 15.37. Length of bronze wire, **15/61** (MEΘ 4135).
Drawing T. Ross, photo I. Coyle

15/61. (MEΘ 4135 [ME 1622]) Fr Bronze Wire   Fig. 15.37

East Hill #274.032043-051, backfill. 20/11/2004. Phase undetermined.

P.H. (as bent) 0.058; Th. (max.) 0.003; Wt. 3.1 g.

Single fr preserving undetermined length of wire.

Shaft mostly square in section, bent and folded onto itself as shown.

Cf., among others, Papadopoulos 2003a, p. 135, fig. 170, nos. 471–473; cf. also pieces such as Kilian-Dirlmeier 2002, pp. 170–171, pl. 175, nos. 2983–2984 (classified as *Spiralscheiben* und *Spiralröllen*).

Bronze rods, strips, and related

Several bronzes, fragmentary in the main, are assembled under this heading, primarily thin rods or strips of bronze. A few of the pieces must be tools. For example, **15/62** resembles an awl or even a drill, such as several from Kastanas and Kalapodi, and **15/63** may be closely related; there is also an iron awl ("punteruolo di ferro") from Pithekoussai tomb 678, which is LG II.[208] Others may possibly be functioning tools. For example, **15/67**, with its sharp point, may be an L-shaped staple of sorts or even an implement for incising organic material, and it, together with the slightly more substantial **15/62** and **15/63**, may be tools for the working of softer organic material, such as bone, ivory, leather, wood, and the like. I can also imagine **15/66**, its blunted tapering point slotted into a handle of bone or wood, exposing the flattened sharp terminal for use as a tool to smooth over or trim excess unwanted material during the working of bone, ivory, or wood. Such tools would be ideal in what was one of the most important industrial activities at Methone, the working of elephant and hippopotamus tusk ivory, as well as local animal bone, especially deer antler.[209]

The more substantial portion of a rod or spike, **15/64**, is the largest of such pieces from the Hypogeion, but not enough of it survives to determine if it was just a rod, or served some other function. As preserved, it is not an obvious tool, like a chisel or awl, and its size precludes it from being a nail. In many ways, **15/65** is one of the more interesting pieces. It is not absolutely clear whether the two non-joining fragments are from one object or from two, but it seems that both pieces belong to the same item, with the central shaft, rectangular in section, and with both terminals hammered flat. The piece is related to the small bronze **15/23** that I have interpreted as a dress pin, but which may prove to be a stylus, but **15/65** does not taper toward a point. As tempting as it would be to regard this piece as a flattened-out pair of tweezers—a *sine qua non* for any self-respecting warrior of the Early Iron Age and Archaic period, and later—and which are common votive dedications at Greek sanctuaries and can also be found in tombs, it is not a convincing pair of tweezers.[210] It is worth adding that such tweezers are also common elsewhere in Macedonia and the Balkans.[211]

Of the eight objects assembled below, three were found in Phase I of the Hypogeion fill (**15/65**, **15/66**, **15/67**), three in Phase II (**15/62**, **15/63**, and **15/68**), one in a post–Phase III context (**15/69**), and one (**15/64**) from Phase II or III. The majority can therefore be assigned to the Late Geometric or early Archaic period.

15/62. (ΜΕΘ 4136 [ME 1143]) Likely Bronze Awl Fig. 15.38
East Hill #274.032054 [7]. 9/8/2004. Phase II.
L. 0.098; W. x Th. (shaft) 0.005 x 0.004; Wt: NR.
Intact.

Bronze rod, mostly rectangular in section, though more square toward the terminals, slightly tapering toward both ends, neither of which appears to be broken or damaged.

Cf., among others, Kilian-Dirlmeier 2002, p. 155, pl. 162, no. 2577, which is smaller than **15/62** (classified under the heading of "Werkstattreste"); cf. also the iron awl ("Pfriem") from Vergina, Bräuning and Kilian-Dirlmeier 2013:161, fig. 38, no. 8.

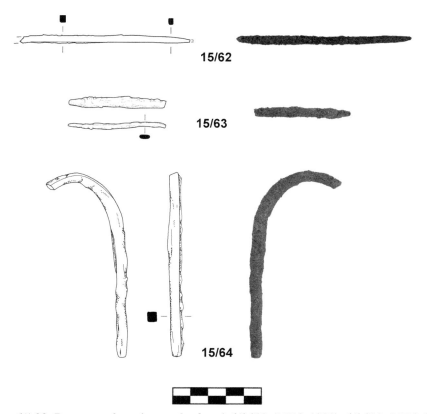

FIGURE 15.38. Bronze rods, strips, and related, **15/62** (ΜΕΘ 4136), **15/63** (ΜΕΘ 1516), **15/64** (ΜΕΘ 4121). Drawings A. Hooton and T. Ross, photos I. Coyle and J. Vanderpool

15/63. (ΜΕΘ 1516 [ME 1427]) Possible Awl(?)   Fig. 15.38
East Hill #274/032065 [7]. 7/9/2004. Phase II.
P.L. 0.055; W. 0.006–0.007; Th. 0.004; Wt. 2.0 g.
Single fr preserving undetermined portion of strip; corroded.
Thin and narrow strip, tapering toward one end, broken at the other.
Cf. **15/62** (ΜΕΘ 4136).

15/64. (ΜΕΘ 4121 [ME 1076]) Bronze Rod Fr   Fig. 15.38
East Hill #274/022, cleaning of Wall 14. 29/7/2004. Phase II.
P.L. (as bent) 0.113; W. x Th. (shaft, max.) 0.007 x 0.007; Wt. 26.7 g.
Single fr, broken at both ends, preserving large portion of shaft, but nothing of the head or tip.
Shaft square in section and clearly from a large object.

15/65. (ΜΕΘ 1490 [ME 3031]) "Spatula"-shaped Object   Fig. 15.39
East Hill #274/022059 [12]. 25/8/2006. Phase I.
Main fr: p.L. 0.059; W. (head) 0.012; L. x W. (shaft) 0.006 x 0.005; Wt. 4.7 g. Smaller fr: p.L. 0.024; Wt. 1.9 g.
Two frr, which do not clearly join, preserving portion of shaft and terminal(s) of spatula-like object.
Shafts of both frr rectangular in section, with terminals hammered flat, as shown.
Cf. the spatulate implement **26/115** from the agora of Methone.

15/66. (ΜΕΘ 1520 [ME 3321]) Bronze Spatula-shaped Object   Fig. 15.39
East Hill #274/032086 [9]. 22/11/2006. Phase I.
P.L. (as bent) 0.038; W. (head) 0.007; Wt. 2.6 g.
Single fr preserving most of object; top of head seems chipped; opposite end clearly broken, but very close to the original terminal; corroded.
Shaft, as preserved at its upper part, plano-convex in section, but almost with a central ridge for part of its length resulting in an almost triangular section, tapering toward point. Head hammered flat to create the spatula-like form, with the straight edge fairly sharp. There is a clear thickening on the concave side, near the broken tip, and another on the convex side near the head.

15/67. (ΜΕΘ 4120 [ME 1247]) Bronze L-shaped Staple   Fig. 15.39
East Hill #274/032060 [7]. 19/8/2004. Phase I. L-shaped Staple
P.H. 0.031–0.034 (depending on orientation); Th. (max.) 0.002–0.003; Wt. 1.4 g.
Intact.
Small rod, square to rectangular in section, tapering noticeably toward both points, one of which is especially sharp.

15/68. (ΜΕΘ 1517 [ME 1445]) Narrow Bronze Strip   Fig. 15.39
East Hill #274/032067 [7]/ 13/9/2004. Phase II.
P.L. (as bent) 0.038; W. 0.005; Th. 0.002–0.003; Wt. 2.5 g.
Single fr preserving undetermined portion of object; somewhat corroded.
Thin and narrow strip of bronze tapering toward a clear point at one end; evidently broken at the opposite end, though this is not perfectly clear.

15/69. (ΜΕΘ 5304 [ME 313]) Thin Bronze Strip   Fig. 15.39
East Hill #274/032010 [3]. 5/8/2003. Post–Phase III.
P.L. 0.080; W. (max.) 0.008; Th. 0.002; Wt. 3.7 g.

Single fr preserving almost complete strip. One terminal clearly preserved; the opposite end, although broken, must be close to the original terminal.

Thin strip hammered flat, widest near midpoint, tapering toward the intact terminal; strip at opposite end also tapers toward a point, itself not preserved.

Other fragmentary bronze strips:

ΜΕΘ 1509 (ΜΕ 2937). East Hill #274/022, fill below Wall 14. 8/8/2006. Phase II. Four frr, P.L. (largest fr) 0.034; Wt. (all frr) 0.6 g.

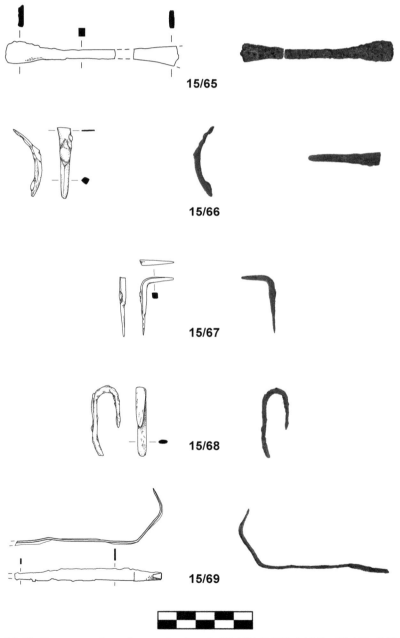

FIGURE 15.39. Bronze rods, strips, and related, **15/65** (ΜΕΘ 1490), **15/66** (ΜΕΘ 1520), **15/67** (ΜΕΘ 4120), **15/68** (ΜΕΘ 1517), **15/69** (ΜΕΘ 5304). Drawings A. Hooton and T. Ross, photos I. Coyle and J. Vanderpool

Bronze sheet and wider strips of bronze

The small bronzes under this heading include thin sheets of bronze, together with wider strips of bronze. The small perforated bronze sheets **15/70** (fragmentary, with a small hole below preserved end) and **15/71** (intact, with a slightly larger hole at either end) could serve any number of functions, such as parts of binding sheaths like those discussed above, as well as binding plates (see **26/150–26/156** below), but would also be ideal patches for the repair of bronze vessels.[212] **15/72** is related, but it remains uncertain whether the circular or apsidal "cutout" is original or the result of post-depositional damage, and **15/73** is a small bronze sheet folded over, with no visible perforations. Of interest is the thicker leaf-shaped bronze sheet, **15/74**. Although the piece as preserved resembles some fibulae, such as those with violin-bow arch (e.g., **15/6** [ΜΕΘ 1390]), the clear terminal at one end, together with its weight, precludes a fibula. Moreover, the constant thickness of the bronze throughout, with no taper in the section toward a cutting edge, means that it cannot be a bronze knife like **15/54** (ΜΕΘ 1505). Although leaf-shaped, **15/74** is not a votive leaf such as those found in sanctuary contexts.[213] An evidently close parallel is offered by a similar leaf-shaped bronze from Ephesos, which is thicker and different from the bona fide bronze leaves.[214] Of the bronzes presented below, two (**15/70**, **15/73**) were encountered in the Phase I fill of the Hypogeion, and two (**15/71**, **15/72**) in Phase II; the precise context of **15/74** was undetermined.

15/70. (ΜΕΘ 4110 [ΜΕ 3010]) Perforated Bronze Sheet Fig. 15.40
East Hill #274/022058 [12]. 22/8/2006. Phase I.
P.L. 0.037; W. 0.012; Th. 0.003; Wt. 2.1 g.
Single fr, broken on one of the short sides, preserving undetermined portion of strip.
Rectangular; one short side nicely finished and clearly an edge, with small perforation below the edge.

15/71. (ΜΕΘ 4115 [ΜΕ 1034]) Small Perforated Sheet Fig. 15.40
East Hill #274/032049 [5]. 19/7/2004. Phase II.
L. 0.021; W. 0.009; Th. 0.001–0.002; Diam. (holes) 0.003; Wt. 0.8 g.
Intact.
Rectangular strip of thin sheet bronze, hammered flat, with two holes, one at each end.
Cf., among others, *Zagora* 2, pl. 275:d.

15/72. (ΜΕΘ 4106 [ΜΕ 782]) Fragmentary Sheet Attachment Fig. 15.40
East Hill #274/022045 [11]. 14/06/2004. Phase II.
P.L. 0.033; W. 0.017; Th. 0.002; Wt. 2.1 g.
Three joining frr preserving portion of thin bronze strip, including both of the longer edges, and portion of one of the shorter edges.
Sheet bronze hammered flat; rectangular. Very slightly bent over at the preserved short edge, as if hinged; the opposite end has what appears to be a circular or apsidal cutout, though this could be the result of breakage.

15/73. (ΜΕΘ 4113 [ΜΕ 1272]) Fr of Bronze Sheet Fig. 15.40
East Hill #274/032063 [9]. 25/8/2004. Phase I.
L. x W. (as folded) 0.027 x 0.023; Wt. 6.1 g.
Single fr, folded over and fused at one end, preserving portion of sheet; corroded.
Roughly rectangular sheet, folded over.

15/74. (ΜΕΘ 1503 [ME 872]) Leaf-shaped Object Fig. 15.40
East Hill #274/022048 [12]. 5/7/2004. Phase undetermined.
P.L. 0.046; W. 0.011; Th. 0.003; Wt. 3.9 g.
Single fr preserving undetermined portion of object; one short end clearly broken, the other intact. Surface corroded.
Leaf-shaped thick sheet bronze, tapering to a point at one end. Although the fr resembles some fibulae (cf. **15/6** [ΜΕΘ 1390]), the clear terminal at one end, plus its weight, precludes a fibula. The fact that the thickness of the bronze is constant throughout precludes it being a bronze knife like **15/54** (ΜΕΘ 1505). Although leaf-shaped, it is not a votive leaf such as those occasionally found in sanctuary contexts.

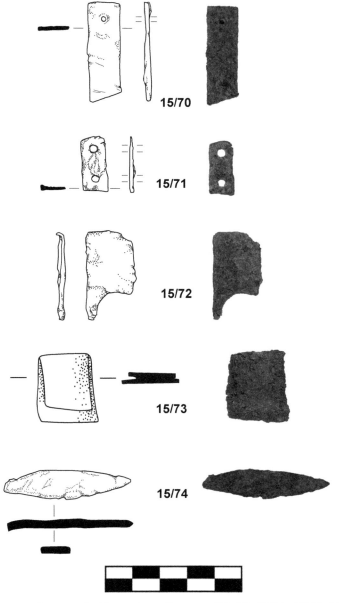

FIGURE 15.40. Bronze sheet and wider strips of bronze, **15/70** (ΜΕΘ 4110), **15/71** (ΜΕΘ 4115), **15/72** (ΜΕΘ 4106), **15/73** (ΜΕΘ 4113), **15/74** (ΜΕΘ 1503).
Drawings T. Ross and F. Skyvalida, photos I. Coyle and J. Vanderpool

Objects of Iron

Iron was the preferred metal for weapons and for many different types of tools.[215] As we have seen, there were few, if any, weapons of bronze from the Hypogeion. I begin the survey of the iron objects from the Hypogeion at Methone with the weapons. There are, demonstrably, no swords (ξίφη) in the fill of the Hypogeion. The only real weapons include a spearhead, together with a couple of fragmentary sockets that probably derive from spearheads, and a solitary arrowhead. I then deal with the blades, the majority of which are from tools rather than weapons, or from objects that could be both tools and weapons. The axe heads are in a similarly liminal category, as they could serve as tools, best associated with the Methonaian timber trade (see Chapter 20), or as battle axes that are not unknown in the Aegean Early Iron Age. The fact that several of the axes may well be adzes indicates that the majority of such objects from Methone are for the working of wood. The tools include chisels, tongs, and tacks, and the account of the iron objects ends with some miscellaneous items, including a ring of sorts, a fragmentary spiral, an attachment, and a roughly square piece of iron. Unfortunately, the state of preservation of the Methone iron objects is not good, and heavy corrosion in virtually all cases has made it difficult to determine details.

Weapons

Spearhead

The only diagnostic spearhead from the Hypogeion, **15/75**, was encountered in the Phase I fill and, as such, a Late Geometric or early Archaic date is assured. Although heavily corroded and only partially preserved, with a cockle shell lodged uncomfortably in its corrosion, **15/75** is a classic example of Anthony Snodgrass's Type M spear, which he describes in the following terms: "A plain, smallish type, with a flat blade . . . but with the socket properly hammered into a tube. It is only known in iron."[216] Snodgrass lists 19 examples, from Crete in the south to Boubousti in the north, and from Athens to Bassai and Olympia. Among those that can be dated by context, the earliest are Protogeometric and the remainder are Geometric, and primarily Late Geometric.[217] This type continues well into the Archaic and later periods and is prominent among the Archaic dedications at the sanctuary of Poseidon at Isthmia, where it is common from the 6th century B.C. on.[218] Ioulia Vokotopoulou illustrates no fewer than 23 examples of Type M from Vitsa Zagoriou, and the type is similarly popular at the Molossian cemetery at Liatovouni in Epirus.[219] Snodgrass lists nine more examples of Type M spearheads from the North Cemetery at Knossos ranging in date from Early Protogeometric to Late Geometric and Early Orientalizing.[220] Closer to home, related examples are known at Vergina and Sindos.[221] Farther north, a broad array of iron spearheads have been found at Trebenište and the Glasinac region,[222] and to the south in Thessaly and Phokis, iron spearheads, including examples of Type M, are well known at Philia and Kalapodi.[223] As for **15/76** and **15/77**, little can be said. Enough survives to suggest that both are probably fragmentary or partial spearhead sockets; the former was encountered in the Phase II fill of the Hypogeion, the latter in Phase I.

In dealing with the incidence of spearheads in Early Iron Age burials in Greece generally, Snodgrass wrote:

> From about 900 B.C. onwards, the practice of including two or three spearheads in a warrior-grave, often with no other arms, gradually became common in Greece. By the late 8th century B.C. this custom was almost universal, and it continued sporadically thereafter. Sometimes there is one larger and one smaller spearhead, but more often, there are two or three of more or less identical size. Such multiple spears cannot be intended as a token of the deceased's wealth, as they were in the graves of Mycenaean kings and nobles. Almost certainly they mean something quite different: namely, that the tactics of long-range warfare had been adopted in Greece, with the spear being thrown as a javelin, so that two or more would be carried.[224]

Snodgrass went on to discuss Late Geometric battle scenes and the testimony of Homer for the use of two spears by warriors.[225]

But are all spears associated with warriors?[226] In the context of Late Bronze and Early Iron Age Epirus and Macedonia, spearheads constitute an essential element of the grave furnishings of the male. At Liatovouni, for example, the deceased male was usually accompanied by two, sometimes more, iron spearheads.[227] Rather than label the entire male population of the cemetery as "warriors," these spears could just as easily be considered indispensable for the farmer/stockbreeder/hunter in his day-to-day activities. The uniformity of the material remains and burial customs that can be observed over a broad region of northern Greece and the southern Balkans in the pre-Classical period is noteworthy. The evidence of spears alone does not, in itself, support the widespread arming of the rural population as an indication of aggressive practice and of intra-social hostilities. In certain contexts, the use of such spears can more easily be seen against the backdrop of hunting practices, as well as in defense from wild animals or from groups of bandits or thieves.[228] Just as Greek iconography furnishes evidence for the use of two spearheads by warriors, so too does it depict hunters with two spears, often with different types of spear. In Mycenaean iconography it is sometimes difficult to distinguish between warriors and hunters, but in the Archaic and Classical periods, the distinctions are sometimes clearly rendered.[229]

15/75. (ΜΕΘ 1533 [ΜΕ 1183]) Iron Spearhead　　　　　　　　　　　　　　　　　　　　Fig. 15.41
　　East Hill #274/032056 [7]. 11/8/2004. Phase I.
　　P.L. 0.101; p.W. (max.) 0.032; Diam. (socket) 0.016; Wt. (including attached shell) 51.4 g.
　　Single fr preserving upper portion of socket and lower part, together with the midpoint of the blade. Seashell adhering to the corrosion.
　　Blade hammered flat, with no clear central rib or thickening. What survives of the socket is comparatively short and rather small.
　　Cf. **26/188** (ΜΕΘ 1746) and **26/189** (ΜΕΘ 1752).

15/76. (ΜΕΘ 1532 [ΜΕ 1290]) Socket Fr Fig. 15.41
　　East Hill #274/022056 [12]. 31/8/2004. Phase II.
　　P.L. 0.039; Diam. 0.024; Wt. 24.2 g.
　　Single fr, heavily corroded, preserving portion of cylinder. One end is clearly broken but the other may be original, although this remains difficult to determine because of corrosion. The ever-so-slight taper of the tube suggests that this should be a spearhead socket.

15/77. (ΜΕΘ 5327 [ΜΕ 3004]) Socket Fr　　　　　　　　　　　　　　　　　　　　　　　Fig. 15.41
　　East Hill #274/022058 [12]. 22/8/2006. Phase I.
　　P.L. 0.060; Diam. 0.025; Wt. 24.3 g.
　　Single fr preserving substantial portion of object; heavily corroded.
　　Iron sheet, hammered flat and rolled into a partial tube, open along the seam.

Arrowhead

The solitary arrowhead from the Hypogeion was found in a post–Phase III context and is thus Archaic. It is a small arrowhead, with a flat, leaf-shaped blade and a short solid tang. As has been repeatedly noted in the literature, the abundance of arrowheads and the evidence they provide for the practice of archery in the Late Bronze Age is matched by their rarity during the Early Iron Age.[230] Nevertheless, the discovery of 15 arrowheads at Vergina by Andronikos, and of more examples by Photios Petsas,[231] the finds from the cemeteries at Lefkandi,[232] 18 arrowheads from one context

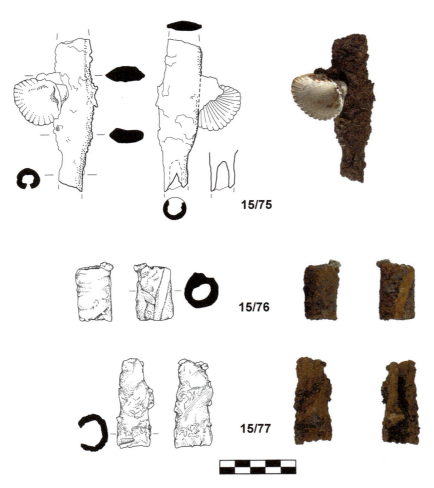

FIGURE 15.41. Iron spearhead, **15/75** (MEΘ 1533), and iron sockets probably associated with spearheads, **15/76** (MEΘ 1532), **15/77** (MEΘ 5327). Drawings A. Hooton and T. Ross, photos I. Coyle and J. Vanderpool

and another 16 from a grave at Kavousi, seven examples from tombs at Knossos, and a solitary iron arrowhead from Torone,[233] another from the Athenian Agora,[234] coupled with the publication or mention of previously overlooked examples,[235] have added significantly to the evidence for the practice of archery in the Early Iron Age. Most recently, at least four of the arrowheads from the Itonia sanctuary near Philia were found in contexts of the Late Geometric to the "hocharchaischer Zeit," with numerous additional iron arrowheads from undated contexts.[236] The sanctuary at Kalapodi has yielded a notable range of arrowheads, ranging in date from LH IIIC through Late Geometric and into the Archaic, Classical, and later periods.[237] The few arrowheads from the cemetery at Sindos are Archaic and Classical, three of bronze, one of iron.[238]

The leaf-shaped tanged arrowhead corresponds to Snodgrass's Type 5, which he describes in the following terms: "This, the most primitive and basic form of arrowhead, is found in almost all civilizations and periods, and can be long and narrow or short and broad, with or without midrib, in bronze or iron. Its survivals, in Greece, mostly in iron and generally when poverty or lack of skill made more efficient types unobtainable, are largely without interest."[239] He goes on to list and discuss examples from Anatolia and the Near East, as well as examples from Greece, including those from Delos, Athens, Olynthos, and a Geometric example of the type from Argos. He concludes the discussion by noting that, among the remaining examples from Greece, "It can only be said of them that, save in Crete, not one can be definitely assigned to a date as early as the eighth century."[240]

FIGURE 15.42. Iron arrowhead, **15/78** (MEΘ 1566).
Drawing T. Ross, photos I. Coyle

15/78. (MEΘ 1566 [ME 328]) Arrowhead   Fig. 15.42
    East Hill #274/032011 [3]. 6/8/2003. Post–Phase III.
    P.L. 0.032; W. (max.) 0.010–0.011; W./Diam. (tang) 0.007; Wt. 1.3 g.
    Single fr, corroded, preserving almost complete arrowhead.
    Small arrowhead, with flat, leaf-shaped blade and short solid tang rather than a socket, thinnest at juncture with blade and splaying out toward its terminal.

Blades (larger and smaller knives)

As noted above, there are no demonstrable swords from the Hypogeion at Methone. In contrast, iron blades from larger and smaller knives are common. Many are probably tools, though a few may represent fragments from weapons, normally referred to as daggers in the literature. All or most of the pieces presented below could be used as both tools and weapons. At nearby Vergina, Andronikos distinguished between μάχαιραι and μαχαιρίδια. The latter are small knives with a length of up to 0.150 m, the former are what he describes as the "proper daggers" ("πραγματικὰς μαχαίρας"), which can reach a length of up to 0.400 m.[241] There is a total of 39 of the smaller μαχαιρίδια and only seven μάχαιραι at Vergina.[242] Similar knives, primarily of the 6th century B.C., a few extending into the Classical period, are also common in tombs at Sindos.[243] In central and southern Greece in the Early Iron Age, the length of most of the small iron knives from the Athenian Agora vary between 0.100 and 0.150.[244] Larger knives are known: the original length of the largest from the Agora is 0.200; a "killed" knife from Kerameikos Protogeometric Grave 28 measures 0.270 in length, and there is another from Lefkandi that is 0.280 m long, but few reaching 0.40 m.[245]

There are two broad types of iron knives at Methone. The most common are those knives characterized by a slightly curved blade, tapering toward a point, which is triangular in section, with the cutting edge usually on the inner concave side. In the case of **15/82** the cutting edge appears to be along the convex side.[246] A few preserve remnants of the haft, but most are fairly heavily corroded and details are difficult to glean. The Methone knives of this type include **15/79–15/84**. In terms of size, the largest of the examples from the Hypogeion are **15/79** and **15/81**; the former only has a preserved length of 0.118 for all of the fragments lined up; the preserved length of the latter is 0.086–0.087. The second broad type of knife is typified by **15/87** and **15/88**. The former, which preserves a substantial portion of the blade and a clear part of the haft, has a preserved length of only 0.101 and its original length is unlikely to exceed 0.150 m. The fragmentary **15/88** is similarly small, with a preserved length of only 0.065 m. Two other knives, **15/85** and **15/86**, share features of both types; the cutting edge of both is on the convex side. I provide a few comparanda for individual knives in the catalogue entries below. The knives assembled below were encountered throughout the fill of the Hypogeion: five were found in the Phase I fill (**15/79**, **15/81–15/82**, **15/86**, **15/88**), three in Phase II (**15/83–15/85**), and two in a post–Phase III context (**15/80**, **15/87**). Consequently, they were in use from the Late Geometric period well into the Archaic.

In dealing with the small iron knives of Middle Protogeometric through Subprotogeometric Lefkandi, Catling noted that such blades are "ideal general purpose implements that would be equally useful for cutting food, cleaning game, whittling, pruning and—conceivably—shaving."[247] In a similar vein, Jane Waldbaum writes: "Knives are defined as one-edged cutting instruments and may serve many functions. They are used as domestic and agricultural cutting tools and may also be used as weapons."[248] What is important to note here is that whenever they are found in tombs in Early Iron Age and Archaic Greece, they are found with both men and women, the classic case being the celebrated "Booties Grave" in the Athenian Agora of a younger female adult aged 20–25 years at death.[249] In his overview of early Greek armor and weapons, Snodgrass referred to various daggers under the heading of "swords," but judiciously included no mention of knives such as those discussed here.[250] In a more recent publication, Snodgrass classifies one-edged iron knives as tools, not weapons.[251] Knives are not gender specific and, like modern knives, ancient knives were used by both men and women in a variety of quotidian activities. In the context of an industrial center like Methone—which was also a thriving settlement—small and larger knives could have been used for many functions.

In addition to Lefkandi, Early Iron Age knives of similar form are common in Crete, especially at Knossos, where Snodgrass distinguished five types, labeled A–E.[252] They are also common in east Lokris,[253] Euboian Kyme,[254] Thessaly,[255] Messenia,[256] the Dodecanese,[257] and on Cyprus.[258] Farther north, they are also common in Macedonia[259] and Thasos.[260] Similar small iron knives are also found in numbers over a wider area of Europe, and a number of scholars have emphasized the relationship of the broader European examples to those of Greece.[261] In dealing, however, with the material from Lefkandi, Catling could find nothing to suggest foreign influence on knife design.[262] A related issue concerns the Bronze Age antecedents of the one-edged bronze knives, normally with riveted handles, and their local Aegean versus European-influenced development, which has an important bearing on the development of Early Iron Age types.[263]

15/79. (ΜΕΘ 1538 [ME 3198]) Fr Larger Blade (Knife/Dagger?)   Fig. 15.43
East Hill #274/022065 [13]. 11/10/2006. Phase I.
P.L. (largest fr) 0.073; p.L. (all frr together) 0.118; W. (max.) 0.027; Wt. 25.3 g.
Main fr made up of two joining frr, with an additional two non-joining frr, preserving small portion of blade; heavily corroded.
Frr clearly from a large blade, slightly curved, as **15/80** (ΜΕΘ 1564) and **15/81** (ΜΕΘ 1537); the cutting edge should be on the concave side, though this is in places unclear due to corrosion.
Cf., among others, Kilian-Dirlmeier 2002, pl. 68, no. 1061; pl. 69, nos. 1095–1096; *Sindos* III, pp. 239–240, 463, fig. 210, no. 453 (ca. 500 B.C.); pp. 241, 464, figs. 214–215, nos. 460 (ca. 410 B.C.) and 461 (end of the 5th century B.C.).

15/80. (ΜΕΘ 1564 [ME 355]) Blade Fr   Fig. 15.43
East Hill #274/032015 [4]. 11/8/2003. Post–Phase III.
P.L. 0.076; W. (max.) 0.020; Wt. 11.7 g.
Two joining frr, corroded, preserving portion of blade.
Blade slightly curved, with cutting edge along the concave side. No clear evidence of a haft.
Cf. **15/79**, and, among others, *Vergina* I, p. 267, fig. 104, Κιβ; *Sindos* III, pp. 237, 461, fig. 199, no. 441 (540–530 B.C.); Kilian-Dirlmeier 2002, pl. 108, no. 1764.

15/81. (ΜΕΘ 1537 [ME 3171]) Fr Larger Blade (Dagger?)   Fig. 15.43
East Hill #274/022064 [13]. 21/9/2006. Phase I.
P.L. 0.086–0.087; W. 0.028; Wt. 35.2 g.

Single fr preserving relatively small portion of large blade; heavily corroded.

Fr clearly from a larger blade, perhaps a dagger. Uncertain whether or not there is a clear cutting edge.

Cf., among others, Kilian-Dirlmeier 2002, pl. 155, no. 2439.

15/82. (ΜΕΘ 1539 [ME 1223]) Blade Fr   Fig. 15.43

East Hill #274/032058 [7]. 16/8/2004. Phase I.

P.L. 0.069–0.070; W. 0.020; Wt. 9.4 g.

Originally single fr, now two joining frr, preserving undetermined portion of blade; corroded.

Blade as **15/80** (ΜΕΘ 1564), but with cutting edge probably along the convex side (unlike **15/80**).

Cf., among others, *Vergina* I, p. 269, fig. 105, TX; *Sindos* III, pp. 237, 461, fig. 200, no. 442 (end of the 6th century B.C.); Kilian-Dirlmeier 2002, pl. 68, no. 1066.

15/83. (ΜΕΘ 1540 [ME 1446]) Fragmentary Blade   Fig. 15.43

East Hill #274/032067 [7]. 13/9/2004. Phase II.

P.L. (three main frr laid out) 0.140; W. (max.) 0.025; Wt. 46.5 g.

Three main frr, two of which clearly join, plus chips of corrosion, preserving small portion of large blade; corroded.

Shape as **15/79** (ΜΕΘ 1538). On the best preserved of the frr, both edges look similar and there was no clear cutting edge.

Cf., among others, Kilian 1975a, pl. 93, no. 10; Kilian-Dirlmeier 2002, pl. 155, no. 2439

15/84. (ΜΕΘ 1534 [ME 1889]) Knife   Fig. 15.44

East Hill #274/022047-051, backfill. 27/5/2005. Probably Phase II.

P.L. 0.075; W. 0.024; Wt. 17.2 g.

Single fr, corroded, preserving portion of blade and point.

Blade tapering toward a point. From what survives, the cutting edge appears to be on the straighter side, which is, nevertheless, slightly curved.

Cf., among others, *Nichoria* III, pp. 303, 310, fig. 5-55, no. 92; Kilian-Dirlmeier 2002, pl. 69, no. 1082.

15/85. (ΜΕΘ 5321 [ME 1447]) Iron Knife/Blade Fr   Fig. 15.44

East Hill #274/032067 [7]. 13/5/2004. Phase II.

P.L. 0.060; p.W. 0.0261 Th. (max.) 0.008; Wt. 13.5 g.

Single fr, corroded, preserving portion of knife.

Blade straight-edged along one side, tapering toward a blunt point as preserved; cutting edge along the convex side.

Cf. esp. Kilian-Dirlmeier 2002, pl. 69, no. 1086; pl. 153, no 2392; Gadolou 2008, p. 203, fig. 153, no. 57; *Sindos* III, pp. 236, 461, fig. 196, no. 435 (last quarter of the 6th century B.C.).

15/86. (ΜΕΘ 1545 [ME 3083]) Knife   Fig. 15.44

East Hill #274/022061 [13]. 5/9/2006. Phase I.

P.L. (all frr strung together) 0.138; Wt. 27.4 g.

Four frr, not clearly joining, preserving greater portion of knife; very heavily corroded.

Blade slightly curved, tapering toward a point, with the cutting edge along the convex side. Frr from opposite end may preserve portion of the haft.

Cf., for example, Brock 1957, pl. 172, no. 1611; Kilian-Dirlmeier 2002, pl. 100, no. 1648; pl. 153, no 2392.

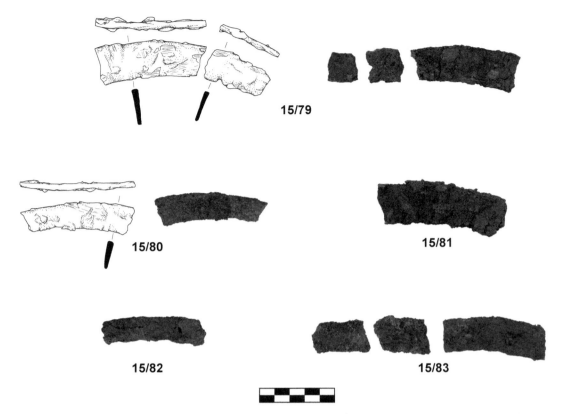

Fig. 15.43. Iron blades (larger and smaller knives), **15/79** (ΜΕΘ 1538), **15/80** (ΜΕΘ 1564), **15/81** (ΜΕΘ 1537), **15/82** (ΜΕΘ 1539), **15/83** (ΜΕΘ 1540). Drawings T. Ross, photos I. Coyle

15/87. (ΜΕΘ 1563 [ME 341]) Long, Narrow Small Blade   Fig. 15.45
East Hill #274/032014 [3]. 7/8/2003. Post–Phase III.
P.L. 0.101; W. 0.016; Wt. 16.2 g.
Two joining frr preserving substantial portion of blade.
Comparatively long, straight-sided blade, almost stiletto-like. Thicker short side clearly portion of the haft, rectangular in section. Cutting surface on the side below the haft articulation.
Cf. **15/88** (ΜΕΘ 1546) and, among others, Brock 1957, pl. 172, no. 1616; Kilian-Dirlmeier 2002, pl. 71, no. 1112.

15/88. (ΜΕΘ 1546 [ME 3361]) Fr Long Narrow Knife   Fig. 15.45
East Hill #274/022061 [13]. 5/9/2006. Phase I.
P.L. 0.065; p.W. (max.) 0.012; Wt. 9.2 g.
Single fr preserving undetermined portion of blade; metal comparatively well preserved.
Comparatively long, straight-sided blade, as **15/87** (ΜΕΘ 1563), almost stiletto-like. Better-preserved short side has a clear edge, which may be part of the haft. Cutting edge along bottom side, as shown.
Cf., among others, Kilian 1975a, pl. 93, no. 3; Kilian-Dirlmeier 2002, pl. 71, no. 1111; pl. 101, no. 1658; pl. 154, no. 2416.

Additional blade, similar to ΜΕΘ 1563 and ΜΕΘ 1546:
ΜΕΘ 1547 (ME 3123). East Hill #274/022062 [13]. 14/9/2006. Phase I. Three frr: p.L. (largest) 0.088; W. (max.) 0.025; Wt. 27.8 g.

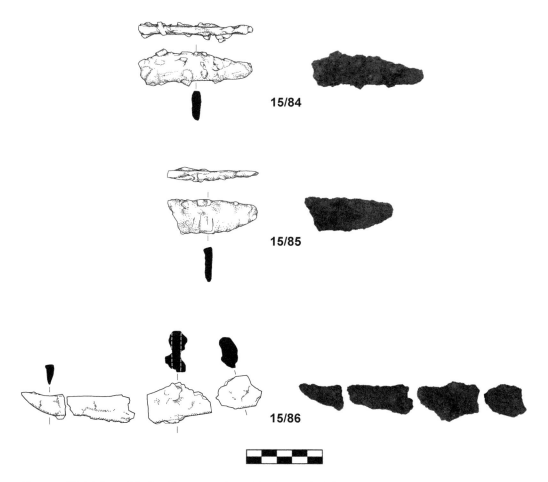

Figure 15.44. Iron blades (larger and smaller knives), **15/84** (MEΘ 1534), **15/85** (MEΘ 5321), **15/86** (MEΘ 1545). Drawings A. Hooton and T. Ross, photos I. Coyle

Axes/adzes/hammers

There are two axes/adzes from the Hypogeion, **15/89** and **15/90**, and a possible third, **15/91**, the state of preservation of which makes it difficult to determine whether it is an axe/adze or a possible hammer head. **15/89** was found in the Phase I fill of the Hypogeion, **15/91** in Phase II, and **15/90** in a post–Phase III context.

Distinguishing between an axe and an adze is not straightforward, especially when the examples are corroded and often fragmentary. An axe is essentially a tool for chopping wood, and is attached at right angles to a wooden handle. An adze is similar to an axe, usually with an arched blade at right angles to the handle, used for cutting, shaping, or carving wood. **15/89** and **15/90** are probably both axes, though they may also have been used for shaping wood once it was chopped. This is especially the case for **15/90**, with its curved or arched profile, allowing both ends of the tool to be used as both an axe and an adze.[264] In their respective publications of the finds from the sanctuary of Apollo Daphnephoros and the "aire sacrificielle" just to the north at Eretria in the Geometric and Archaic periods, Sandrine Huber and Samuel Verdan judiciously refer to related individual iron implements as "haches-herminettes," or axes/adzes.[265] In most contexts, axes and adzes are normally associated with both carpentry and masonry, because it is often difficult to determine from the implement alone whether wood or stone was the intended material to be worked.[266]

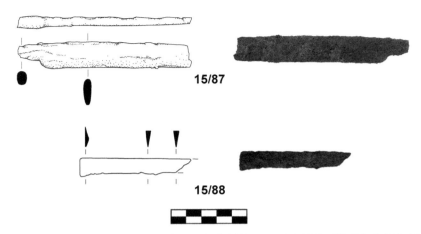

FIGURE 15.45. Narrow iron blades (knives), **15/87** (MEΘ 1563), **15/88** (MEΘ 1546). Drawing A. Hooton and T. Ross, photos I. Coyle and J. Vanderpool

There are several different types of axes in the Early Iron Age of Greece: the trunnion axe with projections on the sides to aid the fastening of the handle;[267] the same basic type, but with no projections; the double axe, usually with a central hole for the insertion of the wooden handle;[268] and the so-called "winged" axe.[269] The Methone examples presented below should all be of trunnion axes without the projections. Similar axes are known from the Early Iron Age tombs at Knossos, ranging in date from Protogeometric B through Late Geometric,[270] and there is a related variant with a more distinct shoulder, instead of the smaller projections, from Kavousi and Eleutherna on Crete, Galaxidi in central Greece, and Philia in Thessaly.[271] Similar iron axes are known from Troy and Istria,[272] and Lefkandi has yielded a somewhat simpler, straight-sided axe, without the projections, and with no close parallels.[273]

In Greek iconography of the Archaic and Classical periods, axes, especially double axes, could be used both as weapons in combat and as implements for the hunt, as well as for sacrificing large animals, especially cattle.[274] Other scholars have claimed that certain types of axes were religious or funerary symbols, or votives for dedication in sanctuaries.[275] I have argued elsewhere that axes in warrior graves, such as Athenian Agora Tomb 13, may be battle axes,[276] and the use of battle axes has been well argued by Snodgrass for the Early Iron Age.[277] But in the context of Late Geometric and earlier Archaic Methone, especially given the shape and size of the Hypogeion axes, it is much more likely—if not assured—that they were used for the chopping and working of timber (see further, Chapter 20).

I have noted in the catalogue below that **15/91** may be an axe or a hammer head, but its fragmentary and corroded state makes it difficult to determine. As Raubitschek notes: "The double axe is differentiated from the hammer by the condition of the ends, which on the axe are sharp for cutting but on hammers are larger flat surfaces for pounding."[278] She goes on to cite the Late Geometric double axe in the shape of a hammer from Philia published by Klaus Kilian.[279] There is also the double hammer and a shafted hammer or anvil from the Athens Acropolis hoard.[280]

15/89. (MEΘ 1556 [ME 3103]) Axe/Adze Head　　　　　　　　　　　　　　　　　　　　　　Fig. 15.46
　　　East Hill #274/032077 [7]. 11/9/2006. Phase I.
　　　L./p.L. 0.117; W. (at peen): 0.048–0.049; Wt. 64.8 g.
　　　Two joining frr, heavily corroded, preserving most of axe head, except for part of the edge of the peen. Axe head, as shown, with broad peen, tapering both toward the cutting edge and toward the haft.
　　　Cf. **15/90** (MEΘ 1565).

15/90. (ΜΕΘ 1565 [ME 212]) Small Axe/Adze Head Fig. 15.46
East Hill #274/022024 [8]. 8/7/2003. Post–Phase III.
L./p.L.0.085; W. (peen) 0.039; Wt. 30.6 g.
Single fr preserving complete or near-complete axe head; corroded.
Broad peen with clear edge, tapering to a comparatively long and slender haft, which is mostly rectangular to square in section.
Cf. **15/89** (ΜΕΘ 1556).

15/91. (ΜΕΘ 1551 [ME 1411]) Possible Axe or Hammer Head Fig. 15.47
East Hill #274/022, fill below Wall 14. 2/9/2004. Phase II.
L./p.L. 0.086; p.W. (max.) 0.049; Wt. 172.4 g.
Single fr preserving undetermined portion of object; heavily corroded and conceivably bent out of shape.
More or less amorphous as preserved, but clearly flat on one side; more convex on the other. Possibly an axe head, or else a hammer head, but impossible to tell due to preservation.

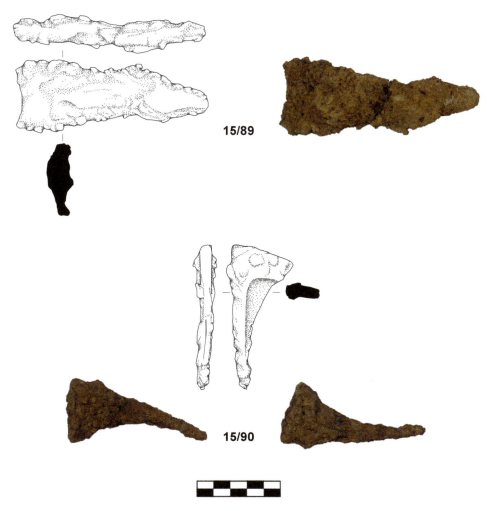

FIGURE 15.46. Iron axes/adzes, **15/89** (ΜΕΘ 1556), **15/90** (ΜΕΘ 1565).
Drawings T. Ross, photos I. Coyle

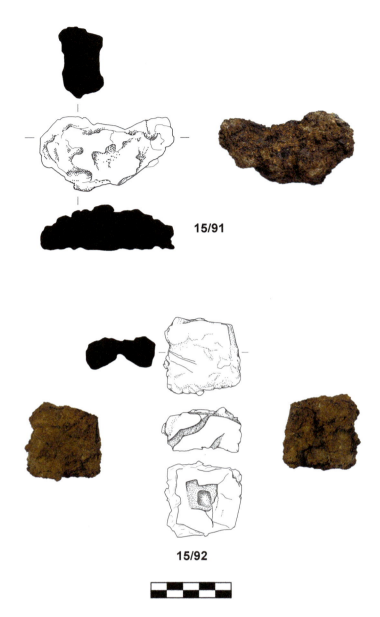

FIGURE 15.47. Iron axes/adzes or hammers, and related, **15/91** (МЕΘ 1551), **15/92** (МЕΘ 1553). Drawings A. Hooton and T. Ross, photos I. Coyle and J. Vanderpool

Related
This piece is essentially unidentified. It is roughly square in shape, mostly flat on one side, with a prominent concavity on the other. Heavily corroded, it is not even clear whether the piece as preserved is fragmentary or almost complete: at least one of the edges appears to be original (the right edge on the left photo), and perhaps also the adjacent edges along the top and bottom of the piece as oriented on the illustration. **15/92** vaguely recalls the bronze cube, **15/53** (МЕΘ 1502), which may have functioned as a possible weight or ingot, even though **15/92** is not a cube. Square weights of roughly the same size as **15/92**, thin in section, and sometimes inscribed, are known from Corinth and Sardis, but these are invariably of lead, and iron seems like a most unlikely metal for a weight.[281] It may well be that **15/92** is a damaged, corroded, and fragmentary hammer or axe/adze such as the pieces presented above.

15/92. (ΜΕΘ 1553 [ME 1121]) Square-shaped Object (Hammer?)   Fig. 15.47
       East Hill #274/032052 [7]. 5/8/2004. Phase II.
       L. x W. x Th. 0.051 x 0.048 x 0.023; Wt. 98.6 g.
       Single piece conceivably preserving undetermined portion of object, perhaps even complete; heavily corroded.
       Roughly square-shaped; mostly flat on one side, with a prominent concavity on the other.

Chisels and related large iron rods

There are five sturdy iron rods from the Hypogeion at Methone that I would classify as chisels. They were found throughout the fill of the Hypogeion (**15/93** from Phase I, **15/96** and **15/97** from Phase II, **15/94** from Phase III, and **15/95** from a post–Phase III context); all are therefore Late Geometric down to ca. 690 B.C., except for **15/95**, which is Archaic. Their dimensions and descriptions are provided in the catalogue entries below. All five are pointed chisels as opposed to the flat chisels that were common in the Bronze Age, that is, chisels with flattened ends that were used to work timber or stone.[282] In this context, it is worth referring to the bronze awls presented above, **15/62** and **15/63**. Among the metal tools from the sanctuary of Poseidon at Isthmia, Raubitchek considered the various iron chisels as tools used primarily by stonemasons.[283] As noted, the five examples from Methone are of the pointed variety. They all lack, or do not preserve, the flat cutting edge that was standard in the bronze chisels of the Late Bronze Age. In her discussion of the pointed chisel, Raubitschek writes: "The pointed chisel has been in use on the Greek mainland at least from the Early Geometric period, and the mastery of this tool, as well as other woodworking instruments, by Corinthian shipwrights must have taken place before the Corinthian expansion into the Greek West in the 7th century B.C."[284] The existence of at least one narrow chisel, together with seven flat or broad chisels in the Athenian Acropolis hoard, together with numerous broad and narrow chisels from Lerna, Malthi, Mycenae, Thebes Arsenal, Orchomenos, Kalydon, Katamachi, Ithaka, Aigina (Oros), Salamis (Kanakia), Anthedon, and Kierion Karditsa, certainly takes the history of the chisel back to the Middle and Late Bronze Age.[285] Nicholas Blackwell quantified no fewer than 75 narrow chisels and 44 broad chisels from the Late Bronze Age Greek mainland.[286] Moreover, although used in carpentry and masonry, chisels—together with tracers, punches, and awls—could also be used in metalworking, as the work of Herbert Maryon and others has shown.[287] These are only a few of the implements in the metalworker's tool set. As Blackwell has noted: "The metallurgical tool set is diverse, reflecting a multi-stage process of ore extraction, crushing, melting, casting, and cold working."[288] This said, the Methone rods classified here as chisels are not for small or fine craft activities, such as the working of ivory or animal bone.

     As Blackwell further notes, although iron tools have been found at many prominent Greek Early Iron Age sites—including Karphi, Kavousi, Knossos, and Eleutherna on Crete; Lefkandi and Eretria on Euboia; Nichoria, Athens, Oropos, and Mitrou on the mainland—their comparative dearth stands out.[289] Moreover, tools like chisels, axes/adzes, and so on, are rarely encountered in tombs of the period, although a number of chisels have been found in Early Iron Age tombs at Kavousi and elsewhere in Crete, and at Pithekoussai in the Bay of Naples.[290] They are also occasionally dedicated at sanctuaries, like the rather numerous iron chisels, no fewer than 26, at the Itonia sanctuary near Philia in Thessaly.[291] Unfortunately, most of the chisels from the Itonia sanctuary were from undated contexts, but in her study of them Kilian-Dirlmeier distinguishes between various types of chisels under the general heading of "Werkzeug," including "Meissel mit Griffangel" (chisel with handle), "Flachtmeissel" (flat chisel), "Holzmeissel bzw. Stemmeisen" (chisel for wood), and the "Tüllenmeissel" (a "spouted" chisel of sorts with an open terminal opposite the cutting edge).[292] These, together with the occurrence of chisels and awls in the settlement at Kastanas on the Axios River, coupled with the new finds from Methone, add a new dimension to Early Iron Age iron tools in the north Aegean.[293]

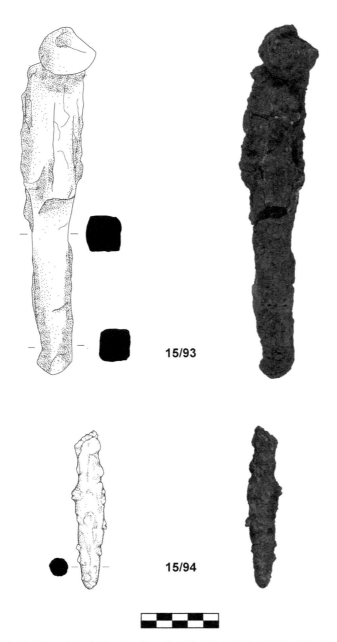

FIGURE 15.48. Iron chisels (and related), **15/93** (MEΘ 1554), **15/94** (MEΘ 1531).
Drawings T. Ross, photos I. Coyle

15/93. (MEΘ 1554 [ME 1190]) Large Pointed Chisel   Fig. 15.48
East Hill #274/032056 [7]. 11/8/2004. Phase I.
L./p.L. 0.235; W. x Th. (shaft) 0.041 x 0.040; Wt. 451.5 g.
Reconstructed from several joining frr almost complete; heavily corroded, especially at thicker end (the apparent extension at the top may be little more than a product of corrosion, though this remains unclear).
Large and heavy rod, with shaft more or less square in section, tapering toward one end, where there is, as preserved, a blunt/rounded point, which cannot be too far from the original point.

15/94. (ΜΕΘ 1531 [ME 853]) Pointed Chisel Fig. 15.48
   East Hill #274/032046 [5]. 30/6/2004. Phase III.
   P.L. 0.111; W. x Th. (shaft) 0.018 x 0.021; Wt. 62.4 g.
   Two joining frr preserving substantial portion of tool; corroded.
   Thick shaft, probably mostly square in section, tapering toward a blunt point at one end, which seems to be original, and where the shaft is more circular in section. Opposite end perhaps broken.

15/95. (ΜΕΘ 1530 [ME 581]) Likely Pointed Chisel Fig. 15.49
   East Hill #274/022, cleaning of Wall 5. Post–Phase III.
   P.L. 0.123; W./Th. 0.013; Wt. 31.4 g.
   Two joining frr preserving almost complete object, except for point; corroded.
   Thick, sturdy rod of iron, with one end rounded and blunt, which appears to be original, tapering at the opposite end toward a point, itself not preserved.

15/96. (ΜΕΘ 1555 [ME 1417]) Rod, Likely Pointed Chisel Fig. 15.49
   East Hill #274/032064 [7]. 6/9/2004. Phase II.
   P.L. 0.146; Th./Diam. 0.015; Wt. 63.7 g.
   Two joining frr preserving substantial portion of original tool; heavily corroded.
   Large rod shaft, probably originally square in section, but difficult to determine due to corrosion, tapering toward a point.
   Cf. **15/95** (ΜΕΘ 1530).

15/97. (ΜΕΘ 1550 [ME 2974]) Fr Large Rod (Perhaps Chisel?) Fig. 15.49
   East Hill #274/022, fill below Wall 14. Phase II.
   P.L. 0.091; W. x Th. (shaft) 0.040 x 0.037; Wt. 210.7 g.
   Single piece, very heavily corroded, preserving undetermined portion of object.
   Large and heavy rod, more or less square in section, in places plano-convex, perhaps from a large chisel.

   Related to the above:
   ΜΕΘ 1549 (ME 3306). East Hill #274/022071 [15]. 17/11/2006. Phase I. Fragmentary iron rod (perhaps large nail) with accretions that have nothing to do with the original object. P.L. (shaft) 0.090; Diam. (shaft) 0.011; Wt. 33.5 g.

Metalworkers' tongs or poker

The two following objects are presented here as interesting pieces, not least for their early date (late 8th or early 7th century B.C.), as both were found in Phase I of the Hypogeion fill. I am fairly sanguine that **15/98** comes from a pair of metalworkers'—blacksmiths'—tongs or else from an iron poker. Although fragmentary and corroded, the preserved length of all the surviving fragments laid out straight is 0.388 m, and the original length would have been greater, something just under half a meter. The surviving fragments essentially preserve one arm of a pair of tongs. The long and sturdy rod is mostly square in section, tapering toward one end. At the opposite end, the shaft is folded back onto itself to form the handle. On one of the non-joining fragments, which preserves the surviving terminal at the other end of the eyelet/handle, the extension of the shaft is hammered to form a crude disk of sorts. Similar disk terminals are sometimes found on Early Iron Age iron oboloi, and had **15/98** not preserved the opposite terminal, it would have been tempting to classify it as an obelos and be done with it.[294] If my interpretation of the object as a metalworkers' tongs is correct, this terminal would have facilitated the purchase of whatever was being held by the tongs. As for **15/99**, despite a little ambivalence on my part—and thus its listing below as "related'—it shares so many features with **15/98** that its fragments should be from a similar pair of tongs or poker. First of all, it is of similar size: its surviving fragments measured out straight have a preserved length of 0.430 m. The iron shaft is similarly square, tapering slightly toward one end, which also has a circular, disk-shaped terminal not unlike that on **15/98** to facilitate purchase. The opposite end, now bent at about 90º, may be post-depositional damage, but it may also represent the damaged looped-over handle. Be that as it may, enough survives of **15/99** to link it with **15/98**, albeit loosely.[295]

Blackwell lists tongs—together with charcoal shovels, furnace spatulas, molds, anvils, and hammers—among metallurgical tools of the Late Bronze Age, but illustrated examples of these are few and far between.[296] Two of the best preserved pairs of tongs of the Late Bronze Age in bronze come from the "Serraglio" on Kos.[297] Both measure just over 0.200 m in length, and are smaller than **15/98** and **15/99** by one-half or more. The two arms are made from a continuous strip of bronze, rectangular in section, rounded at the top and slightly pinched in, resembling a large pair of tweezers. For the Early Iron Age, I know of only one pair of iron tongs from Kavousi of even simpler form, consisting of a long shaft of iron bent in half, not unlike the tongs from the "Serraglio" on Kos, but without the nicely rounded and pinched-in terminal; they, too, resemble a large pair of tweezers.[298]

As for how **15/98** functioned, it is unfortunate that what survives preserves only a portion of the original object, and perhaps only one element of the pair of tongs. On the surviving pieces, there is no clear rivet or screw—nor anywhere where such would have existed—to secure two separate arms into what would amount to a large scissor-like, or pincer-like, pair of tongs, like those from Corinth of Byzantine date.[299] Consequently, the form of **15/98** may well have been close to a standard form of Greek tongs that broadly resembles a figure-of-eight form with one end open to hold in place what would have been held during the working of bronze or iron or gold during its movement to or from a furnace or on the anvil. Two pairs of such tongs are illustrated on the Attic black-figure amphora now in the Museum of Fine Arts in Boston, attributed to the Plousios Painter, dating to ca. 500–490 B.C. (Fig. 15.52).[300] One side of the vessel (Side A: not illustrated), shows a shoemaker's shop with a young woman being fitted for a new pair of sandals. Side B shows the blacksmith's shop. The blacksmith, bearded and standing in the center, is about to strike what resembles a bar of metal with a wedge-shaped hammer (resembling an axe). A beardless younger man—the blacksmith's assistant—partially obscured by the furnace, holds the heated bar on an anvil with a pair of tongs. A second pair of tongs, together with a hammer or mallet, is on the ground in front of the younger man. To the right, two clad men observe the scene, and above a whole series of tools hangs on the shop walls, including various hammers (some resembling axes/adzes), a long straight knife with a clear haft, a saw, a small dagger in a scabbard, and another tool that I cannot identify near the center (drill?). Also hanging on the wall below the saw is a hydria.[301]

What is worth stressing is that **15/98** is, proportionately, the same size, more or less, as the tongs on the amphora. The double-curved tongs depicted on the Boston amphora would have relied on the tensile strength of the iron and their form—replete with a looped-over handle—to hold safely heated metal or a crucible, mold, or melting plate. They would have been far superior to the simpler iron tongs from Kavousi, as well as the smaller bronze tongs from Kos, already noted. Moreover, such a pair of tongs would not require moving parts, like a rivet or screw to keep together two putative arms of an implement, such as the Byzantine example from Corinth already cited. Given the melting points of the metals we know were worked at Methone (see Chapter 14)—gold at 1,064º C, copper 1,085º C, iron 1,538º C[302]—such tongs would have been indispensable for the handling and working of any metal. They would have been especially critical for handling many

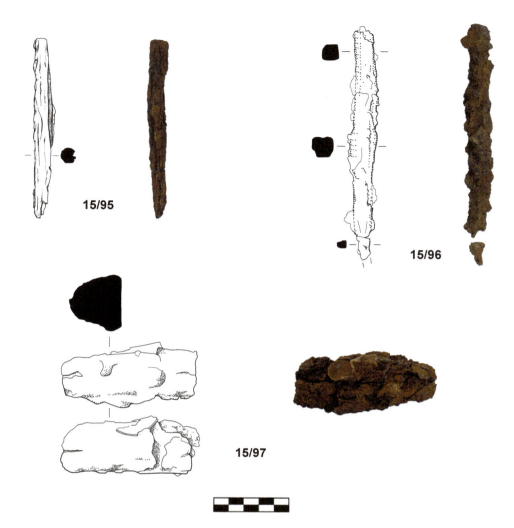

FIGURE 15.49. Iron chisels (and related), **15/95** (MEΘ 1530), **15/96** (MEΘ 1555), **15/97** (MEΘ 1550). Drawings A. Hooton and T. Ross, photos I. Coyle

of the metallurgical ceramics used at the site, such as the bronze crucibles or the heavily vitrified gold melting plates (Chapter 14), the terracotta and stone molds (for the latter, see Chapter 27), as well as maneuvering tuyères into place in a furnace. **15/98** and **15/99** are thus presented here in the hope that further fragments of tongs may be noted and published.

The fragmentary state of both of the pieces presented below is such that it remains difficult to confirm both as metalworkers' tongs with certainty. An alternative interpretation, which would be in keeping with what survives of both **15/98** and **15/99**, is that they are iron pokers, that is, metal rods with a handle, used for prodding and stirring a fire. Moreover, it is not inconceivable that two such pokers might be used to hold in place a heated bar of metal, a small ceramic crucible for bronze or lead, or a gold melting pan.

15/98. (MEΘ 1544 [ME 3053]) Metalworkers' Tongs or Poker   Fig. 15.50
    East Hill #274/022060 [12]. 29/8/2006. Phase I.
        P.L. (main frr, as bent) 0.195; p.L. (reconstructed: all frr laid out straight) 0.388 +; L. (head) 0.075;
          Wt. 121.0 g.

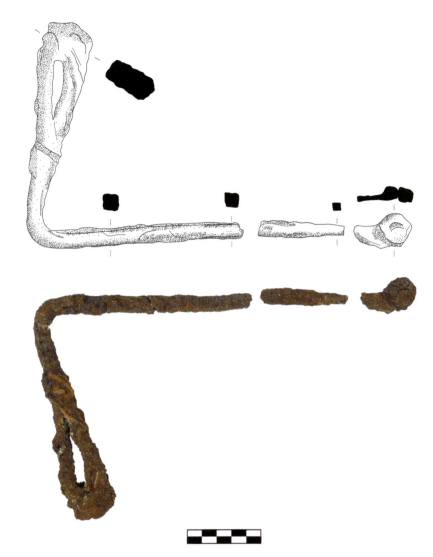

Figure 15.50. Fragmentary iron metalworker's tongs or poker, **15/98** (MEΘ 1544). Drawing F. Skyvalida, photo I. Coyle

Three joining, plus two non-joining, frr preserving greater part of object; heavily corroded.

Long rod of iron, which, although it looks circular in section, is mostly square, tapering toward one end. At the opposite end the shaft is folded back on itself to form a large eyelet which served as a handle of sorts, as well as a possible suspension loop. On one of the non-joining frr (itself made up of two joining frr), the extension of the shaft is hammered and appears almost as a round disk.

There is at least one similar fr of a partially preserved iron rod with an eyelet/handle like **15/98** from the agora of Methone (**26/195** [MEΘ 1755]).

Related

15/99. (MEΘ 1548 [ME 3294]) Large Iron Object   Fig. 15.51

East Hill #274/022070 [14]. 15/11/2006. Phase I.

P.L. (as bent) 0.351; p.L. (original, unbent) ca. 0.430; Wt. 338.0 g.

Two main joining frr, plus a few additional frr preserving greater part of original, but unidentified, object; heavily corroded in places.

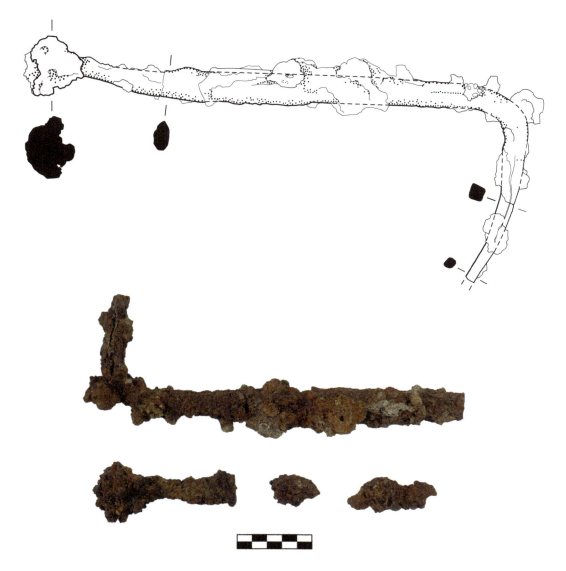

FIGURE 15.51. Related fragmentary iron tongs or poker, **15/99** (ΜΕΘ 1548).
Drawing as reconstructed by A. Hooton, photo I. Coyle

Long and sturdy shaft, rectangular in section, tapering toward one end, where it is more square in section. At the opposite end there appears to be the head, roughly rounded (Diam. ca. 0.042), but extremely corroded. The rectangular shaft is thinnest near the rounded head.

Tack

Tacks, nails, and related bronze and iron shafts are better represented, and much better preserved, among the metal objects from the later deposits at Methone in the area of the agora and on the West Hill (see Chapter 26). From the Hypogeion I present a solitary iron tack, **15/100**, and another, together with a few fragmentary shafts of likely iron nails or pins, are listed. At most sites where they are found in quantity, related nails and tacks are especially common in later periods, ranging in date from the Classical, through Roman, and into Byzantine times, though some are earlier, including Archaic Lydian examples from Sardis, and a variety of iron and bronze nails and tacks from Philia.[303] The importance of the few examples from Methone presented or listed below lies in their early date (8th–7th century B.C.).

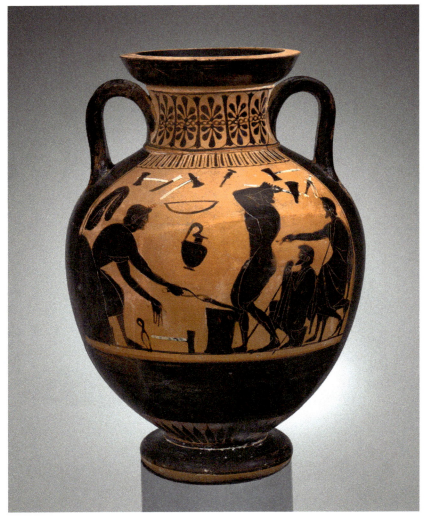

FIGURE 15.52. Athenian black-figure amphora, attributed to the Plousios Painter, Museum of Fine Arts, Boston (MFA 01.8035, BAPD 2188), ca. 500–490 B.C.

15/100. (ΜΕΘ 5319 [ME 3678]) Fragmentary Tack Fig. 15.53

    East Hill #274/032041 [6]. 15/6/2004. Phase II.

    P.L. (main fr) 0.012; L. x W. (head) 0.014 x 0.014; Wt. (main fr) 1.2 g.

    Two non-joining frr, the smaller likely not from the same object; both much corroded (only the main fr is here presented).

    Small tack with square head; shaft, as preserved, round in section.

Similar tacks

ME 1262. East Hill #274/032061 [7]. Phase undetermined. P.L. 0.014; L. x W. (head) 0.020 x 0.017; Wt. 3.3 g.

Possible shafts of iron nails or pins (poorly preserved)
- ΜΕΘ 1541 (ME 717). East Hill #274/022, near Wall 5. Phase III. Thin shaft, circular in section. P.L. (all frr together) 0.130; Diam. (shaft) 0.004; Wt. 3.6 g.
- ΜΕΘ 1542 (ME 2940). East Hill #274/022, fill below Wall 14. Phase II. Shaft circular in section. P.L. 0.074; Diam. (shaft) 0.006; Wt. 2.8 g.

FIGURE 15.53. Iron tack, **15/100** (ΜΕΘ 5319).
Drawing T. Ross, photo I. Coyle

Fragmentary iron wire or iron shaft fragments in the form of spirals and rings
Little can be said about the following two pieces. They are not items of jewelry nor are they full-fledged *krikoi* such as the bronze examples discussed above.[304] Both resemble segments of iron wire of various thickness—**15/101** is thicker and more substantial than **15/102**—the former as preserved coiled into a spiral, the latter more amorphous.

15/101. (ΜΕΘ 1558 [ME 724]) Spiral   Fig. 15.54

    East Hill #274/032, backfill. Phase undetermined.

    Diam. 0.030–0.032; Wt. 18.9 g.

    Reconstructed from a few joining frr preserving what appears to be complete or near-complete spiral. Corroded, but not as badly as other pieces.

    Thick iron shaft, circular in section, perhaps tapering toward a well-preserved but rather blunt rounded point/terminal at both ends, formed into a spiral.

15/102. (ΜΕΘ 5323 [ME 1414]) Fragmentary Ring   Fig. 15.54

    East Hill #274/022, fill below Wall 14. 2/9/2004. Phase II.

    P.L/L. 0.040; Wt. 10.0 g.

    Two joining frr, corroded, preserving much of ring.

    Ring shaft circular in section, with ring, as preserved, more ovoid than round. Possible extension (or corrosion?) on one side, which seems intentional?

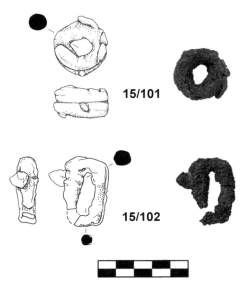

FIGURE 15.54. Fragmentary iron wire or iron shaft fragments in the form of spirals and rings, **15/101** (ΜΕΘ 1558), **15/102** (ΜΕΘ 5323). Drawings A. Hooton and T. Ross, photos I. Coyle and J. Vanderpool

"Fish-shaped" attachment?

I end this overview of the iron objects from the Hypogeion with an enigma, for I have no idea what the purpose of **15/103** might be. It is a single piece, corroded, but conceivably whole. The iron itself is a thick sheet of fairly even thickness throughout, plano-convex in section, with the flat side accounting for its interpretation as an "attachment," although how it was attached to anything remains a mystery. The form is schematically fish-shaped, with a circular element and two splaying "legs" resembling a fish tail. If a fish, there are certainly no telltale details, like an eye or scales, though the surface of the iron is corroded. Isthmia has produced two interesting pieces, including a solid-cast bronze statuette of a dolphin (with a length of only 0.033 m) and, more interestingly, a bronze appliqué, consisting of a flat piece of hammered bronze cut into the shape of a dolphin.[305] The former is dated to the early 5th century B.C., the latter to the Archaic period. But **15/103** resembles neither of the Isthmia bronze dolphins. Another object from Isthmia is a heavy two-pronged piece of iron found with debris from the Archaic temple, identified as a hinge by the flap that is bent at the side over a heavy nail still in situ.[306] None of the cited Isthmia pieces are convincing comparanda.

15/103. (ΜΕΘ 1552 [ΜΕ 628]) "Fish-shaped" Attachment? Fig. 15.55
East Hill #274/032037 [6]. 8/4/2004. Phase II.
L./p.L. 0.072; W. (max.) 0.048; Th. 0.012; Wt. 34.0 g.
Single piece, corroded, preserving conceivably whole, or undetermined, portion of object.
The iron itself is a thick sheet of even thickness throughout, plano-convex in section, with the flat side accounting for its interpretation as an attachment, although how it was attached remains a mystery. Roughly "fish-shaped" as preserved, with a circular element and two splaying legs resembling a fish tail.

Objects of Lead

Fishnet weights

The three fishnet weights from the Hypogeion were all found in the Phase I fill, and are dated to the later 8th or earlier 7th century B.C. The form is standard throughout the Mediterranean and throughout most periods. It consists of a narrow rectangular sheet of lead folded over and easily opened or tightened to serve as a fishnet weight. Similar lead fishnet weights are common in the Greek world from the Bronze Age,[307] through the Early Iron Age and Archaic periods,[308] the Classical and Hellenistic periods,[309] into Byzantine and post-Byzantine times,[310] and are still in use today. A recent discussion of lead fishnet weights, together with useful comments on alternative uses for these weights, is provided by Giorgos Brokallis on the material from Agios Georgios sto Vouno on Kythera.[311]

FIGURE 15.55. Iron "fish-shaped" attachment(?), **15/103** (ΜΕΘ 1552).
Drawing T. Ross, photos I. Coyle

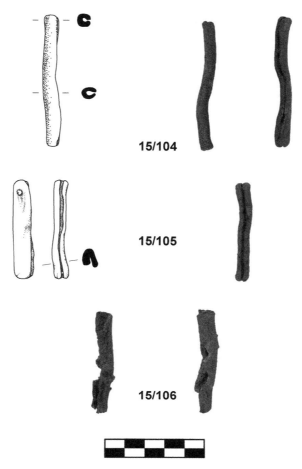

FIGURE 15.56. Lead fishnet weights, **15/104** (MEΘ 1527), **15/105** (MEΘ 1525), **15/106** (MEΘ 1528). Drawings T. Ross, F. Skyvalida, photos I. Coyle

15/104. (MEΘ 1527 [ME 3132]) Fishnet Weight   Fig. 15.56
    East Hill #274/022062 [13]. 14/9/2006. Phase I.
    L. 0.067; H. 0.009; Wt. 16.1 g.
    Intact.
    Narrow rectangular sheet of lead folded over and easily opened or tightened to serve as fishnet weight.
    As **15/105** (MEΘ 1525) and **15/106** (MEΘ 1528).

15/105. (MEΘ 1525 [ME 3252]) Fishnet Weight   Fig. 15.56
    East Hill #274/932982 [10]. 20/10/2006. Phase I.
    P.L. 0.051; H. 0.011; Wt. 16.6 g.
    Intact.
    As **15/104** (MEΘ 1527) and **15/106** (MEΘ 1528).

15/106. (MEΘ 1528 [ME 1488]) Fishnet Weight   Fig. 15.56
    East Hill #274/032071 [7]. 20/9/2004. Phase I.
    L. 0.053; H. 0.009; Wt. 12.1 g.
    Single piece, chipped and slightly pitted, preserving most of weight.
    As **15/104** (MEΘ 1527).

Mending clamp

The solitary lead mending clamp from the Hypogeion was found in the post–Phase III fill and, as such, it could date to either the later Geometric or, most likely, the Archaic period. The form is fairly standard for this type of mending clamp. As oriented on the drawing, the horizontal struts are essentially plano-convex in section, and are connected by one surviving vertical strut, circular in section. Such clamps are normally 0.025–0.045 m long, with two cylindrical struts passed through the drilled mending holes on either side of the break on a broken pot, with the upper and lower connections flattened against the surface of the vessel.[312] The practice of mending broken pots and other types of vessels with lead or bronze rivets/clamps is well attested over a wide area throughout the course of the Bronze Age.[313] Judging by mending holes preserved on a good number of pots, the antiquity of the practice may be traced back to the Early Neolithic, although the binding in the earliest examples would not be of metal.[314] In Macedonia, mending holes are commonly met on vessels assigned as early as the Neolithic, through the Bronze Age, and into the Early Iron Age.[315] In other parts of Greece, pottery of Protogeometric and Geometric date mended with clamps was very common.[316]

15/107. (ΜΕΘ 4369 [ME 72]) Fragmentary Lead Mending Clamp   Fig. 15.57
    East Hill #274/022004 [3]. 3/6/2003. Post–Phase III.
    P.L. 0.036; H. 0.014; Wt. 10.6 g.
    Single fr preserving portion of clamp.
    Horizontal struts roughly plano-convex in section, connected by one surviving vertical strut, circular in section.

Small length of lead wire

From Phase I of the Hypogeion fill comes the short length of lead wire, mostly square in section and, as preserved, coiled to form what now resembles a very small spiral ring. I do not think that the object is a piece of jewelry, but a small length of wire.

15/108. (ΜΕΘ 1529 [ME 3659]) Small Length of Lead Wire   Fig. 15.57
    East Hill #274/032086 [9]. 22/11/2006. Phase I.
    Diam. (max.) 0.011; Th. 0.002; Wt. 0.7 g.
    Single fr preserving portion of spiral ring, somewhat bent out of shape.
    Short length of lead wire, mostly square in section, coiled to form a small spiral ring.

FIGURE 15.57. Lead mending clamp, **15/107** (ΜΕΘ 4369), and small length of lead wire, **15/108** (ΜΕΘ 1529). Drawings T. Ross and F. Skyvalida, photos I. Coyle

NOTES

1. I cannot stress enough that the selection I have made is a representative sample only; to do justice to all the metal objects from the Hypogeion, not to mention those from the entire site explored to date, would require a full volume on its own. I am grateful to Manthos Bessios, Athena Athanassiadou, Sarah Morris, Samuel Verdan, and Adam DiBattista for discussion and assistance with various aspects of this chapter.

2. For gold- and other metalworking activity in the Hypogeion, see Chapter 14; Fig. 14.9, ME 1345 and ME 1346. As Samuel Verdan has argued, the "end product" of the goldworking operation of the late 8th and early 7th centuries B.C. at Methone was the production of pellets of gold, which he compared to examples from Eretria and classified as "ingots."

3. The materials associated with the working of metal and other products, especially from the Hypogeion—the "*ergastiriaka*"—will be published separately by Manthos Bessios.

4. See Chapter 6.

5. Analyses of Late Bronze and Early Iron Age and Archaic metal objects have been the exception, not the rule, though for the later periods (including the Archaic), see Scott et al. 2003 (with further notes in Papadopoulos 2003a); Riederer 2007; Muros and Scott 2014; see also Knox et al. 1983.

6. Kilian-Dirlmeier 1979, pp. 53–61, esp. pp. 56–59.

7. Cf. Kilian-Dirlmeier 1979, p. 57, pl. 21, nos. 348–353. A few of Kilian-Dirlmeier's "Oblong" variety are not dissimilar, see, esp. p. 57, pl. 21, nos. 340, 341.

8. Kilian-Dirlmeier 1979, p. 57, esp. nos. 348, 349, 350, and 353; the two examples from Pherai come from undetermined contexts; that from Thermon was listed as unpublished; for the example from Olympia, see now *OlForsch* XIII, p. 352, pl. 25, no. 1251. The size and plain form of the pendant from Perachora is particularly close, see *Perachora* I, p. 182, pl. 66, no. 17 (listed under "sundries"). In addition to the illustrated example from Aetos in Ithaka, Robertson (1948, p. 119, pl. 50, no. E83) lists two more examples of the same type, E84 and E85.

9. *OlForsch* XIII, pp. 260–324, pls. 59–71.

10. See *Perachora* I; Blinkenberg 1931.

11. See, for example, Sapouna-Sakellarakis 1978, pp. 110–116, where they are classified as "Fibeln nördlicher Form oder nördlicher Herkunft (Type X)." The most detailed study of their origin remains Alexander 1965, esp. pp. 7–8. For an early example from Pateli published by Heurtley, see Heurtley 1939, p. 240, fig. 112:o.

12. E.g., *Vergina* I, pp. 227–230; see further Radt 1974, p. 124, pl. 38, nos. 4–13; with additional examples from Petsas's excavations, see esp. Bräuning and Kilian-Dirlmeier 2013, pp. 37–45.

13. See Blinkenberg 1926, pp. 253–262; for "Spiralplattenfibeln," see Sundwall 1943, pp. 50–54; for "Plattenfibeln," see Sundwall 1943, pp. 170–176, where he distinguishes between "Brillenfibeln (Spiraldisken)" and other types; the term "Brillenfibel" is now most commonly used, see Kilian 1975a, pls. 57–58; Sapouna-Sakellarakis 1978, pp. 110–113, pl. 47, various examples; *OlForsch* XIII, pp. 299–301; Kilian-Dirlmeier 2002, p. 42, pl. 40, esp. nos. 580–582; Felsch 2007, pp. 138–140, 290–291, pls. 31–32, nos. 518; for the "spectacle fibula" in English, see, among others, Alexander 1965; Benton 1950, 1952; for early French usage, see Babelon and Blanchet 1895, pp. 615–616. For the distribution of the type in central, eastern, and southeastern Europe, see Bader 1983, pp. 41–71, pls. 5–23, nos. 25–127, esp. pls. 11–22; Betzler 1974, esp. pls. 20–71; Gedl 2004, pls. 42–48; Gergova 1987, pls. 18, 19; Glogović 2003, pls. 14–34; Laux 1973; Novotná 2001, pls. 14, 15; Říhovský 1993, esp. pl. 12; Vasić 1999, pls. 8–22.

14. For central and southern Greece, see, among others, Blinkenberg 1926, p. 257, fig. 303, XIV 2e (Tanagra); p. 258, fig. 304, XIV 2p (Olympia); Waldstein 1905, p. 240, pl. LXXXV, esp. no. 818 (Argive Heraion); Reichel and Wilhelm 1901 (Lousoi); Voyatzis 1990, p. 280, pl. 170, no. L42; p. 344, pl. 166, nos.

B251, B252 (Lousoi and Tegea or Mavriki); Brock 1957, p. 54, pl. 37, Tomb X, no. 558 (Fortetsa, Knossos); Coldstream and Catling 1996, fig. 171, Tomb 292, f.3 (Knossos KMF); Dawkins et al. 1906–1907, p. 84, fig. 20a; p. 113, fig. 3b (Sparta); Dawkins 1929a, pl. LXXXI (three examples, upper right); pl. LXXXII, c–d, h, m; pl. CXXXIII, a (Sparta); Felsch 2007, pl. 8, nos. 506, 506; pls. 31–32, nos. 503–508 (Kalapodi); *Olympia* IV, pl. XXI, no. 359; *OlForsch* XIII, pl. 21, no. 1070; Onassoglou 1981, pp. 18–19 (Tragana, east Lokris). For Thessaly, see Kilian 1975a, pls. 56–58, nos. 1574–1711; Kilian-Dirlmeier 2002, pl. 40, nos. 580–582. For northern Greece, see, among others, Casson 1923–1925, pl. III, no. 2a–b; Heurtley 1939, p. 240, fig. 112o (Pateli); Rhomiopoulou 1971, p. 39, fig. 2 (three examples); Radt 1974, pp. 124–126, pl. 38, nos. 4–13 (Vergina); Rhomiopoulou and Kilian-Dirlmeier 1989, p. 94, fig. 6, no. 8; p. 95, fig. 7, nos. 1–2, 17, 21; p. 108, fig. 17, nos. 9, 14, 17; p. 109, fig. 18, nos. 6, 14; p. 118, fig. 29, nos. 1–2, 5–7, 31 (Vergina); Bräuning and Kilian-Dirlmeier 2013, pp. 37–45 (Vergina); Rhomiopoulou and Touratsoglou 2002, pp. 48–49, M 1051–1052 (Tomb 6); p. 65 (Tomb 31) (Mieza); Savvopoulou 2004, p. 315, fig. 12 (top and middle) (Axios River region); Chrysostomou 2008, p. 39, fig. 17 (Edessa); Vokotopoulou 1986, fig. 109α–β, ια, ιβ, inv. 2357/T113; inv. 2261/T103; inv. 2323/T46; pl. 211β; pl. 240γ; pl. 247β–γ; pl. 248β (upper right) (Vitsa Zagoriou, Epirus).

15 For Albania, the Adriatic generally, the central Balkans, including Serbia, Kosovo, Bosnia-Herzegovina, North Macedonia (FYROM), Slovenia, the Italian peninsula, and other parts of Europe, see Papadopoulos et al. 2014, pp. 333–334; see also Lo Schiavo 1970, pl. XIII: 17; pl. XXX:2; Kilian 1975b, pl. 36, no. 16; pl. 43, no. 22; pl. 54, no. 10; pl. 65, no. 2.

16 Alexander 1965, pp. 7–11, with ills. 1–2.

17 See Alexander 1965, p. 8, ill. 1.

18 Benton 1950, pp, 17–20, incorporating analysis of spectacle fibulae found at the sanctuary of Artemis Orthia in Sparta, Thera, Tsaousitsa, Delphi, and Marmariani.

19 See Papadopoulos et al. 2014, pp. 332–335, 1015–1016, nos. 10/13–10/17; for the absolute chronology of the Lofkënd phases, see pp. 109–121, esp. p. 111, table 4.1. In addition to the one example from Phase III and the two from Phase Va, two examples belonged to tombs of Phase IV (10th to 9th century B.C.). One other example, 10/18, was encountered in topsoil and could not be dated precisely. The Lofkënd dates are based primarily on AMS ^{14}C dating from human bone collagen derived from the skeletons.

20 See Kilian-Dirlmeier 2002, p. 42, pl. 40, nos. 580–582, "spätgeometrische bis hocharchaische Zeit"; on p. 42, she adds: "Als Grabbeigabe kommen bronzene Brillenfibeln vom Beginn bis zum Ende der geometrischen Zeit vor," with examples cited from Pherai, Vitsa Zagoriou in Epirus, Tragana, Akraipha, and Amphissa.

21 *Vergina* I, pp. 227–230, where almost all of the 104 examples correspond to Alexander's (1965) type Ib.

22 For the terminology in German, see, among others, Sundwall 1943, pp. 8–19, 66–77; Kilian 1975a, pp. 12–18; Sapouna-Sakellarakis 1978, pp. 34–41, pls. 1–3, nos. 1–50.

23 See esp. discussion in Blinkenberg 1926, pp. 41–58; Sapouna-Sakellarakis 1978, pp. 34–35.

24 Sapouna-Sakellarakis 1978, pp. 34–41.

25 Blinkenberg 1926, pp. 50–51.

26 Pendlebury, Pendlebury, and Money-Coutts 1937–1938, p. 72, under 36, pl. 29:2, no. 636 (= Sapouna-Sakellarakis 1978, p. 38, pl. 2, no. 28); although Sapouna-Sakellarakis presents the arch as undecorated, in the original publication it is said to be the "decorated plate of a bronze fibula"; cf. also p. 119, pl. 29:2, no. 200, from the slopes of Mikre Koprana at Karphi (= Sapouna-Sakellarakis 1978, p. 38, pl. 2, no. 27), which is clearly decorated.

27 Kilian 1975a, esp. p. 19, pl. 1, no. 6; cf. also p. 20, pl. 1, no. 7.

28 Vokotopoulou 1986, pp. 69–72, esp. 70–71, no. 5, fig. 109:ζ (2386/T21) bronze, third quarter of the 8th century B.C.; for the iron examples, see pp. 92–93, fig. 114:κγ (6144/T41), 8th century, perhaps first

quarter; pp. 120–122, fig. 114:κε (2260/T129), ca. 750 B.C.; pp. 128–129, fig. 114:κοτ (5688/T175), ca. 750 B.C.; pp. 129–130, fig. 114:κδ (5697/T176), 800–775 B.C.; pp. 157–158, fig. 114:κζ (2265/T114), ca. 800 B.C.; pp. 197–198, fig. 114:κβ (5291/T154), first half of the 8th century B.C. Among the iron versions of the type from Vitsa, the closest to **15/6** (ΜΕΘ 1390) is fig. 114:κοτ.

29 Kilian 1973, p. 35, map 2; see also p. 37, map 4.
30 Blinkenberg 1926, pp. 54–55, Group I (Types mycéniens), Type 11, where three examples are presented, one from Vrokastro (Late Minoan III), one from Kavousi, and a third of unknown provenance. The length of the fibula from Kavousi is virtually identical to that of **15/7** (ΜΕΘ 1387), and should also be of Early Iron Age date. Blinkenberg's Group I, Type 12, is the same, but with the arch decorated.
31 Sapouna-Sakellarakis 1978, pp. 40–41, pl. 2, nos. 43–46.
32 For the general form, cf. Vasić 1999, esp. pl. 2, nos. 18–21, and also no. 25, with more elaborate decoration on the side of both the spring and the catchplate.
33 Blinkenberg 1926, esp. pp. 58–60; Sapouna-Sakellarakis 1978, pp. 41–54; von Eles Masi 1986, pp. 14–40, pls. 3–15.
34 Sapouna-Sakellarakis 1978, esp. p. 42.
35 Of Sapouna-Sakellarakis' (1978, pp. 41–54) eight types, there are at least 38 examples of Type IIa, over 50 of Type IIb, 24 of Type IIc, some 20 examples each of Types IId and IIf, but only a few of the remaining types, IIe (three from Crete and Lefkandi), IIg (two from Crete), and IIh (one from Ialysos on Rhodes).
36 *Lefkandi* I, pp. 233–244, see esp. pls. 247–248, various examples. For the Athena Itonia sanctuary, see Kilian-Dirlmeier 2002, pp. 20–29, pl. 15; for the type elsewhere in Thessaly, see Kilian 1975a, pp. 20–31, pls. 1–5.
37 Müller-Karpe 1959, *passim*; for the type in Italy, see von Eles Masi 1986, pp. 14–40; for southern Germany, Austria, and Switzerland (Urnenfelderzeitliche Typen), see Betzler 1974, pp. 65–74; for the central Balkans, see Vasić 1999, esp. pp. 45–72; for Bulgaria, see Gergova 1987, pp. 19–52, where the type is found in many varieties; for Anatolia, see Caner 1983, pp. 28–35. For further discussion, see *Agora* XXXVI, pp. 910–911.
38 *Vergina* I, pp. 230–233, fig. 69–73.
39 *Agora* XXXVI, pp. 911–914; bronze examples of Agora Type 2 fibulae include: T11-28, T11-29, T15-68, T15-69, T45-9; iron examples: T6-3, T6-4, T49-5, T49-6, T50-3, T50-4, T51-9, T52-4, T52-5, T77-6. Agora Type 2 fibulae = Blinkenberg Type II 19 a–g.
40 Blinkenberg 1926, pp. 60–72 under the broad heading of Types submycéniens.
41 For which, see esp. Kilian 1975a, pp. 29–31, pl. 5, various examples, esp. nos. 191–192, 196–198, 200–210, even though the small no. 193 is not unlike **15/9**; Sapouna-Sakellarakis 1978, pp. 68–85, pls. 19–32. The primary series of the bow fibulae with swollen arches are, however, significantly different from **15/9** in that they are usually decorated with elaborate beaded ornaments.
42 For which see Blinkenberg 1926, pp. 83–87, 100–106; Sapouna-Sakellarakis 1978, pp. 68–85, esp. Type IVa, pp. 68–69, pl. 18, nos. 589–601.
43 Sapouna-Sakellarakis 1978, pp. 54–68, pls. 9–18.
44 Sapouna-Sakellarakis' typology closely followed that of Blinkenberg, who, in the early 1920s, had access to far fewer examples than in the last quarter of the 20th century. Consequently, her Type IIIa corresponds to Blinkenberg's Type III 10 b and III 11 a; her Type IIIb corresponds to his Type III 5 a; III 10 c and f; III 11 b and e; and Type IV 14; her Type IIIc corresponds primarily to his Type III 10-11 f and Type IV 12. It is only really her Types IIIe and IIIf that correspond fully to Blinkenberg's Type IV, the former to Blinkenberg's Type IV 11, the latter to his Type IV 13, and whether these are categorized as Type III or IV is a moot exercise, as the fibulae themselves often defy straightforward classification. It should be noted that among the illustrated examples published by Blinkenberg, the closest to **15/10** is Blinkenberg 1926, p. 83, Type III 10 a (from Vrokastro, Crete).

45 Sapouna-Sakellarakis 1978, p. 54.

46 For the tomb, see Brock 1957, pp. 84–88; for the fibula, see p. 97, pls. 75, 167, no. 1106 (= Sapouna-Sakellarakis 1978, p. 58, pl. 12, no. 339, which corresponds to her Type IIIb).

47 See esp. Brock's drawing of the Fortetsa fibula, Brock 1957, pl. 167, no. 1106. The more schematic rendering of the drawing of the same fibula in Sapouna-Sakellarakis 1978, pl. 12, no. 339, which is, in reality, a drawing after a drawing, does not do complete justice to the original. For Type IIIb fibulae decorated with fillets on the side of the spring or catchplate or both, see, among others, Sapouna-Sakellarakis 1978, pl. 12, nos. 337, 343, 344, 348, 353.

48 Caner 1983, pp. 35–37, esp. his Type IIIb, which are common at Iasos and Didyma.

49 Sapouna-Sakellarakis 1978, pp. 85–90, pls. 32–34.

50 Blinkenberg 1926, pp. 98–99.

51 Sapouna-Sakellarakis 1978, p. 90; for Ephesos, see further Klebinder-Gauss 2007, pls. 3–6, nos. 27–85.

52 Blinkenberg 1926, p. 98 wrote "ce type paraît s'être développé de celui qui précède sur la côte occidentale de l'Asia Mineure."

53 Caner 1983, pp. 43–45, pls. 95–107.

54 Sapouna-Sakellarakis 1978, p. 85, and see also her comments on p. 90.

55 Sapouna-Sakellarakis 1978, pp. 86–87, pls. 32–33, nos. 1064–1144.

56 For the examples from Samos, Chios, and Lesbos, see Sapouna-Sakellarakis 1978, pp. 87–89, nos. 1145–1159 (Samos), nos. 1169–1179 (Chios, Kato Phana, and Emporio), and no. 1181 (Lesbos).

57 Sapouna-Sakellarakis 1978, p. 88, nos. 1161, 1162 (Paros); p. 89, no. 1180 A and B (Thera); p. 88, nos. 1163–1165 (Aigina). For Kythnos, see Mazarakis Ainian 2019, p. 114, fig. 187.

58 For the example from Arkades, see Sapouna-Sakellarakis 1978, p. 88, no. 1160; and for Samothrace, see p. 88, nos. 1166–1168; see also Lehmann 1953, p. 7, pl. 3:d; *Samothrace* 4:1, pp. 151–153, nos. 98–100.

59 Sapouna-Sakellarakis 1978, p. 89.

60 Sapouna-Sakellarakis 1978, pp. 89–90.

61 Blinkenberg 1926, pp. 110–128.

62 Blinkenberg 1926, esp. p. 115, fig. 132, Type VI 8; p. 118, figs. 140–141, Type VI 15; cf. also some of the examples of his Types VI 13 and VI 14.

63 Kilian 1975a, pp. 31–35. I tend to avoid the term "sanguisuga" (or "leech") for this fibula type in order not to confuse it with the broad array of Italian fibulae with a "swollen" arch or bow. For the Italian "fibule rivestite e a sanguisuga e ad arco con staffa lunga," see von Eles Masi 1986, pp. 144–209, pls. 111–162.

64 Kilian-Dirlmeier 2002, p. 22.

65 Sapouna-Sakellarakis 1978, pp. 94–100.

66 Her Type VIIb has a small bird as the decorative element, whereas the sole example listed under her Type VIIc is an idiosyncratic fibula from Naxos with a fuller and more triangular arch surmounted by a small bird.

67 Sapouna-Sakellarakis 1978, p. 97.

68 See *Sindos* III, pp. 177–190, pp. 451–455, figs. 152–172, nos. 324–354; p. 527, fig. 31, no. 324; pp. 601–604, figs. 332–363, nos. 324–354.

69 Blinkenberg 1926, pp. 204–230.

70 Blinkenberg 1926, p. 206, table; see also p. 205, where he reports on Koerte's observations on the finds from Gordion.

71 Muscarella 1967; Sapouna-Sakellarakis 1978, pp. 120–129, where she labeled Blinkenberg's 17 varieties of Type XII fibulae as her Types XII A a–XII A l, with her Gruppe XII B dealing with types from the Near East and Gruppe XII C with fibulae from Cyprus; Caner 1983, pp. 50–175. Where

Muscarella kept Blinkenberg's original 17 subtypes, adding additional varieties as needed, Caner took Blinkenberg's and Muscarella's designations and rearranged them according to his own amended typology, which he broadly labeled "Phrygische bzw. Anatolische Fibeln." See also Boehmer's (1972) study of the fibulae from Boğazköy, which was largely based on Muscarella's typology.

72 Muscarella 1967, p. 23, pl. XVI, nos. 83–84, where he adds: "The mouldings of the fibulae cast in these moulds consist of a single oblong torus at both center and ends."

73 In describing Type XII 14, Muscarella (1967, p. 24) writes: "The arc is like those of type XII, 13 in form and decoration, except for an additional moulding on each arm of the arc between the central and the end mouldings, making a total of five mouldings on the arc."

74 See discussion in Muscarella 1967, p. 26, under Types XII, 15–17. For the recently published fibulae from Kolophon in Asia Minor, see Mariaud 2019; for the fibulae from the city mound at Gordion, see Vassileva 2018.

75 Cf. **26/5** (ΜΕΘ 5278) and **26/6** (ΜΕΘ 5277).

76 Sundwall 1943, pp. 177–231. The Methone fibulae of this type are closest to some of the smaller examples of Sundwall's Group G, see esp. p. 222, fig. 355 (G II β b 2); p. 223, fig. 358 (G II β d 4); p. 224, figs. 359–360 (G III α 1 and G III β a 7); p. 226, fig. 362 (G III β a 22); pp. 228–229, figs. 365–366 (G III β c 9 and G III β c 18).

77 See von Eles Masi 1986, pp. 85–143, pls. 49–111.

78 Blinkenberg 1926, pp. 200–201; Sapouna-Sakellarakis 1978, pp. 118–120, pl. 49.

79 *OlForsch* XIII, pp. 291–293, pls. 20, 64–65, various examples (it is worth noting that Fulvia Lo Schiavo [in *OlForsch* XIII, p. 291] dates the Olympia examples assembled by Hanna Philipp "frühen und mittleren orientalisierenden Periode"); *Perachora* I, pp. 170–171, pl. 73, nos. 5, 7–8, 11; Dawkins 1929a, pl. LXXXIII:f.

80 Kilian 1975a, pp. 80–85, pls. 31–32, nos. 839–869.

81 Lo Schiavo 1983–1984a, pp. 112–113, fig. 37, no. 7; Lo Schiavo 1983–1984b, pp. 130–131, fig. 45, no. 10; see also Papadopoulos 2003a, pp. 79, 81–82, fig. 101a–b, no. 220, which is bigger, with incised decoration on the arch and a long catchplate.

82 See Gergova 1987, pp. 44–51, pls. 13–17, various examples (Bulgaria); Vasić 1999, pp. 55–71, pls. 29, 33–38, various examples of different types (from Vojvodina, Serbia, Kosovo, and North Macedonia).

83 Gergova 1987, pp. 44–51.

84 Vasić 1999, pp. 55–65 for the sanduhrförmiger Fussplatte, and pp. 65–71 for the Schildfuss.

85 Benac and Čović 1957, pl. XXI, no. 6; pl. XXII, nos. 1–4; pl. XXIV, nos. 2–5; pl. XXV, nos. 1–3; pl. XXXIII, nos. 5, 7–9; pl. XXXVI, no. 3; pl. XLVII, no. 30.

86 Gergova 1987, pp. 44–45.

87 Vasić 1999, pp. 55–71.

88 Kilian-Dirlmeier 2002, p. 96, pl. 93, no. 1463; *Perachora* I, p. 171, pl. 73:18 (where it is noted: "the Perachora example is no doubt an import from the Illyrian regions, where the type appears to originate, or from Thrace"); Boardman 1967, pp. 209, 211, no. 240 (Type M), from the Harbor Sanctuary, Period IV, ca. 630–600 B.C. In discussing the latter, Boardman (1967, p. 211) notes: "Thrace or Macedonia might be a source of the finds in Greece."

89 See, among others, Desborough 1972, p. 295; Hood and Coldstream 1968, p. 214.

90 E.g., Desborough 1972, p. 295; Hägg 1967–1968.

91 See, among others, Bouzek 1985, pp. 165–167; Desborough 1964, pp. 53–54; Desborough 1972, pp. 296–298; Hood and Coldstream 1968, pp. 214–218; Hood, Huxley, and Sandars 1958–1959, pp. 235–237.

92 See, esp., Deshayes 1966, pp. 204–207; Snodgrass 1971a, pp. 227–228; Kilian-Dirlmeier 1984a, pp. 80–83.

93   Bielefeld 1968, pp. 38–40; Kilian-Dirlmeier 1984c.

94   See discussion in Alexander and Hopkins 1982, p. 401; and, generally, Alexander 1973a, 1973b.

95   Undset 1889.

96   Tsountas 1899a, cols. 101–102.

97   For Corinth, see Shear 1930, p. 408; *Corinth* XIII, pp. 7–8, grave 2, nos. 5, 10; for Eleusis, see Mylonas 1975, vol. 3, pls. 50–51, χ6, ΜΠ4–χ23, ΛΠ16–χ22, ΖΠ6–χ12.

98   For the Minoan pins, see Hood and Coldstream 1968, p. 214; for the Shaft Graves at Mycenae, see Karo 1930–1933, pp. 173–174, esp. pl. 18, nos. 245–247.

99   Jacobsthal 1956, p. 1.

100   *Sitagroi* 2, p. 305, fig. 8.1f, pl. 8.2a.

101   Kilian-Dirlmeier 1984a, p. 25, pl. 1, no. 20 (Lerna); Milojčić 1961, p. 53, no. 13 (= pl. 50, no. 6); Lamb 1936, pp. 167, 178, fig. 48, pl. XXV, nos. 32.15, 32.35, 32.46 (Thermi); Cherry and Davis 2007, pp. 413–414, fig. 10.4, no. 707 (Phylakopi). For a Middle Bronze Age example from Palamari on Skyros, see Parlama et al. 2010, p. 289, fig. 13 (middle).

102   For the Late Bronze Age, see Kilian-Dirlmeier 1984a, pl. 5, nos. 146–151; see also Felsch 2007, p. 269, pl. 22, nos. 203–204; Karamitrou-Mentesidi 2008, p. 74, fig. 115 (third from the right). For Early Iron Age examples from Greece, including those from Athens, Nichoria, Salamis, Lefkandi, Thessalian Philia, and Halos, see Papadopoulos and Kurti 2014, pp. 342–343; see also the overview by Reinholdt 2008, pp. 123–124, pls. 9–10, nos. 005–008; p. 128, pl. 14; pp. 135–137, pls. 21–23.

103   *Vergina* I, pl. 95, P III η; Radt 1974, p. 126, pl. 38, no. 26; see also Desborough 1952, p. 152. For the example from Kastanas, see Hochstetter 1987, p. 31, pl. 4, no. 26 (same as pl. 27, no. 8).

104   Kilian-Dirlmeier 1984a, pp. 206–207, pl. 84, nos. 3383–3407, illustrates examples from Olympia, Corinth, Bassai, Mantineia, and cites examples outside the Peloponnese; for Arkadia, see Voyatzis 1990, p. 342, pl. 158, no. B237. The type is found at Isthmia from the Archaic well into the Roman period, see *Isthmia* VII, p. 48, pl. 34, nos. 184–188. In dealing with numerous examples of the type from Emporio on Chios, Boardman (1967, pp. 223–224, fig. 145, nos. 377–382) writes: "it is remarkable that most of the straight pins from the archaic deposits are 'roll pins,' a type not hitherto met in Ionia, and rare enough in the rest of Greece." Additional examples from Tegea, Halae, Dodona, Oynthos, Karphi, Knossos (and elsewhere on Crete), Aigina, and Thera are cited in Papadopoulos and Kurti 2014, p. 343; cf. also Maass and Kilian-Dirlmeier 1998, pp. 78, 80–81, fig. 13, no. 61 (Aigina, Aphaia temple), showing that the type is nowhere near as rare as Boardman once thought.

105   See, among others, Furmánek, Veliačik, and Vladár 1999, p. 36, fig. 10, no. 23; p. 87, fig. 39, no. 2; Lo Schiavo 1970, p. 463, pl. XXXVI:17, no. 24; Mason 1996, p. 15, fig. 2, no. 1; Truhelka 1904, pl. XXXVIII, no. 24.

106   For Albania, see Kilian-Dirlmeier 1984b, p. 102, pl. III, nos. 42–46, see also nos. 39–40; for additional examples, see Papadopoulos and Kurti 2014, p. 342, with reference to the one example from Lofkënd Tomb XXVII, which can be dated to Phase II of the tumulus, 12th–11th century B.C. *Rollenkopfnadeln* are the most common type of iron pin at Lofkënd, see Papadopoulos and Kurti 2014, pp. 345–346, nos. 10/33–10/41.

107   The type is especially common in northern and central Italy, see, among others, Åberg 1932, p. 47, fig. 63 (second from left); Montelius 1895, pl. 7, no. 8; pl. 91, no. 4; Montelius 1904, pl. 221, no. 7; Müller-Karpe 1959, pl. 56, A, no. 10; pl. 59, K, no. 2; pl. 71, C, left; pl. 88, no. 11; for the occurrence of the type at Pithekoussai, see Macnamara 2006, p. 271, fig. 2, no. 7. For the ubiquity of the *Rollenköpfnadel* on the Italian peninsula, see Carancini 1975, pp. 7–9, pls. 4–12, 79–80, various examples. For related pin types in northern Italy, esp. in the Bologna region, see Jacobsthal 1956, figs. 352–353, with further bibliography and discussion in Papadopoulos and Kurti 2014, p. 343.

108 See, among others, Beck 1980, pl. 23, no. 9; Childe 1929, pl. XI, no. C1; David 2002, pl. 172, no. 6; pl. 353, nos. 2–3; Gimbutas 1965, p. 115, fig. 75, nos. 10, 16; p. 277, fig. 184, no. 4; p. 289, fig. 195, no. 5; p. 295, fig. 201, no. 3; p. 417, fig. 271, no. 3; Holste 1953, p. 41, fig. 3, no. 2; Müller-Karpe 1959, pl. 116, no. 3; pl. 118, no. 3; pl. 164, no. 4; pl. 166, C, no. 3; pl. 193, nos. 28–31; pl. 196, A, no. 8; pl. 202, C, no. 8; pl. 205, B, no. 12; von Sacken 1868, pl. XVI, nos. 2–3 (with both plain and twisted shaft).

109 Gimbutas 1965, p. 514, fig. 350, no. 11.

110 Vasić 2003, p. 23, with references to the relevant literature.

111 Jacobsthal 1956, p. 122, with full discussion on pp. 122–123, figs. 350–351, 354–356, 360–361.

112 Hetty Goldman (1940, p. 421), for example, stated: "The type is very old, going back to the prehistoric Bronze Age. It is sometimes referred to as of Cypriote origin but, as a matter of fact, it has a very wide distribution throughout Anatolia and is also found in Mesopotamia." The type is well known on Cyprus, cf., for example, Dikaios 1969, pl. 163, nos. 3, 13; *SwCyprusExp* II, p. 35, pl. IX, 1; pl. CLII, 6; Catling 1964, p. 238, fig. 22, nos. 23–24. For the type in Anatolia, see Emre 1978, pp. 119–120, figs. 123–124, Type d, with additional comparanda cited from Boğazköy, Alacahöyük, Beycesultan, Elbistan-Karahöyük, and at the Karum at Kanesh. For additional parallels from Tarsus, Troy, and Alishar Hüyük, see Papadopoulos and Kurti 2014, p. 344.

113 Kaniuth 2006, p. 119, nos. 214–215, Type F-5, with reference to parallels from central Asia, Iran, and Pakistan.

114 Catling 1964, p. 238.

115 Catling 1964, p. 238.

116 Kilian-Dirlmeier 1984a, pp. 147–149, pl. 61, esp. nos. 1857–1860, classified as Geometrische Nadeln, Typengruppe XVIII (T-Nadeln), esp. Type XVIIIB.

117 Cf., among others, Vasić 2003, pp. 11–14, esp. pl. 3, nos. 24–25, referred to "Zyprische Schleifennadel" (unfortunately, the context of nos. 24–25 is unknown).

118 Kilian-Dirlmeier 1984c, pp. 281–283, pls. 112–113, nos. 4872–4903; Voyatzis 1990, p. 342, pl. 162, nos. B242a, B242b.

119 Vasić 2003, pp. 82–86, pls. 31–34, nos. 536–630.

120 See Carancini 1975, pl. 49, nos. 1518–1519, 1521, referred to as "spilloni tipo Iseo" and "spilloni con terminazione superiore non ingrossata," and dated to the Late Bronze Age.

121 Similar incised decoration is occasionally found on violin-bow fibulae from the Balkans and central Europe, see, for example, Betzler 1974, pl. 1, no. 7; Vasić 1999, pl. 1, nos. 7, 9–11, but these fibulae are earlier, Bronze Age, and it seems clear that **15/22** is not a fibula. The same incised decoration is also found on some Italian dress pins of rather different form, see, among others, Carancini 1975, pl. 33, no. 955; pl. 34, no. 968; pl. 35, no. 1003; pl. 41, no. 1238.

122 For related objects normally interpreted as styli, mostly of later date, see, for example, *Corinth* XII, 185–187; in dealing broadly with "writing implements," Gladys Davidson (*Corinth* XII, p. 185), notes that a "comparatively small number of instruments can be definitely identified as styli." Most of the styli at Corinth are made of bronze or bone/ivory, and although all of the bronze examples from Corinth are late—none dating before the Roman period—Davidson cites examples from *Olynthus* X, pp. 357–359 that are Classical, as well as *Délos* XVIII, p. 254, pl. LXXX, nos. 674, 675, which may be Classical or Roman. Davidson dutifully notes that styli are found iconographically in Athenian vase painting as early as the early 5th century B.C., with reference to the Pantaios Painter (*Corinth* XII, p. 185, n. 82) (the example I always like to give is the cup by Douris [Berlin 2285], for which see Sider 2010, esp. p. 542, fig. 1, side B). At least one of the styli from Lindos is of Archaic date, see Blinkenberg 1931, col. 150, pl. 16, nos. 422–423, the former of bronze, the latter of bone. The bronze styli from Isthmia range in date from the Archaic period, through Classical, into the 3rd century B.C., see *Isthmia* VII, pp. 110, 114–115, pl. 62, nos. 386–392, though the distinction

between "spatula" and "stylus" is not always clear. The styli from Olympia and Dodona are somewhat later than those from Lindos and the Archaic examples from Isthmia, see *Olympia* IV, p. 182, pl. LXV, no. 1123; Carapanos 1878, p. 109, pls. LIII, LVII, nos. 8–11. The styli in *Olynthus* X, pp. 357–359, pl. CXIV, nos. 1725–1735 are Classical and are decorated with bands, simplified bead-and-reel ornament, concentric circles, or spirally grooved; note also the one with a molded saurian head at either end, with one protruding tongue pointed for writing, the other flattened for erasing.

123 Papadopoulos and Kurti 2014, pp. 350–353, fig. 10.21, no. 10/55.

124 Kilian-Dirlmeier 1984a, pp, 152–155, esp. her Type XXA, nos. 1933–1948, many of which are assigned to the Middle Geometric period.

125 Schalk 2008, p. 187, fig. 3, Type VII; p. 190, fig. 10, Type VII (Nadeln mit vierkantigem Kolbenkopf); also, p. 187, fig. 3, Type XIII; p. 194, fig. 17; p. 226, fig. 36, no. 330 (Nadeln mit vertikalem Scheibenkopf).

126 Carancini 1975, pp. 212–213, pl. 49, esp. nos. 1511–1513 (Spilloni tipo Vidolasco, Varietà B), most of which are assigned to the Late Bronze Age on the basis of an example from Scoglio del Tonno.

127 See, among others, Vasić 2003, esp. pl. 9, nos. 117–120, 122.

128 Carancini 1975, p. 215, pl. 49, nos. 1529–1530.

129 *Eretria* XIV, p. 52, pl. 120, nos. O 58–O 64, esp. O 60.

130 The closest parallels are Kilian-Dirlmeier 1984a, p. 100, pl. 26, nos. 607–609.

131 *OlForsch* XIII, pp. 46, 48, pls. 27–28, nos. 38, 52; Kilian-Dirlmeier 1984a, p. 156, pl. 64, nos. 1977, 1979.

132 For "vase-headed," see, e.g, Catling 1964, p. 239; Alexander 1964, pp. 167–169, fig. 6, nos. 3–4 (Type II). For "pomegranate" head, see Jacobsthal 1956, pp. 185–200, fig. 48; *Tarsus* III, p. 375, fig. 175, no. 63. For "poppy-headed," see Duru 2008, p. 180, fig. 362.

133 See, among others, Bouzek 1974b, pp. 105–117, figs. 32–33; Bouzek 1987, pp. 91–100, esp. for the distribution of the type; Vickers 1977, pl. III.

134 For Thessaly, see, among others Kilian 1975a, pl. 76, esp. nos. 15, 20–25 (Pherai); pl. 95, nos. 4–6 (Valanida); Kilian-Dirlmeier 2002, p. 102, pl. 97, esp. nos. 1573–1575, and the larger nos. 1578–1979, which are of similar form (Philia).

135 Blinkenberg 1931, cols. 96–98, pl. 10, nos. 210–213; of these, the form of no. 212 is perhaps closest to **15/29**. The only bead that comes close to **15/29** in Beck's standard classifications and nomenclature of beads is a 19th-century ivory bead from Japan, see Beck 1973 [1926], p. 38, fig. 31, A 7).

136 Kilian 1975a, pl. 87, no. 27.

137 Higgins 1980, p. 89.

138 Higgins 1980, pp. 89–90; he also lists a further type, a hoop with an S-spiral bezel, which he refers to as of "northern type"; cf. *Kerameikos* I, p. 85, fig. 4 (right); Müller-Karpe 1962, p. 87, fig. 5:16 (Grave SM 108); see also Gardner and Casson 1918–1919, p. 21, fig. 14 (Aivasil, Grave 3). Desborough (1972, p. 304, illustrated on p. 219, fig. 21:b) refers to this type of ring as one "with double-spiral terminals," noting, in addition to central European examples, pieces from Vergina (e.g., *Vergina* I, pp. 238–240, figs. 78, 79, where central European examples are cited), as are examples from Hexalophos in Thessaly, Elaphotopos in Epirus, and Amphikleia in Lokris; see further Desborough 1965, esp. p. 224; Vokotopoulou 1986, pp. 312–315, fig. 31, Type δ; the fullest discussion of these is now Kilian-Dirlmeier 1980, who lists over 150 examples from France in the west to the former Soviet Union in the east; for additional bibliography, see *Agora* XXXVI, p. 923, n. 169.

139 *Lefkandi* I, p. 247.

140 Lemos went on to add that, unlike the situation in the Argolid, where finger rings are found in large numbers, they lost favor in Athens during PG, see Lemos 2002, pp. 115–117 (this point was first made by Styrenius [1967, p. 109] and echoed by Catling in *Lefkandi* I, p. 248).

141 In *Lefkandi* I, p. 248; see further *Kerameikos* I, p. 85, with nn. 2, 3; Styrenius 1967, pp. 48–70, 109.

142 See Higgins 1980, pp. 88–93, 210–212; Desborough 1972, p. 304. Ruppenstein in *Kerameikos* XVIII, pp. 206–216, distinguishes eight types of bronze rings, many further divided into subtypes: (1) Ringe mit konkaver Aussenseite und halbrundem Querschnitt; (2) Ringe mit bikonischer Aussenseite und dreieckigem Querschnitt; (3) Bandringe; (4) Spiralringe; (5) Ringe mit rundem Querschnitt; (6) Schildringe; (7) Drahtring mit gegenstandigen Spiralenden; and (8) Typologisch nicht zuweisbare Ringe. He also distinguishes four types of iron rings, see *Kerameikos* XVIII, pp. 216–217.

143 See *Kerameikos* I, pp. 33–34, 85, fig. 3 (right), esp. the example from Grave SM 70; Müller-Karpe 1962, p. 86, fig. 4:12 (Grave SM 70); cf. p. 84, fig. 2:13 (Grave SM 24); *Kerameikos* XVIII, p. 24, Beil. 11, Grave SM 136, no. 15; p. 28, Beil. 13, Grave SM 143, no. 8. Parlama and Stampolidis 2000, p. 45, nos. 13, 14 (two examples from a tomb excavated in the course of work on the Acropolis Metro Station).

144 *Lefkandi* I, p. 248. The SM examples are Skoubris Tomb 15B, pl. 95, no. 6; Skoubris Tomb 19, pl. 98, nos. 14, 15; Skoubris Tomb 22, pl. 99, no. 6; Skoubris Tomb 40, no. 9; Skoubris Tomb 53, pl. 107, no. 2. The EPG examples are Skoubris Tomb 16, pl. 95, nos. 14:b, 17. The latest example is Palia Perivolia Tomb 10, pl. 131, no. 21.

145 For Aigina, see Furtwängler 1906, pl. 116, esp. no. 38; for the Argolid see, among others, Daux 1957, pp. 663–664, fig. 55; Verdelis 1963, p. 7, fig. 3, various examples, esp. Types E (Grave VII:1), F (Grave XV:1), and H (Grave XXIII:1); also Beil. 24:4 (Grave II:1–2); Kokkou-Vyridi 1977, p. 177, fig. 4, no. E 1969 (considered EPG). For Elis, see Eder 2001, p. 92, pl. 14:a, nos. e–i. For elsewhere in the Peloponnese, see, e.g., *OlForsch* XIII, pp. 141–142, pl. 42, nos. 515–517; *Nichoria* III, esp. p. 300, fig. 5.10; cf. also Taylour and Janko 2008, p. 446, pl. 52, nos. 7011, 7012 (Agios Stephanos, Late Helladic). For central Greece, see, among others, Vlachogianni 2000, p. 397, fig. 28 (= Morgan et al. 2010, p. 81, fig. 84), several examples from Ellopia; Felsch 2007, pp. 300–303, pl. 37, various examples, esp. nos. 621, 622, 630, 661. For Thessaly, see Batziou-Eustathiou 1984, p. 76, fig. 1 (from Phiki near Trikala); Arachoviti 1994, pp. 132, 134, fig. 11, no. 2, inv. BE 8655 (Pherai); Kilian-Dirlmeier 2002, p. 12, pl. 8, no. 59, cf. no. 64 (Philia). For the north Aegean, see, among others, *Vergina* I, pp. 238–241, fig. 80; Hochstetter 1987, p. 35, pl. 5:1–4 (Kastanas); Papadopoulos 2005, p. 559, fig. 70, no. T11-1 (Torone). For Epirus, see Vokotopoulou 1986, pp. 312–314, fig. 31, Type γ (where it is the most common of the Early Iron Age types). For Crete, see Brock 1957, pp. 71, 199, no. 795; Coldstream and Catling 1996, p. 557; Rethemiotakis and Englezou 2010, pl. 55, ill. 141 (Tomb 5). For the Dodecanese, see, among others, Morricone 1978, pp. 84–85, fig. 78; pp. 166–167, fig. 297 (Serraglio Tombs 10, 22).

146 See, e.g., discussion in *Lefkandi* I, p. 248, where there are 12 examples of closed rings (five Submycenaean, six Early Protogeometric, and one undated; for the type in Athens, see *Kerameikos* I, p. 85, fig. 3 (two examples in the center); Müller-Karpe 1962, p. 84, fig. 2:10 (Grave SM 24); p. 86, fig. 4:5, 13 (Graves SM 52, 70); p. 87, fig. 5:3 (Grave SM 16); *Kerameikos* XVIII, pp. 206–207 (Types 1, 2); Papadopoulos 2005, p. 559.

147 See *Agora* XXXVI, pp. 324–325, 328, figs. 2.226–2.227, T45-10; p. 450, fig. 2.336, T70-10. Both of the Agora rings were associated with children: T70-10 was worn on one of the fingers of the left hand of the deceased, and T45-10 was also associated with the finger bones, evidently of the right hand, of the deceased in that grave.

148 Among many others, cf. Desborough 1972, p. 303, pl. 60:c (right); Kilian 1975a, pl. 70, nos. 33–42 (Pherai), esp. nos. 33–35, which may well be finger rings; *OlForsch* XIII, pp. 150–152, pl. 42, nos. 542–545, 555–556 (Olympia, all classified as "Fingerringe"); Kilian-Dirlmeier 2002, p. 14, pl. 10, nos. 165–168, 172–173, 176 (Philia, Athena Itonia sanctuary, all classified as finger rings); Felsch 2007, pp. 164, 303, pl. 37, nos. 679–688 (Kalapodi, esp. Typ III B, classified simply as "Spiralringe").

149 For Athens, cf. *Kerameikos* I, p. 85, fig. 4 (left) (Grave SM 52), and various other examples from Grave SM 108 (cf. also the gold spiral from Grave PG 5, *Kerameikos* I, p. 183, pl. 76); *Kerameikos* IV, pl. 39, inv. M 24 (Grave PG 39); *Kerameikos* XVIII, p. 24, Beil. 11, Grave SM 136, nos. 16, 17; also Müller-Karpe

1962, p. 84, fig. 2:7 (Grave SM 46); p. 94, fig. 12:3, 4 (Grave PG 39); Styrenius 1967, p. 109. For nearby Salamis, cf. Wide 1910, pp. 29–30, fig. 37. Beyond Athens and Attica, the following list does not pretend to be exhaustive, particularly as many similar spirals cannot be identified as finger rings, hair- or earrings with certainty: for the Argolid, see, among others, Kritzas 1972, p. 205, pl. 148:γ; Courbin 1974, pp. 38–39, pl. 29, B.31, B.32 (Tomb 37); Kokkou-Vyridi 1977, p. 177, fig. 4, pl. 55:ζ, nos. E1958–E1961; for other parts of the Peloponnese, see, among others, *Nichoria* III, pp. 278, 300, figs. 5.12–5.15. For Thessaly, see Wace and Thompson 1912, pp. 212–213, fig. 147:c, k (Theotokou); cf. Theocharis 1960, p. 56, pl. 38:β; for Macedonia, e.g., *Vergina* I, p. 240, fig. 80, ΑΑVδ; the type is also well represented among the Early Iron Age burials on Kos, see Morricone 1978, p. 72, fig. 54; pp. 84–85, fig. 78; p. 226, fig. 453; p. 363, fig. 785.

150   LSJ⁹, s.v. κρίκος.

151   The following list does not aim to be exhaustive, but does try to show the ubiquity of such rings in various contexts. Among many others, see Kilian 1975a, pls. 71–74 (numerous examples from the Enodia sanctuary at Pherai); Felsch 2007, pls. 40–44, nos. 852–1360 (numerous examples from Kalapodi); *Olympia* IV, p. xxiv, nos. 454–456; DeCou 1905, pls. LXXX–LXXXVIII (various examples from "ring fibulae"), pls XC–XCI, various decorative and structural rings from the Argive Heraion; Caskey and Amandry 1952, pl. 46, nos. 91–92 (Argive Heraion); Dawkins 1929a, pl. LXXXV:q–r, u–z (Sparta); Evangelidis 1952, p. 293, fig. 18, nos. 1–10; Evangelidis 1957, pl. 26:β (center top and bottom, from Dodona); Robertson 1948, p. 119, pl. 50, nos. E38–E80 (Ithaka); Palaiokrassa 1991, pp. 170–171, fig. 14, M 8 (sanctuary of Artemis Mounichia at Piraeus); Phaklaris 1990, pl. 79:α–β (Kynourgia); Kardara 1988, pls. 89α, 113α (sanctuary of Aphrodite Erykine); Versakis 1916, p. 97, fig. 42 (bottom row) from the sanctuary of Apollo Korynthos in Messenia; Jacopi 1932–1933, p. 336, fig. 83 (various examples from "la stipe votive" on the acropolis of Kameiros); Kourouniotis 1916, p. 210, fig. 34, *krikoi* from Chios; Lamb 1934–1935, pl. 32, no. 17 (Chios); Klebinder-Gauss 2007, pp. 88–89, 258, pl. 41, nos. 639–650 (Ephesos); Blinkenberg 1931, p. 26, esp. nos. 637, 640 (classified as "anneaux portants" or bearing rings, from Lindos); *Olynthus* X, esp. pp. 231–241, pls. LXII–LXIII, nos. 833–946; Vokotopoulou 1990, pl. 20:δ (lower right); pl. 40:α. See also Dunbabin 1940, pp. 185–186, pl. 84, nos. 11–12, 14, 17, 20, 25 (mostly silver).

152   See, among many others, Kilian 1970, *passim*; Orsi 1926, cols. 41–42, fig. 26 (upper right); col. 119, fig. 113 (bottom); col 140, fig. 137 (left); col. 166, fig. 143; cols. 293–294, fig. 209 (bottom left); de la Genière 1971, p. 453, fig. 17 (upper left); p. 456, fig. 24 (right); Mazzoli 2018, p. 924, nos. PZ M 08-PZ M 11. For further references, from various sites, including Locri Epizefiri, Amendolara, Roccella Ionica, San Leonardo near Metaponto, Ruvo del Monte, Monte Finocchito, Gela, Monte Casaia in Sicily, Calascibetta, Leontinoi, see Papadopoulos 2003a, pp. 156–157, n. 382. Note also the bronze rings of various sizes found in the Muschovitza burial mound in southern Bulgaria, Filow 1934, p. 9, fig. 121, nos. 1–4.

153   Dakoronia 1989.

154   Williams 1997, 21, fig. 11.

155   Williams 1997, 19–21; for further discussion, see Papadopoulos 2002a, 2012.

156   See discussion in Papadopoulos 2012. For tripods and related bronze vessel forms, see, among others, *OlForsch* III; *OlForsch* X; Matthäus 1980, 1985; *FdD* V.3; *FdD* V.1.

157   For pendants with small double spirals (i.e., "spectacle" pendants), see, among others, Kilian 1975a, p. 143, pl. 56, no. 1567 (possible pendant); Papadopoulos and Kurti 2014, pp. 353–354, fig. 10.22; Papadopoulos 2003a, pp. 70–71, figs. 90–91, nos. 178–182.

158   For which see, among others, *Isthmia* VII, p. 48, pl. pl. 35, no. 190; Kilian-Dirlmeier 1984a, p. 208, pl. 84, no. 3408 (Sparta = Droop 1906–1907, pp. 109–111, fig. 1:b); Carancini 1975, pls. 18–21, nos. 577–643, 648, 653 (Italy); Vasić 2003, pls. 9–10, nos. 124–138 (central Balkans).

159 There are other types of objects that spiral ornaments can adorn, such as the double spiral ornament from Nagybátony in northern Hungary used to attach the two ends of a bronze belt, for which see Gimbutas 1965, p. 295, fig. 201, no. 19.

160 For the tutuli, see *Vergina* I, 236–238; Radt 1974, pl. 39, nos. 1–5; for the spectacle fibulae see *Vergina* I, pp. 227–230; for the σύριγγες see pp. 225–227.

161 *Vergina* I, pp. 236–237, figs. 75–77.

162 For a useful reconstruction of how the σύριγγες and the tutuli were worn, see Bräuning and Kilian-Dirlmeier 2013 (not least the cover illustration).

163 Douzougli and Papadopoulos 2010, p. 30, fig. 8, with the tutuli described and discussed more fully on p. 70, under T59-15. There were in fact two types of tutuli for the shoulder pads of the Liatovouni burial: one type, of which there were seven examples, were small tacks with hemispherical heads and a thin shaft on the underside, of the type described by Andronikos under his third type (*Vergina* I, p. 237, fig. 77). The other type at Liatovouni, of which there were 21 examples, also had hemispherical heads, but lacked the shaft on the underside, and were designed to be attached to the organic material of the corselet by means of thin sheet attachments, folded over.

164 *Vergina* I, p. 237; for the Kephallenia tombs, see Marinatos 1932, p. 26.

165 Kilian-Dirlmeier 2002, p. 167, pl. 171, nos. 2886–2893.

166 In addition to the references to Vergina already cited, see also Rhomiopoulou and Kilian-Dirlmeier 1989, p. 115, fig. 26, nos. 11–20; p. 119, fig. 30, nos. 12–24.

167 Kilian-Dirlmeier 2002, p. 167; for Derveni tomb B and tutuli, see Themelis and Touratsoglou 1997, p. 84, pl. 94, B 121.

168 For the tomb at Macchiabate, see Zancani Montuoro 1974–1976, pp. 23–24, pl. 8a, no. 12, with full discussion and comparanda. For references to these types of tutuli in southern Italy and Sicily, see Papadopoulos 2003a, pp. 86–87, 154, n. 320.

169 See Bianco and Tagliente 1985, p. 56, fig. 26 (Tursi, 8th century B.C.); p. 72, fig. 37 (Alianello, 7th century B.C.).

170 *Pithekoussai* I, p. 445, pl. 134, no. 432-7 (inv. 167709).

171 For the small examples, which are referred to as "bottoni tondi di bronzo," as opposed to "bottonicini," see Zancani Montuoro 1983–1984, p. 72; for the larger bosses, see Zancani Montuoro 1977–1979, pp. 59–60, fig. 22.

172 *Olynthus* X, p. 260.

173 See Papadopoulos 2003a, p. 207 for the metallographic analysis.

174 *Vergina* I, pp. 236–237, fig. 75.

175 Kilian-Dirlmeier 2002, p. 164, pl. 169, nos. 2843–2848.

176 Kilian-Dirlmeier 2002, p. 164, with reference to *Olynthus* X, pp. 362–363, nos. 1750–1754 (for the full range of needles from Olynthos, see pp. 361–364); Coldstream 1973, pp. 151–152, fig. 36, nos. 164–172; *Corinth* XII, pp. 173–174, nos. 1234–1247.

177 *Isthmia* VII, pp. 112, 117, pls. 64–65, nos. 415–419.

178 Vasić 2003, pp. 130–133, pl. 48, nos. 963–1000, including publication of a stone mold from Brza Palanka for a needle of this type (p. 131, pl. 48, no. 971). These should not be confused with the decorated eyelet pins, for which see Vasić 2003, p. 35, pl. 12, nos. 173–175.

179 Schalk 2008, p. 187, fig. 3, Type XIa–c; p. 192, fig. 13, Type X; p. 193, fig. 15, Type XI.

180 Kilian-Dirlmeier 1984a, pp. 121–122, pl. 44, nos. 1282–1302.

181 See, among others, the references in Papadopoulos 2003a, pp. 88–90.

182 See full references in Papadopoulos 2003a, pp. 88–90, 154–155.

183 Zancani Montuoro 1983–1984, pp. 14–16, pl. VI, no. 10, with further references in Papadopoulos 2003a, pp. 154–155, n. 330.

184 See, for example, Zancani Montuoro 1983–1984, pl. XVIII:b (left); pl. XXVIII:a–b (various examples); Lo Schiavo 1983–1984a, p. 118, fig. 40, no. 23.

185 *OlForsch* XIII, pp. 371–375, pls. 80–81, nos. 1322–1351; the first variety is characterized by nos. 1322–1332, the second by nos. 1333–1345, and cf. the slightly more substantial and lozenge-shaped in section nos. 1345–1351. A good example of the Boiotian or Dipylon shield miniature double axe is Vokotopoulou 1986, fig. 109:στ.

186 *OlForsch* XIII, p. 372, pl. 81, nos. 333–335; Kilian-Dirlmeier 2002, p. 66, pl. 64, nos. 993–994 (referred to as "Beilanhänger); several of the Philia miniature axes, as well as others elsewhere, are equipped with an axe handle in bronze.

187 *OlForsch* XIII, pp. 373–374, n. 740; to the list one can add several from Arkadia, Voyatzis 1990, p. 279, p. 170, L30, L31; p. 336, pls. 123–125, nos. B164–B169 (Lousoi and Tegea); also two votive double axes at the Artemision at Ephesos, see Klebinder-Gauss 2003.

188 *OlForsch* XIII, p. 373.

189 Kilian-Dirlmeier 2002, p. 66.

190 Such a date is confirmed by several slightly larger miniature bronze axes from Pithekoussai tomb 433, dated to LG I, see *Pithekoussai* I, p. 447, pls. 134 and CLXII, nos. 433-3–433-7.

191 See *OlForsch* XXV, pp. 155–156, pls. 1, 13, 14a. It is considered to be on the Aiginetan standard, and classified by Konrad Hitzl as "Talent Gruppe I Klasse A." Two other bronze cubes are smaller, both with eyelets at the top ("Würfelgewichte," of "Gruppe XIII Klasse A"): *OlForsch* XXV, p. 249, pl. 11, Kat. 465, 466, weighing respectively 307 g and 410 g, and also considered to be on the Aiginetan standard. What is interesting about the Olympia weights is that they are almost exclusively of bronze, except for one of silver. In contrast, lead weights from the Greek era at Olympia have not been found, although it is noted that some lumps of lead may have been used as weights, see *OlForsch* XXV, p. 43.

192 *OlForsch* XXV, pp. 155–156, pls. 1, 13, 14a.

193 *Agora* X, pp. 25–26, pl. 1, BW 1 (B 495), BW 2 (B 492), BW 3 (B 497). In contrast to Olympia, there are only 14 bronze weights in the Athenian Agora, as opposed to at least 109 lead weights, see *Agora* X, pp. 2–33.

194 *Sardis* 8, p. 87, pl. 30, nos. 480–481; cf. *Corinth* XII, pp. 204, 208, pl. 94, nos. 1580–1552.

195 Felsch 2007, p. 382, pl. 63, nos. 2230–2235; for the Geometric or later bronze knives at Kalapodi, see Felsch 2007, pp. 384–385, pl. 64, nos. 2271–2274, esp. 2271–2272.

196 See, among others, Koukouli-Chrysanthaki 1992, pp. 404–408, fig. 90 (Thasos); Morricone 1978, p. 210, fig. 433 (Kos); Bianco Peroni 1976, pl. 39, nos. 346, 354 (bronze knives from 8th–7th century B.C. Italy).

197 Cf., among others, **26/26** (ΜΕΘ 5284) from the West Hill, and the following examples from the agora: **26/122** (ΜΕΘ 1784), **26/123** (ΜΕΘ 295), **26/124** (ΜΕΘ 296), **26/125** (ΜΕΘ 299); there was also a small cone point from the surface survey of Methone, see Morris et al. 2020, p. 675, fig. 16:b.

198 For the Acropolis, see Keramopoullos and Pelekidis 1915, p. 27, fig. 25:β; for Bassai, see Kourouniotis 1910, col. 328, fig. 53 (left), referred to as χαλκαῖ ἐπενδύσεις σκευῶν.

199 *Olynthus* X, pp. 301–306, pls. LXXXVII–LXXXIX, nos. 1309–1336; for the Argive Heraion, see DeCou 1905, pl. CIV, esp. nos. 1803–1804.

200 For the bronze reinforcement, see *Isthmia* VII, p. 27, pl. 22, no. 115; for the iron examples, see p. 101, n. 28 (with references to two-plate clamps from the Kerameikos, see Müller-Karpe 1962, p. 125, fig. 21:13, with further examples from Gordion and the Crimea), pp. 106–108, figs. 18–20, pl. 58, nos. 351–362; p. 171, pl. 95, Appendix H; cf. also an example from Crete published in Boardman 1971, pl. Δ΄ (center left, from Early Iron Age Kavousi).

201 Papadopoulos 2003a, pp. 129–130, fig. 161, nos. 450–454.

202 *Isthmia* VII, p. 140, pl. 77, nos. 499–503; Raubitschek refers here to the large bronze examples as spikes, not nails, see p. 140, p. 78, nos. 507–508 (with further examples listed); for Philia, see Kilian-Dirlmeier 2002, pp. 166–167, pl. 170, nos. 2871–2875, 2881–2882.

203 Blinkenberg 1931, cols. 202–203, pl. 26, nos. 626–629.

204 Klebinder-Gauss 2007, pp. 191–192, pls. 99–102, nos. 979–1000.

205 For small hinged objects of Archaic date, see Papadopoulos 2003a, pp. 130–131, fig. 162, no. 455, with cited comparanda from Bassai, and Francavilla in southern Italy, and later examples from Isthmia and Olynthos. For various hinged objects from the Itonia sanctuary near Philia, see Kilian-Dirlmeier 2002, p. 166, pl. 170, nos. 2863–2870 (of uncertain date); cf. also some of the bronze hinged attachments to helmets of the Classical period, Kilian-Dirlmeier 2002, pp. 115–116, pl. 110, nos. 1782–1785.

206 Such as Blinkenberg 1931, col. 136, pl. 13, no. 343 ("Crochet d'un fuseau," with reference to parallels from Olympia, Praisos, and the Psychro Cave); Kilian-Dirlmeier 2002, pp. 164–165, pl. 169, nos. 2849–2852 ("*Spindelhaken*"); *Isthmia* VII, p. 116, pl. 63, esp. no. 404 (of uncertain date). For a well-preserved bronze spindle hook from the agora of Methone, see **26/121** (ΜΕΘ 1781).

207 Among others, cf. Felsch 2007, pp. 385–386, pls. 64–65, nos. 2280, 2290–2292; Kilian-Dirlmeier 2002, pl. 162, no. 2601 (probably from a bronze vessel).

208 For awls, see Hochstetter 1987, pp. 27–28; there are rather more awls at Kastanas than there are chisels. For awls ("Ahlen und Pfrieme") at Kalapodi, considered to be of Mycenaean date, see Felsch 2007, p. 383, pl. 63, nos. 2238–2246. For the iron awl from Pithekoussai, see *Pithekoussai* I, pp. 657–660, esp. p. 659, pl. 190 (inv. 168668); measuring 0.114, its size is similar to **15/62**.

209 For which see DiBattista 2021.

210 For tweezers at Greek sanctuaries, see, among others, *Olympia* IV, p. 68, pl. XXV, nos. 493–495; Carapanos 1878, p. 95, pl. LI, nos. 20–21 (Dodona, "deux petits pinces"); Furtwängler 1906, pl. 116, no. 61 (= p. 417, no. 126, with further references, from the sanctuary of Aphaia on Aigina); Voyatzis 1990, p. 339, pl. 146, nos. B204, B205 (Tegea, with further references); Lamb 1934–1935, p. 151, pl. 32, no. 29 (Chios); Boardman 1967, p. 226, fig. 147, pl. 93, nos. 397–398 (Archaic Emporio on Chios); Kilian 1975a, pl. 88, no. 14, and cf. also no. 15 (Pherai); Kilian-Dirlmeier 2002, p. 70, pl. 67, nos. 1046–1060 ("spätgeometrische und hocharchaische Zeit Pinzetten" from the Athena Itonia sanctuary near Philia); p. 124, pl. 114, nos. 1898–1899 (Classical examples from Philia); p. 165, pl. 169, nos. 2853–2855 (undated tweezers from Philia); Felsch 2007, pp. 355–356, pl. 49, nos.1940–1956; Pfuhl 1903, p. 233, fig. 78, no. 38 ("Haarzwicken" from Archaic Thera); Mazarakis Ainian 2019, p. 119, fig. 213 (Kythnos); Stais 1917, p. 195, fig. 7 (bottom row, third and fourth from right, two possible examples from the sanctuary of Poseidon at Sounion); Lambrinoudakis 1982, p. 50, fig. 1 (top row, second from left, and another immediately below, from the sanctuary of Apollo Maleatas at Epidauros); Robertson 1948, pl. 50, no. E171 (Ithaka); Papadopoulos 2003a, p. 73, fig. 94, esp. no. 192 (from the extramural sanctuary of Sybaris at Francavilla Marittima); see also the tweezers from the tombs in the Chora of Metaponto, Proházska 1998, p. 807, nos. MT6–MT12. For bronze tweezers in Early Iron Age tombs, see, among others, *Kerameikos* V,1, p. 197, pl. 167, no. M 89 ("Bronzeklammer" from Geometric grave 58). Note also Bronze and Early Iron Age examples from Crete, in Boardman 1961, pp. 31–32, fig. 12, pl. XIII, nos. 127–134 (Diktaian Cave). For Mycenaean tweezers, see Wace 1932, p. 105, pl. VII, no. 28 (Mycenae Tomb 529), and for silver tweezers from the Shaft Graves at Mycenae, see Karo 1930–1933, p. 145, pl. CXXXVI, no. 818. For examples from farther north in the Glasinac region, see, among others, Benac and Čović 1956, pl. XXXII, no. 2; Benac and Čović 1957, pl. XI, no. 28; pl. XV, no. 2; pl. XXI, nos. 5. 13, 15; pl. XXVII, no. 12; pl. XXX, no. 9; pl. XXXVII, no. 2; pl. XXXIX, no. 1.

211 For examples from Macedonia, see Casson 1919–1921, pp. 16–17, fig. 11 (lower left); Casson 1923–1925, pl. II:2, nos. k–l; for the eastern Adriatic, see Lo Schiavo 1970, pl. XLII, nos. 9–11.

212 For binding sheaths or plates, see discussion above under **15/56**, and below, under **26/150–26/158**, and esp. Papadopoulos 2003a, pp. 127–130, figs. 158–160 (binding plates), fig. 161 (binding sheaths). For bronze vessels, many of Corinthian manufacture, but found in Epirus, with bronze repair patches, see Vokotopoulou 1986, figs. 81:α, δ (two jugs with bronze repair patches); Douzougli and Papadopoulos 2010, p. 52, fig. 21 (large cutaway neck jug with bronze repair patch); see further Zachou 2007.

213 Leaves, often found by themselves unattached to a larger whole, are a fairly common dedication in Archaic and later sanctuaries in Greece and southern Italy. In her discussion of the bronze and copper leaves from the sanctuary of Poseidon at Isthmia, Isabelle Raubitschek (*Isthmia* VII, p. 68) noted that some of these may derive from metal crowns dedicated by victorious athletes. Indeed, according to the *scholia* on Pindar, *Odes* 7. 152, bronze garlands of myrtle were common at the festival of Hera. Alternatively, a number of bronze leaves may have adorned bronze statues, otherwise lost, as has been suggested in the case of Olympia (see *OlForsch* IX, pp. 66–68) and Nemea, and perhaps also for Philia (Kilian-Dirlmeier 2002, pp. 128–129, pl. 116, no. 1929). For leaves at sanctuaries in Greece, see de Ridder 1896, p. 138, fig. 91, no. 420 (Athenian Acropolis); Keramopoullos and Pelekidis 1915, p. 30, mention at least two olive and two laurel leaves from the Acropolis; Kourouniotis 1910, col. 329, fig. 54 (φύλλον δάφνης from Bassai); *FdD* V.1, pp. 122–123, figs. 458*bis*–459*bis*, nos. 663–668, esp. figs. 454–456; *Olympia* IV, p. 186, pl. LXVI, nos. 1171–1181; *OlForsch* IX, pp. 67, 129, pl. 60, nos. 348–349; Carapanos 1878, pl. XLIX, no. 6 (leaf) and also nos. 8, 12–14 (various leaves and floral elements from Dodona); Miller 1978, p. 63, pl. 12:e, BR 383; *Isthmia* VII, p. 71, pl. 42, nos. 275–276; *Larisa am Hermos* III, pl. 10, no. 36; Kilian 1975a, pl. 88, nos. 7–10 (Pherai); Klebinder-Gauss 2007, p. 274, pl. 93, nos. 947–948; see also *Olynthus* X, pl. VII, with full discussion and comparanda on pp. 52–53, n. 232. For similar leaves from southern Italy, see *Metaponto* I, p. 45, fig. 23, no. 11; p. 47, figs. 26 (right), 27; Orsi 1914, col. 903, fig. 144 (left, from Kaulonia); Orsi 1933, p. 97, fig. 59 (silver) and p. 114, fig. 71 (bronze and copper), all from the Temple of Apollo Alaios; Adamesteanu and Dilthey 1992, p. 75, fig. 85 (Macchia di Rossano). Note also the gold leaves from the Heraion at Foce del Sele, Zancani Montuoro 1965–1966, color plate B (right). For bronze votive floral sprays, flower rosettes, and votive fruit, together with flower buds, see Papadopoulos 2003a, pp. 117–124 (with references).

214 See Klebinder-Gauss 2007, pp. 187, 274, no. 949.

215 For a recent overview of tools in the Late Bronze and Early Iron Age, see Blackwell 2020.

216 Snodgrass 1964, pp. 125, 127–128, fig. 8:b.

217 The earliest example comes from Tomb UV at Agios Ioannis (Knossos), see Boardman 1960, p. 133, pl. 39 (IV 8) (= Snodgrass 1964, p. 127, M1).

218 Broneer 1958, p. 35, pl. 17:c, nos. 15–24.

219 Vokotopoulou 1986, figs. 100–102 for the Type M spearheads; for the full array of iron spearheads at Vitsa, see Vokotopoulou 1986, pp. 300–304, figs. 93–107; for Liatovouni, see Douzougli and Papadopoulos 2010, p. 41, fig. 15:e–h.

220 Snodgrass 1996, p. 583, under Knossos Type B.

221 *Vergina* I, p. 270, fig. 106, ΑΓ XVI; *Sindos* III, esp. p. 486, figs. 275–277, nos. 626 (540–535 B.C.), 628 (540–530 B.C.), 629 (530–520 B.C.); p. 487, fig. 280, no. 632 (520 B.C.).

222 For iron spearheads and iron swords from the tombs from Trebenište, see Filow 1927, pp. 90–91, figs. 105, 106; cf. p. 88, fig. 103. For the cemetery at Trebenište see further Stibbe 2003. For the Glasinac region, see Benac and Čović 1957, various examples, pls. III 9; IV 7–8, 10, 12; XIII 8; XV 3; XX 11–12; XXII 11; XXIII 7; XXIX 4; XXXI 14–15; XXXVI 16; XXXXI 23–24; XXXXIV 1–4; XXXXV 1–5.

223 For Philia, see Kilian-Dirlmeier 2002, pp. 135–142, pls. 121–147, nos. 2009–2247, for the full array of iron spearheads; for those of, or related to, Type M, cf., among others, pls. 124–126, nos. 2035–2058;

pl. 132, nos. 2102–2103; pl. 141, nos. 2171–2181; pl. 142, nos. 2190–2197. For Kalapodi, see Schmitt 2007, pp. 426–466, 526–543, pls. 67–90, nos. 1–317; those that accord most closely to Type M include pl. 79, nos. 151–153; pl. 86, nos. 269–272.

224 Snodgrass 1967, pp. 38–39; cf. Snodgrass 1964, pp. 136–139; Verdelis 1963, pp. 35–40, esp. p. 35 Beil. 5, 3 (Grave XXIII, Tiryns).

225 Snodgrass 1967, p. 39; cf. Lorimer 1950, pp. 259–260.

226 It is worth noting that, as a category of tombs, "warrior graves" have been studied and problematized by a number of scholars, including James Whitley (2002) and Anna Maria D'Onofrio (2011). In a more recent study, Bernhard Steinmann (2012), in dealing with "Waffengräber" of the Aegean Bronze Age, rightly refers to these tombs as "weapon-graves," as opposed to "warrior graves." He thus shifts the focus away from "warrior graves" to burials that may do no more than claim a status by those burying the deceased.

227 See Douzougli and Papadopoulos 2010, pp. 40–42. This is a pattern that remains standard throughout the period of use of the cemetery, from the 12th century down to the late 5th or early 4th century B.C.

228 Reading between the lines of Hammond 1967, it is clear that even the indefatigable Hammond could have used a spear or two in his travels through northwest Greece and southern Albania, not least for protection against the menacing Albanian (Illyrian) hounds.

229 For representations of Mycenaean warriors/hunters carrying two spears both in frescoes and on pictorial vases, see Buchholz, Foltiny, and Höckmann 1980, pp. 288–290, figs. 73–75 (Höckmann). For the Archaic and Classical periods, several Athenian white-ground lekythoi depict a male warrior with two spears. Often, however, the male is a hunter with two spears, not in heroic nude, but wearing a petasos rather than a helmet; in a similar vein, a lekythos in Taranto depicts Oedipus as traveler, wearing a short tunic, cloak, traveler's boots, and a petasos, leaning against two spears, contemplating the sphinx. For Oedipus and the sphinx, see Oakley 2004, p. 104, fig. 65; for other Athenian white-ground lekythoi depicting hunters with two spears as opposed to warriors, see, among others, Athens, National Museum, inv. 1857, 1828, 1935, 1943.

230 See Snodgrass 1964, pp. 144, 148; Snodgrass 1971a, pp. 274–275; *Lefkandi* I, pp. 256–257; the Bronze Age evidence assembled in Buchholz 1962 is now supplemented by Avila 1983.

231 *Vergina* I, pp. 272–273; Petsas 1961–1962, p. 227, fig. 10, grave LXV BΔ; see further Radt 1974, p. 140.

232 Most notably the "quiverful" of iron arrows from the Late Protogeometric Toumba tomb 26, the possible remains of a bow, and the figurative representation of archers on the Middle Protogeometric hydria in Skoubris tomb 51, 2, see *Lefkandi* I, pp. 256–257. For additional arrowheads from Lefkandi, of bronze and iron, see *Lefkandi* III, pl. 128, T. 79, A 14 and T 79, B 12. The most recent study of bows, arrows, and quivers in the ancient Greek world in the historic period is Bellas 2018.

233 For Kavousi, see Day, Coulson, and Gesell 1986, p. 382, pl. 80:i–j, esp. j, some of which are close to the example from Methone; Gesell, Coulson, and Day 1991, pp. 154–155, pl. 59:e–f (16 iron arrowheads from grave 12); Snodgrass 1996, pp. 584–585 (Knossos); Papadopoulos 2005, p. 562, fig. 112c (Torone).

234 *Agora* XXXVI, p. 962.

235 The earlier list in Snodgrass 1964, pp. 144, 148, which was added to in Snodgrass 1971a, pp. 274–275, is now supplemented by the material from Lefkandi and Torone cited above. A fuller, but still not complete, list was provided by Avila 1983, pp. 146–147, appendix 5, which is especially useful for the previously unpublished examples from Mycenae, Thermon, and Sparta. See also Desborough 1952, p. 133; Béquignon 1937, p. 52 (tombs 85–86, six iron arrowheads).

236 Kilian-Dirlmeier 2002, pp. 16–17, pl. 12, nos. 214–217; for the numerous iron arrowheads from the site that cannot be dated, many of which are similar to **15/78**, see pp. 146–147, pls. 152–153, nos. 2346–2381.

237 Schmitt 2007, pp. 474–492, 544–548, pls. 93–98, nos. 350–422.
238 *Sindos* III, pp. 314–315, 492, figs. 302–304, nos. 658 (540–530 B.C.), 659 (360–350 B.C.), 660 (undated), and 661 (undated); only the latter is of iron.
239 Snodgrass 1964, p. 155.
240 Snodgrass 1964, pp. 154–156.
241 *Vergina* I, pp. 266–269, figs. 104–105.
242 *Vergina* I, p. 266. Although unkind to human skeletal remains, the soil at Vergina was more conducive to the preservation of both bronze and iron objects.
243 *Sindos* III, pp. 232–241, 460–464, nos. 429–461; several of the Sindos knives came in groups of three to five knives, and some were found in scabbards.
244 *Agora* XXXVI, p. 962. Elsewhere in Athens knives of similar form are well represented in the Kerameikos and at the Kynosarges site, see esp. *Kerameikos* I, pl. 76 (Grave PG 17); *Kerameikos* IV, pl. 38, inv. M 52 (Grave PG 28); *Kerameikos* V.1, pl. 166, inv. M 54 (Grave G 38: EG II), M 80 (Grave G 13: MG I), M 96 (Grave G 12: MG I–II), M 120 (Grave G 69: MG II); with further discussion of the Kerameikos and Agora iron knives in Müller-Karpe 1962, p. 105, fig. 23:7; p. 109, fig. 27:5, 7; p. 110, fig. 28:6; p. 111, fig. 29:4. For the Kynosarges site, see Droop 1905–1906, p. 91, fig. 12 (top); Coldstream 2003, pp. 336, 340, fig. 1, pl. 46, no. B7.
245 *Kerameikos* IV, p. 35, pl. 38, inv. M 52; *Lefkandi* I, pl. 170, Toumba Tomb 3, no. 11.
246 It is worth noting two similar small curved knives in *Vergina* I, p. 267, fig. 104 (bottom), ZΠ1α and Kiβ.
247 *Lefkandi* I, p. 257; for the iron knives of Lefkandi, see *Lefkandi* I, pls. 134, 246:h, Palia Perivolia Tomb 16, no. 7; pl. 144, Palia Perivolia Tomb 31, no. 7; pl. 153, Palia Perivolia Pyre 16, no. 2; pl. 170, Toumba Tomb 3, no. 11; *Lefkandi* III, pls. 57, 127, Toumba Tomb 50, no. 4; pls. 61, 127, Toumba Tomb 54, no. 32. Some of the more recent examples at Lefkandi have been found in graves together with weapons (including a sword, spearhead, dagger, axe), see Lemos 2002, p. 123; cf. also the comments in Papadopoulos 2005, pp. 561–562.
248 *Sardis* 8, p. 54.
249 *Agora* XXXVI, pp. 77–83, esp. p. 83; for the iron knife, see pp. 100–101, fig. 2.51, T11-31; for the skeletal remains, see p. 531.
250 For daggers see Snodgrass 1964, pp. 94, 98–99, 103–104, 106.
251 Snodgrass 1996, pp. 585–587. Moreover, the association of a knife or knives in some graves with weapons does not make all knives weapons. Indeed, at a number of sites in various parts of Greece, iron knives are found in the graves of both men and women. At the Molossian sites of Vitsa Zagoriou and Liatovouni, numerous knives have been found in male and female graves, and indeed the all-purpose nature of such implements no doubt have made them indispensable for both sexes (see Vokotopoulou 1986, p. 297; for Liatovouni, Douzougli and Papadopoulos 2010, pp. 43–45, with fig. 16).
252 Snodgrass 1996, pp. 585–587.
253 E.g., Onassoglou 1981, pp. 11–12, fig. 5, nos. 17–19; Dakoronia 1987, several iron knives mentioned from Tombs XIV, XXIII, XXXIII.
254 Sapouna-Sakellarakis 1998, p. 104, fig. 44:31–43, esp. 41–43.
255 See, among others, Heurtley and Skeat 1930–1931, pp. 36–38, fig. 15, no. 23 (various examples, one with wooden hilt) (Marmariani); Wace and Thompson 1912, p. 212, fig. 147:I (Theotokou) (= Wace and Droop 1906–1907, pp. 323, 326, fig. 12:i); Kilian 1975a, pl. 93:3–10 (Pherai); Kilian-Dirlmeier 2002, pp. 71–72, pls. 68–71, nos. 1061–1112 (Philia); Tziaphalias 1983, pp. 204–208, notes at least six iron knives from Tombs 1, 28, 37, 61 (Krannon).
256 *Nichoria* III, p. 310, no. 92; p. 312, fig. 5-55.
257 See, among others, Laurenzi 1936, pp. 164–165, fig. 152 (Ialysos); Morricone 1978, p. 75, fig. 60; p. 311, fig. 665; see also p. 210, fig. 433, which is bronze (Kos).

258 Among many other sites, see, e.g., Karageorghis 1983, pp. 216–221, pl. 143, esp. nos. 23, 96, and cf. no. 26 (sickle) (Tomb 76); p. 279, pl. 174, no. 8 (Tomb 83); p. 285, pl. 174, nos. 70, 72, 77 (Tomb 83); p. 292, pl. 174, no. 15 (Tomb 84); note also the long iron knife, p. 54, pl. 48, no. 2 (Tomb 48).

259 *Vergina* I, pp. 266–269, figs. 104, 105; Radt 1974, p. 139, pl. 42:5–12; *Sindos* III, pp. 232–241; Casson 1923–1925, pp. 21–22, pl. 2:b–d (Tsaousitsa); Savvopoulou 1988, p. 229, fig. 13 (top row) (Palaio Gynaikokastro); Papadopoulos 2005, pp. 561–562, pls. 468–470 (Torone); Chrysostomou 2008, p. 36, fig. 13 (top); p. 45, fig. 29 (bottom) (Edessa).

260 Koukouli-Chrysanthaki 1992, pp. 404–408, figs. 90 (bronze knives), 91 (iron knives), pls. 350–353.

261 Andronikos, in *Vergina* I, pp. 266–269 (with references); Foltiny 1961, pp. 289–290, pl. 95, fig. 1, nos. 4, 5; cf. Randall-MacIver 1927, pl. 6:5. Iron knives were also common in the tombs of both men and women at Sala Consilina in southern Italy; de la Genière 1979, p. 79.

262 In *Lefkandi* I, p. 258.

263 Sandars (1955) stresses local Aegean development, whereas Milojčić (1948–1949) and Harding (1975) emphasize the similarity of Mycenaean and Italian types; see further Bianco Peroni 1976, pl. 39, nos. 342, 343, pl. 40, esp. nos. 346, 354 for bronze examples of the 8th and 7th centuries B.C.

264 Cf. some of the axes and adzes in *Isthmia* VII, pp. 119, 124–125, pls. 67–68, nos. 428–434, including mattocks (tools like a pickaxe, with an adze and a chisel edge as the ends of the heads, used more for digging earth).

265 *Eretria* XXII, vol. 2, pp. 25, 158, pl. 105, nos. 431–434; *Eretria* XIV, p. 67, pl. 133, nos. O 236–O 240.

266 Blackwell 2020, p. 527.

267 The trunnion axe in iron with projections has been found in various parts of the Aegean, including Athens, for which see *Kerameikos* IV, pp. 41–42, pl. 38, inv. M 9 (Grave PG 40), with the projections, although poorly preserved, clearly visible. The solitary axe in Tomb 13 in the Athenian Agora, although classified by Blegen (1952, p. 289, fig. 3, pl. 75:c, no. 6) as an "axe or broad chisel," is considered by both Snodgrass (1964, pp. 166–167) and Catling (in *Lefkandi* I, p. 256) to be an axe, see further *Agora* XXXVI, pp. 114–117, figs. 2.62–2.64, no. T13-13. Several such axes were found at Lefkandi, see *Lefkandi* I, pl. 133, Palia Perivolia Tomb 13, no. 22, with full discussion on p. 256; also *Lefkandi* III, pl. 61, Toumba Tomb 54, no. 33; as well as pl. 43, Toumba Tomb 39, no. 33 (= Popham, Touloupa, and Sackett 1982a, pp. 238, 241, fig. 8). There is an example from Troy (Level VIIb1), see Becks and Thumm 2001, p. 421, fig. 482. For a bronze example from Karphi, referred to as an adze, see Pendlebury, Pendlebury, and Money-Coutts 1937–1938, p. 116, pl. 29:2, no. 455, which is also decorated with incised linear patterns. Cf. also an example from Philia, Kilian 1983, p. 143, fig. 12:16. Additional examples from the Aegean, as well as Italy and Spain, are assembled in Bouzek 1997, pp. 105–106, fig. 100 (with examples from Hephaistia on Lemnos, Herakleion-Mastamba, and Anchialos [Sindos]). A fragmentary mold for a trunnion axe has also been found in a Late Bronze Age context at Assiros Toumba, see Wardle and Wardle 1999, p. 39, fig. 3:2. Trunnion axes in bronze are known over a wide area of Europe and the Near East during the Bronze Age. See esp. Deshayes 1960, pp. 113–131, pls. XIII–XV, LV, and map VII (*lames à moignons*). See also Catling 1964, pp. 87–88, fig. 8:11, pl. 6:g–j (for flat axes and adzes, see pp. 85–87, figs. 8:7, 12; pl. 6:a–f) (both with references). For Boğazköy, see Boehmer 1972, pp. 37–38, pl. II, esp. nos. 26, 27; see also Hamilton 1935, p. 26, no. 130 (with reference to examples from Egypt, e.g., Petrie 1917, pls. XVII, XVIII). For Europe, see further Maryon 1938, pp. 248–249, figs. 18, 19 (from Lusmagh and Pozzuoli); Giardino 2006, esp. p. 63, fig. 1; for the Near East, see Maxwell-Hyslop 1953. Note also the bronze lugged adze from the Uluburun shipwreck, Bass 1986, p. 292, ill. 32. For the axes and adzes of Bronze Age Canaan, see Miron 1992.

268 This type is well known on Crete, especially in the Fortetsa Cemetery (see Brock 1957, pp. 137–138, 202, pl. 172, nos. 1602–1605, 1641, 1642 [six in all]), and probably also from the cemetery at Vrokastro on Crete, see Hall 1914, p. 38, no. 10 (described but not illustrated). There are also two examples from the Geometric tomb at Argos published by Courbin 1957, esp. p. 369, figs. 50, 51, with

discussion on pp. 384–385 (for further discussion of these, see Snodgrass 1964, pp. 166–167). For Euboia, see Popham, Touloupa, and Sackett 1982a, pp. 238, 241–242, fig. 8, Lefkandi, Toumba Pyre 13, no. 1; Sapouna-Sakellarakis 1998, pp. 83–84, 104, fig. 44:47 (Kyme). There are also several from the Athena Itonia sanctuary near Philia in Thessaly, see Kilian 1983, p. 143, fig. 12:14, 15, 23, 27; Kilian-Dirlmeier 2002, pp. 10–11, pl. 7, nos. 37–50. Late Bronze and Early Iron Age examples are also known in Epirus, see esp. Metallinou 2008, p. 47, figs. 44, 45. The type in bronze from Mycenae was first noted by Schliemann (1878, p. 111, fig. 173); for a published bronze example from Aigina, see Felten et al. 2008, p. 52, fig. 7; see also Kanta-Kitsou, Palli, and Anagnostou 2008, p. 17, no. 5. Note also the "axe/adze" from Knossos, Snodgrass 1996, p. 588, fig. 175 (Tomb 75, no. f49), with one peen set vertically, the other horizontally, and a central hole. For Bronze Age double axes, adzes, etc., see Deshayes 1960, pp. 253–262, 279–293; Catling 1964, pp. 88–92; Aravantinos 2010, p. 90 (second row); Boardman 1961, pp. 42–45, fig. 19, pls. XIV–XV, nos. 198–209. Note also the remarkable bronze double axe from Phaistos decorated with relief butterflies, recently restudied by Baldacci 2008; and bronze double axes from the Mitsotakis Collection, Davaras 1992, pp. 262–266, nos. 325–330. For the type in Italy, see Guglielmino and Pagliara 2006, p. 119, pl. 1, no. 6. For the double axes of the Late Bronze Age from the hoard on the Athenian Acropolis, see Blackwell 2020, p. 526, fig. 3.6.1.

269 For the "winged" axe, see the bronze mold at Mycenae of LH IIIB date, published in Stubbings 1954.

270 See discussion in Snodgrass 1996, pp. 587–588, fig. 175 (Tomb 75, nos. f52, f53, f11a, f36).

271 For Kavousi, see Gesell, Day, and Coulson 1988, p. 288, pl. 77:d; Gesell, Coulson, and Day 1991, p. 153, pl. 58:e; Day 2011, p. 756, fig. 7:5; for Eleutherna, see Stampolidis 1996, p. 54, fig. 102:23; for Galaxidi, see Threpsiadis 1972, p. 203, pl. 81:α, no. ε; for Philia, see Kilian 1983, p. 143, fig. 12:7, 8, 17, 18; Kilian-Dirlmeier 2002, p. 10, pl. 6, nos. 32–36.

272 For the example from Troy, see Becks and Thumm 2001, pp. 419–424, fig. 482; for that from Istria, see Mihovilić 2007, p. 344, pl. LXXXVII:j, no. 2 (from the site of Pećina na Gradini).

273 *Lefkandi* I, p. 256, pl. 190, Tomb Pyre 1, no. 3.

274 For battle, see, among others, Boardman 2007, p. 259, fig. 2 (Theseus dispatching Prokroustes with an axe); for the sacrifice of large animals, see, e.g., van Straten 1995, pp. 107–109, figs. 113, 114; for the hunt, see Hampe 1936, pl. 25 (on a Boiotian LG kantharos) and, most recently, Ignatiadou 2002, p. 133, figs. 8, 10 (for the Vergina lion-hunt painting).

275 See, among others, Deonna 1959, esp. pp. 248–250 for the axes; Snodgrass 1964, p. 166. For real votive axes dedicated at sanctuaries, not functional tools/weapons, see, for example, Lambrinoudakis 1981, pp. 64–65, figs. 10, 12; Karetsou 1981, p. 148, fig. 14.

276 *Agora* XXXVI, pp. 104–118, 965–966; see further Snodgrass 1964, p. 166.

277 Snodgrass 1964, pp. 166–167.

278 *Isthmia* VII, p. 120, n. 8.

279 *Isthmia* VII, p. 120, n. 8, with reference to Kilian 1983, p. 143, fig. 32, nos. 14, 15, 23, 27. Raubitschek also noted that the comparative rarity of the metal hammer in the Bronze Age was explained by Deshayes (1960, p. 295) by the preference for stone or wooden mallets.

280 For which, see Blackwell 2020, pp. 525–531, with fig. 3.6.1; see further Blackwell 2011.

281 See *Corinth* XII, pp. 204, 208, pl. 94, nos. 1580–1582 (two of these are 5th or 4th centuries B.C., one is 4th or 3rd century B.C.; *Sardis* 8, p. 87, pl. 30, nos. 480–481; both of these are square and of similar dimensions to **15/92**, and both are thought to be Lydian, with one dated to the 6th century B.C.

282 Blackwell (2018, p. 522) considers the broad chisel as one with a cutting edge of 3 cm or more, the narrow chisel as one with a cutting edge under 3 cm.

283 *Isthmia* VII, p. 120, where she distinguished two types, the flat chisel (four examples), and the pointed chisel (five). For the flat chisel (p. 120, n. 10), she traces its history back to the Bronze Age, through the Early Iron Age (*Nichoria* III, pp. 301, 307, fig. 5-25, no. 34), and Geometric period (Kilian 1983, p. 144,

fig. 13, no. 32), into the Archaic (McClellan 1975, pp. 502, 504–509). The use of the flat chisel in sculpture is normally deduced from the tool marks, for which see Casson 1933, pp. 168, 180–185; Adam 1967, pp. 26–39; and for its general use, see further Orlandos 1966, pp. 42–44, h and i; Palagia 2008, esp. p. 246, fig. 78 (for the various different tools: the punch, point, claw, rounded claw, drove, flat chisel, bull-nosed chisel, fine point). As for the pointed chisel (see *Isthmia* VII, p. 120, n. 11), Raubitschek notes that its history is essentially that of the flat chisel, but the one Early Iron Age example she cites, from the warrior grave, Agora tomb 13, is, as I have argued, an arrowhead (see further Blackwell 2020, p. 533, fig. 3.6.2). She does list, however, some useful illustrations of pointed chisels in Athenian red-figure.

284   *Isthmia* VII, p. 120 (the Early Geometric date is on the basis of tomb 13 in the Athenian Agora, discussed in the previous footnote). Of the pointed chisels from Isthmia, those that can be dated are Archaic, see *Isthmia* VII, pp. 125–127, fig. 25, esp. nos. 441–442.

285   Blackwell 2018, p. 523, table 2; and see also p. 522, fig. 4; p. 525, fig. 5; p. 526, fig. 6.

286   Blackwell 2018, p. 524, table 3.

287   Maryon 1938.

288   Blackwell 2020, p. 528.

289   Blackwell 2020, p. 532.

290   For Kavousi, there is a chisel from tomb 6, see Gesell, Day, and Coulson 1988, p. 288, pl. 77:c (V87.121); another iron object, classified as a "scraper" from tomb 9, may be a broad iron chisel or a scraper, see Gesell, Coulson, and Day 1991, pp. 152–153, pl. 58:g (V88.181). Kilian-Dirlmeier (2002, p. 151, n. 603) also notes a chisel from Mastambas in Crete, Lembesi 1970, p. 292, pl. 403:γ (which also illustrates other iron tools and weapons, including axes). For Pithekoussai, see *Pithekoussai* I, p. 517, pl. 154, no. 515-11 (inv. 168039); p. 555, pls. 165 and CLXXIV, no. 557-7 (inv. 168226); p. 659, pl. 190, no. 678-5 (from tombs 515, 557, and 678, all Late Geometric II).

291   Kilian-Dirlmeier 2002, pp. 151–152, pls. 157–158, nos. 2485–2500.

292   Under the same heading of "Werkzeug," Kilian-Dirlmeier (2002, pp. 151–152) includes a number of related tools, such as several cross-cutting hammers ("kreuzschneider Treibhammer" and "querschneider Treibhammer"), a forge hammer ("Schmiedehammer"), and a small "Steckamboss" (or small plug anvil).

293   For awls and chisels at Kastanas, see Hochstetter 1987, pp. 27–28.

294   See esp. the iron obeloi of Protogeometric to Archaic date from the Itonia sanctuary near Philia in Thessaly, in Kilian-Dirlmeier 2002, p. 31, pl. 4, esp. nos. 15–20. Several of these obeloi (esp. nos. 15–18) also preserve small projections on either side of the shafts around the midpoint of the rod (another, pl. 5, no. 21, has a circular-disk projection at the midpoint of its shaft).

295   I know of no similar object in iron. An idiosyncratic iron object of uncertain function measuring 0.205 is described in *Eretria* XXII, vol. 2, pp. 25, 158, no. 435 simply as "ferrure."

296   Blackwell 2020, p. 527. Blackwell classifies copper-alloy and bronze tools from the Aegean and eastern Mediterranean of the Late Bronze Age into six functional categories, in order of their prominence: 1) carpentry/masonry tools (axes, adzes, chisels, saws, drills, etc.); 2) utilitarian implements (knives, razors, cleavers, undefined blades, scrapers, spatulas); 3) tools for small craft activities (awls, punchers, borers, indeterminable small tools); 4) agricultural tools (sickles, picks, shovels, pruning knives, hoes, and plowshares); 5) the metallurgical tools already noted; 6) tools for prestige or ritual (elaborately decorated implements, tridents, shepherds' crooks, miniature tools).

297   Vitale et al. 2016, p. 271, fig. 25:h, i.

298   Gesell, Day, and Coulson 1988, p. 288, pl. 77:e (V87.114). A few of the later (4th–2nd century B.C.) fragmentary iron objects from the acropolis sanctuary at Stymphalos may be from metalworkers' tongs, see Schaus 2014b, p. 179, fig. 17.15, nos. 198–199. A variety of blacksmith's tools, including tongs and a poker, was found in a hoard at Waltham Abbey, Essex, and dating to the 1st century B.C. or 1st century A.D., see Manning 1980.

299 Such tongs, with two arms riveted together, are known much later. A particularly well-preserved iron pair from Corinth is of Byzantine date, probably no later than the 11th century A.D., see *Corinth* XII, pp. 190, 193, pl. 87, no. 1444. In her discussion of them, Davidson (p. 190) writes: "The exact use of the tongs (No. 1444) is hard to fix: a blacksmith might have found them handy." For such tongs in Roman Britain, see Manning 1980, pp. 88–90, with figs. 1–2.

300 Boston, MFA 01.8035, BAPD 2188; *CVA* Boston 1, pl. 37; pl. 38, 3–4.

301 Whether this was a metal hydria of bronze or silver, or a terracotta hydria containing water, is unclear.

302 The melting point of bronze depends on the ratio of the alloy and what metals were used in the alloy, but it would be typically something around 950º C; silver melts at 961.8º C, lead at 327.5º C, tin at 231.9º C.

303 See, among others, Munaretto and Schaus 2014, pp. 186–190, figs. 8.1 and 8.2 for various nails with large, medium, and small heads, tacks, nails with folded heads, bolts, etc. See further *Corinth* XII, pp. 140–143, pl. 72, nos. 1025–1052 for bronze, iron, and at least one lead nails and tacks; *Sardis* 8, pp. 68–69, pls. 21–22, nos. 295–345, various nails, tacks, and rivets, mostly of iron, including at least six that are of Lydian, 6th-century B.C. date. For the nails and tacks (all referred to as "Nagel") from the Itonia sanctuary at Philia, see Kilian-Dirlmeier 2022, pp. 153-154, pls. 158–159, nos. 2511–2533; pp. 166–167, pl. 170, esp. the tacks or small nails, nos. 2871–2874; virtually all of the iron nails and tacks from Philia derive from undated contexts.

304 For iron rings at the Itonia sanctuary near Philia in Thessaly, see Kilian-Dirlmeier 2002, p. 150, pl. 157, nos. 2464–2478, most of which I would classify as *krikoi*.

305 *Isthmia* VII, pp. 9–10, pl. 7, nos. 34–35; under the appliqué, Raubitschek cites another fragmentary bronze sheet cutout from the Argive Heraion, DeCou 1905, p. 274, pl. CVIII, no. 1837.

306 *Isthmia* VII, p. 136, pl. 74, no. 484; with a length of 0.150 m, this piece is twice the size of **15/103**.

307 For Bronze Age examples from Perati and the Uluburun shipwreck, see, among others, Buchholz, Jöhrens, and Maull 1973, pp. 176–178, n. 680, pl. VI:c; Powell 1992, pl. LXXVI:b; Bass et al. 1989, pp. 7, 9; Pulak 1988, p. 32; Iakovidis 1969–1970, vol. 1, p. 435; vol. 2, pp. 355–356, pl. 135:b, M172 (no fewer than 72 examples in tomb 131 alone). For other Bronze Age sites see, among others, Dimakopoulou 1988, p. 244, nos. 244–245; Doumas 1975, p. 372, pl. 272:γ (Dodekanese); Iakovidis 1989, p. 100, pl. 36:α (Gla); Courtois 1984, p. 47, no. 413, fig. 15:15, pl. 21:19 (Enkomi, Cyprus).

308 There are two fishnet weights from tombs 287 and 292 in the North Cemetery at Knossos that are dated to Late Protogeometric/PGB, see Evely in Coldstream and Catling 1996, p. 634, fig. 193, 292.f10a and 287.f5. For Archaic examples, cf., among others, Pfuhl 1903, p. 237, fig. 80 (right); Friis Johansen 1958, p. 75, figs. 171–172, Z 39–Z 40; *Isthmia* VII, p. 121, n. 16; pp. 127–128, pl. 72, nos. 455–456; Boardman 1967, pp. 202–204, fig. 134, nos. 160–161 (in discussing the Archaic examples from Emporio on Chios, Boardman adds: "Lead fish-net weights are undatable except by context. At Emporio the same type is met in the seventh century A.D."). For Archaic southern Italy, see Hänsel 1973, pp. 421–423, figs. 14–15, with further discussion on p. 425 (some 102 similar lead fishnet weights were found together with various bronze and iron implements in an Archaic cremation tomb at Herakleia); see also Papadopoulos 2003a, pp. 142–143, fig. 178, no. 561.

309 Cf., among many others, *Olynthus* X, p. 475, no. 2504 (121 weights were found together in a small area in House A v 6, room k); cf. *Olynthus* VIII, pp. 92–94, pls. 29–30, 96; *Torone* I, pp. 731–732, fig. 171, no. 18.24; Stavropoullos 1938, p. 21, fig. 22 (26 late Classical or Hellenistic lead fishnet weights); see also Mazzoli 2018, p. 929, no. PZ M 24 (Metaponto).

310 About 40 identical fishnet weights were found together in a Byzantine context in Shop XXVIII of the South Stoa at Corinth, see *Corinth* XII, p. 193, pl. 88, no. 1449.

311 Brokallis 2013, pp. 365–368.

312 The process of mending is described more fully in Iakovidis 1969–1970, vol. 2, pp. 64–65, fig. 5. For mending pottery in the Classical period, see esp. Cook 1972, p. 249; Noble 1988, p. 94, figs. 253–254; *Olynthus* X, pp. 329–334, pl. LXXXIX, and esp. pls. XCVIII–XCIX, for bronze reinforcements/rivets and lead clamps/rivets.

313 For Early Bronze Age clamps, see, among others, Bernabò-Brea 1976, pp. 292–293, pl.234:r–t (Lemnos); Valmin 1938, p. 373 (Messenia). For Middle Bronze Age clamps in the Argolid, see Nordquist 1987.

314 For general comments, see Cleal 1988, p. 139. According to Gazmend Elezi (pers. comm.), the mending of pottery can be traced back to the Early Neolithic period, as early as the 7th millennium at Franchthi Cave (see Vitelli 1989), and even earlier, ca. 7000 B.C., at Knossos (see Tomkins 2007).

315 Heurtley 1939, p. 141, no. 15 (= frontispiece, pl. VI); p. 141, fig. 10:a; p. 145, fig. 12:c; p. 140, fig. 8:c (all Late Neolithic from Servia); p. 159, fig. 28:b (Neolithic from Kritsana); pp. 102, 215, fig. 86:i, f, g (Late Bronze Age, preserving rivets); Wardle 1980, p. 245, fig. 9, no. 1 (Late Bronze Age); Hänsel 1979, p. 187, fig. 14, no. 10; Hochstetter 1984, pl. 45, no. 6; pl. 49, no. 2; pl. 265, no. 2; also the Early Iron Age pithos from Vergina: Snodgrass 1971a, p. 74, fig. 33:a–b.

316 See, among many others, *Kerameikos* I, pl. 63, inv. 532; *Lefkandi* I, pl. 16, nos. 184, 192; pl. 17, no. 219; pl. 23, no. 545; pl. 26, no. 704; pl. 279, no. 1061; pl. 280, no. 1139; pl. 282D (T pyre 4); Popham, Touloupa, and Sackett 1982a, pl. 32:h (T pyre 11.4); Wells 1983a, pp. 80, 72, fig. 49, no. 410; p. 47, fig. 19, no. 101; and the lead clamp, p. 101, fig. 83, no. 740. See also Heurtley and Skeat 1930–1931, pl. 11, no. 149; p. 34, fig. 14 (Marmariani); Choremis 1973, p. 66, pl. 35:γ, no. 622 (Messenia); Andreiomenou 1980, pl. 127:b (Boiotia); *Nichoria* III, pp. 303, 311, figs. 5-60–5.62; Evangelidis 1912, p. 133 (Mycenae); Zapheiropoulou 1969, pl. 400:γ (right) (Donousa).

16

CLAY TEXTILE TOOLS FROM METHONE:
SPINDLEWHORLS AND LOOMWEIGHTS FROM THE HYPOGEION

Sarah P. Morris

Among the artifacts deposited in large numbers in the Hypogeion are clay objects associated with spinning and weaving (Fig. 16.1), and thus termed spindlewhorls (Figs. 16.2–16.3) and loomweights (Figs. 16.4–16.5), respectively. Presumably these objects were collected and discarded with other domestic and industrial debris discussed in other chapters—stone tools (Chapter 13), glass (Chapter 25) and metal (Chapter 15) artifacts, and transport amphoras (Chapter 12), as well as fine wares (Chapter 9) and objects such as the ivory seal (Fig. 1.14)—along with large quantities of organic materials (Chapter 10). Collectively, with their signs of use and wear, they offer an impression of textile production by the inhabitants of Methone in the Early Iron Age through Archaic periods on the East Hill. A selection of these textile-related implements, arranged in five categories by size and shape, represents all levels of the Hypogeion deposits (Fig. 16.1).

SPINDLEWHORLS (FIGS. 16.2–16.3)

These small, vertically pierced clay objects, commonly conical or biconical in shape and made of fine fabric often burnished, were also kept and worn as ornaments or buttons in antiquity (including in prehistoric burials: see Chapter 6), hence they are conventionally called "spindlewhorl, bead, or button" (Fig. 16.2).[1] Larger discoid versions, weighing up to 100 g (Fig. 16.3), are more readily identified as weights for spinning, rather than ornaments. At least eight examples shaped like a rounded loaf or hemisphere with flat underside, deeply grooved across their width, represent a type common in northern Greece since the Middle Bronze Age (Figure 16.6).

From the Late Bronze Age through the Early Iron Age, the same types were in use over time in northern Greece, with biconical and conical types most frequent.[2] Existing typological and functional studies of spinning weights have been amplified by technological analyses of use wear from suspension gestures, string weight, and so on, to reconstruct past techniques of spinning, but are best performed on a full set of contemporary artifacts found in a settlement context.[3] A total of 128 examples of spindlewhorls in various shapes and sizes (including flat, rounded, and pierced "sherd whorls," some perhaps reused to weight thread in spinning:[4] Fig. 16.3; see Chapter 17 for unpierced sherds) were identified and inventoried in the excavation of the Hypogeion, in virtually all of its levels, of which 23 were selected for description and illustration here. A join identified between **16/8**, a bell-shaped whorl found in Trench 22 (pass 74, level [15]), and a fragment from Trench 32 (ME 3641, pass 90, level [10]), both from the earliest phase of the Hypogeion (late 8th–early 7th century B.C.), offers a stratigraphic link that may illuminate deposition processes.

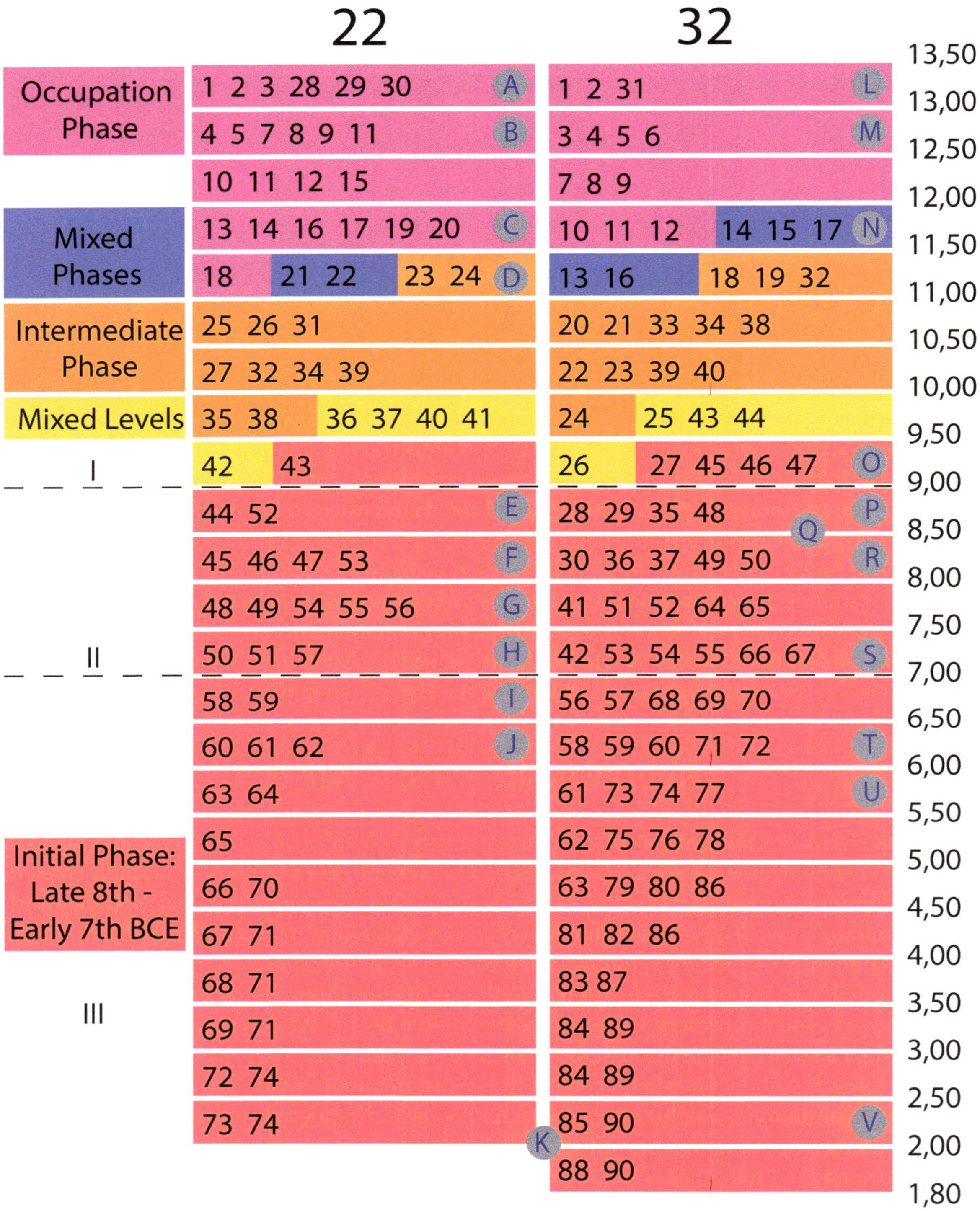

FIGURE 16.1. Distribution of clay textile artifacts across different levels of the Hypogeion. A) **16/29**; B) **16/30**; C) **16/20**, **16/34**; D) **16/33** E) **16/4**, **16/16**; F) **16/12**; G) **16/7**; H) **16/10**; I) **16/37**; J) **16/38**, **16/40**; K) **16/8**; L) **16/21**; M) **16/32**, **16/35**; N) **16/27**; O) **16/31**; P) **16/17**, **16/25**; Q) **16/3**; R) **16/5**, **16/6**, **16/15**; S) **16/18**, **16/24**; T) **16/1**, **16/9**, **16/22**; U) **16/19**, **16/26**; V) **16/28**. (**16/23** [not shown] was found in Unit 22, between 8,50 and 3,00 [masl]; 16/39 [not shown] was found in Unit 32, between 8,00 and 6,00 [masl])
Prepared by Adam DiBattista

Conical and Biconical Variants (Bell-profile, etc.) (Fig. 16.2)
(Size category: larger than 3 x 3 cm, greater than 20 g; total of 110 examples)

16/1. (ΜΕΘ 469 [ME 1489]) Conical Spindlewhorl   Fig. 16.2
#274/032072 [7]. Earliest phase (late 8th–early 7th century B.C.). 22-09-2004.
H. 0.029; Diam. (max, above base) 0.037; Diam. (top) 0.020; Diam. (perforation) 0.007; Wt. 34.5 g.
Conical, slight bell shape (raised base); surface cracked, worn edges (once burnished?).
Dark greenish "sandy" fabric, much white grit, quartz; dark gray surface (10YR 4/1).

16/2. (ΜΕΘ 435 [ME 580]) Conical Spindlewhorl   Fig. 16.2
#274/022 (cleaning Wall 5). 18-03-2004.
H. 0.027–0.032 (top slanting); Diam. (base) 0.025–0.026; Diam. (max) 0.038; Wt. 38 g.
Conical, on raised concave base. Very worn (abraded top end).
Fine dark fabric (2.5Y 5/2), white grit and mica; surface dark, once burnished?

16/3. (ΜΕΘ 472 [ME 677]) Biconical Spindlewhorl   Fig. 16.2
#274/032035-37 (fill). 30-04-2004. Similar example from Korinos, "Toumbes" (Pit 48).
H. 0.024; Diam. (base) 0.026; Diam (top, max, below midpoint) 0.035; Diam. (perforation) 0.008; Wt. 25 g.
Biconical (widest diameter below midpoint); well flattened top and underside; burnished.
Fine hard dark-red fabric (5YR 5/4), fine white grit, mica; surface black, once burnished.

16/4. (ΜΕΘ 438 [ME 762]) Conical Spindlewhorl   Fig. 16.2
#274/022044 [11]. Earliest phase (late 8th–early 7th century B.C.). 04-06-2004.
H. 0.0225; Diam. (base) 0.033; Diam. (top) 0.018; Diam. (perforation) 0.006; Wt. 21 g.
Conical, slight bell-shaped profile; smoothed top surface and underside, sides uneven.
Fine light-red fabric (5YR 5/6), mica; dark patches at lower edge. Once burnished?

16/5. (ΜΕΘ 460 [ME 1059]) Biconical Spindlewhorl   Fig. 16.2
#274/032050 [7]. Earliest phase (late 8th–early 7th century B.C.). 23-07-2004.
H. 0.030; Diam. (base) 0.025; diam. (max. below midpoint) 0.034–0.036 (oval section); Wt. 32.5 g.
Biconical, on raised concave base; widest diameter well below midpoint.
Fabric fine, dark brown with mica, grit (10YR 5/3); surface very worn.

16/6. (ΜΕΘ 459 [ME 1057]) Biconical Spindlewhorl   Fig. 16.2
#274/032050 [7]. Earliest phase (late 8th–early 7th century B.C.). 23-07-2004.
H. 0.035; Diam. (max, at midpoint) 0.040–0.042; Diam. (perforation) 0.006; Wt. 46 g.
Biconical; worn and chipped around both holes.
Semi-coarse fabric, white chips and grit; surface brown (7.5YR 5/6) with black patches.

16/7. (ΜΕΘ 443 [ME 867]) Conical Spindlewhorl   Fig. 16.2
#274/022048 [11]. Earliest phase (late 8th–early 7th century B.C.). 05-07-2004.
H. 0.028; Diam. (base) 0.028; Diam. (top) 0.016; Diam. (perforation) 0.005–0.006; Wt. 18.3 g.
Conical, convex profile; surface very worn, pitted on one side.
Fabric: fine red-brown (2.5YR 4/6), mica, white grit, lime chips; dark surface patches.

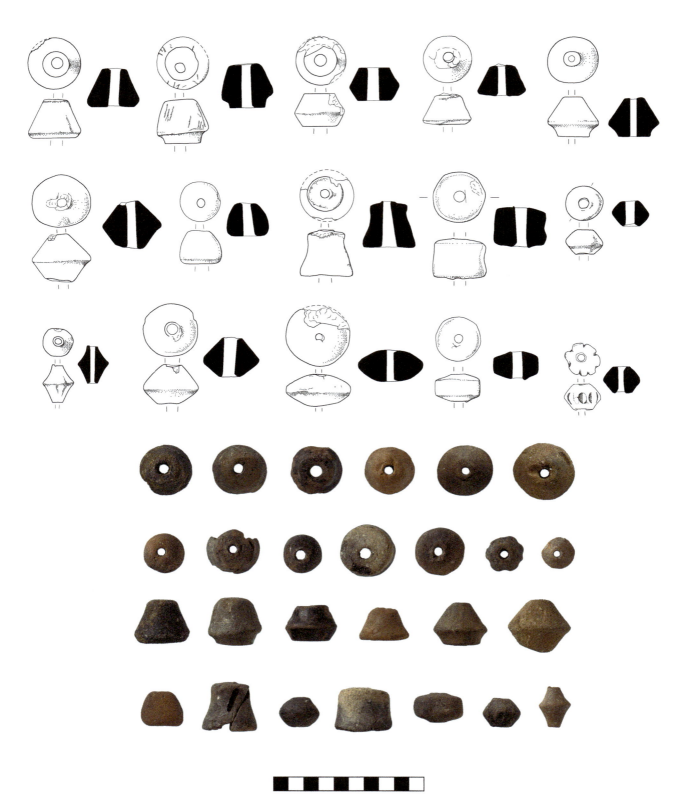

FIGURE 16.2. Clay biconical and conical spindlewhorls from the Hypogeion. a) drawings: top row, left to right: **16/1** (ΜΕΘ 469), **16/2** (ΜΕΘ 435), **16/3** (ΜΕΘ 472), **16/4** (ΜΕΘ 438), **16/5** (ΜΕΘ 460); middle row: **16/6** (ΜΕΘ 459), **16/7** (ΜΕΘ 443), **16/8** (ΜΕΘ 2778), **16/9** (ΜΕΘ 468), **16/10** (ΜΕΘ 447); bottom row: **16/11** (ΜΕΘ 1249), **16/12** (ΜΕΘ 442), **16/13** (ΜΕΘ 457), **16/20** (ΜΕΘ 92), **16/22** (ΜΕΘ 495). b) photos: upper register view from top, lower register side-on view; top row: **16/1**, **16/2**, **16/3**, **16/4**, **16/5**, **16/6**; bottom row: **16/7**, **16/8**, **16/10**, **16/9**, **16/20**, **16/22**, **16/11**. Drawings A. Hooton, photos J. Vanderpool

16/8. (ΜΕΘ 2778 [ME 3698]) Bell-shaped Spindlewhorl   Fig. 16.2

#274/022074 [15], 14-12-2006 + ME 3541 (032090 [10], 08-05-2007). Earliest phase (late 8th–early 7th century B.C.).

H. 0.034; Diam. (base) 0.037; Diam. (top) 0.026; Diam. (perforation, flaring from top to base) 0.005–0.008; Wt. 30 g.

Bell-shaped: flat top, concave faces; two joining frr (preserving 2/3 of whole).

Fabric very fine, red core (5YR 5/6), mica and white grit, dark surface; smooth, once burnished?

16/9. (ΜΕΘ 468 [ME 1479]). Cylindrical Spindlewhorl   Fig. 16.2

#274/032063 [9]. Earliest phase (late 8th–early 7th century B.C.). 23-08-2004.

H. 0.030; Diam. (base) 0.038 Diam. (top) 0.034; Diam. (perforation) 0.007–0.008; Wt. 46 g.

Cylindrical section, with truncated profile (flaring sides).

Dark gray semi-coarse fabric, "sandy" with fine white grit, mica (10YR 3/1); surface fired light brown (10YR 7/3), one side dark brown, underside black (burnt?).

16/10. (ΜΕΘ 447 [ME 897]) Biconical Spindlewhorl   Fig. 16.2

#274/022051 [11]. Earliest phase (late 8th–early 7th century B.C.). 12-07-2004.

H. 0.020; Diam. (max) 0.026; Diam. (perforation) 0.006; Wt. 12.6 g.

Biconical, with small rounded profile (angular sides now worn).

Fine light-brown fabric (core) 7.5YR 6/4, dark surface (7.5YR 3/1); very worn.

16/11. (ΜΕΘ 1249 [ME 2922]) Biconical Spindlewhorl   Fig. 16.2

#274/022 (fill of Wall 14). 07-08-2006.

H./L. 0.029; Diam. (midpoint) 0.022; Diam. (perforation) 0.004; Wt. 7.9 g.

Elegant profile; biconical shape with concave upper and lower surfaces, carefully shaped (tooling marks visible as vertical strokes). Chipped at both ends.

Very fine light red fabric (5YR 5/6); once burnished?

16/12. (ΜΕΘ 442 [ME 856]) Biconical Spindlewhorl   Fig. 16.2

#274/022047 [11]. Earliest phase (late 8th–early 7th century B.C.). 18-06-2004.

H. 0.0285; Diam. (max, midpoint) 0.040; Diam. (perforation) 0.0085; Wt. 34.6 g.

Biconical, with flat angular profile; widest diameter below midpoint.

Fabric: fine, brick red (5YR 5/6), surface smooth, dull (pale brown: 7.5YR 5/3), worn, chipped around holes, on edge.

(Cf. ΜΕΘ 7291: #229, Tr. 1, Unit 37.2: SF 374; 19/08/2015). Early Iron Age? H. 3 cm, Diam. [max] 0.025; Diam. [perforation] 0.003. Fabric fine, brown; very worn, chipped).

16/13. (ΜΕΘ 457 [ME 1044]) Biconical Spindlewhorl   Fig. 16.2

#274/032050 [7]. Earliest phase (late 8th–early 7th century B.C.). 23-07-2004.

Diam. 0.043–0.047; H. 0.022; Diam. (perforation) 0.005; Wt. 45 g.

Biconical (large flattened sphere); worn, one side broken above and below midpoint.

Semi-fine fabric, light red (5YR 7/3); much straw temper, light brown surface; worn.

Discoid, "Doughnut"-shaped and Flat Spindlewhorls (Figs. 16.2–16.3)

16/14. (ΜΕΘ 446 [ME 896]) Biconical Discoid Spindlewhorl   Fig. 16.3

#274/022051 [11]. Earliest phase (late 8th–early 7th century B.C.). 12-07-2004.

H. 0.032; Diam. (max) 0.053; Diam. (perforation) 0.005; Wt. 74.6 g.
Biconical discoid form; pierced perforation off-center.
Fine light-brown fabric (2.5YR 5/4), mica; surface worn, scratched, and dull.

16/15. (ΜΕΘ 456 [ME 1043]) Large Biconical Whorl or Weight — Fig. 16.3
#274/032050 [7]. Earliest phase (late 8th–early 7th century B.C.). 23-07-2004.
Diam. 0.052–0.053; H. 0.036; Diam. (perforation) 0.007; Wt. 73 g.
Large, biconical form; very worn, dented and chipped.
Fabric: light red-yellow clay (7.5YR 5/6), much straw temper, white grit and mica; surface pitted.

16/16. (ΜΕΘ 437 [ME 760]) Discoid Spindlewhorl — Fig. 16.3
#274/022044 [11]. Earliest phase (late 8th–early 7th century B.C.). 04-06-2004.
Diam. 0.052; H. 0.012; Diam. (perforation) 0.011; Wt. 36 g.
Discoid spindlewhorl, very worn.
Once red fabric (5YR 6/6), dark surface (10YR 5/3); small hollows, mica.

16/17. (ΜΕΘ 454 [ME 1012]) Flat Pierced Sherd — Fig. 16.3
#274/032048 [5]. Earliest phase (late 8th–early 7th century B.C.). 15-07-2004.
Diam. 0.059; Th. 0.006; Wt. 28.5 g.
Large flat pierced sherd (thin hard fabric), reused as weight (central drilled hole).
Fine dark red fabric (interior: 5YR 5/6), dark red exterior surface (5YR 4/6).

16/18. (ΜΕΘ 462 [ME 1151]) Flat Pierced Sherd — Fig. 16.3
#274/032054 [7]. Earliest phase (late 8th–early 7th century B.C.). 09-08-2004.
Diam. 0.029–0.031; Th. 0.006; diam. (perforation) 0.004; Wt. 7.2 g.
Small flat round sherd cut from closed vessel, centrally pierced (drilled).
Fabric: fine, bright red (2.5YR 5/6), fine white grit, mica; surface streaky brown, burnished.

16/19. (ΜΕΘ 471 [ME 1507]) Small Discoid Spindlewhorl — Fig. 16.3
#274/032074 [7]. Earliest phase (late 8th–early 7th century B.C.). 24-09-2004.
Diam. 0.024; Th. 0.0095; Diam. (perforation) 0.005; Wt. 7.3 g.
Small discoid spindlewhorl (round, flat, and centrally pierced).
Fabric: fine, white grit, dark yellow to brown clay (10YR 5/2); uneven surfaces.

16/20. (ΜΕΘ 92 [ME 188]). Discoid Spindlewhorl Fig. 16.2
#274/022018 [7]. Occupation phase (fill C). 01-07-2003.
H. 0.020; Diam. 0.033; Diam. (perforation) 0.006; Wt. 23 g.
Discoid form, slightly domed upper and lower surfaces.
Fine dark fabric (7.5YR 5/1), much mica; worn surface.

SMALL BEAD-SIZED SPINDLEWHORLS AND VARIANTS (MELON-SHAPED) (FIGS. 16.2–16.3) (SIZE CATEGORY: SMALLER THAN 3 × 2.5 CM, LESS THAN 20 G IN WEIGHT; TOTAL OF 18).

16/21. (ΜΕΘ 488 [ME 748]) Small Flat Pierced Disk — Fig. 16.3
#274/023002 [1]. Surface layers. 28-05-2004. Found outside Hypogeion.
Diam. 0.024; Th. 0.005; Diam. (perforation) 0.004; Wt. 5 g.

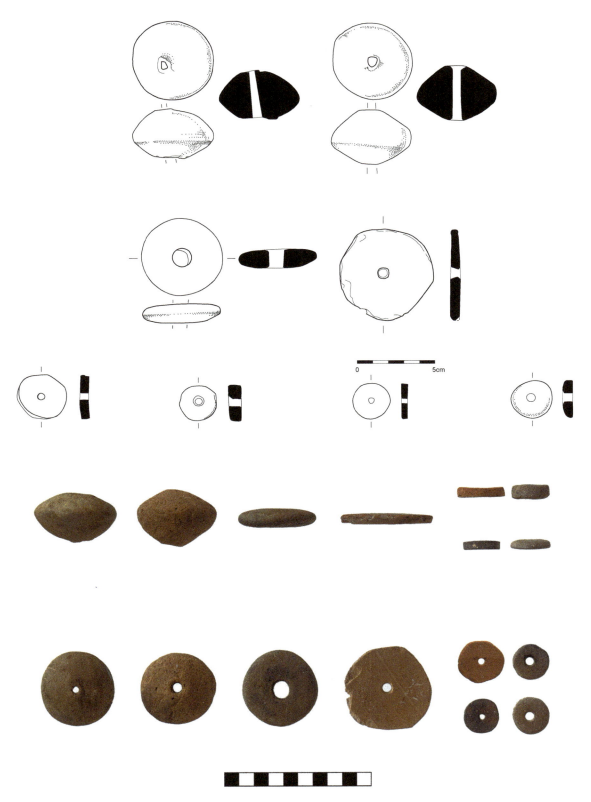

FIGURE 16.3. Discoid, "doughnut," and flat spindlewhorls from the Hypogeion. a) drawings: top row, left to right: **16/14** (ΜΕΘ 446), **16/15** (ΜΕΘ 456), **16/16** (ΜΕΘ 437), **16/17** (ΜΕΘ 454); bottom row: **16/18** (ΜΕΘ 462), **16/19** (ΜΕΘ 471), **16/21** (ΜΕΘ 488), **16/23** (ΜΕΘ 667); b) photos: upper register, side-on view; lower register, view from top; top and bottom, left to right: **16/14**, **16/15**, **16/16**, **16/17**, **16/18**, **16/19**, **16/21**, **16/23**. Drawings A. Hooton, photos J. Vanderpool

Cut from flat sherd; drilled central hole.
Fine dark fabric (7.5YR 4/2–4/3), light in weight, fine white grit; smoothed, worn.

16/22 (MEΘ 495 [ME 1482]) Small Biconical Spindlewhorl Fig. 16.2
#274/032071 [7]. Earliest phase (late 8th–early 7th century B.C.). 20-09-2004.
H. 0.019; Diam. (max, midpoint) 0.025; Diam. (at top and base) 0.013; Diam. (perforation) 0.005; Wt. 10.6 g.
Small biconical spindlewhorl, melon-shaped (vertically fluted: bead?).
Fine dark-brown fabric (10YR 4/3); dull black surface (once burnished?).

16/23. (MEΘ 667 [ME 1885]) Small Discoid Spindlewhorl Fig. 16.3
#274/022047-51 (found in backfill). 27-05-2005.
Diam. 0.026; H. 0.006; Diam. (perforation) 0.006; Wt. 4.8 g.
Small discoid shape, plano-convex in section (flat underside); drilled hole.
Fine light-brown clay (10YR 6/4–5/4), mica; very worn.

LOOMWEIGHTS (FIG. 16.4)

The Hypogeion at Methone contained a sizable number of heavier clay artifacts, of the type usually classified as weights designed to hold in sustained suspension the warp/woof threads of a standing, warp-weighted loom for weaving cloth. The types common in prehistoric Macedonia[5] are well represented in this deposit, including pyramidal shapes pierced horizontally through the upper shaft, before firing (ca. 50 were inventoried), and the larger, heavier kind, irregular in shape as well as size (ca. 12). One particular "doughnut" type, round in shape with a flat underside and rounded upper profile (**16/27**) and made of coarse fabric, heavy with straw, is common at Early Iron Age Lefkandi.[6] Some weights derive from the latest (uppermost) levels of the Hypogeion, and thus could date as late as the 6th century B.C., unlike many of the spindlewhorls and spools. However, very large loomweights of pyramidal shape are known since the Early Bronze Age in northern Greece (e.g., at Torone, 86.391), as well as at Lefkandi in both the Late Bronze and Early Iron Ages, and from the Early Iron Age kiln at Torone (Late Geometric).[7]

A single large flat coarse ware sherd with a central, manmade depression, not pierced (**16/28**, Fig. 16.4: upper right), is more likely to have served another purpose.

PYRAMIDAL LOOMWEIGHTS, SMALL TO MEDIUM (AND MISCELLANEOUS)
(SIZE CATEGORY, CA. 3–4 X 3–4 CM, BASE DIMENSIONS; 5–7 CM, HEIGHT).

16/24. (MEΘ 479 [ME 1160]) Small Pyramidal Loomweight Fig. 16.4
#274/032054 [7]. Earliest phase (late 8th–early 7th century B.C.). 09-08-2004.
H. 0.046; L. x W. (base) 0.030 x 0.031; L. x W. (top) 0.013 x 0.014; Diam. (perforation) 0.006; Wt. 38 g.
Small pyramidal loomweight, rounded top; relatively large pierced horizontal hole.
Fabric: light brown (7.5YR 5/6), fine white chips; much straw temper (surface pitted).

16/25. (MEΘ 478 [ME 1022]) Small Pyramidal Loomweight Fig. 16.4
#274/032048 [5]. Earliest phase (late 8th–early 7th century B.C.). 15-07-2004.
H. 0.044; L. x W. (base) 0.036–0.037; L. x W. (top) 0.016 x 0.018; Diam. (perforation) 0.005; Wt. 47 g.
Small pyramidal loomweight, horizontally pierced at an angle.
Fabric: semicoarse, fine straw temper (surface pitted); light to dark brown (7.5YR 5/4).

16/26. (ΜΕΘ 482 [ME 1500]) Small Pyramidal Loomweight Fig. 16.4
#274/032073 [7]. Earliest phase (late 8th–early 7th century B.C.). 23-09-2004.
P.H. 0.041; L. x W. (base) 0.032 x 0.032; L. x W. (top, at break) 0.014 x 0.015; Diam. (perforations) 0.004; Wt. 42 g (incomplete).
Small pyramidal loomweight, pierced horizontally (twice). The second perforation (drilled after firing?), below the first one (pierced before firing), implies break at first hole (placed too high?), and object re-pierced for continued use as weight.
Fine light brown fabric (7.5YR 5/3), mica; surface darker brown (encrusted, with water-laid deposits).

16/27. (ΜΕΘ 96 [ME 351]) Large Discoid Loomweight Fig. 16.4
#274/032015 [4]. Mixed level (transitional and occupation phases). 08-08-2003.
Diam. 0.090; H. 0.045; Diam. (central hole) 0.015–0.019; Wt. (incomplete) 316 g.
Large discoid ("doughnut") loomweight, badly chipped on one side.
Coarse brick-red fabric (5YR 5/6), heavy straw temper; very worn underside.

16/28. (ΜΕΘ 2794 [ME 3544]) Ceramic Refractory Plate Fr Fig. 16.4
#274/032090 [10]. Earliest phase (late 8th–early 7th century B.C.). 08-05-2007.
L. x W. 0.080 x 0.060 square; Th. 0.020; Wt. 157.3 g.
Large flat rounded coarse ware sherd (pithos wall?) with central hollow (shallow depression) made in exterior wall. Reused (possibly as a metalworking plate? Chapter 14, Figs. 14.5–14.8).
Heavy coarse fabric, white and dark pebbles and chips visible at surface; dark core, surface fired dark gray-brown (10YR 4/1), now cracked.

16/29. (ΜΕΘ 125 [ME 67]) Pyramidal Loomweight Fig. 16.4
#274/022003 [2]. Occupation phase. 03-06-2003.
H. 0.061; L. X W. (base) 0.042 x 0.043; L. x W. (top) 0.020 x 0.023; Diam. (perforation) 0.006; Wt. 111 g.
Pyramidal loomweight, horizontally pierced at angle; uneven profile, faces not smooth.
Fine red clay, white chips, mica; fired dark red (5YR 5/6) with brown, black patches.

16/30. (ΜΕΘ 145 [ME 93]) Pyramidal Loomweight Fig. 16.4
#274/022007 [5]. Occupation phase. 06-06-2003.
H. 0.068; L. x W. (base) 0.039 x 0.041; L. x W. (top) 0.017 x 0.017; Wt. 120.3 g.
Pyramidal loomweight, horizontally pierced; off-center vertical axis.
Fine dark clay (dense black fabric), 10YR 3/1; fine white pebbles, chips, mica.

16/31. (ΜΕΘ 160 [ME 512]) Pyramidal Loomweight Fig. 16.4
#274/032027 [4]. Earliest phase (late 8th–early 7th century B.C.). 07-10-2003.
H. 0.067; L. x W. (base) 0.040 x 0.040; top tapers to small point; Diam. (perforation) 0.005; Wt. 83 g.
Pyramidal loomweight; string wear above suspension hole on both faces.
Fabric fine, light red (dark surface patches), 7.5YR 5/6; much straw temper (hollows).

16/32. (ΜΕΘ 146 [ME 269]) Pyramidal Loomweight Fig. 16.4
#274/032003 [2]. Occupation phase. 24-07-2003.
H. 0.065; L. x W. (base) 0.029 x 0.031; Diam. (perforation) 0.004; Wt. 67 g.
Pyramidal loomweight, horizontally pierced; worn, chipped at lower edge.
Semi-coarse fabric, large white pebbles, chips; light brown (10YR 6/3) with dark surface patches.

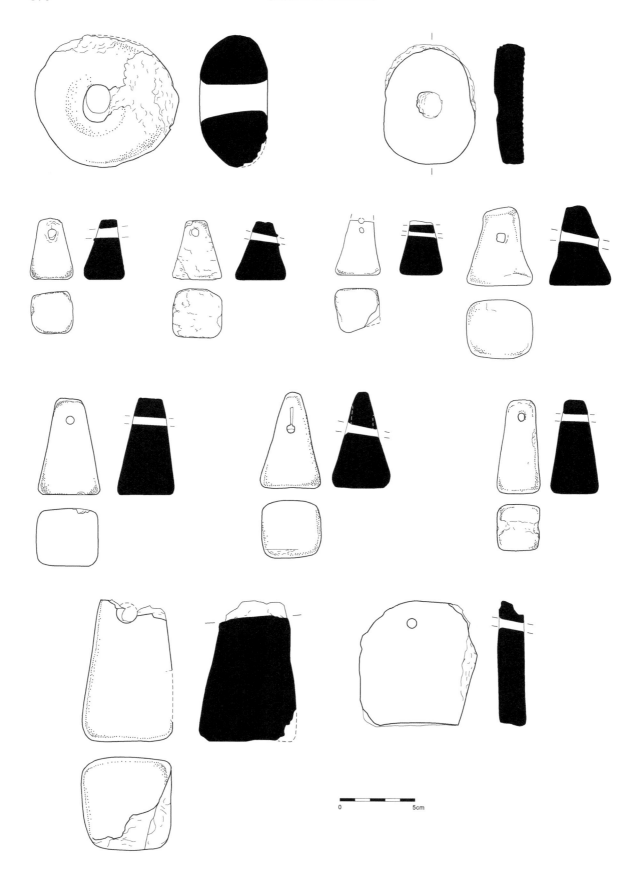

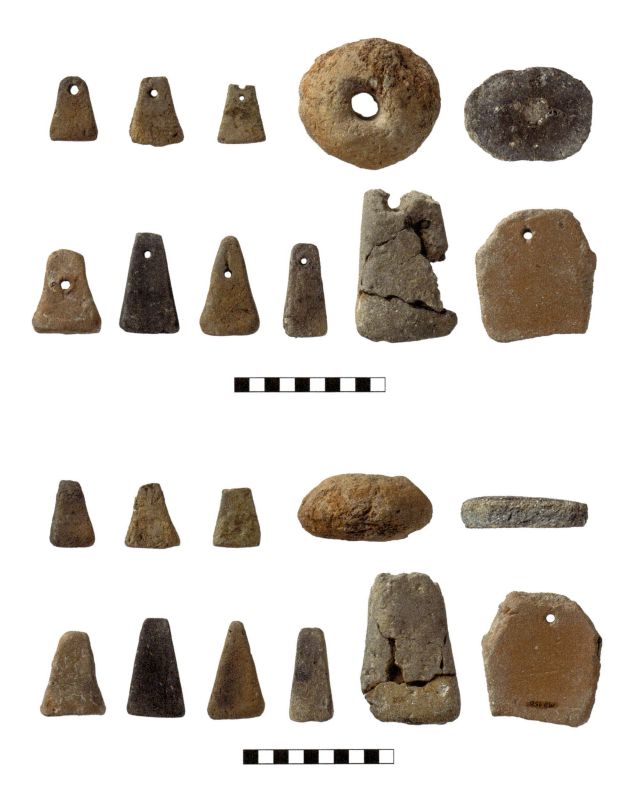

FIGURE 16.4. Pyramidal and large loomweights (and miscellaneous) from the Hypogeion. a) drawings: top row, left to right: **16/27** (ΜΕΘ 96), **16/28** (ΜΕΘ 2794); second row: **16/24** (ΜΕΘ 479), **16/25** (ΜΕΘ 478), **16/26** (ΜΕΘ 482), **16/29** (ΜΕΘ 125); third row: **16/30** (ΜΕΘ 145), **16/31** (ΜΕΘ 160), **16/32** (ΜΕΘ 146); bottom row: **16/33** (ΜΕΘ 1961), **16/34** (ΜΕΘ 158); b) photos (two views, similarly arranged): top row: **16/24**, **16/25**, **16/26**, **16/27**, **16/28** (the latter unpierced, possible refractory plate); bottom row: **16/29**, **16/30**, **16/31**, **16/32**, **16/33**, **16/34**. Drawings A. Hooton, photos J. Vanderpool

LOOMWEIGHTS: LARGE SIZE, IRREGULAR SHAPE, ETC.

16/33. (ΜΕΘ 1961 [ME 209 + ME 3950]) Pyramidal Loomweight　　　　　　　　　　　　　Fig. 16.4
#274/022023 [7], intermediate level, 08-07-2003 + #274/032 (backfill). 05-05-2004.
P.H. 0.090–0.100; L. x W. (base) 0.050 x 0.060; Diam. (perforation) 0.008; Wt. 230.9 g.
Pyramidal loomweight, several joining frr. Broken at perforation, as if top above could not sustain large weight.
Fine, dense, hard fired clay; dark red core (5YR 4/6), surface dull gray-brown (5YR 4/1).

16/34. (ΜΕΘ 158 [ME 169]) Large Pierced Sherd　　　　　　　　　　　　　　　　　　　Fig. 16.4
#274/022014 [6]. Occupation phase. 25-06-2003.
L. x W. x Th. 0.085 x 0.085 x 0.018; Wt. 177.5 g.
Large flat sherd, horizontal drill hole at one end (= top).
Semi-coarse fabric, fine white grit and mica, dark chips, red sandy surface; 5YR 5/4.

SPOOLS (FIG. 16.5)

A less frequent find in the Iron Age, common as a small cylinder in the Early Bronze Age, a more elegant profile in the Middle Bronze Age, and a solid shape in the Late Bronze Age,[8] is a type of clay cylinder with sides flaring at both ends to broad flat terminals, often roughly made and highly variable in size, profile, and perforation. They resemble modern spools for winding thread closely enough to have attracted this name (also called "bobbin" or "waisted weight"); some are pierced horizontally through the central stem (**16/35**: to secure thread wound around the center from a knot fixed through the hole?), or vertically (**16/36**), to be suspended for use as spindlewhorls (if small) or as loomweights, in the case of heavier ones.[9] About 15 examples were inventoried during the excavation of the Hypogeion, of which six are illustrated here. Also common since the post-palatial Late Bronze Age is the spool-shaped, thickened weight (**16/40**), which has been associated with a change to woollier sheep and heavier garments.[10]

16/35. (ΜΕΘ 40 [ME 278]) Clay Spool (Horizontally Pierced)　　　　　　　　　　　　　Fig. 16.5
#274/032005 [3]. Occupation phase. 25-07-2003.
L./H. 0.070; Diam. (at both ends) 0.035–0.042; Diam. (center) 0.023; Diam. (perforation) 0.004; Wt. 54.5 g.
Spool, with flattened ends; perforated horizontally at midpoint; one end heavily worn.
Fine fabric, smoothed, once red (2.5YR 5/6), burnished; very worn; worn smooth.

16/36. (ΜΕΘ 44 [ME 226]) Clay Spool (Vertically Pierced)　　　　　　　　　　　　　　Fig. 16.5
#274/022 (S balk trim). 14-07-2003.
L./H. 0.032; Diam. (end, at top) 0.025; Diam. (end, at base) 0.030; Diam. (central stem) 0.021–0.022; Wt. 17.4 g.
Short spool, asymmetrical (different end diameters), pierced vertically, chipped at ends.
Fine red fabric with mica, quartz, white grit (2.5YR 5/6); brown to black surface; very worn.

16/37. (ΜΕΘ 1236 [ME 3019]) Clay Spool　　　　　　　　　　　　　　　　　　　　　　Fig. 16.5
#274/022058 [12]. Earliest phase (late 8th–early 7th century B.C.). 22-08-2006.
L./H. 0.065; Diam. (ends) 0.046; Diam. (midpoint) 0.031; Wt. 74.5 g.
Coarse heavy spool.
Fabric dark gray-brown (2.5Y 4/3), much white grit, mica; dark surface, encrusted (water damage?).

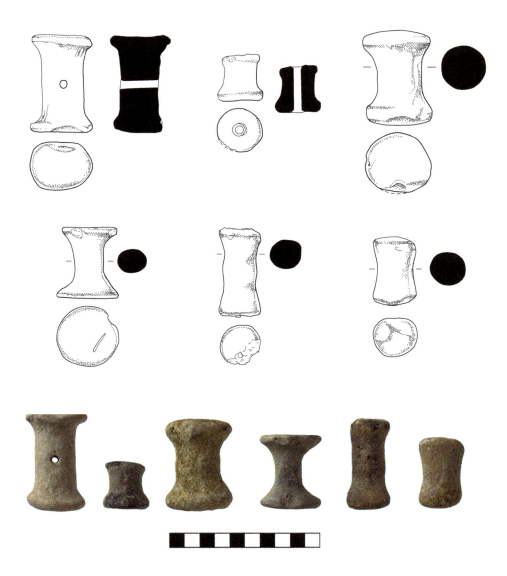

FIGURE 16.5. Clay "spools" from the Hypogeion. a) drawings: top row, left to right: **16/35** (MEΘ 40), **16/36** (MEΘ 44), **16/37** (MEΘ 1236); bottom row: **16/38** (MEΘ 1237), **16/39** (MEΘ 661), **16/40** (MEΘ 1238). b) photos: left to right: **16/35**, **16/36**, **16/37**, **16/38**, **16/39**, **16/40**. Drawings A. Hooton, photos J. Vanderpool

16/38. (MEΘ 1237 [ME 3050]) Clay Spool   Fig. 16.5

#274/022060 [12]. Earliest phase (late 8th–early 7th century B.C.). 29-08-2006.

L./H. 0.050; Diam. (midpoint) 0.018; Diam. (at both ends) 0.037–0.039 and 0.041–0.042; Wt. 33.9 g.

Medium-sized spool, broad flat ends and narrow stem; surface smooth (worn), chipped.

Fine light-brown fabric (10YR 5/3), fine white grit, chips, and mica.

16/39. (MEΘ 661 [ME 1630]) Clay Spool   Fig. 16.5

#274/032052-60 (backfill). 08-12-2004.

L./H. 0.061; Diam. (at ends) 0.027–0.029; Diam. (midpoint) 0.022; Wt. 26.6 g.

Long spool in form of solid cylinder thickened slightly at ends and midpoint (resembling pestle?). Surface rough, much worn, chipped at one end; yellowish (10YR 6/4).

Coarse dark gray fabric (10YR 4/3), heavy quartz and stone grit, pebbles, many hollows.

16/40. (ΜΕΘ 1238 [ME 3092]) Clay Spool   Fig. 16.5
#274/022061 [13]. Earliest phase (late 8th–early 7th century B.C.). 05-09-2006.
L./H. 0.048; Diam. (at ends) 0.029; Diam. (midpoint) 0.023; Wt. 28.3 g.
Short heavy spool, domed ends; very worn (water-worn?) on all surfaces.
Fabric: light red core (5YR 5/6), surface dark gray (5YR 5/1).

HEMISPHERICAL ("LOAF"-SHAPED) WEIGHTS (FIG. 16.6)

A final group of weights or whorls is hemispherical in profile, round to oval in plan, with flat underside, shaped like a "loaf," and bisected vertically at midpoint by a deep groove, rounded in section, to secure string or thread (Fig. 16.6). This type is first found in the Middle Bronze Age in northern Greece, but also at Toumba Thessalonikis and Sindos in the early first millennium.[11] At Methone, examples are found since the earliest phase of the Hypogeion, co-present with other weights and whorls, and presumably used in similar fashion.

16/41. ΜΕΘ 1243 (ME 3355)   Fig. 16.6
#274/022072 [15]. 04-12-2006.
L. 0.042; W. 0.0375; H. 0.021; Diam (groove) 0.025; Wt. 38.3 g.
Irregular oval shape, deep off-center groove, underside has uneven surface.
Fine clay, dark gray core with dull brown surface (7.5YR 6/3)

16/42. ΜΕΘ 1242 (ME 3349)   Fig. 16.6
#274/022072 [15]. 04-12-2006.
L. 0.0442; W. 0.033; H. 0.0175; Diam. (groove) 0.027; Wt. 30.0 g.
Oval shape, groove slightly off-center.
Dark red clay (2.5YR 5/6).

16/43. ΜΕΘ 1244 (ME 3348)   Fig. 16.6
#274/032085 [10]. 01-11-2006.
L. 0.045; W. 0.038; H. 0.016; Diam (groove) 0.029; Wt. 26.6 g.
Round shape, shallow dome, deep groove; cracked and damaged at one edge.
Fine red clay (5YR 5/6), mica sparkles.

16/44. ΜΕΘ 2783 (ME 3647)   Fig. 16.6
#274/032086 [9]. 22-11-2006.
L. 0.032; W. 0.027; H. 0.016; Diam. (groove) 0.02; Wt. 15.4 g.
Small rounded oval shape, deep central groove.
Fine red clay (core: 2.5YR 4/6); surface encrusted (water deposits?).

16/45. ΜΕΘ 1960 (ME 3548). Broken in half at groove.   Fig. 16.6
#274/022074 [15]. 14-12-2006.
P.L. 0.019; W. 0.026; H. 0.0145; Diam. (groove) 0.016; Wt. 7.9 g.
Small oval shape, broken vertically at midpoint of groove.
Fine light red clay (5YR 6/4), smooth surface; worn.

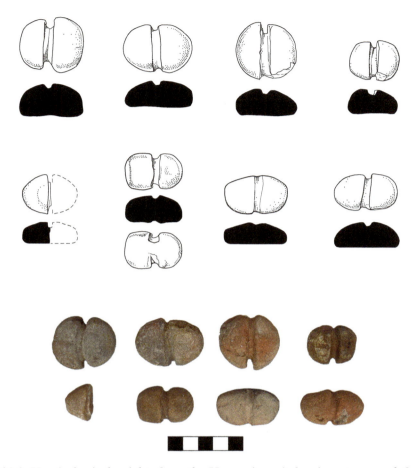

FIGURE 16.6. Hemispherical weights from the Hypogeion: a) drawings, top row, left to right: **16/41** (ΜΕΘ 1243), **16/42** (ΜΕΘ 1242), **16/43** (ΜΕΘ 1244), **16/44** (ΜΕΘ 2783); bottom row: **16/45** (ΜΕΘ 1960), **16/46** (ΜΕΘ 497), **16/47** (ΜΕΘ 498), **16/48** (ΜΕΘ 499); b) photos, top row, left to right: **16/41**, **16/42**, **16/43**, **16/44**; bottom row: **16/45**, **16/46**, **16/47**, **16/48**. Drawings A. Hooton, photos J. Papadopoulos and J. Vanderpool

16/46. ΜΕΘ 497 (ΜΕ 824) Fig. 16.6
#274/022045-46. 24-06-2004.
L. 0.038; W. 0.025; H 0.018; Diam. (groove) 0.019; Wt. 20.5 g.
Lengthened oval shape, deep groove with uneven underside.
Fine hard dense clay, mica sparkles; yellowish brown (10YR 5/4).

16/47. ΜΕΘ 498 (ΜΕ 857) Fig. 16.6
#274/022047 [11]. 18-06-2004.
L. 0.043; W. 0.0255; H. 0.014; Diam. (groove) 0.02; Wt. 18.0 g.
Long oval shape, shallow groove; flat underside.
Fine clay, light brown (10YR 6/3), dark patches on edges, underside. Worn smooth.

16/48. ΜΕΘ 499 (ΜΕ 828) Fig. 16.6
#274/032044 [5]. 25-06-2004.
L. 0.042; W. 0.025; H. 0.016; Diam. (groove) 0.02; Wt. 18.2 g.
Long oval shape (amygdaloid), shallow groove, flat underside.
Fine red clay (firing hollows: straw temper?), mica sparkles; 5YR 5/6.

NOTES

1 On their status as beads, buttons, or ornaments, see Mauel 2009, pp. 99–101; Gimatzidis 2010, p. 296, n. 1863; cf. Iakovidis 1977.

2 Heurtley 1939, p. 213, fig. 83:l–o; p. 231, fig. 104:a–l; Hochstetter 1987, pp. 83–86, figs. 14–15, pls. 18, 20–21; Mauel 2012, p. 140, pl. XXXV for their chronological distribution at Kastanas.

3 Carington Smith 1975; Andersson Strand and Nosch 2015, chapter 4, for experimental tests.

4 Pierced sherds ("sherd whorls": Carington Smith 1975, *passim*), see Sindos (Gimatzidis 2010, p. 297, pl. 126h) and Kastanas (Hochstetter 1984, pp. 86–88; Mauel 2009, pp. 103–106).

5 Vardaroftsa: Heurtley 1939, pp. 213, fig. 83:t; p. 231, fig. 104:q–s; Kastanas (EIA): Mauel 2009, pp. 106–115.

6 Popham and Sackett 1980, pp. 82–83, pl. 64:f, g, h; Mauel 2009, p. 116 (one example at Kastanas). This type was also found on the West Hill at Methone during the 2014–2017 excavations, in Trenches 2 (Pit 46) and 4.

7 Lefkandi: Evely 2006, pp. 297–299, fig. 5.17, 2–3; Torone: Papadopoulos 1989.

8 Pavúk 2012; Gimatzidis 2010, p. 296, fig. 126, k; Midea: Sabatini 2016, pp. 222, 236, Type 8, "concave cylindrical": SW34, pl. 1G; LBA Lerna: Wiencke 1998, p. 163, fig. 23; MO21 (pierced vertically); *Tiryns XVI*, pl. 5, #2105, 1519; 1672?; pl. 90, figs. 5–7; Rahmstorf 2003, 2005; Siennicka and Ulinowska 2016. Cf. the thicker "reels" common at LH IIIC Lefkandi: Evely 2006, pp. 296–297, figs. 5.15–16. Earlier examples (Final Neolithic to Early Bronze Age) at Thasos: Vakirtzi, Koukouli-Chrysanthaki, and Papadopoulos 2014, p. 47, n. 15; Sitagroi (Elster 2003c, pp. 239–240).

9 Gimatzidis and Jung 2008, p. 214, fig. 8, for 10 "spools" from a floor dated to the PG/SubPG period, at Kastro Neokaisareia, probably used as weights; cf. Early Iron Age Kastanas (Schicht 11, Protogeometric): Mauel 2009, pp. 116–119, fig. 41, and Olofsson, Andersson Strand, and Nosch 2015, pp. 92–96, for a reconstruction of their use as loomweights (possibly for tablet weaving or *Brettchenweberei*: Elster 2003c, pp. 239–240; Di Fraia 2017), as suggested by context (often found with other types of loomweights) and experimentation.

10 *Tiryns* XVI, pp. 59–73, pls. 23–32; Rahmstorf et al. 2015, pp. 275–276.

11 Agios Mamas: Heurtley 1939, p. 213, fig. 83q, r; Becker and Kroll 2008, pp. 131–133, fig. 58 ("Knöpfe": fishnet weights?): Torone: Cambitoglou and Papadopoulos 1991, p. 162, pl. 25:1; Toumba Thessalonikis: Anagnostou et al. 1990, pp. 283, 287, fig. 8 (16 examples found on floor near oven in pre-SubPG building); Soueref 1990, p. 313, fig. 21; Sindos: Gimatzidis 2010, p. 297, pl. 106, 126j.

17

CUT SHERD DISKS FROM THE HYPOGEION

John K. Papadopoulos

INTRODUCTION

A common find in the Hypogeion, as in various other areas of Early Iron Age and Archaic date on the East and West Hills at Methone, were cut sherd disks. A selected representative sample of 41 examples from the late 8th and early 7th centuries B.C. Hypogeion is presented below. I do not include cut disk sherds that have been pierced or partially pierced, as these most probably served a different function that necessitated a hole or a partially drilled hole for purchase (see Chapter 16). Immediately noteworthy about the cut sherd disks from Methone is their variety in terms of size—the largest has a diameter of 0.090 m, the smallest 0.021 m, weighing from 125 g to a mere 1.5 g—and the different types of vessels from which they were cut. Of the 41 catalogued pieces, seven derive from wheelmade open vessels (**17/6**, **17/7**, **17/10**, **17/26**, **17/29**, **17/37**, **17/39**);[1] 17 are sherds from wheelmade closed vessels (**17/1**, **17/8**, **17/11**, **17/12**, **17/14**, **17/16**, **17/17**, **17/20**, **17/21**, **17/23**, **17/30**, **17/31**, **17/32**, **17/34**, **17/35**, **17/36**, **17/40**), and of these, four are clearly from transport amphoras, including one Milesian (**17/11**), one north Aegean (**17/14**), one Chian (**17/31**), and one from another imported amphora (**17/34**).[2] Sherd disks cut from handmade vessels, many of them from prehistoric vessel forms predating the Hypogeion, were equally common: eight derive from handmade closed vessels (**17/2**, **17/3**, **17/9**, **17/15**, **17/18**, **17/19**, **17/22**, **17/27**), three from open vessels (**17/5**, **17/25**, **17/28**), some finely burnished, three others are from cooking ware pots (**17/13**, **17/33**, and perhaps also **17/38**); three more are from unidentified handmade shapes (**17/4**, **17/24**, **17/41**). The fact that several of the handmade examples were cut from pottery fragments that were lying around for some time, perhaps even centuries, before they were picked up and fashioned into their current form, is significant, as it is a pattern also seen among the Early Iron Age contexts in the Athenian Agora.[3]

Much has been written about small disks or roundels of clay fashioned from sherds of pottery by chipping and smoothing around the edges.[4] They are common occurrences not only in the Hypogeion at Methone, but in various types of Early Iron Age deposits in the area of the Classical Athenian Agora, and especially common in many of the Late Geometric and Early Archaic wells in Athens.[5] In discussing the possible function of the disks, Eva Brann wrote:

> What they were used for, whether for counters, pucks, covers or plugs, is uncertain. Those with holes . . . may have had a string to serve as the handle of a lid. Remains of plugs have actually

been found in Mycenaean stirrup jars . . . but the 7th century has no common round-mouthed, narrow-necked shape. Some, most likely, were game-counters. Several games requiring sherd disks were played in the streets and public places of Athens (cf. Pauly-Wissowa, *R.E.*, "Spiele") and the Agora even possesses a die of the period (Agora MC 84).[6]

Evelyn Smithson believed that such disks, pierced and unpierced, were common in domestic deposits from earliest times, and that "they were probably stoppers."[7] Of these various functions, however, that of gaming pieces (*pessoi*) has been largely singled out by philologists.[8] Although such disks, cut from fragments of decorated and undecorated pots, are very common in the various well and other deposits in the area of the Athenian Agora, they are exceedingly rare in tombs.[9] In his discussion of a pierced disk from a Late Geometric tomb (Grave XVII-23), Rodney Young wrote:

> The disk from Grave XVII might serve conveniently as a lid for small pots like the amphoriskos XVII-19, or the jars XVII-20–21. The string passed through the holes could serve either for tying it onto the rim, or as a loop by which it could be lifted. Such disks, placed in the mouth of a vase containing liquid, and with clay or wax smeared around the edge, would serve admirably as watertight stoppers.[10]

The fact that disks from at least two of the Athenian Agora Early Iron Age tombs were pierced renders Young's interpretation at least possible, but other contexts in Athens and Attica suggest a very different function for pierced disks. The most important of these is the "Submycenaean" tomb 10 south of the Athenian Acropolis, in the Koukaki district, that contained 35 pierced disks of various sizes. In discussing these, the excavator, Eugenia Tsalkou, noted that they cannot have served as stoppers as there was no pottery in the tomb with which they could be associated; she stressed that we should never assume a single function for such disks, and went on to suggest that they may have served as gaming pieces, though noted that this was only a hypothetical possibility that could not be proved.[11]

As for the stopper function in the Late Bronze Age, this was posited by Alan Wace in dealing with over 80 disks chipped from broken pottery or from stone in a Late Bronze Age storeroom at Mycenae, found together with stirrup jars and pithoi. In discussing these, Wace writes: "Discs like this are not uncommonly found in small numbers on Mycenaean sites, and are usually called counters for playing games. It is hard, however, to see, what game could be played with over eighty counters, and it is not easy to see why they should be in a storeroom with stirrup jars and pithoi. A more probable explanation is that they served as covers for the tops of jars or for spouts of stirrup jars."[12] Although the Bronze Age has seen no shortage of closed vessels stopped with cut sherd disks and other types of stoppers, I do not know of any such disks used as stoppers on closed Early Iron Age vessel forms.

As we have seen, much recent scholarship has become fixated on seeing such disks as gaming pieces (*pessoi*),[13] or as tallies, tokens, or counters.[14] Although the *pessoi* interpretation is possible in the case of some, if not many, of the sherds that were not pierced, it seems less likely that the pierced examples served such a function, and it remains difficult to see *all* these disks, whether in Greece, Africa, or Mesopotamia, as tallies, tokens or counters, especially since so few are clearly linked with standard weights, sizes, or units of measurement.[15] There are, to be sure, exceptions, such as the many hand-shaped clay "counters" (of discoid and conical/pyramidal shape) from the Temple Complex at Mycenae, but these are clearly formed by hand from unbaked clay and fired, not cut from larger fragments of pottery.[16] An alternative explanation, which has not found universal favor, but one that is firmly based on context, sees some of the unpierced examples cut from pottery sherds deriving from Athenian domestic refuse contexts as convenient wipes, that is, as Early Iron Age "toilet paper."[17]

Whatever their function—and it would be wrong to insist on one interpretation for all such objects—pierced and unpierced disks cut from vases are known, in addition to the numerous non-funerary contexts from Methone and the area of the Athenian Agora, from the Neolithic settlement at Knossos,[18] from the Early Bronze Age "Casa a Sud della Rampa" at Phaistos,[19] as well as the Geometric quarter west of the Minoan palace at Phaistos,[20] from various sacrificial and domestic deposits at Eretria,[21] from Lefkandi, both in the Toumba Building and in the Xeropolis settlement,[22] from Late Bronze and Early Iron Age settlement mounds in Macedonia,[23] and there are related examples from numerous Near Eastern contexts.[24] In contrast, funerary contexts that have yielded such disks are exceedingly rare. There is a solitary example from Tomb 36 in the Toumba cemetery at Lefkandi, referred to as a "counter";[25] another example was found in Palia Perivolia Tomb 36;[26] and there is yet another from Grave 1963:3 at Elis.[27] Indeed, one of the few "sets" of such objects from an Early Iron Age burial known to me comes from Tomb 11 at Eretria, where the disks, normally referred to as "jetons" at Eretria, have been interpreted by one commentator as gaming pieces, and their context is such that it is difficult to see them as anything but gaming pieces.[28]

CATALOGUE AND CONTEXT

Contextually, cut sherd disks were found throughout the fill of the Hypogeion, including the later levels (fill B and C) (Fig. 17.1). The vast majority, however, were found in the original Phases I–III fill of the Hypogeion (collectively fill A), with the lion's share in Phases I and II, the deposition of which can be assigned to the late 8th and very early 7th century B.C. Only two pieces were found in Phase III or in the mixed levels at the interface of Phase III and the overlying fill B. The majority of the remainder, no more than ten disks, were encountered in fill B. Consequently, virtually none of the cut sherd disks from the Hypogeion at Methone are demonstrably later than the 7th century B.C.

Dimensions given are the maximum. Unless otherwise noted, the sherds are preserved as single fragments and cut from locally made, north Aegean pottery. In addition to the pieces catalogued below, there are 44 whole or fragmentary additional examples from the Hypogeion.

17/1. ΜΕΘ 346 (ΜΕ 779) Figs. 17.2–17.3
East Hill #274/022045 [11]. 14/6/2004.
Diam. 0.090; Th. 0.006–0.007; Wt. 69.2 g.
WM painted closed vessel.

17/2. ΜΕΘ 348 (ΜΕ 1593) Figs. 17.2–17.3
East Hill #274/022045 [11]. 11/6/2004.
Diam. 0.079; Th. 0.012; Wt. 70.8 g.
Base fr, HM closed vessel; prehistoric.

17/3. ΜΕΘ 354 (ΜΕ 1594) Figs. 17.2–17.3
East Hill #274/022046 [11]. 17/6/2004.
Diam. 0.075; Th. 0.015; Wt. 76.5 g.
HM coarse closed vessel; prehistoric.

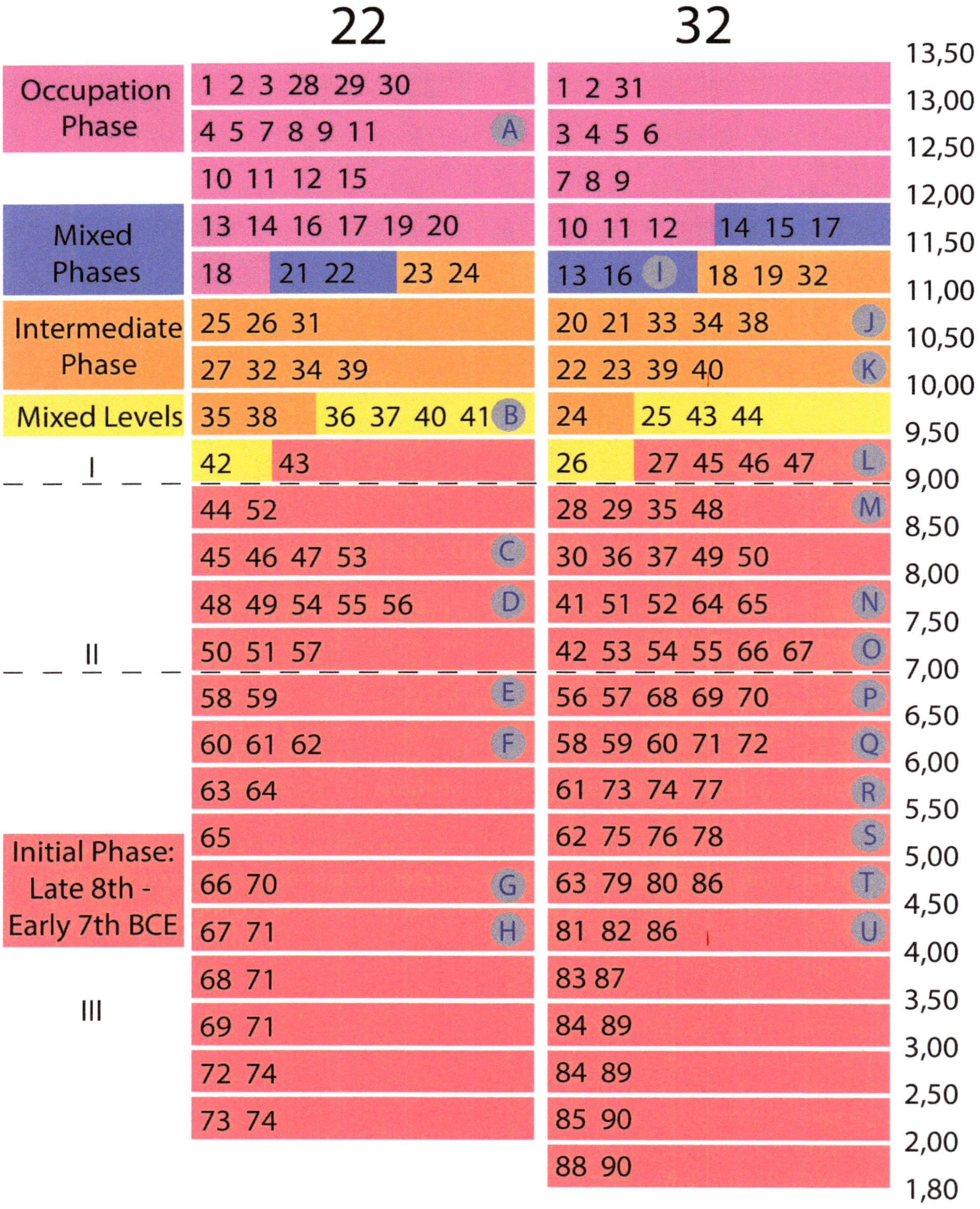

Figure 17.1. The context of the catalogued cut sherd disks from the Hypogeion at Methone. A) **17/4, 17/10, 17/18, 17/19, 17/25, 17/32**; B) **17/27**; C) **17/1, 17/2, 17/3, 17/7, 17/30, 17/34**; D) **17/8**; E) **17/37**; F) **17/12, 17/24, 17/41**; G) **17/26**; H) **17/9**; I) **17/31**; J) **17/6, 17/40**; K) **17/5**; L) **17/16**; M) **17/15, 17/39**; N) **17/36, 17/38**; O) **17/35**; P) **17/14, 17/22**; Q) **17/23**; R) **17/11, 17/21**; S) **17/20**; T) **17/29**; U) **17/13, 17/33**

Prepared by Adam DiBattista

17/4. ΜΕΘ 114 (ME 98)   Figs. 17.2–17.3
East Hill #274/022008 [5]. 6/6/2003.
Diam. 0.077; Th. 0.018; Wt. 125.0 g.
Large HM coarse vessel.

17/5. ΜΕΘ 362 (ME 651)   Figs. 17.2–17.3
East Hill #274/032040 [5]. 19/4/2004.
Diam. 0.062; Th. 0.010; Wt. 34.5 g.
HM burnished open vessel; prehistoric.

17/6. ΜΕΘ 360 (ME 1613)   Figs. 17.2–17.3
East Hill #274/032038 [5]. 15/4/2004.
Diam. 0.049–0.050; Th. 0.007; Wt. 15.6 g.
Three joining frr WM painted open vessel, probably skyphos; Euboian.

17/7. ΜΕΘ 352 (ME 861)   Figs. 17.2–17.3
East Hill #274/022047 [11]. 18/6/2004.
Diam. 0.058; Th. 0.007; Wt. 27.7 g.
WM painted Early Iron Age open vessel, krater or large skyphos; imported.

17/8. ΜΕΘ 358 (ME 1284)   Figs. 17.2–17.3
East Hill #274/022056 [12]. 31/8/2004.
Diam. 0.049; Th. 0.007; Wt. 20.8 g.
Large WM closed vessel.

17/9. ΜΕΘ 1224 (ME 3475)   Figs. 17.2–17.3
East Hill #274/022067 [15]. 23/10/2006.
Diam. 0.059; Th. 0.012; Wt. 37.5 g.
Large HM closed vessel.

17/10. ΜΕΘ 105 (ME 80)   Figs. 17.2–17.3
East Hill #274/022005 [3]. 4/6/2003.
Diam. 0.059; Th. 0.008; Wt. 29.1 g.
WM painted open vessel; perhaps Mycenaean?

17/11. ΜΕΘ 385 (ME 1498)   Figs. 17.2–17.3
East Hill #274/032073 [7]. 23/9/2004.
Diam. 0.065; Th. 0.009; Wt. 45.1 g.
Large WM painted closed vessel; Milesian amphora.

17/12. ΜΕΘ 1218 (ME 3403)   Figs. 17.2–17.3
East Hill #274/022060 [12]. 29/8/2006.
Diam. 0.052; Th. 0.005–0.006; Wt. 14.9 g.
WM painted closed vessel of undetermined type.

17/13. ΜΕΘ 1230 (ME 3500)   Figs. 17.2–17.3
East Hill #274/032086 [9]. 22/9/2006.

Diam. 0.061–0.062; Th. 0.007; Wt. 30.5 g.
HM cooking ware.

17/14. ΜΕΘ 372 (ΜΕ 1209)   Figs. 17.2–17.3
East Hill #274/032057 [7]. 12/8/2004.
Diam. 0.056; Th. 0.015; Wt. 49.6 g.
Large WM painted closed vessel; north Aegean amphora.

17/15. ΜΕΘ 367 (ΜΕ 1010)   Figs. 17.2–17.3
East Hill #274/032048 [5]. 15/7/2004.
Diam. 0.043–0.044; Th. 0.007; Wt. 16.1 g.
HM closed vessel, painted.

17/16. ΜΕΘ 366 (ΜΕ 841)   Figs. 17.2–17.3
East Hill #274/032045 [5]. 29/6/2004.
Diam. 0.042; Th. 0.007; Wt. 13.8 g.
WM closed vessel.

17/17. ΜΕΘ 361 (ΜΕ 648)   Figs. 17.2–17.3
East Hill #274/0320439 [5]. 16/4/2004.
Diam. 0.045; Th. 0.008–0.009; Wt. 18.0 g.
WM closed vessel.

17/18. ΜΕΘ 106 (ΜΕ 114)   Figs. 17.2–17.3
East Hill #274/022009 [5]. 10/6/2003.
Diam. 0.055; Th. 0.007–0.008; Wt. 21.9 g.
HM burnished closed vessel; prehistoric.

17/19. ΜΕΘ 112 (ΜΕ 99)   Figs. 17.2–17.3
East Hill #274/022008 [5]. 6/6/2003.
Diam. 0.041; Th. 0.012; Wt. 21.7 g.
HM burnished closed vessel; prehistoric.

17/20. ΜΕΘ 386 (ΜΕ 1514)   Figs. 17.2–17.3
East Hill #274/032075 [7]. 27/9/2004.
Diam. 0.047; Th. 0.007; Wt. 18.1 g.
Large WM painted closed vessel.

17/21. ΜΕΘ 377 (ΜΕ 1253)   Figs. 17.2–17.3
East Hill #274/032061 [7]. 20/8/2004.
Diam. 0.043; Th. 0.006; Wt. 12.2 g.
WM closed vessel.

17/22. ΜΕΘ 371 (ΜΕ 1197)   Figs. 17.2–17.3
East Hill #274/032057 [7]. 12/8/2004.
Diam. 0.040; Th. 0.008–0.009; Wt. 12.5 g.
HM burnished closed vessel; prehistoric.

17/23. ΜΕΘ 375 (ΜΕ 1243)   Figs. 17.2–17.3
 East Hill #274/032060 [7]. 19/8/2004.
 Diam. 0.039; Th. 0.006; Wt. 10.4 g.
 WM painted closed vessel; imported.

17/24. ΜΕΘ 1217 (ΜΕ 3077)   Figs. 17.2–17.3
 East Hill #274/022060 [12]. 29/8/2006.
 Diam. 0.052; Th. 0.006; Wt. 19.2 g.
 HM burnished vessel (unclear whether open or closed); prehistoric.

17/25. ΜΕΘ 2798 (ΜΕ 4281)   Figs. 17.2–17.3
 East Hill #274/022009 [5]. 10/6/2003.
 Diam. 0.044; Th. 0.008; Wt. 17.4 g.
 HM burnished open vessel; prehistoric.

17/26. ΜΕΘ 1221 (ΜΕ 3393)   Figs. 17.2–17.3
 East Hill #274/022066 [14]. 13/10/2006.
 Diam. 0.043; Th. 0.007; Wt. 12.8 g.
 WM painted open vessel, probably skyphos.

17/27. ΜΕΘ 433 (ΜΕ 709)   Figs. 17.2–17.3
 East Hill #274/022041 [10]. 21/5/2004.
 Diam. 0.037; Th. 0.004; Wt. 6.4 g.
 WM painted closed vessel, probably hydria.

17/28. ΜΕΘ 432 (ΜΕ 695)   Figs. 17.2–17.3
 East Hill #274/022 Area near Wall 5. 13/5/2004.
 Diam. 0.038; Th. 0.005; Wt. 8.4 g.
 HM burnished open vessel; prehistoric.

17/29. ΜΕΘ 1229 (ΜΕ 3407)   Figs. 17.2–17.3
 East Hill #274/032080 [9]. 6/10/2006.
 Diam. 0.034; Th. 0.004; Wt. 5.0 g.
 Two joining frr, WM open vessel.

17/30. ΜΕΘ 355 (ΜΕ 1598)   Figs. 17.2–17.3
 East Hill #274/022047 [11]. 18/6/2004.
 Diam. 0.037; Th. 0.007; Wt. 11.0 g.
 WM closed vessel.

17/31. ΜΕΘ 1956 (ΜΕ 34)   Figs. 17.2–17.3
 East Hill #274/032013 [5]. 7/8/2003.
 Diam. 0.036; Th. 0.008; Wt. 10.7 g.
 Large WM painted closed vessel; Chian amphora.

17/32. ΜΕΘ 2797 (ΜΕ 4280)   Figs. 17.2–17.3
 East Hill #274/022007 [5]. 5–6/6/2003.

Diam. 0.034; Th. 0.008; Wt. 9.7 g.
Large WM closed vessel.

17/33. ΜΕΘ 1241 (ΜΕ 3501)   Figs. 17.2–17.3
East Hill #274/032086 [9]. 22/11/2006.
Diam. 0.033; Th. 0.003; Wt. 4.3 g.
Cooking ware sherd, very worn.

17/34. ΜΕΘ 350 (ΜΕ 799)   Figs. 17.2–17.3
East Hill #274/022046 [11]. 17/6/2004.
Diam. 0.036; Th. 0.006–0.007; Wt. 7.3 g.
Large WM painted closed vessel; imported transport amphora.

17/35 ΜΕΘ 363 (ΜΕ 1079)   Figs. 17b.2–17.3
East Hill #274/032042 [6]. 17/6/2004.
Diam. 0.030–0.031; Th. 0.005–0.006; Wt. 6.4 g.
WM painted closed vessel.

17/36. ΜΕΘ 369 (ΜΕ 1087)   Figs. 17.2–17.3
East Hill #274/032051 [7]. 2/8/2004.
Diam. 0.033–0.034; Th. 0.005; Wt. 6.2 g.
WM closed vessel.

17/37. ΜΕΘ 1216 (ΜΕ 3014)   Figs. 17.2–17.3
East Hill #274/022058 [12]. 22/6/2006.
Diam. 0.037; Th. 0.006; Wt. 8.6 g.
Large WM painted open vessel, large skyphos or krater.

17/38. ΜΕΘ 368 (ΜΕ 1086)   Figs. 17.2–17.3
East Hill #274/032051 [7]. 2/8/2004.
Diam. 0.032; Th. 0.005; Wt. 5.5 g.
Sherd very worn, perhaps cooking ware?

17/39. ΜΕΘ 1959 (ΜΕ 39)   Figs. 17.2–17.3
East Hill #274/032028 [4]. 9/10/2003.
Diam. 0.028; Th. 0.006; Wt. 3.7 g.
WM painted open vessel, skyphos; imported, probably Euboian.

17/40. ΜΕΘ 359 (ΜΕ 582)   Figs. 17.2–17.3
East Hill #274/032033 [5]. 22/3/2004.
Diam. 0.026; Th. 0.005; Wt. 3.6 g.
WM closed vessel, burnished on exterior.

17/41. ΜΕΘ 5328 (ΜΕ 3404)   Figs. 17.2–17.3
East Hill #274/022060 [12]. 28/8/2006.
Diam. 0.021; Th. 0.003; Wt. 1.5 g.
Small HM burnished vessel (unclear whether open or closed).

FIGURE 17.2. Selected cut sherd disks from the Hypogeion, obverse (the order of the disks follows the order of the catalogue, beginning at the top left, and progressing left to right).
Photo I. Coyle

FIGURE 17.3. Selected cut sherd disks from the Hypogeion, reverse (the order of the disks follows the order of the catalogue, beginning at the top left, and progressing left to right).
Photo I. Coyle

NOTES

1. Of these, two (**17/6** and **17/39**) are probably fragments of imported Euboian skyphoi, another (**17/7**) is also imported, while one (**17/10**) may even derive from a Mycenaean open vessel. I am grateful to Antonis Kotsonas and Trevor Van Damme for discussion and assistance with this chapter, and to Adam DiBattista for Figure 17.1.
2. Among the wheelmade closed vessels, not including the transport amphoras, one other piece (**17/23**) is imported. For the transport amphoras from the Hypogeion, see Kotsonas, Chapter 12; for the amphoras from the West Hill, see Kasseri, Chapter 21.
3. See discussion in *Agora* XXXVI, pp. 212–213, fig. 2.125; pp. 940–942, under T20-12 (sherd disk cut and perforated from a Protogeometric pot found in a Middle Geometric I tomb).
4. See, among others, Burr 1933, pp. 546, 603–604; Young 1939, pp. 86, 191–192, figs. 57, 142, nos. XVII 23 and C 163–173; Brann 1961, p. 342, under no. F 62; Lalonde 1968, p. 131; Smithson 1974, p. 362; most recently, D'Onofrio 2007.
5. See Papadopoulos 2002b.
6. Brann 1961, p. 342, no. F 62; with further references to *Corinth* XII, pp. 217–222.
7. Smithson 1974, p. 362, n. 41.
8. Especially by Leslie Kurke (1999a, 1999b), who has written much on Greek board games and how to play—or not play—them; for a more recent and nuanced study, see Kidd 2019. The examples most commonly illustrated from the area of the Classical Agora are those from the so-called Protoattic "votive deposit" published by Dorothy Burr (1933) and recently restudied by Laughy 2018. Not all of these, however, were "ornamented bits of old pottery," as Kurke (1999b, p. 273) maintains.
9. There is mention (but no illustration, nor any details) of seven pot fragments, each with one hole, as well as an orthogonal or squared-off sherd with three holes, in Alexandri 1977, p. 19, from a Submycenaean tomb (Grave 18) at Odos Drakou 19 in Athens. The fragments are described by Alexandri (1977, p. 19) as: "επτά θραύσματα αγγείων με μία τρύπα μέσο το καθένα και ένα ορθογωνισμένο όστρακο με τρεις τρύπες."
10. Young 1939, p. 86, Grave XVII-23.
11. Tsalkou 2020, pp. 576–578, fig. 3, where she also lists other contexts in Athens with similar pierced disks. What makes the 35 pierced disks from Koukaki tomb 3 unlikely as gaming pieces is their number, as it is difficult to imagine—as Alan Wace did (see below, n. 12)—any game played with this number of gaming pieces.
12. Wace 1953, p. 17, with pl. 11:d. Wace goes on to explain the manner in which stirrup jars were sealed with a potsherd disk, clay, and leaves; on this, see further, Dawkins 1909–1910, pp. 9–10, with pl. III. The most recent and fullest discussion of Mycenaean cut sherd disks serving as stoppers for stirrup jars is Van Damme 2019. For the large number of pierced and unpierced cut sherd disks from Bronze Age Tiryns, see *Tiryns* XVI, pp. 37–52, pls. 7–21.
13. See Kurke 1999a, 1999b.
14. Most recently D'Onofrio 2007, which offers a cross-cultural survey of such disks and related pieces, from the Mediterranean to India.
15. For a more nuanced, comprehensive, and cogent study of measurement, see the volume edited by Morley and Renfrew 2010.
16. Conveniently illustrated in D'Onofrio 2007, p. 128, pl. 10 (they are illustrated together with the scale dishes from Loupano Tomb VIII, with which the clay "counters" are not associated).
17. See Papadopoulos 2002b, with full discussion.
18. Evans 1964, pl. 58:1–2.
19. Militello 2001, p. 34, figs. 1–4, 6.

20 Cucuzza 1998, pp. 65–66, fig. 6.3 (illustrating pottery and stone disks, some pierced).

21 Pierced and unpierced disks were found in the sacrificial area north of the sanctuary of Apollo Daphnephoros at Eretria, see *Eretria* XIV, p. 69, pl. 135, nos. O 271–283 (referred to as "jetons en terre cuite"), as well as the Geometric building at Eratomymou Street at Eretria, for which see Andreiomenou 1981, fig. 99, and from other Eretrian contexts, see figs. 84–85.

22 See *Lefkandi* I, pl. 65:a–h; *Lefkandi* II.2, pp. 73, 78, pl. 33, nos. 44–47 (the Toumba Building also yielded larger pierced disks that were shaped from terracotta, some unbaked, referred to as "loomweights").

23 For Late Bronze and Early Iron Age examples from Vardaroftsa and Boubousti, see Heurtley 1939, p. 231, fig. 104:m–p; p. 240, fig. 112:i–j. For earlier examples from prehistoric settlements in Macedonia, see Heurtley 1939, p. 139, fig. 7:k (Early Neolithic Servia); p. 203, fig. 67:gg–ii (Early Bronze Age Vardaroftsa); p. 213, fig. 83:u–v (Middle Bronze Age Vardaroftsa). For the recently published disks—both pierced and unpierced—from Sindos/Anchialos, see Gimatzidis 2010, pl. 126:g–i.

24 See, for example, D'Onofrio 2007, pp. 119–127, esp. pls. 1, 3, 4:a–b, 6.1, 9.1–3.

25 *Lefkandi* I, p. 192, pl. 189, Toumba Tomb 36, no. 32.

26 *Lefkandi* I, p. 155, pl. 145, Tomb 36, no. 6 (cut from an amphora).

27 Eder 2001, p. 95, pl. 4:b, no. 3; pl. 14:a, no. N, who writes: "Die Funktion der Tonscherbe aus Grab 1963:3 is nicht geklärt."

28 See *Eretria* XVII, vol. 1, pp. 89–90; vol. 2, p. 50, pl. 93:6, nos. 12–22 (11 pieces in all, from the tomb of an infant aged 2 years ± 8 months at death); the tomb is dated to ca. 700 B.C. The interpretation that the disks were gaming pieces was first suggested by Bérard in *Eretria* III, p. 33; most recently illustrated in Kaltsas et al. 2010, p. 321, fig. 5 (bottom); p. 361, nos. 357–364. Cf. also the small rounded stones (24 in all, one larger than the rest) from an Early Iron Age tomb at Mycenae, interpreted by Desborough (1956, pp. 129–130, with pl. 34:b) as likely to represent a child's game, such as "Jacks," where "the large stone is thrown into the air, and then as many as possible of the smaller stones are picked up before the large stone is caught again." Desborough goes on to add that such a game was played in Greece by children in his day, as it is throughout many other parts of the world.